Second Edition

MANAGING TODAY!

Stephen P. Robbins

San Diego State University

Prentice Hall

Upper Saddle River, New Jersey 07458

Senior Editor: David Shafer
Editorial Assistant: Shannon Sims
Editor-in-Chief: Natalie Anderson
Assistant Editor: Shane Gemza
Managing Editor (editorial): Jennifer Glennon
Marketing Manager: Michael Campbell
Associate Managing Editor (production): Judith Leale
Permissions Coordinator: Monica Stipanov
Manufacturing Buyer: Diane Peirano
Manufacturing Supervisor: Arnold Vila
Senior Manufacturing Manager: Vincent Scelta
Senior Designer: Cheryl Asherman
Design Manager: Patricia Smythe
Interior Design: Ox + Company, Inc.
Cover Design: Ox + Company, Inc.
Composition: Progressive Publishing Alternatives

Library of Congress Cataloging-in-Publication Data

Robbins, Stephen P.
    Managing today! / Stephen P. Robbins. — 2nd ed.
      p.   cm.
    Includes bibliographical references and index.
    ISBN 0-13-011672-6
    1. Management.   2. Organizational effectiveness.   3. Personnel
management. 4. Management—Problems, exercises, etc.   I. Title.
HD31.R5648 1999
658—dc21   98-50314
                                           CIP

Prentice-Hall International (UK) Limited, London
Prentice-Hall of Australia Pty. Limited, Sydney
Prentice-Hall Canada, Inc., Toronto
Prentice-Hall Hispanoamericana, S.A., Mexico
Prentice-Hall of India Private Limited, New Delhi
Prentice-Hall of Japan, Inc., Tokyo
Prentice-Hall (Singapore) Pte. Ltd.
Editora Prentice-Hall do Brasil, Ltda., Rio de Janeiro

Printed in the United States of America

10 9 8 7 6 5 4 3 2

DEDICATION

for Laura

Brief Contents

Contents

The first edition of *Managing Today!* had two distinct objectives: (1) to introduce a new management paradigm and (2) to effectively combine the basic concepts of management and organizational behavior into a single volume. This second edition continues to seek these same two objectives.

THE NEW MANAGEMENT PARADIGM. The traditional paradigm for organizing management textbooks has been the "functional approach." Using this paradigm, textbooks were divided into sections on planning, organizing, leading, and controlling. This framework did a very good job of describing the manager's job in the 1960s and 1970s. But times changed and the functional approach had difficulty adequately incorporating changes in organizations and the workplace. Topics like diversity, globalization, quality, ethics, social responsibility, entrepreneurship, and organizational learning didn't naturally into the functional paradigm. Moreover, the manager's job had changed from one of "command and control" to creating shared visions, empowering employees, and creating self-managed teams. In response to these changes, the first edition of this book introduced a new, integrative paradigm. It builds managerial competencies by focusing on three knowledge areas: decision, planning, and monitoring systems; organizing tasks, people, and culture; and leading and empowering people. Further, topics such as globalization, diversity, and ethics are integrated throughout the text (see Exhibit 1) rather than isolated in separate chapters. While certainly not perfect, this new paradigm better captures the reality of what today's managers do.

TWO PRIMARY OBJECTIVES OF THIS BOOK

EXHIBIT 1

Integrative Topics
(with specific page references)

Chapter	Globalization	Diversity	Ethics
1	4–5, 9–10	7, 13–14	7–8, 21–22
2		46	
3	91–92		89–90, 94–95
4	102–03, 118–19, 122–25, 125–26		115, 126–28
5	142, 143, 144, 157		
6	170–71		187–88
7	220–21	228–31	
8	254, 256		
9	269–72	269–72, 285, 293–95	285
10	326–27, 328, 329	311, 324–25	
11	338–39, 345, 351	358	
12	387–88, 395–97	397	
13	404–05, 411, 424–25, 427	431–32	
14	440–41, 460–61		
15	470–71	488–89	489–90
16	516–17		502, 504, 507
17	530–32, 543	530	552–53
18	577–78		570–71, 581

COMBINING MANAGEMENT AND ORGANIZATIONAL BEHAVIOR. The second objective of this book is a response to changing curriculum in business schools throughout the world. Until very recently, most schools offered separate introductory courses in "Principles of Management" and "Organizational Behavior." As a result of changes suggested by the primary accrediting body of business programs, as well as the perception by many that the two courses contained considerable overlap, a number of schools have combined the two courses. These blend courses require a text that has more organizational behavior (OB) than does the typical introductory managment book and more management content than does the standard OB text. *Managing Today!* incorporates the basic concepts found in any management course with a comprehensive review of OB topics. Consistent with this blend objective, traditional management topics are given a strong behavioral emphasis and basic OB topics are treated in a managerial context. For instance, chapter 3 on decision making downplays the rational model in order to focus on the behavioral aspects of decision making. And when basic OB topics like personality, perception, and attitudes are discussed in chapter 12, the emphasis is on how an understanding of these topics can help you become a more effective manager.

THE PHILOSOPHY UNDERLYING THIS BOOK: BALANCING KNOWLEDGE AND SKILLS

This second edition of *Managing Today!* balances the acquisition of knowledge with skill applications. Students need to know *about* management. But they also need to be able to *apply* that knowledge on the job.

Readers will find considerable attention paid in this book toward helping them develop their managerial skills. Some examples of skills (with chapter reference in parentheses) include: active listening (17), budgeting (5), coaching (15), conflict management (17), counseling (17), decision making (3), delegation (17), environmental scanning (4), feedback (17), interviewing (9), negotiation (17), problem solving (3), time management (5), and trust building (16).

In addition, I realize that students want to know what works and what doesn't. Most aren't interested in the details of research, the historical evolution of our knowledge, or long discourses on competing ideas. So, in this book, I've downplayed names, historical developments, and research methods. For example, in contrast to most introductory management textbooks, I've organized the chapters on motivation and leadership (chapters 13–15) around issues rather than historical theories. These chapters focus on current issues and draw on the theories to clarify those issues and to provide readers with practical guidelines for applications.

MAINTAINING CONTEMPORARY CONTENT

Many users of this book's first edition commented positively about the inclusion of relevant management topics not found in other introductory texts. This revision continues to provide coverage of contemporary topics. The following list highlights some issues ignored in many other management textbooks:

- Management competencies
- Assessing managerial effectiveness
- Project management
- Environmental scanning
- Competitive intelligence
- Time management
- Externalization of risk
- Privatization

▸ Technology transfer
▸ Visionary leadership
▸ Team leadership
▸ Transforming individuals into team players
▸ Building trust
▸ Understanding emotions

While the objectives of this edition have remained unchanged from the previous one, I've made a number of improvements this time around to help students better achieve these objectives. The following are highlights of the major changes you'll find in this edition:

▶ IN GENERAL

Today? or Tomorrow? boxes. These boxes introduce cutting-edge ideas that are currently being implemented in organizations, on the verge of implementation, or within the realm of near-term possibilities. The intention of these boxes is to focus the reader's attention on the changing world of management and how managing tomorrow may be different than managing today.

If I Were the Manager exercises. These exercises are included at the end of each chapter. They provide students with a real-life problem faced by a practicing manager and ask the student to consider what he or she would do.

Team Activity exercises. Today's successful manager needs to be able to work effectively as part of a team. To help students develop their team-building skills, each chapter concludes with an activity exercise that requires group interplay. These activities are designed as in-class exercises.

Cross-Disciplinary Analysis. College courses typically are taught in isolation. There is usually little effort in an introductory accounting course, for instance, at helping students to see the relationship between accounting and economics or psychology. The result, unfortunately, is that students often fail to see the integrative nature of a business education. *Managing Today!* attempts to address this problem. The end of each section concludes with a discussion that explicitly links management concepts with the content of courses in other business disciplines, as well as in the humanities and social sciences.

▶ BY CHAPTER

▸ *Chapter 1* New material on externalization of risk, privatization, multiple skills, and continual retraining.
▸ *Chapter 4* New material on culture shock.
▸ *Chapter 5* New material on time-management skills.
▸ *Chapters 7 and 8* have been reversed, providing a more logical presentation.
▸ *Chapter 7* New material on cycle-time reduction and technology transfer.
▸ *Chapter 10* New material on virtual teams.
▸ *Chapter 12* New material on the Big-5 personality dimensions and on understanding emotions.
▸ *Chapter 14* New material on the cognitive resource model of leadership.
▸ *Chapter 15* New material on a leader's role in framing issues and self-leadership.
▸ *Chapter 16* New chapter on building trust.
▸ *Chapter 18* New material on downsizing and layoff-survivor sickness.

SUPPLEMENTS

Managing Today! Second Edition, comes with a complete, high-tech support package for faculty and students. This includes a comprehensive instructor's manual and test bank; a dedicated Web site <www.prenhall.com/robbins>; inclusion on PHLIP (Prentice Hall Learning on the Internet Partnership), a faculty-support Web site featuring Instructor's Manual, PowerPoint slides, current news articles, and links to related Internet sites; an on-line student study guide; electronic transparencies; and the Robbins Self-Assessment Library, which provides students with insights into their skills, abilities, and interests.

- **Instructor's Manual:** Designed to guide the educator through the text, each chapter in the instructor's manual includes learning objectives, chapter contents, a detailed lecture outline, questions for discussion, and boxed materials.
- **Instructor's Manual on Disk:** As above but in electronic format.
- **Test Item File:** Each chapter contains true/false, multiple choice, short answer/essay questions, and situation-based questions. Together the questions cover the content of each chapter in a variety of ways providing flexibility in testing the students' knowledge of the text.
- **Windows/Prentice Hall Test Manager version 4.0:** Contains all of the questions in the printed TIF. Test Manager is a comprehensive suite of tools for testing and assessment. Test Manager allows educators to easily create and distribute tests for their courses, either by printing and distributing through traditional methods, or by on-line delivery via a Local Area Network (LAN) server.
- **PowerPoint Electronic Transparencies with Teaching Notes:** A comprehensive package allowing access to all of the figures from the text, these PowerPoint transparencies are designed to aid the educator and supplement in-class lectures. To further enhance the lecture, teaching notes for each slide are included both electronically, and as a printed, punched, and perforated booklet for insertion into a three-ring binder, allowing the educator to customize the lecture.
- **Color Transparencies:** Designed to aid the educator and enhance classroom lectures, 100 of the most critical PowerPoint electronic transparencies have been chosen for inclusion in this package as full-color acetates.
- **Part Integrative Custom Video Cases:** Mad Dogs & Englishmen, a New York City-based advertising firm, is the subject of five part integrative video cases. This small innovative company illustrates a variety of management issues from ethics and social responsibility to horizontal organizational structure.
- **Chapter-Ending Video Cases:** Drawn from the acclaimed public television series Small Business 2000 and ABC News, these videos were chosen to complement the text, enhance classroom lectures, and improve student comprehension of the topics discussed in the text.
- **Study Guide:** Designed to aid student comprehension of the text, the study guide contains chapter objectives, detailed chapter outlines, review, discussion, and study questions.
- **Self-Assessment Library CD-ROM:** Included FREE with each copy of the text, this valuable tool includes 45 individual self-assessment exercises, organized around individuals, groups, and organizations. Each exercise can be taken electronically and scored immediately, giving students individual feedback.
- **PHLIP/CW Web Site:** *Managing Today! 2/e*, is supported by PHLIP, *(Prentice Hall Learning on the Internet Partnership)* the book's companion Web site. An invaluable resource for both instructors and students, **PHLIP** features a wealth of up-to-date, on-line resources at the touch of a button! A research center, current

events articles, an interactive study guide, exercises, and additional resources all combine to give you the most advanced text-specific Web site available.

Visit www.prenhall.com/robbins

ACKNOWLEDGEMENTS

The comments of reviewers helped shape this revision. I want to thank the following for taking the time to offer suggestions on how I could improve the first edition: Lizabeth A. Barclay, Oakland University; Charles M. Byles, Virginia Commonwealth University; James F. Cashman, University of Alabama; William Fenuema, University of Indianapolis; Daniel Kopp, Southwest Missouri State University; Rodley C. Pineda, Tennessee Technological University; William W. Sannwald, San Diego State University; Larry Siebers, Utah State University; Ram Subramanian, Grand Valley State University; S. Stephen Vitucci, University of Central Texas; Marion White, James Madison University; Diana J. Wong-MingJi, University of Massachusetts; and D. Kent Zimmerman, James Madison University.

At Prentice Hall, I want to single out and thank the following people for their contributions on this revision: David Shafer, Michael Campbell, Shannon Sims, Natalie Anderson, Jim Boyd, Sandy Steiner, my production editor Judy Leale, and the book's designer Cheryl Asherman.

Finally, I want to acknowledge and thank my wife, Laura Ospanik. Writing is a lonely profession. Even when you're not in the office putting words on the computer screen, your mind is frequently back in the office thinking of ways to present ideas. Writing is a 24 hours a day, 7 days a week job. Thank heavens, I'm fortunate enough to have a partner who understands and supports what I do. My life is immeasurably enriched because of Laura.

Stephen P. Robbins

STEPHEN P. ROBBINS received his Ph.D. from the University of Arizona. He previously worked for Shell Oil Company and Reynolds Metals Company. Since completing his graduate studies, Dr. Robbins has taught at the University of Nebraska at Omaha, Concordia University in Montreal, the University of Baltimore, Southern Illinois University at Edwardsville, and San Diego State University. Dr. Robbins's research interests have focused on conflict, power, and politics in organizations, as well as the development of effective interpersonal skills. His articles on these and other topics have appeared in such journals as *Business Horizons, California Management Review, Business and Economic Perspectives, International Management, Management Review, Canadian Personnel and Industrial Relations,* and the *Journal of Management Education.*

In recent years, Dr. Robbins has been spending most of his professional time writing textbooks. In addition to *Managing Today!* second edition, these include *Essentials of Organizational Behavior,* sixth edition (Prentice Hall, 2000); *Human Resource Management,* sixth edition, with David DeCenzo (Wiley, 1999); *Management,* sixth edition, with Mary Coulter (Prentice Hall, 1999); *Fundamentals of Management,* second edition with David DeCenzo (Prentice Hall, 1998); *Organizational Behavior,* eighth edition (Prentice Hall, 1998); *Supervision Today!* second edition, with David DeCenzo (Prentice Hall, 1998); *Training in Interpersonal Skills,* second edition, with Philip Hunsaker (Prentice Hall, 1996); and *Organization Theory,* third edition (Prentice Hall, 1990). These books are used at more than a thousand U.S. colleges and universities, as well as hundreds of schools throughout Canada, Latin America, Australia, New Zealand, Asia, and Europe.

In Dr. Robbins's "other life," he participates in masters' track competition. Since turning 50 in 1993, he has set numerous indoor and outdoor age-group world sprint records. He has also won gold medals at the World Veteran Games in the 100-, 200-, and 400-meter dashes. In 1995, Robbins was named the year's outstanding "age 40 and over" male track and field athlete by the Masters Track and Field Committee of USA Track & Field, the governing organization for athletes in the United States. In 1998, he won national indoor titles at 60-, 200-, and 400-meters.

WELCOME TO THE CHANGING WORLD OF WORK

IN TODAY'S WORLD OF DYNAMIC CHANGE, ONLY THE
PARANOID SURVIVE.

A. S. GROVE

LEARNING OBJECTIVES

After studying this chapter, you should be able to:

1 Describe the effects of globalization on the economy and on organizations.

2 Explain the three waves in human history and their implications for the economy and organizations.

3 Describe how organizations externalize risk.

4 Identify the key elements in total quality management.

5 Explain why organizations are reengineering work processes.

6 Define the contingent workforce.

7 Explain the bimodal workforce.

8 Describe what happened to the loyalty-for-job-security arrangement.

Benny Karl-Erik Olsson, Marion Manigo-Truell, and Lillian Hurn provide us with a window into what the contemporary manager's job looks like. These three people, who work for three very different organizations, share one common characteristic—they're adapting to a world undergoing dramatic changes.[1]

Olsson works for the Zurich-based ABB ASEA Brown Boveri, one of the world's largest builders of power plants, industrial factories, and infrastructure projects. Born in South Africa and raised in Sweden, Olsson was recently asked where he's from. He quickly replied, "I'm Mexican." That's because he is currently ABB's country manager in Mexico. However, had you asked him the same question nine months earlier, he was Venezuelan. Before that, he was from Madrid, and before that, the 44-year old executive was from Barcelona. Olsson represents a growing class of managers—individuals who are able to move easily across national borders and help their employers implement global strategies.

Manigo-Truell (see photo) characterizes today's need for mobility. At age 51, she has changed careers six times and has gone back to school an equal number of times. She has moved between jobs in banking, hotel marketing, investor relations, and consulting. Currently she's on a temporary assignment with Anderson Consulting in New York, coordinating conference and special-events planning. "Every time I've changed jobs," Manigo-Truell says, "I've moved into a better position and received a better salary."

Although AT&T has cut its staff by tens of thousands over the past decade, Lillian Hurn has enjoyed a 12-year career with the company. She provides an important lesson in today's work climate: Security and opportunity depend on keeping your skills current. This 48-year-old single mother's first job at AT&T was assembling components at a phone company plant in Massachusetts. But after noting where most of the vacancies in the plant occurred, she began taking courses in material management—on everything from inventory control to scheduling deliveries. That led to a job scheduling component deliveries. Additional courses in inventory control prepared her for her next job—supervising a team of quality-control specialists. Today, as she continues taking courses to prepare herself for new challenges, Hurn is an AT&T product planner in a unit that refurbishes and sells used products.

The three previous examples reflect just a few of the changes affecting today's managers— the rising importance of globalization, more women in management, the value of adaptability in moving between jobs and organizations, and the need to keep skills current. They also reinforce the major theme throughout this book. Managing today is about managing in times of rapid change. We are going to show you that, as we enter the twenty-first century, people like Benny Olsson, Marion Manigo-Truell, and Lillian Hurn are not unique.

This opening chapter provides you with an overview of the changing world of work. We'll show you how changes in the economy are reshaping organizations and redefining people's jobs. The message of this chapter is simple: The world of work today and in the future is nothing like it was just a decade or two ago.

Let's start by looking at the major changes that are reshaping the economy. These include globalization; technological upheavals, especially in the areas of computers, telecommunications, and information; growth and decline among job sectors; cultural diversity; changing societal expectations; expanding interest in entrepreneurship; more-fickle, more-demanding customers; and increased privitization of government businesses (see Exhibit 1-1).

THE NEW ECONOMY

EXHIBIT 1-1

The Changing Economy

Old Economy	New Economy
• National borders limit competition	• National borders are nearly meaningless in defining an organization's operating boundaries
• Technology reinforces rigid hierarchies and limits access to information	• Technological changes in the way information is created, stored, used, and shared have made it more accessible
• Job opportunities are for blue-collar industrial workers	• Job opportunities are for knowledge workers
• Population is relatively homogeneous	• Population is characterized by cultural diversity
• Business is estranged from its environment	• Business accepts its social responsibilities
• Economy is driven by large corporations	• Economy is driven by small, entrepreneurial firms
• Customers get what business chooses to give them	• Customer needs drive business
• State-owned businesses proliferate	• State-owned businesses are being sold off to private interests

▶ Globalization

Twenty-five or thirty years ago, national borders acted to insulate most firms from foreign competitive pressures. They no longer do. National borders have become nearly meaningless today in defining an organization's operating boundaries. It has become increasingly irrelevant, for instance, to label a company's home country. BMW is supposedly a German firm, but it builds cars in South Carolina. Ford, which is headquartered in Detroit, builds its Mercury Tracers in Mexico. And Chrysler, long an American icon, was bought by the German company Daimler-Benz in 1998. So-called U.S. companies such as Exxon, Gillette, Coca-Cola, and IBM now receive more than 60 percent of their sales from outside the United States.[2] And Mitsubishi of Japan, Siemens of Germany, Nestlé of Switzerland, and Royal Dutch/Shell of the Netherlands are just four examples of the hundreds of multibillion dollar corporations that operate in dozens of countries throughout the world.[3] Siemens, for instance, employs 50,000 electronics workers in the United States alone.[4] Even this textbook, published in the United States, is at this very moment being read by students in the United States, Canada, Jamaica, Australia, Singapore, Hong Kong, Malaysia, the Philippines, Great Britain, Sweden, the Netherlands, and across Latin America.

But globalization doesn't just mean doing business across national borders. It also means expanded competition for almost every type of organization. Today's managers must be aware that they face foreign competitors as well as local and national ones. For instance, since 1972, Dennis Marthell has run a profitable business by processing checks for several major banks in the southeastern United States. In recent years, however, he has found himself competing against firms in the Caribbean. Because of computer technology and overnight delivery services, the Caribbean firms can provide the same services Marthell does but at better prices because of lower labor costs in countries such as Jamaica and Trinidad.

The two major forces driving globalization have been the search for expanded markets and efforts to reduce costs. If Sony sold its products only in its home country of Japan, its sales potential would be limited. Japan has a population of only 125 million. By going global, Sony has been able to market its products to billions of people. If an organization wants to grow, expanding operations outside its national borders is a logical strategy. Political barriers to this strategy have been lessened in recent years by the creation of multicountry trading blocs. NAFTA (the North American Free Trade Agreement, which unites Canada, the United States, and Mexico), the European Union (which includes fifteen Western European countries), and the Asia-Pacific Economic Cooperation (a group of 21 Pacific Rim nations that includes NAFTA participants as well as countries such as China, Japan, Australia, and South Korea) are examples of trading blocs that have significantly reduced tariffs and other barriers to cross-national trade among the participating countries. And the creation of trade blocs continue to grow. For instance, active negotiations have already begun to create a Free Trade Area of the Americas by the year 2005. It will include Canada, the United States, and 32 Latin American countries. The current world political climate appears to be moving increasingly toward reducing protectionist policies and opening up international trade.

With the breaking down of national borders and the search for expanded markets has come economic interdependence. Unlike ever before, business firms are finding their financial performance heavily dependent on economic conditions in foreign countries. As a case in point, the Asian financial crisis of the late 1990s severely undermined the performance of companies like Intel and Motorola, which relied heavily on markets in Japan, South Korea, Hong Kong, Singapore, Thailand, and Indonesia for a significant portion of their sales.

Many organizations have also been motivated to expand beyond their national borders in order to gain competitive advantages over rivals. The fact that many North American and European firms manufacture products such as semiconductors and textiles in Southeast Asia can be explained largely in terms of lower labor costs. Competitive advantage also explains the popularity of moving jobs to Mexico (low labor costs), factories to Canada (low-cost energy), developing mines in Australia (abundant raw materials), and running administrative operations out of Hong Kong (low taxes and minimal government regulations). It can explain the recent move by Western companies into central Europe to gain access to its low-cost, high-skilled labor force. When workers in western Germany make more than $33 an hour, and their contemporaries less than $3 an hour in Poland and the Czech Republic, is there any surprise that firms are moving jobs from Germany to places like Warsaw and Prague?

▶ Technological Changes

We often forget that only 20 years ago, almost no one had a fax machine or a cellular phone; the terms *e-mail* and *modem* were in the vocabulary of, perhaps, a couple of hundred people; computers occupied entire rooms rather than 11 inches of lap space; and *networks* referred to the major providers of television programming. How quickly times have changed.

The silicon chip and other advances in information technology have permanently altered the economies of the world and, as we will demonstrate shortly, the way people work. Digital electronics, optical data storage, more powerful and portable computers, and the ability for computers to communicate with each other are changing the way information is created, stored, used, and shared.

▶ Three Waves: Growth and Decline in Job Sectors

Futurist Alvin Toffler argued that human history can be divided into "waves."[5] The first wave was *agriculture*. Until the late nineteenth century, all economies were agrarian. For instance, in the 1890s, approximately 90 percent of people were employed in agriculture-related jobs. The second wave was *industrialization*. From the late 1800s until the 1960s, most developed countries moved from agrarian societies to ones based on machines. The third wave arrived in the 1970s. It is based on *information*. Toffler and others see these waves as essentially revolutions, in which complete "ways of life" are thrown out and replaced by new ones. The second wave, for instance, totally changed the lives of English villagers as they adjusted to life in English factories.[6] And the third wave is eliminating low-skilled, blue-collar jobs while creating abundant job opportunities for educated and skilled technical specialists, professionals, and other "knowledge workers."

Exhibit 1-2 illustrates the changing makeup during the twentieth century of the workforce in developed countries like the United States, Canada, the United Kingdom, Germany, France, Italy, and Japan.[7] Before World War I, farmers composed the largest single group in every developed country. Since that time, the proportion of the population engaged in farming has consistently dropped. Now less than five percent of the workforce is needed to provide our food; in the United States, it's under three percent.

The industrial revolution destroyed the careers of hundreds of thousands of skilled craftsmen. But it created a new group—blue-collar industrial workers. In 1900, this new group represented about 20 percent of the workforce. By the 1950s, industrial workers had become the largest single group in every developed country. They made products such as steel, automobiles, rubber, and industrial equipment. Ironically, "no class in history has ever risen faster than the blue-collar worker. And no class in history has ever fallen faster."[8] Today, blue-collar industrial workers account for less than 20 percent of the U.S. workforce, essentially about the same proportion they held in 1900![9] The shift since World

EXHIBIT 1-2   **Changing Makeup of the Workforce in Industrialized Countries**

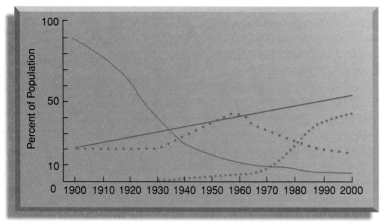

Source: Based on T. M. Godbout, "Employment Change and Sectoral Distribution in 10 Countries, 1970–90, *Monthly Labor Review*, October 1993, pp. 3–12; and "Historical Trends, Current Uncertainties," *Monthly Labor Review*, November 1993, p. 8.

War II has been away from manufacturing work and toward service jobs. Manufacturing jobs today are highest, as a proportion of the total civilian workforce, in Japan—at 24.3 percent. In the United States, manufacturing jobs make up only 18 percent of the civilian workforce. In contrast, services make up 59 percent of jobs in Italy (the lowest percentage of any industrial country) and 72 percent in the United States and Canada.[10]

Job growth in the past 20 years has been in low-skilled service work (such as fast-food employees, clerks, and home health aides) and knowledge work. This latter group includes professionals such as registered nurses, accountants, teachers, lawyers, and engineers. It also includes *technologists*—people who work with their hands and with theoretical knowledge.[11] Computer technicians, physical therapists, and medical technicians are examples of jobs in this category. Knowledge workers currently make up about a third of the U.S. workforce.[12]

Knowledge workers are at the cutting edge of the third wave. Their jobs are designed around the acquisition and application of information. The economy needs people who can fill these jobs, and they will be paid well for their services. Meanwhile, the number of blue-collar jobs has shrunk dramatically. Many blue-collar workers don't have the education and flexibility necessary to exploit the new job opportunities in the information revolution. They don't have the specific skills to move easily into high-paying technology jobs. This situation contrasts with the shift from the first wave to the second. The transition from the farm to the factory floor required little skill, just a strong back and the willingness to work hard.

▶ Diversity

As recently as 1960, only 32 percent of married women were in the U.S. workforce. Today, that figure is close to 60 percent.[13] Approximately 61 percent of all working-age women in the United States currently have jobs, and women make up 47 percent of the total workforce. Currently, women with children under six years of age are the fastest-growing segment of the U.S. workforce.[14] This trend of women's joining the workforce, incidentally, is taking place worldwide in industrialized nations. The percentage of women in the workforce is rapidly approaching that of men in Great Britain, Canada, Australia, Hong Kong, Singapore, and Japan.

The increased participation of women in the workforce is not the only diversity issue reshaping the labor pool. Another is multiculturalism. Globalization has been reducing barriers to immigration. In the United States, the proportion of people of Hispanic, Asian, Pacific Island, and African origin has increased significantly over the past two decades. And this trend will continue. Moreover, multiculturalism is not just a U.S. phenomenon. Countries such as Great Britain, Germany, and Canada are experiencing similar changes. Canada, as a case in point, has large populations of people who have recently emigrated from Hong Kong, Pakistan, Vietnam, and Middle Eastern countries. These immigrants are making Canada's population more diverse and its workforce more heterogeneous.

▶ Changing Societal Expectations

The 1960s gave us the Beatles, hippies, civil rights legislation, and the women's movement. It also gave us the beginning of heightened expectations for business firms. The term *corporate social responsibility* became an established part of our vocabulary. Business firms would increasingly be judged on how good a "citizen" they were as well as on how successful they were at making money.

Today, business firms are expected to act as responsible citizens.[15] Society expects corporations, for instance, to contribute to worthy charities, support community programs, and pursue environmentally friendly policies. Executives of these firms are expected to maintain and promote high ethical standards. A recent survey found that Dow Chemical,

Exxon, and General Electric were rated negatively by consumers largely because of perceptions about their environmental records or ethical practices.[16] In a globally competitive world, few organizations can afford the bad press or potential economic repercussions associated with being seen as socially irresponsible.

Social responsibility includes a broad range of issues including community relations, employee relations, product development and liability, policies to support women and minorities, and not doing business in countries that abuse human rights. Currently, sensitivity to the environment is receiving a great deal of attention. Business is reassessing its forms of packaging, recyclability of products, environmental safety practices, and the like. "The idea of being environmentally friendly, or 'green,' will have an impact on all aspects of the business—from the conception of products and services to use and subsequent disposal by customers."[17]

Corporate executives have gotten the message. Business is accepting society's heightened expectations of its social role. For example, a recent magazine poll of managers found that 76 percent agreed with the statement "Social responsibility *is* good business."[18]

▶ Entrepreneurial Spirit

It's a watershed event in the world of business. People are creating their own businesses at unprecedented rates. It's happening in North America. It's happening in Latin America. It's even taking hold in places such as the Czech Republic, Hungary, Russia, and China. The magnitude of change is impressive: In 1950 there were 90,000 new start-up businesses in the United States; the comparable annual figure today is about 2 million.[19]

Entrepreneurship is the process of initiating a business venture, organizing the necessary resources, and assuming the associated risks and rewards. Because entrepreneurial businesses usually start small, most fall within the definition of a "small business"—one that has fewer than 500 employees.

What explains the increased popularity of individuals starting their own businesses? There has always been a segment of the population that has wanted to control its own destiny. Such people have long chosen entrepreneurship. But recent changes in the economy have stimulated increased interest in being one's own boss. The downsizing of large corporations has displaced millions of workers and managers. Many of these employees have taken the trauma of being laid off and turned it into a self-employment opportunity, frequently financed in large part by severance pay or an early retirement bonus. Other members of the corporate world have seen colleagues, relatives, and friends lose their jobs and have concluded that future opportunities in downsized corporations will be limited. So they have voluntarily cut their corporate ties and chosen self-employment. Another force boosting entrepreneurship is the growing options in franchising. Purchasing a franchise such as Burger King, Merry Maids, Stanley Steamer, or Subway allows an entrepreneur to run his or her own business, but with less risk. Franchises have a lower failure rate than the typical new business because of the marketing, operations, and management support provided by the franchiser.

From a globalization perspective, we should note that entrepreneurship is probably more important to the economic health of developing nations than in countries like the United States, France, or Australia. Developing economies are dependent on small business to create employment opportunities. The road to prosperity can come only through job creation. In Peru, for example, there are over 3 million small businesses, employing more than 5 million people.[20] These small businesses generate up to 40 percent of Peru's GDP. The future of economies in countries such as Peru depend on entrepreneurs starting new business ventures, creating jobs, and putting money in more people's pockets.

Steve Lauer (second from left) has met his entrepreneurial needs by buying a Subway franchise in Colorado.

▶ "The Customer Is King": Quality, Speed, and Low Costs

Henry Ford said his customers could have any color car they wanted "as long as it's black." Stew Leonard, the world's largest dairy store in southern Connecticut, says there are only two rules in its business: "Rule 1—The customer is always right. Rule 2—If the customer is ever wrong, reread Rule 1."[21]

Today's economy is being driven by the Stew Leonards of the world. They realize that long-term success can be achieved only by satisfying the customer.[22] It's the customer who ultimately pays all the bills. And today's customers have more choices than ever and are, therefore, more difficult to please. "We are going to have multiple countries competing in the same businesses," says former vice chairman of Xerox, William F. Glavin. "Fulfilling customer requirements with lower cost will be the driving factor in success."[23] Glavin's viewpoint is widely shared by managers. For instance, a recent survey found that senior executives rated customer satisfaction as the most important issue in determining business success—ahead of financial performance, competitiveness, and marketing.[24]

Customers are demanding quick service, high quality, and value for their money. Mass customization, toll-free service hot lines, the growth of mail order, home shopping via television and the Internet, discount superstores, and managers who have become obsessed with quality are all responses to more-demanding customers. Even the definition of quality reflects this perspective: Experts in the quality movement emphasize that "quality is what the customer says it is."[25]

▶ Privatization

Many federal governments historically owned and operated businesses that, it was widely believed, served the public's interest best when run by the state. These businesses typically included utilities; banks; transportation systems such as airlines, railroads, and bus lines; telecommunication systems; and basic industries like steel and mining. This view of state ownership has been losing popularity over the past 20 years. The new trend is toward **privatization**, that is, the sale of state-run organizations to private business.

In the early 1980s, British prime minister Margaret Thatcher and her conservative government sold a number of Britain's crown corporations to private-sector interests. In recent years, Canada, France, eastern European countries, and much of Latin America have sold off major parts of state-owned businesses. In Latin America, during 1998, for instance, Peru and Venezuela privitized electric and hydroelectric plants, Panama sold off its state-owned sugar corporation, Mexico privatized the Benito Juarez International Airport in Mexico City, Colombia sold off a major part of its rail system, and Brazil sold its state telephone company to private interests.[26]

The move to privatization increases the need for effective management and up-to-date management practices. Profits become expected for shareholders. To achieve those profits, significant improvements in operations leading to improved efficiency are implemented and higher-quality goods and services typically result.

THE NEW ORGANIZATION

The economy has been undergoing changes, and so, too, have organizations. As the following describes, the underlying theme is that the "new organization" is becoming more flexible and more responsive to its environment[27] (see Exhibit 1-3).

Flexibility and Temporariness

Lou Capolzzola worked full-time, for 10 years, at *Sports Illustrated*. He was a photographic lighting specialist. Then his job was eliminated. Well, not exactly eliminated. Capolzzola was given the choice to continue as an independent contractor. But his base pay would be about half what it was as a full-time employee. And he wouldn't be paid most of the overtime pay he previously was entitled to, and he would lose all of his $20,000-a-year benefit package and whatever security goes with a full-time, permanent job. Why did this happen? Time Warner, the publisher of *Sports Illustrated*, decided it could save money and increase its flexibility by converting a lot of jobs like Capolzzola's into temporary positions.[28]

Time Warner's action is not unique. Many large companies are converting permanent jobs into temporary ones. Eight percent of Delta Air Lines' workforce are now temporaries. Hewlett-Packard has stated its intention to keep 10 percent of its workforce as temporaries. And 27 percent of Microsoft's Seattle-area employees are temporaries.[29] Six out of every 10 people who work for the giant British retailer Marks & Spencer are part-timers.[30]

In 1983, there were 619,000 temporary jobs in the United States. Today that number is over 2.6 million.[31] In Europe, companies have shifted overwhelmingly to hiring temporary workers. About 11 percent of all jobs in France, and more than 33 percent of those in Spain, are now filled by temporary workers.[32]

How do employees feel about this growth in temporary work? About a third of all temporary workers claim to prefer their contingent status to permanent employment.[33] Yet the prime reason United Parcel Service's 185,000 workers went on strike in August 1997 was in protest over UPS filling the majority of its new positions with temporaries, who were paid significantly lower wages than full-timers.[34] It's probably accurate to say that the majority of the workforce prefers permanent, full-time employment. But in a world of rapid change, permanent employees limit management's flexibility. A large permanent workforce, for example, restricts management's options and raises costs for firms that suffer the ups and downs of market cycles. So we can expect employers to rely increasingly on temporaries to fill new and vacated positions.

The Changing Organization

EXHIBIT 1-3

Old Organization

- Permanent jobs
- Control your own destiny through independence
- Relatively homogeneous workforce
- Quality is an afterthought

- Large corporations provide job security
- If it ain't broke, don't fix it
- Employers find an abundance of prospective employees with the necessary skills
- Spread risks by being in multiple sets of businesses
- Workdays are defined as 9-to-5
- Managers alone make decisions
- Work is organized around individuals
- Work is defined by jobs

- Pay is stable and related to seniority and job level
- Business decision making is driven by utilitarianism

New Organization

- Temporary jobs
- Externalize risk

- Diverse workforce
- Continuous improvement and customer satisfaction are critical
- Large corporations are cutting overall staff
- Reengineer all processes
- Employers find a serious shortage of prospective employees with proper skills
- Concentrate on core competencies

- Workdays have no time boundaries
- Employees participate in decisions
- Work is organized around teams
- Work is defined in terms of tasks to be done
- Pay is flexible and broadbanded

- Business decision-making criteria are expanded to include rights and fairness

Externalization of Risk

The corporation of the 1960s or 1970s sought to own and control as much of its operating activities as possible. Vertically integrated and largely self-sufficient companies such as General Motors, U.S. Steel, and IBM were role models for the world. They owned the manufacturing plants that built their products. To maintain maximum control, they created powerful centralized departments that carefully monitored the decisions of lower-level managers throughout their companies. For similar control reasons, they often bought or merged with the firms that supplied them with raw materials. Support activities such as accounting and maintenance were done by people employed by the corporation.

The downside of ownership and control is inflexibility and increased risk. Today's organizations are increasingly responding by externalizing risks. Why own when you can rent? Why take all the risk when you can share it with others? So they're subcontracting out work, licensing products to others, and forming joint partnerships.

Outsourcing refers to contracting with outside firms to provide resources or services.[35] It is a natural extension of the move to emphasize core competencies. Organizations can focus on their strengths and buy everything else from the outside. Anything can be fair game for outsourcing. A survey of 100 of the largest U.S. corporations found that 77 percent were outsourcing some aspect of their business support services. These include functions such as warehousing, payroll management, tax administration, mailroom operations, and computer systems management. The pharmaceutical giant Merck & Company outsources its mail and copier needs to Pitney Bowes. To run its information services,

Jen-Hsun Huang, the 33-year-old cofounder and president of Nvidia Corporation relies heavily on outsourcing. His company produces a multimedia platform that handles the 3-D graphics and audio for playing video games on a PC. Nvidia designs in-house the specialized chip that goes into the platform, then contracts its manufacture with SGS-Thomson. Its game-playing circuit board is produced by Diamond Multimedia Systems. Nvidia even outsources marketing. It sells most of its products under the Sega brandname.

Continental Airlines uses EDS Corp. The Presbyterian Medical Center in Philadelphia outsources its food service, environmental services, security, maintenance and engineering, central processing, and transport functions. Keep in mind that outsourcing is not restricted to business services. Three out of ten large U.S. industrial companies now outsource more than half of their manufacturing.[36] Sara Lee Corp., as a case in point, recently sold off most of its factories to concentrate on marketing its brands.

Ralph Lauren's Polo brand clothing is not made by Ralph Lauren. He licenses his name to others and collects a royalty for each garment sold. Disney doesn't make those Mickey Mouse and Donald Duck stuffed animals you find in toy stores. Other companies are manufacturing these products under a licensing agreement with Disney. These examples illustrate another way that organizations are externalizing risk. By licensing products, technologies, and similar proprietary properties, firms can let others assume the downside risk while allowing themselves to capture the upside potential.

Boeing and Europe's Airbus are competitors, but they have joined forces to do research on developing the next generation of commercial aircraft. Apple Computer relied on Sony's expertise in miniaturization to develop its PowerBook. G & F Industries, a maker of plastic components, has an employee who works full-time and on-site for the high-fidelity systems manufacturer Bose Corp. These examples illustrate another way in which organizations are externalizing risk. They're developing partnerships with other companies to share expertise and personnel. Like outsourcing, partnering allows firms to do more with less and to benefit from other organizations' core competencies.

Management is also externalizing risk by creating new kinds of working relationships with its employees.[37] As shown in Exhibit 1-4, this can be best understood if you think of management's commitment to its employees as varying based on *length* of commitment (long-term vs. short-term) and *depth* of commitment (deep versus shallow). Historically, organizations sought deep commitments and hired almost exclusively for the long-term. These employees were expected to make a career commitment to the organization, be loyal, and hold work as their central life interest. And the organization responded by providing them with relatively permanent employment and long-term career opportunities. Organizations still have such *core employees*, but as noted earlier in the chapter, they're a shrinking category. Increasingly, organizations are hiring people that fit the categories on the left side of Exhibit 1-4. Called **contingent workers**, these are temporaries employed by temporary help companies, leased, contract, and part-time workers. And in terms of reducing risk, contingent workers provide management with more flexibility because they

The New Organization's Commitment to Its Employees

EXHIBIT 1-4

	Short-Term	Long-Term
Deep	Part-Timers	Core Employees
Shallow	Temporaries and Independent Contractors	Substitutes and Periodic Employees

Depth of Commitment

Length of Commitment

Source: Based on D. M. Rousseau and K. A. Wade-Benzoni, Changing Individual-Organization Attachments, in A. Howard (ed.), *The Changing Nature of Work* (San Francisco: Jossey-Bass, 1995), pp. 305—14.

can be added and deleted easily and with minimal legal hassles. Substitutes and periodic employees—which would include on-call workers (such as substitute teachers and nurses) and people who share a single job—are a residual category that also increase management flexibility.

Workforce Diversity

We described earlier how cultural diversity is changing the makeup of the workforce. As organizations become more heterogeneous in terms of gender, age, race, sexual orientation, and ethnicity, management has been adapting its human resource practices to reflect those changes. Many organizations today—small ones as well as large ones—have workforce diversity programs. They tend to focus on training employees and modifying benefit programs to make them more "family-friendly."[38]

Training seeks to increase awareness and understanding of diversity. The typical program lasts from half a day to three days and includes role-playing exercises, lectures, and group experiences. Hewlett-Packard, for instance, has a basic three-day program.[39] It covers topics such as awareness of attitudes and prejudices, sexual harassment, workers with disabilities, legal issues, corporate objectives, and management responsibilities. In addition, with the workforce rapidly graying, age-based stereotypes are becoming an important diversity issue.[40] Hartford Insurance has responded by introducing specific training exercises to increase sensitivity to aging.[41] In one, participants are asked to respond to the following four questions: (1) If you didn't know how old you are, how old would you guess you are? In other words, how old do you feel inside? (2) When I was 18, I thought middle age began at age _____ . (3) Today, I think middle age begins at age _____ . (4) What would be your first reaction if someone called you an older worker? Answers to these questions are then used to analyze age-related stereotypes.

Family-friendly benefits is a term that encompasses a wide range of work and family programs such as on-site day care, child-care and elder-care referrals, flexible hours, compressed workweeks, job sharing, telecommuting, temporary part-time employment, unpaid leaves of absence, personal concierge service, and relocation assistance for employees' family members.[42] With more women working and more two-career couples, family-friendly benefits are seen as a means to help employees better balance their per-

Implications from an Aging Workforce

Diversity will be showing itself in all kinds of ways. Consider the implications of baby boomers, those born between 1946 and 1960, who will be clogging the workplace by hanging on to the best-paid jobs and blocking the advancement of younger workers.

The boomers are an anomaly. They are far more numerous than the generations that preceded or will follow them. They are also experiencing pangs of financial insecurity. Add in the change in laws that have, for all intents and purposes, eliminated forced retirement, and you have a large group of people who are likely to be working well past traditional retirement age. Many may work well into their 70s. And new forecasts indicate that by 2020, the workforce participation rates for men and women aged 55 to 64 could be as much as 14 percent higher than originally forecasted, adding 11.5 million additional workers.

We are likely moving to a two-tier workforce. Boomers keep the good jobs and the good pay. The younger generation—particularly the baby busters, born from 1965 to 1985—increasingly will have to accept low-skill jobs (often on a temporary basis) with little prospect of having the income their parents did.

You can already begin seeing the early signs of this trend. For instance, at Cummins Engine Co.'s diesel plant in Columbus, Indiana, which employs 2,800 people, they haven't hired a permanent full-timer since 1978! New hires have all been temps, most of them stuck in low-skill jobs that pay no more than $8 an hour. Meanwhile, within the next decade, all of Cummins's hourly workers will be old enough—65—to retire. But they aren't likely to. Most can't afford or aren't willing to give up their $18 an hour jobs.

What are the implications for management? An older workforce will cost more in direct wages and may significantly increase medical costs. Younger workers are likely to exhibit frustrations over limited opportunities to get the high-skilled, high-pay permanent jobs. And eventually, when the baby

At Cummins Engine, older workers are holding on to the best-paying jobs—so further generations are squeezed out.

boomers do retire, organizations are likely to have a skill deficit because younger workers will not have gained the necessary abilities to handle the more complex jobs.

Source: Based on R. Stodghill II, "The Coming Job Bottleneck," *Business Week*, March 24, 1997, pp. 184–85.

sonal lives with work. And studies indicate that helping employees resolve work and family conflicts boosts morale, increases productivity, reduces absenteeism, and makes it easier for employers to recruit and retain first-class workers.[43] For instance, a study at Johnson & Johnson found that absenteeism among employees who used flexible work hours and family-leave policies was on average 50 percent less than for their workforce as a whole.[44]

▶ Total Quality Management

You've seen the ad: "At Ford, Quality Is Job 1." Well, Ford isn't alone! In organizations engaged in a wide range of endeavors—for example, Motorola, Xerox, Federal Express, Hospital Corporation of America, Oregon State University, and the U.S. Navy—the goal of improving quality has taken on the appearance of something resembling a religion. The term increasingly used to describe this effort is **total quality management**, or **TQM**.[45] The TQM movement is largely a response to global competition and more-demanding customers. And its popularity is confirmed in a recent survey of more than 1,350 firms, all employing 100 or more people. Forty-nine percent indicated they currently had TQM programs under way.[46]

Although TQM became popular in the 1980s, its roots go back 30 years earlier. In 1950, an American quality expert, W. Edwards Deming, went to Japan and advised many top Japanese managers on how to improve production effectiveness. Central to his management methods was the use of statistics to analyze variability in production processes. A well-managed organization, according to Deming, was one in which statistical control reduced variability and resulted in uniform quality and predictable quantity of output. His ideas were largely responsible for the incredible success postwar Japan had in creating high-quality products at very competitive prices.

American managers saw what Japanese companies were doing, and they responded. The result has been TQM. It's a philosophy of management that is driven by the constant attainment of customer satisfaction through the continuous improvement of all organizational processes.

Exhibit 1-5 summarizes the basic elements of TQM. Notice that the term *customer* in TQM is expanded beyond the traditional definition to include everyone who interacts with the organization's products or services either internally or externally. So TQM encompasses employees and suppliers, as well as the people who buy the organization's products or services.

Although TQM has been criticized by some for overpromising and underperforming, its overall record is impressive.[47] Varian Associates Inc., a maker of scientific equipment, used TQM in its semiconductor unit to cut by 14 days the time it took to put out new designs. Another Varian unit, which makes vacuum systems for computer clean rooms, boosted on-time delivery from 42 percent to 92 percent through TQM.

What Is Total Quality Management?

EXHIBIT 1-5

1. **Intense focus on the customer.** The customer includes not only outsiders who buy the organization's products or services but also internal customers (such as shipping or accounts payable personnel) who interact with and serve others in the organization.
2. **Concern for continual improvement.** TQM is a commitment to never being satisfied. "Very good" is not good enough. Quality can always be improved. TQM creates a race without a finish line.
3. **Improvement in the quality of everything the organization does.** TQM uses a very broad definition of quality. It pertains not only to the final product but also to how the organization handles deliveries, how rapidly it responds to complaints, how politely the phones are answered, and the like.
4. **Accurate measurement.** TQM uses statistical techniques to measure every critical variable in the organization's operations. These are compared against standards or benchmarks to identify problems, trace them to their roots, and eliminate their causes.
5. **Empowerment of employees.** TQM involves the people on the line in the improvement process. Teams are used widely in TQM programs as empowerment vehicles for finding and solving problems.

Globe Metallurgical Inc., a small Ohio metal producer, credits TQM for having helped it become 50 percent more productive. The most impressive finding, however, is a recent comparative study contrasting TQM award-winners with a corporate control group. The TQM group posted 37 percent higher sales growth and 44 percent higher stock prices.[48]

Downsizing

The old rule of thumb was that organizations hired in good times and fired in bad times. Since the late 1980s, that rule no longer seems to apply, at least among large companies. Throughout the 1990s, for instance, most of the Fortune 500 made drastic cuts in their overall staff. IBM cut staff by 122,000 people, and AT&T by 83,000. General Motors laid off 74,000, Boeing reduced its staff by 61,000, Sears cut 50,000 jobs, and Eastman Kodak has reduced its workforce by 34,000 positions.[49]

Downsizing has become a dominant management strategy. It refers to the practice of reducing an organization's size through extensive layoffs. The facts are undebatable—large companies have cut millions of jobs—but management's motivation is not always clear.[50] Critics believe that massive downsizing has become a fad. They say it's a way for management to demonstrate to stockholders that it's serious about keeping costs down. Failure to downsize, when everyone else is doing it, signals to investors that management has gotten soft and lazy. To support their case, the critics point out that many of the companies that downsized did so even though they were experiencing healthy profits. Supporters of downsizing maintain that large-scale staff reductions are necessary to maintain competitiveness in a fast-changing global marketplace. Big corporations overstaffed in the decades when competition was less severe. Downsizing is merely an attempt to get their workforces back in balance.

Which is right? Perhaps both. Managers are certainly as susceptible to fads as anybody else, and downsizing does cut costs. But recent evidence suggests that managers are not merely lopping off heads to cut costs.[51] Most organizations are strategically cutting operations that have become overstaffed and, at the same time, are increasing staff in areas that add value. AT&T, for instance, cut 8,000 jobs in 1996—mostly operators being replaced by voice-recognition technology—while, at the same time, adding staff in marketing and networking systems.

Reengineering

In times of rapid and dramatic change, it's sometimes necessary for managers to ask: How would we do things around here if we were starting over from scratch? This question expresses the essence of what **reengineering** is about. It asks managers to reconsider how work would be done and the organization structured if they were starting over.[52] Apparently, a lot of managers are asking that question. A recent survey of large U.S. firms (with 10,000 or more employees) found that 61 percent engaged in reengineering.[53] A similar survey of 600 European companies revealed that 75 percent had implemented at least one reengineering initiative.[54] Even many Japanese firms are replacing their traditional practice of seeking slow and continuous improvements with reengineering efforts. Major companies such as Kao, Kawasaki Steel, Ryoshoku Trading, Seiko Epson, Casio Computer, Fumitsu, and Oki Electric Industry are some of the Japanese companies that have gotten onto the reengineering bandwagon.[55]

The logic underlying reengineering is that organizations develop processes in their early years and then become locked into them despite changing conditions. For instance, most large companies can trace their work practices back to organizing concepts proposed nearly a hundred years ago. Division of labor and the fragmentation of work have been the cornerstones for how all kinds of firms—steel manufacturers, airlines, insurance companies, computer chip makers—have organized work processes. Reengineering argues that, for most firms, these old ways of doing business simply don't work anymore. The old ways are not responsive enough to customers' needs and are inefficient. Managers have to rethink what their organization is about and then reinvent the processes for producing and delivering their goods or services.

An accounts payable department at Ford Motor Company illustrates how reengineering can be applied.[56] This unit employed 500 people in a process that had been in place since the 1930s. Ford's purchasing department would send a purchase order to a supplier, and a copy of the purchase order would go to accounts payable. When the supplier shipped the goods and they arrived at Ford, a clerk at the receiving dock would complete a form describing the goods and would send it to accounts payable. Meanwhile, the supplier would send an invoice to accounts payable. The 500 employees in accounts payable spent most of their time straightening out situations in which purchase orders, receiving tickets, invoices, and other documents didn't match.

Ford radically redesigned the entire process. Accounts payable clerks no longer match purchase order with receiving document because the new process eliminated the invoice entirely. In the new process, when a buyer in the purchasing department issues a purchase order to a vendor, that buyer simultaneously enters the order into an on-line database. When goods are received from the supplier at Ford's receiving dock, someone in receiving checks a computer terminal to see whether the received shipment corresponds to an outstanding purchase order in the database. If it does, the clerk at the dock accepts the goods and pushes a button on the terminal keyboard that tells the database that the goods have arrived. The computer then automatically sends a check to the supplier. If the goods do not correspond to an outstanding purchase order in the database, the clerk on the dock refuses the shipment and sends it back to the supplier.

Under the new system at Ford, the receiving dock now handles payment authorization, so most of the accounts payable department's activities are eliminated. Instead of 500 people in that unit, Ford has just 125 people. And in some Ford units, reengineering has resulted in accounts payable departments that have cut their staff by as much as 95 percent.

The prototype of the new organization is one that is undergoing or has undergone reengineering. This dramatic approach to change, in fact, can explain a large part of how many companies have been able to successfully downsize their operations. Reengineering processes have dramatically reduced waste and inefficiencies. And the number of people needed to do the work that remains has been similarly reduced.

> Reengineering argues that, for most firms, the old ways of doing business simply don't work anymore.

▶ Skill Shortages

Ironically, at the same time that organizations are downsizing, they're also facing a labor shortage. How is it possible to have *too many* people while simultaneously having *too few* people? The answer is: The supply-demand equation has become out of sync. The kinds of skills that people have who are being let go are, for the most part, different from the skills that organizations increasingly need to be competitive.

The changing workplace is putting a premium on workers with strong math, language, and reasoning capabilities.[57] So clerks who predominantly process paper are likely to find themselves "downsized" as their jobs are reengineered. The same fate lies in store for production workers who can't decipher complex instructions, handle basic geometry and calculus, or operate computers.

The demand for people with up-to-date skills will exceed the supply for a number of years into the future. This means management will have to make concerted efforts to hire such people. For instance, they'll need to expand the recruiting net to include older workers and foreigners. And once hired, to keep these in-demand employees they'll need to introduce more flexible work arrangements, provide challenging work assignments, and create a stimulating workplace.

▶ Playing to Strengths: Core Competencies

Many organizations in the past thought they could be all things to all people. The growth of conglomerates such as Gulf & Western, ITT, Textron, Rockwell International, TRW, United Technologies, and Litton Industries in the 1960s reflected a belief that the most effective organizations were ones that spread their risks by being in diverse businesses. At one time, for instance, ITT owned Sheraton Hotels, Federal Electric, Grinnel, Rayonier, Continental Baking, Avis Rent-a-Car, and Eason Oil. Over time, these conglomerates were outperformed by competitors whose strategy was to focus on their unique strengths rather than to "spread the risk."

Today's successful organizations are playing to their strengths. They are focusing on what they do best and what makes them special—their **core competencies**—and are selling off or closing down noncore businesses.[58] Core competencies are the capabilities of an organization that distinguish it from its competitors. They tend to be based on knowledge rather than on current products or assets owned. Examples of capabilities that can be core competencies include superior research and development, a unique technology, manufacturing efficiency, or outstanding customer service. Domino Pizza's strength is not its pizzas. It's the company's super-speedy delivery system. Nordstrom, the Seattle-based retailer, distinguishes itself from its competitors through extraordinary service. Sears has sold off its insurance and brokerage businesses to focus on what it does best—retailing. Similarly, Bausch & Lomb has divested itself of operations peripheral to its core eyewear operations, such as making scientific instruments and dental implants. Now it concentrates on the businesses it knows—sunglasses, contact lenses, and lens-care products.

▶ The Demise of "9-to-5": The Flexible Workday

Organizations are redefining what we call "the workday." The concept of a "9-to-5" job is essentially a residual of the 1950s, when labor could be measured in an office or a factory. Today, especially among professionals and technical specialists, the line is increasingly blurred between work and personal lives.[59] At one time, only doctors were on call 24 hours a day. Now that organizations are pursuing global opportunities and have mobile communication capabilities, employees are increasingly expected to be on call around the clock. Business opportunities in Cape Town, South Africa, may require people in Honolulu to be having phone conversations when most people in Hawaii are sound asleep.

It's the unusual professional that doesn't take work home nowadays. Meanwhile, millions of workers are just staying home, networking their computer to the ones at their employer's offices, and telecommuting. And an increasing number of organizations are keeping their offices open all the time to accommodate the diverse schedules of employees. It's no longer that unusual for employees at Microsoft, Intel, The Princeton Review, and thousands of other organizations to put in 70- or 80-hour weeks, working through the night and on weekends.

Empowered People

Most organizations that were created before the early 1980s were designed around the notion that there should be a clear division of work and responsibility between management and workers. Managers were to do the planning and thinking, and workers were just to do what they were told. This approach made good sense at the turn of the century, but it doesn't work too well anymore. Most organizations today are redesigning work and jobs so as to let workers make many of the job-related decisions that previously were made exclusively by managers. This transfer of job-related authority and responsibility from managers to workers is called **empowerment**.[60]

What explains this move to empower employees? There are at least three forces at work. First, the workforce has changed. Today's workers are far better educated and trained than they were in the early part of this century. In fact, because of the complexity of many jobs, today's workers are often considerably more knowledgeable than their managers about how best to do their jobs. Second, global competitiveness demands that organizations be able to move fast. Companies must be able to make decisions and implement changes quickly. When the people who actually do the work are allowed to make their own job-related decisions, both the speed and quality of those decisions often improve. Finally, there is the effect of dismantling organizational hierarchies. Organizations have eliminated many middle-management positions and have flattened their structures in order to cut costs and improve responsiveness. This process has left many lower-level managers with a lot more people to supervise. A manager who had only six or eight employees to oversee could closely monitor each person's work and micromanage activities. Now that manager is likely to have twenty or thirty people to oversee and can't possibly know everything that is going on. So managers have been forced to let go of some of their authority.

Few organizations have been untouched by the empowerment movement. Its pervasiveness can be seen with a few examples. At a General Electric lighting plant in Ohio, work teams perform many tasks and assume many of the responsibilities once handled by their supervisors. Childress Buick, an automobile dealer in Phoenix, allows their salespeople to negotiate and finalize deals with customers without any approval from management. NCR has instituted a program that cross-trains even part-time employees to do multiple jobs and to take total responsibility for their work.[61] Roger Meade, the chief executive officer of Scitor Corp., a 200-person firm that provides information systems products and services, tells his employees to make all decisions against this simple standard: "Utilize your best judgment at all times. Ask yourself: Is it fair and reasonable? Is it honest? Does it make good business sense in the context of our established objectives? If you can answer yes to all of these, then proceed. Remember, you are accountable against this policy for all your actions."[62]

Organizing Around Teams

Teams are a structural device that allows organizations to increase flexibility. A recent survey found that 73 percent of U.S. organizations have at least some employees working in teams, most of which are cross-functional or interdepartmental.[63] Why are teams so popular? Division of labor created overfragmented work tasks. People began to lose sight of the big picture. And coordinating activities between departments became increasingly

> Most organizations today are redesigning work and jobs so as to let workers make many of the job-related decisions that previously were made exclusively by managers.

difficult. Cross-functional work teams break down both horizontal and vertical hierarchical barriers, and allow the organization to respond more quickly to changing situations.

▶ Dejobbing and the Loss of Traditional Job Security

Organizations are actually eliminating jobs. By that I mean that the whole notion of jobs, as we have come to know them, is rapidly becoming obsolete.[64] Before 1800, very few people had a "job." People worked hard raising food or making things at home. They had no regular hours, no job descriptions, no bosses, and no employee benefits. Instead, they put in long hours on shifting clusters of tasks, in a variety of locations, on a schedule set by the sun and the weather and the needs of the day. It was the industrial revolution and the creation of large manufacturing companies that brought about the concept of what we have come to think of as jobs. But the conditions that created "the job" are disappearing. Customized production is pushing out mass production; most workers now handle information, not physical products; and competitive conditions are demanding rapid response to changing markets.

In a fast-moving economy, jobs are rigid solutions to a fluid problem. In reality, they are no solution at all. Organizations can rewrite a person's job description occasionally, but not every week. When the work that needs doing changes constantly—which increasingly describes today's world—organizations can't afford the inflexibility of traditional jobs, so they are **dejobbing**. That is, they are replacing many of their traditional jobs with part-time and temporary work situations.[65] They are increasingly relying on "hired guns"—members of the contingent workforce (temporaries, part-timers, consultants, and contract workers)—who join project teams created to complete a specific task. When that task is finished, the team disbands. People then move on to new teams within the organization or join teams in another organization. Some people are working on more than one team at a time.

The dejobbing of work is undermining the security that employees of 20 or more years ago enjoyed. Organizations are increasingly offering people flexibility and autonomy in place of security and predictability.

The dejobbed workforce is well under way. For instance, most employees at Boeing, Intel, and Microsoft are typically assigned to a project when they are hired. As the project changes over time, employee responsibilities and tasks change with it. As projects evolve and new projects are developed, employees are added to and dropped from various projects. At any given time, many employees are working on multiple projects, under several team leaders, keeping different schedules, being in various places, and performing different tasks. This model also describes the majority of jobs in advertising, consulting firms, and the largely freelance workforce of creative and technical people in the entertainment industry.

The dejobbing process will take time to fully enmesh itself. As a result, it may be more realistic to envision today's workforce, and the one in place for the next 15 or 20 years, as made up of three classes of employees that vary in degrees of connectedness to the organization.[66] There will be a small core of permanent employees who have the skills and knowledge that allow the organization to maintain its core competencies. These people will have the security typically associated with what employees had a generation ago when working for a large corporation. A second group will essentially be contract workers. The organization will offer them employment for a specified period of time. This will be the bulk of any organization's workforce. As long as their job lasts and their performance is satisfactory, these contracted employees will have full-time work. Finally, a third set of workers will be part-timers. They will work brief periods, on an as-needed basis. These employees will have minimal loyalty to the organization because the organization will make a minimal commitment to them.

▶ Flexible Compensation

The traditional method of compensating people for their work reflected a time of stability. Pay was determined largely by seniority and job level. So the earnings of a grade-3 computer analyst at Dow Chemical had to fall between $4,225 and $4,960 a month because that was the pay range for that grade level. The trend in recent years has been to make pay more flexible and to reduce the number of grade levels.

By linking pay to performance variables such as individual or team productivity or corporate profits, management is able to turn labor expenses into variable rather than fixed costs and consequently has more flexibility in dealing with labor costs. Another, perhaps less desirable, consequence is that employees' pay is less predictable; it can vary significantly from year to year.

In the past, employees typically had to move up in the organization to get major increases in pay. For instance, in our Dow Chemical example, no matter how much a grade-3 computer analyst contributed to the company, he or she was limited to making no more than $4,960 a month. The latest trend is toward **broadbanding compensation**—replacing multiple pay grades with a few wide scales.[67] So, instead of, say, five computer-analyst grade levels, Dow might establish two with considerably larger salary ranges. This arrangement allows management considerably more flexibility in linking compensation to specific skills and contributions. And it gives managers more freedom to award pay raises without having to give a promotion.

▶ Social Responsibility and Ethics

As noted earlier, society's expectations of business have changed. Cornelius Vanderbilt's "the public be damned" attitude might have been acceptable in 1869, but it certainly is not acceptable in 1999. In the 1950s, a Cleveland steel plant could get away with polluting Lake Erie, but it couldn't today. Even the standards in politics have changed. Twenty-five years ago the public was more tolerant of unethical actions of politicians—for example, profiting from insider information, influence peddling, lying, padding expense accounts, or hiring unqualified friends and relatives. Such practices today are likely to end up on the front page of newspapers and result in full-scale investigations.

One of the ironies of these changing social expectations is shown in Exhibit 1-6 on page 22. Business firms today are more socially responsible than at any time in the recent past. Yet they continue to be frequently criticized for their lack of social responsibility. What has happened is that society's expectations of what is considered "proper conduct" have risen faster than the ability of business to raise its standards.[68] So, even though businesses today are more socially conscious, the public's perception is that they still have significant room for improvement.

Most business firms today recognize that their responsibilities go beyond merely obeying the law and earning a competitive financial return for their owners.[69] **Utilitarianism**, which assesses actions in terms of providing the greatest good for the greatest number, no longer is the single criterion by which business decisions can be judged. It prevailed when organizational performance was assessed by narrow goals such as efficiency, productivity, or profit maximization. As managers have become more aware of the number of stakeholders they must satisfy, they have expanded their decision criteria to include respecting and protecting basic rights of individuals (e.g., privacy, speech, due process) and ensuring that rules are enforced fairly and impartially.[70]

Business firms today are more socially responsible than at any time in the recent past. Yet they continue to be frequently criticized for their lack of social responsibility.

EXHIBIT 1-6

Rising Societal Expectations

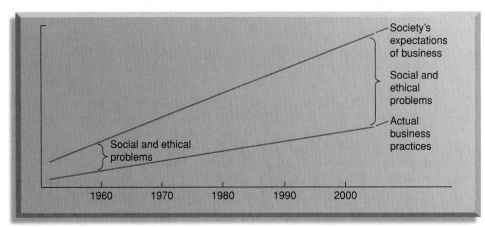

Source: A. B. Carroll, *Social Responsibility of Management*, 1984, p. 14. Reprinted by permission of Prentice Hall, Upper Saddle River, N.J.

Today, companies such as McDonald's, Ben & Jerry's, Timberland Co., Polaroid, and Levi-Strauss have become standard-bearers for responsible and ethical practices. McDonald's is well known for its charitable efforts, including support for Ronald McDonald houses. Ben & Jerry's has become the prototype for a socially responsible firm with its efforts to promote world peace, preserve the environment, and support local businesses. Timberland and Polaroid were both recent recipients of America's Corporate Conscience Awards—the former for community service and the latter for responsiveness to employees. And Levi-Strauss has won accolades for its progressive human resource policies and proactive stance on setting ethical guidelines for doing business with foreign contractors. For instance, the company voluntarily decided to phase out contracts with Chinese clothing manufacturers, citing what it termed "pervasive violations of basic human rights" by the Chinese government.[71]

THE NEW EMPLOYEE

How have all these changes in the economy and in organizations redefined the *employee*? This section answers that question (see Exhibit 1-7).

The Bimodal Split

As recently as 25 years ago, there were plenty of well-paying manufacturing jobs in industries such as steel, automobiles, and rubber for the high school graduate with minimal skills. A young man in Pittsburgh, for example, could graduate from high school and immediately get a relatively high-paying and secure job in a local steel plant. But those jobs have all but disappeared.[72] A good portion of those manufacturing jobs in industrialized countries have been replaced by automated equipment, reconstituted into jobs requiring considerably higher technical skills, or taken by workers in other countries who will do the same work for a fraction of the wages.

The massive decline of blue-collar manufacturing jobs that pay $25,000 to $35,000 a year in current dollars has created a bimodal workforce. As shown in Exhibit 1-8, most

The Changing Employee

EXHIBIT 1-7

Old Employee	New Employee
• Low-skilled jobs in manufacturing pay well	• Low-skilled jobs pay poorly
• Develops narrow, specialized skills	• Develops multiple skills
• Receives job security in return for loyalty	• Job security is minimal
• Organization takes responsibility for career development	• Employee is responsible for career development
• Training occurs before employment	• Retraining is continual
• Is an individual performer	• Is a team player
• Predictability and stability minimize alienation and stress	• Unpredictability and instability heighten alienation and stress

low-skilled workers are at an income level just a few dollars above the minimum wage. High-skilled workers—professionals and technical or knowledge workers who program computers, conduct laboratory tests, fix office machines, and the like—make up almost a completely separate income group whose pay level is almost three times as high as that of most low-skilled workers. These two separate classes of employees differ on more than just their immediate wage levels. They also differ in their potential for future earnings, their mobility, and their job security. Low-skilled workers face a future of permanent low wages, minimal promotion opportunities, and limited bargaining power with employers. In contrast, the high-skilled group will be able to convert the demand for their skills into financial security and career opportunities.

The Bimodal Workforce

EXHIBIT 1-8

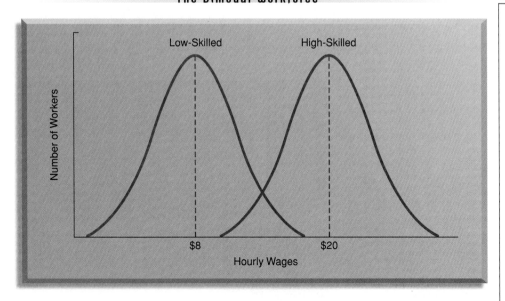

▶ Multiple Skills

Yesterday's successful employee was someone who had perfected a narrow set of specific skills. This made sense when organizations were essentially stable and the skills needed from week to week or year to year stayed relatively constant. The most efficient organizations were ones that relied heavily on work specialization and employees with a narrow set of skills.

Today's ever-changing workplace has significantly cut the useful "shelf life" of an employee's skills. While it might have taken thirty or more years for your grandfather's skills to become obsolete, today's employee is likely to find his or her skills obsolete in just a few years or less.

Employers today are substituting higher-skilled jobs for lower-skilled ones. And they're looking for employees who have multiple skills rather than a narrow specialization. Most of the 5.5 million jobs added in the United States during the first thirty months of the 1990s were in occupations with above-average pay.[73] More than two-thirds of the new jobs created in the past several years have been managerial and professional, especially in health care, education, business services, banking, retailing, and telecommunications. At the same time, manufacturing jobs have generally declined.[74] The need for people to do low-skilled, repetitive tasks on an assembly line dropped considerably in the 1990s. New factory workers rely more on brains than brawn, are able to perform a wide range of high-skilled tasks, and keep their skills current and up to date.[75]

Today's employee needs a multiple set of skills to handle a variety of job tasks. He or she has to be able to move fluidly from one new task to another and between an ever-changing group of projects. The more skills you have, the better able you are to help an organization achieve its goals and the more valuable you are in the job market.

▶ Impermanence

Regardless of skill level, all employees face a world that provides less permanence and predictability than existed just 10 to 20 years ago. The unwritten loyalty contract that previously existed between employees and employers has been irrevocably broken.[76]

John Warner, 44, put in 25 years at Acme Metals, Inc., outside Chicago. Most of that time he was a pipe fitter. When Acme introduced high-tech equipment, it offered employees the opportunity to learn new skills and new jobs. Warner jumped at the chance to become a maintenance technician. To upgrade his skills, the company paid for him to spend nine months, full-time, learning everything from metallurgy, math, and computers to a piece-by-piece study of the new machinery.

Downsizing, reengineering, outsourcing, and dejobbing are major reasons why the vast majority of individuals no longer can expect to have career-long employment with a single large organization. An increasingly large number of employees have entered the contingent workforce.

If the loyalty-for-job-security arrangement is dead, what has taken its place? The new deal essentially says to employees: "We don't owe you anything. We make no promises because we don't know what the future holds. But we have shared economic interests. So you have a job here as long as your contribution to the organization's goals exceeds your cost." And employees are responding by reprioritizing their loyalties. As one expert described it, a worker's first loyalty is to his or her team or project, second to his or her profession, and only third to the place where he or she works.[77]

The new deal is both good news and bad news for employees. First the bad news. Paternalism is on its last legs. So, too, is loyalty, as we came to know it. Employers are no longer responsible for your future. The old notion that you joined an organization when you were young, worked hard for a while, built up substantial credits, then coasted into retirement no longer applies. Job security now is almost completely a function of your keeping your skills current and marketable. When or if your "value added" is less than your cost, your employment is in jeopardy. Now the good news. You have choices. You have the right to demand interesting work, the freedom and resources to perform it well, pay that reflects your contribution, and opportunities to learn skills that increase your market value. Moreover, persons who work hard and make a valuable contribution are less likely to have to tolerate working with unproductive colleagues than they would have been in the old, more-permanent structure.

Self-Directed Careers

The new compact between employers and employees transfers responsibility for career development from the organization to the employee.[78] So today's employees are becoming more concerned than ever with keeping skills current and developing new skills. They see learning as a lifelong process. At one time, a skill learned in youth could provide a living for life. Now technology changes so rapidly that as soon as you have learned something, that "something" becomes obsolete. In this climate, employees are increasingly recognizing that "if you snooze, you lose." There will always be other people out there who are keeping current and who are ready to assume your work responsibilities if you show signs of falling behind.

Some analysts say that workers can expect to change careers—not just jobs, but careers—three or four times during their working lives.[79] If they are right, today's worker must be prepared to go back to school and learn new skills at a minimum of every 5 to 10 years. Since fewer and fewer employers are providing this retraining, most employees will be balancing current work responsibilities with taking courses during their off hours. In the same way that TQM emphasizes continuous improvement, self-directed careers require continuous training.

Continual Retraining

The changing workplace, obsolescence and the need for multiple skills, self-directed careers, and dejobbing are forcing employees to become continual learners. "Going back to school" is becoming commonplace for workers of all types.

In previous generations, skill updating and retraining tended to take place after a job or industry suffered a major setback. For most workers, this wasn't likely to happen more than once or twice during their working lifetime. The automobile, for example, required a lot of horseshoers to retrain for new employment opportunities. Automated equipment similarly forced hundreds of thousands of U.S. coal miners to retrain for other jobs. And almost everyone over age 40 who makes a living as an accountant has had to update his or her skills with computers.

Today, technical colleges, community colleges, universities, and private training organizations find their classrooms filled with individuals who have come to terms with the new workplace mantra: "Keep current to keep employed." Some organizations are providing in-house training for their people. But for those individuals whose employers aren't taking the initiative, the responsibility falls back on workers to find out what future skills they'll need and then to develop those skills.

▶ Being a Team Player

With work being increasingly organized around teams, employees have had to become team players.[80] This means developing the kind of skills necessary for being able to contribute to high-performance teams—especially problem-solving and group decision-making skills and good listening, feedback, conflict resolution, and other interpersonal skills.

Being a team player is a particular challenge for people who have grown up in cultures that encourage and reward individual achievement. They typically find it difficult to think like a team player and to sublimate their personal ambitions for the good of the team. Consequently, team-training programs are popular in companies such as AT&T, Ford, and Motorola (which historically grew and prospered by fostering individual initiative) and among employees raised in the United States, Canada, Great Britain, and Australia (countries that instill individualism in their citizens from an early age).

▶ Coping with Alienation and Stress

For an increasing number of people, especially professionals, the changing world of work means long hours, little time for family, and increased feelings of alienation and stress. Take the case of Brad Slutsky.[81] A partner in the Atlanta law firm of King & Spaulding, he regularly puts in 60 to 80 hours a week. He rarely gets home for dinner, and he works many weekends. During one recent summer, he went five months without a day off. On his "free" nights, he works on outside activities that might help build his practice.

While not typical, more and more professionals' lives are looking like Slutsky's. And alienation and stress are not the sole provinces of professionals. It's affecting workers in all types of jobs. Downsizing and reengineering have resulted in many employees having to take on new tasks and, very often, having to work harder. To reduce costs, for instance, companies are frequently increasing overtime among their high-skilled employees. By so doing, the companies don't have to find new workers, train them, or provide additional costly benefits.

A major source of alienation and stress has been the downsizing movement. Layoffs have become a permanent part of today's economy, in good times as well as bad.

Brad Slutsky rarely sees his three kids. But he has photos to remind him.

For instance, through November 1996, even after more than five years of economic recovery, the number of layoffs announced by U.S. companies had increased 14 percent from a year earlier.[82] In 1996, 49 percent of workers polled said they were somewhat worried or very worried that someone in their household might be laid off within two or three years.[83] And among those who do get laid off, only a minority do as well as they had been. Among one study of long-tenured workers who had been laid off, only 34 percent were earning as much as or more than in their previous jobs. The rest were still looking for a job, were working part-time, were self-employed, or were working full-time for less money than before.[84]

And survivors of downsizing are experiencing alienation and stress as well.[85] Studies confirm that survivors of downsizing experience similar feelings of frustration, anxiety, and loss that people who are laid off do. They feel the strain from having to take on new tasks and learn new skills, the stress from increased workloads imposed when they assume the work of those laid off, and the insecurity about their job future. So even those who survive layoffs are experiencing increased levels of alienation and stress.

There is a variety of additional material available on the CD-ROM and companion Web site that accompany this text. You can access this information through the CD-ROM or by visiting the Web site at <**www.prenhall.com/robbins**>.

SUMMARY

(This summary is organized by the chapter-opening learning objectives on page 2.)

1. Globalization has increased competition. Rivals can now come from the other side of the world as well as the other side of town, so organizations must be flexible and responsive if they are to survive. Globalization also creates tremendously expanded opportunities for organizations to offer their products and services worldwide.

2. The first wave was agriculture (up to the 1890s). The second was industrialization (about 1900 to the 1960s). The third wave is information technology (beginning in the 1970s). Today, agriculture represents less than 5 percent of employment in industrialized countries. Meanwhile, the information age has significantly reduced low-skilled, blue-collar jobs in manufacturing, but it has created abundant opportunities for educated and skilled technical specialists, professionals, and other knowledge workers.

3. Organizations externalize risk through subcontracting out work, licensing products to others, and forming joint partnerships.

4. The key elements in total quality management are intense focus on the customer, concern for continual improvement in the quality of everything the organization does, accurate measurement, and empowerment of employees.

5. Organizations are reengineering work processes in order to maintain competitiveness. New technologies can bring about dramatic improvements in productivity. Reengineering encompasses looking at all work processes from scratch. It offers opportunities for improvements of far greater magnitude than the traditional approach of incremental change.

6. The contingent workforce includes temporaries, part-timers, consultants, contract workers, and others who are employed on a nonpermanent basis.

7. The bimodal workforce represents low-skilled workers earning little above minimum wage and high-skilled professional, technical, and knowledge workers who earn solid middle-class wages. The low-skilled workers not only earn low wages, but they have little opportunity to improve their economic status, have restricted mobility, and have weak job security.

8. The loyalty-for-job-security arrangement has been irrevocably broken. Employers need flexibility today, and long-term job security is inconsistent with that objective. As a result, employees are increasingly placing loyalty to their work group and to their profession ahead of loyalty to their employer.

REVIEW QUESTIONS

1. Describe the shift in types of jobs in the workforce during the twentieth century.

2. What explains the increased popularity of entrepreneurship in the past 20 years?

3. What is the role of the customer in TQM? In reengineering?

4. How has workforce diversity affected the manager's job?

5. Do you think downsizing is a fad or a permanent organizational strategy? Support your position.

6. How has a focus on core competencies changed the ways in which organizations are structured and managed?

7. What are the implications of outsourcing for large corporations? For small businesses?

8. If organizations "dejob," what employment opportunities might the displaced employees have?

9. What caused the bimodal workforce?

10. What kind of things can you do if you accept responsibility for your own career development?

IF I WERE THE MANAGER . . .

Can Outsourcing Be Carried Too Far?

I can't pick up a business magazine that doesn't have something about outsourcing. To improve efficiency, it seems like every company is going to outsiders to buy products and services that once were made by their own employees. I run a small business that manufactures bath and kitchen faucets. Our primary market is builders and contractors. Specifically, we provide economy products for those putting up low-cost single-family homes and modestly priced apartments.

I took over the business last year from my father, who started it in 1964. I not only inherited the factory, but I also became responsible for the 75 people that my dad had employed. Most have been with us for at least 25 years. But my dad was a control freak. So we did everything we could in-house. That includes the actual manufacturing process, all purchasing, accounting, human resources, warehousing, and transportation coordination.

And we have a sales staff of ten people who call on clients throughout the southeastern part of the United States.

Our employees aren't unionized, so I have a great deal of discretion on employee matters. I've been thinking that I should give serious consideration to outsourcing some of our activities. For instance, I think I could save more than $100,000 a year by eliminating our in-house sales force and using outside representatives. The downside: Many of these sales people have been with us for a very long time. They have good relations with our customers. And would outside reps work as hard for our customers as our inside people? I think we could also save serious money by selling our warehouse and using an outside facility. Similarly, I could outsource much of our accounting, transportation/distribution, and human resource functions, but it could hurt internal morale by cutting the number of people in our administrative office in half. I have even given some thought to selling the factory and having our products manufactured in Southeast Asia or Latin America. I think we could cut our hourly labor costs from $15 an hour to under $4. Per-worker productivity would be a lot lower, but labor costs would still be much less.

How do I make the choice of what functions we continue to do in-house and which ones we outsource? At the extreme, with a staff of maybe three or four, I could run the whole company by outsourcing. We could do the design and market plans, then job the rest out. But we would be giving up a lot of control. An outside manufacturer, for instance, could easily rip off our designs and proprietary technology. And what price do I put on loyalty? Can I expect people in outsource firms to be as conscientious and dependable as my own people?

If you were me, what would you do?

SKILL EXERCISE

Identifying Cross-Cultural Differences

The people of Great Britain and the United States speak the same language. But their use of that language varies considerably. Break into groups of four or five. You have 20 minutes to complete this exercise.

Review the following two lists of words. List A is a list of British words and phrases. For each term, write the American word or phrase that means the same thing. List B is a list of American words and phrases. For each term, write the British word or phrase that means the same thing. When you have completed the exercise, your instructor will provide you with the correct answers. Then discuss the implications of this exercise for cross-cultural understanding and managing people from diverse cultures.

List A		List B	
roundabout	fifty "p"	subway	elevator
bonnet	braces	restroom	sweater
boot	"Old Bill"	check in a	cookie
plasters	queue	restaurant	knives, forks,
seven stone	pram	police officer	spoons
		truck	parking lot

Source: Based on G. D. Klein, "Introducing the Largely Land-Locked to Cross-Cultural Differences," *Journal of Management Education*, February 1995, pp. 119–21.

TEAM ACTIVITY

Past, Present, and Future

Break the class into groups of approximately 5 members each. The groups have 40 minutes to complete the following exercise:

Describe your perception of the world of work in 1960. Look at the following issues:

1. What did successful organizations look like?
2. What did a successful career in these organizations look like?
3. What was the role of clerical personnel?
4. What was the role of knowledge workers?
5. How would you characterize the demographics of the workforce (age, race, gender, family status, education)?

Now look ahead to the year 2020. Answer the same questions, only now in the future:

1. What will successful organizations look like?
2. What will a successful career in these organizations look like?
3. What will be the role of clerical personnel?
4. What will be the role of knowledge workers?
5. What will the workforce's demographics look like?

When finished, select someone from your group to be its spokesperson. This individual should be prepared to make a five-minute presentation to the class on your group's analysis.

Is This Anyway to Treat Customers?

In an era when successful companies believe they have to coddle their customers, Fry's Electronics treats their customers with disdain. Customers have to deal with a security system that treats them as a potential thief, salespeople who know almost nothing about the products they sell, and a management attitude that frowns on returns. Yet these customers keep coming back.

In 1985, John Fry built his first electronics superstore in northern California. There are now 16 of these stores. While competitors like Circuit City, Best Buy, and the Good Guys endure falling sales and profits, Fry's just keeps getting bigger and selling more. Fry's turns over its entire inventory once a month—more than twice as fast as its competitors. And per-store annual gross of $85 million is among the highest in the industry. From its California base, Fry's has recently acquired six Incredible Universe megastores and expanded into Arizona, Texas, and Oregon.

Walk into a Fry's Electronics store. You'll have to run a gauntlet of security guards, who look for anything suspicious. If you look up, you'll see rows of security cameras. They cover the ceiling in a grid, spaced just 15 to 20 feet apart. Now go over and ask a salesperson a question. Don't expect too much information. Instead of hiring knowledgeable salespeople, Fry's hires neophytes for about $6 an hour, paying few commissions. If you buy something and then try to return it for a refund, good luck! Employees at the return desk are given bonuses based on the number of customers they talk into taking store credit instead of cash. Getting a refund can take weeks. The company overtly makes getting a refund hard to discourage the practice. The point is to wear customers down until they give up.

Who shops at Fry's? And why do they keep coming when they're treated like dirt? Fry's customers tend to be hard-core techies. They know about the products they want to buy and don't require much information from sales staff. And they keep coming back because the stores offer one-stop shopping with the best prices and selection in their communities. Fry's beats the competition's prices by seeking innovative revenue sources and keeping its costs down. For instance, like supermarkets, it charges suppliers fees for freestanding placements at the end of aisles. A single Fry's store may contain more than 400 premium selling spots for which it receives hundreds of thousands of dollars. In addition to brand names, it sells a lot of no-name brands with slick features. These no-name products generate a higher margin. And Fry's Orwellian security system keeps theft levels to a fraction of those of its competitors.

QUESTIONS

1. Why does Fry's approach to customers work?
2. Do you think it will continue to work? Why or why not?
3. What does this case say to those who argue that "the customer is king"?
4. Do you think Fry's management is unethical? Explain.

Source: Based on A. Marsh and S. Woolley, "The Customer Is Always Right? Not at Fry's," *Forbes*, November 3, 1997, pp. 86–89.

The Changing World of Corporate Loyalty

ABCNEWS

The list of blue chip companies handing out pink slips continues to grow. Sears announces 50,000 jobs will be eliminated; IBM says it will cut 63,000 jobs; Kodak plans to lay off 10,000 employees. And entire job categories have disappeared before our eyes. For example, between 1986 and 1994, banks eliminated 41,000 tellers, most of whom were replaced by ATMs. Increasingly, there is no such thing as job security. The following comments by Albert Dunlap, former CEO of Scott Paper Company and Sunbeam Corporation, although harsh, capture the essence of the new employer-employee arrangement. Dunlap, incidentally, has built a reputation for cutting jobs: hence his nickname, Chainsaw Al. He begins by defending his nickname.

"It's not offensive because I've gone into companies that have had very poor results. The company, before I joined Scott, they lost $277 million and were on credit watch, and I was forced to fire about 35 percent of the people, but 65 percent of the people had a more secure future than they've ever had before, and that's what people don't realize. I'm the doctor. I didn't create the problem."

"The reason to be in business is to make money for your shareholders. The shareholders own the company. They take all the risks. No company ever gives the shareholders their money back when they go bust, and you have an awesome responsibility to see that they get the proper return for their risk."

"The free enterprise system is very efficient when it's allowed to perform. America was becoming unproductive in global economies. American companies were failing. Because people have come in and made the tough decisions, American companies are now becoming successful. They're becoming global giants. And over time, they will create considerably more employment. And yes, some people have to lose their jobs, but as I said before, that's a lot better than everyone losing their jobs."

"The world has changed over the last 20 years. But business is not a social experiment. You exist in business to be competitive, to come out with the best products, the best facilities, and to create a future for your people, and the companies that do well must have good products, must have good employee relations, because it all figures into the future of the company."

"The business role is to provide as secure a future for its employees as it can, and within doing that, some people lose their job. That has happened since the beginning of time. And because people didn't take their responsibilities to run efficient

corporations seriously, we're in the situation we are now. And the last person that should arbitrate it is the government, the largest business in America with the worst balance sheet, the poorest management, services people don't want, and a bloated cost structure."

QUESTIONS

1. Do you think Albert Dunlap is accurately describing today's business climate? Why or why not?

2. Do you believe that there's a difference between downsizing for organizational survival and downsizing for "economic reasons"? Discuss.

3. What are the implications of Dunlap's comments for managers? For employees?

4. Dunlap was fired from his job at Sunbeam in 1998. If you were on the board of directors of a company in serious financial trouble would you consider hiring Dunlap? Why or why not?

Source: Based on "Corporate Layoffs and the Fate of American Workers," *ABC News Nightline*, aired February 14, 1996.

NOTES

1. Based on J. Guyon, "ABB Fuses Units with One Set of Values," *Wall Street Journal*, October 2, 1996, p. A12; A. Saltzman, "You, Inc.," *U.S. News & World Report*, October 28, 1996, pp. 66–71; and S. G. Thomas, "No Deadwood Here," *U.S. News & World Report*, October 28, 1996, pp. 83–84.
2. "Buying American," *Forbes*, July 28, 1997, pp. 218–20.
3. See E. S. Hardy, "The Forbes Foreign Rankings," *Forbes*, July 17, 1995, pp. 226–58.
4. Cited in *Business Week*, July 1, 1996, p. 1.
5. A. Toffler, *The Third Wave* (New York: Bantam, 1984).
6. W. Bridges, *JobShift* (Reading, MA: Addison-Wesley, 1994), p. xi.
7. This section is based on T. M. Godbout, "Employment Change and Sectoral Distribution in 10 Countries, 1970–90," *Monthly Labor Review*, October 1993, pp. 3–10; "Historical Trends, Current Uncertainties," *Monthly Labor Review*, November 1993, p. 8; K. H. Hammonds, "The New World of Work," *Business Week*, October 17, 1994, pp. 76–87; and J. Greenwald, "The New Service Class," *Time*, November 14, 1994, pp. 72–74.
8. P. F. Drucker, "The Age of Social Transformation," *Atlantic Monthly*, November 1994, p. 56.
9. Ibid.
10. *Monthly Labor Review*, October 1993, p. 9.
11. Drucker, "The Age of Social Transformation," p. 56.
12. Ibid., p. 62.
13. See H. N. Fullerton, "The 2005 Labor Force: Growing, But Slowly," *Monthly Labor Review*, November 1995, pp. 29–44; J. J. Friedman and N. DiTomaso, "Myths about Diversity: What Managers Need to Know about Changes in the U.S. Labor Force," *California Management Review*, Summer 1996, pp. 54–72; and R. W. Judy and C. D'Amico, *Workforce 2020: Work and Workers in the 21st Century* (Indianapolis: Hudson Institute, 1997), pp. 52–53.
14. Cited in V. Elliott and A. Orgera, "Competing for and with Workforce 2000," *HR Focus*, June 1993, p. 3.
15. See, for example, R. N. Kanungo and J. A. Conger, "Promoting Altruism as a Corporate Goal," *The Executive*, August 1993, pp. 37–48.
16. J. Martin, "Good Citizenship Is Good Business," *Fortune*, March 21, 1994, pp. 15–16.
17. C. K. Prahalad and G. Hamel, "Strategy as a Field of Study: Why Search for a New Paradigm?" *Strategic Management Journal*, Summer 1994, p. 8.
18. C. Caggiano, "Is Social Responsibility a Crock?" *INC.*, May 1993, p. 15.
19. C. Vesper, *Entrepreneurship and National Policy* (Chicago: Heller Institute, 1983); D. L. Birch, "The Truth about Start-Ups," *Inc.*, January 1988, pp. 14–15; B. O'Reilly, "The New Face of Small Business," *Fortune*, May 2, 1992, p. 82; and M. Selz, "Entrepreneurship in U.S. Is Taking Off," *Wall Street Journal*, December 13, 1996, p. B5B.

20. Cited in *Peru Inc.*, March–April 1997, p. 5.

21. S. Leonard, "Love That Customer," *Management Review*, October 1987, pp. 36–39.

22. See J. Lorinc, "Now the Customer Is Job One," *Canadian Business*, July 1997, pp. 22–28; and J. DeYoung and G. Jidoun, "Service Is Alive and Well," *Working Woman*, November 1997, pp. 18–20.

23. Quoted in J. S. McClenahen, "Can You Manage in the New Economy?" *Industry Week*, April 5, 1993, p. 28.

24. Cited in "A Matter of Priorities," *New York Times*, February 19, 1995, p. F23.

25. A. V. Feigenbaum, quoted in *Boardroom Reports*, April 1, 1991, p. 16.

26. See, for example, "Trends: Bids & Privatization," *Latin Trade*, April 1998, pp. 96–97.

27. See, for example, "Workplace Trends," *Training*, October 1994, p. 60.

28. C. Ansberry, "Workers Are Forced to Take More Jobs with Few Benefits," *Wall Street Journal*, March 11, 1993, p. A1.

29. Cited in S. Caudron, "Contingent Work Force Spurs HR Planning," *Personnel Journal*, July 1994, p. 54; and L. Helm, "Microsoft Testing Limits on Temp Worker Use," *Los Angeles Times*, December 7, 1997, p. D14.

30. D. Bentley, "Part Works," *International Management*, July/August 1994, p. 12.

31. Cited in E. L. Andrews, "Only Employment for Many in Europe Is Part-Time Work," *New York Times*, Sepember 1, 1997, p. A1 and B7.

32. Ibid.

33. Cited in R. W. Judy and C. D'Amico, *Workforce 2020*, p. 56.

34. L. Uchitelle, "Strike Points to Inequalities in a Two-Tier Job Market," *New York Times*, August 8, 1997, p. A15.

35. This section on outsourcing is based on "Outsourcing," *Fortune*, December 12, 1994, pp. 52–92; S. Lubove, "Fixing the Mix," *Forbes*, April 10, 1995, pp. 86–87; and P. Klebnikov, "Focus, Focus, Focus," *Forbes*, September 11, 1995, pp. 42–44. For a discussion of the downside of outsourcing, see S. Leibs, "Outsourcing's No Cure-All," *Industry Week*, April 6, 1998, pp. 20–28.

36. Cited in T. A. Stewart, "Welcome to the Revolution," *Fortune*, December 13, 1993, p. 76.

37. See, for example, D. M. Rousseau and K. A. Wade-Benzoni, "Changing Individual-Organization Attachments: A Two-Way Street," in A. Howard (ed.), *The Changing Nature of Work* (San Francisco: Jossey-Bass, 1995), pp. 305–14; S. R. Cohany, "Workers in Alternative Employment Arrangements," *Monthly Labor Review*, October 1996, pp. 31–45; and T. Aeppel, "Full Time, Part Time, Temp—All See the Job in a Different Light," *Wall Street Journal*, March 18, 1997, p. A1.

38. See, for instance, J. K. Ford and S. Fisher, "The Role of Training in a Changing Workplace and Workforce: New Perspectives and Approaches," and S. A. Lobel and E. E. Kossek, "Human Resource Strategies to Support Diversity in Work and Personal Lifestyles: Beyond the 'Family-Friendly' Organization," both in E. E. Kossek and S. A. Lobel (eds.), *Managing Diversity* (Cambridge, MA: Blackwell Publishers, 1996), pp. 164–93 and 221–44, respectively.

39. "Hewlett-Packard Discovers Diversity Is Good for Business," *Los Angeles Times*, May 17, 1993, p. 16.

40. G. Capowski, "Ageism: The New Diversity Issue," *Management Review*, October 1994, pp. 10–15; and "Valuing Older Workers: A Study of Costs and Productivity," prepared for the American Association of Retired Persons by ICF Incorporated, 1995.

41. B. Hynes-Grace, "To Thrive, Not Merely Survive," in Textbook Authors Conference Presentations (Washington, DC: American Association of Retired Persons, 1992), p. 12.

42. See, for instance, M. N. Martinez, "An Inside Look at Making the Grade," *HRMagazine*, March 1998, pp. 61–66.

43. A. Fisher, "The 100 Best Companies to Work for in America," *Fortune*, January 12, 1998, pp. 69–70; and L. Grant, "Happy Workers, High Returns," *Fortune*, January 12, 1998, p. 81.

44. M. Galen, "Work & Family," *Business Week*, June 28, 1993, p. 82.

45. See, for instance, R. R. Gehani, "Quality Value-Chain: A Meta-Synthesis of Frontiers of Quality Movement," *The Executive*, May 1993, pp. 29–42; M. Sashkin and K. J. Kiser, *Putting Total Quality Management to Work* (San Francisco: Berrett-Koehler, 1993); D. Greising, "Quality: How to Make It Pay," *Business Week*, August 8, 1994, pp. 54–59; J. R. Hackman and R. Wageman, "Total Quality Management: Empirical, Conceptual, and Practical Issues," *Administrative Science Quarterly*, June 1995, pp. 309–42; and R. Reed, D. J. Lemak, and J. C. Montgomery, "Beyond Process: TQM Content and Firm Performance," *Academy of Management Review*, January 1996, pp. 173–202.

46. Cited in "Workplace Trends," *Training*, October 1996, p. 68.

47. M. Frohman, "Remything Management," *Industry Week*, March 21, 1994, p. 24; and M. J. Zbaracki, "The Rhetoric and Reality of Total Quality Management," *Administrative Science Quarterly*, September 1998, pp. 602–36.

48. Cited in "Innovations," *Business Week*, September 7, 1998, p. 111.

49. See "Happy Labor Day," *Time*, September 4, 1995, p. 21; "Loser Layoffs," *U.S. News & World Report*, November 25, 1996, pp. 73–81; and A. Bernstein, "Who Says Job Anxiety Is Easing?" *Business Week*, April 7, 1997, p. 38.

50. M. F. R. Kets de Vries and K. Balazs, "The Downside of Downsizing," *Human Relations*, January 1997, pp. 11–50.

51. J. A. Byrne, "Why Downsizing Looks Different These Days," *Business Week*, October 10, 1994, p. 43.

52. M. Hammer and J. Champy, *Reengineering the Corporation: A Manifesto for Business Revolution* (New York: HarperBusiness, 1993); and J. Champy, *Reengineering Management: The Mandate for New Leadership* (New York: HarperBusiness, 1995).

53. Cited in *Training*, October 1996, p. 68.

54. Cited in "Business Process Reengineering," *Industrial Management*, September 1994, p. 62.

55. J. Teresko, "Japan: Reengineering vs. Tradition," *Industry Week*, September 5, 1994, pp. 62–70.

56. Hammer and Champy, *Reengineering the Corporation*.

57. R. W. Judy and C. D'Amico, *Workforce 2020*, pp. 8, 81–83.

58. G. Hamel and C. K. Prahalad, "The Core Competence of the Corporation," *Harvard Business Review*, May–June 1990, pp. 79–91; C. Long and M. Vickers-Koch, "Using Core Capabilities to Create Competitive Advantage," *Organizational Dynamics*, Summer 1995, pp. 7–22; and D. Lei,

M. A. Hitt, and R. Bettis, "Dynamic Core Competencies Through Meta-Learning and Strategic Context," *Journal of Management*, vol. 22, no. 4, 1996, pp. 549–69.

59. See, for instance, S. Greengard, "Workers Go Virtual," *Personnel Journal*, September 1994, p. 71.

60. See K. W. Thomas and B. A. Velthouse, "Cognitive Elements of Empowerment: An 'Interpretive' Model of Instrinsic Task Motivation," *Academy of Management Review*, October 1990, pp. 666–81; J. L. Cotton, *Employee Involvement* (Newbury Park, CA: Sage, 1993); and R. E. Quinn and G. M. Spreitzer, "The Road to Empowerment: Seven Questions Every Leader Should Consider," *Organizational Dynamics*, Autumn 1997, pp. 37–50.

61. T. Catchpole, "Empowering Part-Time Workers," *Industry Week*, March 16, 1992, pp. 18–24.

62. M. A. Verespej, "Roger Meade: Running on People Power," *Industry Week*, October 18, 1993, pp. 13–18.

63. Cited in "Teams," *Training*, October 1996, p. 69.

64. This section is largely based on W. Bridges, *JobShift: How to Prosper in a Workplace Without Jobs* (Reading, MA: Addison-Wesley, 1994).

65. B. Ettorre, "The Contingent Workforce Moves Mainstream," *Management Review*, February 1994, pp. 11–16.

66. See B. O'Reilly, "The New Deal: What Companies and Employees Owe One Another," *Fortune*, June 13, 1994, p. 52.

67. See, for instance, K. Jacobs, "The Broad View," *Wall Street Journal*, April 10, 1997, p. R10.

68. A. B. Carroll, *Social Responsibility of Management* (New York: Macmillan, 1984).

69. See, for example, R. A. Buchholz, *Essentials of Public Policy for Management*, 2nd ed. (Upper Saddle River, NJ: Prentice Hall, 1990).

70. G. F. Cavanagh, D. J. Moberg, and M. Valasquez, "The Ethics of Organizational Politics," *Academy of Management Journal*, June 1981, pp. 363–74.

71. J. Impoco, "Working for Mr. Clean Jeans," *U.S. News & World Report*, August 2, 1993, pp. 49–50.

72. See S. Dentzer, "The Vanishing Dream," *U.S. News & World Report*, April 22, 1991, pp. 39–43; A. Bernstein, "The Global Economy: Who Gets Hurt," *Business Week*, August 10, 1992, pp. 48–53; P. T. Kilborn, "For High School Graduates, a Job Market of Dead Ends," *New York Times*, May 30, 1994, p. 1; L. S. Richman, "The New Worker Elite," *Fortune*, August 22, 1994, pp. 56–66; and H. Schachter, "The Dispossessed," *Canadian Business*, May 1995, pp. 30–40.

73. A. Howard (ed.), *The Changing Nature of Work*, p. 94.

74. Ibid.

75. S. Baker, "The New Factory Worker," *Business Week*, September 30, 1996, pp. 59–68.

76. See, for example, S. Sherman, "A Brave New Darwinian Workplace," *Fortune*, January 25, 1993, pp. 50–56; "Jobs in an Age of Insecurity," *Time*, November 22, 1993, pp. 32–39; O'Reilly, "The New Deal"; T. Brown, "Life Without Job Security," *Industry Week*, August 15, 1994, pp. 24–32; H. Lancaster, "A New Social Contract to Benefit Employer and Employee," *Wall Street Journal*, November 29, 1994, p. B1; and P. T. Kilborn, "Even in Good Times, It's Hard Times for Workers," *New York Times*, July 3, 1995, p. A1.

77. Cited in C. Rapoport, "Charles Handy Sees the Future," *Fortune*, October 31, 1994, p. 168.

78. See, for example, B. Filipczak, "You're On Your Own: Training, Employability, and the New Employment Contract," *Training*, January 1995, pp. 29–36; D. T. Hall and P. H. Mirvis, "Careers as Lifelong Learning," in A. Howard (ed.), *The Changing Nature of Work*, pp. 323–61; and M. Arthur and D. Rousseau, eds., *The Boundaryless Career* (New York: Oxford University Press, 1996).

79. Cited in M. Calabresi, J. Van Tassel, M. Riley, and J. R. Szczesny, "Jobs in an Age of Insecurity," *Time*, November 22, 1993, p. 38.

80. This section is based on J. R. Katzenbach and D. K. Smith, *The Wisdom of Teams* (Boston: Harvard Business School Press, 1993), pp. 43–64; and T. D. Schellhardt, "To Be a Star Among Equals, Be a Team Player," *Wall Street Journal*, April 20, 1994, p. B1.

81. B. Morris, "Is Your Family Wrecking Your Career?" *Fortune*, March 17, 1997, pp. 71–90.

82. Cited in "Though Upbeat on Economy, Americans Still Fear for Their Jobs," *Manpower Argus*, February 1997, p. 2. See also A. Bernstein, "Who Says Job Anxiety Is Easing?" *Business Week*, April 7, 1997, p. 38.

83. Ibid.

84. Ibid.

85. See S. P. Robbins, "Layoff Survivor Syndrome: A Missing Topic in OB," *Journal of Management Education*, February 1999, pp. 31–43.

Chapter

MANAGING ORGANIZATIONS AND PEOPLE: WHO, WHAT, AND WHY?

MANAGING IS LIKE HOLDING A DOVE IN YOUR HAND.
IF YOU SQUEEZE TOO TIGHT, YOU KILL IT. OPEN
YOUR HAND TOO MUCH, YOU LET IT GO.

T. LASORDA

LEARNING OBJECTIVES

After studying this chapter, you should be able to:

1. Define who managers are.

2. Explain why there are managers.

3. Define an organization.

4. Contrast management and organizational behavior.

5. Describe four management functions.

6. Identify four general and six specific skills needed by managers.

7. Contrast the managerial role of coach versus boss.

8. Explain how chaos and ambiguity can be turned into an opportunity.

9. Contrast effectiveness and efficiency.

10. Assess an organization's effectiveness.

Julie Herendeen and Richard Thibeault probably don't know it, but their jobs represent what many managers' work lives will probably look like in the very near future. Herendeen (see photo) is a group product manager at Netscape, the company that dominates the Internet browser software market, at their headquarters in Mountain View, California.[1] Her team is responsible for Netscape Navigator Personal Edition 2.0—a program that helps users find what they're looking for on the Internet. What makes Herendeen's managerial job "cutting-edge" is that while she holds ultimate responsibility for her product's success, she has limited authority. The engineers and marketers who work on her product, for instance, don't report directly to her. They report to their respective managers in engineering and marketing. So one of the major challenges in Herendeen's job is "managing" people over whom she has no formal authority. Instead of being able to tell people what to do, she has to rely on her ability to persuade and influence. In the recent past and certainly in the coming years, more and more managers are going to find themselves like Julie Herendeen—overseeing project or product teams and managing people who don't directly report to them.

Richard Thibeault is the 46-year-old manager of an Au Bon Pain bakery café in Boston. He oversees a small staff. He hires people. He does performance appraisals. He worries about falling sales. But Thibeault represents a rapidly growing breed of individuals. They carry the title of manager, but they essentially lead a blue-collar work life.[2] They put in long hours, have little power or autonomy, and earn modest pay. Richard Thibeault, for instance, regularly works 70 hours a week. He spends a good part of his time baking muffins, preparing soups, hauling around racks of croissants, and doing similar nonmanagerial tasks that are also done by those he employs. He has little input into major decisions at the café. Those are made by higher-level executives in the Au Bon Pain organization. Thibeault is assigned productivity quotas, told which products to push and which to drop, and who and how many to hire. He earns about $35,000 to $37,000 a year, including bonus. This, as he notes, equates to about $8 an hour. The part-time college students he employs are making only a dollar an hour less! In the past decade, the percentage of U.S. workers classified as "managers" has increased from 11 percent to 14.5 percent. For many of them—such as the manager at your local McDonald's, the assistant manager at your neighborhood discount drugstore, the manager of a nearby travel agency, the head of your branch bank—their jobs are far from the white-collar status positions normally associated with the term *manager*.

The jobs performed by managers have undergone a dramatic change in recent years. What most managers do today looks quite a bit different from what managers were doing only 15 years ago. As Julie Herendeen is finding at Netscape, the manager's job is increasingly working with people over whom she has little or no authority. Similarly, as we saw with Richard Thibeault, the line between managerial and nonmanagerial tasks is becoming increasingly blurred for many people in management positions.

In chapter 1 we described how change is reshaping the economy, organizations, and employees' jobs. Those changes, of course, are also radically reshaping the manager's job. In this chapter, we lay the groundwork for understanding who managers are, what they do, and how their jobs are changing. We conclude this chapter with a model of the manager's job. This model shows how chapters 3 through 18 of this book tie together to capture the challenges and opportunities facing today's and tomorrow's managers.

Who are managers? What, if anything, differentiates managers from other employees in an organization? And, for that matter, what is an organization? We'll answer those questions in this section.

MANAGERS AND THEIR TERRAIN

▶ What Is a Manager?

Walter Shipley is the chief executive officer (CEO) of Chase Manhattan Corp. Michael Walsh is an elementary school principal in Tempe, Arizona. Mary Jean Giroux is a retirement-products supervisor at Canada's London Life Insurance Co. Theresa Gonzalez works as a regional director with the U.S. Internal Revenue Service. And Yong-Chang Chu is a construction foreman with Hong Kong–based Hutchison Whampoa. Despite the fact that these people have jobs with different titles and work in organizations that do very different things, they all have one thing in common—they're managers. But as we saw with Richard Thibeault, merely calling someone a manager doesn't mean he or she does only managerial tasks or even a common set of tasks.

Until very recently, we were safe in defining managers as "individuals who oversee the activities of others."[3] We could also confidently differentiate "managers" from "operatives"; the latter term describes people who work directly on a job or task and have no managerial responsibilities. This is no longer true.[4] Today's manager may have no direct subordinates. He or she is likely to be viewed as the team coach, facilitator, or even as a co-equal member of the team, with no more authority than anyone else on the team. Additionally, while an increasing number of managers are also performing nonmanagerial tasks, more and more so-called *operative employees* are assuming responsibilies that traditionally were deemed as belonging to management. So definitions we've used in the past no longer apply.

Any definition today must reflect that many traditional workers' jobs now include managerial activities, especially on teams. For instance, team members are developing plans, making decisions, and monitoring their own performance. And on self-directed teams—a rapidly growing way to organize groups of workers—no one person oversees the group or is singularly accountable for the team's performance.

So how do we define *manager*? A **manager** is a person who integrates the work of others. That might mean direct responsibility for a group of people. It might mean supervising a single person. It might be coordinating individuals in other departments or working with people from other organizations. And it includes facilitators or leaders who integrate work-team activities.

▶ Why Do We Have Managers?

What would a company such as Eastman Kodak, with more than 100,000 employees, look like without any managers? Can you imagine what your local McDonald's might be like without managers?

One of the first words that probably comes to your mind is *chaotic*. If so, you would be right, because one of the things that managers do is give a group or organization direction. They typically provide formal leadership by clarifying for people what they are supposed to do. They also facilitate coordination. Managers act as a communication conduit by coordinating their unit's activities with the activities of other units in an organization. Still another thing that managers provide is accountability. Organizations reduce ambiguity over performance outcomes by appointing managers who become accountable for achievement of performance goals.

Managers add overhead or additional expense to the operation of any organization. So they must justify their existence by providing "value added," that is, by creating benefits that exceed their costs. Eastman Kodak, for example, will employ 5,000 or more managers and pay them in excess of half a billion dollars a year (including benefits) because without them Kodak could not accomplish its goals. Similarly, the managers at your local McDonald's hire operating personnel; train them; assign their work schedules; order supplies; ensure that food is prepared appropriately; check to make sure that health, cleanliness, and safety standards are maintained; and handle a wide assortment of problems that can arise. In fact, when you have a bad meal in a restaurant or incur poor service in a retail store, you are likely to comment: "This place is poorly managed." As you will see, good managers make a real difference in the quality of an organization's operations. They can spell the difference between mediocre and excellent service, profits and losses for stockholders of corporations, and winning or losing in the athletic arena. The success of organizations such as Microsoft, Southwest Airlines, Sony, General Electric, Mitsubishi, and the Utah Jazz basketball team is largely due to the quality of their management.

▶ How Do We Typically Classify Managers?

As shown by the shaded portions in Exhibit 2-1, we typically classify managers as either first-line, middle, or top. But be aware that managers come packaged in a variety of titles. **First-line managers** are the lowest level of management and are frequently called supervisors. In a manufacturing plant, the first-line manager may be called a foreman. On an athletic team, this job carries the title of coach. An increasingly popular title for first-line managers in high-tech and professional organizations is project or team leader. **Middle managers** have titles such as department or agency head, unit chief, district manager, dean, bishop, or division manager. At or near the top of an organization, **top managers** typically have titles such as vice president, president, chancellor, managing director, chief operating officer, chief executive officer, or chairman of the board.

Classifying Managers

EXHIBIT 2-1

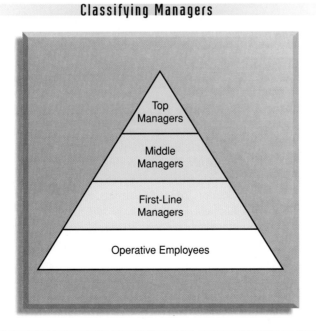

▶ What Is an Organization?

So far, we have thrown around the term *organization* as if we all understood and agreed on what the term means. This may not be the case. For instance, when does a new business become an organization? Can you be a one-person organization? Would you define your family as an organization?

An **organization** is a systematic arrangement of two or more people who fulfill formal roles and share a common purpose. Your college or university is an organization. So are fraternities, government agencies, churches, Eastman Kodak, your neighborhood grocery store, the United Nations, the Toronto Blue Jays baseball team, and the Salvation Army. These are all organizations because they all have three common characteristics.

First, each has a distinct purpose. This purpose is typically expressed in terms of a goal or set of goals. Second, each is composed of people. Third, all organizations develop a systematic structure that defines formal roles and limits the behavior of its members. Development of a structure might include, for example, creating rules and regulations, defining teams, identifying formal leaders and giving them authority over other members, and writing up job descriptions so that members know what they are supposed to do. The term *organization* therefore refers to an entity that has a distinct purpose, includes people or members, and has a systematic structure.

Now we can answer the questions proposed at the beginning of this section. A business becomes an organization when it has formal goals, employs more than a single person, and develops a formal structure that defines the relationships between members. One person alone isn't an organization. And a family is not an organization in the sense that we treat it here. In contrast to a family, an organization is less personal and is designed to accomplish specific tasks rather than to meet personal needs.[5]

▶ Why Do We Have Organizations?

We have organizations because they are more efficient than individuals acting independently. This fact can best be understood by looking at two concepts—markets and hierarchies—and demonstrating how they act as alternative ways to coordinate economic activity.[6]

Markets are defined as a means for allocating resources on the basis of bargaining for prices. This, for example, would describe the process you would probably use if you needed to hire someone for a couple of days to paint your house. Because there is competition among painters, the transaction is likely to be perceived as efficient, with both you and the painter feeling that an equitable bargain has been struck.

But markets become too costly, and hence inefficient, when transactions become overly complex or ill-defined. Such might be the case if you owned forty or fifty buildings and needed the ongoing services of dozens of painters, electricians, plumbers, and similar tradespeople. What if you happened to be a large chemical manufacturer or owned a dozen car dealerships? To reduce uncertainty, you would seek the services of accountants, marketing professionals, and personnel specialists, and you would want a sophisticated information system to minimize transaction costs. Under high uncertainty, then, **hierarchies** often become more efficient and replace markets by allocating resources through rules and authority relationships. Rules create job classifications, outline compensation schedules, identify people in authority, determine who can interact with whom, and the like. So hierarchical organizations arise because they reduce costs by establishing rules and coordinating positions that are not found in markets.

College fraternities and sororities are organizations because they have a distinct purpose, multiple members, and a systematic structure.

▶ Linking Managers and Organizations to Organizational Behavior

Managers work in a place we call an organization. The organization is the "playing field" upon which managers perform. A critical tool of effective managers is the ability to understand and predict the behavior of people in organizations. Why? Look back at our definition of managers. They integrate the work of others. If the key element of management is working with other people, then managers need a solid understanding of human behavior. The field of **organizational behavior** (frequently referred to as OB) has developed to help us better understand the behavior of individuals and groups. OB is defined as the systematic study of how people behave in organizations. It draws on the disciplines of psychology, sociology, anthropology, and other social sciences, and then uses these findings to explain and predict employee performance factors (such as productivity, absenteeism, and turnover) and employee attitudes (such as job satisfaction and organizational loyalty).[7]

The content of this book draws heavily from the field of organizational behavior. For instance, OB research has given us a wealth of insights into how managers can be more effective leaders and offers important suggestions on how to best motivate different types of employees. But management isn't synonymous with organizational behavior. Rather, OB is a management tool. Just as a knowledge of accounting can help managers more effectively utilize their organization's financial resources, an understanding of organizational behavior can provide insights into how to best utilize an organization's human resources.

People who study and write about management have long argued over the best way to categorize the manager's job.[8] This debate is not purely academic. If you are going to learn to be an effective manager, you need to understand what the job entails. In this section we review various perspectives on the manager's job.

◀ **MULTIPLE PERSPECTIVES ON WHAT MANAGERS DO**

▶ Management Functions

In the early part of this century, a French industrialist by the name of Henri Fayol (see Appendix A) wrote that all managers perform five functions: They plan, organize, command, coordinate, and control.[9] Today, the use of **management functions** as a way to classify the manager's job is still very popular.[10] Now, however, they are usually condensed to four: planning, organizing, leading, and controlling. Let's briefly define what each of these functions encompasses.

Since organizations exist to achieve some purpose, someone has to define that purpose and the means for its achievement. Management is that someone. The **planning function** encompasses defining an organization's goals, establishing an overall strategy for achieving those goals, developing a comprehensive hierarchy of plans to integrate and coordinate activities, and scheduling tasks.

Managers are also responsible for designing an organization's structure. This is called the **organizing function**. It includes the determination of what tasks are to be done, who is to do them, how the tasks are to be grouped, who reports to whom, and where in the organization decisions are to be made.

Every organization contains people, and it is management's job to direct and coordinate those people. This is the **leading function**. When managers motivate employees, direct the activities of others, select the most effective communication channel, or resolve conflicts among members, they are engaging in leading.

The final function managers perform is controlling. After the goals are set, the plans formulated, the structural arrangements delineated, and the people hired, trained, and motivated, something may still go amiss. To ensure that things are going as they should, management must monitor the organization's performance. Actual performance must be compared with the previously set goals. If there are any significant deviations, it is management's job to get the organization back on track. This process of monitoring, comparing, and correcting constitutes the **controlling function**.

▶ Management Roles

In the late 1960s, Henry Mintzberg undertook a careful study of five chief executives at work. On the basis of diaries kept by these executives and his own observations, Mintzberg concluded that the functional approach did a poor job of describing what managers do. He found, for instance, that managers spend only small amounts of their time in long-term planning activities, engage in little dispassionate analysis of information, and react to events at least as frequently as they initiate them. Based on the data he collected, Mintzberg redefined the manager's job as performing ten different but highly interrelated roles.[11] The term **management roles** refers to specific categories of managerial behavior. Mintzberg's ten roles can be grouped around three themes: interpersonal relationships, the transfer of information, and decision making (see Exhibit 2-2).

INTERPERSONAL ROLES All managers are required to perform duties that are ceremonial and symbolic in nature. When the president of a college hands out diplomas at commencement or a factory supervisor gives a group of high school students a tour of the plant, he or she is acting in a *figurehead* role. All managers have a role as a *leader*. This role includes hiring, training, motivating, and disciplining employees. The third role within the interpersonal grouping is the *liaison* role. Mintzberg described this activity as contacting external sources who provide the manager with information. These sources are individuals or groups outside the manager's unit, and they may be inside or outside the organization. The sales manager who obtains information from the human resources manager in his or her same company has an internal liaison relationship. When that sales manager has con-

EXHIBIT 2-2

Mintzberg's Categories of Managerial Roles

General Role	Specific Role
Interpersonal	Figurehead
	Leader
	Liaison
Informational	Monitor
	Disseminator
	Spokesperson
Decisional	Entrepreneur
	Disturbance handler
	Resource allocator
	Negotiator

tact with other sales executives through a marketing trade association, he or she has an outside liaison relationship.

INFORMATIONAL ROLES   All managers will, to some degree, receive and collect information from organizations and institutions outside their own. Typically, they do this by reading magazines and talking with others to learn of changes in the public's tastes, what competitors may be planning, and the like. Mintzberg called this the *monitor* role. Managers also act as a conduit to transmit information to organizational members. This is the *disseminator* role. When they represent the organization to outsiders, managers also perform a *spokesperson* role.

DECISIONAL ROLES   Finally, Mintzberg identified four roles that revolve around the making of choices. As *entrepreneurs*, managers initiate and oversee new projects that will improve their organization's performance. As *disturbance handlers*, managers take corrective action in response to unforeseen problems. As *resource allocators*, managers are responsible for distributing human, physical, and monetary resources. Last, managers perform as *negotiators* when they discuss and bargain with other groups to gain advantages for their own units.

Management Skills

Proponents of the skills perspective argue that it's not enough to *know about* managing organizations and people. You need to be prepared to *do it*! **Management skills** identify those abilities or behaviors that are crucial to success in a managerial position. This approach began with the identification of general skills and then moved to the search for specific skills related to managerial effectiveness.

GENERAL SKILLS   There seems to be overall agreement that effective managers must be proficient in four general skill areas.[12] *Conceptual skills* refer to the mental ability to analyze and diagnose complex situations. They help managers see how things fit together and facilitate making good decisions. *Interpersonal skills* encompass the ability to work with, understand, and motivate other people, both individually and in groups. Since managers integrate the work of others, they must have good interpersonal skills to communicate, motivate, and delegate. All managers need *technical skills*. These are abilities to apply specialized knowledge or expertise. For top-level managers these abilities tend to be related to knowledge of the industry and a general understanding of the organization's processes and products. For middle and lower-level managers, they are related to the specialized knowledge required in the areas in which they work—finance, human resources, manufacturing, computer systems, law, marketing, and the like. Finally, managers need *political skills*. This area is related to the ability to enhance one's position, build a power base, and establish the right connections. Organizations are political arenas in which people compete for resources. Managers with good political skills tend to be better at getting resources for their group than are managers with poor political skills. They also receive higher evaluations and get more promotions.[13]

SPECIFIC SKILLS   Research has identified six sets of behaviors that explain a little bit more than 50 percent of a manager's effectiveness.[14]

1. *Controlling the organization's environment and its resources.* This includes demonstrating, in planning and allocation meetings as well as in on-the-spot decision making, the ability to be proactive and stay ahead of environmental changes. It also involves basing resource decisions on clear, up-to-date, accurate knowledge of the organization's objectives.

2. *Organizing and coordinating.* In this skill, managers organize around tasks and then coordinate interdependent relationships among tasks wherever they exist.

3. *Handling information.* This set of behaviors comprises using information and communication channels for identifying problems, understanding a changing environment, and making effective decisions.

4. *Providing for growth and development.* Managers provide for their own personal growth and development, as well as for the personal growth and development of their employees, through continual learning on the job.

5. *Motivating employees and handling conflicts.* So that employees feel impelled to perform their work, managers enhance the positive aspects of motivation while eliminating those conflicts that may inhibit employees' motivation.

6. *Strategic problem solving.* Managers take responsibility for their own decisions and ensure that employees effectively use their decision-making skills.

► Management Competencies

The most recent approach to defining the manager's job focuses on **management competencies**.[15] These are defined as a cluster of related knowledge, skills, and attitudes related to effective managerial performance. One of the most comprehensive competency studies has come from the United Kingdom.[16] It's called the *management charter initiative (MCI)*. Based on an analysis of management functions and focusing on what effective managers should be able to do, rather than on what they know, the MCI sets generic standards of management competence. Currently, there are two sets of standards. Management I is for first-line managers. Management II is for middle managers. Standards for top management are under development.

Exhibit 2-3 lists standards for middle management. For each area of competence there is a related set of specific elements that define effectiveness in that area. For instance, one area of competence is recruiting and selecting personnel. Successful development of this competence requires that managers be able to define future personnel requirements, to determine specifications to secure quality people, and to assess and select candidates against team and organizational requirements.

The MCI standards are attracting global interest. The Australian Institute of Management, for example, has already started using the standards, and the Management Development Center of Hong Kong is considering introducing them to help managers become more mobile after China's recent takeover of Hong Kong. However, despite the generic nature of these standards—the developers of MCI believe that the standards can be applied to management jobs in any industry—there is recognition that national differences can require adjustments. As a case in point, family-run businesses are still common in Italy. So references to superiors or teams have had to be modified for use with Italian managers.

► The Manager As Decision Maker

Almost everything managers do involves making decisions. Selecting the organization's objectives requires making decisions. So, too, do such varied activities as designing the best organization structure, selecting among alternative technologies, choosing among job

Management Charter Initiative Competencies for Middle Managers

EXHIBIT 2-3

Basic Competence	Specific Associated Elements
1. Initiate and implement change and improvement in services, products, and systems	1.1. Identify opportunities for improvement in services, products, and systems 1.2. Evaluate benefits and disadvantages of proposed changes 1.3. Negotiate and agree on the introduction of change 1.4. Implement and evaluate changes in services, products, and systems 1.5. Introduce, develop, and evaluate quality-assurance systems
2. Monitor, maintain, and improve service and product delivery	2.1. Establish and maintain the supply of resources into the organization/department 2.2. Establish and agree on customer requirements 2.3. Maintain and improve operations against quality and functional specifications 2.4. Create and maintain the necessary conditions for productive work
3. Monitor and control the use of resources	3.1. Control costs and enhance value 3.2. Monitor and control activities against budgets
4. Secure effective resource allocation for activities and projects	4.1. Justify proposals for expenditure on projects 4.2. Negotiate and agree on budgets
5. Recruit and select personnel	5.1. Define future personnel requirements 5.2. Determine specifications to secure quality people 5.3. Assess and select candidates against team and organizational requirements
6. Develop teams, individuals, and self to enhance performance	6.1. Develop and improve teams through planning and activities 6.2. Identify, review, and improve developmental activities for individuals
7. Plan, allocate, and evaluate work carried out by teams, individuals, and self	7.1. Set and update work objectives for teams and individuals 7.2. Plan activities and determine work methods to achieve objectives 7.3. Allocate work and evaluate teams, individuals, and self against objectives 7.4. Provide feedback to teams and individuals on their performance
8. Create, maintain, and enhance effective working relationships	8.1. Establish and maintain the trust and support of one's subordinates 8.2. Establish and maintain the trust and support of one's immediate manager 8.3. Establish and maintain relationships with colleagues 8.4. Identify and minimize interpersonal conflict

(continued)

Basic Competence	Specific Associated Elements
	8.5. Implement disciplinary and grievance procedures
	8.6. Counsel staff
9. Seek, evaluate, and organize information for action	9.1. Obtain and evaluate information to aid decision making
	9.2. Forecast trends and developments that will affect objectives
	9.3. Record and store information
10. Exchange information to solve problems and make decisions	10.1. Lead meetings and group discussions
	10.2. Contribute to discussions to solve problems and make decisions
	10.3. Advise and inform others

Source: "MCI Launches Standards for First Two Levels," *Personnel Management*, November 1990, p.13.

candidates, or determining how to motivate low-performing employees. In fact, the decision-making process is seen by some commentators as the core of the manager's job.[17] Nobel laureate Herbert Simon, a strong advocate of this position, even went so far as to say that decision making is synonymous with managing.[18]

This decision-making approach looks at the manager's job and addresses such questions as: How do managers identify problems? Are decision makers rational? How do managers make judgments under uncertainty? What general biases surface in the decision-making process? When are groups better for making decisions than individuals? To what degree should managers empower employees to make operating decisions?

▶ The Manager As Change Agent

The last approach we'll present is the agent-of-change perspective. This approach answers the question "What do managers do?" by proposing that they bring about change. They are catalysts and assume the responsibility for managing the change process.[19]

The change-agent perspective has evolved through three stages. In its preliminary stage, which began in the 1950s, proponents argued that managers needed to design and execute planned change programs.[20] These intervention programs included attempts to improve interpersonal interactions in organizations, change work processes and methods, and redesign organization structures. The second stage arose in the 1980s and evolved out of efforts to improve quality.[21] It sought to bring about change through continual improvement. The manager's job was to seek out and implement continual incremental changes to improve everything about the organization. In the past decade, a third view on this perspective has developed. The manager's job is no longer conceived as initiating incremental changes. Rather, managers need to implement quantum, or radical, change.[22] This theme argues that in a world that is undergoing dramatic change, organizations that attempt to adjust by making only small incremental changes are doomed to fail. Managers, therefore, need to completely reinvent their organizations. They need to start with a blank sheet and rebuild their organizations from scratch. Moreover, this is not a one-shot effort. Effective managers will be continually reinventing their organizations to adapt to a changing world.

The manager-as-change-agent perspective is consistent with our discussion, in chapter 1, on the changing world of work. That is, not only are the economy, organizations, and employee's jobs undergoing change, but so, too, is the manager's job. But the manager is on both the receiving end and the giving end. Managers have to adjust to change, and they also must be the catalyst for initiating change within their organizations. Exhibit 2-4 highlights some of the recent changes in the manager's job.

THRIVING ON CHAOS   The new economy and new organization do not cause stress only for employees. They have a similar effect on many managers. Reports of high stress levels and job burnout among managers have risen as the work climate has become more chaotic and ambiguous.[23]

Management guru Tom Peters captured the challenge for managers in his best-selling book *Thriving on Chaos: Handbook for a Management Revolution*.[24] In that book he argued that successful managers, in today's unpredictable environment, must be able to thrive on change and uncertainty.

The manager's job is increasingly one of juggling a dozen balls at once, in the dark, on the deck of a boat, during a typhoon! It requires turning an environment of chaotic change into an opportunity—the chance for well-managed organizations to gain a competitive advantage over rivals by being smarter, more flexible, quicker, more efficient, and better at responding to customer needs.

BEING A COACH   The manager-as-boss model dominated organizations for the first 80 years or so of the twentieth century. Managers were assumed to be smarter than their employees and to know each employee's job better than the employee did. It was the boss's job to tell employees what to do, how to do it, and when to do it, and to make sure they did it right. Managers made all the relevant decisions, provided direction, gave orders, and carefully controlled activities to minimize mistakes and ensure that the rules were followed.

Today's manager is increasingly more like a coach than a boss.[25] Coaches don't play the game. They create a climate in which their players can excel. They define the overall objectives, set expectations, define the boundaries of each player's role, ensure that players are properly trained and have the resources they need to perform their roles, attempt to enlarge each player's capabilities, offer inspiration and motivation, and evaluate results. Contemporary managers look much more like coaches than bosses as they guide, listen to, encourage, and motivate their employees.

The Changing Manager

EXHIBIT 2-4

Old Manager	New Manager
• Operates in climate of predictability and stability	• Thrives on chaos
• The boss	• The coach
• Covets authority	• Empowers employees
• Hoards information	• Shares information
• Treats people as all the same	• Is sensitive to differences
• Oversees on-site employees	• Oversees on-site and virtual employees

EMPOWERING EMPLOYEES Consistent with their coaching role, today's managers are increasingly giving up authority and empowering their employees. As described in our discussion of the new organization, the trend to empowerment has become widespread. Managers are having to adjust their leadership styles to reflect this trend. That is, they are having to expand their leadership options to include empowerment. Empowering employees isn't the only leadership style a manager needs, nor is it the appropriate style for every situation, but those situations in which it is the preferred choice have expanded significantly in recent years.

For most younger managers, the transition to an empowering style has been relatively painless. But that hasn't been the case for many experienced managers. They came of age when effective managers were perceived as "take-charge" people. Letting employees make independent, job-related decisions—even sharing decision-making authority with employees—was seen as a sign of weakness. These managers have had difficulty giving up control.[26] In some cases, managers have been unable to give up "being boss" and have subsequently lost their jobs.

SHARING INFORMATION Another characteristic of the manager-as-boss model was maintaining control of information. If information is power, then a manager who shared information with employees would increase the employees' power. Managers did not see that outcome as desirable.

But now, individual employees and teams need to make critical, job-related decisions, and to do so they require accurate and up-to-date information. So managers are increasingly sharing with these empowered employees information they used to keep closely guarded. Contemporary managers are acting as conduits. They gather information from horizontal units, upper levels of management, and external sources; then they share that information with members of their unit.

Some managers are having difficulty giving up control of information. They are threatened by sharing power with their staff. Most managers, however, are learning that their unit's performance is enhanced through information sharing. And when their unit does better, they're perceived as more effective managers.

SENSITIVITY TO DIFFERENCES Workforce diversity requires managers to be increasingly sensitive to differences. The values, needs, interests, and expectations of workers have never been homogeneous. But when the work population was dominated by married white males of European extraction, managers could quite accurately generalize about employees. They could, for instance, assume that "my employees are like me. We prefer similar foods; we have common responsibilities; we celebrate the same holidays; we enjoy similar social and recreational interests." This assumption may never have been true, but the range of variation before the 1970s was considerably narrower than it is today.

The true minority employee in today's workforce is a white male who has school-age children and a wife who is not gainfully employed outside the home. Managers now have to understand that it is very difficult for some employees to put in overtime hours without substantial notice, to work weekends, to be gone overnight on business, or to accept a transfer to a new location. Similarly, physical barriers such as narrow doorways or stairs can be troublesome for some employees. Nor can managers assume that all employees share a common understanding of language. In addition, managers have to be sure that employees are sensitive to co-workers who are different. That means being observant of expressions of sexism, racism, ageism, and more subconscious biases within the work group.

COORDINATING VIRTUAL EMPLOYEES Managers historically oversaw and coordinated employees who were physically in their presence. They could keep in touch with their people by merely walking the halls. They could monitor activities through direct observation.

Carolina Fine Snacks in Greensboro, North Carolina, has only eight employees, but half of them are disabled. The company's president says hiring disabled employees has improved both operating efficiency and employee attendance rates.

Direct coordination has become increasingly difficult as employees telecommute, work at geographically disbursed locations, or do their jobs during flexible hours when their manager may not be present. Today, managers are increasingly overseeing "virtual" employees as well as on-site personnel. In extreme cases, managers are actually responsible for people who they've never met! An Airbus project manager in France, for instance, oversees team members in Britain, Germany, Spain, and Belgium, several of whom he knows only from phone conversations and e-mail. They've never met face-to-face.

The new manager accepts the fact that employees don't work standardized 40-hour workweeks nor do they do their jobs in a single location. The new manager increasingly relies on electronic communications to stay in touch with his or her people, as a motivation vehicle, and for monitoring and controlling activities.

▶ Synthesis and a Look Ahead

Don't let these varied views on the manager's job confuse you. For the most part, they are not in conflict. What they are is just different ways of looking at the same thing. As such, they all have some truths to them. And a close look shows that there is considerable overlap among them. For instance, Mintzberg's decisional roles and the emphasis on conceptual and information-handling skills are all consistent with the view that managers are decision makers. The leading function encompasses Mintzberg's interpersonal roles and the specific skills of motivating employees and handling conflict. The first competency identified in the MCI middle-manager standards—initiate and implement change—is totally consistent with the manager-as-change-agent perspective.

As you read through the chapters in this book, you'll see that we draw on all of the various perspectives. Chapter 3 acknowledges the importance of decision making. Chapters 5 and 6 and parts III and IV—covering planning, control systems, organizing tasks, and leading and empowering people—evolved out of considerations of management functions. In-chapter guidelines on how to apply quantitative decision techniques, competitive intelligence, benchmarking, budgets, control charts, empowering employees, and interpersonal skills are all an effort to help you develop your management skills. Chapters 1 and 18 on the changing world of work and managing change and innovation reflect the belief that managers are catalysts of change. Finally, a review of this text's detailed table of contents reveals that almost all of the competencies listed in Exhibit 2-3 are touched upon within the book's eighteen chapters.

A primary objective of this book is to help you to be an *effective manager*. In the preceding sections we addressed what a manager is and does, and we used the term *effective* several times. So now we turn to the question: How do we know if a manager is *effective*? In this section, we define managerial and organizational effectiveness, identify the primary organizational stakeholders who judge effectiveness, and review the various criteria they use.

◀ ASSESSING MANAGERIAL EFFECTIVENESS

▶ Definitions

Early writers took a somewhat simplistic view when they sought to determine whether a manager was doing a good job. They focused on two concepts: *efficiency* and *effectiveness*.

Efficiency refers to the relationship between inputs and outputs. If you get more output for a given input, you have increased efficiency. Similarly, if you can get the same output from less input, you again increase efficiency. Managers are concerned with the efficient use of input resources—money, people, equipment. For instance, Nissan's auto plant in Tennessee requires 2.23 workers to assemble each vehicle. In contrast, General Motors' U.S. plants average 3.47 workers per vehicle. So Nissan is considerably more efficient in auto manufacturing than is GM.

It is not enough to be efficient. Managers must also be concerned with getting activities completed; that is, they must achieve **effectiveness**. Managers who achieve their organizations' goals are said to be effective. Or, as one management expert put it, "Efficiency means *doing things right*, and effectiveness means *doing the right thing*."[27] Doing things right means minimizing the cost of resources needed to achieve goals. Doing the right thing means selecting appropriate goals and then achieving them.

Is managerial effectiveness the same as organizational effectiveness? No, but the concepts are closely related. Managerial effectiveness is concerned with the achievement of a manager's goals, whereas organizational effectiveness addresses the organization's goals. Yet, because a manager's success is essentially defined in terms of how well his or her organizational unit performs, it is difficult to separate the two concepts. As such, the following discussion is really applicable to both.

▶ Organizational Stakeholders

Effectiveness may sound like a straightforward concept, but it isn't. The problem is that effectiveness, like beauty, is in the eye of the beholder. Different groups judge organizations by different criteria. Employees, for instance, may think that the right thing for an organization to do is to provide workers with good pay and benefits. They would then judge the organization's effectiveness by how well those goals are achieved. In contrast, stockholders typically think that the right thing for an organization to do is to increase stockholder wealth by improving earnings per share. If we want to more fully understand the concept of effectiveness, we need to take a look at the various groups who evaluate managers and organizations.

An organization's **stakeholders** are those groups within or outside the organization that have an interest in it. These typically include employees, customers, management, boards of directors, investors, competitors, suppliers, creditors, media, government agencies, and special interest groups.[28]

Each stakeholder has a set of criteria to which it expects the organization to respond. Unfortunately, because stakeholders have different interests in the organization, the criteria they use for judging the organization's effectiveness also differ[29] (see Exhibit 2-5). As you will see shortly, multiple stakeholders and multiple criteria require managers to emphasize different effectiveness criteria to different audiences.

▶ Popular Effectiveness Criteria

In 1983, the head of General Motors announced, with great fanfare, the creation of Saturn Corp. He said Saturn would prove that GM could profitably build a small automobile in the United States that would beat Japanese competition. More than fifteen years have passed since GM created Saturn. So it seems fair to ask: Well, were they successful? The answer is Yes, No, or Maybe.[30] It depends on how you define success. Initial sales were strong, but recent sales figures have been declining. Surveys indicate that Saturn has achieved quality, reliability, and customer satisfaction that are every bit as good as what

EXHIBIT 2-5

Common Stakeholders and Their Typical Effectiveness Criteria

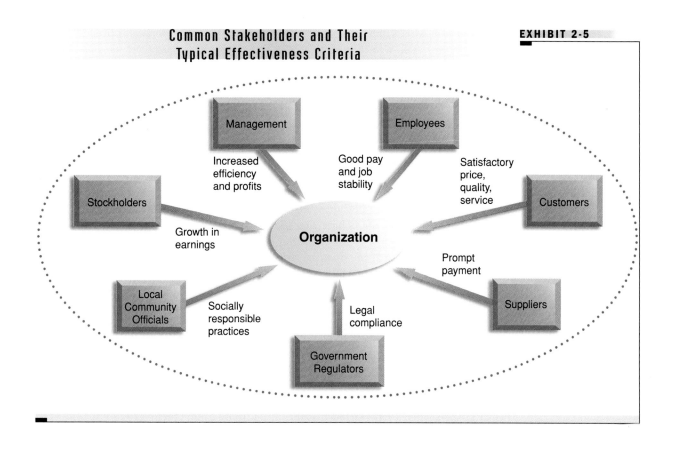

Japanese automakers have achieved. But in terms of productivity, costs, and profits, Saturn has been a major disappointment. Saturn is much less productive than comparable Honda and Toyota plants in the United States. GM lost billions of dollars during Saturn's first decade in operation. In recent years, Saturn has been breaking even, although this has largely been achieved through creative accounting.

Saturn Corporation illustrates the problem of defining organizational effectiveness. Saturn has been very effective at building strong customer satisfaction. It's been less effective at making money. So is the company effective or isn't it?

Saturn illustrates the major problem in defining organizational effectiveness. Effectiveness is essentially determined by how well the organization achieves its goals. But we must know *what* goals and *whose* goals.[31] Let's take a brief look at a few of the more popular effectiveness goals or criteria and show how different stakeholders emphasize different criteria.

FINANCIAL MEASURES The best-known criteria for measuring organizational effectiveness are financial measures, especially among profit-seeking business firms. Surveys of large multinational corporations found that in the late 1960s, the dominant financial goal that these companies sought was maximizing market share. By the mid-1970s, attention shifted to earnings per share. By the early 1980s, return on equity had become the dominant goal. Since the early 1990s, cash flow measures have become the most popular.[32]

Although specific criteria have changed over time, business firms still rely heavily on financial measures to assess how well they're doing. Among publicly held corporations, satisfactory performance on financial criteria is necessary to maintain legitimacy and credibility with investors and lenders.

PRODUCTIVITY Productivity criteria are synonymous with measures of organizational efficiency. The more output an organization can generate from a given input, the more productive it is. A few years back, each Toyota employee produced 57.7 vehicles a year, while his or her Ford counterpart turned out only 16.1 vehicles.[33] Toyota was more productive because it generated more cars per employee.

Examples of efficiency criteria include output per employee labor-hour, costs per patient, and scrap as a percentage of steel shipped. Each of those criteria overlaps with financial measures when a criterion such as rate of return on capital or assets is used.

GROWTH In the 1960s, a popular measure of organizational effectiveness was expansion of payrolls. The more people an organization hired, the more successful many people believed that organization to be. Nowadays it's quite the opposite. Those organizations that can increase production and sales by holding their workforce in check or by actually reducing jobs are seen as the most effective.

Growth in payrolls is no longer a valued effectiveness measure, but growth in sales units, total revenues, and net profits continue to have a wide following. In the investment community, high stock prices are frequently justified for firms with modest profits solely on the basis that the firm is expanding and growing rapidly. For instance, in 1998, the stocks of most restaurant chains were selling for about twenty times earnings. But Starbucks, the rapidly growing coffee retailer, was selling for better than fifty times earnings.

CUSTOMER SATISFACTION As competition has increased for producers of almost every product and service, no organization is safe in taking its customer or client base for granted. This fact of business life explains the recent obsession by management in many organizations with achieving high customer satisfaction.

Studies consistently indicate that it's a lot more expensive to attract new customers than it is to spend whatever is necessary to keep the customers you have. So organizations are doing things such as spending substantial sums of money to train employees who interact with customers, establishing toll-free numbers for customers to get help or register complaints, introducing "no-questions-asked" return policies, and conducting comprehensive after-sale surveys.

As Saturn Corp. has learned, high customer satisfaction is no assurance that an organization will achieve its financial goals. However, the long-term viability of an organization will be severely tested if customers are not satisfied and look to competing organizations to meet their needs. The success of companies such as Nordstrom, L.L. Bean, Lexus, Singapore Airlines, and Federal Express is regularly attributed to their obsession with doing whatever is necessary to satisfy their customers.

QUALITY Closely linked with the criterion of customer satisfaction is the concern for quality. But the goal of quality encompasses internal operations and processes as well as judgments by customers. So the search for quality means cutting out unnecessary steps in the processing of accounts payable, keeping inventory costs down, and maintaining spotless floors in the production areas, as well as ensuring that external customers are satisfied. Part of McDonald's phenomenal success is due to management's commitment to provide high quality at low cost and having restaurants that meet the most stringent standards for cleanliness.

FLEXIBILITY A flexible organization is one that can shift resources from one activity to another quickly and easily. In an era of global competition and rapid social, economic, and technological change, the survival of many organizations depends on their ability to adapt quickly. Companies such as the Cable News Network, Charles Schwab, and Southwest Airlines have succeeded against much larger competitors because they have internal systems that were designed, and employees who were selected and trained, to adapt rapidly to change.

EMPLOYEE GROWTH AND SATISFACTION An organization's employees are its heart and soul. Unfortunately, in recent years, a lot of organizations have lost sight of that fact. Employee loyalty has declined as many employers have laid off workers and undermined the job security of those who remain.[34] Many organizations have considered this a price that has had to be paid in order to increase flexibility and productivity.

There is no question that a number of organizations had overstaffed during the 1970s and 1980s, thus requiring employee cutbacks. But goals such as high quality and improved customer service depend on a well-trained and motivated workforce. Therein lies a dilemma: How does an organization achieve high productivity and flexibility while, at the same time, maintaining committed and motivated employees?

Richard Branson, the billionaire founder and head of the Virgin Group, doesn't think there's a problem. Counter to most executives who say that the customer or profits should come first, Branson says, "Almost 100 percent of running a business is motivating your

In stark contrast to what most CEO's say, Richard Branson of the Virgin Group puts his staff first. He believes that by putting the emphasis on motivating employees, everything else will naturally fall into place.

In The News

A New Class of Corporation?

Can government induce corporations to look beyond stockholders, broaden their stakeholder constituencies, and act more responsibly? Some U.S. senators think so. They're proposing a new kind of federally chartered corporation—the R (or Responsible) Corp. It is specifically designed to enhance the stakeholder role that employees and communities play in corporation decision making.

The senators propose replacing the corporate income tax with a "business activity tax," which would be applied at a fixed rate to all receipts, subtracting payments for most inputs. Employee training and research-and-development costs would be tax-deductible, while wages, dividends, and interest would not. An R Corp. would be taxed at 11 percent versus 18 percent for conventional corporations.

To qualify as an R Corp., a firm would have to meet a number of criteria. It would be required to contribute 3 percent of payroll to a general multiemployer pension plan, devote 2 percent to employee training, pay half the costs of a qualifying health program, have a profit-sharing or employee stock ownership plan, keep the ratio of the highest-to-lowest-paid employee to no more than 50 to 1, agree to restrictions on relocations and layoffs, and insure that at least half of its new investment and employment would be in the United States.

The idea of a separate corporate charter that uses the tax structure to encourage or discourage certain practices is controversial. But it acknowledges the growing belief that corporations need to strike a new balance between the need to cut costs to be globally competitive and the need to be more responsible corporate citizens.

Based on R. Kuttner, "Rewarding Corporations That Really Invest in America," *Business Week*, February 26, 1996, p. 22.

staff and the people around you. And if you can motivate them, then you can achieve anything. And too many companies have put shareholders first, customers second, staff way last. If you reverse that and you put your staff first, very quickly you find that the customers come first as well, and the shareholders come first, as well."[35]

SOCIAL ACCEPTANCE Organizations need to be good citizens. When they aren't, they can suffer at the hands of stakeholders such as government agencies, consumer advocate groups, or a critical media. Dow Corning's reputation and financial integrity were severely damaged by its manufacture of defective silicone breast implants. Investigations by newspapers, the U.S. Food and Drug Administration, and congressional subcommittees found company memos indicating that Dow Corning was in such a rush to gets its implants on the market that it either dismissed or short-circuited animal studies showing that silicone leaked from the implants.[36] The company eventually got out of the breast implant business and was required to contribute hundreds of millions of dollars into a fund against future liabilities. In contrast, companies such as Levi Strauss and Ben & Jerry's Homemade Inc. have gained a strong following for their socially responsible practices and efforts to preserve the environment.

An Integrative Framework

Managers are judged by a diverse set of stakeholders. Moreover, because these stakeholders have different interests, they don't necessarily agree on when managers are doing a good job or when an organization is effective. So what can managers do? How can they satisfy different and even conflicting demands from multiple stakeholders? One answer is that they can prioritize criteria in terms of the power of various stakeholders and emphasize different achievements to different audiences.

The tobacco industry offers an illustration. A study of the major tobacco companies found that the public evaluated the firms in terms of not harming smokers' health, while stockholders evaluated the firms' ability to produce cigarettes efficiently and profitably. Not surprisingly—using such diverse criteria—the public rated the tobacco firms as ineffective, and stockholders rated the same firms as highly effective.[37] Effectiveness of a tobacco company, therefore, can be said to be determined by management's ability to identify the company's critical stakeholders, assess their preference patterns, and satisfy their demands. Stockholders and consumers might be satisfied with tobacco firms, but if the public, through its legislative representatives, outlaws the sale of cigarettes, then the tobacco companies lose big!

The long-term viability of an organization requires that management not overlook the demands of any powerful stakeholder. So management needs to carefully and systematically identify critical organizational stakeholders, assess their relative power, and identify what each expects of the organization. Then management should attempt to satisfy the goals of those stakeholders with the greatest power or, at least, make the effort to persuade those stakeholders that significant progress is being made toward meeting their goals.

Let's apply this integrative framework at Goodyear Tire & Rubber. Goodyear's stakeholders include suppliers of critical petroleum products used in the tire-manufacturing process; officers of the United Rubber Workers union; unionized employees; officials at banks where Goodyear has sizable short-term loans; government regulatory agencies that grade tires and inspect facilities for safety violations; city officials and community leaders in Akron, Ohio, where Goodyear is headquartered; security analysts at major brokerage firms who specialize in the tire and rubber industry; mutual fund managers who have large holdings of Goodyear stock; regional tire jobbers and distributors; and purchasing agents responsible for the acquisition of tires at GM, Mack Truck, Caterpillar, and other vehicle manufacturers.

Goodyear's management could evaluate this list to determine the relative power of each. Basically, this means looking at each stakeholder in terms of how dependent on it Goodyear is. Does it have considerable power over Goodyear? Are there alternatives for what this stakeholder provides? How do these stakeholders compare in the impact they have on Goodyear's operations?

Next, Goodyear's management needs to identify the expectations that these stakeholders hold for the organization. What goals does each seek to impose on the organization? Stockholders' goals may be in terms of profit or appreciation in the stock's price; the union's goals may be in acquiring job security and high wages for its members; the U.S. Environmental Protection Agency will want Goodyear's manufacturing plants to meet all minimum air-, water-, and noise-pollution requirements; the Akron City Council is likely to be concerned with preserving jobs.

Finally, Goodyear's management needs to compare the various expectations, determine common goals and those that are incompatible, assign relative weights to the various stakeholders, and prioritize these various goals for the benefit of the organization as a whole. The resulting preference order, in effect, represents the relative power of the various stakeholders. Goodyear's effectiveness will then be assessed in terms of its ability to satisfy those goals.

One last point: Whether an organization is meeting a stakeholder's goals is not a fully objective determination. Subjective judgments will be made by stakeholders. For instance,

Goodyear employees tend to assess their company's effectiveness by how well Goodyear's management responds to their needs for job security and high wages.

TODAY ? or TOMORROW ?

Balanced Scorecards

Imagine a pilot who flew his or her plane using only a single instrument that measured air speed. There's no altimeter to meaure altitude; no guage to show fuel status; no compass for direction; and no radar to identify airports or other aircraft. This pilot would be prone to make a lot of errors! Even if the pilot did a terrific job on air speed, he or she could still run into a mountain, run out of fuel, end up in the wrong place, or collide with another plane.

In many ways, managers are like this pilot when they use a single indicator—traditional financial measures—to assess how well they're "flying" their organization. When they focus on a limited set of measures to assess how effective their organization is, they are likely to miss a lot of other important factors. This logic has led to the development of the balanced scorecard.[38] In addition to basic financial measures, three additional areas are assessed:

Customers—Includes factors such as customer satisfaction, customer retention, new customer acquisition, and market share in targeted segments.

Internal business processes—Includes new product development, speed of response, quality assessment, and cycle time.

Learning and growth—Includes employee skill updating, employee job satisfaction, enhancing information technology and systems.

These three criteria don't replace financial measures. They complement them. By combining financial and nonfinancial measures, management achieves a more balanced picture of the organization's effectiveness. Specifically, financial measures focus on the past and short-term performance. A balanced scorecard directs management's attention to what is necessary to assure long-term future growth and success.

Is the corporate scoreboard the "organizational effectiveness" approach of the future? Maybe. A recent study by the Institute of Management Accountants found 64 percent of U.S. companies are experimenting with multiple measures of performance like the corporate scorecard. Analog Devices, for instance, is strongly committed to this approach. Once a quarter, Analog's 12 senior managers meet for a full day to discuss results from their scorecards. Management attributes this approach to identifying problems much earlier than would occur with single reliance on traditional financial measures.

Not every organization, however, is enamored with veering from the single focus on financial performance. Shell Oil, as a case in point, continues to be strongly devoted to number crunching. Shell's executives see the balanced scorecard as confusing and hard to implement. Shell managers acknowledge that you have to have a sophisticated way to measure organizational performance but that those measurements should be purely financial. As one finance professor commented, in support of Shell's views, "How do you know the cost of gaining or losing a customer, for example? Maybe you can use the balanced scorecord after you've done the financial analysis, but you have to begin with the financial measurements to decide what's on the scorecard."

suppose that investors are looking for an increase in profits of 15 percent over the previous year, but actual profits rise only 11 percent. If it's crucial to appease these investors, management can take the offensive. It can argue its case for the adequacy of the 11 percent increase. In actual practice, managers are doing this all the time. Like good lawyers, they shape facts and use persuasive language to present the organization in the most favorable light.[39] So when executives are talking to a group of security analysts, the emphasis will be on how successful management has been at improving profitability. When those same executives meet with union officials, they'll emphasize management's efforts to create jobs and improve working conditions. And when those executives have to appear before a local zoning commission to get approval for a plant expansion, the focus will be on what a caring and responsible citizen the company has been in the community.

If you're going to embark on a journey, it helps to have a plan or guide so you can see where you're going and where you've been. Exhibit 2-6 is your guide to this book. The objectives of this book are to help you understand management and to help you become an effective manager. To achieve either, you need to build management competencies. Those competencies are organized into two groups: knowledge and applicable skills. Knowledge builds understanding. Applicable skills apply that understanding. For the most part, our knowledge base is derived from the management functions: planning, organizing, leading, and controlling. Our skills build from, and elaborate upon, the six specific management skills mentioned earlier.

COMING ATTRACTIONS: A GUIDE TO THE BOOK

Managers and organizations must respond to forces of change, the subject of chapters 1 and 18. These forces for change operate on the organization by way of the environment to determine the organizational boundaries.

The core of Exhibit 2-6 on page 56 (and of this book) is made up of three competency areas. Part I—decision, planning, and monitoring systems—is covered in chapters 3 through 6. Those chapters cover conceptual issues such as making decisions, assessing the environment, creating plans, and developing control systems. Applicable skills presented in chapters 3 through 6 include creativity stimulation, environmental scanning, objective setting, and budget formulation.

Part III, chapters 7 through 11, addresses organizing tasks and people and shaping the organization's culture. You'll learn about technology and the design of work processes, organization design, managing human resources, groups and teams, and the organization's culture. Skills developed in these chapters include designing motivating jobs, choosing the proper organizational structure, conducting effective interviews, assessing team effectiveness, and reading an organization's culture.

Chapters 12 through 17 in part IV develop your knowledge of leading and empowering people. Applicable skills covered in those chapters include shaping employee behavior, motivating professionals, choosing an effective leadership style, coaching, building trust, and active listening.

Note the inclusion of organizational effectiveness in Exhibit 2-6. As we pointed out previously in this chapter, this is the determinant of whether managers are doing a good job. Therefore, managerial competencies are shown as leading to organizational effectiveness.

There is a variety of additional material available on the CD-ROM and companion Web site that accompany this text. You can access this information through the CD-ROM or by visiting the Web site at <**www.prenhall.com/robbins**>.

EXHIBIT 2-6   Managerial Competencies in a Changing World

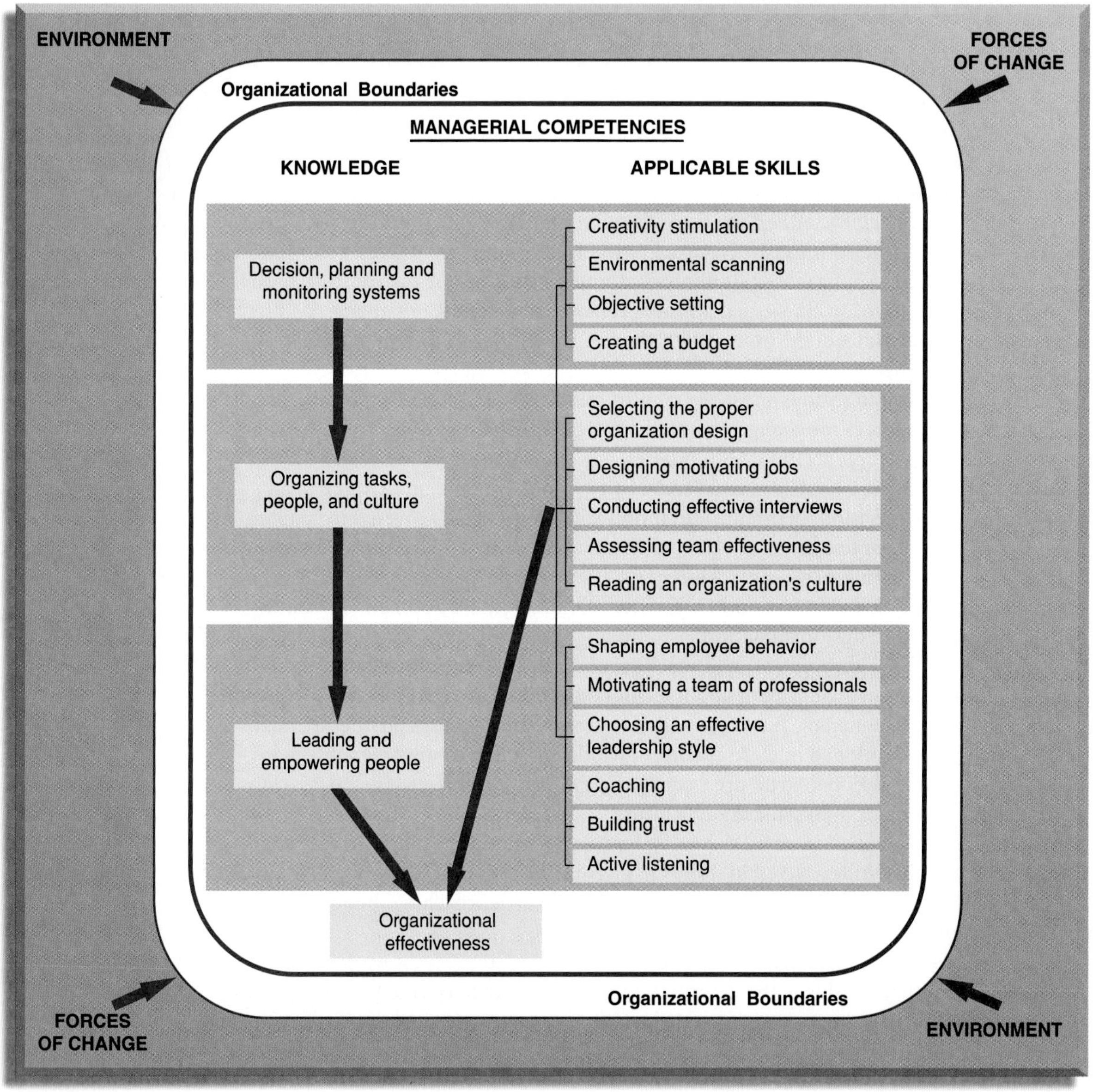

ENVIRONMENT

FORCES OF CHANGE

Organizational Boundaries

MANAGERIAL COMPETENCIES

KNOWLEDGE

APPLICABLE SKILLS

Decision, planning and monitoring systems

Creativity stimulation

Environmental scanning

Objective setting

Creating a budget

Organizing tasks, people, and culture

Selecting the proper organization design

Designing motivating jobs

Conducting effective interviews

Assessing team effectiveness

Reading an organization's culture

Leading and empowering people

Shaping employee behavior

Motivating a team of professionals

Choosing an effective leadership style

Coaching

Building trust

Active listening

Organizational effectiveness

Organizational Boundaries

FORCES OF CHANGE

ENVIRONMENT

SUMMARY

(This summary is organized by the chapter-opening learning objectives on page 34.)

1. Managers are individuals who integrate the work of others. That might mean direct responsibility for a group of people. It might mean supervising a single person. It might be coordinating individuals in other departments or working with people from other organizations. And it includes facilitators or leaders who integrate work-team activities.

2. Managers give an organizational unit direction, coordinate their unit's activities with the activities of other units, and provide accountability for unit outcomes.

3. An organization is a systematic arrangement of two or more people who fulfill formal roles and share a common purpose. It is designed to accomplish specific tasks rather than to meet personal needs.

4. Organizational behavior (OB) systematically studies how people behave in organizations. Managers use their knowledge of OB to help them work with others and to get high levels of performance from employees.

5. Four management functions are planning, organizing, leading, and controlling. Planning includes goal setting and establishing the organization's strategy. Organizing identifies tasks to be done, who is to do them, how the tasks are to be grouped, who reports to whom, and where in the organization decisions are to be made. Leading refers to directing and coordinating people. Controlling is the process of monitoring, comparing, and correcting performance.

6. Four general skill areas needed by managers are conceptual, interpersonal, technical, and political. Six specific skills are controlling the organization's environment and its resources, organizing and coordinating, handling information, providing for growth and development, motivating employees and handling conflict, and strategic problem solving.

7. Bosses covet authority and control. They tell employees what to do, how to do it, and when to do it, and they make sure they do it right. In contrast, coaches create a climate that supports employee high performance. They guide, listen to, encourage, and motivate their employees.

8. Chaos and ambiguity can be turned into an opportunity because they allow managers who can adapt to gain a competitive advantage. Rapid change is an opportunity for the quick and adept to outsmart or outmaneuver their rivals.

9. Effectiveness is concerned with goal attainment: "doing the right thing." Efficiency is a relationship between inputs and outputs: "doing things right."

10. To assess an organization's effectiveness you need to identify its key stakeholders; determine each stakeholders' interest in the organization in terms of goals and expectations; translate these goals and expectations into effectiveness criteria; prioritize critieria in terms of the power of the various stakeholders; identify which stakeholder(s) you represent; determine the degree of power your stakeholder's group has over the organization; and evaluate the organization's performance against the criteria with which you are concerned. The more power your stakeholder group has over the organization, the greater emphasis the organization is likely to give to your effectiveness criteria.

REVIEW QUESTIONS

1. Can you conceive of an organization of 100 people that has no managers? What problems would you expect it to have?

2. If managers are so important to an organization, why do you think there has been a trend in recent years toward having fewer middle managers and more self-managed teams?

3. Why do you think that managers typically are better paid than nonmanagers?

4. Senior executives in major U.S. corporations routinely earn more than $2 million a year. Are these managers overpaid? Build a case to defend your position.

5. American CEOs typically earn two or three times as much as their counterparts in Canada and Europe. Why do you think this is?

6. Contrast markets and hierarchies.

7. Reconcile the four managerial functions, Mintzberg's three role categories, and the four general skills.

8. Introductory university courses often have lecture sections of 200 or more students. Is this practice efficient? Is it effective? Explain.

9. Who are the key stakeholders for (a) IBM, (b) the University of Michigan, and (c) the New York Museum of Modern Art?

10. "For a business firm, the bottom line is profit. You don't need any other measures of effectiveness." Do you agree or disagree with this statement? Support your position.

Trying to Fill Anita Roddick's Shoes

Anita Roddick and her husband, Gordon, opened their first Body Shop in 1976 in Brighton, England. Their concept was unique at the time—soaps and lotions that were made primarily from natural ingredients. They would merge cosmetics with environmental activism. The company supported and promoted a wide range of environmental and human-rights projects—from Greenpeace's Save-the-Whales campaign, to Survival International's rain-forest project, to boycotting Shell Oil for its human-rights abuses in Nigeria.

The concept worked. Twenty years later, Body Shop International had 1,366 stores in 46 countries. But recent problems have forced the Roddicks to bring in Stuart Rose, a professional manager, as the company's managing director. Here are the major challenges Rose is concerned with:

➤ The company's image has been tarnished. A 1992 television documentary charged that Body Shop made false claims about its stand against animal testing. (The Roddicks sued for libel and won.) A 1994 article broadened the charge of hypocrisy to include Body Shop's environmental standards, charitable contributions, and efforts to buy materials from third world countries. (An independent research group later concluded these charges were "broadly unfair.") Nevertheless, the company's "do-gooder" reputation was hurt.

➤ The Limited has aggressively expanded its Body Shop competitor, Bath & Body Works. Between 1992 and 1996, it opened 412 stores in the United States, mostly in high-rent malls. With its aggressive marketing and The Limited's deep pockets, they have cut into Body Shop's growth.

➤ U.S. operations have suffered badly. The 272 stores in the United States are losing money. Part of the problem is that 113 of these stores are owned by the Body Shop, unlike other countries, where stores are franchised. Another part of the problem is that costs have risen as new stores have been located in malls to gain a foothold against Bath & Body Works.

All is not gloomy for Rose. The Body Shop's Asian market has grown rapidly and is profitable. Although the British market is nearly saturated, and generates 44 percent of the company's revenues, profits there are solid.

Rose has plenty of options. He can retreat in the United States, or he can expand. For instance, expansion could include putting more stores in small towns, mail order, or developing in-home sales (like Avon). He can deemphasize the company's environmental focus. What Rose can't do is continue on the company's current course. It is clearly losing momentum. Assume you're Rose. You have some immediate challenges to confront. What do you do?

Source: Based on C. P. Wallace, "Can the Body Shop Shape Up?" *Fortune*, April 15, 1996, pp. 118–20.

Evaluating the Effectiveness of U.S. Colleges

Every year, *U.S. News & World Report* publishes rankings of U.S. colleges.* These rankings have become well known, and college administrators have begun to pay attention to the results and to the criteria that the magazine uses in establishing the rankings.

The most recent rankings were calculated by asking college presidents, deans, and admissions directors to rate other colleges in their same category (i.e., national universities, national liberal arts colleges, regional universities, regional liberal arts colleges, specialized institutions) on six attributes:

1. Academic reputation. Respondents were asked to rank each institution from a list (e.g., 228 national universities were listed) into one of four quartiles based on its reputation.
2. Student selectivity. Determined by applicant acceptance rates, percentage of those accepted who actually enrolled, enrollees' high school class standings, and national aptitude test scores.
3. Faculty resources. Based on student-faculty ratio, percentage of full-time faculty with doctorates, percentage of part-time faculty, faculty salaries, and class size data.
4. Financial resources. Total expenditures for its education program divided by number of students enrolled.

5. Graduation rates. Average percentage of students who graduated within six years of the year in which they enrolled.
6. Alumni giving. Average percentage of a school's living alumni who made a donation to the college during the previous two years.

Data for each of the six attributes were converted into percentiles. The highest raw score for any attribute or subattribute was valued at 100 percent. Next, all the other scores were taken as a percentage of that top score and totaled. The six attributes for each institution were then numerically ranked in ascending order and weighted: alumni satisfaction (5 percent), graduation rates (25 percent), financial resources (10 percent), faculty resources (20 percent), student selectivity (15 percent), and academic reputation (25 percent). The weighted numbered ranks for each institution were totaled and compared with the weighted totals for all the others in its category. The highest-ranking institution in a given category was the one with the lowest total. Its overall score was converted into a percentile of 100. The totals for the other institutions in the catagory were then translated into a percentage of the top score.

The previously described procedure, in 1998, determined that the top-ten-rated national universities were Harvard (100.0), Princeton (100.0), Yale (100.0), Massachusetts Institute of Technology (98.0), Stanford (98.0), Cornell (97.0), Duke (97.0), University of Pennsylvania (97.0), California Institute of Technology (96.0), and Dartmouth (95.0).

Class members should form into groups of three to five and answer the following questions.

1. What stakeholders are these rankings legitimizing?
2. What important stakeholders, if any, do you think are being excluded?
3. What is your opinion of the criteria that *U.S. News* has chosen?
4. How might a particular institution improve each of these rankings?
5. What does this exercise tell you about measuring organizational effectiveness?

*See, for example, "America's Best Colleges," *U.S. News & World Report*, August 31, 1998, pp. 61–98.

TEAM ACTIVITY

Federal Express's Nine Faces of Leadership

According to Federal Express, its best leaders share nine personal attributes.* These include:

1. *Charisma.* Instills faith, respect, and trust. Conveys a strong sense of mission.
2. *Individual consideration.* Coaches, advises, and teaches people who need it. Actively listens and gives indications of listening.
3. *Intellectual stimulation.* Gets others to use reasoning and evidence, rather than unsupported opinion. Encourages creative thinking in others.
4. *Courage.* Willing to stand up for ideas even if they are unpopular. Does not give in to pressure or to others' opinions in order to avoid confrontation.
5. *Dependability.* Follows through and keeps commitments. Takes responsibility for actions and accepts responsibility for mistakes.

6. *Flexibility.* Functions effectively in changing environments. Changes course when the situation warrants it.
7. *Integrity.* Does what is morally and ethically right. Does not abuse management privileges.
8. *Judgment.* Reaches sound and objective evaluations of alternative courses of action through logic, analysis, and comparison. Puts facts together rationally and realistically.
9. *Respect for others.* Honors and does not belittle the opinions or work of other people, regardless of their status or position.

Break into groups of three. Your task is to determine to what degree FedEx's nine leadership attributes fit with (a) the four management functions, (b) Mintzberg's ten management roles, (c) the set of six specific management skills, and (d) the 10 basic competencies listed in Exhibit 2-3.

*Source: H. Row, "Is Management for Me? *That* Is the Question," *Fast Company*, February/March 1998, p. 52.

UPS: Where Efficiency Is an Obsession

United Parcel Service claims to run "the tightest ship in the shipping business." And they probably do. For decades, UPS has stood as a model of corporate efficiency. It truly "sweats the details." Its management methodically trains its employees to do their jobs as efficiently as possible. For instance, consider the job of a delivery driver—the person who drives that familiar boxy brown truck.

The company's 3,000 industrial engineers have time-studied each driver's route and set standards for each delivery, stop, and pickup. These engineers have recorded every second taken up by stoplights, traffic, detours, doorbells, walkways, stairways, and coffee breaks. Even bathroom stops are put into the standards. All of this information is then fed into company computers to provide detailed time standards for every driver, every day.

To meet their objective of 400 packages to pick up and deliver each day, drivers must follow the engineers' procedures exactly. As they approach a delivery stop, drivers shed their seat belts, toot their horns, and cut their engines. In one seamless motion, they are required to yank up their emergency brakes and push their gearshifts into first. They're now ready for take-off after their deliveries. The drivers slide to the ground with their clipboards under their right arms and their packages in their left hands. Their keys, teeth up, are in their right hands. They take one look at the package to fix the address in their minds. Then they walk to the customer's door at the prescribed 3 feet per second and knock first to avoid lost seconds searching for the doorbell. After making the delivery, they do the paperwork on the way back to the truck.

UPS's obsession with efficiency has paid off for the company and its employees. UPS is the largest transportation company in the United States. It delivers 10 million packages a day and has annual revenues of $19.6 billion, or twice that of its chief rival, Federal Express. Delivery drivers, who are members of the International Brotherhood of Teamsters union, earn between $40,000 and $50,000 a year and enjoy outstanding benefits and a generous profit-sharing plan.

But UPS is facing challenges to its system. Heated competition is putting pressure on profits, and employees are increasingly complaining about job stress.

In the past, UPS's high labor costs could be offset in part by price increases. But increased competition from nonunion rivals such as Roadway Package Services have made price freezes the norm in the industry. To maintain profitability, UPS has sought to additionally improve efficiency. And employees are increasingly complaining. Some complain about increased workloads. But a bigger problem is the new breed of employee that UPS is hiring—more highly skilled and college-educated—to handle delivery jobs that have become more complex. As a result of new technologies introduced by UPS, drivers now have to learn an array of codes and billing systems. More and more packages have special-handling and time-sensitive requirements. These better-educated workers are less tolerant of the company's work rules and controls. So the union has begun to demand limits on driver supervision, workloads, and harassment by managers. In support of these demands, the union claims that UPS employees scored in the ninety-first percentile of U.S. workers for job stress, and that many suffer from anxiety, phobias, and back strain. A labor strike by UPS employees, in August 1997, focused on the excessive use of part-timers, high productivity expectations, and work pressures.

UPS's management is considering revising its long-held practices. For instance, the company is using its entire operation in Alabama as a test site for experimenting with giving employees more freedom and responsibility. It is considering eliminating many of its precise measurement practices. And rather than having managers or computers tell the drivers which packages to deliver first and when, the company is allowing the drivers to design their own routes.

QUESTIONS

1. Do you think UPS's detailed training and control of employees is inappropriate today? Explain your position.
2. Why do you think so few organizations today program employee behavior the way UPS has done?
3. Both the company and the union call UPS drivers "the highest-paid truck drivers in the United States." Doesn't money compensate these drivers for the stress they experience? Explain your position.
4. "If it ain't broke, don't fix it." Does this phrase apply to UPS? Explain.

Source: Based on D. Machalaba, "UPS Gets Deliveries Done by Driving Its Workers," *Wall Street Journal*, April 22, 1986, p. 1; R. Frank, "As UPS Tries to Deliver More to Its Customers, Labor Problems Grow," *Wall Street Journal*, May 23, 1994, p. A1; and R. Frank, "Efficient UPS Tries to Increase Efficiency," *Wall Street Journal*, May 24, 1995, p. B1.

Caring Management

Although caring may not be a word many people would normally associate with management, Cheryl Womack of Kansas City, Missouri, has built a $45 million company by caring about her customers *and* her 75 employees. She started her business—VCW Inc.—in 1981 in the basement of her home with one telephone and call-waiting. What does VCW Inc. do? The company oversees the National Association of Independent Truckers. VCW offers cost-effective insurance coverage, retirement benefit plans, low-interest credit cards, and other benefits to approximately 8,000 (out of 300,000 total) independent truck drivers who belong to this association. In addition, many large motor carriers who hire independent drivers also are her customers.

Womack's customers are a unique breed, indeed! Independent truck drivers "move the world" as they haul across the United States in their 18-wheelers most of the products we use every day. Independent truck drivers also are businessmen and must run their businesses effectively or they won't survive in this intensely competitive industry. How does VCW show that it cares about its customers—these independent truckers? It provides an answer to a problem that many of them face: where to find cost-effective insurance coverage and other types of financial coverage that other insurance companies refuse to carry. Womack subscribes to the belief that if you can help solve a customer's problem, you'll be successful. She and her employees *have* been successful at solving their customers' problems and caring about them by providing outstanding customer service. But Womack's caring management doesn't stop with her customers. It extends to her employees, as well.

Her most telling statement about her management philosophy is that "everything I do here is designed to cultivate and grow employees." From the beautifully designed offices to the formal dinners and travel experiences she provides, Womack sees her role as a mentor for employees, not as a boss. She wants her employees to not only do their jobs but also to recreate, redesign, and expand them. Employees can earn $1,000 for proposing suggestions that help them do their job better. VCW Inc. also has a profit-sharing plan that gives employees a stake in the company's ability to make a profit. Womack also recognizes that employees need more than financial caring. To that end, she implemented on-site day care for employees' children, and employees enjoy inexpensive, delicious home-cooked meals at the office prepared by an employee who started at VCW in customer service but who had always dreamed of a job cooking for others. Cheryl strongly believes in the power of such benefits to show employees that she cares about them and wants them to be committed and productive at their jobs.

QUESTIONS

1. At which of the four management functions does Cheryl Womack seem to be particularly strong? Which of the management skills? Provide examples supporting your choices.
2. What can you learn about being a manager from Cheryl Womack? Be specific.
3. What do you think it means to be a mentor, not a boss?
4. Assess VCW's effectiveness as might be assessed by (a) banks, (b) employees, and (c) customers.

Source: Based on *Small Business 2000, Show 110.*

NOTES

1. Based on S. Sherman, "A Day in the Life of a Netscape Exec," *Fortune*, May 13, 1996, pp. 124–30.
2. Based on J. Kaufman, "For Richard Thibeault, Being a 'Manager' Is a Blue-Collar Life," *Wall Street Journal*, October 1, 1996, p. A1.
3. Almost all current management textbooks continue to define managers this way.
4. For a discussion of the antiquated views on hierarchy and how knowledge "technicians" blur the line between managerial and nonmanagerial work, see S. R. Barley, "Techni-

cians in the Workplace: Ethnographic Evidence for Bringing Work into Organization Studies," *Administrative Science Quarterly*, September 1996, pp. 404–41. For a discussion of "quasi-managerial roles," where individuals perform managerial functions but do not have hierarchical authority, see S. A. Mohrman and S. G. Cohen, "When People Get Out of the Box," in A. Howard (ed.), *The Changing Nature of Work* (San Francisco: Jossey-Bass, 1995), pp. 389–91.

5. J. J. Macionis, *Sociology*, 5th ed. (Englewood Cliffs, NJ: Prentice Hall, 1995), p. 188.

6. See O. E. Williamson, *Markets and Hierarchies: Analysis and Antitrust Implications* (New York: Free Press, 1975); and G. Miller, *Managerial Dilemmas* (London: Cambridge, 1992).

7. See B. M. Staw, "Organizational Behavior: A Review and Reformulation of the Field's Outcome Variables," in M. R. Rosenzweig and L. W. Porter (eds.), *Annual Review of Psychology*, vol. 35 (Palo Alto, CA: Annual Reviews, 1984), pp. 627–66; and S. P. Robbins, *Organizational Behavior*, 8th ed. (Upper Saddle River, NJ: Prentice Hall, 1998), pp. 22–28.

8. See, for instance, H. Koontz (ed.), *Toward a Unified Theory of Management* (New York: McGraw-Hill, 1964); and C. P. Hales, "What Do Managers Do? A Critical Review of the Evidence," *Journal of Management Studies*, January 1986, pp. 88–115.

9. H. Fayol, *Industrial and General Administration* (Paris: Dunod, 1916).

10. See, for instance, S. P. Robbins and M. K. Coulter, *Management*, 6th ed. (Upper Saddle River, NJ: Prentice Hall, 1999); J. R. Schermerhorn Jr., *Management*, 6th ed. (New York: Wiley, 1999); and R. L. Daft, *Management*, 4th ed. (Fort Worth, TX: Dryden, 1997).

11. H. Mintzberg, *The Nature of Managerial Work* (New York: Harper & Row, 1973). See also L. B. Kurke and H. E. Aldrich, "Mintzberg Was Right! A Replication and Extension of the Nature of Managerial Work," *Management Science*, August 1983, pp. 975–84; and G. R. Carroll and A. C. Teo, "On the Social Networks of Managers," *Academy of Management Journal*, April 1996, pp. 421–40.

12. The first three were originally proposed in R. L. Katz, "Skills of an Effective Administrator," *Harvard Business Review*, September–October 1974, pp. 90–102. The fourth was added by C. M. Pavett and A. W. Lau, "Managerial Work: The Influence of Hierarchical Level and Functional Specialty," *Academy of Management Journal*, March 1983, pp. 170–77.

13. F. Luthans, R. M. Hodgetts, and S. A. Rosenkrantz, *Real Managers* (Cambridge, MA: Ballinger, 1988); and D. A. Gioia and C. O. Longnecker, "Delving into the Dark Side: The Politics of Executive Appraisal," *Organizational Dynamics*, Winter 1994, pp. 47–58.

14. J. J. Morse and F. R. Wagner, "Measuring the Process of Managerial Effectiveness," *Academy of Management Journal*, March 1978, pp. 23–35.

15. See S. B. Parry, "The Quest for Competencies," *Training*, July 1996, pp. 48–56; "The Challenges in Applying Competencies," *Compensation & Benefits Review*, March–April 1997, pp. 64–75; P. A. McLagan, "Competencies: The Next

Generation," *Training & Development Journal*, May 1997, pp. 40–47; and S. B. Parry, "Just What Is a Competency?" *Training*, June 1998, pp. 58–64.

16. "Management Charter Initiative Issues Competence Standards," *Personnel Management*, October 1990, p. 17; "MCI Launches Standards for First Two Levels," *Personnel Management*, November 1990, p. 13; and L. Carrington, "Competent to Manage?" *International Management*, September 1994, p. 17.

17. See, for example, H. A. Simon, *Administrative Behavior* (New York: Macmillan, 1945); E. F. Harrison, *The Managerial Decision-Making Process*, 4th ed. (Boston: Houghton Mifflin, 1995); and M. H. Bazerman, *Judgment in Managerial Decision Making*, 3rd ed. (New York: Wiley, 1994).

18. H. A. Simon, *The New Science of Management Decision* (New York: Harper & Row, 1960), p. 1.

19. See J. R. Katzenbach, *Real Change Leaders* (New York: Times Books, 1997).

20. See, for example, K. Lewin, *Field Theory in Social Science* (New York: Harper & Row, 1951); N. Margulies and J. Wallace, *Organizational Change: Techniques and Applications* (Glenview, IL.: Scott, Foresman, 1973); and W. L. French and C. H. Bell Jr., *Organization Development*, 4th ed. (Upper Saddle River, NJ: Prentice Hall, 1990).

21. See, for example, M. Walton, *The Deming Management Method* (New York: Putnam/Perigee, 1986).

22. M. Hammer and J. Champy, *Reengineering the Corporation: A Manifesto for Business Revolution* (New York: HarperBusiness, 1993).

23. L. Smith, "Burned-Out Bosses," *Fortune*, July 25, 1994, p. 44.

24. T. Peters, *Thriving on Chaos: Handbook for a Management Revolution* (New York: Knopf, 1988). See also J. Huey, "Managing in the Midst of Chaos," *Fortune*, April 5, 1993, pp. 38–48.

25. See, for instance, C. D. Orth, H. E. Wilkinson, and R. C. Benfari, "The Manager's Role as Coach and Mentor," *Organizational Dynamics*, Spring 1987, pp. 66–74; and R. D. Evered and J. C. Selman, "Coaching and the Art of Management," *Organizational Dynamics*, Autumn 1989, pp. 16–31.

26. See, for example, J. Weber, "Letting Go Is Hard to Do," *Business Week*, November 1, 1993, pp. 218–19.

27. P. Drucker, *The Effective Executive* (New York: Harper & Row, 1967).

28. See T. Donaldson and L. E. Preston, "The Stakeholder Theory of the Corporation: Concepts, Evidence, and Implications," *Academy of Management Review*, January 1995, pp. 65–91; and R. K. Mitchell, B. R. Agle, and D. J. Wood, "Toward a Theory of Stakeholder Identification and Salience: Defining the Principle of Who and What Really Counts," *Academy of Management Review*, October 1997, pp. 853–86.

29. N. C. Roberts and P. J. King, "The Stakeholder Audit Goes Public," *Organizational Dynamics*, Winter 1989, pp. 63–79.

30. R. R. Rehder, "Is Saturn Competitive?" *Business Horizons*, March–April 1994, pp. 7–15.

31. See M. W. Meyer and V. Gupta, "The Performance Pardox," in B. M. Staw and L. L. Cummings (eds.), *Research in Organizational Behavior*, vol. 16 (Greenwich, CT: JAI, 1994), pp. 309–69.

32. Ibid., p. 322.

33. Cited in T. Moore, "Make-or-Break Time for General Motors," *Fortune*, February 15, 1988, p. 35.

34. B. O'Reilly, "The New Deal: What Companies and Employees Owe One Another," *Fortune*, June 13, 1994, pp. 44–52; and H. Lancaster, "A New Social Contract to Benefit Employer and Employee," *Wall Street Journal*, November 29, 1994, p. B1.

35. From "Richard Branson," *ABC News Business World*, November 22, 1992.

36. S. Fink, "Dow Corning's Moral Evasions," *New York Times*, February 16, 1992, p. F13.

37. R. H. Miles, *Coffin Nails and Corporate Strategies* (Upper Saddle River, NJ: Prentice Hall, 1982).

38. This box is based on R. S. Kaplan and D. P. Norton, "Using the Balanced Scoreboard As a Strategic Management System," *Harvard Business Review*, January–February 1996, pp. 75–85; R. S. Kaplan and D. P. Norton, "Linking the Balanced Scoreboard to Strategy," *California Management Review*, Fall 1996, pp. 53–78; and J. Kurtzman, "Is Your Company Off Course? Now You Can Find Out Why," *Fortune*, February 17, 1997, pp. 128–30.

39. C. K. Warriner, "The Problem of Organizational Purpose," *Sociological Quarterly*, Spring 1965, pp. 139–46.

MANAGEMENT: FROM A CROSS-DISCIPLINARY PERSPECTIVE

A few years ago, a student told me a story. At the end of every semester he liked to go through the same routine. After each final exam he would stop by the closest open garbage can, position his head over the can, tilt his head to the left, then slam the palm of his hand as hard as he could against his right ear. He considered this a necessary cleansing process to "free up brain space" for future courses he'd have to take.

While this story was meant to be a joke, there is a kernel of truth in it. College courses often seem to be independent bodies of knowledge. Because little of what is taught in one course tends to be linked to past or future courses, there isn't much need to hold on to what you've previously learned. This has certainly been true in most business curriculums. There is a lack of connectedness between core business courses and between courses in business and the liberal arts. Accounting classes, for instance, make little reference to marketing; and marketing classes typically make little reference to courses in economics or political science. The reality is that college curriculums have developed into something looking a lot like silos, each silo representing a separate and distinct discipline.

Management educators have begun to recognize the need to build bridges between these silos—to integrate courses across the college curriculum. But how is this to be accomplished? Actually, there are a number of ways for faculty to facilitate integration. Some examples include case analyses, organizational simulations, team activities, field trips, and capstone courses. This book takes a direct approach—specifically describing, at the end of each part, how issues and concepts in other courses are applicable to the management topics just presented.

You'll find these sections organized around two blocks of courses. The first covers the *humanities and social sciences*. The purpose of this section will be to help you see how your courses in disciplines such as economics, psychology, sociology, political science, philosophy, and speech communications relate to topics in management.

The second section addresses core *business disciplines* such as accounting, finance, marketing, and operations. Although often overlooked or underemphasized because of the "silo effect," these disciplines have direct relevance to management. You'll see, for example, that accounting isn't just for accountants. Today's managers require a basic understanding of accounting concepts and techniques in order to do their jobs effectively.

The "big picture" is often lost when management and organizational behavior concepts are studied in isolation. By adding this cross-disciplinary perspective, you'll gain a greater appreciation of how general-education classes and other business courses are useful to students of organizations. This, in turn, will help you to be a more effective manager and leader.

Humanities and the Social Sciences

ECONOMICS Economics is concerned with the allocation and distribution of scarce resources. It provides us with an understanding of the changing economy as well as the role of competition and free markets in a global context.

For example, why are most athletic shoes made in Asia? Or why does Mexico now have more automobile plants than Detroit? Economists provide the answers to these questions when they discuss comparative advantage. Similarly, an understanding of free trade and protectionist policies is absolutely essential to any manager operating in the global marketplace.

PSYCHOLOGY Psychology is the science that seeks to measure, explain, and sometimes change the behavior of humans and other animals. Psychologists concern themselves with studying and attempting to understand individual behavior.

The field of psychology is leading the way in providing managers with insights into human diversity. Today's managers confront both a diverse customer base and a diverse set of employees. Psychologists' efforts to understand gender and cultural diversity provide managers with a better understanding of the needs of their changing customer and employee populations.

SOCIOLOGY Sociology studies people in relation to their fellow human beings. What are some of the issues that sociologists have investigated that have relevance to managers? Here's a few. How are societal changes such as globalization, cultural diversity, gender roles, and family life affecting organizational practices? What are the implications of schooling practices and education trends on future employees' skills and abilities? How are changing demographics altering customer and employment markets? What will the postindustrial society look like?

ANTHROPOLOGY Anthropology is the study of societies to learn about human beings and their activities. Anthropologists' work on cultures and environments, for instance, has helped us understand differences in fundamental values, attitudes, and behavior between people in different countries and within different organizations.

PHILOSOPHY Philosophy courses inquire into the nature of things, particularly values and ethics.

Ethics are standards governing human conduct. Ethical concerns go directly to the existence of organizations and what constitutes proper behavior within them. For instance, the liberty ethic (John Locke) proposed that freedom, equality, justice, and private property were legal rights; the Protestant ethic (John Calvin) encouraged individuals to be frugal, work hard, and attain success; and the market ethic (Adam Smith) argued that the market and competition, not government, should be the sole regulators of economic activity. These ethics have shaped today's organizations by providing a basis for legitimate authority, linking rewards to performance, and justifying the existence of business and the corporate form.

POLITICAL SCIENCE Political science studies the behavior of individuals and groups within a political environment. Specific topics of concern to political scientists include structuring of conflict, allocation of power, and how people manipulate power for individual self-interest.

Capitalism is just one form of economic system. The former Soviet Union and much of Eastern Europe, for example, were based on socialistic concepts. Planned economies were not free markets. Rather, government owned most of the goods-producing businesses. And organizational decision makers essentially carried out dictates from government-established policies. Efficiency had little meaning in such economies. There was no competition in most of the basic industries because they were government controlled. In many cases, effectiveness was defined by how many people a plant employed rather than by any basic financial criteria.

Management is affected by a nation's form of government, whether it allows its citizens to hold property, by the ability to engage in and enforce contracts, and by the appeal mechanisms available to redress grievances. In a democracy, for instance, people typically have the right of private property, the freedom to enter or not to enter into contracts, and an appeal system for justice. A nation's stand on property, contracts, and justice, in turn, shapes the type, form, and policies of its organizations.

Business Disciplines

MARKETING Marketing is a process by which individuals and groups obtain what they need and want through creating, offering, and exchanging products (goods, services, ideas) of value with others.

Today's customers are placing greater weight on quality and value in making their purchasing decisions. Managers play a crucial role in this by their efforts to increase quality and bring down their costs through increasing efficiency. Efforts at continuous improvement, for instance, allow organizations to better satisfy customer needs and wants.

Marketing is playing a major role in helping organizations to pursue markets beyond their borders. Globalization requires managers to drop their traditional assumptions about market behavior and adapt their offerings to other countries' cultures.

OPERATIONS The discipline of production-and-operations management (POM) is concerned with the efficient transformation of the organization's inputs into outputs. It focuses on the conversion process by which physical and human resources are transformed into goods and services. General topics within POM that have clear links to management include introducing new technologies and improving quality, productivity, and competitiveness.

From the late 1800s until about the mid-1950s, the field of management was essentially shaped by what we, today, would call manufacturing or production management. The early "research" in management focused on means for improving the production process. Today's students of operations management study subjects such as work layout, time-and-motion study, and job design. A hundred years ago, that was the essence of management theory! The field of management is built on the solid foundation originally laid down by the discipline that today we call production-and-operations management.

MAKING DECISIONS

THE DECISION NOT TO DECIDE IS STILL A DECISION.
IT'S A DECISION TO MAINTAIN THE STATUS QUO.

ANONYMOUS

LEARNING OBJECTIVES

After studying this chapter, you should be able to:

1 ▶ Explain the six-step rational decision-making model and its assumptions.

2 ▶ Contrast risk with uncertainty.

3 ▶ Demonstrate increased creativity in your decisions.

4 ▶ Identify and describe popular quantitative techniques for improving decision making.

5 ▶ Contrast the conditions favoring individual decisions with those favoring groups.

6 ▶ Describe actions of the boundedly rational decision maker.

7 ▶ Identify four decision-making styles.

8 ▶ Explain how managers can improve their decision making.

They say that necessity is the mother of invention. For Bill Bartmann, it proved to be absolutely true.[1]

It was 1985. Bartmann was in the business of manufacturing pipes for oil rigs in Oklahoma. Out of the blue, OPEC's oil cartel collapsed and, with it, the price of crude. Almost immediately, drilling in Oklahoma came to a near halt. Within three months, sales of his pipe went from $1 million a month to zero. Bartmann was forced to close out his business. If that wasn't bad enough, he was $1 million in debt.

Bill collectors hounded Bartmann for their money. He was getting telephone calls from collection agents at all hours of the day and night. They were threatening lawsuits, hurling insults, and demanding money he didn't have. In the eyes of these collectors, he had become a deadbeat. Wanting to avoid bankruptcy, Bartmann decided he needed a truly outsized risk, an absurd long shot, to get himself out of his financial hole. Risk, he knew, was the reciprocal of reward, and the reward he required was very, very large.

Bartmann investigated all types of new business ventures. Nothing seemed right. Then one day he saw an unusual advertisement. The Federal Deposit Insurance Corporation was auctioning off the delinquent loans it had inherited from a failed bank in Tulsa. Maybe this was the high-reward opportunity he was looking for. He went to the auction. Only one other bidder showed up. Obviously this "opportunity" wasn't so self-evident to others! Some 200 portfolios of bad loans were for sale, ranging from the mildly delinquent to the long-since-considered-unredeemable. Bartmann began inspecting the latter. As he reviewed the files, he saw the collectors' records of their unsuccessful efforts. Their most common comment: "This deadbeat won't pay." And then it struck him: "I realized, *This is me*." He thought of the angry voices on the phone pestering and intimidating him for their money. He was convinced their style was unproductive. He thought he could do better. So he scraped up what little money he could get his hands on and bought those delinquent loans for two cents on the dollar.

Out of that decision, Commerical Financial Services (CFS) was born. In just 12 years, Bartmann has turned CFS into the world's biggest repository of bad consumer debt. In one recent year, with a staff of 2,500 highly trained collection agents, CFS made nearly half a billion dollars in income on a billion dollars in sales. His 80 percent stake in the firm is worth a startling $2.4 billion. Bill Bartmann is now one of the 25 wealthiest people in America—just ahead of Rupert Murdoch and Ross Perot. This all came about because he saw an opportunity others didn't, and he made the decision to act on it.

Making decisions is a critical element of organizational life. In this chapter, we focus on two different approaches to understanding decision making. First we describe how decisions should be made. Then, we review a large body of evidence to show you how decisions actually are made in organizations. Finally, we present some specific suggestions on how managers can improve their decision-making effectiveness.

Let's begin our discussion of decision making by describing how individuals should behave in order to maximize or optimize a certain outcome.

HOW SHOULD DECISIONS BE MADE?

The Rational Decision-Making Process

The optimizing decision maker is **rational**. That is, he or she makes consistent, value-maximizing choices within specified constraints.[2] These choices are made following a six-step model.[3] Moreover, specific assumptions underlie this model.[4]

THE RATIONAL MODEL The six steps in the rational decision-making model are illustrated in Exhibit 3-1. The model begins by *defining the problem*. A problem exists when there is a discrepancy between an existing and a desired state of affairs.[5] Many poor decisions can be traced to the decision maker's overlooking a problem or defining the wrong problem.

Once a decision maker has defined the problem, he or she needs to *identify the decision criteria* that will be important in solving the problem. In this step, the decision maker is determining what is relevant in making the decision. This step brings the decision maker's interests, values, and personal preferences into the process. Identifying criteria is important because what one person thinks is relevant, another may not. Also keep in mind that any factors not identified in this step are considered irrelevant to the decision maker.

The criteria identified are rarely all equal in importance. So the third step requires that the decision maker *weight the previously identified criteria* in order to give them correct priority in the decision.

The fourth step requires the decision maker to *generate possible alternatives* that could succeed in resolving the problem. No attempt is made in this step to appraise these alternatives, only to list them.

Once the alternatives have been generated, the decision maker must critically analyze and evaluate each one. This is done by *rating each alternative on each criterion*. The strengths and weaknesses of each alternative become evident as they are compared with the criteria and weights established in the second and third steps.

The final step in this model requires *computing the optimal decision*. How is this done? By using something called "expected value," which we will describe in the next section. In essence, it requires the decision maker to multiply the expected effectiveness of each choice times the weighting of each criterion times the rating of each criterion for each alternative. The alternative with the highest expected value then becomes the optimal or optimizing choice.

EXHIBIT 3-1   **The Six-Step Rational Decision-Making Model**

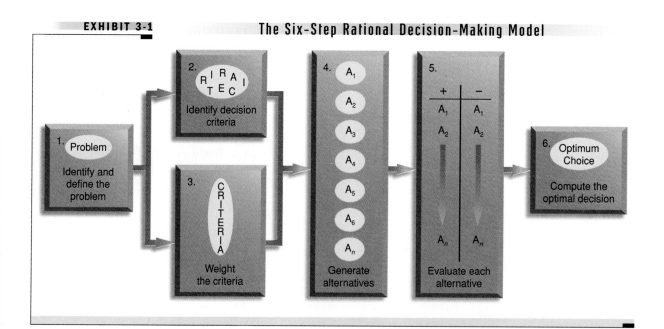

We can use this six-step model to describe how someone *should* make a decision. For instance, take the college-selection decision as an example. If you used the rational model, the process would look something like this: Your graduation from high school creates a problem. What do you do *now*? Let's assume that you've chosen to attend college (versus other, noncollege options). So you begin listing the criteria that will be relevant in your decision. These might include factors such as availability of financial aid, school's reputation, annual cost, degree offerings, geographical location, quality of social life, and the like. After listing these criteria, you weight them in order to prioritize their importance. For instance, using a 1-to-10 scale (with 10 being most important), you might determine that availability of financial aid rates a 10, while quality of social life rates 4. In other words, financial aid is considered 2.5 times as important as social life in your decision. After weighting your criteria, you list all the viable colleges that could possibly be in your decision set. For some people, this list might include dozens of colleges. Then you need to evaluate each of these college options. The strengths and weaknesses of each alternative become evident when they are compared against the criteria and weights previously established. Finally, if you are following the rational decision model, you will choose the college that scored the highest expected value. And you will have made an optimal decision.

ASSUMPTIONS OF THE MODEL The rational decision-making model we just described contains six assumptions:

1. *Problem clarity*. The problem is clear and unambiguous. The decision maker is assumed to have complete information regarding the decision situation.
2. *Known options*. The decision maker can identify all the relevant criteria and can list all the viable alternatives. Further, the decision maker is aware of all the possible consequences of each alternative.
3. *Clear preferences*. The criteria and alternatives can be ranked and weighted to reflect their importance.
4. *Constant preferences*. The specific decision criteria are constant, and the weights assigned to them are stable over time.
5. *No time or cost constraints*. The rational decision maker can obtain full information about criteria and alternatives because it is assumed that there are no time or cost constraints.
6. *Maximum payoff*. The rational decision maker will choose the alternative that yields the highest perceived value.

Rationality is enhanced by understanding uncertainty and risk, creative problem solving, and quantitative analysis. The following sections review those topics.

▶ Uncertainty and Risk

One of the more challenging tasks facing a decision maker is analyzing alternatives. This analysis is done under one of three sets of conditions. In some cases, decisions are made under the conditions of **certainty**. This means that the decision maker knows in advance the outcome of the decision. For instance, the treasurer of Alcoa recently received $100 million from the sale of bonds but didn't need the money for 6 months. He invested it in 6-month Treasury bills that paid 5.20 percent annual interest. The treasurer was certain that when the T-bills matured he would receive $102.6 million. Unfortunately, few decisions are made under conditions of certainty.

EXHIBIT 3-2

Expected Value of Two Retail Locations

Alternative	Possible Outcome	Probability	Expected Value
Ft. Lauderdale	$40,000 profit	0.6	$24,000
	10,000 loss	0.4	(4,000)
			$20,000
Palm Beach	$25,000 profit	0.5	$12,500
	10,000 profit	0.5	5,000
			$17,500

A far more typical situation is one of risk. **Risk** refers to those conditions in which the decision maker is able to estimate the likelihood of alternatives or outcomes. This ability to assign probabilities may be the result of personal experience or secondary information. One of the more visible illustrations of dealing with risk conditions are military leaders who have to make decisions during times of war. For instance, during the Persian Gulf War, General Schwarzkopf had to decide when to begin the ground assault to free Kuwait. Schwarzkopf and his aides calculated probabilities for various scenarios and used those calculations in making the final decision.

A rational approach to evaluating alternatives under risk conditions is the use of expected value. **Expected value** is a concept that allows decision makers to place a numerical value on the positive and negative consequences likely to result from the selection of a particular alternative. It equals the summation of various possible outcomes multiplied by the benefit or cost from each outcome. If you are thinking about opening a small retail business and have narrowed your alternatives down to two locations, you could use expected value to help you make your final choice. As shown in Exhibit 3-2, assume you've calculated two possible outcomes for each store location. You can ascertain that the expected value of locating your store in Palm Beach is $17,500, and in Ft. Lauderdale, it's $20,000. On the basis of expected value analysis alone, locating in Ft. Lauderdale is your better choice.

The most difficult condition to make decisions under is **uncertainty**. In this situation, decision makers don't have enough information to be clear about alternatives or to estimate their risk. So what do they do? They rely on their intuition or creativity. Many decisions currently being made in the telecommunications industry fall into this category. For instance, Bill Gates (Microsoft co-founder), Craig McCaw (founder of McCaw Cellular), and Boeing are each committing huge sums of money to build a $9 billion satellite network. They're gambling that their company, Teledesic, will become a worldwide information transfer system that can successfully compete against established phone, cellular, and cable companies.[6]

▶ Creativity

The rational decision maker needs **creativity**, that is, the ability to produce a product, service, idea, procedure, or process that is both novel or unusual and useful.[7] To illustrate, consider an executive at Revlon, the cosmetic giant, who is concerned with developing a new item to add to the company's product line. The suggestion that the company sell sugar cookies is novel but not useful. And the idea to sell a new shade of red lipstick is useful but not creative.

Why is this ability so important? Creativity allows a decision maker to more fully appraise and understand a problem and to see problems others can't see. However, creativity's most obvious value is in helping the decision maker identify all viable alternatives.

CREATIVE POTENTIAL Most people have unused creative potential that they can call upon when confronted with a decision-making problem. But to unleash that potential, they have to get out of the psychological ruts most of us get into and learn how to think about a problem in divergent ways.

We can start with the obvious. People differ in their inherent creativity. Einstein, Edison, Picasso, and Mozart were individuals of exceptional creativity. By definition, however, exceptional creativity is scarce. A study of lifetime creativity of 461 men and women found that fewer than 1 percent were exceptionally creative.[8] But 10 percent were highly creative, and about 60 percent were somewhat creative. This result suggests that most of us have creative potential, if we can learn to unleash it.[9]

THE HIGHLY CREATIVE INDIVIDUAL What, if anything, can we say about highly creative people? What qualities differentiate them from the more typical individual?

Studies indicate a number of characteristics associated with high creativity.[10] These include self-confidence, independence of judgment, intuition, broad interests, curiosity, ability to tolerate ambiguity and complexity, willingness to take risks and make mistakes, and persistence in the face of obstacles. Interestingly, contrary to what many believe, creative people aren't necessarily super intelligent.[11] Creative individuals are intelligent— they have above-average IQs. But beyond a certain point, higher scores don't appear to be related to higher creativity. The cutoff seems to be around 120.

THE CREATIVE CLIMATE Even individuals with strong creative characteristics can have their creativity sapped by an unsupportive work climate. That said, what kind of workplace is likely to bring creativity out of people? We can identify five organizational characteristics associated with stimulating employee creativity.[12]

Kim Bromley, visual effects producer for Industrial Light & Magic, oversees special effects creative teams. Her challenge is to allow each team member to follow his or her creative instincts while, at the same time, insuring projects are finished on time.

The first is a culture that encourages and rewards risk taking. People have to feel that holding unorthodox views is acceptable. Very importantly, individuals can't be penalized for mistakes. Being creative, by definition, means fostering ideas that are unusual. As soon as such behavior is penalized, you can expect it to decline.

Second, creative work climates are characterized by porous boundaries. Rigid barriers between departments and other organizational units are minimized. Why? Because rigid boundaries limit interactions. Porous boundaries encourage spontaneity and face-to-face interactions, which stimulate creative thinking.

Third, creativity is fostered when individuals have considerable autonomy. This freedom allows creative juices to flow and gives people choices in how to go about accomplishing their tasks.

The fourth is an abundance of slack resources. It's hard to be creative where there isn't adequate money, equipment, or people. Slack resources also allow room for mistakes, which reinforces employees' willingness to take risks.

Finally, creative work climates are characterized by moderate levels of workload and time pressures. Some degree of pressure seems to stimulate creativity by encouraging a sense of urgency. However, extreme levels of pressure create stress and act to retard creativity.

> The mere action of telling yourself that you're going to try to think "outside the box" and avoid obvious approaches to problems has shown to lead to more creative ideas.

METHODS FOR STIMULATING INDIVIDUAL CREATIVITY To stimulate creativity, the place to begin is with having a *supportive work climate*. It should possess the five characteristics noted in the previous section. Once the right climate exists, what else can be done to enhance creativity? Here are some suggestions you can use to increase your creativity and help you develop unique decision alternatives.[13]

Believe that you *can* be creative. The mere action of telling yourself that you're going to try to think "outside the box" and avoid obvious approaches to problems has shown to lead to more creative ideas.

Don't begin by searching for the one "right" answer to a problem. Keep your mind open to the fact that there is rarely a single best answer to any given dilemma. Even when you quickly come up with what you believe is the best answer, keep searching for other alternatives.

Avoid being too logical and rational. It's OK to use random or what may appear to be "irrelevant" information. And you don't have to think sequentially. It's OK, for example, to begin with a solution and, working backward, create alternative beginning states. You often have to get off the main highway and take some unchartered side roads if you're going to discover something new.

Don't be concerned with always developing practical solutions. What may appear as impractical, even silly, at first glance can, on closer examination, be the thrust to get you out of the box or to see the problem in a different light.

Ask "what if" questions. Avoid the status quo and "tried and true" solutions by continually challenging yourself with questions.

Finally, don't be afraid to fail. Creative solutions don't always work. The safest routes are usually to continue to do what you've always been doing. If you're going to go down a road that hasn't been taken before, you're likely to run into a dead end. But you may also find a wonderful new shortcut that no one else knows about.

▶ Quantitative Analysis

Students of management typically spend considerable time learning quantitative decision techniques in courses with titles such as "Operations Research," "Decision Sciences," and "Quantitative Methods." These courses are meant to help students develop rational, analytical tools for objectively appraising decision alternatives. In this section, we'll briefly introduce the more popular of these quantitative techniques. Our objective here is simply to make you aware of what they are and what they can generally do, so our discussion will be descriptive rather than technical.

BREAK-EVEN ANALYSIS   How many units of a product must an organization sell in order to break even—that is, to have neither profit nor loss? A decision maker might want to know the minimum number of units that must be sold to achieve his or her profit objective or whether a current product should continue to be sold or be dropped from the organization's product line. **Break-even analysis** is a widely used financial decision-making technique that enables decision makers to determine whether a particular sales volume will result in losses or profits.[14]

Break-even analysis is a simplistic formulation, yet it is valuable to decision makers because it points out the relationship between revenues, costs, and profits. To compute the break-even point (BE), the decision maker needs to know the unit price of the product being sold (P), the variable cost per unit (VC), and total fixed costs (TFC).

An organization breaks even when its total revenue is just enough to equal its total costs. But total costs has two parts: a fixed component and a variable component. *Fixed costs* are expenses that do not change, regardless of volume. Examples include insurance premiums and property taxes. Fixed costs, of course, are fixed only in the short-term because, in the long run, commitments terminate and thus are subject to variation. *Variable costs* change in proportion to output and include raw materials, labor costs, and energy costs.

The break-even point can be computed graphically or by using the following formula:

$$BE = \frac{TFC}{P-VC}$$

This formula tells us that (1) total revenue will equal total cost when we sell enough units at a price that covers all variable unit costs and (2) the difference between price and variable costs, when multiplied by the number of units sold, equals the fixed costs.

For example, assume that Dave's Copy Center charges 10 cents per photocopy. If fixed costs are $27,000 a year and variable costs are 4 cents per copy, Dave can compute his break-even point as follows: $27,000 ÷ ($0.10–$0.04) = 450,000 copies, or when annual revenues are $45,000. This same relationship is shown graphically in Exhibit 3-3.

RETURN ON INVESTMENT   Another financial decision tool is **return on investment** (ROI). Among business firms, ROI is a highly popular single criterion by which to measure productivity of assets. By computing profits as a percentage of capital invested, an organization can determine how well the investment is being utilized to generate profits. Thus, ROI can be used to compare firms within industries and between industries.

For example, Checkpoint Systems and Code Alarm are two companies that are both in the electronic security control systems business. In one recent year, Checkpoint had net profits of $1.62 million, while Code Alarm's net profits were a bit lower at $1.54 million. But in terms of return on investment, Code Alarm was much more impressive. Code Alarm's ROI was 6.4 percent against Checkpoint Systems' 1.8 percent.[15] Checkpoint Systems required considerably more investment than did Code Alarm to generate similar profits. As this example illustrates, ROI directs attention away from absolute profits and focuses on how efficient a company is in using its assets.

EXHIBIT 3-3

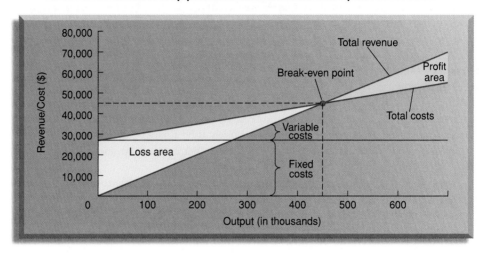

Dave's Copy Center Break-Even Analysis

MARGINAL ANALYSIS The concept of marginal, or incremental, analysis helps decision makers optimize returns or minimize costs. **Marginal analysis** deals with the additional cost in a particular decision rather than the average cost. Specifically, it analyzes decisions by focusing on incremental costs. Your author had a recent experience where a major U.S. airline failed to properly use marginal analysis. The end result was that the airline passed up a profit opportunity and angered a potential customer.

My wife and I were flying from Rome to Seattle by way of New York. Our Delta flight from Rome arrived an hour late into New York, and we missed our United connection to Seattle. Fortunately, TWA had a nonstop flight leaving for Seattle in an hour, and United offered to endorse our tickets over to TWA. Unfortunately for us and TWA, the TWA ticket agent we dealt with and her supervisor didn't understand marginal analysis. The flight to Seattle had empty seats. We had paid $199 each for our United tickets to Seattle. The added cost to put my wife and me on that TWA flight was less than $9 a passenger (the cost of a dinner, some peanuts, and a couple of beverages). Yet TWA demanded full price from us—$899 each!—to allow us on that flight. They wouldn't budge from this listed full fare. We passed on their offer, and the TWA flight left with two more empty seats than it needed to. By not having us on that flight, TWA reduced its profits by around $380 $[2 \times (199 - 9)]$. An understanding of marginal analysis would have permitted the ticket agent and her supervisor to understand that the decision should not have focused on the full cost of flying passengers from New York to Seattle. The decision should have been made on the basis of whether the revenue from two additional passengers would cover the incremental costs of flying them.

GAME THEORY Game theory is currently one of the hottest techniques in quantitative analysis. Its major developers won the 1994 Nobel Prize in economics. And it is being used to help decision makers bid on contracts, negotiate labor agreements, develop expansion plans, and make a host of other decisions. For instance, executives at Pacific Telesis recently relied on game theory experts to help the company submit winning bids for wireless communications rights auctioned off by the Federal Communications Commission.[16]

Game theory uses mathematical models to analyze the outcomes that will emerge in multiparty decision-making contexts if all parties act rationally.[17] To analyze a game, the decision maker outlines specific conditions that define how decisions are to be made and then attaches outcome probabilities to every possible combination of player response. The actual analysis focuses on predicting whether an agreement will be reached and, if one is reached, what the specific nature of that agreement will be. The following illustrates how game theory works.

Say you have two competitors, Ace and Smith. Ace expects Smith to enter the market and is trying to understand Smith's likely pricing strategy. To do so, Ace uses something called a "payoff matrix" (see Exhibit 3-4). Each quadrant in the matrix contains the "payoffs"—or financial impact—to each player for each possible strategy. If both players maintain prices at current levels, they will both be better off: Ace will earn $100 million, and Smith will earn $60 million (quadrant A). Unfortunately for both Ace and Smith, however, they have perverse incentives to cut prices.

Ace calculates that if he maintains prices, Smith will cut prices to increase earnings to $70 million from $60 million. (See arrow moving from quadrant A to

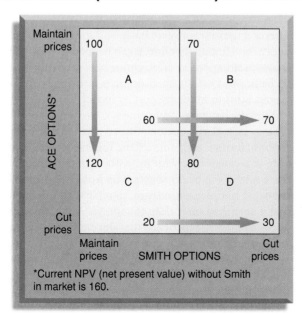

Game Theory Payoff Matrix (in millions of NPV)

Source: McKinsey & Co. Reproduced in F.W. Barnett, "Making Game Theory Work in Practice," *Wall Street Journal*, February 13, 1995, p. A14. Reprinted by permission of the *Wall Street Journal*, © 1995, Dow Jones & Company, Inc. All rights reserved worldwide.

EXHIBIT 3-4

quadrant B.) Smith makes a similar calculation that if she maintains prices, Ace will cut. The logic eventually drives them both to quadrant D, with both cutting prices and both earning lower returns than they would with current prices in place. This "equilibrium" is unattractive for both parties. If each party perceives this, then there is some prospect that each will separately determine to try to compete largely on other factors, such as product features, service levels, sales force deployment, or advertising.[18]

LINEAR PROGRAMMING **Linear programming** uses graphical or algebraic techniques to optimally solve resource allocation dilemmas. It requires competition between two or more activities for limited resources and assumes a linear relationship in the problem and the objective. For example, if we assume that spending depends on income, then a linear relationship exists when we say that if income goes up 10 percent, spending also increases by 10 percent. Linear programming is especially useful when input data can be quantified and objectives are subject to definite measurement.[19] What kind of problems would these be? Selecting transportation routes that minimize shipping costs, allocating a limited advertising budget among various product brands, making the optimum assignment of personnel among projects, and determining how much of each product to make with a limited number of resources are a few.

For example, assume that an automobile manufacturer that makes both cars and trucks seeks to maximize its profits. Also assume that we know the profit generated by each truck or car produced. If the manufacturer has scarce resources—for example, a given production space and a given number of available labor hours—and if resources expended to manufacture trucks are at the expense of resources expended to manufacture cars, we could utilize linear programming techniques to determine how many cars and how many trucks should be produced to maximize profit.

QUEUING THEORY Whenever a decision involves balancing the cost of having a waiting line against the cost of service to maintain that line, it can be made easier with queuing theory. This includes such common situations as determining how many gas pumps are needed at gas stations, tellers at bank windows, or check-in lines at airline ticket counters. In each situation, decision makers want to minimize cost by having as few stations open as possible, yet not so few as to test the patience of customers.

A simple example may help clarify queuing theory. Assume that you are a bank supervisor. One of your responsibilities is assigning tellers. You have five teller windows, but you want to know whether you can get by with only one window open during an average morning. You consider 6 minutes to be the longest you would expect any customer to wait patiently in line. If it takes 2 minutes, on average, to serve each customer, the line should not be permitted to get longer than three deep (6 minutes ÷ 2 minutes per customer = 3 customers). If you know from past experience that during the morning people arrive at the average rate of 24 an hour, you can calculate the probability (P) that the line will become longer than any number (n) of customers as follows:

$$P_n = (1 - \text{arrival rate/service rate}) \times (\text{arrival rate/service rate})^n$$

where n = 6 customers; arrival rate = 24 an hour, and service rate = 2 minutes (or 30 per hour) per customer. Putting these numbers into the above formula generates the following:

$$P_3 = (1 - 24/30) \times (24 \neq 30)^3 = (1/5)(13,824/27,000 = (.20) \times (.512) = .1024$$

What does a P_6 of 0.1024 mean? It tells you that the likelihood of having more than three customers in line during the morning is about one chance in 10. Are you willing to live with four or more customers in line 10 percent of the time? If so, keeping one teller window open will be enough. If not, you'll need to add windows and assign additional personnel to staff them.

We're not interested in all decision making. Our focus is on decisions in organizations. Therefore, we need to address the issue of who makes decisions. First, we look at individuals versus groups to learn when one is preferable. Then we look at level in the organization. When should decisions be made by top managers, middle managers, first-level supervisors, or the operating employees themselves?

▶ The Individual Versus Groups

The belief—characterized by juries—that two heads are better than one has long been accepted as a basic component of North American and many countries' legal systems. This belief has expanded to the point that, today, many decisions in organizations are made by groups (sometimes also called *teams* or *committees*). But groups aren't always preferable to individuals as decision makers. Let's review the strengths of each.[20]

STRENGTHS OF INDIVIDUAL DECISION MAKING A major plus with individual decision making is *speed*. An individual doesn't have to convene a meeting and spend time discussing various alternatives. So when a decision is needed quickly, individuals have the advantage. Individual decisions also have *clear accountability*. You know who made the decision and, therefore, who is responsible for the decision's outcome. Accountability is more ambiguous with group decisions. A third strength of individual decisions is that they tend to convey *consistent values*. Group decisions can suffer from intragroup power struggles. This disadvantage is best illustrated by decisions of the U.S. Congress. Decisions can vary by as much as 180 degrees from one session to the next, reflecting the makeup of members and their ability to influence their peers on any specific issue. Individuals are not perfectly consistent in their decision making, but they do tend to be more consistent than groups.

STRENGTHS OF GROUP DECISION MAKING Groups generate *more complete information and knowledge*. By aggregating the resources of several individuals, groups bring more input into the decision process. In addition to more input, groups can bring heterogeneity to the decision process. They offer *increased diversity of views*. This opens up the opportunity for more approaches and alternatives to be considered. The evidence indicates that a group will almost always outperform even the best individual. So groups generate *higher-quality decisions*. Finally, groups lead to *increased acceptance of a solution*. Many decisions fail after the final choice is made because people don't accept the solution. Group members who participated in making a decision are more likely to enthusiastically support the decision and encourage others to accept it.

BALANCING PROS AND CONS There are times when decisions are best handled by individuals. For example, evidence indicates that individuals are preferred when the decision is relatively unimportant and does not require employee commitment to its success. Similarly, individuals should make the decision when they have sufficient information and when others will be committed to the outcome even if they're not consulted.[21]

> Individuals are not perfectly consistent in their decision making, but they do tend to be more consistent than groups.

Silicon Graphics is one company that relies heavily on groups for decision making.

Overall, whether individuals or groups should make a decision essentially comes down to weighing effectiveness against efficiency. In terms of effectiveness, groups are superior. They generate more alternatives, are more creative, more accurate, and produce higher-quality decisions than do individuals. But individuals are more efficient than groups. Group efficiency suffers because they consume more time and resources to achieve their solution.

Decision-Making Level

In chapter 2, we provided a pyramid-shaped figure that identified four organizational levels. They included three levels of formal management—top, middle, and first-line—plus operative employees. We return to these four levels to ask: At which of these levels should decisions be made? The answer is: It depends. Let's briefly review what it *depends upon* and which decisions are best made at which level.[22]

Generally speaking, recurring and routine decisions (often referred to as **programmed decisions**) are best handled at lower levels of management and by the workers themselves. Conversely, nonrecurring and unique decisions (also frequently called **nonprogrammed decisions**) are better handled by top management. Similarly, top management is better qualified to make long-term strategic decisions—such as determining what the organization's business is, the organization's overall strategic direction and objectives, and where to allocate key resources of capital and people. Middle-level managers are best equipped to handle coordinating decisions that have medium-term implications. First-line managers should focus on more-routine departmental decisions. They typically make "what" decisions—determining *what* needs to be done. Finally, operative employees are best able to make job-related operating decisions. These are "how" decisions—determining *how* to get the work done.

These guidelines need to be tempered to reflect the delegating of decision-making authority to lower levels in the organization. In all but the smallest organizations, top management cannot make all the decisions. There would be too many to make. Decision making would become incredibly slow and laborious, bogged down at the top. So managers push decisions down to lower levels. Even strategic decisions may filter down to middle and lower-level managers for ideas. These managers might even actively participate in evaluating alternatives and choosing a final course of action. But the final responsibility for strategic decisions stays with top management.

EXHIBIT 3-5

Source: *Non Sequitur*, by Wiley, September 4, 1995. © 1995, Washington Post Writers Group. Reprinted with permission.

Two recent trends are significantly influencing who makes decisions in organizations. First, middle management positions are being reduced in many large organizations.[23] Middle managers historically existed to channel information between upper management and operating departments. They gathered information, processed it, interpreted it, and passed it either up or down. Computerized management information systems, however, now allow top executives to bypass middle management and communicate directly with supervisors, project teams, and individual employees. So many of the decisions previously made by middle managers are now either being made by top managers or being pushed down to the lowest levels. The second relevant trend is toward empowering operating employees with decision authority.[24] As noted in chapter 2, individuals and teams are increasingly being given greater discretion over work-related decisions. In contrast to 15 or 20 years ago, many of the decisions that had been the province of managers have been turned over to employees. As a result, having effective decision-making skills is becoming increasingly important for all employees—not just for managers.

HOW ARE DECISIONS ACTUALLY MADE IN ORGANIZATIONS?

Are decision makers in organizations rational? Do they carefully assess problems, identify all relevant criteria, use their creativity to identify all viable alternatives, and painstakingly evaluate every alternative to find an optimizing choice? In some situations they do. When decision makers are faced with a simple problem having few alternative courses of action, and when the cost of searching out and evaluating alternatives is low, the rational model provides a fairly accurate description of the decision process.[25] But such situations are the exception. Most decisions in the real world do not follow the rational model.[26] For instance, people are usually content to find an acceptable or reasonable solution to their problem rather than an optimizing one.[27] So decision makers generally make limited use of their creativity. Choices tend to be confined to the neighborhood of the problem symptom and to the neighborhood of the current alternative.[28] Moreover, even though an increasing number of decision makers are aware of and capable of using quantitative analysis, they rarely do.[29] And when they do, it's a good bet that it's to objectively support decisions that were made subjectively. As one expert in decision making recently concluded: "Most significant decisions are made by judgment, rather than by a defined prescriptive model."[30] The following sections review a large body of evidence to provide you with a description of how most decisions in organizations are actually made.

▶ Bounded Rationality

When you considered which college to attend, did you look at every viable alternative? Did you carefully identify all the criteria that were important in your decision? Did you calculate the expected value of each alternative against the criteria in order to find the optimum college? I expect the answer to all those questions is no. Well, don't feel bad. Most people chose their college in the same way you did. Instead of optimizing, they "satisficed."

When faced with a complex problem, most people respond by reducing the problem to a level at which it can be readily understood. They do so because the limited information-processing capability of human beings makes it impossible to assimilate and understand all the information necessary to optimize. So people *satisfice*; that is, they seek solutions that are *satisfactory* and *sufficient*.

Because the capacity of the human mind for formulating and solving complex problems is far too small to meet the requirements for full rationality, individuals operate within the confines of **bounded rationality**. They construct simplified models that extract the essential features from problems without capturing all their complexity.[31] Individuals can then behave rationally within the limits of the simple model.

How does bounded rationality work for the typical individual? Once a problem is identified, the search for criteria and alternatives begins. But the list of criteria is likely to be far from exhaustive. The decision maker will identify a limited list made up of the more conspicuous choices. These are the choices that are easy to find and that tend to be highly visible. In most cases, they will represent familiar criteria and tried-and-true solutions. Once this limited set of alternatives is identified, the decision maker will begin reviewing them. But the review will not be comprehensive—not all the alternatives will be evaluated carefully. Instead, the decision maker will begin with alternatives that differ only in a relatively small degree from the choice currently in effect. Following along familiar and well-worn paths, the decision maker will proceed to review alternatives only until he or she identifies an alternative that is "good enough"—one that meets an acceptable level of performance. The first alternative that meets the "good enough" criterion ends the search. So the final solution represents a satisficing choice rather than an optimum one. (See Exhibit 3-6.)

One of the more interesting aspects of bounded rationality is that the order in which alternatives are considered is critical in determining which alternative is selected. Remember, in the fully rational optimizing model, all alternatives are eventually listed in a hierarchy of preferred order. Since all alternatives are considered, the initial order in which they are evaluated is irrelevant. Every potential solution gets a full and complete evaluation. But this isn't the case with bounded rationality. If a problem has more than one potential solution, the satisficing choice will be the first acceptable one the decision maker encounters. Because decision makers use simple and limited models, they typically begin by identifying alternatives that are obvious, ones with which they are familiar, and those not too far from the status quo. Those solutions that depart least from the status quo and meet the decision criteria are most likely to be selected. So a unique and creative alternative may present an optimizing solution to the problem, but it's unlikely to be chosen because an acceptable solution will be identified well before the decision maker is required to search very far beyond the status quo.

A Model of Bounded Rationality

EXHIBIT 3-6

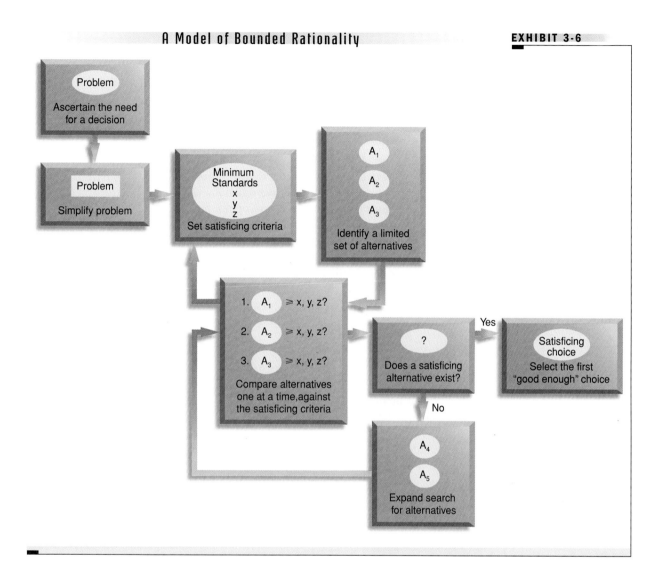

Intuition

"Sometimes you've just got to go with your gut feeling," the manager said as he tried to explain how he chose between two qualified job applicants. Was this manager wrong to use his "gut feeling"? Is using gut feelings a sign of being a poor manager? Does it necessarily result in an inferior outcome? The anwer to all these questions is no. Managers regularly use their intuition, and it may actually help improve decision making.[32]

DEFINITION First, let's define what we mean by intuitive decision making. There are several ways to conceptualize intuition.[33] For instance, some consider it a form of extrasensory power or sixth sense, and some believe it is a personality trait that a limited number of people are born with. For our purposes, we'll define **intuitive decision making** as an unconscious process created out of distilled experience. It doesn't necessarily operate independently of rational analysis; rather, the two complement each other.

Research on chess playing provides an excellent illustration of how intuition works.[34] Novice chess players and grand masters were shown an actual, but unfamiliar, chess game with about twenty-five pieces on the board. After 5 or 10 seconds, the pieces were removed and each player was asked to reconstruct the board. On average, the grand master could put twenty-three or twenty-four pieces in their correct squares, whereas the novice was able to replace only six. Then the exercise was changed. This time the pieces were placed randomly on the board. Again, the novice got only about six correct, but so did the grand master! The second exercise demonstrated that the grand master didn't have any better memory than the novice. What he did have was the ability, based on the experience of having played thousands of chess games, to recognize patterns and clusters of pieces that occur on chessboards in the course of games. Studies further show that chess professionals can simultaneously play fifty or more games in which decisions must be made in only seconds and exhibit only a moderately lower level of skill than when playing one game under tournament conditions, in which decisions often take half an hour or longer. The expert's experience allows him or her to recognize a situation and draw upon previously learned information associated with that situation to quickly arrive at a decision. The result is that the intuitive decision maker can decide rapidly with what appears to be very limited information.

IMAGE THEORY Image theory offers a comprehensive explanation of how most people use intuition in making decisions.[35] The theory is quite complex, so we'll extract its key elements and show you how people use it to make decisions such as: Should I adopt a certain course of action?

There are three basic elements to image theory: images, tests, and frames. Decision makers are guided by three different views, called **images**. One image represents a decision maker's basic *principles*, or values. The second represents the *goals,* or ends, to which a decision maker aspires. The third image represents the *plans*, or means for achieving those goals.

There are two *tests* by which decisions are made. The *compatibility test* determines whether an alternative fits with your principles and existing goals. The *profitability test* compares potential consequences of one alternative against those of other alternatives. The object of the compatibility test is to screen out the unacceptable. The object of the profitability test is to seek the best option.

The game of chess relies heavily on intuitive decision-making skills. Garry Kasparov recently received considerable attention when he challenged an IBM computer to a chess match.

Image Theory Applied to Adoption Decisions

EXHIBIT 3-7

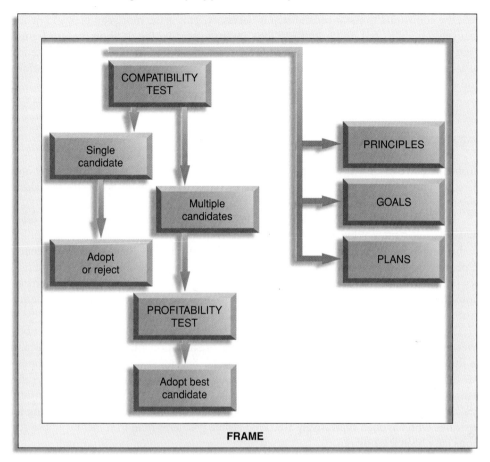

FRAME

Source: Based on T. R. Mitchell and L. R. Beach, "'. . . Do I Love Thee? Let Me Count . . .' Toward an Understanding of Intuitive and Automatic Decision Making," *Organizational Behavior and Human Decision Processes*, October 1990, p. 11; and L. R. Beach and T. R. Mitchell, "Image Theory: A Behavioral Theory of Decision Making in Organizations," in B. M. Staw and L. L. Cummings, eds., *Research in Organizational Behavior*, vol. 12 (Greenwich, Conn.: JAI Press, 1990), p. 13.

Frames refers to the context of a decision or how information is presented. The proverbial question "Is the glass half-empty or half-full?" is a framing issue. Framing is important because image theory argues that the context in which decisions occur gives them meaning and that past successes and failures in the same or similar contexts provide guidance about what to do about the current decision. So framing allows the decision maker to draw on his or her intuition to decide what to do this time.

Given the above concepts and definitions, here's what image theory proposes (see Exhibit 3-7). Decision making is essentially an automatic and intuitive process, requiring a minimal amount of thinking. Individuals make adoption decisions on the basis of a simple two-step process. First an option needs to pass the compatibility test. Does it fit with the decision maker's principles, goals, and plans? If it does, and no other competing candidates also fit, this option is adopted. This, incidentally, is synonymous with a "satisficing" choice. If the option fails the compatibility test, it's rejected. Most decisions do not go any further than this step. That is, there is only one alternative being considered, and either it's "good enough" or it isn't! In cases where there are multiple alternatives and two or more pass the compatibility test, a second step is necessary. This is the more complex and deliberative profitability test. But both these tests are influenced by the decision maker's frame. That is, he or she assesses information in the context of past experiences. So framing tends to taint objectivity. It encourages decision makers to rapidly size up a decision situation, and then quickly develop and assess an alternative on the basis of their intuition.

▶ Problem Identification

Problems don't come with flashing neon lights identifying them as problems. And one person's *problem* is another person's *acceptable status quo*. So how do decision makers identify and select problems?

Problems that are visible tend to have a higher probability of being selected than ones that are important.[36] Why? We can offer at least two reasons. First, it's easier to recognize visible problems. They are more likely to catch a decision maker's attention. This tendency explains why politicians are more likely to talk about the "crime problem" than the "illiteracy problem." Second, remember that we are concerned with decision making in organizations. Decision makers want to appear competent and "on top of problems." This desire motivates them to focus on problems that are visible to others.

Don't ignore the decision maker's self-interest. If a decision maker faces a conflict between selecting a problem that is important to the organization and one that is important to the decision maker, self-interest tends to win out.[37] Self-interest also is related to the issue of visibility. It is usually in a decision maker's best interest to attack high-profile problems. It conveys to others that things are under control. Moreover, when the decision maker's performance is later reviewed, the evaluator is more likely to give a high rating to someone who has been aggressively attacking visible problems than to someone whose actions have been less obvious.

Finally, when a problem is identified it is also framed. And framing has a large bearing on how the problem will be approached. For instance, consider the following problem.[38] A large car manufacturer has recently been hit with economic difficulties; it appears as if three plants will have to be closed and 6,000 employees laid off. The vice president of production has been exploring alternative ways to avoid this crisis. She has developed two plans:

Plan A: This plan will save 1 of the 3 plants and 2,000 jobs.

Plan B: This plan has a one-third probability of saving all 3 plants and all 6,000 jobs, but it has a two-thirds probability of saving none of the 3 plants and none of the 6,000 jobs.

If you were the vice president, which plan would you choose? If you're like most people, you would choose A. We'll explain why in a moment. But let's reconsider the problem with two more alternative plans. Which of these would you choose?

Plan C: This plan will result in the loss of 2 of the 3 plants and 4,000 jobs.

Plan D: This plan has a two-thirds probability of resulting in the loss of all 3 plants and all 6,000 jobs, but it has a one-third probability of losing none of the 3 plants and none of the 6,000 jobs.

Most people choose Plan D.

The two sets of alternative plans are exactly the same. Plans A and C both result in the loss of 4,000 jobs and the saving of 2,000 jobs. Plans B and D offer the same probabilities—a 1-in-3 chance that all the plants and jobs will be saved and a 2-in-3 chance that all the plants and jobs will be lost.

The reason people typically choose differently between these options is that they were framed differently in terms of gains and losses. And a substantial body of evidence indicates that decision makers tend to be risk-averse when facing a positively framed problem and risk-seeking when facing a negatively framed problem.[39] If you're offered the choice of *losing* $1,000 or taking a gamble with an equal expected value, you're likely to take the gamble (be risk-seeking). However, if you're offered the choice of *being given* $1,000 or taking a gamble with an equal expected value, you'll probably take the $1,000 (be risk-averse). Apparently, avoiding the pain of losing $1,000 is the deciding factor. So problems framed to emphasize positive gains encourage decision makers to select conservative choices, whereas problems framed to emphasize potential losses encourage risk-seeking choices.

> Problems framed to emphasize positive gains encourage decision makers to select conservative choices, whereas problems framed to emphasize potential losses encourage risk-seeking choices.

Alternative Development

Because decision makers rarely seek an optimum solution, but rather a satisficing one, we should expect to find a minimal use of creativity in the search for alternatives. And that expectation is generally on target.

Efforts will be made to try to keep the search process simple. It will tend to be confined to the neighborhood of the current alternative. More complex search behavior, which includes the development of creative alternatives, will be resorted to only when a simple search fails to uncover a satisfactory alternative. Or, in image theory terms, one satisfactory alternative frequently exists that meets the compatibility test. So this is chosen, and the decision maker rarely needs to go to the profitability test.

Rather than formulating new and unique problem definitions and alternatives, with frequent journeys into unfamiliar territory, the evidence indicates that most decision makers behave incrementally rather than comprehensively.[40] This means that decision makers avoid the difficult task of considering all the important factors, weighing their relative merits and drawbacks, and calculating the expected value for each alternative. Instead, they make successive limited comparisons. This incremental approach simplifies decision choices by comparing only those alternatives that differ in relatively small degree from the choice currently in effect. This approach also makes it unnecessary for the decision maker to thoroughly examine an alternative and its consequences. Instead, one need investigate only those aspects in which the proposed alternative and its consequences differ from the status quo.

What emerges is a decision maker who takes small steps toward his or her objective. It acknowledges the noncomprehensive nature of choice selection; in other words, decision makers make successive comparisons because decisions are never made forever and engraved in stone, but rather they are made and remade endlessly in small comparisons between narrow choices.

Making Choices

We've already noted that biases can creep into decisions. For instance, positively framed problems lead to different choices than negatively framed problems. But there are other biases. In order to avoid information overload, we rely on **heuristics**, or judgmental shortcuts, in decision making.[41] There are two common categories of heuristics—availability and representativeness. Another bias that decision makers confront is the tendency to escalate commitment to a failing course of action.

AVAILABILITY HEURISTIC A lot more people suffer from fear of flying than fear of driving a car. The reason is that many people think that flying is more dangerous than driving. It isn't, of course. With apologies ahead of time for this graphical example, if flying on a commercial airline were as dangerous as driving, the equivalent of two 747s filled to capacity would have to crash every week, killing all aboard, to match the risk of being killed in a car accident. But the media give a lot more attention to air accidents, so we tend to overstate the risk in flying and understate the risk in driving.

This illustration is an example of the **availability heuristic**, which is the tendency to assess probabilities on the basis of how easily instances of the events in question can be brought to mind. Events that evoke emotions, that are particularly vivid, that are familiar, or that have occurred recently tend to be most available in our memory. As a result, we tend to be prone to overestimating unlikely events such as an airplane crash. The availability heuristic can also explain why managers, when doing annual performance appraisals, tend to give more weight to recent behaviors of an employee than to those of 6 or 9 months ago.

REPRESENTATIVE HEURISTIC A recent survey found that 66 percent of all African-American males between the ages of 13 and 18 believe they can earn a living playing professional sports.[42] In reality, the odds that any high school athlete will play a sport on the professional level are about 10,000 to 1!

These young men are suffering from a **representative heuristic**. They are assessing the likelihood of an event based on how closely it resembles some other event or set of events. The media and advertisers bombard these young men with stories of kids who grew up in the black community, just like them, and who now earn tens of millions of dollars in the NBA, NFL, or playing professional baseball. So they begin to believe they, too, can become professional athletes. They are drawing analogies and seeing identical situations where they don't exist.

We all are guilty of using this heuristic at times. Managers, for example, frequently predict the performance of a new product by relating it to a previous product's success. Or they hired three graduates from the same college who turned out to be poor performers, so they predict that a current job applicant from that college won't be a good employee.

ESCALATION OF COMMITMENT Another bias that creeps into decisions in practice is a tendency to escalate commitment when a course of action represents a decision stream (a series of decisions).[43] **Escalation of commitment** is an increased commitment to a previous decision despite negative information. For example, a friend of mine had been dating a woman for about 4 years. Although he admitted that things weren't going too well in the relationship, he informed me that he was going to marry the woman. A bit surprised by his decision, I asked him why. He responded: "I have a lot invested in the relationship!" Similarly, another friend was explaining why she was working on a doctorate in education even though she disliked teaching and didn't want to continue her career in education. She told me she really wanted to be a software programmer. Then she hit me with her escalation of commitment explanation: "I already have a master's in education and I'd have to go back and complete some deficiencies if I changed to work on a degree in software programming now."

It has been well documented that individuals escalate commitment to a failing course of action when they view themselves as responsible for the failure. That is, they "throw good money after bad" to demonstrate that their initial decision wasn't wrong and to

The representative heuristic explains why African American boys believe they have a 66 percent chance of making a living in professional sports when, in fact, the odds are more like 10,000 to 1.

avoid having to admit they made a mistake. Escalation of commitment is also congruent with evidence that people try to appear consistent in what they say and do. Increasing commitment to previous actions conveys consistency.

Escalation of commitment has obvious implications for managerial decisions. Many an organization has suffered large losses because a manager was determined to prove that his or her original decision was right by continuing to commit resources to what was a lost cause from the beginning. In addition, as we'll elaborate on in our discussion of leadership in chapters 14 and 15, effective leaders are perceived as consistent. So managers, in an effort to appear effective, may be motivated to be consistent even when switching to another course of action may be preferable. In actuality, effective managers are those who are able to differentiate between situations in which persistence will pay off and situations where it won't.

Solution Implementation

"Good decisions" often fail because of poor implementation. So, in addition to understanding how decisions are made, we need to know something about how they are implemented.[44] Interestingly, the rational decision-making model speaks little to this issue. It essentially assumes that the people who have to carry out a decision will enthusiastically endorse and support it. That, of course, is an idealistic assumption.

In practice, three sets of variables will largely determine the success of a solution's implementation—leadership, communication, and political support. Leaders make choices about how decisions will be made. The popularity in recent years of the use of participative decision making, empowerment, and self-managed teams reflects the belief that people are most likely to support decisions in which they actively participated.[45]

People need to understand the reasons underlying decisions that will affect them. Major changes can be particularly disruptive for employees. Change brings uncertainty and ambiguity. Opening channels of communication and explaining why a decision was made and how it will affect people will go a long way toward lessening resistance and increasing support.

Failure to gain political support for a decision often leads to its downfall.[46] People with power can use it to support or undermine a decision, so successful implementation requires support from individuals and groups who have the power to thwart the decision if they do not agree with it. One of the most potent techniques that powerful people use to stymie a decision they don't like is to do nothing. This is what happens in the U.S. Congress when a bill "dies in committee." Many an organizational decision has died because it lacked political support among those who had to carry it out.

Individual Differences

Put Chad and Sean into the same decision situation and Chad almost always seems to take longer to come to a solution. Chad's final choices aren't necessarily always better than Sean's; he's just slower in processing information. In addition, if there's an obvious risk dimension in the decision, Sean seems consistently to prefer a riskier option than does Chad. What this description illustrates is that we all bring personality and other individual differences to the decisions we make. Two of these individual variables seem particularly relevant to decision making in organizations—an individual's decision-making style and level of moral development.

DECISION-MAKING STYLES The decision-styles model identifies four different individual approaches to making decisions.[47] It was designed to be used by managers and aspiring managers, but its general framework can be used by any individual decision maker.

The basic foundation of the model is the recognition that people differ along two dimensions. The first is their *way of thinking*. Some people are logical and rational. They process information serially. In contrast, some people are intuitive and creative. They perceive things as a whole. Note that these differences are above and beyond the general human characteristics—specifically, bounded rationality and image theory—discussed earlier. The other dimension addresses a person's *tolerance for ambiguity*. Some people have a high need to structure information in ways that minimize ambiguity, whereas others are able to process many thoughts at the same time. When these two dimensions are diagrammed, they form four styles of decision making: directive, analytical, conceptual, and behavioral (see Exhibit 3-8).

People using the *directive style* have low tolerance for ambiguity and seek rationality. They are efficient and logical. But their efficiency concerns result in their making decisions using minimal information and assessing few alternatives. Directive types make decisions fast, and they focus on the short run.

The *analytical type* has a much greater tolerance for ambiguity than do directive decision makers. This trait leads to the desire for more information and consideration of more alternatives than is true for directives. Analytical managers would best be characterized as careful decision makers with the ability to adapt or cope with new situations.

Individuals with a *conceptual style* tend to be very broad in their outlook and consider many alternatives. Their focus is long-range, and they are very good at finding creative solutions to problems.

The final category—those with a *behavioral style*—characterizes decision makers who work well with others. They are concerned with the achievements of peers and subordinates. They are receptive to suggestions from others and rely heavily on meetings for communicating. This type of manager tries to avoid conflict and seeks acceptance.

Although these four categories are distinct, most managers have characteristics that fall into more than one. So it's probably best to think in terms of a manager's dominant

EXHIBIT 3-8

Decision-Style Model

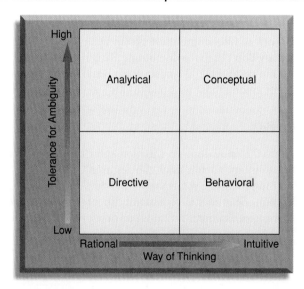

Source: A. J. Rowe, J. D. Boulgarides, and M. R. McGrath, *Managerial Decision Making*, Modules in Management Series (Chicago: SRA, 1984), p. 18.

style and his or her backup styles. Some managers rely almost exclusively on their domi-nant style; more-flexible managers can make shifts depending on the situation.

Business students, lower-level managers, and top executives tend to score highest in the analytical style. That's not surprising, given the emphasis that formal education, par-ticularly business education, gives to developing rational thinking. For instance, courses in accounting, statistics, and finance all stress rational analysis.

In addition to providing a framework for looking at individual differences, focusing on decision styles can be useful for helping you understand how two equally intelligent people, with access to the same information, can differ in the ways in which they approach decisions and in the final choices they make.

▶ Level of Moral Development

Moral development is relevant because many decisions have an ethical dimension. An un-derstanding of this concept can help you see how different people apply different ethical standards to their decisions.

There is a substantial body of research that confirms the existence of three levels of moral development, each comprising two stages.[48] At each successive stage, an individual's moral judgment grows less and less dependent on outside influences. The three levels and six stages are described in Exhibit 3-9.

The first level is labeled *preconventional*. At this level, individuals respond to notions of right or wrong only when there are personal consequences involved, such as physical punishment, reward, or exchange of favors. Reasoning at the *conventional level* indicates that moral value resides in maintaining the conventional order and the expectations of

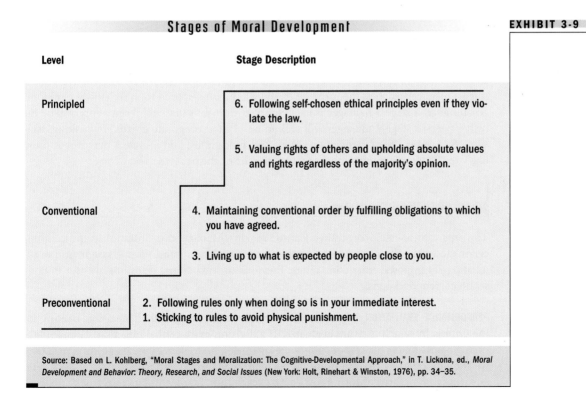

Stages of Moral Development

EXHIBIT 3-9

Level	Stage Description
Principled	6. Following self-chosen ethical principles even if they vio-late the law.
	5. Valuing rights of others and upholding absolute values and rights regardless of the majority's opinion.
Conventional	4. Maintaining conventional order by fulfilling obligations to which you have agreed.
	3. Living up to what is expected by people close to you.
Preconventional	2. Following rules only when doing so is in your immediate interest.
	1. Sticking to rules to avoid physical punishment.

Source: Based on L. Kohlberg, "Moral Stages and Moralization: The Cognitive-Developmental Approach," in T. Lickona, ed., *Moral Development and Behavior: Theory, Research, and Social Issues* (New York: Holt, Rinehart & Winston, 1976), pp. 34–35.

The Increasing Importance of Moral Judgment

Organizations need to raise their employees' level of moral development. This conclusion comes through loud and clear from a recent survey of 1,324 selected U.S. operative employees and managers from a diverse set of industries.

The survey found that ethical and legal lapses are common at all levels of the American workforce. Nearly half, 48 percent, of the respondents admitted to having taken unethical or illegal actions during the preceding 12 months. These include one or more from a list of 25 actions, including cutting corners on quality control, covering up incidents, cheating on an expense account, discriminating against co-workers, paying or accepting kickbacks, lying to or deceiving customers, secretly forging signatures, trading sex for sales, calling in sick when they're feeling well, stealing from their employer, and looking the other way when environmental laws are violated.

These results are actually more damning than they even first appear. Workers were asked only to list violations that they attributed to "pressure" due to such things as long hours, sales quotas, job insecurity, balancing work and family, and personal debt. It didn't ask about unethical or illegal action for other reasons such as greed, revenge, or blind ambition. Moreover, the survey was taken during good economic times. Pressure, and resulting ethics violations, would undoubtedly increase during an economic slump. Finally, the trend isn't encouraging. Fifty-seven percent of the respondents said they felt more pressure to be unethical than they had five years earlier, and 40 percent said it had gotten worse over the previous year.

Source: Based on D. Jones, "48% of Workers Admit to Unethical or Illegal Acts," *USA Today*, April 4–6, 1997, p. 1A.

others. In the *principled level*, individuals make a clear effort to define moral principles apart from the authority of the groups to which they belong or society in general.

Research on these stages of moral development allows us to draw several conclusions.[49] First, people proceed through the six stages in a lock-step fashion. They gradually move up a ladder, stage by stage. They don't jump steps. Second, there is no guarantee of continued development. Development can terminate at any stage. Third, the majority of adults are at stage 4. They are limited to obeying the rules and laws of society. Finally, the higher the stage a manager reaches, the more he or she will be predisposed to make ethical decisions. For instance, a stage 3 manager is likely to make decisions that will receive approval by his or her peers; a stage 4 manager will seek to be a "good corporate citizen" by making decisions that respect the organization's rules and procedures; and a stage 5 manager is more likely to challenge organizational practices that he or she believes to be wrong.

Organizational Constraints

The organization itself constrains decision makers. Managers, for instance, shape their decisions to reflect the organization's performance evaluation and reward system and organizationally imposed time constraints. Previous organizational decisions also act to constrain current decisions.

PERFORMANCE EVALUATION Managers are strongly influenced in their decision making by the criteria by which they are evaluated. If a division manager believes that the manufacturing plants under his responsibility are operating best when he hears nothing negative, we shouldn't be surprised to find that his plant managers spend a good part of their time ensuring that negative information doesn't reach him. Similarly, if a college dean believes that an instructor should never fail more than 10 percent of her students—to fail more reflects on the instructor's ability to teach—we should expect that new instructors, who want to receive favorable evaluations, will decide not to fail too many students.

REWARD SYSTEMS The organization's reward system influences decision makers by suggesting to them which choices are preferable in terms of personal payoff. For example, if the organization rewards risk aversion, managers are likely to make conservative decisions. From the 1930s through the mid-1980s, General Motors consistently gave out promotions and bonuses to those managers who kept a low profile, avoided controversy, and were good team players. The result was that GM managers became very adept at dodging tough issues and passing controversial decisions on to committees.

SYSTEM-IMPOSED TIME CONSTRAINTS Organizations impose deadlines on decisions. For instance, department budgets need to be completed by next Friday. Or the report on new product development has to be ready for the executive committee to review by the first of the month. A host of decisions have to be made quickly in order to stay ahead of the competition and keep customers satisfied. And almost all important decisions come with explicit deadlines. These conditions create time pressures on decision makers and often make it difficult, if not impossible, to gather all the information they might like before having to make a final choice. The rational model ignores the reality that, in organizations, decisions come with time constraints.

HISTORICAL PRECEDENTS Rational decision making takes an unrealistic, closed-system perspective. It views decisions as independent and discrete events. But that isn't the way it is in the real world! Decisions aren't made in a vacuum. They have a context. In fact, individual decisions are more accurately characterized as points in a stream of decisions.

Decisions made in the past are ghosts that continually haunt current choices. For instance, commitments made in the past constrain current options. We can use a social situation as an example. The decision you might make after meeting "Mr. (or Ms.) Right" is more complicated if you're married than if you're single. A prior commitment—in this case, the marriage vow—constrains your options. In a business context, Eastman Kodak is a good example of a firm that has had to live with its past mistakes.[50] Starting in the early 1970s, Kodak's management concluded that the days of silver halide photography were numbered. They predicted that other technologies, such as electronic photography, would soon replace it. But instead of approaching the problem deliberately, Kodak management panicked. They took off in all directions. Today, virtually all of Kodak's problems can be traced to the decisions made and not made since then. Government budget decisions also offer an illustration of this point. It is common knowledge that the largest determining factor of the size of any given year's budget is last year's budget.[51] Choices made today, therefore, are largely a result of choices made over the years.

▶ Cultural Differences

The rational model does not acknowledge cultural differences. But Arabs, for instance, don't necessarily make decisions the same way that Canadians do. Therefore, we need to recognize that the cultural background of the decision maker can significantly influence selection of problems, depth of analysis, the importance placed on logic and rationality, whether organizational decisions will be made autocratically by an individual manager or collectively in groups, time orientation, and belief in the ability of people to solve problems.[52]

Differences in time orientation help us understand why managers in Egypt will make decisions at a much slower and more deliberate pace than their American counterparts. Although rationality is valued in North America, it isn't valued everywhere in the world. A North American manager might make an important decision intuitively, but he or she knows that it's important to appear to proceed in a rational fashion. This is because rationality is highly valued in the West. In countries such as Iran, where rationality is not deified, efforts to appear rational are not necessary.

Some cultures—the United States is one—emphasize solving problems; others, such as Thailand and Indonesia, focus on accepting situations as they are. Because problem-solving managers believe they can and should change situations to their benefit, American managers might identify a problem long before their Thai or Indonesian counterparts would even recognize it as such.

Decision making by Japanese managers is much more group-oriented than in the United States. The Japanese value conformity and cooperation. So before Japanese CEOs make an important decision, they collect a large amount of information, which is then used in consensus-forming group decisions.

WHAT CAN MANAGERS DO TO IMPROVE THEIR DECISION MAKING?

If you're a manager, what can you do to become a more effective decision maker? Here are a few suggestions.

▶ Analyze the Situation

You can improve your decision-making effectiveness by assessing the decision context, including the national culture you're operating in, the characteristics of your organization's culture, and your organization's political climate.

National culture is a key variable in determining whether you should use groups and the importance you should place on rationality. In countries that score high on individualism, you should expect much more resistance to group decision processes than in highly collectivist cultures. Great care needs to be shown in relying on group decision-making practices in individualistic countries such as the United States, Sweden, Italy, France, England, Canada, and Australia. In contrast, managers and employees alike will be willing to accept group decision making in such countries as Greece, Japan, Mexico, Singapore, and Venezuela.

Decision making at the daily newspaper Asahi Shinbun *illustrates the Japanese preference for consensus seeking.*

TODAY ? or TOMORROW ?

Software That Thinks

You run a small auto-body repair shop. You rely on recommendations from insurance companies for business: A person has an accident, calls his or her insurance company, reports the claim, and the insurance company suggests a body shop to do the repairs. This system has been in place for many years. The problem for a manager of a small body shop is that this system makes you dependent on the insurance companies. Because they initiate the recommendation, you have to "dance to their tune" to get on and stay on their referral lists. That doesn't have to be the case anymore![53]

New artificial intelligence software has been designed to approach problems the way the human brain does—by trying to recognize the patterns that underlie a complex set of data. Like people, this software "learns" to pick out subtle patterns. In so doing, it can perform a number of decision-making tasks—including identifying future customers for a small auto-body repair shop.

Atlanta-based Marketing Arsenal has created software that allows body shop managers to bypass referral lists entirely and appeal directly to the drivers—even before accidents happen!

Marketing Arsenal has developed a database of more than 40 million accidents. Using this database and its artificial intelligence software, it can create profiles of likely accident types. For instance, a profile might show that the most likely people to get in an accident are 26-year-old females who own sports cars, have three corporate credit cards, and spend at least $1,000 a month on each card. Then the auto repair shop can create a list of people who fit the profiles and produce a direct-mail piece to get their business. So far, test runs with this software have yielded highly accurate results—about 25 percent more accurate than statistical modeling.

Imagine the potential of this kind of software in the hands of chiropractors or lawyers? It could also be valuable to help law-enforcement agencies analyze travel patterns and pinpoint likely drug dealers or to assist hospitals in determining a patient's likelihood of contracting specific diseases.

As previously noted, rationality is widely accepted among Western cultures, but it's not a universal standard. So if you're in a country that doesn't value rationality, don't feel compelled to follow the rational decision-making model or even to try to make your decisions appear rational. In fact, you may be more effective by purposely avoiding the appearance of following rational processes.

Organizational cultures differ in terms of the importance they place on factors such as risk, the use of groups, reliance on formalized procedures, and the need for decisions to closely follow the chain of command. Adjust your decision style to ensure that it's compatible with the organization's culture.

Finally, don't ignore the organization's political climate. Don't confuse optimization and pragmatism. The "best" choice is not necessarily the one that can be implemented successfully. So, after deciding what's optimally best, make sure it can pass the reality test. Will others find it acceptable, and can it be realistically implemented? If not, show flexibility and adapt the decision to increase the likelihood that it will be accepted.

▶ Be Aware of Biases

We all bring biases to the decisions we make. Unfortunately, however, we typically don't recognize what our biases are. And we fail to differentiate situations in which biases cause minimal problems from those in which they can have a catastrophic impact. If you understand the biases influencing your judgment, you can begin to change the way you make decisions to reduce those biases.

▶ Combine Simplified Rational Analysis with Intuition

Don't forget that rational analysis and intuition are not conflicting approaches to decision making. By using both, you can actually improve your decision effectiveness. As you gain managerial experience, you should feel increasingly confident in imposing your intuitive processes on top of your rational analysis.

▶ Match Decision-Making Style to Job Requirements

Don't assume that your specific decision style is appropriate for every job. Just as cultures differ, so too do jobs within an organization. And your effectiveness as a decision maker will increase if you match your decision style to the requirements of the job.

All management jobs are not alike. Managing a group of creative copywriters in an advertising agency, for instance, is different from supervising clerical personnel in a retail store. If you're a directive style of decision maker, you'll be more effective working with people whose jobs require quick action. This style, for instance, would match up well with managing stockbrokers. An analytical style would work well managing accountants, market researchers, or financial analysts. A conceptual style fits well with managing corporate planners, forecasters, or creative types. And jobs that require managers to spend a large portion of their time as a team leader are compatible with individuals who use a behavioral style.

▶ Use Creativity-Stimulation Techniques

We all have the tendency to get in mental ruts. We see a problem that we've confronted before and quickly scan our memory for how we handled it in the past. Unless our previous experience was memorably negative, we tend to handle the problem the same way we did before. In many cases, this approach is perfectly satisfactory. If nothing else, it makes life a lot simpler. We don't have to invent a totally new solution to solve an old problem. The downside, however, is that there might be a far better solution available if only you'd take the time to search for it.

You can improve your overall decision-making effectiveness by searching for novel solutions to problems. Your inspiration for finding them can be as elementary as telling yourself to think creatively and to look specifically for unique alternatives. In addition, you should avoid searching for one right answer, avoid being too logical or rational, ignore practicality, ask "what if" questions, and don't fear failing.

▶ Apply Ethical Decision Guides

Your decisions should consider ethical implications. Although there is no simple credo that will ensure that you won't err in your ethical judgments, the following questions can help guide you. Ask yourself these questions when making important decisions or ones with obvious ethical implications.[54]

1. How did this problem occur in the first place?
2. Would you define the problem differently if you stood on the other side of the fence?
3. To whom and to what do you give your loyalty as a person and as a member of your organization?
4. What is your intention in making this decision?
5. What is the likelihood that your intentions will be misunderstood by others in the organization?

6. How does your intention compare with the probable result?
7. Whom could your decision injure?
8. Can you discuss the problem with the parties who will be affected before you make the decision?
9. Are you confident that your position will be as valid over a long period of time as it seems now?
10. Could you disclose your decision to your boss or your immediate family?
11. How would you feel if your decision was described, in detail, on the front page of your local newspaper?

There is a variety of additional material available on the CD-ROM and companion Web site that accompany this text. You can access this information through the CD-ROM or by visiting the Web site at <**www.prenhall.com/robbins**>.

SUMMARY

(This summary is organized by the chapter-opening learning objectives on page 66.)

1. The six-step rational decision-making model is (1) define the problem; (2) identify the decision criteria; (3) weight the decision criteria; (4) generate possible alternatives; (5) rate each alternative on each criterion; and (6) compute the optimal decision. The assumptions of this model include: the problem is clear and unambiguous; all options are known; preferences are clear and constant; there are no time or cost constraints; and the decision maker will choose the maximum payoff.

2. Risk assumes that a decision maker can estimate the likelihood of alternatives or outcomes. With uncertainty, no probabilities can be estimated, so the decision maker must rely on intuition or creativity.

3. You can demonstrate increased creativity in your decisions by explicitly searching for creative alternatives, avoiding the belief that there is one right answer, avoiding being too logical or rational, ignoring practicality, asking "what if" questions, and not being afraid to fail.

4. Popular quantitative techniques include break-even analysis (identifies profit or loss at various sales volumes); return on investment (measures productivity of assets); marginal analysis (compares the additional cost in a particular decision rather than average cost); game theory (mathematical models that analyze multiparty decision contexts); linear programming (for optimally solving resource allocation problems); and queuing theory (for calculating waiting lines).

5. Individual decision making is best when decisions are relatively unimportant, employee commitment isn't necessary for success, sufficient information is available, and speed is important.

6. The boundedly rational decision maker simplifies the problem, creates a limited set of "satisficing" criteria that a solution must meet, reviews a limited set of familiar options, and chooses the first solution that meets the "satisficing" criteria.

7. There are four decision making styles: directive, analytical, conceptual, and behavioral.

8. Managers can improve their decision making by: modifying the process to reflect national culture, the organization's culture, and the organization's political climate; recognizing biases; using both rational and intuitive processes; matching their style to the job; using creativity-stimulation techniques; and by applying ethical guides.

REVIEW QUESTIONS

1. What is rationality? Are decision makers rational?
2. Explain how the type of decision changes with levels of management.
3. What is image theory? What value does it have in explaining decision-making behavior?
4. What is a decision frame? How does it affect problem selection?
5. What is a heuristic? Describe two common categories.
6. Why might a manager escalate commitment to a losing cause?

7. Describe the six stages in the level of moral development model. At what stage are most people? What, if anything, can an organization do to raise the level of moral development among its employees?

8. How do historical precedents influence a decision?

9. On the basis of your decision style, what type of job fits you best? Explain.

10. Describe an ethical dilemma you have faced. How did you resolve it? What, if anything, did you learn from that dilemma?

IF I WERE THE MANAGER . . .

Grand Junction Networks

You're Howard Charney. As a co-founder of 3Com, a leader in computer-networking systems, you've earned a sizable fortune. But at the age of 47, and having spent ten years with 3Com, you'd had enough. It wasn't fun anymore. You resigned. That was 1991.

A year and a half passed. You couldn't shake the entrepreneurial bug. You missed the action, the thrill of creating something. You missed working with real smart people. So you called up some of those smart people and asked them to come to your house and talk. Six or seven people showed up. The group began meeting every few weeks. The purpose? To find a product you could create and develop. One night your group stumbled on it: software that can make the Ethernet go 10 times faster. With $1.5 million of seed money from a venture capital firm, Grand Junction Networks was born in Silicon Valley. It was February 1992.

Your reputation in Silicon Valley was solid. People described you as optimistic, sincere, genuine. One Grand Valley employee described you as "the kind of guy people walk through walls for." You had no trouble putting together a great team.

Fast forward now to summer of 1995. Your little start-up company is thriving. First-year sales were $4.5 million. Second-year sales, in 1994, increased to $7 million. You're forecasting sales of $120 million for 1996. You've got 80 people working for you. Seventy- and eighty-hour weeks have become pretty normal for everyone on staff. But no one is complaining. It's exciting to be associated with a company that's growing so fast.

But growth is expensive. You and your venture capital investors think it's time to take Grand Junction public. You've hired Goldman Sachs to oversee your initial public offering (IPO).

You've notified the SEC of your intentions. Then you get a call from executives at Cisco Systems, one of the richest companies in Silicon Valley. They want to expand their business and need low-end, fast-Ethernet switching products. They want you to rethink your decision to go public. They want to buy your company.

You secretly meet with Cisco executives. Cisco is ready to offer $200 million in their stock for Grand Junction. You really don't want to sell out to Cisco. You'd be back where you were at 3Com—part of a huge organization. But there are factors to consider. What if Cisco bought a rival company, armed it to the teeth, and tried to blow Grand Junction out of the water? Moreover, Cisco has deep pockets. Grand Junction wouldn't have anymore cash flow worries. And Grand Junction would gain considerably wider distribution channels. But you'd be giving up your autonomy. You know that most of the people working for you are here because they like the feel of a small firm. As part of Cisco, that would all change.

Cisco is determined to acquire your firm. They keep upping the offer—$225 million, $275 million. Their final offer is very tempting—Cisco stock worth a minimum of $345 million. If you accept, half of your employees will become instant millionaires. But you know that the people who work for you aren't energized by the strategic advantages that Cisco offers. They care about what it feels like to be at the office. They share one all-consuming goal: to ship great products. And shipping products would be different if you're part of Cisco.

What would you do? Would you recommend to your board of directors that you go forward with the IPO? Or would you recommend accepting Cisco's offer?

Source: Based on P. Dillon, "Is Selling Out 'Selling Out'?" *Fast Company*, February/March 1998, pp. 87–94.

SKILL EXERCISE

Creativity Simulation

1. Take out a couple of sheets of paper. You have 20 minutes to list as many medical or health care–related jobs as you can that begin with the letter "r." For example: radiologist, registered nurse, rheumatologist. If you run out of listings before the time expires, it's OK to quit early.

When the exercise is complete: (a) Identify the range (most to fewest) of how many jobs class members were able to list. (b) Identify unusual or novel jobs that no more than one student in class listed.

2. List on a piece of paper some common terms that apply to both *water* and *finance*.[55] How many were you able to come up with? Compare your list with the lists of others in your class.

TEAM ACTIVITY

Winter Survival

Form into groups of 5 to 9 members each. Then, when instructed, read the situation and do Step 1 without discussing it with the rest of your group.

The Situation. You have just crash-landed in the woods of northern Minnesota and southern Manitoba. It is 11:32 A.M. in mid-January. The light plane in which you were traveling crashed on a lake. The pilot and copilot were killed. Shortly after the crash, the plane sank completely into the lake with the pilot's and copilot's bodies inside. None of your group were seriously injured and you are all dry.

The crash came suddenly, before the pilot had time to radio for help or inform anyone of your position. Because your pilot was trying to avoid a storm, you know the plane was considerably off course. The pilot announced shortly before the crash that you were twenty miles northwest of a small town, which is the nearest known habitation.

You are in a wilderness area made up of thick woods broken up by many lakes and streams. The snow depth varies from above the ankles in windswept areas to knee-deep where it has drifted. The last weather report indicated that the temperature would reach minus twenty-five degrees Fahrenheit in the daytime and minus forty at night. There is plenty of dead wood and twigs in the immediate area. You are dressed in winter clothing appropriate for city wear—suit, pantsuits, street shoes, and overcoats.

While escaping from the plane, members of your group salvaged 12 items. Your task is to rank these items according to their importance to your survival, starting with "1" for the most important item and ending with "12" for the least important one.

You may assume that the number of passengers is the same as the number of persons in your group and that the group has agreed to stick together.

Step 1. Each member of the group is to individually rank each item. Do not discuss the situation or problem until each member has finished the individual ranking.

Step 2. After everyone has finished the individual ranking, rank the 12 items as a group. Once discussion begins, do not change your individual ranking. Your instructor will inform you as to how much time you have to complete this step.

Items	Step 1: Your individual ranking	Step 2: The group ranking	Step 3: Survival expert's ranking	Step 4: Difference between steps 1 and 3	Step 5: Difference between steps 2 and 3
Ball of steel wool	_____	_____	_____	_____	_____
Newspapers (one per person)	_____	_____	_____	_____	_____
Compass	_____	_____	_____	_____	_____
Hand ax	_____	_____	_____	_____	_____
Cigarette lighter (without fluid)	_____	_____	_____	_____	_____
Loaded .45-caliber pistol	_____	_____	_____	_____	_____
Sectional air map made of plastic	_____	_____	_____	_____	_____
Twenty-by-twenty-foot piece of heavy-duty canvas	_____	_____	_____	_____	_____
Extra shirt and pants for each survivor	_____	_____	_____	_____	_____
Can of shortening	_____	_____	_____	_____	_____
Quart of 100-proof whiskey	_____	_____	_____	_____	_____
Family-size chocolate bar (one per person)	_____	_____	_____	_____	_____

Please complete the following steps and insert the scores under your group's number.

	Group Number							
	1	**2**	**3**	**4**	**5**	**6**	**7**	**8**
Step 6. Average Individual Score Add up all the individual scores (Step 4) in the group and divide by the number in the group.	___	___	___	___	___	___	___	___
Step 7. Group Score The difference between the Group Score and the Average Individual Score. If the Group Score is lower than the Average Individual Score, then gain "+". If Group Score is higher than Average Individual Score, then gain is "−".	___	___	___	___	___	___	___	___
Step 8. Lowest Individual Score in the Group	___	___	___	___	___	___	___	___
Step 9. Number of Individual Scores Lower Than the Group Score.	___	___	___	___	___	___	___	___

Source: Adapted from D. Johnson and F. Johnson, *Joining Together*, 3rd edition, Prentice Hall. Used with permission.

CASE EXERCISE

Steve Case and AOL

Steve Case built America Online from nil to 8 million customers in barely a decade. It's a true success story. That is, until December 1996. That's when Case made a decision that caused havoc among his customers. He replaced his company's pay-per-minute fee schedule with a flat-rate $19.95 monthly charge. Suddenly AOL became the busy signal heard around the world as users logged on and kept all the company's lines filled.

How did this happen? Eager to expand his market share, Case decided he would introduce a fixed-rate pay plan. He knew ahead of time what the result would be. The new demand would exceed his system's capability. He expected that users would confront a busy signal. But this occasionally happens in business. Airlines, for instance, regularly oversell their seats. Case figured this would be only temporary, as AOL was making huge investments in new lines. And on-line services had always had occasional service breakdowns. However, in AOL's case, people were trying for days on end to get on-line, with no success.

Case also sought to get more customers while the ones he had were screaming that they couldn't get through. The company ran advertisements on TV, pitching for new customers. They provided a toll-free number in those ads. Ironically, you could get through to sign up, but not to log on.

Compounding Case's problem was the effect the constant busy signal had on businesses that used AOL. Millions of businesspeople had come to depend on the service to some degree for e-mail, customer contacts, and other information needs.

When they couldn't get through to AOL, their communication capabilities were suddenly severely curtailed.

Critics argue that Case and AOL have betrayed the trust of customers. They even think that Case has acted unethically, knowingly selling a product he couldn't deliver. They say that Case flooded America with arresting come-ons and free sign-up software in his effort to significantly increase growth. Only two months before the flat-rate fiasco, Case had taken pains to assure customers of AOL's "single-minded focus" and "obsession" with service. "We will make whatever changes — do whatever we need to do — to keep that commitment to you," he had said.

QUESTIONS

1. Contrast Case's decision with airline practices of overselling seats. Are these decisions similar? Discuss.

2. "What Case has done is just good business. He was out to dramatically increase revenue. And he did. Change agents have to expect to take heat." Do you agree or disagree with this statement? Explain.

3. "Don't recruit customers if you harbor the slightest doubt about your ability to serve them." Do you agree or disagree with this statement? Explain.

4. Can you excuse a company from offering a product it knows it cannot reliably deliver? Is this unethical?

Source: Based on T. Petzinger Jr., "'Gunning for Growth,' AOL's Steve Case Shot Himself in the Foot," *Wall Street Journal*, January 24, 1997, p. B1; and N. K. Austin, "What Do America Online and Dennis Rodman Have in Common?" *INC.*, July 1997, pp. 52–54.

VIDEO CASE EXERCISE

Grace Under Fire

You probably wouldn't know quite what to expect from a business named Pyro Media, but you'd figure it was going to be something pretty unusual. Grace Tsjuikawa Boyd's business, Pyro Media, has pursued a pretty unusual direction, but the decision to do something different wasn't made randomly.

Boyd's Pyro Media started off as a manufacturer of huge ceramic glazed pots such as the ones you might see holding trees or plants in the lobbies of big hotels. Using her degree in art, Boyd herself initially made the high-quality glazed pots, which sold for about $1,500 each. As her business grew to the point at which it had backorders of 8 to 12 weeks, Boyd decided it was time to move to a bigger facility and invest in equipment and employees. She says, "We were in business making money and assumed that business was going to grow at the same rate it had been." Grace soon found, however, that Pyro Media's revenues didn't keep increasing by 30 percent as they had been, but instead were dropping off. Upon investigating the situation, Boyd found out that huge corporations had begun importing and distributing terra cotta planters, essentially stealing away her business.

Boyd knew that she had to do something. She had this equipment, this 56,000-square-foot facility, and employees who knew ceramics. She called in some consultants to see what other markets her business might pursue. Their study, which took about six months, recommended that Pyro Media look into high-tech ce-ramic applications: in other words, using the same technology that Boyd had developed and used in making ceramic pots and applying it to a new area. On the basis of that information, Boyd hired a ceramics engineer and went after the ceramics "castables" market. The company's decision to move into this new market has been so successful that the one engineer has since been joined by seven others!

Recognizing that business was falling off and analyzing the reason behind the loss of revenue were instrumental in Pyro Media's continued success. Boyd says that being able to recognize a problem is critical, especially for small businesses. Why? Because small businesses have no money to waste and no time to waste. If problems are ignored and not analyzed, the business might face quick failure.

QUESTIONS

1. A decision to move into a new market as Boyd's Pyro Media did is a major decision. How could Boyd have used the decision-making process to help her make this decision?

2. Would you call declining revenues a problem or a symptom of a problem? Why?

3. Using Exhibit 3-8, identify the type of decision-making style you think Boyd exhibits. Explain your choice.

4. Is the ability to recognize a problem any less critical to a large corporation than a small business? Support your answer.

Source: Based on *Small Business 2000, Show 108.*

NOTES

1. This opening vignette is based on J. Useem, "The Richest Man You've Never Heard Of," *Inc.*, September 1997, pp. 43–59. For an update, see W. Zellner, "How CFS Made Bad Debts Pay So Well," *Business Week,* November 9, 1998, p. 48.

2. See H. A. Simon, "Rationality in Psychology and Economics," *Journal of Business*, October 1986, pp. 209–24; and A. Langley, "In Search of Rationality: The Purposes Behind the Use of Formal Analysis in Organizations," *Administrative Science Quarterly*, December 1989, pp. 598–631.

3. For a review of the rational model, see E. F. Harrison, *The Managerial Decision-Making Process*, 4th ed. (Boston: Houghton Mifflin, 1995), pp. 75–113.

4. J. G. March, *A Primer on Decision Making* (New York: Free Press, 1994), pp. 2–7.

5. W. Pounds, "The Process of Problem Finding," *Industrial Management Review*, Fall 1969, pp. 1–19.

6. "Boeing-Teledesic Aims for the Stars," *Business Week*, May 12, 1997, p. 50.

7. See R. W. Woodman, J. E. Sawyer, and R. W. Griffin, "Toward a Theory of Organizational Creativity," *Academy of Management Review*, April 1993, pp. 293–321; and C. M. Ford, "A Theory of Individual Creative Action in Multiple Social Domains," *Academy of Management Review*, October 1996, pp. 1112–42.

8. Cited in C. G. Morris, *Psychology: An Introduction*, 9th ed. (Upper Saddle River, NJ: Prentice Hall, 1996), p. 344.

9. See R. Epstein, "Capturing Creativity," *Psychology Today*, July–August 1996, pp. 41–43 and 75–78.

10. H. G. Gough, "A Creative Personality Scale for the Adjective Check List," *Journal of Personality and Social Psychology*, August 1979, pp. 1398–1405; F. B. Barron and D. M. Harrington, "Creativity, Intelligence, and Personality," in M. R. Rosenzweig and L. W. Porter (eds.), *Annual Review of Psychology*, vol. 32 (Palo Alto, CA: Annual Reviews, 1981), pp. 439–76; C. Martindale, "Personality, Situation, and Creativity," in J. A. Glover, R. R. Ronning, and C. R. Reynolds (eds.), *Handbook of Creativity* (New York: Plenum, 1989), pp. 211–32; and R. J. Sternberg and T. I. Lubbart, "An Investment Theory of Creativity and Its Development," *Human Development*, January–February 1991, pp. 1–31.

11. M. Csikszentmihalyi, "The Creative Personality," *Psychology Today*, July–August 1996, p. 38.

12. Based on T. M. Amabile, R. Conti, H. Coon, J. Lazenby, and M. Herron, "Assessing the Work Environment for Creativity," *Academy of Management Journal*, October 1996, pp. 1154–84.

13. Based on R. von Oech, *A Whack on the Side of the Head* (New York: Warner, 1983); M. Stein, *Stimulating Creativity*, vol. 1 (New York: Academic Press, 1974); and E. deBono, *Lateral Thinking: Creativity Step by Step* (New York: Harper & Row, 1971).

14. See, for example, S. Stiansen, "Breaking Even," *Success*, November 1988, p. 16.

15. From Standard & Poor's, June 24, 1994.

16. R. Koselka, "Playing Poker with Craig McCaw," *Forbes*, July 3, 1995, pp. 62–64.

17. M. Bazerman, *Judgment in Managerial Decision Making* (New York: Wiley, 1994), p. 124.

18. F. W. Barnett, "Making Game Theory Work in Practice," *Wall Street Journal*, February 13, 1995, p. A14.

19. For details on using linear programming, see R. S. Russell and B. W. Taylor III, *Production and Operations Management* (Upper Saddle River, NJ: Prentice Hall, 1995), pp. 61–84.

20. This section is based on N. R. F. Maier, "Assets and Liabilities in Group Problem Solving: The Need for an Integrative Function," *Psychological Review*, April 1967, pp. 239–49; G. W. Hill, "Group Versus Individual Performance: Are N + 1 Heads Better Than One?" *Psychological Bulletin*, May 1982, pp. 517–39; R. A. Cooke and J. A. Kernaghan, "Estimating the Difference Between Group Versus Individual Performance on Problem-Solving Tasks," *Group & Organization Studies*, September 1987, pp. 319–42; and L. K. Michaelsen, W. E. Watson, and R. H. Black, "A Realistic Test of Individual Versus Group Consensus Decision Making," *Journal of Applied Psychology*, October 1989, pp. 834–39.

21. V. H. Vroom and A. G. Jago, *The New Leadership: Managing Participation in Organizations* (Englewood Cliffs, NJ: Prentice Hall, 1988).

22. Based on A. L. Delbecq, "The Management of Decision-Making Within the Firm: Three Strategies for Three Types of Decision-Making," *Academy of Management Journal*, December 1967, pp. 329–39; P. F. Drucker, *Management: Tasks, Responsibilities, Practices* (New York: Harper & Row, 1974), pp. 449–50, 465–80; and H. A. Simon, *The New Science of Management Decision*, rev. ed. (Upper Saddle River, NJ: Prentice Hall, 1977), pp. 45–49.

23. See, for instance, R. Zemke, "The 'New' Middle Manager," *Training*, August 1994, pp. 42–46.

24. See, for instance, J. Pfeffer, *Competitive Advantage Through People: Unleashing the Power of the Work Force* (Boston: Harvard Business School Press, 1994).

25. D. L. Rados, "Selection and Evaluation of Alternatives in Repetitive Decision Making," *Administrative Science Quarterly*, June 1972, pp. 196–206.

26. See, for example, March, *A Primer on Decision Making*, pp. 8–25; A. Langley, H. Mintzberg, P. Pitcher, E. Posada, and J. Saint-Macary, "Opening Up Decision Making: The View from the Black Stool," *Organization Science*, May–June 1995, pp. 260–79; and L. R. Beach, *The Psychology of Decision Making* (Thousand Oaks, CA: Sage, 1997).

27. J. G. March and H. A. Simon, *Organizations* (New York: Wiley, 1958).

28. H. A. Simon, *Administrative Behavior*, 3rd ed. (New York: Macmillan, 1976).

29. See, for instance, T. B. Green, W. B. Newsom, and S. R. Jones, "A Survey of the Application of Quantitative Techniques to Production/Operation Management in Large Corporations," *Academy of Management Journal*, December 1977, pp. 669–76; D. J. Isenberg, "How Senior Managers Think," *Harvard Business Review*, November–December 1984, pp. 81–90; Y. Kathawala, "Application of Quantitative Techniques in Large and Small Organizations

in the United States: An Empirical Analysis," *Journal of Operations Research*, July 1988, pp. 981–89; and S. S. K. Lam, "Applications of Quantitative Techniques in Hong Kong: An Empirical Analysis," *Asia Pacific Journal of Management*, October 1993, pp. 229–36.

30. Bazerman, *Judgment in Managerial Decision Making*, p. 5.

31. See Simon, *Administrative Behavior*, 3rd ed., and J. Forester, "Bounded Rationality and the Politics of Muddling Through," *Public Administration Review*, January–February 1984, pp. 23–31.

32. See K. R. Hammond, R. M. Hamm, J. Grassia, and T. Pearson, "Direct Comparison of the Efficacy of Intuitive and Analytical Cognition in Expert Judgment," *IEEE Transactions on Systems, Man and Cybernetics*, SMC-17, 1987, pp. 753–70; W. H. Agor (ed.), *Intuition in Organizations* (Newbury Park, CA.: Sage, 1989); and R. C. Blattberg and S. J. Hoch, "Data Models and Managerial Intuition: 50% Model + 50% Manager," *Management Science*, August 1990, pp. 887–99.

33. O. Behling and N. L. Eckel, "Making Sense Out of Intuition," *The Executive*, February 1991, pp. 46–54; J. Parikh, F. Neubauer, and A. G. Lank, *Intuition: The New Frontier of Management* (Santa Cruz, CA: Blackwell Business, 1994); and S. Shapiro and M. T. Spence, "Managerial Intuition: A Conceptual and Operational Framework," *Business Horizons*, January–February 1997, pp. 63–68.

34. As described in H. A. Simon, "Making Management Decisions: The Role of Intuition and Emotion," *The Executive*, February 1987, pp. 59–60.

35. See L. R. Beach, *Image Theory: Decision Making in Personal and Organizational Contexts* (Chichester, England: Wiley, 1990); L. R. Beach and T. R. Mitchell, "Image Theory: A Behavioral Theory of Decision Making in Organizations," in B. M. Staw and L. L. Cummings (eds.), *Research in Organizational Behavior*, vol. 12 (Greenwich, CT.: JAI, 1990), pp. 1–41; T. R. Mitchell and L. R. Beach, "'. . . Do I Love Thee? Let Me Count . . .' Toward an Understanding of Intuitive and Automatic Decision Making," *Organizational Behavior and Human Decision Processes*, October 1990, pp. 1–20; L. R. Beach, *The Psychology of Decision Making*, pp. 164–81; S. M. Richmond, B. L. Bissell, and L. R. Beach, "Image Theory's Compatibility Test and Evaluations of the Status Quo," *Organizational Behavior and Human Decision Processes*, January 1998, pp. 39–53; and C. Seidl and S. Traub, "A New Test of Image Theory," *Organizational Behavior and Human Decision Processes*, August 1998, pp. 93–116.

36. See, for example, M. D. Cohen, J. G. March, and J. P. Olsen, "A Garbage Can Model of Organizational Choice," *Administrative Science Quarterly*, March 1972, pp. 1–25.

37. See J. G. Thompson, *Organizations in Action* (New York: McGraw-Hill, 1967), p. 123.

38. Bazerman, *Judgment in Managerial Decision Making*, pp. 54–55.

39. A. Tversky and D. Kahneman, "The Framing of Decisions and the Psychology of Choice," *Science*, January 1981, pp. 453–63.

40. C. E. Lindholm, "The Science of 'Muddling Through,'" *Public Administration Review*, Spring 1959, pp. 79–88.

41. A. Tversky and D. Kahneman, "Judgment Under Uncertainty: Heuristics and Biases," *Science*, September 1974, pp. 1124–31.

42. Cited in J. Simons, "Improbable Dreams," *U.S. News & World Report*, March 24, 1997, p. 46.

43. See B. M. Staw, "The Escalation of Commitment to a Course of Action," *Academy of Management Review*, October 1981, pp. 577–87; D. R. Bobocel and J. P. Meyer, "Escalating Commitment to a Failing Course of Action: Separating the Roles of Choice and Justification," *Journal of Applied Psychology*, June 1994, pp. 360–63; and F. D. Schoorman and P. J. Holahan, "Psychological Antecedents of Escalation Behavior: Effects of Choice, Responsibility, and Decision Consequences," *Journal of Applied Psychology*, December 1996, pp. 786–94.

44. See J. Pfeffer, "Understanding Power in Organizations," *California Management Review*, Winter 1992, p. 37.

45. See, for instance, C. E. Larson and F. M. J. LaFasto, *TeamWork* (Newbury Park, CA.: Sage, 1989); and J. L. Cotton, *Employee Involvement* (Newbury Park, CA.: Sage, 1993).

46. See J. Pfeffer, *Organizational Design* (Arlington Heights, IL: AHM, 1978).

47. A. J. Rowe, J. D. Boulgarides, and M. R. McGrath, *Managerial Decision Making*, Modules in Management Series (Chicago: SRA, 1984), pp. 18–22.

48. See, for instance, L. Kohlberg, *Essays in Moral Development: The Philosophy of Moral Development*, vol. 1 (New York: Harper & Row, 1981); L. Kohlberg, *Essays in Moral Development: The Psychology of Moral Development*, vol. 2 (New York: Harper & Row, 1984); and R. S. Snell, "Complementing Kohlberg: Mapping the Ethical Reasoning Used by Managers for Their Own Dilemma Cases," *Human Relations*, January 1996, pp. 23–49.

49. See, for example, J. Weber, "Managers' Moral Reasoning: Assessing Their Responses to Three Moral Dilemmas," *Human Relations*, July 1990, pp. 687–702; and S. B. Knouse and R. A. Giacalone, "Ethical Decision-Making in Business: Behavioral Issues and Concerns," *Journal of Business Ethics*, May 1992, pp. 369–77.

50. S. N. Chakravarty and A. Feldman, "The Road Not Taken," *Forbes*, August 30, 1993, pp. 40–41.

51. A. Wildavsky, *The Politics of the Budgetary Process* (Boston: Little, Brown, 1964).

52. F. Kluckhohn and F. L. Strodtbeck, *Variations in Value Orientations* (Evanston, IL: Row, Peterson, 1961); G. Hofstede, *Cultures and Organizations: Software of the Mind* (New York: McGraw-Hill, 1991); G. Hofstede, "Cultural Constraints in Management Theories," *The Executive*, February 1993, pp. 81–94; and N. J. Adler, *International Dimensions of Organizational Behavior*, 3rd ed. (Cincinnati, OH: Southwestern, 1997) pp.166–73).

53. See S. Schafer, "Software That Thinks," *Inc. Technology*, December 2, 1996, pp. 109–10; and J. A. Byrne, "Virtual Management," *Business Week*, September 21, 1998, pp. 80–82.

54. Adapted from L. L. Nash, "Ethics Without the Sermon," *Harvard Business Review*, November–December 1981, p. 81.

55. D. A. Whetton and K. S. Cameron, *Developing Management Skills*, 2nd ed. (New York: HarperCollins, 1991), p. 182. Common answers: banks, currency, solvent, washed up, liquid assets, deposits, float a loan.

MONITORING THE ENVIRONMENT

DON'T OVERLOOK THE IMPORTANCE OF
WORLDWIDE THINKING. A COMPANY THAT KEEPS ITS
EYE ON TOM, DICK, AND
HARRY IS GOING TO MISS PIERRE,
HANS, AND YOSHIO.

A. RIES

LEARNING OBJECTIVES

After studying this chapter, you should be able to:

1 Define the environment.

2 Explain the importance of environmental scanning and identify four environmental-scanning techniques.

3 Describe the typical benchmarking process.

4 Describe how managers can reduce environmental uncertainty.

5 Identify and describe the five dimensions for analyzing national culture.

6 Compare the classical and socioeconomic views on social responsibility.

7 Contrast social responsibility and social responsiveness.

8 Define ISO 9000 and its implications for management practice.

In 1997, executives at Boeing of Seattle, Washington, and defense contractor McDonnell Douglas, based in St. Louis, Missouri, agreed to a merger.[1] The two companies sought, and received, approval by U.S. antitrust authorities. However, they still had a formidable hurdle to jump before the merger could go through. They had to get approval from the 20-member European Commission. And this commission had the right to reject the agreement. Surprised? You're not alone. A congressman from Missouri was outraged: "The European Union can't tell the American people how to do business." A lot of Americans were similarly mystified: "They can't do that, can they?" they asked. The answer is: They *can* do that!

The EU's right to review a major merger between two U.S. companies is a fact in today's globalized life, as is the United States's right to pass on big intra-European deals. In 1991, the United States and the EU signed an agreement to consult on antitrust actions. Each has already meddled across the sea—the Europeans forced changes in the merger between Scott Paper and Kimberly-

Clark, and the United States won modifications in the all-European agreement between drug makers Sandoz and Ciba-Geigy that created Novartis.

The Boeing-McDonnell marriage would create one of the world's largest arms makers and give the combined firm 70 percent of the world commercial aviation market. The other 30 percent of that market is held by Airbus, the four-nation consortium based in Toulouse, France. Clearly, this merger of American firms was a genuine threat to Airbus's survival.

The concerns of the European Union to the Boeing-McDonnell merger were eventually resolved and the deal was finalized. But the EU had the legal clout to make things rough on the American company if it didn't respond to those concerns. The merged company could be hit with an EU fine equal to 10 percent of Boeing-McDonnell's combined annual revenue, or a cool $4.8 billion! And to satisfy their claim, the EU could seize Boeing planes being delivered in Europe, and European firms could be barred from doing business with the new company. With 25 percent of its sales in Europe, Boeing could not take the EU's threat lightly.

This Boeing-McDonnell example illustrates the power of environmental factors to effect managerial decisions. Effective management requires scanning the environment; keeping close contact with key constituencies such as customers, competitors, and government agencies; and making proactive efforts to positively shape the environment so as to make it more favorable for the organization. As you'll see in this chapter, the organization-environment relationship is a two-way street. The environment influences, shapes, and constrains organizations. But there are strategies management can pursue that allow the organization also to exert some control on its environment.

DEFINING THE ENVIRONMENT

An organization's **environment** is composed of the institutions and forces that are outside the organization and can affect the organization's performance. As noted in chapter 2, the environment typically includes suppliers, customers, competitors, unions, government regulatory agencies, and public pressure groups.

Every organization's environment is different. The exact nature of an organization's environment at any given time depends on the "niche" that the organization has staked out for itself with respect to the range of products or services it offers and the markets it serves. Ferrari and Suzuki both manufacture cars. But they appeal to very different customers. Nucor and Bethlehem Steel both produce steel, but because Bethlehem's employees are unionized and Nucor's aren't, labor unions are not part of Nucor's environment. Similarly, the University of Massachusetts is a state-supported institution. Harvard University is private. As a result, the Massachusetts State Legislature is a key environmental constituent of UMass but not of Harvard. On the other hand, wealthy alumni are a much more powerful environmental force at Harvard than at UMass. Why? Because UMass depends on the state for much of its funding, whereas Harvard relies heavily on alumni contributions.

The key thing to understand about an organization's environment is that it creates potential uncertainty. Some organizations are fortunate to face relatively certain or static environments—few forces in their environment ever change. There are, for example, no new competitors, no new technological breakthroughs by current competitors, and little activity by public pressure groups to influence the organization. Other organizations face dynamic environments—rapidly changing government regulations affecting their business, new competitors, difficulties in acquiring raw materials, continually changing product preferences by customers, and so on. Ideally, management would prefer to operate in a static environment. There would be no uncertainty, and decision making would be simple and highly accurate. But there are few static environments nowadays. Environmental uncertainty characterizes the world that most organizations currently face. And since uncertainty is a threat to an organization's effectiveness, management will try to limit environmental uncertainty through activities such as market research, advertising, lobbying, benchmarking, forecasting, and creating joint ventures with other firms.

Research has helped clarify what is meant by environmental uncertainty. It has been found that there are three key dimensions to any organization's environment. They are labeled capacity, volatility, and complexity.[2]

The *capacity* of an environment refers to the degree to which it can support growth. Rich and growing environments generate excess resources, which can buffer the organization in times of relative scarcity. Abundant capacity, for example, leaves room for an organization to make mistakes; scarce capacity does not. In the late-1990s, firms operating in the multimedia software business had relatively abundant environments, whereas those in the full-service brokerage business faced relative scarcity.

The degree of instability in an environment is captured in the *volatility* dimension. A high degree of unpredictable change creates a dynamic environment in which it is difficult for management to predict accurately the outcomes of various decisions. At the other extreme is a stable environment. The accelerated changes in eastern Europe and the ending of the Cold War had dramatic effects on the U.S. defense industry in the early 1990s. The environment of major defense contractors such as Lockheed Martin, General Dynamics, and Northrop Grumman moved from relatively stable to dynamic.

Finally, the environment needs to be assessed in terms of *complexity*; that is, the degree of heterogeneity and concentration among environmental elements. Simple environments are homogeneous and concentrated. The tobacco industry is one example, because there are relatively few players. It is easy for firms in this industry to keep a close eye on the competition. In contrast, environments characterized by heterogeneity and dispersion are called complex, a term that aptly describes the current environment in the on-line computer data-services business. Every day there seems to be another "new kid on the block" with whom established data-services firms have to deal.

Exhibit 4-1 summarizes our definition of the environment along its three dimensions. The arrows in this figure indicate movement toward higher uncertainty. So organizations that operate in environments characterized as scarce, dynamic, and complex face the greatest degree of uncertainty. Why? Because they have little room for error, high unpredictability, and a diverse set of elements in the environment to constantly monitor.

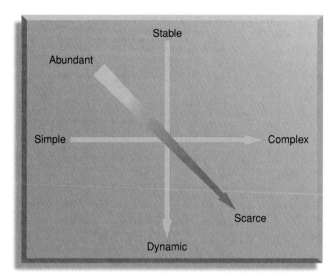

Three-Dimensional Model of the Environment

EXHIBIT 4-1

MAJOR SOURCES OF ENVIRONMENTAL UNCERTAINTY

In chapter 2, we identified key stakeholders that organizations need to satisfy. In this section, we revisit the concept of stakeholders. But this time, we look at only external stakeholders and specifically assess how each creates uncertainty for management.

Customers

Customers' tastes and preferences change. And those changes represent uncertainty to management and organizations. In the 1980s, for instance, conspicuous consumption was in. Manufacturers and retailers of expensive designer clothes, jewelry, and luxury automobiles did well. But the purchase of high-status items went out of fashion in the early 1990s. Suddenly, consumers were looking for value. This change in consumer preference was good news to firms such as Wal-Mart, Home Depot, and Ikea. It was bad news, however, for Rolls-Royce, Rolex, and Ralph Lauren.

Competitors

In a static environment, competitors offer the same products and services at the same prices today that they did yesterday and that they will tomorrow. Unfortunately for managers, competitors change strategies. They introduce new products, for instance, with improved features. Motorola, as a case in point, is continually bombarded by Intel's introduction of ever more powerful microprocessors.

Organizations also face the possibility that new competitors will surface. That is, the players will change. Ten years ago, cable companies could concentrate their attention on other cable rivals. Not today. Telephone companies and firms that sell home-satellite dishes are aggressive competitors for cable service.

Suppliers

Organizations depend on raw materials, labor, and capital to operate. If availability of those resources is restricted, if their prices increase, or if their quality suffers, the ability of the organization to continue operating can be threatened.

The price of coffee beans escalated more than 150 percent in 1997. For organizations like Folger's, Maxwell House, and coffee retailer Starbucks, this was a serious problem. Although part of the cost increase was passed on to customers in higher prices, some of the higher supply costs had to be absorbed, resulting in lower profits.

All organizations rely on people to accomplish goals. They're dependent, therefore, on the availability of labor inputs. The growth of many software companies, in recent years, has been restricted solely because of the limited supply of high-caliber software engineers. Of course, labor uncertainty is most visible when a firm's workforce is unionized, because a strike can cut off the organization's labor supply. For instance, when a coalition of Hyundai unions called a general strike against nine Hyundai companies in Ulsan, South Korea, 60,000 of its workers refused to come to work and caused a complete shutdown of Hyundai plants.[3]

In addition to materials and labor, organizations need capital to operate. Capital can come from internally generated profits, investors who buy equity in the firm, or lenders who loan the organization money. Highly profitable and well-regarded companies have no trouble obtaining money to operate. And they can secure funds at favorable terms. Other companies, however, depend on suppliers, banks, and other financial institutions for capital. To the degree that those sources withhold support, they create uncertainty for management.

Government

Government creates uncertainty for organizations through changes in regulations, the degree to which it enforces regulations, and through its actions that can create economic and political instability.

The Americans with Disabilities Act (ADA) became law in the United States in 1992. In ADA's first year, complaints against companies averaged 1,200 a month. Half of those charges were for wrongful discharge, and another 22 percent were for failure to accommodate an individual to an existing job.[4]

Executives at Office Depot and Staples, the two largest office supply retailers in the United States, spent much of 1997 trying to convince the U.S. Department of Justice that their planned merger would not restrict competition. Why was this necessary? Because the Justice Department had the power to block the deal by virtue of its responsibility to enforce U.S. antitrust laws.[5] The Justice Department didn't buy the argument and challenged the merger in federal court. The court sided with the government, and the merger plans were terminated.

In January 1991, the U.S. Congress added a 10 percent luxury tax on boats costing more than $100,000. This action dramatically cut sales of high-priced boats. Industry sales dropped from $18 billion to under $11 billion, and many small boat builders went out of business. Sales rebounded after August 1993, when Congress repealed the luxury tax, but it was too late for some firms.[6]

Economic and political actions of governments can also play havoc with organizations. In early 1995, for example, when the Mexican government devalued the peso relative to the dollar, it created problems for every global firm operating in Mexico. For instance, 2,600 workers at the Ciudad Juarez plant of French giant Thomson Consumer Electronics walked off the job to protest the 40 percent cut in the value of their wages caused by the peso's devaluation.[7] Along similar lines, no business operating in Hong Kong was able to ignore the ramifications of the colony's return to Chinese rule in 1997.[8]

▶ Media

You've probably heard this joke before: What's the worst thing a secretary can say to his or her boss? "Mike Wallace and the camera crew from *60 Minutes* are here and would like to talk with you."

A bold headline in the *Arizona Daily Star* read, "Econo Lube Cited in 68 Bureau Complaints."[9] The article then proceeded to describe how the Better Business Bureau had received an unusually high number of claims for poor workmanship, unnecessary repairs, incomplete work, and excessive bills at six Econo Lube shops in Tucson. This publicity seriously damaged the company's local reputation and resulted in a significant loss of business.

These examples illustrate how television, newspapers, and other media create uncertainty for organizations by their power to influence consumers and regulatory agencies. Unflattering exposés on national television programs or in publications such as the *Wall Street Journal* or *Fortune* magazine have caused dramatic declines in a company's stock, derailed plans to sell new securities, precipitated legal action and multimillion-dollar fines, and even resulted in an occasional corporate bankruptcy. On the other hand, favorable media publicity can do just the opposite. When Oprah Winfrey reviews a novel on her talk show, sales of that book always explode. It's not unusual for a review on her show to require a publisher to print a million extra copies just to meet the increased demand that follows an Oprah selection.

▶ Special Interests

Organizations are vulnerable to bad publicity, boycotts, and consumer pressures from special interest groups. We can highlight a few examples. Mothers Against Drunk Drivers attacks beer manufacturers such as Miller and Anheuser-Busch for advertising to young people. The American Association of Retired Persons lobbies restaurants and cinemas to offer senior discounts. The Christian Coalition promotes its pro-life agenda by picketing in front of facilities that perform abortions. Meanwhile, women's groups boycott Domino's Pizza because its owner, Tom Monaghan, financially supports pro-life advocates.

MADD is a special interest group that has successfully fought beer and alcohol producers to restrict teenage drinking and increase penalties for drunk driving.

Maria Iriti, who runs a glass company in Massachusetts, put in a bid of $18,000 to repair stained glass windows in a church. She won the bid but lost a bundle. She later found out that the next lowest bid had come in at $76,000. Iriti learned a valuable lesson from her mistake. She now keeps a folder on each competitor, socializes with them at trade shows, and has friends write to competitors for price lists and brochures.[10]

Managers in both small and large organizations are increasingly turning to **environmental scanning** to anticipate and interpret changes in their environment.[11] The term, as we'll use it, refers to screening large amounts of information to detect emerging trends, monitoring the actions of others, and creating a set of scenarios.

The importance of environmental scanning was first recognized (outside of the national security community) by firms in the life insurance industry in the late 1970s.[12] Life insurance companies found that the demand for their product was declining. Yet all the key environmental signals they were receiving strongly favored the sale of life insurance. The economy and population were growing. Baby boomers were finishing school, entering the labor force, and taking on family responsibilities. The market for life insurance should have been expanding. But it wasn't. What the insurance companies had failed to recognize was a fundamental change in family structure in the United States.

Young families, who represented the primary group of buyers of new insurance policies, tended to be dual-career couples who were increasingly choosing to remain childless. The life insurance needs of a family with one income, a dependent spouse, and a houseful of kids are much greater than those of a two-income family with few, if any, children. That a multibillion-dollar industry could overlook such a fundamental social trend underscored the need to develop techniques for monitoring important environmental developments.

There are four main environmental-scanning techniques: competitive intelligence, scenario development, forecasting, and benchmarking.

Competitive Intelligence

One of the fastest-growing tools of environmental scanning is **competitive intelligence**.[13] It seeks basic information about competitors. Who are they? What are they doing? How will what they're doing affect us? As Maria Iriti learned the hard way, accurate information on the competition can allow managers to anticipate competitor actions rather than merely react to them.

One expert on competitive intelligence emphasizes that 95 percent of the competitor-related information an organization needs to make crucial strategic decisions is available and accessible to the public.[14] In other words, competitive intelligence isn't organizational espionage. Advertisements, promotional materials, press releases, reports filed with government agencies, annual reports, employment want ads, newspaper reports, and industry studies are examples of readily available sources of information. Specific information on your industry and competitors is increasingly available through electronic databases. Managers can literally tap into a wealth of competitive information through purchasing access to databases sold by companies such as Nexus and Knight-Ridder. And managers can find plenty of information on competitors by visiting Internet Web sites (see Exhibit 4-2). Trade

Searching the Internet for Information on Competitors

EXHIBIT 4-2

There is plenty of information on the Web about competitors. You just have to know where to look. The following are examples of sites where managers can gain competitive intelligence:

Alta Vista <www.altavista.digital.com>. Powerful index tool used to locate information about products and companies.

Avenue Technologies <www.avetech.com/avenue>. News and numbers from 11,000 private and 9,000 public companies as well as 5,000 international companies.

CareerPath.com <www.careerpath.com>. Newspaper employment ads from major U.S. cities. A good place to find out how the competition plans to expand.

Company Sleuth <www.companysleuth.com>. Select a publicly traded company and this Web service will scan the Internet and report daily on most recent insider trades, trademark registrations, and patent applications.

Competitive Intelligence Guide <www.fuld.com/>. Fuld & Co.'s competitive intelligence site. Offers analytical tools, links to other intelligence sites, and an "Internet Intelligence Index" of company resources.

Exporting <www.exporthotline.com>. Contains thousands of market research reports, a trade library, and market intelligence on 80 countries.

Hoover's Online <www.hoovers.com>. Provides income-statement and balance-sheet numbers in detailed profiles of nearly 2,500 public companies.

IBM Patent Server <www.patents.ibm.com>. The ultimate resource for tracking technology. This site archives 2 million U.S. patent citations from the past 27 years.

I-Net Intelligence <www.eiu.com>. Global business-intelligence information including country and regional publications, market conditions, economic developments, industry trends, and corporate strategies in more than 180 countries.

Inquisit <www.inquisit.com>. Notifies you whenever there's news about companies, customers, markets, or trends that you've asked it to track.

MediaFinder <www.mediafinder.com>. Provides an index and description of thousands of newsletters, catalogs, and magazines.

U.S. Securities and Exchange Commission <www.sec.gov>. Offers 10-K and reports filed by public companies.

Source: Based on material supplied by Fuld & Co. and described in "Search and Employ," *Forbes ASAP*, June 3, 1996, p. 88; S. Greco, "The On-Line Sleuth," *Inc.*, October 1996, pp. 88–89; and G. Imperato, "Competitive Intelligence—Get Smart!" *Fast Company*, April/May 1998, p. 274.

Marc Friedman is manager of market research at Andrew Corp., a fast-growing manufacturer of wireless-telecommunications equipment. Friedman is his company's go-to guy for getting the goods on the competition and he relies heavily on the Web. "The Net isn't my only source of information, but it's a major one. It's where I start."

shows and the debriefing of your own sales force can be other good sources of information on competitors. Many firms even regularly buy competitors' products and have their own engineers break them down to learn about new technical innovations.

If you're in any segment of the computer business, the annual Comdex trade show in Las Vegas is a dream come true for engaging in competitive intelligence.[15] Computer firm representatives, many posing as customers, eavesdrop on conversations, examine competitors' products, and elicit information about pricing, performance, shipping dates, what chips are used, and who supplies key components. Michael Dell of Dell Computer says that checking out exhibits at Comdex a few years earlier helped convince him that the notebooks he had on the drawing board weren't competitive with products already on the showroom floor. So he scrapped his plans and started over from scratch.

► Scenario Development

Extensive environmental scanning is likely to reveal issues and concerns that could affect an organization's current or planned operations. They are not likely to be equally important, so it's usually necessary to focus on a limited set—say, three or four—that are most important and to develop scenarios based on each.

A **scenario** is a consistent view of what the future is likely to be.[16] For instance, in 1998, the province of Quebec was contemplating another election on whether it should separate from the rest of Canada. The previous election, held in 1995, saw the separatists lose by less than 30,000 votes. The results of this election would have serious implications for companies, like the Royal Bank of Canada, that have operations in Quebec. So Royal Bank's management has created a multiple set of scenerios to assess the possible implications of separation. What, for example, would be the implications if Quebec were to become a separate country with its own monetary system? What if Quebec were to separate and successfully negotiate an agreement with the rest of Canada to continue to use the Canadian dollar? Based on scenarios like these, the Royal Bank was prepared to initiate changes in strategy under a variety of conditions.

► Forecasting

Environmental scanning creates the foundation for forecasts. Information obtained through scanning is used to form scenarios. These, in turn, establish parameters for **forecasts**, which are predictions of outcomes.

TYPES OF FORECASTS   Probably the two most popular outcomes for which management is likely to seek forecasts are future revenues and new technological breakthroughs. However, virtually any component in the organization's environment can be the focus of forecasting attention.

Mitsubishi Corporation's sales level drives purchasing requirements, production goals, employment needs, inventories, and numerous other decisions. Similarly, the University of Michigan's income from tuition, donations, grants, and state appropriations will determine course offerings, staffing needs, salary increases for faculty, and the like. Both of these examples illustrate that predicting future revenues—**revenue forecasting**—is a critical activity for both profit and not-for-profit organizations.

Where does management get the data for developing revenue forecasts? Typically, it begins with historical revenue figures. For example, what were last year's revenues? This figure can then be adjusted for trends. What revenue patterns have evolved over recent years? What changes in social and economic factors or actions of rivals might alter the pattern in the future? Answers to questions such as these provide the basis for revenue forecasts.

You probably haven't given much thought to the subject of college textbooks, but it's a fairly good bet that texts, as you know them, will soon look very different. College textbook publishers know that change is in the air, but there is little agreement among decision makers at these firms as to what form the content will take and when these changes are likely to be realized. CD-ROM technology, for instance, could permit students to purchase interactive texts on disks. Some "books" are already being produced in this format. The major barrier to CD-ROM texts is the high cost of the hardware needed to play them.

TODAY ? or TOMORROW ?

Scanning Agents

Imagine software programs that can make judgments, learn from their mistakes, and can make intelligent decisions for you. They're coming. They're called **scanning agents**.[17]

Scanning agents help managers find and process information. They're able to sift through a wealth of information on any topic without any further instruction from you and bring back only what is of specific interest to you. They're able to identify patterns and preferences. These agents, in essence, become your personal assistant. One could, for instance, scan your e-mail for important messages, roam the Net and alert you when there is news on a topic you've identified as important, remind you of an upcoming meeting, find the project reports you'll need in preparation for that meeting, and review the reports for information that are specifically relevant to you. What's unique and exciting about scanning agents is that they improve over time. They become more helpful as they learn about your specific work activities and preferences.

Bill Gates of Microsoft envisions having a scanning agent that will scan every project schedule, note the changes, and distinguish the ones he has to pay attention to from the others. It would learn the critieria for what needs his attention: the size of the project, what other projects are dependent on it, or the cause and the length of any delay. It would learn when a two-week slip could be ignored, and when such a slip indicates real trouble.

In the near future, scanning agents will be doing many of the tasks managers and their support staff now spend considerable time on. These agents will be scanning newspapers, magazines, Internet sites, and a host of other sources looking for trends, actions of competitors, or any other relevant information—then alert you to it. And as your needs and priorities change, so will the information that your scanning agent provides.

The faster the price of this hardware declines, the sooner most students will own computers with CD-ROM players. But CD-ROM is only one technological alternative among many. Another option could be nonpaper texts that are bought directly from publishers through on-line services. Some publishers think the future might have students purchasing digital "books" by downloading texts on their personal computers via modem hookup to the publisher's central data bank. You could call the publisher's toll-free number, use your credit card for payment, and then download the texts you need for your courses onto your personal computer. You could do all this in just minutes, and you would never have to step inside a bookstore. The point of these scenarios is that technology is very likely to change textbook publishing sometime in the near future. Those publishers that can accurately forecast when the market will be ready for these changes, what format the changes will take, and their specific structure, will be able to score big in the market.

Technological forecasting attempts to predict changes in technology and the time frame in which new technologies are likely to be economically feasible. The rapid pace of technological change has seen innovations in lasers, biotechnology, robotics, and data communications dramatically change surgery practices, pharmaceutical offerings, the processes used for manufacturing almost every mass-produced product, and the practicality of networked computers and cellular telephones. Few organizations are exempt from the possibility that technological innovation might dramatically change the demand for their current products or services. Those organizations that do a better job of technological forecasting will have a leg up on their competitors.

EXHIBIT 4-3

Forecasting Techniques

Technique	Description	Example
Quantitative		
Time-series analysis	Fits a trend line to a mathematical equation and projects into the future by means of this equation	Predicting next quarter's sales of Dove Bars based on 3 years of previous sales data
Regression models	Predicts one variable on the basis of known or assumed other variables	Predicting level of sales for Marlboro cigarettes on basis of different advertising outlays
Econometric models	Uses a set of regression equations to simulate segments of the economy	Predicting change in sales of Hatteras yachts as a result of changes in tax law
Economic indicators	Uses one or more economic indicators to predict a future state of the economy	Using change in gross domestic product to predict discretionary income
Substitution effect	Uses a mathematical formulation to predict how, when, and under what circumstances a new product or technology will replace an existing one	Managers at Banca Inbursa of Mexico predicting the effect of ATMs on the employment of bank personnel
Qualitative		
Jury of opinion	Combines and averages the opinions of experts	Executives polling all of Sony's purchasing agents to predict future price increases in various raw materials
Sales-force composition	Combines estimates from field sales personnel of customers' expected purchases	Predicting next year's sales of GE industrial lasers
Customer evaluation	Combines estimates from established customers of expected purchases	Surveys of major retailers to determine types and quantities of Nintendo games desired

FORECASTING TECHNIQUES Forecasting techniques fall into two general categories: quantitative and qualitative. **Quantitative forecasting** applies a set of mathematical rules to a series of past data to predict future outcomes. These techniques are preferred when management has sufficient "hard" data from which to work. **Qualitative forecasts**, on the other hand, use the judgment and opinions of knowledgeable individuals. Qualitative techniques typically are used when precise data are scarce or difficult to obtain. Exhibit 4-3 lists some of the better-known quantitative and qualitative forecasting techniques.

FORECASTING EFFECTIVENESS In the early 1980s, when Alain Gomez became chairman of Thomson Group, the state-owned French conglomerate, he decided to take advantage of the growing trend toward a unified Europe to build a powerful European high-tech company.[18] His strategy was based on forecasts of a continued worldwide defense buildup and a rapid movement to a European Union. Unfortunately for Gomez and his company, his forecasts missed the mark. Just as he had all the pieces in place to dominate world defense and consumer electronics markets, the environment changed. The Cold War started winding down, and military budgets around the world began shrinking. Powerful U.S. defense companies also began competing harder for shares of the diminished market. Meanwhile, movement toward greater European unity stalled, and what progress had been made in creating a single market allowed Asian competitors to initiate aggressive price wars in consumer electronics. The result: Thomson's defense revenues have been steadily declining, and its consumer electronics group has become a money loser. We can generalize from the Thomson example. In spite of the importance of forecasting to effective decision making and planning, managers have had mixed success in forecasting events and outcomes accurately.[19]

Forecasting techniques are most accurate when the environment is static. The more dynamic the environment, the greater the uncertainty and the more likely management is to develop inaccurate forecasts. Forecasting has a relatively unimpressive record in predicting nonseasonal turning points such as recessions, unusual events, discontinuities, and the actions or reactions of competitors.

Although forecasting has a mixed record, there are some things managers can do to improve forecasting effectiveness.[20] First, they should rely on simple forecasting techniques. They tend to do as well as, and often better than, complex methods that tend to mistake random data for meaningful information. Second, they need to compare every forecast with "no change." A no-change forecast is very accurate approximately half the time. Third, they should not rely on any single forecasting method. Accuracy is increased by using several models and averaging them, especially for longer-range forecasts. Fourth, they should not assume that they can accurately identify turning points in a trend. What is typically perceived as a significant turning point is most often an unusual random event. Finally, accuracy declines with expanding time frames. By shortening the length of forecasts, managers can improve their accuracy.

▶ Benchmarking

In school, you'd probably be in big trouble if you sought out the student with the best grades and intentionally tried to copy his or her work. It might surprise you to learn, then, that one of the hottest and fastest-growing techniques in business encourages companies to do essentially that. The technique is called *benchmarking*. In this section, we describe the benchmarking process in detail and show how it has helped managers keep on top of the best practices used by competitors and others.

Benchmarking is the practice of comparing, on some measurable scale, the performance of a key business operation in-house vis-à-vis a similar operation in other organizations.[21] It is an essential element in any organization's TQM (total quality management) program. The basic idea underlying benchmarking is that management can improve quality by analyzing and copying the methods of the leaders in various fields. And because benchmarking focuses on practices outside an organization, it is appropriately classified as an environmental-scanning tool.

The typical benchmarking process follows four steps (see Exhibit 4-4):

1. The organization forms a benchmarking planning team. The team's initial task is to identify what is to be benchmarked, identify "best practices" used by other organizations, and determine data collection methods. To maximize efficiency, the team benchmarks only functions or processes that are critical to their organization's success.

2. The team collects data internally on its own operations and externally from other organizations. Teams often err in paying too little attention to self-assessment—to uncover performance gaps, they must first understand and measure their own processes.

3. The data are analyzed to identify performance gaps and to determine the cause of differences.

4. An action plan is prepared and implemented that will result in meeting or exceeding the standards of others.[22]

How does a manager or benchmarking team get external data on other organizations?[23] First you need to decide who you're going to benchmark against. Use your network of contacts among customers, suppliers, and employees for organizations they think are best at the process you're trying to improve. Trade associations and industry experts often know who has breakthrough practices. And watch for organizations that may have won local, regional, or national quality awards as potential benchmarking targets. Then go to the Internet. Check out the Benchmarking Exchange (www.benchnet.com). It helps organizations share information from surveys, market studies, and lists of best-practice companies. Also, the Web sites of rivals can be a rich source of information. For example, it's not unusual for an organization to describe new products or services that it's currently developing on its Web site. And detailed financial data on rivals is often readily available at their site. This can help you analyze their key financial ratios, inventory turnover rates, and the like. Experts suggest that you don't overlook the possibility of developing partnerships with other organizations, even rivals, in order to share benchmarking data. Obviously, this will work only if you have something to trade that others want. But, for example, if you're looking to improve your customer satisfaction process and you already have a great order system, you may be able to arrange to swap data with another organization that has complementary needs.

EXHIBIT 4-4   **The Benchmarking Process**

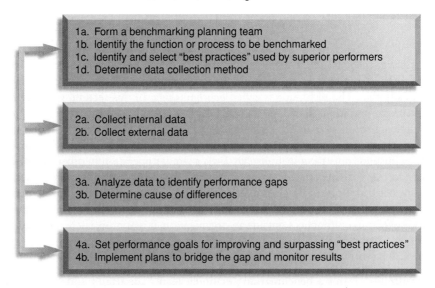

1a. Form a benchmarking planning team
1b. Identify the function or process to be benchmarked
1c. Identify and select "best practices" used by superior performers
1d. Determine data collection method

2a. Collect internal data
2b. Collect external data

3a. Analyze data to identify performance gaps
3b. Determine cause of differences

4a. Set performance goals for improving and surpassing "best practices"
4b. Implement plans to bridge the gap and monitor results

Source: Based on Y. K. Shetty, "Aiming High: Competitive Benchmarking for Superior Performance," *Long Range Planning*, February 1993, p. 42.

Let's look at a few functions and processes that have been identified as "best practices" for benchmarking. Xerox, an early proponent of benchmarking, has identified a long list of best-practice companies covering a variety of areas. They use Toyota and Komatsu for their manufacturing operations; American Express for billing and collection; AT&T and Hewlett-Packard for research and product development; L.L. Bean, Hershey Foods, and Mary Kay Cosmetics for distribution; Procter & Gamble for marketing; and Deere & Co. for computer operations.[24] To improve its ability to empty its planes of passengers and baggage and ready the plane for another flight, Southwest Airlines benchmarked the pit crews at Indy 500 car races. IBM used the operations of Las Vegas casinos to find ways to reduce the risk of employee theft.[25] And Giordano Holdings Ltd., a Hong Kong–based manufacturer and retailer of mass-market casual wear, borrowed its "good quality, good value" concept from Marks & Spencer, used The Limited to benchmark its point-of-sales computerized information system, and modeled its simplified product offerings on McDonald's menu.[26]

When environmental scanning relies exclusively on data readily available to the public, there's little debate about its propriety. But what about practices such as hiring competitors' employees, planting spies in rival firms, or lying to gain competitive information?[27] Consider the following situations, and judge for yourself whether environmental scanning is ethical or not.

ETHICAL ISSUES IN ENVIRONMENTAL SCANNING

Texas Instruments hires a senior engineering executive from Intel. The new executive is well qualified for the position, but so were a dozen or more other candidates. They, however, did not work for Intel, and they did not have up-to-date knowledge of what new microchip products Intel was developing. Is it unethical for TI, one of Intel's primary microchip competitors, to hire this executive? Is it acceptable to hire this executive but unacceptable to question him about Intel's plans?

The vice president at a major book publishing company encourages one of her editors to interview for an editorial vacancy at a competing book publisher. The editor is not interested in the position. The sole purpose of the interview will be to gain as much information as possible on the competitor's near-term publishing list and relay that information back to the vice president. Is going to such an interview unethical? Is asking an employee to engage in this intelligence mission wrong?

At a recent Comdex computer trade show, Compaq Computer sent a senior executive to the Hewlett-Packard booth. Keeping his badge in his pocket, he never let on how much he knew about the business, and to conceal his position, he wore a sweater and slacks instead of a business suit. He asked numerous questions of the HP sales representative about a specific new product. The sales rep explained how it was built, who supplied the communication technology, and HP's future plans. Has this Compaq executive been deceitful? Has he done anything wrong?

Environmental uncertainty is, in varying degrees, a fact of life for most managers.[28] Although managers would prefer to operate in a completely predictable and autonomous environment, almost all organizations face some uncertainty, and many environments are quite dynamic. Is there anything managers can do to reduce uncertainty? The answer is yes. Managers and organizations are not totally captive to their environment.[29] In this section, we'll briefly review strategies for managing the uncertainties presented by various forces in the environment.

STRATEGIES FOR MANAGING THE ENVIRONMENT

Classifying Strategies

> **Managers and organizations are not totally captive to their environment.**

In very simplistic terms, managers have two general strategies they can take in their attempt to lessen environmental uncertainty. They can respond by adapting and changing their actions to fit the environment, or they can attempt to alter the environment to fit better with the organization's capabilities. The former approach we call **internal strategies**, and the latter, **external strategies**.[30]

When management selectively cuts prices or recruits executives from its competitors, it is making internal adjustments to its environment. The environment doesn't change, but the fit between the organization and the environment is improved. The result is that the organization's dependence on the environment is reduced.

External strategies are designed to actually change the environment. If competitive pressures are cutting an airline's profitability, it can merge with another airline to gain a synergistic network of routes. If changes suggested in a federal tax reform proposal threaten a small life insurance company, it might use its membership in a trade association to lobby against those changes.

Internal Strategies

The following internal strategies demonstrate actions that almost any organization can take to better match its environment and, in so doing, lessen the impact of the environment on the organization's operations.

CHANGING DOMAINS Although there are few environments with no uncertainty, astute management can change domains to shift the organization into a niche with less uncertainty! Safeco Insurance of California provides an example of changing domains. California has given Safeco's balance sheet a couple of heavy "jolts" in recent years. First was the San Francisco earthquake, followed a few years later by an even larger earthquake in Los Angeles. After absorbing hundreds of millions of dollars in losses, Safeco's management decided to stop writing earthquake insurance in California.

When faced with an unfavorable environment, management chose to change its business focus to areas with less environmental uncertainty. Managers in many firms have pursued this strategy when faced with a hostile environment. They have, for instance, staked out a niche that has fewer or less-powerful competitors or that has barriers, such as high entry costs, economies of scale, or regulatory approval, to keep other competitors out. Or they have moved to a domain where the environment is more favorable because, for instance, there is little regulation, there are numerous suppliers, there are no unions, or public pressure groups are less powerful. Unfortunately, because there aren't many opportunities for organizations to become unregulated monopolies, most decisions to change domains substitute one set of environmental uncertainties for another.

RECRUITMENT During the heyday of the Cold War—from the 1950s through the 1980s—major defense contractors such as Boeing and Northrop Grumman regularly recruited high-ranking officers when they retired from military service. Why? These officers had information and contacts that could significantly improve the defense firms' likelihood of securing lucrative government contracts.

A few years back, when the governor of Tennessee retired, he was immediately hired as president of the University of Tennessee. Why? You can bet it wasn't because he was the most knowledgeable about academic administration or the problems facing higher education. He was selected because the board thought he was the best candidate for dealing with the university's primary uncertainty—obtaining increased funding from the state.

The practice of selective hiring to reduce environmental uncertainty is widespread. For instance, corporations hire executives from competing firms to acquire information about their competitor's future plans. High-tech firms entice scientists from competitive firms with large salary increases and stock options to gain the technical expertise held by their competition. However, the greatest media attention tends to be reserved for private organizations that recruit former government officials. Business and legal firms regularly hire such officials, often at exorbitant salaries, to acquire their favorable ties with influencial decision makers and their knowledge of government operations. The major New York and Washington law firms, for instance, are full of former influential members of Congress and high-ranking presidential appointees.

BUFFERING In early 1995, with paper prices escalating and shortages developing, book publisher Simon & Schuster didn't sit idly by. Managers placed massive orders with paper suppliers—for quantities three or four times the amount typically ordered. Their strategy was to use stockpiled inventory to reduce the possibility of running out of paper and to cushion the blow from higher prices.

Buffering reduces the possibility that the organization's operations will be disturbed by reduction of supplies or depletion of outputs. On the input side, buffering is evident when organizations stockpile raw materials and supplies, use multiple suppliers, or engage in preventive maintenance. Buffering at the output level allows fewer options. The most obvious method is through the use of inventories. If an organization creates products that can be carried in inventory without damage, then maintaining warehouse inventories allows the organization to produce its goods at a constant rate regardless of fluctuation in sales demand. Toy manufacturers such as Mattel, for example, typically ship most of their products to retailers in the early fall for selling during the Christmas season. These manufacturers, of course, produce their toys year-round and merely stockpile them for shipping during the fall.

SMOOTHING Hertz will rent you a full-size car in Chicago on a weekday for $59 a day. But Hertz will rent you that same car on a Saturday or Sunday for only $42 a day. Why the difference in price? Hertz's management is smoothing demand. Businesspeople are heavy

Like almost all car rental firms, Hertz uses smoothing as a means to reduce fluctuations in the demand for their cars.

users of rental cars, and their primary demand is during the week. Rather than have the cars sit idle on weekends, Hertz cuts prices to attract nonbusiness customers.

Smoothing seeks to level out the impact of fluctuations in the environment. Organizations that use this technique, in addition to car rental agencies, include telephone companies, retail stores, magazines, and sports teams.

The heaviest demand on telephone equipment is by business between the weekday hours of 8:00 A.M. and 5:00 P.M. Telephone companies have to have enough equipment to meet peak demand during this period. But the equipment is still there during the rest of the time. So they smooth demand by charging the highest prices during their peak period and low rates during the evenings and on weekends. Managers of retail clothing stores in North America know that their slowest months are January (after the Christmas "blitz") and August (before the "back-to-school" blitz). To reduce this "trough" in the revenue curve, they typically run their semiannual sales at these times of the year. Magazine publishers give you a substantial discount—often 50 percent or more off newsstand prices—if you become a mail subscriber. As a subscription holder, you are now a guaranteed customer for the length of your subscription. Finally, we observe that sports teams usually give fans reduced prices when they buy season tickets covering all the home games. Even if the team has a very poor win-loss record, management has assured itself of a certain amount of income.

RATIONING The Mesa Grill in New York City requires dinner reservations. Moreover, you have to call before 2:00 P.M. on the day of your reservation to confirm; otherwise, it will be canceled. The manager of the Mesa Grill has only a fixed number of seats in his restaurant, and he wants to be as certain as possible that every one is filled. His reservation system essentially rations those seats.

When uncertainty is created by way of excess demand, management may consider **rationing** products or services, that is, allocating output according to some priority system. In addition to restaurants, examples of rationing can be found in many organizations. Hospitals, for instance, often ration beds for nonemergency admissions. And when a disaster strikes—fire, flood, earthquake, plane crash—beds are made available only to the most serious cases. The U.S. Postal Service resorts to rationing, particularly during the peak Christmas rush. First-class mail takes priority, and lesser classes are handled on an "as-available" basis. Have you ever called a mail-order firm or the ticket office for a major airline? If you have, you probably heard something like: "Currently all our agents are busy. But please hold. Your call will be answered in the order in which it was received." This is an illustration of management's rationing the time of their telephone agents.

GEOGRAPHIC DISPERSION Japanese car manufacturers Toyota, Nissan, and Honda have all built plants in the United States. So, too, have German manufacturers BMW and Mercedes. By building plants in the United States, these companies have lessened their dependence on fluctuating currency rates and have reduced potential criticism that they are making profits in the United States but not creating jobs.

Environmental uncertainty sometimes varies with location. There is clearly more political uncertainty for a business firm operating in Iraq or Bosnia than for one operating in Switzerland. To lessen location-induced uncertainty, organizations can move to a different community or operate in multiple locations.

Historically, unions were strongest in the northeastern United States and weakest in the South. Many business firms responded by moving their operations to the South. In so doing, they reduced one uncertainty—union-induced strikes or walkouts—from their environment. One of the major advantages of being a global company is that it spreads risk and uncertainty. Christie's International PLC is a British firm, but it runs auctions in New York, Paris, Geneva, Sydney, and Tokyo, as well as London. By globally dispersing its operations, Christie's is less vulnerable to economic recessions in any one country.

▶ External Strategies

Now we turn to strategies that directly seek to change the environment to make it more favorable for an organization. These include everything from the use of advertising to shape consumer tastes to illegal agreements with a rival to restrict competition.

ADVERTISING Wrigley, the chewing gum maker, advertised its products in the United States throughout World War II. What's interesting about this fact is that the company didn't sell chewing gum in the United States during those years! All its output was being bought by the military for use by service personnel overseas. But Wrigley's management wanted to be sure that civilian demand for its products would still be there when the war was over. So it continued its advertising campaigns.

Nestlé, the giant Swiss consumer products firm, spends hundreds of millions of dollars each year to promote Kit Kat candy bars, Friskies pet food, Carnation ice cream, Buitoni pasta, and dozens of other Nestlé products. Through extensive advertising, Nestlé's management seeks to reduce competitive pressures, stabilize demand, and allow it the opportunity to set prices with less concern for the response of its competitors.

The organization that can build brand loyalty reduces uncertainty. Advertising, then, is a device that management uses to lessen its dependence on fickle consumers and new alternatives offered by the competition.

Maybe the classic example of advertising's creating a following and sustaining demand for a product over time is Bayer aspirin. The content of aspirin is the same regardless of brand name. Yet Bayer AG, the aspirin's maker, has convinced a significant segment of the aspirin-buying public that Bayer's "pure aspirin" is superior to its rivals' aspirin and justifies a price from two to five times higher than that of generic brands.

CONTRACTING A major soap manufacturer—whose products are household names—contracts to sell 10,000 cases a month of its standard detergent to discount operator Price/Costco, that will be sold under Price/Costco's private label. This strategy assures the soap manufacturer of a certain amount of sales and reduces its dependency on the fluctuating preferences of consumers. Similarly, Boeing signs long-term agreements with Continental, Delta, and American Airlines to be their exclusive supplier of aircraft. The effect of this agreement is to reduce the uncertainty imposed by Airbus Industrie (Boeing's key competitor) over future sales.

Contracting protects the organization from changes in quantity or price on either the input or the output side. We see this strategy used when management agrees to a long-term fixed contract to purchase materials and supplies or to sell a certain part of the organization's output. This strategy is also being pursued when organizations sign long-term leases with specific rental rates locked in.

CO-OPTING Look at the makeup of the board of directors of any major corporation. External members are likely to be prominent names from finance, politics, the media, and industry. The selection of external board members is not a random process. Astute management chooses individuals who can reduce uncertainty for their organization.[31]

> Advertising is a device that management uses to lessen its dependence on fickle consumers and new alternatives offered by the competition.

Managers resort to **co-opting** uncertainties when they absorb those individuals or organizations in the environment that threaten their organization's stability. If an organization's primary need is capital, expect to find a high percentage of directors from banks, insurance companies, mutual funds, and other financial institutions. Regulated industries such as public utilities are overseen by government agencies, and these industries respond by disproportionately loading their boards with lawyers. Following this theme, you can expect organizations facing labor uncertainties to appoint union officers to their boards; those vulnerable to public sentiment to appoint board members who are consumer advocates, prominent women, or minority spokespersons; those whose legitimacy is in question to include on the board winners of the Nobel Prize, prominent military heroes, or similarly accomplished individuals.

COALESCING Du Pont and Phillips joined forces to develop, produce, and sell optical-storage disks. Caterpillar and Mitsubishi teamed up to manufacture giant earthmovers. Lufthansa is working with Deutsche Telekom on a multimedia program to speed aircraft repairs. Suzuki is manufacturing GEOs, and General Motors is distributing them under the Chevrolet nameplate. These are examples of **coalescing**—combining with one or more other organizations for the purpose of joint action. It includes mergers, joint ventures, and cooperative (though illegal) agreements to fix prices or split markets.

Mergers and joint ventures are legal means for organizations to manage their environment. They frequently reduce environmental uncertainty by lessening interorganizational competition and dependency. For instance, Chevron's acquisition of Gulf Oil created one less player in the big-oil game. In contrast, while illegal cooperative activities for managing the environment are certainly not condoned here, we do need to acknowledge their existence. For example, many states make it illegal for real estate agents to conspire to set a fixed sales commission rate. Yet within these states, agents' commissions almost never deviate from the 6 or 7 percent "norm." Selling real estate requires cooperation among many agents. Most use multiple-listing services, which create the opportunity for implicit cooperative agreements to develop. Moreover, any agent who undercuts the norm will find other agents uncooperative. The result is that the real estate sales industry essentially operates with fixed prices.

Marie-Josee Lapointe is spokesperson for the Canadian Tobacco Manufacturers' Council. She speaks for this lobbying group which represents the interests of the $3 billion-a-year Canadian tobacco industry.

LOBBYING Since the early 1990s, Microsoft's competitors have been ganging up to attack what they believe are unfair practices by the software giant. Apple Computer, Novell, Lotus Development, Oracle, Sun Microsystems, Sybase, Borland International, and America Online have lobbied the U.S. Federal Trade Commission and the Department of Justice to restrain Microsoft's allegedly monopolistic practices.[32] Microsoft's position is that it has done nothing wrong and that these competitors are merely looking for government to do what these firms have been unable to do in the free market. To the degree that Microsoft's competitors succeed in influencing government in restraining Microsoft and reducing its control of the software industry, these competitors will have effectively reduced environmental uncertainty.

Lobbying—using influence to achieve favorable outcomes—is a widespread practice used by organizations to manage their environment. For instance, many companies and industry groups have formed political action committees (PACs). These PACs are a major source of funds for political candidates. And organizations that seek particular advantages can direct money through PACs to those candidates who will support their interests. In addition, trade and professional associations actively lobby on behalf of their members. The Tobacco Institute and the National Rifle Association fight hard in Washington and in state capitals to reduce uncertainties that might affect tobacco and gun interests, respectively. Similarly, in Canada, the Canadian Tobacco Manufacturers' Council and the Fur

EXHIBIT 4-5

Matching Sources of Uncertainty with Strategic Actions

Source	Examples of Strategic Actions
Government	Lobby for favorable treatment
	Recruit former government officials
	Relocate to a different governmental jurisdiction
Competitors	Advertise to build brand loyalty
	Select a less competitive domain
	Merge with competition to gain larger market share
Unions	Negotiate a long-term collective-bargaining agreement
	Build facilities in countries with a large, low-cost labor supply
	Appoint prestigious union officials to board of directors
Suppliers	Use multiple suppliers
	Inventory critical supplies
	Negotiate long-term contracts
Financial institutions	Appoint financial executives to board
	Establish a line of credit to draw upon when needed
	Use multiple financial sources
Customers	Advertise
	Use a differentiated price structure
	Change domain to where there are more customers
Special interest groups	Appoint critics to board
	Engage in visible activities that are socially conscious
	Use trade association to counter criticism

Source: Adapted from S. P. Robbins, *Organization Theory: Structure, Design, and Applications,* 3rd ed., 1990, p. 377. Reprinted by permission of Prentice Hall, Upper Saddle River, NJ.

Institute are powerful lobbies that promote the interests of tobacco and fur trade. Some organizations also use the power of the government to stabilize relationships in an industry. Doctors, chiropractors, and other professionals lobby state licensing boards to restrict entry, regulate competition, and keep their professions more stable.

Selecting Strategic Actions

Success in managing the environment requires managers to analyze the source of uncertainty and then select a strategy that the organization can effectively implement. Exhibit 4-5 presents some responses managers can make to reduce environmental uncertainty. The strategic actions listed are only examples. They do not purport to be all or the only options available to management.

We close this chapter by addressing five current issues that deal with the organization-environment interface. First, we consider how managers need to adjust their actions when dealing with people from different national cultures. Second, we discuss the problem of culture shock when people move from one culture to another. Third, we look at how organizations can become more socially conscious and responsive. Fourth, we describe what some

CONTEMPORARY ORGANIZATION-ENVIRONMENT ISSUES

managements are doing to more effectively "satisfy the customer." And finally, we discuss the rise of global quality standards and their implications for management practice.

▶ Adjusting Management Practices to Different National Cultures

When Corning and giant Mexican glass manufacturer Vitro created a joint venture in the early 1990s, it seemed a blessed union.[33] But within three years, the honeymoon was over. Corning gave back Vitro's $130 million investment and called off the joint venture. The reason for failure illustrates the challenges of merging different national cultures. Business in Mexico is done on a consensus basis, is sensitive to the concerns of others, and often is slow by U.S. standards. Corporate style is also more formal in Mexico than in the United States.

Employees at Corning and Vitro took a different approach to work, reflected in everything from scheduling to decision making to etiquette. Corning managers were sometimes left waiting for important decisions about marketing and sales because in the Mexican culture only top managers make them, and at Vitro those people were busy with other matters. The Mexicans frequently thought Corning moved too fast; the Americans felt Vitro was too slow. The Mexicans sometimes saw the Americans as too direct, while Vitro managers, in their dogged pursuit of politeness, often seemed to the Americans as unwilling to acknowledge problems and faults. Executives at the two firms even responded to the failure of their venture differently. Corning people openly discussed what went wrong and tried to learn from the experience. Their counterparts at Vitro were reluctant to criticize anyone and wanted to focus on positive aspects of the venture.

The United States and Mexico share a common border, but their cultures are different. Therefore, it's often difficult for them to work together or to manage individuals from the other's culture. But this fact is generalizable to interactions between people from many different nations.[34] So we ponder these two questions: How do cultures differ? And what are the implications of these differences to management practice?

CULTURAL DIFFERENCES   The most comprehensive and accepted framework for analyzing national cultures identifies five dimensions along which they can differ:[35]

1. *Power distance.* The degree to which people in a country accept that power in institutions and organizations is distributed unequally. Ranges from relatively equal (low power distance) to extremely unequal (high power distance).
2. *Individualism versus collectivism.* Individualism is the degree to which people in a country prefer to act as individuals rather than as members of groups. Collectivism is the opposite, or the equivalent of low individualism.
3. *Quantity of life versus quality of life.* Quantity of life is the degree to which values such as assertiveness, the acquisition of money and material goods, and competition prevail. Quality of life is the degree to which people value relationships and show sensitivity and concern for the welfare of others.[36]
4. *Uncertainty avoidance.* The degree to which people in a country prefer structured over unstructured situations. People with high uncertainty avoidance prefer structured situations. In countries that score high on uncertainty avoidance, people have a higher level of anxiety, which manifests itself in greater nervousness, stress, and aggressiveness.
5. *Long-term versus short-term orientation.* People in long-term countries look to the future and value thrift and persistence. A short-term orientation values the past and present and emphasizes respect for tradition and fulfilling social obligations.

EXHIBIT 4-6

Examples of Cultural Dimensions

Country	Power distance	Individualism*	Quantity of life**	Uncertainty avoidance	Long-term orientation***
China	High	Low	Moderate	Moderate	High
France	High	High	Moderate	High	Low
Germany	Low	High	High	Moderate	Moderate
Hong Kong	High	Low	High	Low	High
Indonesia	High	Low	Moderate	Low	Low
Japan	Moderate	Moderate	High	Moderate	Moderate
Netherlands	Low	High	Low	Moderate	Moderate
Russia	High	Moderate	Low	High	Low
United States	Low	High	High	Low	Low
West Africa	High	Low	Moderate	Moderate	Low

Note: *A low score is synonymous with collectivism. **A low score is synonymous with high quality of life. ***A low score is synonymous with a short-term orientation.
Source: Adapted from G. Hofstede, "Cultural Constraints in Management Theories," *The Executive,* February 1993, p. 91.

Exhibit 4-6 provides a summary of how ten countries rate on these five dimensions. For instance, not surprisingly, most Asian countries are more collectivist than individualistic. On the other hand, the United States ranked highest among all countries surveyed on individualism.

IMPLICATIONS FOR MANAGEMENT PRACTICE A country's score on the five cultural dimensions can go a long way toward helping you understand what management practices are considered normal and desirable in a specific country. For instance, a high power-distance society accepts wide differences in power in organizations. Employees show a great deal of respect for those in authority. Titles, rank, and status carry a lot of weight. When negotiating in high power-distance countries, companies find that it helps to send representatives with titles at least as high as the title of those with whom they are bargaining. In contrast, low power-distance societies play down inequalities as much as possible. Superiors will still have authority, but employees are not fearful or in awe of the boss.

Performance evaluation and reward systems look different in countries that score high on individualism than in high-collectivism countries. As might be expected, managers in high-individualism countries emphasize and reward individual contribution. Managers in high-collectivist societies tend to stress being part of the work group and to evaluate and reward groups of employees rather than any specific individual.

Countries that score high on quantity of life almost all have strong capitalistic economic systems. They value materialism and achievement. Managers in these countries encourage competition among individuals and teams. Organizations in these countries also tend to place high importance on status differences between managerial levels, pay differentials, performance bonuses, and other visible material symbols.

Employees in high uncertainty avoidance countries are threatened by uncertainty and ambiguity. So organizations in these countries tend to create mechanisms to provide security and reduce risk. Their organizations are likely to have formal rules and there will be little tolerance for deviant ideas and behaviors. In organizations in countries with high

Doing Business in Vietnam

Vietnam is likely to become a major growth market in the coming years and a place where foreign investors will find abundant opportunities. This country of 73 million people is populated with workers/consumers who are young and well-educated. Eighty percent of the population is under the age of 40; and the literacy rate is nearly 90 percent. Add in the fact that it has low labor costs—the average annual per capita income is only about $250—and it's easy to see why foreign businesses and investors are going to be attracted to Vietnam.

However, North Americans and Europeans need to understand that Vietnam's culture is very different from what they are used to. And adjusting for these differences is critical to successful business relations. Consider attitudes toward time, personal relationships, individual and group dynamics, and age. In most of these areas, Vietnamese attitudes are very different from those of North Americans and Europeans. The following highlights those differences as they apply to individuals raised in the United States.

Concepts of time. The Vietnamese have a more extended concept of time than that of most Americans. Americans measure time by the clock and think in terms of days or weeks. The Vietnamese focus on seasons. As a result, you should expect the Vietnamese to take a longer view of time and to be suspicious of the need for urgency in making decisions or culminating a business deal. Patience is the ultimate virtue in the Vietnamese personal life as well as in business.

Personal relationships. In Vietnam, developing trust plays a major role in personal relationships. And, like most Asian cultures, the Vietnamese focus on building relationships before they are ready to do business. During initial meetings with Vietnamese officials, you can expect little real business to be accomplished. The Vietnamese will concentrate on getting to know you. Americans need to be sensitive to the serious nature of what may seem to them to be casual business relations. Failure to do so can easily lead to a loss of trust or credibility.

Individual and group dynamics. The Vietnamese consider themselves part of a larger collective, generally centered on the family or clan. Individual needs are considered subordinate to those of their family or organization. In contrast, Americans are highly individualistic. These differences are especially relevant when offering praise or criticism, and in dealing with conflicts.

In Vietnam, praise or singling out an individual for attention or reward in public is embarrassing to the individual concerned and will likely be counterproductive. Public rewards are best given to groups, not individuals. Since Vietnamese culture considers "face" extremely important, any overt public criticism or disparaging remarks can cause extreme embarrassment. Criticism of a Vietnamese is best handled privately and, if possible, indirectly.

The Vietnamese don't like direct confrontation and try to avoid conflict. Because a direct refusal or negative answer is considered impolite, the Vietnamese will often agree to something even if they have no intention of carrying it out. They aren't devious; rather, they are just trying to maintain a harmonious relationship. This Vietnamese attribute offers great potential for cross-cultural misunderstandings in negotiations with Americans, for whom disagreement and negative responses are just part of the negotiating process and have nothing to do with interpersonal relationships.

Age. The Vietnamese believe that respect for the elderly is a cardinal virtue. Age carries experience and wisdom. This attitude extends into the business arena. The oldest member of a foreign delegation is often treated with great deference, regardless of his official position or rank. Americans should defer to older members of Vietnamese groups by being especially respectful and solicitous. Conversely, Americans should not be surprised that Vietnamese don't take young people seriously, especially when it comes to having business expertise or making important decisions.

Source: Based on E. D. Smith Jr. and C. Pham, "Doing Business in Vietnam: A Cultural Guide," *Business Horizons*, May–June 1996, pp. 47–51.

uncertainty avoidance, employees demonstrate relatively low job mobility, and lifetime employment is a widely practiced policy.

Managers in long-term orientation countries are likely to focus on the future. They feel comfortable with implementing change, pursuing new markets, and introducing new policies and practices. In short-term cultures, the emphasis is on preserving traditional ways of doing things and respecting historical precedents. Managers are expected to support and maintain those traditions.

In summary, there is substantial evidence that national cultures differ in terms of the fundamental values held by the majority. These values, in turn, shape employee expectations and managerial practices. Effective managers, therefore, realize the need to modify their behavior when dealing with people from different cultures or when managing in a country significantly different in values from the one in which they grew up.

▶ Culture Shock

An American manager accepted a transfer to France. Unfamiliar with French culture, she is surprised to find that the French evaluate others by who you know, where you were educated, and your style of elocution. She was used to the American perspective of evaluating individuals on how good they were and what they had accomplished.[37] Similarly, Japanese executives running a new Mazda plant in Michigan were totally perplexed when the first fall season came around, production slowed to a crawl, and half the plant's line workers and supervisors requested time off to go deer hunting.[38] Taking time off work for personal pursuits is unheard of in Japan.

Any move from one country to another will create a certain amount of confusion, disorientation, and emotional upheaval. We call this **culture shock**. The transfer of an executive from the United States to Canada, for example, would require as little adjustment as one could possibly make. Why? Because the United States and Canada have relatively similar profiles in terms of cultural dimensions. Even so, there would be some culture shock. The executive would still have to adjust to differences that would include the form of representative government (Canadians have a parliamentary system, much like the one in Great Britain); language (Canada is a bilingual—English- and French-speaking—country); and even holidays (the Canadian Thanksgiving is in early October). However, culture shock will obviously be more severe when individuals move to cultures that are most unlike their old environment.

The adjustment to a foreign country has been found to follow a U-shaped curve that contains four distinct stages.[39] This is shown in Exhibit 4-7.

Stage I is one of novelty. The newcomer is excited and optimistic. His or her mood is high. For the temporary visitor to a foreign country, this stage is all that is experienced. A person who spends a week or two on vacation in a strange land considers cultural differences to be interesting, even educational. However, the employee who makes a permanent, or relatively permanent, move experiences euphoria and then disillusionment. In Stage II, the "quaint" quickly becomes obsolete, and the "traditional," inefficient. The opportunity to learn a new language turns into the reality of struggling to communicate. After a few months, the newcomer hits bottom. At Stage III, any and all of the culture's differences have become blatantly clear. The newcomer's basic interpretation system, which worked fine at home, now no longer functions. He or she is bombarded by millions of sights, sounds, and other cues that are uninterpretable. Frustration and confusion are highest and mood lowest in Stage III. Finally, the newcomer begins to adapt, and the negative re-

EXHIBIT 4-7

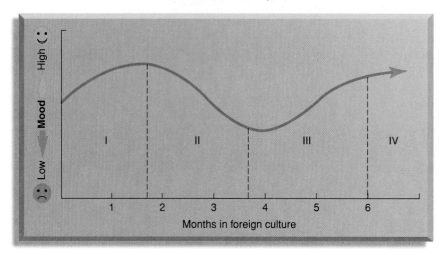

sponses related to culture shock dissipate. In Stage IV, the newcomer has learned what is important and what can be ignored about the new culture.

What are the implications of this model? There are at least two. First, if you're a newcomer in a foreign land or you are managing a newcomer, expect culture shock. It's not abnormal. To some degree, everyone goes through it. Second, culture shock follows a relatively predictable pattern. Expect early euphoria, followed by depression and frustration. However, after about four to six months, most people adjust to their new culture. What was previously different and strange becomes understandable.

▶ Social Responsiveness

An increasing number of business firms are finding that doing good and doing well are not mutually exclusive goals. Take a look at the following examples:[40]

▶ Harley-Davidson gives its employees an interest-free loan of $2,500 if they agree to buy a house in the inner-city neighborhood around the company's Milwaukee headquarters. And the loan will be forgiven entirely if the employee stays in the house for three years.

▶ If you telephone the Kentucky Fried Chicken restaurant on Kuala Lumpur's Jalan Ipoh, you'll get a recorded message. That's because all twenty workers are deaf. Hiring the hearing-impaired is part of the company's policy to help people in the area who normally have difficulty finding work.

▶ On a six-month test basis, UPS agreed to hire dozens of welfare recipients to fill part-time jobs at its Philadelphia distribution center. The company ended up retaining 88 percent of the welfare employees, compared with its 60 percent average in Philadelphia.

▶ Workers at the clothing company Esprit of Australia are given time off work to engage in philanthropic activities in the community. The average employee gets involved in about three projects a year.

▶   Patagonia, a maker of outerwear, has converted all of its production to organic cotton. As a result, the company estimates that it has kept 10,000 pounds of pesticides out of the farm fields.

▶   Hanna Andersson, a children's clothing mail-order company in Portland, Oregon, asks customers to recycle its products. Any used piece of the company's clothing that isn't torn or stained can be sent back, and 20 percent of the returned item's original price will be applied to the customer's next purchase. The company washed and donated 107,000 garments to needy children over a 9-year period.

CLASSICAL VERSUS SOCIOECONOMIC VIEW Not every manager or organization accepts that business has a responsibility to the larger society in which it operates. You can put the issue of social responsibility into perspective once you understand the underlying debate. Two polar positions capture the essence of that debate. On one side, there's the classical—or purely economic—view that management's only social responsibility is to maximize profits. On the other side stands the socioeconomic position, which holds that management's responsibility goes well beyond making profits to include protecting and improving society's welfare.

The most outspoken advocate of the **classical view of social responsibility** is economist and Nobel laureate Milton Friedman.[41] He argues that most managers today are professional managers, which means they don't own the businesses they run. They are employees, responsible to the stockholders. Their primary charge is therefore to conduct the business in the interests of the stockholders. And what are those interests? Friedman says that the stockholders have a single concern: financial return.

According to Friedman, when managers take it upon themselves to spend their organization's resources for the "social good," they undermine the market mechanism. Someone has to pay for this redistribution of assets. If socially responsible actions reduce profits and dividends, stockholders are the losers. If wages and benefits have to be reduced to pay for social action, employees lose. If prices are raised to pay for social actions, consumers lose. If higher prices are rejected by the market and sales drop, the business might not survive—in which case, all the organization's stakeholders lose.

The **socioeconomic view of social responsibility** counters that times have changed and with them so have society's expectations of business. This view is best illustrated in the legal formation of corporations. Corporations are chartered by governments. The same government that creates a charter can take it away. So corporations are not independent entities, responsible only to stockholders. They also have a responsibility to the larger society that creates and sustains them.

According to proponents of the socioeconomic perspective, a major flaw in the classicists' view is their time frame. Supporters of the socioeconomic view contend that managers should be concerned with maximizing financial returns over the *long run*. To do that, they must accept some social obligations and the costs that go with them. They must protect society's welfare by *not* polluting, *not* discriminating, *not* engaging in deceptive advertising, and the like. They must also play an affirmative role in improving society by involving themselves in their communities and contributing to charitable organizations.

Proponents of the socioeconomic position also point out that the classical view flies in the face of reality. Modern business firms are no longer merely economic institutions. They lobby, form political action committees, and engage in other activities to influence the political process for their benefit. Society accepts and even encourages business to become involved in its social, political, and legal environment. That might not have been true 30 or 40 years ago, but it is the reality of today.

FROM OBLIGATIONS TO RESPONSIVENESS In order to provide more clarity to this debate, we will differentiate three related concepts: social obligation, social responsibility, and social responsiveness.[42] This discussion should help you see how different organizations actually handle the question: How socially active should we be?

As Exhibit 4-8 depicts, social obligation is the foundation of business's social involvement. A business has fulfilled its **social obligation** when it meets its economic and legal responsibilities and no more. It does the minimum that the law requires. A firm pursues social goals only to the extent that they contribute to its economic goals. In contrast to social obligation, both social responsibility and social responsiveness go beyond merely meeting basic economic and legal standards.

Social responsiveness refers to the capacity of a firm to adapt to changing societal conditions. As such, it's guided by social norms. Organizations that are socially responsive scan the environment to identify changing mores and attitudes. Then management modifies its practices to align with the prevailing standard.

Social responsibility adds an ethical imperative to do those things that make society better and *not* to do those that could make it worse. It's a business firm's efforts, beyond those required by the law and economics, to pursue long-term goals that are good for society. Note that social responsibility views business as a moral agent. In its effort to do *good* for society, it must differentiate between right and wrong.

A U.S. company that meets pollution control standards established by the federal government or doesn't discriminate against employees over the age of 40 in promotion decisions is meeting its social obligation and nothing more. The law says that the company may not pollute or practice age discrimination. Consider, on the other hand, Du Pont, which now provides on-site child-care facilities for employees; Procter & Gamble, which declares that Tide "is packaged in 100 percent recycled paper"; and the world's largest tuna canner, whose head says, "StarKist will not purchase, process, or sell any tuna caught in association with dolphins." These firms are being socially responsive. Why? Pressure from working mothers and environmentalists make their practices pragmatic. If these same companies had provided child care, offered recycled packaging, or sought to protect dolphins back in the early 1970s, they would have been accurately characterized as socially responsible.

Advocates of social responsiveness believe that the concept replaces philosophical discourse with pragmatism. They see it as a more tangible and achievable objective than social responsibility. Rather than assessing what is good for society in the long-term, a socially responsive management scans the environment, identifies the prevailing social norms, and then changes its social involvement to respond to changing societal conditions.

EXHIBIT 4-8

Levels of Social Involvement

Social responsibility | Social responsiveness

Social obligation

Satisfying the Customer

Why is it that Federal Express can "absolutely, positively" deliver a package overnight, but Delta, American, and United Airlines have trouble keeping your bags on your plane? Why is it that Lands' End remembers your last order and your family members' sizes, but after 10 years of membership, you are still being solicited by American Express to join? Why is it you can get patient help from a Home Depot clerk when selecting a $2.70 package of screws, but you can't get any advice when purchasing a $2,700 personal computer from IBM's direct ordering service?[43] The answer to these questions is that Federal Express, Lands' End, and Home Depot are committed to satisfying the customer.

It's a truism that organizations can't exist without customers. It's ironic, then, that during the 1970s and 1980s, a lot of managers seemed to take this critical constituency for granted. Instead of focusing on doing what was necessary to keep customers satisfied, managers became obsessed with financial numbers. Business organizations weren't treated as producers of products and services. Rather, they were seen as bundles of assets that were to be bought, sold, merged, leveraged, or closed down—whichever would increase their value the most. During those decades, organizations were dancing to the tunes played by financial institutions and markets. Since the early 1990s, as we noted in chapter 1, managers have increasingly returned the customer to his or her rightful place as the primary determinant of an organization's success.

A select group of companies have made customer service an obsession. And their solid profit record suggests they have been rewarded for this obsession. This group includes—in addition to Federal Express, Lands' End, and Home Depot—Toyota's Lexus, Singapore Airlines, Southwest Airlines, Banc One, Hertz, Dell Computer, Four Seasons Hotels, and United Parcel Service.

Quality and ISO 9000

In today's global economy, the ISO 9000 family of standards is becoming the world measure for quality management. If a company wants to be able to convey to its customers that its products meet the highest quality standards, they can obtain ISO 9000 certification. And companies throughout the world are doing just that.[44]

What is **ISO 9000**? It's a certificate attesting that an organization's factory, laboratory, or office has met quality management requirements determined by the International Organization for Standardization in Geneva. It's a way of demonstrating process quality and consistency. Certification doesn't focus on end products. A company, for instance, can meet ISO 9000 standards and still make shoddy products (although it's not likely). Meeting the standards means that an organization is following rigid procedures for inspecting production processes, updating engineering drawings, maintaining machinery, calibrating equipment, training workers, and dealing with customer complaints. ISO 9000 standards are becoming to quality what generally accepted accounting principles have become to financial data. They are becoming an internationally recognized system for documenting quality procedures.

Getting a certificate is not an easy process. For most firms it takes between 18 months and 2 years. But when they get it, their quality standards have instant global credibility. And for some firms, meeting ISO 9000 standards is becoming an absolute necessity to do business. For instance, British Telecom, Du Pont, Eastman Kodak, General Electric, Hewlett-Packard, Motorola, and Philips Electronics are among the big-name companies that insist that their suppliers adopt ISO 9000.

IPL Inc., a 500-worker plastics fabricator in Quebec, Canada, spent 2 years and about $350,000 for its certificate. But its efforts translated into new contracts with General Motors, Bell Canada, and Frigidaire Canada. Those companies knew that IPL could be depended upon to manufacture quality products. "Once you're certified," says IPL's quality manager, "customers know you can contract to perform at a high level of quality." Tadao Okabe, president of Canon Virginia, Inc., offered a similar analysis. Since his company achieved ISO certification, it's no longer necessary for a customer such as Hewlett-Packard "to come to this plant to check all the details of our quality-control systems, again and again."

The number of companies meeting ISO 9000 standards is expanding rapidly as certification is increasingly being regarded as the price of entry into international markets. In 1998, there were more than 120,000 ISO 9000–registered sites worldwide. In the United States, there were fewer than 1,000 registered sites in 1992. By 1998, that number was up to 17,000.

There is a variety of additional material available on the CD-ROM and companion Web site that acompany this text. You can access this information through the CD-ROM or by visiting the Web site at **<www.prenhall.com/robbins>**.

SUMMARY

(This summary is organized by the chapter-opening learning objectives on page 102.)

1. The environment is composed of those institutions or forces that are outside the organization and potentially can affect the organization's performance, including customers, competitors, suppliers, government, media, and special interest groups.

2. Environmental scanning is important if managers are to be aware of changing tastes of customers, future actions of competitors, and similar changes taking place in their environment. Four environmental-scanning techniques are competitive intelligence, scenario development, forecasting, and benchmarking.

3. The typical benchmarking process is made up of four steps: (1) forming a planning team; (2) collecting internal and external data; (3) analyzing data to identify performance gaps and the cause of differences; and (4) preparing and implementing an action plan.

4. Managers can reduce environmental uncertainty by adapting to the environment through internal strategies such as changing domains, recruitment, buffering, smoothing, rationing, or geographical dispersion. They also can attempt to alter the environment through external strategies such as advertising, contracting, co-opting, coalescing, or lobbying.

5. The five dimensions for analyzing national culture are (1) power distance, which is a measure of power distribution; (2) preference for individual versus collective activities; (3) quantity versus quality of life, which contrasts values of materialism against concern for others; (4) uncertainty avoidance, which measures preference for structure; and (5) long-term versus short-term orientation.

6. The classical view of social responsibility argues that management's only responsibility is to maximize profits. The socioeconomic view says that management's responsibility goes well beyond making profits to include protecting and improving society's welfare.

7. Social responsibility portrays business as a moral agent, deciding what is right and wrong for society. Social responsiveness is pragmatic—managers scan the environment, identify changing mores and attitudes, and modify organizational practices to align with the prevailing standards.

8. ISO 9000 is a certificate attesting that an organization's processes have met universal quality standards. By achieving these standards, management makes it easier for its firm to compete globally because other firms interpret the standards as reducing their environmental uncertainty as related to quality.

REVIEW QUESTIONS

1. Define and describe the three dimensions of environmental uncertainty.
2. Who are external stakeholders?
3. What are forecasts, and how accurate are they?
4. Is environmental scanning unethical? Explain.
5. Contrast internal and external strategies for managing the environment.
6. How might managing in China be different from managing in the United States?
7. Describe the typical responses a person can be expected to exhibit when he or she is transferred to a job in a country with a very different culture than he or she is used to.
8. "The business of business is business." What does this statement mean to you? What are its implications for socially conscious management?
9. Are most business firms socially responsible? Explain.
10. Why might a small firm producing electronic components seek ISO 9000 certification?

IF I WERE THE MANAGER . . .

Put Yourself in Andy's Shoes

Andy Jehl joined Ford Motor Co. in 1989, after a short stint as a management consultant. His original assignment at Ford was as a productivity analyst at company headquarters in Detroit. From there he was transferred to a Mazda plant outside Toledo, Ohio (Ford owns a major portion of Mazda and frequently interchanges personnel). At Mazda, Andy began as a production supervisor. Two promotions later, Andy was assistant plant superintendent.

In the fall of 1998, Andy was informed of his next assignment, effective January 1, 1999. He was to become plant manager at the large Ford plant in Hermisillo, Mexico. Andy had mixed feelings about this assignment. It was a high-profile and coveted position within the company. But he didn't know much about Mexico and had little idea what it would be like to manage a labor force of people from a different culture. Andy grew up in Connecticut, and his total knowledge of Mexico and its people came from a couple of vacations in Cancun and Cabo San Lucas.

To prepare for his new assignment, Andy went to the local university library to see if he could get a quick education on Mexican culture. He found an informative article that discussed the struggle many U.S. executives have in adjusting to the Mexican workplace.* The following highlights some of the facts presented in the article:

➤ Many U.S. managers have considerable difficulty understanding the motivations and values of Mexican staff members. Many become exasperated when they can't find ways to encourage their Mexican colleagues and employees to work according to what they perceive as "commonly accepted" professional standards.

➤ Mexicans tend to accept the inherent worth of friends and colleagues without demanding specific performance or achievement. Americans, on the other hand, believe that one demonstrates integrity or dignity through action. Americans view performance situations in terms of winners and losers, and the one who wins is obviously the "better person." For the Mexican, the individual is special, whether the winner or not.

➤ Americans believe that all people are created equal. A person shouldn't look for any special favors or exemptions from the rules. No one is above the law. Rules, policies, and procedures are sometimes overlooked by the Mexican worker. Given the belief in the uniqueness of each individual, it stands to reason that people, rather than abstract principles or concepts, should be respected. Americans' insistence on "playing by the rules" is often received with amused, yet polite, disregard by Mexicans. Following the rules is often considered the most ineffective way to get things done.

➤ There is a strong tendency in Mexico to shun open confrontation because of fear of losing face and having to acknowledge disagreements. Negative or disappointing information is either withheld or modified to avoid being offensive or irritating. In contrast, Americans place great emphasis on stating the facts, regardless of the impact.

➤ Within Mexican society, there is a tendency to respect those in power. Title and position are usually sufficient to enforce authority. Americans believe respect is earned, not given.

➤ When a U.S. executive agrees to do something, it is a matter of personal honor and professional integrity to fulfill that commitment. For many Mexicans, a commitment is more of an intention to do something than a firm decision. A commitment is a statement of a desirable outcome, not a promise to fulfill an agreed-upon arrangement.

► Mexicans and Americans have a different perception of time. For Mexicans, there is a loose notion of what being "on time" means, interruptions are handled without undue stress, and there is little expectation that plans will proceed in a logical order. In the U.S. culture, appointments and deadlines are scheduled tightly and respected as much as possible; interruptions are annoying and inefficient; and "on time" literally means "on time."

As Andy read the article, he pondered some of the challenges that awaited him in Hermisillo. If you were Andy, what changes, if any, would you make to your management style and practices to improve your chances that you'll be effective in this new assignment?

Source: *M. I. Erlich, "Making Sense of the Bicultural Workplace," Business Mexico, August 1993, pp. 16–18.*

SKILL EXERCISE

Environmental Scanning

Tina Irwin owns Friendship Cards, a small firm that designs greeting cards and sells them directly to retailers. Last year, her company had sales of a little over $300,000. She employs three full-time people and another five on a part-time basis. Because Friendship is small, Tina makes almost all key managerial decisions.

Tina has an idea for a new line of cards that combine humor and environmental issues. She knows that none of her competitors—which include Hallmark, American Greetings, and dozens of small producers like herself—have yet intro-

duced a line exactly like what she has in mind. But she doesn't know what her competitors have planned for the coming card season. Tina is very sensitive to her competitors' actions because most are much larger than she is and command considerably more clout with retailers. Her existence depends on filling niches that competitors pass over.

If you were Tina, what sources would you utilize to find out what your competitors have planned for the coming season? Would your sources be different if you wanted to assess your competitors' plans for a year or more ahead? Be specific in your answer, and identify what information you would expect to get from each source.

TEAM ACTIVITY

Internet Intelligence

Form into teams of four or five students each. You are to research and prepare a report *using only the Internet* that summarizes sources you used to find:

1. Listings of job opportunities for high school teachers in Melbourne, Australia.
2. The number of firms in the United Kingdom that have successfully achieved ISO 9000 certification.

3. The most recent annual compensation for the CEOs at (a) DaimlerChrysler, (b) Disney, (c) Grand Metropolitan, (d) Seagrams, and (e) Sony.
4. The most recent inflation rates for Brazil, Israel, Japan, and the Philippines.
5. The names of colleges and universities in Hong Kong that have graduate programs in business administration or management.

CASE EXERCISE

Philip Morris and the Tobacco Industry Environment

Over the past 30 years, tobacco companies have used a number of strategies in an effort to reduce the uncertainty created by lawsuits and government regulations.

Since the late 1960s, several tobacco firms expanded their domain through diversification. R. J. Reynolds Industries pur-

chased Nabisco Brands and became RJR Nabisco. Philip Morris bought General Foods and Kraft. These merged companies are now more food companies than cigarette manufacturers. Meanwhile, the Liggett Group changed domains by selling off its tobacco division to a British firm.

Tobacco firms also spent heavily on lobbying. They fought hard to defeat any legislation that sought to limit smoking in public areas and at the workplace. Additionally, individual to-bacco firms and the Tobacco Institute (which is supported by tobacco companies) contributed funds for research on the rela-tionship between smoking and cancer. The companies realized that it was statistically unlikely that the research would "prove" that smoking causes cancer, thus giving the tobacco firms more data to cloud the controversy. Further, if such research were unfavorable to tobacco interests, the researchers had no strong motivations to publicize their findings widely. Why kill the goose that lays the golden eggs?

Finally, tobacco firms aggressively used advertising and pro-motional events to protect their interests. Since the early 1990s, tobacco ads were specifically directed at countering the strong antismoking forces. Emphasis in these ads was on framing the decision to smoke as a "right" and laws to restrict smoking as an attack on individual freedom.

These efforts worked for decades. But the public has grown increasingly suspicious of the tobacco industry, and pressures to penalize tobacco firms for their past actions have escalated. In July 1997, the tobacco industry reached a $368 billion agree-ment with forty state general attorneys. The money, to be paid over 25 years, was to pay compensatory damages to settle law-suits, and to help finance an antitobacco advertising program and a campaign to reduce smoking by youths. The agreement also barred tobacco advertising on billboards and sporting events. In return, the tobacco firms were promised immunity from future class-action suits and limits on individual compen-sation claims.

The 1997 agreement would have cost Philip Morris $50 bil-lion. That's about half what the company is worth. Yet com-pany management supported the agreement. Congress, how-ever, didn't like the agreement. They wanted stronger controls on tobacco companies. Their proposal raised the ante for to-bacco firms. Congress demanded $500 billion in payments, forcing the price of cigarettes up at least $1.10 a pack. It also ex-acts stiff penalties from tobacco firms if teen smoking doesn't decline sharply, strips away the companies' protection against lawsuits, and places regulation of tobacco under the Food and Drug Administration.

Needless to say, the public response from tobacco companies was highly vocal to this new proposal. Tobacco representatives say the huge increase in cigarette prices could bankrupt some firms. The industry also said it could not accept any legislation that didn't grant companies immunity from health-related lawsuits.

QUESTIONS

1. Contrast Philip Morris's environment in 1999 with that en-vironment in 1969.

2. Explain why Philip Morris's management might actually de-sire to negotiate an agreement with the government that would cost the company billions of dollars.

3. If you were on the Philip Morris management team, what suggestions would you make that could help the company manage its environment over the next ten to twenty years?

Source: T. Noah, "A Hit or a Miss for Mr. Butts?" *U.S. News & World Report*, June 30, 1997, pp. 22–24; R. Lowenstein, "Even with Settlement, Big To-bacco Can't Lose," *Wall Street Journal*, July 3, 1997, p. C1; and D. Gergen, "Getting Real on Tobacco," *U.S. News & World Report*, April 13, 1998, p. 84.

VIDEO CASE EXERCISE

When You Care Enough to Send the Very Best

Although "caring enough to send the very best" may be the marketing slogan for the world's largest man-ufacturer of greeting cards, caring and compassion also are fitting descriptions of Judi Jacobsen's Madison Park Greeting Card Company of Seattle, Washington. The slogan, however, would have to be changed to "caring enough to *do* the very best." Jacobsen's compassion is directed at the com-munity where her business is located and at the people she employs.

At the age of 30, Jacobsen decided to pursue her desire to paint. People who saw and bought her paintings told her that they would make good greeting cards. Taking that advice to heart, together with a partner, Jacobsen started Madison Park Greeting Card Company. Today she sells her greeting cards in more than 4,000 specialty shops around the United States. Madison Park employs 25 people and has reached the $3 million sales mark. The admirable part of this story is not just the fact that Jacobsen was able to pursue her dream but also that she had a strong commitment to helping others. Her community involvement started with her decision to locate her business in a rundown section of town and to help revitalize the area. In addition, she has a strong and specific concern for her employees.

Jacobsen's management philosophy is that one of the best things you can do for your people is to give them meaningful work. To put this philosophy into practice, she has hired Cam-bodian refugees who couldn't speak English but who could pack cards into boxes. She has hired hearing-impaired employ-ees and displaced mothers for other jobs at Madison Park. Ja-cobsen strongly believes that people count more than the bottom line and that, although she understands that businesses must do well to be able to help others, having a balance between profits and people is important. She says, "If I had to choose people or profits, I'd put people first."

QUESTIONS

1. Would you call Judi Jacobsen socially responsive or socially responsible? Explain your choice.
2. What's your opinion of Judi's statement, "If I had to choose people or profits, I'd put people first"? What would this type of philosophy imply as far as management decisions and actions?
3. If Judi approached you about investing in her firm, would you be interested? Why or why not?
4. What role, if any, does the customer play in Judi's management philosophy?

Source: Based on *Small Business 2000, Show 104.*

NOTES

1. Based on J. Branegan, "They Might Be Giants," *Time*, July 28, 1997, pp. 52–53.
2. See G. G. Dess and D. W. Beard, "Dimensions of Organizational Task Environments," *Administrative Science Quarterly*, March 1984, pp. 52–73; E. A. Gerloff, N. K. Muir, and W. D. Bodensteiner, "Three Components of Perceived Environmental Uncertainty: An Exploratory Analysis of the Effects of Aggregation," *Journal of Management*, December 1991, pp. 749–68; and O. Shenkar, N. Aranya, and T. Almor, "Construct Dimensions in the Contingency Model: An Analysis Comparing Metric and Non-Metric Multivariate Instruments," *Human Relations*, May 1995, pp. 559–80.
3. L. Nakarmi, "Showdown at Hyundai," *Business Week*, July 19, 1993, p. 19.
4. "The ADA Scorecard," *Inc.*, January 1994, p. 11.
5. "Justice Department Acts Aggressively," *Seattle Times*, January 7, 1998, p. A7.
6. Cited in P. Mao, "Why Warren Luhrs Gave Up Ocean Racing," *Forbes*, March 13, 1995, pp. 120–21.
7. "Peso's Plunge Spurs Walkout at Factory in Northern Mexico," *New York Times*, February 1, 1995, p. A11.
8. N. McGrath, "Prospering in a Sea of Change," *Asian Business*, November 1994, pp. 28–30.
9. L. Brooks, "Econo Lube Cited in 68 Bureau Complaints," *Arizona Daily Star*, March 5, 1995, p. B1.
10. M. Robichaux, "'Competitor Intelligence': A Grapevine to Rivals' Secrets," *Wall Street Journal*, April 12, 1989, p. B2.
11. See B. K. Boyd and J. Fulk, "Executive Scanning and Perceived Uncertainty: A Multidimensional Model," *Journal of Management*, vol. 22, no. 1, 1996, pp. 1–21; L. M. Fuld, *The New Competitor Intelligence* (New York: Wiley, 1995); and L. Kahaner, *Competitive Intelligence* (New York: Simon & Schuster, 1996).
12. W. L. Renfro and J. L. Morrison, "Detecting Signals of Change," *The Futurist*, August 1984, p. 49.
13. See, for instance, T. A. Stewart, "The Information Wars: What You Don't Know Will Hurt You," *Fortune*, June 12, 1995, pp. 119–21; S. Crock, "They Snoop to Conquer," *Business Week*, October 28, 1996, pp. 172–76; J. M. Hannon, "Leveraging HRM to Enrich Competitive Intelligence," *Human Resource Management*, Winter 1997, pp. 409–22; H. McBride, "They Snoop to Conquer," *Canadian Business*, July 1997, pp. 45–47; W. Green, "I Spy," *Forbes*, April 20, 1998, pp. 90–100; and G. Imperato, "Competitive Intelligence—Get Smart!" *Fast Company*, April/May 1998, pp. 268–79.
14. Cited in Robichaux, "'Competitor Intelligence'," p. B2.
15. S. McCartney, "'Go to IBM's Booth. Avoid Recognition. Skulk,'" *Wall Street Journal*, November 17, 1994, p. B1.
16. See, for instance, M. Werner, 'Planning for Uncertain Futures: Building Commitment through Scenario Planning," *Business Horizons*, May–June 1990, pp. 55–58; P. J. H. Schoemaker, "Scenario Planning: A Tool for Strategic Thinking," *Sloan Management Review*, Winter 1995, pp. 25–39; and J. R. Garber, "What if . . . ?" *Forbes*, November 2, 1998, pp. 76–80.
17. Based on B. Gates, *The Road Ahead* (New York: Viking, 1995), pp. 83–85; and D. Lyons, "The Buzz About Firefly," *New York Times Magazine*, June 29, 1997, pp. 37–40.
18. W. Echikson, "When You Can't Control History," *Fortune*, December 13, 1993, p. 170.
19. See, for example, A. B. Fisher, "Is Long-Range Planning Worth It?" *Fortune*, April 23, 1990, pp. 281–84; and P. Schwartz, *The Art of the Long View* (New York: Doubleday/Currency, 1991).
20. P. N. Pant and W. H. Starbuck, "Innocents in the Forest: Forecasting and Research Methods," *Journal of Management*, June 1990, pp. 433–60.
21. See S. Greengard, "Discover Best Practices through Benchmarking," *Personnel Journal*, November 1995, pp. 62–73.
22. See M. J. Spendolini, *The Benchmarking Book* (New York: AMACOM, 1992); J. Main, "How to Steal the Best Ideas Around," *Fortune*, October 19, 1992, pp. 102–06; and T. B. Kinni, "Measuring Up," Industry Week, December 5, 1994, pp. 27–28.
23. This section is based on T. Gutner, "Better Your Business: Benchmark It," *Business Week*, April 27, 1998, pp. ENT 4–6.
24. Shetty, "Aiming High," p. 43.
25. "Benchmarkers Make Strange Bedfellows," *Industry Week*, November 15, 1993, p. 8.
26. A. Tanzer, "Studying at the Feet of the Masters," *Forbes*, May 10, 1993, pp. 43–44.
27. This section is partially based on M. Galen, "These Guys Aren't Spooks. They're "Competitive Analysts'," *Business Week*, October 14, 1991, p. 97; and McCartney, "Go to IBM's Booth."
28. W. R. Dill, "Environment as an Influence on Managerial

Autonomy," *Administrative Science Quarterly*, March 1958, pp. 409–43.

29. See, for instance, J. S. Harrison and C. H. St. John, "Managing and Partnering with External Stakeholders," *The Executive*, May 1996, pp. 46–60.

30. S. P. Robbins, *Organization Theory: Structure, Design, and Applications*, 3rd ed. (Upper Saddle River, NJ: Prentice Hall, 1990), pp. 361–77.

31. See, for instance, J. Pfeffer, "Size and Composition of Corporate Boards of Directors: The Organization and Its Environment," *Administrative Science Quarterly*, March 1972, pp. 218–28; and M. S. Mizruchi and L. B. Stearns, "A Longitudinal Study of the Formation of Interlocking Directorates," *Administrative Science Quarterly*, June 1988, pp. 194–210.

32. B. R. Schlender and D. Kirkpatrick, "The Valley vs. Microsoft," *Fortune*, March 20, 1995, pp. 84–90.

33. A. DePalma, "It Takes More Than a Visa to Do Business in Mexico," *New York Times*, June 26, 1994, p. F5.

34. See, for instance, P. R. Harris and R. T. Moran, *Managing Cultural Differences*, 4th ed. (Houston: Gulf, 1996).

35. See G. Hofstede, *Culture's Consequences: International Differences in Work-Related Values* (Beverly Hills, CA: Sage, 1980); G. Hofstede, *Cultures and Organizations: Software of the Mind* (New York: McGraw-Hill, 1991); and G. Hofstede, "Cultural Constraints in Management Theories," *The Executive*, February 1993, pp. 81–94. Hofstede's findings have been recently criticized for failing to reflect major environmental changes that have had an impact on work-related values. See D. R. Fernandez, D. S. Carlson, L. P. Stepina, and J. D. Nicholson, "Hofstede's Country Classification 25 Years Later," *Journal of Social Psychology*, February 1997, pp. 43–54.

36. Hofstede called this dimension masculinity versus femininity; but I have changed it because of the strong sexist connotation in his choice of terms.

37. C. Gouttefarde, "American Values in the French Workplace," *Business Horizons*, March–April 1996, pp. 60–69.

38. D. Stamps, "Welcome to America: Watch Out for Culture Shock," *Training*, November 1996, pp. 22–30.

39. This section is based on the work of J. T. Gullahorn and J. E. Gullahorn, "An Extension of the U-Curve Hypothesis," *Journal of Social Sciences*, January 1963, pp. 34–47.

40. Based on N. McGrath, "Drawing Morals from Morality," *Asian Business*, March 1995, pp. 20–26; J. H. Green and S. Perman, "Doing Well By Doing Good," *Business Week*, May 20, 1996, p. 42; M. R. Moskowitz, "Company Peformance Roundup," *Business and Society Review*, no. 98, 1997, pp. 57–59; and R. Furchgott, "UPS's Package Deal for Workers," *Business Week*, June 1, 1998, p. 104.

41. M. Friedman, *Capitalism and Freedom* (Chicago: University of Chicago Press, 1962); and "The Social Responsibility of Business Is to Increase Its Profits," *New York Times Magazine*, September 13, 1970, p. 33.

42. This discussion is based on S. L. Warwick and P. L. Cochran, "The Evolution of the Corporate Social Performance Model," *Academy of Management Review*, October 1985, pp. 758–69; D. J. Wood, "Corporate Social Performance Revisited," *Academy of Management Review*, October 1991, pp. 703–08; D. L. Swanson, "Addressing a Theoretical Problem by Reorienting the Corporate Social Performance Model," *Academy of Management Review*, January 1995, pp. 43–64; and M. B. E. Clarkson, "A Stakeholder Framework for Analyzing and Evaluating Corporate Social Performance," *Academy of Management Review*, January 1995, pp. 92–117.

43. Cited in M. Treacy and F. Wiersema, *The Discipline of Market Leaders* (Reading, MA: Addison-Wesley, 1995), pp. 3–4.

44. See, for instance, R. Henkoff, "The Hot New Seal of Quality," *Fortune*, June 28, 1993, pp. 116–20; J. Southerst, "The Gold Standard," *Canadian Business*, December 1993, p. 27; A. Zuckerman, *ISO 9000 Made Easy: A Cost-Savings Guide to Documentation and Registration* (New York: AMACOM, 1994); "ISO 9000 Series Vital for Smaller Korean Firms," *Business Korea*, August 1994, pp. 34–35; M. V. Uzumeri, "ISO 9000 and Other Metastandards: Principles for Management Practice," *The Executive*, February 1997, pp. 21–36; and H. R. Meyer, "Small Firms Flock to Quality System," *Nation's Business*, March 1998, pp. 66–68.

PLANNING SYSTEMS

I LOOK TO THE FUTURE BECAUSE I'M GOING TO SPEND
THE REST OF MY LIFE THERE.

C. KETTERING

LEARNING OBJECTIVES

After studying this chapter, you should be able to:

1 Explain the benefits that can accrue from planning.

2 Describe the value of SWOT analysis.

3 Contrast cost-leadership, differentiation, and focus strategies.

4 Identify the elements in successful strategy implementation.

5 Explain what is unique about the concept of project management.

6 Define entrepreneurship.

7 Describe the personality characteristics of an entrepreneur.

8 Explain why an organization's stated objectives might not be its real objectives.

9 Set up an MBO program.

10 Better manage your time.

Jeff Bezo created "the better mousetrap." And, as the proverb predicted, people are beating a path to his door. Now his job is to keep every other mousetrap builder from ripping him off.[1]

In the summer of 1994, at the age of 30, Bezo quit his job as a Wall Street trader and began methodically analyzing opportunities for Internet commerce. He concluded that on-line retailing was the next big thing and that selling books over the Web was the first big retail opportunity. After a year of planning, Bezo launched his Amazon.com Books, or what he called "Earth's Biggest Bookstore." The following briefly traces the history of Amazon.com and Bezo's initial efforts to keep others from stealing his customers.

Bezo decided on the book business for essentially three reasons. First, the number of books in print is huge. There are 1.5 million English-language titles and 3 million in all languages worldwide. No bookstore could physically stock more than a small percentage of this inventory. Second, the biggest phenomenon in retailing had become the "category killer." Stores like Toys "R" Us, Home

Depot, and Tower Records were destroying their smaller competitors by offering consumers huge selections. And third, the book business did not lend itself to traditional catalog sales. A book catalog with a million titles would be the size of seven New York City phone books. These three factors led Bezo to believe that the Internet was ripe for creation of an on-line bookstore.

As a virtual business, Amazon.com could have been located anywhere. Bezo chose Seattle because it met a rigorous set of criteria. It has a lot of technical talent. It's near a major book distributor who warehouses a large number of books. It's a desirable place to live, making it easy to attract employees. Finally, it's in a small state. Because you have to charge sales tax to customers who live in-state, it made no sense to locate in a large population state requiring Amazon to charge those customers an additional tax.

Within two years, Bezo's Amazon.com was a success. He offered readers 1.5 million titles and discounted prices. Its low cost structure and high inventory turnover allowed the company to discount books deeper than physical bookstores were able. And its obsession with innovation (for example, Amazon pioneered reader-produced reviews and topic-related chat rooms) and customer service resulted in a solid base of satisfied customers.

But Amazon's success was not going unnoticed by the big book chains like Barnes & Noble and Borders. In the summer of 1997, for instance, B&N opened its own on-line bookshop. Hiring hot designers from Silicon Valley, B&N offers a Web shopfront that is just as inviting and useful as Amazon's, with easy-to-use subject indexes, on-line author events every day, book forums, and book reviews. Bezo countered by increasing his stock of titles to 2.5 million and slashing prices up to 40 percent to surpass B&N's 30 percent hardcover discount. This, however, may be only a short-term solution. Because B&N sells more than 20 times as many books as Amazon, B&N can extract lower prices from publishers and pass them on to customers. Unfortunately for Bezo, B&N may be only the beginning of aggressive competition. He also has to deal with entrepreneurs who want to emulate Amazon's success. After all, if it was so easy for Bezo to create an Internet bookstore with little capital, shouldn't it be equally easy for others to enter his market niche?

The Amazon example illustrates the role of planning—not only in creating a business and establishing a competitive advantage, but in acting to sustain that advantage against aggressive competitors. In this chapter, we present the essential elements that you need to know about creating plans and formulating an effective organizational strategy.

WHAT IS PLANNING?

What do we mean by the term *planning*? As we stated in our description of management functions in chapter 1, planning encompasses defining an organization's goals, establishing an overall strategy for achieving those goals, and developing a comprehensive hierarchy of plans to integrate and coordinate activities. It is concerned, then, with *ends* (what is to be done) as well as with *means* (how it is to be done).

Planning can be further defined in terms of whether it is informal or formal. All managers engage in planning, but it might be only the informal variety. For instance, when I asked the owner-manager of a door-manufacturing firm whether he did planning or not, he answered: "Yeah, I have a rough vision in my mind of where we're going." This is an example of informal planning.

The primary factors that differentiate formal from informal planning are the extent of written documentation and a multiyear time frame.[2] Formal plans typically are written down and cover at least 3 years into the future. So when we use the term *planning* in this chapter, we're implying *formal* planning. We'll assume that specific objectives are formulated, that they cover a period of years, that they are committed to writing, and that specific action programs exist for the achievement of those objectives.

TYPES OF PLANS

The most popular way for managers to classify plans is by their breadth—*strategic* versus *operational*—and by their time frame—*short-*, *intermediate-*, and *long-term*. As we will show, these planning classifications are not independent of one another. For instance, there is an overlapping relationship between strategic and long-term plans.

Strategic Versus Operational Plans

Plans that apply to the entire organization, that establish the organization's overall objectives, and that seek to position the organization in terms of its environment are called **strategic plans**. Those that specify the details of how the overall objectives are to be achieved are called **operational plans**.

> Generally speaking, the higher a manager is in an organization, the more he or she is involved with strategic plans.

Strategic and operational plans differ in their time frame and their scope.[3] Operational plans tend to cover shorter periods of time. For instance, an organization's monthly, weekly, and day-to-day plans are almost all operational. Strategic plans tend to include an extended time period—usually 5 years or more. They also cover a broader area and deal less with specifics. Operational plans have a narrower and more limited scope.

Generally speaking, the higher a manager is in an organization, the more he or she is involved with strategic plans. Conversely, the focus of most lower-level managers is on operational plans. But this generalization between level in the organization and type of planning needs to be qualified to reflect the size of the organization. For owner-managers of small businesses and for entrepreneurs like Jeff Bezo, the difference between strategic and operational plans is essentially academic because they'll typically be working on both types of plans simultaneously.

Short-, Intermediate-, and Long-Term Plans

Financial analysts traditionally describe investment returns as *short-*, *intermediate-*, and *long-term*. The short-term covers less than 1 year. The intermediate-term covers from 1 year up to 5 years. And any time frame beyond 5 years is classified as long-term. Managers have adopted the same terminology to describe plans.

Why is time frame important in classifying plans? The answer lies in the **commitment concept**. The more current plans affect future commitments, the longer the time frame for which managers need to plan. So the commitment concept states that plans should extend far enough to see through those commitments that are made today. Planning for too long or too short a period is inefficient.

Why do executives at large public utilities such as Hydro Quebec or Arizona Public Service develop plans that cover 50 years or more into the future, whereas the managers of convenience marts typically have no formal plans that extend beyond a year or two? These differences don't have to do with the quality of management. They have to do with the future impact of the decisions that these managers currently make. The decision to build a hydroelectric plant entails an investment of hundreds of millions or even billions of dollars that will take decades to recoup. The convenience store turns over its entire inventory every 2 weeks and may have only a 1-year renewable lease.

The commitment concept can also provide insights into why the length of the planning horizon tends to increase at higher levels of management. The decisions that top management typically make imply a greater commitment of resources and contain greater uncertainty than do those of lower-level management. To justify this resource commitment and to help reduce uncertainty, top management engages in long-term planning. A supervisor, on the other hand, rarely makes decisions that commit the organization well into the future. So the plans developed by supervisors tend to be of the short-term variety.

Harlan Accola swears by the value of planning. His firm, American Images, is in the aerial photography business.[4] It started in 1980, but by 1986 it was on the verge of bankruptcy. Today his business has fifty-four employees, has annual sales of nearly $5 million, and generates profits of over $300,000 a year. What happened? According to Accola, "We grew too fast and it was simply from lack of planning." Now American Images has identified its unique market niche, introduced formal planning sessions, sets annual sales goals, conducts monthly planning meetings, and generates comprehensive weekly reports on performance.

PLANNING IN AN UNCERTAIN ENVIRONMENT

Harlan Accola has turned religious about planning, but not all managers are so enthusiastic. In fact, formalized planning has come under increased criticism in recent years. In this section, we outline the potential benefits of planning, describe the primary arguments that critics have made, and review the research evidence to determine whether planning actually enhances an organization's performance.

▶ Why Managers Plan

Why should managers plan? We can propose at least four reasons. Planning gives direction, reduces the impact of change, minimizes waste and redundancy, and sets the standards to facilitate control.

Planning establishes coordinated effort. It gives direction to managers and nonmanagers alike. When all concerned know where the organization is going and what they must contribute to reach the objective, they can begin to coordinate their activities, cooperate with each other, and work in teams. A lack of planning can foster "zigzagging" and thus prevent an organization from moving efficiently toward its objectives.

By forcing managers to look ahead, anticipate change, consider the impact of change, and develop appropriate responses, planning reduces uncertainty. It also clarifies the consequences of the actions managers might take in response to change.

Planning also reduces overlapping and wasteful activities. Coordination before the fact is likely to uncover waste and redundancy. Further, when means and ends are clear, inefficiencies become more obvious.

Finally, planning establishes objectives or standards that facilitate control. If we are unsure of what we are trying to achieve, how can we determine whether we have achieved it? In planning, we develop the objectives. And, as we illustrate in chapter 6, the control process compares actual peformance against the objectives, identifies any signficiant deviations, and takes the necessary corrective action. Without planning, there can be no control.

▶ Criticisms of Planning

Formalized and strategic planning became popular in the 1960s. And it still is. There's an intuitive appeal to planning—"the plannning urge remains powerful because it is so tied up with man's notion of himself as an intelligent and rational creature. Everybody makes plans."[5] But critics of planning are accumulating. The following summarizes the major arguments that have recently been offered against formalized and strategic planning.

Planning creates too much rigidity.[6] Formalized planning systems lock people and organizational units into specific goals with specific time periods. The plans assume that conditions will remain relatively stable during that time period, which is almost never the case.

You can't plan for change in a turbulent environment.[7] Most organizations face dynamic, changing, and unpredictable environments. "Setting oneself on a predetermined course in unknown waters is the perfect way to sail straight into an iceberg."[8] Turbulence can be turned into an opportunity for those flexible enough to seize it. But if you're locked into formal plans, every unpredictable change is seen only as a problem.

Systems can't replace intuition and creativity.[9] Formalized strategic planning systems tried to do for management what scientific management (see Appendix A) tried to do a century ago for production work—program and routinize it. But formal procedures will never be able to forecast discontinuities. Developing strategy is a complex and demanding task that depends as much, if not more, on intuition and creativity as on formal analysis. Most successful strategies are visions, not plans. Pedestrian thinkers can't become incisive merely by following some systematic strategic framework.

Planning focuses management's attention on competing within today's industry structure rather than on competing for tomorrow's.[10] Strategic planning has directed too much attention on how to position products and businesses within existing industry structures. The real attention should be toward changing the industry's rules or creating tomorrow's industries. The inability of many managers to look ahead for ways to reinvent their industries has led to both costly blunders and monumental catch-up costs.

Planning reinforces successful organizations to become overly preoccupied with the factors responsible for their success, setting up the conditions that can lead to failure.[11] Ironically, success breeds failure. Managers in successful organizations tend to develop perceptual biases that encourage them to maintain the status quo. Since managers are most likely to assess and change their views of the world when they run into problems, long-term success provides little opportunity for managers to evaluate or change their strategic framework. They tend to become overconfident and more entrenched in the strategy they have created.

> ## Looking at the Bottom Line:
> ## Does Planning Improve Organizational Performance?

Does planning pay off? Who's right—the proponents of planning or the critics? Let's look at the evidence. Dozens of studies have been undertaken to test the relationship between planning and organizational performance.[12] Contrary to arguments made by critics, the overall evidence is generally positive. In fact, the evidence allows us to draw the following conclusions. First, generally speaking, formal planning is associated with increased growth in sales and earnings, higher profits, higher return on assets, and other positive financial results. Second, the quality of the planning process and the appropriate implementation of the plans probably contribute more to high performance than does the extent of planning. Third, managers have learned to build in flexibility by creating contingency plans covering alternative scenarios and by treating planning as an ongoing process rather than as a once-a-year activity. This approach counters the tendency for planning to become overly rigid. Fourth, consistent with the discussion of decision making in chapter 3, no planning system or strategic framework can substitute for creative and intuitive insight. Well-conceived strategies are unlikely to evolve from mediocre minds using sophisticated frameworks. But an absence of strategic planning is also no evidence that management has a creative vision. Finally, in those studies in which formal planning hasn't led to higher performance, the environment is typically the culprit. When strong government regulations, powerful labor unions, and similar environmental forces constrain management's options, planning will have less of an impact on an organization's performance than when those constraints are weak. Why? Because management will have fewer choices for which planning can propose viable alternatives. For example, planning might suggest that General Motors should produce some of its key parts in Asia in order to keep costs down. But if GM's U.S. labor contracts specifically forbid transferring the manufacturing of these parts outside the United States, the value of the company's planning effort is significantly reduced. Dramatic shocks from the environment can also undermine the best-laid plans. The rapid and unexpected rise in bond interest rates in 1994 undermined the formal plans previously developed by administrators in Orange County, California. The county's assets were heavily invested in bond-sensitive options that collapsed in value as interest rates rose; the result was a loss to the county of over $1 billion. In conditions of such environmental uncertainty, there is no reason to expect that planners will necessarily outperform nonplanners.

> **The quality of the planning process and the appropriate implementation of the plans probably contribute more to high performance than does the extent of planning.**

THE PLACE TO START: DEFINING AN ORGANIZATION'S PURPOSE

The best statements of an organization's purpose are short, clear, and easy to understand. For instance, Sony Music Canada states: "Our passion is music. Our commitment is to our artists. Our focus is customer service. Our edge is innovation. Our success is in our attitude!" Newport Shipping Company proclaims, "We will build great ships. At a profit if we can. At a loss if we must. But we will build great ships!"[13] Haworth, Inc., a manufacturer of office furniture with annual sales of more than $800 million, simply says that the company seeks "to be world class in the eyes of our customers at creating well-designed, effective, and exciting work environments."[14] What are we talking about? We're referring to the **mission statement** or vision that defines an organization's purpose and answers such questions as: What business are we in? and What are we trying to accomplish? It also provides important guidance to both managers and employees. Gary Simmons, president of Healthtex, a children's-clothing company, says his firm's mission statement has been valuable for getting different groups of people within the company to focus on a strategic direction.[15]

A recent survey found that more than 50 percent of large companies have formal mission statements.[16] And an increasing number of small firms are realizing that the time required to thrash out a written mission statement is worth the effort.[17] When key people in the organization sit down and attempt to define what the company is about, they are forced to clarify and find common agreement on what the organization's values are and what differentiates it from other organizations. And when complete, the finalized product provides focus and direction for all organizational members.

No organization can be all things to all people. As we'll discuss in the next section, every organization has its strengths and weaknesses. The best managers are able to capitalize on the strengths in order to make their organization more effective. And a clear mission statement can help in this process. How? By focusing on those strengths that give the organization its competitive advantages. Sony Music Canada's management, for instance, understands that it's "edge" is innovation. Management doesn't believe that the company can succeed if it merely tries to copy the success of others.

CREATING A STRATEGY

Sanyo Electric and Sharp Corp. are two Japanese companies, of similar size, with partly overlapping product lines. But they are worlds apart in corporate strategy, and that difference has resulted in very different levels of performance.[18]

Both companies make computers, minidisk players, TVs, and refrigerators. Sanyo thrived until the mid-1980s selling low-end products in overseas markets. But it never developed a quality image and was slow in new product introductions. Sanyo has tried to be a low-cost producer, but its prices have often been higher than those of its rivals. In contrast, Sharp has a more focused strategy. It emphasizes using key devices such as color liquid crystal displays to produce distinctive products that stand out in mature markets. Sharp is so good at focusing its research and development that it often develops more new products each year than a competitor such as Hitachi, which spends nearly five times as much. Sharp's management is also good at keeping personnel costs down. Its sales per employee, for example, are about 30 percent higher than Sanyo's. These differences show themselves on the bottom line. In the most recent fiscal year, Sanyo reported a loss of $11.7 million, while Sharp earned $269 million.

The Sharp-Sanyo comparison illustrates the value and importance of a well-thought-out strategy. In this section, we describe four general or grand strategies, an overall framework for approaching strategy, and some specific strategy applications.

Types of Strategies

Enterprise Rent-A-Car, outdoor clothier Patagonia, Inc., and drug producer Marion Merrell Dow (MMD) are successful, profitable companies. In recent years, however, each seems to be going in a different direction.[19] Enterprise is rapidly expanding its operations and is now number one in the United States—bigger than Hertz Corp. Patagonia's management is content to maintain the status quo. Meanwhile, MMD is cutting staff and downsizing its operations. The different directions of these companies can be explained by the fact that their managements have chosen different grand strategies.[20]

GROWTH The pursuit of growth has long had appeal to managers, especially in North America. If bigger is better, than biggest is best! In our terms, a growth strategy means increasing the level of the organization's operations. Typical measures of growth would be

Enterprise Rent-A-Car has pursued a growth strategy by capitalizing on its niche in the low-budget insurance-replacement market.

expanding revenues, adding employees, and increasing market share. Popular means for achieving growth include aggressive direct expansion, development of new products or services, mergers and acquisitions, joint ventures, and expansion into global markets.

Enterprise has pursued aggressive direct expansion by capitalizing on its niche in the low-budget insurance-replacement market. Its growth has come mainly at the expense of the fragmented collection of independents that compete for insurance-replacement dollars. Barnes & Noble's growth has been fueled by the development of superstores that provide entertainment and coffee as well as books. When British Telecommunications bought MCI, it chose the merger route to growth. Union Carbide has been able to grow in a highly capital-intensive industry, despite limited funds, by using joint ventures. For instance, it is doubling the size of its ethylene glycol plant in Alberta, Canada, by taking on partners from Japan and Taiwan, and building a $2 billion glycol and polyethylene plant in Kuwait in partnership with the Kuwait Petroleum Corp. And Bausch & Lomb is expanding its optics business by moving into new markets in China, India, and Poland.

STABILITY Not every organization deifies growth. Some managers see their organization's future as being best assured through the pursuit of a stability strategy. A stability strategy is characterized by an absence of significant change.

Why would management choose a stability strategy? For Patagonia, management purposely chose to halt growth for environmental reasons. "Everything we make pollutes. Polyester, because it's made from petroleum, is an obvious villain, but cotton and wool are not any better. To kill the boll weevil, cotton is sprayed with pesticides so poisonous they gradually render cotton fields barren; cotton fabric is often treated with formaldehyde. Wool relies on large flocks of sheep that denude fragile, arid areas of the earth."[21] The number of styles offered in Patagonia's catalogue has been cut by 30 to 40 percent, and those styles are now available in only half the colors. In addition, Patagonia's customers receive new catalogues only twice, rather than four times, a year.

WD-40 represents a more traditional pursuit of stability. The company's highly profitable niche product, a petroleum-based lubricant, has had its own unique niche and little competition since the 1950s, so management has little interest in changing the status quo.[22] Management is perfectly happy keeping its good thing going.

RETRENCHMENT As we've pointed out numerous times, many organizations—particularly large corporations—have been downsizing their operations. These include firms such as Mobil Oil, Eastman Kodak, Chase Manhattan Bank, IBM, Olivetti, R.R. Donnelley, and

Marion Merrell Dow. Downsizing, along with divestitures and liquidation, are examples of retrenchment. The common factor in this strategy is that the organization reduces the size or diversity of its operations.

MMD offers a good example of why a company would pursue a retrenchment strategy.[23] MMD enjoyed growth throughout the 1980s, but then two things happened. First, several high-profile products suffered market declines. The public became concerned about possible adverse side effects from Seldane, its popular antihistamine. And there was a sharp drop in demand for its Nicoderm antismoking patches. But the bigger problem was the rise of managed-care services and mail-order prescriptions. To better compete, MMD's management reduced its workforce by 1,300 people.

COMBINATION A combination strategy is the simultaneous pursuit of two or more of the preceding strategies. This option recognizes that units of large organizations are often going in different directions. Raychem, for instance, is a plastics and electronics company that had become heavily dependent on the defense industry. As the defense business declined, Raychem's management responded by closing plants, selling businesses, and terminating 8 percent of its workforce in its electronics group. At the same time, however, Raychem was expanding its commercial plastics business to take advantage of new technologies it had developed.[24]

SWOT Analysis

The essence of any strategic-planning effort is referred to as **SWOT analysis** because it requires managers to assess the organization's strengths, weaknesses, opportunities, and threats in order to identify a niche that the organization can exploit. Because an organization's environment, to a large degree, defines management's options, a successful strategy will be one that aligns well with the environment. So we begin by assuming that management has an accurate grasp of what is taking place in its environment and is aware of important trends that might affect its operations (see chapter 4). Then it is ready to identify internal strengths and weaknesses and external opportunities and threats. It will then be able to specify a niche that the organization can exploit.

IDENTIFY EXTERNAL OPPORTUNITIES AND THREATS Management also needs to evaluate what it has learned from its environmental scanning in terms of opportunities that the organization can exploit and threats that the organization faces.[25] Keep in mind that the same environment can present opportunities to one organization and pose threats to another in the same industry because of their different resources. Consider the European market for computers. The environment has recently been characterized by cutthroat competition and aggressive price cutting.[26] More efficient producers such as Motorola, Matsushita, and Compaq have used their leaner cost structures to significantly increase their European market shares. Meanwhile, companies such as Olivetti and Groupe Bull, which are burdened with heavy overhead costs, have lost market share and absorbed huge operating losses. So what an organization considers an opportunity or a threat depends on the resources it controls.

IDENTIFY THE ORGANIZATION'S STRENGTHS AND WEAKNESSES After analyzing the environment, management needs to look inside its organization.[27] What skills and abilities do the organization's employees have? What is the organization's cash position? Has it been successful at developing new and innovative products? How do consumers perceive the organization and the quality of its products or services?

This step forces management to recognize that every organization, no matter how large and powerful, is constrained in some way by the resources and skills it has available. A small automobile manufacturer, such as Porsche, cannot independently start making sport utility vehicles simply because management sees opportunities in that market. Porsche does not have the resources to successfully compete in the SUV market against the likes of DaimlerChrysler, Ford, and Toyota. Similarly, managers of a six-person computer software firm with annual sales of less than $2 million might see a huge market for on-line services. But their minimal resources limit their ability to act on this opportunity. In contrast, Microsoft's management was able to create the Microsoft Network because it had the access, people skills, name recognition, and financial resources to pursue this market.

Analysis of the organization's resources should lead management to a clear assessment of its organization's strengths and weaknesses. Then management can identify the organization's **distinctive competence**, or the unique skills and resources that determine the organization's competitive weapons. Black & Decker, for instance, bought General Electric's small appliance division—which made coffeemakers, toasters, irons, and the like—renamed them, and capitalized on Black & Decker's reputation for quality and durability to make these appliances far more profitable than they had been under the GE name.

CHOOSING A NICHE Exhibit 5-1 illustrates the objective of SWOT analysis. A successful analysis identifies a niche in which the organization's products or services can have some competitive advantage. The area in which the opportunities in the environment overlap with the organization's resources represents the niche wherein the organization's opportunities lie.

Using SWOT Analysis to Identify the Organization's Niche

Organization's resources

Opportunities in the environment

Organization's niche

EXHIBIT 5-1

▶ A Strategic Framework

How do managers actually choose a specific strategy for their organization? For instance, how do they achieve growth if that is their grand strategy? There are a number of frameworks available for managers to follow.[28] The most widely accepted and validated framework has been developed by Michael Porter of Harvard University.[29]

Porter proposes that no firm can successfully perform at an above-average level by trying to be all things to all people. Management, therefore, must select a strategy that will give its organization a **competitive advantage**. This is a capability or circumstance that gives an organization an edge over its rivals. For instance, Home Depot has proved to be very competitive in every market it has entered because of its broad selection of merchandise and commitment to service. These qualities, which are highly valued by customers, make it difficult for rivals to compete against Home Depot.

Porter has identified three strategies from which management can choose: cost leadership, differentiation, and focus. Which one management chooses depends on the organization's strengths and its competitors' weaknesses. According to Porter, management should avoid a position in which it has to slug it out with everybody in its industry. Management's objective should be to put its organization's strength where the competition isn't.

When an organization sets out to be the low-cost producer in its industry, it is following a **cost-leadership strategy**. Success with this strategy requires that the organization be the cost leader and not merely one of the contenders for that position. In addition, the product or service being offered must be perceived as comparable to that offered by rivals, or, at least, it must be acceptable to buyers.

How does a firm gain such a cost advantage? Typical means include efficiency of operations, economies of scale, technological innovations, low-cost labor, or preferential access to raw materials. Examples of firms that have used this strategy successfully include PC-maker Acer Inc., Price/Costco, and Gallo wines.

The firm that seeks to be unique in its industry in ways that are widely valued by buyers is following a **differentiation strategy**. The list of attributes by which an organization can differentiate itself would include high quality, speed, state-of-the-art design, techno-

Porsche has succeeded by pursuing a differentiation strategy based on high performance.

logical capability, expert advice, convenience, breadth of selection, extraordinary service, or an unusually positive brand image. The key is that the attribute chosen must be different from those offered by rivals and significant enough to justify a price premium that exceeds the cost of differentiating.

There is no shortage of firms that have found at least one attribute that allows them to differentiate themselves from competitors. Intel (technology), Maytag (reliability), Mary Kay Cosmetics (distribution), Singapore Airlines (service), Armani (prestige brand), McKesson drugs (delivery system), and Porsche (high performance) are a few.

The first two strategies sought a competitive advantage in a broad range of industry segments. The **focus strategy** aims at a cost advantage (cost focus) or differentiation advantage (differentiation focus) in a narrow segment. That is, management will select a segment or group of segments in an industry (such as product variety, type of end buyer, distribution channel, or geographical location of buyers) and tailor the strategy to serve them to the exclusion of others. The goal is to exploit a narrow segment of a market. Of course, whether a focus strategy is feasible depends on the size of a segment and whether it can support the additional cost of focusing. Stouffer's used a cost-focus strategy in its Lean Cuisine line to reach calorie-conscious consumers seeking both high-quality products and convenience. The University of Phoenix has more than 55,000 students enrolled at 51 campuses in 13 states. It appeals to busy working students who need flexibility by offering its courses in four-hour-a-week sessions, lasting only five or six weeks. The University of Phoenix is pursuing a differentiation-focus strategy.

In The News

Strategic Planning Pays Off at MRM

In September 1995, Tony Rigato did something that few CEOs would have the courage to do. He "fired" his biggest supplier, a valve manufacturer. Rigato's company, MRM, distributes pneumatic industrial components in Michigan. And while this supplier accounted for 40 percent of MRM's business, Rigato felt confident he was doing the right thing. Why? It fit with his firm's strategic plan.

Rigato discovered strategic planning at a management seminar in 1991. "I knew that our planning was inconsistent and abbreviated," he says. "And when I saw that there was a complete process that covered all aspects of business, I was really excited." He scheduled the first planning session three weeks later. In attendance were Rigato and four key employees. They recorded a company history, composed a mission statement, and conducted a SWOT analysis. Their final plan contained 12 objectives. By 1993, MRM, with $7.2 million in sales, was well on its way to attaining the most ambitious of its 12 objectives—to increase sales from $4 million to $10 million in 3 years.

These strategic-planning sessions became an annual company ritual. By 1995, it had expanded to include a detailed analysis of customers and suppliers—MRM was using strategic planning tools to analyze its products and the way they were distributed. And it was this analysis, in 1995, that led to Rigato's decision to drop its largest supplier. He found that MRM was spending 70 percent of its resources on that supplier's product line, while the line accounted for only 40 percent of MRM's revenues. Even though this supplier had been with MRM for 25 years, it was time for a divorce.

Two years passed and Rigato has no regrets. MRM's sales have rebounded to $13.5 million. And since 1991, when he initiated the first strategic planning session, sales have more than tripled and profitability has increased substantially. "None of what we've been able to accomplish would have been possible without strategic planning," Rigato claims.

Based on D. Fenn, "No More Business as Usual," *Inc.*, November 1997, pp. 114–19.

IMPLEMENTING A STRATEGY

A well-designed strategy means little if it isn't effectively implemented. In this section, we briefly review the factors that determine implementation success.

Characteristics of Successful Strategy Implementation

The consulting firm of McKinsey & Co. has developed a "checklist" for successful strategy implementation.[30] This **7-S model** provides a useful summary of the key factors that managers need to address (see Exhibit 5-2).

Strategy. Management obviously must begin by having the right strategy. The strategy needs to reflect an accurate assessment of the environment, particularly the current and future actions of rivals.

Superordinate goals. This factor translates the strategy into overarching goals that unite the organization in some common purpose. It is typically synonymous with the organization's mission statement.

Skills. This refers to the organization's core competencies. What does the organization do best? The strategy chosen must be congruent with the organization's inherent skill resources.

EXHIBIT 5-2

The 7-S Model

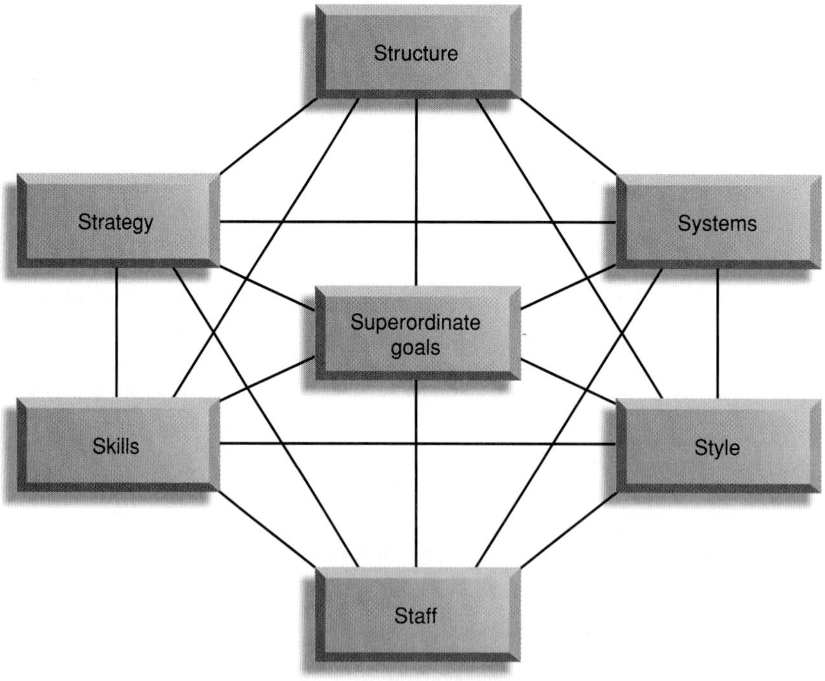

Source: H. Waterman Jr., T. J. Peters, and J. R. Phillips. "Structure Is Not Organization," reprinted from *Business Horizons*, June 1980. Copyright © 1980 by the Foundation for the School of Business at Indiana University. Used with permission.

Structure. Strategy determines structure. The organization's structural design is a vehicle to help the organization achieve its goals. If the organization's strategy changes, so too typically does its structure.

Systems. Systems also need to align with, and support, the strategy chosen. Systems include all the formal policies and procedures such as capital budgeting, accounting, and information systems.

Style. Top management acts as a role model. Its substantive and symbolic actions communicate to everyone in the organization what the priorities are and the organization's true commitment to the strategy.

Staff. It is people who execute a strategy. The organization's selection process and training programs need to support the strategy by ensuring that the right people are hired and that employees have the abilities and skills to carry out the strategy.

The Importance of Sustaining a Competitive Advantage

Jeff Bezo of Amazon.com is quickly learning a basic tenet of strategy development. Long-term success with any strategy requires that its competitive advantage be sustainable. That is, it must resist erosion by the actions of competitors or by evolutionary changes in the industry. Yet, sustaining a competitive advantage is no simple task.

Technology changes, as do tastes of customers. Most important, some advantages can be imitated by competitors. Management needs to create barriers that make imitation difficult or that reduce competitive opportunities. Many of the techniques for managing the environment, discussed in chapter 4, tend to create barriers for rivals. For example, the use of patents and copyrights reduces opportunities for imitation. When there are strong economies of scale, reducing price to gain volume is a useful tactic. Tying up suppliers with exclusive contracts limits their ability to supply rivals. And encouraging government policies that impose import tariffs can limit foreign competition.

Southwest Airlines provides an excellent illustration of how to effectively sustain a competitive advantage.[31] Southwest has consistently made money, in an industry that lost $12 billion over the past 5 years, by pursuing a cost-leadership strategy. It has no meals, no reserved or first-class seats, no computerized reservation systems, no baggage transfers to other airlines, and it uses standardized aircraft and reusable boarding passes. It costs Southwest 7.1 cents per available seat mile to operate. Comparable figures for American, Delta, TWA, and USAir are 10.6, 9.1, 8.5, and 10.1, respectively. But Southwest recently faced aggressive price competition from major carriers and low-cost copycats such as Reno Air, Kiwi, and Shuttle by United. So what did Southwest do? It took advantage of the excellent relationship it has with its employees to persuade its 2,000-strong pilots' union to accept an unprecedented 10-year contract that provides no wage increases in the first 5 years and then only three 3 percent increases in the second 5 years. In exchange, the pilots will be granted options to acquire as many as 1.4 million shares of Southwest stock each year during the life of the contract. And what's the bottom line? This deal virtually assures Southwest of maintaining its cost advantage over rival airlines.

Managing a production department at Chrysler's Windsor, Ontario, minivan plant is different from managing a design team at Chrysler's Technology Center in Auburn Hills, Michigan. The former involves an ongoing process. The latter, however, is an example of project management. In this section, we briefly describe project management, why it has

PROJECT MANAGEMENT: A CONTEMPORARY TOOL

become so popular, outline the project planning process, and assess the challenges that project managers face.

What Is Project Management?

A **project** is a one-time-only set of activities with a definite beginning and ending point in time.[32] Projects vary in size and scope—from a NASA space shuttle launch to arranging a wedding. **Project management** is the task of getting the activities done on time, within budget, and according to specifications.[33]

Chris Higgins has become "Mr. Project" at BankAmerica. He joined BankAmerica in 1993 as a vice president in charge of project management in the payment-services division. He oversaw a team of eight project managers. Within three years, he was running a team of 140 project managers. Says Higgins, "Management today is about managing change. The skills you learn in project management are relevant to every aspect of business."

There is no shortage of project-management cheerleaders. For instance, William Dauphinais, a partner at PriceWaterhouseCoopers, says: "Project management is going to be huge in the next decade."[34] Project management is "the wave of the future," according to a General Motors in-house newsletter.[35] "Project management is the way the business world is going," says Michael Strickland, a manager with Bell South.[36]

Project management has actually been around for a long time in industries such as construction and moviemaking. But now it has expanded into almost every type of business. For instance, one of the last places you might expect to find project management is the mortgage business. But the Federal National Mortgage Association, which processes more than $1 billion in mortgage purchases every day, uses it. Says Fannie Mae's chief information officer, "Automation and empowerment take away the need to have managers oversee the day-to-day work. Everything has become projects. This is the way Fannie Mae does business today."[37]

What explains the growing popularity of project management? It fits well with a dynamic environment and the need for flexibility and rapid response. Organizations are increasingly undertaking projects that are somewhat unusual or unique, have specific deadlines, contain complex interrelated tasks requiring specialized skills, and are temporary in nature. These types of projects don't lend themselves well to the standardized operating procedures that guide routine and continuous organizational activities.

In the typical project, team members are temporarily assigned and report to a project manager. This manager coordinates the project's activities with other departments and reports directly to a senior executive. But the project is seen as temporary. It exists only long enough to complete its specific objectives. Then it's wound down and closed up; members move on to other projects, return to their permanent departments, or leave the organization.

The Project Planning Process

The essential features of the project planning process have been summarized as follows:[38]

Define the project's objectives.

Identify activities and the resources needed to achieve them.

Establish sequencing relationships for activities.

Make time estimates for activities.

Determine project completion time.

Compare project schedule objectives.

Determine resource requirements to meet objectives.

The planning process begins by clearly defining the project's objectives. This step is necessary because the manager and team members need to know what's expected. All activities in the project and the resources needed to accomplish them must then be identified. That is, what labor and materials are needed to complete the project? This task is often time-consuming and complex because the project is unique, so there aren't the history and experience that typically exist in planning most tasks.

Once the activities have been identified, their sequential relationship needs to be determined. That is, what activities must be completed before others can begin? And which can be undertaken simultaneously? This step typically is done using flowchart-type diagrams.

Next, the project activities need to be scheduled. The manager estimates the time required for each activity and then uses these estimates to develop an overall project schedule and completion date. Then the project schedule is compared with the objectives, and adjustments are made. For example, if the project time estimate is too long, the manager can assign more resources to critical activities so they can be completed faster. In recent years, a number of PC-based software tools have been created to help coordinate projects. For instance, smart scheduling software can calculate just how many people will be needed at any point in a project's life cycle. Several manually calculated scheduling techniques used in project planning are described in chapter 6.

The Role of the Project Manager

The temporary nature of projects makes managing them different from, say, overseeing a production line and preparing a weekly tally of costs on an ongoing basis. The one-shot nature of the work makes project managers the organizational equivalent of a hired gunman. There's a job to be done. It has to be defined—in detail, with much haggling. And the project manager is responsible for how it's done.

Inspite of the availability of sophisticated computerized scheduling programs and other project management tools, the role of project manager remains difficult because he or she is managing people who are still linked, authority-wise, to their permanent department. "You have to know how to work with people who have different priorities, who march to a different tune than you," says Ian Benson, a vice president with Chase Manhattan Bank.[39] Janine Coleman, a project manager for AT&T's global business communications systems, which installs equipment for large corporate clients, says, "The company tells the client, 'We assign you a project manager, and she's in charge.' If it fails, it's my fault. But does this put real authority there? No. If a VP won't go along, it's up to the project manager to get him to."[40] The only real influence project managers have is their power of persuasion. To make matters worse, team members seldom work on just one project. They're usually assigned two or three at any given time. So project managers often end up competing with each other to focus a worker's attention on his or her particular undertaking.[41]

ENTREPRENEURSHIP: A SPECIAL CASE OF STRATEGIC PLANNING

You've heard the story dozens of times. With only an idea and a few hundred dollars, someone starts what eventually becomes a multimillion-dollar business. For Cherrill Farnsworth, it's getting to be a habit. At age 44, she's already working on her fifth start-up company![42]

Farnsworth has a talent for exploiting opportunities. At age 25, she spotted her first. After her husband was transferred from Indianapolis to Houston, she noticed that people had no way to get downtown from her northwestern suburb. Despite opposition from major bus operators, she secured a bus line franchise. After 2 years, she sold it for a profit. "I realized at that point what value you could get by working hard and creating something

Cherrill Farnsworth loves being an entrepreneur. At age 44, she is working on her fifth start-up company.

new—especially if there's no competition," Farnsworth says. Her next three ventures leased equipment—luxury vehicles, office equipment, and oil field equipment. Then, at age 35, she identified another opportunity. Magnetic resonance imaging machines were beginning to appear. "The equipment seemed to have so much merit," she says. But many hospitals couldn't afford the $1.5 million to $2 million it would cost to buy their own MRI machines. The hospitals knew that offering MRI services could be profitable, but they couldn't borrow to buy the machines because Medicare had not yet approved reimbursements from insurers for the service. Thus the seed was planted for her current company, TME, which provides MRI services for hospitals. She convinced a set of investors that there was money to be made—big money—in her idea. Today her company operates twenty imaging centers in nine U.S. states, serving thirty-six hospitals and four universities. TME employs 164 people and is adding about eighteen a year. Annual revenues are up to $28 million and growing at about 30 percent a year.

Strategic planning tends to carry a "big business" bias. It implies a formalization and structure that fits well with large, established organizations that have abundant resources. But the primary interest of many people is not in managing large and established organizations. Like Cherrill Farnsworth, Phil Knight of Nike, or Dave Thomas of Wendy's, they're excited about the idea of starting their own businesses from scratch. In this section, we'll demonstrate that entrepreneurship is actually just a special case of strategic planning.

▶ What Is Entrepreneurship?

There is no shortage of definitions of entrepreneurship.[43] Some, for example, apply the term to the creation of any new business. Others focus on intentions, claiming that entrepreneurs seek to create wealth, which is different from starting a business merely as a means of income substitution (i.e., working for yourself rather than working for someone else). When most people describe entrepreneurs, they use adjectives such as bold, innovative, venturesome, and risk-taking. They also tend to associate entrepreneurs with small business. We'll define **entrepreneurship** as a process by which individuals pursue opportunities, fulfilling needs and wants through innovation, without regard to the resources they currently control.[44]

It's important not to confuse managing a small business with entrepreneurship. Why? Because not all small business managers are entrepreneurs.[45] Many don't innovate. A great many managers of small businesses are merely scaled-down versions of the conservative, stability-seeking individuals who staff many large corporations and public agencies.

Can entrepreneurs exist in large, established organizations? The answer to that question depends on one's definition of entrepreneur. The noted management guru Peter Drucker, for instance, argues that they can.[46] He describes an entrepreneurial manager as someone who is confident of his or her ability, who seizes opportunities for innovation, and who not only expects surprises but capitalizes on them. He contrasts that with what he calls a "trustee type" of manager who feels threatened by change, is bothered by uncertainty, prefers predictability, and is inclined to maintain the status quo.

Drucker's use of the term entrepreneurial, however, is misleading. By almost any definition of good management today, his entrepreneurial type would be preferred over his trustee type. Moreover, the term **intrapreneurship** is now widely used to describe the effort to create the entrepreneurial spirit in large organizations.[47] Yet intrapreneurship can never capture the autonomy and riskiness inherent in true entrepreneurship. Because intrapreneurship takes place within a large organization, all financial risks are carried by the

Sean Nguyen's Rise from Vietnamese Refugee to Honored Entrepreneur

It was 1981. Sean Nguyen left his South Vietnamese village with his father, brother, and thirty-six other refugees in a crude wooden boat. Sean was all of 16 years of age. After a year in a Thai refugee camp, he arrived in the United States. He had no marketable skills, and the only job he could get was as a $4-an-hour assembly-line worker at Multi-Tech, a Minneapolis modem manufacturer. By day he worked at Multi-Tech. By night he dreamed of starting his own company. He acted on that dream in 1986.

Sean launched Nguyen Electronics Inc. (NEI) in a basement office while continuing to work full-time at Multi-Tech. NEI assembled printed circuit boards and other electromechanical equipment. During its first year of operations, with 15 part-time employees, NEI made $10,000 profit on sales of $50,000. His only major customer, in those days, was his daytime employer, Multi-Tech. Today, NEI has a roster of 35 customers, including Sun Microsystems and Unisys. It assembles, tests, services, and programs computer circuit boards. Annual sales are in excess of $6 million.

NEI's success is largely due to Sean's obsessive commitment to service. Customers praise the attention they receive from NEI's salespeople and the company's prompt delivery. "NEI provides exactly what we need and builds exactly when we need it, which is a tremendous competitive advantage to us," says the purchasing manager at Multi-Tech. The plant manager at Bermo Corp., a computer-parts maker, adds: "Their pricing and service are always good, and they're able to turn things around very quickly."

Less than 15 years after fleeing Vietnam, Sean Nguyen is an American success story. And his achievements haven't gone unnoticed. He was recently chosen as the U.S. Small Business Association's National Young Entrepreneur of the Year, and *Inc.* magazine has selected NEI as one of America's fastest-growing private companies.

Source: Based on B. Ojo, "His Land of Opportunity," *Asia, Inc.*, May 1996, pp. 74–76.

parent company; rules, policies, and other constraints are imposed by the parent; intrapreneurs have to report to bosses or superiors; and the payoff for success is not financial independence but rather career advancement.[48]

Are You an Entrepreneurial Type?

Does entrepreneurship lie in your future? An increasing proportion of new business graduates, as well as experienced managers who have lost their jobs in large companies as a result of downsizing, are pursuing entrepreneurial opportunities.[49] In this section we look at the personality characteristics of entrepreneurs and other factors related to entrepreneurial pursuits.

THE ENTREPRENEURIAL PERSONALITY One of the most researched topics in entrepreneurship has been the question of what, if any, psychological characteristics entrepreneurs have in common. Some common characteristics have been found: hard work, self-confidence, optimism, determination, and a high energy level.[50] But three factors regularly sit on the top of most lists and profile the entrepreneurial personality—a high need for achievement, a strong belief that you can control your own destiny, and a desire to take only moderate risks.[51]

The research allows us to draw a general description of entrepreneurs. They tend to be independent types who prefer to be personally responsible for solving problems, for setting goals, and for reaching those goals by their own efforts. They value independence and particularly don't like being controlled by others. While they're not afraid to take chances, they're not wild risk takers either. They prefer to take calculated risks in which they feel they have some control over the outcome.

The evidence on entrepreneurial personalities leads us to two obvious conclusions. First, people with this personality makeup are not likely to be contented, productive employees in the typical large corporation or government agency. The rules, regulations, and controls that these bureaucracies impose on their members frustrate entrepreneurs. Second, the challenges and conditions inherent in starting one's own business mesh well with the entrepreneurial personality. Starting a new venture, which they control, appeals to their desire to determine their own destinies and their willingness to take risks. But because entrepreneurs believe that their future is fully in their own hands, they perceive the risk as moderate, whereas nonentrepreneurs often see it as high.

OTHER FACTORS RELATED TO BEING AN ENTREPENEUR Besides certain personality characteristics, other forces have been found to be associated with becoming an entrepreneur.[52] Entrepreneurship tends to flourish in supportive environments. American culture, for instance, places a high value on being your own boss and achieving personal success. These cultural values help explain the wide popularity of entrepreneurial activities in the United States. In contrast, in other countries—including Ireland and Norway—less value is placed on personal achievement and a greater stigma is attached to failure. In addition, some areas of a country often become pockets of entepreneurial subcultures. In the United States, the Route 128 area surrounding Boston; Silicon Valley and northern San Diego County in California; Austin, Texas; and the Research Triangle area in North Carolina are examples of communities that encourage and support entrepreneurs.

Supportive parents seem to play an important part in influencing the entrepreneurial tendencies of their offspring. Entrepreneurs typically have parents who encouraged them to achieve, be independent, and take responsibility for their actions.

Entrepreneurs usually have role models whom they have attempted to emulate. Seeing someone else do something innovative and succeed makes innovation and success seem more realistically achievable. Not surprisingly, given this evidence, one or both parents of entrepreneurs tend to have been self-employed or entrepreneurial themselves.

A final variable related to entrepreneurial activity is previous entrepreneurship. Past behavior is the best predictor of future behaviors. Because it's generally easier to start a second, third, or fourth venture than it is to start the first one, beginning an entrepreneurial business tends to be a recurring activity for certain individuals, as we saw in the case of Cherrill Farnsworth. TME is her fifth start-up venture.

▶ How Entrepreneurs and Traditional Managers Differ

Exhibit 5-3 summarizes some key differences between entrepreneurs and traditional managers in large organizations. The latter tend to be custodial, whereas entrepreneurs actively seek change by exploiting opportunities. When searching for these opportunities, entrepreneurs often put their personal financial security at risk. The hierarchy in large organizations typically insulates traditional managers from these financial wagers and rewards them for minimizing risks and avoiding failures.

Comparing Entrepreneurs and Traditional Managers

EXHIBIT 5-3

Characteristic	Traditional Managers	Entrepreneurs
Primary motivation	Promotion and other traditional corporate rewards such as office, staff, and power	Independence, opportunity to create, financial gain
Time orientation	Achievement of short-term goals	Achievement of 5- to 10-year growth of business
Activity	Delegation and supervision	Direct involvement
Risk propensity	Low	Moderate
View toward failures and mistakes	Avoidance	Acceptance

Source: Based on R. D. Hisrich, "Entrepreneurship/Intrapreneurship," *American Psychologist*, February 1990, p. 218.

In addition, as shown in Exhibit 5-4, entrepreneurs approach strategy differently than typical bureaucratic managers do. Their key strategic questions may focus on the same general areas—resources, structure, control, and opportunity—but they address those questions in a different order, from a different perspective, and with a different emphasis.

The entrepreneur's strategic emphasis is driven by perception of opportunity rather than by availability of resources.[53] The entrepreneur's inclination is to monitor the environment closely in search of opportunities. The resources at his or her disposal take a back seat to identifying an idea that can be capitalized upon.

Once an opportunity is spotted, the entrepreneur begins to look for ways to take advantage of it. Because of his or her personality makeup, the entrepreneur is confident that the opportunity can be exploited. Moreover, the entrepreneur is not afraid to risk financial security, career opportunities, family relations, or psychic well-being to get the new venture off the ground. Entrepreneurs tend to ignore the hard statistics against success—about 42 percent of new businesses aren't around after 5 years.[54] The entrepreneur who

The Order of Strategic Questions

EXHIBIT 5-4

Typical Bureaucratic Manager	Typical Entrepreneur
What resources do I control?	Where is the opportunity, and how do I capitalize on it?
What structure determines our organization's relationship to its market?	What resources do I need?
How can I minimize the impact of others on my ability to perform?	How do I gain control over those resources?
What opportunity is appropriate?	What structure is best?

Source: Used by permission of *Harvard Business Review*; an excerpt from "The Heart of Entrepreneurship" by H. H. Stevenson and D. E. Gumpert, March–April 1985, pp. 86–87. Copyright © 1985 by the President and Fellows of Harvard College; all rights reserved.

sees an opportunity has the confidence and determination to believe that he or she will be on the winning side of those statistics.

Only after the entrepreneur has identified an opportunity and a way to exploit it does he or she begin to feel concerned about resources. But the entrepreneur's priorities are first to find out what resources are needed and then to determine how they can be obtained. This order is in contrast to that of the typical bureaucratic managers, who focus on the resources that are at their disposal. Entrepreneurs are often able to make imaginative and highly efficient use of very limited resources. Finally, when the resource obstacles have been overcome, the entrepreneur will put together the organizational structure, people, systems, marketing plan, and other components necessary to implement the overall strategy.

OBJECTIVES: THEIR USE AND MISUSE IN PLANNING

Creating an organization's strategy tends to be an exercise restricted to top-level managers. Similarly, entrepreneurial planning is restricted to people who are starting up new businesses. But one element of planning permeates just about every manager's job—from CEOs to project managers and first-line supervisors. That's setting objectives.

Objectives or goals (we use the terms interchangeably), refer to desired outcomes for individuals, groups, or entire organizations. In this section we present the key concepts you need to know in order to use objectives effectively.

▶ Organizations Have Multiple Objectives

At first glance, you might assume that each organization has a singular objective—business firms want to make a profit; not-for-profit organizations want to provide a service efficiently. But closer examination demonstrates that all organizations have multiple objectives. Businesses also seek to increase market share, develop new products, move into new markets, satisfy employee welfare, and be responsible citizens.[55] For instance, Haworth, Inc., the office furniture manufacturer, states that in addition to seeking a fair return on investment, the company's objectives include complete customer satisfaction, the pursuit of quality, and employee development.[56]

Or consider the objectives of a church. A church provides a "road to heaven through absolution." But it also assists the underprivileged in its community and acts as a place for church members to congregate socially.

No one measure can evaluate effectively whether an organization is performing successfully. And because organizations seek to satisfy multiple constituencies, it's only logical that they also have multiple objectives.

▶ Real Versus Stated Objectives

Allstate says, "Our goal is to be known by consumers as the best insurer in America." Bell Atlantic's annual report states that the company is "responding to the imperative of global competition with greater personal responsibility and the power of teamwork." Southern Illinois University's catalogue says that it "emphasizes a commitment to quality education."

The statements you find in an organization's charter, annual report, mission statement, brochures, public relations announcements, or in public statements made by managers are **stated objectives**. They are official announcements of what an organization says—and what it wants various constituencies to believe—are its objectives. However, they are often conflicting and excessively influenced by what society believes organizations *should* do.

The conflict in stated goals exists because organizations respond to a vast array of constituencies or stakeholders. And, as we noted in chapter 2, these stakeholders typically evaluate the organization by different criteria. As a result, management is forced to say different things to different audiences. For example, in the summer of 1995, as part of a U.S. effort to force the Japanese to open their markets to U.S. products, President Bill Clinton imposed a short-lived 100 percent tariff on thirteen luxury automobile models sold by the Japanese.[57] This tariff put executives at Lexus, Infiniti, Acura, Mazda, and Mitsubishi in an unpleasant situation as they sought to get the tariff lifted. To Clinton, trade officials, and legislators, the auto executives were saying that the tariff would throw many U.S. workers out of work and that dealerships would go out of business. At the same time, attempting to reassure their dealers, owners, and potential customers, these same executives were saying that they were committed to the U.S. market for the long haul and would provide financial support to their dealers. These Japanese auto executives had explicitly presented themselves in one way to the government and another way to their dealers and the public. Was one true and the other false? No. Both were true, but they were in conflict.

Or consider a couple of recent quotes by CEOs, pulled from their company's annual report, on their firm's commitment to their employees.[58] Henry Duques of First Data Corp. said, "I would like to thank all of the 22,000 employees of FDC for their exceptional efforts. . . . It is the dedication and skill of many people working very hard that creates the type of success that we have enjoyed. We are committed to creating an environment where talented people come to work and stay with our company." John Stafford of American Home Products said, "Our skilled, dedicated, and hard-working employees remain our most important asset." The irony of these comments is that in the preceding year, First Data had cut 1,400 jobs and American Home Products had laid off 6,500. These CEOs may state that employees are their firm's most important asset but their behavior suggests otherwise.

The objectives we described previously from Allstate, Bell Atlantic, and Southern Illinois University all contain considerable ambiguity and social desirability. And these organizations' objectives are not unique. Stated objectives tend to be vague, and they are more likely to represent management's public relations skills than to act as meaningful guides to what the organization is actually seeking to accomplish. What executives, for example, would admit that their organization sought "mediocrity," "to meet minimal quality standards," or "to treat our employees as disposable resources"?

The fact is that an organization's stated objectives are often quite irrelevant to what actually goes on in that organization.[59] In a corporation, for instance, one statement of objectives is issued to stockholders, another to customers, and still others to employees and to the public.[60]

The overall objectives stated by top management should be treated for what they are: "fiction produced by an organization to account for, explain, or rationalize to particular audiences rather than as valid and reliable indications of purpose."[61] The content of objectives is substantially determined by what constituencies want to hear. Moreover, it is simpler for management to state a set of consistent, understandable objectives than to explain a multiplicity of objectives.

If you want to know what an organization's **real objectives** are, closely observe what members of the organization actually do. Actions define priorities. The university that proclaims the objectives of limiting class size, facilitating close student-faculty relations, and actively involving students in the learning process, and then puts its students into lecture halls of 300 or more, is not unusual. Nor is the automobile service center that pro-

> The fact is that an organization's stated objectives are often quite irrelevant to what actually goes on in that organization.

motes high-quality, low-cost repairs and then gives mediocre service at high prices. An awareness that real and stated objectives can deviate is important, if for no other reason than because it can help you explain what might otherwise seem to be management inconsistencies.

The Value of Objectives

The previous discussion shouldn't be interpreted as a blanket indictment of stated objectives. Overall organizational objectives might be more style than substance, but unit objectives and those established for individual employees are more substance than style. For instance, there is an overwhelming amount of evidence to demonstrate that people perform better with goals than without them.

The case for the value of objectives was proposed 30 years ago.[62] Known as **goal-setting theory**, it claimed that specific goals increase performance; that difficult goals, when accepted, result in higher performance than do easy goals; and that feedback leads to higher performance than does the lack of feedback. The evidence strongly supports those three claims.[63]

Specific hard goals produce a higher level of output than does a generalized goal of "do your best." The specificity of the goal itself seems to act as an internal stimulus and encourages people to strive to meet the goal. If factors such as ability and acceptance of the goals are held constant, the evidence also demonstrates that the more difficult the goal, the higher the level of performance. Of course, it's logical to assume that easier goals are more likely to be accepted. But once an employee accepts a hard task, he or she will exert a high level of effort until the goal is achieved, lowered, or abandoned. Finally, people will do better when they get feedback on how well they are progressing toward their goals because feedback helps to identify discrepancies between what they have done and what they want to do.

From Concepts to Skills: Management by Objectives (MBO)

How do you apply goal-setting theory? You implement a **management by objectives (MBO)** program.[64] MBO converts overall organizational objectives into specific objectives for organizational units and individual members. It provides a process by which objectives cascade down through the organization. The organization's overall objectives are translated into specific objectives for each succeeding level—division, department, individual—in the organization. When in place, MBO creates a hierarchy of objectives that links objectives at one level to those at the next level.

The following eight-step process captures the essential features of an MBO program. You can improve your employees' performance by helping them set goals using this process.

1. *Identify an employee's key job tasks.* Begin by defining what it is you want your employee to accomplish. This definition is derived from your unit's goals. When all the employees in your unit achieve their individual goals, your unit should achieve its overall goals.
2. *Establish specific and challenging goals for each key task.* This step should include both quantity and quality dimensions of performance. Examples: to deliver the project within 3 percent of budget; to process all telephone orders within 24 hours of receipt; to keep returns to less than 1 percent of sales.
3. *Specify the deadline for each goal.* Putting a realistic deadline on each goal reduces ambiguity. Example: to deliver the project within 3 percent of budget by November 1, 1999.

Scott Grocki, president of Grocki Magic Studios (with business manager, Jennifer Brown), believes in the power of goals to make things happen. He sets weekly, monthly, six-month, and long-term goals—and takes care to insure that they all interrelate. Every Monday, he posts new weekly goals next to the office telephone. And he reviews monthly and six-month goals every couple of weeks. Two of his long-term goals include appearing on national television and creating a Broadway show revolving around magic.

4. *Have the employee actively participate.* Having employees participate in defining goals increases acceptance of goals. However, the request for participation must be sincere. Employees need to believe that you are truly interested in their input.

5. *Prioritize goals.* Presumably, employees have multiple goals. Prioritizing encourages employees to take action and expend effort on each goal in proportion to its importance.

6. *Rate goals for difficulty and importance.* Goals should not be chosen because they're easy to achieve. By rating goals for their difficulty and importance, individuals can be given credit for trying difficult goals, even if they don't fully achieve them.

7. *Build in feedback mechanisms to assess goal progress.* Feedback lets employees know whether or not their level of effort is sufficient to attain the goal. Feedback should be frequent.

8. *Link rewards to goal attainment.* Goal progress or attainment should be reinforced by performance-based rewards. These rewards should reflect goal difficulty as well as goal outcomes.

▶ The Downside of Objectives

Despite the strong evidence linking specific goals and high employee performance, not everyone enthusiastically endorses the value of objectives. The loudest critic was undoubtedly the late quality guru W. Edwards Deming.[65] He argued that specific numerical goals do more harm than good. Since people tend to focus on the goals by which they will be judged, Deming claimed quantitative goals encourage employees to direct their effort toward quantity of output and away from quality. In addition, people treat specific goals as ceilings rather than as floors. They set a goal, achieve it, and then tend to rest on their laurels. So specific goals tend to limit people's potential by deterring efforts for continual improvement. At the other extreme, overly demanding goals, especially when unilaterally dictated from above, put pressure on individuals to cheat or misrepresent data in order to achieve the goals. For instance, an investigation of Bausch & Lomb found division managers engaging in numerous questionable practices—such as inflating revenues by faking sales, shipping products that were never ordered, and forcing distributors to take unwanted merchandise—largely because the company's CEO insisted that managers achieve double-digit annual growth objectives and fired those who didn't.[66]

These criticisms of specific goals are potentially correct. But they can be overcome.[67] One answer is for managers to ensure that employees have multiple goals and that they address quality of output as well as quantity. A production worker or team should be evaluated on number of rejects as well as on total output. Similarly, assessing the number of complaints registered against service employees adds a quality goal to their performance evaluation. Another solution is to treat goal setting as an ongoing activity. Goals should be regularly reviewed and updated. Further, individuals should be rewarded for setting difficult goals even if they aren't fully achieved. Goals are more likely to limit individual effort when people believe they'll be punished for not reaching them. So employees should be encouraged to set ambitious goals that stretch their capabilities, and they should not be made to fear repercussions if they fail.[68]

It's well substantiated that the work lives of senior executives is pressure-packed.[69] They have far more demands on them than they have time. They're kept constantly busy with meetings, phone calls, e-mail, reviewing paperwork, road trips, conferences, and the like. But time pressures aren't the sole province of executives. Many nonexecutives feel similar

PERSONAL PLANNING: BUILDING YOUR TIME MANAGEMENT SKILLS

Timex CEO Mike Jacobi downloads his daily schedule onto a special Data Link watch. This watch allows him to always have his schedule for the next 30 days on his wrist.

pressures and could benefit from having effective time-management skills. In this section, some suggestions to help you better manage your time are presented. You will see that **time management** is actually a personal form of scheduling. Managers who use their time effectively know what activities they want to accomplish, the best order in which to do the activities, and when they want to complete those activities.

Do time-management skills work? Most of the evidence is positive. Studies indicate, for instance, that positive time-management practices by students lead to higher grade point averages.[70] These practices also lead to higher employee performance and satisfaction.[71] Although the benefits of good time-management skills don't appear to be experienced universally,[72] it appears reasonably safe to conclude that you can get more done, and do it better, if you practice effective time-management skills.

Time As a Scarce Resource

Time is a unique resource in that, if it's wasted, it can *never* be replaced. People talk about *saving time*, but time can never actually be saved. It can't be stockpiled for use in some future period. If lost, it can't be retrieved. When a minute is gone, it's gone forever.

The positive side of this resource is that all managers have it in equal amount. Although money, labor, and other resources are distributed unequally, thus putting some managers at a disadvantage, *every* manager is allotted 24 hours every day, 7 days a week. Some just use their allotments better than others.

Focusing on Discretionary Time

Managers can't control all their time. They are routinely interrupted and must respond to unexpected crises. It's necessary, therefore, to differentiate between response time and discretionary time.[73]

The majority of a manager's time is spent responding to requests, demands, and problems initiated by others. We call this **response time** and treat it as uncontrollable. The portion that *is* under a manager's control is called **discretionary time**. Most suggestions

Analyzing Activities for Importance and Urgency

EXHIBIT 5-5

Rate each activity for

Importance
- A. Very important: must be done
- B. Important: should be done
- C. Not so important: may be useful
- D. Unimportant: doesn't accomplish anything

Urgency
- A. Very urgent
- B. Urgent: should be done now
- C. Not urgent: can be done sometime later
- D. Time not a factor

offered to improve time management apply to its discretionary component. Why? Because this is the only part that is manageable!

Unfortunately, for most managers, particularly those in the lower and middle ranks of organizations, discretionary time makes up only about 25 percent of their work hours.[74] Moreover, discretionary time tends to be available in small segments—5 minutes here, 5 minutes there. Thus it's extremely difficult to use effectively. The challenge, then, is to know what time is discretionary and then to organize activities so as to accumulate discretionary time in blocks large enough to be useful. Managers who are good at identifying and organizing their discretionary time accomplish significantly more, and the things they accomplish are more likely to be high-priority activities (thus contributing to their performance effectiveness).

▶ How Do You Use Your Time?

How do managers, or any individual for that matter, determine how well they use their time? The answer is that they should keep a log or journal of daily activities for a short period of time, and then evaluate the data they gather.

Try keeping such a journal. When it's complete, you'll have a detailed time and activity log. Then you can analyze how effectively you use your time. Rate each activity in terms of its importance and urgency (see Exhibit 5-5 for a sample rating you can use). If you had a number of activities receiving C's or D's, you'll find the next section valuable, as it provides detailed guidelines for better time management.[75]

▶ Toward Effective Time-Management Skills

The essence of time management is to use your time *effectively*. This means you must know the objectives you want to accomplish, the activities that will lead to the accomplishment of those objectives, and the importance and urgency of each activity. The following describes a five-step process for time management and some suggestions for how to use your time most effectively.

A FIVE-STEP PROCESS   Where do you begin? You can use this five-step process as a guide:

1. *List your objectives.* What specific objectives have you set for yourself and the unit you manage? If you're using MBO, these objectives are already in place.
2. *Rank the objectives according to their importance.* Not all objectives are of equal importance. Given the limitations on your time, you want to make sure you give highest priority to the most important objectives.
3. *List the activities necessary to achieve your objectives.* What specific actions do you need to take to achieve your objectives? Again, if you're using MBO, these action plans are already defined.
4. *For each objective, assign priorities to the various activities required to reach the objective.* This step imposes a second set of priorities. Here, you need to emphasize both importance and urgency. If the activity is not important, you should consider delegating it to someone else. If it's not urgent, it can usually wait. This step will identify activities you *must* do, those you *should* do, those you'll get to *when you can*, and those that can be *delegated to others.*
5. *Schedule your activities according to the priorities you've set.* The final step is to prepare a daily plan. Every morning, or at the end of the previous workday, make a list of the five or so most important things you want to do for the day. If the list grows to ten or more activities, it becomes unmanageable and ineffective. Then set priorities for the activities listed on the basis of importance and urgency.

FOLLOW THE 10-90 PRINCIPLE   Most managers produce 90 percent of their results using only 10 percent of their time. It's easy for managers to get caught up in the activity trap and confuse actions with accomplishment. Those who use their time well make sure that the crucial 10 percent gets highest priority.

KNOW YOUR PRODUCTIVITY CYCLE   Each of us has a daily energy cycle that influences when we feel most productive or unproductive. Some of us are morning people, whereas others are late-afternoon or evening people. Don't fight your natural cycle. Understand it and use it to your advantage. Handle your most demanding problems during the high part of your energy cycle, when you are most alert and productive. Relegate routine and undemanding tasks to your low periods.

REMEMBER PARKINSON'S LAW   Parkinson's law says that work expands to fill the time available. The implication for time management is that you can schedule *too* much for a task. If you give yourself an excess amount of time to perform an activity, you're likely to pace yourself so that you use up the entire time allocation even though it may not have needed that much time to complete.

GROUP LESS IMPORTANT ACTIVITIES TOGETHER   Set aside a regular time period each day to make phone calls, respond to e-mail, do follow-ups, and perform other kinds of "busy work." Ideally, this should be during your low cycle. This avoids duplication, waste, and redundancy; it also prevents trivial matters from crowding out high-priority tasks.

MINIMIZE DISRUPTIONS When possible, try to minimize disruptions by setting aside as a block of discretionary time that part of the day when you are most productive. Then try to insulate yourself from interruptions. During this time, you should limit access to your work area. Refuse phone calls or visits during this time. You can set aside other blocks of time each day when your door is open for unexpected visits and when you can initiate or return all your calls.

There is a variety of additional material available on the CD-ROM and companion Web site that accompany this text. You can access this information through the CD-ROM or by visiting the Web site at <**www.prenhall.com/robbins**>.

SUMMARY

(This summary is organized by the chapter-opening learning objectives on page 136.)

1. Planning gives direction and coordinates effort, reduces uncertainty and the impact of change, reduces overlapping and wasteful activities, and establishes objectives or standards that facilitate control.

2. SWOT analysis matches the internal strengths and weaknesses of the organization with opportunities and threats in the environment. Its value lies in finding opportunities in the environment that can be exploited with the distinctive competencies possessed by the organization.

3. Cost-leadership strategies seek to be the lowest-cost operator, while still providing an adequate product or service. A differentiation strategy allows an organization to charge more, but the higher price must be justified by customers in terms of value added. A focus strategy is a narrowly segmented cost-leadership or differentiation strategy.

4. Successful strategy implementation encompasses: (1) the choice of a correct strategy; (2) superordinate goals to unite organizational members; (3) a strategy that is congruent with the organization's core competencies or skills; (4) a supportive structure; (5) supportive systems; (6) top management style that provides substantive and symbolic commitment to the strategy; and (7) a staff with the ability and skills to carry out the strategy.

5. Project management involves specific programs that are temporary in nature and that have definitive deadlines. Planning and scheduling are critical to the success of each project.

6. Entrepreneurship is a process by which individuals pursue opportunities, fulfilling needs and wants through innovation, without regard to the resources they currently control.

7. Entrepreneurs have a high need for achievement, a strong belief they can control their own destiny, and a desire to take only moderate risks.

8. Stated and real objectives may differ because organizations try to satisfy multiple stakeholders who evaluate the organization using different criteria. In addition, organizations are under pressure to state objectives that are socially desirable. These factors often lead to stated objectives that differ significantly from what the organization is actually doing.

9. To set up an MBO program, you need to identify an employee's key job tasks; establish specific and challenging goals for each key task; specify the deadline for each goal; have employees participate; prioritize goals; rate goals for difficulty and importance; build in feedback; and link rewards to goal attainment.

10. To better manage your time, you should: (a) make a list of objectives, (b) rank the objectives in order of importance, (c) list the activities necessary to achieve the objectives, (d) assign priorities to each activity, and (e) schedule your activities according to the priorities established.

REVIEW QUESTIONS

1. Contrast strategic and operational plans.
2. What is the commitment concept, and why is it important?
3. What is the relationship between planning and organizational performance?
4. What advice would you give Jeff Bezo for helping him sustain Amazon.com's competitive advantage?
5. How do entrepreneurs and traditional managers differ?
6. What is goal-setting theory?

7. What criticisms have been made against the use of specific objectives?

8. "Business firms have one and only one objective—to maximize profit." Do you agree or disagree? Support your answer.

9. If stated objectives are often "fiction produced by an organization," what value is there in a formal mission statement that defines an organization's purpose?

10. How might a manager use his or her discretionary time more effectively?

IF I WERE THE MANAGER . . .

"Take This Project and Run with It"

After finishing your degree in business, you spent four years on Wall Street working in mergers and acquisition. Then you spent nearly two years as a marketing consultant with a major consulting firm. Three months ago you joined XelBio, a biotechnology firm. Started in 1992, XelBio is one of the fastest growing companies in America. Last year, sales hit $132 million. This year, that number will exceed $200 million. Your job title is "Assistant to the CEO." Since joining XelBio, you've spent most of your time helping the VP of marketing reorganize the sales staff. Yesterday, your boss called you in and gave you a new assignment.

"Our production needs are rapidly outgrowing our present facilities. Our two plants, the one here in Berkeley and the other in Fremont [both in the San Francisco Bay area], will meet our sales projections through next year. Then we're in trouble. I want

you to head up a project to solve this problem. I don't know if we should build a new plant or outsource the production. If we have to build a new facility, I want you to coordinate the whole thing. I figure this job is going to take you at least three or four months. I'm sending an e-mail to everyone to let them know your assignment and to ask them to give you any help you need. I consider this project your responsibility, so run with it."

You spent a restless night. Where do you begin? XelBio employs nearly 600 people. There are three vice presidents (marketing, administration, and research and development) and a director of plant operations. Each of the VPs have a small staff; the director of plant operations has two plant managers and a facilities engineer reporting to him.

You figure you should start with a meeting. But who do you invite? And what should the agenda cover? And what kind of a structure should this project have?

SKILL EXERCISE

Time Management

Complete the following questionnaire. Check the answer that best describes your behavior:

	Always	Frequently	Sometimes	Infrequently	Never
1. I make lists of the things I have to do each day.	_____	_____	_____	_____	_____
2. I plan my day before it starts.	_____	_____	_____	_____	_____
3. I make a schedule of the activities I have to do on workdays.	_____	_____	_____	_____	_____
4. I write a set of goals for myself each day.	_____	_____	_____	_____	_____
5. I usually keep my desk clear of everything other than what I am currently working on.	_____	_____	_____	_____	_____
6. I have a set of goals for the entire quarter.	_____	_____	_____	_____	_____

7. The night before a major project
   is due, I am usually still working
   on it.

How would you rate your time-management skills? Based on the results from this questionnaire, write down some specific actions you can do to make more efficient use of your time in the future. Put a note in your day planner one month from now to review these actions to assess your progress.

This exercise is based on an instrument described in J. Barling, E. K. Kelloway, and D. Cheung, "Time Management and Achievement Striving Interact to Predict Car Sales Performance," *Journal of Applied Psychology*, December 1996, p. 823.

TEAM ACTIVITY

Building a Sustainable Competitive Advantage for the Stone Oven

Tatianna and John Emerman were both engineers by background, living in Cleveland, Ohio. Having had enough of the corporate life, Tatianna decided in 1991 to become an entrepreneur. She began baking specialty breads in their home and wholesaling them to restaurants and local grocery stores. Response to their Assiago Cheese, Pugliese, Raisin Walnut, and similar breads was favorable. The business grew. In 1995, John quit his job and joined Tatianna full-time. That year, they expanded by opening up a retail bread bakery and café, the Stone Oven in Cleveland Heights. Within a few months, the bakery and café were generating approximately 40 percent of the business's overall revenue.

The Stone Oven bakery and café developed a strong local following. The products were high quality, the café was enticingly well designed, and the Emermans were on the front end of the growing popularity of specialty breads. The latter point, however, was bad news as well as good. The Stone Oven, which opened to almost no serious competition, was in 1998 facing several new competitors. Great Harvest, a chain of bread shops, had opened on the same block. And several independent bread bakeries were scouting for locations in the neighborhood. Suddenly, everyone seemed to be wanting to capitalize on the speciality bread market.

Tatianna and John have a problem. They have created a solid business. But their historical competitive advantage—unique quality breads—is under siege. If the Stone Oven is to survive, it is going to have to react to these new competitors.

Break into teams of four or five. Review the Stone Oven's business strategy. Then develop a plan that will provide them with a sustainable competitive advantage.

CASE EXERCISE

Hamburger Habit

When Michael Richman graduated from the University of Connecticut in 1991, he turned his part-time job at McDonald's into a full-time one. Starting off as assistant manager in Hartford, he quickly became a manager and then a district supervisor.

One day, in spring of 1998, Michael saw a "For Sale" sign on a piece of property he passed every day on his way to work. The property was on a major street with high traffic volume. He envisioned the site as an ideal location for a fast-food hamburger restaurant. Michael thought that this vacant property might be "opportunity knocking." Maybe it was time to strike out on his own. But instead of working through a major franchisor—such as McDonald's or Burger King—Michael wanted to go it alone. He figured the big money and future would be in creating his own chain.

With money from a small trust fund left to him by a grandfather and financial help from his parents, Michael opened Hamburger Habit in June 1999. As Michael quickly found out, in contrast to buying a franchise, he had to build his business from scratch. He had to, for example, oversee the design and the internal layout of his building, create the menu, find suppliers, select uniforms, hire staff, and develop procedures and systems.

QUESTIONS

1. Contrast Michael's planning efforts for Hamburger Habit with how planning might have been done if Michael had bought a McDonald's franchise.

2. Build a strategic plan that Michael might use for his new business. Begin with a mission statement.

VIDEO CASE EXERCISE

Not Just Toying Around

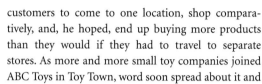

The toy industry, like all others, has its good points and its bad points. One person who's trying to take advantage of the good points—that is, what he sees as the many growth opportunities in the toy industry—is Charlie Woo of Los Angeles.

Woo and his family came to the United States from Hong Kong in the late 1970s. To support the family, his mother and father initially started a restaurant but found that venture to be too time consuming. They looked to start another business and settled on the toy industry. By using their contacts in Hong Kong and by bringing their four sons into the business, the Woo family opened ABC Toys. The company's initial goal was to manufacture and distribute toys to small wholesalers who could not get products from the large toy makers because they weren't big enough customers; that is, they didn't buy in enough volume. ABC Toys had identified a specific niche and wasn't even attempting to compete with the likes of Mattel or the other large toy manufacturers. Charlie, who was just about to complete his Ph.D. in physics from UCLA, found himself making a major career switch—from physics to toys.

ABC Toys purchased several run-down warehouse buildings on a blighted corner of downtown Los Angeles. Charlie's vision was to encourage other small toy manufacturers and distributors to rent from them and together create a "toy town." He recalls that in the beginning ABC Toys was located there by itself. But Charlie reasoned that this wholesale district would enable customers to come to one location, shop comparatively, and, he hoped, end up buying more products than they would if they had to travel to separate stores. As more and more small toy companies joined ABC Toys in Toy Town, word soon spread about it and customers began coming from all over. Now there are more than 500 wholesale toy dealers within a few blocks of each other in Toy Town.

In 1989, Charlie and one other brother spun out of ABC Toys to form Megatoys. This company now employs 30 people and has hit $15 million in sales. And Charlie isn't finished yet! He believes that there is still good potential for growth in his business. Why? The changing global trade environment is opening up many potentially profitable areas. After all, in this business, if you want to be successful, you can't just toy around!

QUESTIONS

1. Charlie wants to continue Megatoys' growth. How might he use strategic management concepts to help him achieve his goals?

2. Would SWOT analysis be useful to Charlie in managing Megtoys? Why or why not? Explain your choice.

3. Charlie has asked you to make a presentation to his employees about competitive advantage. Draw up a list of the main ideas you'd want to tell them.

Source: Based on *Small Business Today, Show 107*.

NOTES

1. W. C. Taylor, "Who's Writing the Book on Web Business?" *Fast Company*, October/November 1996, pp. 132–33; M. Krantz, "Amazonian Challenge," *Time*, April 14, 1997, p. 71; R. E. Stross, "Why Barnes & Noble May Crush Amazon," *Fortune*, September 29, 1997, pp. 248–50; C. Willis, "Does Amazon.com Really Matter?" *Forbes ASAP*, April 6, 1998, pp. 55–58; and R. D. Hof, "A New Chapter for Amazon.com," *Business Week*, August 17, 1998, p. 39.

2. See, for instance, M. A. Lyles, I. S. Baird, J. B. Orris, and D. F. Kuratko, "Formalized Planning in Small Business: Increasing Strategic Choices," *Journal of Small Business Management*, April 1993, pp. 38–50.

3. R. Ackoff, "A Concept of Corporate Planning," *Long Range Planning*, September 1970, p. 3.

4. J. Finegan, "Everything According to Plan," *Inc.*, March 1995, pp. 78–85.

5. P. Foster, "By-the-Book Brilliance," *Canadian Business*, May 1994, p. 78.

6. H. Mintzberg, *The Rise and Fall of Strategic Planning* (New York: Free Press, 1994).

7. Ibid.

8. H. Mintzberg, "The Strategy Concept II: Another Look at Why Organizations Need Strategies," *California Management Review*, Fall 1987, p. 26.

9. Mintzberg, *The Rise and Fall of Strategic Planning*.

10. G. Hamel and C. K. Prahalad, *Competing for the Future* (Boston: Harvard Business School Press, 1994).

11. D. Miller, "The Architecture of Simplicity," *Academy of Management Review*, January 1993, pp. 116–38.

12. See, for instance, K. B. Boyd, "Strategic Planning and Financial Performance: A Meta-Analytic Review," *Journal of Management Studies*, July 1991, pp. 353–74; N. Capon, J. U. Farley, and J. M. Hulbert, "Strategic Planning and Financial Performance: More Evidence," *Journal of Management Studies*, January 1994, pp. 105–10; and C. C. Miller and L. B. Cardinal, "Strategic Planning and Firm Performance: A Synthesis of More Than Two Decades of Research," *Academy of Management Journal*, December 1994, pp. 1649–65.

13. The Sony Music Canada and Newport Shipping Co. examples are cited in C. K. Bart, "Sex, Lies, and Mission Statements," *Business Horizons*, November–December 1997, p. 11.

14. S. Nelton, "Put Your Purpose in Writing," *Nation's Business*, February 1994, p. 62.

15. Ibid., p. 63.

16. G. Fuchsberg, "'Visioning' Missions Becomes Its Own Mission," *Wall Street Journal*, January 7, 1994, p. B1.

17. Nelton, "Put Your Purpose in Writing," pp. 61–64.

18. G. Eisenstodt, "Unidentical Twins," *Forbes*, July 5, 1993, p. 42; and D. Hulme, "The Sharp End of Innovation," *Asian Business*, February 1995, pp. 6–7.

19. B. O'Reilly, "The Rent-a-Car Jocks Who Made Enterprise #1," *Fortune*, October 28, 1996, pp. 125–28; "Sustainability, Not Growth, at Patagonia," *At Work*, May/June 1993, p. 1; and R. Henkoff, "Getting beyond Downsizing," *Fortune*, January 10, 1994, pp. 58–60.

20. See T. T. Herbert and H. Deresky, "Generic Strategies: An Empirical Investigation of Typology Validity and Strategy Content," *Strategic Management Journal*, March–April 1987, pp. 135–47.

21. "Sustainability, Not Growth, at Patagonia," p. 20.

22. W. P. Barrett, "Johnny One-Note," *Forbes*, March 8, 1999, pp. 76–77.

23. Henkoff, "Getting beyond Downsizing."

24. Ibid.

25. See S. E. Jackson and J. E. Dutton, "Discerning Threats and Opportunities," *Administrative Science Quarterly*, September 1988, pp. 370–87.

26. J. Rossant, "Olivetti Tries to Stagger to Its Knees," *Business Week*, March 22, 1993, p. 19.

27. J. B. Barney, "Looking Inside for Competitive Advantage," *Academy of Management Executive*, November 1995, pp. 49–61; J. M. Higgins, "Achieving *the* Core Competence— It's as Easy as 1,2,3, . . . 47,48,49," *Business Horizons*, March–April 1996, pp. 27–32; and W. J. Duncan, P. M. Ginter, and L. E. Swayne, "Competitive Advantage and Internal Organizational Assessment." *Academy of Management Executive*, August 1998, pp. 6–16.

28. See, for instance, R. E. Miles and C. C. Snow, *Organizational Strategy, Structure, and Process* (New York: McGraw-Hill, 1978); M. E. Porter, *Competitive Strategy: Techniques for Analyzing Industries and Competitors* (New York: Free Press, 1980); D. C. Hambrick, I. C. Macmillan, and D. L. Day, "Strategic Attributes and Performance in the BCG Matrix: A PIMS-Based Analysis of Industrial Product Businesses," *Academy of Management Journal*, September 1982, pp. 510–31; and M. Treacy and F. Wiersema, *The Discipline of Market Leaders* (Reading, MA: Addison-Wesley, 1995).

29. M. E. Porter, *Competitive Advantage: Creating and Sustaining Superior Performance* (New York: Free Press, 1985); E. Mosakowski, "A Resource-Based Perspective on the Dynamic Strategy–Performance Relationship: An Empirical Examination of the Focus and Differentiation Strategies in Entrepreneurial Firms," *Journal of Management*, Winter 1993, pp. 819–39; A. Miller and G. G. Dess, "Assessing Porter's (1980) Model in Terms of Its Generalizability, Accuracy, and Simplicity," *Journal of Management Studies*, July 1993, pp. 553–82.

30. R. H. Waterman Jr., T. J. Peters, and J. R. Phillips, "Structure Is Not Organization," *Business Horizons*, June 1980, pp. 14–26.

31. B. O'Brian, "Southwest Wins Pilots' Accord Offering No Wage Boost in First Five of 10 Years," *Wall Street Journal*, November 18, 1994, p. A2; "Southwest's New Deal," *Fortune*, January 16, 1995, p. 94; and D. Jones, "Low-Cost Carrier Still Challenges Industry," *USA Today*, July 10, 1995, p. 5B.

32. E. E. Adam Jr. and R. J. Ebert, *Production & Operations Management*, 5th ed. (Upper Saddle River, NJ: Prentice Hall, 1992), p. 333.

33. See, for instance, J. W. Weiss and R. K. Wysocki, *5-Phase Project Management* (Reading, MA: Addison-Wesley, 1992); J. K. Pinto, "The Power of Project Management," *Industry Week*, August 18, 1997, pp. 138–40; and T. D. Conkright, "So You're Going to Manage a Project," *Training*, January 1998, pp. 62–67.

34. T. A. Stewart, "The Corporate Jungle Spawns a New Species: The Project Manager," *Fortune*, July 10, 1995, pp. 179–80.

35. Ibid.

36. D. Stamps, "Lights! Camera! Project Management!" *Training*, January 1997, p. 52.

37. T. A. Stewart, "The Corporate Jungle Spawns a New Species."

38. This discussion is based on R. S. Russell and B. W. Taylor III, *Production and Operations Management* (Upper Saddle River, NJ: Prentice Hall, 1995), p. 827.

39. D. Stamps, "Lights! Camera! Project Management!" p. 52.

40. T. A. Stewart, "The Corporate Jungle Spawns a New Species."

41. D. Stamps, "Lights! Camera! Project Management!" p. 52.

42. C. Burck, "The Real World of the Entrepreneur," *Fortune*, April 5, 1993, pp. 64–65.

43. See, for example, J. B. Cunningham and J. Lischeron, "Defining Entrepreneurship," *Journal of Small Business Management*, January 1991, pp. 45–61.

44. Adapted from H. H. Stevenson, M. J. Roberts, and H. I. Grousbeck, *New Business Ventures and the Entrepreneur* (Homewood, IL: Irwin, 1989).

45. See, for instance, T. M. Begley and D. P. Boyd, "A Comparison of Entrepreneurs and Managers of Small Business Firms," *Journal of Management*, Spring 1987, pp. 99–108.

46. P. F. Drucker, *Innovation and Entrepreneurship* (New York: Harper & Row, 1985).

47. G. Pinchot III, *Intrapreneuring: Or, Why You Don't Have to Leave the Corporation to Become an Entrepreneur* (New York: Harper & Row, 1985).

48. K. H. Vesper, *New Venture Strategies* (Englewood Cliffs, NJ: Prentice Hall, 1980), p. 14.

49 See, for instance, J. P. Kotter, *The New Rules: How to Succeed in Today's Post-Corporate World* (New York: Free Press, 1995).

50. J. A. Hornaday, "Research about Living Entrepreneurs," in C. A. Kent, D. L. Sexton, and K. H. Vesper (eds.), *Encyclopedia of Entrepreneurship* (Englewood Cliffs, NJ: Prentice Hall, 1982), p. 28.

51. R. H. Brockhaus, "The Psychology of the Entrepreneur," in Kent, Sexton, and Vesper (eds.), *Encyclopedia of Entrepreneurship*, pp. 41–49; and M. Oneal, "Just What Is an Entrepreneur?," *Business Week/Enterprise* 1993, November 1, 1993, pp. 104–12.

52. This section is based on R. D. Hisrich, "Entrepreneurship/Intrapreneurship," *American Psychologist*, February 1990, pp. 209–22; and O. Port, "Starting Up Again—And Again and Again," *Business Week*, August 25, 1997, pp. 99–102.

53. H. H. Stevenson and D. E. Gumpert, "The Heart of Entrepreneurship," *Harvard Business Review*, March–April 1985, pp. 85–94.

54. E. M. Friedman (ed.), "Almanac," *Inc. The State of Small Business, 1997*, p. 112.

55. See Y. K. Shetty, "New Look at Corporate Goals," *California Management Review*, Winter 1979, pp. 71–79.

56. Nelton, "Put Your Purpose in Writing," p. 62.

57. J. Bennet, "A Case of Nerves at the High End," *New York Times*, June 24, 1995, p. Y17.

58. Cited in T. A. Stewart, "Watch What We Did, Not What We Said," *Fortune*, April 15, 1996, p. 140.

59. See, for instance, C. K. Warriner, "The Problem of Organizational Purpose," *Sociological Quarterly*, Spring 1965, pp.

139–46; and J. Pfeffer, *Organizational Design* (Arlington Heights, IL: AHM, 1978), pp. 5–12.

60. Warriner, "The Problem of Organizational Purpose."

61. Ibid.

62. E. A. Locke, "Toward a Theory of Task Motivation and Incentives," *Organizational Behavior and Human Performance*, May 1968, pp. 157–89.

63. G. P. Latham and G. A. Yukl, "A Review of Research on the Application of Goal Setting in Organizations," *Academy of Management Journal*, December 1975, pp. 824–45; E. A. Locke, K. N. Shaw, L. M. Saari, and G. P. Latham, "Goal Setting and Task Performance," *Psychological Bulletin*, January 1981, pp. 125–52; A. J. Mento, R. P. Steel, and R. J. Karren, "A Meta-Analytic Study of the Effects of Goal Setting on Task Performance: 1966–1984," *Organizational Behavior and Human Decision Processes*, February 1987, pp. 52–83; M. E. Tubbs, "Goal Setting: A Meta-Analytic Examination of the Empirical Evidence," *Journal of Applied Psychology*, August 1986, pp. 474–83; E. A. Locke and G. P. Latham, *A Theory of Goal Setting and Task Performance* (Upper Saddle River, NJ: Prentice Hall, 1990); D. E. Terpstra and E. J. Rozell, "The Relationship of Goal Setting to Organizational Profitability," *Group & Organization Management*, September 1994, pp. 285–94; and T. D. Ludwig and E. Scott Geller, "Assigned versus Participative Goal Setting and Response Generalization: Managing Injury Control among Professional Pizza Deliverers," *Journal of Applied Psychology*, April 1997, pp. 253–61.

64. This section is based on S. P. Robbins and P. L. Hunsaker, *Training in InterPersonal Skills: TIPS for Managing People at Work*, 2nd ed. (Upper Saddle River, NJ: Prentice Hall, 1996), pp. 52–57.

65. W. E. Deming, *Out of the Crisis* (Cambridge, MA: MIT Center for Advanced Engineering Study, 1986).

66. M. Maremont, "Blind Ambition," *Business Week*, October 23, 1995, pp. 78–92; and M. Maremont, "Judgment Day at Bausch & Lomb," *Business Week*, December 25, 1995, p. 39.

67. See, for instance, P. P. Carson and K. D. Carson, "Deming versus Traditional Management Theorists on Goal Setting: Can Both Be Right?" *Business Horizons*, September–October 1993, pp. 79–84.

68. S. Tully, "Why to Go for Stretch Targets," *Fortune*, November 14, 1994, pp. 145–58.

69. See, for instance, H. Mintzberg, *The Nature of Managerial Work* (New York: Harper & Row, 1973); and S. Branch, "So Much Work, So Little Time," *Fortune*, February 3, 1997, pp. 115–17.

70. B. K. Britton and A. Tesser, "Effects of Time Management Practices on College Grades," *Journal of Educational Psychology*, September 1991, pp. 405–10.

71. F. J. Landy, H. Rastegary, J. Thayer, and C. Colvin, "Time Urgency: The Construct and Its Measurement," *Journal of Applied Psychology*, October 1991, pp. 644–57; and Y. M. Lim, "Time Dimensions of Work: Relationships with Perceived Organizational Performance," *Journal of Business and Psychology*, Spring 1993, pp. 91–102.

72. J. Barling, E. K. Kelloway, and D. Cheung, "Time Management and Achievement Striving Interact to Predict Car

Sales Performance," *Journal of Applied Psychology*, December 1996, pp. 821–26.

73. P. F. Drucker, *The Effective Executive* (New York: Harper & Row, 1967), pp. 47–51.

74. R. A. Webber, *To Be a Manager* (Homewood, IL: Irwin, 1981), p. 373.

75. For a more detailed discussion of these time-management suggestions, see J. T. McCay, *The Management of Time* (Englewood Cliffs, NJ: Prentice Hall, 1995); G. Griessman, *Time Tactics of Very Successful People* (New York: McGraw-Hill, 1996); and S. Rechtschaffen, *Time Shifting: Creating More Time for Your Life* (New York: Doubleday, 1996).

MONITORING PERFORMANCE THROUGH CONTROL SYSTEMS

WHY IS THERE SO MUCH MONTH LEFT AT THE END
OF THE MONEY?

ANONYMOUS

LEARNING OBJECTIVES

After studying this chapter, you should be able to:

1 ▸ Describe the steps in the control process.

2 ▸ Identify the various behavioral control devices available to managers.

3 ▸ Describe the objectives of the EOQ model.

4 ▸ Contrast data and information.

5 ▸ Trace the evolution of modern MIS.

6 ▸ Contrast incremental and zero-base budgets.

7 ▸ Create a PERT network.

8 ▸ Develop a workable control chart.

Ito-Yokado Co., the majority owner of 7-Eleven, is shipping the control system it uses in its more than 6,800 Japanese stores across the Pacific to the United States.[1] And American managers at 7-Eleven aren't too excited about the changes the new system will bring.

The system has been in place in Japan's 7-Elevens for several decades. Toshifumi Suzuki, Ito-Yokado's CEO, credits the system with doubling unit sales in Japan and dramatically cutting inventory costs. The average Japanese store currently turns over its inventory every 7 days, down from 25 days in the 1970s. Now Suzuki wants to bring this technology to the United States to improve the efficiency of the company's American operations.

What does this system look like? It essentially uses a "point-of-sale" computer to let headquarters know every time a clerk records a sale. To understand how it works, consider the life of Michiharu Endo, a manager of a Tokyo 7-Eleven. The computer schedules most of Endo's activities. It monitors how much time he spends using the analytical tools built into the cash register to track product sales. He's expected to spend his days reviewing sales data, demographic trends, and local weather forecasts graphed out on the computer screen. The idea is to help Endo fine-tune orders to a daily deadline. Based on his sales, he'll receive deliveries three times a day. The precise timing ensures that sandwiches, deli dishes, and other perishables are fresh and that none is wasted.

But the system also imposes a strict regimen on Endo. Headquarters ranks stores by how often their operators use the computer. Endo's store was recently accessing the computer to check on an average of about 600 products a week. An inspector from headquarters told Endo that wasn't enough. The inspector warned him "to shape up and use the computer more." As a backup computer beeps a high-pitched alarm that warns him it's 15 minutes before the 10:00 A.M. deadline for ordering, Endo says, "Sometimes I don't know who's running the store. It's like being under 24-hour surveillance; it's like being enslaved."

American 7-Eleven managers aren't looking forward to the new system. A Newark, New Jersey, owner says the system goes against American workers' desire for independence, and talks of a deep "philosophical difference" between America and Japan. Many experienced U.S. managers feel that they know how to stock their shelves and adjust their orders to reflect changes in the weather or special events. They bristle at the idea that "Big Brother" knows what's best for them and will be constantly monitoring their every action.

Regardless of how thoughtful and insightful management is in developing plans, there is no guarantee that people in the organization are carrying them out properly. For example, objectives give people specific direction. However, just stating objectives or having employees accept your objectives is no guarantee that the necessary actions will be accomplished. The effective manager, therefore, needs to follow up to ensure that the actions that others are supposed to take and the objectives they are supposed to achieve are, in fact, being taken and achieved. This follow-up is referred to as *control*. It needn't be as intrusive or threatening as those used by 7-Eleven. But every organization needs controls.

In this chapter, we describe the control process, identify those elements in the organization that management seeks to control, demonstrate the role of computerized information systems in control, discuss the downsides of controls, and present some basic control tools for effective management.

THE CONTROL PROCESS

Control is the process of monitoring activities to ensure that they are being accomplished as planned and of correcting any significant deviations. Managers can't really know whether their units are performing properly until they've evaluated what activities have been done and have compared the actual performance with the desired standard.[2]

It helps to think of the **control process** as consisting of three separate and distinct steps: (1) *measuring* actual performance, (2) *comparing* actual performance against a standard, and (3) taking *managerial action* to correct deviations or inadequate standards (see Exhibit 6-1).

EXHIBIT 6-1

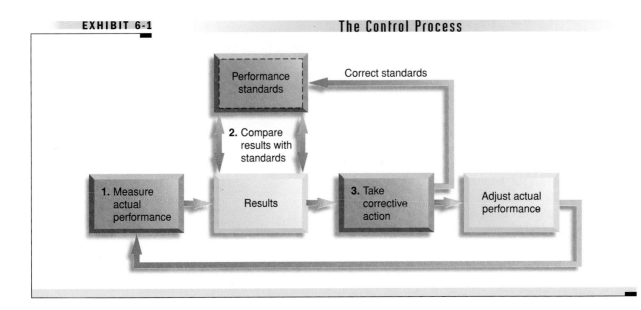

Notice from Exhibit 6-1 that the control process assumes that standards of performance *already* exist. These standards are the specific objectives against which progress can be measured. If managers use MBO, then objectives are, by definition, tangible, verifiable, and measurable. In such instances, these objectives are the standards by which progress is measured and against which it is compared. If MBO isn't practiced, then standards are the specific performance indicators that management uses. In either case, keep in mind that planning must precede the setting of controls because it is in planning that the standards are established.

Measuring

To determine what actual performance is, a manager must acquire information about it. The first step in control, then, is measuring. Let's consider *how* we measure and *what* we measure.

The most frequently used sources of information for measuring actual performance are personal observation, statistical reports, oral reports, written reports, and computer-accessed databases. The effective manager tends to use multiple sources, recognizing that different sources provide different types of information. Personal observations obtained by walking around and talking with employees, for instance, can be a rich source of detailed performance data. A manager can pick up important clues about potential problems from an employee's facial expression or casual comment that might never be evident from reviewing a statistical report. On the other hand, statistical reports typically contain more comprehensive and objective data.

What we measure is probably more critical to the control process than *how* we measure it. Selecting the wrong criteria can have serious dysfunctional consequences. Besides, what we measure determines, to a great extent, what people in the organization will attempt to excel at.[3]

Some control criteria are applicable to any management situation. For instance, because managers direct the activities of others, criteria such as employee attendance or turnover rates can be measured. Most managers have budgets for their area of responsibility set in monetary costs. Keeping costs within budget is therefore a fairly common control measure. Any comprehensive control system, however, needs to recognize the diversity of activities among managers. A production manager in a manufacturing plant might use measures of the quantity of units produced per day, number of units produced per labor-hour, or percent of units rejected by customers because of inferior quality. The manager of an administrative department in a government agency might use number of orders processed per hour or average time required to process service calls. Marketing executives often use measures such as percentage of market captured, average dollar value per sale, or number of customer visits per salesperson.

The performance of some activities is difficult to quantify. It's more difficult, for instance, for an administrator to measure the performance of a research chemist or an elementary school teacher than of a person who sells life insurance. But most activities can be broken down into objective segments that allow for measurement. A manager needs to determine what value a person, department, or unit contributes to the organization and then convert the contribution into standards. When a performance indicator can't be stated in quantifiable terms, subjective measures are always preferable to having no standards at all.

Comparing

The comparison step determines the degree of variation between actual performance and the standard. Some variation in performance can be expected in all activities; it is therefore critical to determine the acceptable range of variation (see Exhibit 6-2). Deviations in excess of this range become significant and receive the manager's attention. In the comparison stage, managers should be particularly concerned with the size and direction of the variation. An example should make this process clearer.

Todd Cruz is new-car sales manager for Dixon Jeep-Eagle in Seattle, Washington. The first week of each month, Todd prepares a report based on sales from the previous month, classified by model. Exhibit 6-3 displays both the standard and actual sales figures for the month of July.

Defining an Acceptable Range of Variation   EXHIBIT 6-2

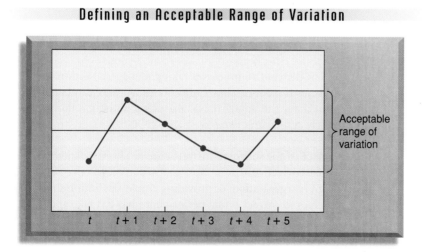

EXHIBIT 6-3

Dixon Jeep-Eagle's July Sales Performance
(in number of units sold)

Model	Standard	Actual	Over (Under)
Wrangler	8	13	5
Cherokee	11	11	0
Grand Cherokee	10	14	4
Grand Wagoneer	6	7	1
Talon	13	9	(4)
Vision	10	8	(2)
Summit	4	3	(1)
Total	62	65	3

Should Todd be concerned about the July performance? Sales were a bit higher than he had originally targeted, but does that mean that there were no significant deviations? Even though overall performance was generally quite favorable, several models might deserve Todd's attention. However, which models deserve attention depends on what Todd believes to be *significant*. How much variation should Todd allow before he takes corrective action?

The deviation on several models is very small and undoubtedly not worthy of special attention. These include the Grand Wagoneer and the Summit. Is the shortfall for Vision significant? That's a judgment Todd must make. Talon sales were 30 percent below Todd's goal. Sales performance for this model needs attention. Todd should look for the cause of the shortfall. In this case, Todd attributed the lower sales to price cuts by competitors on comparable models. If this decline in Talon sales is more than a temporary slump, Todd will need to reduce his orders with Chrysler and lower his inventory stock.

Understating sales goals can be as troublesome as overstating them. For instance, is the popularity of the Jeep Wrangler and Grand Cherokee a 1-month aberration, or are these models increasing their market share? As our example illustrates, both overvariance and undervariance require managerial attention.

► Taking Managerial Action

The third and final step in the control process is taking managerial action. Managers can choose among three courses of action: They can do nothing; they can correct the actual performance; or they can revise the standard. Because doing nothing is fairly self-explanatory, let's look more closely at the latter two.

CORRECT ACTUAL PERFORMANCE If the source of the variation has been deficient performance, managers will want to take corrective action. Examples of such corrective action might include a change in strategy, reorganization, or providing employees with training.

A manager who decides to correct actual performance has to make another decision: Should he or she take immediate or basic corrective action? **Immediate corrective action** corrects problems at once and gets performance back on track. **Basic corrective action** asks how and why performance has deviated and then proceeds to correct the source of deviation.

It's not unusual for managers to rationalize that they don't have time to take basic corrective action and therefore must be content to perpetually "put out fires" with immediate corrective action. Effective managers, however, analyze deviations and, when the benefits justify it, take the time to permanently correct significant variances between standard and actual performance.

In our example of Dixon Jeep-Eagle, Todd Cruz might take basic corrective action on the negative variance for the Talon. He might increase advertising for this model, run a price-cutting promotion, offer bonuses to his salespeople to encourage them to push this model, or reduce future orders with the manufacturer.

REVISE THE STANDARD It's possible that the variance is a result of an unrealistic standard— that is, the goal may be too high or too low. In such cases it is the standard that needs corrective attention, not the performance. In our example, Todd Cruz might need to raise the standard for the Grand Cherokee to reflect its increasing popularity. Athletes revise their standards when, for example, they adjust their performance goals upward during a season if they achieve their season goal early.

Todd Cruz at Dixon Jeep-Eagle relies on controls to manage his automobile inventory.

The more troublesome problem is the revising of a performance standard downward. If an employee or unit falls significantly short of reaching its target, the natural response is to shift the blame for the variance to the standard. Students, for example, who make a low grade on a test often attack the grade cutoff points as too high. Rather than accept the fact that their performance was inadequate, students argue that the standards are unreasonable. Similarly, salespeople who fail to meet their monthly quota may attribute the failure to an unrealistic quota. It may be true that standards are too high, resulting in a significant variance and acting to demotivate those employees being assessed against it. But keep in mind that if employees or managers don't meet the standard, the first thing they are likely to attack is the standard itself. If you believe the standard is realistic, hold your ground. Explain your position, reaffirm to the employee or manager that you expect future performance to improve, and then take the necessary corrective action to turn that expectation into reality.

WHAT MANAGERS SEEK TO CONTROL

What do managers control? Most control efforts are directed at one of four areas: human behavior, finances, operations, or information.

Human Behavior

It may sound manipulative, but managers seek to control their employees' behavior. Remember, managers accomplish goals by integrating the work of other people. They depend on these people to achieve their unit goals. And they are accountable for the results, or lack of results, that these people achieve. To ensure that employees are performing as they're supposed to, managers rely on a wide range of behavioral control devices. The following discussion briefly identifies some of the more powerful behavioral control mechanisms available to managers.

SELECTION The hiring process offers managers an opportunity to impose controls. How? By identifying and selecting people whose values, attitudes, and personality fit with what management desires. If, for example, managers want only employees who are assertive and risk-taking, individuals who don't have those qualities can be screened out of the job applicant pool.

NEW-EMPLOYEE ORIENTATION Once new employees are hired, they are given an initial orientation. In some organizations, this may be several weeks of formal training. In others, it may be nothing more than a brief talk with an immediate supervisor. However, even the most informal orientation typically includes implicit communication by managers to the new employee on what behaviors the organization considers acceptable and unacceptable. So the new-employee orientation acts to fine-tune behavioral expectations of individuals who have already been selected because they appear to fit into the organization.

MENTORING Some organizations have formal mentoring programs for new employees. Mentors act as guides and role models for new employees—showing them "the ropes to skip and the ropes to know." For instance, when mentors show protégés how to do certain tasks or provide insight into job behaviors that can get them into "trouble with the big boss," they are contributing to standardizing the protégé's behavior. The selection of formal mentors should not be random. Managers should judiciously select mentors who will convey to new employees the attitudes and behaviors it wants these new employees to exhibit.

GOALS As described in chapter 5, goals guide and constrain employees by clarifying what behaviors are likely to lead to goal attainment. Once employees accept specific goals, the goals then direct and limit employee behavior.

JOB DESIGN The way jobs are designed determines, to a large degree, the tasks the jobholder does, the pace of the work, the people with whom he or she interacts, and similar activities. For example, assembly-line work tends to constrain behavioral options far more than do traveling sales positions. The latter jobs give employees considerable autonomy, thus allowing them greater control over their daily activities. So managers can influence employee behavior by the way they design their employees' jobs.

FORMAL REGULATIONS Almost all organizations have formal rules, policies, job descriptions, and other regulations that define acceptable practices and constrain behavior. These can range from a short list of Do's and Don'ts to large and detailed policy manuals. The more formal regulations management creates, the greater the visibility of those regulations, and the more managers require employees to adhere to them, the greater control regulations will have over employees.

Managers at Intel's plant in Santa Clara, California, use the assembly line as a means to control the behavior of workers.

DIRECT SUPERVISION On a day-to-day basis, managers oversee employees' work, identify deviant employee behavior, and correct problems as they occur. The manager who spots an employee taking an unnecessary risk when operating his or her machine may point out the correct way to perform the task and tell the employee to do it the correct way in the future. In so doing, the manager constrains the employee's behavioral options.

TRAINING Most organizations encourage or even require employees to undergo training in order to keep their skills current. These formal training programs teach employees desired work practices and, in so doing, act to shape the employees' on-the-job behaviors.

PERFORMANCE APPRAISAL Managers formally assess the work of their employees through performance appraisals. An employee's recent performance is evaluated. If performance is positive, the employee's behavior can be rewarded. If performance is below standard, managers can seek to correct it or, depending on the nature of the deviation, discipline the employee. Performance appraisals become control devices because employees tend to behave in ways so as to look good on the criteria by which they will be appraised.

ORGANIZATIONAL REWARDS Rewards such as pay increases, promotions, desirable job assignments, and recognition awards act as reinforcers to encourage desired behaviors and to extinguish undesirable ones. So by the choices managers make in terms of the critieria they reward—for example, loyalty, dependability, risk-taking, openness, deceitfulness, collegial support—they encourage or discourage certain behaviors.

Finances

Business firms seek to earn a profit. Not-for-profit organizations seek efficiencies through cost control. In pursuit of these objectives, managers of these organizations introduce financial controls. These include budgets, the use of financial ratios, and audits.

BUDGETS Few of us are unfamiliar with budgets. Most of us learned about them at an early age, when we discovered that unless we allocated our "revenues" carefully, we would consume our weekly allowance before half the week was out.

A **budget** is a numerical plan for allocating resources to specific activities. Budgets provide managers with quantitative standards against which to measure and compare resource consumption. And, by pointing out deviations between standard and actual consumption, they become control devices.[4] As shown in Exhibit 6-4, the typical manager is most likely to use budgets to control revenues, expenses, profits, cash usage, and capital expenditures.

The popularity of budgets as a financial control mechanism lies largely in their applicability across different countries, types of organizations, and functions and levels within organizations. We live in a world in which almost everything is expressed in monetary units. Dollars, pesos, yen, marks, francs, and the like are used as a common denominator within a country. Controlling monetary allocations is as important to hospitals and school districts as it is to business firms. And budgets make a useful common denominator for controlling activities in a research lab as well as a production department. Budgets seem to be one device that most managers, regardless of level in the organization, use on a regular basis.

> The popularity of budgets as a financial control mechanism lies largely in their applicability across different countries, types of organizations, and functions and levels within organizations.

EXHIBIT 6-4   Popular Types of Budgets

Revenue budgets. Project future sales. Determined by multiplying estimated sales volume by sales price.

Expense budgets. List the primary activities undertaken by a unit and allocate a monetary value to each.

Profit budgets. Used by separate units of an organization that combines revenue and expense budgets to determine the unit's profit contribution.

Cash budgets. Forecast how much cash an organization will have on hand and how much it will need to meet expenses.

Capital expenditure budgets. Estimate investments in property, buildings, and major equipment.

FINANCIAL RATIOS Exhibit 6-5 summarizes some of the most popular **financial ratios** used in organizations. Taken from the organization's financial statements (the balance sheet and income statement), they compare two significant figures and express them as a percentage, or ratio. Because you undoubtedly have encountered these ratios in introductory accounting and finance courses, or you will in the near future, we needn't elaborate on them. We mention them, however, to remind you that managers use such ratios as internal control devices for monitoring how efficiently the organization uses its assets, debt, inventories, and the like.

AUDITS An **audit** is a formal verification of an organization's accounts, records, operating activities, or performance. Audits can generally be characterized as either external or internal.

An *external audit* is a verification of an organization's financial statements by an outside and independent accounting firm. The organization creates its own financial statements using its own accountants. The external auditor's job is then to review the various accounts on the financial statements in respect to their accuracy and conformity with generally accepted accounting practices.

For publicly held corporations, the primary purpose of the external audit is to protect stockholders. The external audit's value to management, in terms of a control device, is generally indirect because the audits are meant only to verify that which management already knows. They are an indirect control device, however, in the sense that their existence serves as a deterrent against abuses or misrepresentations by those who develop the financial statements.

The *internal audit*, as its name implies, is done by members of the organization. It encompasses verifying the financial statements, just as the external audit does, but additionally includes an evaluation of the organization's operations, procedures, and policies, plus recommendations for improvement. So, in terms of control, the internal audit is a more comprehensive evaluation. It goes beyond merely verifying financial statements, seeks to uncover inefficiencies, and offers suggested actions for their correction.

▶ Operations

The success of an organization depends to a large extent on its ability to produce goods and services effectively and efficiently. Operations control is designed to assess how effectively and efficiently an organization's transformation processes are working—that is, how effective and efficient the organization is in turning inputs into outputs.[5]

Popular Financial Ratios

EXHIBIT 6-5

Objective	Ratio	Calculation	Meaning
Liquidity test	Current ratio	$\dfrac{\text{Current assets}}{\text{Current liabilities}}$	Tests the organization's ability to meet short-term obligations
	Acid test	$\dfrac{\text{Current assets} - \text{inventories}}{\text{Current liabilities}}$	Tests liquidity most accurately when inventories turn over slowly or are difficult to sell
Leverage test	Debt-to-assets	$\dfrac{\text{Total debts}}{\text{Total assets}}$	The higher the ratio, the more leveraged the organization
	Times-interest-earned	$\dfrac{\text{Profits before interest and taxes}}{\text{Total interest charges}}$	Measures how far profits can decline before the organization is unable to meet its interest expenses
Operations test	Inventory turnover	$\dfrac{\text{Sales}}{\text{Inventory}}$	The higher the ratio, the more efficiently inventory assets are being used
	Total asset turnover	$\dfrac{\text{Sales}}{\text{Total assets}}$	The fewer assets used to achieve a given level of sales, the more efficiently management is using the organization's total assets
Profitability	Profit margin on sales	$\dfrac{\text{Net profits after taxes}}{\text{Total sales}}$	Identifies the profits that various products are generating
	Return on investment	$\dfrac{\text{Net profits after taxes}}{\text{Total assets}}$	Measures how efficiently assets generate profits

Operations control typically encompasses monitoring production activities to ensure that they're on schedule, assessing purchasing's ability to provide the proper quantity and quality of supplies needed at the lowest cost possible, monitoring the quality of the organization's products or services to ensure that they meet preestablished standards, and making sure that equipment is well maintained.

SCHEDULING When managers engage in **scheduling**, they determine what activities have to be done, the order in which they are to be done, who is to do each, and when they are to be completed. As such, scheduling involves both planning and control of operational activities. When they focus on prioritizing activities, then they are planning devices. When they are used to determine whether work is being completed on time, then they become control devices.

One of the simplest and best illustrations of a scheduling technique is something called the **Gantt chart**.[6] It was developed in the early 1900s by Henry Gantt. The Gantt chart is essentially a bar graph with time on the horizontal axis and activities to be scheduled on the vertical axis. The bars show output, both planned and actual, over a period of time. The Gantt chart visually shows when each task is supposed to be done and compares that with the actual progress on each. It's a simple device that allows managers to detail easily what has yet to be done to complete a job or project and to assess whether the project is ahead of, behind, or on schedule.

Exhibit 6-6 depicts a Gantt chart that was developed by a production manager at Simon & Schuster publishers. Time is expressed in months across the top of the chart. The major activities are listed down the left side. The planning comes in deciding what activities need to be done to get the book finished, the order in which they need to be done, and the time that should be allocated to each activity. Where a box sits within a time frame reflects its planned sequence. The shading represents actual progress. The chart becomes a control device when the manager looks for deviations from the plan. For instance, in Exhibit 6-6, the production manager has given her team 9 months to go from getting the manuscript copyedited to having bound copies complete. But after 3 months (reporting date), she has two control problems. The people responsible for selecting photos and getting permissions for their use are a full month behind schedule. Similarly, the first pages are 2 weeks behind schedule. If the book is to be completed on time, the production manager is going to have to take some immediate action to pick up lost time on those two activities.

The latest wrinkle in scheduling tools is the use of scheduling-system software.[7] Recent breakthroughs in constraint-based scheduling software allows managers to increase their production efficiency and flexibility. By taking into account such factors as equipment shutdowns, labor shortages, bottlenecks, and shortfalls in materials, this software helps managers

EXHIBIT 6-6

A Gantt Chart for Book Production

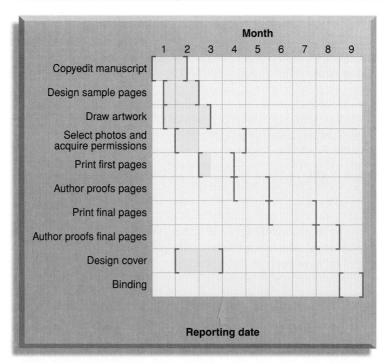

determine when and where resources should be allocated in order to best respond to customer orders. While not cheap—these systems can easily cost $500,000 for a large corporation—they often can pay for themselves in literally a few months. QUALCOMM, Inc., a maker of digital cellular telephones, and Herman Miller, Inc., the officer furniture manufacturer, are two companies commited to the new software. QUALCOMM went to scheduling software when sales exploded in a 6-month period from 10,000 phones a month to 300,000. The complexity of scheduling this volume overwhelmed the company's production planners. The new software improved the company's available-to-promise capability, as well as its ability to assign inventory to specific orders. Herman Miller has used the new software to improve its on-time delivery from 65 percent to 98.4 percent. In a three-year period, HM went from over $10 million in late orders to just $300,000.

PURCHASING It has been said that human beings *are* what they eat. Metaphorically, the same applies to organizations. Their processes and outputs depend on the inputs they "eat." It's difficult to make quality products out of inferior inputs. Highly skilled leatherworkers need quality cowhides if they're going to produce high-quality wallets. Gas station operators depend on a regular and dependable inflow of certain octane-rated gasolines from their suppliers in order to meet their customers' demands. If the gasoline isn't there, they can't sell it. If the gasoline is below the specified octane rating, customers may be dissatisfied and take their business elsewhere. Management must therefore monitor the delivery, performance, quality, quantity, and price of inputs from suppliers. Purchasing control seeks to ensure availability, acceptable quality, continued reliable sources, and, at the same time, reduced costs.

What can managers do to facilitate control of inputs? They need to gather information on the dates and conditions in which supplies arrive. They need to gather data about the quality of supplies and the compatibility of those supplies with operations processes. Finally, they need to obtain data on supplier price performance. Are the prices of the delivered goods the same as those quoted when the order was placed?

This information can be used to rate suppliers, identify problem suppliers, and guide management in choosing future suppliers. Trends can be detected. Suppliers can be evaluated, for instance, on responsiveness, service, reliability, and competitiveness. In recent years, an increasing proportion of manufacturers have reduced the number of vendors they deal with.[8] The reason? It is easier to monitor relations and develop close ties with only two suppliers than it is with twenty-two. Specific purchasing-control techniques range from the simple to the very complex. The following discussion briefly describes several of these techniques.

In the 1800s, economist Vilfredo Pareto found that 80 percent of the wealth was controlled by only 20 percent of the population. Managers typically find that just a few of their employees cause most of their problems. This concept, the vital few and the trivial many, has been applied to inventory control. It's called the **ABC system**. It is not unusual for a company to have thousands of items in inventory. However, evidence indicates that roughly 10 percent of the items in most organizations' inventory account for 50 percent of the annual dollar inventory value. Another 20 percent of the items account for 30 percent of the value. The remaining 70 percent of the items appear to account for only 20 percent of the value. These have been labeled as A, B, and C categories, respectively. Consistent with the idea that managers should direct attention to those areas where their effort can achieve the greatest result, A items should receive the tightest control, B items moderate control, and C items the least control. A items, for example, might be monitored weekly, B items monthly, and C items quarterly.

When you ordered checks from the bank, did you notice that the reorder form was placed about two-thirds of the way through your supply of checks? This is a simple exam-

EXHIBIT 6-7

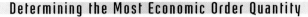

Determining the Most Economic Order Quantity

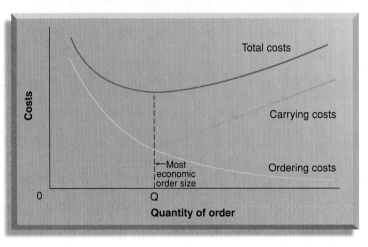

ple of a **fixed-point reordering system**. At some preestablished point in a process, the system is designed to "flag" the fact that the inventory needs to be replenished. The objective is to minimize inventory carrying costs while, at the same time, limiting the probability of *stocking out* of the inventory item. In recent years, retail stores have increasingly been using their computers to perform this control activity. Their cash registers are connected to store computers, and each sale automatically adjusts the store's inventory record. When the inventory of an item hits the critical point, the computer tells management to reorder.

One of the most sophisticated and well-known quantitative techniques for managing purchasing and inventories is the **economic order quantity (EOQ) model**. The EOQ model seeks to balance four costs involved in ordering and carrying inventory: the purchase costs (purchase price plus delivery charges less discounts); the ordering costs (paperwork, follow-up, inspection when the item arrives, and other processing costs); carrying costs (money tied up in inventory, storage, insurance, taxes, and so forth); and stockout costs (profits foregone from orders lost, the cost of reestablishing goodwill, and additional expenses incurred to expedite late shipments). As shown in Exhibit 6-7, the objective of the EOQ model is to minimize the total costs of two of these four costs — carrying costs and ordering costs. As the amount ordered gets larger and larger, average inventory increases, and so do carrying costs. But placing larger orders means fewer orders and thus lowers ordering costs. The lowest total cost — and thus the most economic order quantity — is reached at the lowest point on the total cost curve. A detailed mathematical equation is available for specifically identifying the optimal order quantity.[9]

Information

The quality of any managerial decision is largely dependent on the quality of information that the manager has at his or her disposal. This principle is illustrated in the well-worn computer phrase GIGO (garbage in, garbage out). In today's increasingly complex world, where the ability to make quick and intelligent decisions is an absolute necessity for survival, information control has gained significantly enhanced importance.

GE Pushes Its Quality-Control Plan

Good managers understand that you can't rest on your past successes. Jack Welch (center in photo), chairman of General Electric Co., is one of those managers. He has turned GE into the most profitable company in the United States. To keep GE ahead, Welch and his executive team are implementing a quality-control program that they hope will prevent costly snafus and save $7 billion to $10 billion over the next decade.

In spite of GE's incredible success throughout the 1990s, it had its share of embarrassing quality problems. It's locomotive unit in Erie, Pennsylvania, built defective electric motors for a major transit line in Montreal. The motors shorted out and broke down in heavy snows. An innovative GE gas turbine sold to utility power plants around the world began cracking because of faulty design. And a new jet engine that GE created for the Boeing 777 failed in a test only four months before it was to be delivered. The engine had to be redesigned.

In the new program, GE is training people to become quality experts—called "Black Belts." They train for four months in statistical and other quality-enhancing measures. Then they spend full-time roaming GE plants and setting up quality-improvement projects.

Welch has told young managers that they haven't much future at GE unless they are selected to become Black Belts. So far, the company has trained 2,000 of them and plans to increase that number to 10,000 by the year 2000. To reinforce

the importance that Welch places on the program's success, he has modified the executive bonus program to highlight quality. Forty percent of GE executive bonuses, which run as high as $1 million, now will depend on implementation of the program. Previously, bonuses were based only on profit and cash flow.

In all, GE is investing hundreds of millions of dollars in training, in specific projects, and in computer systems to analyze and run the quality-control program.

Based on W. M. Carley, "To Keep GE's Profits Rising, Welch Pushes Quality-Control Plan," *Wall Street Journal*, January 13, 1997, p. A1.

Managers in the city of Mississauga, Ontario, for instance, are using their computerized executive information system (EIS) to keep costs down.[10] The EIS gives the city's commissioners and managers the key information they need, when they need it, displayed in a user-friendly format. A sophisticated software program analyzes data that individual managers have deemed critical to their specific jobs, and then the system delivers the analyses to the manager's computer screen in an easy-to-read graphics and text format. Managers can find out at any point in time exactly what they have spent and how much they have left. This information allows them to react instantly to financial changes. The system, which has been in place for just 3 years, has enabled the city to operate for the past 2 years without increasing taxes.

Today, information control is typically subsumed under the topic of management information systems. Because this issue is now so important to almost every manager's daily activities, let's proceed to a discussion of how management information systems are changing control systems in organizations.

**HOW MIS IS
CHANGING
CONTROL SYSTEMS**
What is MIS? How has information control changed over the past 35 years? And what ethical implications should we be concerned about regarding computer-based controls? We answer those three questions in this section.

▶ What Is a Management Information System?

A **management information system** (MIS) is a system used to provide management with needed information on a regular basis.[11] In theory, this system can be manual or computer-based, although all current discussion, including ours, focuses on computer-supported applications.

The term *system* in MIS implies order, arrangement, and purpose. Further, an MIS focuses specifically on providing management with *information*, not merely *data*. These two points are important and need elaboration.

A library provides a good analogy. Although it can contain millions of volumes, a library doesn't do users much good if they can't *find* what they want *quickly*. That's why libraries spend a lot of time cataloging their collections and ensuring that volumes are returned to their proper locations. Organizations today are like well-stocked libraries. There is no lack of data. There is, however, a lack of ability to process that data so that the right information is available to the right person when he or she needs it.[12] A library is almost useless if it has the book you want, but either you can't find it or the library takes a week to retrieve it from storage. An MIS, on the other hand, has organized data in some meaningful way and can access the information in a reasonable amount of time. **Data** are raw, unanalyzed facts, such as numbers, names, or quantities. But as data, these facts are relatively useless to managers.[13] When data are analyzed and processed, they become **information**. An MIS collects data and turns them into relevant information for managers to use. Exhibit 6-8 summarizes these observations.

▶ The Evolution of MIS

Exhibit 6-9 describes the four-stage evolution of modern MIS. Beginning in the mid-1960s, it reflects extraordinary changes. In fact, only in stages 3 and 4 has MIS reached its full potential as an integrated and coordinated information system.

STAGE 1: MANAGEMENT-FOCUSED DATA PROCESSING Beginning around 1965, organizations began to convert the centralized data processing systems that had been created for accounting and clerical activities to providing support information for management and operational personnel. Information systems were redesigned specifically to help managers in diverse functions to make better decisions. Not only were managers in the accounting area involved with information control, but so were managers in purchasing, human resources, marketing, engineering, research and development, and production and operations.

Managers of every type began to see how computers could help them do their jobs better and more efficiently. Computers could accumulate and analyze large quantities of data that could never be analyzed economically on a manual basis. Marketing executives, for instance, could now not only review weekly sales reports broken down by each salesperson, but they also could have those data analyzed by product groups. If the sales of a particular product line suddenly dropped, computer-generated information could alert management quickly and allow for rapid corrective action.

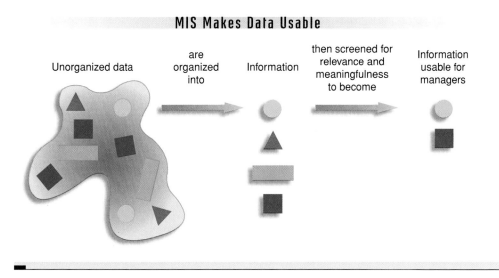

MIS Makes Data Usable

EXHIBIT 6-8

Unorganized data → are organized into → Information → then screened for relevance and meaningfulness to become → Information usable for managers

The major constraint on managers during stage 1 was that managers were dependent on others for information access and control. Computer-generated reports, for the most part, were produced by MIS specialists who worked in departments with titles like Data Systems or Information Systems. When managers had an information control problem, they had to go to the MIS specialists for a solution.

STAGE 2: DECENTRALIZED END-USER COMPUTING By 1980, centralized data processing was being rapidly replaced by decentralized systems in which part or all of the computer logic functions were performed outside a single, centralized computer. In stage 2, managers became end users, personal computers became overwhelmingly popular, and data systems departments evolved into information support centers.

When a manager becomes an **end user**, he or she takes responsibility for information control.[14] It is no longer delegated to some other department or staff assistant. As end users, managers had to become knowledgeable about their own needs and the systems that were

The Evolution of Management Information Systems

EXHIBIT 6-9

Stage	Approximate Time Period	Description
1. Mangement-focused data processing	1965–1979	Direct support for management and operational functions
2. Decentralized end-user computing	1980–1985	Personal computers under the direct control of users
3. Fixed-location interactive networks	1986–1995	Linking of individual end users at their fixed work locations
4. Mobile interactive networks	1996–	Linking of individual end users through mobile personal communicators

available to meet those needs, and they had to accept responsibility for their systems' failures. If they didn't have the information they wanted, there was no one to blame but themselves.

A major explanation of why end-using computing became popular was the creation of powerful, low-cost personal computers. By the 1980s, a $5,000 desktop personal computer could do tasks that 15 years earlier required a roomful of equipment that cost millions of dollars.

With decentralized data processing and user-friendly software, the need for centralized data systems departments declined. Most remade themselves into support centers that could help managers become more effective end users. For instance, they could help managers select appropriate software as well as create executive information systems like the one put into place in the city of Mississauga, Ontario.

STAGE 3: FIXED-LOCATION INTERACTIVE NETWORKS   The third stage of MIS development built on communication software packages to fully achieve the system objective of MIS. In stage 3, the emphasis was on creating and implementing mechanisms to link end users. By means of an interactive network, a manager's computer can communicate with other computers.[15]

Networking interconnects computer hardware. By networking, the user of a personal computer can communicate with other users, turn the computer into a terminal and gain access to an organization's mainframe system, share the use of sophisticated printers, and tap into outside databases.

Networks are reshaping the manager's job. Electronic mail, for instance, is lessening the manager's dependence on the telephone and traditional mail delivery service.[16] Networks permit some employees, including managers, to **telecommute**—to do their jobs at home and connect to the workplace by means of a personal computer. Networks also enable managers to monitor their employees' work closely. For employees who perform their tasks on a terminal, software packages are available that can summarize, in detail, each employee's hourly productivity, error rate, and the like.

We also should not overlook the effect that networks are having on interorganizational communications. Interorganizational networks are widening the scope of database management. If you want to know what other companies are doing in regard to strategic planning, for instance, you can get your answer through a computer search of outside databases. Companies such as Dow Jones, Mead Corporation, and Knight-Ridder have developed extensive databases that are available on a fee basis. On-line services such as Prodigy, CompuServe, and America Online also provide easy access to massive databases to anyone with a personal computer and a modem.

STAGE 4: MOBILE INTERACTIVE NETWORKS   In the mid-1990s, computer technology progressed to a fourth stage. Managers could now network into other computers while maintaining complete mobility. This ability has become possible through personal digital assistants (PDAs), or personal communicators.[17] These palm-sized communicators are combining phone, fax, and computing capability in a completely portable package. They allow users to enter information and commands by writing with a special pen instead of tapping on a keyboard. They feature special software that makes it easy to keep track of appointments and schedules. And they can incorporate faxes, modems, and cellular phones so that users can communicate in a multitude of ways, anytime and anywhere.

Although PDAs are currently in the early stage of development, they are likely to be as common as cellular phones in just a few years. And when that day comes, managers will be able to easily communicate with people above and below them in their organization, as well as with outside suppliers and customers. Moreover, PDAs will allow managers to monitor and control activities to a degree that was never thought possible just a decade ago.

TODAY ? or TOMORROW ?

Never Out of Touch

The ultimate vision (Stage 5?) for personal communications is something that Bill Gates calls a "wallet PC."[18] It will be about the same size as a wallet. And it will essentially encompass all the things you might carry in your pocket or purse. It'll take the place of your house and car keys, checkbook, address book, appointment calendar, notepad, reading material, camera, pocket tape recorder, cellular phone, pager, compass, calculator, electronic entry card, and photographs. The wallet PC will display messages and schedules and let you read or send e-mail and faxes; monitor weather, stock reports, and highway traffic; and store digital money. For managers, it will allow you to go to meetings, take notes, while at the same time, you check your appointments, respond to e-mail or faxes, and review the latest productivity statistics in your department. It will also give you instantaneous access to powerful databases from all over the world (from such providers as Dow-Jones News Retrieval, Lexis, Nexis, and the Internet).

We're well on the road toward Gates's vision. Japan's Sharp Corp., for instance, has developed a PDA—the Color Zaurus—that does many of the functions envisioned by Gates's wallet PC.[19] The one-pound device reads handwriting, surfs the Web, offers street maps, and transmits snapshots over the Internet. It also has a built-in camera and plug-in access for a cell phone. The price? Under $1,000.

▶ Ethical Implications of Computer-Based Controls

Computerized information controls create opportunities for ethical abuses that were never possible a decade or two ago.[20] Consider the following actual examples.

The U.S. Internal Revenue Service's internal audit group monitors a computer log that shows employee access to taxpayer's accounts. This monitoring activity allows management to check and see what employees are doing on their computers.[21]

The mayor of Colorado Springs, Colorado, read the electronic mail messages that city council members sent to each other from their homes. He defended his actions by saying he was making sure that e-mail was not being used to circumvent his state's "open meeting" law that requires most council business to be conducted publicly.[22]

American Express has an elaborate system for monitoring telephone calls. Daily reports are provided to supervisors that detail the frequency and length of calls made by employees, as well as how quickly incoming calls are answered.[23]

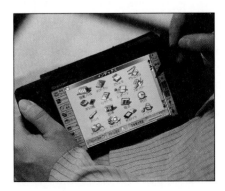

Sharp's Zaurus surfs the Web, takes photos, and reads handwriting.

Management at Midland Bank's branch in Newark, New Jersey, have defined forty-eight everyday tasks that employees do, and each task has a spot on every employee's computer screen. Every time workers complete a task, they make a record of it by touching the appropriate box on the screen. Custom software then tabulates reports for management that classify which tasks people do and exactly how long it takes to do them.[24]

These examples illustrate a growing trend. Technology is increasing the capability of managers to monitor employees, and managers seem to be taking advantage of this new-found capability. Electronic monitoring systems "provide managers with access to their employees' computer terminals and telephones, allowing managers to determine at any moment throughout the day the pace at which employees are working, their degree of accuracy, log-in and log-off times, and even the amount of time spent on bathroom breaks."[25] In the United States alone, it's been estimated that more than 26 million workers are subject to electronic monitoring on the job.[26] A variety of surveillance "snoopware" is currently available to managers. WinVista, Inc., for instance, sells a product that tracks the files that employees open, the Web sites they visit, and e-mails they send. Should an employee decide to join an unapproved Internet chat group or visit a porn site, it can flash an "Access not allowed" message on the employee's screen and inform his or her boss with an instant message.[27]

Managers typically defend their actions in terms of ensuring quality, productivity, and proper employee behavior. An IRS audit of its southeastern regional offices, as a case in point, found that 166 employees took unauthorized looks at the tax returns of friends, neighbors, and celebrities.

When does management's need for information about employee performance cross over the line and interfere with a worker's right to privacy? For example, is any action by management acceptable as long as employees are notified ahead of time that they will be monitored? And what about the demarcation between monitoring work and nonwork behavior? When employees do work-related activities at home during evenings and weekends, does management's prerogative to monitor employees remain in force? Answers to questions such as these have become increasingly relevant as technology has redefined management's ability to monitor the most minute details of employees' behavior.

THE DOWNSIDE OF CONTROLS

Managing without controls is abdication of responsibility. Because managers are accountable for the actions of the people in their unit and the overall performance of that unit, it is imperative that proper controls are established to ensure that activities are being accomplished as planned. But controls can produce unproductive behaviors.[28] Consider the following examples.

Larry Boff called the Dallas Fire Department's emergency number to get immediate help for his stepmother, who was having trouble breathing.[29] The nurse-dispatcher, Billie Myrick, spent 15 minutes arguing with Boff because he wouldn't bring his stepmother to the phone. He repeatedly told Myrick that his stepmother was in the bedroom and couldn't speak. Myrick insisted that she was required to talk to the person in question so she could determine if the situation was a true emergency. Boff insisted that his stepmother was unable to speak on the phone and pleaded with Myrick to send an ambulance. Myrick continually responded that she could not send an ambulance until she spoke to Boff's stepmother. After getting nowhere for 15 minutes, Boff hung up the phone. His stepmother was dead.

Three managers at a big General Motors truck plant in Michigan installed a secret control box in a supervisor's office to override the control panel that governed the speed

As students frequently learn, college rules often have a downside.

of the assembly line.[30] The device allowed the managers to speed up the assembly line—a clear violation of GM's contract with the United Auto Workers union. When caught, the managers explained that, although they knew what they had done was wrong, the pressure from higher-ups to meet unrealistic production goals was so great that they felt the secret control panel was the only way they could meet their targets. As described by one manager, senior GM executives would say, "I don't care *how* you do it—*just do it.*"

Did you ever notice that the people who work in the college registrar's office often don't seem to care much about the problems of students? They become so fixated on ensuring that every rule is followed that they lose sight of the fact that their job is to *serve* students, not to *hassle* them!

These examples illustrate what can happen when controls are inflexible or control standards are unreasonable. People lose sight of the organization's overall goals.[31] Instead of the organization running the controls, sometimes the controls run the organization.

Because any control system has imperfections, problems occur when individuals or organizational units attempt to look good exclusively in terms of the control devices. The result is dysfunctional in terms of the organization's goals. More often than not, this dysfunctionality is caused by incomplete measures of performance. If the control system evaluates only the quantity of output, people will tend to ignore quality. Similarly, if the system measures activities rather than results, people will spend their time attempting to look good on the activity measures. For instance, public employment agencies exist to match up workers searching for jobs with employers who have job vacancies. But when agency interviewers were evaluated by the number of employment interviews they conducted, they focused on activities rather than results. The interviewers emphasized the number of interviews they conducted rather than the number of clients they placed in jobs.[32]

To avoid being reprimanded by managers because of the control system, people can engage in behaviors that are designed solely to influence the information system's data output during a given control period. Rather than actually performing well, employees can manipulate measures to give the appearance that they are performing well. Evidence indicates that the manipulation of control data is not a random phenomenon. It depends on the importance of an activity. Organizationally important activities are likely to make a difference in a person's rewards; therefore, there is a great incentive to look good on those particular measures.[33] When rewards are at stake, individuals tend to manipulate data to appear in a favorable light by, for instance, distorting actual figures, emphasizing successes, and suppressing evidence of failures. On the other hand, only random errors occur when the distribution of rewards is unaffected.[34]

Controls have both an upside and a downside. Failure to design flexibility into a controls system can create problems more severe than those the controls were implemented to prevent.

CONTROL TOOLS

We conclude our discussion of control systems by describing three control tools that can help you be a more effective manager. These are budgets, PERT network analysis, and control charts.

Budgets

We briefly introduced budgets earlier in this chapter in our discussion of financial controls. Because almost every manager is involved in expense budgets, we'll focus on them. You should be aware of the difference between incremental and zero-base budgets, the advantages to bottom-up budgeting, the growing popularity of activity-based budgeting, and the steps in preparing a budget. In this section, we look at those four topics.

INCREMENTAL VERSUS ZERO-BASED BUDGETS   The traditional budget is incremental in nature. It develops out of the previous budget. In the **incremental budget**, each period's budget begins by using the last period as a reference point. Then adjustments are made to individual items within the budget.

The major problems with the incremental approach are that it tends to hide inefficiencies and waste, encourages continual increases, and hinders change. Inefficiencies tend to grow because, in the typical incremental budget, nothing ever gets cut. Each budget begins with the funds allocated for the last period—to which are added a percentage for inflation and requests for new or expanded activities. So this approach to budgeting often provides money for activities long after the need is gone. And because incrementalism builds on the past, this type of budget also tends to constrain bold or radical changes.

An alternative, which directly deals with the incremental budget's limitations, is the **zero-base budget** (**ZBB**). With the ZBB, the entire budget begins from scratch, and each budget item must be justified. No reference is made to previous appropriations.[35] The major advantage of the ZBB is that all programs, projects, and activities going on within every unit of the organization are assessed in terms of benefits and costs. The primary drawbacks to ZBB include increased paperwork and preparation time, the tendency of managers to inflate the benefits of activities they want funded, and the negative effect on intermediate- and long-term planning. On this last point, for example, when departmental budgets have to be completely justified every year, the potential for dramatic ups and downs in funding can create chaos for managers and make intermediate and long-term planning almost impossible.

Most organizations rely on incremental budgeting. But the zero-base approach is increasingly appealing. ZBB is particularly relevant when organizations are developing new strategies, undertaking a significant reorganization, or introducing similar organization-wide change programs.[36] Under these conditions, ZBB will lessen the likelihood that outdated or less important activities will continue to receive their prior level of funding.

TOP-DOWN VERSUS BOTTOM-UP BUDGETING   Another choice that has to be made on budgets is where it will initially be prepared.[37] **Top-down budgeting** originates at the upper levels of the organization. Budgets are initiated, controlled, and directed by top management. This approach assumes that top management is best able to allocate resources among alternative uses within the organization. These budgets are then given to middle-level and lower-level managers whose responsibilities are to carry them out. This method has the advantage of simplifying the budgeting process and focusing on the organization's overall strategy and goals. However, the top-down approach has some huge disadvantages. It assumes that top management has comprehensive data on all activities within the organization. This assumption is rarely valid, especially in relatively large organizations. Since operating personnel and lower-level managers have no input into their budgets, the top-down approach also does nothing to build support and commitment for budgets.

Most organizations today have moved to **bottom-up budgeting**, in which the initial budget requests are prepared by those who must implement them. Then they are sent up for approval to higher levels of management, where modifications may be suggested. Differences are negotiated, and the process is followed upward until an organizationwide budget is developed.

Essentially, the bottom-up approach to budgeting has the opposite advantages and disadvantages of top-down budgeting. Because lower-level managers are more knowledgeable about their needs than are managers at the top, they are less likely to overlook important funding requirements. And a very important advantage is that lower-level managers are much more likely to enthusiastically accept and try to meet budgets they had a hand in shaping.

ACTIVITY-BASED BUDGETING Activity-based budgeting allocates costs for producing a good or service on the basis of the activities performed and services employed.[38] Instead of concentrating on the cost of such budget items as salaries, supplies, or insurance, activity-based budgeting focuses on the processes integral to an organization's operations. In addition, activity-based budgeting redirects the budget's focus from departmental costs to organizational processes. Unlike cost-based budgets, which prompt managers to play numbers games with costs, activity-based budgets force managers to focus on what work needs to be accomplished in the organization and how that work contributes to the overall strategy.

National Forge Co., a Pennsylvania-based firm, used activity-based budgets to review its product lines. One was pipe molds—hunks of precision-engineered steel 30 feet long and up to 42 inches in diameter. "We export about 40 percent of our pipe mold production," said the company's CEO, "and we had a vague notion that these sales were less profitable than our domestic sales. Export items have to be coated to resist water corrosion and specially packed. It also costs a lot more to send an engineer to Singapore than to Ohio. But it wasn't until we used [activity-based budgeting] that we realized how great the disparity in profitability was."[39] The end result: Some products that National Forge thought were breaking even were, in fact, money losers and have been dumped.

Activity-based budgeting is a natural complement to reengineering and TQM efforts. Why? Because it helps management distinguish between those actions that add value for customers and those that do not. Take, as an example, the response of a senior bank executive to this new form of budgeting. His primary complaint about traditional cost-based budgeting was that it left him with very little understanding of the business the bank was in. "As a manager, I can begin [now] to look at . . . performance and I can target improvements, because I now have names to attach" to the actions. "What I'm doing is moving from a cost-control perspective to a cost-reduction perspective."

> Activity-based budgeting helps management distinguish between those actions that add value for customers and those that do not.

THE BUDGET PROCESS If you were a new manager and were asked to submit your first budget, what would you do? The following steps provide some guidance.[40] They assume a bottom-up approach.

EXHIBIT 6-10

THE GOOD MANAGEMENT PENALTY

Source: Scott Adams, *Dogbert's Big Book of Business* (KC: Andrews & McMeel, 1991) p. 29. © Universal Press Syndicate. With permission.

1. *Review the organization's overall strategy and goals.* Understanding your organization's strategy and goals will help you focus on where the overall organization is going and your unit's role in that plan.

2. *Determine your unit's goals and the means to attain them.* What activities will you do to reach your departmental goals and help the organization achieve its overall goals? What resources will you require to achieve these goals? Think in terms of things such as staffing requirements, workloads, and the materials and equipment you'll need. This is also your opportunity to formulate new programs and propose new responsibilities for your unit.

3. *Gather cost information.* You'll need accurate cost estimates of those resources you identified in step 2. Old budgets may be of some help. But you'll also want to talk with your immediate manager, colleagues, and key employees and to use other contacts you have developed inside your organization and out.

4. *Share your goals and cost estimates with your manager.* Your immediate manager typically will need to approve your budget, so his or her support is necessary. Discuss your goals, costs estimates, and other ideas with your immediate manager before you include them in your budget. Preliminary discussion will assure that your goals are aligned with the goals of the unit above yours and will build consensus for your proposed submission.

5. *Draw up your proposed budget.* Once your goals and costs are in place, constructing the actual budget is fairly simple. But be sure to show the linkage between your budget items and your unit's goals. You need to justify your requests. And be prepared to explain and sell your budget to your immediate manager and others on the management team. Assume that there will be other managers competing for some of the same resources that you want.

6. *Be prepared to negotiate.* It is unlikely that your budget will be approved exactly as you submitted it. Be prepared to negotiate changes that senior management suggests and revise your original budget. Recognize that there are politics in the budget process, and negotiate from the perspective of building credits for future budgets. If certain projects aren't approved this time, use this point in the budget process to build support for them in the next budget period.

7. *Monitor your budget.* Once your budget has been approved and implemented, you will be judged on how well you carry it out. Set variance targets that include both percentages and dollars. For instance, you might set a decision rule that says you will investigate all monthly variances of 15 percent or larger if the actual dollar variance is $200 or more.

8. *Keep superiors informed of your progress.* Keeping your immediate manager and other relevant parties advised on how close you are to meeting your budget is likely to help protect you if you exceed your budget for reasons beyond your control. Also, do not expect to be rewarded for underspending your budget. In incremental budgets, underspending only means that you will be allocated fewer funds in the next budget period!

▶ PERT Network Analysis

PERT is an acronym for *p*rogram *e*valuation and *r*eview *t*echnique. It is an important scheduling technique that is widely used by project managers. A Gantt chart can help you schedule simple work projects. But what would you do if you had to manage a large project such as a reorganization, a cost-reduction campaign, or the development of a new product that requires coordinating inputs from marketing, production, and product design personnel? Such projects require coordinating hundreds of thousands of activities, some of which must be done simultaneously and some of which cannot begin until earlier activities have been completed. For instance, if you're overseeing the construction of a building, you obviously can't have your people start to erect walls until after the foundation has been laid. PERT was developed to help manage such complex projects.

DEFINITION The **program evaluation and review technique** (more typically called just **PERT** or PERT network analysis) was originally developed in the late 1950s for coordinating the more than 3,000 contractors and agencies working on the *Polaris* submarine weapon system.[41] This project was incredibly complicated; hundreds of thousands of activities had to be coordinated. PERT is reported to have cut 2 years off the completion date for the *Polaris* project.

The PERT network is a flowchart-like diagram that depicts the sequence of activities needed to complete a project and the time or costs associated with each activity. With a PERT network, a manager must think through what has to be done on a given project, determine which events depend on one another, and identify potential trouble spots. PERT is a valuable control tool because it makes it easy to compare the effects that alternative actions will have on scheduling and costs. Thus PERT allows managers to monitor a project's progress, identify possible bottlenecks, and shift resources as necessary to keep the project on schedule.

To understand how to construct a PERT network, you need to know three terms: *events*, *activities*, and *critical path*. Let's define these terms, outline the steps in the PERT process, and then develop an example.

Events are end points that represent the completion of major activities. **Activities** represent the time or resources required to progress from one event to another. The **critical path** is the longest or most time-consuming sequence of events and activities in a PERT network.

THE PERT PROCESS Developing a PERT network requires a manager to identify all key activities needed to complete a project, rank them in order of dependence, and estimate each activity's completion time. This process can be translated into five specific steps.

1. *Identify every significant activity* that must be achieved for a project to be completed. The accomplishment of each activity results in a set of events or outcomes.
2. *Ascertain the order* in which these events must be completed.
3. *Diagram the flow* of activities from start to finish, identifying each activity and its relationship to all other activities. Use circles to indicate events and arrows to represent activities. The result is a flowchart diagram called the **PERT network**.
4. *Compute a time estimate* for completing each activity. This computation is done with a weighted average that employs an *optimistic* time estimate (t_o) of how long the activity would take under ideal conditions, a *most-likely* estimate (t_m) of the time the activity normally should take, and a *pessimistic* estimate (t_p) that represents the time that an activity should take under the worst possible conditions. The formula for calculating the expected time (t_e) is then

$$t_e = \frac{t_o + 4t_m + t_p}{6}$$

5. Finally, using a network diagram that contains time estimates for each activity, *determine a schedule* for the start and finish dates of each activity and for the entire project. Any delays that occur along the critical path require the most attention because they delay the entire project. That is, the critical path has no slack in it; therefore, any delay along that path immediately translates into a delay in the final deadline for the completed project.

AN APPLICATION As we noted, most PERT projects are quite complicated and may be composed of hundreds or thousands of events. Such complicated computations are best done with a computer using specialized PERT software.[42] But for our purposes, let's work through a simplified example.

Charley Williams is the production supervisor in the casting department at a Reynolds Metals aluminum mill in upstate New York. Charley has proposed and received approval from corporate management to replace one of the massive furnaces that are part of his responsibilities with a new, state-of-the-art electronic furnace. This project will seriously disrupt operations in his department, so he wants to complete it as quickly and as smoothly as possible. He has carefully separated the entire project into activities and events. Exhibit 6-11 outlines the major events in the furnace modernization project and Charley's estimate of the expected time required to complete each activity. Exhibit 6-12 depicts the PERT chart Charley created on the basis of the data in Exhibit 6-11.

Charley's PERT chart tells him that if everything goes as planned, it will take 21 weeks to complete the modernization program. This figure is calculated by tracing the chart's criti-

EXHIBIT 6-11

A PERT Network for the Furnace Modernization Project

Event	Description	Expected Time (in weeks)	Preceding Event
A	Approve design	8	None
B	Get construction permits	4	None
C	Take bids on new furnace and its installation	6	A
D	Order new furnace and equipment	1	C
E	Remove old furnace	2	B
F	Prepare site	3	E
G	Install new furnace	2	D, F
H	Test new furnace	1	G
I	Train workers to handle new furnace	2	G
J	Final inspection by company	2	H
K	Bring furnace on line into production flow	1	I, J

cal path: A-C-D-G-H-J-K. Any delay in completing the events along that path will delay the completion of the entire project. For example, if it took 6 weeks instead of 4 to get construction permits (event B), this delay would have no effect on the final completion date. Why? Because Start-B + B-E + E-F + F-G equals only 11 weeks, whereas Start-A + A-C + C-D + D-G equals 17 weeks. However, if Charley wanted to cut the 21-week time frame, he would give attention to those activities along the critical path that could be speeded up.

Control Charts

Control charts are a tool that grew out of the quality movement.[43] When a manager wants to ensure that a process is being done within an acceptable quality range, control charts can be of valuable assistance.

PERT Chart for Furnace Modernization Project

EXHIBIT 6-12

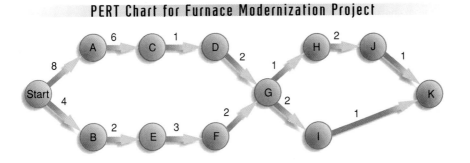

EXHIBIT 6-13

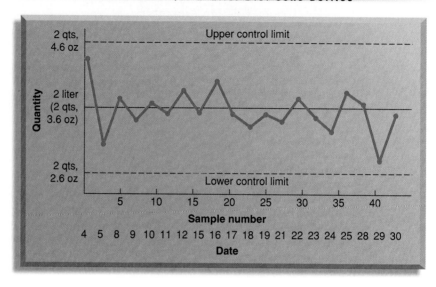

Control Chart for 2-Liter Diet Coke Bottles

As shown in Exhibit 6-13, **control charts** are diagrams that show plottings of results over a period of time, with statistically determined upper and lower limits. For instance, Coca-Cola samples its 2-liter bottles after they have been filled to determine their exact quantity and then plots the data on a control chart. This process tells management when the filling equipment needs adjustment. As long as the process variables fall within the predefined limits, as shown in Exhibit 6-13, the system is said to be "in control." When a point falls outside the limits, then the variation is unacceptable.

TYPES OF CONTROL CHARTS There are two basic types of control charts. One measures attributes and the other measures variables. **Attribute charts** measure a product characteristic in terms of whether it is good or bad. You might use this approach to judge the quality of a bicycle's paint color or the physical appearance of potato chips. **Variable charts** measure a characteristic such as length, weight, or volume on a continuous scale. So the measurement involves a range rather than a dichotomy. Variable charts require the setting of a standard and an acceptable range of deviation around that standard. Our example of filling bottles at Coca-Cola is a variable measure. The following discussion focuses on variable control charts.

SOURCES OF VARIATION There are two sources of variability in any process—one is controllable, the other is not. **Chance causes** of variation are due to random variations in the process. These exist in every process and are impossible to control unless you fundamentally change the process. For instance, no matter how finely tuned a photo-processing machine is, there will still be some minute and random variations among photographs. But control charts are directed at identifying assignable causes. These are due to nonchance variations and, thus, are capable of being identified and controlled.

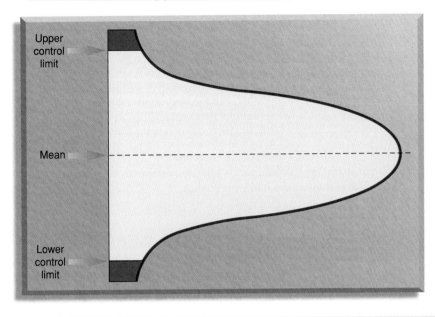

A Conrol Chart Using Three Standard
Deviations as Limits

EXHIBIT 6-14

CALCULATING VARIABILITY A basic knowledge of a few statistical concepts is needed to create a control chart and calculate variability. First is the **central limit theorem**. This states that a sampling distribution approaches normality as the size of the sample increases. Second is the concept of a **normal distribution**. This assumes that variations from a standard follow a bell-shaped curve. When a college instructor gives out grades that are 10 percent each of A's and F's, 20 percent each of B's and D's, and 40 percent C's, she is grading "on a curve" that follows a normal distribution. Third is the term **standard deviation**. This is a measure of variability in a group of numerical values. In a normal distribution, most of the measures will be close to the mean or average. But there will be some deviation. The *typical* difference from the mean is the standard deviation. In a normal distribution, approximately 68 percent of a set of values will fall between +1 and −1 standard deviation from the mean. Ninety-five percent will fall in the range of +2 and −2 standard deviations.

In developing a control chart, you define the upper and lower limits by the degree of deviation you are willing to accept. Typically, managers will set the limits at three standard deviations. This means that 99.7 percent of the mean values sampled should lie between the control limits (see Exhibit 6-14). When a sample average falls outside the limits, that is, above the upper control limit or below the lower limit, the process is very likely out of control. This result should then initiate a search for the cause of the problem.

STEPS IN DEVELOPING A CONTROL CHART The five actual steps that need to be followed to develop a control chart can be summarized as follows.[44]

1. *Gather historical data.* A control chart is constructed from historical data; future performance is compared with past performance. You need two distinctly different data sets, one to construct the control chart and a second to reflect the most recent performance.

2. Using the data for control chart construction, *calculate a process average and upper and lower control limits*. The control limits are based on the sampling distribution.

3. *Draw the control chart*, placing the variable measurement on one axis and the sequence of samples on the other axis.

4. *Plot the current or most recent sample average* on the chart.

5. *Interpret the chart* to see if (a) the process is in control and no action is required, (b) the process is out of control and a cause should be sought, or (c) the process is in control but trends are occurring that should alert you to possible nonrandom conditions.

 There is a variety of additional material available on the CD-ROM and companion Web site that accompany this text. You can access this information through the CD-ROM or by visiting the Web site at <**www.prenhall.com/robbins**>.

SUMMARY

(This summary is organized by the chapter-opening learning objectives on page 170.)

1. The control process consists of three separate and distinct steps: (1) measuring actual performance, (2) comparing actual performance against a standard, and (3) taking managerial action to correct deviations or inadequate standards. The control process assumes that standards of performance already exist.

2. The following behavioral control devices are available to managers: selection, new-employee orientation, mentoring, goals, job design, formal regulations, direct supervision, training, performance appraisal, and organizational rewards.

3. The economic order quantity (EOQ) model seeks to balance four costs involved in ordering and carrying inventory: purchasing, ordering, carrying, and stockout.

4. Data are raw, unanalyzed facts. Information is data that have been analyzed and processed. Managers rely on information, not on data, to make decisions.

5. Modern MIS can be separated into four stages: (1) management-focused data processing, in which centralized MIS units provided reports to management; (2) decentralized end-user computing, in which managers took responsibility for information control; (3) fixed-location interactive networks, when computers became linked and able to communicate with each other; and (4) mobile interactive networks, in which personal digital assistants allow information access and communication in multiple ways, anytime and anywhere.

6. Incremental budgets begin by using the last period as a reference point. Zero-base budgets create each new budget from scratch, and every item must be justified. Incremental budgets tend to limit bold or radical changes by reinforcing the past.

7. To create a PERT network, you need to: identify all significant activities and events, determine the order that events must be completed, diagram the flow of activities from start to finish, compute a time estimate for completing each activity, and determine a schedule for the start and finish dates for each activity and for the entire project.

8. To develop a workable control chart, you need to gather historical data, calculate a process average and upper and lower control limits, draw the control chart, plot the current or most recent sample average on the chart, and interpret the chart.

REVIEW QUESTIONS

1. What is the relationship between planning and control?

2. What critieria would be most effective for controlling (a) a stockbroker in a remote location; (b) a production supervisor; and (c) the membership sales office for a prominent museum?

3. A department manager achieves his unit's goals, yet spends only 70 percent of his allocated budget. Discuss the pluses and minuses of this outcome.

4. Specifically explain how each of the following controls hu-

man behavior: (a) employee selection; (b) mentoring; (c) goals; (d) training; and (e) organizational rewards.

5. What problems do you think might occur if a division manager is judged solely on his or her financial performance—for example, on return on investment or profit per dollar of sales revenue?

6. What is a Gantt chart? Why is it a control tool?

7. Explain the ABC system of inventory control.

8. Contrast the typical manager's control options in 1999 with control options in 1959.

9. When do electronic surveillance devices such as computers, video cameras, and telephone monitoring step over the line from "effective management controls" to "intrusions on employee rights"?

10. Contrast the advantages of control against its disadvantages.

IF I WERE THE MANAGER . . .

Nick's Parking

Nick Vignelli had parked cars to make extra money when he was in high school. Since his high school days, he's made his living running a small construction business. He recently decided he needed to diversify. He thought back to his teen years and thought he could get into the car parking business. Nick took over the parking concession for Mr. C's Italian restaurant three months ago.

As one of the most popular and successful restaurants in Fort Lee, New Jersey, Mr. C's customers almost all come by car, and it is the responsibility of Nick's staff to valet park each. The arrangement that Nick has with the restaurant is that he pays them $900 a month for the exclusive valet rights and his revenues are based completely on tips from Mr. C's customers. When Nick bid for this job, he calculated that his staff would park, on average, 120 cars a day, 6 days a week. He also projected that the average tip would be $3. Mr. C's provided the estimate of the number of cars he'd have each night. His $3 per car figure was derived from discussions with several other restaurant valet parkers.

Nick isn't able to be at the restaurant more than about two hours each evening. So the two or three attendants he's hired essentially work on their own from 11:00 A.M. to midnight.

In the first three months that Nick has had the concession, he's been pleased that the average number of cars parked has exceeded his estimate. The number has consistently been above 130. But the average tip has only been $2.15. When Nick is at the restaurant, tips average better than $3, but the overall numbers are way below his expectations. He's convinced that one or more of his attendants is pocketing some of the tip money, in spite of his rule that all tips go into a box he has set aside in the kiosk. Attendants are paid a flat hourly rate and are not allowed to keep any tip money.

If you were Nick, what could you do to improve controls at your parking lot?

SKILL EXERCISE

Creating a Budget

You have recently been appointed as advertising manager for a new monthly health and diet magazine, *Fitness 1*, being developed by the Magazine Division at Hearst Corporation. You were previously an advertising manager on one of the company's established magazines. You will report to the new magazine's publisher, Molly Tymon.

Estimates of first-year subscription sales for *Fitness 1* are 125,000. Magazine-stand sales should add another 40,000 a month to that number. But your concern is with developing advertising revenue for the magazine.

You and Molly have set a goal of selling advertising space totaling $6 million during *Fitness 1*'s first year. You think you can do this with a staff of about ten people.

Because this is a completely new publication, there is no previous budget for your advertising group. You've been asked by Molly to submit a preliminary budget for your group.

Write up a report, not to exceed three pages in length: (1) Describe in detail how you would go about this assignment. For example, where would you get budget categories? Whom would you contact? (2) Present your best effort at creating a budget for your department.

The Library Addition

Form groups of 4 to 5 students each. You are a project team created to oversee the design and building of a 30,000-square-foot addition to your college's library. Identify at least 15 events that your team considers relevant to this project; then develop realistic estimates of time to complete each. Finally, create a PERT network. Calculate the time for completion. What, if anything, could your team do to cut 3 months from this completion date?

Would You Want to Work for Ron Edens?

Ron Edens runs a company called Electronic Banking System Inc. located outside Baltimore, Maryland, EBS provides outsourcing clerical services. It handles the clerical tasks involved in processing donations for groups such as Mothers Against Drunk Driving, Greenpeace, and the National Organization for Women. Most of Edens's employees earn $7 an hour or less doing repetitive tasks such as opening envelopes or recording donation data on a computer. Ron Edens is especially proud of the control system he has created to closely monitor his employees.

Walking around EBS, you see long lines of people sitting at spartan desks, slitting open envelopes, sorting contents, and filling out "control cards" that record how many letters they have opened and how long it has taken them. These letter openers must process three envelopes a minute. Nearby, other workers tap keyboards, keeping pace with a quota that demands 8,500 strokes an hour. Jobs are highly specialized and involve extensive repetition. Letter openers only open envelopes and sort contents. Workers in the audit department just compute figures. Data-entry clerks punch in the information that the others have collected.

The workroom is silent. Talking is forbidden. The windows are covered. Coffee mugs, personal photos, and other adornments are barred from workers' desks. Edens wants to remove anything that might distract his workers from the job at hand. For example, commenting on the blocked windows, Edens says, "I don't want them looking out—it's distracting. They'll make mistakes."

In his office upstairs, Edens sits before a TV monitor that flashes images from eight cameras posted throughout the plant.

"There's a little bit of Sneaky Pete to it," he admits, using a remote control to zoom in on a document atop a worker's desk. "I can basically read that and figure out how someone's day is going." In addition, his system's software generates daily reports recording the precise number of keystrokes tapped by each data-entry worker and the number of errors made by each worker.

The work floor at EBS resembles an enormous classroom in the throes of exam period. Desks point toward the front, where a manager keeps watch from a raised platform. Other supervisors are positioned toward the back of the room. "If you want to watch someone," Edens explains, "it's easier from behind because they don't know you're watching." There's also a black globe hanging from the ceiling, in which cameras are positioned.

At EBS, workers handle thousands of dollars in checks and cash. That's one reason, Edens says, for the cameras. It can help deter would-be thieves. But Edens concedes that tight observation also helps EBS monitor productivity and weed out workers who don't keep up. "There are multiple uses," Edens says of surveillance.

Edens is unapologetic about his control system, including the rule that forbids all talk unrelated to the completion of each task. "I'm not paying people to chat. I'm paying them to open envelopes," he says.

Edens offers considerable insight into his philosophy of management when he says, "We don't ask these people to think—the machines think for them. They don't have to make decisions." His words could have come directly out of the mouth of Frederick Taylor. In fact, EBS is living proof that today's technology can allow managers to monitor workers more closely than a turn-of-the-century foreman with a stopwatch ever could.

QUESTIONS

1. What kind of people do you think Edens is able to find to work in his firm? (Clue: Think in terms of matching individual personalities and job preferences with the work climate at EBS.)

2. List both the advantages and the disadvantages you see in Edens's control system.

3. What ethical issues, if any, would you be concerned about at EBS and why?

Source: Based on T. Horwitz, "Mr. Edens Profits from Watching His Workers' Every Move," *Wall Street Journal*, December 1, 1994, p. A11.

VIDEO CASE EXERCISE

Keeping the Coffee Coming

At the Port of New Orleans, the largest coffee port in the United States, one company is handling an old-fashioned product in a new-fashioned way. Frederico Pacorini's SiloCaf, a fully computerized bulk coffee storage, handling, and processing facility, is a place where tradition meets technology.

SiloCaf was founded in 1933 as a forwarding company: in other words, a company that takes any type of product and moves it from any location to any other location. Today, the company specializes in forwarding commodities, primarily coffee, and the way it handles coffee is about as high-tech as it can get. Why has SiloCaf invested in technology for such a seemingly simple product? The main reason is that consumers want the same flavor from each and every can of coffee they buy. Coffee, however, is a natural product, with impurities and defects, and coffee crops are never the same, so getting a consistent flavor is difficult without some way to control the coffee blend. SiloCaf is addressing this challenge by using information systems technology and computer technology.

Mossimo Toma is SiloCaf's systems and resources manager. He is responsible for overseeing the coffee-blending process. Coffee beans come into SiloCaf's warehouse from all over the world. Each week 10 million pounds of coffee are blended (about 4 million bags per year). The coffee never stays in SiloCaf's plant more than one week. Once it's been processed and blended, it's loaded into bags or in bulk and shipped to a coffee roasting company. At any one time, SiloCaf has from 35 million to 40 million pounds of coffee in its facility for processing. If you consider the price of a pound of coffee, SiloCaf has an extremely valuable resource in its possession. Actually, SiloCaf never owns the coffee; it's owned by the roasting company or the dealer who delivers the coffee to the roasting company.

All the mechanical parts in SiloCaf's New Orleans facility have been brought from Italy, which is where the company first developed the technology. Frederico Pacorini, the son of the founder and the manager of the New Orleans facility, says that technology in a business like theirs is important because it allows them to make all the blends they need for their customers (coffee roasters), to optimize the way they do blends, and to control blends. SiloCaf's employees receive continual statistical reports for each one of the scales used to blend the coffee. The reports enable them to check the consistency of the scale's performance, which is important for achieving the consistency of the product that the end user (consumer) wants.

You'd think that all this high-tech control would be expensive, but it's not. The nice thing about SiloCaf's solution to the blend consistency challenge is that the technology they're using is relatively simple. In fact, the company's investment was a mere 1 percent of all plant investment dollars spent.

QUESTIONS

1. What types of controls do you see in this example? Be specific.

2. How could you use this case to demonstrate the link between planning and control?

3. SiloCaf never owns the coffee it blends. Considering this fact, why would controls be important?

4. Do controls have to be expensive to be effective? Explain.

Source: Based on *Small Business 2000, Show 109.*

NOTES

1. Based on N. Shirouzu and J. Bigness, "7-Eleven Operators Resist System to Monitor Managers," *Wall Street Journal*, June 16, 1997, p. B1.

2. For a comprehensive review of control systems, see R. Anthony and V. Govindarajan, *Management Control Systems*, 8th ed. (Homewood, IL: Irwin, 1994).

3. See, for instance, E. E. Lawler III and J. G. Rhode, *Information and Control in Organizations* (Pacific Palisades, CA: Goodyear, 1976).

4. See R. Rachlin and A. H. W. Sweeny (eds.), *Handbook of Budgeting* (New York: Wiley, 1993); R. G. Finney, *Basics of Budgeting* (New York: AMACOM, 1993); and J. K. Shim and J. G. Siegel, *Budgeting Basics and Beyond* (Englewood Cliffs, NJ: Prentice Hall, 1995).

5. See R. S. Russell and B. W. Taylor III, *Production & Operations Management* (Englewood Cliffs, NJ: Prentice Hall, 1995).

6. W. Clark, *The Gantt Chart: A Working Tool of Management* (New York: Ronald Press, 1922).

7. D. Bartholomew, "MRP Upstaged," *Industry Week*, February 3, 1997, pp. 39–41.

8. T. M. Rohan, "Supplier-Customer Links Multiplying," *Industry Week*, April 17, 1989, p. 20.

9. See, for instance, Russell and Taylor, *Production & Operations Management*, pp. 591–601.

10. J. Hampton, "Friends of the People," *Canadian Business*, November 1994, p. 43.

11. J. T. Small and W. B. Lee, "In Search of an MIS," *MSU Business Topics*, Autumn 1975, pp. 47–55.

12. H. A. Simon, *Administrative Behavior*, 3rd ed. (New York: Free Press, 1976), p. 294.

13. J. C. Carter and F. N. Silverman, "Establishing an MIS," *Journal of Systems Management*, January 1980, p. 15.

14. See G. L. Boyer and D. McKinnon, "End-User Computing Is Here to Stay," *Supervisory Management*, October 1989, pp. 17–22.

15. See, for example, B. Filipczak, "The Ripple Effect of Computer Networking," *Training*, March 1994, pp. 40–47.

16. "Electronic Mail: Neither Rain, Nor Sleet, Nor Software . . . ," *Business Week*, February 20, 1989, p. 36.

17. See, for example, J. Teresko, "Tripping Down the Information Superhighway," *Industry Week*, August 2, 1993, pp. 32–40; G. Brockhouse, "I Have Seen the Future . . . ," *Canadian Business*, August 1993, pp. 43–45; and C. Newsome, "Executives Can Work on the Move," *Asian Business*, January 1996, pp. 51–55.

18. B. Gates, *The Road Ahead* (New York: Viking, 1995), pp. 73–77.

19. S. V. Brull, "A Digital Jack-of-All Trades," *Business Week*, November 26, 1996, p. 68; and L. Armstrong, "Assistants for the Digital Life," *Business Week*, November 16, 1998, pp. 176–78.

20. See, for instance, T. L. Griffith, "Teaching Big Brother to Be a Team Player: Computer Monitoring and Quality," *The Executive*, February 1993, pp. 73–80; and D. Hawkins, "Who's Watching Now?," *U.S. News & World Report*, September 15, 1997, pp. 56–58.

21. G. Bylinksy, "How Companies Spy on Employees," *Fortune*, November 4, 1991, pp. 131–40.

22. J. Markoff, "The Snooping Mayor," *New York Times*, May 4, 1990, p. B1.

23. J. Rothfeder, "Memo to Workers: Don't Phone Home," *Business Week*, January 25, 1988, pp. 88–90.

24. J. R. Hayes, "Memo Busters," *Forbes*, April 24, 1995, pp. 174–75.

25. J. R. Aiello and K. J. Kolb, "Electronic Performance Monitoring and Social Context: Impact on Productivity and Stress," *Journal of Applied Psychology*, June 1995, p. 339.

26. K. B. DeTienne, "Big Brother or Friendly Coach? Computer Monitoring in the 21st Century," *The Futurist*, February 1993, pp. 33–37.

27. N. Hutheesing, "What Are You Doing on That Porn Site?" *Forbes*, November 3, 1997, pp. 368–69.

28. See, for instance, Lawler and Rhode, *Information and Control in Organizations*; B. J. Jaworski and S. M. Young, "Dysfunctional Behavior and Management Control: An Empirical Study of Marketing Managers," *Accounting, Organizations and Society*, January 1992, pp. 17–35; and S. Kerr, "On the Folly of Rewarding A, While Hoping for B," *The Executive*, February 1995, pp. 7–14.

29. Based on a tape recording made by the Dallas Fire Department and made available under the Texas Open Records Act.

30. Cited in A. B. Carroll, "In Search of the Moral Manager," *Business Horizons*, March–April 1987, p. 7.

31. See, for instance, Jaworski and Young, "Dysfunctional Behavior and Management Control," pp. 17–35.

32. P. M. Blau, *The Dynamics of Bureaucracy*, rev. ed. (Chicago: University of Chicago Press, 1963).

33. Lawler and Rhode, *Information and Control in Organizations*, p. 108.

34. J. D. Thompson, *Organizations in Action* (New York: McGraw-Hill, 1967), p. 124.

35. P. A. Pyhrr, "Zero-Base Budgeting," *Harvard Business Review*, November–December 1970, pp. 111–18; and M. Dirsmith and S. Jablonski, "Zero Base Budgeting as a Management Technique and Political Strategy," *Academy of Management Review*, October 1979, pp. 555–65.

36. See, for instance, J. V. Pearson and R. J. Michael, "Zero-Base Budgeting: A Technique for Planned Organizational Decline," *Long Range Planning*, June 1981, pp. 68–76.

37. N. C. Churchill, "Budget Choice: Planning vs. Control," *Harvard Business Review*, July–August 1984, pp. 150–64.

38. J. A. Miller, *Implementing Activity-Based Management in Daily Operations* (New York: Wiley, 1996); K. M. Kroll, "The ABC's Revisited," *Industry Week*, December 2, 1996, pp. 19–21; and S. S. Rao, "ABC's of Cost Control," *Inc. Technology*, July 1997, pp. 79–81.

39. S. S. Rao, "Overhead Can Kill You," *Forbes*, February 10, 1997, p. 98.

40. See R. N. Anthony, J. Dearden, and N. M. Bedford, *Management Control Systems*, 5th ed. (Homewood, IL: Irwin, 1984), chapters 5–7.

41. See Russell and Taylor, *Production and Operations Management*, p. 830.

42. For a discussion of software and application to a project for restructuring a large retail chain, see P. A. Strassmann, "The Best-Laid Plans," *Inc.*, October 1988, pp. 135–38.

43. See, for instance, M. Sashkin and K. J. Kiser, *Putting Total Quality Management to Work* (San Francisco: Berrett-Koehler, 1993), pp. 12–15.

44. Adapted from Russell and Taylor, *Production & Operations Management*, pp. 153–72.

Humanities and Social Sciences

ECONOMICS It can arguably be said that the foundations for any manager's understanding of rational decision making is based on microeconomic principles, that is, related to the functioning of individual industries and the behavior of individual decision-making units. Business decision makers who lack an understanding of basic microeconomic concepts such as opportunity costs, the marginal principle, sunk costs, price elasticity of demand, or the law of diminishing returns place themselves at a severe disadvantage.

PSYCHOLOGY What economics is to rational decision making, psychology is to an understanding of actual decision making. Bounded rationality, image theory, heuristics, and escalation of commitment are just a few concepts whose roots lay in psychology. And much of what we know about how to use groups effectively in decision making comes from psychology.

POLITICAL SCIENCE Topics such as quotas, tariffs, subsidies, and protectionism—frequently addressed in political science courses—reinforce the role that governments play in an organization's environment. Additionally, our understanding of the increasing power of lobbies and other interest groups on the actions of organizations comes from political scientists.

PHILOSOPHY For students of business, capitalism and socialism provide two very different philosophies of how economic resources should be owned, produced, distributed, and consumed. But philosophy provides something important to anyone who makes decisions in organizations. It helps develop critical thinking and introduces the role of ethics in decision making. Critical thinking facilitates the ability to reason clearly primarily through inductive and deductive logic. It can help you, for example, to identify fallacious reasoning, unclear or misleading language, and manipulative communicative techniques. You can also apply philosophic methods to problem solving, decision making, and strategic thinking. Because ethics moves from beyond black or white to shades of gray, philoso-

phy can also help managers to analyze their values, apply moral reasoning to business conflicts, and deal with ethical issues and the morality of business activities.

Business Disciplines

ACCOUNTING Accounting is the system that measures business activities, processes that information into reports, and communicates these findings to decision makers. Of particular relevance to us is managerial accounting (in contrast to financial accounting), because it serves internal users of an organization's financial information. These internal users are often managers.

Decision makers use accounting information to develop sound business plans. For instance, accounting information determines whether your organization is making a profit. It can tell you if a product is covering its costs. It can guide individual managers in keeping their department costs in line.

An organization's accounting system collects information used by decision makers. Accounting systems, through their use of budgets and reports, are the primary means by which management controls financial resources. The design of an organization's accounting system, in terms of the data generated and who controls information, will also affect the distribution of power within the organization and the structure itself.

Budgets are both planning and control documents. Managers at every level use budgets to numerically specify expectations in terms of revenues and expenditures over a period of time. In addition, financial statements prepared by accountants are used by managers to analyze costs and assess financial performance.

FINANCE Financial statements are documents that report on an organization's performance in monetary terms.

Finance is one area that makes its dependence on other business disciplines explicit. Specifically, knowledge of financial issues are inextricably linked to accounting concepts. Financial analysis relies on accounting data. As such, a course in basic accounting is almost always a prerequisite for any course in finance.

Every organization's strategy should address strengths, weaknesses, opportunities, and threats. Certainly this must include sources and availability of capital. Limits on the availability of short-term or long-term funds, for instance, can completely nullify the most encouraging opportunities.

BUSINESS LAW A course in business law introduces the legal environment in which organizations must operate. Managers don't need to be lawyers, but depending on the type of business you're in, you often do need to understand regulatory law, tort law, contracts, and agency. From a strategic standpoint, laws constrain and limit opportunities. A great business idea, for instance, may not be realistic if it infringes on someone else's copyright, trademark, or patent. Similarly, in the United States at least, there are a host of federal agencies—including the Equal Employment Opportunity Commission, the Food and Drug Administration, the Federal Trade Commission, and the Occupational Safety and Health Administration—that regulate business practices. Failure to understand the laws that these agencies impose upon your business can mean the quick demise of that business.

MARKETING Strategic planning must encompass marketing plans. How are our customers' needs and wants changing? What are the best ways to reach potential customers? For instance, database technology and the Internet now allow many companies to rely less on wholesale and retail intermediaries. They can use direct mail more effectively; and they can sell their products on-line. Amazon.com, as a case in point, has totally reinvented the way consumers can purchase books and forced traditional booksellers, like Barnes and Noble, to develop new strategies.

Much of our knowledge about scanning the environment, identifying competitors, designing competitive intelligence systems, and differentiating an organization's products comes from marketing's contributions. More specifically, every marketing course allocates a considerable amount of time to explaining that plans, decisions, and strategies are strongly influenced by the external environment.

OPERATIONS Organizations often look to operations as a source of sustainable competitive advantage. These can include: a low-cost product, product-line breadth, technical superiority, customized product offerings, and quicker deliveries.

Operational planning tools include budgets and schedules; and planning of capacity, layout, material requirements, and inventory levels.

Statistical process control, inventory control, and quality control are covered in depth in courses on operations management. Similarly, operations provides detailed discussion of forecasting—types, approaches, and techniques. It's in this course, for example, where you'll learn how to do moving averages, exponential smoothing, and trend projections.

A course in operations will spend considerable time covering project management—describing project planning, scheduling, and controlling. Specific issues will include setting time and cost estimates, allocating personnel resources, and learning how to develop PERT networks for large and complex projects.

Finally, operations uses decision science and operations-research techniques developed by mathematicians and statisticians to help with complex decisions. Techniques covered typically include expected value, decision trees, linear programming, queuing theory, and computerized simulations.

MANAGEMENT INFORMATION SYSTEMS MIS describes systems for transmitting and transforming data into information that can be used in decision making. Many students take a separate course in computers or information systems. This course typically covers topics such as database management, software applications, data communication networks, expert systems, and executive information systems. The clearest link of this material to management lies in decision making and communication. Much of the material in chapters 3 and 7 of this book, for example, evolves out of studies in MIS and information technology.

TECHNOLOGY AND THE DESIGN OF WORK PROCESSES

TODAY, A GREETING CARD THAT PLAYS "HAPPY
BIRTHDAY" WHEN YOU OPEN IT HAS MORE COMPUTING
POWER THAN EXISTED IN THE WORLD BEFORE 1950.

J. HUEY

LEARNING OBJECTIVES

After studying this chapter, you should be able to:

1 Explain how technology can improve productivity.

2 Describe the advantages of computer-aided design.

3 Identify why management might consider introducing flexible manufacturing systems.

4 Define and describe the three key elements in reengineering.

5 Explain how information technology is providing managers with decision support.

6 Identify the five key dimensions in a job.

7 Design individual jobs to maximize employee performance.

8 Explain how flextime, job sharing, and telecommuting increase organizational flexibility.

How do you grow and prosper in an industry where you need to offer customers a new product line nearly every six months? Compaq Computer Inc.'s answer is to build two types of factories.[1]

Compaq's management has developed a system that enables the company to respond nimbly to retailers and businesses. Some of its computers are made using "cell manufacturing" technology (see photo). Others are produced using traditional assembly-line technology. Which technology management chooses depends on where a product is in it's life cycle and demand at any specific time.

Cell manufacturing is grounded in the way people built products in their homes before the industrial revolution. Groups of three people operate a workstation "cell," where computers are built, tested, and shipped. Since cells are independent, each one is capable of producing a different computer model. With 48 cells equaling one traditional assembly line, this technology enables Compaq to produce hundreds of different models in any given week.

"Cell manufacturing gives us the ability to make changes when we need to," says Compaq senior vice president Ross Cooley. But not without added expense. A typical assembly line at Compaq costs approximately $2.5 million to set up. "Cellularizing" that same work space costs $10 million because full sets of tools have to be deployed at each workstation and cell workers must be better trained and paid than assembly-line workers.

Currently, Compaq is using a combination of assembly-line and cell manufacturing. The company's Presario computers were produced using the less costly assembly-line methods in the first few months of their shelf life, when demand was exceptionally strong. When orders tapered off, Compaq switched over to cell manufacturing and converted the assembly line for its next generation of products—the Armada line of notebook computers.

In its quest to be the world leader in all product categories—notebooks, servers, consumer and commerical desktops—Compaq faces stiff competition from manufacturers that specialize in certain market segments. Gateway 2000 and Dell, for example, build to order without retail sales. This requires Compaq to be both fast on its feet and efficient. By adding cell manufacturing technology to the more traditional assembly line, Compaq is better able to meet the demands of an ever-changing marketplace.

In recent years, the term *technology* has been widely used by economists, managers, consultants, and business analysts to describe machinery and equipment that utilizes sophisticated electronics and computers. In actuality, **technology** is merely a generic term to describe how an organization transforms its inputs into outputs. Compaq's cell manufacturing and assembly lines are examples of *manufacturing* technologies. But every organization uses some type of technology for converting financial, human, and physical resources into products or services. Colleges, as a case in point, use a number of *instruction* technologies—lectures, case analysis, experiential case methods, programmed learning—to convert the unlearned into the educated.

In this chapter, we focus on how operations and information technologies are influencing management and work processes, the effect of technology on worker obsolescence, and how managers can design jobs and work schedules to maximize employee performance.

The common theme among new technologies in the workplace is that they substitute machinery for human labor in transforming inputs into outputs. This substitution of capital for labor has been going on essentially nonstop since the industrial revolution began in the mid-1800s. For instance, the introduction of electricity allowed textile factories to

TECHNOLOGY AND PRODUCTIVITY

introduce mechanical looms that could produce cloth far faster and more cheaply than was previously possible when the looms were powered by individuals. But it has been the computerization of equipment and machinery in the past 30 years that has reshaped the current workplace. Automated teller machines, for example, have replaced tens of thousands of human tellers in banks. Ninety-eight percent of the spot-welds on new Ford Tauruses are performed by robots, not by people. Many cars now come equipped with onboard computers that diagnose in seconds problems that used to take mechanics hours to diagnose. IBM has built a plant in Austin, Texas, that can produce laptop computers without the help of a single worker. Everything from the time parts arrive at the IBM plant to the final packing of finished products is completely automated. An increasing number of companies, small and large alike, are turning to multimedia and interactive technology for employee training. And literally millions of organizations have utilized personal computers to decentralize decision making and generate enormous increases in productivity.

Productivity is the name of the game! It is technology's ability to significantly increase productivity that is driving the technology bandwagon. In its simplest form, productivity can be expressed in the following ratio:

$$\text{Productivity} = \frac{\text{Outputs}}{\text{Labor} + \text{Capital} + \text{Materials}}$$

This formula can be applied in its total form or broken down into subcategories.[2] For instance, output per labor hour is perhaps the most common partial measure of productivity. Industrial engineers, who conduct time-and-motion studies in factories, are largely focused on generating increases in labor productivity. IBM's automated plant in Austin, Texas, is an example of increasing productivity by substituting capital (i.e., machinery and equipment) for labor. Materials productivity is concerned with increasing the efficient use of material inputs and supplies. A meatpacking plant, as an illustrative case, improves its materials productivity when it finds additional uses for by-products that were previously treated as waste.

Productivity can also be applied at three different levels—the individual, the group, and the total organization. Word-processing software, fax machines, and e-mail have made secretaries more productive by allowing them to generate more output during their workdays. The use of self-managed teams has increased the productivity of many work groups at companies such as Honeywell, Coors Brewing, and Aetna Life. And Southwest Airlines is, overall, a more productive organization than rivals such as American Airlines or USAir because Southwest's cost per available seat-mile is 30 to 60 percent lower than that of these competitors.

This analysis brings us to the following conclusion: Because technology is the means by which inputs are turned into outputs, it is the primary focus of any management's efforts to improve productivity.

OPERATIONS TECHNOLOGY

High-tech manufacturing is going global. Satyan Pitroda, for instance, believes that developing countries such as India and Mexico can leapfrog into the upper ranks of high-tech manufacturing.[3] By using technology developed elsewhere, these countries can bypass stages of development. To illustrate, Pitroda used an all-Indian team to design a phone switch suited to India's heat, humidity, dust, and frequent power failures. Inside the switch are chips from Motorola, Intel, and Texas Instruments. But by using technology transfer, Indian firms are now designing and exporting switches.

In this section, we look at key issues related to operations technology—design, production, customer service, distribution, continuous improvement processes, and reengineering work processes.

Design

Technology is redefining how the design of products is done. For instance, computer-aided design is generating substantial improvements in design productivity. And sophisticated computer networks are allowing designers to collaborate as never before.

Computer-aided design (CAD) essentially has made manual drafting obsolete. With computational and graphics software, the geometry of a product or component can be graphically displayed and manipulated on video monitors. Alternative designs can be created and evaluated quickly, and the cost of developing mock-ups and prototypes is often eliminated.[4] CAD enables engineers to develop new designs in as little as a third of the time required for manual drafting. Eagle Engine Manufacturing, for instance, used its CAD system to design a new race car engine in 9 months instead of the traditional 2+ years.[5]

The best CAD software lets engineers plan products, test them on-screen, and even design tools to make them. Designers at Caterpillar have one of the most sophisticated design systems anywhere—a virtual reality proving ground where designers can test-drive huge earthmoving machines before they are built.[6] The system is a surround-screen, surround-sound cube about 10 feet on each side that creates the illusion of reality for anyone inside by projecting supercomputer-generated 3-D graphics onto the walls. Designers operate imaginary controls and make adjustments as needed. A recent Caterpillar backhoe and wheel loader incorporate visibility and performance improvements based on data from these virtual test-drives. Boeing used CAD to design its 777 jet.[7] Engineers were able to design and preassemble the entire plane and its more than 3 million parts on-screen.

Ford Motor Co. has developed an international network that allows its designers around the world to work together as if they were in the same room.[8] Ford's corporate design organization combines design sites in Dearborn, Michigan; Dunton, England; Cologne, Germany; Turin, Italy; Valencia, California; Hiroshima, Japan; and Melbourne, Australia. The network enables a Ford engineer in Dunton, for example, to transmit to Dearborn massive CAD files of 3-D drawings for a future model car. In Michigan, a designer can bring up the drawings on a workstation, phone his English colleague, and work simultaneously with that colleague in making on-screen revisions, even rotating the 3-D images to view them from all sides. A few hours later, the data files might be sent through satellite or fiber-optic circuits to Turin, where a computerized milling machine can turn out a clay or plastic-foam model in a matter of hours. The Ford Contour, the Mercury Mystique, and Ford's European Mondeo were all designed using this network approach.

Production

Technological advances over the past 20 years have completely reinvented the way products are manufactured. First there were robotics, just-in-time systems, cycle-time reduction efforts. Today, we have entered the stage of mass customization called flexible manufacturing systems. Of course, there have also been important breakthroughs in the basic technologies of manufacturing. For instance, consider the success Finarvedi SpA has had with its new sheet steel plant in Cremona, Italy.[9]

By designing and pre-assembling the entire Boeing 777 on screen, engineers were able to reduce parts interference and rework by up to 90 percent.

Traditional steelmaking uses a technology, called hot and cold rolling, that wastes a lot of energy and floor space. For instance, coils of steel about a twelfth of an inch thick are made by casting steel slabs, lugging them to giant ovens for reheating, and then flattening them under a series of monstrous rollers that stretch for up to 2 miles. The whole process takes about 3 hours. The Cremona mill uses a revolutionary technology that gets the same results in 15 minutes and uses one-third the energy on a line that measures a little under 600 feet! The new technology allows the company to roll molten metal directly into thin steel. The mill employs only 400 people compared with 1,200 workers needed to generate comparable volume in a traditional plant. And not only does this new technology provide Finarvedi with a $25-a-ton cost advantage over its rivals, it also enables the company to produce steel to order. Management can guarantee delivery within 3 days, versus the industry norm of about 3 weeks.

ROBOTICS **Robots** are machines that act like human beings. By the late 1970s, manufacturing firms began adding robots to assembly lines. General Dynamics, for instance, used a robot in its Fort Worth, Texas, plant to drill more than 500 holes in the tail fins of its F-16 jet fighter. The robot was able to do in 3 hours what previously took workers 24 hours![10] From those basic robots came **industrial robotics**—computer-controlled machines that manipulate materials and perform complex functions. The leaders in this move to industrial robotics have been the Japanese.

But robots weren't without their problems. They were good at handling simple jobs, but they failed when tasks became more complicated. Today, robots are playing more of a support role in a larger computer-based manufacturing system.

JUST-IN-TIME INVENTORY SYSTEMS In chapter 6, we discussed the importance of controlling inventories. Large companies such as Boeing, Toyota, and General Electric have literally billions of dollars wrapped up in inventories. It's not unusual for even small firms to have a million dollars or more tied up in inventories. So anything management can do to significantly reduce the size of its inventory will improve its organization's productivity.

Just-in-time (JIT) inventory systems change the technology around which inventories are managed. Inventory items arrive when they are needed in the production process instead of being stored in stock.[11] In Japan, JIT systems are called **kanban**. The derivation of the word gets to the essence of the just-in-time concept. *Kanban* is Japanese for "card" or "sign." Japanese suppliers pack parts into containers and ship them to manufacturers. Each container has a card, or *kanban*, slipped into a side pocket. When a production worker opens a container, he or she takes out the card and sends it back to the supplier. Receiving the card signals the supplier to ship a second container of parts that, ideally, reaches the production worker just as the last part in the first container is being used up. The ultimate goal of a JIT inventory system is to eliminate raw material inventories by coordinating production and supply deliveries precisely. When the system works as designed, it results in a number of positive benefits for a manufacturer: reduced inventories, reduced setup time, better work flow, shorter manufacturing time, less space consumption, and even higher quality. Of course, suppliers who can be depended on to deliver quality materials on time must be found. Because there are no inventories, there is no slack in the system to absorb defective materials or delays in shipments.

How JIT works in the United States can be seen in the relationship that has developed between Lear Seating Corp. and Chrysler.[12] Lear is a rapidly growing manufacturer of car seats. They make seats for most of the major automakers. To supply Chrysler's Detroit "Dodge City" plant with seats for Dodge pickup trucks, Lear built a 200-worker facility 38 miles away in Romulus, Michigan. When a pickup starts down "Dodge City's" line, an

---

In The News

VW Builds the Factory of the Future

It's being described as a revolution in the way cars are built. It is likely to be the model for new car factories all around the world. And it's being done by VW at its new Resende truck plant outside Rio de Janeiro, Brazil.

Cars have traditionally been built on assembly lines. Suppliers deliver parts to the car manufacturer's loading dock, then they are moved to the appropriate place on the assembly line where they're needed, and final assembly is done by the carmaker's workers.

At Resende, VW has essentially outsourced the assembly of its vehicles to its suppliers. The $250 million plant—which builds 7- to 35-ton trucks—uses hundreds of suppliers who channel their materials through just seven final assemblers. Each of these assemblers is allocated in an area in the plant and is responsible for putting together one of the seven modules that makes up a finished truck. German instrument maker VDO Kienzle, for instance, starts with the steel shell of a truck cab. Up to 200 VDO workers install everything from seats to the instrument panels. Then, they attach the finished cab to a chasis moving down the assembly line through the various suppliers'

spaces. In all, Resende will have 1,400 workers when it reaches full speed, but only 200 will be VW employees.

VW saves in a number of ways. It has fewer employees for which it's directly reponsible. Suppliers pay for their own tools and fixtures. And individual suppliers are responsible for their inventory costs. However, these are kept to a minimum, since the plant uses a just-in-time inventory system. Parts arrive just an hour or so before they're needed. Finally, management gains the advice and cooperation of its suppliers in cutting costs and boosting productivity. The net result is that VW expects this plant to use 12 percent fewer labor hours than a typical auto factory.

Other automakers are following VW's lead. For instance, a joint venture between Mercedes Benz and watchmaker SMH Swatch will be relying on a modular approach to build the Smart, a $10,000 city car. The car, to be built in a new factory in western France, is split into seven modules. All will be assembled inside the plant by suppliers.

Source: D. Woodruff, I. Katz, and K. Naughton, "VW's Factory of the Future," *Business Week*, October 7, 1996, pp. 52–56.

---

electronic message calling for the particular seats for that truck is flashed to Romulus, which can produce the seats and deliver them to Chrysler in 90 minutes. The seats are built and shipped in the sequence in which they will be used, saving both Chrysler and Lear large amounts of working capital that was once tied up in seat inventories. In essence, Lear's Romulus plant has become an extension of the "Dodge City" plant. And Chrysler's concentrating its seat orders with Lear gives the seat manufacturer efficiencies of scale that it can pass on to Chrysler in lower costs.

CYCLE TIME REDUCTION If you think of an organization's operations as being a set of steps making up a complete process or cycle, productivity can be increased by eliminating one or more steps, dropping barriers between steps, and/or completing the steps more quickly. These efforts at increasing efficiency reduce **cycle time**. It's the unusual organization today where management isn't focusing on cycle time reduction to lower costs and facilitate faster customer response.[13]

How does an organization reduce cycle time? By using a variety of technical tools, including: TQM techniques, layout redesign, movement flowcharts, supplier certification, just-in-time inventory systems, and redesigning work around teams. And results have been impressive.[14] U.S. Steel reduced cycle time for making hot-rolled sheet steel by 60 percent over 2 years. Schindler Elevator Corp. cut the cycle time by 80 percent over a 5-year period in its escalator production plant in North Carolina. L. L. Bean used layout and movement flowcharts to allow its mail-order unit to respond with a correct shipment rate of 99.9 percent within only a few hours after an order is received.

FLEXIBLE MANUFACTURING SYSTEMS They look like something out of a science fiction movie in which remote-controlled carts deliver a basic casting to a computerized machining center. With robots positioning and repositioning the casting, the machining center calls upon its hundreds of tools to perform various operations that turn the casting into a finished part. Completed parts, each a bit different from the others, are finished at a rate of one every 90 seconds. Neither skilled machinists nor conventional machine tools are used. Nor are there any costly delays for changing dies or tools in this factory. A single machine can make dozens or even hundreds of different parts in any order management wants. This is the world of **flexible manufacturing systems**.[15]

In a global economy, those manufacturing organizations that can respond rapidly to change have a competitive advantage. They can, for instance, better meet the diverse needs of customers and deliver products faster than their competitors. When customers were willing to accept standardized products, fixed assembly lines made sense. But nowadays, flexible technologies are increasingly necessary to compete effectively.

The unique characteristic of flexibile manufacturing systems is that by integrating computer-aided design, engineering, and manufacturing, they can produce low-volume products for customers at a cost comparable to what had previously been possible only through mass production. Flexible manufacturing systems are, in effect, repealing the laws of economies of scale. Management no longer has to mass produce thousands of identical products to achieve low per-unit production costs. With flexible manufacturing, when management wants to produce a new part, it doesn't change machines—it just changes the computer program. So management is able to respond to each customer's unique taste, specification, and budget.

Some automated plants can build a wide variety of flawless products and switch from one product to another on cue from a central computer. John Deere, for instance, has a $1.5 billion automated factory that can turn out ten basic tractor models with as many as 3,000 options without plant shutdowns for retooling. National Bicycle Industrial Co., which sells its bikes under the Panasonic brand, uses flexible manufacturing to produce any of 11,231,862 variations on eighteen models of racing, road, and mountain bikes in 199 color patterns and an almost unlimited number of sizes. Panasonic can provide almost customized bikes at mass-produced prices.[16]

▶ Customer Service

In the midst of the Christmas rush, a frazzled customer came into Silverman's, a men's apparel chain in North and South Dakota.[17] "Do you know Stan Donnelly?" she asked the saleswoman. "What does he like? What size does he wear? Help!" From a computer terminal on the sales floor, the saleswoman confidently checked Stan Donnelly's file. He wears size extra large tall, looks best in Gant rugby shirts and Levi Dockers (items he looked at recently but didn't buy), works as a lawyer, and plays golf. "No problem," the saleswoman said. "I can take care of this gift for you. Sit down and have a cup of coffee." A few minutes later the relieved customer left the store with her gift and the satisfaction of knowing that Stan Donnelly was going to get a Christmas gift he wanted and in the right size.

Consistent with the quality movement, technology can be used to revitalize customer service.[18] It can provide the ability to identify and track individual customers, to monitor service levels by company representatives, and to assist customers in specifying, acquiring, fixing, or returning products.

Managers are using technology to improve their customer service strategies in three ways.[19] First, technology can personalize service that previously was standardized. It can allow management to individualize service for each customer's unique needs. For instance, if you are a previous customer of Domino's Pizza or Land's End, when you call to give an order, their computer system already has data about your personal preferences. When I call Domino's, they will ask for my phone number. With that information, they'll say, "Mr. Robbins?" After confirming who I am, they'll typically ask, "Did you want a medium with pepperoni and mushrooms with extra cheese?" (My usual!) After I agree or modify my order, they'll ask if I'm still at the address they have. This whole process treats me like a person rather than an object and speeds order taking.

Second, technology can augment service by providing the customer with additional support related to the acquisition or use of the product. Hertz used this strategy when it created its Gold Card service. Their computer system has your credit card number for billing, your car style and size preference, insurance data, and driver's license information. One short phone call makes your car reservation. Then when you arrive at your destination, an electronic sign with your name on it indicates where your car is located. The paperwork is already done, and your contract is sitting in your awaiting car. When your trip is complete and you drop the car off, you bypass the line at the checkout counter. All you have to do is hand the keys and contract to the lot attendant, who records the time, date, and mileage in his hand-held computer, and you're off to your next destination in a matter of a couple of minutes.

Third, technology can transform your business. That is, it can allow an organization to fundamentally develop new business practices and reinvent itself. This is what Brenda French did with her business, French Rags.[20] A woman's knitwear manufacturer, she replaced hand knitters with computerized knitting machines, changed her primary distribution from retailers to "at-home" representatives, and now sells mass-produced custom-made knitwear at off-the-rack prices directly to customers.

Brenda French's French Rags uses 11 high-tech computerized knitting machines to offer her customers 50,000 possible style and color combinations, allowing them to wear custom-made outfits that fit perfectly and are exactly like no other, but at mass-produced prices. What used to take a skilled craftsperson 12 hours to knit by hand, her machines can produce in less than an hour.

Distribution

Traditional distribution technology relied heavily on sales agents or brokers, wholesalers, and retailers. It wasn't unusual for a product to go through two or three intermediaries before getting into the consumer's hands. New technologies are increasingly cutting out those intermediaries.[21] Management has been investing heavily in multiple-distribution technologies to get closer to the customer, while also cutting costs, providing quicker deliveries and better service, and better meeting the needs of a diverse customer base. The two most recent breakthroughs in distribution technology are home shopping through television and electronic shopping via the Internet. Each of these technologies allows manufacturers to reach customers directly.

Cable television channels such as the Home Shopping Network, Cable Value Network, and the QVC channel have created a multibillion dollar industry. Because these channels buy most of the products from manufacturers, they merely create a new mechanism for manufacturers to reach customers. However, some manufacturers use these channels to directly sell their products to customers; they pay the channels a commission for airtime. Joan Rivers, for example, can sell tens of thousands of dollars worth of her jewelry products in a few minutes by appearing on one of these cable channels.

Infomercials are another vehicle by which manufacturers can directly take their product to the consumer. These programs—typically lasting a half-hour and presenting product testimonials in an entertainment format—allow makers of products as diverse as car waxes, kitchen appliances, cosmetics, and self-help courses to sell merchandise without having to go through wholesalers or retailers.

The latest and potentially most exciting distribution channel made possible by computer technology is marketing products directly to customers on the Internet.[22] Just about every major business firm, educational institution, and not-for-profit organization has set up sites on the World Wide Web and created a home page. Why? Because it's a relatively cheap way to reach over 20 million consumers. If you want to evaluate mortgage options at Toronto Dominion, learn about the new models from General Motors, review the latest exhibits at the Smithsonian Institute, or buy a Dell Computer, you can merely tap into their Web site. Toronto Dominion, for instance, has turned its Web site into a one-stop financial shopping center. It contains 300 "pages" of general financial information about savings plans, mortgages, and other financial products and services. And Dell Computer is selling more than $1.5 million worth of computers every day through its Web site.[23]

▶ Continuous Improvement Processes

In chapter 1, we described total quality management as a philosophy of management that is driven by the constant attainment of customer satisfaction through the continuous improvement of all organizational processes. Managers in many organizations, especially in North America, have been criticized for accepting a level of performance that is below perfection. TQM, however, argues that good isn't good enough! This point is easy to dramatize: Assume that a 99.9 percent error-free performance represents the highest standard of excellence. Using this standard, the U.S. Post Office would lose 2,000 pieces of mail per hour, or U.S. doctors would perform 500 incorrect surgical operations per week, or there would be two plane crashes a day at O'Hare Airport in Chicago![24] Maybe good isn't good enough.

TQM programs seek to achieve continuous process improvements so that variability is constantly reduced. When you eliminate variations, you increase the uniformity of the product or service. Increased uniformity, in turn, results in lower costs and higher quality. For instance, Advanced Filtration Systems Inc., of Champaign, Illinois, recently cut the number of product defects—as determined by a customer quality audit—from 26.5 per 1,000 units to zero over 4 years. And that reduction occurred during a period when monthly unit production tripled and the number of workers declined by 20 percent.

Continuous improvement runs counter to the more typical American management approach of seeing work projects as being linear—with a beginning and an end. For example, American managers have traditionally looked at cost cutting as a short-term project. They set a goal of cutting costs by 20 percent, achieve it, and then say: "Whew! Our cost cutting is over." The Japanese, on the other hand, have regarded cost control as something that never ends. The search for continual improvement creates a race without a finish line.

The search for never-ending improvement requires a circular approach rather than a linear one, as is illustrated in the Plan-Do-Check-Act (PDCA) cycle shown in Exhibit 7-1.[25] Management plans a change, does it, checks the results, and, depending on the outcome, acts to standardize the change or begin the cycle of improvement again with new information. This cycle treats all organizational processes as being in a constant state of improvement.

Dana Corporation's manufacturing plant in Stockton, California, has adopted the PDCA cycle.[26] The plant builds truck chassis for only one customer—Toyota Motor Co. To win Toyota's business, Dana had to promise to shoot for a 2 percent price cut every

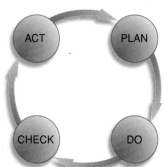

EXHIBIT 7-1

The PDCA Cycle

year. This forced management to commit to finding constant productivity gains. To achieve these gains, management has taken some innovative steps. For instance, it specifically hired welders with no experience, reasoning that unconditioned hands would be freer to explore new and improved ways of welding. Another technique for finding improvements has been demanding that every employee submit two improvement ideas in writing each month. Management considers no change too small. Surprisingly, 81 percent of these ideas have proved sufficiently worthwhile to implement.

Reengineering Work Processes

We also introduced reengineering in chapter 1. We described it as considering how things would be done if you could start all over from scratch. The term *reengineering* comes from the historical process of taking apart an electronics product and designing a better version. Michael Hammer coined the term for organizations. When he saw that companies were using computers simply to automate outdated processes, rather than to find fundamentally better ways of doing things, he realized that the same principles of reengineering electronics products could be applied to business. So, as applied to organizations, reengineering means that management should start with a clean sheet of paper—rethinking and redesigning those processes by which the organization creates value and does work and ridding itself of operations that have become antiquated.[27]

KEY ELEMENTS Three key elements of reengineering are identifying an organization's distinctive competencies, assessing core processes, and reorganizing horizontally by process. As discussed in chapter 5, an organization's distinctive competencies are the unique skills and resources that determine its competitive weapons. They are those things that the organization is better at delivering than its competition is. Examples might include superior store locations, a more efficient distribution system, higher-quality products, more-knowledgeable sales personnel, or superior technical support. Why is identifying distinctive competencies so important? Because it guides decisions regarding what activities are crucial to the organization's success.

Management also needs to assess the core processes that clearly add value to the organization's distinctive competencies. These are the processes that transform materials, capital, information, and labor into products and services that the customer values. When the organization is viewed as a series of processes, ranging from strategic planning to after-sales customer support, management can determine to what degree each adds value. Not surprisingly, this **process value analysis** typically uncovers a whole lot of activities that add little or nothing of value and whose only justification is "we've always done it this way."

Reengineering requires management to reorganize around horizontal processes. This means cross-functional and self-managed teams. It means focusing on processes rather than on functions. So, for instance, the vice president of marketing might become the "process owner of finding and keeping customers."[28] And it also means cutting out levels of middle management. As Hammer points out, "Managers are not value-added. A customer never buys a product because of the caliber of management. Management is, by definition, indirect. So, if possible, less is better. One of the goals of reengineering is to minimize the necessary amount of management."[29]

EXPLAINING REENGINEERING'S POPULARITY Isn't reengineering something management should have been doing all along? What explains why it became popular only in the 1990s? The answers, according to Hammer, are a changing global environment and organizational structures that had gotten top heavy.[30]

Traditionally structured bureaucratic organizations worked fine in times of stable growth. Activities could be fragmented and specialized to gain economic efficiencies. This described the environment faced by most North American organizations in the 1950s, 1960s, and much of the 1970s. But most organizations today operate in global conditions of overcapacity. Customers are much more informed and sophisticated than they were 30 years ago. Moreover, markets, production, and capital are all globally mobile. Investors in Australia, for example, can put their money into opportunities in Japan, Canada, or anywhere else in the world if they see better returns than they can get at home. Global customers now demand quality, service, and low cost. If *you* can't provide it, they'll get it from someone else.

Breaking up work into specialized tasks that were performed in narrowly defined functional departments drove down direct labor costs, but the bureaucracies they created had massive overhead costs. That is, to coordinate all the fragmentation and specialization, the organization had to create numerous levels of middle management to glue together the fragmented pieces. So, although bureaucracies drove down costs at the operating level, they required increasingly expensive coordinating systems. Those organizations that introduced teams, decentralized decisions, and flattened structures became more efficient and challenged the traditional ways of doing things.

REENGINEERING VERSUS TQM Is reengineering just another term for TQM? No! They do have some common characteristics.[31] They both, for instance, emphasize processes and satisfying the customer. After that, they diverge radically, as is evident in their goals and the means they use for achieving them.

TQM seeks incremental improvements; reengineering looks for quantum leaps in performance. That is, the former is essentially about improving something that is basically OK; the latter is about taking something that is irrelevant, throwing it out, and starting over. And the means the two approaches use are totally different. TQM relies on bottom-up, participative decision making in both the planning of a TQM program and its execution. Reengineering, on the other hand, is initially driven by top management. When reengineering is complete, the workplace is largely self-managed. But getting there is a very autocratic, nondemocratic process. Reengineering's supporters argue that it has to be done this way because the level of change that the process demands is highly threatening, and people aren't likely to accept it voluntarily. When top management commits to reengineering, employees have no choice. As Hammer is fond of saying, "You either get on the train, or we'll run over you with the train."[32]

Advances in equipment and software technology have made telemedicine a reality. For instance, emerging information technologies have created a whole new way for rural hospitals to offer radiology services that were previously not financially feasible.[33] In Durham, North Carolina, Team Radiology is able to analyze medical scans delivered over telephone lines from anywhere in the United States, 24 hours a day. Just a decade ago, this wasn't possible. But recent breakthroughs in compression technology now allow the sending of accurate x-ray images over phone lines, and laser technology allows the scanning of images to be more accurate. Rural hospitals can now offer patients fast and competent readings of x-rays without having a radiologist on staff. Similarly, Team Radiology's outsourcing service provides a backup alternative for big-city hospitals' in-house radiologists. In this section, we'll highlight how technology is reshaping office work flows, changing the way internal communications are handled, and providing high-tech support for organizational decision making.

Office Work Flow

In the typical office, information spends most of its life moving from desk to desk.[34] For instance, consider the creation of a marketing plan. The marketing director approves the creation of the plan. A product manager oversees the development of the plan. Staff researchers gather the necessary data. A senior researcher then writes a first draft and sends it to the product manager for review. This whole process requires documents to be passed along from one desk to another as the plan is approved, researched, developed, reviewed, edited, revised, and finally agreed upon and implemented. This process can take weeks or even months because the document can sit on someone's desk for days. One insurance company, for example, estimated that a life insurance application in its firm spent *22 days* in process for only *17 minutes* of actual work![35]

Workflow automation can solve much of this delay. It greatly improves the process of creating and transferring documents by automating the flow of information. Workflow

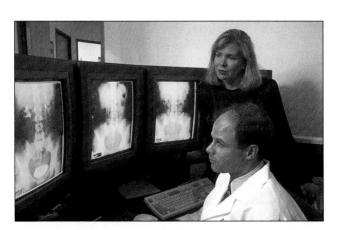

Advances in equipment and software technology have made telemedicine a reality at Team Radiology in Durham, North Carolina.

EXHIBIT 7-2   **Workflow Automation Applied to Expense Reimbursement**

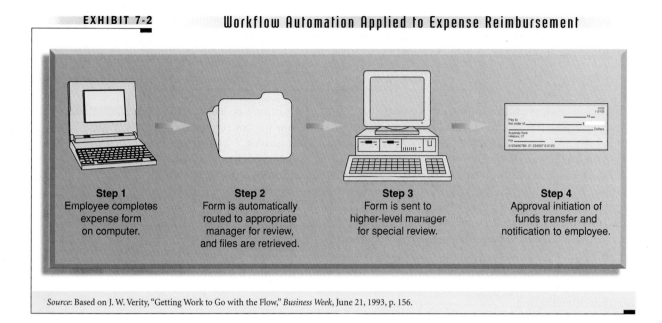

Step 1	Step 2	Step 3	Step 4
Employee completes expense form on computer.	Form is automatically routed to appropriate manager for review, and files are retrieved.	Form is sent to higher-level manager for special review.	Approval initiation of funds transfer and notification to employee.

Source: Based on J. W. Verity, "Getting Work to Go with the Flow," *Business Week*, June 21, 1993, p. 156.

automation begins by examining how documents, business forms, and other information wend their way through an organization. It looks for bottlenecks and outdated procedures that slow things down and add to costs. Once new routes are laid out, workflow software is installed on computer networks to convey information instantly to the right desk—whether it's a digital image of an invoice or an e-mail question from a customer. This software makes the movement of documents automatic, eliminating the need for a human to figure out who should get the information next, collapsing the travel times, and avoiding misrouting. The system can also be programmed to send documents along different paths, depending on content.

Exhibit 7-2 illustrates how workflow automation has improved one firm's information flow in the processing of an employee's expense reimbursement request. In step 1, the employee fills out an expense form on her computer. The form then routes itself over a network to the appropriate decision maker for initial review (step 2). The form's arrival also triggers the retrieval of employee files that might be needed. In step 3, the software recognizes that the transaction involves more than $5,000, so the form is automatically sent to an upper-level manager for special review. Upon final sign-off, in step 4, the form sends a copy of itself to another computer, which processes payment; an electronic note is sent to remind the employee that her reimbursement check is ready (or that an automatic transfer of funds to her bank account has been completed); then the form stores itself on an archival laser disk.

Internal Communications

Information technology is reshaping communications within organizations by, for example, significantly improving management's ability to monitor performance data and allowing employees to bypass hierarchical levels and thereby making structures more porous and flexible. But if we had to identify the two *most* important developments in information technology, in terms of their impact on internal organizational communications, it would probably be digitalization and the wireless phenomena.[36]

Organizations are converting internal information from analog language to digital. Telephones, for instance, have historically used an analog signal—an electrical wave-form representation of sound. Computers, on the other hand, use a digital language—combinations of 1's and 0's—to communicate. Organizations are aggressively changing all their internal communication systems to the digital format. Why? Analog is slower, less accurate, and prone to interruptions and distortions. Moreover, *any* information can be digitized—numbers, words, voice, or pictures. So, by converting to a completely digital format, organizations will have put in place a system that can permit managers and employees to communicate in any form. Anything can be delivered to any instrument capable of displaying it. A television, for instance, can receive and display computer text, or a radio can receive a phone call.

Now combine digitalization with wireless networks and you have revolutionized internal communications within organizations. Wireless products such as personal digital assistants are going to make it possible for people in organizations to be fully accessible to each other, at any time, regardless of where they are. Employees won't have to be at their desk with their computer plugged in in order to communicate with others in the organization. "I think wireless communications is probably the last communications breakthrough in our lifetimes," says Kenneth Forbes III, president and CEO of MobileDigital Corp. "The ability to reach anyone while I'm mobile in real time without it being intrusive is the closest to thought projection we're going to get."[37] Or, as another executive put it, "The last 100 years have been the wireline century. We have just embarked upon the wireless century."[38]

At the current rate of technological advancement, the digital-wireless organization is not very far away. For some organizations, it exists today. For the rest, we are probably talking about less than a half-dozen years.

▶ Decision-Making Support

Information technology is providing managers with a wealth of decision support systems. These include expert systems, neural networks, groupware, and specific problem-solving software. **Expert systems** use software programs to encode the relevant experience of a human expert and allow a system to act like that expert in analyzing and solving unstructured problems.[39] The essence of expert systems is that they (1) use specialized knowledge about a particular problem area rather than general knowledge that would apply to all problems, (2) use qualitative reasoning rather than numerical calculations, and (3) perform at a level of competence that is higher than that of nonexpert humans.[40] They guide users through problems by asking them a set of sequential questions about the situation and drawing conclusions based on the answers given. The conclusions are based on programmed rules that have been modeled on the actual reasoning processes of experts who have confronted similar problems before. Once in place, these systems are allowing operative employees and lower-level managers to make high-quality decisions that previously could have been made only by senior managers. Expert systems are being used in such diverse areas as medical diagnosis, mineral and oil exploration, equipment-fault locating, credit approvals, and financial planning.[41] For instance, IDS Financial Services has encoded the expertise of its best financial-planning account managers in an expert-systems program. "Now even the worst of our 6,500 planners is better than our average planner used to be," said the company's chairman.[42]

Neural networks are the next step beyond expert systems.[43] They use computer software to imitate the structure of brain cells and connections among them. Neural networks have the ability to discern patterns and trends too subtle or complex for human beings. For instance, people cannot easily assimilate more than two or three variables at once, but neural networks can perceive correlations among hundreds of variables. As a result, they can perform many operations simultaneously, recognizing patterns, making associations, generalizing about problems they haven't been exposed to before, and learning through experience. For instance, Mellon Bank uses neural networks to flag potential credit card fraud.[44] The bank previously had an expert system to keep track of its 1.2 million Visa and MasterCard accounts. But this system could look at only a few factors, such as the size of a transaction, so it would frequently generate as many as a thousand potential defrauding incidences a day, most of which were false positives. Meanwhile, all these potential fraud cases were overwhelming Mellon's investigative staff. Since Mellon replaced its expert system with a neural network, it deals with only one-tenth as many suspicious transactions, and they are much more likely to be actual cases of fraud. And with the expert system, investigators usually didn't get around to checking on a questionable transaction for a couple of days. With the new neural network system, investigators are on top of most problems in less than 2 hours.

We briefly discussed group decision making in chapter 3. Most of us, when we think of group decisions, picture a group of people sitting around a conference table sharing ideas, developing alternatives, analyzing those alternatives, debating differences, and arriving at some common solution. This is a pretty good description of how group decision making took place until just a few years ago. However, technology again has changed that description. Nowadays, groups are increasingly interacting electronically.[45]

Groupware is a term used to describe the multitude of software programs that have developed to facilitate group interaction and decision making. For instance, groupware allows management to conduct electronic meetings in which people make decisions on computers that are networked together. Up to fifty people can sit around a table that is empty except for a series of computer terminals. Issues are presented to participants, and they type their responses onto their computer screens. Individual comments, as well as aggregate votes, are then displayed on a projection screen in the room. These electronic meetings allow participants to be brutally honest and still maintain their anonymity. Other applications of groupware are videoconferencing and on-line, real-time conferences. VeriFone, for instance, uses videoconferencing for group meetings, presentations, augmenting face-to-face customer visits, and even for preliminary interviews of job candidates.[46] Conferencing allows participants to communicate over networks or telephone lines with others at different locations at the same time.[47] If you have participated in chat sessions on the Internet or on one of the commercial on-line services, you are already familiar with conferencing.

Executives from Intel and Fuji use videoconferencing to conduct meetings between California and Japan.

The latest wrinkle in decision-support software is the growing supply of unique problem-solving programs to help managers do their jobs more effectively. Consider a few of the latest offerings: Forecast Pro analyzes data and enables managers with minimal background in statistics to run simple forecasts. Business Insight helps managers brainstorm about "big picture" issues such as strategic planning. Performance Now! provides a framework for managers to evaluate an employee's performance and then guides the manager through the steps in writing up a specific performance review. Negotiator Pro prepares a manager for any negotiation by creating a psychological profile of the manager and the opponent and then helps the manager create a detailed negotiation plan.[48]

TECHNOLOGY TRANSFER   Globe Silk Store, a Malaysian company that originally was in the clothing business, decided to diversify. One such project was to buy the technology to make crash helmets for cyclists from an Australian firm. Globe Silk's management then added a feature to the helmets: a flashing light. By combining foreign technology with internal innovation, the company was able to create a highly successful and profitable new product.[49]

In today's global economy, both countries and individual organizations are concerned with **technology transfer**. This is the transfer of knowledge from one country to another for the development of new products or for improvements in the production process.[50] Globe Silk's purchase of crash-helmet technology is an example of a company creating a new product. When a manufacturer in Taiwan hires a Japanese firm to install state-of-the-art robotic equipment in the Taiwanese manufacturing plant, you have an example of improvements in the production process.

Developing countries have a vested interest in stimulating technology transfer. Why? Without it, a country can be stuck in labor-intensive industries—with low-paying jobs and modest growth. Where government policies have fostered technology transfer, economies have blossomed.[51] In Asia, Singapore is a model example of a country whose industrial development policies have encouraged foreign companies to settle and sow the seeds of technology transfer. In contrast, Malaysia and Indonesia have suffered from government policies that obsess on ownership and insist on local equity participation for new investments. When German industrial giant Siemens sought a site for its Asia-Pacific microelectronics design center, it looked at seven Asian cities, but settled on Singapore because of its supportive climate for foreign investments. To jump-start its semiconductor industry, the Singapore government also provided Texas Instruments with tax incentives and industrial infrastructure to set up the country's first water fabrication plant. As competition heats up for new investments, countries like Singapore that provide a supportive climate for technology transfer are going to have faster growth rates and higher-paying jobs than their counterparts that create transfer barriers.

Managers of companies, especially in developing countries, will be increasingly seeking strategies that will facilitiate acquisition of new technologies. This will include mergers, joint ventures, contractual royalty agreements, hiring of foreign consultants, and sending staff to foreign markets to acquire new technological expertise. And they are likely to locate in those countries where government policies are most supportive.

Rob Hanc is only 28, but he has already come face-to-face with the new reality—his skills don't match what employers need.[52] Rob graduated from high school and followed in his father's footsteps by taking a job at the Dofasco steel foundry in Hamilton, Ontario. His job? He was a heavy laborer—doing lifting and carrying. At age 21, Rob was making $47,000 a year. But Do-

TECHNOLOGY AND WORKER OBSOLESCENCE

fasco couldn't compete paying those kind of wages for someone to do unskilled labor. He lost his job. "My biggest problem is lack of education," says Rob. "Me and school don't go together. I need to work with my hands." But, as Rob now knows, "heavy labor is a dying breed."

Glenna Cheney also has only a high school education.[53] But, unlike Rob Hanc, Glenna has been changing with the times. Glenna went to work for Fingerhut Cos., a Minneapolis-based catalogue company, in 1965. She answered telephones, took orders, and wrote customer orders and payment schedules on index cards. When Fingerhut replaced the index cards with a mainframe computer, Glenna learned about computers. She learned so well, in fact, that she got promoted to supervisor. When the mainframe system was recently replaced with a group of workstations, Glenna enthusiastically took training classes to learn the new technology. She was recently promoted to a business analyst position; she advises Fingerhut's computer specialists on how to further develop the workstations to fit workers' needs.

Changes in technology have cut the shelf life of most employees' skills. A factory worker or clerical employee in the 1950s could learn one job and be reasonably sure that his or her skills would be adequate to do that job for most of his or her work life. That certainly is no longer true. New technologies driven by computers, reengineering, TQM, and flexible manufacturing systems are changing the demands of jobs and the skills employees need to do them.

Repetitive tasks—those traditionally performed on assembly lines and by low-skilled office clerks—will continue to be automated. And a good number of jobs will be upgraded. For instance, as most managers and professionals take on the task of writing their own memos and reports using word-processing software, the traditional secretary's job will be upgraded to become more of an administrative assistant. Those secretaries who are not equipped to take on these expanded roles will be displaced. In addition to secretaries, other white-collar jobs that are disappearing or being reshaped as a result of technology include bank teller, telephone operator, meter reader, and travel agent.

Reengineering, as we previously noted, is producing significant increases in employee productivity. The redesign of work processes is achieving higher output with fewer workers. And these reengineered jobs require different skills. Employees who are computer illiterate, have poor interpersonal skills, or cannot work autonomously will increasingly find themselves ill-prepared for the demands of new technologies.

Keep in mind that the obsolescence phenomenon does not exclude managers. Those middle managers who merely acted as conduits in the line between top management and the operating floor are being eliminated. And new skills—for example, coaching, negotiating, and building teams—are becoming absolute necessities for every manager.

Finally, software is changing the jobs of many professionals, including lawyers, doctors, accountants, financial planners, and librarians.[54] Software programs will allow laypeople to use specialized knowledge to solve routine problems themselves or opt for a software-armed paraprofessional. Particularly vulnerable are those professionals who do standardized jobs. A lot of legal work, for instance, consists of writing standard contracts and other routine activities. These tasks will be done inside law firms by computers or paralegals; they might even be done by clients themselves, using software designed to prepare wills, trusts, incorporations, and partnerships. Software packages, such as TurboTax, will continue to take a lot of work away from professional accountants. And hospitals are using software to help doctors make their diagnoses. Punch in a patient's age, sex, lab results, and symptoms; answer a set of structured questions; and a $995 program called Iliad will draw on its knowledge of nine subspecialties of internal medicine to diagnose the patient's problem. These examples demonstrate that even the knowledge of highly trained professionals can become obsolete. As the world changes, professionals will also need to change if they're to survive.

WORK DESIGN

If you walk into the headquarters of the Chiat/Day advertising agency in Venice, California, you might be surprised.[55] There are no executive suites, permanent work cubicles, desks, filing cabinets, or other trappings typically associated with an office. Why? Because Chiat/Day has redesigned its offices into a virtual workplace. Employees are free to work where they please. Nearly half of them choose to telecommute either from home or from the road. The only space at headquarters that employees can call their own are the high-school-style lockers where they can stow their personal belongings. Employees who choose to go into the office on any given day stop in the lobby and pick up laptop computers and portable phones, which can be programmed with their extension number. Then they head for any one of a dozen or so open spaces, pull over a desk-on-wheels, plug into nearby modem jacks, and begin their work. All documents once stored in filing cabinets are now available only electronically. And for the occasional meetings of work groups, a few conference rooms are scattered around the building.

Chiat/Day's virtual office, staffed by mobile employees, is just one way that business firms can redesign work to meet changing demands. The message in this example is that in times of dynamic change, don't expect the design of jobs, work spaces, and work schedules to remain intact. In this section, we'll identify the primary dimensions of jobs, describe how these dimensions can be mixed and matched to maximize employee performance, and review innovative work-scheduling options that managers might consider to further improve employee performance.

► Defining the Key Dimensions in a Job

What differentiates one job from another? Intuitively we know that a traveling salesperson's job is different from that of an emergency room nurse. And we know that both of those jobs have little in common with the job of an editor in a newsroom or a component assembler on a production line. But what is it that allows us to draw these distinctions? Currently, the best answer is something called the **job characteristics model (JCM)**.[56] According to the researchers who developed the JCM, any job can be described in terms of five core job dimensions, or characteristics, defined as follows:

1. *Skill variety.* The degree to which the job requires a variety of different activities so the worker can use a number of different skills and talents.
2. *Task identity.* The degree to which the job requires completion of a whole and identifiable piece of work.
3. *Task significance.* The degree to which the job has a substantial impact on the lives or work of other people.
4. *Autonomy.* The degree to which the job provides substantial freedom, independence, and discretion to the individual in scheduling the work and in determining the procedures to be used in carrying it out.
5. *Feedback.* The degree to which carrying out the work activities required by the job results in the individual's obtaining direct and clear information about the effectiveness of his or her performance.

Exhibit 7-3 on page 224 offers examples of job activities that rate high and low for each characteristic.

Exhibit 7-4 on page 225 presents the model. Notice how the first three dimensions—skill variety, task identity, and task significance—combine to create meaningfulness of the work. That is, if these three characteristics exist in a job, we can predict that the incum-

The Chiat/Day agency has created a virtual office that facilitates open communication and flexibility.

EXHIBIT 7-3

Examples of High and Low Job Characteristics

Characteristic	Example
Skill variety	
High	A garage owner-operator who does electrical repair, rebuilds engines, does body work, and interacts with customers
Low	A body shop worker who sprays paint 8 hours a day
Task identity	
High	A cabinetmaker who designs a piece of furniture, selects the wood, builds the object, and finishes it to perfection
Low	A worker in a furniture factory who operates a lathe solely to make table legs
Task significance	
High	Nursing the sick in a hospital intensive care unit
Low	Sweeping hospital floors
Autonomy	
High	A police detective who schedules his or her own work for the day, makes contacts without supervision, and decides on the most effective techniques for solving a case
Low	A police telephone dispatcher who must handle calls as they come in according to a routine, highly specified procedure
Feedback	
High	An electronics factory worker who assembles a modem and then tests it to determine if it operates properly
Low	An electronics factory worker who assembles a modem and then routes it to a quality-control inspector who tests it for proper operation and makes needed adjustments

Source: Adapted from G. Johns, *Organizational Behavior: Understanding and Managing Life at Work*, 4th ed. (New York: HarperCollins, 1996), p. 204. With permission.

---

bent will view the job as being important, valuable, and worthwhile. Notice, too, that jobs that possess autonomy give the job incumbent a feeling of personal responsibility for the results and that, if a job provides feedback, the employee will know how effectively he or she is performing. Further, the model says that internal rewards are obtained by an individual when she *learns* (knowledge of results) that she *personally* (experienced responsibility) has performed well on a task that she *cares* about (experienced meaningfulness).[57] The more that these three psychological states are present, the greater will be the employee's motivation, performance, and satisfaction, and the lower his or her absenteeism and likelihood of leaving the organization. Exhibit 7-4 shows that the relation between the job dimensions and the outcomes is moderated by the strength of the individual's growth need; that is, the employee's desire for self-esteem and self-actualization. Individuals with a high growth need, for instance, are more likely to respond positively to enriched jobs where they have increased control than are individuals with a low growth need. Enrichment, presumably, enhances the psychological states that are important to individuals with a high growth need.

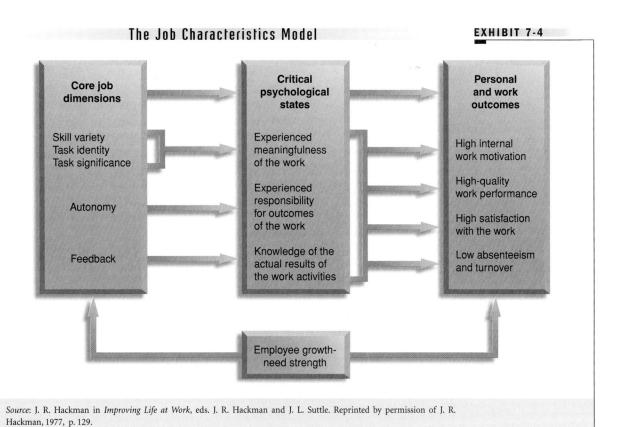

The Job Characteristics Model

EXHIBIT 7-4

Core job dimensions	Critical psychological states	Personal and work outcomes
Skill variety Task identity Task significance	Experienced meaningfulness of the work	High internal work motivation
Autonomy	Experienced responsibility for outcomes of the work	High-quality work performance High satisfaction with the work
Feedback	Knowledge of the actual results of the work activities	Low absenteeism and turnover

Employee growth-need strength

Source: J. R. Hackman in *Improving Life at Work*, eds. J. R. Hackman and J. L. Suttle. Reprinted by permission of J. R. Hackman, 1977, p. 129.

The job characteristics model has been well researched. Most of the evidence supports the general framework of the theory—that is, there is a set of definable job characteristics, and those characteristics affect behavioral outcomes.[58] But there is considerable debate around the five specific core dimensions in the JCM and the validity of growth-need strength as a moderating variable.

There is some question as to whether task identity adds to the model's predictive ability,[59] and there is evidence suggesting that skill variety may be the equivalent of autonomy.[60] In addition, the strength of an individual's growth needs as a meaningful moderating variable has recently been called into question.[61] Other variables—such as the presence or absence of social cues, perceived equity with comparison groups, and propensity to assimilate work experience[62]—may be more valid in moderating the job characteristics–outcome relationship. Given the current state of research on moderating variables, one should be cautious in unequivocally accepting growth-need strength as originally included in the JCM.

Where does this leave us? Given the current state of evidence, we can make the following statements with relative confidence: (1) The JCM provides a reasonably valid framework for defining the core characteristics in a cross section of jobs. (2) People whose jobs rate high on the core job dimensions are generally more motivated, satisfied, and productive than are people whose jobs rate low. (3) Job dimensions influence personal and work outcome by operating through the critical psychological states rather than by influencing the outcomes directly.[63]

▶ Job Dimensions: Perception or Reality?

Jan Chomsky teaches science classes at Lakeside High School. She has been teaching the same chemistry, biology, and physics courses at the same school for 12 years. "This job is driving me crazy," says Jan. "It's boring. I talk about the same concepts, to a similar bunch of 16- and 17-year-olds, semester after semester. I know the answer to their questions before they get the fifth word out of their mouths. I've heard it all before. I can teach these classes with my brain turned off! I'm burned out! I'm sick of this job. I've made the decision that this is my last year of teaching."

Cathy Sharp also teaches science classes at Lakeside High School. She and Jan joined the faculty at the same time, right out of college. But listening to Cathy, you would think she was doing an entirely different job than Jan. "I've loved my job from day one," Cathy told me. "It's as interesting and challenging this term as it was the first. The students change every year, but they're still young and optimistic. I have a unique opportunity to shape their attitudes about science. In less than 10 years, some of these young people will be working in labs, hospitals, and classrooms—changing the world! And I'll have had a major part in that! I don't think I'll ever tire of what I do."

This illustration shows that people can look at the same job and evaluate it differently. The fact that people respond to their jobs as they perceive them rather than to the objective jobs themselves is the central thesis of the **social information processing (SIP) model**.[64] The SIP model argues that employees adopt attitudes and behaviors in response to the social cues provided by others with whom they have contact. These others can be co-workers, supervisors, friends, family members, or customers. For instance, Gary Ling got a summer job working in a sawmill in British Columbia. Jobs were scarce and this one paid particularly well, so Gary arrived on his first day of work highly motivated. Two weeks later, however, his motivation was quite low. What had happened? His co-workers consistently bad-mouthed their jobs. They said the work was boring, that having to clock in and out proved that management didn't trust them, and that supervisors never listened to their opinions. The objective characteristics of Gary's job had not changed in the 2-week period, but Gary had reconstructed his perception of reality on the basis of messages he had received from others.

A number of studies generally confirm the validity of the SIP model.[65] For instance, employee motivation and satisfaction can be manipulated by actions as subtle as a co-worker's commenting that your job is very difficult, or not challenging, or you have no autonomy. So managers should give as much (or more) attention to employees' perceptions of their jobs as they give to the actual characteristics of those jobs. They might spend more time telling employees how interesting and important their jobs are. And managers should also not be surprised that newly hired employees and people transferred or promoted to a new position are more likely to be receptive to social information than are those with greater seniority.

▶ Designing Individual Jobs to Maximize Employee Performance

As a manager, how can you design jobs so as to maximize your employees' performance? On the basis of the JCM and SIP models, we suggest that you improve the five core job dimensions (this process is frequently referred to as **job enrichment**) and attempt to shape employees' perceptions by speaking positively about their jobs. But exactly how do you enrich a job? The following suggestions, which are derived from the JCM, specify the types

The Job Characteristics Model

EXHIBIT 7-5

Suggested Action	Core Job Dimension
Combining Tasks	Skill Variety
Forming Natural Work Units	Task Identity
Establishing Client Relationships	Task Significance
Vertical Loading	Autonomy
Opening Feedback Channels	Feedback

Source: J. R. Hackman, in *Improving Life at Work*, eds. J. R. Hackman and J. L. Suttle. Reprinted by permission of J. R. Hackman, 1977.

of changes in jobs that are most likely to lead to improvements in each of the five core dimensions (see Exhibit 7-5):

1. *Combine tasks.* Putting existing fractionalized tasks back together to form a new, larger module of work increases skill variety and task identity.
2. *Create natural work units.* Designing tasks that form an identifiable and meaningful whole increases employee "ownership" of the work and encourages employees to view their work as meaningful and important rather than as irrelevant and boring.
3. *Establish client relationships.* The client is the user of the product or service that the employee works on. Establishing direct relationships between workers and their clients whenever possible increases skill variety, autonomy, and feedback for the employee.
4. *Expand jobs vertically.* Vertical expansion—giving employees responsibilities and controls that were formerly reserved for management—partially closes the gap between the "doing" and "controlling" aspects of the job, and it increases employee autonomy.
5. *Open feedback channels.* Feedback tells employees not only how well they are performing their jobs but also whether their performances are improving, deteriorating, or remaining at a constant level. Ideally, employees should receive performance feedback directly as they do their jobs rather than from management on an occasional basis.[66]

Group-Based Work Design

Increasingly, people are doing work in groups and teams. What, if anything, can we say about the design of group-based work to try to improve employee performance in those groups? We know a lot more about individual-based job design than we do about design at the group level,[67] mostly because the wide popularity of teams—specifically assigning tasks to a group of individuals instead of to a single person—is a relatively recent phenomenon. That said, the best work in this area offers two sets of suggestions.[68]

First, the JCM recommendations seem to be as valid at the group level as they are at the individual level. Managers should expect a group to perform at a high level when (1) the group task requires members to use a variety of relatively high-level skills; (2) the group task is a whole and meaningful piece of work, with a visible outcome; (3) the outcomes of the group's work on the task have significant consequences for other people; (4) the task provides group members with substantial autonomy for deciding how they do the work; and (5) work on the task generates regular, trustworthy feedback about how well the group is performing.

Second, group composition is critical to the success of the work group. Managers should try to ensure that the following four conditions are met: (1) Individual members have the necessary task-relevant expertise to do their work, (2) the group is large enough to perform the work, (3) members possess interpersonal as well as task skills, and (4) membership is moderately diverse in terms of talents and perspectives. In chapter 10, we'll elaborate on these group-composition factors.

▶ Work Schedule Options

Susan Ross is your classic "morning person." She rises each day at 5:00 A.M. sharp, full of energy. On the other hand, as she puts it, "I'm usually ready for bed right after the 7 P.M. news." Susan's work schedule as a claims processor at Hartford Insurance is flexible. It allows her some degree of freedom as to when she comes to work and when she leaves. Her office opens at 6:00 A.M. and closes at 7:00 P.M. It is up to her how she schedules her 8-hour day within this 13-hour period. Because Susan is a morning person and also has a 7-year-old son who gets out of school at 3:00 P.M. every day, she opts to work from 6:00 A.M. to 3:00 P.M. "My work hours are perfect. I'm at the job when I'm mentally most alert, and I can be home to take care of Sean after he gets out of school."

Most people work an 8-hour day, 5 days a week. They are full-time employees who report to a fixed organizational location and start and leave at a fixed time. But consistent with managers' attempting to increase their organizations' flexibility, a number of new scheduling options are being introduced.[69] In addition to an increased use of temporary workers, which has been around for a long time, these include flextime, job sharing, and telecommuting.

FLEXTIME Flextime is a scheduling option that allows employees, within specific parameters, to decide when to go to work. Susan Ross's work schedule at Hartford Insurance is an example of flextime. But what specifically is flextime?

Flextime is short for flexible work hours. It allows employees some discretion over when they arrive and leave work. Employees have to work a specific number of hours a week, but they are free to vary the hours of work within certain limits. As shown in Exhibit 7-6, each day consists of a common core, usually 6 hours, with a flexibility band surrounding the core. For example, exclusive of a 1-hour lunch break, the core may be 9:00 A.M. to 3:00 P.M., with the office actually opening at 6:00 A.M. and closing at 6:00 P.M. All employees are required to be at their jobs during the common core period, but they are allowed to accumulate their other 2 hours before or after the core time. Some flextime programs allow extra hours to be accumulated and turned into a free day off each month.

Flextime has become an extremely popular scheduling option. For instance, a recent study of firms with more than 1,000 employees found that 53 percent offered employees the option of flextime.[70]

The potential benefits from flextime are numerous. They include improved employee motivation and morale, reduced absenteeism as a result of enabling employees to better balance work and family responsibilities, and the ability of the organization to recruit higher-quality and more-diverse employees.[71]

A Flextime Schedule

EXHIBIT 7-6

Flexible Hours	Common Core	Lunch	Common Core	Flexible Hours

6 A.M.   9 A.M.   12 NOON 1 P.M.   3 P.M.   6 P.M.

Time During the Day

Flextime's major drawback is that it is not applicable to every job. It works well with clerical tasks where an employee's interaction with people outside his or her department is limited. It is not a viable option when key people must be available during standard hours, when work flow requires tightly determined scheduling, or when specialists are called upon to maintain coverage of all functions in a unit.[72]

JOB SHARING **Job sharing** is a special type of part-time work. It allows two or more individuals to split a traditional 40-hour-a-week job. So, for example, one person might perform the job from 8:00 A.M. to noon, and another will perform the same job from 1:00 P.M. to 5:00 P.M.; or the two could work full, but alternate, days.

Although job sharing is growing in popularity, it is less widespread than flextime. Only about 36 percent of large organizations offer this option.[73] NOVA Corp. in Calgary, Canada, is one organization that does. Kim Sarjeant and Lorraine Champion, for instance, are staff lawyers who divide one position in the company's human resource department.[74] Both have young children and wanted the flexibility that job sharing provides. Sarjeant works Monday through Wednesday, whereas Champion is on the job Wednesday to Friday. The arrangement allows them one day a week to work side by side, to share information, and to make joint decisions.

Job sharing allows the organization to draw upon the talents of more than one individual for a given job. A bank manager who oversees two job sharers describes it as an opportunity to get two heads, but "pay for one."[75] It also opens up the opportunity to acquire skilled workers—for instance, women with young children and retirees—who might not be available on a full-time basis.[76] The major drawback, from management's perspective, is finding compatible pairs of employees who can successfully coordinate the intricacies of one job.[77]

TELECOMMUTING It might be close to the ideal job for many people. No commuting, flexible hours, freedom to dress as you please, and few or no interruptions from colleagues. It is called **telecommuting** and refers to employees who do their work at home on a computer that is linked to their office.[78] Currently, between 9 million and 14 million people work at home in the United States doing things such as taking orders over the phone, filling out reports and other forms, and processing or analyzing information.[79] In Great Britain and France, the comparable numbers are 563,000 and 215,000, respectively.[80]

What kind of jobs lend themselves to telecommuting? Writers, attorneys, analysts, and other professionals who are relatively autonomous. And, of course, employees who spend the majority of their time working on computers or on the telephone are natural candidates for telecommuting. For instance, telemarketers, customer-service representa-

Kim Sarjeant and Lorraine Champion, two part-time lawyers, happily share one position at NOVA Corporation.

tives, reservation agents, and product-support specialists spend most of their time on the phone. As telecommuters, they can access information on their computer screens at home as easily as the computer screen in any office.

The extent to which telecommuting may someday permeate global organizations is illustrated in the experience of Liz Codling, a senior manager at Bank of Montreal in Toronto.[81] After running the bank's staff education center for four years and overseeing a team of eight people, she and her husband decided to return to their British homeland. But her bosses didn't want to lose her. So she became the bank's first transatlantic telecommuter. Although separated from her staff by five time zones and more than 3,000 miles, she is able to manage her team by relying on communication technology—phone, fax, computer, e-mail, videoconferencing, and the Internet. Some adjustments were needed. For instance, Codling has had to adjust her workday to align with Toronto hours, and her colleagues have had to learn to schedule meetings in the mornings so she can be included. But after more than two years, this long-distance telecommute seems to be a success.

TODAY ? or TOMORROW ?

Will We Be Saying Goodbye to the 40-Hour Workweek?

The Fair Labor Standards Act (FLSA), passed in 1938, established the 40-hour workweek in the United States, with time-and-a-half for overtime. One of the original purposes of the law, not surprising because it was passed during the Great Depression, was to force employers into hiring more workers. The 40-hour workweek has since become a basic standard in the American workplace. Its days, however, may be numbered.[83] The U.S. Congress is considering several bills that will change the FLSA and give employers and employees more flexibility. Central to the various bills is allowing individuals to work more than 40-hours in a given week without having to be paid overtime.

About one in five U.S. workers get overtime in a given week. Although new work scheduling options, like flextime, have gained in popularity, they have been restricted by current labor laws. Employers who use flextime, for instance, must go to great lengths not to violate the 40-hour week established by the FLSA. In today's more fluid workplace, strict compliance with the 40-hour week doesn't fit the needs of either employers or employees.

If Congress is successful in modifying the FLSA, what changes are likely to occur? Any changes almost certainly will be made optional for employees. That is, new flexibility would apply only if both the employer and the employee agreed. The changes themselves would likely include letting workers put in longer days in exchange for more three-day weekends, save up paid time for days off, or opt for time-and-a-half compensatory time instead of time-and-a-half pay for overtime work.

The primary resistance to these suggested changes come from labor unions. They fear that employees would be coerced into working longer hours and giving up premium pay. Says one union official, planned legislation "totally destroys the concept of the 40-hour workweek." Although acknowledging the success of flextime for federal employees (exempt from the FLSA, flextime has been in place for federal workers since 1978 and is used by about half of them), the same union official added, federal workers "don't have the profit motive driving employers to squeeze the last dollar out of employees."

In spite of labor union resistance, the rigid 40-hour workweek and its required overtime pay seems to have outlived its usefulness. It doesn't fit well with the future workplace and the changing needs of both employers and employees.

Not all employees embrace the idea of telecommuting. After the massive Los Angeles earthquake in January 1994, many L.A. firms began offering telecommuting for their workers.[82] It was popular for a week or two, but its popularity soon faded. Many workers complained they were missing out on important meetings and informal interactions that led to new policies and ideas. The vast majority were willing to put up with 2- and 3-hour commutes, while bridges and freeways were being rebuilt, in order to maintain their social contacts at work.

The long-term future of telecommuting depends on some questions for which there aren't yet definitive answers. For instance, will employees who do their work at home be at a disadvantage in office politics? Might they be less likely to be considered for salary increases and promotions? Is being out of sight equivalent to being out of mind? Will non-work-related distractions such as children, neighbors, and the proximity of the refrigerator significantly reduce productivity for those without superior willpower and discipline?

There is a variety of additional material available on the CD-ROM and companion Web site that accompany this text. You can access this information through the CD-ROM or by visiting the Web site at **<www.prenhall.com/robbins>**.

SUMMARY

(This summary is organized by the chapter-opening learning objectives on page 206.)

1. By substituting computerized equipment and machinery for human labor and traditional machinery, technology allows organizations to achieve increased levels of output with less labor, capital, and materials.

2. Computer-aided design has essentially made manual drafting obsolete. It allows designers to create and evaluate alternative designs quickly and dramatically cut the costs of developing prototypes.

3. Flexible manufacturing systems provide management with the technology to meet customers' unique demands by producing nonstandardized products, but with the efficiency associated with standardization.

4. The three key elements of reengineering are: (1) identifying an organization's distinctive competencies—the unique skills and resources that determine an organization's competitive weapons; (2) assessing core processes—these are the processes that customers value; and (3) reorganizing horizontally by process—flattening the structure and relying more on teams.

5. Expert systems, neural networks, groupware, and specific managerial problem-solving software are examples of information technologies that have been created to support and improve organizational decision making.

6. The five key dimensions in a job are skill variety, task identity, task significance, autonomy, and feedback.

7. You can design individual jobs to maximize employee performance by combining tasks, creating natural work units, establishing client relationships, expanding jobs vertically, and opening feedback channels.

8. Flextime, job sharing, and telecommuting increase organizational flexibility. Flextime allows employees some discretion in choosing their work hours. Job sharing allows the organization to hire people who might not be available on a full-time basis and gives the organization two heads for the price of one. Telecommuting cuts the costs of maintaining a permanent work area for an employee and increases employee flexibility by cutting out commuting time and allowing workers to better balance work and family responsibilities.

REVIEW QUESTIONS

1. Explain how just-in-time systems improve productivity.
2. Describe how technology can improve an organization's customer service.
3. How might the Internet change organizations and management practice?
4. Contrast reengineering and TQM.

5. How do you think information technology will have re-shaped the office by the year 2010?

6. What downside, if any, do you see for (a) the organization and (b) employees from using computerized technology to replace the human element?

7. What are the implications of worker obsolescence on (a) society, (b) management practice, and (c) you, as an individual, planning a career?

8. "Everyone wants a job that scores high on the five JCM dimensions." Build an argument to support this statement. Then negate that argument.

9. What can management do to improve employees' perceptions that their jobs are interesting and challenging?

10. Why would technology transfer be relevant to a large, European-based, global company?

IF I WERE THE MANAGER . . .

Virtual Grocery Shopping

Judy Belasco thought she had a great idea. Wouldn't it be great to pick out her groceries from an on-line catalog and have them delivered promptly?

You're Judy Belasco. You're in the final term of your business degree. You've considered dozens of ideas around which you could create a business. About a week ago, while you were in the supermarket doing your weekly shopping, you realized how much you hated this task. You were certain others felt the same. Why couldn't you develop a business that took advantage of the Internet to provide home-delivered groceries?

Your idea is only in its preliminary stages. You envision a warehouse that is conveniently located near a large, urban community. Your target market would be single professionals and two-career couples. Customers could access your catalogue on-line by visiting your Web site. It would be laid out like a supermarket. They would "walk" the aisles, see prices and specials, select items and put them in their "basket," but avoid going through the checkout line. When they were finished making their selections, they would provide their protected ID number. This would provide you with their name, address, and credit card data. Depending on the preference of the customer, you would deliver their selected groceries that afternoon, evening, or early the next morning.

You wondered: Could this work? What would be necessary—technology-wise—to make this a success? What operations and information problems would you have to overcome?

SKILL EXERCISE

Designing Motivating Jobs

Break into groups of four or five. You are a consulting team that has been hired by Banc One to help solve a motivation/performance problem.

Banc One employs several hundred people in this specific back office. These employees process all the company's financial transactions in its region. Their jobs have been split up so that each person performs a single, routine task over and over again. Employees have become dissatisfied with these mundane jobs, and their dissatisfaction shows in their work. Severe backlogs have developed, and error rates are unacceptably high. Your team's task is to (a) redesign these jobs in order to resolve the problems and (b) identify how your changes are likely to affect the jobs of supervisors in this department.

Your team has 30 minutes to complete this task.

TEAM ACTIVITY

Designing Tomorrow's University

Break into groups of four or five. Your team's task is to assess how technology will change the way colleges and universities disseminate information a decade from now. Specifically, what will the typical college's teaching technologies look like in the year 2010? Things to ponder: Will there still be college campuses, sprawled over hundreds of acres? Will every student have a laptop? Will there be computers in every classroom? Will students physically come to campus or telecommute from their office or home?

You have 30 minutes to discuss this issue and develop your response. Appoint someone in your group to be prepared to make a presentation to the class on your findings.

CASE EXERCISE

Terry Galinsky Looks Back to the Future

Terry Galinsky joined Hewlett-Packard in 1985, fresh out of college with her B.S. in electrical engineering. By 1989, she was a production supervisor. Today she heads up a design team. I asked Terry to look back to 1989 and describe how technology had influenced her job and to compare her job then with her job in 1999.

"We were a hierarchical company back then. I ran a department with fifteen people. I spent a lot of time in meetings and committees. Communications tended to closely follow the chain of command. We got weekly newsletters from upper management that kept us informed of the lastest happenings. And, since changes came slower in those days, we were better able to prepare for them. For instance, the life of an HP printer model in those days was probably 4 years. Today it's more like 12 to 18 months. We had a lot more time back in the 1980s to adjust to anticipated changes. Now they come at us a mile a minute.

Back in 1989, I was a production manager. Now I'm a project team leader. Membership on my team is fluid. People come and go. Some months I have twenty people on my team; other months there are only ten or twelve. And the biggest difference is undoubtedly due to the networking of our computers. It was very different back in the 1980s. Our individual computers weren't networked. I relied heavily on weekly reports that the centralized systems department created for me. Now I can get that information myself, in less than a minute, by accessing our central databases. And people who worked for me in those days were geographically consolidated together so I could directly supervise them. Today, my team members are spread all over the place. But we are able to communicate as if we're all in the same room because of the development of linking software."

QUESTIONS

1. Project into the future. Describe the technological advances you think will realistically develop by the year 2009 that could reshape the manager's job.
2. Now specifically describe how those technological advances in 2009 might likely change Terry Galinsky's job.

NOTES

1. D. McGraw, "Staying Loose in a Tense Tech Market," *U.S. News & World Report*, July 8, 1996, p. 46.
2. E. E. Adam Jr. and R. J. Ebert, *Production & Operations Management*, 5th ed. (Upper Saddle River, NJ: Prentice Hall, 1992), p. 46.
3. P. Engardio, "There's More Than One Way to Play Leapfrog," in "21st Century Capitalism," *Business Week*, special issue, November 18, 1994, pp. 162–65.
4. Adam and Ebert, *Production & Operations Management*, 5th ed., p. 137.
5. J. Teresko, "Speeding the Product Development Cycle," *Industry Week*, July 18, 1988, p. 41.
6. G. Bylinsky, "The Digital Factory," *Fortune*, November 14, 1994, pp. 96–100.
7. G. Taninecz, "Blue Sky Meets Blue Sky," *Industry Week*, December 18, 1995, p. 48–52.
8. J. E. Halpert, "One Car, Worldwide, with Strings Pulled from Michigan," *New York Times*, August 29, 1993, p. F7.
9. P. Fuhrman, "New Way to Roll," *Forbes*, April 24, 1995, pp. 180–82.
10. G. Bock, "Limping Along in Robot Land," *Time*, July 13, 1987, p. 55.
11. See, for instance, E. H. Hall Jr., "Just-in-Time Management: A Critical Assessment," *The Executive*, November 1989, pp. 315–18.
12. J. Flint, "King Lear," *Forbes*, May 22, 1995, pp. 43–44.
13. See, for example, P. Northey and N. Southway, *Cycle Time Management: The Fast Track to Time-Based Productivity Improvement* (Portland, OR: Productivity Press, 1994); and W. L. Douchkoff, T. Petroski, and T. E. Petroski, *Reengineering Through Cycle Time Management* (Boston: Pt. Publications, 1996).
14. O. Port, "Quality: Small and Midsize Companies Seize the Challenge Not a Moment Too Soon," *Business Week*, November 30, 1992, pp. 68–72; and "America's Best Plants," *Industry Week*, October 21, 1996, pp. 54–58 and 68–70.
15. See, for instance, O. Port, "Moving Past the Assembly Line," in "Reinventing America," *Business Week*, special issue, November 1992, pp. 177–80; D. M. Upton, "The Management of Manufacturing Flexibility," *California Management Review*, Winter 1994, pp. 72–89; Bylinsky, "The Digital Factory"; and N. Gross and P. Coy, "The Technology Paradox," *Business Week*, March 6, 1995, pp. 76–84.
16. S. Moffat, "Japan's New Personalized Production," *Fortune*, October 22, 1990, p. 44.
17. S. M. Silverman, "Retail Retold," *Inc. Technology*, Summer 1995, pp. 23–24.
18. See B. Ives and R. O. Mason, "Can Information Technology Revitalize Your Customer Service?" *The Executive*, November 1990, pp. 52–69; and K. Kane, "L. L. Bean Delivers the Goods," *Fast Company*, August/September 1997, pp. 104–13.

19. Ibid.

20. H. Plotkin, "Riches to Rags," *Inc. Technology*, Summer 1995, pp. 62–67.

21. See, for instance, S. Dentzer, "Death of the Middleman?" *U.S. News & World Report*, May 22, 1995, p. 56.

22. See, for instance, J. W. Verity, "Planet Internet," *Business Week*, April 3, 1995, pp. 118–24; and B. Ziegler, "In Cyberspace the Web Delivers Junk Mail," *Wall Street Journal*, June 13, 1995, p. B1.

23. "The Internet: Instant Access to Information," *Canadian Business*, May 1995, pp. 41–43; and D. McGraw, "Shootout at PC Corral," *U.S. News & World Report*, June 23, 1997, p. 38.

24. See, for example, T. H. Berry, *Managing the Total Quality Transition* (New York: McGraw-Hill, 1991); D. Ciampa, *Total Quality* (Reading, MA: Addison-Wesley, 1992); W. H. Schmidt and J. P. Finnegan, *The Race without a Finish Line* (San Francisco: Jossey-Bass, 1992); and T. B. Kinni, "Process Improvement," *Industry Week*, January 23, 1995, pp. 52–58.

25. M. Sashkin and K. J. Kiser, *Putting Total Quality Management to Work* (San Francisco: Berrett-Koehler, 1993), p. 44.

26. T. Petzinger Jr., "A Plant Manager Keeps Reinventing His Production Line," *Wall Street Journal*, September 19, 1997, p. B1.

27. M. Hammer and J. Champy, *Re-engineering the Corporation: A Manifesto for Business Revolution* (New York: HarperBusiness, 1993). See also J. Champy, *Reengineering Management: The Mandate for New Leadership* (New York: HarperBusiness, 1995); and M. Hammer and S. A. Stanton, *The Reengineering Revolution* (New York: HarperBusiness, 1995).

28. R. Karlgaard, "ASAP Interview: Mike Hammer," *Forbes ASAP*, September 13, 1993, p. 70.

29. Ibid.

30. "The Age of Reengineering," *Across the Board*, June 1993, pp. 26–33.

31. Ibid., p. 29.

32. Ibid., p. 33.

33. R. Hotch, "In Touch through Technology," *Nation's Business*, January 1994, pp. 33–35.

34. This section is based on J. W. Verity, "Getting Work to Go with the Flow," *Business Week*, June 21, 1993, pp. 156–61.

35. M. Hammer, "Reengineering Work: Don't Automate, Obliterate," *Harvard Business Review*, July–August 1990, p. 106.

36. See, for example, R. Hotch, "Communications Revolution," *Nation's Business*, May 1993, pp. 20–28.

37. Ibid., pp. 21–22.

38. B. Ziegler, "Building a Wireless Future," *Business Week*, April 5, 1993, p. 57.

39. See, for example, B. Enslow, "The Payoff from Expert Systems," *Across the Board*, January–February 1989, pp. 54–58; and E. I. Schwartz, "Smart Programs Go to Work," *Business Week*, March 2, 1992, pp. 97–105.

40. F. L. Luconi, T. W. Malone, and M. S. S. Morton, "Expert Systems: The Next Challenge for Managers," *Sloan Management Review*, Summer 1986, pp. 3–14.

41. M. W. Davis, "Anatomy of Decision Support," *Datamation*, June 15, 1985, p. 201.

42. Cited in T. A. Stewart, "Brainpower," *Fortune*, June 3, 1991, p. 44.

43. G. Bylinsky, "Computers That Learn by Doing," *Fortune*, September 6, 1993, pp. 96–102; R. E. Calem, "To Catch a Thief," *Forbes ASAP*, June 5, 1995, pp. 44–45; and O. Port, "Computers That Think Are Almost Here," *Business Week*, July 17, 1995, pp. 68–73.

44. G. Bylinsky, "Computers That Learn by Doing."

45. J. Bartimo, "At These Shouting Matches, No One Says a Word," *Business Week*, June 11, 1990, p. 78; M. S. Poole, M. Holmes, and G. DeSanctis, "Conflict Management in a Computer-Supported Meeting Environment," *Management Science*, August 1991, pp. 926–53; A. R. Dennis and J. S. Valacich, "Computer Brainstorms: More Heads Are Better Than One," *Journal of Applied Psychology*, August 1993, pp. 531–37; R. B. Gallupe and W. H. Cooper, "Brainstorming Electronically," *Sloan Management Review*, Fall 1993, pp. 27–36; and R. B. Gallupe, W. H. Cooper, M. L. Grise, and L. M. Bastianutti, "Blocking Electronic Brainstorms," *Journal of Applied Psychology*, February 1994, pp. 77–86.

46. W. R. Pape, "Beyond E-Mail," *Inc. Technology*, Summer 1995, p. 28.

47. M. E. Flatley and J. Hunter, "Electronic Mail, Bulletin Board Systems, Conferences: Connections for the Electronic Teaching/Learning Age," in N. J. Groneman (ed.), *Technology in the Classroom* (Reston, VA: National Business Education Association, 1995), pp. 73–85.

48. A. L. Sprout, "Surprise! Software to Help You Manage," *Fortune*, April 17, 1995, pp. 197–202.

49. D. Hulme and P. Janssen, "Struggling to Acquire Expertise," *Asian Business*, July 1996, pp. 58–62.

50. See, for example, N. F. Sullivan, *Technology Transfer: Making the Most of Your Intellectual Property* (London: Cambridge University Press, 1996); and A. A. Lado and G. S. Vozikis, "Transfer of Technology to Promote Entrepreneurship in Developing Countries: An Integration and Proposed Framework," *Entrepreneurship Theory and Practice*, Winter 1996, pp. 55–72.

51. This section is based on D. Hulme and P. Janssen, "Struggling to Acquire Expertise."

52. H. Schachter, "The Dispossessed," *Canadian Business*, May 1995, pp. 30–40.

53. J. E. Rigdon, "Give and Take," *Wall Street Journal*, November 14, 1994, p. R24.

54. P. E. Ross, "Software as Career Threat," *Forbes*, May 22, 1995, pp. 240–46.

55. This description is based on L. Jaroff, "Age of the Road Warrior," *Time*, Spring 1995, pp. 38–40.

56. See J. R. Hackman and G. R. Oldham, "Motivation through the Design of Work: Test of a Theory," *Organizational Behavior and Human Performance*, August 1976, pp. 250–79; Y. Fried and G. R. Ferris, "The Validity of the Job Characteristics Model: A Review and Meta-Analysis," *Personnel Psychology*, Summer 1987, pp. 287–322; S. J. Zaccaro and E. F. Stone, "Incremental Validity of an Empirically Based Measure of Job Characteristics," *Journal of Applied Psychology*, May 1988, pp. 245–52; and R. W. Renn and R. J. Vandenberg, "The Critical Psychological States: An Underrepresented Component in Job Charac-

teristics Model Research," *Journal of Management*, vol. 21, no. 2, 1995, pp. 279–303.

57. J. R. Hackman, "Work Design," in J. R. Hackman and J. L. Suttle (eds.), *Improving Life at Work* (Glenview, IL: Scott, Foresman, 1977), p. 129.

58. See "Job Characteristics Theory of Work Redesign," in J. B. Miner, *Theories of Organizational Behavior* (Hinsdale, IL: Dryden Press, 1980), pp. 231–66; Fried and Ferris, "The Validity of the Job Characteristics Model," and Zaccaro and Stone, "Incremental Validity of an Empirically Based Measure of Job Characteristics;" and J. R. Rentsch and R. P. Steel, "Testing the Durability of Job Characteristics as Predictors of Absenteeism Over a Six-Year Period," *Personnel Psychology*, Spring 1998, pp. 165–90.

59. See R. B. Dunham, "Measurement and Dimensionality of Job Characteristics," *Journal of Applied Psychology*, August 1976, pp. 404–09; J. L. Pierce and R. B. Dunham, "Task Design: A Literature Review," *Academy of Management Review*, January 1976, pp. 83–97; D. M. Rousseau, "Technological Differences in Job Characteristics, Employee Satisfaction, and Motivation: A Synthesis of Job Design Research and Sociotechnical Systems Theory," *Organizational Behavior and Human Performance*, October 1977, pp. 18–42.

60. R. B. Dunham, "Measurement and Dimensionality of Job Characteristics," J. L. Pierce and R. B. Dunham, "Task Design: A Literature Review;" D. M. Rousseau, "Technological Differences in Job Characteristics, Employee Satisfaction, and Motivation," and Y. Fried and G. R. Ferris, "The Dimensionality of Job Characteristics: Some Neglected Issues," *Journal of Applied Psychology*, August 1986, pp. 419–26.

61. R. B. Tiegs, L. E. Tetrick, and Y. Fried, "Growth Need Strength and Context Satisfactions as Moderators of the Relations of the Job Characteristics Model," *Journal of Management*, September 1992, pp. 575–93.

62. C. A. O'Reilly and D. F. Caldwell, "Informational Influence as a Determinant of Perceived Task Characteristics and Job Satisfaction," *Journal of Applied Psychology*, April 1979, pp. 157–65; R. V. Montagno, "The Effects of Comparison Others and Prior Experience on Response to Task Design," *Academy of Management Journal*, June 1985, pp. 491–98; and P. C. Bottger and I. K.-H. Chew, "The Job Characteristics Model and Growth Satisfaction: Main Effects of Assimilation of Work Experience and Context Satisfaction," *Human Relations*, June 1986, pp. 575–94.

63. Fried and Ferris, "The Validity of the Job Characteristics Model"; and Hackman, "Work Design," pp. 132–33.

64. G. R. Salancik and J. Pfeffer, "A Social Information Processing Approach to Job Attitudes and Task Design," *Administrative Science Quarterly*, June 1978, pp. 224–53; J. G. Thomas and R. W. Griffin, "The Power of Social Information in the Workplace," *Organizational Dynamics*, Autumn 1989, pp. 63–75; and M. D. Zalesny and J. K. Ford, "Extending the Social Information Processing Perspective: New Links to Attitudes, Behaviors, and Perceptions," *Organizational Behavior and Human Decision Processes*, December 1990, pp. 205–46.

65. See, for instance, J. Thomas and R. W. Griffin, "The Social Information Processing Model of Task Design: A Review of the Literature," *Academy of Management Review*, October 1983, pp. 672–82; R. W. Griffin, T. S. Bateman, S. J. Wayne, and T. C. Head, "Objective and Social Factors as Determinants of Task Perceptions and Responses: An Integrated Perspective and Empirical Investigation," *Academy of Management Journal*, September 1987, pp. 501–23; and G. W. Meyer, "Social Information Processing and Social Networks: A Test of Social Influence Mechanisms," *Human Relations*, September 1994, pp. 1013–45.

66. Hackman, "Work Design," pp. 136–40.

67. R. W. Griffin and G. C. McMahan, "Motivation through Job Design," in J. Greenberg (ed.), *Organizational Behavior: The State of the Science* (Hillsdale, NJ: Lawrence Erlbaum Associates, 1994), pp. 36–38.

68. J. R. Hackman, "The Design of Work Teams," in J. W. Lorsch (ed.), *Handbook of Organizational Behavior* (Upper Saddle River, NJ: Prentice Hall, 1987), pp. 324–27.

69. See, for instance, D. Stamps, "Taming Time with Flexible Work," *Training*, May 1995, pp. 60–66; and A. Saltzman, "Companies in a Family Way," *U.S. News & World Report*, May 12, 1997, pp. 64–73.

70. Cited in C. M. Solomon, "Job Sharing: One Job, Double Headache?" *Personnel Journal*, September 1994, p. 90.

71. D. R. Dalton and D. J. Mesch, "The Impact of Flexible Scheduling on Employee Attendance and Turnover," *Administrative Science Quarterly*, June 1990, pp. 370–87; and K. S. Kush and L. K. Stroh, "Flextime: Myth or Reality?" *Business Horizons*, September–October 1994, p. 53.

72. Kush and Stroh, "Flextime."

73. Cited in E. M. Friedman (ed.), "Almanac: A Statistical and Informational Snapshot of the Business World Today," *Inc's The State of Small Business 1997*, p. 121.

74. H. Schachter, "Slaves of the New Economy," *Canadian Business*, April 1996, p. 89.

75. S. Shellenbarger, "Two People, One Job: It Can Really Work," *Wall Street Journal*, December 7, 1994, p. B1.

76. "Job-Sharing: Widely Offered, Little Used," *Training*, November 1994, p. 12.

77. Shellenbarger, "Two People, One Job."

78. See, for example, R. Maynard, The Growing Appeal of Telecommuting," *Nation's Business*, August 1994, pp. 61–62; and F. A. E. McQuarrie, "Telecommuting: Who Really Benefits?" *Business Horizons*, November–December 1994, pp. 79–83.

79. Cited in "America's Stay-at-Home Workers," *Manpower Argus*, January 1998, p. 2.

80. "Telecommuting in Europe," *Manpower Argus*, April 1997, p. 9.

81. R. Hearn, "First Banker in Space," *Canadian Business*, August 1997, p. 15.

82. S. Silverstein, "Telecommuting Boomlet Has Few Follow-Up Calls," *Los Angeles Times*, May 16, 1994, p. A1.

83. R. A. Zaldivar, "Republicans Push for Alternatives to 40-Hour Weeks," *Seattle Times*, February 2, 1997, p. A8.

ORGANIZATION DESIGN

GUIDELINES FOR BUREAUCRATS: (1) WHEN IN CHARGE,
PONDER; (2) WHEN IN TROUBLE, DELEGATE;
(3) WHEN IN DOUBT, MUMBLE.

J. H. BOREN

LEARNING OBJECTIVES

After studying this chapter, you should be able to:

1　Define the six key elements of organization structure.

2　Contrast mechanistic and organic designs.

3　Identify the four contingency variables that explain structural differences.

4　Explain how environmental uncertainty affects an organization's structure.

5　Describe the bureaucracy and its strengths.

6　Explain the advantages and disadvantages of a matrix structure.

7　Describe the virtual organization and its strengths.

The Trufresh Marketing Group has a unique product and a unique organization structure for producing and delivering that product.[1]

Trufresh harvests and distributes "fresh frozen" Atlantic salmon. Using a patented freezing technology from Japan, the company is able to sell salmon that is indistinguishable from fresh. As a case in point, when Trufresh salmon was tested against freshly harvested salmon by the Culinary Institute of America, its expert tasters couldn't tell them apart. Trufresh harvests its farm-raised salmon in Maine. Within hours of being plucked from a pen, the salmon is boned, skinned, cleaned, sealed in airtight plastic, and then plunged into a patented cryogenic brine at −40°F. The fish are frozen so quickly that, unlike conventional frozen fish, Trufresh salmon lose very little moisture. The result is a product that can be served by upscale restaurants as well as institutional food-service operators.

To run this rapidly growing business, Trufresh's management has chosen an unusual form of structural design. It's sort of a no-structure structure! There are no headquarters, a bare-bones sales staff, and a very small set of managers spread over a five-state region. The majority owners of Trufresh, who are real estate executives, oversee the company's finances from their real estate offices in New York City. A retired ocean tanker captain handles Trufresh's production in rented space in Maine that once was a sardine canning plant. The national sales manager works at home in Pittsburgh, "managing" five freelance sales representatives. The only Trufresh office with overhead is in Connecticut. With a couple of secondhand desks, a computer, a fax machine, a telephone, and a filing cabinet, the company's CEO works here, along with his marketing team made up of two sons— one an 18-year-old high school senior and the other a 21-year-old college junior. The rest of Trufresh's organization is a warehouse, leased in Massachusetts, and a distribution network that is contracted out to a small trucking company.

Trufresh's "virtual organization" enables it to focus on technology and sales, without diverting resources. It also allows the company maximum flexibility while minimizing costs. In today's ever-changing business world, a lot of managers are talking about outsourcing those functions that are not part of their company's core competency. Trufresh is actually walking the talk!

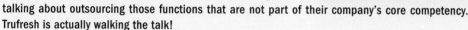

No topic in management has undergone more change in the past decade than the area of organization design. The reason is quite simple—the environment has become considerably more chaotic. In times of relative environmental stability, organizational effectiveness tends to focus on achieving high efficiency. How do you achieve high efficiency in a stable environment? Through standardization. So organizations created rigid structures, with lots of rules and regulations and tight controls. Rigid structures, however, are unable to respond rapidly to change. In dynamic times, organizations with rigid structures become vulnerable to more-flexible competitors. To meet and beat their rivals, managers have had to aggressively redesign their structures in ways that can make their organizations more adaptive. As a case in point, recent evidence indicates that more than 75 percent of large companies have significantly altered their structures in the past decade to make them more flexible.[2]

In this chapter, we'll describe the key structural dimensions that managers control, show how those dimensions can be combined to create different structural options, and discuss the conditions that favor different options. We'll also present a description of how organization designs have evolved from efficiency machines to technology-based structures that better balance efficiency with flexibility.

An **organization structure** defines how job tasks are formally divided, grouped, and coordinated. For instance, Johnson & Johnson groups activities into 168 semiautonomous companies organized around products (making everything from Tylenol to contact lenses) and allows managers of those companies considerable decision-making latitude. In

WHAT IS ORGANIZATION STRUCTURE?

EXHIBIT 8-1

Six Key Questions That Managers Need to Answer in Designing the Proper Organization Structure

The Key Question Is	The Answer Is Provided By
1. To what degree are tasks subdivided into separate jobs?	*Work specialization*
2. On what basis will jobs be grouped together?	*Departmentalization*
3. To whom do individuals and groups report?	*Chain of command*
4. How many individuals can a manager efficiently and effectively direct?	*Span of control*
5. Where does decision-making authority lie?	*Centralization and decentralization*
6. To what degree will there be rules and regulations to direct employees and managers?	*Formalization*

contrast, Trufresh has grouped activities into parcels that can be easily outsourced and then coordinates them from a small central office.

There are six key elements that managers need to address when they design their organization's structure: work specialization, departmentalization, chain of command, span of control, centralization and decentralization, and formalization.[3] Exhibit 8-1 presents each of those elements as an answer to an important structural question. The following sections describe the six elements of structure.

Work Specialization

Early in the twentieth century, Henry Ford became rich and famous by building automobiles on an assembly line. Every Ford worker was assigned a specific, repetitive task. For instance, one person would put on the right front wheel, and someone else would install the right front door. By breaking jobs up into small standardized tasks that could be performed over and over again, Ford was able to produce cars at the rate of one every 10 seconds using employees who had relatively limited skills.

Ford demonstrated that work can be performed more efficiently if employees are allowed to specialize. Today we use the term **work specialization**, or *division of labor*, to describe the degree to which tasks in the organization are subdivided into separate jobs.

The essence of work specialization is that an entire job is not done by one individual; it is broken down into steps, and each step is completed by a different person. Individuals specialize in doing part of an activity rather than the entire activity.

By the late 1940s, most manufacturing jobs in industrialized countries were being done with high work specialization. Management saw this as a means to make the most efficient use of its employees' skills. In most organizations, some tasks require highly developed skills; others can be performed by unskilled personnel. If all workers were engaged in each step of, say, an organization's manufacturing process, all would have to have the skills necessary to perform both the most demanding and the least demanding jobs.

The result would be that, except when performing the most skilled or highly sophisticated tasks, employees would be working below their skill levels. And, since skilled workers are paid more than unskilled workers and their wages tend to reflect their highest level of skill, it represents an inefficient usage of organizational resources to pay highly skilled workers to do simple tasks.

Managers also looked for other efficiencies that could be achieved through work specialization. Employee skills at performing a task successfully increase through repetition. Less time is spent in changing tasks, in putting away one's tools and equipment from a prior step in the work process, and in getting ready for another. Equally important, training for specialization is more efficient from the organization's perspective. It is easier and less costly to find and train workers to do specific, repetitive, limited tasks than to find and train workers to do all the tasks. This is especially true of highly sophisticated and complex operations. For example, could Cessna produce one Citation jet a year if one person had to build the entire plane alone? Not likely! Finally, work specialization increases efficiency and productivity by encouraging the creation of special inventions and machinery.

For much of the first half of the twentieth century, managers viewed work specialization as an unending source of increased productivity. And it probably was. Because specialization was not widely practiced, its introduction almost always generated higher productivity. But, by the 1960s, evidence was increasing that a good thing can be carried too far. The point had been reached in some jobs at which the human diseconomies from specialization—such as boredom, fatigue, stress, low productivity, poor quality of work, increased absenteeism, and high turnover—more than offset the economic advantages (see Exhibit 8-2). In such cases, productivity could be increased by enlarging, rather than narrowing, the scope of job activities. In addition, a number of companies found that employees who were given a variety of activities to do, allowed to do a complete job, and put into teams with interchangeable skills often achieved significantly higher output and were more satisfied with their jobs than were specialized employees.

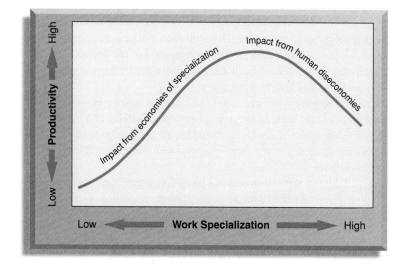

Economies and Diseconomies of Work Specialization

EXHIBIT 8-2

Surgical teams in hospitals rely on specialization and coordination to get their jobs done effectively.

Most managers today see work specialization as neither obsolete nor an unending source of increased productivity. Rather, managers recognize the economies it provides in certain types of jobs and the problems it creates when it is carried too far. McDonald's, for example, uses high work specialization to efficiently make and sell hamburgers and fries. And an increasing number of hospitals are cutting health care costs by focusing on a narrow specialization—such as stroke victims or people with back problems.[4] On the other hand, companies such as the Saturn Corporation and Aetna Life and Casualty have had success by broadening the scope of jobs and reducing specialization.

► Departmentalization

Once you have divided jobs up through work specialization, you will need to group the jobs together so that common tasks can be coordinated. The basis on which jobs are grouped is called **departmentalization**.

Historically, one of the most popular ways to group activities is by *function* performed. A manufacturing manager might organize his or her plant by separating engineering, accounting, manufacturing, personnel, and purchasing specialists into common departments. Of course, departmentalization by function can be used in all types of organizations, but the functions change to reflect the organization's objectives and activities. A hospital might have departments devoted to research, patient care, accounting, and so forth. A professional football franchise might have departments entitled Player Personnel, Ticket Sales, and Travel and Accommodations. The major advantage to this type of grouping is obtaining efficiencies from putting like specialists together. Functional departmentalization seeks to achieve economies of scale by placing people with common skills and orientations into common units.

Tasks can also be departmentalized by the type of *product* the organization produces. This is essentially the structural foundation at Johnson & Johnson. Each of J&J's 168 companies focuses on a narrow set of products (for example, baby oil, artificial optic lenses, blood-testing machines, adhesive bandages). The head of each company is responsible for everything having to do with his or her product line. Each, for example, has his or her own manufacturing and marketing group. The advantage of the product grouping is that it increases accountability for product performance, since all activities related to a specific product are under the direction of a single manager. If an organization's activities were service- rather than product-related, each service would be autonomously grouped. For instance, an accounting firm could have departments for tax preparation, management consulting, auditing, and the like. Each department would offer an array of related services under the direction of a service manager.

Another way to departmentalize is on the basis of *geography* or territory. The sales function, for instance, may have western, southern, midwestern, and eastern regions. Each of these regions is, in effect, a department organized around geography. If an organization's customers are scattered over a large geographical area, then this form of departmentalization can be valuable.

At a Reynolds Metals aluminum tubing plant in upstate New York, production is organized into five departments: casting, press, tubing, finishing, and inspect, pack, and ship. This is an example of *process* departmentalization because each department specializes in one specific phase in the production of aluminum tubing. The metal is cast in huge furnaces, and then sent to the press department, where it is extruded into aluminum pipe. The pipe is transferred to the tube mill, where it is stretched into various sizes and shapes of tubing, and then moved to finishing, where it is cut and cleaned. Finally, it arrives in the inspect, pack, and ship department. Since each process requires different skills, this method offers a basis for the homogeneous categorizing of activities.

Process departmentalization can be used for processing customers as well as products. If you've ever been to a state motor vehicle office to get a driver's license, you probably went through several departments before receiving your license. In one state, applicants must go through three steps, each handled by a separate department: (1) validation, by motor vehicles division; (2) processing, by the licensing department; and (3) payment collection, by the treasury department.

A final category of departmentalization is to use the particular type of *customer* the organization seeks to reach. The sales activities in an office supply firm, for instance, can be broken down into three departments to service retail, wholesale, and government customers. A large law office can segment its staff on the basis of whether they service corporate or individual clients. The assumption underlying customer departmentalization is that customers in each department have a common set of problems and needs that can best be met by having specialists for each.

Large organizations often combine many of the forms of departmentalization that we described in this section. A major Japanese electronics firm, for instance, organizes each of its divisions along functional lines and organizes its manufacturing units around processes; it departmentalizes sales around seven geographical regions; and it divides each sales region into four customer groupings. Two general trends, however, have surfaced over the past decade. First, customer departmentalization has grown in popularity. In order to better monitor the needs of customers and to be better able to respond to changes in those needs, many organizations have given greater emphasis to customer departmentalization. Xerox, for example, has eliminated its corporate marketing staff and placed marketing specialists out in the field.[5] This arrangement allows the company to better understand who their customers are and to respond faster to their requirements. The second trend is that rigid functional departmentalization has become complemented by teams that cross over traditional departmental lines. As tasks have become more complex and more-diverse skills are needed to accomplish those tasks, management has turned to cross-functional teams.

> In order to better monitor the needs of customers and to be better able to respond to changes in those needs, many organizations have given greater emphasis to customer departmentalization.

Chain of Command

Twenty-five years ago, the chain-of-command concept was a basic cornerstone in the design of organizations. As you will see, it has far less importance today. But contemporary managers should still consider its implications when they decide how best to structure their organizations.

The **chain of command** is an unbroken line of authority that extends from the top of the organization to the lowest echelon and clarifies who reports to whom. It answers questions for employees such as "Who do I go to if I have a problem?" and "Who am I responsible to?"

You can't discuss the chain of command without discussing two complementary concepts: authority and unity of command. **Authority** refers to the rights inherent in a managerial position to give orders and expect the orders to be obeyed.[6] To facilitate coordination, the organization gives each managerial position a place in the chain of command and each manager a degree of authority in order to meet his or her responsibilities. The **unity of command** principle helps preserve the concept of an unbroken line of authority. It states that a person should have one and only one superior to whom he or she is directly responsible. If the unity of command is broken, an employee might have to cope with conflicting demands or priorities from several superiors.

Times change and so do the basic tenets of organization design. The concepts of chain of command, authority, and unity of command have substantially less relevance today because of advancements in computer technology and the trend toward empowering employees. Just how different things are today is illustrated in the following excerpt from a recent article in *Business Week*:

> Puzzled, Charles Chaser scanned the inventory reports from his company's distribution centers one Wednesday morning in mid-March. According to the computer printouts, stocks of Rose Awakening Cutex nail polish were down to three days' supply, well below the three-and-a-half week stock Chesebrough-Pond's Inc. tries to keep on hand. But Chaser knew his Jefferson City (Missouri) plant had shipped 346 dozen bottles of the polish just two days before. Rose Awakening must be flying off store shelves, he thought. So Chaser turned to his terminal next to the production line and typed in instructions to produce 400 dozen more bottles on Thursday morning.
>
> All in a day's work for a scheduling manager, right? Except for one detail: Chaser isn't management. He's a line worker—officially a "line coordinator"—one of hundreds who routinely tap the plant's computer network to track shipments, schedule their own work loads, and generally perform functions that used to be the province of management.[7]

A low-level employee today can access information in seconds that, 20 years ago, was available only to top managers. Similarly, computer technology increasingly allows employees anywhere in an organization to communicate with anyone else without going through formal channels. Moreover, the concepts of authority and maintaining the chain of command are increasingly less relevant as operating employees are being empowered to make decisions that previously were reserved for management. Add to this the popularity of self-managed and cross-functional teams and the creation of new structural designs that include multiple bosses, and the unity-of-command concept takes on less relevance. There are, of course, still many organizations that find they can be most productive by enforcing the chain of command. There just seem to be fewer of them nowadays.

▶ Span of Control

How many employees can a manager efficiently and effectively direct? This question of **span of control** is important because, to a large degree, it determines the number of levels and managers an organization has. All things being equal, the wider or larger the span, the more efficient the organization. An example can illustrate the validity of this statement.

Assume that we have two organizations, both of which have approximately 4,100 operative-level employees. As Exhibit 8-3 illustrates, if one has a uniform span of four and the other a span of eight, the wider span would have two fewer levels and approximately 800 fewer managers. If the average manager made $45,000 a year, the wider span would save $36 million a year in management salaries! Obviously, wider spans are more efficient in terms of cost. However, at some point wider spans reduce effectiveness. That is, when the span becomes too large, employee performance suffers because supervisors no longer have the time to provide the necessary leadership and support.

Small spans have their advocates. By keeping the span of control to five or six employees, a manager can maintain close control.[8] But small spans have three major drawbacks. First, as already described, they are expensive because they add levels of management. Second, they

Contrasting Spans of Control

EXHIBIT 8-3

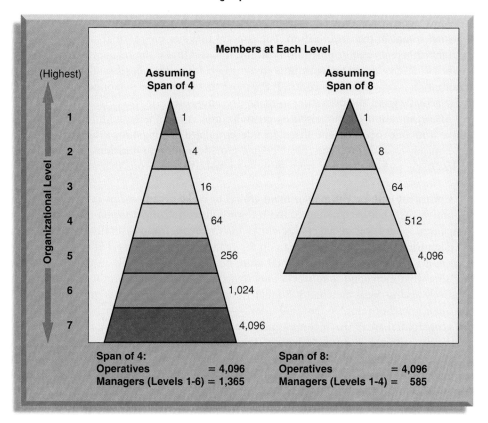

Members at Each Level

(Highest)

Organizational Level

Assuming Span of 4

Level	Members
1	1
2	4
3	16
4	64
5	256
6	1,024
7	4,096

Assuming Span of 8

Level	Members
1	1
2	8
3	64
4	512
5	4,096

Span of 4:
Operatives = 4,096
Managers (Levels 1-6) = 1,365

Span of 8:
Operatives = 4,096
Managers (Levels 1-4) = 585

make vertical communication in the organization more complex. The added levels of hierarchy slow down decision making and tend to isolate upper management. Third, small spans of control encourage overly tight supervision and discourage employee autonomy.

The trend in recent years has been toward larger spans of control. For example, Tom Smith, a regional manager with Carboline Co., today oversees twenty-seven people. His counterpart of 20 years ago would have typically managed twelve employees.[9]

Wide spans of control are consistent with recent efforts by companies to reduce costs, cut overhead, speed up decision making, increase flexibility, get closer to customers, and empower employees. However, to ensure that performance doesn't suffer because of these wider spans, organizations have been investing heavily in employee training. Managers recognize that they can handle a wider span when employees know their jobs inside and out or can turn to their co-workers when they have questions.

Centralization and Decentralization

In some organizations, top managers make all the decisions. Lower-level managers merely carry out top management's directives. At the other extreme, there are organizations in which decision making is pushed down to those managers who are closest to the action.

> **The more that lower-level personnel provide input or are actually given the discretion to make decisions, the more decentralization there is.**

The former organizations are described as highly centralized, and the latter as decentralized.

The term *centralization* refers to the degree to which decision making is concentrated at a single point in the organization. The concept includes only formal authority, that is, the rights inherent in one's position. Typically, it is said that if top management makes the organization's key decisions with little or no input from lower-level personnel, then the organization is centralized. In contrast, the more that lower-level personnel provide input or are actually given the discretion to make decisions, the more decentralization there is.

An organization characterized by centralization is an inherently different structural animal from one that is decentralized. In a decentralized organization, action can be taken more quickly to solve problems, more people provide input into decisions, and employees are less likely to feel alienated from those who make the decisions that affect their work lives.

Consistent with recent management efforts to make organizations more flexible and responsive, there has been a marked trend toward decentralizing decision making. In large companies, lower-level managers are closer to "the action" and typically have more detailed knowledge about problems than do top managers. For instance, big retailers such as Sears and J. C. Penney have given their store managers considerably more discretion in choosing what merchandise to stock. This structure allows those stores to compete more effectively against local merchants. Similarly, the Bank of Montreal has grouped its 1,164 Canadian branches into 236 "communities"—that is, a group of branches within a limited geographical area.[10] Each community is led by a community area manager, who typically works within a 20-minute drive of the other branches. This area manager can respond faster and more intelligently to problems in his community than could some senior executive in Montreal. IBM Europe's chairman, Renato Riverso, has sliced the Continent into some 200 autonomous business units, each with its own profit plan, employee incentives, and customer focus. "We used to manage from the top, like an army," says Riverso. "Now, we're trying to create entities that drive themselves."

▶ Formalization

Formalization refers to the degree to which jobs within the organization are standardized. If a job is highly formalized, then the job incumbent has a minimum amount of discretion over what is to be done, when it is to be done, and how he or she should do it. Employees can be expected always to handle the same input in exactly the same way, resulting in a consistent and uniform output. There are explicit job descriptions, lots of organizational rules, and clearly defined procedures covering work processes in organizations that have high formalization. Where formalization is low, job behaviors are relatively nonprogrammed and employees have a great deal of freedom to exercise discretion in their work. Because an individual's discretion on the job is inversely related to the amount of behavior in that job that is preprogrammed by the organization, the greater the standardization, the less input the employee has into how his or her work is to be done. Standardization not only eliminates the possibility that employees will engage in alternative behaviors, but it even removes the need for employees to consider alternatives.

The degree of formalization can vary widely between organizations and within organizations. Certain jobs, for instance, are well known to have little formalization. College book travelers—the representatives of publishers who call on professors to inform them of their company's new publications—have a great deal of freedom in their jobs. They have no standard sales "spiel," and the extent of rules and procedures governing their behavior may

Three CEOs Speak Out on Delegating Authority

How hard is it to delegate? How much should you delegate? What tasks should be delegated? Three CEOs give their views on these issues.

Joseph Liemandt; CEO, Trilogy Development Group

You always have to delegate something that you like to do, but you have no choice if the company is going to grow. I loved development and sales. I loved to sit down and work on product direction, but it created a bottleneck. So I had to take myself out of the equation.

To help make delegation easier, I put together a framework: If you can delegate a task to somebody who can do it 75 percent to 80 percent as well as you can today, you delegate it immediately.

For example, I used to write the entire marketing plan myself. When I handed it over, I knew the person could do a good job, but not as good as I could because I had more information. The expectation was that by the second or third plan she'd be doing it better than I because she could focus entirely on it.

Michael Merriman; CEO, Royal Appliance Manufacturing Co., Dirt Devil Inc.

We chief executives don't delegate enough. That was a lesson I learned pretty quickly after I became chief executive. The mission in the first two months was to get out and see all the major retailers.

Then, about a month later, I went to see them again with the vice president of sales. Later he said to me, "You know, Mike, you can keep doing this if you want to, but if you see them too often, there is no role for me."

He was right. I was too gung ho. You can't undermine your people's authority. Nor can our business rely solely on my relationship with a couple key retailers.

Kim Polese; CEO, Marimba Inc.

For Marimba, the need to delegate is absolute. I haven't found it difficult to master because I tend to like organizations that give people the rope to go and really prove themselves.

When I became the product manager of Java—then called Oak—there was little management involved. We were a spinoff unit and for the first time I had the autonomy to make key decisions.

It was scary but exhilarating because it convinced me of my own ability. There's a parallel with the Internet, which represents distribution rather than centralization.

Source: S. Bistayi, "Delegate—Or Not?" *Forbes*, April 21, 1997, pp. 20–22.

be little more than the requirement that they submit a weekly sales report and some suggestions on what to emphasize for the various new titles. At the other extreme, there are clerical and editorial positions in the same publishing houses where employees are required to "clock in" at their workstations by 9:00 A.M. or be docked a half-hour of pay and, once at that workstation, to follow a set of precise procedures dictated by management.

THE CONTINGENCY APPROACH TO ORGANIZATION DESIGN

All organizations are not structured exactly the same way. That's not surprising, you're probably thinking. After all, a company with 30 employees is not going to look like one with 30,000 employees. But even companies of comparable size do not necessarily have similar structures. What works for one organization may not work for another.

Structural differences among organizations are not random or happenchance. Senior executives of most organizations typically put a great deal of time and thought into designing the right structure. What that right structure is depends upon four contingency variables: the organization's strategy, size, technology, and degree of environmental uncertainty. Using these variables to select the proper structure is referred to as the **contingency**

approach to organization design.[11] In this section, we'll present two generic models of organization design and then consider when the contingency variables favor one design over the other.

Mechanistic and Organic Designs: Efficiency versus Flexibility

Exhibit 8-4 describes two diverse organizational forms.[12] The **mechanistic organization** is a rigid and tightly controlled structure. It is characterized by high specialization, extensive departmentalization, narrow spans of control, high formalization, a limited information network (mostly downward communication), and little participation by low-level members in decision making.

In the mechanistic structure, work specialization creates jobs that are simple, routine, and standardized. Further specialization through the use of departmentalization increases impersonality and the need for multiple layers of management to coordinate the specialized departments. There is also strict adherence to the unity-of-command principle. This ensures the existence of a formal hierarchy of authority, with each person controlled and supervised by one superior. Narrow spans of control, especially at increasingly higher levels in the organization, create tall, impersonal structures. And, as the distance between the top and the bottom of the organization expand, top management tends to impose rules and regulations. Why? Because top managers can't control lower-level activities through direct observation and ensure the use of standard practices, so they substitute high formalization.

In its ideal form, the mechanistic organization becomes an *efficiency* machine, well oiled by rules, regulations, routinization, and similar controls. This organizational form tries to minimize the impact of personalities, human judgments, and ambiguity because these are seen as imposing inefficiencies and inconsistencies. Although there exists no pure form of the mechanistic organization in practice, almost all large corporations and government agencies as recently as 25 or 30 years ago had most of these mechanistic characteristics. And a number of large organizations today still have many mechanistic properties.

EXHIBIT 8-4

Mechanistic versus Organic Designs

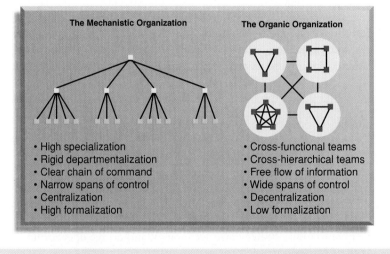

The Mechanistic Organization

The Organic Organization

- High specialization
- Rigid departmentalization
- Clear chain of command
- Narrow spans of control
- Centralization
- High formalization

- Cross-functional teams
- Cross-hierarchical teams
- Free flow of information
- Wide spans of control
- Decentralization
- Low formalization

The **organic organization** is a direct contrast to the mechanistic form. It is a highly adaptive form that is as loose and flexible as the mechanistic organization is rigid and stable. The organic structure is flat, uses teams to cut across functional departments and hierarchical levels, has low formalization, possesses a comprehensive information network (utilizing lateral and upward communication as well as downward), and actively involves all employees in decision making.

Rather than having standardized jobs and regulations, the organic structure's *flexibility* allows it to change rapidly as needs require. The organic form has division of labor, but the jobs people do are not standardized. Employees are highly trained and empowered to make job-related decisions. And organic structures tend to rely heavily on teams. The net effect is that employees in this form require a minimal degree of formal rules and little direct supervision—their high skills, training, and the support provided by other team members tend to make high formalization and tight managerial controls unnecessary.

With these two models in mind, we're now prepared to address the question: Why are some organizations structured along more mechanistic lines while others lean toward organic characteristics?

Strategy

An organization's structure is a means to help management achieve its objectives. Since objectives are derived from the organization's overall strategy, it's only logical that strategy and structure should be closely linked. More specifically, structure should *follow* strategy. If management makes a significant change in its organization's strategy, the structure will need to be modified to accommodate and support this change.[13]

Most current strategy-structure frameworks focus on three strategy dimensions—innovation, cost minimization, and imitation—and the structural design that works best with each.[14]

To what degree does an organization introduce major new products or services? An **innovation strategy** does not mean a strategy merely for simple or cosmetic changes from previous offerings but rather one for meaningful and unique innovations. Obviously, not all firms pursue innovation. This strategy may appropriately characterize 3M Co., but it certainly is not a strategy pursued by the publisher of *Reader's Digest*.

An organization that is pursuing a **cost-minimization strategy** tightly controls costs, refrains from incurring unnecessary innovation or marketing expenses, and cuts prices in selling a basic product. This would describe the strategy pursued by Wal-Mart or the sellers of generic grocery products.

Organizations following an **imitation strategy** try to capitalize on the best of both of the previous strategies. They seek to minimize risk and maximize opportunity for profit. Their strategy is to move into new products or new markets only after viability has been proved by innovators. They take the successful ideas of innovators and copy them. Manufacturers of mass-marketed fashion goods that are knockoffs of designer styles follow the imitation strategy. This label also characterizes Matsushita Electric, one of the world's largest corporations.[15] Matsushita is never first to pioneer a product or technology. But once it enters a market, its offerings are almost always better and/or cheaper than its innovation-driven competitors.

Exhibit 8-5 describes the structural option that best matches each strategy. Innovators need the flexibility of the organic structure, whereas cost minimizers seek the efficiency and stability of the mechanistic structure. Imitators combine the two structures. They use a mechanistic structure in order to maintain tight controls and low costs in their current

EXHIBIT 8-5

The Strategy-Structure Thesis

Strategy	Best Structural Option
Innovation	*Organic*: A loose structure; low specialization, low formalization, decentralized
Cost minimization	*Mechanistic*: Tight control; extensive work specialization, high formalization, high centralization
Imitation	*Mechanistic and organic*: Mix of loose with tight properties; tight controls over current activities and looser controls for new undertakings

activities, while, at the same time, they create organic subunits in which to pursue new undertakings.

Organization Size

A quick glance at the organizations we deal with regularly in our lives would lead most of us to conclude that size would have some bearing on an organization's structure. The more than 800,000 employees of the U.S. Postal Service, for example, do not neatly fit into one building or into several departments supervised by a couple of managers. It's pretty hard to envision 800,000 people being organized in any manner other than one that contains a great deal of specialization and departmentalization, uses a large number of procedures and regulations to ensure uniform practices, and follows a high degree of decentralized decision making. On the other hand, a local messenger service that employs ten people and generates less than $300,000 a year in service fees is not likely to need decentralized decision making or formalized procedures and regulations.

There is considerable evidence to support the idea that an organization's size significantly affects its structure.[16] For instance, large organizations—those typically employing 2,000 or more people—tend to have more specialization, more departmentalization, more vertical levels, and more rules and regulations than do small organizations. But the relationship is not linear. Rather, size affects structure at a *decreasing* rate; the impact of size becomes less important as an organization expands. Why? Essentially, once an organization has around 2,000 employees, it is already fairly mechanistic. An additional 500 employees will not have much impact. On the other hand, adding 500 employees to an organization that has only 300 members is likely to result in a shift toward a more mechanistic structure.

Technology

The initial interest in technology as a determinant of structure can be traced to the mid-1960s and the work of Joan Woodward.[17] Her research, which focused on production technology, was the first major attempt to view organization structure from a technological perspective.

Woodward studied nearly 100 small manufacturing firms in the south of England to determine the extent to which organization-design principles such as unity of command

The U.S. Postal Service, because of its huge size, has to rely on standardization and other mechanistic properties to accomplish its objectives.

and span of control were related to firm success. She was unable to derive any consistent pattern from her data until she segmented her firms into three categories based on the size of their production runs. The three categories, representing three distinct technologies, had increasing levels of complexity and sophistication. The first category, unit production, comprised unit or small-batch producers that manufactured custom products such as tailor-made suits and turbines for hydroelectric dams. The second category, mass production, included large-batch or mass-production manufacturers that made items such as refrigerators and automobiles. The third and most technically complex group, process production, included continuous-process producers such as oil and chemical refiners.

Woodward found that (1) distinct relationships existed between these technology classifications and the subsequent structure of the firms and (2) the effectiveness of the organizations was related to the "fit" between technology and structure.

For example, the number of vertical levels increased with technical complexity. The median number of vertical levels for firms in the unit, mass, and process categories were three, four, and six, respectively. More important, from an effectiveness standpoint, the more successful firms in each category clustered around the median for their production group. But not all the relationships were linear. As a case in point, the mass-production firms scored high on formalization, whereas the unit and process firms rated low on this structural characteristic. Woodward found that imposing rules and regulations was impossible with the nonroutine technology of unit production and unnecessary in the highly standardized process technology.

EXHIBIT 8-6

Source: Scott Adams, *Dogbert's Big Book of Business*, (Kansas City; Andrews & McMeel, 1991), p. 41.

After carefully analyzing her findings, Woodward concluded that specific structures were associated with each of the three categories and that successful firms met the requirements of their technology by adopting the proper structural arrangements. Within each category, the firms that most nearly conformed to the median figure for each structural component were the most effective. She found that there was no one best way to organize a manufacturing firm. Unit and process production were most effective when matched with an organic structure, whereas mass production was most effective when matched with a mechanistic structure.

Since Woodward's initial work, numerous studies have been carried out on the technology-structure relationship. And these studies generally demonstrate that organization structures adapt to their technology.[18] The details of those studies are quite complex, so we'll go straight to "the bottom line" and attempt to summarize what we know. The common theme that differentiates technologies is their degree of routineness. By this we mean that technologies tend toward either routine or nonroutine activities. The former are characterized by automated and standardized operations. Nonroutine activities are customized. They include such varied operations as furniture restoring, custom shoemaking, and genetic research.

> The common theme that differentiates technologies is their degree of routineness.

What relationships have been found between technology and structure? Although the relationship is not overwhelmingly strong, we find that routine tasks are associated with taller and more departmentalized structures. The relationship between technology and formalization, however, is stronger. Studies consistently show routineness to be associated with the presence of rule manuals, job descriptions, and other formalized documentation.

Environmental Uncertainty

As we described in chapter 4, an organization's environment is composed of those institutions or forces that are outside the organization and potentially affect the organization's performance. The environment has acquired a large following as a key determinant of structure.

Why should an organization's structure be affected by its environment? Because of environmental uncertainty. Again, as noted in chapter 4, some organizations face relatively static environments, whereas other organizations face very dynamic environments. Static environments create significantly less uncertainty for managers than do dynamic ones. And because uncertainty is a threat to an organization's effectiveness, management will try to minimize it. One way to reduce environmental uncertainty is through adjustments in the organization's structure.[19]

There is substantial evidence that relates the degrees of environmental uncertainty to different structural arrangements. Essentially, the more scarce, dynamic, and complex the environment—that is, the greater the environmental uncertainty—the greater the need for flexibility. Hence, the organic structure will lead to higher organizational effectiveness. Conversely, in abundant, stable, and simple environments, the mechanistic form will be the structure of choice.

Explaining the Increasing Popularity of the Organic Structure

Why are managers increasingly restructuring their organizations and trying to make them more organic? The answer substantially lies in the contingency approach to organization design.

The most powerful force today driving the restructuring of organizations toward the organic form is, arguably, increased environmental uncertainty. Global competition, accelerated product innovation by all competitors, and increased demands from customers for higher quality and faster deliveries are examples of dynamic environmental forces that confront today's managers. Mechanistic organizations tend to be ill-equipped to respond to such rapid environmental change.

An argument can be made that the other contingency variables are also increasingly favoring the organic structure. For the first two-thirds of the twentieth century, most large corporations chose to pursue cost minimization or imitation strategies. They tended to leave innovation to the little guys. But many of those "little guys" became hugely successful, took business away from the big companies, and became big companies themselves. The result? Large and small companies alike increasingly have been pursuing innovation strategies. Consistent with a dynamic environment and the need to innovate, large organizations have also been breaking themselves up into smaller and more flexible subunits. Instead of being one large company, management is creating a bunch of autonomous minicompanies. Finally, increased competition and demand by customers for more-customized products and services is requiring organizations to rely more heavily on nonroutine technologies. In aggregate, then, these forces—more innovation strategies, smaller-sized units, and the expanded use of nonroutine technologies—when combined with increased environmental uncertainty, explain why managers are restructuring their organizations to make them more organic.

DESIGN OPTIONS

The contingency approach to organization design provides a basic theoretical framework for labeling structures and explaining why organizations are structured differently. But placing organizations into only two categories—mechanistic and organic—fails to capture the nuances and realities of today's organizations. We need to make the leap from the theoretical to the applied. In this section, we present a number of practical organization-design options. We start with the simple structure—the form that almost all new organizations begin with and that continues to be widely used by managers of small business firms.

The Simple Structure

What do a small grocery store, a software design firm run by a hard-driving entrepreneur, and a new furniture-manufacturing company have in common? They probably all utilize the **simple structure**.[20]

In structural terms, the simple structure has a low degree of departmentalization, wide spans of control, authority centralized in a single person, and little formalization. It is a "flat" organization—with typically only two or three vertical levels, a loose body of employees, and one individual in whom the decision-making authority is centralized.

The simple structure is most widely practiced in small businesses in which the manager and the owner are one and the same. This structure, for example, is illustrated in Exhibit 8-7 on page 252—an organization chart for a two-year-old software-design firm in the Boston area. Kevin Jordan owns and manages the firm. Although Kevin employs five full-time people, he "runs the show."

The strength of the simple structure lies in its simplicity. It's fast, flexible, and inexpensive to maintain, and accountability is clear. It is an ideal structure for small organizations and new start-ups. Its major weakness is that it is difficult to maintain in anything

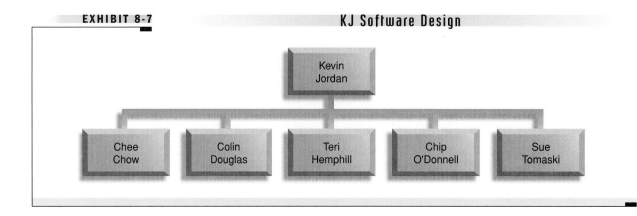

other than small organizations. It becomes increasingly inadequate as an organization grows because its low formalization and high centralization tend to create information overload at the top. As size increases, decision making typically becomes slower and can eventually come to a standstill as the single executive tries to continue making all the decisions. This structural weakness often proves to be the undoing of many small businesses. When an organization begins to employ fifty or a hundred people, it's very difficult for the owner-manager to make all the choices. If the structure is not changed and made more elaborate, the firm often loses momentum and can eventually fail. The simple structure's other weakness is that it is risky—everything depends on one person. One heart attack can literally destroy the organization's information and decision-making center.

The simple structure isn't strictly limited to small organizations; it's just harder to make it work effectively in larger firms. One large company that seems to have succeeded with the simple structure is Nucor Corp., a $4.2 billion steel company that operates minimills in Indiana and Arkansas.[21] Its headquarters in Charlotte, North Carolina, employs just twenty-five people. And there are only three levels between the company's president and mill workers. This lean structure has helped Nucor to become the most profitable steelmaker in the United States.

The Bureaucracy

Thirty years ago it was the model for structuring large organizations.[22] We're talking about the **bureaucracy**. The bureacracy is characterized by highly standardized operating tasks achieved through specialization, very formalized rules and regulations, tasks that are grouped into functional departments, centralized authority, narrow spans of control, and decision making that follows the chain of command.

The primary strength of the bureaucracy lies in its ability to perform standardized activities in a highly efficient manner. Putting like specialties together in functional departments results in economies of scale, minimum duplication of personnel and equipment, and employees who have the opportunity to talk "the same language" among their peers. Further, bureaucracies can function smoothly with less-talented—and, hence, less costly—middle- and lower-level managers. The pervasiveness of rules and regulations substitute for managerial discretion. Standardized operations, coupled with high formalization, allow decision making to be centralized. So there is little need for creative and experienced decision makers below the level of senior executives.

Nucor Corporation's lean structure has helped it to become the most profitable steel maker in the United States.

One of the major weaknesses of bureaucracy is illustrated in the following dialogue among four executives in one company:

Production executive: Ya know, nothing happens in this place until we produce something.

Director of research and development: Wrong, nothing happens until we design something!

Marketing executive: What are you talking about? Nothing happens here until we sell something!

Exasperated accounting manager: It doesn't matter what you produce, design, or sell. No one knows what happens until we tally up the results!

That conversation points up the fact that specialization creates jurisdictional disputes and subunit conflicts. Functional unit goals often override the overall goals of the organization. And accountability for outcomes is muddied. When problems occur, managers in bureaucracies can be very quick to point to someone else or some other department as the cause.

The other major weakness of bureaucracy is its resistance to change. The rules and standardized operations work fine as long as today is just like yesterday. But when cases arise that do not precisely fit the rules, the system breaks down. The bureaucracy is efficient only as long as employees confront problems that they have previously encountered and for which programmed decision rules have already been established.

The peak of bureaucracy's popularity was probably in the 1950s and 1960s. At that time, for instance, just about every major corporation in the world—firms such as IBM, General Electric, Volkswagen, Matsushita, and Royal Dutch Shell—was organized as a bureaucracy. Although the bureaucracy is out of fashion today—critics argue that it can't respond rapidly to change and hinders employee initiative[23]—don't assume that bureaucracies have gone the way of the dinosaur. Formal procedures, systems, and specialization are still the hallmarks of large organizations.[24] But executives have taken action in recent years to make their organizations less rigid and more entrepreneurial—such as decentralizing decision making, designing work around teams, and developing strategic alliances with other firms.[25]

The Matrix Structure

The **matrix** is a structural design that assigns specialists from specific functional departments to work on one or more interdisciplinary teams, which are led by project leaders. Essentially, the matrix combines two forms of departmentalization—functional and product.[26]

The matrix evolved in the 1960s, initially among aerospace firms, as a way for organizations to gain flexibility while still maintaining bureaucracy's economies of specialization. In the late 1980s, many multinationals went to a modified matrix—having country managers report to both a regional boss and a product-group executive.[27] Today, you'll find the matrix still used in the aerospace industry and in many advertising agencies, research and development laboratories, construction companies, hospitals, government agencies, universities, management consulting firms, and entertainment companies.

The strength of functional departmentalization lies in putting like specialists together. This strategy minimizes the number of specialists necessary, while it allows the pooling and sharing of specialized resources across products. Its major disadvantage is the difficulty of coordinating the tasks of diverse functional specialists so that their activities are completed on time and within budget. Product departmentalization, on the other hand, has exactly the opposite benefits and disadvantages. It facilitates coordination among specialties to achieve on-time completion and meet budget targets. Further, it provides clear responsibility for all activities related to a product, but with duplication of activities and costs. The matrix attempts to gain the strengths of each, while avoiding their weaknesses.

The most obvious structural characteristic of the matrix is that it breaks the unity-of-command concept. Employees in the matrix have two bosses—their functional department managers and their product managers. Therefore, the matrix has a dual chain of command.

Exhibit 8-8 shows the matrix form as used in a college of business administration. The academic departments of accounting, economics, marketing, and so forth are functional units. In addition, specific programs (that is, products) are overlaid on the functions. In this way, members in a matrix structure have a dual assignment—to their functional department and to their product groups. For instance, a professor of accounting teaching an undergraduate course reports to the director of undergraduate programs as well as to the chairperson of the accounting department.

The strength of the matrix lies in its ability to facilitate coordination when the organization has multiple complex and interdependent activities. As an organization gets larger, its information-processing capacity can become overloaded. In a bureaucracy, complexity results in increased formalization. The direct and frequent contact between different specialties in the matrix can make for better communication and more flexibility. In-

EXHIBIT 8-8

Matrix Structure for a College of Business Administration

Academic Departments	Programs					
	Undergraduate	Master's	Ph.D.	Research	Executive Programs	Community-Service Programs
Accounting						
Administrative Studies						
Economics						
Finance						
Marketing						
Organizational Behavior						
Quantitative Methods						

formation permeates the organization and more quickly reaches those people who need to take account of it.

There is also another advantage to the matrix. It facilitates the efficient allocation of specialists. When individuals with highly specialized skills are lodged in one functional department or product group, their talents are monopolized and underutilized. The matrix achieves the advantages of economies of scale by providing the organization with both the best resources and an effective way of ensuring their efficient deployment.

The major disadvantages of the matrix lie in the confusion it creates, its propensity to foster power struggles, and the stress it places on individuals.[28] When you dispense with the unity-of-command concept, ambiguity is significantly increased, and ambiguity often leads to conflict. For example, it is frequently unclear who reports to whom, and it is not unusual for product managers to fight over getting the best specialists assigned to their products. Confusion and ambiguity also create the seeds of power struggles. Bureaucracy reduces the potential for power grabs by defining the rules of the game. When those rules are "up for grabs," power struggles between functional and product managers result. For individuals who desire security and absence from ambiguity, this work climate can produce stress. Reporting to more than one boss introduces role conflict, and unclear expectations introduce role ambiguity. The comfort of bureaucracy's predictability is replaced by insecurity and stress.

Overall, the matrix has met with mixed success. Some companies swear by it. For instance, L. M. Ericsson, Sweden's $18 billion telecommunications equipment maker, successfully used the matrix as a means to get the company's often fractious business units to work as a team.[29] In Ericsson's matrix, unit managers report to both product divisions and corporate headquarters. Management gives the matrix credit for facilitating the sharing of information among the company's forty research and development labs around the globe and getting products to market faster. In contrast, Digital Equipment Corp.'s CEO blames the matrix for delaying for years his company's needed shift from minicomputers to PCs. While manufacturing, engineering, marketing, and other groups debated the decision, competitors aggressively moved way ahead.[30]

Team-Based Structures

As we will describe extensively in chapter 10, organizing work activities around teams has become extremely popular. When management uses teams as its focus of coordination, it is using a **team structure**.[31] The primary characteristics of the team structure are that it breaks down departmental barriers, makes the organization more horizontal than vertical, and decentralizes decision making to the level of the work team. Team structures also require employees to be generalists as well as specialists.[32]

In smaller companies, the team structure can define the entire organization. For instance, Imedia, a thirty-person marketing firm in New Jersey, is organized completely around teams that have full responsibility for most operational issues and client services.[33] Whole Foods Market, Inc., the largest natural-foods grocer in the United States, is structured entirely around teams.[34] Every one of Whole Foods' 43 stores is an autonomous profit center composed of an average of 10 self-managed teams, each with a designated team leader. The team leaders in each store are a team; store leaders in each region are a team; and the company's six regional presidents are a team.

More often, particularly among larger organizations, the team structure complements what is typically a bureaucracy. This arrangement allows the organization to achieve the efficiency of bureaucracy's standardization while gaining the flexibility that teams provide.

Northeast Region President of Whole Foods, Chris Hitt, fields questions from his store leaders during a team meeting.

To improve productivity at the operating level, for instance, companies such as Chrysler, Saturn, Motorola, and Xerox have made extensive use of self-managed teams. On the other hand, when companies such as Boeing, Baxter International, or Hewlett-Packard need to design new products or coordinate major projects, they will structure activities around cross-functional teams.

▶ Autonomous Internal Units

Autonomous internal units could well be the heir apparent to the monolithic pyramid for large organizations.[35] The primary characteristic of this structural form is that management breaks the organization up into decentralized business units with their own products, clients, competitors, and profit goals; it then creates a market-oriented infrastructure of performance measures, financial incentives, communication systems, and the like so that units can be evaluated just as if they were free-standing companies.[36]

It has been estimated that about 15 percent of large corporations have moved to this structural form.[37] Some of the most noteworthy of these include ABB ASEA Brown Boveri, Magna International, Thermo Electron Corp., and Dover Corp.

We briefly mentioned ABB at the opening of chapter 1. It's a monstrous global company that makes electric power generation and transmission equipment, high-speed trains, automation and robotics, and environmental-control systems. Even though the company has 210,000 employees, its typical profit center has only 50 people! How is this possible? ABB is actually 1,300 companies divided into almost 5,000 profit centers located in 140 countries. The whole operation is overseen by just eight top executives in Zurich, Switzerland. This structure allows ABB remarkable flexibility—to acquire new businesses, to respond to competitors, and to exploit opportunities.[38]

You have probably never heard of Magna International. This Canadian auto parts manufacturer makes everything from air bags to bumpers, has sales in excess of $4.5 billion, and has been growing very rapidly.[39] Magna has structured each of its eighty-eight plants, located in ten different countries, as a separate profit center. Plant managers are given almost total control of their operations, and they are motivated to maintain an entrepreneurial spirit by receiving 3 percent of their plant's gross profits. These managers are paid an average of $60,000 a year, but their annual bonuses can add an additional $500,000!

Thermo Electron is another large company that has perfected the ability to create autonomous internal units.[40] This high-tech firm—it makes a diverse set of products including sophisticated instruments, bomb detectors, and artificial hearts—is actually fifteen distinct companies. When a manager or engineer invents something or finds a new market for a technology, Thermo often creates a whole new autonomous company to manage it. But Thermo always retains a majority of the equity in the new company. This structure has allowed Thermo to retain its entrepreneurial spirit while accelerating the growth of new businesses.

Dover Corp. is a $3 billion a year company that has introduced autonomous internal units because it is engaged in more than seventy diverse businesses, from elevators and garbage trucks to valves and welding torches. Top management wanted maximum flexibility—to be able to acquire and divest businesses with a minimal amount of disruption.[41] Each of its businesses is run as if it were almost a completely autonomous unit. Headquarters management—which is just twenty-two employees—limits itself to defining corporate strategy and handling support activities such as finance and legal affairs. Top management's philosophy is to free up its business heads to manage their companies as if they owned them.

The Virtual Organization

Why own when you can rent? That question captures the essence of the **virtual organization** (also sometimes called the *network* or *modular organization*)—a small, core organization that outsources major business functions.[42] In structural terms, the virtual organization is highly centralized, with little or no departmentalization. The Trufresh Marketing Group, described at the opening of this chapter, is a virtual organization.

The prototype of the virtual structure is today's moviemaking organization. In Hollywood's golden era, movies were made by huge vertically integrated corporations. Studios such as MGM, Warner Brothers, and 20th Century-Fox owned large movie lots and employed thousands of full-time specialists—set designers, camera people, film editors, directors, and even actors. Nowadays, most movies are made by a collection of individuals and small companies who come together and make films project by project.[43] This structural form allows each project to be staffed with the talent most suited to its demands, rather than having to choose just from those people the studio employs. It minimizes bureaucratic overhead because there is no lasting organization to maintain. And it lessens long-term risks and their costs because there is no long-term—a team is assembled for a finite period and then disbanded.

Wendy Rickard runs a virtual organization. She, her assistant, and one part-time employee produce a wide range of magazines and marketing materials, but Wendy's firm, Rickard Associates, is run out of an old house in Hopewell, New Jersey. This virtual firm contracts art from someone in Arizona; uses editors in Florida, Georgia, and Michigan; and employs dozens of freelancers from all over North America. Using the Internet and America Online, these people are able to work together as if they were in the same office.

When large organizations use the virtual structure, they frequently use it to outsource manufacturing. Companies such as Nike, Reebok, L. L. Bean, and Dell Computer are just a few of the thousands of companies that have found that they can do hundreds of millions of dollars in business without owning manufacturing facilities. Dell Computer, for instance, owns no plants and merely assembles computers from outsourced parts. But National Steel Corp. contracts out its mailroom operations, AT&T farms out its credit-card processing, and Mobil Corp. has turned over maintenance of its refineries to another firm.

What's going on here? A quest for maximum flexibility. These "virtual" organizations have created networks of relationships that allow them to contract out manufacturing, distribution, marketing, or any other business function that management feels others can do better or more cheaply.

The virtual organization stands in sharp contrast to the typical bureaucracy that has many vertical levels of management and where control is sought through ownership. In such organizations, research and development are done in-house, production occurs in company-owned plants, and sales and marketing are performed by the company's own employees. To support this structure, management has to employ extra personnel including accountants, human resource specialists, and lawyers. The virtual organization, however, outsources many of these functions and concentrates on its core competencies. For most U.S. firms, that means focusing on design or marketing.

Exhibit 8-9 on page 258 shows a virtual organization in which management outsources all of the primary functions of the business. The core of the organization is a small group of executives. Their job is to oversee directly any activities that are done in-house and to coordinate relationships with the other organizations that manufacture, distribute, and perform other crucial functions for the virtual organization. The dotted lines in Exhibit 8-9 represent those relationships, typically maintained under contracts. In

Tony Whitman is part of Hollywood's mobile, free agent-like workforce. He's a key grip—"I'm in charge of everything possible that needs to be done for the camera and lighting"—and is required to move fluidly from one film to the next.

EXHIBIT 8-9

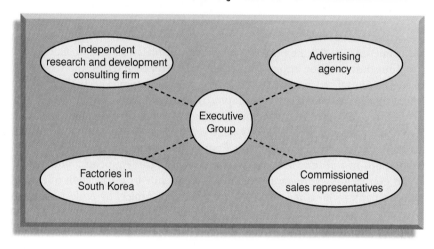

A Virtual Organization

essence, managers in virtual structures spend most of their time coordinating and controlling external relations, typically by way of computer network links.

The major advantage to the virtual organization is its flexibility. For instance, it allowed someone with an innovative idea and little money—such as Michael Dell and his Dell Computer firm—to successfully compete against large companies such as IBM. The primary drawback to this structure is that it reduces management's control over key parts of its business.

TODAY ? or TOMORROW ?

The Boundaryless Organization

General Electric chairman Jack Welch coined the term **boundaryless organization** to describe his idea of what he wanted GE to become. Welch wanted to turn his company into a "$60 billion family grocery store."[44] That is, in spite of its monstrous size, he wanted to eliminate vertical and horizontal boundaries within GE and break down external barriers between the company and its customers and suppliers. The boundaryless organization seeks to eliminate the chain of command, have limitless spans of control, and replace departments with empowered teams. And because it relies so heavily on information technology, some have turned to calling this structure the *T-form* (or technology-based) organization.[45]

Although GE has not yet achieved this boundaryless state—and probably never will—it has made significant progress toward that end. So have other companies such as Hewlett-Packard, AT&T, Motorola, and Oticon A/S. Let's take a look at what a boundaryless organization would look like and what some firms are doing to try to make it a reality.[46]

By removing vertical boundaries, management flattens the hierarchy. Status and rank are minimized. Cross-hierarchical teams (which includes top executives, middle managers, supervisors, and operative employees), participative decision-making practices, and the use of 360-degree performance appraisals (where peers and others above and below the employee evaluate his or her performance) are examples of what GE is doing to break down vertical boundaries. At Oticon A/S, a $160 million a year Danish hearing aid manufacturer, all traces of hierarchy have disappeared. Everyone works at uniform mobile workstations. And project teams, not functions or departments, are used to coordinate work.

Functional departments create horizontal boundaries. And these boundaries stifle interaction between functions, product lines, and units. The way to reduce these barriers is to replace functional departments with cross-functional teams and to organize activities around processes. For instance, Xerox now develops new products through multidisciplinary teams that work in a single process instead of around narrow functional tasks. Similarly, some AT&T units are now doing annual budgets based not on functions or departments but on processes such as the maintenance of a worldwide telecommunications network. Another way management can cut through horizontal barriers is to use lateral transfers and rotate people into and out of different functional areas. This approach turns specialists into generalists.

When fully operational, the boundaryless organization also breaks down barriers to external constituencies (suppliers, customers, regulators, etc.) and barriers created by geography. Globalization, strategic alliances, customer-organization linkages, and telecommuting are all examples of practices that reduce external boundaries. Coca-Cola, for instance, sees itself as a global corporation, not as a U.S. or Atlanta company. Firms such as NEC Corp., Boeing, and Apple Computer each have strategic alliances or joint partnerships with dozens of companies. These alliances blur the distinction between one organization and another as employees work on joint projects. Companies such as AT&T and TWA are allowing customers to perform functions that previously were done by management. For instance, some AT&T units are receiving bonuses based on customer evaluations of the teams that serve them. TWA's Royal Ambassador frequent flyers get "Something Good" coupons to give to outstanding TWA employees. Recipients can turn the coupons in for prizes and will be featured in company ads. This practice, in essence, allows TWA's customers to participate in employee appraisals. Finally, we suggest that telecommuting is blurring organizational boundaries. The security analyst with Merrill Lynch who does his job from his ranch in Montana or the software designer who works for a San Francisco company but does her job in Boulder, Colorado, are just two examples of the millions of workers who are now doing their jobs outside the physical boundaries of their employers' premises.

The one common technological thread that makes the boundaryless organization possible is networked computers. They allow people to communicate across intraorganizational and interorganizational boundaries.[47] Electronic mail, for instance, enables hundreds of employees to share information simultaneously and allows rank-and-file workers to communicate directly with senior executives. Additionally, many large companies, including Federal Express, AT&T, and 3M, are developing private nets or "intranets." Using the infrastructure and standards of the Internet and the World Wide Web, these private nets are internal communication systems, protected from the public Internet by special software. And interorganizational networks now make it possible for Wal-Mart suppliers such as Procter & Gamble and Levi Strauss to monitor inventory levels of laundry soap and jeans, respectively, because P&G and Levi's computer systems are networked to Wal-Mart's system.

There is a variety of additional material available on the CD-ROM and companion Web site that accompany this text. You can access this information through the CD-ROM or by visiting the Web site at <**www.prenhall.com/robbins**>.

SUMMARY

(This summary is organized by the chapter-opening learning objectives on page 236.)

1. The six key elements of organization structure are (1) work specialization, the degree to which tasks in the organization are subdivided into separate jobs; (2) departmentalization, the basis by which jobs are grouped together; (3) chain of command, an unbroken line of authority that extends from the top of the organization to the lowest echelon and clarifies who reports to whom; (4) span of control, the number of employees directly reporting to a manager; (5) centralization/decentralization, where decision making is concentrated; and (6) formalization, the degree to which jobs are standardized.

2. Mechanistic structures are rigid. They are characterized by high specialization, departmentalization, narrow spans of control, high formalization, and centralized decision making. Organic structures are the opposite. They are flexible and adaptive. They have wide spans of control, fewer levels of vertical hierarchy, fluid communications, decentralized decision making, and low formalization.

3. The four contingency variables that explain structural differences are the organization's strategy, size, technology, and degree of environmental uncertainty.

4. The greater the degree of environmental uncertainty, the more susceptible an organization is to shocks from the environment. Because management does not like uncertainty, it tries to reduce it. One means for reducing uncertainty is through the organization's structure. If uncertainty is high, a flexible and adaptive structure is better at allowing the organization and its members to respond quickly.

5. The bureaucracy is characterized by highly routine operating tasks achieved through specialization, very formalized rules and regulations, tasks that are grouped into functional departments, centralized authority, narrow spans of control, and decision making that follows the chain of command. It is effective and efficient when the organization's technology is routine and standardized. It also matches up well with a stable environment, where there is little change.

6. The advantages of the matrix are that it facilitates coordination across functional specialties, provides for clear responsibility for all activities related to a product or project, and facilitates the efficient allocation of specialists. Its primary disadvantages are increased confusion and ambiguity, the tendency to foster power struggles, and increased stress for organizational members.

7. The virtual organization has a small permanent staff that oversees operations, focuses on the organization's core competencies, and coordinates relations with external constituencies. This structure relies heavily on outsourcing for noncore functions. The strength of this structure is that it provides tremendous flexibility for management. It facilitates using the resources of other organizations to allow the virtual organization to do more with less.

REVIEW QUESTIONS

1. Contrast how the typical large corporation is organized today against how it was organized in the 1960s.
2. Why isn't work specialization an unending source of increased productivity?
3. In what ways can management departmentalize?
4. What is the relationship between span of control and vertical levels of hierarchy?
5. Contrast the value of formalization for management with its value for employees.
6. When would the simple structure be the preferred organization design?
7. How could management of a large bureaucracy maintain their efficiencies but also increase the organization's flexibility?
8. What could management do to make a bureaucracy more like a boundaryless organization?
9. Would you rather work in a bureaucracy or a virtual organization? What are the implications of your answer to your career plans?
10. Refer back to question 1. What factor(s) do you think explain the design of the typical large corporation today? Be specific.

IF I WERE THE MANAGER . . .

Finding a Place for Product Planning

You're Douglas Harrison, president of Ontario Electronics.

Your firm is one of the largest and fastest electronic component manufacturers in Canada. Between 1993 and 1998, your company achieved a 45 percent per year compounded growth rate.

At its current pace, Ontario Electronics will have sales in excess of $400 million (Canadian) by 2000. Its growth is fueled primarily by heavy outlays for research that have resulted in an ever-expanding product line.

At last Wednesday's board of directors meeting, the board gave unanimous approval to your suggestion that the company establish a product-planning group. No decision was made as to where this new group would be located. You've decided to use today's executive committee meeting (they're held every Monday morning) to hear arguments from your vice presidents of marketing, production, and corporate planning as to who's jurisdiction product planning should be placed.

"I have a major decision to make," you said to begin the meeting. "As you know, the board has approved the creation of a product-planning group. It will be the general mission of this group to identify customer needs and develop product prototypes. Exactly how far they go in terms of market research or design has not been established by the board. They left that to me. My preliminary budget for the next year includes $950,000 for this new group. I expect when they're fully operable there will be more than a dozen people in this group."

"I think it's obvious to each of you that product planning belongs in the marketing function," said Veronica Duval, vice president of marketing. "The major thrust of product planning is environmental scanning. It must work closely with current and potential customers to identify their product requirements. This is a marketing activity. Since we work with our customers on a daily basis, we know them and are in the best position to interpret and understand their needs."

"I agree with you, Veronica, when you say that the major thrust of product planning is environmental scanning," replied Claude Fortier, head of corporate planning. "And environmental scanning is precisely what we in corporate planning do on a full-time basis. It's our job to assess where the company is going. Clearly, product planning should be part of our area. Planning is planning, regardless of whether it's at the organization or product level. Our expertise, and I think the company's solid growth is a tribute to our efforts, is in scanning the environment—reading trends, assessing economic changes, evaluating the actions of competitors, and the like. The identification of customer needs is a natural extension of our current activities."

"I can't agree with either of you," was the opening comment of Mitch Jenkins, vice president of production. "The primary emphasis of this company is in production and research. Both these activities are closely related as demonstrated by the fact that production, engineering, and product-research activities are all currently under my direction. This company's success is not due to marketing or corporate planning! Our success has come about because we have shown the ability to develop innovative products that meet high-quality standards. I'm not going to get in a fight over whose function is more important here. The bottom line is that this is a manufacturing firm in a high-technology industry. Its success depends predominantly on generating new quality products, and that's precisely what my people do. Doug, I think the decision of where we locate product planning is self-evident. It belongs under production."

As Douglas Harrison, this decision is yours. Where will you put product planning? And why? Be sure to consider how the activities of product planning might differ based on where you place it.

SKILL EXERCISE

Selecting the Proper Organization Design

Kitchen Stuff is growing like crazy. And Anne Turrin isn't sure how to control the monster she has created. Anne started Kitchen Stuff out of her three-room Milwaukee apartment in 1994. It was to be a mail-order business that carried everything people would need for their kitchens. She used her savings and a $10,000 loan from her parents to fund her first catalogue. That catalogue contained only twenty pages and generated sales of $65,000. Today, the Kitchen Stuff catalogue is a slick 170 pages and is expected to bring in revenues in excess of $10 million.

The Kitchen Stuff operations comprise essentially three functions: buying/ordering, warehousing, and taking orders. Until 1997, Anne and her sister ran the whole business out of Anne's apartment. Then she hired her first real employee to handle telephone orders. Recently Anne moved her business into a 6,000-square-foot warehouse in a suburb of Milwaukee. She and her sister do all the buying, although the task has become far too cumbersome for the two to handle by themselves. Anne plans to add at least two additional full-time buyers. Anne also recognizes that her staff of six telephone operators are overburdened. She plans to triple the size of this group over the next 6 months. But by doing so, she realizes that she will not be able to directly oversee everything anymore. Her managerial demands are now pushed beyond her ability. Finally, the warehouse itself is grossly understaffed. Currently, one person is responsible for all shipping. He is assisted by four college students who work part-time.

In 1994, Kitchen Stuff had two employees. At the time this was written, it had nine full-time employees (including Anne and her sister) and four part-timers. Anne runs everything and makes all the decisions. Within 6 months, the company will very likely employ twenty-five to thirty people. Anne realizes that she will not be able to single-handedly manage the firm as it moves to this new level. Moreover, if Anne succeeds in reaching her 5-year plan, Kitchen Stuff will be doing more than $50 million a year and employing between sixty and seventy-five people by the year 2005.

If you were Anne, what organization design options would you consider viable? Which one would you choose? Why?

TEAM ACTIVITY

Assessing Boundarylessness

Listed below are 16 statements that describe a boundaryless organization. Break into groups of 3 or 5 members each and discuss (a) specific conditions under which these attributes would be desirable and when they might hinder an organization's performance and (b) the applicability of the boundaryless organization to a cross section of business firms.

1. Most decisions are made on the spot by those closest to the work, and they are acted on in hours rather than weeks.
2. Managers at all levels routinely take on frontline responsibilities as well as broad strategic assignments.
3. Key problems are tackled by multilevel teams whose members operate with little regard to formal rank in the organization.
4. New ideas are screened and decided on without fancy overheads and multiple rounds of approvals.
5. New products or services are getting to market at an increasingly fast pace.
6. Resources quickly, frequently, and effortlessly shift between centers of expertise and operating units.
7. Routine work gets done through end-to-end process teams; other work is handled by project teams drawn from shared centers of experience.
8. Ad hoc teams representing various stakeholders spontaneously form to explore new ideas.
9. Customer requests, complaints, and needs are anticipated and responded to in real time.
10. Strategic resources and key managers are often "on loan" to customers and suppliers.
11. Supplier and customer reps are key players in teams tackling strategic initiatives.
12. Suppliers and customers are regular and prolific contributors of new product and process ideas.
13. Best practices are disseminated and leveraged quickly across country operations.
14. Business leaders rotate regularly between country operations.
15. There are standard product platforms, common practices, and shared centers of experience across countries.
16. New product ideas are evaluated for viability beyond the country where they emerged.

Source: R. Ashkenas, D. Ulrich, T. Jick, and S. Kerr, *The Boundaryless Organization* (San Francisco: Jossey-Bass, 1995), pp. 28–29. With permission.

CASE EXERCISE

Visa International: The Invisible Organization

Dee Ward Hock created an organization that has grown by something like 10,000 percent since 1970. It continues to grow at roughly 20 percent a year. It operates in some 200 countries worldwide. And it serves about half a billion clients. Annual sales volume exceeds $1 trillion! The organization is Visa International.

From the beginning, Hock envisioned a business that was organized according to the principles of distributed power, diversity, and ingenuity. "In Visa, we tried to create an invisible organization and keep it that way. It's the results, not the structure or management that should be apparent," he says.

Hock believed that the command-and-control model of organization that evolved to support the industrial revolution didn't work anymore. When he reached the point in his life where he could influence an organization's complete design, he would create a more fluid and democratic organization. And he did that with Visa International. It's a nonstock, for-profit membership corporation with ownership in the form of nontransferable rights of participation. Hock designed the organization according to his philosophy: highly decentralized and highly collaborative. Authority, decision making, power—everything possible is pushed out to the periphery of the organization, to the members. The members are those financial institutions that issue Visa cards.

Visa members are in the unusual position of being competitors who must cooperate. They compete by going after each other's customers—for instance, in some communities, six or more different banks may be issuing competing Visa cards. But at the same time, members also have to cooperate with each other. For the system to work, participating merchants must be able to take any Visa card issued by any bank, anywhere. So banks must abide by certain standards on issues such as card layout; and agree to participate in a common clearinghouse that handles all merchant-bank transactions.

"Members are free to create, price, market, and service their own products under the Visa name," Hock says. "At the same time, in a narrow bank of activity essential to the success of the whole, they engage in the most intense cooperation."

Hock created Visa with a structure that distributes power and function to the lowest level possible. "No function should be performed by any part of the whole that could reasonably be done by any other more peripheral part, and no power should be vested in any part that might reasonably be exercised by any lesser part." Additionally, Hock says Visa doesn't have a chain of command. "Authority comes from the bottom up, not the top down. The U.S. federal system is designed so authority rises from the people to local, state, and federal governments; in Visa, which contains elements of the federal system, the member banks send representatives to a system of national, regional, and international boards. Although the system appears to be hierarchical, the Visa hierarchy is not a chain of command. Instead, each board is supposed to serve as a forum for members to raise common issues, debate them, and reach some kind of consensus and resolution."

Hock calls Visa an organization that is "based on biological concepts"—able to evolve and invent and organize itself. He sees the company as living proof that a large organization can be effective without being centralized and coercive. "Visa has elements of Jeffersonian democracy, it has elements of the free market, of government franchising—almost every kind of organization you can think about. But it's none of them. Like the body, the brain, and the biosphere, it's largely self-organizing." It's adaptable and responsive to changing conditions, while preserving overall cohesion and unity of purpose. Hock further describes Visa as a corporation whose product is coordination and as a model for how networked organizations of the future could be managed. "Inherent in Visa is the archetype of the organization of the twenty-first century."

QUESTIONS

1. Describe this organization using the variables discussed in this chapter.
2. What kind of organization is this?
3. What factors do you think explain why management has chosen this design?
4. What are the strengths of this structure? Its limitations?

Source: Based on M. M. Waldrop, "The Trillion-Dollar Vision of Dee Hock," *Fast Company*, October–November 1996, pp. 75–86.

VIDEO CASE EXERCISE

Rules, Regulations, and You Say What?

ABCNEWS

Rules and regulations often help to keep order in an organization by establishing the parameters in which organizational members operate. In most organizations, rules and regulations help members plan, organize, control, and make decisions. And, depending on the size of the organization, these same rules and regulations can help to coordinate activities by keeping employees' work focused on goal attainment. But sometimes, rules become unwieldy and end up creating an amazing and inefficient runaround. Let's look at two such situations involving the Environmental Protection Agency (EPA) and the Department of Transportation (DOT).

The concern in the EPA situation revolved around testing for clean water at a site in Phoenix, Arizona. To do this testing, the EPA places flathead minnows and waterfleas into stormwater drains. These small creatures are then tracked as they float in the stormwater making its way into streams and rivers. When the stormwater reaches its destination, if the minnows and waterfleas are alive, the water is considered to be not contaminated. If, however, the animals die en route, the water is considered to be polluted. Simple enough, right? Well, maybe not?

The problem in Phoenix is that the riverbed being tested is dry; there's absolutely no water in it, and there hasn't been any for years. The EPA spends about $500,000 annually on this aquatic life test—in a riverbed where no aquatic life exists. The EPA defends its actions on the grounds that they're charged with protecting the groundwater, which will ultimately become drinking water for citizens in the general vicinity. Although no one says that this goal isn't important, the EPA regulations, ironically, don't focus on drinking water, just on protecting aquatic life. So the test they're performing in Phoenix is worthless.

If you think testing a dry riverbed for aquatic life is counterproductive, just look at the rule imposed by the Department of Transporation and the Occupational Safety and Health Administration. These two government agencies require lumber companies to have specially designed gas cans to hold the fuel used in chainsaws. Each gas container (they usually hold five gallons of gasoline) is required to have "a double roll bar on top, double-walled steel sides, and a screw filter on top, and it must be vented." A gas can that meets these regulations costs about $230. And, if the extra costs aren't enough, there are also the maddening results. The filler neck on the government-approved gas can won't fit into the chainsaw, so about half of the gas poured spills out on the ground. But then, when it contaminates the ground it's not really the DOT's responsibility. That would fall under the jurisdiction of the EPA.

QUESTIONS

1. How would you describe the rules and regulations at such government agencies as the EPA and the DOT?
2. For rules and regulations to be effective, they must be enforced. At times, however, they are not applicable, as in the case of the dry riverbed in Phoenix. Can an organization have contingencies built into its rules and regulations and still effectively coordinate and control member actions? Explain your position.
3. Build an argument in support of a government agency's requirement that organizations abide by its rules and regulations. Now build an argument against it. Which of the two arguments do you feel is stronger? Discuss.

Source: "Rules, Regs, and Runaround," *ABC Primetime*, June 7, 1995.

NOTES

1. G. Sandler, "Trufresh: A Company That's Truly Virtual," *Business Week Enterprise*, April 28, 1997, pp. ENT 8–9.
2. Cited in T. Lester, "Balancing Act," *International Management*, September 1994, p. 30.
3. See, for instance, R. L. Daft, *Organization Theory and Design*, 6th ed. (St. Paul, MN: West, 1998).
4. See, for instance, K. H. Hammonds and N. Harris, "Medical Lessons from the Big Mac," *Business Week*, February 10, 1997, pp. 94–98.
5. J. H. Sheridan, "Sizing Up Corporate Staffs," *Industry Week*, November 21, 1988, p. 47.
6. For a discussion of authority, see W. A. Kahn and K. E. Kram, "Authority at Work: Internal Models and Their Organizational Consequences," *Academy of Management Review*, January 1994, pp. 17–50.
7. J. B. Treece, "Breaking the Chains of Command," *Business Week/The Information Revolution 1994*, special issue, p. 112.
8. See, for instance, L. Urwick, *The Elements of Administration* (New York: Harper & Row, 1944), pp. 52–53.
9. J. R. Brandt, "Middle Management: Where the Action Will Be," *Industry Week*, May 2, 1994, p. 31.
10. A. Ross, "BMO's Big Bang," *Canadian Business*, January 1994, pp. 58–63.
11. See, for instance, G. Schreyogg, "Contingency and Choice in Organization Theory," *Organization Studies*, no. 3, 1980, pp. 305–26; and H. L. Tosi Jr. and J. W. Slocum Jr., "Contingency Theory: Some Suggested Directions," *Journal of Management*, Spring 1984, pp. 9–26.
12. T. Burns and G. Stalker, *The Management of Innovation* (London: Tavistock, 1961); and J. A. Courtright, G. T. Fairhurst, and L. E. Rogers, "Interaction Patterns in Organic and Mechanistic Systems," *Academy of Management Journal*, December 1989, pp. 773–802.
13. The strategy-structure thesis was originally proposed in A. D. Chandler Jr., *Strategy and Structure: Chapters in the History of the Industrial Enterprise* (Cambridge, MA: MIT Press, 1962). For an updated analysis, see T. L. Amburgey and T. Dacin, "As the Left Foot Follows the Right? The Dynamics of Strategic and Structural Change," *Academy of Management Journal*, December 1994, pp. 1427–52.
14. See R. E. Miles and C. C. Snow, *Organizational Strategy, Structure, and Process* (New York: McGraw-Hill, 1978); D. Miller, "The Structural and Environmental Correlates of Business Strategy," *Strategic Management Journal*, January–February 1987, pp. 55–76; and D. C. Galunic and K. M. Eisenhardt, "Renewing the Strategy-Structure-Performance Paradigm," in B. M. Staw and L. L. Cummings (eds.), *Research in Organizational Behavior*, vol. 16 (Greenwich, CT: JAI, 1994), pp. 215–55.
15. J. P. Kotter, "Matsushita: The World's Greatest Entrepreneur?" *Fortune*, March 31, 1997, pp. 105–11.
16. See, for instance, P. M. Blau and R. A. Schoenherr, *The Structure of Organizations* (New York: Basic Books, 1971); D. S. Pugh, "The Aston Program of Research: Retrospect and Prospect," in A. H. Van de Ven and W. F. Joyce (eds.), *Perspectives on Organization Design and Behavior* (New York: Wiley, 1981), pp. 135–66; R. Z. Gooding and J. A. Wagner III, "A Meta-Analytic Review of the Relationship between Size and Performance: The Productivity and Efficiency of Organizations and Their Subunits," *Administrative Science Quarterly*, December 1985, pp. 462–81; and A. C. Bluedorn, "Pilgrim's Progress: Trends and Convergence in Research on Organizational Size and Environments," *Journal of Management*, Summer 1993, pp. 163–92.
17. J. Woodward, *Industrial Organization: Theory and Practice* (London: Oxford University Press, 1965).
18. See C. Perrow, "A Framework for the Comparative Analysis of Organizations," *American Sociological Review*, April 1967, pp. 194–208; J. D. Thompson, *Organizations in Action* (New York: McGraw-Hill, 1967); J. Hage and M. Aiken, "Routine Technology, Social Structure, and Organi-

zational Goals," *Administrative Science Quarterly*, September 1969, pp. 366–77; C. C. Miller, W. H. Glick, Y. Wang, and G. P. Huber, "Understanding Technology-Structure Relationships: Theory Development and Meta-Analytic Theory Testing," *Academy of Management Journal*, June 1991, pp. 370–99; and H. Kolodny, M. Liu, B. Stymne, and H. Denis, "New Technology and the Emerging Organizational Paradigm," *Human Relations*, December 1996, pp. 1457–88.

19. F. E. Emery and E. Trist, "The Causal Texture of Organizational Environments," *Human Relations*, February 1965, pp. 21–32; P. Lawrence and J. W. Lorsch, *Organization and Environment: Managing Differentiation and Integration* (Boston: Harvard Business School, Division of Research, 1967); M. Yasai-Ardekani, "Structural Adaptations to Environments," *Academy of Management Review*, January 1986, pp. 9–21; and Bluedorn, "Pilgrim's Progress."

20. This discussion is based on H. Mintzberg, *Structure in Fives: Designing Effective Organizations* (Englewood Cliffs, NJ: Prentice Hall, 1983), pp. 157–62. See also M. A. Seabright and J. Delacroix, "The Minimalist Organization as a Postbureaucratic Form," *Journal of Mangement Inquiry*, June 1996, pp. 140–54.

21. J. H. Sheridan, "Tale of a 'Maverick,'" *Industry Week*, June 8, 1998, pp. 22–28.

22. See, for example, C. J. Loomis, "Dinosaurs?" *Fortune*, May 3, 1993, pp. 36–42; and R. E. Hoskisson, C. W. L. Hill, and H. Kim, "The Multidivisional Structure: Organizational Fossil or Source of Value?" *Journal of Management*, Summer 1993, pp. 269–98.

23. See, for instance, the interview with E. Lawler in "Bureaucracy Busting," *Across the Board*, March 1993, pp. 23–27; and R. M. Kanter, "Can Giants Dance in Cyberspace?" *Forbes ASAP*, December 2, 1996, pp. 247–48.

24. C. K. Bart, "Gagging on Chaos," *Business Horizons*, September–October 1994, pp. 26–36.

25. B. Harrison, *Lean and Mean: The Changing Landscape of Corporate Power in the Age of Flexibility* (New York: Basic Books, 1994).

26. See, for instance, K. Knight, "Matrix Organization: A Review," *Journal of Management Studies*, May 1976, pp. 111–30; L. R. Burns and D. R. Wholey, "Adoption and Abandonment of Matrix Management Programs: Effects of Organizational Characteristics and Interorganizational Networks," *Academy of Management Journal*, February 1993, pp. 106–38; and R. E. Anderson, "Matrix Redux," *Business Horizons*, November–December 1994, pp. 6–10.

27. P. Dwyer, "Tearing Up Today's Organization Chart," *Business Week*, November 18, 1994, pp. 81–82.

28. See, for instance, S. M. Davis and P. R. Lawrence, "Problems of Matrix Organization," *Harvard Business Review*, May–June 1978, pp. 131–42.

29. J. Flynn, "An Ever-Quicker Trip from R&D to Customer," *Business Week*, November 18, 1994, p. 88.

30. Dwyer, "Tearing Up Today's Organization Chart," p. 82.

31. S. A. Mohrman, S. G. Cohen, and A. M. Mohrman Jr., *Designing Team-Based Organizations* (San Francisco: Jossey-Bass, 1995).

32. M. Kaeter, "The Age of the Specialized Generalist," *Training*, December 1993, pp. 48–53.

33. L. Brokaw, "Thinking Flat," *Inc.*, October 1993, p. 88.

34. C. Fishman, "Whole Foods Is All Teams," *Fast Company*, Greatest Hits, vol. 1, 1997, pp. 102–13.

35. W. E. Halal, "From Hierarchy to Enterprise: Internal Markets Are the New Foundation of Management," *The Executive*, November 1994, pp. 69–83.

36. Ibid.

37. Cited in *At Work*, May–June 1993, p. 3.

38. M. F. R. Kets de Vries, "Making a Giant Dance," *Across the Board*, October 1994, pp. 27–32.

39. W. C. Symonds, "Frank Stronach's Secret? Call It Empower Steering," *Business Week*, May 1, 1995, pp. 63–65; and D. Berman, "Car and Striver," *Canadian Business*, September 1996, pp. 92–101.

40. H. Kahalas and K. Suchon, "Managing a Perpetual Idea Machine: Inside the Creator's Mind," *The Executive*, May 1995, pp. 57–66; and N. Alster, "Making the Kids Stand on Their Own," *Forbes*, October 9, 1995, pp. 49–56.

41. S. Woolley, "Who Says the Conglomerate Is Dead?" *Business Week*, January 23, 1995, pp. 92–93.

42. See E. A. Gargan, "'Virtual' Companies Leave the Manufacturing to Others," *New York Times*, July 17, 1994, p. F5; D. W. Cravens, S. H. Shipp, and K. S. Cravens, "Reforming the Traditional Organization: The Mandate for Developing Networks," *Business Horizons*, July–August 1994, pp. 19–27; J. W. Verity, "A Company That's 100% Virtual," *Business Week*, November 21, 1994, p. 85; R. E. Miles and C. C. Snow, "The New Network Firm: A Spherical Structure Built on a Human Investment Philosophy," *Organizational Dynamics*, Spring 1995, pp. 5–18; G. G. Dess, A. M. A. Rasheed, K. J. McLaughlin, and R. L. Priem, "The New Corporate Architecture," *Academy of Management Executive*, August 1995, pp. 7–20; and J. Huey, The Atlanta Game," *Fortune*, July 22, 1996, pp. 42–56.

43. J. Bates, "Making Movies and Moving On," *Los Angeles Times*, January 19, 1998, p. A1.

44. "GE: Just Your Average Everyday $60 Billion Family Grocery Store," *Industry Week*, May 2, 1994, pp. 13–18.

45. H. C. Lucas Jr., *The T-Form Organization: Using Technology to Design Organizations for the 21st Century* (San Francisco: Jossey-Bass, 1996).

46. See L. Grant, "The Management Model That Jack Built," *Los Angeles Times Magazine*, May 9, 1993, pp. 20–22 and 34–36; P. LaBarre, "The Seamless Enterprise," *Industry Week*, June 19, 1995, pp. 22–34; D. D. Davis, "Form, Function and Strategy in Boundaryless Organizations," in A. Howard (ed.), *The Changing Nature of Work* (San Francisco: Jossey-Bass, 1995), pp. 112-38; R. Ashkenas, D. Ulrich, T. Jick, and S. Kerr, *The Boundaryless Organization: Breaking the Chains of Organizational Structure* (San Francisco: Jossey-Bass, 1995); and P. Roberts, "We Are One Company, No Matter Where We Are. Time and Space Are Irrelevant," *Fast Company*, April/May 1998, pp. 122–28.

47. See J. Lipnack and J. Stamps, *The TeamNet Factor* (Essex Junction, VT: Oliver Wight Publications, 1993); J. Fulk and G. DeSanctis, "Electronic Communication and Changing Organizational Forms," *Organization Science*, July–August 1995, pp. 337–49; and A. Cortese, "Here Comes the Intranet," *Business Week*, February 26, 1996, pp. 76–84.

Chapter

MANAGING HUMAN RESOURCES

I FAILED TO GET THIS JOB I WANTED BECAUSE I
ANSWERED ONE OF THE QUESTIONS ON THE
APPLICATION WRONG. THE QUESTION ASKED, "DO YOU
ADVOCATE THE OVERTHROW OF THE UNITED STATES
GOVERNMENT BY REVOLUTION OR VIOLENCE?"
I CHOSE VIOLENCE!

D. CAVETT

LEARNING OBJECTIVES

After studying this chapter, you should be able to:

1 Contrast job analysis, job descriptions, and job specifications.

2 Explain why selection devices must be valid and reliable.

3 Describe the relationship between IQ and job performance.

4 Identify places to find job applicants.

5 Describe the strengths and weaknesses of the interview as a selection device.

6 Conduct effective interviews.

7 Describe the four general skills that training can improve.

8 Explain the primary methods for appraising employee performance.

9 Define *sexual harassment* and how organizations can limit its occurrence.

10 Help employees develop their careers.

Once an organization's structural design is in place, it needs people with the right skills, knowledge, and abilities to fill positions in that structure. And no matter how well designed the structure, the organization is going to have serious problems if it hires poorly. Toward improving the quality of the people they hire, a number of companies—including Microsoft, Silicon Graphics, the consulting firm of Booz, Allen & Hamilton, and the newsmagazine *The Economist*—have begun relying heavily on brain-teasers in interviews.[1] These companies openly admit to wanting to hire the best and the brightest—people who are smart, creative, and flexible. Here are some examples of questions these companies' interviewers might ask job candidates:

- Why are manhole covers round?
- How many barbers are there in Chicago?
- How many gas stations are there in the United States?
- How much water flows through the Mississippi daily?
- How many golf balls does it take to fill the swimming pool that was used at the 1996 Olympics?
- Why do Coke cans have an indent at the bottom?

The interviewers asking the questions don't expect job candidates to know the specific answers. What they're looking for is their thinking process and verbal skills. Is the candidate logical and pragmatic? Intuitive? Verbally agile? Does he or she respond deftly when challenged? Can he or she think quickly and creatively?

In a knowledge-based economy, where brainpower and intellectual flexibility are increasingly critical to an employee's success, organizations can't afford to make mistakes. Microsoft's director of recruiting puts it succinctly when he says, "The best thing we can do for our competitors is hire poorly. If I hire a bunch of bozos, it will hurt us, because it takes time to get rid of them. They start infiltrating the organization and then they themselves start hiring people of lower quality."

In today's organizations, where 70 percent of workers are engaged in service jobs and management is aggressively redesigning work to expand employee responsibilities, human resource management (HRM) becomes a critical determinant of an organization's effectiveness. Finding, selecting, and keeping highly qualified employees can become a source of sustained competitive advantage.[2]

In this chapter we'll describe the HRM process, provide you with some specific guidelines for managing human resources, and discuss a number of contemporary HRM issues currently challenging many managers. First, however, let's look at the role of the everyday manager in HRM.

MANAGERS AND THE HUMAN RESOURCES DEPARTMENT

Some of you may be thinking, "Sure, human resource decisions are important, but aren't they made by people in human resources departments? These aren't decisions that *all* managers are involved in!" It's true that, in large organizations, a number of the activities grouped under the label of HRM often are done by specialists in human resources (or personnel) departments. However, not all managers work in organizations that have formal HR departments, and even those who do still have to be engaged in some human resource activities.

Small-business managers are an obvious example of individuals who frequently must do their own hiring without the assistance of an HR department. But even managers in billion-dollar corporations are involved in recruiting candidates, reviewing application forms, interviewing applicants, inducting new employees, appraising employee performance, and making decisions about employee training. Whether or not an organization has an HR department, *every* manager is involved with human resource decisions in his or her unit.

THE HUMAN RESOURCE MANAGEMENT PROCESS

Exhibit 9-1 depicts the HRM process in organizations. All HRM policies and practices must comply with the laws and regulations of the country, state, or province in which the organization operates. This aspect is shown in Exhibit 9-1 as the regulatory environment, which is an integral part of the organizational boundaries.

The HRM process actually begins with human resource planning. It is here where management learns whether it will need to hire additional employees (recruitment) or, if overstaffed, lay off employees (decruitment). Recruitment leads to attempting to select the best applicant from among those recruited. Decruitment leads to having some people leave the organization.

The need for training tends to be identified in the selection stage ("This candidate appears capable of doing the job but requires some additional training") or as a result of the performance appraisal ("Jason's appraisal indicates that he needs some additional training to bring his performance level up"). Effective managers should link rewards to performance. But we'll leave that issue until chapter 13, in our discussion of motivation and rewards.

EXHIBIT 9-1   HRM Process in Organizations

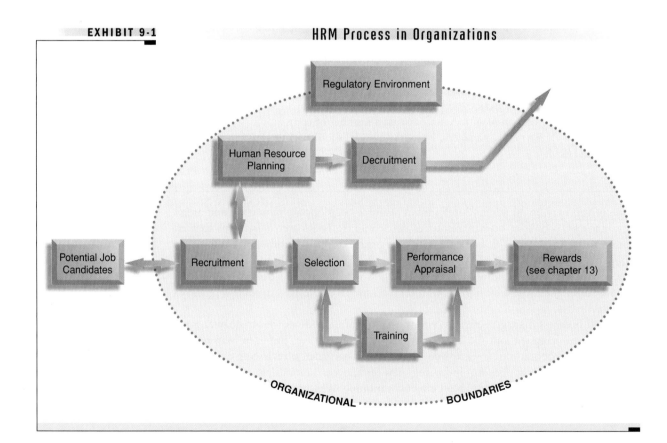

From a manager's standpoint, HRM's primary issues can be seen as answers to seven questions:

1. What laws and regulations shape HRM practices? (Answered by an understanding of the *regulatory environment.*)
2. What are our HRM needs? (Answered by a knowledge of *human resource planning.*)
3. Where do I find qualified job candidates? (Answered by *recruitment practices.*)
4. How can I choose the best-qualified job candidates? (Answered by *selection techniques.*)
5. How can I ensure employee skills are current? (Answered by *training.*)
6. What is the best way to evaluate an employee's performance? (Answered by *performance appraisal.*)
7. What options exist to handle overstaffing? (Answered by *decruitment options.*)

This chapter will provide managers with answers to each of these seven questions. In addition, we'll present several contemporary HRM issues with which managers are increasingly being required to deal—sexual harassment, career development of employees, and unions. Let's begin by reviewing major laws and regulations that guide and shape current HRM practices.

Laws and regulations affecting HRM practices differ from country to country. And, within countries, there are state or provincial and local regulations that further influence specific practices. Consequently, it is impossible to provide you with a full description of the relevant regulatory environment you will face as a manager.

What we can do is remind you that you need to know the laws and regulations that apply in your locale. And, to illustrate our point that laws and regulations shape HRM practices, we can highlight some of the federal legislation that influences HRM practices in selected countries—the United States, Canada, Mexico, Australia, and Germany.

THE REGULATORY ENVIRONMENT: WHAT LAWS AND REGULATIONS SHAPE HRM PRACTICES?

▶ The United States

You are a manager of a small machine shop operating in Buffalo, New York. Because you're concerned with keeping workers' compensation costs down, you want to know if a job applicant has a history of workers' compensation claims. But did you know you can't ask about previous claims until a conditional job offer is made? And the question can be asked only to determine whether a prior injury may prevent the applicant from carrying out the job. The Americans with Disabilities Act (ADA) defines these rules.[3]

In the United States, there's a long list of federal laws that managers need to know and follow that apply to human resource practices. They influence management decisions on such issues as hiring procedures, working conditions, pay practices, requests for leaves of absence, layoff notifications, retirement policies, and responses to union-organizing efforts. The following examples illustrate this point.

National Labor Relations Act (1935). Requires employers to recognize a union chosen by the majority of their employees and established procedures governing collective bargaining.

Equal Pay Act (1963). Prohibits pay differences based on sex for equal work.

Civil Rights Act (1964, amended in 1972). Prohibits discrimination based on race, color, religion, national origin, or sex.

Occupational Safety and Health Act (1970). Establishes mandatory safety and health standards in organizations.

Vocational Rehabilitation Act (1973). Prohibits discrimination on the basis of physical or mental disabilities.

Vietnam-Era Veterans' Readjustment Assistance Act (1974). Prohibits discrimination against disabled veterans and Vietnam-era veterans.

Age Discrimination in Employment Act (1967, amended in 1978 and 1986). Prohibits age discrimination against employees between 40 and 65 years of age and restricts mandatory retirement.

Pregnancy Discrimination Act (1978). Prohibits dismissal of women because of pregnancy alone and protects job security during maternity leaves.

Mandatory Retirement Act (1978). Prohibits the forced retirement of most employees before the age of 70.

Immigration Reform and Control Act (1986). Prohibits employers from knowingly hiring illegal aliens and prohibits employment on the basis of national origin or citizenship.

Worker Adjustment and Retraining Notification Act (1988). Requires employers to provide 60 days' notice before a facility closing or mass layoff.

Employee Polygraph Protection Act (1988). Limits an employer's ability to use lie detectors.

Americans with Disabilities Act (1990). Prohibits employers from discriminating against individuals with physical or mental disabilities or the chronically ill, and requires that "reasonable accommodations" be provided for the disabled.

Civil Rights Act (1991). Reaffirms and tightens prohibition of discrimination; permits individuals to sue for punitive damages in cases of intentional discrimination; and shifts the burden of proof to the employer.

Family and Medical Leave Act (1993). Permits employees in organizations with fifty or more workers to take up to 12 weeks of unpaid leave for family or medical reasons each year.

This list conveys our point that there are a large number of federal laws that affect HRM practices in the United States. A closer look at this list also reveals that these regulations are in a constant state of flux. New laws, as well as court and federal agency interpretations, continually add to, modify, and delete the list of things managers can and cannot legally do. For instance, in 1997, the Equal Employment Opportunity Commission clarified ADA's relevance to mental illness.[4] It declared that employers may not ask job applicants if they have ever been mentally ill and they must take "reasonable steps" to accommodate employees with psychiatric or emotional problems—including depression, schizophrenia, obsessive-compulsive disorder, and personality disorders. Behaviors that previously might have been considered as poor work habits—such as chronic lateness, poor impulse control, curt and rude behavior, or hostility to co-workers or supervisors—now may be symptoms of a mental impairment that is a disability. And to accommodate these problems, employers might have to provide time off from work, reassign the employee to a different supervisor, alter work schedules or assignments, or make physical changes in the workplace.

The message is clear: Organizational practices in the United States relating to personnel issues must be conducted within the laws of the land; there are a large number of these laws, and they change over time; and it is management's responsibility to keep current on these laws and to ensure that they are followed within their organization.

Canada

Canadian laws pertaining to HRM practices closely parallel those in the United States. But Canada's HRM environment is somewhat different from that in the United States. For instance, there is more decentralization of lawmaking to the provincial level in Canada. Approximately 90 percent of labor and human rights issues fall within the jurisdiction of the individual 12 provinces, with the remaining 10 percent falling under federal jurisdiction.[5] In addition, unions are more powerful in Canada. Less than 15 percent of nonagricultural workers in the United States belong to labor unions. In Canada, the comparable figure is 37 percent.[6] Moreover, Canadian unions tend to be more militant than their U.S. counterparts.

The Canadian Human Rights Act provides federal legislation that prohibits discrimination on the basis of race, religion, age, marital status, sex, physical or mental disability, or national origin. This act governs practices throughout the country. Discrimination on the basis of sexual orientation, however, is permissible in Alberta and the Northwest Territories but not in the rest of Canada. Similarly, although employers in Canada cannot discriminate on the basis of marital status, four provinces have laws to limit nepotism. Alberta, New Brunswick, Prince Edward Island, and Newfoundland allow employers to refuse employment to all near relatives except a spouse. And discrimination on the basis of language is not prohibited anywhere in Canada except in Quebec.[7]

> Less than 15 percent of nonagricultural workers in the United States belong to labor unions. In Canada, the comparable figure is 37 percent.

Mexico

As in Canada, Mexican employees are more likely to be unionized than in the United States.[8] About 25 to 30 percent of Mexico's labor force is unionized. But all labor matters are governed by the Mexican Federal Labor Law. For instance, after hiring, an employer has 28 days to evaluate the employee's work performance. After that period, the employee is granted job security, and termination becomes very expensive. And infractions of the Mexican Federal Labor Law are subject to severe penalties, including criminal action. For example, high fines and even jail sentences can be imposed on employers who fail to pay the minimum wage.

Hiring in Mexico is strongly influenced by Mexican law and history that view the employer as having a moral and family responsibility for all employees. Recruitment is done primarily by approaching people and asking them to apply. Most often this results in many family members working at the same plant. Advertisements are useless in recruitment because the high relative cost of newspapers makes them inaccessible to the masses. When it comes to layoffs, seniority carries great weight. Employees who have long tenure in the organization are given protection because it is assumed that they embrace the company's values and have demonstrated that they can uphold its traditions.

Australia

Equal employment opportunity legislation is much more recent in Australia than in the United States.[9] For instance, the United States enacted antidiscrimination legislation with the passage of the Civil Rights Act in 1964. Its origin was essentially to protect American blacks from discriminatory practices, but it also protected women. Australia did not introduce similar antidiscrimination legislation until decades later with the Sex Discrimination Act (1984) and the Affirmative Action (Equal Employment Opportunity for Women) Act (1986). And, although discrimination on racial grounds is outlawed in Australia, the main body of federal laws on discrimination and affirmative action apply only to women. Yet Australia continues to lag behind the United States in widening gender opportunities. As recently as 1990, 59 percent of female workers in Australia were employed in only three job categories: clerical, sales/service, and sport/recreation.

Labor laws pertaining to unions have been more important in Australia than in the United States largely because of the heavy influence of labor unions. Approximately 41 percent of Australian workers are unionized. The high percentage of unionized laborers has placed increased importance on industrial relations specialists in Australia and reduced the control of line managers over workplace labor issues. However, Australia overhauled its labor and industrial laws with the objective of increasing productivity and reducing union power. The Workplace Relations Bill (1997) gives employers greater flexibility to negotiate directly with employees on pay, hours, and benefits. It also simplifies federal regulation of labor-management relations.

► Germany

> **The goal of representative participation is to redistribute power within an organization, putting labor on a more equal footing with the interests of management and stockholders.**

Almost every country in Western Europe has some type of legislation requiring companies to practice **representative participation**. It has been called "the most widely legislated form of employee involvement around the world."[10] The goal of representative participation is to redistribute power within an organization, putting labor on a more equal footing with the interests of management and stockholders.

The two most common forms that representative participation takes are works councils and board representatives. **Works councils** link employees with management. They are groups of nominated or elected employees who must be consulted when management makes decisions involving personnel. **Board representatives** are employees who sit on a company's board of directors and represent the interests of the firm's employees. By German law, elected labor representatives have the right to half the seats on big companies' supervisory boards, which ratify all major strategic decisions.[11]

Labor unions are very strong in Germany and provide workers with many more rights than in most other countries. Workers, for example, get six weeks' paid vacation every year, and most put in only a 30-hour workweek. And even when German employees are considered redundant, restrictive work laws make it impossible to lay them off. Union strength is also demonstrated in the high wage rates they've achieved for their members. Germany's wage costs are the world's highest. The average German autoworker earns $48 an hour—considerably higher than his or her U.S. and Japanese counterparts, who earn $25 and $27, respectively.[12]

Tough German unions, restrictive work laws, and problems incurred by merging East and West Germany have pushed Germany's unemployment rate to 12 percent. This is putting pressure on government and business to support the country's weakening apprenticeship program.[13] In the past, two-thirds of Germany's secondary-school graduates participated in a multiyear program that combined academic studies and on-the-job training in one of 400 occupations, from electrician to dental assistant. Companies paid 80 percent of these costs. This program thrived when labor was in short supply and companies needed to attract workers for a booming manufacturing economy. But big German companies have moved jobs abroad in search of lower labor costs and less-restrictive government policies. Today, there are far more applicants than there are available apprenticeships. And Germany's largest union association is pushing for companies to pay more into a fund that will allow for an expansion of apprenticeships. Not surprisingly, management is opposed to this union effort.

German autoworkers are among the world's highest paid industrial workers. This partly explains why German car manufacturers like Mercedes and BMW have begun building cars in the United States.

Human resource planning is the process by which management ensures that it has the right number and kinds of people in the right places, and at the right times, who are capable of effectively and efficiently completing those tasks that will help the organization achieve its overall objectives. Human resource planning, then, translates the organization's objectives into the quantity and mix of workers needed to meet those objectives.[14]

Human resource planning can be condensed into three steps: (1) assessing current human resources, (2) assessing future human resource needs, and (3) developing a program to meet future human resource needs.

Current Assessment

Management typically begins by doing a **job analysis**. This defines the jobs within the organization and the behaviors that are necessary to perform those jobs. For instance, what are the duties of a purchasing specialist, grade 3, who works for International Paper? What minimal knowledge, skills, and abilities are necessary for the adequate performance of a grade 3 purchasing specialist's job? How do the requirements for a purchasing specialist, grade 3, compare with those for a purchasing specialist, grade 2, or a purchasing analyst? These are questions that job analysis can answer.

Information gathering through job analysis allows management to draw up a **job description** and **job specification**. The former is a written statement of what a jobholder does, how it's done, and why it's done. It typically portrays job content, environment, and conditions of employment. The job specification states the minimum acceptable qualifications an incumbent must possess to perform a given job successfully. It identifies the knowledge, skills, and abilities needed to do the job effectively.

The job description and job specification are important documents when managers begin recruiting and selecting new hires. The job description can be used to describe the job to potential candidates. The job specification keeps the manager's attention on the list of qualifications necessary for an incumbent to perform a job and assists in determining whether candidates are qualified.

Future Assessment

Future human resource needs are determined by the organization's objectives and strategies. Demand for human resources is a result of demand for the organization's products or services and levels of productivity. On the basis of its estimate of total revenue, management can attempt to establish the number and mix of human resources needed to reach those revenues. This information is then adjusted to reflect gains or losses in productivity based on changes in technology. For instance, a great deal of the recent personnel cutbacks initiated by large corporations has come about as a result of new technologies. Automated equipment, computerization, reengineering, and process redesign have made it possible for companies to generate greater outputs with less labor input.

Developing a Future Program

After it has assessed both current capabilities and future needs, management is able to estimate shortages—both in number and in kind—and to highlight areas in which the organization will be overstaffed. A program can then be developed that matches these estimates with forecasts of future labor supply. So human resource planning not only provides information to guide current staffing needs but also provides projections of future personnel needs and availability.

RECRUITMENT: WHERE DO MANAGERS FIND QUALIFIED JOB CANDIDATES?

If managers find they are understaffed, they need to begin looking for qualified candidates to fill vacancies. **Recruitment** is the process of locating, identifying, and attracting capable applicants.[15] A recent survey found that finding qualified employees is the greatest challenge facing managers of small businesses.[16] And as labor markets got tighter in the late 1990s, organizations of all types and sizes were expanding their nets to find capable applicants.[17]

Where does a manager look to recruit potential candidates? Exhibit 9-2 offers some guidance. Which sources management uses depends on the type or level of the job and the state of the economy.[18] The greater the skill required or the higher the position in the organization's hierarchy, the more the recruitment process will expand to become a regional or national search. In recent years, for instance, with a drastic shortage of skilled computer engineers, software and computer chip companies have been casting their recruitment net worldwide to find new hires.[19] And when the unemployment rate is high, organizations find it easier to attract qualified applicants. When unemployment is low, more recruitment sources will typically be needed to fill the applicant pool.

Three recruiting trends have surfaced in the past decade. First, organizations are showing more creativity and using more alternative sources in order to increase the diversity of applicants.[20] For instance, to hire more Latinos, Alpine Banks of Colorado ran help-wanted ads printed in Spanish. Fussy Cleaners in Akron, Ohio, works with the local Jewish Center to help Russian immigrants start new lives in the United States, and gets good job candidates in the process. Other organizations have placed ads in minority papers and magazines, expanded recruiting at women's and historically black colleges, sought the services of minority professional groups, and paid small bonuses to current employees who refer a new minority hire. The second trend is the increased reliance on temporary help firms as a source of new employees.[21] By using temps from companies such as Manpower Inc. to fill positions, an organization increases its flexibility and gets an opportunity to assess a potential permanent employee with minimal commitment. Robertshaw Controls, for instance, selects all its permanent hires from its pool of experi-

Major Sources of Potential Job Candidates

EXHIBIT 9-2

Source	Advantages
Current employees	Low cost; build employee morale; candidates are familiar with the organization
Employee referrals	Knowledge about the organization provided by the current employee
Former employees	Rehires know the organization; the organization has historical data about the person's previous performance level
Advertisements	Wide distribution; can be targeted to specific groups
Employment agencies	Wide contacts; careful screening; short-term guarantees often given
College recruiting	Large, centralized body of candidates; good source for entry-level and future-management candidates
Customers and suppliers	Specific industry knowledge; knowledge of your organization; previous contacts might provide insights into candidates' skills and abilities

enced temporaries. Robertshaw's human resources department has taken itself out of the hiring business—anyone walking into the company looking for a job is handed a Manpower application![22] An increasing set of organizations are using temporary positions as the ultimate "job performance test" before hiring anyone as a permanent member of the organization.[23] The final trend is the use of the Internet as a recruiting device. Particularly in the search for candidates with technical and computer-related skills, posting a job vacancy on the Internet can provide wide access to potential candidates. As an illustration, Geometrics Corp., a small imaging-software firm in Wisconsin, posted a job listing for a software engineer on a worldwide electronic-mail bulletin board. The company received 200 résumés—some from as far away as Israel, Germany, and Hong Kong.[24]

Are certain recruiting sources superior to others? More specifically, do certain recruiting sources produce superior candidates? The answer is no. It was long believed that employee referrals were the best candidates because these applicants had more accurate knowledge about organizations and jobs.[25] It was also thought that current employees would only refer others who they were reasonably confident would perform well and thereby make them look good. The most recent research suggests that employee referrals are no more productive, stable, or satisfied with their jobs than recruits obtained from other sources.[26] At this time, the best advice we can give you, once a final applicant pool has been generated, is to ignore recruitment sources.[27]

You have developed a set of applicants for your job opening. Now the task before you is to figure out who, among this set, would be the best-qualified candidate so that you can offer him or her a job. This is no easy task. Fortunately, there is a large body of research to help guide you in screening and selecting candidates.[28]

SELECTION: HOW CAN MANAGERS CHOOSE THE BEST-QUALIFIED JOB CANDIDATE?

▶ Foundations of Selection

Selection is a prediction exercise. It seeks to predict which applicants will be successful if hired. *Successful* in this case means performing well on the critieria management uses to

TODAY ? or TOMORROW ?

Internet Recruitment

Newspaper advertisements and employment agencies may be on their way to extinction as primary sources for finding job candidates. The reason: Internet recruiting.[29]

One in five companies currently uses the Internet to recruit new employees—increasingly by adding a recruitment section to their Web sites. As almost every organization—small as well as large—creates its own Web site, these become natural extensions for finding new employees.

Those organizations planning to do a lot of Internet recruiting will develop dedicated sites—specifically designed for recruitment. They'll have the typical information you might find in an employment advertisement—qualifications sought, experience desired, benefits provided. But they'll also allow the organization to showcase its products, services, corporate philosophy, and mission statement. This information will increase the quality of applicants, as those whose values don't mesh with the organization tend to self-select themselves out. The best designed of these Web sites will include an on-line response form, so applicants won't need to send a separate résumé by e-mail or fax. Applicants will only need to fill in a résumé page and hit a "submit" button.

Facilitating the growth of Internet recruitment will be commercial job-posting services that will provide essentially electronic classified ads. A few examples include CareerWeb <*www.cweb.com*>, CareerMosaic <*www.careermosaic.com*>; CareerPath <*www.careerpath.com*>, JobCenter <*www.jobcenter.com*>, Online Career Center <*www.occ.com*>, and The Monster Board <*www.monster.com*>. As a case in point, Monster Board lists more than 50,000 jobs from over 4,000 companies including Intel, Fidelity Investments, Nike, MCI Communications, and Arthur Andersen. Ads on these Web sites will typically cost considerably less than a comparable ad in a large metropolitan newspaper and can reach candidates worldwide.

Aggressive job candidates will also be using the Internet. They'll be setting up their own Web sites to "sell" their job candidacy. When they learn of a possible job opening, they'll encourage potential employers to "check me out at my Web site." There, applicants will have standard résumé information, support documentation, and possibly a video where they introduce themselves to potential employers.

Internet recruiting provides a low-cost means for small businesses to gain unprecedented access to potential employees worldwide. It's also a way to increase diversity and find people with unique talents. Job-posting services will create subgroup categories for employers looking, for example, to find bilingual workers, female lawyers, or black engineers. Expect to find professions and industries, such as dentistry or fashion, setting up dedicated recruitment Web sites with their own job listings.

Finally, Internet recruitment won't be merely the choice of those looking to fill high-tech jobs. As computer prices fall and the majority of working people become comfortable with the Internet, on-line recruitment will be used for all kinds of nontechnical jobs—from those paying thousands of dollars a week to those paying $8 an hour.

evaluate personnel. In filling a sales position, for example, the selection process should be able to predict which applicants will generate a high volume of sales. For a position of software programmer, the criterion might be which applicants will produce the highest quantity of error-free code.

PREDICTION Consider, for a moment, that any selection decision can result in four possible outcomes. As shown in Exhibit 9-3, two of these outcomes would be correct decisions, but

Selection Decision Outcomes

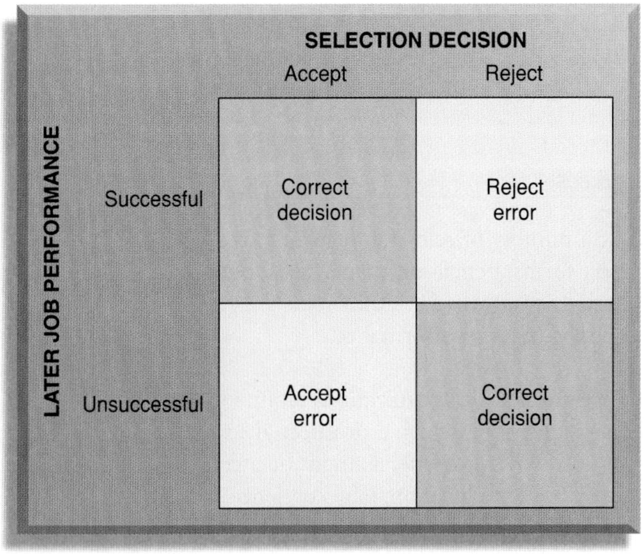

EXHIBIT 9-3

	SELECTION DECISION	
	Accept	Reject
Successful	Correct decision	Reject error
Unsuccessful	Accept error	Correct decision

(Vertical axis label: **LATER JOB PERFORMANCE**)

two would be errors. A decision is correct when the applicant was accepted and later proved to be successful on the job or when the applicant was rejected and would have performed unsuccessfully if hired.

Problems occur when we make errors by rejecting candidates who would later have performed successfully on the job (reject errors) or by accepting those who subsequently perform poorly (accept errors). These problems are, unfortunately, far from insignificant. Selection techniques that result in reject errors can open the organization to charges of discrimination, especially if applicants from protected groups are disproportionately rejected. Accept errors, on the other hand, have very obvious costs to the organization, including the cost of training the employee, the costs generated or profits forgone because of the employee's incompetence, and the cost of severance and the subsequent costs of further recruiting and selection screening. The major thrust of any selection activity is therefore to reduce the probability of making reject errors or accept errors while increasing the probability of making correct decisions.

VALIDITY Any selection device that a manager uses—such as tests or interviews—must demonstrate **validity**. That is, there must be a proven relationship between the selection device and some relevant criterion. For example, U.S. laws prohibit management from using a test score as a selection device unless there is clear evidence that, once on the job, individuals with high scores on this test outperform individuals with low test scores. Thus handwriting analysis is not a valid screening device. Results aren't correlated with job performance criteria![30]

RELIABILITY In addition to being valid, a selection device must also demonstrate reliability. **Reliability** indicates whether the device measures the same thing consistently. For example, if a test is reliable, any single individual's score should remain fairly stable over time, assuming the characteristics it is measuring are also stable.

The importance of reliability should be evident. No selection device can be effective if it is unreliable. Using an unreliable selection device is equivalent to weighing yourself every day on an erratic scale. If the scale is unreliable—randomly fluctuating, say, 5 to 10 pounds every time you step on it—the results won't mean much. To be effective predictors, selection devices must possess an acceptable level of consistency.

▶ Selection Devices

Managers can use a number of selection devices to reduce accept and reject errors. These include application forms, pencil-and-paper tests, performance-simulation tests, and interviews.   Let's briefly review each of these devices, giving particular attention to the validity of each in predicting job performance.

THE APPLICATION FORM   Almost all organizations require job candidates to fill out an application. It may be only a form on which a prospect gives his or her name, address, and telephone number. At the other extreme, it might be a comprehensive personal history profile, detailing the applicant's education, job experience, skills, and accomplishments.

Hard and relevant biographical data that can be verified—for example, rank in high school graduating class—have shown to be valid measures of performance for some jobs.[31] In addition, when application form items have been appropriately weighted to reflect job relatedness, the device has proved to be a valid predictor for such diverse groups as salesclerks, engineers, factory workers, district managers, clerical employees, and technicians.[32] But, typically, only a couple of items on the application prove to be valid predictors, and then only for a specific job. Use of weighted applications for selection purposes is difficult and expensive because the weights have to be validated for each specific job and must be continually reviewed and updated to reflect changes in weights over time.

PENCIL-AND-PAPER TESTS   Typical pencil-and-paper tests include tests of intelligence, personality, aptitude, ability, interest, and integrity. Three types of tests arguably have gotten the most attention in recent years—integrity, personality, and intelligence. Integrity tests measure factors such as dependability, carefulness, responsibility, and honesty. But can a pencil-and-paper test really identify people who might, for instance, steal from the organization? The evidence is impressive that these tests are powerful in predicting supervisory ratings of job performance and counterproductive employee behavior on the job such as theft, discipline problems, and excessive absenteeism.[33]

Personality tests are problematic. General personality inventories tend to be weak predictors of an applicant's future job performance when the tests are used with a broad section of jobs.[34] The only personality trait that tends to predict job performance regardless of occupation is *conscientiousness* (reflected in traits such as responsibility, dependability, and persistence).[35] Other personality dimensions can predict job performance, but they need to be used selectively for specific jobs. For instance, an extroverted personality is a valid predictor of job performance in managerial and sales positions; and attention to detail has been found to be related to the performance of accountants.[36] Personality inventories that have been carefully validated for specific jobs can be meaningful screening devices.

The issue of intelligence as a job predictor became a headline topic in the fall of 1994 with the publication of Richard Herrnstein and Charles Murray's *The Bell Curve*.[37] This book became one of the most controversial social science books of all time largely because of the authors' claim that economic inequality between racial groups is related to differences in average IQ levels between different races. Unfortunately, that section of the book drowned out the authors' excellent review of the relationship between intelligence and job performance.[38] In the following paragraphs, we'll summarize what we know about this relationship. And as you will see, we know quite a lot!

Certain facts are beyond significant technical dispute. For instance: (1) IQ scores closely match whatever it is that people mean when they use the word *intelligent* or *smart* in ordinary language; (2) IQ scores are stable, although not perfectly so, over much of a person's life; (3) properly administered IQ tests are not demonstrably biased against social, economic, ethnic, or racial groups; and (4) smarter employees, on average, are more proficient employees.[39]

All jobs require the use of intelligence or cognitive ability. Why? For reasoning and decision making. A high IQ is generally necessary to perform well in jobs that are novel, ambiguous, changing, or multifaceted. This category would include professional occupations such as accountants, engineers, scientists, architects, and physicians. But IQ is also a good predictor in moderately complex jobs such as crafts, clerical, and police work. IQ is a less valid predictor for unskilled jobs that require only routine decision making or simple problem solving.

Intelligence clearly is not the only factor affecting job performance, but it is often the most important! It is, for example, a better predictor of job performance than a job interview, reference checks, or college transcripts. Unfortunately, many U.S. employers have become fearful of using intelligence tests for selecting professional and managerial employees because the courts have generally criticized such tests for lacking job relevance. But the evidence cannot be ignored. As Herrnstein and Murray noted, biographical data, reference checks, and college transcripts are "valid predictors of job performance in part because they imperfectly reflect something about the applicant's intelligence. Employers who are forbidden to obtain test scores nonetheless strive to obtain the best possible work force, and it so happens that the way to get the best possible work force, other things equal, is to hire the smartest people they can find."[40]

PERFORMANCE-SIMULATION TESTS Performance-simulation tests have increased significantly in popularity during the past two decades. Undoubtedly the enthusiasm for these tests comes from the fact that they are based on job analysis data and, therefore, should more easily meet the requirement of job relatedness than do written tests. Performance-simulation tests are made up of actual job behaviors rather than surrogates, as are written tests. The two best-known performance-simulation tests are work sampling and assessment centers. The former is suited to routine jobs, whereas the latter is relevant for the selection of managerial personnel.

Work sampling is an effort to create a miniature replica of a job. Applicants demonstrate that they possess the necessary talents by actually doing the tasks. Carefully devised work samples based on job analysis data determine the knowledge, skills, and abilities needed for each job. Then each work sample element is matched with a job performance element. For instance, at BMW's factory in South Carolina, job candidates for production jobs are given 90 minutes to perform a variety of typical work tasks on a specially built simulated assembly line.[41] The overall results from work sample experiments are impressive. Studies almost consistently demonstrate that work samples yield validities superior to written aptitude and personality tests.[42]

A more elaborate set of performance-simulation tests, specifically designed to evaluate a candidate's managerial potential, is administered in assessment centers. In **assessment centers**, line executives, supervisors, or trained psychologists evaluate candidates as they go through exercises that simulate real problems that they would confront on the job. Based on a list of descriptive dimensions that the actual job incumbent has to meet, activities might include interviews, in-basket problem-solving exercises, group discussions, and

> Smarter employees, on average, are more proficient employees.

A Cessna Aircraft manager (background) goes through an assessment center exercise while watched by four evaluators.

business decision games. For instance, managerial candidates at a Cessna airplane factory in Independence, Kansas, go through an assessment center that simulates a typical day for a harried Cessna executive.[43] Candidates spend up to 12 hours in an office with a phone, a fax, and an in-basket stuffed with files and letters. Throughout the day, the prospect works through memos and handles problems such as responding to an irate customer.

How valid is the assessment center as a selection device? The evidence on the effectiveness of assessment centers is extremely impressive. They have consistently demonstrated results that accurately predict later job performance in managerial positions.[44]

INTERVIEWS In Korea, Japan, and many other Asian countries, employee interviews traditionally have not been part of the selection process. Decisions were made almost entirely on the basis of exam scores, scholastic accomplishments, and letters of recommendation. This is not the case, however, throughout most of the world. It's probably correct to say that most of us don't know anyone who has gotten a job without at least one interview. You may have an acquaintance who got a part-time or summer job through a close friend or relative without having to go through an interview, but such instances are rare. Of all the selection devices that organizations use to differentiate candidates, the interview continues to be the one most frequently used.[45] Even companies in Asian countries have begun to rely on employee interviews as a screening device.[46]

Not only is the interview widely used, it also seems to carry a great deal of weight. That is, its results tend to have a disproportionate amount of influence on the selection decision. The candidate who performs poorly in the employment interview is likely to be cut from the applicant pool, regardless of his or her experience, test scores, or letters of recommendation. Conversely, "all too often, the person most polished in job-seeking techniques, particularly those used in the interview process, is the one hired, even though he or she may not be the best candidate for the position."[47]

These findings are important because of the unstructured manner in which the selection interview is frequently conducted. The unstructured interview—short in duration, casual, and made up of random questions—has been proven to be an ineffective selection device.[48] The data gathered from such interviews are typically biased and often unrelated to future job performance. Without structure, a number of biases can distort results. These biases include interviewers' tending to favor applicants who share their attitudes, giving unduly high weight to negative information, and allowing the order in which applicants are interviewed to influence evaluations.[49] Having interviewers use a standardized set of questions, providing interviewers with a uniform method of recording information, and standardizing the rating of the applicant's qualifications reduce the variability in results among applicants and enhance validity of the interview as a selection device. In fact, structured interviews yield validities comparable to weighted applications, paper-and-pencil ability tests, or assessment centers.[50] (See Exhibit 9-4 on page 282.)

The evidence indicates that interviews are particularly valuable for assessing an applicant's intelligence, level of motivation, and interpersonal skills.[51] When these qualities are related to job performance, the validity of the interview as a selection device is increased. For example, these qualities have demonstrated relevance for performance in upper managerial positions. This relationship may explain why applicants for senior management positions typically undergo dozens of interviews with executive recruiters, board members, and other company executives before a final decision is made. It can also explain why organizations that design work around teams may similarly put applicants through an unusually large number of interviews.

One final benefit from selection interviews needs to be mentioned—they offer the opportunity for management to give prospective employees a realistic preview of the organization and the job vacancy.[52] The typical interviewer tends to paint an overly positive image of a job when he or she is trying to "sell" it to an attractive candidate. Unfortunately, this tendency often builds unrealistic expectations that lead to disappointment and premature resignations. To improve applicants' future job satisfaction and reduce turnover, interviewers should give them a **realistic job preview**—that is, provide candidates with both unfavorable and favorable information before an offer is made. For example, in addition to positive comments, the candidate might be told that there are limited opportunities to talk with co-workers during work hours or that erratic fluctuations in work load create considerable stress on employees during rush periods. Comparisons of turnover rates between organizations that use the realistic job preview versus either no preview or presentation of only positive job information show that those not using the realistic job preview have, on average, almost 29 percent higher turnover.[53]

Worldwide, organizations spend hundreds of *billions* of dollars each year on training. Companies in the United States, with 100 or more employees, alone spend in excess of $60 billion annually.[54] This training covers everything from basic computer skills to teaching new work methods and procedures, to management development, to employee health-improvement programs.

TRAINING: HOW CAN MANAGERS ENSURE EMPLOYEE SKILLS ARE CURRENT?

▶ The Increasing Importance of Training

Money spent on training can provide big returns to an organization.[55] This may be truer today than at any time in the past century. Intensified competition, technological changes, and the search for improved productivity are increasing skill demands on employees. A recent U.S. study, for instance, found that 57 percent of employers reported that employee skill requirements had increased over a 3-year period and that only 20 percent of employees were fully proficient in their jobs.[56] Skills deteriorate and can become obsolete. Engineers need to update their knowledge of mechanical and electrical systems. Hourly workers, many now working in teams, require problem-solving, quality improvement, and team-building skills. Clerical personnel need to take courses to learn how to fully utilize the latest software programs on their computers. And executives recognize that they have to become more effective leaders and planners. These developments explain why Xerox

EXHIBIT 9-4

Selection Interviewing Skills

The interview is made up of four stages. *Preparation* is followed by the *opening*, a period of *questioning and discussion*, and a *conclusion*.

1. *Preparation*. Before meeting the applicant, you should review his or her application form and résumé. You also should review the job description and job specification for the position for which the applicant is interviewing.

   Next, structure the agenda for the interview. Specifically, use the standardized questions provided to you, or prepare a set of questions you want to ask the applicant. Choose questions that can't be answered with merely a yes or a no. Inquiries that begin with *how* or *why* tend to stimulate extended answers. Avoid leading questions that telegraph the desired response (such as "Would you say you have good interpersonal skills?") and bipolar questions that require the applicant to select an answer from only two choices (such as "Do you prefer working with people or working alone?"). Don't ask questions that aren't relevant to the job. In most cases, questions relating to marital and family status, age, race, religion, gender, ethnic background, credit rating, and arrest record are prohibited by law in the United States unless you can demonstrate that they are in some way related to job performance. So avoid them. In place of asking "Are you married?" or "Do you have children?", you might ask "Are there any reasons why you might not be able to work overtime several times a month?" Of course, to avoid discrimination, you have to ask this question of both male and female candidates. Since the best predictor of future behavior is past behavior, the best questions tend to be those that focus on previous experiences that are relevant to the current job. Questions should be designed to get people to say what they *have done* in the past rather than what they *would do* in the future. Examples might include: "What have you done in previous jobs that demonstrates your creativity?" "On your last job, what was it that you most wanted to accomplish but didn't? Why didn't you?"

2. *Opening*. Assume that the applicant is tense and nervous. If you're going to get valid insights into what the applicant is really like, you'll need to put him or her at ease. Introduce yourself. Be friendly. Begin with a few simple questions or statements that can break the ice: for example, "Did you run into much traffic coming over?"

   Once the applicant is fairly relaxed, you should provide a brief orientation. Preview what topics will be discussed, how long the interview will take, and explain if you'll be taking notes. Encourage the applicant to ask questions.

3. *Questioning and discussion*. The questions you developed during the preparation stage will provide a general road map to guide you. Make sure you cover them all. Additional questions should arise from the answers to the standardized questions. Select follow-up questions that naturally flow from the answers given.

   Follow-up questions should seek to probe deeper into what the applicant says. If you feel that the applicant's response is superficial or inadequate, seek elaboration. Ask a question such as, "Tell me more about that issue." To clarify information, you could say, "You said working overtime was OK *sometimes*. Can you tell me specifically when you'd be willing to work overtime?" If the applicant doesn't directly answer your question, follow up by repeating the question or paraphrasing it. Finally, never underestimate the power of silence in an interview. One of the biggest errors that inexperienced interviewers make is that they talk too much. You're not learning anything about the candidate when you're doing the talking. Pause for at least a few seconds after the applicant appears to have finished an answer. Your silence encourages the applicant to continue talking.

4. *Concluding*. Once you're through with the questions and discussions, you're ready to wrap up the interview. Let the applicant know this fact with a statement like, "Well, that covers all the questions I have. Do you have any questions about the job or our organization that I haven't answered for you?" Then let the applicant know what's going to happen next. When can he or she expect to hear from you? Will you write or phone? Are there likely to be more follow-up interviews?

   Before you consider the interview complete, write your evaluation while it is fresh in your mind. Ideally, you kept notes or recorded the applicant's answers to your questions and made comments of your impressions. Now that the applicant is gone, take the time to assess the applicant's responses.

Source: Based on W. C. Donaghy, *The Interview: Skills and Applications* (Glenview, IL: Scott, Foresman, 1984), pp. 245–80; and J. M. Jenks and B. L. P. Zevnik, "ABCs of Job Interviewing," *Harvard Business Review*, July–August 1989, pp. 38–42.

spends over $300 million a year on training and retraining its employees,[57] or why Motorola has made a commitment to lifelong employee learning and introduced a fourfold increase (from 40 hours a year to 160) that a typical Motorola employee spends in training.[58]

Assessing Training Needs

Norton Manufacturing Co., a metalworking and machining firm that employs 400 people, recently assessed the skills of its machine operators. One assessment covered math, and Norton found that some of its operators had mastered the subject only to a seventh-grade level. "That scared the heck out of us," says the vice president of operations, "because math is what this is all about." The company responded by giving the low scorers 20 hours of classroom training. When the workers were retested, they scored at a college freshman level.[59]

Ideally, employees and managers alike should be continually undergoing training to keep their skills current. In reality, few organizations have made a commitment to providing their staff with continual learning, nor do employees voluntarily take the initiative to seek out training opportunities. In most organizations, training is provided on an "as-needed" basis, and the decision as to when that need arises lies with individual managers. So, if you're a manager, what signals do you look for that might suggest an employee is in need of training? Here are a few suggestions:

- New equipment or processes are introduced that may affect an employee's job.
- A change is made in the employee's job responsibilities.
- There is a drop in an employee's productivity or in the quality of his or her output.
- There is an increase in safety violations or accidents.
- The number of questions employees ask you or their colleagues increases.
- Complaints by customers or co-workers increases.

If you see any of these signs, should you automatically assume that the solution is increased training? Not necessarily! Training is only one response to a performance problem. If the problem is lack of motivation, a poorly designed job, or external conditions, training is not likely to offer much help. For example, training is not likely to be the answer if a performance deficiency is caused by low salaries, inadequate benefits, a lingering illness, or the trauma of layoffs associated with corporate downsizing.

When you have determined that training is necessary, specify training goals.[60] What explicit changes or results do you expect the training to achieve? These goals should be clear to both you and the employee. For instance, the new service assistant at a Kinko's Copy Center is expected to be able to (1) use all photocopying equipment, (2) be able to enlarge and reduce copies, (3) send and receive domestic and international facsimiles, (4) operate the passport photo machine, (5) operate and answer technical questions about the Macintosh computer rentals, (6) answer all technical questions regarding photo processing and differences in paper quality, and (7) operate the cash register and make change. These goals then guide the design of the training program and can be used after the program is complete to assess its effectiveness.

Norton Manufacturing is concerned with the skills of its workers. Here, A. J. Hoover, right, vice president of operations, talks with employee Robert Tasker. Hoover says, "We're trying like heck to train our own people, because the schools are not getting the job done for us."

Types of Training

Training can include everything from teaching employees basic reading skills to advanced courses in executive leadership. The following summarizes four general skill categories—basic literacy, technical, interpersonal, and problem solving—where most training is focused. In addition, we briefly discuss ethics training and diversity training.

BASIC LITERARY SKILLS A recent report by the U.S. Department of Education found that 90 million American adults have limited literacy skills, and about 40 million can read little or not at all![61] Most workplace demands require a tenth- or eleventh-grade reading level, but about 20 percent of Americans between the ages of 21 and 25 can't read at even an eighth-grade level.[62] And in many third world countries, few workers can read or have gone beyond the equivalent of the third grade.

Organizations are increasingly having to provide basic reading and math skills for their employees. For instance, William Dudek runs a small manufacturing firm on Chicago's North Side.[63] His thirty-five employees make metal clips, hooks, and clasps used in household appliances and automotive components. When Dudek tried to introduce some basic quality-management principles in his plant, he noticed that many of his employees seemed to disregard the written instructions. Checking further, he discovered that the workers couldn't read the instructions, and only a few could calculate percentages or plot a simple graph. Dudek conducted a needs assessment, hired an instructor, and had classes in English and mathematics taught to his employees in the firm's cafeteria. Dudek says that this training, which cost him $15,000 in its first year, made his employees more efficient and that they now work better as a team.

TECHNICAL SKILLS Most training is directed at upgrading and improving an employee's technical skills—in both white-collar and blue-collar jobs. Technical training has become increasingly important today for two reasons—new technology and new structural designs.

Jobs change as a result of new technologies and improved methods. For instance, many auto repair personnel have had to undergo extensive training to fix and maintain recent models with computer-monitored engines, electronic stabilizing systems, and other innovations. Similarly, computer-controlled equipment has required millions of production employees to learn a whole new set of skills.

In addition, technical training has become increasingly important because of changes in organization structures. As organizations flatten their structures, expand their use of teams, and break down traditional departmental barriers, employees need to learn a wider variety of tasks. Management has responded by significantly increasing opportunities for cross-functional training.[64] For instance, Graphic Control Corp. in Buffalo, New York, is using cross-functional training to increase its workforce's versatility. By teaching its manufacturing employees to perform the jobs of at least one other person, management can move people around more easily and reduce the need to hire skilled temporary help.[65]

INTERPERSONAL SKILLS Almost all employees belong to a work unit. To some degree, their work performance depends on their ability to effectively interact with their co-workers and their boss. Some employees have excellent interpersonal skills, but others require training to improve theirs. This includes learning how to be a better listener, how to communicate ideas more clearly, and how to be a more effective team player.[66]

PROBLEM-SOLVING SKILLS Managers, as well as many employees who perform nonroutine tasks, have to solve problems on their job. When people require these skills, but are deficient, they can participate in problem-solving training. This would include activities to sharpen their logic, reasoning, and problem-defining skills, as well as their abilities to assess causation, develop alternatives, analyze alternatives, and select solutions. Problem-solving training has become a basic part of almost every organizational effort to introduce self-managed teams or implement TQM.

WHAT ABOUT ETHICS TRAINING? Approximately 80 percent of the largest U.S. corporations have formal ethics programs, and 44 percent of these provide ethics training.[67] What do proponents of ethics training expect to achieve? They claim that training can stimulate moral thought, help people recognize ethical dilemmas, create a sense of moral obligation, and help employees learn to tolerate or reduce ambiguity. But the evidence is not clear on whether you can teach ethics.

Critics argue that ethics are based on values, and value systems are fixed at an early age. By the time employers hire people, their ethical values have already been established. The critics also claim that ethics cannot be formally "taught," but must be learned by example. Leaders set ethical examples by what they say and do. If this claim is true, then ethics training is relevant only as part of leadership training.

Supporters of ethics training argue that values can be learned and changed after early childhood. And even if they couldn't, ethics training would be effective because it gets employees to think about ethical dilemmas, become more aware of the ethical issues underlying their actions, and reaffirms the organization's expectations that members will act ethically.

THE GROWING POPULARITY OF DIVERSITY TRAINING Arguably one of the fastest growing areas of training is helping employees to cope with an increasingly diverse workforce.[68] Diversity training has become an essential element of almost all diversity programs.

The two most popular types of diversity training focus on increasing awareness and building skills. *Awareness training* tries to create an understanding of the need for, and meaning of, managing and valuing diversity. *Skill-building training* educates employees about specific cultural differences in the workplace. Companies leading the way in diversity training include American Express, Avon, Corning, Hewlett-Packard, Monsanto, Motorola, Pacific Gas & Electric, U.S. West, and Xerox.

In The News

Diversity Training at EDS

EDS, a global leader in information services, employs 95,000 men and women in 43 countries. And more than 9,000 of these employees have gone through the company's diversity awareness workshops. They are specifically designed to help employees work in teams composed of individuals with diverse backgrounds and to deal with a variety of diverse customers.

"Our workshop goes beyond race and gender to include religion, age, disabilities, social status, and more," says one manager. "And instead of merely teaching white males how to manage women and minorities, we help all employees learn to work with others different from themselves."

Are the workshops effective? The company's diversity director in the Customer Service Technologies group thinks so. For instance, he points out that one group who went through the diversity awareness workshop saw their ratings on customer satisfaction surveys improve by 24 percent. In addition, the director noted that the training enlarged the pool of professional resources from which the company can draw to support its fast growth.

Source: "Diversity Helps Recruitment and Customer Satisfaction," *Business Week*, December 9, 1996, p. 13 (special section).

Training Methods

Most training takes place on the job. This preference can be attributed to the simplicity and, usually, lower cost of on-the-job training methods. However, on-the-job training can disrupt the workplace and result in an increase in errors as learning proceeds. Also, some skill training is too complex to learn on the job. In such cases, it should take place outside the work setting.[69]

ON-THE-JOB TRAINING Popular on-the-job training methods include job rotation and mentor relationships. *Job rotation* involves lateral transfers that enable employees to work at different jobs. Employees get to learn a wide variety of jobs and gain increased insight into the interdependency between jobs and a wider perspective on organizational activities. New employees frequently learn their jobs under the guidance of a seasoned veteran. In the trades, this is usually called an *apprenticeship*. In white-collar jobs, it is called a *coaching*, or *mentor*, relationship. In each, the new employee works under the observation of an experienced worker, who acts as a model whom the newcomer attempts to emulate.

Both job rotation and mentoring apply to the learning of technical skills. Interpersonal and problem-solving skills are acquired more effectively by training that takes place off the job.

OFF-THE-JOB TRAINING There are a number of off-the-job training methods that managers may want to make available to employees. The more popular are classroom lectures, videos, and simulation exercises. *Classroom lectures* are well suited for conveying specific information. They can be used effectively for developing technical and problem-solving skills. *Videos* can also be used to explicitly demonstrate technical skills that are not easily presented by other methods. Interpersonal and problem-solving skills may be best learned through *simulation exercises* such as case analyses, experiential exercises, role playing, and group interaction sessions. Complex computer models (virtual training!), such as those used by airlines in the training of pilots, are another kind of simulation exercise, which in this case is used to teach technical skills. So, too, is *vestibule training*, in which employees learn their jobs on the same equipment they will be using, only the training is conducted away from the actual work floor.

In addition, there are new technologies that some progressive companies are using to facilitate training on the employees' own computers.[70] Hewlett-Packard, for instance, is encouraging its employees to use their workstations to gain access to peer-based training over the company's Local Area Network, to take entire courses on the World Wide Web, and to utilize HP's library of video courses available for broadcast via satellite for viewing through workers' desktop terminals.

Off-the-job training can rely on outside consultants, local college faculty, or in-house personnel. Most of you are probably familiar with the fact that McDonald's has been training thousands of its managers and future managers since 1961 at its Hamburger University.[71] The heart of Hamburger U's curriculum is a 2-week program that combines operations enhancement, equipment management, and interpersonal skills training for restaurant managers and franchisees. But you don't have to be a multibillion-dollar corporation to make a major commitment to in-house training. Granite Rock, Inc., a producer of construction and paving materials, spends nearly 1 percent of gross sales and a whopping 4.2 percent of payroll on training, in its own internal university.[72] Granite Rock University offers more than fifty courses and seminars for company employees on everything from enhancing self-esteem to the mechanics of mobile hydraulic equipment.

Training circles, being updated by Leland Millsaps, serve as a visual record of who is learning what jobs and how quickly the learning is progressing at the Mercedes-Benz plant outside Tuscaloosa, Alabama.

▶ Individualizing Training: Different Strokes for Different Folks

The way that you process, internalize, and remember new and difficult material isn't necessarily the same way that someone else does. This fact means that effective training should be individualized to reflect the learning style of the employee.[73]

Some examples of different learning styles include reading, watching, listening, and participating. Some people absorb information better when they read about it. They're the kind of people who can learn to use computers by sitting in their study and reading manuals. Some people learn best by observation. They watch others and then emulate the behaviors they've seen. Such people can watch someone use a computer for a while, and then copy what they've seen. Listeners rely heavily on their auditory senses to absorb information. They would prefer to learn how to use a computer by listening to an audiotape. People who prefer a participating style learn by doing. They want to sit down, turn on the computer, and gain hands-on experience by practicing.

You can translate these styles into different learning methods to maximize learning. Readers should be given books or other reading material to review; watchers should get the opportunity to observe individuals demonstrating the new skills either in person or on video; listeners will benefit from hearing lectures or audiotapes; and participants will benefit most from experiences in which they can simulate and practice the new skills.

These different learning styles are obviously not mutually exclusive. In fact, good teachers recognize that their students learn differently and, therefore, provide multiple learning methods. They assign readings before class; give lectures; use visual aids to illustrate concepts; and have students participate in group projects, case analyses, role plays, and experiential learning exercises. If you know the preferred style of an employee, you can design his or her training program to optimize this preference. If you don't have that information, it's probably best to design the program to use a variety of learning styles. Overreliance on a single style places individuals who don't learn well from that style at a disadvantage.

PERFORMANCE APPRAISAL: WHAT'S THE BEST WAY TO EVALUATE AN EMPLOYEE'S PERFORMANCE?

One of a manager's most important responsibilities is appraising his or her employees' performance. Why is performance appraisal so important? Because it serves several critical purposes.[74] Appraisals are used to make key personnel decisions such as promotions, transfers, and terminations; to identify training needs; to provide feedback to employees on how the organization views their performance; and often as the basis for pay adjustments. In this section, we'll discuss appraisal criteria, the choice of appraisers, methods of appraisal, the performance feedback interview, and the issue of appraising employees when they're part of a team.

▶ What Do We Appraise?

What should management appraise? The three most popular sets of criteria are individual task outcomes, behaviors, and traits.

INDIVIDUAL TASK OUTCOMES If ends count, rather than means, then management should appraise an employee's task outcomes. Task outcomes could be used to judge a plant manager on criteria such as quantity produced, scrap generated, and cost per unit of production. Similarly, a salesperson could be assessed on overall sales volume in his or her territory, dollar increase in sales, and number of new accounts established.

BEHAVIORS It often is difficult to identify specific outcomes that can be directly attributable to one employee's actions. This is particularly true of personnel in staff positions and individuals whose work assignments are intrinsically part of a group effort. In the latter case, the group's performance may be readily evaluated, but the contribution of each group member may be difficult or impossible to identify clearly. In such instances, management still will want to appraise the employee's behavior. Behaviors of a plant manager that could be used for performance appraisal purposes might include promptness in submitting his or her monthly reports or the leadership style that the manager exhibits. Pertinent salesperson behaviors could be average number of contact calls made per day or sick days used per year.

TRAITS The weakest set of criteria, yet one that is still widely used by organizations, is individual traits.[75] We say they're weaker than either task outcomes or behaviors because they're furthest removed from the actual performance of the job itself. Traits such as having "a good attitude," showing "confidence," being "dependable" or "cooperative," "looking busy," or possessing "a wealth of experience" may or may not be highly correlated with positive task outcomes, but only the naive would ignore the reality that such traits are frequently used in organizations as criteria for assessing an employee's level of performance.

► Who Should Do the Appraising?

Who should appraise an employee's performance? The obvious answer would seem to be his or her immediate boss! By tradition, a manager's authority typically has included appraising subordinates' performance. The logic behind this tradition seems to be that, since managers are held responsible for their employees' performance, it only makes sense that those managers evaluate that performance. But that logic may be flawed. Others may actually be able to do the task better, or at least contribute to the task.

IMMEDIATE SUPERIOR About 95 percent of all performance appraisals at the lower and middle levels of the organization are conducted by the employee's immediate boss.[76] Yet a number of organizations are recognizing the drawbacks to using this source of evaluation. For instance, many bosses feel unqualified to evaluate the unique contributions of each of their employees. Others resent being asked to "play God" with their employees' careers. In addition, today, when many organizations are using self-managed teams, telecommuting, and other organizing devices that distance bosses from their employees, an employee's immediate superior may not be a reliable judge of that employee's performance.

> **Peer evaluations are one of the most reliable sources of appraisal data.**

PEERS Peer evaluations are one of the most reliable sources of appraisal data. Why? First, peers are close to the action. Daily interactions provide them with a comprehensive view of an employee's job performance. This is especially true where work is performed in teams. Second, using peers as raters results in several independent judgments, whereas a boss can offer only a single evaluation. And the average of several ratings is often more reliable than a single evaluation. On the downside, peer appraisals can suffer from co-workers' unwillingness to evaluate one another, from biases based on friendship or animosity, and their inapplicability where peers are geographically distanced (as, for example, exists among telecommuters).

SELF-APPRAISALS Having employees appraise their own performance is consistent with values such as self-management and empowerment. Self-appraisals get high marks from employees themselves; they tend to lessen employees' defensiveness about the appraisal process; and they make excellent vehicles for stimulating job performance discussions between employees and their superiors. However, as you might guess, they suffer from over-inflated assessment and self-serving bias. Moreover, self-evaluations are often low in agreement with superiors' ratings.[77] Because of these serious drawbacks, self-evaluations are probably better suited to guiding employee development than for appraisal purposes.

IMMEDIATE SUBORDINATES A fourth judgment source is an employee's immediate subordinate. For instance, Datatec Industries, a maker of in-store computer systems, uses this form of appraisal.[78] The company's president says that it is consistent with the firm's core values of honesty, openness, and employee empowerment.

Immediate subordinates' appraisals can provide accurate and detailed information about a manager's behavior because the evaluators typically have frequent contact with the evaluatee. The obvious problem with this form of rating is fear of reprisal from bosses given unfavorable evaluations. Therefore, respondent anonymity is crucial if these appraisals are to be accurate.

CUSTOMERS For some jobs, customers are in a unique position to judge employee performance. This would include, for instance, salespeople, customer relations personnel, and similar positions that interface with customers and clients. Although customer evaluations are probably one of the least used appraisal sources, it matches well with two current trends—the move to a service economy and the increased importance management is placing on customer satisfaction.[79]

THE COMPREHENSIVE APPROACH: 360-DEGREE FEEDBACK The latest approach to performance evaluation is the use of 360-degree feedback appraisals.[80] It provides for performance feedback from the full circle of daily contacts that an employee might have, ranging from mailroom personnel to customers to bosses to peers. The number of appraisals can be as few as three or four evaluations or as many as twenty-five; most organizations collect five to ten for each employee.

Studies show that about 12 percent of U.S. companies are using full 360-degree feedback programs.[81] This group includes companies such as Alcoa, Du Pont, Levi Strauss, Honeywell, UPS, Sprint, Amoco, AT&T, and W. L. Gore & Associates.

What's the appeal of 360-degree feedback appraisals? They fit well into organizations that have introduced teams, employee involvement, and TQM programs. By relying on feedback from co-workers, customers, and subordinates, these organizations are hoping to give everyone more of a sense of participation in the review process and gain more accurate readings on employee performance.

▶ Methods of Performance Appraisal

Now that we have explained *what* we evaluate and *who* should do the appraising, we can ask, *How* do we appraise an employee's performance? That is, what are the specific techniques for appraisal? This section reviews the major performance appraisal methods.

WRITTEN ESSAYS Probably the simplest method of appraisal is to write a narrative describing an employee's strengths, weaknesses, past performance, potential, and suggestions for improvement. The written essay requires no complex forms or extensive training to complete. But the results often reflect the ability of the writer. A good or bad appraisal may be determined as much by the evaluator's writing skill as by the employee's actual level of performance.

CRITICAL INCIDENTS **Critical incidents** focus the appraiser's attention on those behaviors that are key in making the difference between executing a job effectively and executing it ineffectively. With this method, the appraiser writes down anecdotes that describe what the employee did that was especially effective or ineffective. The key here is that only specific behaviors, not vaguely defined personality traits, are cited. A list of critical incidents provides a rich set of examples from which the employee can be shown those behaviors that are desirable and those that call for improvement.

GRAPHIC RATING SCALES One of the oldest and most popular methods of appraisal is the use of **graphic rating scales**. In this method, a set of performance factors, such as quantity and quality of work, depth of knowledge, cooperation, loyalty, attendance, honesty, and initiative, are listed. The appraiser then goes down the list and rates each on incremental scales. The scales typically specify five levels, so a factor such as *job knowledge* might be rated from 1 ("poorly informed about work duties") to 5 ("has complete mastery of all phases of the job").

Why are graphic ratings scales so popular? Though they don't provide the depth of information that essays or critical incidents do, they are less time-consuming to develop and administer. They also allow for quantitative analysis and comparison.

BEHAVIORALLY ANCHORED RATING SCALES **Behaviorally anchored rating scales** (BARS) combine major elements from the critical incident and graphic rating scale approaches: The appraiser rates the employees on items along a continuum, but the points are examples of actual behavior on the given job rather than general descriptions or traits.

BARS specify definite, observable, and measurable job behavior. Examples of job-related behavior and performance dimensions are found by asking participants to give specific illustrations of effective and ineffective behavior regarding each performance dimension. These behavioral examples are then translated into a set of performance dimensions, each dimension having varying levels of performance. The results of this process are behavioral descriptions, such as *anticipates*, *plans*, *executes*, *solves immediate problems*, *carries out orders*, and *handles emergency situations*.

MULTIPERSON COMPARISONS Multiperson comparisons evaluate one individual's performance against the performance of one or more others. It is a relative rather than an absolute measuring device. The three most popular comparisons are group order ranking, individual ranking, and paired comparisons.

The **group order ranking** requires the appraiser to place employees into a particular classification, such as top one-fifth or second one-fifth. This method is often used in recommending students to graduate schools. Appraisers are asked whether the student ranks in the top 5 percent of the class, the next 5 percent, the next 15 percent, and so forth. But when managers use this method to appraise employees, they deal with all their employees. Therefore, if a rater has twenty employees, only four can be in the top fifth and, of course, four must also be relegated to the bottom fifth.

The **individual ranking** approach rank-orders employees from best to worst. If the manager is required to appraise thirty employees, this approach assumes that the difference between the first and second employee is the same as that between the twenty-first and twenty-second. Even though some of the employees may be closely grouped, this approach allows for no ties. The result is a clear ordering of employees, from the highest performer down to the lowest.

The **paired comparison** approach compares each employee with every other employee and rates each as either the superior or the weaker member of the pair. After all paired comparisons are made, each employee is assigned a summary ranking based on the number of superior scores he or she achieved. This approach ensures that each employee is compared against every other, but it can obviously become unwieldy when many employees are being compared.

Multiperson comparisons can be combined with one of the other methods to blend the best from both absolute and relative standards. For example, a college might use the graphic rating scale and the individual ranking method to provide more-accurate information about its students' performance. The student's relative rank in the class could be noted next to an absolute grade of A, B, C, D, or F. A prospective employer or graduate school could then look at two students who each got a B in their different financial accounting courses and draw considerably different conclusions about each because next to one grade it says "ranked fourth out of twenty-six," whereas next to the other it says "ranked seventeenth out of thirty." Obviously, the latter instructor gives out a lot more high grades!

▶ Providing Performance Feedback

For many managers, few activities are more unpleasant than providing performance feedback to employees.[82] In fact, unless pressured by organizational policies and controls, managers are likely to ignore this responsibility.[83]

Why the reluctance to give performance feedback? There seem to be at least three reasons. First, managers are often uncomfortable discussing performance weaknesses with employees. Given that almost every employee could stand to improve in some areas, managers fear a confrontation when presenting negative feedback. Second, many employees tend to become defensive when their weaknesses are pointed out. Instead of accepting the feedback as constructive and a basis for improving performance, some employees challenge the evaluation by criticizing the manager or redirecting blame to someone else. Finally, employees tend to have an inflated assessment of their own performance. Statistically speaking, half of all employees must be below-average performers. But the evidence indicates that the average employee's estimate of his or her own performance level generally falls around the seventy-fifth percentile.[84] So even when managers are providing *good news*, employees are likely to perceive it as *not good enough*!

The solution to the performance feedback problem is not to ignore it, but to train managers in how to conduct constructive feedback sessions. An effective review—one in which the employee perceives the appraisal as fair, the manager as sincere, and the climate as constructive—can result in the employee's leaving the interview in an upbeat mood, informed about the performance areas in which he or she needs to improve, and determined to correct the deficiencies.[85] In addition, the performance review should be designed more as a counseling activity than a judgment process. This can best be accomplished by allowing the review to evolve out of the employee's own self-appraisal.

> Even when managers are providing *good news,* employees are likely to percieve it as *not good enough!*

EXHIBIT 9-5

Source: *Dilbert* reprinted by permission of United Feature Syndicate, Inc.

Team Performance Appraisals

Performance appraisal concepts have been almost exclusively developed with only individual employees in mind. This fact reflects the historical belief that individuals are the core building blocks around which organizations are built. But as described throughout this book, more and more organizations are restructuring themselves around teams. How should organizations using teams appraise performance? Four suggestions have been offered for designing a system that supports and improves the performance of teams.[86]

1. *Tie the team's results to the organization's goals.* It's important to find measurements that apply to important goals that the team is supposed to accomplish.
2. *Begin with the team's customers and the work process the team follows to satisfy their needs.* The final product the customer receives can be appraised in terms of the customer's requirements. The transactions between teams can be appraised on the basis of delivery and quality, and the process steps on the basis of waste and cycle time.
3. *Measure both team and individual performance.* Define the roles of each team member

in terms of accomplishments that support the team's work process. Then assess each member's contribution and the team's overall performance.

4. *Train the team to create its own measures.* Having the team define its objectives and those of each member ensures that every member understands his or her role on the team and helps the team develop into a more cohesive unit.

In the past decade, many large corporations, as well as many government agencies, not-for-profit organizations, and small businesses, have found themselves overstaffed. Because of market changes, implementation of new technologies, foreign competition, mergers, and the like, management concludes that it has a surplus of employees and needs to reduce the labor supply within the organization. These organizations need to engage in **decruitment**.

Decruitment is not a pleasant task for any manager to perform. But as many organizations are forced to shrink the size of their workforce or restructure their skill composition, decruitment is becoming an increasingly important part of human resource management.

What are a manager's decruitment options? Obviously, people can be fired. But other choices may be more beneficial to the organization or the employee or both.[87] For instance, Honda of America "rents" some of its engineers to other companies when it finds itself overstaffed.[88] Exhibit 9-6 summarizes a manager's major options.

DECRUITMENT: WHAT OPTIONS EXIST TO HANDLE OVERSTAFFING?

We close this chapter by addressing three specific human resource issues that managers are currently facing: (1) How can managers limit sexual harassment? (2) What role should organizations play in employee career development? (3) What effect do labor unions have on HRM practices?

CONTEMPORARY ISSUES IN HUMAN RESOURCE MANAGEMENT

How Can Managers Limit Sexual Harassment?

Few workplace topics have received more attention in recent years than that of sexual harassment.[89] In the United States, there were 6,000 sexual harassment complaints made in 1990. Five years later that number was 15,000.[90] Since 1980, U.S. courts generally have

---

Decruitment Options

EXHIBIT 9-6

Option	Description
Firing	Permanent involuntary termination
Layoffs	Temporary involuntary termination; may last only a few days or extend to years
Attrition	Not filling openings created by voluntary resignations or normal retirements
Transfers	Moving employees either laterally or downward; usually does not reduce costs but can reduce intraorganizational supply-demand imbalances
External loans	Providing employees' services to other organizations temporarily, on a contract basis, while still keeping them on the payroll
Reduced workweeks	Having employees work fewer hours per week, share jobs, or perform their jobs on a part-time basis
Early retirements	Providing incentives to senior employees for retiring before their normal retirement date

Sexual harassment is complicated by the fact that men and women often perceive behavior differently. A man may think a touch on the hand or neck is innocent, but a woman may view it as a prelude to an assault.

defined **sexual harassment** as encompassing sexually suggestive remarks, unwanted touching and sexual advances, requests for sexual favors, and other verbal and physical conduct of a sexual nature. Such conduct is illegal in the United States and Canada—a violation of civil rights law. And other countries are quickly moving to enact legislation to protect workers from sexual harassment.[91] Mexico, for example, is a country that values masculinity characteristics and where men hold the overwhelming majority of positions of power. Yet the country passed federal legislation in 1990 that criminalizes sexual harassment.[92]

In a 1993 ruling, the U.S. Supreme Court widened the test for sexual harassment under U.S. civil rights law to include comments or behavior in a work environment that "would reasonably be perceived, and is perceived, as hostile or abusive." Now individuals need not show that they have been psychologically damaged to prove sexual harassment in the workplace. They merely need to show that they are working in a hostile or abusive environment.

From a manager's standpoint, sexual harassment is a growing concern because it intimidates employees, interferes with job performance, and exposes the organization to liability. The first step toward reducing an organization's potential liability and limiting sexual harassment behavior is for senior management to establish a written sexual harassment policy (see Exhibit 9-7). This statement should define sexual harassment,

---

EXHIBIT 9-7

Management Guidelines for Reducing Potential Liability for Sexual Harassment

The following guidelines reduce the potential liability of a sexual harassment suit:

- ► Establish a written policy prohibiting sexual harassment.
- ► Communicate the policy and train employees in what constitutes sexual harassment.
- ► Establish an effective organizational complaint procedure.
- ► Promptly investigate all claims and demonstrate that complaints will be examined fairly and objectively.
- ► Take remedial action to correct past harassment.
- ► Follow up to ensure that no further harassment occurs and that retaliation does not occur.

Source: Reproduced with permission from CCH *Sexual Harassment Manual for Managers and Supervisors*, published and © by CCH, Inc., 2700 Lake Cook Rd., Riverwoods, IL 60016.

make clear that it will not be tolerated, describe disciplinary measures that will be taken if the policy is violated, and tell employees how to make a complaint. The policy should be reinforced by regular discussion sessions in which employees are reminded of the rule and carefully instructed that even the slightest sexual overture to another employee will not be tolerated. At AT&T, for instance, all employees have been specifically advised that they can be fired for making repeated unwelcome sexual advances, using sexually degrading words to describe someone, or displaying sexually offensive pictures or objects at work.

What Role Should Organizations Play in Employee Career Development?

Management's role in career development has undergone significant change in the past decade. It has gone from paternalism—in which the organization took responsibility for managing its employees' careers—to supporting individuals as they take personal responsibility for their future.[93] And careers, themselves, have gone from a series of upward moves with increasing income, authority, status, and security to one where people adapt quickly, learn continuously, and change their work identities over time.

For much of the twentieth century, companies recruited young workers with the intent that they would spend their entire career inside that single organization. For those with the right credentials and motivation, they created promotion paths dotted with ever-increasing responsibility. Employers would provide the training and opportunities; and employees would respond by demonstrating loyalty and hard work. The changes we described in chapter 1 changed those rules. High uncertainty now limits the ability of organizations to accurately forecast future needs. Management seeks flexibility over permanence. Meanwhile, flattened hierarchies have reduced promotion opportunities. The result is that, today, career planning is something increasingly being done by individual employees rather than by their employers. It has become the employee's responsibility to keep his or her skills, abilities, and knowledge current and to prepare for tomorrow's new tasks.

What, if any, responsibility does management have for career development under these new rules? Amoco Corp.'s career development program is a model for modern companies.[94] It is designed around employee self-reliance and to help employees reflect on their marketability both inside and outside the Chicago-based oil company. All workers are encouraged to participate in a half-day introduction to the program and a full day of self-assessment and self-development sessions. The company supports its employees by providing information—a worldwide electronic job-posting system, a network of career advisers, and a worldwide directory of Amoco employees and their skills from which company managers can search for candidates for job openings. But the whole program is voluntary and assumes that it is the employees' responsibility to maintain their employability.

The essence of a progressive career development program is built on providing support for employees to continually add to their skills, abilities, and knowledge. This support includes:

1. *Clearly communicating the organization's goals and future strategies.* When people know where the organization is headed, they are better able to develop a personal plan to share in that future.
2. *Creating growth opportunities.* Employees should have the opportunity to get new, interesting, and professionally challenging work experiences.
3. *Offering financial assistance.* The organization should offer tuition reimbursement to help employees keep current.

> Today, career planning is something increasingly being done by individual employees rather than by their employers.

4. *Providing the time for employees to learn.* Organizations should be generous in providing paid time off from work for off-the-job training. In addition, work loads should not be so demanding that they preclude employees from having the time to develop new skills, abilities, and knowledge.

What Effect Do Labor Unions Have on HRM Practices?

Some managers will be working with employees who belong to a labor union. How does unionization affect the manager in the performance of his or her job?

Labor unions are a vehicle by which employees act collectively to protect and promote their interests. They use the collective bargaining process to negotiate wage levels and conditions of employment with management.

Where a union represents a portion of an organization's workforce, many of the management decisions we have discussed in this chapter are spelled out in the collective bargaining contract. For instance, recruitment sources, hiring criteria, work schedules, safety rules, redress procedures, and eligibility for training programs are typical issues addressed in the contract. The most obvious and pervasive area of union influence, of course, is wage rates and working conditions. Where unions exist, performance appraisal systems tend to be less complex than in nonunion organizations because they play a relatively small part in reward decisions. Seniority usually takes priority over performance in decisions regarding job preferences, work schedules, and layoffs. Wage rates, when determined by collective bargaining, also tend to emphasize seniority and downplay performance differences.

The bottom line is that when employees are represented by a union and are covered by a collective bargaining contract, managers need to familiarize themselves with the details of that contract. And if problems surface from the contract that make it difficult to effectively manage unionized members, managers should convey these problems to the organization's labor relations specialist or senior management. This information can then be used to correct those problems in future negotiations. And there's good news on this front! In contrast to the past, when labor and management negotiations were typically adversarial in nature, unions are now increasingly taking the initiative to become partners with management.[95] Many unions are openly cooperating with management to increase productivity, maintain organizational competitiveness, and in the process protect jobs.

There is a variety of additional material available on the CD-ROM and companion Web site that accompany this text. You can access this information through the CD-ROM or by visiting the Web site at <**www.prenhall.com/robbins**>.

SUMMARY

(This summary is organized by the chapter-opening learning objectives on page 266.)

1. Job analysis defines the jobs within the organization and the behaviors that are necessary to perform them. Job descriptions and specifications come out of the job analysis.

They describe the job and qualifications needed by the jobholder.

2. A selection device must be valid because validity assures that it will be an accurate predictor. If it is not valid, then it will not contribute to identifying effective candidates.

Selection devices must be reliable to ensure that results will be consistent over time. If results are erratic, managers can't depend on them in the selection process.

3. The general evidence linking IQ to job performance is impressive. Specifically, the greater a job's ambiguity and complexity, the better IQ is in predicting a candidate's performance in that job.

4. Sources for job applicants include current employees, employee referrals, former employees, advertisements, employment agencies, college recruiting, and customers and suppliers.

5. The major strength of the interview as a selection device is that it is reasonably effective for tapping a candidate's intelligence, level of motivation, and interpersonal skills. Unstructured interviews tend to be biased in favor of similar attitudes between interviewer and applicant, biased against negative information, and influenced strongly by the order in which applicants are interviewed.

6. Effective interviews begin with preparation. You need to review the candidate's application and résumé, the position's job description and job specification, and structure the agenda for the interview. When the candidate arrives, put him or her at ease with a few simple questions or ice-breaking statements. Then provide a brief orientation. Ask

questions and use follow-up questions for clarification. Ask questions that require elaboration. Use silence to encourage the candidate to talk. Conclude the interview with a clear indication that the interview is over, ask the candidate if he or she has any questions, and then tell the candidate what will happen next. Write your evaluation of the candidate as soon as the interview is over.

7. Training can improve an employee's basic literacy, technical, interpersonal, and problem-solving skills.

8. The primary methods for appraising employee performance include written essays, critical incidents, graphic rating scales, behaviorally anchored rating scales (BARS), and multiperson comparisons.

9. Sexual harassment is defined as sexually suggestive remarks, unwanted touching and sexual advances, requests for sexual favors, and other verbal and physical contact of a sexual nature. To reduce its occurrence, management needs a written policy statement that is well communicated, training, specific penalties for breaking the policy, and strong enforcement of the policy.

10. To help employees develop their careers, you should: clearly communicate the organization's goals and future strategies, create growth opportunities, offer financial assistance, and provide the time for employees to learn.

REVIEW QUESTIONS

1. Give some examples of HRM practices that are governed by laws and regulations in your country.

2. What pluses and minuses for the organization do you see in using temporary employees as a pool from which to select permanent employees? Are there any pluses from the temporary employee's standpoint?

3. What are the costs of reject errors? Of accept errors?

4. What is an assessment center? Why do you think it has proved to be a valid selection predictor?

5. Describe the proper way to conduct a selection interview.

6. Explain why training has gained increased importance in the HRM process during the past decade.

7. Why is it better to appraise employee behaviors rather than traits?

8. Besides firing employees, what other options does management have if it finds its organization overstaffed?

9. Contrast current career development programs in most large organizations with those programs 20 years ago.

10. How does the existence of a labor union affect HRM practices?

IF I WERE THE MANAGER . . .

Hiring Criteria

You decided to take the entrepreneurial plunge. You opened up a retail bath and beauty store in a local shopping mall.

One of your earliest decisions was hiring. Your selection criteria? People you knew and felt you could trust. And who were these? Family members and close friends. So the first five people you hired were your sister, a sister-in-law, and three long-time friends.

After less than two months, problems have begun to appear. Your "staff" finds it hard to see you as the boss. When you would tell them to do something, they'd treat it as a suggestion rather than an order. No one acknowledged your authority. Your employees also seemed lackidaisical. You kept telling them to approach customers promptly when they entered the store. More often than not, customers spent several minutes looking around before anyone approached them. Many left without ever having had anyone speak to them. The few rules you had established were essentially ignored. For instance, the 15-minute morning and afternoon breaks typically lasted more than 30 minutes. And instead of staggering their 45-minute lunch period between 11:00 A.M. and 1:30 P.M., they tended to take lunches together. The result has been that you're often understaffed during this time each day. To make matters even worse, your employees seem regularly to call in on short notice

to tell you they're taking the day off. Just last Thursday, while you were out of the store visiting a supplier, no one showed up to open the store until 1:00 P.M. Stores in the mall are supposed to be open at 9 A.M.

Had you made a mistake hiring friends and family? What should you do now?

Conducting Effective Interviews

1. Break into groups of three.
2. Take up to 10 minutes to compose five challenging job interview questions that you think would be relevant in the hiring of new college graduates for a sales-management training program at Procter & Gamble. Each hiree will spend 18 to 24 months as a sales representative calling on retail grocers. After this training period, successful candidates can be expected to be promoted to the position of district sales supervisor.
3. Exchange your five questions with another group.

4. Each group should allocate one of the following roles to their three members: interviewer, applicant, and observer. The person playing the applicant should rough out a brief résumé of his or her background and experience, and then give it to the interviewer.
5. Role play a job interview. The interviewer should include, but not be limited to, the questions provided by the other group.
6. After the interview, the observer should evaluate the interviewer's behaviors in terms of the selection-interviewing skills box presented earlier in the chapter.

Developing a Class Sexual-Harassment Policy

Break into groups of five or six. Your task is to create a sexual-harassment policy for your classmates and instructor that can guide them in their classroom behavior. Do not refer to any formal college or university policies on this subject. You are to develop yours from scratch. Make sure that it is in writing and clearly legible for others to read.

You have 45 minutes to complete this exercise. When completed, exchange your written policy statement with another group in your class. Evaluate their statement. What are its strengths and weaknesses? What did you learn from evaluating their statement that can help you improve the one your group developed?

Hiring at Southwest Airlines

At Southwest Airlines, the People Department is one of the company's most important functions. This 125-member department handles all the company's hiring. And they keep busy. In 1996, for example, they received more than 150,000 applications for about 4,500 job openings.

What are Southwest's recruiters looking for in a candidate?

"An attitude," says one. "A genuineness—a sense of what it takes to be one of us." They have to be people who match up with the company's famously offbeat and customer-obsessed culture. The vice president of the People Department, Libby Sartain, only half-jokingly says that taking a job with Southwest is like joining a cult. The ultimate employee is someone whose devotion to customer and company amounts to "a sense of mission, a sense that 'the cause' comes before their own needs."

Southwest's CEO is on record as having said that his company can find lots of people with the technical skills that are necessary to serve customers on the ground or in the air. But the characteristics that are critical to being a good Southwest employee—like energy and humor—are innate. The company has to hire people who already have those qualities.

Southwest's management favors an informal approach to job interviews. Take, for example, how Rita Bailey, the firm's manager of corporate employment, chose to handle the initial interviews for an opening in the airline's "special marketing" department. This department seeks to attract more business-women, elderly, and young people as passengers.

Four female applicants, led by Bailey, sit around talking amicably about everything from their childhoods to tough problems they've faced on the job. For 2 hours, the four applicants chat while Bailey evaluates. In this case, Bailey considers the marketing background of the four women as important. But she is more intent on finding a self-starter who has a willingness to pitch in on any job, even blowing up balloons for festive events. Bailey also is looking for subtler clues—how the candidates interact. "We just want the kind of person who can relate to everybody and everything." For this marketing position, Bailey has already interviewed twenty-two applicants. None of the four candidates in this session quite fits the bill, so there will be no callbacks.

Bailey admits that this is a time-consuming process. But she insists that the company won't compromise quality to speed up its hiring process. Because Southwest is growing so fast and insists on this lengthy hiring process, the People Department's staff is taxed to its limits. In actuality, if Southwest followed more traditional hiring procedures, it might be able to fill positions much more quickly and with a far smaller human resources department.

QUESTIONS

1. Contrast Southwest's hiring process with your personal experiences in getting a job.
2. "In a dynamic industry, where firms must respond quickly, Southwest's approach to employment selection is neither effective nor efficient." Do you agree or disagree with this statement? Discuss.
3. On the basis of your knowledge of hiring, what suggestions would you make to help Southwest increase the probability of finding successful candidates?
4. What suggestions would you make to Bailey to help her increase the probability of finding the right person to fit the marketing vacancy?

Source: Based on W. Zellner, "Southwest," *Business Week*, February 13, 1995, p. 69; P. Carbonara, "Hire for Attitude, Train for Skill," *Fast Company*, Greatest Hits, vol. 1, 1997, pp. 64–66; and J. Martin, "So, You Want to Work for the Best . . . ," *Fortune*, January 12, 1998, pp. 77–78.

VIDEO CASE EXERCISE

The Fine Art of Managing People

Every business has three basic components, or the three Ps: the *product*, or service being provided; the *process*, or the way the product or service is being delivered; and the *people*. Of those three components, the most crucial is the people. Successful business owners are likely to say that the single most important factor in their business's success is the people. Although there's some science behind managing people, there's a lot of art as well. What do some successful businesspeople have to say about the fine art of managing people? Let's take a look!

Jeff Gordon, owner of an ad agency in Washington, D.C., says that recruitment is the single most important task of any business leader. He recruits full time, and he may have to sift through 150–300 people to get that one outstanding person. However, in his business, he has to put that kind of effort into recruiting to identify the "gems" who are so critical to his company's success.

Jill and Doug Smith approached people management somewhat differently than what experts advise. They have developed their business, Buckeye Beans and Herbs of Spokane, Washington, using friends and family. And as Jill says, this approach can be either a tremendous negative or a tremendous positive. It's been a tremendous positive for their business because they all share similar values. In fact, she describes her business as a value-added people company.

When Dale Crownover, owner of Texas Name-Plate of Dallas, Texas, implemented a quality improvement program, he found that his employees wanted more communication opportunities. At the company's monthly meetings, regular employees (not just managers) get involved. Crownover says it's really all about sharing and communicating; letting employees know the goals, the plans, why we're doing what we're doing, and how we're doing. Very simply, he's found that employees want to be part of something.

Finally, Greg Thurman of Hartford Communication in Priest River, Idaho, says he doesn't tell people what to do but asks them what they think they should do to solve a problem. His goal was to create an environment in which people didn't feel stifled. As Thurman says, "I don't know every job as well as the people doing the job." Therefore, instead of telling them how to do their jobs, he encourages employees to look for answers and then together they "polish" a solution.

QUESTIONS

1. What "people" advice did each of the four business owners profiled give?

2. What's your opinion of the advice these business owners gave?

3. How could the advice that each of these business owners described help in the design of an organization's HRM programs and actions? Be specific.

Source: Based on *Small Business 2000, Show 413*.

NOTES

1. See R. Lieber, "Wired for Hiring: Microsoft's Slick Recruiting Machine," *Fortune*, February 5, 1996, pp. 123–24; R. E. Stross, "Microsoft's Big Advantage–Hiring Only the Supersmart," *Fortune*, November 25, 1996, pp. 160–62; and N. Munk and S. Oliver, "Think Fast!" *Forbes*, March 24, 1997, pp. 146–51.

2. J. Pfeffer, "Producing Sustainable Competitive Advantage through the Effective Management of People," *Academy of Management Executive*, February 1995, pp. 55–69; and M. A. Huselid, S. E. Jackson, and R. S. Schuler, "Technical and Strategic Human Resource Management Effectiveness as Determinants of Firm Performance," *Academy of Management Journal*, February 1997, pp. 171–88.

3. This example is based on L. M. Litvan, "The Disabilities Law: Avoid the Pitfalls," *Nation's Business*, January 1994, pp. 26–27.

4. R. Pear, "Employers Told to Accommodate the Mentally Ill," *New York Times*, April 30, 1997, p. A1; and E. J. Pollock and J. S. Lublin, "Employers Are Wary of Rules on Mentally Ill," *New York Times*, May 1, 1997, p. B1.

5. Cited in K. A. Kovach, "Comparable Worth: The Canadian Legislation," *Business Horizons*, January–February 1996, p. 42.

6. Cited in P. C. Wright, R. W. Mondy, and R. M. Noe III, *Human Resource Management in Canada* (Scarborough, Ontario: Prentice Hall Canada, 1996).

7. Ibid.

8. This section is based on C. R. Greer and G. K. Stephens, "Employee Relations Issues for U.S. Companies in Mexico," *California Management Review*, Spring 1996, pp. 121–44; and R. S. Schuler, S. E. Jackson, E. Jackofsky, and J. W. Slocum Jr., "Managing Human Resources in Mexico: A Cultural Understanding," *Business Horizons*, May–June 1996, pp. 55–61.

9. This section is based on R. S. Schuler, P. J. Dowling, J. P. Smart, and V. L. Huber, *Human Resource Management in Australia*, 2nd ed. (New South Wales: HarperEducational, 1992), pp. 117, 119, 142; and "Australia Is Set to Reduce Power of Unions," *New York Times*, October 31, 1996, p. C5.

10. J. L. Cotton, *Employee Involvement* (Newbury Park, CA: Sage, 1993), p. 114. See also M. Poole, "Industrial Democracy: A Comparative Analysis," *Industrial Relations*, Fall 1979, pp. 262–72.

11. P. R. Harris and R. T. Moran, *Managing Cultural Differences*, 4th ed. (Houston: Gulf Publishing, 1996), p. 323.

12. P. Klebnikov, "Bringing Back the Beetle," *Forbes*, April 7, 1997, pp. 42–44; and D. Woodruff, "'The German Worker Is Making a Sacrifice,'" *Business Week*, July 28, 1997, pp. 46–47.

13. K. L. Miller, "'Without Training, I Can't Start My Real Life,'" *Business Week*, September 16, 1996, p. 60.

14. See, for instance, J. Walker, *Human Resource Management Strategy* (New York: McGraw-Hill, 1992).

15. See S. L. Rynes, "Recruitment, Job Choice, and Post-Hire Consequences: A Call for New Research Directions," in M. D. Dunnette and L. M. Hough (eds.), *Handbook of Industrial & Organizational Psychology*, 2nd ed. (Palo Alto, CA: Consulting Psychologists Press, 1991), pp. 399–444.

16. Cited in E. M. Friedman, "Almanac: A Statistical and Informational Snapshot of the Business World Today," *Inc: The State of Small Business, 1997*, p. 108.

17. See L. Uchitelle, "Employers Hustle to Fill Job Rolls, Without Pay Raises," *New York Times*, April 6, 1998, p. A1; and C. Caggiano, "Recruiting Secrets," *Inc.*, October 1998, pp. 30–42.

18. L. R. Gomez-Mejia, D. B. Balkin, and R. L. Cardy, *Managing Human Resources*, 2nd ed. (Upper Saddle River, NJ: Prentice Hall, 1998), p. 154.

19. K. A. Dolan, "Help Wanted: Urgent!" *Forbes*, October 7, 1996, pp. 18–20; and S. Baker and A. Barrett, "Calling All Nerds," *Business Week*, March 10, 1997, pp. 36–37.

20. See, for example, L. M. Litvan, "Casting a Wider Net," *Nation's Business*, December 1994, pp. 49–51; and D. D. Buss, "Help Wanted Desperately," *Nation's Business*, April 1996, p. 19.

21. See, for example, R. Resnick, "Leasing Workers," *Nation's Business*, November 1992, pp. 20–28; T. G. Block, "Brains for Rent," *Forbes*, July 31, 1995, pp. 99–100; and J. Aley, "The Temp Biz Boom: Why It's Good," *Fortune*, October 16, 1995, pp. 53–56.

22. D. L. Boroughs, "Business Gives in to Temptation," *U.S. News & World Report*, July 4, 1994, pp. 56–57.

23. V. Frazee, "The Try-Before-You-Buy Method of Hiring," *Personnel Journal* (supplement), August 1996, pp. 6–8.

24. Cited in M. Klimas, "How to Recruit a Smart Team," *Nation's Business*, May 1995, p. 26.

25. See J. C. Ullman, "Employee Referrals: Prime Tool for Recruiting Workers," *Personnel*, May–June 1966, pp. 30–35;

and J. P. Kirnan, J. A. Farley, and K. F. Geisinger, "The Relationship between Recruiting Source, Applicant Quality, and Hire Performance: An Analysis by Sex, Ethnicity, and Age," *Personnel Psychology*, Summer 1989, pp. 293–308.

26. C. R. Williams, C. E. Labig Jr., and T. H. Stone, "Recruitment Sources and Posthire Outcomes for Job Applicants and New Hires: A Test of Two Hypotheses," *Journal of Applied Psychology*, April 1993, pp. 163–72; and R. P. Vecchio, "The Impact of Referral Sources on Employee Attitudes: Evidence from a National Sample," *Journal of Management*, vol. 21, no. 5, 1995, pp. 935–65.

27. Williams, Labig, and Stone, "Recruitment Sources and Posthire Outcomes for Job Applicants and New Hires," p. 171.

28. For instance, see R. L. Dipboye, *Selection Interviews: Process Perspectives* (Cincinnati, OH: South-Western Publishing, 1992); and W. F. Cascio, *Applied Psychology in Human Resource Management*, 5th ed. (Upper Saddle River, NJ: Prentice Hall, 1998).

29. This box is based on information from R. Maynard, "Casting the Net For Job Seekers," *Nation's Business*, March 1997, pp. 28–29; V. Pospisil, "Recruitment Added to Web Sites," *Industry Week*, April 21, 1997, p. 12; E. I. Schwartz, "A New Reality," *Business Week*, February 9, 1998, p. ENT 7; and J. Martin, "Changing Jobs? Try the Net," *Fortune*, March 2, 1998, pp. 205–08.

30. See A. Rafaeli and R. J. Klimoski, "Predicting Sales Success through Handwriting Analysis: An Evaluation of the Effects of Training and Handwriting Sample Content," *Journal of Applied Psychology*, May 1983, pp. 212–17; and A. Fowler, "An Even-Handed Approach to Graphology," *Personnel Management*, March 1991, pp. 40–43.

31. J. J. Asher, "The Biographical Item: Can It Be Improved?" *Personnel Psychology*, Summer 1972, p. 266.

32. G. W. England, *Development and Use of Weighted Application Blanks*, rev. ed. (Minneapolis: Industrial Relations Center, University of Minnesota, 1971).

33. D. S. Ones, C. Viswesvaran, and F. L. Schmidt, "Comprehensive Meta-Analysis of Integrity Test Validities: Findings and Implications for Personnel Selection and Theories of Job Performance," *Journal of Applied Psychology*, August 1993, pp. 679–703; and P. R. Sackett and J. E. Wanek, "New Developments in the Use of Measures of Honesty, Integrity, Conscientiousness, Dependability, Trustworthiness, and Reliability for Personnel Selection," *Personnel Psychology*, Winter 1996, pp. 787–829.

34. R. M. Guion and R. F. Gottier, "Validity of Personality Measures in Personnel Selection," *Personnel Psychology*, Summer 1965, pp. 135–63.

35. M. R. Barrick and M. K. Mount, "The Big Five Personality Dimensions and Job Performance: A Meta-Analysis," *Personnel Psychology*, Spring 1991, pp. 1–26.

36. Ibid.

37. R. J. Herrnstein and C. Murray, *The Bell Curve: Intelligence and Class Structure in American Life* (New York: Free Press, 1994).

38. Ibid., pp. 51–89. See also the statement, signed by fifty-two experts in intelligence and allied fields, "Mainstream Science on Intelligence," *Wall Street Journal*, December 13,

1994, p. A18. For further critiques, see R. Jacoby and N. Glauberman (eds.), *The Bell Curve Debate* (New York: Times Books, 1995); and J. L. Kincheloe, S. R. Steinberg, and A. D. Gresson III (eds.), *Measured Lies: The Bell Curve Examined* (New York: St. Martin's, 1996).

39. Herrnstein and Murray, *The Bell Curve*; and M. J. Ree, J. A. Earles, and M. S. Teachout, "Predicting Job Performance: Not Much More Than *g*," *Journal of Applied Psychology*, August 1994, pp. 518–24; and W. Borman, M. Hanson, and J. Hedges, "Personnel Selection," in J. T. Spence, J. M. Darley, and D. J. Foss (eds.), *Annual Review of Psychology*, vol. 48, 1997, pp. 299–337.

40. Herrnstein and Murray, *The Bell Curve*, p. 88.

41. P. Carbonara, "Hire for Attitude, Train for Skill," *Fast Company*, Greatest Hits, vol. 1, 1997, p. 68.

42. J. J. Asher and J. A. Sciarrino, "Realistic Work Sample Tests: A Review," *Personnel Psychology*, Winter 1974, pp. 519–33; and I. T. Robertson and R. S. Kandola, "Work Sample Tests: Validity, Adverse Impact and Applicant Reaction," *Journal of Occupational Psychology*, Spring 1982, pp. 171–82.

43. P. Carbonara, "Hire for Attitude, Train for Skill," p. 68.

44. G. C. Thornton, *Assessment Centers in Human Resource Management* (Reading, MA: Addison-Wesley, 1992).

45. Dipboye, *Selection Interviews*, p. 6.

46. L. Yoo-Lim, "More Companies Rely on Employee Interviews," *Business Korea*, November 1994, pp. 22–23.

47. T. J. Hanson and J. C. Balestreri-Spero, "An Alternative to Interviews," *Personnel Journal*, June 1985, p. 114. See also T. W. Dougherty, D. B. Turban, and J. C. Callender, "Confirming First Impressions in the Employment Interview: A Field Study of Interviewer Behavior," *Journal of Applied Psychology*, October 1994, pp. 659–65.

48. See A. I. Huffcutt and W. Arthur Jr., "Hunter and Hunter (1984) Revisited: Interview Validity for Entry-Level Jobs," *Journal of Applied Psychology*, April 1994, pp. 184–90; M. A. McDaniel, D. L. Whetzel, F. L. Schmidt, and S. D. Maurer, "The Validity of Employment Interviews: A Comprehensive Review and Meta-Analysis," *Journal of Applied Psychology*, August 1994, pp. 599–616; and J. M. Conway, R. A. Jako, and D. F. Goodman, "A Meta-Analysis of Interrater and Internal Consistency Reliability of Selection Interviews," *Journal of Applied Psychology*, October 1995, pp. 565–79.

49. Dipboye, *Selection Interviews*, pp. 42–44.

50. W. C. Borman, M. A. Hanson, and J. W. Hedge, "Personnel Selection," in J. T. Spence, J. M. Darley, and D. J. Foss, eds., *Annual Review of Psychology*, vol. 48, 1997, pp. 314–17; and M. A. Campion, D. K. Palmer, and J. E. Campion, "A Review of Structure in the Selection Interview," *Personnel Psychology*, Autumn 1997, pp. 655–702.

51. Cascio, *Applied Psychology in Human Resource Management*, p. 149.

52. See, for instance, R. R. Reilly, B. Brown, M. R. Blood, and C. Z. Malatesta, "The Effects of Realistic Previews: A Study and Discussion of the Literature," *Personnel Psychology*, Winter 1981, pp. 823–34; J. A. Breaugh, "Realistic Job Previews: A Critical Appraisal and Future Research Direction," *Academy of Management Review*, October 1983, pp. 612–19; R. J. Vandenberg and V. Scarpello, "The Matching

Model: An Examination of the Processes Underlying Realistic Job Previews," *Journal of Applied Psychology*, February 1990, pp. 60–67; and R. D. Bretz Jr. and T. A. Judge, "Realistic Job Previews: A Test of the Adverse Self-Selection Hypothesis," *Journal of Applied Psychology*, April 1998, pp. 330–37.

53. Reilly, Brown, Blood, and Malatesta, "The Effects of Realistic Previews."

54. Cited in *Training*, October 1998, p. 48.

55. W. F. Cascio, *Costing Human Resources: The Financial Impact of Behavior in Organizations*, 3rd ed. (Boston: PWS/Kent, 1991); and C. C. Morrow, M. Q. Jarrett, and M. T. Rupinski, "An Investigation of the Effect and Economic Utility of Corporate-Wide Training," *Personnel Journal*, Spring 1997, pp. 91–119.

56. Cited in W. H. Miller, "The Future? Not Yet," *Industry Week*, April 17, 1995, p. 73.

57. Cited in J. C. Szabo, "Training Workers for Tomorrow," *Nation's Business*, March 1993, pp. 22–32.

58. See K. Kelly, "Motorola: Training for the Millennium," *Business Week*, March 28, 1994, pp. 158–63; and L. Grant, "A School for Success," *U.S. News & World Report*, May 22, 1995, pp. 53–55.

59. M. Barrier, "Closing the Skills Gap," *Nation's Business*, March 1996, p. 26.

60. See I. L. Goldstein, *Training in Organizations: Needs Assessment, Development, and Evaluation*, 2nd ed. (Monterey, CA: Brooks/Cole, 1986); and K. M. Nowack, "A True Training Needs Analysis," *Training and Development Journal*, April 1991, pp. 69–73.

61. Cited in M. Hequet, "The Union Push for Lifelong Learning," *Training*, March 1994, p. 31.

62. Reported in *From School to Work* (Princeton, NJ: Educational Testing Service, 1990).

63. J. C. Szabo, "Honing Workers' Basic Skills," *Nation's Business*, May 1994, p. 69.

64. See M. Messmer, "Cross-Discipline Training: A Strategic Method to Do More with Less," *Management Review*, May 1992, pp. 26–28.

65. J. E. Santora, "Keep Up Production through Cross-Training," *Personnel Journal*, June 1992, pp. 162–66.

66. See S. P. Robbins and P. Hunsaker, *Training in InterPersonal Skills: TIPS for Managing People at Work*, 2nd ed. (Upper Saddle River, NJ: Prentice Hall, 1996).

67. This section is based on P. F. Miller and W. T. Coady, "Teaching Work Ethics," *Education Digest*, February 1990, pp. 54–55; D. Rice and C. Dreilinger, "Rights and Wrongs of Ethics Training," *Training and Development Journal*, May 1990, pp. 103–08; J. Weber, "Measuring the Impact of Teaching Ethics to Future Managers: A Review, Assessment, and Recommendations," *Journal of Business Ethics*, March 1990, pp. 183–90; and R. Goodell, "Ethics in American Business: Policies, Programs, and Perceptions." Report of the Ethics Resource Center, Washington, DC, 1994.

68. H. B. Karp, "Choices in Diversity Training," *Training*, August 1994, pp. 73–74; S. Nelton, "Nurturing Diversity," *Nation's Business*, June 1995, pp. 25–27; S. Rynes and B. Rosen, "A Field Survey of Factors Affecting the Adoption and Perceived Success of Diversity Training," *Personnel Psychology*, Spring 1995, pp. 247–70; and J. K. Ford and

S. Fisher, "The Role of Training in a Changing Workplace and Workforce: New Perspectives and Approaches," in E. E. Kossek and S. A. Lobel (eds.), *Managing Diversity* (Cambridge, MA: Blackwell, 1996), pp. 164–93.

69. For an extended discussion of on-the-job and off-the-job training methods, see D. DeCenzo and S. P. Robbins, *Human Resource Management*, 6th ed. (New York: Wiley, 1999), pp. 230–32. See also M. A. Verespej, "Formal Training: 'Secondary' Education?" *Industry Week*, January 5, 1998, pp. 42–46.

70. "Training That U.S. Businesses Do Not Need," *Manpower Argus*, July 1996, p. 7; and A. Field, "Class Act," *Inc. Technology*, vol. 1, 1997, pp. 55–59.

71. D. Schaaf, "Inside Hamburger University," *Training*, December 1994, pp. 18–24.

72. Cited in N. Austin, "Where Employee Training Works," *Working Woman*, May 1993, p. 23.

73. D. A. Kolb, "Management and the Learning Process," *California Management Review*, Spring 1976, pp. 21–31; and B. Filipczak, "Different Strokes: Learning Styles in the Classroom," *Training*, March 1995, pp. 43–48.

74. J. N. Cleveland, K. R. Murphy, and R. E. Williams, "Multiple Uses of Performance Appraisal: Prevalence and Correlates," *Journal of Applied Psychology*, February 1989, pp. 130–35.

75. A. H. Locher and K. S. Teel, "Appraisal Trends," *Personnel Journal*, September 1988, pp. 139–45.

76. G. P. Latham and K. N. Wexley, *Increasing Productivity through Performance Appraisal* (Reading, MA: Addison-Wesley, 1981), p. 80.

77. See review in R. D. Bretz Jr., G. T. Milkovich, and W. Read, "The Current State of Performance Appraisal Research and Practice: Concerns, Directions, and Implications," *Journal of Management*, June 1992, p. 326.

78. "Appraisals: Reverse Reviews," *Inc.*, October 1992, p. 33.

79. See H. J. Bernardin, "An 'Analytic' Framework for Customer-Based Performance Content Development and Appraisal," *Human Resource Management*, Summer 1992, pp. 81–102; and J. W. Hedge and W. C. Borman, "Changing Conceptions and Practices in Performance Appraisal," in A. Howard (ed.), *The Changing Nature of Work* (San Francisco: Jossey-Bass, 1995), pp. 458–59.

80. See, for instance, J. E. Jones and W. L. Bearley, *360° Feedback: Strategy, Tactics, and Techniques for Developing Leaders* (Amherst, MA: HRD Press, 1996); R. Lepsinger and A. D. Lucia, "360° Feedback and Performance Appraisal," *Training*, September 1997, pp. 62–70; A. Furnham and P. Stringfield, "Congruence in Job-Performance Ratings: A Study of 360° Feedback Examining Self, Manager, Peers, and Consultant Ratings," *Human Relations*, April 1998, pp. 517–30; D. A. Waldman, L. E. Atwater, and D. Antonioni, "Has 360 Degree Feedback Gone Amok?" *Academy of Management Executive*, May 1998, pp. 86–94; and W. W. Tornow and M. London, *Maximizing the Value of 360-Degree Feedback* (San Francisco: Jossey-Bass, 1998).

81. D. Antonioni, "Designing an Effective 360-Degree Appraisal Feedback Process," *Organizational Dynamics*, Autumn 1996, pp. 24–38.

82. C. Lee, "Performance Appraisal: Can We 'Manage' Away the Curse?" *Training*, May 1996, pp. 44–59.

83. Much of this section is based on H. H. Meyer, "A Solution to the Performance Appraisal Feedback Enigma," *The Executive*, February 1991, pp. 68–76.

84. R. J. Burke, "Why Performance Appraisal Systems Fail," *Personnel Administration*, June 1972, pp. 32–40.

85. B. R. Nathan, A. M. Mohrman Jr., and J. Milliman, "Interpersonal Relations as a Context for the Effects of Appraisal Interviews on Performance and Satisfaction: A Longitudinal Study," *Academy of Management Journal*, June 1991, pp. 352–69.

86. J. Zigon, "Making Performance Appraisal Work for Teams," *Training*, June 1994, pp. 58–63.

87. See, for example, L. Greenhalgh, A. T. Lawrence, and R. I. Sutton, "Determinants of Work Force Reduction Strategies in Declining Organizations," *Academy of Management Review*, April 1988, pp. 241–54.

88. B. S. Moskal, "Want to 'Rent' an Engineer?" *Industry Week*, March 7, 1994, p. 68.

89. See, for example, L. F. Fitzgerald and S. L. Shullman, "Sexual Harassment: A Research Analysis and Agenda for the 1990s," *Journal of Vocational Behavior*, February 1993, pp. 5–27; and "Sexual Harassment Complaints on the Rise," *HRMagazine*, February 1998, p. 28.

90. Cited in "Cost of Sexual Harassment in the U.S.," *Manpower Argus*, January 1997, p. 5.

91. A. R. Karr, "Issue of Sex Harassment at Workplace Is Getting More Attention World-Wide," *Wall Street Journal*, December 1, 1992, p. A2.

92. "Mexico: Sexual Harassment in the Workplace," *Manpower Argus*, March 1997, p. 8.

93. This section is based on D. T. Hall, "Protean Careers of the 21st Century," *Academy of Management Executive*, November 1996, pp. 8–16; M. B. Arthur and D. Rousseau, "A New Career Lexicon for the 21st Century," *Academy of Management Executive*, November 1996, pp. 28–39; D. T. Hall and Associates (eds.), *The Career Is Dead—Long Live the Career* (San Francisco: Jossey-Bass, 1996); M. Cianni and D. Wnuck, "Individual Growth and Team Enhancement: Moving Toward a New Model of Career Development," *Academy of Management Executive*, February 1997, pp. 105–15; and D. Bencivenga, "Employers & Workers Come to Terms," *HRMagazine*, June 1997, pp. 91–97.

94. M. Hequet, "Flat and Happy?" *Training*, April 1995, pp. 29–34.

95. A. Bernstein, "Look Who's Pushing Productivity," *Business Week*, April 7, 1997, pp. 72–75.

UNDERSTANDING GROUPS AND DEVELOPING EFFECTIVE TEAMS

A LOT OF ATHLETES SAY THEY WANT TO BE PART OF A
COHESIVE TEAM—BUT THEY ALSO WANT THEIR NAME
PRINTED ON THE BACK OF THEIR JERSEYS IN
6-INCH-HIGH BLOCK LETTERS.

S. P. ROBBINS

LEARNING OBJECTIVES

After studying this chapter, you should be able to:

1 Contrast groups with teams and describe three types of teams.

2 Explain how roles and norms shape employee behavior.

3 Describe the relationship between group cohesiveness and productivity.

4 Explain the work-related implications of social loafing.

5 Identify the main characteristics of the grapevine.

6 Define *groupthink* and *groupshift* and discuss how they can affect group decision making.

7 List characteristics of high-performing teams.

8 Explain how management can transform individuals into team players.

9 Describe when teams may hinder organizational effectiveness.

The way people's tasks are organized can have a major influence on their productivity. Take the case of Custom Research Inc., a Minneapolis-based market-research firm.[1]

Custom Research had been organized around a traditional structure of functional departments. But in the early 1990s, the company's two partners, Jeffrey Pope and Judith Corson (see photo), became convinced that their organization no longer was well adapted to meet the changing needs of their clients and their own growth objectives. "Our clients were downsizing and asking more of us," recalled Corson. "We were also experiencing a flattening of growth, and we wanted to have a more consistent selling effort." The solution? Pope and Corson reorganized their firm's 100 employees into account teams, each headed by an account manager and a research manager with equal authority. By having every aspect of a client's work handled within the team rather than by separate departments, communication and tracking of work improved.

But this reorganization had a major drawback. Team members had become limited, learning only about the clients or the business categories handled by their team. So after a couple of years, Corson and Pope introduced another change: Once or twice a year staff members are reorganized into new teams, their size determined by the volume of work at hand.

Changing to a team approach has been a resounding success at Custom Research. Revenue per full-time employee has increased 70 percent. The firm's billings in 1996 totaled $22 million, up from just $10 million in 1985. Additionally, feedback from clients indicates improvement in project performance. Survey results show that the firm now meets or exceeds clients' expectations on 97 percent of its projects and that 92 percent of its clients rated the firm as better than the competition on level of service.

Teams are being introduced worldwide as a means to increase productivity, quality, and employee job satisfaction. In this chapter, we will describe various types of teams, some of the problems teams can create, and what management can do to increase the likelihood that teams in their organization will be high-performing.

Our current understanding of teams builds on a half-century of research on work groups. So let's begin this chapter by contrasting groups and teams and providing a brief review of basic group concepts.

GROUPS VERSUS TEAMS

Groups and teams are not the same thing.[2] A **group** is two or more individuals, interacting and interdependent, who have come together to achieve particular objectives. A **work group** is a group who interact primarily to share information and to make decisions to help each other perform within their separate areas of responsibility.

Work groups have no need or opportunity to engage in collective work that requires joint effort. So their performance is merely the summation of all the group members' individual contributions. There is no positive synergy that would create an overall level of performance that is greater than the sum of the inputs.

A **work team** generates positive synergy through coordinated effort. Their individual efforts result in a level of performance that is greater than the sum of those individual inputs. Exhibit 10-1 highlights the differences between work groups and work teams.

These definitions help clarify why so many organizations have recently restructured work processes around teams. Management is looking for that positive synergy that will allow their organization to increase performance. The extensive use of teams creates the *potential* for an organization to generate greater outputs with no increase in inputs. Note,

EXHIBIT 10-1   Comparing Work Groups and Work Teams

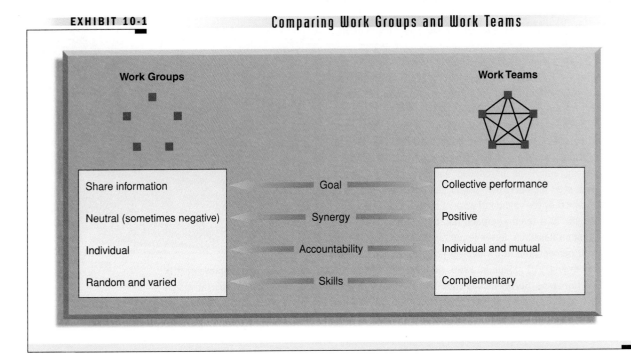

however, we said "potential." There is nothing inherently magical in the creation of teams that assures the achievement of this positive synergy. Merely calling a *group* a *team* does not automatically increase its performance. As we'll show later in this chapter, successful or high-performing teams have certain common characteristics. If management hopes to gain increases in organizational performance through the use of teams, it will need to ensure that the teams possess these characteristics.

BASIC GROUP CONCEPTS

The following review of basic group concepts builds on the recognition that groups are not unorganized mobs. They have a structure that shapes the behavior of their members.

Roles

Laura Campbell is a buyer with Marks & Spencer, the large British retailer. Her job requires her to play a number of **roles**, that is, to engage in a set of expected behavior patterns that are attributed to occupying a given position in a social unit. For instance, Laura plays the role of a Marks & Spencer employee, a member of the headquarter's buying group, a member of the cost-improvement task force, and an adviser to the committee on diversity. Off the job, Laura Campbell finds herself in still more roles: wife, mother, Methodist, member of the Labor Party, board member at her daughter's school, singer in the St. Andrews Chapel choir, and a member of the Surrey women's soccer league. Many of these roles are compatible; some create conflicts. For instance, a recent offer of a promotion would require Laura to relocate from London to Manchester, yet her husband and daughter want to remain in London. Can the role demands of her job be reconciled with the demands of her roles as wife and mother?

Like Laura Campbell, we all are required to play a number of roles, and our behavior varies with the role we are playing. The concept of roles can help us explain why Laura's behavior at her soccer league match on Saturday, for instance, is different from her behavior when participating in a meeting of her cost-improvement task force at work—the groups impose different identities and expectations on Laura.

The understanding of role behavior would be dramatically simplified if each of us chose one role and played it out regularly and consistently. Unfortunately, we don't. We can better understand an individual's behavior in specific situations if we know what role that person is playing.

On the basis of decades of role research, we can make the following conclusions:[3] (1) People play mulitple roles. (2) People learn roles from the stimuli around them—friends, books, movies, television. For instance, many current lawyers had their roles shaped by role models such as Perry Mason or cast members on *L.A. Law.* (3) People have the ability to shift roles rapidly when they recognize that the situation and its demands clearly require major changes. (4) And people often experience role conflict when compliance with one role requirement is at odds with another. An increasing number of people, for instance, are experiencing the stress that Laura Campbell is experiencing as a result of trying to reconcile work and family roles.[4]

If you're a manager, what value is a knowledge of roles? When you're dealing with employees, it helps to think in terms of what group they are predominantly identifying with at the time and what behaviors would be expected of them in that role. This perspective can often allow you to more accurately predict the employee's behavior and guide you in determining how best to handle situations with that employee.

▶ Norms

Did you ever notice that golfers don't speak while their partners are putting on the green or that most employees don't criticize their bosses in public? These behaviors are the result of **norms**—acceptable standards of behavior within a group that are shared by the group's members.[5]

All groups have norms. They tell members what they ought and ought not to do under certain circumstances. When agreed to and accepted by the group, norms act as a means of influencing the behavior of group members with a minimum of external

Golfing norms dictate that players don't speak while another is putting.

controls. Employees don't need a supervisor to tell them that throwing paper airplanes or gossiping at the water cooler are unacceptable behaviors when the big boss from New York is touring the office. The group norms that are operating tell them. A key point to remember about norms is that groups exert pressure on members to bring members' behavior into conformity with the group's standards. Group members can be expected to act to correct or even punish people in the group who violate its norms.

Because individuals desire acceptance by the groups to which they belong, they are susceptible to conformity pressures. The impact that group pressures for conformity can have on an individual member's judgment and attitudes was demonstrated in the now-classic studies by Solomon Asch.[6] Asch made up groups of seven or eight people who sat in a classroom and were asked to compare two cards held by the experimenter. One card had one line, the other had three lines of varying length. As shown in Exhibit 10-2, one of the lines on the three-line card was identical to the line on the one-line card. Also as shown in Exhibit 10-2, the difference in line length was quite obvious; under ordinary conditions, subjects made fewer than 1 percent errors. The object was to announce aloud which of the three lines matched the single line. But what would happen if the members in the group began to give incorrect answers? Would the pressures to conform cause an unsuspecting subject (USS) to alter his or her answer to align with the others? That was what Asch wanted to know. He arranged the group so that only the USS was unaware that the experiment was "fixed." The seating was prearranged: The USS was placed so as to be the last to announce his or her decision.

The experiment began with several sets of matching exercises. All the subjects gave the right answers. On the third set, however, the first subject gave an obviously wrong answer—for example, saying that "C" in Exhibit 10-2 matched "X". The next subject gave the same wrong answer, and so did the others. The USS knew that "B" was the same as "X," yet everyone had said "C." The decision confronting the USS was this: Do I publicly state a perception that differs from the preannounced position of the others in the group? Or do I give an answer that I strongly believe is incorrect in order to have my response agree with that of the other group members? Over many experiments and many trials, Asch's subjects conformed in about 35 percent of the trials; that is, the subjects gave answers that they knew were wrong but that were consistent with the replies of other group members.

Asch's findings suggest that people desire to be one of the group, to avoid being visibly different, and thus they feel pressure to conform. We can generalize these findings fur-

EXHIBIT 10-2

Examples of Cards Used in Asch Study

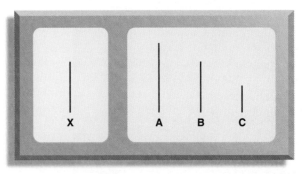

ther to say that when an individual's opinion of objective data differs significantly from that of others in the group, especially if the person has a strong need for acceptance, he or she feels extensive pressure to align his or her opinion to conform with that of the others.

Each group will establish its own set of norms. For instance, group norms might determine appropriate dress, when it's acceptable to goof off, with whom group members eat lunch, and friendships on and off the job. However, probably the most widespread norms—and the ones managers tend to be most concerned with—deal with performance-related processes. Work groups typically provide their members with explicit cues on how hard they should work, how to get the job done, their level of output, appropriate communication channels, and the like. These norms are extremely powerful in affecting an individual employee's performance. In fact, it's not unusual to find cases in which an employee with strong abilities and high personal motivation performs at a very modest level because of the overriding influence of group norms that discourage members from producing at high levels.

▶ Cohesiveness

Groups differ in their **cohesiveness**, that is, the degree to which members are attracted to each other and are motivated to stay in the group. For instance, some work groups are cohesive because the members have spent a great deal of time together, or the group's small size facilitates higher interaction, or the group has experienced external threats that have brought members closer together. Cohesiveness is important because it has been found to be related to the group's productivity.[7]

Studies consistently show that the relationship of cohesiveness and productivity depends on the performance-related norms established by the group. The more cohesive the group, the more its members will follow its goals. If performance-related norms are high (for example, high output, quality work, cooperation with individuals outside the group), a cohesive group will be more productive than will a less cohesive group. But if cohesiveness is high and performance norms are low, productivity will be low. If cohesiveness is low and performance norms are high, productivity increases, but less than in the high cohesiveness–high norms situation. Where cohesiveness and performance-related norms are both low, productivity will tend to fall into the low-to-moderate range. These conclusions are summarized in Exhibit 10-3 on page 310.

What can you, as a manager, do to encourage group cohesiveness? You might try one or more of the following suggestions:[8]

1. Make the group smaller.
2. Encourage agreement with group goals.
3. Increase the time members spend together.
4. Increase the status of the group and the perceived difficulty of attaining membership in the group.
5. Stimulate competition with other groups.
6. Give rewards to the group rather than to members.
7. Physically isolate the group.

▶ Size

Does the size of a group affect the group's overall behavior? The answer is a definite yes.[9] The evidence indicates, for instance, that smaller groups are faster at completing tasks than are larger ones. However, if the group is engaged in problem solving, large groups

EXHIBIT 10-3

Relationship Between Group Cohesiveness, Performance Norms, and Productivity

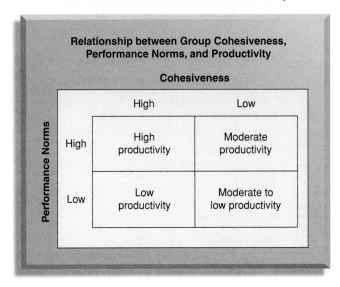

Relationship between Group Cohesiveness, Performance Norms, and Productivity

		Cohesiveness	
		High	Low
Performance Norms	High	High productivity	Moderate productivity
	Low	Low productivity	Moderate to low productivity

Research on social loafing demonstrates that increases in group size are inversely related to individual performance. So adding individuals to a tug-of-war contest will typically increase the team's pulling intensity at a decreasing rate.

consistently get better marks than their smaller counterparts. Translating these results into specific numbers is a bit more hazardous, but we can offer some parameters. Large groups—with a dozen or more members—are good for gaining diverse input. So if the goal of the group is fact finding, larger groups should be more effective. On the other hand, smaller groups are better at doing something productive with that input. Groups of approximately seven members, therefore, tend to be more effective for taking action.

One of the most important findings related to the size of a group has been labeled **social loafing**. Social loafing is the tendency for individuals to expend less effort when working collectively than when working individually. It directly challenges the logic that the productivity of the group as a whole should at least equal the sum of the productivity of all the individuals in that group.

A common stereotype about groups is that the sense of team spirit spurs individual effort and enhances the group's overall productivity. In the late 1920s, a German psychologist named Max Ringelmann compared the results of individual and group performance on a rope-pulling task.[10] He expected that the group's effort would be equal to the sum of the efforts of individuals within the group. That is, three people pulling together should exert three times as much pull on the rope as one person, and eight people should exert eight times as much pull. Ringelmann's results, however, did not confirm his expectations. Groups of three people exerted a force only two and a half times the average individual performance. Groups of eight collectively achieved less than four times the solo rate.

Replications of Ringelmann's research with similar tasks have generally supported his findings.[11] Increases in group size are inversely related to individual performance. More may be better in the sense that the total productivity of a group of four is greater than that of one or two people, but the individual productivity of each group member declines.

What causes this social loafing effect? It may be due to a belief that others in the group are not carrying their fair share. If you see others as lazy or inept, you can establish equity by reducing your effort. Another explanation is the dispersion of responsibility. Because the results of the group cannot be attributed to any single person, the relationship between an individual's input and the group's output is clouded. In such situations, individuals may be tempted to become "free riders" and coast on the group's efforts. In other words, there will be a reduction in efficiency when individuals think that their contribution cannot be measured.

The implications for managers of this effect on work groups is significant. Managers who utilize collective work situations to enhance morale and teamwork must also provide means by which individual efforts can be identified. If they don't, they must weigh the potential losses in productivity from using groups against any possible gains in worker satisfaction.[12] However, this conclusion has a Western bias. It is consistent with individualistic cultures, such as the United States and Canada, that are dominated by self-interest. It is not consistent with collective societies in which individuals are motivated by in-group goals. For instance, in studies comparing employees from the United States with employees from the People's Republic of China and Israel (both collectivist societies), the Chinese and Israelis showed no propensity to engage in social loafing. In fact, the Chinese and Israelis actually performed better in a group than when working alone.[13]

Composition

Most group activities require a variety of skills and knowledge. Given this requirement, it would be reasonable to conclude that heterogeneous groups—those composed of dissimilar individuals—would be more likely to have diverse abilities and information and should be more effective than homogeneous groups. Research studies generally substantiate that conclusion.[14]

When a group is heterogeneous in terms of gender, personalities, opinions, abilities, skills, and perspectives, there is an increased probability that the group will possess the needed characteristics to complete its tasks effectively.[15] The group may be more conflict-laden and less expedient as diverse positions are introduced and assimilated, but the evidence generally supports the conclusion that heterogeneous groups perform more effectively than do homogeneous ones.

What are the effects of diversity created by racial or national differences? The evidence indicates that these elements of diversity interfere with group processes, at least in the short-term.[16] Cultural diversity seems to be an asset on tasks that call for a variety of viewpoints. But culturally heterogeneous groups have difficulty in learning to work with each other and solving problems. The good news is that these difficulties seem to dissipate with time. Newly formed culturally diverse groups do not perform as well as newly formed culturally homogeneous groups, but the differences disappear after about 3 months. The reason is that it takes diverse groups a while to learn how to work through disagreements and different approaches to solving problems.

The managerial implications here are related to staffing formal groups and using groups to make decisions. To increase the performance of work groups, you should try to choose as members individuals who can bring a diverse perspective to problems and issues. But don't be surprised if these differences negatively affect the group's performance in the short-term. Be patient. As members learn to work with these differences, the group's performance will improve.

▶ Informal Communication: The Grapevine

When you put employees into groups, their communication is not limited to the formal channels as defined by their job descriptions or the chains of command. They also develop informal channels to share information. We call these informal channels the **grapevine**. All groups have them. They are a natural phenomenon whenever people get together. Regardless of how conscientious management is in using formal channels—official memos, press releases, supervisory announcements—the grapevine will still flourish. It helps bind people together, lets the powerless blow off steam, conveys concerns of employees, and fills in voids within the formal communication system.

> **The grapevine is perceived by most employees as being more believable and reliable than formal communiqués issued by top management.**

The grapevine has three main characteristics.[17] First, it is not controlled by management. Second, it is perceived by most employees as being more believable and reliable than formal communiqués issued by top management. Third, it is largely used to serve the self-interests of those people within it.

One of the most famous studies of the grapevine investigated the communication pattern among sixty-seven managerial personnel in a small manufacturing firm.[18] The basic approach used was to learn from each communication recipient how he first received a given piece of information and then trace it back to its source. It was found that, although the grapevine was an important source of information, only 10 percent of the executives acted as liaison individuals—that is, passed the information on to more than one other person. For example, when one executive decided to resign to enter the insurance business, 81 percent of the executives knew about it, but only 11 percent had transmitted the information to others.

Two other conclusions from this study are also worth noting. Information on events of general interest tended to flow between the major functional groups (that is, production and sales) rather than within them. Also, no evidence surfaced to suggest that members of any one group consistently acted as liaisons; rather, different types of information passed through different liaison persons.

An attempt to replicate this study among employees in a small state government office also found that only a small percentage (10 percent) acted as liaison individuals.[19] This finding is interesting because the replication contained a wider spectrum of employees—including rank-and-file and managerial personnel—than did the original study. However, the flow of information in the government office took place within, rather than between, functional groups. It was proposed that this discrepancy might be due to comparing an executive-only sample against one that also included rank-and-file workers. Managers, for example, might feel greater pressure to stay informed and thus cultivate others outside their immediate functional group. Also, in contrast to the findings of the original study, the replication found that a consistent group of individuals acted as liaisons by transmitting information in the government office.

Is the information that flows along the grapevine accurate? The evidence indicates that about 75 percent of what is carried is accurate.[20] But what conditions foster an active grapevine? What gets the rumor mill rolling?

It is frequently assumed that rumors start because they make titillating gossip. Such is rarely the case. Rumors have at least four purposes: to structure and reduce anxiety; to make sense of limited or fragmented information; to serve as a vehicle to organize group members, and possibly outsiders, into coalitions; and to signal a sender's status ("I'm an insider and, with respect to this rumor, you're an outsider") or power ("I have the power to make you into an insider").[21] Research indicates that rumors emerge as a response to situations that are important to us, where there is ambiguity, and under conditions that

---

EXHIBIT 10-4

Suggestions for Reducing the Negative Consequences of Rumors

1. Announce timetables for making important decisions.
2. Explain decisions and behaviors that may appear inconsistent or secretive.
3. Emphasize the downside, as well as the upside, of current decisions and future plans.
4. Openly discuss worst-case possibilities—discussing the worst possible case is almost never as anxiety-provoking as silently imagining it.

Source: Adapted from L. Hirschhorn, "Managing Rumors," in L. Hirschhorn (ed.), *Cutting Back* (San Francisco: Jossey-Bass, 1983), pp. 54–56. Reprinted with permission of L. Hirschhorn.

---

arouse anxiety.[22] Work situations frequently contain these three elements, which explains why rumors flourish in organizations. The secrecy and competition that typically prevail in large organizations—around such issues as the appointment of new bosses, the relocation of offices, and the realignment of work assignments—create conditions that encourage and sustain rumors on the grapevine. A rumor will persist either until the wants and expectations creating the uncertainty underlying the rumor are fulfilled or until the anxiety is reduced.

What can we conclude from this discussion? Certainly the grapevine is an important part of any group or organization's communication network and is well worth understanding.[23] It identifies for managers those confusing issues that employees consider important and anxiety-provoking. It acts, therefore, as both a filter and a feedback mechanism, picking up the issues that employees consider relevant. Maybe more important, again from a managerial perspective, it seems possible to analyze grapevine information and to predict its flow, given that only a small set of individuals (around 10 percent) actively passes on information to more than one other person. By assessing which liaison individuals will consider a given piece of information to be relevant, we can improve our ability to explain and predict the pattern of the grapevine.

Can management entirely eliminate rumors? No! What management should do, however, is minimize the negative consequences of rumors by limiting their range and impact. Exhibit 10-4 offers a few suggestions for minimizing those negative consequences.

Status

Status—that is, a socially defined position given to groups or group members by others—permeates most of the societies in which we live. Despite efforts to make many of them more egalitarian, we have made little progress toward creating classless societies. Even the smallest group will develop roles, rights, and rituals to differentiate its members. Status is an important factor in understanding human behavior primarily because it has major behavioral consequences when individuals perceive a disparity between what they believe their status to be and what others perceive it to be.

CHANGING SOURCES OF STATUS As recently as 20 years ago, status hierarchies tended to be largely defined by an individual's formal location in the organization. The higher your rank in the structure, the more status you were accorded. That's no longer completely true.[24] Today, an employee's degree of permanence within the organization and his or her level of expertise tend to be the prime sources of status.

As we noted in chapter 1, the need for flexibility has created different types of workers with various degrees of attachment to the organization. And greater status tends to be given to employees who have longer-term and more permanent ties to the organization. Permanent core employees are likely to be held in higher esteem than temporaries or independent contractors.

In the information age, where organizations covet knowledge workers, expertise carries enhanced status. Holding key information connotes status. As one author suggests, "you can tell how much you matter to an organization by counting the number of questions you're asked, e-mail messages or calls you receive, and decisions you're involved in."[25]

STATUS EQUITY It's important for group members to believe that the status hierarchy is equitable. When inequity is perceived, it creates disequilibrium that results in various types of corrective behavior.[26]

People expect rewards to be proportionate to costs incurred. If Dana and Anne are the two finalists for the head nurse position in a hospital, and it is clear that Dana has more seniority and better preparation for assuming the promotion, Anne will view the selection of Dana to be equitable. However, if Anne is chosen because she is the daughter-in-law of the hospital director, Dana will believe an injustice has been committed.

The trappings that go with formal positions are also important elements in maintaining equity. When we believe there is an inequity between the perceived ranking of an individual and the status accoutrements that person is given by the organization, we are experiencing status incongruence. This kind of incongruence occurs, for example, when the more desirable office location is held by a lower-ranking individual or when paid country club membership is provided by the company for division managers but not for vice presidents. Pay incongruence has long been a problem in the insurance industry, where top sales agents often earn two to five times more than senior corporate executives. The result is that it is very hard for insurance companies to entice agents into management positions. The importance of maintaining status equity is more problematic, but certainly as relevant, among specialized professionals. Although they may not hold managerial rank, their expertise is often highly coveted by the organization. Those with high status resulting from this expertise should, to maintain equity, receive higher pay, more stock options, more desirable offices, and the like. Our point is that employees expect the things an individual has and receives to be congruent with his or her status.

A person's status is often reflected in his or her office. Signs of high status include a large office on a high floor, paneled walls, a large and expensive desk, thick carpeting, an impressive view, and a private bathroom.

Groups generally agree within themselves on status criteria, and hence, there is usually high concurrence in group rankings of individuals. However, individuals can find themselves in a conflict situation when they move between groups whose status criteria are different or when they join groups whose members have heterogeneous backgrounds. For instance, business executives may use personal income or the growth rate of their companies as determinants of status. Government bureaucrats may use the size of their budgets. Professional employees may use the degree of autonomy that comes with their job assignment. Blue-collar workers may use years of seniority. Academics may use the number of grants received or articles published. In groups made up of heterogeneous individuals or when heterogeneous groups are forced to be interdependent, status differences may initiate conflict as the group attempts to reconcile and align the differing hierarchies. As we'll see later in this chapter, this can be a particular problem when mangement creates organizational teams made up of employees from varied functions or with varied expertise.

Conflict

Group members don't always see eye to eye on issues. Groups, therefore, can experience conflict. For our purposes, we'll define **conflict** as perceived incompatible differences that result in interference or opposition. This definition encompasses a wide range of actions—from overt and violent acts to subtle forms of disagreement.

Conflict can have obvious negative ramifications on a group's functioning. Disagreements and infighting can hurt the group when they misdirect members' efforts away from accomplishing goals to trying to resolve differences. At the extreme, conflict can breed discontent, can dissolve common ties, and can lead to the eventual demise of the group.

But all group conflicts aren't bad! Low and moderate levels of conflict have been shown to have positive influences on group performance.[27] How? By reducing apathy, stagnation, and resistance to change. The existence of some conflict keeps a group viable, self-critical, and creative. It improves the quality of decisions, stimulates creativity and innovation, encourages interest and curiosity among group members, provides the medium through which problems can be aired and tensions released, and fosters an environment of self-evaluation and change.

When conflicts become too great and hurt the group's effectiveness, managers need to reduce it. In chapter 17, when we discuss interpersonal skills, we'll present some specific suggestions to help you better manage conflict.

Group Decision-Making Revisited

Our last topic in this section is group decision making. In chapter 3, we briefly compared individual and group decisions. We also identified situations in which group decisions are better than those made by individuals. In this section, we take a closer look at groups as decision makers. Specifically we discuss internal group processes that deter decision-making groups from achieving their full potential. Then we review four group decision-making techniques and how well each does at addressing these limiting internal processes. Finally, we conclude by offering some guidelines for helping you conduct group meetings.

GROUPTHINK A number of years ago I had a peculiar experience. During a faculty meeting, someone made a motion stipulating each faculty member's responsibilities in regard to counseling students. The motion was seconded, and the floor was opened for questions. There were none. After about 15 seconds of silence, the chairman asked if he could "call for the question" (fancy terminology for permission to take the vote). No objections were voiced. When the chairman asked for those in favor, a vast majority of the thirty-two faculty members in attendance raised their hands. The motion was passed, and the chairman proceeded to the next item on the agenda.

Nothing in the process seemed unusual, but the story is not over. About 20 minutes after the meeting, a professor came roaring into my office with a petition. The petition said that the motion on counseling students had been rammed through and requested the chairman to again place the motion on the next month's agenda for discussion and a vote. When I asked this professor why he had not spoken up less than an hour earlier, he gave me a frustrated look. He then proceeded to tell me that in talking with people after the meeting, he realized there actually had been considerable opposition to the motion. He didn't speak up, he said, because he thought he was the only one opposed. Conclusion: The faculty meeting we had attended had been attacked by the deadly "disease" called groupthink.

> Groupthink involves a deterioration in an individual's mental efficiency, reality testing, and moral judgment as a result of group pressures.

Have you ever felt like speaking up in a meeting, classroom, or informal group, but decided against it? One reason may have been shyness. On the other hand, you may have been a victim of **groupthink**, the phenomenon that occurs when group members become so enamored of seeking concurrence that the norm for consensus overrides the realistic appraisal of alternative courses of action and the full expression of deviant, minority, or unpopular views. It involves a deterioration in an individual's mental efficiency, reality testing, and moral judgment as a result of group pressures.[28]

How do you know if a group is showing symptoms of groupthink? It tends to exhibit four characteristics: (1) Group members rationalize any resistance to the assumptions they have made; (2) members pressure any doubters to support the alternative favored by the majority; (3) doubters keep silent about misgivings and even minimize to themselves the importance of their doubts; and (4) the group interprets members' silence as a yes vote for the majority.[29] These symptoms lead to several decision-making deficiencies: incomplete assessment of the problem, poor information search, selective bias in processing information, limited development of alternatives, incomplete assessment of alternatives, failure to examine risks of preferred choice, and failure to reappraise initially rejected alternatives.[30]

Studies of decision making in U.S. government agencies have found deficient outcomes frequently preceded by symptoms of groupthink. These include unpreparedness at Pearl Harbor in 1941, the invasion of North Korea in the 1950s, the Bay of Pigs fiasco in the early 1960s, the escalation of the Vietnam War, the failed Iran hostage rescue in the late 1970s, and the decisions preceding the launch of the ill-fated space shuttle *Challenger*.[31]

Are all groups equally vulnerable to groupthink? The evidence suggests not.[32] Researchers have focused on five variables that seem to influence when groupthink is likely to surface — the group's cohesiveness, its leader's behavior, its insulation from outsiders, time pressures, and failure to follow methodical decision-making procedures. This list leads to the following suggestions for managers who, when leading a decision-making group, want to minimize the influence of groupthink. First, cohesiveness can be an asset because highly cohesive groups have more discussion and bring out more information than do loose groups. But cohesiveness can also discourage dissent. So managers should be vigilant when working with a cohesive group. Second, managers should strive for an open leadership style. This includes encouraging member participation, refraining from stating their opinions at the beginning of the meeting, encouraging divergent opinions from all group members, and emphasizing the importance of reaching a wise decision.[33] Third, managers should avoid allowing the group to detach itself from external sources. Insulated groups tend to lose perspective and objectivity. Fourth, managers need to downplay time constraints. When group members feel severe time pressures on them to reach a decision, they resort to shortcuts that inevitably lead to false or superficial consensus. Finally, managers should encourage the use of methodical decision-making procedures. Following the rational decision-making process described in chapter 3 will promote constructive criticism and a full analysis of decision options.

GROUPSHIFT   Comparisons of group decisions with the individual decisions of members within the group suggest that there are differences.[34] In some cases, the group decisions are more cautious than the individual decisions. More often, they involve greater risk.[35]

What appears to happen in groups is that the discussion leads to a significant shift in the positions of members. They move in the direction toward which they were already leaning before the discussion, but to a more extreme position. So conservative types become more cautious, and the more aggressive types take on more risk. The group discussion tends to exaggerate the initial position of the group.

The **groupshift** can be viewed as actually a special case of groupthink. The decision of the group reflects the dominant decision-making norm that develops during the group's discussion. Whether the shift in the group's decision is toward greater caution or more risk depends on the dominant prediscussion norm.

The greater occurrence of the shift toward risk has generated several explanations for the phenomenon.[36] For instance, it has been suggested that the discussion creates familiarization among the members. As they become more comfortable with one another, they also become bolder and more daring. Arguably, the most plausible explanation of the shift toward risk seems to be that the group diffuses responsibility. Group decisions free any single member from accountability for the group's final choice. Greater risk can be taken because even if the decision fails, no one member can be held wholly responsible.

So, as a manager, how should you use the findings on groupshift? You should recognize that group decisions exaggerate the initial position of the individual members, that the shift has been shown most often to be toward greater risk, and that whether a group will shift toward greater risk or caution is a function of the members' prediscussion inclinations.

SELECTING THE BEST GROUP DECISION-MAKING TECHNIQUE   The most common form of group decision making takes place in face-to-face **interacting groups**. But as our discussion of groupthink demonstrated, interacting groups often censor themselves and pressure individual members toward conformity of opinion. Brainstorming, the nominal group technique, and electronic meetings have been proposed as ways to reduce many of the problems inherent in the traditional interacting group.

Brainstorming is meant to overcome pressures for conformity in the interacting group that retard the development of creative alternatives.[37] It does this by utilizing an idea-generation process that specifically encourages any and all alternatives, while withholding any criticism of those alternatives.

In a typical brainstorming session, a half-dozen to a dozen people sit around a table. The group leader states the problem in a clear manner so that it is understood by all participants. Members then "free-wheel" as many alternatives as they can in a given length of time. No criticism is allowed, and all the alternatives are recorded for later discussion and analysis. That one idea stimulates others and that judgments of even the most bizarre suggestions are withheld until later encourages group members to "think the unusual."

Employees at St. Joseph's Rehabilitation Hospital in Providence, Rhode Island, use brainstorming to generate ideas and improve creativity.

Brainstorming, however, is merely a process for generating ideas. The following two techniques go further by offering methods of actually arriving at a preferred solution.[38]

The **nominal group technique** restricts discussion or interpersonal communication during the decision-making process; hence, the term *nominal*. Group members are all physically present, as in a traditional committee meeting, but members operate independently. Specifically, a problem is presented, and then the following steps take place:

1. Members meet as a group, but before any discussion takes place, each member independently writes down his or her ideas on the problem.
2. After this silent period, each member presents one idea to the group. Each member takes his or her turn, presenting a single idea until all ideas have been presented and recorded (typically on a flip chart or chalkboard). No discussion takes place until all ideas have been recorded.
3. The group now discusses the ideas for clarity and evaluates them.
4. Each group member silently and independently rank-orders the ideas. The idea with the highest aggregate ranking determines the final decision.

The chief advantage of the nominal group technique is that it permits the group to meet formally but does not restrict independent thinking, as does the interacting group.

The most recent approach to group decision making blends the nominal group technique with sophisticated computer technology. This is the **electronic meeting** and is based on the technology of groupware discussed in chapter 8. As we noted in that discussion, these electronic meetings promote anonymity, honesty, and speed. Moreover, if we ignore the additional hardware and software costs, electronic meetings have proven to be more effective than other methods for generating unique alternatives.[39] The future of group meetings undoubtedly will include extensive use of this technology.

Each of these four group decision techniques has its own set of strengths and weaknesses. The choice of one technique over another will depend on what criteria you want to emphasize and the cost-benefit trade-off. For instance, as Exhibit 10-5 indicates, the interacting group is good for building group cohesiveness, brainstorming keeps social pressures to a minimum, the nominal group technique is an inexpensive means for generating high-quality ideas, and electronic meetings process ideas fast.

EXHIBIT 10-5

Evaluating Group Effectiveness

Effectiveness Criterion	Type of Group			
	Interacting	Brainstorming	Nominal	Electronic
Number of ideas	Low	Moderate	Moderate	High
Quality of ideas	Low	Moderate	High	High
Social pressure	High	Low	Moderate	Low
Money costs	Low	Low	Low	High
Speed	Moderate	Moderate	Moderate	High
Task orientation	Low	High	High	High
Potential for interpersonal conflict	High	Low	Moderate	Low
Feelings of accomplishment	High to low	High	High	High
Commitment to solution	High	Not applicable	Moderate	Moderate
Development of group cohesiveness	High	High	Moderate	Low

Source: Based on J. K. Murnighan, "Group Decision Making: What Strategies Should You Use?" *Management Review*, February 1981, p. 61.

CONDUCTING GROUP MEETINGS Group decision making typically takes place in meetings. Given that most managers will spend at least 25 to 30 percent of their time in meetings,[40] and that managers often have responsibility for chairing these meetings, let's review what you can do as chair to run more effective meetings.[41]

1. *Prepare a meeting agenda.* An agenda defines what you hope to accomplish at the meeting. It should state the meeting's purpose; who will be in attendance; what, if any, preparation is required of each participant; a detailed list of items to be covered; the specific time and location of the meeting; and a specific finishing time.
2. *Distribute the agenda in advance.* Participants should have the agenda enough ahead of time so they can adequately prepare for the meeting.
3. *Consult with participants before the meeting.* An unprepared participant can't contribute to his or her full potential. As chair, it's your responsibility to ensure that members are prepared, so check with them ahead of time.
4. *Get participants to go over the agenda.* The first thing to do at the meeting is to have participants review the agenda, make any changes, and then approve the final agenda.
5. *Establish specific time parameters.* Meetings should begin on time and have a specific time for completion. It's your responsibility to specify these time parameters and to hold to them.
6. *Maintain focused discussion.* It's your responsibility to give direction to the discussion; to keep it focused on the issues; and to minimize interruptions, disruptions, and irrelevant comments.
7. *Encourage and support participation of all members.* To maximize the effectiveness of problem-oriented meetings, each participant must be encouraged to contribute. Quiet or reserved personalities need to be drawn out so their ideas can be heard.
8. *Maintain a balanced style.* The effective chair pushes when necessary and is passive when need be.
9. *Encourage the clash of ideas.* You need to encourage different points of view, critical thinking, and constructive disagreement.
10. *Discourage the clash of personalities.* An effective meeting is characterized by the critical assessment of ideas, not attacks on people. When running a meeting, you must quickly intercede to stop personal attacks or other forms of verbal insult.
11. *Be an effective listener.* You need to listen with intensity, empathy, objectivity, and do whatever is necessary to get the full intended meaning from each participant's comments.
12. *Bring proper closure.* You should close a meeting by summarizing the group's accomplishments; clarifying what actions, if any, need to follow the meeting; and allocating follow-up assignments. If any decisions are made, you also need to determine who will be responsible for communicating and implementing them.

Let us return now to the topic of teams. We begin with an explanation of why teams have recently become so popular.

Twenty-five years ago, when companies such as Volvo, Toyota, and General Foods introduced teams into their production processes, they made news because no one else was doing it. Today, it's just the opposite. The organization that *doesn't* use teams is the one that has become newsworthy. Pick up almost any business periodical today and you will read how teams have become an essential part of the way business is being done in companies such as General Electric, AT&T, Hewlett-Packard, Motorola, Shiseido, Federal Express, DaimlerChrysler, Saab, 3M Co., John Deere, Texas Instruments, Australian Airlines,

WHAT EXPLAINS THE RECENT POPULARITY OF TEAMS?

Johnson & Johnson, Dayton Hudson, Shenandoah Life Insurance Co., Florida Power & Light, and Emerson Electric. Even the world-famous San Diego Zoo has restructured its native habitat zones around cross-departmental teams. A recent survey of more than 1,400 U.S. organizations found that 73 percent had at least some employees working in teams.[42] How do we explain the current popularity of teams? The major force seems to be the desire of management to increase flexibility and quality.

The evidence suggests that teams typically outperform individuals when the tasks being done require multiple skills, judgment, and experience.[43] As organizations have restructured themselves to compete more effectively and efficiently, they have turned to teams as a way to better utilize employee talents. Management has found that teams are more flexible and responsive to changing events than are traditional departments or other forms of permanent groupings. Teams have the capability to quickly assemble, deploy, refocus, and disband.

Teams are also a fundamental part of TQM programs. The essence of TQM is process improvement, and employee involvement is the linchpin of process improvement. In other words, TQM requires management to give employees the encouragement to share ideas and act on what they suggest. As one author put it, "None of the various TQM processes and techniques will catch on and be applied except in work teams. All such techniques and processes require high levels of communication and contact, response and adaptation, and coordination and sequencing. They require, in short, the environment that can be supplied only by superior work teams."[44]

| In The News |

Getting a Career Boost from Working on a Temporary Team

There is both power and peril on a temporary team. These are typically teams made up from members from different departments and different levels to handle a specific project—such as developing new policies, reengineering operations, or designing a new product. Handled properly, such teams can give you the opportunity to showcase your skills to people from across your organization, often including influential senior executives. The downside is that because these team assignments are often critical and closely watched, if the team flops, you flop, regardless of how good your contribution may have been.

Take the case of Shaunna Sowell at Texas Instruments. Her team experience led to a promotion and a better career path than she ever envisioned, but she also burned some bridges with a boss. Sowell was leading a plant design group when she was tapped for a product-quality steering team that was loaded with bosses. She was intimidated at first, but her confidence grew with her experience.

"I left one meeting thinking, my God, I've ruined my career," she recalls. "I'd just told a guy four levels above me he was wrong."

Actually, she impressed several powerful executives on the team. And her corporate visibility skyrocketed. Her team involvement earned her recognition and mentoring from senior executives that she never would have gotten in the days before TI emphasized teams.

Sowell admits that her team experience also created friction. "My visibility was getting wider than my boss's," she says. "It was pretty uncomfortable." As her relationship with her boss cooled, she used her new visibility and contacts to arrange a move to another, and higher, position in the company.

Source: Based on H. Lancaster, "That Team Spirit Can Lead Your Career to New Victories," *Wall Street Journal*, January 14, 1997, p. B1.

Teams can be structured on the basis of a number of criteria. For instance, organizations can create teams on the basis of *purpose* (problem-finding, cost-cutting, new product, quality); *degree of self-management* (self-managed versus hierarchically led); *nature of membership* (permanent, project, task); *interskill variety* (single function versus cross-function); or *level* (operating versus management).[45] Many organizations, in fact, have been quite inventive in coming up with labels to describe their "unique" teams. A closer examination indicates that most can be subsumed under one of three labels: *problem-solving teams*, *self-managed work teams*, and *cross-functional teams* (see Exhibit 10-6).

Problem-Solving Teams

If we look back to about 1980, teams were just beginning to grow in popularity. And the form most of these teams took was similar. They were typically composed of five to twelve hourly employees from the same department who met for a few hours each week to discuss ways of improving quality, efficiency, and the work environment.[46] We call these **problem-solving teams**.

In problem-solving teams, members share ideas or offer suggestions on how work processes and methods can be improved. Rarely, however, are these teams given the authority to unilaterally implement any of their suggested actions.

Self-Managed Work Teams

Problem-solving teams were on the right track, but they didn't go far enough in getting employees involved in work-related decisions and processes. This weakness led to experimentations with truly autonomous teams that could not only solve problems but could also implement solutions and take full responsibility for outcomes.

Self-managed work teams are groups of interdependent individuals that can self-regulate their behavior on relatively whole tasks.[47] Typically, their responsibilities include setting work schedules, developing performance goals, dealing directly with external customers, and

Three Types of Teams

EXHIBIT 10-6

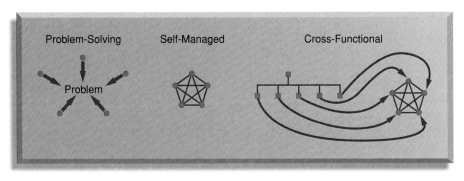

Problem-Solving   Self-Managed   Cross-Functional

Problem

purchasing necessary equipment and services. Fully self-managed work teams even select their own members and have the members evaluate one another's performance. As a result, supervisory positions take on decreased importance and may even be eliminated. At GE's locomotive-engine plant in Grove City, Pennsylvania, there are about 100 teams, and they make most of the plant's decisions. They arrange the maintenance, schedule the work, and routinely authorize equipment purchases. One team spent $2 million, and the plant manager never flinched. At the L-S Electrogalvanizing Co. in Cleveland, the entire plant is run by self-managed teams. They do their own scheduling, rotate jobs on their own, establish production targets, set pay scales that are linked to skills, fire co-workers, and do the hiring. "I never meet a new employee until his first day on the job," says the plant's general manager.[48]

Xerox, General Motors, Coors Brewing, PepsiCo, Hewlett-Packard, Honeywell, M&M/Mars, and Aetna Life are just a few familiar names that have implemented self-managed work teams. Overall, about 30 percent of U.S. employers now use this form of teams.[49]

Recent business periodicals have been chock full of articles describing successful applications of self-managed teams. For instance, Aid Association for Lutherans, one of the largest insurance and financial service companies in the United States, claims that self-managed teams were primarily responsible for helping increase employee satisfaction and allowing the company to increase business volume by 50 percent over a 4-year period while cutting workforce staff by 15 percent.[50]

Despite the upbeat press, a word of caution needs to be offered here. The overall research on the effectiveness of self-managed work teams has not been uniformly positive.[51] For example, individuals on these teams do tend to report higher levels of job satisfaction. However, counter to conventional wisdom, employees on self-managed work teams seem to have higher absenteeism and turnover rates than do employees working in traditional work structures. The specific reasons for these findings are, at this point, still unclear.

Cross-Functional Teams

Cross-functional teams are made up of employees from about the same hierarchical level, but from different work areas, who come together to accomplish a task.[52] In most cases, the employees come from different levels and all work in a single organization. But cross-functional teams can also be composed of a select cadre of senior executives within a single firm who are responsible for coordinating a number of subunits or they may include members from other organizations.

Many organizations have used horizontal, boundary-spanning groups for years. For example, IBM created a large task force in the 1960s—made up of employees from across departments in the company—to develop the highly successful System 360. And a **task force** is really nothing other than a temporary cross-functional team. **Committees** composed of members from across departmental lines are another example of cross-functional teams.

But the popularity of cross-discipline work teams exploded in the late 1980s. All the major automobile manufacturers—including Toyota, Honda, Nissan, BMW, GM, Ford, and DaimlerChrysler—have turned to this form of team in order to coordinate complex projects. Cross-functional teams seem to be particularly attractive as a means to facilitate product development. For instance, a typical product team at Caterpillar's tractor division in Peoria, Illinois, consists of a product designer; manufacturing engineers; representatives from assembly, purchasing, and materials processing; the customer, either directly or through marketing services groups; and suppliers.[53] Black & Decker attributes a large part of its success in continually introducing new products to its cross-functional teams that are drawn from marketing, sales, manufacturing, engineering, and finance.[54]

Black & Decker research and development teams, made up from employees across the organization, are a rich source of innovative products.

Motorola's Iridium Project illustrates why so many companies have turned to cross-functional teams.[55] This project is developing a huge network that will contain sixty-six satellites. "We realized at the beginning that there was no way we could manage a project of this size and complexity in the traditional way and still get it done on time," says the project's general manager. For the first year and a half of the project, a cross-functional team of twenty Motorola people met every morning. This team has since been expanded to include diverse experts from dozens of other companies as well, such as Raytheon, Russia's Khrunichev Enterprise, Lockheed-Martin, Scientific-Atlanta, and General Electric.

In summary, cross-functional teams are an effective means for allowing people from diverse areas within an organization or between organizations to exchange information, develop new ideas and solve problems, and coordinate complex projects. Of course, cross-functional teams are no picnic to manage.[56] Their early stages of development are often very time-consuming as members learn to work with diversity and complexity. It takes time to build trust and teamwork, especially among people from different backgrounds, with different experiences and perspectives.

TODAY ? or TOMORROW ?

Virtual Teams

It's an extension of the electronic meeting. It's called the *virtual team*. It allows groups to meet without concern for space or time. Team members use communication links like conference calls, video conferencing, or e-mail to solve problems—even though they may be geographically dispersed or a dozen time zones away. VeriFone, a California-based manufacturer of in-store credit-card authorization terminals, provides a glimpse at the possible future of virtual teams.[57]

The VeriFone sales rep in Greece knew he was in big trouble when he left the offices of an Athens bank at 4:30 P.M. A competitor had challenged VeriFone's ability to deliver a new payment-service technology. The sales rep knew his company was the main supplier of this technology in the United States and many other countries, but it was unproven in Greece. The rep needed to convince bank executives that this technology would work but he had no details on its effectiveness by users in other countries.

So what did the VeriFone rep do? He created a virtual team. He found the nearest phone and hooked up his laptop to it. Then he sent an SOS e-mail to all VeriFone sales, marketing, and technical-support staff worldwide.

In San Francisco, an international marketing staffer who was on duty to monitor such distress calls got the message at home when he checked his e-mail at 6:30 A.M. He organized a conference call with two other marketing staffers, one in Atlanta and one in Hong Kong, where it was 9:30 A.M. and 10:30 P.M., respectively. Together, they decided how to handle the data coming in from everyone who'd received the message. A few hours later, the two U.S. team members spoke on the phone again while they used the company's wide area network to fine-tune a sales presentation. Before leaving for the day, the leader passed the presentation on to the Hong Kong team member so he could add Asian information to the detailed account of experiences and references when he arrived at work.

The Greek sales rep awakened a few hours later. He retrieved the presentation from the network, got to the bank at 8 A.M., and showed the customer the data. Impressed by the speedy and informative response, the customer's apprehensions about VeriFone's technology were alleviated. The sales rep got the order.

VeriFone uses virtual teams in every aspect of its operations—from groups of facility managers who determine how to reduce toxins in their offices, to manufacturing purchasing groups that seek hard-to-find semiconductors, to marketing and development groups that brainstorm new products.

CREATING HIGH-PERFORMANCE TEAMS

We've learned a lot over the past few years on how to create high-performing teams. Although many specific recommendations need to be qualified to reflect the type of team being discussed,[58] there are still a number of observations we can make about teams in general.[59]

Size of Work Teams

The best work teams tend to be small. When they have more than about ten to twelve members, it becomes difficult for them to get much done. They have trouble interacting constructively and agreeing on much. Large numbers of people usually cannot develop the cohesiveness, commitment, and mutual accountability necessary to achieve high performance. So, in designing effective teams, managers should keep them to under a dozen. If a natural working unit is larger and you want a team effort, consider breaking the group into subteams.

Abilities of Members

To perform effectively, a team requires three different types of skills. First, it needs people with *technical expertise*. Second, it needs people with the *problem-solving and decison making skills* required to identify problems, generate alternatives, evaluate those alternatives, and make competent choices. Finally, teams need people with good listening, feedback, conflict resolution, and other *interpersonal skills*.

No team can achieve its performance potential without developing all three types of skills. The right mix is crucial. Too much of one at the expense of others will result in lower team performance. Management can, and should, take responsibility for creating the right mix through selection and making training in team skills available as needed.

Allocating Roles and Promoting Diversity

Teams have different needs, and people should be selected for a team on the basis of their personalities and preferences. High-performing teams properly match people to various roles. For example, the basketball coaches who continually win over the long-term have learned how to size up prospective players, identify their strengths and weaknesses, and then assign them to positions that best fit with their skills and allow them to contribute most to the overall team's performance. They recognize that winning teams need a variety of skills—for example, ball handlers, power scorers, three-point shooters, defensive specialists, and shot blockers.

Successful work teams have people to fill all the key roles (see Exhibit 10-7) and have selected people to play in these roles according to their skills and preferences. (On many teams, individuals will play multiple roles.) Managers need to understand the individual strengths that each person can bring to a team, select members with their strengths in mind, and allocate work assignments that fit with members' preferred styles. By matching

Key Roles on Teams

EXHIBIT 10-7

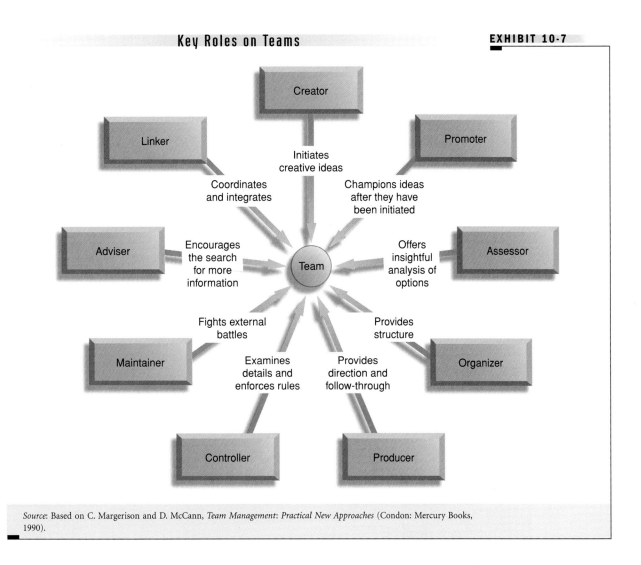

Source: Based on C. Margerison and D. McCann, *Team Management*: *Practical New Approaches* (Condon: Mercury Books, 1990).

individual preferences with team role demands, managers increase the likelihood that the team members will work well together.

Having a Commitment to a Common Purpose

Does the team have a meaningful purpose to which all members aspire? This purpose is a vision. It's broader than specific goals. Effective teams have a common and meaningful purpose that provides direction, momentum, and commitment for members. Production teams at Saturn Corp., for example, are driven and united by the common purpose of building an American automobile that can successfully compete in terms of quality and price with the best of Japanese cars.

Members of successful teams put a tremendous amount of time and effort into discussing, shaping, and agreeing upon a purpose that belongs to them both collectively and individually. This common purpose, when accepted by the team, becomes the equivalent of what celestial navigation is to a ship captain—it provides direction and guidance under any and all conditions.

Establishing Specific Goals

Successful teams translate their common purpose into specific, measurable, and realistic performance goals. Just as we demonstrated in chapter 5 how goals lead individuals to higher performance, goals also energize teams. These specific goals facilitate clear communication. They also help teams maintain their focus on getting results.

Social Loafing and Accountability

We learned earlier in this chapter that individuals can hide inside a group. They can engage in social loafing and coast on the group's effort because their individual contributions cannot be identified. High-performing teams undermine this tendency by holding themselves accountable at both the individual and the team levels.

Successful teams make members individually and jointly accountable for the team's purpose, goals, and approach. They are clear on what they are individually responsible for and what they are jointly responsible for.

Appropriate Performance Appraisal and Reward Systems

How do you get team members to be both individually and jointly accountable? The traditional individually oriented appraisal and reward system must be modified to reflect team performance.[60]

Individual performance appraisals, fixed hourly wages, individual incentives, and the like are not consistent with the development of high-performance teams. So in addition to appraising and rewarding employees for their individual contribution, management should consider group-based appraisals, profit-sharing, small-group incentives, and other system modifications that will reinforce team effort and commitment.

TRANSFORMING INDIVIDUALS INTO TEAM PLAYERS

So far, we've made a strong case for the value and growing popularity of teams. But many people are not inherently team players. They are loners or people who want to be recognized for their individual achievements. There are also a great many organizations that have historically nurtured individual accomplishments. They have created competitive work environments where only the strong survive. If these organizations adopt teams, what can they do about the "I have to look out for me" employees that they created? And finally, as we discussed in chapter 4, countries differ in terms of how they rate on individualism and collectivism. Teams fit well with countries that score high on collectivism. It's

EXHIBIT 10-8

"No, but I think I could *learn* to be a team player."

Source: *Training*, February 1997, p. 10. Reprinted by permission of the artist Mike Shapiro.

not by chance, for instance, that teams have been so widely accepted in Japan. As Exhibit 10-9 illustrates, the Japanese culture is more conducive to teams than is the U.S. culture. But what if an organization wants to introduce teams into a work population that is made up largely of individuals born and raised in a highly individualistic society? As one writer so aptly put it, in describing the role of teams in the United States: "Americans don't grow up learning how to function in teams. In school we never receive a team report card or learn the names of the team of sailors who traveled with Columbus to America."[61] This limitation would obviously be just as true of Canadians, Britons, Australians, and others from highly individualistic societies.

EXHIBIT 10-9

Cultural Differences Between the United States and Japan That Influence the Success of Teams

United States	Japan
► Core of performance is the individual	► Core of performance is the group
► Preservation of individual rights is key	► Preservation of harmony is key
► Conflict and competition are allowed	► Conflict and competition are discouraged
► Equality of membership is important	► Status within group is important
► Focus is on present and quick results	► Focus is on past and long-term future
► Dynamic actions are preferred	► Slow progress is preferred
► Cultural values are heterogeneous	► Cultural values are homogeneous

Source: Adapted from A. Nahavandi and E. Aranda, "Restructuring Teams for the Re-Engineered Organization," *The Executive*, November 1994, p. 60. With permission.

The Challenge

The previous points are meant to dramatize that one substantial barrier to using work teams is individual resistance. An employee's success is no longer defined in terms of individual performance. To perform well as team members, individuals must be able to communicate openly and honestly, to confront differences and resolve conflicts, and to sublimate personal goals for the good of the team. For many employees, these are difficult—sometimes impossible—tasks. The challenge of creating team players will be greatest where (1) the national culture is highly individualistic and (2) the teams are being introduced into an established organization that has historically valued individual achievement. These conditions describe, for instance, what faced managers at AT&T, Ford, Motorola, and other large U.S.-based companies. These firms prospered by hiring and rewarding corporate stars; they created a competitive climate that encouraged individual achievement and recognition. Employees in these types of firms can be jolted by a sudden shift to the importance of team play.[62] One veteran employee of a large company, who had done very well by working alone, described the experience of joining a team. "I'm learning my lesson. I just had my first negative performance appraisal in 20 years."[63]

On the other hand, the challenge for management is less demanding when teams are introduced where employees have strong collectivist values—such as in Japan or Mexico—or in new organizations that use teams as their initial form for structuring work. Mercedes-Benz's new plant in Alabama, for instance, was designed around teams from its inception. Everyone at the plant was initially hired with the knowledge that they would be working in teams. And the ability to be a good team player was a basic hiring qualification that all new employees had to meet.

> The challenge of creating team players will be greatest where (1) the national culture is highly individualistic and (2) the teams are being introduced into an established organization that has historically valued individual achievement.

Shaping Team Players

The following list summarizes the primary options managers have for trying to turn individuals into team players.

- *Selection.* Some people already possess the interpersonal skills to be effective team players. When hiring team members, in addition to the technical skills required to fill the job, care should be taken to ensure that candidates can fulfill their team roles as well as technical requirements.
- *Training.* A large proportion of people raised on the importance of individual accomplishment can be trained to become team players. Training specialists conduct exercises that allow employees to experience the satisfaction that teamwork can provide. They typically offer workshops to help employees improve their problem-solving, communication, negotiation, conflict-management, and coaching skills. And employees are instructed in the importance of patience—because teams take longer to make decisions than do employees acting alone.[64]
- *Rewards.* The reward system needs to be reworked to encourage cooperative efforts rather than competitive ones. Promotions, pay raises, and other forms of recognition should be given to individuals for how effective they are as a collaborative team member. This doesn't mean individual contribution is ignored; rather, it is balanced with selfless contributions to the team. Examples of behaviors that should be rewarded include training new colleagues, sharing information with teammates, helping resolve team conflicts, and mastering new skills that your team needs but in which it is deficient.

Unfortunately, in organizations that are undergoing the transformation to teams, there will be some current employees who will resist team training or prove untrainable. Your options with such individuals are essentially two. You can transfer them to another unit within the organization that does not have teams, if this possibility exists. The other choice is obvious and acknowledges that some employees may become casualties of the team approach.

We close this chapter by providing a caveat: Teams are not a universal panacea! They don't always work. Sometimes their costs exceed their benefits. And there are conditions where individuals, operating independently, will outperform teams.[65]

TEAMS ARE NOT A PANACEA! WHEN TO SHOW CAUTION

We see increased reports of incidences where team results have been disappointing. For instance, a study of 30 quality programs, each of which relied on teams, found two-thirds either stalled or failed to produce the desired results.[66] A number of factors seem to influence the acceptability and success of teams. The following list highlights situations or conditions that can undermine team effectiveness. Reviewing these factors before you introduce teams into your work unit or organization could save you a great deal of grief.

The wrong national culture. Teams work best in countries that score low on individualism and power distance.[67] This doesn't mean that teams *can't* succeed in alien cultures. It just means there are higher barriers to overcome.

The wrong organizational culture. It's difficult for teams to succeed in organizations characterized by extensive interpersonal conflicts, lack of trust, and strong individualistic values.[68]

The wrong work tasks. Some tasks are better done by individuals than by teams. Teams work best where there's a need for change and innovation. But for routine activities, where speed and cost minimization are dominant determinants of success, authoritative, nonparticipative, nonteam approaches may be more effective.[69]

The wrong staff. For teams to work, team members must have the right skills.[70] Specifically, if employees have weak communication and other interpersonal skills, team performance is going to suffer.

The use of teams provides a number of challenges to managers.[71] These include not letting the team atmosphere drive out creative, independent individuals; avoiding groupthink within teams; maintaining accountability; and finding the proper balance between rewarding individual performance and rewarding team performance. These challenges *can* be met, resulting in high-performance teams. But it should not be lost on managers that teams are merely a device to facilitate organizational performance. They are a means, not an end. In spite of the current popularity of teams, they are not right for every occasion.

There is a variety of additional material available on the CD-ROM and companion Web site that accompany this text. You can access this information through the CD-ROM or by visiting the Web site at <**www.prenhall.com/robbins**>.

SUMMARY

(This summary is organized by the chapter-opening learning objectives on page 304.)

1. All teams are groups. But teams create a synergy that results in a level of performance greater than the sum of individual inputs. Three types of teams are problem-solving (small groups that discuss ways of improving quality, efficiency, and the work environment); self-managed (teams that take on responsibilities of their former supervisors); and cross-functional (teams made up of individuals from different work areas).

2. Roles shape behavior by creating expected behavior patterns that people enact in different situations. Norms shape behavior by imposing acceptable group standards on individual members.

3. The cohesiveness-productivity relationship is moderated by performance-related norms of the group. For instance, if the norms are high, a cohesive group will be more productive. If cohesiveness is high and norms are low, productivity will be low.

4. The most important work-related implication of social loafing is that managers need to have measures of individual effort in collective work situations. Otherwise, members can be "free riders" without being detected.

5. The main characteristics of the grapevine are that (1) it is not controlled by management, (2) it is perceived by most employees as being more reliable and believable than formal communiqués, and (3) it is largely used to serve the self-interests of the people within it.

6. Groupthink is a condition whereby consensus-seeking drives out deviant, minority, or unpopular positions. Groupthink retards critical evaluation of options and leads to poorer-quality decisions. Groupshift is a movement of the group to a more extreme position from that held by individuals. It tends to be toward greater risks in group decisions.

7. High-performing teams are characterized by small size, diverse skills, people properly matched to roles, a meaningful purpose to which all members aspire, specific goals, individual and joint accountability, and an appraisal and reward system modified to reflect team performance.

8. Management can transform individuals into team players through selecting individuals with a collectivist orientation, team training, and reworking the reward system to encourage cooperative efforts.

9. Teams can undermine organizational effectiveness when they don't mesh with the national or organizational culture, when the work tasks are routine and speed and cost minimization are of primary importance, and when staff lacks the necessary interpersonal skills.

REVIEW QUESTIONS

1. Would you prefer a job that is designed around you as an individual or one that places you on a self-managed work team? Why?

2. What are the implications of the Asch findings for managers?

3. Should managers seek cohesive groups? If they want cohesive groups, what can they do to encourage them?

4. What predictions would you make regarding the effect of racial or national diversity on a group's performance?

5. Is conflict among employees good or bad? Explain.

6. How can managers minimize the influence of groupthink in decision-making groups?

7. Contrast the effectiveness of four group decision-making techniques.

8. How do you explain the recent popularity of teams in organizations?

9. Contrast the advantages of self-managing and cross-functional teams.

10. Should pay systems be modified when organizations move to teams? Explain.

IF I WERE THE MANAGER . . .

Starting Up a Low-Fare Airline

You're CEO of US Airways Group. Your company is the sixth-largest carrier in the United States. After spending nearly a decade as CEO of United Airlines, you've been in your current job for two years.

After considerable discussion with your senior executive group, you've decided that US Air needs to respond to Southwest Airlines' expansion into the East—where the bulk of US Air's routes are. Southwest is a low-cost carrier that has created major headaches for competitors in almost every market it has entered. Your executive group has ruled out merely cutting prices on current US Air routes. The decision has been made to create a new, low-fare airline. Code named US2, you'd like to have this new airline up and flying within eight months.

There is some disagreement among your staff as to the best way to implement this decision. Three perspectives came out of a recent discussion. One way would be to appoint an individual executive to oversee this new-business start-up. He or she would be the new company's CEO and would unilaterally make the key implementation decisions. A second approach would be to create a management team, made up of current US Air executives, to make key decisions. A third perspective would be to empower a team of US Air employees—pilots, ramp super-

visors, reservation agents, mechanics, flight attendants, office staffers, and the like—to put this new airline together.

Whichever way you go, the list of decisions to be made will be enormous. They'll include everything from interior layouts of the aircraft, to how fast to fly the planes, to methods for fueling, cleaning, and loading.

Is this the type of decision that would lend itself to a team? Could a single person do this job better? Or if a team is the best way to go, what type of team would be most effective?

Source: Based on S. Carey, "U.S. Air 'Peon' Team Pilots Start-Up of Low-Fare Airline," *Wall Street Journal*, March 24, 1998, p. B1.

SKILL EXERCISE

Assessing Team Effectiveness

Think of a team of which you were a part. Did you think it was effective? To objectively assess whether that team was effective, complete the following questionnaire. Using the scale below, rate your assessment of the extent to which each statement is true about your team.

5 = Strongly agree; 4 = Agree; 3 = Neutral; 2 = Disagree; 1 = Strongly disagree

1. Everyone on my team knows exactly why the team does what it does.	5	4	3	2	1
2. The team leader consistently lets the team members know how we're doing on meeting our customers' expectations.	5	4	3	2	1
3. Everyone on my team has a significant amount of say or influence on decisions that affect his or her job.	5	4	3	2	1
4. If outsiders were to describe the way we communicate within our team, they would use words such as "open," "honest," "timely," and "two-way."	5	4	3	2	1
5. Team members have the skills they need to accomplish their roles within the team.	5	4	3	2	1
6. Everyone on the team knows and understands the team's priorities.	5	4	3	2	1
7. As a team, we work together to set clear, achievable, and appropriate goals.	5	4	3	2	1
8. I would rather have the team decide how to do something rather than have the team leader give step-by-step instructions.	5	4	3	2	1
9. As a team, we are able to work together to solve destructive conflicts rather than ignoring conflicts.	5	4	3	2	1
10. The role each member of the team is expected to play makes sense to the whole team.	5	4	3	2	1
11. The team understands how it fits into the organization.	5	4	3	2	1
12. If my team doesn't reach a goal, I'm more interested in finding out why we have failed to meet the goal than I am in reprimanding the team members.	5	4	3	2	1
13. The team has so much ownership of the work that, if necessary, we would offer to stay late to finish a job.	5	4	3	2	1
14. The team leader encourages every person on the team to be open and honest, even if people have to share information that goes against what the team leader would like to hear.	5	4	3	2	1
15. There is a good match between the capabilities and responsibilities of each person on the team.	5	4	3	2	1
16. Everyone on the team is working toward accomplishing the same thing.	5	4	3	2	1
17. The team has the support and resources it needs to meet customer expectations.	5	4	3	2	1

18. The team knows as much about what's going on in the organization as the team leader does, because the team leader always keeps everyone up-to-date.	5	4	3	2	1
19. The team leader believes that everyone on the team has something to contribute that is valuable to all.	5	4	3	2	1
20. Team members clearly understand the team's unwritten rules of how to behave within the group.	5	4	3	2	1

Total up your score. The highest score possible is 100. You can rate your team's effectiveness by how close it comes to achieving the ideal score. Look specifically at items that you rated at 3 or less. These are areas where your team fell down in performance. You can use this twenty-item inventory to help you manage current and future teams of which you're a part.

Source: The questionnaire is from V. A. Hoevemeyer, "How Effective Is Your Team?" *Training & Development Journal*, September 1993, pp. 67–71.

TEAM ACTIVITY

Building Effective Work Teams

Objective: This exercise is designed to allow class members (a) to experience working together as a team on a specific task and (b) to analyze this experience.

Time: Teams will have 90 minutes to engage in steps 2 and 3 below. Another 45–60 minutes will be used in class to critique and evaluate the exercise.

Procedure:

1. Class members are assigned to teams of about six people.
2. Each team is required to:
   a. Determine a team name.
   b. Compose a team song.
3. Each team is to try to find the following items on their scavenger hunt:
   a. A picture of a team
   b. A newspaper article about a group or team
   c. A piece of apparel with the college name or logo
   d. A set of chopsticks
   e. A ball of cotton
   f. A piece of stationery from a college department
   g. A bottle of Liquid Paper
   h. A floppy disk
   i. A cup from McDonald's
   j. A dog leash
   k. A utility bill
   l. A calendar from last year
   m. A book by Ernest Hemingway
   n. An ad brochure for a Ford product
   o. A test tube
   p. A pack of gum
   q. An ear of corn
   r. A Garth Brooks tape or CD
4. After 90 minutes, all teams are to be back in the classroom. (A penalty, determined by the instructor, will be imposed on late teams.) The team with the most items on the list will be declared the winner. The class and instructor will determine whether the items meet the requirements of the exercise.
5. Debriefing of the exercise will begin by having each team engage in self-evaluation. Specifically, it should answer the following:
   a. What was the team's strategy?
   b. What roles did individual members perform?
   c. How effective was the team?
   d. What could the team have done to be more effective?
6. Full class discussion will focus on issues such as:
   a. What differentiated the more effective teams from the less effective?
   b. What did you learn from this experience that is relevant to the design of effective teams?

Source: Adapted from M. R. Manning and P. J. Schmidt, "Building Effective Work Teams: A Quick Exercise Based on a Scavenger Hunt," *Journal of Management Education*, August 1995, pp. 392–98. With permission.

The Boeing 777 Program

As Boeing Corp.'s management prepared to develop its 777 commercial jet, it decided it could no longer do business as usual. Times had changed and so must the development process. The 777 had to be cost-efficient to compete against Airbus Industrie. And it had to be customer-focused in response to the increasing demands made by airlines. Boeing was still suffering from the disappointing reception given to the company's proposed 150-seat jetliner called the 7J7. It failed to sell in the 1980s.

Senior management wrote up a brief statement of what they wanted in the 777:

> In order to launch on time a truly great airplane we have a responsibility to work together to design, produce and introduce an airplane that exceeds the expectations of flight crews, cabin crews, maintenance and support teams and ultimately our passengers and shippers.
>
> From day one: best dispatch reliability in the industry; greatest customer appeal in the industry and user-friendly and everything works.

To achieve this ambitious goal, management committed itself to designing the plane using the latest computer-aided design technology. Similarly, high-tech manufacturing techniques would be utilized to cut costs and increase quality. For instance, laser beams would be used to align big parts and eliminate costly reworking. But the most significant change would be in the use of teams and the inclusion of customers in the design stage. By getting customer input up front, airlines could select features they wanted, thus allowing Boeing to standardize many items and reduce costly customization.

As development began, Boeing set up about 240 design teams representing every company unit, from engineers, to machinists, to marketing personnel, to suppliers and customers. They dictated open communication among employees who never before had worked together or with customers. But learning to work together instead of maintaining turf was difficult for some. Many were reluctant to share information or mistakes. Financial managers, for instance, who were brought in to consult on costs, had difficulty in being forthright. And there was concern by upper-level managers that if too many people knew a lot about a process, design, or plan, word would get out to competitors.

Boeing came up with more efficient ways of doing things by bringing together workers from different areas of the company to problem-solve. They learned, for example, that it's faster and better to fill fuselage sections with wires, ducts, tubes, and insulation before joining them together than to do it after. Once the sections are joined, it's easier to connect the systems instead of having a lot of people getting in one another's way trying to install all of the interior parts at once.

The early evidence indicates that the 777 project is going to be a major success for Boeing. It is highly cost-competitive, largely because traditional production time has been cut from 18 months to 10 months. And it is proving to be just what customers want. United Airlines has placed orders or options for sixty-eight planes, and other airlines are rapidly getting in line to place orders.

QUESTIONS

1. Why do you think the use of teams was novel for the design of a complex project like an airplane?
2. How valid do you think upper management's concern is that teams could provide competitors with critical information on their new plane, especially with customers actively involved in its design?
3. What happened to the advantages from work specialization? Don't teams undermine the benefits that come from developing planes sequentially—with each department providing its contribution as the project evolves?

Source: Based on P. Lane, "Boeing 777: Delivering on a Promise," *Seattle Times*, May 7, 1995, p. F1.

Group Pressures Inside the FAA

ABCNEWS

Gregory May was a man with influence and power. He had a $1.5 million contract to provide diversity training for the Federal Aviation Administration. Approximately 4,000 people, including hundreds from management, had taken his course. He was perceived to be very close to senior FAA managers and was believed to share personal information with those managers about FAA employees. More important, doing well in May's training program was required to get ahead in the organization. If you didn't get May's approval for completing the course in good standing, your career could be derailed, and if you objected to some of the things in May's course, you might even get fired.

Given the importance of this course to FAA employees, you'd assume that the course would have been well thought out and professionally conducted. Well, that assumption would have been wrong! Air traffic controllers, for instance, were subjected to sessions in which they were forced to share their innermost sexual secrets. People would be expected to share details of painful experiences from their youth, which often brought them to the point of being in tears. They had to undergo weird rituals. For instance, May would bark out orders such as "sit down," "stand up," "sit down," for hours on end. He wanted complete obedience from participants. In another exercise, he would tie individuals of the same sex together and make them go to the bathroom and shower together. When one complained that the exercise embarrassed him, May tossed it off and said, "Learn from it." In still an-

other exercise, May made male air traffic controllers run a gauntlet of women who were told to grope the men's private parts. All of this was in the name of teaching diversity.

Did anyone complain? A few did. Did they disobey? Not many. One former FAA employee said, "I was a single parent with two small children, and they're 100 percent dependent on me, and my income. And there was no way I was going to give up a 12-year career working with the FAA." So they did what they were told for fear of losing their jobs.

May is no longer doing diversity training for the FAA. A government investigation was undertaken to find out what went on and to ensure it wouldn't happen again. But, meanwhile, thousands of FAA employees spent several years being tormented by Gregory May under the guise of sensitizing workers to diversity issues.

QUESTIONS

1. What does this case say about group pressures to conform?
2. Can you make any argument favoring this type of diversity training done in a group setting? Explain your position.
3. What, if anything, does this case say about group influences on training effectiveness?

Source: Based on "A Cult and Its Influence within the FAA," *ABC Nightline*, February 21, 1995.

1. Based on R. Maynard, "A Client-Centered Firm's Lessons in Teamwork," *Nation's Business*, March 1997, p. 32.
2. This section is based on J. R. Katzenbach and D. K. Smith, *The Wisdom of Teams* (Boston: Harvard Business School Press, 1993), pp. 21, 45, 85; D. C. Kinlaw, *Developing Superior Work Teams* (Lexington, MA: Lexington Books, 1991), pp. 3–21; and S. A. Mohrman, S. G. Cohen, and A. M. Mohrman Jr., *Designing Team-Based Organizations* (San Francisco: Jossey-Bass, 1995), pp. 39–40.
3. See, for example, R. K. Merton, *Social Theory and Social Structure* (New York: Free Press, 1968); and S. E. Jackson and R. S. Schuler, "A Meta-Analysis and Conceptual Critique of Research on Role Ambiguity and Role Conflict in Work Settings," *Organizational Behavior and Human Decision Processes*, August 1985, pp. 16–78.
4. See M. P. O'Driscoll, D. R. Ilgen, and K. Hildreth, "Time

Devoted to Job and Off-Job Activities, Interrole Conflict, and Affective Experiences," *Journal of Applied Psychology*, April 1992, pp. 272–79.
5. D. C. Feldman, "The Development and Enforcement of Group Norms," *Academy of Management Review*, January 1984, pp. 47–53; and J. R. Hackman, "Group Influences on Individuals in Organizations," in M. D. Dunnette and L. M. Hough (eds.), *Handbook of Industrial & Organizational Psychology*, 2nd ed., vol. 3 (Palo Alto, CA: Consulting Psychologists Press, 1992), pp. 235–50.
6. S. E. Asch, "Effects of Group Pressure upon the Modification and Distortion of Judgments," in H. Guetzkow (ed.), *Groups, Leadership and Men* (Pittsburgh, PA: Carnegie Press, 1951), pp. 177–90.
7. I. Summers, T. Coffelt, and R. E. Horton, "Work-Group Cohesion," *Psychological Reports*, October 1988, pp.

627–36; and B. Mullen and C. Copper, "The Relation between Group Cohesiveness and Performance: An Integration," *Psychological Bulletin*, March 1994, pp. 210–27.

8. Based on J. L. Gibson, J. M. Ivancevich, and J. H. Donnelly Jr., *Organizations* (Burr Ridge, IL: Irwin, 1994), p. 323.

9. E. J. Thomas and C. F. Fink, "Effects of Group Size," *Psychological Bulletin*, July 1963, pp. 371–84; A. P. Hare, *Handbook of Small Group Research* (New York: Free Press, 1976); and M. E. Shaw, *Group Dynamics: The Psychology of Small Group Behavior*, 3rd ed. (New York: McGraw-Hill, 1981).

10. W. Moede, "Die Richtlinien der Leistungs-Psychologie," *Industrielle Psychotechnik*, 4 (1927), pp. 193–207. See also D. A. Kravitz and B. Martin, "Ringelmann Rediscovered: The Original Article," *Journal of Personality and Social Psychology*, May 1986, pp. 936–41.

11. See, for example, J. A. Shepperd, "Productivity Loss in Performance Groups: A Motivation Analysis," *Psychological Bulletin*, January 1993, pp. 67–81; and S. J. Karau and K. D. Williams, "Social Loafing: A Meta-Analysis Review and Theoretical Integration," *Journal of Personality and Social Psychology*, October 1993, pp. 681–706.

12. S. G. Harkins and K. Seymanski, "Social Loafing and Group Evaluation," *Journal of Personality and Social Psychology*, December 1989, pp. 934–41.

13. See P. C. Earley, "Social Loafing and Collectivism: A Comparison of the United States and the People's Republic of China," *Administrative Science Quarterly*, December 1989, pp. 565–81; and P. C. Earley, "East Meets West Meets Mideast: Further Explorations of Collectivistic and Individualistic Work Groups," *Academy of Management Journal*, April 1993, pp. 319–48.

14. See, for example, P. S. Goodman, E. C. Ravlin, and L. Argote, "Current Thinking about Groups: Setting the Stage for New Ideas," in P. S. Goodman and Associates (eds.), *Designing Effective Work Groups* (San Francisco: Jossey-Bass, 1986), pp. 15–16; and R. A. Guzzo and G. P. Shea, "Group Performance and Intergroup Relations in Organizations," in Dunnette and Hough (eds.), *Handbook of Industrial & Organizational Psychology*, 2nd ed., vol. 3, pp. 288–90.

15. M. E. Shaw, *Contemporary Topics in Social Psychology* (Morristown, NJ: General Learning Press, 1976), p. 356.

16. W. E. Watson, K. Kumar, and L. K. Michaelsen, "Cultural Diversity's Impact on Interaction Process and Performance: Comparing Homogeneous and Diverse Task Groups," *Academy of Management Journal*, June 1993, pp. 590–602.

17. See, for instance, J. W. Newstrom, R. E. Monczka, and W. E. Reif, "Perceptions of the Grapevine: Its Value and Influence," *Journal of Business Communication*, Spring 1974, pp. 12–20; and S. J. Modic, "Grapevine Rated Most Believable," *Industry Week*, May 15, 1989, p. 14.

18. K. Davis, "Management Communication and the Grapevine," *Harvard Business Review*, September–October 1953, pp. 43–49.

19. H. Sutton and L. W. Porter, "A Study of the Grapevine in a Governmental Organization," *Personnel Psychology*, Summer 1968, pp. 223–30.

20. K. Davis, cited in R. Rowan, "Where Did That Rumor Come From?" *Fortune*, August 13, 1979, p. 134.

21. L. Hirschhorn, "Managing Rumors," in L. Hirschhorn (ed.), *Cutting Back* (San Francisco: Jossey-Bass, 1983), pp. 49–52.

22. R. L. Rosnow and G. A. Fine, *Rumor and Gossip: The Social Psychology of Hearsay* (New York: Elsevier, 1976).

23. See, for instance, J. G. March and G. Sevon, "Gossip, Information and Decision Making," in J. G. March (ed.), *Decisions and Organizations* (Oxford: Blackwell, 1988), pp. 429–42; M. Noon and R. Delbridge, "News from Behind My Hand: Gossip in Organizations," *Organization Studies* 14, no. 1 (1993), pp. 23–36; N. Difonzo, P. Bordia, and R. L. Rosnow, "Reining in Rumors," *Organizational Dynamics*, Summer 1994, pp. 47–62; and P. LaBarre, "The Other Network," *Industry Week*, September 19, 1994, pp. 33–36.

24. D. M. Rousseau and K. A. Wade-Benzoni, "Changing Individual-Organizational Attachments," in A. Howard (ed.), *The Changing Nature of Work* (San Francisco: Jossey-Bass, 1995), pp. 301–05.

25. S. Berglas, "The Death of Status," *Inc.*, October 1996, p. 36.

26. J. Greenberg, "Equity and Workplace Status: A Field Experiment," *Journal of Applied Psychology*, November 1988, pp. 606–13.

27. See S. P. Robbins, *Managing Organizational Conflict: A Nontraditional Approach* (Englewood Cliffs, NJ: Prentice Hall, 1974).

28. I. L. Janis, *Groupthink* (Boston: Houghton Mifflin, 1982).

29. Ibid.

30. I. L. Janis and L. Mann, *Decision Making* (New York: Free Press, 1977).

31. I. L. Janis, *Groupthink*; S. Smith, "Groupthink and the Hostage Rescue Mission," *British Journal of Political Science* 15 (1984), pp. 117–23; and G. Moorhead, R. Ference, and C. P. Neck, "Group Decision Fiascoes Continue: Space Shuttle Challenger and a Revised Framework," *Human Relations*, May 1991, pp. 539–50.

32. C. R. Leana, "A Partial Test of Janis' Groupthink Model: Effects of Group Cohesiveness and Leader Behavior on Defective Decision Making," *Journal of Management*, Spring 1985, pp. 5–17; G. Moorhead and J. R. Montanari, "An Empirical Investigation of the Groupthink Phenomenon," *Human Relations*, May 1986, pp. 399–410; and C. P. Neck and G. Moorhead, "Groupthink Remodeled: The Importance of Leadership, Time Pressure, and Methodical Decision-Making Procedures," *Human Relations*, May 1995, pp. 537–57.

33. Neck and Moorhead, "Groupthink Remodeled," p. 550.

34. See D. J. Isenberg, "Group Polarization: A Critical Review and Meta-Analysis," *Journal of Personality and Social Psychology*, December 1986, pp. 1141–51; J. L. Hale and F. J. Boster, "Comparing Effect Coded Models of Choice Shifts," *Communication Research Reports*, April 1988, pp. 180–86; and P. W. Paese, M. Bieser, and M. E. Tubbs, "Framing Effects and Choice Shifts in Group Decision Making," *Organizational Behavior and Human Decision Processes*, October 1993, pp. 149–65.

35. See, for example, N. Kogan and M. A. Wallach, "Risk Taking as a Function of the Situation, the Person, and the Group," in N. Kogan and M. A. Wallach (eds.), *New Directions in Psychology*, vol. 3 (New York: Holt, Rinehart and

Winston, 1967); and M. A. Wallach, N. Kogan, and D. J. Bem, "Group Influence on Individual Risk Taking," *Journal of Abnormal and Social Psychology* 65 (1962), pp. 75–86.

36. R. D. Clark III, "Group-Induced Shift toward Risk: A Critical Appraisal," *Psychological Bulletin*, October 1971, pp. 251–70.

37. See R. I. Sutton and A. Hargadon, "Brainstorming Groups in Context: Effectiveness in a Product Design Firm," *Administrative Science Quarterly*, December 1996, pp. 685–718.

38. See A. L. Delbecq, A. H. Van deVen, and D. H. Gustafson, *Group Techniques for Program Planning: A Guide to Nominal and Delphi Processes* (Glenview, IL: Scott, Foresman, 1975); and W. M. Fox, "Anonymity and Other Keys to Successful Problem-Solving Meetings," *National Productivity Review*, Spring 1989, pp. 145–56.

39. R. B. Gallupe, W. H. Cooper, M.-L. Grise, and L. M. Bastianutti, "Blocking Electronic Brainstorms," *Journal of Applied Psychology*, February 1994, pp. 77–86.

40. E. A. Michaels, "Business Meetings," *Small Business Reports*, February 1989, pp. 82–88; and E. Wakin, "Make Meetings Meaningful," *Today's Office*, May 1991, pp. 68–69.

41. See S. P. Robbins and P. L. Hunsaker, *Training in InterPersonal Skills: TIPS for Managing People at Work*, 2nd ed. (Upper Saddle River, NJ: Prentice Hall, 1996), pp. 180–82.

42. Cited in "Teams," *Training*, October 1996, p. 69.

43. See, for example, D. Tjosvold, *Team Organization: An Enduring Competitive Advantage* (Chichester, England: Wiley, 1991); J. Lipnack and J. Stamps, *The TeamNet Factor* (Essex Junction, VT: Oliver Wight, 1993); Wellins, Byham, and Dixon, *Inside Teams*, pp. 338–46; and R. D. Banker, J. M. Field, R. G. Schroeder, and K. K. Sinha, "Impact of Work Teams on Manufacturing Performance: A Longitudinal Field Study," *Academy of Management Journal*, August 1996, pp. 867–90.

44. Kinlaw, *Developing Superior Work Teams*, p. 43.

45. Based on D. Dunphy and B. Bryant, "Teams: Panaceas or Prescriptions for Improved Performance?" *Human Relations*, May 1996, pp. 677–99.

46. J. H. Shonk, *Team-Based Organizations* (Homewood, IL: Business One Irwin, 1992); and M. A. Verespej, "When Workers Get New Roles," *Industry Week*, February 3, 1992, p. 11.

47. S. G. Cohen, G. E. Ledford Jr., and G. M. Spreitzer, "A Predictive Model of Self-Managing Work Teams," *Human Relations*, May 1996, p. 644.

48. M. A. Verespej, "Workers-Managers," *Industry Week*, May 16, 1994, p. 30.

49. "Teams," *Training*, October 1996, p. 69.

50. "A Conversation with Charles Dull," *Organizational Dynamics*, Summer 1993, pp. 57–70.

51. See, for instance, T. D. Wall, N. J. Kemp, P. R. Jackson, and C. W. Clegg, "Outcomes of Autonomous Workgroups: A Long-Term Field Experiment," *Academy of Management Journal*, June 1986, pp. 280–304; and J. L. Cordery, W. S. Mueller, and L. M. Smith, "Attitudinal and Behavioral Effects of Autonomous Group Working: A Longitudinal Field Study," *Academy of Management Journal*, June 1991, pp. 464–76.

52. See D. R. Denison, S. L. Hart, and J. A. Kahn, "From Chim-

neys to Cross-Functional Teams: Developing and Validating a Diagnostic Model," *Academy of Management Journal*, August 1996, pp. 1005–23.

53. G. Taninecz, "Team Players," *Industry Week*, July 15, 1996, pp. 28–32.

54. Cited in *Forbes*, September 23, 1996, p. 47.

55. T. B. Kinni, "Boundary-Busting Teamwork," *Industry Week*, March 21, 1994, pp. 72–78.

56. "Cross-Functional Obstacles," *Training*, May 1994, pp. 125–26.

57. W. R. Pape, "Group Insurance," *Inc. Technology*, July 1997, pp. 29–31. For more on virtual teams, see B. Geber, "Virtual Teams," *Training*, April 1995, pp. 36–40; M. E. Warkentin, L. Sayeed, and R. Hightower, "Virtual Teams versus Face-to-Face Teams: An Exploratory Study of a Web-Based Conference System," *Decision Sciences*, Fall 1997, pp. 975–93; S. V. Brull, "Networks That Do New Tricks," *Business Week*, April 6, 1998, p. 100; and A. M. Townsend, S. M. DeMarie, and A. R. Hendrickson, "Virtual Teams: Technology and the Workplace of the Future," *Academy of Management Executive*, August 1998, pp. 17–29.

58. S. G. Cohen and D. E. Bailey, "What Makes Teams Work: Group Effectiveness Research from the Shop Floor to the Executive Suite," *Journal of Management*, vol. 23, no. 3, 1997, pp. 239–90.

59. The suggestions in this discussion come from K. Hess, *Creating the High-Performance Team* (New York: Wiley, 1987); Katzenbach and Smith, *The Wisdom of Teams*, pp. 43–64; Wellins, Byham, and Dixon, *Inside Teams*, pp. 299–337; M. A. Campion, G. J. Medsker, and A. C. Higgs, "Relations Between Work Group Characteristics and Effectiveness: Implications for Designing Effective Work Groups," *Personnel Psychology*, Winter 1993, pp. 823–50; K. D. Scott and A. Townsend, "Teams: Why Some Succeed and Others Fail," *HRMagazine*, August 1994, pp. 62–67; and M. A. Campion, E. M. Papper, and G. J. Medsker, "Relations Between Work Team Characteristics and Effectiveness: A Replication and Extension," *Personnel Psychology*, Summer 1996, pp. 429–52.

60. S. T. Johnson, "Work Teams: What's Ahead in Work Design and Rewards Management," *Compensation & Benefits Review*, March–April 1993, pp. 35–41; and A. M. Saunier and E. J. Hawk, "Realizing the Potential of Teams through Team-Based Rewards," *Compensation & Benefits Review*, July–August 1994, pp. 24–33.

61. D. Harrington-Mackin, The Team Building Tool Kit (New York: AMACOM, 1994), p. 53.

62. T. D. Schellhardt, "To Be a Star among Equals, Be a Team Player," *Wall Street Journal*, April 20, 1994, p. B1.

63. Ibid.

64. Ibid.

65. See, for instance, H. Robbins and M. Finley, *Why Teams Don't Work* (Princeton, NJ: Pacesetter Books, 1995); D. Dunphy and B. Bryant, "Teams: Panaceas or Prescriptions for Improved Performance?" *Human Relations*, May 1996, pp. 677–99; and A. B. Drexler and R. Forrester, "Teamwork—Not Necessarily the Answer," *HRMagazine*, January 1998, pp. 55–58.

66. Cited in R. Zemke, "Rethinking the Rush to Team Up," *Training*, November 1993, p. 56.

67. See, for instance, P. R. Harris and R. T. Moran, *Managing Cultural Differences*, 4th ed. (Houston: Gulf Publishing, 1996), pp. 105–08; and B. L. Kirkman and D. L. Shapiro, "The Impact of Cultural Values on Employee Resistance to Teams: Toward a Model of Globalized Self-Managing Work Team Effectiveness," *Academy of Management Review*, July 1997, pp. 730–57.

68. See, for instance, A. C. Amason, K. R. Thompson, W. A. Hochwarter, and A. W. Harrison, "Conflict: An Important Dimension in Successful Management Teams," *Organizational Dynamics*, Autumn 1995, pp. 20–35.

69. R. Zemke, "Rethinking the Rush to Team Up," p. 58.

70. S. G. Cohen, G. E. Ledford Jr., and G. M. Spreitzer, "A Predictive Model of Self-Managing Work Team Effectiveness."

71. J. Gordon, "The Team Troubles That Won't Go Away," *Training*, August 1994, pp. 25–34.

Chapter

11

CREATING AND SUSTAINING THE ORGANIZATION'S CULTURE

CULT-LIKE CULTURES ARE GREAT PLACES TO WORK, BUT
ONLY FOR THOSE WHO BUY INTO THE CORE IDEOLOGY.
THOSE WHO DON'T FIT WITH THE IDEOLOGY ARE
EJECTED LIKE A VIRUS.

J. C. COLLINS AND J. I. PORRAS

LEARNING OBJECTIVES

After studying this chapter, you should be able to:

1 Define *organizational culture.*

2 Identify the seven primary characteristics that describe an organization's culture.

3 Define the qualities that characterize a strong culture.

4 Explain the ultimate source of an organization's culture.

5 Describe how employees learn their organization's culture.

6 Explain the primary forces that sustain a culture.

7 Identify the situational factors that favor cultural change.

8 Describe how to minimize cultural clash in mergers and acquisitions.

The merger of Pharmacia AB and Upjohn Co. in 1995 was seen by many as the perfect marriage.[1] Both were second-tier players fighting for survival in a world of global drug giants. Pharmacia, based in Sweden, had a solid roster of drugs, including allergy medicines and human-growth hormones. But its distribution in the United States was weak and its product line was aging. Upjohn, based in Kalamazoo, Michigan, owned such household name brands as Rogaine and Motrin, yet it had no likely breakthroughs in its product pipeline and suffered from stagnant sales. The merger was seen as a way to cut costs, improve worldwide market penetration, and allow the combined company to better compete against global heavyweights like Merck, Bristol-Myers Squibb, Pfizer, and Warner-Lambert. Two years into the marriage, few of the hoped-for benefits have emerged. Pharmacia & Upjohn's earnings have plummeted. The company's stock has tanked. Many of P&U's senior executives have quit. John Zabriskie (see photo), CEO of Upjohn, the man who engineered the merger and assumed the top

338

spot in the new company, has been fired by the directors. And employee morale has hit bottom. The problem? Most experts point to the incompatibility between Pharmacia and Upjohn's organizational cultures.

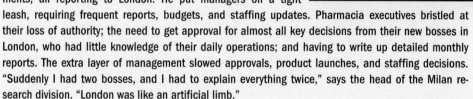

Pharmacia's primary operations were in Sweden and Italy. It's managers were used to a loose structure and a great deal of autonomy. Upjohn managers, in contrast, had become comfortable with Zabriskie's tightly centralized management style. As a geographic compromise, Zabriskie set up P&U's headquarters in London. But the organization structure he created was very similar to what he had created at Upjohn. London executives were given much of the responsibility for the financial and operating performance of the local units. Pharmacia people were used to an open system, in which small teams were left largely on their own. Managers preferred getting a whole group's approval before making a big decision. Upjohn, however, was used to commanding captains. Zabriskie combined the new company into departments, all reporting to London. He put managers on a tight leash, requiring frequent reports, budgets, and staffing updates. Pharmacia executives bristled at their loss of authority; the need to get approval for almost all key decisions from their new bosses in London, who had little knowledge of their daily operations; and having to write up detailed monthly reports. The extra layer of management slowed approvals, product launches, and staffing decisions. "Suddenly I had two bosses, and I had to explain everything twice," says the head of the Milan research division. "London was like an artificial limb."

Differences in work rules also created problems. Upjohn, for instance, had strict policies requiring all employees to undergo drug and alcohol tests, including top management. At Pharmacia's Italian business center, waiters poured wine freely every afternoon in the company dining room. Upjohn also banned smoking; Pharmacia's boardrooms were stocked with humidors for executives who liked to light a cigar during long meetings.

The Upjohn and Pharmacia case illustrates an important issue in any merger decision. Even if the financial and marketing criteria indicate a good match, the merger may still encounter major difficulties if the two organizations' cultures aren't compatible.

In this chapter, we define organizational culture, show how cultures differ, describe the powerful influence they can have on organizational members, explain how they're created and transmitted, and offer some techniques for managing them.

WHAT IS ORGANIZATIONAL CULTURE?

A few years back, I asked an executive to tell me what he thought *organizational culture* meant. He gave me essentially the same answer that a U.S. Supreme Court justice once gave in attempting to define pornography: "I can't define it, but I know it when I see it." This executive's approach to defining organizational culture is not acceptable for our purposes. We need a basic definition to provide a point of departure for our quest to better understand the phenomenon. In this section, we will propose a specific definition and review several peripheral issues that revolve around that definition.

▶ A Definition

There seems to be wide agreement that **organizational culture** refers to a system of shared meaning held by members that distinguishes the organization from other organizations.[2] This system of shared meaning is, on closer examination, a set of key characteristics that the organization values. The most recent research suggests that there are seven primary characteristics that, in aggregate, capture the essence of an organization's culture.[3]

1. *Innovation and risk taking.* The degree to which employees are encouraged to be innovative and take risks.
2. *Attention to detail.* The degree to which employees are expected to exhibit precision, analysis, and attention to detail.
3. *Outcome orientation.* The degree to which management focuses on results or outcomes rather than on the techniques and processes used to achieve those outcomes.
4. *People orientation.* The degree to which management decisions take into consideration the effect of outcomes on people within the organization.
5. *Team orientation.* The degree to which work activities are organized around teams rather than individuals.
6. *Aggressiveness.* The degree to which people are aggressive and competitive rather than easygoing.
7. *Stability.* The degree to which organizational activities emphasize maintaining the status quo in contrast to growth.

Each of these characteristics exists on a continuum from low to high. Appraising the organization on these seven characteristics, then, gives a composite picture of the organization's culture. This picture becomes the basis for feelings of shared understanding that members have about the organization, how things are done in it, and the way members are supposed to behave. Exhibit 11-1 demonstrates how these characteristics can be mixed to create highly diverse organizations.

▶ Do Organizations Have Uniform Cultures?

Organizational culture represents a common perception held by the organization's members. This aspect of a culture was made explicit when we defined a culture as a system of *shared* meaning. We should expect, therefore, that individuals with different backgrounds or at different levels in the organization will tend to describe the organization's culture in similar terms.[4]

Acknowledgment that organizational culture has common properties does not mean, however, that there cannot be subcultures within any given culture. Most large organizations have a dominant culture and numerous sets of subcultures.[5] A **dominant culture** expresses the core values that are shared by a majority of the organization's members. When we talk about an *organization's culture*, we are referring to its dominant culture. It is this macro view of culture that gives an organization its distinct personality. **Subcultures** tend to develop in large organizations to reflect common problems, situations, or experiences that members face. These subcultures are likely to be defined by department designations and geographical separation.[6] The purchasing department, for example, can have a subculture that is uniquely shared by members of that department. It will include the core values

Contrasting Organizational Cultures

EXHIBIT 11-1

Organization A

This organization is a manufacturing firm. Managers are expected to fully document all decisions, and "good managers" are those who can provide detailed data to support their recommendations. Creative decisions that incur significant change or risk are not encouraged. Because managers of failed projects are openly criticized and penalized, they try not to implement ideas that deviate much from the status quo. One lower-level manager quoted an often-used phrase in the company: "If it ain't broke, don't fix it."

There are extensive rules and regulations in this firm that employees are required to follow. Managers supervise employees closely to ensure there are no deviations. Management is concerned with high productivity, regardless of the impact on employee morale or turnover.

Work activities are designed around individuals. There are distinct departments and lines of authority, and employees are expected to minimize formal contact with other employees outside their functional area or line of command. Performance evaluations and rewards emphasize individual effort, although seniority tends to be the primary factor in the determination of pay raises and promotions.

Organization B

This organization is also a manufacturing firm. Here, however, management encourages and rewards risk taking and change. Decisions based on intuition are valued as much as those that are well rationalized. Management prides itself on its history of experimenting with new technologies and its success in regularly introducing innovative products. Managers or employees who have a good idea are encouraged to "run with it," and failures are treated as "learning experiences." The company prides itself on being market-driven and rapidly responsive to the changing needs of its customers.

There are few rules and regulations for employees to follow, and supervision is loose because management believes that its employees are hardworking and trustworthy. Management is concerned with high productivity but believes that this comes through treating its people right. The company is proud of its reputation as being a good place to work.

Job activities are designed around work teams, and team members are encouraged to interact with people across functions and authority levels. Employees talk positively about the competition between teams. Individuals and teams have goals, and bonuses are based on achievement of outcomes. Employees are given considerable autonomy in choosing the means by which the goals are attained.

---

of the dominant culture plus additional values unique to members of the purchasing department. Similarly, an office or unit of the organization that is physically separated from the organization's main operations may take on a different personality. Again, the core values are essentially retained but modified to reflect the separated unit's distinct situation.

If organizations had no dominant culture and were composed only of numerous subcultures, the importance of organizational culture would be significantly lessened because there would be no uniform interpretation of what represented appropriate and inappropriate behavior. It is the "shared meaning" aspect of culture that makes it such a potent device for guiding and shaping behavior. But we cannot ignore the reality that many organizations also have subcultures that can influence the behavior of members.

▶ Strong Versus Weak Cultures

It has become increasingly popular to differentiate between strong and weak cultures.[7] The argument is that strong cultures have a greater impact on employee behavior and a more positive effect on the organization's performance.

In a strong culture, the organization's core values are both intensely held and widely shared.[8] The more members who accept the core values and the greater their commitment to those values, the stronger the culture is. Consistent with this definition, a strong culture will have a great influence on the behavior of its members because the high degree of sharedness and intensity creates an internal climate of high behavioral control. For example, Seattle-based Nordstrom has developed one of the strongest service cultures in the retailing industry. Nordstrom employees know in no uncertain terms what is expected of them, and these expectations go a long way in shaping their behavior. This message is communicated on a single 5-by-8-inch card that the company distributes (see Exhibit 11-2).

An increasing body of evidence indicates that strong cultures are associated with high organizational performance.[9] For instance, one study comparing eighteen high-performing companies—which included Procter & Gamble, Nordstrom, Hewlett-Packard, and Walt Disney—against a control group of eighteen lesser-performing firms found that a strong culture was the key factor in explaining the high-performers' long-term success.[10] Similarly, another study of more than 200 companies in 22 different industries found that those with strong cultures consistently outperformed their weak-culture counterparts.[11]

Why should strong cultures be positively linked to higher organizational performance? We can offer several reasons. A strong culture gives everyone in the organization a clear and focused vision. Employees tend to "march to the same drummer" when there is high goal alignment.[12] Strong cultures also increase employee commitment and loyalty. People feel better about where they work when they know what their organization stands for. And finally, a strong culture gives an organization a sustainable competitive advantage because competitors can't easily replicate it. "The evidence suggests that it is much more difficult to duplicate an organization's culture and way of operating than its technology, its strategy, or even its products or services. That is why culture and organizational capability are increasingly important sources of organizational success."[13]

Don't, however, ignore the downside of strong cultures. Although they help employees to march to the same drummer, they can also lead intelligent people to march, in con-

---

EXHIBIT 11-2

The Essence of Nordstrom's Organizational Culture

WELCOME TO NORDSTROM

We're glad to have you with our Company.
Our number one goal is to provide
outstanding customer service.
Set both your personal and professional goals high.
We have great confidence in your ability to achieve them.

Nordstrom Rules
Rule #1: **Use your good judgment in all situations.**
There will be no additional rules.

Please feel free to ask your department manager,
store manager, or division general manager
any questions at any time.

Source: Courtesy of Nordstrom. With permission.

cert, off a cliff.[14] And strong cultures that don't value adaptability are apt to *lower* organizational performance in today's dynamic environment. IBM, as a case in point, has a strong culture. But that culture hindered the company's ability to respond to the growth in PCs because the organization was rigidly attached to viewing computers through a mainframe mentality. Large mainframes had built IBM, and for a long time its executives resisted changes that threatened that world.

▶ Culture as the Organization's Personality

In many organizations, especially those with strong cultures, one cultural dimension will rise above the others and essentially shape the organization. 3M Co., for instance, is dominated by its focus on innovation. The company "lives and breathes" new product generation. Let's take a look at how different organizations have chosen different cultural themes. This discussion will illustrate that strong cultures don't have to be similar to be successful.

STRONG RISK-TAKING PERSONALITIES Companies such as Microsoft, Coca-Cola, and Physio-Control Corp. pride themselves on risk taking and tolerance (even encouragement) of failure. Microsoft seeks out people who have taken chances and failed.[15] But management looks to see whether people have learned from their mistakes. In hiring, for instance, interviewers always ask: What was a major failure you had? What did you learn from it? Microsoft wants employees who are willing to take risks, fail, and learn from their mistakes. Bill Gates, the company's CEO, says, "The way people deal with things that go wrong is an indicator of how they deal with change." [16]

Coca-Cola is changing itself to be more risk seeking.[17] Says its CEO, "We became uncompetitive by not being tolerant of mistakes." As an example, the company hired back as its chief global marketing executive the man who was behind New Coke—the most disastrous product launch in the company's history. Sergio Zyman left Coca-Cola, wounded, a year after he oversaw the introduction of New Coke. Seven years later, the company brought him back with a promotion. The company's CEO saw rehiring Zyman as visible evidence that Coca-Cola believes you "can stumble only if you're moving."

People have to see that it's worthwhile to take risks. "People will only take risks if supported by the culture," observes an executive at Physio-Control Corp., a Redmond, Washington, maker of medical devices. "To facilitate this behavior, we moved toward reward structures that promote more individual risk-taking." [18]

STRONG ATTENTION-TO-DETAIL PERSONALITIES Organizations that have made quality their driving theme have attention-to-detail personalities. Maybe the most visible example is Motorola. It's "Six Sigma" program has been instrumental in achieving a dramatic improvement in quality. In one six-year period, Motorola went from 6,000 defects per million to 3.4 defects per million (equal to 99.999 percent defect-free manufacturing). The company, a world leader in achieving quality, is a past winner of the Malcolm Baldrige National Quality Award.

STRONG OUTCOME-ORIENTATION PERSONALITIES Some organizations succeed by focusing on outcomes such as customer service. This orientation, for example, would describe Nordstrom. It would also characterize Disney's commitment to treating its theme-park customers as guests. Other organizations have achieved success by focusing on internal processes. Companies with a strong ethical emphasis would fall into this category. The

Ben & Jerry's Homemade has made social responsibility and high ethical standards a part of its culture from the company's very beginnings. It continues to try to maintain these values in spite of recent financial setbacks.

culture of Ben & Jerry's Homemade, for instance, is tightly woven around maintaining high ethical standards and behaving in a socially responsible fashion.

STRONG PEOPLE-ORIENTATION PERSONALITIES Corporations such as Hewlett-Packard and Adobe Systems have made their employees central to their culture. HP is committed to recognizing and respecting the personal worth of employees and allowing them to share in the success of the company.[19] It has a long history of progressive personnel policies. For instance, it had employee profit sharing in the 1940s and automatic stock grants for all employees in the 1950s. It has kept layoffs to a minimum by requiring divisions to hire HP insiders first before looking to the outside and by asking all employees to cut their pay and hours so no one has to lose his or her job. HP was one of the first American companies to introduce flextime, and the company is currently a leader in creating a family-friendly work environment.

Adobe Systems is the third-largest manufacturer worldwide of personal-computer software. Its 1,700 employees all receive stock options and are eligible for company-paid sabbaticals. The company's culture emphasizes openness, teamwork, and respect for the individual. "Every capital asset we have at Adobe gets into an automobile and drives home at night," says one of the company's co-founders. "Without them, there is nothing of substance in this company. It is the creativity of individuals—not machines—that determines the success of this company."[20]

STRONG TEAM-ORIENTATION PERSONALITIES An increasing number of smaller organizations and divisions of larger organizations are defining their cultures around the team concept. Many law firms now organize their operations around teams. For instance, the largest law firm in the Pacific Northwest, Perkins Coie, has its 300-plus lawyers operating in teams defined around litigation, business, personal planning, and environmental law. All 200 employees at Colgate-Palmolive's Cambridge, Ohio, liquid-detergent plant are members of self-managed or cross-functional teams.[21] And the 8,300 employees at Eastman Chemical Company's Tennessee Eastman Division are all members of teams.[22] The common theme through these examples is that these organizations or divisions use their commitment to teams to define the essence of their unit's identity.

STRONG AGGRESSIVENESS PERSONALITIES Some people argue, and maybe correctly, that Microsoft's culture is more dominated by aggressiveness than by risk taking. The company, and its CEO, are regularly characterized as epitomizing the best and worst characteristics of the entrepreneurial spirit. Microsoft's aggressiveness in fighting competitors, protecting its copyrights, and using the court system against rivals has created a long list of adversaries (including the U.S. federal government) that continue to try to rein in the software behemoth.[23]

Siemens is another company whose culture is being shaped by aggressiveness.[24] The company, which produces everything from hearing aids to power plants, has recently undergone a revolution to replace its engineering-driven culture with an aggressive, entreprenurial culture. Toward this end, a new executive team is giving local managers almost complete freedom to cut costs, bid for projects, and do whatever is necessary to service customers.

General Electric represents still another example of an organization with a strong aggressiveness culture. Senior management sets very demanding goals for its division managers and pays more attention than most organizations to its bottom line.[25] Moreover, GE's strategy to be either the number one or the number two player in each of its markets (in terms of market share), or exit from those markets, is consistent with aggressiveness.

STRONG NONSTABILITY PERSONALITIES Finally, there are organizations that define their culture by their overwhelming emphasis on growth. Few companies better illustrate this type of culture than the Samsung Group.[26] The company is already South Korea's largest business group, with operations in electronics, chemicals, finance, and heavy machinery. But Samsung has very ambitious plans. Its seven-year plan, for instance, includes the goal of quadrupling annual sales. Management plans to achieve this goal by expanding into new industries including automobiles, aerospace, transportation, and entertainment. For instance, Samsung is spending $4.5 billion to develop cars with Nissan and is leading a Sino-Korean joint venture to create a 100-seat jetliner. Meanwhile, all Samsung employees are being indoctrinated in the company's growth culture. Inside the Samsung Human Resources Center, where thousands of new hires undergo monthlong training, lecture halls are draped with banners proclaiming the company's commitment to become "The Leader for the 21st Century the World Will Notice."

▶ Organizational Culture Versus National Culture

Organizational culture and national culture are not the same thing. The former focuses at the level of the specific organization. The latter is concerned with intracountry similarities and intercountry differences. We have pointed out in numerous places, for instance, how differences in national culture can explain differences in management practices between organizations in Japan and those in the United States.

How do these two concepts compare in terms of strength? More specifically, does national culture override an organization's culture? Is an IBM facility in Germany, for example, more likely to reflect German ethnic culture or IBM's corporate culture?

The research indicates that national culture has a greater impact on employees than does their organization's culture.[27] German employees at an IBM facility in Munich, therefore, will be influenced more by German culture than by IBM's culture. This means that as influential as organizational culture is in shaping managerial practices and employee behavior, national culture is even more influential.

This conclusion has to be qualified to reflect the self-selection that goes on at the hiring stage.[28] A British multinational corporation, for example, is likely to be less concerned with hiring the "typical Italian" for its Italian operations than in hiring an Italian who fits with the corporation's way of doing things. We should expect, therefore, that the employee selection process will be used by multinationals to find and hire job applicants who are a good fit with their organization's dominant culture, even if such applicants are somewhat atypical for members of their country.

An organization's current customs, traditions, and general way of doing things are largely due to what it has done before and the degree of success it has had with those endeavors. This principle leads us to the ultimate source of an organization's culture: its founders.[29]

HOW IS CULTURE CREATED?

The founders of an organization traditionally have a major impact on that organization's early culture. They have a vision of what the organization should be. They are unconstrained by previous customs or ideologies. The small size that typically characterizes new organizations further facilitates the founders' imposition of their vision on all organizational members.

The process of culture creation occurs in three ways.[30] First, founders only hire and keep employees who think and feel the way they do. Second, they indoctrinate and

Chris Hassett is the former CEO and cofounder of PointCast, Inc. This hot Internet media company went from 3 employees to 220 in less than five years. And Hassett made sure new hires understood his company's culture. He interviewed as many as 25 people for every vice presidency position and demanded that every vice president be able to communicate PointCast's cultural values to their employees.

socialize these employees to their way of thinking and feeling. And finally, the founders' own behavior acts as a role model that encourages employees to identify with them and thereby internalize their beliefs, values, and assumptions. When the organization succeeds, the founders' vision becomes seen as a primary determinant of that success. At this point, the founders' entire personality becomes embedded in the culture of the organization.

McDonald's founder Ray Kroc died in 1984. But his philosophy of providing customers with quality, service, cleanliness, and value continue to shape managerial decisions. Other contemporary examples of founders who have had an immeasurable impact on their organization's culture are Akio Morita at Sony, Ted Turner at Turner Broadcasting Systems, Bill Gates at Microsoft, Fred Smith at Federal Express, Mary Kay at Mary Kay Cosmetics, Chung Ju Yung at Hyundai, Steve Jobs at Apple Computer, David Packard at Hewlett-Packard, Richard Branson at the Virgin Group, and Chris Hassett at PointCast.

HOW DO EMPLOYEES LEARN THEIR ORGANIZATION'S CULTURE?

Success breeds success. It also breeds cultural values. Those things that work tend to become repeated, ritualized, and even deified. Solutions that continually solve reappearing problems thus become a part of the organization's culture. The longer the solutions seem to work, the more deeply they tend to become embedded in the culture.[31] This helps explain how dominant cultural personality types—like high risk-taking or aggressive cultures—develop. It also helps explain how a company like IBM could, for years, dismiss the growth of PCs and continually focus on large mainframe computers.

Once in place, how do people learn their organization's culture? The most potent means by which culture is transmitted to employees is through stories, rituals, material symbols, and language.

Stories

During the days when Henry Ford II was chairman of the Ford Motor Co., one would have been hard-pressed to find a manager who hadn't heard the story about Mr. Ford's reminding his executives, when they got too arrogant, that "it's my name that's on the building." The message was clear: Henry Ford II ran the company!

Nordstrom employees are fond of the following story. It strongly conveys the company's policy toward customer returns: When this specialty retail chain was in its infancy, a customer came in and wanted to return a set of automobile tires. The salesclerk was a bit uncertain how to handle the problem. As the customer and salesclerk were speaking, Mr. Nordstrom walked by and overheard the conversation. He immediately interceded, asking the customer how much he had paid for the tires. Nordstrom then instructed the clerk to take the tires back and provide a full cash refund. After the customer had received his refund and left, the perplexed clerk looked at the boss. "But, Mr. Nordstrom, we don't sell tires!" "I know," replied the boss, "but we do whatever we need to do to make the customer happy. I mean it when I say we have a no-questions-asked return policy." Nordstrom then picked up the telephone and called a friend in the auto parts business to see how much he could get for the tires.

Stories such as these circulate through many organizations. They typically contain a narrative of events about the organization's founders, rule breaking, rags-to-riches successes, reductions in the workforce, relocation of employees, reactions to past mistakes, and organizational coping.[32] These stories anchor the present in the past and provide explanations and legitimacy for current practices.[33]

> The most potent means by which culture is transmitted to employees is through stories, rituals, material symbols, and language.

▶ Rituals

Rituals are repetitive sequences of activities that express and reinforce the key values of the organization, what goals are most important, which people are important and which are expendable.[34] College faculty members undergo a lengthy ritual in their quest for permanent employment, or tenure. Typically, the faculty member is on probation for 6 years. At the end of that period, the member's colleagues must make one of two choices: extend a tenured appointment or issue a 1-year terminal contract. What does it take to obtain tenure? It usually requires satisfactory teaching performance, service to the department and university, and scholarly activity. But, of course, what satisfies the requirements for tenure in one department at one university may be appraised as inadequate in another. The key is that the tenure decision, in essence, asks those who are tenured to assess whether the candidate has demonstrated, on the basis of 6 years of performance, whether he or she fits in. Colleagues who have been socialized properly will have proved themselves worthy of being granted tenure. Every year, hundreds of faculty members at colleges and universities are denied tenure. In some cases, this action is a result of poor performance across the board. More often, however, the decision can be traced to the faculty member's not doing well in those areas that the tenured faculty believe are important. The instructor who spends dozens of hours each week preparing for class and achieves outstanding evaluations by students but neglects his or her research and publication activities may be passed over for tenure. What has happened, simply, is that the instructor has failed to adapt to the norms set by the department. The astute faculty member will assess early on in the probationary period what attitudes and behaviors his or her colleagues want and will then proceed to give them what they want. And, of course, by demanding certain attitudes and behaviors, the tenured faculty have made significant strides toward standardizing tenure candidates.

One of the best-known corporate rituals is Mary Kay Cosmetics' annual award meeting.[35] Looking like a cross between a circus and a Miss America pageant, the meeting takes place over a couple of days in a large auditorium, on a stage in front of a large, cheering audience, with all the participants dressed in glamorous evening clothes. Saleswomen are rewarded with an array of flashy gifts—gold and diamond pins, fur stoles, pink

A ritual at Mary Kay Cosmetics is the annual sales meeting. Recognizing high achievement is an important part of the company's culture, which values hard work and determination. The ritual of praise and recognition honors the beauty contestants' accomplishments in meeting their sales quotas, which contribute to the success of the company.

Cadillacs—in recognition of their success in achieving sales goals. This "show" acts as a motivator by publicly acknowledging outstanding sales performance. In addition, the ritual aspect reinforces Mary Kay's determination and optimism, which enabled her to overcome personal hardships, found her own company, and achieve material success. It conveys to her salespeople that reaching their sales goals is important and that through hard work and encouragement they too can achieve success.

Material Symbols

Fullers and Lampreia are two of Seattle's most highly rated and expensive restaurants. Geographically, they are less than ten blocks apart, but culturally the two restaurants are miles apart. Fullers is formal to the point of being "stuffy." It has a museum-level decor. The staff is formally attired, serious, focused, and stiff. In contrast, Lampreia is casual and low-key. It has a stylish but minimalist decor. The staff's casual dress and style are consistent with the decor.

Both Fullers and Lampreia consistently receive honors for their food and service; they both require reservations be made days, and sometimes weeks, ahead of time; and they both cost at least $80 for dinner for two. Yet the restaurants' distinct cultures, as reflected in material symbols such as the decor and the attire worn by employees, are conveyed to customers, new employees, and current employees. At Fullers, that message is that we're serious, formal, and conservative. The message at Lampreia is that we're relaxed and open.

Did you ever notice that some corporations provide their top executives with chauffeur-driven limousines and, when they travel by air, unlimited use of the corporate jet? Executives at other firms may not get to ride in limousines or private jets, but they might still get a car and air transportation paid for by the company. The car, however, is a Chevrolet (with no driver), and the jet seat is in the economy section of a commercial airliner.

The layout of an organization's facilities, dress attire, the types of automobiles top executives are given, and the presence or absence of corporate aircraft are examples of material symbols. Others include the size of offices, the elegance of furnishings, executive perks, the existence of employee lounges or on-site dining facilities, and the presence of reserved parking spaces for certain employees. These material symbols convey to employees who is important, the degree of egalitarianism desired by top management, and the kinds of behavior (for example, risk-taking, conservative, authoritarian, participative, individualistic, social) that are appropriate.

► Language

Many organizations and units within organizations use language as a way to identify members of a culture or subculture. By learning this language, members attest to their acceptance of the culture and, in so doing, help to preserve it.

The following are examples of terminology used by employees at Knight-Ridder Information, a California-based data redistributor: *accession number* (a number assigned each individual record in a database); *KWIC* (a set of key-words-in-context); and *relational operator* (searching a database for names or key terms in some order). Librarians are a rich source of terminology foreign to people outside their profession. They sprinkle their conversations liberally with acronyms such as ARL (Association for Research Libraries), OCLC (a center in Ohio that does cooperative cataloguing), and OPAC (for on-line patron accessing catalogue). When Louis Gerstner left RJR Nabisco to head up IBM, he had to learn a whole new vocabulary, which included: *the Orchard* (IBM's Armonk, New York, corporate headquarters, which was once an apple orchard); *big iron* (mainframe computers); *hypo* (a high-potential employee); *a one performer* (an employee with IBM's top performance rating); and *PROFS* (Professional Office Systems, IBM's internal electronic mail system).[36]

Organizations, over time, often develop unique terms to describe equipment, locations, key personnel, suppliers, customers, or products that are related to its business. New employees are frequently overwhelmed with acronyms and jargon that, after 6 months on the job, have become fully part of their language. Once assimilated, this terminology acts as a common denominator that unites members of a given culture or subculture.

HOW DO YOU READ AN ORGANIZATION'S CULTURE?

The ability to read and assess an organization's culture can be a valuable skill. If you're looking for a job, you'll want to choose an employer whose culture is compatible with your values and in which you'll feel comfortable. If you can accurately assess a prospective employer's culture before you make your decision, you may be able to save yourself a lot of grief and reduce the likelihood of making a poor choice. Similarly, you'll undoubtedly have business transactions with numerous organizations during your career. You'll be trying to sell a product or service, negotiate a contract, arrange a joint venture, or merely be seeking out who in the organization controls certain decisions. The ability to assess another organization's culture can be a definite plus in successfully completing these pursuits.

Getting an accurate read on an organization's culture is no easy task.[37] Essentially you are limited to getting your information by making observations and asking questions. And one of the major problems in asking direct questions is that you tend to get socially desirable answers. Regardless of the real culture, it's tempting for managers to *say* their organization is "family-friendly," "practices empowerment," or "values teamwork." Additionally, because you're trying to tap into information that members of the organization generally take for granted and haven't given much thought to, you need multiple observations and you need to ask many members the same questions. Only in this way can you increase the reliability of your data. The use of multiple sources also allows you to identify and differentiate both an organization's dominant culture and its subcultures.

To illustrate, consider the problem of reading an organization's culture from the perspective of a job applicant. Assume that you're interviewing for a job. Here are some things you can do to learn about a potential employer's culture:

► *Observe the physical surroundings.* Pay attention to signs, pictures, style of dress, length of hair, degree of openness between offices, and office furnishings and arrangements.

➤ *Ask to sit in on a team meeting.* In addition to showing you're interested in the position and organization, you'll see how different ranks of employees are treated and the degree of openness in communication.

➤ *Listen to the language that people use.* Managers who use words like *care, family,* and *intuition* are describing a very different organization from one who, for instance, talks in aggressive metaphors such as "take no prisoners," "SWAT teams," and "beat their brains out."

➤ *With whom did you meet?* Just the person who would be your immediate supervisor, or also with potential colleagues, managers from other departments, senior executives? On the basis of what they revealed, to what degree do people other than the immediate supervisor have input into the hiring decision?

➤ How would you characterize the style of the people you met? Formal? Casual? Serious? Jovial?

➤ Does the organization have formal rules and regulations set out in a personnel policy manual? If so, how detailed are these policies?

➤ Ask questions of the people with whom you meet. The most valid and reliable information tends to come from asking the same questions of many people (to see how closely their responses align) and by talking with internal boundary spanners. These are employees whose work links them to the external environment and includes jobs such as human resource interviewer, salesperson, purchasing agent, labor negotiator, public relations specialist, and company lawyer. Questions that will give you insights into organizational processes and practices might include:

What is the background of the founders?

What is the background of current senior managers? What are their functional specializations? Were they promoted from within or hired from outside?

How does the organization integrate new employees? Is there an orientation program? Training? If so, could you describe them?

How does your boss define job success? (Amount of profit? Serving customers? Meeting deadlines? Acquiring budget increases?)

What is the basis for reward allocations? Seniority? Performance?

Who is on the "fast track"? How did they get there?

Who seems to be considered a deviant in the organization? How has the organization responded to him or her?

Can you describe a decision that someone made here that was well received?

Can you describe a decision that didn't work out well? What were the consequences for the decision maker?

Could you describe a crisis or critical event that has occurred recently in the organization? How did top management respond? What was learned from this experience?

➤ *Make use of outside contacts and ask them questions like those just mentioned.* Talk with former employees, especially the job's previous encumbent; customers; and suppliers. Executive recruiters, who have completed assignments for the organization, can be a particularly rich source of information. They're always evaluating whether candidates fit a specific organization's culture.

TECHNIQUES FOR MANAGING AN ORGANIZATION'S CULTURE

German manufacturing efficiency is world-renowned. But Germany's service organizations are another story.[38] Telecommunications, finance, transportation, and retailing are industries in which most German firms are competitive only with themselves. Take the case of Deutsche Telekom AG, Germany's phone monopoly. Potential customers regularly wait years for a hookup. The company's equipment is decades behind the times, re-quiring two to three times as much labor to operate than comparative systems in France or the United Kingdom. Indifferent employees and obsolete equipment translate into an avalanche of billing errors, high phone charges, limited service options, calls that get improperly routed, and listening quality that often is not much better than you would get with two tin cans connected by a string. Telekom's new chief executive, Ron Sommer, hired away from Sony Corp., is determined to modernize the company's network, increase service options, cut costs, and make the company's culture more service-oriented. With 37 million customers and 225,000 employees, Sommer has quite a challenge ahead of him.

Can management change a culture that is hindering the organization's performance? If yes, then how? In this section, we look at techniques for managing culture. Specifically, we look at what managers can do to (1) sustain an appropriate culture, (2) change a culture that is no longer compatible with the organization's direction, and (3) successfully blend their culture with the cultures of other organizations in response to mergers, strategic alliances, or other interorganizational arrangements.

► Sustaining an Organization's Culture

Once a culture is in place, there are practices within the organization that act to maintain and reinforce it by giving employees a set of similar experiences.[39] For example, many of the human resource practices discussed in chapter 10 reinforce the organization's culture. The selection process, performance appraisal criteria, training activities, and promotion procedures ensure that those hired fit in with the culture, reward those who support it, and penalize (and even expel) those who challenge it. Three forces, controllable by management, play a particularly important part in sustaining an appropriate culture—selection practices, the actions of top management, and socialization methods.

SELECTION PRACTICES The explicit goal of the selection process is to identify and hire individuals who have the knowledge, skills, and abilities to perform the jobs within the organization successfully. But, typically, more than one candidate will be identified who meets any given job's requirements. It would be naive to ignore the fact that, when that point is reached, the final decision as to who is hired will be significantly influenced by the decision maker's judgment of how well the candidates will fit into the organization. This attempt to ensure a proper match, whether purposely or inadvertently, results in the hiring of people who have values essentially consistent with those of the organization.[40] In addition, the selection process provides information to applicants about the organization. Candidates learn about the organization, and if they perceive a conflict between their values and those of the organization, they can self-select themselves out of the applicant pool. Selection, therefore, becomes a two-way street, allowing either employer or applicant to refuse a marriage if there appears to be a mismatch. In this way, the selection process sustains an organization's culture by selecting out those individuals who might attack or undermine its core values.

Applicants for entry-level positions in brand management at Procter & Gamble undergo an exhaustive application and screening process. Their interviewers are part of an elite cadre who have been selected and trained extensively via lectures, videotapes, films, practice interviews, and role plays to identify applicants who will successfully fit in at P&G. Applicants are interviewed in depth for such qualities as their ability to "turn out high volumes of excellent work," "identify and understand problems," and "reach

These forces play a particularly important part in sustaining an appropriate culture — selection practices, the actions of top management, and socialization methods.

thoroughly substantiated and well-reasoned conclusions that lead to action." P&G values rationality and seeks applicants who think rationally. College applicants receive two interviews and a general knowledge test on campus before being flown to Cincinnati for three more one-on-one interviews and a group interview at lunch. Each encounter seeks corroborating evidence of the traits that the firm believes are highly correlated with "what counts" for success at P&G.[41] At Eaton Corp.'s Forge Division in South Bend, Indiana, all work is done in teams.[42] To insure that new hires fit this team-oriented culture, all job applicants must go through a rigorous selection process that includes 10 to 12 interviews with four- to six-person peer teams. This process assures the selection of new people who are team-oriented and who co-workers are commited to working with.

TOP MANAGEMENT BEHAVIOR The actions of top management also have a major impact on the organization's culture.[43] Through what they say and how they behave, senior executives establish norms that filter down through the organization as to whether risk taking is desirable; how much freedom managers should give their employees; what is appropriate dress; what actions will pay off in terms of pay raises, promotions, and other rewards; and the like.

For example, look at Xerox Corp.[44] Its chief executive from 1961 to 1968 was Joseph C. Wilson. An aggressive, entrepreneurial type, he oversaw Xerox's staggering growth on the basis of its 914 copier, one of the most successful products in American history. Under Wilson, Xerox had an entrepreneurial environment, with an informal, high-camaraderie, innovative, bold, risk-taking culture. Wilson's replacement as CEO was C. Peter McColough, a Harvard MBA with a formal management style. He instituted bureaucratic controls and a major change in Xerox's culture. By the time McColough stepped down in 1982, Xerox had become stodgy and formal, with lots of politics and turf battles and layers of watchdog managers. His replacement was David T. Kearns. He believed that the culture he had inherited hindered Xerox's ability to compete. To increase the company's competitiveness, Kearns trimmed Xerox down by cutting 15,000 jobs, delegating decision making downward, and refocusing the organization's culture around a simple theme: boosting the quality of Xerox products and services. By his actions and those of his senior managerial cadre, Kearns conveyed to everyone at Xerox that the company valued and rewarded quality and efficiency. When Kearns retired in 1990, Xerox still had its problems. The copier business was mature, and Xerox had fared badly in developing computerized office systems. The current CEO, Paul Allaire, has again sought to reshape Xerox's culture. Specifically, he has reorganized the corporation around a worldwide marketing department, has unified product development and manufacturing divisions, and has replaced half of the company's top-management team with outsiders. Allaire seeks to reshape Xerox's culture to focus on innovative thinking and out-hustling the competition.

SOCIALIZATION METHODS No matter how good a job the organization does in recruiting and selection, new employees are not fully indoctrinated in the organization's culture. Maybe most important, because they are unfamiliar with the organization's culture, new employees are potentially likely to disturb the beliefs and customs that are in place. The organization will, therefore, want to help new employees adapt to its culture. This adaptation process is called **socialization**.[45]

All U.S. Marines must go through boot camp, where they "prove" their commitment. Of course, at the same time, the Marine trainers are indoctrinating new recruits in the "Marine way." New Sanyo employees go through an intensive 5-month training program (trainees eat and sleep together in company-subsidized dorms and are required to vacation together at company-owned resorts), in which they learn the Sanyo way of doing everything—from how to speak to superiors to proper grooming and dress.[46] The company considers this program essential for transforming young employees, fresh out of school, into dedicated *kaisha senshi*, or "corporate warriors."

As we discuss socialization, keep in mind that the most critical socialization stage is at the time of entry into the organization. This is when the organization seeks to mold the outsider into an employee "in good standing." Those employees who fail to learn the essential or pivotal role behaviors risk being labeled "nonconformists" or "rebels," labels that often lead to expulsion. But the organization will be socializing every employee, though maybe not as explicitly, throughout his or her entire career in the organization. This continued socialization further contributes to sustaining the culture.

Socialization can be conceptualized as a process made up of three stages: prearrival, encounter, and metamorphosis.[47] The first stage encompasses all the learning that occurs before a new member joins the organization. In the second stage, the new employee sees what the organization is really like and confronts the possibility that expectations and reality may diverge. In the third stage, the relatively long-lasting changes take place. The new employee masters the skills required for his or her job, successfully performs his or her new roles, and makes the adjustments to his or her work group's values and norms.[48]

The **prearrival stage** explicitly recognizes that each individual arrives with a set of values, attitudes, and expectations. These cover both the work to be done and the organization. For instance, in many jobs, particularly professional work, new members will have undergone a considerable degree of prior socialization in training and in school. One major purpose of a business school, for example, is to socialize business students to the attitudes and behaviors that business firms want. If business executives believe that successful employees value the profit ethic, are loyal, will work hard, and desire to achieve, they can hire individuals out of business schools that are known to premold students in that pattern. But prearrival socialization goes beyond the specific job. The selection process is used in most organizations to inform prospective employees about the organization as a whole. In addition, as noted previously, the selection process also acts to ensure the inclusion of the "right type"—those who will fit in. "Indeed, the ability of the individual to present the appropriate face during the selection process determines his ability to move into the organization in the first place. Thus, success depends on the degree to which the aspiring member has correctly anticipated the expectations and desires of those in the organization in charge of selection."[49]

Upon entry into the organization, the new member enters the **encounter stage**. In this stage, the individual confronts the possible dichotomy between her expectations—about her job, her co-workers, her boss, and the organization in general—and reality. If expectations prove to have been more or less accurate, the encounter stage merely provides for a reaffirmation of the perceptions gained earlier. Expectations, however, are not always accurate. When expectations and reality differ, the new employee must undergo socialization that will detach her from her previous assumptions and replace them with another set that the organization deems desirable. At the extreme, a new member may become totally disillusioned with the actualities of her job and resign. Proper selection should significantly reduce the probability of the latter occurrence.

Finally, the new member must work out any problems discovered during the encounter stage. This process may mean going through changes—hence, we call this the **metamorphosis stage**. The options presented in Exhibit 11-3 are alternatives designed to bring about the desired metamorphosis. Note, for example, that the more management relies on socialization programs that are formal, collective, fixed, serial, and that emphasize divestiture, the greater the likelihood that newcomers' differences and perspectives will be stripped away and replaced by standardized and predictable behaviors. Careful selection by management of newcomers' socialization experiences can—at the extremes—

> The organization will be socializing every employee throughout his or her entire career in the organization.

EXHIBIT 11-3

Entry Socialization Options

Formal Versus Informal. The more a new employee is segregated from the ongoing work setting and differentiated in some way to make explicit his or her newcomer's role, the more formal socialization is. Specific orientation and training programs are examples. Informal socialization puts the new employee directly into his or her job, with little or no special attention.

Individual Versus Collective. New members can be socialized individually, as in many professional offices. They can also be grouped together and processed through an identical set of experiences, as in military boot camp.

Fixed Versus Variable. This refers to the time schedule in which newcomers make the transition from outsider to insider. A fixed schedule establishes standardized stages of transition. This schedule characterizes rotational training programs. It also includes probationary periods, such as the 8- to 10-year "associate" status used by accounting and law firms before deciding on whether a candidate is made a partner. Variable schedules give no advanced notice of their transition timetable. Variable schedules describe the typical promotion system, in which one is not advanced to the next stage until he or she is "ready."

Serial Versus Random. Serial socialization is characterized by the use of role models who train and encourage the newcomer. Apprenticeship and mentoring programs are examples. In random socialization, role models are deliberately withheld. The new employee is left on his or her own to figure things out.

Investiture Versus Divestiture. Investiture socialization assumes that the newcomer's qualities and qualifications are the necessary ingredients for job success, so those qualities and qualifications are confirmed and supported. Divestiture socialization tries to strip away certain characteristics of the recruit. Fraternity and sorority "pledges" go through divestiture socialization to shape them into the proper role.

Sources: Based on J. Van Maanen, "People Processing: Strategies of Organizational Socialization," *Organizational Dynamics*, Summer 1978, pp. 19–36; and E. H. Schein, "Organizational Culture," *American Psychologist*, February 1990, p. 116.

---

create rigid conformists who maintain traditions and customs or creative individualists who consider no organizational practice to be sacred.

We can say that metamorphosis and the entry socialization process are complete when the new member has become comfortable with the organization and his or her job. She has internalized the norms of the organization and her work group, and she understands and accepts those norms. She feels accepted by her peers as a trusted and valued individual, is self-confident that she has the competence to complete the job successfully, and understands the system—not only her own tasks, but the rules, procedures, and informally accepted practices as well. Finally, she knows how she will be appraised, that is, what criteria will be used to measure and evaluate her work. She knows what is expected and what constitutes a "job well done."

▶ Changing an Organization's Culture

The fact that an organization's culture is made up of relatively stable and permanent characteristics—and is reinforced by its selection process, top management behavior, and socialization methods—tends to make most cultures very resistant to change.[50] A culture takes a long time to form, and once it has been established it tends to become entrenched.

Shaping the Starbucks Employee

Imagine paying $1,400 a year to maintain a daily latte and scone habit. Millions do at Starbucks. This coffee purveyor, with more than a thousand locations and opening a new one every business day, plans on turning the world on to "triple-tall nonfat mochas."

What's the secret to Starbucks amazing success? A quality product and a culture focused on customer service. Every one of Starbucks' 20,000 employees has gone through a set of formal classes during his or her first six weeks with the company. When this socialization is complete, employees have become coffee experts.

The indoctrination begins with a history of the company. It's followed by a session on what customers need to know to brew a perfect cup of coffee at home. These include purchasing new beans weekly, the right type of water to use, and tips like never letting coffee sit on a hot plate for more than 20 minutes. The specific techniques for drink making are learned in an eight-hour class on retail skills. Here, new employees learn such varied skills as how to steam milk for a latte, how to clean an espresso machine, and the proper way to fill one-pound sacks with coffee. There are also classes that teach new employees how to explain Starbucks' Italian drink names to baffled customers and coffee-tasting classes so employees understand why Sanani is described as "winey" and Costa Rica as "tangy and bright."

Starbucks' socialization program turns out employees who are seeped in the company's culture and understand manage-

ment's obsession with "elevating the coffee experience," as the company's senior vice president of marketing puts it.

Comprehensive training, pay that exceeds most entry-level food service jobs, and comprehensive benefits (including health insurance even for part-timers and stock options), have produced a skilled and loyal workforce. Annual turnover among Starbucks employees is 60 percent. That compares with 140 percent for hourly workers in the fast-food business.

Source: Based on J. Reese, "Starbucks: Inside the Coffee Cult," *Fortune*, December 9, 1996, pp. 190–200.

Strong cultures at firms such as General Motors, AT&T, IBM, Digital Equipment, and Eastman Kodak have been found to be particularly resistant to change because employees have become so committed to them. If, over time, a given culture becomes inappropriate to an organization and a handicap to management, there might be little management can do to change it, especially in the short run. Even in the most favorable conditions, cultural changes have to be measured in years, not in weeks or months.

UNDERSTANDING THE SITUATIONAL FACTORS What "favorable conditions" might facilitate cultural change? The evidence suggests that cultural change is most likely to take place when most or all of the following conditions exist:

A dramatic crisis occurs. This is the shock that undermines the status quo and calls into question the relevance of the current culture.[51] Examples might be a surprising financial setback, the loss of a major customer, a serious decline in market share, or a dramatic breakthrough by a competitor. Executives at Pepsi-Cola and Ameritech even admit to creating crises in order to stimulate change in their cultures.[52]

Turnover in leadership. New top leadership, which can provide an alternative set of key values, may be perceived as being needed to respond to the crisis. New leadership would definitely include the organization's chief executive but also might need to include all senior management positions. The hiring of outside CEOs at IBM (Louis Gerstner), General Motors (Jack Smith), and Kodak (George Fisher) illustrates attempts to introduce new leadership.

Young and small organization. The younger the organization is, the less entrenched its culture will be. Similarly, it is easier for management to communicate its new values when the organization is small. This relationship helps explain the difficulty that multibillion-dollar corporations have in changing their cultures.

Weak culture. The more widely held a culture is and the higher the agreement among members on its values, the more difficult it will be to change. Weak cultures are more amenable to change than strong ones.

These situational factors help to explain why a company like General Motors has had such difficulty in reshaping its culture. For the most part, employees didn't see GM's day-to-day problems as being of crisis proportions. Until just a couple of years ago, top management positions were always filled by internal candidates who were steeped in the company's established culture. And, finally, GM was neither young nor small, and its culture was not weak.

HOW CAN CULTURAL CHANGE BE ACCOMPLISHED? If the situational factors are favorable, how does management go about enacting the cultural change? The challenge is to "unfreeze" the current culture. No single action is likely to have the impact necessary to unfreeze something that is entrenched and highly valued. Therefore there needs to be a comprehensive and coordinated strategy for managing culture.

The best place to begin is with a cultural analysis.[53] This would include a cultural audit to assess the current culture, a comparison of the present culture with the culture that is desired, and a gap evaluation to identify what cultural elements specifically need changing.

Next, management needs to make it clear to employees that the organization's survival is legitimately threatened if change is not forthcoming. This is where exploiting a dramatic crisis comes in. If a crisis exists but isn't visible to all members of the organization, then management needs to raise the alarm. If there isn't any crisis to exploit, it may be necessary to invent one. Remember, if employees don't see the urgency for change, apathy is likely to win out over any change efforts.

The appointment of a new top executive is likely to dramatize that major changes are going to take place. He or she can offer a new role model, a new vision, and new standards of behavior. The change effort is more likely to succeed if the new executive moves quickly to introduce his or her new vision and to staff key management positions with individuals who are similarly committed to this vision.

The new leadership will also want to move quickly to create new stories, symbols, and rituals to replace those that were previously used to convey to employees the organization's dominant values. This change needs to be done rapidly. Delays will allow the current culture to become associated with the new leadership, thus closing the window of opportunity for change.

Finally, management will want to change the selection and socialization processes and the appraisal and reward systems to support employees who espouse the new values that are sought.

These suggestions, of course, provide no guarantee that change efforts will succeed. Organizational members do not quickly let go of values that they understand and that have worked well for them in the past. Managers must therefore show patience. Change, if it comes, will be painfully slow. And management must keep on constant alert to protect against reversion to old, familiar practices and traditions. Yet, there is an expanding set of success stories. For instance, Bankers Trust, British Airways, First Chicago, and GE have effectively achieved dramatic cultural change.[54] Three points about these success stories are worth noting. First, these turnarounds tended to take 4 to 10 years, confirming our call for patience. Second, in every case of successful cultural change, the CEOs who provided the leadership were essentially outsiders. They were brought in either from outside the organization or from a division not in the corporate mainstream. And, finally, all of the CEOs started their new jobs by trying to create an atmosphere of perceived crisis.

▶ Blending Organizational Cultures

The Pharmacia and Upjohn merger, described at the opening of this chapter, represents an example of blending organizational cultures. In this section, our objective is to see if we can derive some lessons from previous experiences with mergers, acquisitions, and joint ventures that can guide managers in making future interorganizational linkage decisions.

A review of major mergers and acquisitions leads us to the obvious conclusion that not all marriages are made in heaven! In fact, studies repeatedly indicate that, at best, only half of all mergers and acquisitions meet initial financial expectations.[55]

The motive behind almost all corporate marriages is to gain positive synergy by merging financial, marketing, or strategic advantages. For instance, AT&T bought McCaw Cellular as part of its strategy to become a power in wireless communications.[56] Consistent with this synergy motive, when assessing marriage partners, acquirers have historically focused the bulk of their attention on financial and strategic factors. The evidence, however, suggests that cultural incompatibility breaks up more marriages than those traditional factors.[57] For instance, a survey of more than 200 European chief executives found that the ability to integrate the new company was ranked as the most important factor for acquisition success.[58] Cultural fit is probably the most important determinant of whether mergers, acquisitions, or joint ventures succeed.

The landscape is littered with corporate marriages in which management failed to accurately assess the downside from culture clash. Wells Fargo acquired First Interstate Bancorp for $11.3 billion in 1996. But Wells Fargo's culture sought to efficiently execute customers' transactions through the most convenient, low-cost channel. First Interstate focused on spoiling its customers with personalized service. The result has been difficulty in integrating the two firms and high turnover among First Interstate management. In the first year following the acquisition, 386 of the firm's 506 senior managers had left.[59] The joint venture to develop a revolutionary computer memory chip by Siemens AG, Toshiba Corp., and IBM has been plagued with problems, as researchers try, unsuccessfully, to reconcile disparate organizational and national cultures.[60] Waterford Crystal's takeover of Wedgwood China, billed originally as "the perfect marriage," has been a financial disaster.[61]

What can management do to improve its odds when acquiring another firm? First, consistent with the previous discussion of cultural change, management should conduct a cultural audit of the acquisition candidate. This is *in addition to* the more traditional financial and strategic analysis. The results of the cultural analysis should be used to determine the degree of integration the acquiring firm will introduce and to guide communication with the takeover candidate. Southwest did just this in its purchase of Morris Air in

A review of major mergers and acquisitions leads us to the conclusion that not all marriages are made in heaven!

Angry with what they call the company's "racist" culture, Hispanic and black protesters picket Texaco's refinery in Los Angeles, California.

December 1993.[62] Southwest spent two months exploring its cultural compatibility with Morris before acquiring its smaller rival. Southwest was particularly concerned that Morris employees had Southwest's same customer focus and friendly esprit de corps. "We can train you to do any job, but we can't give you the right spirit," explained a Southwest spokesman. Southwest's "due diligence" paid off. The integration of Morris, which was expected to take three years, was accomplished in only 11 months.

Corporate marriages fall into one of three types based upon the degree of integration and culture change necessary.[63] The least disruptive are *extension mergers*, in which the acquiring organization takes a relatively "hands-off" approach. The newly acquired firm is allowed to operate essentially independently of the acquirer. *Collaborative mergers* integrate operations or involve exchange of technology or other expertise. Collaborative efforts should be pursued only when the different organizational cultures are highly compatible. The final category encompasses *redesign mergers*. This type characterizes organizations that intend to introduce wide-scale change in the firm they are acquiring. The acquired firm is expected to totally adopt the practices, procedures, and culture of the dominant merger partner.

Any of these three typologies *can* be successful. The key factor is gaining consensus between the combining organizations and their members as to the desired mode of acculturation. When corporate marriages fail because of cultural incompatibility, the typical culprit is that the parties did not recognize, share, or accept each other's perception of the marriage terms. It is important, therefore, to invite employees of the acquired company or both merger partners to participate in a series of group meetings so that they can discuss results of the culture analysis and expectations. This effort to open communications, of course, provides no guarantee that cultural clashes can be avoided, but it improves the odds.

THREATS TO DIVERSITY: THE DOWNSIDE OF STRONG CULTURES

We conclude this chapter by acknowledging one additional drawback to strong cultures: They create a real barrier to achieving workforce diversity and capitalizing on its benefits. Hiring new employees who, because of race, gender, ethnicity, or other differences, are not like the majority of the organization's members creates a paradox.[64] Management wants new employees to accept the organization's core cultural values. Otherwise, these employees are unlikely to fit in or be accepted. But at the same time, management wants to openly acknowledge and demonstrate support for the differences these employees bring to the workplace.

Strong cultures put considerable pressure on employees to conform. They limit the range of values and styles that are acceptable. Obviously, this emphasis creates a dilemma. Organizations hire diverse individuals because of the alternative strengths these people bring to the workplace. Yet these diverse behaviors and strengths are likely to diminish in strong cultures as people attempt to fit in. Strong cultures, therefore, can be liabilities when they effectively eliminate those unique strengths that people of different backgrounds bring to the organization. Strong cultures can also block efforts at expanding diversity. Strong cultures that have historically valued homogeneity can be major barriers in efforts to eliminate workplace discrimination and sexual harassment. For example, Texaco's antiminority culture has hindered its diversity efforts and cost it $176.1 million to settle a racial-discrimination lawsuit.[65]

There is a variety of additional material available on the CD-ROM and companion Web site that accompany this text. You can access this information through the CD-ROM or by visiting the Web site at <**www.prenhall.com/robbins**>.

SUMMARY

(This chapter summary is organized by the chapter-opening learning objectives on page 338.)

1. Organizational culture is a system of shared meaning held by members that distinguishes the organization from other organizations.

2. The seven primary characteristics that define an organization's culture are: (1) innovation and risk taking, (2) attention to detail, (3) outcome orientation, (4) people orientation, (5) team orientation, (6) aggressiveness, and (7) stability.

3. A strong culture is characterized by core values that are intensely held and widely shared.

4. The ultimate source of an organization's culture is the organization's founder. He or she is unconstrained by previous ideologies, and the organization's typical small size in its early years facilitates communication of the founder's vision.

5. Employees learn their organization's culture through stories, rituals, material symbols, and language.

6. The primary forces that sustain a culture are the organization's selection practices, top management behavior, and socialization methods.

7. The situational factors that favor cultural change are a dramatic crisis, turnover in top leadership, a young and small organization, and a weak culture.

8. To minimize cultural clash in mergers and acquisitions, management of the acquiring organization should conduct a cultural audit, choose a degree of integration consistent with compatibility, and use open communications to share expectations.

REVIEW QUESTIONS

1. Contrast dominant cultures and subcultures and compare their influence on shaping the behavior of organizational members.

2. Demonstrate how one individual dimension of organizational culture can rise above the others and essentially shape the organization.

3. Contrast the strength of organizational culture with that of national culture. Explain your conclusion.

4. How do stories shape cultures?

5. What do the material symbols in offices and classrooms at your college convey about its culture?

6. Think of a large organization you know. Develop a list of jargon used in that organization that would differentiate its members and the organization from other organizations.

7. How do you read and assess an organization's culture?

8. Describe various socialization options and how they shape new organizational members.

9. "To survive in today's dynamic environment, organizations need to have an innovative, risk-taking, team-oriented, and aggressive culture." Do you agree or disagree with this statement? Support your answer.

10. "You can't change an organization's culture." Build an argument to support this statement; then negate your argument.

IF I WERE THE MANAGER . . .

Responding to the Nordstrom Challenge

You've recently been promoted by the department store chain Dillards from store manager in St. Louis to the company's flagship store in Cleveland. You've moved from a store with fewer than 200 employees to one that is more than twice as large. But with the new job comes a major challenge. In St. Louis, there was no Nordstrom to compete against. In Cleveland, Nordstrom has recently opened a large store in the Beachwood Place Mall. You know Nordstrom's reputation for service. The corporate culture obsesses on doing whatever is necessary to make customers happy. When Nordstrom comes into a community,

they strike fear into competitors. And the Dillard customer is exactly the person that Nordstrom is seeking as *its* customer.

It's the first week in your new position as store manager in Cleveland. It's late in the afternoon on Saturday. You usually don't work on weekends. Your assistant manager oversees the store's operations on Saturdays and Sundays. But you wanted your spouse and two daughters to see your new workplace. Your spouse also mentioned the need to buy a couple of pieces of furniture for your new house. So you and the family drive over to the store. You take the escalator up to the third floor where furniture is sold. It's quiet. There are only a couple of customers walking around the floor, looking around. You're looking for a salesperson. After about 5 minutes, you realize there is only one salesperson on the entire floor and he's helping a customer looking at recliners. The salesman sees you from afar, but doesn't recognize who you are. Your spouse, getting impatient, walks over to the salesman and asks for some help. "Listen, lady, I'm the only person up here. And I'm helping this customer right now. Why don't you come back another day when we have more help on the floor?"

When you heard the salesperson's comment, your jaw dropped. Is this an aberration or is this the way the employees in your store treat potential customers? How are you going to compete against a high-service-mentality firm like Nordstrom with employees like this?

SKILL EXERCISE

Reading an Organization's Culture

Select an organization where you have worked. If you have no work experience, choose an organization with which you have had regular contact and to which you can gain access.

Visit the organization and take the time to talk with as many people as possible and observe employees executing their jobs. Ask pertinent questions. The answers will give you insights into the organization's culture.

After gathering your data (a) describe the organization's culture using the seven characteristics described in the chapter, and (b) list some probable preferred employee behaviors in this organization based on your data.

TEAM ACTIVITY

Assessing Your College's Culture

Break into teams of four or five. You have 30 minutes to assess your college's culture using the seven primary characteristics presented earlier in this chapter. As your team attempts to categorize your college in each category, pay particular attention to the criteria various members use in order to draw their individual conclusions.

When the 30 minutes is up, each team should present its findings. The class will then compare the various teams' conclusions. How much agreement was there? What explains differences? Where there were differences between individuals on a team, how did the group reconcile these differences to arrive at a final conclusion? The exercise can conclude by having students who have attended other colleges contrast the perceptions of the class with the culture of these other colleges. To what degree do colleges and universities have common cultures (consider factors such as size, age, mission, state versus private, and religious versus nonsectarian affiliation)?

CASE EXERCISE

Mitsubishi: The Downside of a Strong Culture

Mitsubishi Motors Corp. president Katsuhiko Kawasoe was the bearer of bad news. In the fiscal year of 1997, his company had lost $846 million. His company, the fourth largest automaker in Japan, was suffering from weak truck and bus markets at home. Additionally, it has been slow to take on Toyota and Honda in the hot minivan and sport-utility sectors.

Closer analysis suggests that Kawasoe's problems go a lot deeper than merely its product line. The major problem lies in the roots of the larger system of which it is part, Mitsubishi Corp. This super-conglomerate owns Mitsubishi Motors, Bank of Tokyo (the world's largest bank), Mitsubishi Heavy Industries, and dozens of other businesses. The group's recent annual revenues of $370 billion equaled 10 percent of Japan's gross domestic product.

Much of the Mitsubishi empire is cloistered in many ways from the real world of competition. Mitsubishi companies do things the way they've been doing them for more than a century. Long and close relationships with customers and suppliers preclude dropping loss-making product lines. Executives, for the most part, pay little attention to the market. And the culture focuses on the past. New recruits, for instance, are told about the company's special place in history and duty to country. When a reporter asked a senior Mitsubishi executive why his company didn't follow U.S.-style management practices like downsizing, the executive barked, "Employment is more important than profits! We are not concerned with return on equity. . . . If foreign investors don't see merit in our stock, they can sell it." Mitsubishi executives believe it would be un-Japanese to fire anyone or close plants. And these same executives seem to lack incentives or respond to market pressures that might make their counterparts in North America or Europe change.

Almost all the Mitsubishi companies are bleeding red ink. In addition to the auto group's recent losses, Mitsubishi Electric expected to lose $538 million in 1998. And the Bank of Tokyo had to absorb more than $5.8 billion in losses during the same year. These results suggest that managers have paid no attention to the lessons learned years ago by American companies—that no one company can do everything. *Focus* does not seem to be a word in the Mitsubishi rule book. One consultant says that Mitsubishi needs a top executive with the courage to downsize and restructure the company. "Unfortu-

nately," he adds, "such people are virtually nonexistent in traditional Japanese companies."

QUESTIONS

1. What does this case say about strong cultures?
2. How could the same culture that was so effective for Mitsubishi in the 1970s become a huge negative in the 1990s?
3. "Employment is more important than profits!" Do you agree or disagree with this statement? Explain.
4. What, if anything, can the board of directors at Mitsubishi do to change the company's culture?

Source: Based on N. Weinberg, "A Setting Sun?" *Forbes*, April 20, 1998, pp. 118–24.

VIDEO CASE EXERCISE

The Bean Queen

There's the Bean Queen. There are Bean Counters. And there are Human Beans. All can be found at Buckeye Beans and Herbs in Spokane, Washington. Jill Smith is the Bean Queen. She's a self-proclaimed hippie artist turned entrepreneur who started her company in 1983 with an investment of $1,000. From that small, inauspicious beginning, Buckeye Beans now has sales revenues approaching $8 million and employs 50 people (human beans). Buckeye Beans has been innovative in expanding its product line, which started out with one product, Buckeye Bean Soup, and now includes a line of all-natural soups, chili, bread mixes, and pasta. Buckeye Beans also pioneered special-occasion-shaped pasta: that is, pasta shaped like Christmas trees, hearts, bunnies, dolphins, leaves, grapes, baseballs, and even golf balls. But what strikes you most about Buckeye Beans isn't its unique products, it's the unusual organizational culture that melds this company together.

That unusual organizational culture is reflected in the company's simple mission statement: Make people smile. Smith's belief is that cooking should be fun and that the experience of cooking can be a fun escape, not a drudgery. That's why the first ingredient listed on all Buckeye's product packages is a cup of good wine for the cook. Buckeye's strategy—that its products go beyond just a simple bag of beans and instead serve as entertainment—is also seen in the company's HEHE principle: humor, education, health, and environment. That's what Jill Smith, husband Doug, and other Buckeye employees believe in and value.

Shared values are very important to Smith and her employees. Not only are many of Buckeye's employees family and long-time friends, but they all share like values. As Smith built Buckeye Beans, she felt it was important that her employees have the same value systems. And although she admits that her approach wouldn't work for every organization, she does think it's important for managers to identify their basic values and what they're trying to accomplish. Smith suggests asking what kinds of values are important and what kind of organization is desired. For Buckeye Beans, the approach has been to create a "different" type of company—a new model—in which the business is run and employee and customer relationships operate on the basis of trust, confidence, loyalty, and working hard together to get something done. As Smith so earnestly stresses, it's easier to work hard when you have a philosophy like that.

QUESTIONS

1. How would you describe Buckeye Beans' organizational culture?
2. If Buckeye Beans and Herbs continues to grow in size, what challenges will it face in maintaining its organizational culture? What advice would you give Jill Smith about maintaining the culture?
3. How could Buckeye Beans use stories, rituals, material symbols, and language to transmit its culture to employees? Give specific examples.

Source: Based on *Small Business 2000, Show 203.*

NOTES

1. Based on J. Flynn and K. Naughton, "A Drug Giant's Allergic Reaction," *Business Week*, February 3, 1997, pp. 122–25; and R. Frank and T. M. Burton, "Cross-Border Merger Results in Headaches for a Drug Company," *Wall Street Journal*, February 4, 1997, p. A1.

2. See, for example, H. S. Becker, "Culture: A Sociological View," *Yale Review*, Summer 1982, pp. 513–27; E. H. Schein, *Organizational Culture and Leadership*, 2nd ed. (San Francisco: Jossey-Bass, 1992); and J. P. Kotter and J. L. Heskett, *Corporate Culture and Performance* (New York: Free Press, 1992).

3. C. A. O'Reilly III, J. Chatman, and D. F. Caldwell, "People and Organizational Culture: A Profile Comparison Approach to Assessing Person-Organization Fit," *Academy of Management Journal*, September 1991, pp. 487–516; and J. A. Chatman and K. A. Jehn, "Assessing the Relationship between Industry Characteristics and Organizational Culture: How Different Can You Be?" *Academy of Management Journal*, June 1994, pp. 522–53.

4. The view that there will be consistency among perceptions of organizational culture has been called the "integration" perspective. For a review of this perspective and conflicting approaches, see D. Meyerson and J. Martin, "Cultural Change: An Integration of Three Different Views," *Journal of Management Studies*, November 1987, pp. 623–47; and P. J. Frost, L. F. Moore, M. R. Louis, C. C. Lundberg, and J. Martin (eds.), *Reframing Organizational Culture* (Newbury Park, CA: Sage, 1991).

5. See S. A. Sackmann, "Culture and Subcultures: An Analysis of Organizational Knowledge," *Administrative Science Quarterly*, March 1992, pp. 140–61; and G. Hofstede, "Identifying Organizational Subcultures: An Empirical Approach," *Journal of Management Studies*, January 1998, pp. 1–12.

6. J. P. Kotter and J. L. Heskett, *Corporate Culture and Performance*, pp. 5–6.

7. See, for example, G. G. Gordon and N. DiTomaso, "Predicting Corporate Performance from Organizational Culture," *Journal of Management Studies*, November 1992, pp. 793–98; and J. P. Kotter and J. L. Heskett, *Corporate Culture and Performance* (New York: Free Press, 1992), pp. 15–27.

8. Y. Wiener, "Forms of Value Systems: A Focus on Organizational Effectiveness and Cultural Change and Maintenance," *Academy of Management Review*, October 1988, p. 536.

9. See, for example, D. R. Denison, *Corporate Culture and Organizational Effectiveness* (New York: Wiley, 1990); Gordon and DiTomaso, "Predicting Corporate Performance from Organizational Culture," pp. 784–98; J. C. Collins and J. I. Porras, *Built to Last* (New York: HarperBusiness, 1994); and D. R. Denison and A. K. Mishra, "Toward a Theory of Organizational Culture and Effectiveness," *Organization Science*, March–April 1995, pp. 204–23.

10. Collins and Porras, *Built to Last*.

11. Kotter and Heskett, *Corporate Culture and Performance*.

12. Ibid., p. 16.

13. J. Pfeffer, "Will the Organization of the Future Make the Mistakes of the Past?," in F. Hesselbein, M. Goldsmith, and R. Beckhard, (eds.), *The Organization of the Future* (San Francisco: Jossey-Bass, 1997), p. 48.

14. Kotter and Heskett, *Corporate Culture and Performance*, p. 8.

15. B. McMenamin, "The Virtue of Making Mistakes," *Forbes*, May 9, 1994, pp. 192–94; and B. Gates, "Failure Is a Part of the Game and Should Be Used," *Seattle Post-Intelligence*, April 26, 1995, p. B5.

16. B. Gates, "Failure Is a Part of the Game and Should Be Used."

17. P. Sellers, "So You Fail . . . Now Bounce Back!" *Fortune*, May 1, 1995, p. 49.

18. J. H. Sheridan, "Culture-Change Lessons," *Industry Week*, February 17, 1997, p. 20.

19. Collins and Porras, *Built to Last*, pp. 207–08.

20. M. A. Verespej, "Empire without Emperors," *Industry Week*, February 5, 1996, pp. 13–16.

21. R. S. Wellins, W. C. Byham, and G. R. Dixon, *Inside Teams: How 20 World-Class Organizations Are Winning Through Teamwork* (San Francisco: Jossey-Bass, 1994), pp. 164–78.

22. Ibid., pp. 234–47.

23. K. Rebello, "Inside Microsoft," *Business Week*, July 15, 1996, pp. 56–67.

24. K. L. Miller, "Siemens Shapes Up," *Business Week*, May 1, 1995, pp. 52–53.

25. See J. Castro, T. McCarroll, J. Moody, and W. McWhirter, "Jack in the Box," *Time*, October 3, 1994, pp. 56–58.

26. S. Glain, "Korea's Samsung Plans Very Rapid Expansion into Autos, Other Lines," *Wall Street Journal*, March 2, 1995, p. A1.

27. See N. J. Adler, *International Dimensions of Organizational Behavior*, 3rd ed. (Cincinnati, OH: Southwestern, 1997), pp. 61–63.

28. S. C. Schneider, "National vs. Corporate Culture: Implications for Human Resource Management," *Human Resource Management*, Summer 1988, p. 239.

29. E. H. Schein, "The Role of the Founder in Creating Organizational Culture," *Organizational Dynamics*, Summer 1983, pp. 13–28.

30. E. H. Schein, "Leadership and Organizational Culture," in F. Hesselbein, M. Goldsmith, and R. Beckhard (eds.), *The Leader of the Future* (San Francisco: Jossey-Bass, 1996), pp. 61–62.

31. Kotter and Heskett, *Corporate Culture and Performance*, pp. 6–7.

32. D. M. Boje, "The Storytelling Organization: A Study of Story Performance in an Office-Supply Firm," *Administrative Science Quarterly*, March 1991, pp. 106–26; and C. H. Deutsch, "The Parables of Corporate Culture," *New York Times*, October 13, 1991, p. F25.

33. A. M. Pettigrew, "On Studying Organizational Cultures," *Administrative Science Quarterly*, December 1979, p. 576.

34. Ibid.

35. Cited in J. M. Beyer and H. M. Trice, "How an Organization's Rites Reveal Its Culture," *Organizational Dynamics*, Spring 1987, p. 15.

36. "LOB, Anyone?" *Business Week*, October 4, 1993, p. 94.

37. A number of the ideas in this section were influenced by A. L. Wilkins, "The Culture Audit: A Tool for Understanding Organizations," *Organizational Dynamics*, Autumn 1983, pp. 24–38; H. M. Trice and J. M. Beyer, *The Cultures of Work Organizations* (Englewood Cliffs, NJ: Prentice Hall, 1993), pp. 358–62; and H. Lancaster, "You Have Your Values; How Do You Identify Your Employer's?" *Wall Street Journal*, April 8, 1997, p. B1.

38. G. Steinmetz, "Customer-Service Era Is Reaching Germany Late, Hurting Business," *Wall Street Journal*, June 1, 1995, p. A1.

39. See, for example, J. R. Harrison and G. R. Carroll, "Keeping the Faith: A Model of Cultural Transmission in Formal Organizations," *Administrative Science Quarterly*, December 1991, pp. 552–82.

40. B. Schneider, "The People Make the Place," *Personnel Psychology*, Autumn 1987, pp. 437–53; J. A. Chatman, "Matching People and Organizations: Selection and Socialization in Public Accounting Firms," *Administrative Science Quarterly*, September 1991, pp. 459–84; and D. M. Cable and T. A. Judge, "Interviewers' Perceptions of Person-Organization Fit and Organizational Selection Decisions," *Journal of Applied Psychology*, August 1997, pp. 546–61.

41. R. Pascale, "The Paradox of 'Corporate Culture': Reconciling Ourselves to Socialization," *California Management Review*, Winter 1985, pp. 26–27.

42. J. H. Sheridan, "Culture-Change Lessons," p. 24.

43. D. C. Hambrick and P. A. Mason, "Upper Echelons: The Organization as a Reflection of Its Top Managers," *Academy of Management Review*, April 1984, pp. 193–206; B. P. Niehoff, C. A. Enz, and R. A. Grover, "The Impact of Top-Management Actions on Employee Attitudes and Perceptions," *Group & Organization Studies*, September 1990, pp. 337–52; and H. M. Trice and J. M. Beyer, "Cultural Leadership in Organizations," *Organization Science*, May 1991, pp. 149–69.

44. "Culture Shock at Xerox," *Business Week*, June 22, 1987, pp. 1, 6–10; T. Vogel, "At Xerox, They're Shouting 'Once More into the Breach,'" *Business Week*, July 23, 1990, pp. 62–63; and <www.xerox.com> (April 1999).

45. See, for instance, R. L. Falcione and C. E. Wilson, "Socialization Processes in Organizations," in G. M. Golhar and G. A. Barnett (eds.), *Handbook of Organizational Communication* (Norwood, NJ: Ablex, 1988), pp. 151–70; V. D. Miller and F. M. Jablin, "Information Seeking During Organizational Entry: Influences, Tactics, and a Model of the Process," *Academy of Management Review*, January 1991, pp. 92–120; C. L. Adkins, "Previous Work Experience and Organizational Socialization: A Longitudinal Examination," *Academy of Management Journal*, June 1995, pp. 839–62; and R. Ganzel, "Putting Out the Welcome Mat," *Training*, March 1998, pp. 54–62.

46. J. Impoco, "Basic Training, Sanyo Style," *U.S. News & World Report*, July 13, 1992, pp. 46–48.

47. J. Van Maanen and E. H. Schein, "Career Development," in J. R. Hackman and J. L. Suttle (eds.), *Improving Life at Work* (Santa Monica, CA: Goodyear, 1977), pp. 58–62.

48. D. C. Feldman, "The Multiple Socialization of Organization Members," *Academy of Management Review*, April 1981, p. 310.

49. Van Maanen and Schein, "Career Development," p. 59.

50. See T. H. Fitzgerald, "Can Change in Organizational Culture Really Be Managed?" *Organizational Dynamics*, Autumn 1988, pp. 5–15; and B. Dumaine, "Creating a New Company Culture," *Fortune*, January 15, 1990, pp. 127–31.

51. C. R. Day, Jr., "Go Find Yourself a Crisis!" *Industry Week*, July 4, 1994, pp. 20–24; and J. P. Kotter, "Kill Complacency," *Fortune*, August 5, 1996, pp. 168–70.

52. B. Dumaine, "Times Are Good? Create a Crisis," *Fortune*, June 28, 1993, pp. 123–30.

53. M. Albert, "Assessing Cultural Change Needs," *Training and Development Journal*, May 1985, pp. 94–98.

54. Kotter and Heskett, *Corporate Culture and Performance*, pp. 94–106.

55. See J. Kitching, "Why Do Mergers Miscarry," *Harvard Business Review*, March–April 1970, pp. 84–101; and J. Fairburn and P. Geroski, "The Empirical Analysis of Market Structure and Performance," in J. A. Fairburn and J. A. Kay (eds.), *Mergers and Merger Policy* (Oxford: Oxford University Press, 1989).

56. A. Kupfer, "AT&T's $12 Billion Cellular Dream," *Fortune*, December 12, 1994, pp. 100–12.

57. A. F. Buono and J. L. Bowditch, *The Human Side of Mergers and Acquisitions: Managing Collisions between People, Cultures, and Organizations* (San Francisco: Jossey-Bass, 1989); P. W. Zweig, "The Case against Mergers," *Business Week*, October 30, 1995, pp. 122–30; and J. R. Carleton, "Cultural Due Diligence," *Training*, November 1997, pp. 67–75.

58. Booz, Allen & Hamilton, Inc., "Diversification: A Survey of European Chief Executives," *Executive Summary*, 1985.

59. L. Himelstein, "Why Wells Fargo Is Circling the Wagons," *Business Week*, June 9, 1997, pp. 92–93.

60. E. S. Browning, "Computer Chip Project Brings Rivals Together, But the Cultures Clash," *Wall Street Journal*, May 3, 1994, p. A1.

61. Cited in S. Cartwright and C. L. Cooper, "The Role of Culture Compatibility in Successful Organizational Marriage," *The Executive*, May 1993, p. 59.

62. J. S. Lublin and B. O'Brian, "When Disparate Firms Merge, Cultures Often Collide," *Wall Street Journal*, February 14, 1997, p. B7B.

63. This section is based on Cartwright and Cooper, "The Role of Culture Compatibility in Successful Organizational Marriage," pp. 57–70.

64. See C. Lindsay, "Paradoxes of Organizational Diversity: Living within the Paradoxes," in L. R. Jauch and J. L. Wall (eds.), *Proceedings of the 50th Academy of Management Conference* (San Francisco: Academy of Management, 1990), pp. 374–78; and T. Cox, Jr., *Cultural Diversity in Organizations: Theory, Research & Practice* (San Francisco: Berrett-Koehler, 1993), pp. 162–70.

65. M. A. Verespej, "Zero Tolerance," *Industry Week*, January 6, 1997, pp. 24–28.

Humanities and Social Sciences

ECONOMICS Managers have long benefited from economic theories. For instance, the advantages that accrue from substituting capital for labor has its roots in early economic theory. Similarly, much of what currently is called *industrial relations* or *labor-management relations* have developed from economic theories of labor and trade unions.

In the past dozen years, organizational economics has provided fresh insights to our understanding of organizations. The two most relevant contributions of organizational economics to management have been agency theory and transaction-cost economics. Out of this work, for instance, managers have gained new insights into governance, contracting, and the efficiency trade-offs between markets and hierarchies.

PSYCHOLOGY Every introductory psychology course spends some time on industrial/organizational psychology. The issues that are addressed—job analysis, recruitment, selection interviews, employment tests, training, performance evaluation—are the foundation for the content of our chapter 9 on "Managing Human Resources."

SOCIOLOGY Most of our knowledge of organization design has its roots in sociology. Specifically, sociologist Max Weber's bureaucracy set the design standard for most large organizations from the 1920s through the 1980s. He created a means for combining large size with efficiency through standardization and formalization. Similarly, recognition of the role that technology and environment play in the design of organizations was established and elaborated upon by sociologists.

Much of our knowledge of groups—for example, norms, roles, status, and conformity—is essentially from the area of social interaction within sociology. Similarly, much of the recent research on teams has its origins in sociology.

We discussed socialization within the larger topic of organizational cultures. Most of everything we know about socialization is derived from the work of sociologists. They address the issue at a societal level, but organizational sociologists have extended this work to illustrate how people adjust to new work situations.

ANTHROPOLOGY Several classic research studies of the 1930s and 1940s, undertaken at Western Electric and Sears Roebuck, were done by anthropologists. The studies at Western Electric, for instance, used the same techniques employed to uncover social structure and belief systems in tribal societies to assess group behavior in a manufacturing plant. In addition, much of what we know about organizational cultures—such as rites, rituals, ceremonies, and taboos—comes from anthropologists studying informal groups within organizations.

PHILOSOPHY A philosophical perspective has helped managers to conceptualize organizations in new ways. For instance, consider the use of metaphors. Managers who see organizations as psychic prisons or as instruments of domination will view their roles differently than managers who perceive organizations as a set of social contracts. In addition, philosophers are asking managers to reassess their perspectives through their work in critical theory and postmodernism. Critical theory, for instance, describes business organizations as exploiting labor and destroying third world cultures and values through global operations. Postmodernism is, among other things, seeking to redefine equality and reorder power relationships in organizations.

POLITICAL SCIENCE The notion of private ownership and corporations has its roots in political science. Capitalism is just one economic system. And there is no manifest destiny to the corporate form. In the United States, for instance, individual states authorize the creation of corporations. A Delaware corporation must abide by the laws of the state of Delaware. And with the right to create corporations, states also have the right to dissolve them.

Business Disciplines

ACCOUNTING An organization's accounting system and structure are closely intertwined. Both accounting and organization design are caught up in control. Accounting systems, through their use of budgets and reports, are the primary means by which management controls financial resources. Further, the design of an organization will influence what data is collected and how it is disseminated. Of course, the reverse is also true. The design of an organization's accounting system, in terms of the data generated and who controls information, will affect the distribution of power within the organization and the structure itself.

BUSINESS LAW Human resource practices are largely guided by employment law. No manager can effectively do his or her job today without an understanding of the laws that affect issues such as equal opportunity, discrimination, and sexual harassment.

OPERATIONS Courses in operations cover a wide range of design and production technology topics. These include quality management, product design, process design, flexible manufacturing, computer-integrated manufacturing, location selection, layout design, supply-chain management, inventory management, scheduling, and maintenance. Work design is also covered in operations, with the focus on specialization versus expansion, the use of teams, and ergonomics.

UNDERSTANDING THE BASICS OF HUMAN BEHAVIOR

YOU CAN OBSERVE A LOT BY JUST WATCHING.

Y. BERRA

LEARNING OBJECTIVES

After studying this chapter, you should be able to:

1 Identify the personality dimensions in the Myers-Briggs Type Indicator.

2 Describe the personality-job fit model.

3 Explain attribution theory.

4 Discuss the implications of the self-fulfilling prophecy.

5 Contrast the three components of an attitude.

6 Explain the theory of cognitive dissonance.

7 Describe the relationship between satisfaction and productivity.

8 Contrast operant conditioning and social-learning theory.

Today's "politically correct" management style includes being sensitive to others' needs and treating people with respect. But not all managers follow this model. For some, showing sensitivity and respect for others is not part of their personality. One such manager is Linda Wachner, chief executive of the Warnaco Group.[1]

Wachner is one of the few female chief executives at a Fortune 500 company. And her somewhat abrasive personality hasn't seemed to deter her from doing her job. Her record at Warnaco, in fact, is sterling. Since leading a leveraged buyout and becoming head of the giant apparel maker (the company's annual sales now exceed $800 million) in 1986, profits and the company's stock price have skyrocketed. Warnaco stock, for instance, continually outperforms others in its industry and the Standard & Poor's 500. Wachner's strong management skills have made money for her stockholders and for herself (her original $3 million investment is now worth more than $100 million). But would you want to work for Linda Wachner? You decide.

"I've been called controlling in my business style—and I am," Wachner admits. But then she quickly adds: "That's what delivers 43 percent [return on equity] for shareholders, not laissez-faire."

Former employees describe Wachner as a smart boss, but someone who is so impatient to achieve results that she will do almost anything, including frequently humiliating employees in front of their peers. She has a fiery temper, which she readily admits to. "I'm not very long on patience. I've yelled at people," she says, "and I'm not ashamed of it. We have to run this company efficiently and without a bunch of babies who say, 'Mommy yelled at me today.' If you don't like it, leave. It's not a prison."

How does Wachner see herself? "Effective and good, with an excellent record. You don't achieve that without focus, strategy, and having people do it your way." When *Fortune* magazine named her one of the seven toughest bosses in American business, she made no apologies. "It was not the best glimpse of me," Wachner says of the article. "But if you've got to run a company and improve the results and the image, you're not going to come out being a darling."

For people who have to work with Linda Wachner, having insights into her personality can help them better understand and predict her behavior. But this is true for all of us, because our personality goes a long way in shaping our behavior. In this chapter, we look at five psychological concepts—personality, perception, expectations, attitudes, and learning—and demonstrate how these concepts can help managers to better understand the behavior of those people with whom they have to work.

PERSONALITY: CLASSIFYING INDIVIDUAL DIFFERENCES

Some people are quiet and passive; others are loud and aggressive. When we describe people in terms such as *quiet, passive, loud, aggressive, ambitious,* or *persistent,* we are categorizing them in terms of *personality traits.* An individual's **personality** is the combination of the psychological traits we use to classify that person.

Predicting Behavior from Personality Traits

There are literally dozens of personality traits, but a small number have been found to be particularly valuable in providing insights into employee behavior. We review those traits in this section.

LOCUS OF CONTROL Some people believe that they are masters of their own fate. Other people see themselves as pawns of fate, believing that what happens to them in their lives is due to luck or chance. The first type, those who believe that they control their destinies, have been labeled **internals**, whereas the latter, who see their lives as being controlled by outside forces, have been called **externals**.[2]

Comparisons of internals with externals have consistently shown that individuals who rate high in externality are less satisfied with their jobs, have higher absenteeism rates, are more alienated from the work setting, and are less involved in their jobs than are internals.[3] Why are externals more dissatisfied? The answer is probably because they perceive themselves as having little control over those organizational outcomes that are important to them. Internals, facing the same situation, attribute organizational outcomes to their own actions. If the situation is unattractive, they believe that they have no one to blame but themselves. Also, the dissatisfied internal is more likely to quit a dissatisfying job.

The effect of **locus of control** on absenteeism is an interesting one. Internals believe that health is substantially under their own control through proper habits, so they take more responsibility for their health and have better health habits. Consequently, internals have lower incidences of sickness and, hence, lower absenteeism than externals.[4]

The overall evidence indicates that internals generally perform better on their jobs, but that conclusion should be moderated to reflect differences in jobs. Internals search more actively for information before making a decision, are more motivated to achieve, and make a greater attempt to control their environment. Externals, however, are more compliant and willing to follow directions. Therefore, internals do well on jobs that involve sophisticated tasks—which include most managerial and professional positions—that require complex information processing and learning. In addition, internals are more suited to jobs that require initiative and independence of action. In contrast, externals should do well on jobs that are well structured and routine and in which success depends heavily on complying with the directions of others.

ACHIEVEMENT ORIENTATION We noted that internals are motivated to achieve. This achievement orientation has also been singled out as a personality characteristic that varies among employees and that can be used to predict certain behaviors.

People with a high **need to achieve (nAch)** continually strive to do things better.[5] They want to overcome obstacles, but they want to feel that their successes (or failures) are due to their own actions. This means that they like tasks of intermediate difficulty. If a task is very easy, it will lack challenge. High achievers receive no feelings of accomplishment from doing tasks that fail to challenge their abilities. Similarly, they avoid tasks that are so difficult that the probability of success is very low and where, even if they do succeed, it's more apt to be due to luck than to ability. Given the high achiever's propensity for tasks where the outcome can be attributed directly to his or her efforts, the high-*nAch* person looks for challenges having approximately a 50-50 chance of success.

What can we say about high achievers on the job? In jobs that provide intermediate difficulty and rapid performance feedback and that give the employee control over his or her results, the high-*nAch* individual will perform well.[6] So high achievers should do better in sales or professional sports than on an assembly line or in clerical tasks. That is, those individuals with a high *nAch* will not *always* outperform those who are low or intermediate in this characteristic. The tasks that high achievers undertake must provide the challenge, feedback, and responsibility they look for if the high-*nAch* personality is to be positively related to job performance.

MACHIAVELLIANISM   The personality characteristic of **Machiavellianism (Mach)** is named after Niccolo Machiavelli, who wrote in the sixteenth century on how to gain and manipulate power. An individual high in Machiavellianism is pragmatic, maintains emotional distance, and believes that ends can justify means.

A considerable amount of research has been directed toward relating high- and low-Mach personalities to certain behavioral outcomes.[7] High-Machs manipulate more, win more, are persuaded less, and persuade others more than do low-Machs.[8] Yet these high-Mach outcomes are moderated by situational factors. It has been found that high-Machs flourish (1) when they interact face-to-face with others rather than indirectly; (2) when the situation has a minimum number of rules and regulations, thus allowing latitude for improvisation; and (3) when emotional involvement with details irrelevant to winning distracts low-Machs.[9]

Should we conclude that high-Machs make good employees? That answer depends on the type of job and whether you consider ethical implications in evaluating performance. In jobs that require bargaining skills (such as labor negotiation) or that offer substantial rewards for winning (as in commissioned sales), high-Machs will be productive. But if ends can't justify the means, if there are absolute standards of behavior, or if the three situational factors noted in the preceding paragraph are not in evidence, our ability to predict a high-Mach's performance will be severely curtailed.

SELF-ESTEEM   People differ in the degree to which they like or dislike themselves. This trait is called **self-esteem**.[10] The research on self-esteem (SE) offers some interesting insights into employee behavior. For example, self-esteem is directly related to expectations for success. High-SEs believe that they possess the ability they need in order to succeed at work. High-SEs will take more risks in job selection and are more likely to choose unconventional jobs than low-SEs.

The most generalizable finding on self-esteem is that low-SEs are more susceptible to external influence than are high-SEs. Low-SEs depend on positive evaluations from others. As a result, they are more likely to seek approval from others and more prone to conform to the beliefs and behaviors of those they respect than are high-SEs. In managerial positions, low-SEs will tend to be concerned with pleasing others and, therefore, are less likely to take unpopular stands than are high-SEs.

Not surprisingly, self-esteem has also been found to be related to job satisfaction. A number of studies confirm that high-SEs are more satisfied with their jobs than are low-SEs.[11]

SELF-MONITORING   A personality trait that has recently received increased attention is called **self-monitoring**.[12] It refers to an individual's ability to adjust his or her behavior to external, situational factors. Individuals high in self-monitoring show considerable adaptability in adjusting their behavior to external situational factors. They are highly sensitive to external cues and can behave differently in different situations. High self-monitors are capable of presenting striking contradictions between their public persona and their private self. Low self-monitors can't disguise themselves in this way. They tend to display their true dispositions and attitudes in every situation; hence, there is high behavioral consistency between who they are and what they do.

The evidence suggests that high self-monitors tend to pay closer attention to the behavior of others and are more capable of conforming than are low self-monitors.[13] High self-monitors also seem to get more promotions than individuals who score low on this characteristic.[14] We might additionally hypothesize that high self-monitors will be more successful in managerial positions, in which individuals are required to play multiple, and

> Individuals high in self-monitoring are highly sensitive to external cues and can behave differently in different situations.

Individuals with a high-risk-taking personality are well matched to the job of a stock trader at a brokerage firm because this job typically demands rapid decision making.

even contradicting, roles. Why? Because the high self-monitor is capable of putting on different "faces" for different audiences.

RISK TAKING   People differ in their willingness to take chances. This propensity to assume or avoid risk has been shown to have an impact on how long it takes managers to make a decision and how much information they require before making their choice. For instance, seventy-nine managers worked on simulated personnel exercises that required them to make hiring decisions.[15] High-risk-taking managers made decisions more rapidly and used less information in making their choices than did the low-risk-taking managers. Interestingly, the decision accuracy was the same for both groups.

It makes sense to recognize this personality variable by aligning risk-taking propensity with specific job demands.[16] For instance, a high-risk-taking propensity may lead to more effective performance for a stock trader in a brokerage firm because this type of job demands rapid decision making. On the other hand, this personality characteristic might prove to be a major obstacle to an accountant who performs auditing activities. The latter job might be better filled by someone with a low-risk-taking propensity.

PERSONALITY TYPE   Do you know any people who are excessively competitive and always seem to be experiencing a chronic sense of time urgency? It's a good bet that these people have a **Type A personality**.[17] A Type A individual is "aggressively involved in a *chronic, incessant* struggle to achieve more and more in less and less time, and if required to do so, against the opposing efforts of other things or other persons."[18] In the North American culture, such characteristics tend to be highly prized and positively associated with ambition and the successful acquisition of material goods. Type A's can be recognized by some behavioral traits. Type A's have the following characteristics:

1. They are always moving, walking, and eating rapidly.
2. They feel impatient with the rate at which most events take place.
3. They strive to think or do two or more things simultaneously.
4. They cannot cope with leisure time.
5. They are obsessed with numbers, measuring their success in terms of how much of everything they acquire.

In contrast to the Type A personality is the **Type B personality**, who is exactly the opposite. Type B's are "rarely harried by the desire to obtain a wildly increasing number of things or participate in an endless growing series of events in an ever decreasing amount of time."[19] Type B's have the following characteristics:

1. They never suffer from a sense of time urgency with its accompanying impatience.
2. They feel no need to display or discuss either their achievements or accomplishments unless such exposure is demanded by the situation.
3. They play for fun and relaxation, rather than to exhibit their superiority at any cost.
4. They can relax without guilt.

Type A's operate under moderate to high levels of stress. They subject themselves to more or less continuous time pressure, creating for themselves a life of deadlines. These characteristics result in some rather specific behavioral outcomes. For example, Type A's are fast workers, because they emphasize quantity over quality. In managerial positions, Type A's demonstrate their competitiveness by working long hours and, not infrequently, making poor decisions because they make them too fast. Type A's are also rarely creative. Because of their concern with quantity and speed, they rely on past experiences when faced with problems. They will not allocate the time that is necessary to develop unique solutions to problems. They rarely vary in their responses to specific challenges in their milieu; hence their behavior is easier to predict than is that of Type B's.

Are Type A's or Type B's more successful in organizations? Despite the hard work of Type A's, the Type B's are the ones who appear to make it to the top. Great salespersons are usually Type A's, but senior executives are usually Type B's. Why? The answer lies in the tendency of Type A's to trade off quality of effort for quantity. Promotions in corporate and professional organizations "usually go to those who are wise rather than to those who are merely hasty, to those who are tactful rather than to those who are hostile, and to those who are creative rather than to those who are merely agile in competitive strife."[20]

The Myers-Briggs Framework

One of the most widely used personality frameworks is called the **Myers-Briggs Type Indicator (MBTI)**.[21] It is essentially a 100-question personality test that asks people how they usually feel or act in particular situations.

On the basis of the answers individuals give to the test, they are classified as extroverted or introverted (E or I), sensing or intuitive (S or N), thinking or feeling (T or F), and perceiving or judging (P or J). These are then combined into sixteen personality types. To illustrate, let's take several examples. INTJs are visionaries. They usually have original minds and great drive for their own ideas and purposes. They are characterized as skeptical, critical, independent, determined, and often stubborn. ESTJs are organizers. They are practical, realistic, matter-of-fact, and have a natural head for business or mechanics. They like to organize and run activities. The ENTP type is a conceptualizer. He or she is quick, ingenious, and good at many things. This person tends to be resourceful in solving challenging problems but may neglect routine assignments. A recent book that profiled thirteen contemporary businesspeople who created super-successful firms such as Apple Computer, Federal Express, Honda Motors, Microsoft, Price Club, and Sony found that all thirteen are intuitive thinkers (NTs).[22] This finding is particularly interesting, since intuitive thinkers represent only about 5 percent of the population. Thinking and judging types (TJs) have been found to be most prevalent among managers in general, suggesting logical decision makers are attracted to management positions.[23] Additionally, the evidence indicates that N's are predominant among top managers, while S's are most common in middle and lower-level managers. Moreover, S's are more effective in lower positions, while N's excel in the upper levels.[24]

More than 3 million people a year take the MBTI.[25] Organizations using the MBTI include AT&T, Exxon, GE, 3M Co., plus many hospitals, educational institutions, and even the U.S. armed forces.

What value does the MBTI have for managers? One obvious use is in matching people with jobs. Since results provide insights into what individuals enjoy doing, using the MBTI in employee selection can lessen the likelihood that someone will be put into a job that conflicts with his or her personality. For instance, ENFPs are well matched to jobs such as copywriter or psychologist. They are not well suited to being office managers, accountants, or insurance underwriters. These latter jobs might be better filled by ISTJs. Similarly, the MBTI suggests that the personality type that is most effective in lower managerial jobs (S's) are not necessarily the best choices for top managerial positions. S's are well suited for routine and detailed activities, while N's excel at nonroutine tasks and creative problem solving.

▶ The "Big Five" Framework

Although the MBTI is widely used in corporations, another model of personality appears to offer a more comprehensive and unifying framework for identifying personality dimensions. This is the **five-factor model of personality**—more typically called the "Big Five."[26] Recent research provides impressive evidence that five basic personality dimensions underlie all others. The Big Five factors are:

- **Extraversion**. This dimension captures one's comfort level with relationships. Extraverts (high in extroversion) tend to be sociable, friendly, and outgoing. They maintain a large number of relationships. Introverts tend to be reserved and to have fewer relationships, and they are more comfortable with solitude than most people are.
- **Agreeableness**. This dimension refers to an individual's propensity to defer to others. Highly agreeable people value harmony more than they value having their say or their way. They are cooperative and trusting of others. People who score low on agreeableness focus more on their own needs than on the needs of others.
- **Conscientiousness**. This dimension refers to the number of goals on which a person focuses. A highly conscientious person pursues fewer goals, in a purposeful way, and tends to be responsible, persistent, dependable, and achievement-oriented. Those who score low on this dimension tend to be more easily distracted, pursuing many goals, and more hedonistic.
- **Emotional stability**. This dimension taps a person's ability to withstand stress. People with positive emotional stability tend to be characterized as calm, enthusiastic, and secure. Those with high negative scores tend to be nervous, anxious, and insecure.
- **Openness to experience**. The final dimension addresses one's range of interests. Extremely open people are fascinated by novelty and innovation. They tend to be imaginative, artistically sensitive, and intellectual. Those at the other end of the openness category appear more conventional and find comfort in the familiar.

In addition to providing a unifying framework, important relationships have been found between Big Five dimensions and job performance.[27] A broad spectrum of occupations have been studied: professionals (including engineers, architects, accountants, attorneys), police, managers, salespeople, and semiskilled and skilled workers. Job performance was defined in terms of professional ratings, training proficiency (performance during training programs), and personnel data such as salary level. The results showed that conscientiousness predicted job performance for all occupational groups. "The preponderance of evidence shows that individuals who are dependable, reliable, careful, thorough, able to plan, organized, hardworking, persistent, and achievement-oriented tend to have higher job performance in most if not all occupations."[28] For the other personality dimensions, predictability depends upon both the performance criterion and the occupational group. For instance, extraversion predicted performance in managerial and sales positions. This finding makes sense because those occupations involve high social interaction. Similarly, openness to experience was found to be important in predicting training proficiency, which, too, seems logical. What wasn't so clear was why positive emotional stability wasn't related to job performance. Intuitively, it would seem that people who are calm and secure would do better on almost all jobs than people who are anxious and insecure. The most plausible explanation is that only people who score fairly high on emotional stability retain their jobs. So the range among those people studied, all of whom were employed, would tend to be quite small.

Do these conclusions transfer across national cultures? The evidence previously cited is based on studies done in the United States and Canada. However, a recent evaluation of similar studies all conducted with employees in European Union countries also found that conscientiousness was positively related to job performance regardless of occupational group.[29] So these conclusions do appear to have generalizability across national boundaries.

Finally, we suggest that the conclusions drawn concerning the Big Five dimensions could be dated.[30] As described in chapter 10, today's workplace is increasingly being organized around work teams. And effective job performance on teams emphasizes strong interpersonal skills such as communication, conflict resolution, and the ability to empathize with others. The evidence from which these conclusions were drawn came from studies undertaken *before* teams became so popular. We suggest, therefore, that future studies might find increased importance placed on extraversion and agreeableness as predictors of job performance. These two personality dimensions would appear to be important for job success among employees who have to work in teams.

> **The evidence shows that conscientiousness predicts job performance for all occupational groups.**

▶ Matching Personalities and Jobs

Another approach to matching personalities and jobs—one that has substantial evidence to back it up—is J. L. Holland's **personality-job fit model**.[31] This model is based on the notion of fit between an individual's personality characteristics and his or her occupational environment. Holland identified six personality types and proposed that satisfaction and the propensity to leave a job depend on the degree to which individuals successfully match their personalities to a compatible occupational environment.

Each one of the six personality types has a congruent occupational environment. Exhibit 12-1 on page 374 describes the six types and their personality characteristics and gives examples of congruent occupations.

Holland developed a Vocational Preference Inventory questionnaire that contains 160 occupational titles. Respondents indicate which of these occupations they like or dislike, and their answers are used to form personality profiles. Utilizing this procedure, research strongly supports the hexagonal diagram in Exhibit 12-2.[32] This figure shows that the closer two fields or orientations are in the hexagon, the more compatible they are. Adjacent categories are quite similar, whereas those diagonally opposite are highly dissimilar.

Holland's Typology of Personality and Sample Occupations

Type	Description	Personality Characteristics	Sample Occupations
Realistic	Prefers physical activities that require skill, strength, and coordination	Shy, genuine, persistent, stable, conforming, practical	Mechanic, drill press operator, assembly-line worker, farmer
Investigative	Prefers activities involving thinking, organizing, and understanding	Analytical, original, curious, independent	Biologist, economist, mathematician, news reporter
Social	Prefers activities that involve helping and developing others	Sociable, friendly, cooperative, understanding	Social worker, teacher, counselor, clinical psychologist
Conventional	Prefers rule-regulated, orderly, unambiguous activities	Conforming, efficient, practical, unimaginitive, inflexible	Accountant, corporate manager, bank teller, file clerk
Enterprising	Prefers verbal activities where there are opportunities to influence others and attain power	Self-confident, ambitious, energetic, domineering	Lawyer, real estate agent, public relations specialist, small business manager
Artistic	Prefers ambiguous and unsystematic activities that allow creative expression	Imaginative, disorderly, idealistic, emotional, impractical	Painter, musician, writer, interior decorator

Hexagonal Diagram of the Relationship Among Occupational Personality Types

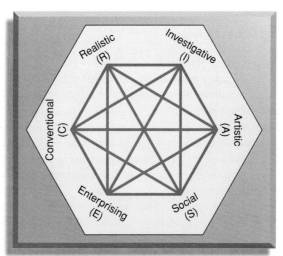

What does all this mean? The theory argues that satisfaction is highest and turnover lowest when personality and occupation are in agreement. Social individuals should be in social jobs, conventional people in conventional jobs, and so forth. A realistic person in a realistic job is in a more congruent situation than is a realistic person in an investigative job. A realistic person in a social job is in the most incongruent situation possible.

Implications for Managers

A review of the personality literature offers general guidelines that can lead to effective job performance. As such, it can improve hiring, transfer, and promotion decisions. Because personality characteristics create the parameters for people's behavior, they give us a framework for predicting behavior. For example, individuals who are shy, introverted, and uncomfortable in social situations would probably be ill suited as salespeople. Individuals who are submissive and conforming might not be effective as advertising "idea" people.

Can we predict which people will be high performers in sales, research, or assembly-line work on the basis of their personality characteristics alone? The answer is no. But a knowledge of an individual's personality can aid in reducing mismatches, which, in turn, can lead to greater job stability and higher job satisfaction.

We can look at certain personality characteristics that tend to be related to job success, test for those traits, and use the data to make selection more effective. It may not even be necessary to use personality tests. The Big Five traits, for instance, have been found to be easily and accurately observed, even by strangers.[33] So recruiters and managers may be able to make accurate personality assessments during employment interviews. Regardless, the evidence allows us to conclude, for instance, that a person who accepts rules, conformity, and dependence and rates low on risk taking is likely to feel more comfortable in, say, a structured assembly-line job, as an admittance clerk in a hospital, or as an administrator in a large public agency than as a researcher or an employee whose job requires a high degree of creativity.

PERCEPTION AND ATTRIBUTIONS: INTERPRETING THE WORLD AROUND US

One of the basic tenets of human behavior is that people act on their perceptions, not on reality. The world as it is perceived is the world that is behaviorally important. And because there are a number of forces acting to distort perceptions, people often misinterpret events and activities. As we will show, the message for managers is that if you are going to try to explain or predict someone's behavior, it is important to try to see the world the way he or she sees it.

Perception can be defined as a process by which individuals organize and interpret their sensory impressions in order to give meaning to their environment. However, as we have noted, what one perceives can be substantially different from objective reality. It need not be, but there is often disagreement. For example, it's possible that all employees in a firm may view it as a great place to work—favorable working conditions, interesting job assignments, good pay, an understanding and responsible management—but, as most of us know, it's very unusual to find such agreement.

Factors Influencing Perception

How do we explain the fact that people can perceive the same thing differently? A number of factors operate to shape and sometimes distort perception. These factors can reside in

EXHIBIT 12-3

Perception Illustration

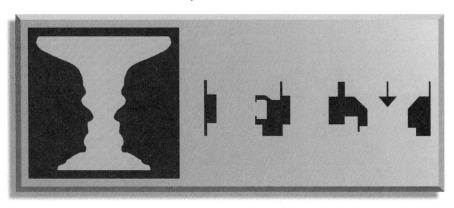

The object on the left may at first look like a violet vase. However, if violet is taken as the background, we see two dark profiles. Similarly, at first observation, the group of objects on the right appears to be some modular figure against a violet background. Closer inspection will reveal the word "FLY" once the background is defined as the darker color.

the *perceiver*; in the object, or *target*, being perceived; or in the context of the *situation* in which the perception is made.

When an individual looks at a target and attempts to interpret what he or she sees, the individual's personal characteristics are going to heavily influence the interpretation. These personal characteristics include attitudes, personality, motives, interests, past experiences, and expectations. For instance, it shouldn't surprise you that a plastic surgeon is more likely to notice an imperfect nose than is a plumber. Similarly, the supervisor who has just been reprimanded by her boss for the excessive amount of tardiness among her staff is more likely to notice lateness by an employee tomorrow than she was last week. And if you are preoccupied with a personal problem, you may find it hard to be attentive in class. These examples illustrate that the focus of our attention is influenced by our interests. Because our individual interests differ considerably, what one person notices in a situation can differ from what others perceive.

The characteristics of the target being observed can affect what is perceived. Loud people are more likely than quiet people to be noticed in a group. So, too, are extremely attractive or unattractive individuals. Because targets are not looked at in isolation, the relationship of a target to its background also influences perception (see Exhibit 12-3), as does our tendency to group close things together and similar things together. Employees in a specific department, for example, are seen as a group. If two people in a four-member department suddenly resign, we tend to assume that their departures were related when, in fact, they may have been totally unrelated.

The context in which we see objects or events is also important. The time at which an object or event is seen can influence attention, as can location, light, heat, and any number of other situational factors. For instance, you probably wouldn't take particular notice of a couple in formal evening attire at an exclusive London club on a Saturday night. But that same couple, dressed similarly, walking down a residential street in London at 10:00 A.M. the following Monday morning would undoubtedly turn your head. Notice that the only thing that changed was the situational context in which you saw the couple.

Attribution Theory

Our perceptions of people differ from our perceptions of inanimate objects such as desks, machines, or buildings because we make inferences about the actions of people that we don't make about inanimate objects. Nonliving objects are subject to the laws of nature, but they have no beliefs, motives, or intentions. People do. The result is that when we observe people, we attempt to develop explanations of why they behave in certain ways. Our perception and judgment of a person's actions, therefore, will be significantly influenced by the assumptions we make about the person's internal state.

Attribution theory has been proposed to develop explanations of the ways in which we judge people differently, depending on what meaning we attribute to a given behavior.[34] Basically, the theory suggests that when we observe an individual's behavior, we attempt to determine whether it was internally or externally caused. Internally caused behaviors are those that are believed to be under the personal control of the individual. Externally caused behavior results from outside causes; that is, the person is seen as having been forced into the behavior by the situation. That determination, however, depends largely on three factors: distinctiveness, consensus, and consistency.

Distinctiveness refers to whether an individual displays different behaviors in different situations. Is the employee who arrives late today also the source of complaints by co-workers for being a "goof-off"? What we want to know is whether this behavior is unusual. If it is, the observer is likely to give the behavior an external attribution. If this action is not unusual, it will probably be judged as internal.

If everyone who is faced with a similar situation responds in the same way, we can say the behavior shows *consensus*. Our late employee's behavior would meet this criterion if all employees who took the same route to work were also late. From an attribution perspective, if consensus is high, you would be expected to give an external attribution to the employee's tardiness, whereas if other employees who took the same route made it to work on time, you would conclude that the cause was internal.

Finally, an observer looks for *consistency* in a person's actions. Does the person respond the same way over time? Coming in 10 minutes late for work is not perceived in the same way for an employee who is rarely late (she hasn't been late for several months) as it is for an employee who is routinely late (she is late two or three times a week). The more consistent the behavior, the more the observer is inclined to attribute it to internal causes.

Exhibit 12-4 on page 378 summarizes the key elements in attribution theory. It would tell us, for instance, that if your employee, Kim Randolph, generally performs at about the same level on other related tasks as she does on her current task (low distinctiveness), if other employees frequently perform differently—better or worse—than Kim does on that current task (low consensus), and if Kim's performance on this current task is consistent over time (high consistency), you or anyone else who is judging Kim's work is likely to hold her primarily responsible for her task performance (internal attribution).

One of the more interesting findings from attribution theory is that there are errors or biases that distort attributions. For instance, there is substantial evidence that when we make judgments about the behavior of other people, we have a tendency to underestimate the influence of external factors and overestimate the influence of internal or personal factors.[35] This is called the **fundamental attribution error** and can explain why a sales manager is prone to attribute the poor performance of her sales agents to laziness rather than to the innovative product line introduced by a competitor. There is also a tendency for individuals to attribute their own successes to internal factors such as ability or effort while putting the blame for failure on external factors such as luck (see Exhibit 12-5 on page 379).

EXHIBIT 12-4

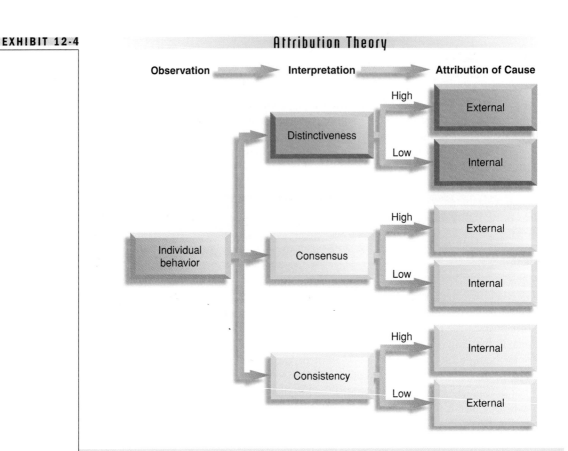

Attribution Theory

This is called the **self-serving bias** and suggests that feedback provided to employees in performance reviews will be predictably distorted by recipients depending on whether it is positive or negative.

Perceptual Shortcuts or Errors We Make in Judging Others

We use a number of shortcuts when we judge others. Perceiving and interpreting what others do is burdensome. As a result, we all develop techniques for making the task more manageable. These techniques are frequently valuable—they allow us to make accurate perceptions rapidly and provide valid data for making predictions. But they are not fool-proof. They can and do get us into trouble. An understanding of these shortcuts can be helpful toward recognizing when they can result in significant distortions.

Individuals cannot assimilate all they observe, so they engage in selectivity. They take in bits and pieces. These bits and pieces are not chosen randomly; rather, they are selectively chosen depending on the interests, background, experience, and attitudes of the observer. **Selective perception** allows us to "speed read" others, but not without the risk of drawing an inaccurate picture.

It's easy to judge others if we assume that they are similar to us. In **assumed similarity**, or the "like-me" effect, the observer's perception of others is influenced more by the observer's own characteristics than by those of the person observed. For example, if you want challenge and responsibility in your job, you will assume that others want the same.

EXHIBIT 12-5

Source: *Non Sequitur*, by Wiley, © 1996, Washington Post Writers Group. Reprinted with permission.

People who assume that others are like them can, of course, be right, but most of the time they are wrong.

When we judge someone on the basis of our perception of a group to which he or she belongs, we are using the shortcut called **stereotyping**. "Married people are more stable employees than singles" and "union people expect something for nothing" are examples of stereotyping. To the degree that a stereotype is based on fact, it may produce accurate judgments. However, many stereotypes have no foundation in fact. In such cases, they distort judgments.

When we form a general impression about an individual on the basis of a single characteristic such as intelligence, appearance, or sociability, we are being influenced by the **halo effect**. This effect frequently occurs when students evaluate their classroom instructor. Students may isolate a single trait such as enthusiasm and allow their entire evaluation to be tainted by their perception of this one trait. An instructor might be quiet, assured, knowledgeable, and highly qualified, but if his style lacks zeal, he will be rated lower on a number of other characteristics.

▶ Implications for Managers

Managers need to recognize that their employees react to perceptions, not to reality. So whether a manager's appraisal of an employee is *actually* objective and unbiased or whether the organization's salary levels are *actually* among the highest in the industry is less relevant than what employees perceive them to be. If individuals perceive appraisals as biased or salary levels as low, they'll behave as if those conditions actually exist. Employees organize and interpret what they see; and this becomes *their reality*.

The message to managers should be clear: Close attention needs to be paid to how employees perceive their jobs and management practices. Remember, the valuable employee who quits because of an *incorrect perception* is just as great a loss to an organization as the valuable employee who quits for a *valid reason*.

Expectations exert a powerful force on behavior. Take the case of 105 Israeli soldiers who were participating in a combat command course.[36] The four course instructors were told that one-third of the specific incoming trainees had high potential, one-third had normal potential, and the potential of the rest was unknown. In reality, the trainees were randomly placed into these categories by researchers conducting the study. Consistent with the power of expectations, those trainees whom instructors were told had high potential scored significantly higher on objective achievement tests, exhibited more positive attitudes, and held their leaders in higher regard than did the others. The instructors of the supposedly high-potential trainees got better results from them because the instructors expected it!

The terms **self-fulfilling prophecy** and *pygmalion effect* have evolved to characterize the fact that an expectation about how someone is likely to act causes that person to fulfill the expectation.[37] From an organizational standpoint, managers get the performance they expect.

How does the self-fulfilling prophecy work in manager-employee relations? Exhibit 12-6 provides an explanation. First, a manager forms an impression of the employee. From this perception, the manager further develops expectations about the employee's future behavior. When those expectations are high, the manager will behave in ways consistent with high expectations. For instance, the manager will tend to be supportive, friendly, offer helpful feedback, and provide more opportunities for the employee. The employee, in turn, responds positively to his or her manager's behavior. He or she will take advantage of the support and opportunities offered. In addition, the confidence that the manager exhibits toward the employee builds that employee's self-esteem, and the employee then behaves in ways that fulfill the manager's high expectations.

EXHIBIT 12-6

Development of the Self-Fulfilling Prophecy

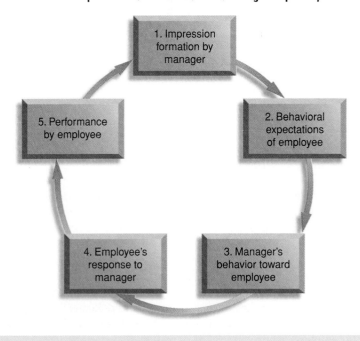

1. Impression formation by manager
2. Behavioral expectations of employee
3. Manager's behavior toward employee
4. Employee's response to manager
5. Performance by employee

We can draw two conclusions from the self-fulfilling prophecy: (1) Misperceptions of a situation can evoke actions that make the original misperception come true; and (2) managers who set high expectations for their employees—but not so high as to be intimidating or impossible—will initiate a process that can lead to the fulfillment of those high expectations.

BP Exploration conducts annual attitude surveys among its 12,000 employees. And it's not alone. Many organizations regularly survey their employees to learn how they feel about their job, their bosses, company pay practices, and the like. Why do organizations do this? Because managers recognize that attitudes have a significant bearing on employee behavior. An increase in complaints about working conditions or benefits, for instance, is often followed by an increase in resignations.

Attitudes are evaluative statements—either favorable or unfavorable—concerning objects, people, or events. They reflect how one feels about something. When I say "I like my job," I am expressing my attitude about work.

To better understand the concept of attitudes, we should look at an attitude as being made up of three components: cognition, affect, and behavior.[38] The **cognitive component** of an attitude makes up the beliefs, opinions, knowledge, or information held by a person. The belief that "discrimination is wrong" illustrates a cognition. It sets the stage for the more critical part of an attitude—the **affective component**. Affect is the emotional, or feeling, segment of an attitude and is reflected in the statement "I don't like Jon because he discriminates against minorities." Finally, affect can lead to behavioral outcomes. The **behavioral component** of an attitude refers to an intention to act in a certain way toward someone or something. So, to continue our example, I might choose to avoid Jon because of my feelings about him.

Viewing attitudes as made up of three components—cognition, affect, and behavior—is helpful toward understanding their complexity and the potential relationship between attitudes and behavior. But for clarity's sake, keep in mind that the term *attitude* essentially refers to the affect part of the three components.

▶ Popular Work-Related Attitudes

A person can have thousands of attitudes, but managers aren't interested in every attitude an employee might hold. They are interested in job-related attitudes. The three most popular of these are job satisfaction, job involvement, and organizational commitment.[39]

JOB SATISFACTION   The term **job satisfaction** refers to an individual's general attitude toward his or her job. A person with a high level of job satisfaction holds positive attitudes toward the job, whereas a person who is dissatisfied with his or her job holds negative attitudes about the job. When people speak of employee attitudes, more often than not they mean job satisfaction. In fact, the two terms are frequently used interchangeably.

JOB INVOLVEMENT   Although there is not complete agreement over what the term **job involvement** means, a workable definition states that it measures the degree to which a person identifies psychologically with his or her job and considers his or her perceived performance level to be important to self-worth.[40] Employees with a high level of job involvement strongly identify with and really care about the kind of work they do.

Norm Sears characterizes a model of organizational commitment. Here he accepts several awards at his retirement ceremony after 41 years at Draper Labs in Cambridge, Massachusetts.

High levels of job involvement have been found to be related to fewer absences and lower resignation rates.[41] However, it seems to more consistently predict turnover than absenteeism.[42]

ORGANIZATIONAL COMMITMENT The third job attitude we shall discuss is **organizational commitment**. It's defined as a state in which an employee identifies with a particular organization and its goals and wishes to maintain membership in the organization.[43] So, high *job involvement* means identifying with one's specific job, whereas high *organizational commitment* means identifying with one's employing organization.

As with job involvement, the research evidence demonstrates negative relationships between organizational commitment and both absenteeism and turnover.[44] In fact, studies demonstrate that an individual's level of organizational commitment is a better indicator of turnover than is the far more frequently used job satisfaction predictor.[45] Organizational commitment is probably a better predictor because it is a more pervasive and enduring response to the organization as a whole than is job satisfaction.[46] An employee may be dissatisfied with his or her particular job and consider it a temporary condition yet not be dissatisfied with the organization as a whole. But when dissatisfaction spreads to the organization itself, individuals are likely to consider resigning.

▶ Coping with Cognitive Dissonance

Did you ever notice how people change what they say so that it doesn't contradict what they do? The reason is that people seek consistency among their attitudes and between their attitudes and their behavior. They try to reconcile divergent attitudes and align their attitudes and behavior so they appear to be rational and consistent. When there are inconsistencies, people will typically alter the attitude, change their behavior, or develop a rationalization to explain the discrepancy.

Given this tendency for people to seek consistency, can we assume that an individual's behavior can always be predicted if we know his or her attitude on a subject? The answer to this question is, unfortunately, more complex than merely a yes or a no.

The theory of **cognitive dissonance** helps explain the relationship between attitudes and behavior.[47] Dissonance means an inconsistency. Cognitive dissonance refers to any incompatibility that an individual might perceive between two or more of his or her attitudes, or between his or her behavior and attitudes. The theory proposes that any form of inconsistency is uncomfortable and that individuals will attempt to reduce the dissonance and, hence, the discomfort. Therefore, individuals will seek a stable state where there is a minimum of dissonance.

Of course, no individual can completely avoid dissonance. You know that cheating on your income tax is wrong, but you "fudge" the numbers a bit every year and hope that you won't be audited. Or you tell your children to brush after every meal, but *you* don't. So how do people cope? The theory states that the desire to reduce dissonance will be determined by the *importance* of the elements creating the dissonance, the degree of *influence* the individual believes he or she has over the elements, and the *rewards* that may be involved in dissonance.

If the elements creating the dissonance are relatively unimportant, the pressure to correct this imbalance will be low. However, say that a corporate manager—Clara Smith—believes strongly that no company should pollute the air or water. Unfortunately, Smith, because of the requirements of her job, is placed in the position of having to make decisions that would trade off her company's profitability against her attitudes on pollution. She knows that dumping the company's sewage into the local river (which we'll assume is legal) is in the best economic interest of her firm. What will she do? Clearly, Smith is experiencing a high degree of cognitive dissonance. Because of the importance of the elements in this example, we cannot expect Smith to ignore the inconsistency. There are several paths that she can follow to deal with her dilemma. She can change her behavior (stop polluting the river). Or she can reduce dissonance by concluding that the dissonant behavior is not so important after all ("I have to make a living, and in my role as a corporate decision maker, I often have to place the good of my company above that of the environment or society"). A third alternative would be for Smith to change her attitude ("There is nothing wrong in polluting the river"). Still another choice would be to seek out more consonant elements to outweigh the dissonant ones ("The benefits to society from our products more than offset the cost to society of the resulting water pollution").

The degree of influence that individuals believe they have over the elements will have an impact on how they will react to the dissonance. If they perceive the dissonance to be uncontrollable—something about which they have no choice—they are not likely to be receptive to attitude change. If, for example, the dissonance-producing behavior were required as a result of the boss's directive, the pressure to reduce dissonance would be less than if the behavior were performed voluntarily. Although dissonance exists, it can be rationalized and justified.

Rewards also influence the degree to which individuals are motivated to reduce dissonance. When high rewards accompany high dissonance, the tension inherent in the dissonance tends to be reduced. The rewards act to reduce dissonance by increasing the consistency side of the individual's balance sheet.

These moderating factors suggest that just because individuals experience dissonance they will not necessarily move directly toward consistency, that is, toward reduction of this dissonance. If the issues underlying the dissonance are of minimal importance, if an individual perceives that the dissonance is externally imposed and is substantially uncontrollable by him or her, or if rewards are significant enough to offset the dissonance, the individual will not be under great tension to reduce the dissonance.

What are the organizational implications of the theory of cognitive dissonance? It can help to predict the propensity to change attitudes and behavior. If individuals are required, for example, by the demands of their job to say or do things that contradict their personal attitude, they will tend to modify their attitude in order to make it compatible with the cognition of what they have said or done. In addition, the greater the dissonance—after it has been moderated by importance, choice, and reward factors—the greater the pressures to reduce it.

▶ Is a Happy Worker a Productive Worker?

One of the most studied relationships in the disciplines of management and organizational behavior is that between satisfaction and productivity.[48] It tends to be addressed by the question: Is a happy worker a productive worker?

As far back as the 1930s, researchers in industry were studying the satisfaction-productivity relationship.[49] Those early studies prematurely concluded that happy workers were indeed productive workers. As a result, managers in the 1930s, 1940s, and 1950s became enamored with the idea of increasing employee job satisfaction. One outcome was corporate paternalism. In order to make workers happy, managers formed company bowling teams and credit unions, held company picnics, and trained supervisors to be sensitive to the concerns of employees. However, the early research findings supporting the happy worker thesis were flawed. Let's briefly summarize what we now know about this relationship.

A careful review of the research indicates that if there is a positive relationship between satisfaction and productivity, the correlations are consistently low.[50] However, introduction of moderating variables has improved the strength of the relationship.[51] For example, the relationship is stronger when the employee's behavior is not constrained or controlled by outside factors. An employee's productivity on machine-paced jobs, for instance, is going to be much more influenced by the speed of the machine than by his or her level of satisfaction. Similarly, a stockbroker's productivity is largely constrained by the general movement of the stock market. When the market is moving up and volume is high, both satisfied and dissatisfied brokers are going to ring up lots of commissions. Conversely, when the market is in the doldrums, the level of broker satisfaction is not likely to mean much. Job level also seems to be an important moderating variable. The satisfaction-performance correlations are stronger for higher-level employees. Thus, we might expect the relationship to be more relevant for individuals in professional, supervisory, and managerial positions.

Another point of concern in the satisfaction-productivity issue is the direction of the causal arrow. Most of the studies on the relationship used research designs that could not prove cause and effect. Studies that have controlled for the direction of the relationship indicate that the more valid conclusion is that productivity leads to satisfaction rather than the other way around.[52] If you do a good job, you intrinsically feel good about it. In addition, assuming that the organization rewards productivity, your higher productivity should increase verbal recognition, your pay level, and probabilities for promotion. These rewards, in turn, increase your level of satisfaction with the job.

The most recent evidence provides renewed support for the original satisfaction-productivity relationship.[53] When satisfaction and productivity data are gathered for the organization as a whole, rather than at the individual level, we find that organizations with more-satisfied employees tended to be more effective than organizations with less-satisfied employees. This evidence may explain why we haven't gotten strong support for the satisfaction-causes-productivity thesis. Studies have focused on individuals rather than on the organization, and individual-level measures of productivity fail to take into consideration all the interactions and complexities in the work process.

How Can Organizations Keep Employees Satisfied?

Most employers want to have satisfied workers. What can they do to achieve that end?

One approach has focused on work design (see chapter 7). By enriching jobs, employees would find work more interesting and challenging. Although this had some success, not *all* employees found enriched jobs more satisfying. Additionally, enriching jobs is expensive and frequently difficult to implement. For instance, some jobs, such as those performed by fast-food workers, are more efficiently done by relying on narrow work specialization.

Another approach toward increasing satisfaction has focused on rewards. On the assumption that money can buy happiness, some employers have given employees high salaries, pay increases, and bonuses in the belief that this will increase satisfaction. Unfortunately, this approach has rarely been successful. The motivating elements of money quickly dissipate. And the rich are no significantly happier than those with moderate incomes. For instance, when asked how happy they were, the super rich averaged 5.82 on a 7-point scale (7 meant "delighted" and 1 was "terrible"), whereas the average population scored

5.34. International studies generate similar conclusions. Except for the very poorest countries such as India and Bangladesh, most people in most countries are at least mildly happy.

The most powerful explanation of job satisfaction may simply be: Whether a person is happy or not is largely genetically determined. You either have happy genes or you don't. Approximately 80 percent of people's differences in happiness, or subjective well-being, is attributable to their different genes.

If employers want satisfied employees, their most effective approach is probably to focus on hiring people who are already happy. Although interesting work and money may have some influence, employers are better advised to try to identify and hire upbeat job applicants. And the message in this data for *you* may be—if you're depressed and negative, and think that'll all change if you were just rich, you're probably wrong.

Source: Based on D. Lykken and A. Tellegen, "Happiness Is a Stochastic Phenomenon," *Psychological Science*, May 1996, pp. 186–89; and D. Seligman, "Does Money Buy Happiness?" *Forbes*, April 21, 1997, pp. 394–96.

▌ Understanding Emotions

On a recent Friday, a 37-year old U.S. postal worker in Milwaukee walked into his place of work. He pulled out a gun and shot and killed a co-worker he had argued with, wounded a supervisor who had scolded him, and injured another worker. He then killed himself.[54] For this worker, anger had led to violence.

Going on a shooting rampage at work is an extreme example, but it dramatically illustrates the theme of this section: Emotions are a critical factor in employee behavior.

Given the obvious role that emotions play in our everyday life, it might surprise you to learn that, until very recently, the topic of emotions had been given little or no attention within the field of management. How could this be? We can offer two possible explanations. The first is the *myth of rationality*.[55] Since the late nineteenth century and the rise of scientific management, organizations have been specifically designed with the objective of trying to control emotions. A well-run organization was one that successfully eliminated frustration, anger, love, hate, joy, grief, and similar feelings. Such emotions were the antithesis of rationality. So although researchers and managers knew that emotions were an inseparable part of everyday life, they tried to create organizations that were emotion-free. That, of course, was not possible. The second factor was the belief that *emotions of any kind were disruptive*.[56] When emotions were considered, the discussion focused on

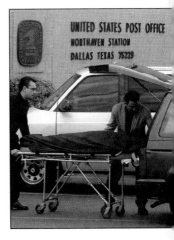

In recent years, U.S. Post Offices have been the scene of a number of violent acts by current or former employees of the U.S. Postal Service.

strong negative emotions—especially anger—that interferred with an employee's ability to do his or her job effectively. Emotions were rarely viewed as being constructive or able to stimulate performance-enhancing behaviors.

Certainly some emotions, particularly when exhibited at the wrong time, can reduce employee performance. But this doesn't change the reality that employees bring an emotional component with them to work everyday and that no study of workplace behavior could be comprehensive without considering the role of emotions.

> No study of workplace behavior could be comprehensive without considering the role of emotions.

WHAT ARE EMOTIONS? Although we don't want to obsess on definitions, before we can proceed with our analysis, we need to clarify three terms that are closely intertwined. These are *affect*, *emotions*, and *moods*.

Affect is a generic term that covers a broad range of feelings that people experience. It's an umbrella concept that encompasses both emotions and moods.[56] **Emotions** are intense feelings that are directed at someone or something.[57] Finally, **moods** are feelings that tend to be less intense than emotions and they lack a contextual stimulus.[58]

Emotions are reactions to an object, not a trait. They're object-specific. You show your emotions when you're "happy about something, angry at someone, afraid of something."[59] Moods, on the other hand, aren't directed at an object. Emotions can turn into moods when you lose focus on the contextual object. So when a work colleague criticizes you for the way you spoke to a client, you might become angry at him. That is, you show emotion (anger) toward a specific object (your colleague). But later in the day, you might find yourself just generally dispirited. You can't attribute this feeling to any single event; you're just not your normal, upbeat self. This affect state describes a mood.

A related affect term is *emotional labor*. Every employee expends physical and mental labor when they put their bodies and cognitive capabilities, respectively, into their job. But most jobs also require **emotional labor**. This is when an employee expresses organizationally desired emotions during interpersonal transactions.[60] The concept of emotional labor originally developed in relation to service jobs. Airline flight attendants, for instance, are expected to be cheerful, funeral counselors sad, and doctors emotionally neutral. But today, the concept of emotional labor seems relevant to almost every job. You're expected, for example, to be courteous and not hostile in interactions with co-workers. And leaders are expected to draw on emotional labor to "charge the troops." Almost every great speech, for instance, contains a strong emotional component that stirs feelings in others.

FELT VERSUS DISPLAYED EMOTIONS Emotional labor creates dilemmas for employees when their job requires them to exhibit emotions that are incongruous with their actual feelings. Not surprisingly, this is a frequent occurrence. You find it very difficult to be friendly with some people that you have to work with. Maybe you consider someone's personality abrasive. Maybe you know someone who has said negative things about you behind your back. Regardless, your job requires you to interact with these people on a regular basis. So you're forced to feign friendliness.

To better understand emotions, let's separate them into *felt* versus *displayed*.[61] **Felt emotions** are an individual's actual emotions. In contrast, **displayed emotions** are those that are organizationally required and considered appropriate in a given job. They're not innate; they're learned. "The ritual look of delight on the face of the first runner-up as the new Miss America is announced is a product of the display rule that losers should mask their sadness with an expression of joy for the winner."[62] Similarly, most of us know that we are expected to act sad at funerals regardless of whether we consider the person's death to be a loss, and to pretend to be happy at weddings even if we don't feel like celebrating.[63] Effective managers have learned to be serious when giving an employee a negative performance evaluation and to cover-up their anger when they've been passed over for promotion. And the salesperson who hasn't learned to smile and appear friendly, regardless of his or her true feelings at the moment, isn't typically going to last long on most sales jobs.

The key point here is that felt and displayed emotions are often different. In fact, many people have problems working with others simply because they naively assume that the emotions they see others display is what those others actually feel. This is particularly true in organizations, where role demands and situations often require people to exhibit emotional behaviors that mask their true feelings.

THE SIX UNIVERSAL EMOTIONS There have been numerous efforts to limit and identify the fundamental or basic set of emotions.[64] Research has identifed six universal emotions: anger, fear, sadness, happiness, disgust, and surprise.[65]

Exhibit 12-7 illustrates that these six emotions can be conceptualized as existing along a continuum.[66] The closer any two emotions are to each other on this continuum, the more people are likely to confuse them. For instance, happiness and surprise are frequently mistaken for each other, whereas happiness and disgust are rarely confused. In addition, as we'll elaborate on later in this section, cultural factors can also influence interpretations.

Do these six basic emotions surface in the workplace? Absolutely. I get *angry* after receiving a poor performance appraisal. I *fear* that I could be laid off as a result of a company cutback. I'm *sad* about one of my co-workers leaving to take a new job in another city. I'm *happy* after being selected as employee of the month. I'm *disgusted* with the way my supervisor treats women on our team. And I'm *surprised* to find out that management plans a complete restructuring of the company's retirement program.

EMOTIONS VARY IN INTENSITY People give different responses to identical emotion-provoking stimuli. In some cases this can be attributed to the individual's personality. Other times it is a result of the job requirements.

People vary in their inherent ability to express intensity. You undoubtedly know individuals who almost never show their feelings. They rarely get angry. They never show rage. In contrast, you probably also know people who seem to be on an emotional rollercoaster. When they're happy, they're ecstatic. When they're sad, they're deeply depressed. And two people can be in the exact same situation—with one showing excitement and joy, and the other being calm and collected.

Jobs make different intensity demands in terms of emotional labor. For instance, air traffic controllers and trial judges are expected to be calm and controlled, even in stressful situations. Conversely, the effectiveness of television evangelists, public-address announcers at sporting events, and lawyers can depend on their ability to alter their displayed emotional intensity as the need arises.

EMOTIONS AND NATIONAL CULTURE Cultural norms in the United States dictate that employees in service organizations should smile and act friendly when interacting with customers.[67]

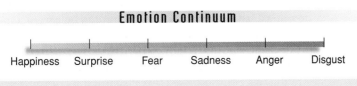

Emotion Continuum

Happiness   Surprise   Fear   Sadness   Anger   Disgust

EXHIBIT 12-7

Source: Based on R. D. Woodworth, *Experimental Psychology* (New York: Holt, 1938).

But this norm doesn't apply worldwide. In Israel, smiling by supermarket cashiers is seen as a sign of inexperience, so cashiers are encouraged to look somber.[68] In Moslem cultures, smiling is frequently taken as a sign of sexual attraction, so women are socialized not to smile at men.[69]

> **Cultures differ in terms of the interpretation they give to emotions.**

These examples illustrate the need to consider cultural factors as influencing what is or isn't considered emotionally appropriate. What's acceptable in one culture may seem extremely unusual or even dysfunctional in another. And cultures differ in terms of the interpretation they give to emotions.

There tends to be high agreement on what emotions mean *within* cultures but not between. For instance, one study asked Americans to match facial expressions with the six basic emotions.[70] The range of agreement was between 86 percent and 98 percent. When a group of Japanese were given the same task, they correctly labeled only surprise (with 97 percent agreement). On the other five emotions, their accuracy ranged from only 27 percent to 70 percent. In addition, studies indicate that some cultures lack words for such standard emotions as *anxiety, depression,* or *guilt.* Tahitians, as a case in point, don't have a word directly equivalent to sadness. When Tahitians are sad, their peers typically attribute their state to a physical illness.[71]

▶ Implications for Managers

Managers should be interested in their employees' attitudes because attitudes give warnings of potential problems and because they influence behavior. Satisfied and committed employees, for instance, have relatively low rates of turnover and absenteeism. Given that managers want to keep resignations and absences down—especially among their more productive employees—they will want to do those things that will generate positive job attitudes.

Managers should recognize that employees will try to reduce cognitive dissonance. More important, dissonance can be managed. If employees are required to engage in activities that appear to be inconsistent or are at odds with their attitudes, the pressures to reduce the resulting dissonance are lessened when the employee perceives the dissonance as being externally imposed and beyond his or her control or if the rewards are significant enough to offset the dissonance.

Can managers control the emotions of their colleagues and employees? No. Emotions are a natural part of an individual's make up. Where managers err is when they ignore the emotional elements in employee behavior and assess individuals as if they were completely rational. As one consultant aptly put it, "You can't divorce emotions from the workplace because you can't divorce emotions from people."[72] Managers who understand the role of emotions will significantly improve their ability to explain and predict individual behavior.

Do emotions affect job performance? Yes. They can *hinder* performance, especially negative emotions. That's probably why organizations, for the most part, try to extract emotions out of the workplace. But emotions can also *enhance* performance. How? Two ways.[73] First, emotions can increase arousal levels, thus acting as motivators to higher performance. Second, emotional labor recognizes that feelings can be part of a job's required behavior. So, for instance, the ability to effectively manage emotions in leadership and sales positions may be critical to success in those positions.

What differentiates functional from dysfunctional emotions at work? Although there is no precise answer to this, it's been suggested that the critical moderating variable is the complexity of the individual's task.[74] The more complex a task, the lower the level of arousal that can be tolerated without interfering with performance. Whereas a certain minimal level of arousal is probably necessary for good performance, very high levels interfere with the ability to function, especially if the job requires calculative and detailed cognitive processes. Given that the trend is toward jobs becoming more complex, you can see why organizations are likely to go to considerable efforts to discourage the overt display of emotions—especially intense ones—in the workplace.

No basic review of human behavior would be complete without a discussion of learning. Why? Because almost all complex behavior is learned. If we want to understand human behavior, we need to understand how people learn.

LEARNING: HOW PEOPLE ADAPT

What is learning? It's more than "what we did when we went to school." Learning occurs all the time. We continually learn from our experiences. So we'll define **learning** as any relatively permanent change in behavior that occurs as a result of experience.

Ways People Learn

How do we learn such varied skills as riding a bicycle, writing a memo, or using a computer spreadsheet? Psychologists have developed two explanations for how we learn—*operant conditioning* and *social learning theory*.

OPERANT CONDITIONING **Operant conditioning** argues that behavior is a function of its consequences. People learn to behave to get something they want or avoid something they don't want. Operant behavior means voluntary or "learned" behavior in contrast to reflexive or "unlearned" behavior. The tendency to repeat such behavior is influenced by the reinforcement or lack of reinforcement brought about by the consequences of the behavior. Reinforcement, therefore, strengthens a behavior and increases the likelihood that it will be repeated.[75]

Operant conditioning proposes that behavior is determined from "without"—that is, it is learned—rather than from "within"—that is, reflexive or unlearned. Creating pleasing consequences that follow specific forms of behavior increases the frequency of that behavior. People will most likely engage in desired behaviors if they are positively reinforced for doing so. Rewards, for example, are most effective if they immediately follow the desired response. In addition, behavior that isn't rewarded, or is punished, is less likely to be repeated.

You see illustrations of operant conditioning everywhere. For example, any situation in which it is either explicitly stated or implicitly suggested that reinforcements are contingent on some action on your part involves the use of operant learning. Your instructor says that if you want a high grade in the course, you must supply correct answers on the test. A commissioned salesperson wanting to earn a sizable income finds that this is contingent on generating high sales in her territory. Of course, the linkage can also work to teach the individual to engage in behaviors that work against the best interests of the organization. Assume that your boss tells you that if you will work overtime during the next 3-week busy season, you will be compensated for it at the next performance appraisal. However, when performance appraisal time comes, you find that you are given no positive reinforcement for your overtime work. The next time your boss asks you to work overtime, what will you do? You'll probably decline! Your behavior can be explained by operant conditioning: If a behavior fails to be positively reinforced, the probability that the behavior will be repeated declines.

New employee Shari Pharr receives positive feedback from a manager at Aldrich Chemical as part of her training. This is consistent with reinforcement in social learning.

SOCIAL LEARNING Individuals can also learn by observing what happens to other people and just by being told about something, as well as by direct experiences. So, for example, much of what we have learned comes from watching models—parents, teachers, peers, motion picture and television performers, bosses, and so forth. This view that we can learn through both observation and direct experience has been called **social-learning theory**.[76]

Although social-learning theory is an extension of operant conditioning—that is, it assumes that behavior is a function of consequences—it also acknowledges the existence of observational learning and the importance of perception in learning. People respond to how they perceive and define consequences, not to the objective consequences themselves.

The influence of models is central to the social-learning viewpoint. Four processes have been found to determine the influence that a model will have on an individual:

1. *Attentional processes.* People learn from a model only when they recognize and pay attention to its critical features. We tend to be most influenced by models that are attractive, repeatedly available, important to us, or similar to us in our estimation.
2. *Retention processes.* A model's influence will depend on how well the individual remembers the model's action after the model is no longer readily available.
3. *Motor reproduction processes.* After a person has seen a new behavior by observing the model, the watching must be converted to doing. This process then demonstrates that the individual can perform the modeled activities.
4. *Reinforcement processes.* Individuals will be motivated to exhibit the modeled behavior if positive incentives or rewards are provided. Behaviors that are reinforced will be given more attention, learned better, and performed more often.

▶ Managing Learning through Shaping

Because learning takes place on the job as well as before it, managers will be concerned with how they can teach employees to behave in ways that most benefit the organization. When managers attempt to mold individuals by guiding their learning in graduated steps, they are **shaping behavior**.

Consider the situation in which an employee's behavior is significantly different from that sought by management. If management reinforced the individual only when he or she showed desirable responses, there might be very little reinforcement taking place. In such a case, shaping offers a logical approach toward achieving the desired behavior.

Managers *shape* behavior by systematically reinforcing each successive step that moves the employee closer to the desired response. If an employee who has chronically been a half-hour late for work comes in only 20 minutes late, we can reinforce this improvement. Reinforcement would increase as responses more closely approximate the desired behavior.

METHODS OF SHAPING BEHAVIOR There are four ways in which to shape behavior: through positive reinforcement, negative reinforcement, punishment, and extinction.

Following a response with something pleasant is called **positive reinforcement**. This would describe, for instance, the boss who praises an employee for a job well done. Following a response by the termination or withdrawal of something unpleasant is called **negative reinforcement**. If your college instructor asks a question and you don't know the answer, looking through your lecture notes is likely to preclude your being called on. This is a negative reinforcement because you have learned that looking busily through your notes prevents the instructor from calling on you. **Punishment** is causing an unpleasant condition in an attempt to eliminate an undesirable behavior. Giving an employee a 2-day suspension without pay for showing up drunk is an example of punishment. Eliminating any reinforcement that is maintaining a behavior is called **extinction**. When the behavior is not reinforced, it tends to gradually be extinguished. College instructors who wish to discourage students from asking questions in class can eliminate this behavior by ignoring students who raise their hands to ask questions. Hand raising will become extinct when it is invariably met with an absence of reinforcement.

Both positive and negative reinforcement result in learning. They strengthen a response and increase the probability of repetition. In the preceding illustrations, praise strengthens and increases the behavior of doing a good job because praise is desired. The behavior of "looking busy" is similarly strengthened and increased by its terminating the undesirable consequence of being called on by the teacher. Both punishment and extinction, however, weaken behavior and tend to decrease its subsequent frequency.

Reinforcement, whether it is positive or negative, has an impressive record as a shaping tool. Our interest, therefore, is in reinforcement rather than in punishment or extinction. A review of the evidence on the impact of reinforcement upon behavior in organizations has concluded that:

1. Some type of reinforcement is necessary to produce a change in behavior.
2. Some types of rewards are more effective for use in organizations than others.
3. The speed with which learning takes place and the permanence of its effects will be determined by the timing of reinforcement.[77]

Point 3 is extremely important and deserves elaboration.

SCHEDULES OF REINFORCEMENT   The two major types of reinforcement schedules are continuous and intermittent. A **continuous reinforcement** schedule reinforces the desired behavior each and every time it is demonstrated. For example, in the case of someone who has historically had trouble arriving at work on time, every time he is not tardy his manager might compliment him on his desirable behavior. In an intermittent schedule, on the other hand, not every instance of the desirable behavior is reinforced, but reinforcement is given often enough to make the behavior worth repeating. This latter schedule can be compared to the workings of a slot machine, which people will continue to play even when they know that it is adjusted to give a considerable return to the gambling house. The intermittent payoffs occur just often enough to reinforce the behavior of slipping in coins and pulling the handle. Evidence indicates that the intermittent or varied form of reinforcement tends to promote more resistance to extinction than does the continuous form.[78]

An **intermittent reinforcement** can be of a ratio or interval type. *Ratio schedules* depend upon how many responses the subject makes. The individual is reinforced after giving a certain number of specific types of behavior. *Interval schedules* depend upon how much time has passed since the last reinforcement. With interval schedules, the individual is reinforced on the first appropriate behavior after a particular time has elapsed. A reinforcement can also be classified as fixed or variable. Intermittent techniques for administering rewards can, therefore, be placed into four categories, as shown in Exhibit 12-8.

When rewards are spaced at uniform time intervals, the reinforcement schedule is of the **fixed-interval** type. The critical variable is time, and it is held constant. This is the predominant schedule for almost all salaried workers in North America. When you get your paycheck on a weekly, semimonthly, monthly, or other predetermined time basis, you are rewarded on a fixed-interval reinforcement schedule.

EXHIBIT 12-8

Schedules of Reinforcement

	Interval	Ratio
Fixed	Fixed-interval	Fixed-ratio
Variable	Variable-interval	Variable-ratio

If rewards are distributed in time so that reinforcements are unpredictable, the schedule is of the **variable-interval** type. When an instructor advises her class that there will be a number of pop quizzes given during the term (the exact number of which is unknown to the students), and the quizzes will account for 20 percent of the term grade, she is using such a variable-interval schedule. Similarly, a series of randomly timed unannounced visits to a company office by the corporate audit staff is an example of a variable-interval schedule.

In a **fixed-ratio schedule**, after a fixed or constant number of responses are given, a reward is initiated. For example, a piece-rate incentive plan is a fixed-ratio schedule—the employee receives a reward based on the number of work pieces generated. If the piece rate for a zipper installer in a dressmaking factory is $5.00 a dozen, the reinforcement (money in this case) is fixed to the number of zippers sewn into garments. After every dozen is sewn in, the installer has earned another $5.00.

When the reward varies relative to the behavior of the individual, he or she is said to be reinforced on a **variable-ratio** schedule. Salespeople on commission are examples of individuals on such a reinforcement schedule. On some occasions, they may make a sale after only two calls on potential customers. On other occasions, they might need to make twenty or more calls to secure a sale. The reward, then, is variable in relation to the number of successful calls the salesperson makes.

REINFORCEMENT SCHEDULES AND BEHAVIOR Continuous reinforcement schedules can lead to early satiation, and under this schedule, behavior tends to weaken rapidly when reinforcers are withheld. However, continuous reinforcers are appropriate for newly emitted, unstable, or low-frequency responses. In contrast, intermittent reinforcers preclude early satiation because they don't follow every response. They are appropriate for stable or high-frequency responses.

In general, variable schedules tend to lead to higher performance than fixed schedules. For example, as noted previously, most employees in organizations are paid on fixed-interval schedules. But such a schedule does not clearly link performance and rewards. The reward is given for time spent on the job rather than for a specific response (performance). In contrast, variable-interval schedules generate high rates of response and more stable and consistent behavior because of a high correlation between performance and reward and because of the uncertainty involved—the employee tends to be more alert since there is a surprise factor.

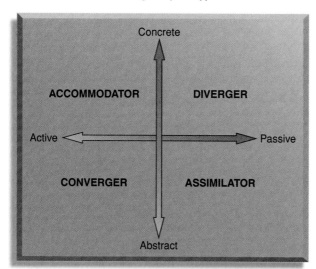

Learning-Style Types

EXHIBIT 12-9

Learning Styles

Not everyone learns the same way. Each of us has a preferred means by which learning is best accomplished. For instance, some people don't gain much from lectures. They prefer reading about an issue or discussing it with others. Chris Turner, of Xerox Business Services, says she found that only 17 percent of the people in her organization learn best by reading texts, listening to lectures, and through the traditional school experience. The majority of XBS people learn by doing. She concludes that we have to "teach the way people learn; don't make them learn the way you teach."[79]

It has been proposed that learning is a recurring process that cycles through four stages: concrete experience, reflective observation, abstract conceptualization, and active experimentation.[80] But individuals develop preferences for particular stages according to their abilities, previous experiences, and current goals. These preferences are called *learning modes.*

Four learning modes have been identified. Some people learn best by involving themselves in new experiences. They don't do well with abstract theories. These people learn through *concrete experience.* A second category includes those who prefer *reflective observation.* They like to observe things passively and then reflect on their experiences. A third category describes people who learn best through impersonal situations directed by authorities who emphasize theory. These people rely on *abstract conceptualization* to develop workable theories of phenomena. Finally, there are those people who use *active experimentation.* They learn by doing—by actively involving themselves in projects.

A close examination of these learning modes reveals that they contain four underlying dimensions—concrete versus abstract and active versus passive. By mixing these dimensions, it is possible to identify four learning-style types (see Exhibit 12-9):

▶ *The Accommodator (concrete and active).* This type of learner relies on intuition and trial and error. Accommodators prefer to go with other people's opinions rather than to do their own analysis. The accommodator is a hands-on learner who might be well matched to learning by way of participating in simulation exercises or in group discussion led by an expert.

▶ *The Diverger (concrete and passive)*. This type of learner has an open mind and likes to tackle problems from many perspectives. He or she learns well through examples. So divergers might be well matched to training sessions using lectures in which the instructor relies heavily on examples rather than on abstract theories.

▶ *The Converger (abstract and active)*. This type of learner is a thinker and doer. He or she prefers things over people and learns best through training techniques such as computer simulations or case analysis.

▶ *The Assimilator (abstract and passive)*. This type of learner likes to observe and think about abstract concepts. He or she values logic and factual data. An assimilator might prefer lectures or videos that focus on theoretical presentations.

Efforts to match individual training methods to learning styles have proved to increase training effectiveness. For instance, this framework has been used to successfully teach people to use a complex computer system.[81] Results demonstrated that performance was enhanced by tailoring instructional methods to reflect individual differences in learning styles.

▶ Implications for Managers

Managers can very clearly benefit from understanding the learning process.[82] Because employees continually learn on the job, the only issue is whether managers are going to let employee learning occur randomly or whether they are going to manage learning through the rewards they allocate and the examples they set. If marginal employees are rewarded with pay raises and promotions, they will have little reason to change their behavior. If managers want a certain type of behavior but reward a different type of behavior, it shouldn't surprise them to find that employees are learning to engage in the other type of behavior.[83] Similarly, managers should expect that employees will look to them as models. Managers who are constantly late to work, or take 2 hours for lunch, or help themselves to company office supplies for personal use should expect employees to read the message they are sending and model their behavior accordingly.

An understanding of learning concepts additionally provides managers with insights in designing human resource programs—for instance, sick-leave policies and training programs. Most organizations provide their salaried employees with paid sick leave as part of the employees' benefit package. But, ironically, organizations with paid sick-leave programs experience almost twice the absenteeism of organizations without such programs.[84] The reality is that sick leave reinforces the wrong behavior—absence from work.

Organizations should have programs that encourage employees to be on the job by discouraging unnecessary absences. When employees receive ten paid sick days a year, most employees will use them all up, regardless of whether they are sick or not. Managers who understand how rewards shape behavior will modify their organization's sick-leave policy to reward attendance, not absence.

Similarly, the design of training programs can benefit from an understanding of learning concepts. It is estimated that more than 90 percent of all private organizations have some type of systematic training program and more than $60 billion a year is spent on training initiatives.[85] That money can be better spent if managers apply their knowledge of learning. For instance, social-learning theory tells us that training should offer a model to grab the trainee's attention; provide motivational properties; help the trainee file away what he or she has learned for later use; provide opportunities to practice new behaviors; offer positive rewards for accomplishments; and, if the training has taken place off the job, allow the trainee some opportunity to transfer what he or she has learned to the job. In addition, given that people have different preferences for learning modes, managers should design training programs to fit individual preferences. Doing so allows training dollars to be more efficiently allocated.

Does where you were born and raised have any significant bearing on explaining and predicting your behavior? Absolutely! For example, there are a lot more Type A personalities in the United States than in Mexico; Canadian and Chinese workers have different attitudes toward pay systems designed around collective efforts; and workers from India are more likely to prefer passive learning methods than are Australian employees.

CULTURAL DIFFERENCES IN HUMAN BEHAVIOR

So we conclude our discussion of basic concepts in human behavior by returning to the issue of cultural differences. As you'll remember, national cultures vary along five dimensions—power distance, individualism versus collectivism, quantity of life versus quality of life, uncertainty avoidance, and long-term versus short-term orientation. If you're not comfortable with the meaning of those terms, you might want to refresh your memory by reviewing our discussion in chapter 4.

Contrasting Cultures

To illustrate the differences between countries, the following describes some of the unique characteristics you might find when working in a foreign land or with individuals from another country. We have chosen for our illustration the United States, Japan, and Australia.

THE UNITED STATES Americans score high on individualism, below average on power distance, well below average on uncertainty avoidance, well above average on quantity of life, and they have a short-term orientation. These results are not inconsistent with the world image of the United States.

The below-average score on power distance aligns with what one might expect in a country with a representative type of government with democratic ideals. The well-below-average ranking on uncertainty avoidance is also consistent with a democracy. Americans perceive themselves as being relatively free from threats of uncertainty. The individualistic ethic is one of the most frequently used stereotypes to describe Americans, and that stereotype seems well founded. In one contrast of forty countries, the United States ranked as the single most individualistic.[86] Finally, the well-above-average score on quantity of life and the short-term focus are not surprising. Capitalism—which values aggressiveness, materialism, and immediate gratification—is consistent with quantity of life and short-term characteristics.

JAPAN Japanese workers like being part of a group. They prefer to sublimate their individual contribution to that of the group or team of which they are a part. Their high score on collectivism is consistent with this preference.[87]

The Japanese culture has long valued lifetime employment security. Employees were traditionally hired right out of school. These employees were expected to show absolute loyalty to their employer, and the employer responded reciprocally. Until very recently, it was unusual for a worker to switch employers. And Japanese managers are expected to show patience. Promotions come slowly. It's not uncommon for an employee to wait 10 years or more for his or her first promotion. All these organizational practices fit with trying to offset a society that scores high on uncertainty avoidance.

The Japanese also practice a form of consultative decision making that fits well with their moderate score on power distance. Japanese managers are not autocratic. But they also do not actively involve their employees in the decision-making process. What they do is informally discuss and consult with all those people who may be affected by the decision. When all are familiar with the proposal, a formal request for a decision is made, and, as a result of the previous informal preparations, it is almost always ratified. The key is not so much agreement with a decision but that those concerned are advised about it and have their views fairly heard.

AUSTRALIA Much of the world's impression of Australians is based on the Crocodile Dundee character. His words — "Put another shrimp on the barbee" and "You call that a knife? THIS is what we call a knife!" — gave the image of Australians as down-to-earth, straightforward, no-frills, honest people, with a wry sense of humor.[88] Is this characterization accurate? Partly. Australians are very casual and direct. They are also competitive, especially in sports, and they are leisure-oriented and known for betting on almost anything.[89]

Contrasts between U.S. and Australian managers reveal that although there are wide similarities, there are also a few interesting differences.[90] Australian managers are less extroverted, tend to be more dominating and assertive, and are more forthright and moralistic.

These descriptions can be reconciled with research on Australian attitudes. For instance, Australians score high on both individualism and quantity of life. This score would suggest a population of people who are competitive, risk-taking, and assertive — which Australians are.

Implications for Managers

Differences in employees' cultural backgrounds have wide implications for many, if not most, managerial practices. As a result, managers need to make sure they consider cultural differences when they choose a leadership or communication style, select motivation tech-

Paul Hogan, in Crocodile Dundee, captures the image that most North Americans have of Australians.

niques, design a compensation system, decide on training methods, or consider the re-design of jobs.

This chapter introduced a number of principles and concepts that can be applied to people in general. But we also underscored the importance of acknowledging individual differences. Managers, for instance, who do not recognize the existence of personality differences and use that information in making hiring or job-placement decisions are going to be less effective than their counterparts who do. Similarly, people from different cultures present challenges to managers. In a world where workforce diversity has become the norm, effective managers are increasing their knowledge of different cultures and using that information to better lead their work units.

There is a variety of additional material available on the CD-ROM and companion Web site that accompany this text. You can access this information through the CD-ROM or by visiting the Web site at <**www.prenhall.com/robbins**>.

SUMMARY

(This summary is organized by the chapter-opening learning objectives on page 366.)

1. The personality dimensions in the Myers-Briggs Type Indicator (MBTI) are: extroverted or introverted, sensing or intuitive, thinking or feeling, and perceiving or judging.

2. The personality-job fit model identifies six personality types—realistic, investigative, social, conventional, enterprising, and artistic. The better the fit between an individual's personality type and occupational environment, the higher will be the individual's satisfaction and the less likely he or she will be to quit.

3. Attribution theory proposes that we judge people differently depending on whether we attribute their behavior to internal or external causes. We hold people responsible in internal attributions.

4. As a result of the self-fulfilling prophecy, managers should set high expectations for their employees because doing so will initiate a process that leads to the fulfillment of those high expectations.

5. The cognitive component of an attitude makes up the beliefs, opinions, knowledge, or information held by a person. The affective component is the emotional or feeling segment of an attitude. The behavioral component is the intent to behave in a certain way.

6. The theory of cognitive dissonance says that people will try to reduce inconsistencies that might arise between multiple attitudes or between behavior and attitudes.

7. At the individual level, findings on the relationship between satisfaction and productivity report a positive but low correlation. It may well be that satisfaction does not lead to productivity but the other way around. At the organizational level, the evidence indicates that more-satisfied employees tend to be more effective.

8. Operant conditioning states that learning occurs as a result of reinforcement or lack of reinforcement after a given behavior. Social-learning theory states that learning can take place as a result of observation as well as direct experience.

REVIEW QUESTIONS

1. What work-related predictions would you make about an employee who had each of the following: (a) an internal locus of control, (b) a high nAch, (c) a high-Mach score, (d) low-SE, (e) a high self-monitoring score, or (f) a Type A personality?

2. Which personality type would fit best in the job of (a)

management professor? (b) physician? (c) aerobics instructor?

3. How is it possible for two people to see the same phenomenon, yet perceive it differently?

4. The acquisition editor at Simon & Schuster was frustrated because one of her authors was extremely late in turning in

a highly prized book manuscript. Assume that you are that author. Using attribution theory, develop a plausible explanation that might satisfy your editor.

5. What is the self-serving bias? What are its implications for managers?

6. You strongly dislike large cities. However, you have been offered a promotion by your employer that requires you to move to Chicago. How might you reconcile your attitude toward large cities and the decision to accept the move to Chicago?

7. Is a happy worker a productive worker?

8. How can managers read employee emotions? Why should the ability to "read emotions" be a valuable managerial skill?

9. Using social-learning theory, how could you maximize the effectiveness of an employee training program?

10. Contrast schedules of reinforcement.

IF I WERE THE MANAGER . . .

Transfer to Ohio

You are a manager with Honda, born and raised in Japan. You attended a prestigious Japanese university and have degrees in both engineering and business. After more than 20 years with the company, you have been transferred to the United States to run one of Honda's plants in Ohio. Several of your unit managers at the Ohio plant were also transferred from Japan, but most of your managers and almost all your employees are Americans.

What differences in personality, attributions, and attitudes do you think you'll have compared to your American counterparts? What adjustments, if any, do you think you will have to make in your management style?

SKILL EXERCISE

Shaping Employee Behavior

You are a new supervisor at a large dry-cleaning plant located in a large city. You directly oversee five people who operate pressing equipment.

Your company's senior management is committed to hiring young minority employees. Part of this commitment is related to management's social conscience. Another part just reflects reality: Pay is generally low for entry jobs, minimal skills are needed, and plenty of young minority applicants live near the company's inner-city plant.

You recently hired a young man to fill one of your press jobs. Charlie is a 20-year-old high school graduate whose prior job experience includes delivering pizza and working part-time in a warehouse stacking shelves. Charlie impressed you as conscientious and motivated, although you recognized that he had little relevant experience. You expected that you would have to spend at least 20 to 30 hours training Charlie on the press equipment before he would be able to perform his job independently.

Charlie started working for you last Monday. Today is Thursday. He arrived 20 minutes late on Monday, an hour late on Tuesday, and 45 minutes late yesterday. You are specifically aware of his lateness because you've been directly overseeing his training. This morning, Charlie has just arrived. You look at your watch. He's almost 2 hours late for work. You briefly mentioned his tardiness on each of the prior 3 days. He acknowledged his lateness and said he wasn't used to using an alarm clock and getting up so early. But he promised to try harder. You can't allow this behavior to continue. You have to take some action.

Specifically describe what you plan to do to change Charlie's behavior. Assume that you have letters of recommendation from each of his former employers and that they do not mention any tardiness problems.

TEAM ACTIVITY

Focusing on Cultural Differences

Form into groups of four or five. Your group has 15 minutes to complete the following sentence:

Characteristics that differentiate Americans from other nationalities are . . .

Now take another 15 minutes and do the same thing, except substitute "Mexicans"* for "Americans."

When your group has finished its sentence-completion exercises, consider your results in terms of (a) common personalities within cultures, (b) stereotypes, and (c) cultural differences.

*Your instructor may substitute other nationalities to focus on diverse cultural differences.

CASE EXERCISE

Can a Computer Program Learn Your Job?

"Among high-level people, a common misperception is that they think that whatever they do is so creative or involved that it can't possibly be put in a computer when in fact it usually can." With that statement, the CEO at a leading maker of electronic performance support systems (EPSS) software has drawn the somewhat controversial conclusion: Educational attainment and job experience may not be important for doing most white-collar jobs. Computer software can allow less-educated workers to effectively do what historically required a college degree or even graduate training.

EPSS programs are distinguished by their ability both to automate many job-related mental skills and to provide instant instructions to help users make whatever human judgments are still necessary. They are already widely used in many blue-collar and clerical settings. Chrysler mechanics, for instance, can use this software to diagnose car troubles. Now, however, EPSS programs are making incursions into professional jobs. They may make it possible for someone with a high school education and experience limited to working the counter at McDonald's to be a nurse, financial analyst, or psychotherapist.

One such program has been developed by the National As-

sociation of Securities Dealers, one of Wall Street's largest self-regulatory organizations, to dramatically reduce the training time and skill levels needed to conduct an audit of a securities firm. The program features step-by-step instructions on what information and procedures are needed. Meanwhile, embedded spreadsheets automatically calculate key ratios that might indicate securities violations, and the program's internal logic looks for other clues. Once the program has the information it requests, its word processor automatically writes up an examination report. This specific program has cut the time required to create a fully competent auditor from $2\frac{1}{2}$ years to 1 year, and cut NASD's training costs by $413,500 annually.

QUESTIONS

1. What are the implications of this case to human learning?
2. Will EPSS change the nature of white-collar jobs and the importance of a college education? Explain.
3. What aspects of a manager's job do you think could be effectively handled by a computer program? Which aspects would not?

Source: Based on P. J. Longman, "The Janitor Stole My Job," *U.S. News & World Report*, December 1, 1997, pp. 50–52.

VIDEO CASE EXERCISE

Age and Attitudes

ABCNEWS

Did you know that U.S. federal laws consider anyone 40 years of age or more as an older worker? You probably know that, because of laws against age discrimination, no organization has the right to discriminate against older workers. Despite the law, however, as companies continue to downsize and millions of 40+ workers look for work, examples of age discrimination are happening every day in every profession across the United States. Statistics show that it takes older job seekers 64 percent longer to find work than younger ones. Even though age discrimination is illegal, it appears to be such an ingrained part of our culture that we may not even recognize it or when we're doing it.

Think about your perception of older workers. Would you say they're sick more often, they can't work as hard, and they don't stay with a company as long as younger workers do? Well,

if that is what you think, you're wrong! A study by Days Inn Corporation, which deliberately recruits older workers, found that older workers stay with the company longer, take fewer sick days, and are just as productive as their younger counterparts. In fact, the president of Days Inn says that older workers are actually *less* expensive than the average U.S. worker.

Do the attitudes we may subconsciously have about older workers affect the way we behave? Yes. They often have subtle influences on the way we treat older persons. For instance, in job interviews, differences can be seen in the treatment of younger and older applicants. In several staged interviews with pairs of applicants—one older woman and one younger woman—the younger women were accommodated more by the interviewer. The older women were subtly discouraged. In fact, in one-third of these 24 staged interviews, a startling difference in the way older and younger job applicants were treated could be seen. In another staged interview situation, one individual was made up to look young one time and older another in interviews at the same company. His "younger" self was offered a job at a brokerage firm even though this "person" had less job experience than his "older" self and didn't follow up on the interview with a letter or phone call. Although the interviewers didn't appear to purposely discriminate (after all, it *is* illegal) against the older job applicants in the way they acted and in the questions they asked, differences could still be seen. Attitudes that we have about elderly people in general, and older workers in particular, appear to influence the way we act.

QUESTIONS

1. Describe the three components of an attitude—cognitive, affective, and behavioral—in relation to the attitudes often held about older workers as shown in this video clip.
2. What role do you think perception plays in the way we subtly behave toward older persons?
3. Is stereotyping part of the problem with attitudes about age? Explain.

Source: "Age and Attitudes," *ABC News Primetime,* June 9, 1994.

NOTES

1. Based on B. Drumaine, "America's Toughest Bosses," *Fortune,* October 18, 1993, pp. 38–50; M. Mallory, "What Do Women Want?" *U.S. News & World Report,* November 6, 1995, p. 75; and "Linda Wachner," *Working Woman,* December 1996, pp. 107–08.
2. J. B. Rotter, "Generalized Expectancies for Internal versus External Control of Reinforcement," *Psychological Monographs* 80, no. 609 (1966).
3. See P. E. Spector, "Behavior in Organizations as a Function of Employee's Locus of Control," *Psychological Bulletin,* May 1982, pp. 482–97; and G. J. Blau, "Locus of Control as a Potential Moderator of the Turnover Process," *Journal of Occupational Psychology,* Fall 1987, pp. 21–29.
4. R. T. Keller, "Predicting Absenteeism from Prior Absenteeism, Attitudinal Factors, and Nonattitudinal Factors," *Journal of Applied Psychology,* August 1983, pp. 536–40.
5. D. C. McClelland, *The Achieving Society* (New York: Van Nostrand Reinhold, 1961); and J. W. Atkinson and J. O. Raynor, *Motivation and Achievement* (Washington, DC: Winston, 1974).
6. D. C. McClelland and D. G. Winter, *Motivating Economic Achievement* (New York: Free Press, 1969).
7. R. G. Vleeming, "Machiavellianism: A Preliminary Review," *Psychological Reports,* February 1979, pp. 295–310.
8. R. Christie and F. L. Geis, *Studies in Machiavellianism* (New York: Academic Press, 1970), p. 312; and N. V. Ramanaiah, A. Byravan, F. R. J. Detwiler, "Revised Neo Personality Inventory Profiles of Machiavellian and Non-Machiavellian People," *Psychological Reports,* October 1994, pp. 937–38.
9. Ibid.
10. Based on J. Brockner, *Self-Esteem at Work* (Lexington, MA: Lexington Books, 1988), chapters 1–4.
11. Ibid.
12. See M. Snyder, *Public Appearances/Private Realities: The Psychology of Self-Monitoring* (New York: W. H. Freeman, 1987).
13. Ibid.
14. M. Kilduff and D. V. Day, "Do Chameleons Get Ahead? The Effects of Self-Monitoring on Managerial Careers," *Academy of Management Journal,* August 1994, pp. 1047–60.
15. R. N. Taylor and M. D. Dunnette, "Influence of Dogmatism, Risk-Taking Propensity, and Intelligence on Decision-Making Strategies for a Sample of Industrial Managers," *Journal of Applied Psychology,* August 1974, pp. 420–23.
16. N. Kogan and M. A. Wallach, "Group Risk Taking as a Function of Members' Anxiety and Defensiveness," *Journal of Personality,* March 1967, pp. 50–63.
17. M. Friedman and R. H. Rosenman, *Type A Behavior and Your Heart* (New York: Knopf, 1974).
18. Ibid., p. 84.
19. Ibid., pp. 84–85.
20. Ibid., p. 86.
21. R. R. McCrae and P. T. Costa Jr., "Reinterpreting the Myers-Briggs Type Indicator from the Perspective of the Five-Factor Model of Personality," *Journal of Personality,* March 1989, pp. 17–40.
22. G. N. Landrum, *Profiles of Genius* (New York: Prometheus, 1993).
23. W. L. Gardner and M. J. Martinko, "Using the Myers-Briggs Type Indicator to Study Managers: A Literature Review and Research Agenda," *Journal of Management,* vol. 22, no. 1, 1996, p. 64.
24. Ibid., p. 76.
25. Ibid., p. 45.
26. See J. M. Digman, "Personality Structure: Emergence of the Five-Factor Model," in M. R. Rosenzweig and L. W. Porter (eds.), *Annual Review of Psychology,* vol. 41 (Palo Alto, CA: Annual Reviews, 1990), pp. 417–70; M. K. Mount and M. R. Barrick, "The Big Five Personality Dimensions: Implications for Research and Practice in Human Resource Management," in K. M. Rowland and G. Ferris (eds.), *Research in Personnel and Human Resource Management,* vol. 13 (Greenwich, CT: JAI Press, 1995), pp. 153–200; and J. S. Wiggins (ed.), *The Five-Factor Model of Personality: Theoretical Perspectives* (New York: Guilford, 1996).
27. M. R. Barrick and M. K. Mount, "The Big Five Personality Dimensions and Job Performance: A Meta-Analysis," *Personnel Psychology,* Spring 1991, pp. 1–26; and M. R. Barrick and M. K. Mount, "Autonomy as a Moderator of the Relationships between the Big Five Personality Dimensions and Job Performance," *Journal of Applied Psychology,* February 1993, pp. 111–18.

28. M. K. Mount, M. R. Barrick, and J. P. Strauss, "Validity of Observer Ratings of the Big Five Factors," *Journal of Applied Psychology*, April 1994, p. 272.

29. J. F. Salgado, "The Five Factor Model of Personality and Job Performance in the European Community," *Journal of Applied Psychology*, February 1997, pp. 30–43.

30. Suggested in F. J. Landy, L. Shankster-Cawley, and S. Kobler Moran, "Advancing Personnel Selection and Placement Methods," in A. Howard (ed.), *The Changing Nature of Work* (San Francisco: Jossey-Bass, 1995), p. 265. See also T. A. Judge and D. M. Cable, "Applicant Personality, Organizational Culture, and Organization Attraction," *Personnel Psychology*, Summer 1997, pp. 359–94 for evidence linking the Big Five personality dimensions to contemporary cultures.

31. J. L. Holland, *Making Vocational Choices: A Theory of Vocational Personalities and Work Environments*, 2nd ed. (Upper Saddle River, NJ: Prentice Hall, 1985).

32. See, for instance, A. R. Spokane, "A Review of Research on Person-Environment Congruence in Holland's Theory of Careers," *Journal of Vocational Behavior*, June 1985, pp. 306–43; J. L. Holland and G. D. Gottfredson, "Studies of the Hexagonal Model: An Evaluation (or, The Perils of Stalking the Perfect Hexagon)," *Journal of Vocational Behavior*, April 1992, pp. 158–70; and T. J. Tracey and J. Rounds, "Evaluating Holland's and Gati's Vocational-Interest Models: A Structural Meta-Analysis," *Psychological Bulletin*, March 1993, pp. 229–46.

33. D. Watson, "Strangers' Ratings of the Five Robust Personality Factors: Evidence of a Surprising Convergence with Self-Report," *Journal of Personality and Social Psychology*, July 1989, pp. 120–28. See also M. K. Mount, M. R. Barrick, and J. Perkins Strauss, "Validity of Observer Ratings of the Big Five Personality Factors," *Journal of Applied Psychology*, April 1994, pp. 272–80.

34. H. H. Kelley, "Attribution in Social Interaction," in E. Jones et al. (eds.), *Attribution: Perceiving the Causes of Behavior* (Morristown, NJ: General Learning Press, 1972).

35. See L. Ross, "The Intuitive Psychologist and His Shortcomings," in L. Berkowitz (ed.), *Advances in Experimental Social Psychology*, vol. 10 (Orlando, FL: Academic Press, 1977), pp. 174–220; and A. G. Miller and T. Lawson, "The Effect of an Informational Option on the Fundamental Attribution Error," *Personality and Social Psychology Bulletin*, June 1989, pp. 194–204.

36. D. Eden and A. B. Shani, "Pygmalion Goes to Boot Camp: Expectancy, Leadership, and Trainee Performance," *Journal of Applied Psychology*, April 1982, pp. 194–99.

37. See D. Eden, "Self-Fulfilling Prophecy as a Management Tool: Harnessing Pygmalion," *Academy of Management Review*, January 1984, pp. 64–73; and D. Eden, "Leadership and Expectations: Pygmalion Effects and Other Self-Fulfilling Prophecies in Organizations," *Leadership Quarterly*, Winter 1992, pp. 271–305.

38. S. J. Breckler, "Empirical Validation of Affect, Behavior, and Cognition as Distinct Components of Attitude," *Journal of Personality and Social Psychology*, May 1984, pp. 1191–1205; and S. L. Crites Jr., L. R. Fabrigar, and R. E. Petty, "Measuring the Affective and Cognitive Properties of Attitudes: Conceptual and Methodological Issues," *Personality and Social Psychology Bulletin*, December 1994, pp. 619–34.

39. P. P. Brooke Jr., D. W. Russell, and J. L. Price, "Discriminant Validation of Measures of Job Satisfaction, Job Involvement, and Organizational Commitment," *Journal of Applied Psychology*, May 1988, pp. 139–45.

40. Based on G. J. Blau and K. R. Boal, "Conceptualizing How Job Involvement and Organizational Commitment Affect Turnover and Absenteeism," *Academy of Management Review*, April 1987, p. 290.

41. G. J. Blau, "Job Involvement and Organizational Commitment as Interactive Predictors of Tardiness and Absenteeism," *Journal of Management*, Winter 1986, pp. 577–84; and K. Boal and R. Cidambi, "Attitudinal Correlates of Turnover and Absenteeism: A Meta Analysis," paper presented at the meeting of the American Psychological Association, Toronto, Canada, 1984.

42. G. Farris, "A Predictive Study of Turnover," *Personnel Psychology*, Summer 1971, pp. 311–28.

43. Blau and Boal, "Conceptualizing How Job Involvement and Organizational Commitment Affect Turnover and Absenteeism," p. 290.

44. See, for instance, P. W. Hom, R. Katerberg, and C. L. Hulin, "Comparative Examination of Three Approaches to the Prediction of Turnover," *Journal of Applied Psychology*, June 1979, pp. 280–90; H. Angle and J. Perry, "Organizational Commitment: Individual and Organizational Influence," *Work and Occupations*, May 1983, pp. 123–46; and J. L. Pierce and R. B. Dunham, "Organizational Commitment: Pre-Employment Propensity and Initial Work Experiences," *Journal of Management*, Spring 1987, pp. 163–78.

45. Hom, Katerberg, and Hulin, "Comparative Examination of Three Approaches to the Prediction of Turnover;" and R. T. Mowday, L. W. Porter, and R. M. Steers, *Employee Organization Linkages: The Psychology of Commitment, Absenteeism, and Turnover* (New York: Academic Press, 1982).

46. L. W. Porter, R. M. Steers, R. T. Mowday, and P. V. Boulian, "Organizational Commitment, Job Satisfaction, and Turnover among Psychiatric Technicians," *Journal of Applied Psychology*, October 1974, pp. 603–09.

47. L. Festinger, *A Theory of Cognitive Dissonance* (Stanford, CA: Stanford University Press, 1957).

48. See, for example, E. A. Locke, "The Nature and Causes of Job Satisfaction," in M. D. Dunnette (ed.), *Handbook of Industrial and Organizational Psychology* (Chicago: Rand McNally, 1976), pp. 1319–28; R. A. Katzell, D. E. Thompson, and R. A. Guzzo, "How Job Satisfaction and Job Performance Are and Are Not Linked," in C. J. Cranny, P. C. Smith, and E. F. Stone (eds.), *Job Satisfaction* (New York: Lexington Books, 1992), pp. 195–217; and T. A. Wright and B. M. Staw, "In Search of the Happy/Productive Worker: A Longitudinal Study of Affect and Performance," in D. P. Moore (ed.), *Academy of Management Proceedings* (Dallas: Academy of Management, 1994), pp. 274–78.

49. E. Mayo, *The Human Problems of an Industrial Civilization* (New York: Macmillan, 1939); and F. J. Roethlisberger and W. J. Dickson, *Management and the Worker* (Cambridge, MA: Harvard University Press, 1939).

50. V. H. Vroom, *Work and Motivation* (New York: Wiley, 1964); and M. T. Iaffaldano and P. M. Muchinsky, "Job Sat-

isfaction and Job Performance: A Meta-Analysis," *Psychological Bulletin*, March 1985, pp. 251–73.

51. See, for example, J. B. Herman, "Are Situational Contingencies Limiting Job Attitude–Job Performance Relationship?" *Organizational Behavior and Human Performance*, October 1973, pp. 208–24; and M. M. Petty, G. W. McGee, and J. W. Cavender, "A Meta-Analysis of the Relationship between Individual Job Satisfaction and Individual Performance," *Academy of Management Review*, October 1984, pp. 712–21.

52. C. N. Greene, "The Satisfaction-Performance Controversy," *Business Horizons*, February 1972, pp. 31–41; E. E. Lawler III, *Motivation in Organizations* (Monterey, CA.: Brooks/Cole, 1973); and Petty, McGee, and Cavender, "A Meta-Analysis of the Relationship between Individual Job Satisfaction and Individual Performance."

53. C. Ostroff, "The Relationship between Satisfaction, Attitudes, and Performance: An Organizational Level Analysis," *Journal of Applied Psychology*, December 1992, pp. 963–74; and A. M. Ryan, M. J. Schmit, and R. Johnson, "Attitudes and Effectiveness: Examining Relations at an Organizational Level," *Personnel Psychology*, Winter 1996, pp. 853–82.

54. Cited in the *Los Angeles Times*, January 3, 1998, p. A3.

55. See, for example, L. L. Putnam and D. K. Mumby, "Organizations, Emotion and the Myth of Rationality," in S. Fineman (ed.), *Emotion in Organizations* (Thousand Oaks, CA: Sage, 1993), pp. 36–57.

56. J. M. George, "Trait and State Affect," in K. R. Murphy (ed.), *Individual Differences and Behavior in Organizations* (San Francisco: Jossey-Bass, 1996), p. 145.

57. See N. H. Frijda, "Moods, Emotion Episodes and Emotions," in M. Lewis and J. M. Haviland (eds.), *Handbook of Emotions* (New York: Guildford, 1993), pp. 381–403.

58. H. M. Weiss and R. Cropanzano, "Affective Events Theory," in B. M. Staw and L. L. Cummings, *Research in Organizational Behavior*, vol. 18 (Greenwich, CT: JAI Press, 1996), pp. 17–19.

59. N. H. Frijda, "Moods, Emotion Episodes and Emotions," p. 381.

60. See J. A. Morris and D. C. Feldman, "The Dimensions, Antecedents, and Consequences of Emotional Labor," *Academy of Management Review*, October 1996, pp. 986–1010; and C. S. Hunt, "Although I Might Be Laughing Loud and Hearty, Deep Inside I'm Blue: Individual Perceptions Regarding Feeling and Displaying Emotions at Work," paper presented at the Academy of Management National Conference, Cincinnati, OH, August 1996.

61. A. R. Hochschild, "Emotion Work, Feeling Rules, and Social Structure," *American Journal of Sociology*, November 1979, pp. 555–75.

62. B. M. DePaulo, "Nonverbal Behavior and Self-Presentation," *Psychological Bulletin*, September 1992, pp. 203–43.

63. C. S. Hunt, "Although I Might Be Laughing Loud and Hearty," p. 3.

64. See, for example, P. Shaver, J. Schwartz, D. Kirson, and C. O'Connor, "Emotion Knowledge: Further Exploration of a Prototype Approach," *Journal of Personality and Social Psychology*, June 1987, pp. 1061–86; P. Ekman, "An Argument for Basic Emotions," *Cognition and Emotion*, May–July

1992, pp. 169–200; C. E. Izard, "Basic Emotions, Relations among Emotions, and Emotion-Cognition Relations," *Psychological Bulletin*, November 1992, pp. 561–65; and R. Plutchik, *The Psychology and Biology of Emotion* (New York: HarperCollins, 1994).

65. H. M. Weiss and R. Cropanzano, "Affective Events Theory," pp. 20–22.

66. R. D. Woodworth, *Experimental Psychology* (New York: Holt, 1938).

67. A. Rafaeli and R. I. Sutton, "The Expression of Emotion in Organizational Life," in L. L. Cummings and B. M. Staw, *Research in Organizational Behavior*, vol. 11 (Greenwich, CT: JAI Press, 1989), p. 8.

68. A. Rafaeli, "When Cashiers Meet Customers: An Analysis of Supermarket Cashiers," *Academy of Management Journal*, June 1989, pp. 245–73.

69. Ibid.

70. Described in S. Emmons, "Emotions at Face Value," *Los Angeles Times*, January 9, 1998, p. E1.

71. R. I. Levy, *Tahitians: Mind and Experience in the Society Islands* (Chicago: University of Chicago Press, 1973).

72. S. Nelton, "Emotions in the Workplace," *Nation's Business*, February 1996, p. 25.

73. H. M. Weiss and R. Cropanzano, "Affective Events Theory," p. 55.

74. D. O. Hebb, "Drives and the CNS (Conceptual Nervous System)," *Psychological Review*, July 1955, pp. 243–54.

75. B. F. Skinner, *Contingencies of Reinforcement* (East Norwalk, CT: Appleton-Century-Crofts, 1971).

76. A. Bandura, *Social Learning Theory* (Englewood Cliffs, NJ: Prentice Hall, 1977).

77. T. W. Costello and S. S. Zalkind, *Psychology in Administration* (Englewood Cliffs, NJ: Prentice Hall, 1963), p. 193.

78. F. Luthans and R. Kreitner, *Organizational Behavior Modification and Beyond*, 2nd ed. (Glenview, IL: Scott, Foresman, 1985).

79. "The Fast Company Unit of One Anniversary Handbook," *Fast Company*, February–March 1997, p. 106.

80. This section is based on D. A. Kolb, *The Learning Style Inventory*. Technical Manual (Boston: McBer, 1976); and D. A. Kolb, I. M. Rubin, and J. M. McIntyre, "Learning and Problem Solving," in *Organizational Psychology: An Experiential Approach*, 3rd ed. (Englewood Cliffs, NJ: Prentice Hall, 1979), pp. 27–54.

81. M. K. Sein and D. Robey, "Learning Style and the Efficacy of Computer Training Methods," *Perceptual and Motor Skills*, February 1991, pp. 243–48.

82. See, for instance, R. Zemke and S. Zemke, "Adult Learning: What Do We Know for Sure?" *Training*, June 1995, pp. 31–40.

83. S. Kerr, "On the Folly of Rewarding A, While Hoping for B," *Academy of Management Journal*, December 1975, pp. 769–83.

84. D. Willings, "The Absentee Worker," *Personnel and Training Management*, December 1968, pp. 10–12.

85. Cited in *Training*, October 1998, p. 48.

86. G. Hofstede, *Culture's Consequences: International Differences in Work Related Values* (Beverly Hills, CA: Sage, 1980).

87. This discussion of Japanese organizational practices is

based on N. Hatvany and V. Pucik, "An Integrated Management System: Lessons from the Japanese Experience," *Academy of Management Review*, July 1981, pp. 469–80.

88. S. P. Robbins, T. Waters-Marsh, R. Cacioppe, and B. Millett, *Organizational Behavior: Australia and New Zealand*, 2nd ed. (Sydney: Prentice Hall of Australia, 1998).

89. H. MacKay, *Australia Reinvented: The Mind and Mood of Australia in the '90s* (Sydney: Angus & Robertson, 1993).

90. B. Barry and P. Dowling, "Towards an Australian Management Style? A Study of the Personality Characteristics and Management Style of Australian Managers," *The Australian Institute of Management* (Victoria, 1984).

Chapter

WORK MOTIVATION AND REWARDS

BY THE TIME YOU MAKE ENDS MEET,

THEY MOVE THE ENDS.

A N O N Y M O U S

L E A R N I N G   O B J E C T I V E S

After studying this chapter, you should be able to:

1 Explain why a highly motivated worker may not necessarily be a high-performing employee.

2 Define *motivation*.

3 Contrast the hierarchy of needs with ERG theory.

4 Describe the motivational implications of Theory X and Theory Y.

5 Explain the motivation implications of motivation-hygiene theory.

6 Identify how goals motivate.

7 Describe the motivation implications of inequitable rewards.

8 Explain expectancy theory.

9 Define *employee involvement* and describe why it can increase motivation.

10 Contrast variable- and skill-based pay programs.

Anyone who thinks that "people are the same, no matter where they come from" or that everybody wants more money should contrast the work lives of two people who have comparable jobs for comparable pay at two department stores—one is from the United States, and the other is from Germany.[1]

Angie Clark is a 50-year-old merchandising manager at a J. C. Penney store in suburban Washington, D.C. She earns $32,000 a year plus bonus. Andreas Drauschke is a 29-year-old floor supervisor at Karstadt, Germany's largest department-store chain. Drauschke works at the chain's Berlin store, earning $28,000 a year plus bonus and holiday pay. Clark and Drauschke have very different attitudes toward work and leisure. But their attitudes essentially reflect those of their countrymen.

Clark puts in 44 hours a week on her job, including evening shifts and frequent Saturdays and Sundays. Her typical workday wraps up at about 7:00 P.M., and then she brings a couple of hours of paperwork home with her. She never takes more than a week of vacation at a time. In contrast,

Drauschke works only 37 hours a week. He has no extended hours. His store, like all stores in Germany, closes for weekends at 2:00 P.M. on Saturday and is open only one evening, Thursday. He comes in 20 minutes earlier than the rest of his staff, but otherwise he has no interest in working beyond his 37 hours, even if it means more money. "Free time can't be paid for," he says.

The desire to keep short hours is an obsession in Germany. For instance, Drauschke finds it hard to staff the extra 2 hours on Thursday evening, even though the late shift is rewarded with an hour less overall on the job. He can't relate to the American habit of taking a second job to earn extra money, "I already get home at seven. When should I work?" he asks. Clearly, Drauschke reflects the German attitude that leisure comes first and work second.

Clark has no problem staffing her store on weekends or evenings. Her employees reflect the American attitude that work is more important than leisure. In fact, she estimates that between 25 percent and 35 percent of her Penney's sales staff hold second jobs. When given the chance to earn more money or have more free time, her workers are quick to take the money.

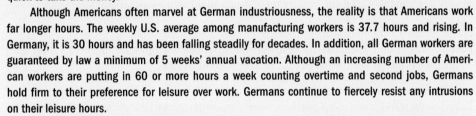

Although Americans often marvel at German industriousness, the reality is that Americans work far longer hours. The weekly U.S. average among manufacturing workers is 37.7 hours and rising. In Germany, it is 30 hours and has been falling steadily for decades. In addition, all German workers are guaranteed by law a minimum of 5 weeks' annual vacation. Although an increasing number of American workers are putting in 60 or more hours a week counting overtime and second jobs, Germans hold firm to their preference for leisure over work. Germans continue to fiercely resist any intrusions on their leisure hours.

The cultural differences between the United States and Germany toward the work-leisure trade-off can largely explain why Clark spends far more time than Drauschke interviewing job candidates and training new workers. The annual turnover rate at the German store is negligible. At Clark's Penney's store, it's 40 percent a year!

This example explodes the misconception that everybody wants more money. Interestingly, there is no shortage of erroneous notions when it comes to the subject of motivation and rewards. There are probably more misconstrued ideas on this subject than any other in management, with the possible exception of leadership. So let's start our discussion by debunking a few of these myths.

We offer the following to open your mind to the challenges in motivating today's workforce and to show you how preconceived notions can limit your ability to get the most out of your people.

SOME POPULAR MISCONCEPTIONS ABOUT MOTIVATION AND REWARDS

Myth: Motivation is individual-specific.

Fact: Motivation is situation-specific.

Many people assume that some people are highly motivated and others are lazy. Managers who follow this assumption spend a lot of time in the selection process trying to find job candidates who are "motivated." The fact is, few of us are highly motivated all of the time, regardless of the task. Similarly, almost everyone is highly motivated occasionally.

If you want to get the most out of people, stop looking for the "super" individual. Your time will be better spent, and employee motivation will increase, if you learn what is important to each individual and (recognizing that this will change with times and conditions) match people to jobs that fit their interests and personality. You should also ensure that rewards are linked to performance and focus on similar situational factors.

Myth: A motivated worker is a high-performing employee.

Fact: High employee performance requires ability and support as well as motivation.

Motivation is only one element in getting employees to perform at their highest level. Just as important are ability and support.[2] Individuals need to have the skills and talent necessary to do the job properly. If they are underskilled or undertrained, their performance will suffer. They also need to have the tools, equipment, supplies, favorable working conditions, helpful colleagues, sufficient information, and similar supportive resources so that they can do their best work. Nothing is more demotivating than to want to do a good job but to be incapable of it because you have outdated computer software, a poorly designed workstation, shabby tools, or unqualified co-workers.

Myth: Young people today aren't motivated.

Fact: Young people today are more unorthodox, rebellious, and have different values than baby boomers; but they aren't necessarily less motivated.

Young workers today, the so-called Generation X, have different work values than baby boomers.[3] Generation X workers value flexibility, job satisfaction, and loyalty to relationships. They are much more individualistic than boomers. They value family and relationships. Money is important as an indicator of career performance, but they are willing to trade off salary increases, titles, security, and promotions for expanded lifestyle options and work that challenges them. And Xers are not loyal to a single employer. Consistent with the growth of the contingent workforce, they want to build a diverse set of skills that will maintain their marketability.

Young people today can be highly motivated workers. But managers have to accommodate their needs.

Myth: Most people are interested in absolute rewards.

Fact: People are more sensitive to relative differences than to absolute differences.

Beginning salaries, pay increases, and office furnishings are important factors in motivation. But not in the way that most people think. Most employees are sensitive to inequities.[4] They compare what they get from the organization with what others get. And even though the absolute amount might be considerable, if it's relatively less than what others receive, it acts as a demotivator. Think of the professional athlete who, although earning $5 million a year, refuses to report to his team until his contract is renegotiated. His agent's argument is never that the player can't live on $5 million a year. Rather, the argument is that other players, of lesser or equal qualifications, have more lucrative contracts.

Myth: Everyone wants a challenging job.

Fact: Not everyone values a challenging job.

EXHIBIT 13-1

"I RESENT BEING CALLED 'LAZY.' THE CORRECT TERM IS 'MOTIVATIONALLY IMPAIRED.'"

Source: Reprinted by permission of Harley Schwadron.

Behavioral scientists, consultants, professors, and many others who study organizations have been arguing, for years, that employees want jobs that are interesting and challenging and that allow them to experience meaningfulness and responsibility. Well, not everyone wants a job like that! There are still a lot of people who prefer jobs that make minimal psychological demands. Work to them is merely a means to some other end; it is not an end in itself. They use their hours *off the job* to fulfill their needs for responsibility, achievement, growth, and recognition.

The belief that everyone wants a challenging job has been promoted by individuals who have projected their own needs onto the work population as a whole. Work for most behavioral scientists, consultants, and professors is their central life interest. And they value challenging jobs. But they have projected their values onto others. Certainly an increasing portion of the workforce is seeking work that is interesting and that challenges them.[5] But you can't generalize to the entire workforce.

Having cleared up some misconceptions about motivation and rewards, it's time to make sure you have a uniform understanding of just what is meant by the term *motivation*.

What is motivation? What does a motivated worker look like? **Motivation** is the willingness to exert a persistent and high level of effort toward organizational goals, conditioned by the effort's ability to satisfy some individual need.[6] General motivation is concerned with

DEFINING MOTIVATION

effort toward *any* goal; we narrow the focus to organizational goals in order to reflect our singular interest in work-related behaviors. The key elements in our definition are intensity of effort, persistence, direction toward organizational goals, and needs.

The *effort* element is a measure of intensity. Someone who is motivated tries hard. *Persistence* is follow-through, or stick-to-itiveness. People who are persistent sustain their high level of effort despite barriers or difficulties. Of course, persistence and effort are unlikely to lead to favorable job performance outcomes unless the effort is channeled in a *direction* that benefits the organization. Therefore, the quality of the effort must be considered as well. Effort that is directed toward, and consistent with, the organization's goals is the kind of effort we should be seeking. Finally, we treat motivation as a need-satisfying process. A **need**, in our terminology, means some internal state that makes certain outcomes appear attractive. An unsatisfied need creates tension that stimulates drives within the individual. These drives generate a search behavior to find particular goals that, if attained, will satisfy the need and lead to the reduction of tension.

So we can say that motivated employees are in a state of tension. To relieve this tension, they exert effort. The greater the tension, the higher the effort level. If this effort successfully leads to the satisfaction of the need, tension is reduced. But since we are interested in work behavior, this tension-reduction effort must also be directed toward organizational goals. Therefore, inherent in our definition of motivation is the requirement that the individual's needs be compatible and consistent with the organization's goals. When they are not, individuals might exert high levels of effort that actually run counter to the interests of the organization. This, incidentally, is not so unusual. For example, some employees regularly spend a lot of time talking with friends at work in order to satisfy their social needs. There is a high level of effort, only it's being unproductively directed.

BASIC MOTIVATION AND REWARD ISSUES

In this section, we address in a question format some of the basic issues managers need to be concerned with if they are going to design motivation and reward systems that will maximize employee performance. We begin by considering the different needs that drive human behavior.

▶ What Basic Needs Do People Seek to Satisfy?

Four specific theoretical frameworks have sought to identify basic needs that individuals seek to satisfy. The common theme among these frameworks is that motivation is caused by deficiencies in one or more needs or need groups.

MASLOW'S HIERARCHY OF NEEDS Probably the best-known approach to motivation is Abraham Maslow's **hierarchy of needs**.[7] He hypothesized that within every human being there exists a hierarchy of the following five sets of needs.

1. *Physiological needs.* Includes hunger, thirst, shelter, sex, and other survival needs.
2. *Safety needs.* Includes security, stability, and protection from physical and emotional harm.
3. *Belongingness needs.* Includes the need for social interaction, affection, companionship, and friendship.
4. *Esteem needs.* Includes internal esteem factors such as self-respect, autonomy, and achievement; and external esteem factors such as status, recognition, and attention.
5. *Self-actualization needs.* Includes growth, self-fulfillment, and achieving one's potential.

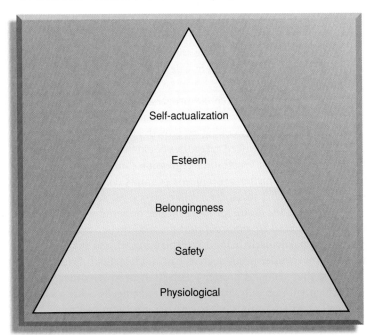

Maslow's Hierarchy of Needs

EXHIBIT 13-2

Self-actualization

Esteem

Belongingness

Safety

Physiological

Source: Data for diagram based on "Hierarchy of Needs" from *Motivation and Personality*, 3rd ed. by Abraham H. Maslow. Revised by Roger Frager, James Fadiman, Cynthia McReynolds, and Ruth Cox. © 1954, © 1987 by Harper & Row. © 1970 by Abraham H. Maslow. Reprinted by permission of HarperCollins Publishers, Inc.

Maslow described the first three sets as *deficiency needs* because they must be satisfied if the individual is to be healthy and secure. The last two were called *growth needs* because they are related to the development and achievement of one's potential. These groups are also frequently referred to as **lower-order needs** and **higher-order needs**, respectively.

Maslow proposed that these needs were inherent in all people, that they were genetically determined, and that the five need-sets existed in a hierarchy (see Exhibit 13-2). Although all people have the same need structure, according to Maslow, they can be at different levels on the hierarchy. And as each of these needs becomes substantially satisfied, the next higher need becomes dominant. From the standpoint of motivation, Maslow was arguing that, although no need is ever fully gratified, a substantially satisfied need no longer motivates. So if you want to motivate someone, you need to understand what level of the hierarchy that person is currently on and focus on satisfying the needs at or above that level.

ERG THEORY Despite the popularity of Maslow's hierarchy of needs framework, efforts to support it with substantive research evidence have met with little success.[8] In an attempt to deal with some of its limitations, Clayton Alderfer proposed a condensed version with some modified assumptions.[9] As you will see, this modification of Maslow's framework has proved to more accurately describe the relationship between needs and motivation.

Alderfer argued that there are three groups of core needs—existence, relatedness, and growth—hence the label **ERG theory**. The *existence* group is concerned with providing our basic material existence requirements. It includes the items that Maslow considered physiological and safety needs. The second group includes needs of *relatedness*—the desire we have for maintaining interpersonal relationships. These social and status desires require interaction with others if they are to be satisfied, and they align with Maslow's belongingness need and the external component of his esteem classification. Finally, Alderfer isolated *growth* needs—an intrinsic desire for personal development. These include the internal component from Maslow's esteem category and the characteristics included under self-actualization.

In contrast to Maslow's rigid steplike progression, ERG theory does not assume a rigid hierarchy where a lower need must be substantially gratified before one can move on. A person can, for instance, be working on growth even though existence or relatedness needs are unsatisfied, or all three need categories could be operating at the same time.

ERG theory also contains a frustration-regression dimension. Essentially, Alderfer argued that the frustration of higher-order needs prompts demands for greater satisfaction of lower-order needs. Inability to satisfy a relatedness need such as social interaction, for instance, tends to increase the desire for more money or better working conditions.

Tests have demonstrated far more support for ERG theory than for Maslow's theory.[10] ERG theory has been particularly helpful in explaining why so many people become singularly focused on lower-order needs such as pay and benefits.[11] Frustrated by unsatisfied higher-order needs, they demand greater satisfaction of lower-order needs. Because pay and benefits—which substantially gratify lower-order needs—are visible and relatively easy for management to administer, managers rely on them too much to motivate employees. And this overreliance on lower-order needs creates a vicious circle of deprivation, regression, and temporary gratification—deprived of higher-order need gratification, employees come to expect more and more lower-order-focused rewards.

THEORY OF MANIFEST NEEDS Sixty years ago, Henry Murray developed his **theory of manifest needs**.[12] Despite the passing of years, Murray's work still provides us with some important insights into the link between needs and motivation.

First, Murray gets credit for identifying needs as having two components—direction and intensity. You will remember those terms as part of our earlier definition of motivation. Second, he identified more than twenty needs that individuals can possess. Some of his examples included the need for achievement, affiliation, autonomy, change, order, and power. Third, in direct contrast to Maslow, Murray argued that most needs were learned, rather than inherited, and that they are activated by cues from an individual's environment. So an employee with a high need for achievement would pursue that need only when the environmental conditions were appropriate (such as when he or she was assigned a challenging job). Only then would the need surface or become manifest. If not cued, the need would be latent. Finally, Murray's theory provides more flexibility in describing people. Unlike Maslow, Murray didn't assume that people were at a single level on a rigid hierarchy. He proposed that multiple needs motivate behavior simultaneously rather than in some preset order. So people could have high needs for achievement and affiliation and a low need for power—all at the same time.

How well has the theory of manifest needs held up in terms of providing managers with insights into employee motivation? Specific tests of the full theory do not exist. But certain elements seem valid. For instance, many needs appear to be learned; and individuals regularly demonstrate the capability of pursuing multiple needs at the same time. Murray's work is also important for providing the foundation for research conducted by David McClelland in the 1960s through the 1970s. As we show in the next section, McClelland extended and expanded on Murray's ideas, with specific focus on the needs for achievement, affiliation, and power.

In The News

Lower-Order Needs Dominate in Eastern Europe

If employees don't have some basic job security, other needs are not likely to be very important to them. This fact has become evident as executives try to turn around inefficient, formerly state-owned businesses in Eastern Europe.

Take the case of boiler manufacturer Alstrom Fakop in Poland. Managers of the 400-employee company initially tried to increase motivation and morale by offering employees incentive pay. It didn't work. So management tried something different. It offered to maintain staffing at current levels if sales targets were met. To management's pleasant surprise, this commitment resulted in an increase in morale and sales.

Because of the chaos inherent in changing to a market economy, many eastern European employees are more concerned with keeping their jobs than with getting a bonus. And, while this may be an obvious point, notes Ted Snyder of the University of Michigan, it's one most Western managers just don't get. Western managers rush in with new incentives, downsizing targets, and cost-accounting systems, but that isn't enough, says Snyder: "There's real fear. You need a growth strategy. You need to say, 'If we achieve this, we won't have to cut.'"

Ironically, this advice may have more relevance to managing in the West than many managers want to admit. Cost-cutting, downsizing, and reengineering efforts in the United States,

Employees at this boiler plant in Poland want job security, not incentive pay.

Canada, and Western Europe have left many employees feeling insecure about their jobs. People whose jobs are in jeopardy are not likely to be motivated by efforts to redesign work into teams or by offers of more-flexible work schedules.

Source: Based on R. Jacob, "Secure Jobs Trump Higher Pay," *Fortune*, March 20, 1995, p. 24.

LEARNED NEEDS THEORY David McClelland spent much of his career studying three learned needs that he considered to be particularly important sources of motivation.[13] As noted, they are achievement, affiliation, and power. He defined them as follows:

- **Need for achievement (nAch).** The drive to excel, to achieve in relation to a set of standards, to strive to succeed.
- **Need for affiliation (nAff).** The desire for friendly and close interpersonal relationships.
- **Need for power (nPow).** The need to make others behave in a way that they would not have behaved otherwise.

McClelland believed that these needs are acquired from the culture of a society— hence, the label **learned needs theory**. For instance, he argued that the *nAch* is nurtured early in life through children's books, parental styles, and social norms. Some societies stimulate it a lot more in their young than do others. In fact, McClelland has had considerable success in making people from low-achievement cultures exhibit high-achievement behaviors.

As noted in chapter 12, McClelland found that high achievers differentiate themselves from others by their desire to do things better.[14] They seek situations in which: they can attain personal responsibility for finding solutions to problems; they can receive rapid feedback on their performance so that they can tell easily whether they are improving; and they can set moderately challenging goals. High achievers are not gamblers; they dislike succeeding by chance. They prefer the challenge of working at a problem and accepting the personal responsibility for success or failure rather than leaving the outcome to chance or the actions of others. Importantly, they avoid what they perceive to be very easy or very difficult tasks. They want to overcome obstacles, but they want to feel that their success (or failure) is due to their own actions. This means they like tasks of intermediate difficulty.

The need for power is the desire to have an impact, to be influential, and to control others. Individuals high in *nPow* enjoy being "in charge," strive for influence over others, prefer to be placed into competitive and status-oriented situations, and tend to be more concerned with prestige and gaining influence over others than with effective performance.

The third need considered by McClelland is affiliation. This need has received the least attention from researchers. Affiliation can be likened to Dale Carnegie's goals—the desire to be liked and accepted by others. Individuals with a high affiliation motive strive for friendship, prefer cooperative situations rather than competitive ones, and desire relationships involving a high degree of mutual understanding.

Relying on an extensive amount of research, we can make some reasonably well-supported predictions on the relationship between achievement need and job performance. Although less research has been done on power and affiliation needs, there are consistent findings on those dimensions, too.

First, as shown in Exhibit 13-3, individuals with a high need to achieve prefer job situations with personal responsibility, feedback, and an intermediate degree of risk. When these characteristics are prevalent, high achievers will be strongly motivated. The evidence consistently demonstrates, for instance, that high achievers are successful in entrepreneurial activities such as running their own businesses and managing a self-contained unit within a large organization.[15]

Second, a high need to achieve does not necessarily lead to being a good manager, especially in large organizations. People with a high achievement need are interested in how well they do personally and not in influencing others to do well. High-*nAch* salespeople do

---

EXHIBIT 13-3

Matching Achievers and Jobs

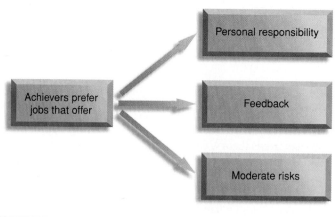

not necessarily make good sales managers, and the good general manager in a large organization does not typically have a high need to achieve.[16]

Third, the needs for affiliation and power tend to be closely related to managerial success. The best managers are high in their need for power and low in their need for affiliation.[17] In fact, a high power motive may be a requirement for managerial effectiveness.[18] Of course, what is the cause and what is the effect is arguable. It has been suggested that a high power need may occur simply as a function of one's level in a hierarchical organization.[19] The latter argument proposes that the higher the level an individual rises to in the organization, the greater is the incumbent's power motive. As a result, powerful positions would be the stimulus to a high power motive.

CONCLUSIONS What conclusions can we draw from these studies of needs that might help you better motivate others? Despite its popularity, Maslow's hierarchy of needs seems to offer little of value for managers. There is no evidence, for instance, that there is a rigid hierarchy of needs that would be applicable to a diverse workforce. Which needs dominate in an individual seem to change with the situation and time. So managers need to become adept at "reading" their employees' needs. How? Ask questions and pay attention to employee behaviors. Don't be afraid to ask people what would motivate them to do a good job. And watch what on-the-job activities employees choose to do when they have free time. This is a window into what currently interests them and drives their actions.

On a more positive note, there does appear to be value in differentiating lower-order and higher-order need sets. Why? If lower-order needs are not substantially met, employees are unlikely to respond to management efforts to stimulate higher needs. For instance, employees are unlikely to respond positively to the introduction of self-managed teams (which can help satisfy autonomy, achievement, and recognition needs) if they are afraid of layoffs and losing their jobs.

▶ Are People Basically Responsible or Irresponsible?

After watching the way managers dealt with employees, psychologist Douglas McGregor made an interesting observation.[20] Managers, he said, hold either of two sets of assumptions about human nature. And those assumptions shape the way the managers treat their employees. He then proceeded to list the assumptions. The first set McGregor called **Theory X**, which basically sees people as irresponsible and lazy. Theory X assumes that:

1. Employees inherently dislike work and, whenever possible, will attempt to avoid it.
2. Since employees dislike work, they must be coerced, controlled, or threatened with punishment to achieve goals.
3. Employees will avoid responsibilities and seek formal direction whenever possible.
4. Most workers place security above all other factors associated with work and will display little ambition.

The second set of assumptions McGregor called **Theory Y**, which basically views people as responsible and conscientious. Theory Y assumes that:

1. Employees can view work as being as natural as rest or play.
2. People will exercise self-direction and self-control if they are committed to the objectives.
3. The average person can learn to accept, even seek, responsibility.
4. The ability to make innovative decisions is widely dispersed throughout the population and is not necessarily the sole province of those in management positions.

What are the motivational implications of McGregor's analysis? Theory X assumes that lower-order needs dominate individuals. Theory Y assumes that higher-order needs dominate individuals. And, because McGregor himself held to the belief that Theory Y assumptions were more valid, he proposed such ideas as participative decision making, responsible and challenging jobs, and good group relations as approaches that would maximize an employee's job motivation.

Unfortunately, there is no evidence to confirm that either set of assumptions is universally valid or that managers who accept Theory Y assumptions and alter their actions accordingly have more-motivated workers. Either Theory X or Theory Y assumptions may be appropriate depending on the particular situation.

The lack of supporting evidence does not negate the value of McGregor's analysis. Quite the contrary. You should familiarize yourself with his terminology because it is frequently used (or misused) by people in organizations. Autocratic executives, for instance, are frequently described as Theory X managers. Although this is not the correct usage of McGregor's terminology—remember, he was describing assumptions about human nature, not management styles—it has nonetheless become a popular way to describe how managers relate to their employees.

▶ What Leads to Satisfaction or Dissatisfaction?

What do people want from their jobs? That was the question psychologist Frederick Herzberg asked that led to one of the most frequently cited theories of motivation.

Herzberg asked people to describe, in detail, situations in which they felt exceptionally good and bad about their jobs. The responses were tabulated and categorized. His findings, shown in Exhibit 13-4, represent the essence of what he called **motivation-hygiene theory**.[21]

Herzberg found that the replies people gave when they felt good about their jobs were significantly different from the replies given when they felt bad. This finding led to motivation-hygiene theory's primary conclusion: Intrinsic factors are related to job satisfaction, whereas extrinsic factors are associated with dissatisfaction.

According to Herzberg, the factors leading to job satisfaction are separate and distinct from those that lead to job dissatisfaction. Therefore, managers who seek to eliminate factors that create job dissatisfaction can bring about peace, but not necessarily motivation. They will be placating their employees rather than motivating them. As a result, such characteristics as company policy and administration, supervision, interpersonal relations, working conditions, and salary have been characterized by Herzberg as hygiene factors. When they are adequate, people will not be dissatisfied; however, neither will they be satisfied. If we want to motivate people on their jobs, Herzberg suggests emphasizing achievement, recognition, the work itself, responsibility, and growth. These are the characteristics that people find intrinsically rewarding.

This theory has had more than its fair share of criticism.[22] The most relevant of these criticisms, at least from our perspective, is that it is actually more a theory of job satisfaction than of motivation. Yet Herzberg's findings have been widely used by managers to justify efforts at job enrichment (see chapter 7). Many organizations have combined job tasks, expanded employee responsibility, and introduced work teams with the intention of increasing employee satisfaction and motivation.

If you want a more accurate and comprehensive explanation of what leads to employee satisfaction, we would offer four recommendations based on an extensive review of the job satisfaction literature.[23] But there is no assurance that these recommendations will automatically lead to increased motivation or employee performance.

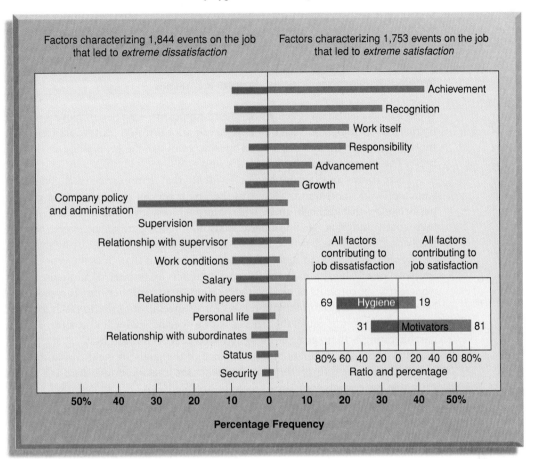

EXHIBIT 13-4

Comparison of Satisfiers (Motivators) and Dissatisfiers (Hygiene Factors)

Factors characterizing 1,844 events on the job that led to *extreme dissatisfaction*

Factors characterizing 1,753 events on the job that led to *extreme satisfaction*

Achievement
Recognition
Work itself
Responsibility
Advancement
Growth
Company policy and administration
Supervision
Relationship with supervisor
Work conditions
Salary
Relationship with peers
Personal life
Relationship with subordinates
Status
Security

50% 40 30 20 10 0 10 20 30 40 50%
Percentage Frequency

All factors contributing to job dissatisfaction

All factors contributing to job satisfaction

69 Hygiene 19
31 Motivators 81

80% 60 40 20 0 20 40 60 80%
Ratio and percentage

1. *Give employees mentally challenging jobs.* Consistent with Herzberg's recommendations, employees tend to prefer jobs that give them opportunities to use their skills and abilities and offer a variety of tasks, freedom, and feedback on how well they're doing. These characteristics make work mentally challenging.
2. *Provide equitable rewards.* Employees want pay systems and promotion policies that they perceive as being just, unambiguous, and in line with their expectations. When pay or other rewards are seen as fair, satisfaction is likely to result.
3. *Offer supportive working conditions.* Employees are concerned with their work environment for both personal comfort and facilitating doing a good job. They prefer physical surroundings, for instance, that are not dangerous or uncomfortable. Most employees also prefer working relatively close to home, in clean and relatively modern facilities, and with adequate tools and equipment.
4. *Encourage supportive colleagues.* People get more out of work than merely money or

tangible achievements. For most employees, work also fills the need for social interaction. Not surprisingly, therefore, having friendly and supportive co-workers leads to increased job satisfaction. Satisfaction is also increased when employees perceive that their immediate supervisor is understanding and friendly, offers praise for good performance, listens to employees' opinions, and shows a personal interest in them.

▶ Does Having "Specific Goals" Improve Motivation?

Dawn Sanders felt she was being honest and supportive with her employees when she told them, "Just do your best. That's all anyone can ask from you." But would Dawn have been more effective if she had substituted specific goals for the generalized goal of "do your best"? The answer is probably yes. Here's why.

There is now an extensive body of evidence that demonstrates that goals are a major source of work motivation.[24] More to the point, we can say that specific goals increase performance; that difficult goals, when accepted, result in higher performance than do easy goals; and that goal feedback leads to higher performance than does lack of feedback.[25] We call these principles **goal-setting theory**.

Specific hard goals produce a higher level of output than does the generalized goal of "do your best." The specificity of the goal itself acts as an internal stimulus. For instance, when a trucker commits to making twelve round-trip hauls between Toronto and Buffalo, New York, each week, this intention gives him a specific objective to reach for. We can say that, all things being equal, the trucker with a specific goal will outperform his counterpart operating with no goals or the generalized goal of "do your best."

If factors such as ability and acceptance of the goals are held constant, we can also state that the more difficult the goal, the higher the level of performance. It is logical to assume that easier goals are more likely to be accepted. But once an employee accepts a hard task, he or she will exert a high level of effort until it is achieved, lowered, or abandoned.

People do best when they get feedback on how well they are progressing toward their goals, because feedback helps to identify discrepancies between what they have done and what they want to do; that is, feedback acts to guide behavior. But all feedback is not equally potent. Self-generated feedback—in which the employee is able to monitor his or her own progress— has been shown to be a more powerful motivator than externally generated feedback.[26]

If employees have the opportunity to participate in the setting of their own goals, will they try harder? The evidence is mixed regarding the superiority of participative over assigned goals.[27] In some cases, participatively set goals elicited superior performance; in other cases, individuals performed best when assigned goals by their boss. But a major advantage of participation may be in increasing acceptance of the goal itself as a desirable one to work toward.[28] As we noted, resistance is greater when goals are difficult. If people participate in goal setting, they are more likely to accept even a difficult goal than if they are arbitrarily assigned it by their boss. The reason is that individuals are committed to choices in which they have a part. Thus, although participative goals may have no superiority over assigned goals when acceptance is taken as a given, participation does increase the probability that more difficult goals will be agreed to and acted upon.

Are there any contingencies in goal-setting theory, or can we take it as a universal truth that difficult and specific goals will always lead to higher performance? In addition to feedback, three other factors have been found to influence the goals-performance relationship. These are goal commitment, adequate self-efficacy, and national culture. Goal-setting theory presupposes that an individual is *committed* to the goal, that is, is determined not to lower or abandon the goal. Commitment is most likely to occur when goals are made public, when the individual has an internal locus of control, and when the goals are self-set rather than assigned.[29] **Self-efficacy** refers to an individual's belief that he or she is capable of performing a task.[30] The higher your self-efficacy, the more confidence you have in your ability to succeed in a task. So, in difficult situations, we find that people with low self-efficacy are likely to lessen their effort or give up altogether, whereas those with high self-efficacy will try harder to master the challenge.[31] In addition, individuals high in self-efficacy seem to respond to negative feedback with increased effort and motivation, whereas those low in self-efficacy are likely to lessen their effort when given negative feedback.[32] Last, goal-setting theory is culture-bound. It is well adapted to countries such as the United States and Canada because its key components align reasonably well with North American cultures. It assumes that employees will be reasonably independent (not too high a score on power distance), that managers and employees will seek challenging goals (low in uncertainty avoidance), and that performance is considered important by both (high in quantity of life). So don't expect goal setting to necessarily lead to higher employee performance in countries such as Portugal or Chile, where the opposite conditions exist.

Pole vaulters epitomize the central role that goals play in most competitive sports.

How Does Reinforcement Affect Motivation?

A counterpoint to goal-setting theory is **reinforcement theory**. The former is a cognitive approach, proposing that an individual's purposes direct his or her action. Reinforcement theory is a behavioristic approach that argues that reinforcement conditions behavior. The two are clearly at odds philosophically. Reinforcement theorists see behavior as being environmentally caused. You needn't be concerned, they would argue, with internal cognitive events; what controls behavior are reinforcers—any consequence that, when immediately following a response, increases the probability that the behavior will be repeated.

Reinforcement theory ignores the inner state of the individual and concentrates solely on what happens to a person when he or she takes some action. Because it doesn't concern itself with what initiates behavior, it is not, strictly speaking, a theory of motivation. But it does provide a powerful means of analysis of what controls behavior, and it is for this reason that it is typically considered in discussions of motivation.[33]

In the previous chapter, we discussed the reinforcement process in detail. We showed how using reinforcers to condition behavior gives us considerable insight into how people learn. Yet we can't ignore the fact that reinforcement has a wide following as a motivational device. In its pure form, however, reinforcement theory ignores feelings, attitudes, expectations, and other cognitive variables that are known to affect behavior.

Reinforcement is undoubtedly an important influence on behavior, but it is not the only influence. The behaviors employees engage in at work and the amount of effort they allocate to each task are affected by the consequences that follow from those behaviors and efforts. So, for instance, if an employee's colleagues consistently reprimand him for outproducing them, he is likely to reduce his productivity. But the lower productivity may also be explained in terms of goals, inequity, or expectancies.

What Happens When Employees Believe That They Are Being Unfairly Rewarded?

Do the concepts of *fairness* and *equity* have relevance to employee motivation? Absolutely! As we noted earlier in this chapter, in our discussion of popular misconceptions, people are sensitive to relative differences in rewards. Specifically, they make comparisons of their job inputs and outcomes relative to those of others. They perceive what they get from a

---

EXHIBIT 13-5		**Equity Theory**

| Outcome-Input Ratio Comparison* | | Perception |
Employee	**Relevant Other**	
O/I_A <	O/I_B	Inequity due to being underrewarded
O/I_A =	O/I_B	Equity
O/I_A >	O/I_B	Inequity due to being overrewarded

* O = Outcome; I = Input; A = Employee; B = Relevant Other.

job situation (outcomes) in relation to what they put into it (inputs), and then they compare their outcome-input ratio with the outcome-input ratio of relevant others. As shown in Exhibit 13-5, there are three possible perceptions. If the ratio is equal to that of the relevant others, a state of equity exists. That is, an individual would perceive the situation as fair. But when the ratio is unequal, there is equity tension. **Equity theory** proposes that this state of negative tension provides the motivation to do something to correct it.[34]

Evidence indicates that the referent chosen is an important element in equity theory.[35] There are four referent comparisons an employee can use:

1. *Self-inside.* An employee's experiences in a different position inside his or her current organization
2. *Self-outside.* An employee's experiences in a situation or position outside his or her current organization
3. *Other-inside.* Another individual or group of individuals inside the employee's organization
4. *Other-outside.* Another individual or group of individuals outside the employee's organization

So employees might compare themselves with friends, neighbors, co-workers, colleagues in other organizations, or past jobs they themselves have had. Which referent an employee chooses will be influenced by the information the employee holds about referents as well as by the attractiveness of the referent.

Equity theory predicts that when employees perceive an inequity, they will make one of six choices:[36]

1. Change their inputs (for example, don't exert as much effort)
2. Change their outcomes (for example, individuals paid on a piece-rate basis can increase their pay by producing a higher quantity of units of lower quality)
3. Distort perceptions of self (for example, "I used to think I worked at a moderate pace, but now I realize that I work a lot harder than everyone else.")
4. Distort perceptions of others (for example, "Mike's job isn't as desirable as I previously thought it was.")
5. Choose a different referent (for example, "I may not make as much as my brother-in-law, but I'm doing a lot better than my dad did when he was my age.")
6. Leave the field (for example, quit the job)

Equity theory recognizes that individuals are concerned not only with the absolute amount of rewards they receive for their efforts but also with the relationship of that amount to what others receive. They make judgments as to the relationship between their inputs—such as effort, experience, education, and competence—and outcomes—such as salary levels, raises, recognition, and other factors—and the inputs and outcomes of others. When people perceive an imbalance in their outcome-input ratio relative to others, tension is created. This tension provides the basis for motivation, as people strive for what they perceive as equity and fairness.

Specifically, the theory establishes four propositions relating to inequitable pay:

1. *Given payment by time, overrewarded employees will produce more than will equitably paid employees.* Hourly and salaried employees will generate high quantity or quality of production in order to increase the input side of the ratio and bring about equity.
2. *Given payment by quantity of production, overrewarded employees will produce fewer, but higher-quality, units than will equitably paid employees.* Individuals paid on a piece-rate basis will increase their effort to achieve equity, which can result in greater quality or quantity. However, increases in quantity will only increase inequity, since every unit produced results in further overpayment. Therefore, effort is directed toward increasing quality rather than increasing quantity.
3. *Given payment by time, underrewarded employees will produce less or poorer quality of output.* Effort will be decreased, which brings about lower productivity or poorer quality output than equitably paid subjects.
4. *Given payment by quantity of production, underrewarded employees will produce a large number of low-quality units in comparison with equitably paid employees.* Employees on piece-rate pay plans can bring about equity because trading off quality of output for quantity will result in an increase in rewards with little or no increase in contributions.

These propositions have generally been supported, with a few minor qualifications.[37] First, inequities created by overpayment do not seem to have a very significant impact on behavior in most work situations. Apparently, people have a great deal more tolerance of overpayment inequities than of underpayment inequities, or they are better able to rationalize them. Second, not all people are equity-sensitive. For example, there is a small part of the working population who actually prefer that their outcome-input ratio be less than the referent comparison. Predictions from equity theory are not likely to be very accurate with these "benevolent types."

It's also important to note that, although most studies on equity theory have focused on pay, employees seem to look for equity in the distribution of other organizational rewards. For instance, it has been shown that the use of high-status job titles as well as large and lavishly furnished offices may function as outcomes for some employees in their equity equation.[38]

How Do Expectations Influence Motivation?

Currently, one of the most widely accepted explanations of motivation is provided by **expectancy theory**.[39] This theory argues that the strength of a tendency to act in a certain way depends on the strength of an expectation that the act will be followed by a given outcome and on the attractiveness of that outcome to the individual. In more practical terms, expectancy theory says that an employee will be motivated to exert a high level of effort when he or she believes that the effort will lead to a good performance appraisal; that a good appraisal will lead to organizational rewards such as a bonus, a salary increase, or a promotion; and that the rewards will satisfy the employee's personal goals. The theory, therefore, focuses on three relationships (see Exhibit 13-6).

In the fall of 1996, basketball star Shawn Kemp engaged in a 22-day holdout from the Seattle Sonics training camp. His objective was to get his contract renegotiated. Although he was currently making $3 million a year and $40 million over the next seven years, he felt he was underpaid because other teams were now handing out $50 million contracts to run-of-the-mill players. "After you play for seven years, and you've been an All-Star for four or five years, and you see these guys signing contracts that are more than you make, unproven players, then it is upsetting," said Kemp. In fall of 1997, Kemp was traded to Cleveland, who gave him a much more lucrative contract.

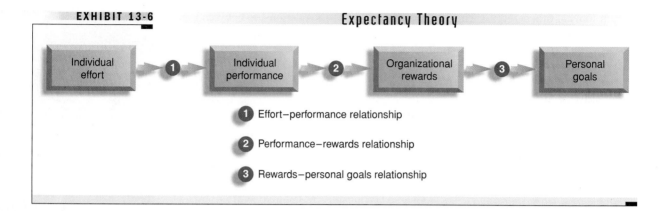

EXHIBIT 13-6

Expectancy Theory

Individual effort → ① → Individual performance → ② → Organizational rewards → ③ → Personal goals

① Effort–performance relationship

② Performance–rewards relationship

③ Rewards–personal goals relationship

1. *Effort–performance relationship.* The probability perceived by the individual that exerting a given amount of effort will lead to performance.
2. *Performance–rewards relationship.* The degree to which the individual believes that performing at a particular level will lead to the attainment of a desired outcome.
3. *Rewards–personal goals relationship.* The degree to which organizational rewards satisfy an individual's personal goals or needs and the attractiveness of those potential rewards for the individual.

Expectancy theory helps explain why a lot of workers aren't motivated on their jobs and merely do the minimum necessary to get by. This attitude is evident when we look at the theory's three relationships in a little more detail. We present them as questions employees need to answer in the affirmative if their motivation is to be maximized.

First, *if I give a maximum effort, will it be recognized in my performance appraisal?* For a lot of employees, the answer is no. Why? Their skill level may be deficient, which means that no matter how hard they try, they are not likely to be high performers. Or, if the organization's performance appraisal system is designed to assess nonperformance factors such as loyalty, initiative, or courage, more effort won't necessarily result in a higher evaluation. Still another possibility is that the employee, rightly or wrongly, perceives that her boss doesn't like her. As a result, she expects to get a poor appraisal regardless of her level of effort. These examples suggest that one possible source of low employee motivation is the employee's belief that no matter how hard she works, the likelihood of getting a good performance appraisal is low.

Second, *if I get a good performance appraisal, will it lead to organizational rewards?* Many employees see the performance-rewards relationship in their job as weak. The reason is that organizations reward a lot of things besides just performance. For example, when pay is allocated to employees on the basis of factors such as seniority, being cooperative, or "kissing up" to the boss, employees are likely to see the performance-rewards relationship as being weak and demotivating.

Last, *if I'm rewarded, are they the rewards that I find personally attractive?* The employee works hard in hope of getting a promotion, but gets a pay raise instead. Or the employee wants a more interesting and challenging job, but receives only a few words of praise. Or the employee puts in extra effort to be relocated to the company's Paris office but instead is transferred to Chicago. These examples illustrate the importance of the rewards' being tailored to individual employee needs. Unfortunately, many managers are limited in the rewards they can distribute, so it is difficult for them to individualize rewards. Moreover, some managers incorrectly assume that all employees want the same thing and thus overlook the motivational effects of differentiating rewards. In either case, employee motivation is not maximized.

In summary, the key to expectancy theory is the understanding of an individual's goals and the linkage between effort and performance, between performance and rewards, and, finally, between the rewards and individual goal satisfaction.

Does expectancy theory work? The overall evidence is generally supportive.[40] But one important caveat should be noted. The theory assumes that employees have few constraints on their decision discretion. For major decisions, such as accepting or resigning from a job, expectancy theory works well because people do not rush into those kinds of decisions. They are prone to take the time to carefully consider the costs and benefits of all alternatives. However, expectancy theory is not a very good explanation for more typical types of work behavior, especially for individuals in lower-level jobs, because such jobs come with considerable limitations imposed by work methods, supervisors, and company policies. Expectancy theory's power in explaining employee productivity increases as the complexity and level in the organization increase, that is, as discretion increases.

In The News

Practicing Expectancy Theory at Lucent Technologies

Managers at Lucent Technologies' Microelectronics Division in Pennsylvania may not be aware of it, but the incentive program they have introduced for employees clearly builds off expectancy theory. And that may be a major reason why it's been successful.

The program was designed to increase employee recognition and generate cost-saving and revenue-generating ideas for the division. Consistent with expectancy theory, these goals are used in the appraisal process. Those individuals and teams that are top performers in any given quarter, or who generate improvement ideas that are implemented, are recognized in their evaluations. Then, consistent with expectancy theory, they are rewarded for their contributions by receiving recognition points. The amount of these points range from 50 to 250,000, depending on the scope of the idea and its value to the business. Finally, the points can be turned in for a variety of rewards, the choice of which is left to the individual employee. Among the rewards available to employees are paid vacations, golf clubs, and home appliances.

In the first year of the incentive program, employees submitted 6,000 ideas, of which 2,100 were approved for implementation. These included ideas for reducing recycling scrap, improving plant safety, reducing the costs of overnight mail, and improving the efficiency of the e-mail system. One team of factory workers, for example, devised a way to eliminate waste that saved the company $45,000. For their efforts, the employees each received enough points to take a trip to Jamaica. In total, the division achieved $20 million worth of cost savings and new revenue in the first year that could be directly attributable to the new incentive program.

Could the program be improved? According to expectancy theory, the answer is probably yes. For instance, management could consider widening the reward choices, and therefore tailor them more closely to the diverse needs of employees. So, in addition to trips and merchandise, management might consider adding paid time off, cash, or educational vouchers.

Source: S. Caudron, "Spreading Out the Carrots," *Industry Week*, May 19, 1997, pp. 20–24.

▶ What Are the Motivation Implications of the New Employee-Employer Covenant?

As introduced in chapter 1 and reiterated in many subsequent chapters, today's employee-employer relationship is very different from the one that existed just 20 years ago. In most organizations, the "loyalty-for-security" bond has been irreparably broken.[41] *Security* and *stability* are increasingly something that "my father and grandfather had" but that "don't relate much to me." The majority of employees today face a working world characterized by temporariness, little job security, and limited promotion opportunities (created by flatter structures). The question is: What are the motivation implications for this new employee-employer covenant?

There's no simple answer to that question. To better focus the issue, let's look at some of the fastest-growing segments of the new workforce. These include independent contractors, contingent workers, professionals, minimum-wage service workers, and people required to do highly repetitive tasks.

INDEPENDENT CONTRACTORS An increasing number of employees are acting as independent contractors. They have no permanent ties to a specific organization. Rather, they contract on an individual basis to work on a specific project or set of projects. Some examples of these jobs include an accounting expert who *contracts* with a small trucking firm to install a cost-control system; an electrical engineer who *contracts* with Intel to help in the design of the next generation of microchips; or a training specialist who *contracts* with Boeing to provide an in-house course to improve diversity awareness.

The common characteristics of these "employees" is that, because of the temporary nature of their work, they have no loyalty to the organization. So how can managers who have to work with these people motivate them? Money should be one factor that is important. Since the "relationship" is designed to be short-lived, good pay can be a meaningful and sustainable stimulus to high performance. Other factors that should provide motivation to these people are challenging assignments and opportunities to develop new skills. An independent contractor's future employment is essentially determined by his or her ability to meet employers' needs. Doing so requires keeping skills highly tuned and current. Managers who can provide independent contractors with jobs that fulfill this requirement should have motivated workers.

CONTINGENT WORKERS Temporary and part-time workers, especially those who choose this status voluntarily, tend to place a high value on flexibility. They should be particularly receptive to flexible work schedules and other options that increase their autonomy. For instance, companies such as Lancaster Laboratories and Ridgeview Hosiery find that they can cut turnover and improve motivation by providing employees with on-site day care.[42] For single parents and dual-career parents, quality day care may make the difference between staying home or being able to come to work. It also allows employees to concentrate on their job once they're at work.

Going beyond day care, organizations such as American Bankers Insurance Group, Barnett Banks, and Hewlett-Packard are sponsoring public schools at their work sites.[43] American Bankers, for instance, spent $2.4 million to build a satellite public school on its 84-acre corporate campus. The school serves 225 children. And parents are encouraged to visit their children at lunchtime and after school.

Starbucks Coffee, Hemmings Motor News, and G. T. Water Products have found that they can get more out of part-time employees by providing them with the same benefits offered full-timers.[44] For instance, Starbucks offers health and dental insurance, stock options, and matching retirement plan benefits to part-timers as well as full-timers.

Other motivators for contingent workers include company-paid training and opportunities for permanent status. For instance, Performark, Inc., a Bloomington, Minnesota, marketing-services company, offers its temporary workers the same training as its other employees. And two-thirds of the firm's full-time employees began as temporary staffers.[45]

PROFESSIONALS Professionals are typically different from nonprofessionals. They have a strong and long-term commitment to their field of expertise. Their loyalty is more often to their profession than to their employer. To keep current in their field, they need to regularly update their knowledge. And their commitment to their profession means they rarely define their workweek in terms of 9-to-5 and 5 days a week.

So what motivates professionals? Money and promotions into management typically are low on their priority list. Why? They tend to be well paid, and they enjoy what they do. In contrast, job challenge tends to be ranked high. They like to tackle problems and find solutions. Their chief reward in their job is the work itself. Professionals also value support. They want others to think that what they are working on is important.

This implies that managers should provide professionals with new assignments and challenging projects. Give them autonomy to follow their interests and allow them to structure their work in ways they find productive. Reward them with educational opportunities—training, workshops, attending conferences—that allow them to keep current in their field. Also reward them with recognition. And managers should ask questions and engage in other actions that demonstrate to their professional employees that they're sincerely interested in what they're doing.

Because professionals often work long hours, they frequently have limited time to do typical household chores and errands. As a result, they put a high value on organizational efforts to simplify their nonwork lives. Employees at Wilton Connor Packaging in Charlotte, North Carolina, can bring their laundry to work and have it washed, dried, and folded courtesy of the company. In addition to on-site laundry service, Wilton Connor has a handyman on staff who does free minor household repairs for employees while they're at work.[46]

An increasing number of companies are creating alternative career paths for their technical people. These allow employees to earn more money and status, without assuming managerial responsibilities. At Merck & Co., IBM, and AT&T, the best scientists, engineers, and researchers gain titles such as Fellow and Senior Scientist. Their pay and prestige are comparable to those of managers, but without the corresponding authority.[47]

MINIMUM-WAGE SERVICE WORKERS One of the most challenging motivation problems facing managers in industries such as retailing, hotels, and fast food is: How do you motivate individuals who are making very low wages and who have little opportunity to significantly increase their pay in either their current jobs or through promotions? These jobs are typically filled with people who have limited education and skills, and pay levels are little above minimum wage.

Traditional approaches for motivating these people have focused on providing more flexible work schedules and filling these jobs with teenagers and retirees whose financial needs are relatively low. These approaches have met with less than overwhelming success. For instance, annual turnover rates of 200 percent or more are not uncommon for businesses such as McDonald's. Taco Bell, the Mexican fast-food chain, has tried to enrich some of its service jobs but with limited results.[48] It has experimented with incentive pay and stock options for cashiers and cooks. These employees also have been given broader responsibility for inventory, scheduling, and hiring. But over a 4-year period, this experiment has reduced annual turnover only from 223 percent to 160 percent.

> Money and promotions into management typically are low on the priority list of motivators for professionals.

Turnover rates run high at fast-food restaurants like Taco Bell. Pay levels tend to be at or near minimum wage; there is little opportunity for advancement; and job challenge tends to be low.

What choices are left for managers? Unless pay and benefits are significantly increased, high turnover probably has to be expected in these jobs. This can be somewhat offset by widening the recruiting net, making these jobs more appealing, and raising pay levels.[49] Managers might also try some nontraditional approaches as well. Aramark, a services-contracting company, offers free English-as-a-second-language classes to its hospital staffers and school dining-service employees. Conagra built a 100-unit on-site housing project to cut Arkansas workers' transportation costs. The Opryland Hotel gives employees free bus service and one free meal a day.[50] And Judy Wicks has found that celebrating employees' outside interests has dramatically cut turnover among waiters at her White Dog Cafe in Philadelphia.[51] For instance, to help create a close and familylike work climate, Wicks sets aside one night a year for employees to exhibit their art, read their poetry, explain their volunteer work, and introduce their new babies.

PEOPLE REQUIRED TO DO HIGHLY REPETITIVE TASKS   Our final category considers employees who do standardized and repetitive jobs. For instance, working on an assembly line or transcribing court reports are jobs that incumbents often find boring and even stressful.

Motivating individuals in these jobs can be made easier through careful selection. People vary in their tolerance for ambiguity. A great many individuals prefer jobs that have a minimal amount of discretion and variety. Such individuals are obviously a better match to standardized jobs than are individuals with strong needs for growth and autonomy. Standardized jobs should also be the first considered for automation.

Many standardized jobs, especially in the manufacturing sector, pay well. This factor makes it relatively easy for employers to fill vacancies. Although high pay can ease recruitment problems and reduce turnover, it doesn't necessarily lead to highly motivated workers. And realistically, there are jobs that don't readily lend themselves to enrichment or redesign. Some tasks, for instance, are just far more efficiently done on assembly lines than in teams. These jobs leave managers with limited options. They may not be able to do much more than try to make a bad situation tolerable by creating a pleasant work climate. They might provide clean and attractive work surroundings, ample work breaks, the opportunity to socialize with colleagues during breaks, and empathetic supervisors.

▶ How Do Cultural Differences Influence Employee Motivation?

Most Americans place high importance on professional accomplishments.[52] Their self-esteem and social status are largely derived from their accomplishments. They're motivated to work hard to earn money, because job and social position depend on such efforts. To the French, on the other hand, industriousness and devotion to work are not highly valued attributes. What is highly valued is *qualite de la vie*—quality of life. The French place a great deal of importance on free time and vacations. They're seldom willing to sacrifice this enjoyment of life to achieve work-related accomplishments.

Differences between American and French needs may be expanded to comparisons across many cultures. That is, what motivates people in one country doesn't necessarily motivate people somewhere else. The problem is exasperated because most current motivation theories were developed in the United States by Americans and about Americans.[53] And they reflect American biases. Goal-setting and expectancy theories, for instance, emphasize goal accomplishment as well as rational and individual thought. They reflect the importance Americans place on individualism, achievement, and material acquisitions. When a country's values don't align with Americans', as we saw with our French example, then theories like goal setting and expectancy are unlikely to transfer very successfully. To further dramatize our point, let's look at how American biases are weaved into conclusions about Maslow's need hierarchy and the achievement need.

Maslow's need hierachy argues that people start at the physiological level and then move progressively up the hierarchy in this order: physiological, safety, social, esteem, and self-actualization. This hierarchy, if it has any application at all, aligns with American culture. In countries like Japan, Greece, and Mexico, where uncertainty avoidance characteristics are strong, security needs would be on top of the need hierarchy. And in countries that score high on quality-of-life characteristics—Denmark, Sweden, Norway, the Netherlands, and Finland—social needs would be on top.[54] We could predict, for instance, that group work will motivate employees more when the country's culture scores high on the quality criterion.

The view that a high achievement need acts as an internal motivator presupposes two cultural characteristics—a willingness to accept a moderate degree of risk (which excludes countries with strong uncertainty avoidance characteristics) and a concern with performance (which applies almost singularly to countries with strong quantity-of-life characteristics). This combination is found in Anglo-American countries like the United States, Canada, and Great Britain.[55] On the other hand, these characteristics are relatively absent in countries such as Chile and Portugal.

In spite of the previous comments, don't assume there aren't *any* cross-cultural consistencies. For instance, the desire for interesting work seems important to almost all workers, regardless of their national culture. In a study of seven countries, employees in Belgium, Britain, Israel, and the United States ranked "interesting work" number one among 11 work goals. And this factor was ranked either second or third in Japan, the Netherlands, and Germany.[56] Similarly, in a study comparing job-preference outcomes among graduate students in the United States, Canada, Australia, and Singapore, growth, achievement, and responsibility were rated the top three and had identical rankings.[57] Both of these studies suggest that the importance placed on intrinsic factors in motivation-hygiene theory may be applicable to a number of national cultures.

We have presented a number of ideas and theories so far in this chapter. Let's try to tie them together so you can better see their interrelationships.

Exhibit 13-7 on page 426 presents a model that integrates much of what we know about motivation. Its basic framework is organized around the expectancy-theory variables shown in Exhibit 13-6.

We begin by explicitly recognizing that supportive resources facilitate individual effort. The Individual Effort box also has another arrow leading into it. This arrow flows out of the person's goals. Consistent with goal-setting theory, this goals-effort loop is meant to remind us that goals direct behavior.

Expectancy theory predicts that an employee will exert a high level of effort if he or she perceives that there is a strong relationship between effort and performance, performance and rewards, and rewards and satisfaction of personal goals. Each of these relationships, in turn, is influenced by certain factors. For effort to lead to good performance, the individual must have the requisite ability to perform, and the performance appraisal system that measures the individual's performance must be perceived as being fair and objective. The performance-rewards relationship will be strong if the individual perceives that it is performance (rather than seniority, personal favorites, or other criteria) that is rewarded. The final link in expectancy theory is the rewards-goals relationship.

AN INTEGRATIVE MODEL OF MOTIVATION

EXHIBIT 13-7   Integrative Model of Motivation

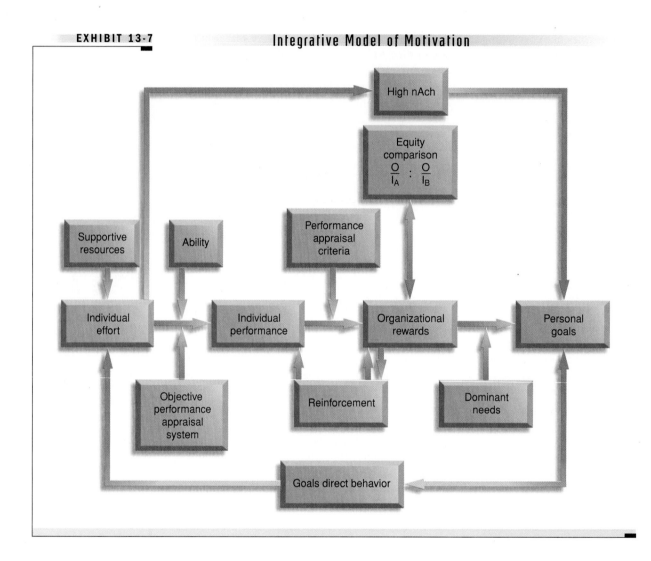

Motivation would be high to the degree that the rewards an individual received for his or her high performance satisfied the dominant needs consistent with his or her individual goals.

A closer look at Exhibit 13-7 will also reveal that the model considers the achievement need and reinforcement and equity theories. The high achiever is not motivated by the organization's assessment of his or her performance or organizational rewards, hence, the jump from effort to personal goals for those with a high *nAch*. Remember, high achievers are internally driven as long as the jobs they are doing provide them with personal responsibility, feedback, and moderate risks. So they are not concerned with the effort-performance, performance-rewards, or rewards-goal linkages.

Reinforcement theory enters our model by recognizing that the organization's rewards reinforce the individual's performance. If management has designed a reward system that is seen by employees as "paying off" for good performance, the rewards will reinforce and encourage continued good performance. Rewards also play the key part in equity theory. Individuals will compare the rewards (outcomes) they receive from the inputs they make with the outcome-input ratio of relevant others ($O/I_A : O/I_B$), and inequities may influence the effort expended.

Of course, like any model, our motivation model is an abstraction. It provides a *general* integration of the concepts we've discussed in this chapter. But it has clear limitations. It does not, for example, reflect differences across cultures. Since the theories in this chapter are, for the most part, Anglo-American in derivation, you would need to exhibit considerable care when applying them in non-Anglo-American cultures.

CONTEMPORARY APPLICATIONS

Today's managers are experimenting with a number of applications in order to increase their employees' motivation. We conclude our discussion of motivation and rewards by briefly reviewing the more popular of these applications.

Employee Involvement

Employee involvement has become a convenient catchall term to cover a variety of techniques.[58] For instance, it encompasses such popular ideas as employee participation or participative management, empowerment, workplace democracy, and employee ownership. We define **employee involvement** as a participative process that uses the entire capacity of employees and is designed to encourage increased commitment to the organization's success.[59] The underlying logic is that by involving workers in those decisions that affect them and by increasing their autonomy and control over their work lives, employees will become more motivated, more committed to the organization, more productive, and more satisfied with their jobs. Exhibit 13-8 describes four forms of employee involvement.

Germany, France, Holland, and the Scandinavian countries have firmly established the principle of industrial democracy in Europe, and other nations, including Japan and Israel, have traditionally practiced some form of representative participation for decades. Participative management and representative participation were much slower to gain ground in North American organizations. But nowadays employee-involvement programs that stress participation have become the norm. Quality circles were very popular in the 1980s. Many have since been replaced by more-comprehensive team-based structures as part of TQM programs. And employee stock ownership programs (ESOPs) in the United

Popular Employee-Involvement Programs

EXHIBIT 13-8

Type	Description
Participative management	Joint decision making. Employees share a significant degree of decision-making power with their immediate superiors.
Representative participation	Workers are represented by a small group of employees who participate in organizational decision making. Redistributes power by putting labor on a more equal footing with the interests of management and stockholders.
Quality circles	Work groups of eight to ten employees and supervisors who have a shared area of responsibility. These groups meet regularly to discuss their quality problems, investigate causes of the problems, recommend solutions, and take corrective actions.
Employee stock ownership plans	ESOPs are company-established benefit plans in which employees acquire stock as a part of their benefits.

States have now been implemented in about 10,000 companies, including such well-known firms as United Airlines, Anheuser-Busch, Procter & Gamble, and Polaroid.[60]

Open-Book Management

In 1980, a long strike had nearly forced the closing of Missouri-based Springfield ReManufacturing Co. (SRC), a subsidiary of then International Harvester.[61] To cut losses, Harvester sold SRC, which reassembles diesel engines, to a group of investors. The new management needed to radically change the company if it was going to survive. That radical change came in the form of what has become known as **open-book management** (**OBM**). Essentially, OBM seeks to get every employee to think and behave like an owner.[62] It throws out the notion that bosses run things and employees do what they're told. In the open-book approach, employees are given the information that historically was strictly kept within the management ranks. The result is that employees understand *why* they're being called upon to solve problems, cut costs, reduce defects, and give the customer better service. And they have a reason to do so. Exhibit 13-9 lists the ten principles underlying OBM.

At SRC, management trained employees to understand the company's financials, shared those numbers routinely with the workforce, and provided bonuses and incentive pay based on profit improvement. For instance, each week SRC shuts down its machines for 30 minutes while its 800 employees break into small groups and study the latest financial statements. Every employee at SRC can now interpret profit and loss statements as well as most accountants. In fact, SRC employees sound a lot like accountants. For instance, when a visitor to the SRC plant asked a worker what the price was of the crankshaft he was working on, he looked up and said, "List price or dealer net?" He then went on to explain both prices, how they compared with SRC's cost, and what his own component of the cost was.[63]

The result of open-book management has been nothing short of sensational at SRC. In 1981, the company lost $61,000 on sales of $16 million. Currently, the company is earning around $6 million a year on sales of $135 million.

Hundreds of companies, from Allstate Insurance to Amoco Canada to sportswear maker Patagonia, have implemented OBM. Allstate's Business Insurance Group, for instance, used OBM to boost return on equity from 2.9 percent to 16.5 percent in just three years.

How does OBM act as a motivator? By turning employees into businesspeople, it makes their work more interesting and increases their involvement in organizational decision mak-

---

EXHIBIT 13-9   Principles of Open-Book Management

1. Turn the management of a business into a game that employees can win.
2. Open the books and share financial and operating information with employees.
3. Teach employees to understand the financial statements of the company.
4. Show employees how their work influences financial results.
5. Link nonfinancial measures to financial results.
6. Target priority areas and empower employees to make improvements.
7. Review results together and keep employees accountable.
8. Post results and celebrate successes.
9. Distribute bonus awards based on employee contributions to financial outcomes.
10. Share the ownership of the company with employees.

Source: T. R. V. Davis, "Open-Book Management: Its Promise and Pitfalls," *Organizational Dynamics*, Winter 1997, p. 12. With permission.

ing. Every employee, not just managers, gets to experience the challenge of matching wits with the marketplace, toting up the score, and sharing in their organization's success.

▶ Variable-Pay Programs

In 1996, Robert J. Eaton, chairman of Chrysler Corp., earned a salary and bonus of $5.9 million. In 1997, that figure dropped to $4.6 million. Why? Did he put in fewer hours or not work as hard? No! The company's profits dropped 20 percent, and the majority of Eaton's compensation is tied to Chrysler's profits.[64]

For over 30 years, Nucor Steel has had an incentive compensation plan in place that pays bonuses to employees on the basis of the company's profitability.[65] Originally intended to provide workers with an additional 15 percent to 20 percent on top of their base wages, actual bonus payouts have been as high as 80 percent to 150 percent of base.

These two examples illustrate **variable-pay programs**. What differentiates these forms of compensation from more traditional programs is that pay is not based only on a person's time on the job or seniority; a portion of an employee's pay is based on some individual or organizational measure of performance. Exhibit 13-10 on page 430 describes four of the more widely used variable-pay programs.

Variable pay has been around a long time. It has been the typical way that entrepreneurs, salespeople, piecework factory workers, and rock stars have been compensated. But it is now reaching the masses—at banks, in factories, within marketing teams, even at whole companies—replacing the relatively fixed paycheck that grew a little bit every year.[66] A recent survey indicates that 14 percent of U.S. companies are using some form of variable pay, another 6 percent are installing such a program, and 26 percent report they are giving the matter serious study.[67]

The fluctuation in variable pay has made these programs attractive to management. It turns part of an organization's fixed labor costs into a variable cost, thus reducing expenses when performance declines. In addition, by tying pay to performance, earnings recognize contribution rather than being a form of entitlement. Low performers find, over time, that their pay stagnates; high performers enjoy pay increases commensurate with their contribution.

▶ Skill-Based Pay Plans

The highest pay that machine operators at Polaroid Corporation can earn is $14 an hour. But if they can broaden their competencies to include additional skills such as material ac-

Eugene Vasser, a factory worker who has been at Lincoln Electric for 25 years, works long hours. A typical workweek includes five 10-hour days plus 8 hours on Saturday. Vasser has only a high school education but he earns in excess of $100,000 a year because of Lincoln's lucrative incentive pay plan.

EXHIBIT 13-10

Popular Variable-Pay Programs

Type	Description
Piece-rate wages	Long used to compensate production employees. Workers are paid a fixed sum for each unit of production completed.
Bonuses	Onetime payments that can be paid on the basis of individual, group, or organization-wide performance variables.
Profit-sharing	Organization-wide programs that distribute compensation based on some established formula designed around a company's profitability. These can be direct cash outlays, or, particularly popular for compensating top executives, they can be allocated as stock options.
Gainsharing	A formula-based group incentive plan. Improvements in group productivity—from one period to another—determine the total amount of money allocated. Typically, the division of productivity savings is split 50-50 between the company and the employees.

counting, equipment maintenance, and quality inspection, they can earn up to 10 percent more.[68] At Xel Communications, a maker of telecommunications transmission equipment, its 300 employees can earn an additional 50 cents an hour for each new task they master.[69] Workers at American Steel & Wire can boost their annual salaries by up to $12,480 by acquiring as many as ten skills. And new employees at a Quaker Oats' pet food plant in Topeka, Kansas, start at $8.75 an hour, but they can reach a top rate of $14.50 when they master ten to twelve skills such as operating lift trucks and factory computer controls.[70]

These examples illustrate **skill-based pay**. Rather than having an individual's job title define his or her pay category, skill-based pay rewards employees for the job skills and competencies they can demonstrate.[71] It provides an incentive for individuals to learn new tasks and broaden their skills. It facilitates communication across the organization because people gain a better understanding of others' jobs. And it helps meet the needs of ambitious employees who confront minimal advancement opportunities. These people can increase their earnings and knowledge without a promotion in job title.

Skill-based pay meshes nicely with the new world of work. As one expert noted, "Slowly, but surely, we're becoming a skill-based society where your market value is tied to what you can do and what your skill set is. In this new world where skills and knowledge are what really count, it doesn't make sense to treat people as jobholders. It makes sense to treat them as people with specific skills and to pay them for those skills."[72]

▶ Broadbanding Compensation

We briefly mentioned broadbanding compensation in chapter 1 during our discussion of flexible compensation. We described it as replacing multiple job levels or salary grades with a few broad bands.

A typical large organization may have 25 or more salary grades. Under broadbanding, those categories are slashed to as few as two—but more typically five to ten—with a much wider range of pay within the reduced number of grades. For example, General Electric reduced its 29 pay grades to six bands. Now, rather than climbing through a series of levels, employees may spend a major portion of their career in a single band. But that band is much wider—say $32,000 to $60,000, in contrast to more traditional salary grades such as $41,500 to $47,000.

The popularity of broadbanding is rapidly growing. A recent survey of 380 large companies, for instance, found that 29 percent were using or implementing broadbanding, up from less than 17 percent only two years earlier. And 27 percent of respondents indicated they were considering making the change.[73]

As noted in chapter 1, a large part of the interest in broadbanding is that it increases organizational flexibility. Managers have more freedom to award pay raises without having to promote workers. Moreover, broadbanding helps employees to stop thinking that success is defined as a steady progression up an artificial ladder. As such, broadbanding is more consistent with new organizational structures. Traditional vertical pay systems, with their vast number of grades, don't fit well with the new, flatter, team-oriented structures. Broadbanding does.[74]

What about broadbanding's motivation implications? First, there is a potential downside. The typical narrow-banded system creates a visible status hierarchy. Some employees miss the existence of clear multiple-grades against which they can mark career progress. But on the upside, broadbanding reinforces lateral and personal development rather than vertical career progress. Employees can focus on enhancing their long-term skills. Broadbanding also allows managers more discretion to reward individual competence and performance. Since there are fewer pay grades, there are also fewer pay "ceilings" to limit salary increases. So there should be a tighter link between an employee's contribution and his or her pay. The GE employee, who was earning $45,500 in a tight pay grade that topped out at $47,000, had to get a promotion to get anything beyond a $1,500 raise. When that employee is in a broad band that goes to $60,000, there is still ample room for pay increases without the promotion.

Family-Friendly Workplaces

Forty-six percent of the U.S. workforce is now female. More and more fathers want to actively participate in the care and raising of their children. As baby boomers age, many are finding themselves having to care for elderly parents. These three facts translate into an increasing number of employees who are attempting to juggle family obligations along with their job responsibilities. In response, companies such as MBNA America, Motorola, First Tennessee Bank, Hewlett-Packard, DuPont, Baxter International, and Sequent Computer Systems are leading the way in establishing themselves as **family-friendly workplaces**.[75] These are organizations that have instituted programs to reduce the conflict between work and family obligations.[76] They offer an umbrella of programs such as paid paternity and adoption leave, on-site day care, child-care and elder-care referrals, use of sick leave for chil-

Jackie Demo, an operations analyst at Baxter International, uses flexible hours and telecommutes at least one day a week to reduce work-family conflicts created by caring for her young daughter and terminally-ill mother-in-law.

dren's illnesses, flexible work hours, 4-day workweeks, job sharing, telecommuting, temporary part-time employment, and relocation assistance for employees' family members.[77]

Creating a family-friendly work climate was initially introduced by management because of concern with improving employee morale and productivity and to reduce absenteeism. It has been estimated that the cost to U.S. businesses of time lost through breakdowns in child-care arrangements alone is about $3 billion annually.[78] At Quaker Oats, for instance, 60 percent of employees admitted being absent at least 3 days a year because of children's illnesses, and 56 percent said they were unable to attend company-related functions or to work overtime because of child-care problems.[79]

Has it worked? Yes and no! There are few data to support any significant increase in productivity. But the evidence does indicate that creating a family-friendly workplace makes it easier for employers to recruit and retain first-class workers.[80] There are also substantial observational data to suggest that it limits family-related distractions and reduces absenteeism.[81]

Employee Recognition Programs

A few years back, 1,500 employees were surveyed in a variety of work settings to find out what they considered to be the most powerful workplace motivator. Their response? Recognition, recognition, and more recognition![82] Another study found that employees rated personal thanks from a manager for a job well done as the most motivating of a variety of incentives offered.[83] But, unfortunately, 58 percent of the workers in this latter study said their managers didn't typically give such thanks.

In today's highly competitive global economy, most organizations are under severe cost pressures. That makes recognition programs particularly attractive. In contrast to most other motivators, recognizing an employee's superior performance often costs little or no money. Maybe that's why a recent survey of 3,000 employers found that two-thirds use or plan to use special recognition awards.[84] Recognition has been found to be especially relevant in the motivation of low-wage workers.[85] It costs little and helps to build employee self-esteem. Fine Host Corp., a food service firm in Connecticut, gives out quality awards and posts workers'

EXHIBIT 13-11

Source: From the *Wall Street Journal*, October 21, 1997. Reprinted by permission of Cartoon Features Syndicate.

names in company buildings to recognize good work. All Metro Health Care in Lynnbrook, New York, sponsors an award for home health caregiver of the year and also gives employees gifts, such as watches and blenders, for scoring high in quarterly training exercises.

Consistent with reinforcement theory, rewarding a behavior with recognition immediately following that behavior is likely to encourage its repetition. How can managers use this technique? They can personally congratulate an employee in private for a good job. They can send a handwritten note or an e-mail message acknowledging something positive that the employee has done. For employees with a strong need for social acceptance, managers can publicly recognize accomplishments. And to enhance group cohesiveness and motivation, managers can celebrate team successes. They can use meetings to recognize the contributions and achievements of successful work teams.

There is a variety of additional material available on the CD-ROM and companion Web site that accompany this text. You can access this information through the CD-ROM or by visiting the Web site at <**www.prenhall.com/robbins**>.

SUMMARY

This summary is organized by the chapter-opening learning objectives on page 404.

1. High performance is not just a function of high motivation. It also requires that an employee have the requisite ability to do a job and the necessary supportive resources.

2. Motivation is the willingness to exert a persistent and high level of effort toward organizational goals, conditioned by the effort's ability to satisfy some individual need.

3. The hierarchy of needs identifies five needs categories—physiological, safety, belongingness, esteem, and self-actualization—that exist in a hierarchy of steps. As a need is substantially satisfied, the individual moves on to the next. ERG theory condenses these into three groups of core needs—existence, relatedness, and growth. Existence equals physiological and safety needs. Relatedness equals belongingness and the external component of esteem. Growth equals the internal component of esteem and self-actualization. ERG theory proposes that individuals can be working on all three core needs at the same time and can regress from higher-order needs to lower-order needs.

4. Theory X assumes that lower-order needs dominate individuals. So a manager who holds Theory X assumptions is likely to motivate by focusing on physiological and safety needs. This manager is likely to believe that "fear is a great motivator." Theory Y assumes that higher-order needs dominate. Managers holding Theory Y assumptions will try to motivate employees through using participation, creating challenging jobs, and developing good group relations.

5. According to motivation-hygiene theory, extrinsic hygiene factors such as company policy, supervision, pay, and working conditions don't motivate workers. They merely placate them. Motivation comes from achievement, growth, responsibility, and similar intrinsic factors in a job.

6. Goals motivate by providing individuals with specific and challenging targets to reach for. Goal feedback further tells a person how well he or she is progressing so adjustments can be made.

7. For people who are equity-sensitive, inequitable rewards (specifically, underrewarding) create tension. People compare the rewards (outcomes) they receive with their inputs; then they compare their outcome-input ratio with the ratios of relevant others. If they perceive inequity, they will try to reestablish equity through actions such as exerting less effort, reducing quality of work, increasing absences, distorting perceptions of self or others, changing referents, or quitting their jobs.

8. Expectancy theory essentially says that for employees to exert high levels of effort, they must believe that the effort will result in a favorable performance appraisal, that the favorable appraisal will lead to increased organizational rewards, and that those rewards will satisfy their personal goals or needs.

9. Employee involvement is a participative process that uses the entire capacity of employees and is designed to encourage increased commitment to the organization's success. Employees are more likely to work hard on a task or job if they have more control over it.

10. Variable-pay programs tie pay to performance. Skill-based programs tie pay to the number of skills or competencies an employee masters. The former focuses on outcomes, and the

latter, on means. Skill-based pay encourages learning, growth, and teamwork. Variable pay encourages individuals to do whatever is necessary to achieve the individual, group, and organizational criteria used for measuring performance.

REVIEW QUESTIONS

1. Contrast the belief that motivation is individual-specific with the belief that it is situation-specific.
2. "Everyone wants a challenging job." Build an argument in favor of this statement. Then build an argument negating the statement.
3. Integrate the two components of a need—direction and intensity—identified by Murray with this chapter's definition of motivation.
4. What characteristics do high achievers prefer in a job?
5. What can managers do to increase employee satisfaction?
6. Does employee participation in goal setting lead to higher performance? Explain your answer.
7. In what ways can you use reinforcement theory to improve employee motivation?
8. How can you motivate (a) contingent workers? (b) professionals? (c) minimum-wage service workers?
9. Explain Exhibit 13-7 (page 426) in terms of how it can help a manager motivate his or her staff.
10. What are "family-friendly workplaces"? How might they influence employee motivation?

IF I WERE THE MANAGER . . .

Motivating Millionaires

You had to laugh. You're sitting at your desk, looking at a list of company stock options held by your Microsoft team. No one on your nine-person team was older than 33. Yet everyone was a millionaire, at least on paper. The value of their individual options, on this given day, ranged from $1.7 million to $18.4 million.

Your team wasn't unusual. More than 4,000 of Microsoft's 27,000 employees are millionaires—all created by the incredible rise in the value of the company's stock. So your problem isn't unique at Microsoft or, for that matter, at a number of fast-growing, high-tech companies. Your problem? How do you motivate multimillionaires to come to work every day?

SKILL EXERCISE

The Murray Group

You opened your first car dealership in 1984. That small Toyota dealership has since grown into the Murray Group: four dealerships selling seven different auto makes. Your four dealerships sit, side-by-side, just outside Miami, Florida. Business has been fairly good in recent years. You've been able to pay off almost all your loans. Unfortunately, your employees seem to think you're getting rich at their expense. You're hearing increasing criticism about pay. Just yesterday, one of your longest tenured mechanics took you aside: "Since I joined this company, we're selling five times as many cars. Our service shops are now always packed. This place is making you a bundle. Meanwhile, most of us are barely scraping by. Morale has really tanked in

recent months. We need some serious pay raises around here or you're gonna see a lot of people leaving."

You're very concerned with this criticism. You're concerned because it's undermining motivation. And you value these employees. You don't want them leaving! But you're most concerned with their misinterpretation of your financial situation. Yes, the business has grown quite a bit. And you are making money. But you're not getting rich! Your overhead has gone up a lot in recent years. And competitive pressures have squeezed your profit margins.

You've read about open-book management and decided that this might be exactly the solution to your problem. Describe exactly how you would implement open-book management in your business.

TEAM ACTIVITY

Determining Pay Increases

Step 1: This exercise begins by each class member reading the following scenario and deciding on pay increases for each of the eight employees. You have 20 minutes to complete this part of the exercise.

You have to make salary increase recommendations for eight managers that you supervise. They have just completed their first year with the company and are now to be considered for their first annual raise. Keep in mind that you may be setting precedents and that you need to keep salary costs down. However, there are no formal company restrictions on the kind of raises you can give. Indicate the size of the raise that you would like to give each manager by writing a dollar amount next to their names. You have a total of $34,000 available in your salary budget to use for pay raises.

$_____ *A. J. Adams.* Adams is not, as far as you can tell, a good performer. You have checked your view with others, and they do not feel that Adams is effective either. However, you happen to know that Adams has one of the toughest work groups to manage. Adams's subordinates have low skill levels, and the work is dirty and hard. If you lose Adams, you are not sure whom you could find as a replacement. *Salary: $40,000.*

$_____ *B. K. Berger.* Berger is single and seems to live a carefree lifestyle. In general, you feel that Berger's job performance is not up to par, and some of Berger's "goofs" are well known to the other employees. *Salary: $45,000.*

$_____ *C. C. Carter.* You consider Carter to be one of your best managers. However, it is quite apparent that other people don't agree. Carter has married into wealth and, as far you know, doesn't need additional money. *Salary: $49,200.*

$_____ *D. Davis.* You happen to know from your personal relationship that Davis badly needs more money because of certain personal problems. As far you are concerned, Davis also happens to be one of your best managers. For some reason, your enthusiasm is not shared by your other managers, and you have heard them make joking remarks about Davis's performance. *Salary: $45,400.*

$_____ *E. J. Ellis.* Ellis has been very successful so far. You are particularly impressed by this, since it is a hard job. Ellis needs money more than many of the other people and is respected for good performance. *Salary: $47,000.*

$_____ *F. M. Foster.* Foster has turned out to be a very pleasant surprise to you, has done an excellent job, and is seen by peers as one of the best people in your group. This surprises you because Foster is generally frivolous and doesn't seem to care very much about money and promotion. *Salary: $43,600.*

$_____ *G. K. Gomez.* Your opinion is that Gomez just isn't cutting the mustard. Surprisingly enough, however, when you check with others to see how they feel about Gomez, you discover that Gomez is very highly regarded. You also know that Gomez badly needs a raise. Gomez was just recently divorced and is finding it extremely difficult to support a house and a young family of four as a single parent. *Salary: $41,000.*

$_____ *H. A. Hunt.* You know Hunt personally. This employee seems to squander money continually. Hunt has a fairly easy job assignment, and your own view is that Hunt doesn't do it particularly well. You are, therefore, quite surprised to find that several of the other new managers think that Hunt is the best of the new group. *Salary: $42,000.*

Step 2: Form teams of three to five members each. Each team member should report his or her pay increase, and the team should reach consensus on a pay increase for the eight employees. Your team should justify these raises, explaining the criteria for these choices.

Step 3: Each team's results will be posted on the board. Class discussion will focus on differences in results, critiera used to affect pay raise decisions, and the behavioral effects of basing pay on factors chosen.

Source: Adapted from R. J. Lewicki, D. D. Bowen, Douglas T. Hall, and F. S. Hall, *Experiences in Management and Organizational Behavior*, 3rd ed. (New York: Wiley, 1988), pp. 49–51.

CASE EXERCISE

Lantech: Incentive Pay Ignites Gang Warfare

Lantech is a privately owned company of 325 employees that manufactures packaging machinery in Louisville, Kentucky. Founded in 1972, the company was a pioneer in incentive pay.

In the mid-1970s, workers were asked to rate one another's job performance, and bonuses were distributed accordingly. That program caused too much anxiety and was scrapped. But

the company's CEO, Pat Lancaster, was still determined to make incentive pay work. So he sought other incentive ideas.

At one point, each of the company's five manufacturing divisions was given a bonus determined by how much profit it made. Employees could earn up to 10 percent of their regular pay in bonus money. But the divisions are interdependent, so it was very difficult to sort out which was entitled to what profits. "That led to so much secrecy, politicking, and sucking noise that you wouldn't believe it," says the present CEO, Jim Lancaster, Pat's son. For example, the division that built standard machines and the one that added custom design features to those machines depended on each other for parts, engineering expertise, and such. So inevitably the groups clashed, each one trying to assign costs to the other and claim credit.

Pat recalls that, by the early 1990s, "I was spending 95 percent of my time on conflict resolution instead of on how to serve our customers." The divisions fought so long over who would get charged for overhead cranes to haul heavy equipment around the factory floor that Lantech couldn't install those useful machines until 1992, several years later than planned. At the end of each month, the divisions would rush to fill orders from other parts of the company. Such actions created profits for the divisions filling the order but generated piles of costly and unnecessary inventory in the receiving division. Some employees even argued over who would pay for the

toilet paper in the common restrooms. One person suggested that toilet paper costs should reflect the gender makeup of the division, on the questionable theory that one gender uses more tissue than the other.

Given all these problems, Lantech has abandoned individual and division performance pay.

QUESTIONS

1. What, if anything, did Lantech do wrong in setting up its incentive pay plan?
2. What suggestions would you make for a new incentive system?
3. What lessons could managers draw from this case?

Source: Based on P. Nulty, "Incentive Pay Can Be Crippling," *Fortune*, November 13, 1995, p. 235.

VIDEO CASE EXERCISE

Pedaling Your Way to Fame

ABCNEWS

Three weeks of constant pain and punishment that demands extreme levels of courage, endurance, and motivation. This is how participants in the Tour de France describe what they go through. It's called the greatest bicycle race in the world. It's a race in which every participant must be incredibly strong, have a signficant amount of courage, and possess a phenomenal endurance level.

The cyclists who race in the Tour belong to teams sponsored by commercial companies. These teams exist, however, to help their "star" win the race. Usually only one or two members of a team are capable of winning. The other riders are there to help them. They push the leaders to pick up the pace and support each other to keep going. Not surprisingly, the winner of the Tour traditionally donates the $400,000 prize to his teammates. However, the winner doesn't go home empty handed! Corporate sponsors pay their star athletes million dollar salaries, and a winner of the Tour stands to earn millions more in commercial endorsements.

What sets the Tour de France apart as one of the greatest sporting spectacles in the world and as a test of individual motivation and endurance? First of all, there's the speed. These bicyclists on two thin wheels can reach speeds of more than 60 miles an hour. One racer says that's the ultimate thrill—going fast. But, there's also the danger of a crash. The uncertainty and potential danger associated with speed and equipment failure

give participants the thrill of "living on the edge." However, what really sets the Tour apart is its almost inhuman test of endurance. For three weeks, the Tour rolls on and on through cities and small villages. The riders push themselves to the limit and sometimes beyond—through a race course that covers a total of 2,500 miles. Racers pedal up to 150 miles each day, six hours a day, until they reach the finish line in Paris. Some describe the experience to be like running a marathon, then getting up and having to run it again the next day, and the next, and so on. It takes enormous levels of athletic skill and stamina, as well as mental discipline and experience. It also takes knowing yourself very well. Successful racers must know their bodies, their state of mind, and what they can and cannot do. It's a challenge that those who participate in the race gladly take.

QUESTIONS

1. In this situation, what role does the team play in motivating extraordinary levels of performance from individuals? What implications can you see for managing?
2. Use expectancy theory to explain an individual's motivation to compete in the Tour de France.
3. Explain the motivation of Tour participants using (a) goal-setting theory, (b) reinforcement theory, and (c) pay-for-performance.

Source: Based on "Test of Courage—Tour de France," *ABC News Nightline*, July 21, 1994.

NOTES

1. D. Benjamin and T. Horwitz, "German View: 'You Americans Work Too Hard—and For What?'" *Wall Street Journal*, July 14, 1994, p. B1.

2. See, for instance, M. Blumberg and C. D. Pringle, "The Missing Opportunity in Organizational Research: Some Implications for a Theory of Work Performance," *Academy of Management Review*, October 1982, pp. 560–69; and J. Hall, "Americans Know How to Be Productive If Managers Will Let Them," *Organizational Dynamics*, Winter 1994, pp. 33–46.

3. S. Ratan, "Generational Tension in the Office: Why Busters Hate Boomers," *Fortune*, October 4, 1993, pp. 56–70; B. Filipczak, "It's Just a Job: Generation X at Work," *Training*, April 1994, pp. 21–27; and P. Sellers, "Don't Call Me Slacker!" *Fortune*, December 12, 1994, pp. 181–96.

4. See E. W. Miles, J. D. Hatfield, and R. C. Huseman, "The Equity Sensitive Construct: Potential Implications for Worker Performance," *Journal of Management*, December 1989, pp. 581–88; and R. T. Mowday, "Equity Theory Predictions of Behavior in Organizations," in R. M. Steers and L. W. Porter (eds), *Motivation and Work Behavior*, 5th ed. (New York: McGraw-Hill, 1991), pp. 111–31.

5. A study comparing the importance of work goals in seven countries found that interesting and challenging work was the overall preeminent goal. See I. Harpaz, "The Importance of Work Goals: An International Perspective," *Journal of International Business Studies*, First Quarter 1990, pp. 75–93.

6. Based on C. Pinder, *Work Motivation: Theory, Issues, and Applications* (Glenview, IL: Scott, Foresman, 1984).

7. A. Maslow, *Motivation and Personality* (New York: Harper & Row, 1954).

8. M. A. Wahba and L. G. Bridwell, "Maslow Reconsidered: A Review of Research on the Need Hierarchy Theory," *Organizational Behavior and Human Performance*, April 1976, pp. 212–40; and J. Rauschenberger, N. Schmitt, and J. E. Hunter, "A Test of the Need Hierarchy Concept by a Markov Model of Change in Need Strength," *Administrative Science Quarterly*, December 1980, pp. 654–70.

9. C. P. Alderfer, "An Empirical Test of a New Theory of Human Needs," *Organizational Behavior and Human Performance*, May 1969, pp. 142–75.

10. C. P. Schneider and C. P. Alderfer, "Three Studies of Measures of Need Satisfaction in Organizations," *Administrative Science Quarterly*, December 1973, pp. 489–505.

11. As described in G. Johns, *Organizational Behavior: Understanding and Managing Life at Work*, 4th ed. (New York: HarperCollins, 1996), p. 165.

12. H. A. Murray, *Explorations in Personality* (New York: Oxford University Press, 1938).

13. D. C. McClelland, *The Achieving Society* (New York: Van Nostrand Reinhold, 1961); D. C. McClelland, "Toward a Theory of Motive Acquisition," *American Psychologist*, May 1965, pp. 321–33; D. C. McClelland and D. G. Winter, *Motivating Economic Achievement* (New York: Free Press, 1969); D. C. McClelland, *Power: The Inner Experience* (New York: Irvington, 1975); and D. Miron and D. C. McClelland, "The Impact of Achievement Motivation Training on Small Businesses," *California Management Review*, Summer 1979, pp. 13–28.

14. McClelland, *The Achieving Society*.

15. McClelland and Winter, *Motivating Economic Achievement*.

16. McClelland, *Power*; D. C. McClelland and D. H. Burnham, "Power Is the Great Motivator," *Harvard Business Review*, March–April 1976, pp. 100–10; and R. E. Boyatzis, "The Need for Close Relationships and the Manager's Job," in D. A. Kolb, I. M. Rubin, and J. M. McIntyre, *Organizational Psychology: Readings on Human Behavior in Organizations*, 4th ed. (Upper Saddle River, NJ: Prentice Hall, 1984), pp. 81–86.

17. See note 16.

18. J. B. Miner, *Studies in Management Education* (New York: Springer, 1965).

19. D. Kipnis, "The Powerholder," in J. T. Tedeschi (ed), *Perspectives in Social Power* (Chicago: Aldine, 1974), pp. 82–123.

20. D. McGregor, *The Human Side of Enterprise* (New York: McGraw-Hill, 1960).

21. F. Herzberg, B. Mausner, and B. Snyderman, *The Motivation to Work* (New York: Wiley, 1959); and F. Herzberg, "One More Time: How Do You Motivate Employees?" *Harvard Business Review*, January–February 1968, pp. 54–63.

22. R. J. House and L. A. Wigdor, "Herzberg's Dual-Factor Theory of Job Satisfaction and Motivations: A Review of the Evidence and Criticism," *Personnel Psychology*, Winter 1967, pp. 369–89; D. P. Schwab and L. L. Cummings, "Theories of Performance and Satisfaction: A Review," *Industrial Relations*, October 1970, pp. 403–30; and R. J. Caston and R. Braito, "A Specification Issue in Job Satisfaction Research," *Sociological Perspectives*, April 1985, pp. 175–97.

23. E. A. Locke, "The Nature and Causes of Job Satisfaction," in M. D. Dunnette (ed), *Handbook of Industrial and Organizational Psychology* (Chicago: Rand McNally, 1976), pp. 1319–28.

24. E. A. Locke, "Toward a Theory of Task Motivation and Incentives," *Organizational Behavior and Human Performance*, May 1968, pp. 157–89.

25. G. P. Latham and G. A. Yukl, "A Review of Research on the Application of Goal Setting in Organizations," *Academy of Management Journal*, December 1975, pp. 824–45; E. A. Locke, K. N. Shaw, L. M. Saari, and G. P. Latham, "Goal Setting and Task Performance," *Psychological Bulletin*, January 1981, pp. 125–52; A. J. Mento, R. P. Steel, and R. J. Karren, "A Meta-Analytic Study of the Effects of Goal Setting on Task Performance: 1966–1984," *Organizational Behavior and Human Decision Processes*, February 1987, pp. 52–83; M. E. Tubbs, "Goal Setting: A Meta-Analytic Examination of the Empirical Evidence," *Journal of Applied Psychology*, August 1986, pp. 474–83; P. C. Earley, G. B. Northcraft, C. Lee, and T. R. Lituchy, "Impact of Process

and Outcome Feedback on the Relation of Goal Setting to Task Performance," *Academy of Management Journal*, March 1990, pp. 87–105; and E. A. Locke and G. P. Latham, *A Theory of Goal Setting and Task Performance* (Upper Saddle River, NJ: Prentice Hall, 1990).

26. J. M. Ivancevich and J. T. McMahon, "The Effects of Goal Setting, External Feedback, and Self-Generated Feedback on Outcome Variables: A Field Experiment," *Academy of Management Journal*, June 1982, pp. 359–72.

27. See, for example, G. P. Latham, M. Erez, E. A. Locke, "Resolving Scientific Disputes by the Joint Design of Crucial Experiments by the Antagonists: Application to the Erez-Latham Dispute Regarding Participation in Goal Setting," *Journal of Applied Psychology*, November 1988, pp. 753–72.

28. M. Erez, P. C. Earley, and C. L. Hulin, "The Impact of Participation on Goal Acceptance and Performance: A Two-Step Model," *Academy of Management Journal*, March 1985, pp. 50–66.

29. J. R. Hollenbeck, C. R. Williams, and H. J. Klein, "An Empirical Examination of the Antecedents of Commitment to Difficult Goals," *Journal of Applied Psychology*, February 1989, pp. 18–23. See also J. C. Wofford, V. L. Goodwin, and S. Premack, "Meta-Analysis of the Antecedents of Personal Goal Level and of the Antecedents and Consequences of Goal Commitment," *Journal of Management*, September 1992, pp. 595–615; and M. E. Tubbs, "Commitment as a Moderator of the Goal-Performance Relation: A Case for Clearer Construct Definition," *Journal of Applied Psychology*, February 1993, pp. 86–97.

30. A. Bandura, "Self-Efficacy: Toward a Unifying Theory of Behavioral Change," *Psychological Review*, May 1977, pp. 191–215; M. E. Gist, "Self-Efficacy: Implications for Organizational Behavior and Human Resource Management," *Academy of Management Review*, July 1987, pp. 472–85; and A. Bandura, *Self-Efficacy: The Exercise of Control* (New York: W. H. Freeman, 1997).

31. E. A. Locke, E. Frederick, C. Lee, and P. Bobko, "Effect of Self-Efficacy, Goals, and Task Strategies on Task Performance," *Journal of Applied Psychology*, May 1984, pp. 241–51; and M. E. Gist and T. R. Mitchell, "Self-Efficacy: A Theoretical Analysis of Its Determinants and Malleability," *Academy of Management Review*, April 1992, pp. 183–211.

32. A. Bandura and D. Cervone, "Differential Engagement in Self-Reactive Influences in Cognitively Based Motivation," *Organizational Behavior and Human Decision Processes*, August 1986, pp. 92–113.

33. R. M. Steers and L. W. Porter (eds), *Motivation and Work Behavior*, 2nd ed. (New York: McGraw-Hill, 1979), p. 13.

34. J. S. Adams, "Inequity in Social Exchanges," in L. Berkowitz (ed), *Advances in Experimental Social Psychology* (New York: Academic Press, 1965), pp. 267–300.

35. P. S. Goodman, "An Examination of Referents Used in the Evaluation of Pay," *Organizational Behavior and Human Performance*, October 1974, pp. 170–95; S. Ronen, "Equity Perception in Multiple Comparisons: A Field Study," *Human Relations*, April 1986, pp. 333–46; and T. P. Summers and A. S. DeNisi, "In Search of Adams' Other: Reexamination of Referents Used in the Evaluation of Pay," *Human Relations*, June 1990, pp. 497–511.

36. See, for example, E. Walster, G. W. Walster, and W. G. Scott, *Equity: Theory and Research* (Boston: Allyn & Bacon, 1978); and J. Greenberg, "Cognitive Reevaluation of Outcomes in Response to Underpayment Inequity," *Academy of Management Journal*, March 1989, pp. 174–84.

37. P. S. Goodman and A. Friedman, "An Examination of Adams' Theory of Inequity," *Administrative Science Quarterly*, September 1971, pp. 271–88; R. P. Vecchio, "An Individual-Differences Interpretation of the Conflicting Predictions Generated by Equity Theory and Expectancy Theory," *Journal of Applied Psychology*, August 1981, pp. 470–81; J. Greenberg, "Approaching Equity and Avoiding Inequity in Groups and Organizations," in J. Greenberg and R. L. Cohen (eds), *Equity and Justice in Social Behavior* (New York: Academic Press, 1982), pp. 389–435; E. W. Miles, J. D. Hatfield, and R. C. Huseman, "The Equity Sensitive Construct: Potential Implications for Worker Performance," *Journal of Management*, December 1989, pp. 581–88; and Mowday, "Equity Theory Predictions of Behavior in Organizations," pp. 111–31.

38. J. Greenberg and S. Ornstein, "High Status Job Title as Compensation for Underpayment: A Test of Equity Theory," *Journal of Applied Psychology*, May 1983, pp. 285–97; and J. Greenberg, "Equity and Workplace Status: A Field Experiment," *Journal of Applied Psychology*, November 1988, pp. 606–13.

39. V. H. Vroom, *Work and Motivation* (New York: Wiley, 1964).

40. See, for example, L. W. Porter and E. E. Lawler III, *Managerial Attitudes and Performance* (Homewood, IL: Richard D. Irwin, 1968); D. F. Parker and L. Dyer, "Expectancy Theory as a Within-Person Behavioral Choice Model: An Empirical Test of Some Conceptual and Methodological Refinements," *Organizational Behavior and Human Performance*, October 1976, pp. 97–117; P. M. Muchinsky, "A Comparison of Within- and Across-Subjects Analyses of the Expectancy-Valence Model for Predicting Effort," *Academy of Management Journal*, March 1977, pp. 154–58; H. J. Arnold, "A Test of the Multiplicative Hypothesis of Expectancy-Valence Theories of Work Motivation," *Academy of Management Journal*, April 1981, pp. 128–41; and W. Van Eerde and H. Thierry, "Vroom's Expectancy Models and Work-Related Criteria: A Meta-Analysis," *Journal of Applied Psychology*, October 1996, pp. 575–86.

41. See, for instance, W. J. Byron, "Coming to Terms with the New Corporate Contract," *Business Horizons*, January–February 1995, pp. 8–15.

42. M. P. Cronin, "One Life to Live," *Inc.*, July 1993, p. 57.

43. K. A. Dolan, "When Money Isn't Enough," *Forbes*, November 18, 1996, pp. 167–68.

44. Cronin, "One Life to Live;" and D. Hage and J. Impoco, "Jawboning for Jobs," *U.S. News & World Report*, August 9, 1993, p. 53.

45. "Motivating Temps," Inc., November 1996, p. 84.

46. Dolan, "When Money Isn't Enough," pp. 165, 168.

47. G. Fuchsberg, "Parallel Lines," *Wall Street Journal*, April 21, 1993, p. R4; and A. Penzias, "New Paths to Success," *Fortune*, June 12, 1995, pp. 90–94.

48. Hage and Impoco, "Jawboning for Jobs," p. 53.
49. R. Maynard, "How to Motivate Low-Wage Workers," *Nation's Business*, May 1997, pp. 35–39.
50. C. Yang, "Low-Wage Lessons," *Business Week*, November 11, 1996, pp. 108–16.
51. Cronin, "One Life to Live," pp. 56–60.
52. This French-American comparison is from P. R. Harris and R. T. Moran, *Managing Cultural Differences*, 4th ed. (Houston: Gulf Publishing, 1996), p. 319.
53. N. J. Adler, *International Dimensions of Organizational Behavior*, 3rd ed. (Cincinnati, OH: Southwestern, 1997), p. 158.
54. G. Hofstede, "Motivation, Leadership, and Organization: Do American Theories Apply Abroad?" *Organizational Dynamics*, Summer 1980, p. 55.
55. Ibid.
56. I. Harpaz, "The Importance of Work Goals: An International Perspective," *Journal of International Business Studies*, First Quarter 1990, pp. 75–93.
57. G. E. Popp, H. J. Davis, and T. T. Herbert, "An International Study of Intrinsic Motivation Composition," *Management International Review*, January 1986, pp. 28–35.
58. J. L. Cotton, *Employee Involvement* (Newbury Park, CA: Sage, 1993), pp. 3, 14.
59. Ibid., p. 3.
60. See, for instance, J. L. Pierce and C. A. Furo, "Employee Ownership: Implications for Management," *Organizational Dynamics*, Winter 1990, p. 32; and S. Kaufman, "ESOPs' Appeal on the Increase," Nation's Business, June 1997, pp. 43–44.
61. Based on J. Stack, *The Great Game of Business* (New York: Doubleday, 1992); and J. A. Byrne, "Management Meccas," *Business Week*, September 18, 1995, pp. 126–80.
62. See J. Case, *The Open-Book Experience* (Reading, MA: Addison-Wesley, 1997); T. R. V. Davis, "Open-Book Management: Its Promise and Pitfalls," *Organizational Dynamics*, Winter 1997, pp. 7–20; E. J. Stendardi and T. Tyson, "Maverick Thinking in Open-Book Firms: The Challenge for Financial Executives," *Business Horizons*, September–October 1997, pp. 35–40; and J. Case, "HR Learns How to Open the Books," *HRMagazine*, May 1998, pp. 71–76.
63. J. Case, "The Open-Book Revolution," *Inc.*, June 1995, p. 29.
64. A. B. Henderson, "Chrysler Cuts 1997 Executive Bonuses, Reflecting 20% Profit Drop Last Year," *Wall Street Journal*, April 20, 1998, p. B8.
65. S. E. Gross and J. P. Bacher, "The New Variable Pay Programs: How Some Succeed, Why Some Don't," *Compensation & Benefits Review*, January–February 1993, p. 52.
66. B. Wysocki Jr., "Unstable Pay Becomes Ever More Common," *Wall Street Journal*, December 4, 1995, p. A1.
67. Ibid.
68. M. Rowland, "For Each New Skill, More Money," *New York Times*, June 13, 1993, p. F16.
69. H. Gleckman, "Bonus Pay: Buzzword or Bonanza?" *Business Week*, November 14, 1994, p. 64.
70. These examples are cited in A. Gabor, "After the Pay Revolution, Job Titles Won't Matter," *New York Times*, May 17, 1992, p. F5; "Skill-Based Pay Boosts Worker Productivity and Morale," *Wall Street Journal*, June 23, 1992, p. A1; and L. Wiener, "No New Skills? No Raise," *U.S. News & World Report*, October 26, 1992, p. 78.
71. E. E. Lawler III, G. E. Ledford Jr., and L. Chang, "Who Uses Skill-Based Pay, and Why," *Compensation & Benefits Review*, March–April 1993, p. 22; and G. E. Ledford Jr., "Paying for the Skills, Knowledge, and Competencies of Knowledge Workers," *Compensation & Benefits Review*, July–August 1995, pp. 55–62.
72. M. Rowland, "It's What You Can Do That Counts," *New York Times*, June 6, 1993, p. F17.
73. Cited in K. Jacobs, "The Broad View," *Wall Street Journal*, April 10, 1997, p. R10.
74. See, for instance, D. Brown, "Broadbanding: A Study of Company Practices in the United Kingdom," *Compensation & Benefits Review*, November/December 1996, pp. 41–49.
75. K. H. Hammonds, "Work and Family," *Business Week*, September 15, 1997, pp. 96–99.
76. Based on R. G. Netemeyer, J. S. Boles, and R. McMurrian, "Development and Validation of Work-Family Conflict and Family-Work Conflict Scales," *Journal of Applied Psychology*, August 1996, pp. 400–10.
77. See, for instance, S. Nelton, "Adjusting Benefits for Family Needs," *Nation's Business*, August 1995, pp. 27–28; S. A. Lobel and E. E. Kossek, "Human Resource Strategies to Support Diversity in Work and Personal Lifestyle: Beyond the 'Family-Friendly' Organization," in E. E. Kossek and S. A. Lobel, *Managing Diversity* (Cambridge, MA: Blackwell, 1996), pp. 221–44; and M. N. Martinez, "An Inside Look at Making the Grade," *HRMagazine*, March 1998, pp. 61–66.
78. E. Klein, "Is Your Company Family-Friendly?" *Dun & Bradstreet Reports*, November–December 1991, p. 34.
79. Cited in M. A. Verespej, "People-First Policies," *Industry Week*, June 21, 1993, p. 20.
80. S. Shellenbarger, "Data Gap," *Wall Street Journal*, June 21, 1993, p. R6.
81. Hand and Zawacki, "Family-Friendly Benefits"; and R. Dogar, "Corporate Relief for Desperate Parents," *Working Woman*, March 1995, pp. 15–16.
82. Cited in S. Caudron, "The Top 20 Ways to Motivate Employees," *Industry Week*, April 3, 1995, p. 14.
83. Cited in B. Nelson, "Try Praise," *Inc.*, September 1996, p. 115.
84. "Look, Movie Tickets: With Budgets Tight, Alternatives to Pay Increases Emerge," *Wall Street Journal*, September 27, 1994, p. A1.
85. R. Maynard, "How to Motivate Low-Wage Workers."

BASIC ISSUES IN LEADERSHIP

IT OFTEN HAPPENS THAT I WAKE AT NIGHT AND BEGIN
TO THINK ABOUT A SERIOUS PROBLEM AND DECIDE I
MUST TELL THE POPE ABOUT IT. THEN I WAKE UP
COMPLETELY AND REMEMBER THAT *I AM THE POPE.*

POPE JOHN XXIII

LEARNING OBJECTIVES

After studying this chapter, you should be able to:

1. Contrast leadership and management.

2. Identify the five key variables that have shaped our understanding of leadership.

3. Explain what is meant by leadership effectiveness.

4. List the traits that have been found to regularly explain perceptions of leadership.

5. Describe the three primary leadership styles.

6. Explain the leader-participation model.

7. Describe the leader-member exchange model and its implications.

8. Contrast the Fiedler and path-goal models of leadership.

Hiroshi Okuda (see photo) is a leader who isn't afraid to speak his mind and impose radical change.[1] He sticks out at his company, Toyota, where, as president, he is the first nonfamily member in three decades to run the company. He also sticks out in Japan, where executives are supposed to blend into the woodwork. Okuda justifies his outspoken and aggressive style as necessary to change a company that has become lethargic and overly bureaucratic.

Okuda moved ahead at Toyota by taking jobs other people didn't want. In the early 1980s, for instance, the company was trying to build a plant in Taiwan. But the Taiwanese government's demands for high local content, technology transfer, and guaranteed exports convinced many at Toyota that the project should be dropped. Okuda thought otherwise. He successfully fought for the plant, and it's now highly profitable. "Everyone wanted to give up," says Okuda. "But I restarted the project and led it to success." It was this drive and ability to overcome obstacles that were central to his rise in Toyota's hierarchy.

When Okuda took over as president in early 1995, the company was losing market share at home to Mitsubishi and Honda. Okuda attributed this problem to several factors. Toyota had been losing touch with customers in its home market for several years. For instance, when engineers redesigned the Corolla in 1991, they made it too big and expensive. Then, four years later, they stripped out so many costs that the Corolla looked cheap. Competitors had also done a much better job at identifying the boom in recreational vehicles and developing product for that market niche. Toyota's burdensome bureaucracy, staffed with a lot of dead wood, additionally irked Okuda. It took Suzuki Motor Corp. just five minutes to convey a top executive's decision to the whole company, whereas it took weeks at Toyota.

In his first 18 months on the job, Okuda led a major shake-up at Toyota. In a country where lifetime employment is the norm and seniority is revered, he replaced a third of Toyota's highest-ranking executives with new managers. He revamped Toyota's long-standing promotion system based on seniority and added a new emphasis on merit. In many cases, Okuda promoted managers several levels, a previously unheard of action at Toyota. To further increase the amount of new blood in the managerial ranks, he also introduced a policy that strips general managers of their titles at age 55 and managers at age 50. They can stay on the payroll, but with reduced responsibilities.

To speed product development, Okuda instructed that vehicle designers be given a freer hand in reading the market and be less subject to input from market studies or the whims of top executives. He challenged engineers to complete their new models within 18 months instead of 27.

Okuda even established casual-dress days on Friday—in this least casual of companies—with the hope that employees might be more creative if they were more relaxed.

Finally, Okuda is using the visibility of his job to take the leadership on larger issues facing Japanese business. He's recently accused Japan's finance ministry of trying to destroy the auto industry by driving up the yen. And he has condemned the lax lending practices that forced Japanese banks to write off billions in bad loans.

It's too early to determine if all of Okuda's changes will pay off. However, without new leadership at the top, Toyota seemed to be destined to continue to lose market share to more aggressive competitors.

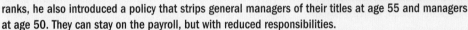

Successful organizations require leadership. But what is leadership? What differentiates effective leaders from ineffective leaders? In this chapter and in chapter 15, we will review what we have come to learn about leadership and provide you with some specific guidelines for selecting and training leaders.

| Few terms have stimulated as much debate about definition as *leadership* has. Everyone seems to agree about its importance. And experts generally agree that Bill Gates at Microsoft, Linda Wachner of Warnaco, Michael Eisner at Disney, and Richard Branson of the Virgin Group are effective leaders. But are leaders born or made? Do leaders have common personality characteristics? On questions such as these, there is little agreement. | **WHAT IS LEADERSHIP?** |

A review finds that common to all definitions of **leadership** is the notion that leaders are individuals who, by their actions, facilitate the movement of a group of people toward a common or shared goal.[2] This definition implies that leadership is an influence process.

The distinction between *leader* and *leadership* is important, but potentially confusing. The leader is the individual; leadership is the function or activity the individual performs. Do all leaders exercise leadership? It depends on what *you* mean by the term *leader*. The word *leader* is often used (interchangeably with the word *manager*) to describe those individuals in an organization who have positions of formal authority, regardless of how they actually act in those jobs. But just because someone is supposed to be a formal leader in an organization might not mean that he or she exercises leadership.

In fact, one of the most debated issues related to this topic is whether leadership is a different function and activity from management.[3] Do some formal leaders exercise leadership while others exercise management? Arguably, the best analysis of this question has been provided by Harvard's John Kotter.[4] He says that management is about coping with complexity. Good management brings about order and consistency by drawing up formal plans, designing organization structures, and monitoring results against the plans. Leadership, in contrast, is about coping with change. Leaders establish direction by developing a vision of the future; then they align people by communicating this vision and inspiring them to overcome hurdles. Kotter sees both strong leadership and strong management as necessary for optimum organizational effectiveness. But he believes that most organizations are underled and overmanaged. He claims we need to focus more on developing leadership in organizations because the people in charge today are too concerned with keeping things on time and on budget and with doing what was done yesterday, only doing it a little bit better.

In contrasting management and leadership, it may also help to think of the latter as involving the ability to inspire people. Management focuses on inanimate objects, whereas leadership focuses on raising human potential. Or, as the late Admiral Grace Murray Hopper put it, "You cannot manage men into battle. You manage things; you lead people."[5]

So we have learned that formal leaders—those in positions of authority—may exhibit behaviors that we would call leadership, but not in every case. On the other hand, we often use the word *leader* to describe people in organizations who are exhibiting leadership, even though they don't hold formal leader positions. These people are typically referred to as informal leaders, or **emergent leaders**. The discussion in this chapter and the next will encompass both formal and emergent leaders.

IDENTIFYING THE BASIC ISSUES IN LEADERSHIP

Leadership can best be understood by looking at its key variables: *leadership effectiveness, leader characteristics and style, follower characteristics, leader behavior,* and *leadership context* (see Exhibit 14-1). As you'll see, all the basic issues that have shaped the direction of leadership study in the last century can be subsumed within these five variables.

Our discussion in this chapter will begin with leadership effectiveness. This is, after all, the final test of whether a leader is successfully doing his or her job. Much of the difficulty in making generalizations about leadership is directly due to different definitions given to the term *leadership effectiveness.*

Then we move to the individual leader—specifically, his or her characteristics and style. This variable is central to almost all leadership frameworks because it is the individual leader who is at the heart of any leadership effort. Two issues directly address *leader characteristics.* First, do effective leaders have common traits that differentiate them from others? Second, does experience make leaders more effective? Two issues focus on *leader*

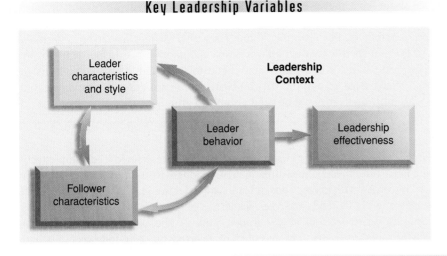

Key Leadership Variables

EXHIBIT 14-1

style: Do effective leaders use a common leadership style? And are leadership styles fixed, or can leaders change them to fit the situation? We also deal with the role of perceptions. Specifically, we answer the question, If someone can't *be* a leader, can he or she at least *look* like one?

Leaders can't be leaders without *followers*. Surprisingly, this self-evident truth was ignored until somewhat recently. So we need to take a look at the role of followership. Do followers really matter? What characteristics of followers seem to be important? Can great leadership overcome mediocre followers? Do leaders treat all followers alike?

The next variable brings leader characteristics and style and follower characteristics together to discuss choices leaders face about the *behaviors* they should exhibit. Our focus is to find whether there is something unique in the way effective leaders behave. How do follower characteristics influence the effectiveness of a leader's style? How much should leaders involve followers in their decisions? Answers to these questions look more closely at interaction—and fit—*between* the leader and the follower.

Finally, the *leadership context* influences not only what leadership characteristics and style, follower characteristics, and leader behavior emerge, but it also affects whether a particular leader will be effective. An overwhelming amount of evidence demonstrates that leader actions that work well under *some* circumstances don't necessarily work well under *all* circumstances. And in some situations, leadership doesn't seem to have much effect at all on a group's goal efforts. Specifically, we'll address two issues: What situational variables might make a leader effective sometimes and ineffective other times? And under what conditions are leaders relatively unimportant?

LEADERSHIP EFFECTIVENESS

In chapter 2, we described the problems in defining organizational effectiveness. Studies of leadership too have been guilty of using inconsistent definitions of effectiveness. Part of the trouble, undoubtedly, is due to the fact that leaders have to do different things to be effective. It may also reflect different interests of researchers.

Our concern may seem inconsequential—relevant to researchers but not to practitioners—but it isn't! Why? Because the quality of any generalizations we are able to stipulate about what makes an effective leader depends heavily on the quality of leadership research used to draw those generalizations and the consistency of definitions used by those researchers. For example, if one researcher defines leadership effectiveness in terms of how satisfied individual followers are, and another researcher defines it in terms of group productivity, it becomes very difficult to make any generalizations about what makes an effective leader. Productivity and satisfaction are different outcomes. And what works with individuals may not be generalizable to groups.

A review of the leadership literature finds researchers using at least five different ways of assessing effectiveness.

1. *Objective versus perceptual measures.* Some studies have defined leadership effectiveness using hard and objective measures such as productivity. Others, however, have merely been concerned with perceptions of leadership effectiveness. In other words, do followers say that an individual *looks* like a leader?

2. *Acceptance versus rejection of the leader.* Some studies have defined effectiveness in terms of whether leaders are accepted or rejected by their followers. No hard performance measures are utilized. A leader who is accepted by the followers is considered to be effective.

3. *Individual versus group performance measures.* Although most studies emphasize performance outcomes, they are not uniform in whether they measure the leader's effect on individual performance or on group performance. The focus on different levels can create very different and noncomparable outcomes.

4. *Productivity versus satisfaction.* Some studies have emphasized follower or group satisfaction rather than productivity. The actions a leader takes to increase productivity may be very different from the actions that would increase satisfaction.

5. *Level of analysis.* Most studies focus on the leader's influence on his or her group. Others, however, focus on the organization or even on specific societies. When we say that a Jack Welch at GE or a George W. Bush in the Texas state house is an effective leader, we are using organizational-level measures of effectiveness. And when the discussion centers on the effectiveness of presidents or prime ministers, the level of analysis jumps to how well they lead their countries.

It isn't our intention to suggest an easy synthesis of these differences. Rather, we have introduced the issue to make two points. First, leadership effectiveness is important. It is the ultimate critierion upon which we determine whether a leader succeeds or fails. Second, the people who study leadership have not defined effectiveness in a consistent manner. So care needs to be taken in making generalizations about what contributes to leadership effectiveness.

As you proceed through this and the following chapter, we'll repeatedly refer to leadership effectiveness. And when we do, we'll attempt to clarify how the researchers defined the term, along with their research evidence.

LEADER CHARACTERISTICS AND STYLE

Every 4 years, Americans vote to elect a president. Since 1960, these elections have been preceded by widely televised debates. Presidential candidates spend 90 minutes or so discussing issues, responding to questions, and trying to "look presidential." Looking good in this "beauty contest" is viewed by the candidates and their staffs as critical to a campaign's success. The losses by Richard Nixon (1960), Gerald Ford (1976), and Michael Dukakis (1988) are often attributed to their inability to project the leadership traits that the television audience was looking for in their next president.[6] Voters seem to look for certain

Many political experts believe that Richard Nixon lost the 1960 presidential election because he came across as stoic and rigid in his televised debate with John F. Kennedy.

leader characteristics in their presidents—such as confidence, determinedness, decisiveness, and trustworthiness—and they use the debates as an important indicator of whether candidates have those characteristics.

Debates may be a poor means for assessing leadership traits, but the question still remains: Do effective presidents have common traits? The American voting public seems to think so. Since presidents are chosen for their leadership qualities, let's broaden the question to look at all leaders. Specifically, what traits, if any, differentiate leaders from nonleaders or effective from ineffective leaders?

Do Leaders Have Common Traits?

The media have long believed that leaders share common traits. They identify people such as South Africa's Nelson Mandela, Virgin Group CEO Richard Branson, Apple co-founder Steve Jobs, New Jersey governor Christine Todd Whitman, U.K. prime minister Tony Blair, and General Colin Powell as leaders and then describe them in terms such as *charismatic*, *enthusiastic*, and *courageous*. Well, the media aren't alone. The search for personality, social, physical, and intellectual attributes that would describe leaders and differentiate them from nonleaders has been going on among management and leadership researchers for more than half a century.[7]

A full review of the evidence leads us to the familiar good news–bad news scenario. First the good news. A number of traits seem to regularly appear that differentiate leaders from others. These include ambition and energy, the desire to lead, self-confidence, and intelligence.[8] In addition, there is strong evidence that people who are high self-monitors (see chapter 12)—that is, highly flexible in adjusting their behavior in different situations—are much more likely to emerge as leaders in groups than are low self-monitors.[9] Overall, it appears that these traits are relatively powerful at explaining people's perceptions of leadership.[10]

Now for the bad news. First, traits provide no guarantees. Rather than being applicable across *all* situations, they appear to predict leadership in *selective* situations.[11] Second, traits predict behavior more in "weak" situations than in "strong" situations.[12] Strong situations are those in which there are strong behavioral norms, strong incentives for specific types of behaviors, and clear expectations as to what behaviors are rewarded and punished. Such strong situations create less opportunity for leaders to express their inherent

| In The News | ## Jack Welch at GE: A Leader's Leader |

Jack Welch, CEO at General Electric, is near the top of everyone's list of the best leaders in corporate America. In *Industry Week's* 1996 survey of his peers, he was rated as the "most respected CEO." This was the third time since 1993 that he had received this honor.

What differentiates Jack Welch from less effective leaders? Part of the answer is that he, himself, dedicates a major part of his time to developing executive talent at GE. "My most important job is to choose and develop business leaders who are bright enough to grasp the elements of their game, creative enough to develop a simple vision, and self-confident enough to liberate and inspire people," Welch says. So Jack Welch is not only a leader—he also successfully builds leaders.

Welch believes a good leader must have situational flexibility. Effective leaders can't be rigidly locked into a way of behaving or a source of information. He also believes leaders can't operate without a moral compass. That's why he has established a set of "management values" to guide leaders in the company. At GE, leaders:

▶ Create a clear, simple, reality-based, customer-focused vision and are able to communicate it straightforwardly to all constituencies.

▶ Set aggressive goals and recognize and reward progress, while understanding accountability and commitment.

▶ Have a passion for excellence and hate bureaucracy and all the nonsense that comes with it.

▶ Have the self-confidence to empower others and behave in a boundaryless fashion and are open to ideas from anywhere.

▶ Have, or have the capacity to develop global brains and global sensitivity, and are comfortable building diverse and global teams.

▶ Have enormous energy and the ability to energize and invigorate others, stimulate and relish change, and see change as an opportunity not a threat.

▶ Possess a mindset that drives quality, cost, and speed for a competitive advantage.

Welch's record at creating leaders is stunning. The list of ex-GE executives that have gone on to successful CEO roles with other companies include: Lawrence Bossidy, AlliedSignal Inc.; Stanley Gault, Goodyear Tire & Rubber Co.; Glen Hiner, Owens Corning Inc.; Norman Blake, USF&G Corp.; Harry Stonecipher, McDonnell Douglas Corp.; and Michael Lockhart, General Signal Corp.

Source: Based on T. Stevens, "Follow the Leader," *Industry Week*, November 18, 1996, p. 16.

dispositional tendencies. Since highly formalized organizations and those with strong cultures fit the description of strong situations, the power of traits to predict leadership in many organizations is probably limited. Third, the evidence is unclear in separating cause from effect. For example, are leaders self-confident, or does success as a leader build self-confidence? Finally, traits do a better job at predicting the appearance of leadership than in actually distinguishing between *effective* and *ineffective* leaders.[13] That an individual exhibits the traits and that others consider that person to be a leader does not necessarily mean that the "leader" is successful at getting his or her group to achieve its goals. Remember, as we noted earlier, having a leader doesn't automatically mean having effective leadership.

Does Experience Make Leaders More Effective?

Those same American voters who are looking for leadership traits also assume that there is a relationship between experience and effectiveness. Presidential candidates typically have been U.S. senators or state governors. Why? Voters tend to believe that these jobs prepare individuals to be effective presidents.

This belief in the power of experience is very strong and widespread. Organizations, for instance, carefully screen outside candidates for senior management positions on the basis of their experience. Similarly, organizations usually require several years of service at one managerial level before a person can be considered for promotion. And have you ever filled out an employment application that *didn't* ask about previous experience or job history? In many instances, experience is the single most important factor in hiring and promotion decisions.[14] Obviously, organizations attribute considerable importance to experience. But does experience translate into leader effectiveness? The answer may surprise you.

Experience per se doesn't seem to necessarily contribute to leadership effectiveness. "Some inexperienced leaders have been outstandingly successful, while many experienced leaders have been outstanding failures. Among the most highly regarded former presidents are Abraham Lincoln and Harry Truman, who had very little previous leadership experience, while the highly experienced Herbert Hoover and Franklin Pierce were among the least successful."[15] Studies of military officers, research and development teams, shop supervisors, post office administrators, and school principals indicate that experienced managers tend to be no more effective than the managers with little experience.[16] How could this be? Doesn't experience create learning opportunities that would translate into improved on-the-job leadership skills? The problems seem to be twofold. First, quality of experience and time in the job are not necessarily the same thing. Second, there is variability between situations that influence the transferability of experience.

Most studies that have looked at the experience-performance relationship have used length of time on the job (tenure) as the measure of experience. However, the relationship has been found to be considerably stronger when experience is defined as the number of times an individual has performed a given task and the variety of tasks he or she has performed.[17] The fact that one person has 20 years' experience while another has two years' says nothing about the quality of that experience. As the old joke goes, "He doesn't have twenty years' experience. He has one year of experience twenty times!"

The situation in which experience is obtained is rarely comparable to new situations. But this fact is rarely taken into account in leadership selection. It's true that past behavior is the best predictor of future behavior; perhaps that is why experience is so popular as a selection criterion. But it is critical to take into consideration the *relevance* of past experience to a new situation. Jobs differ, support resources differ, organizational cultures differ, follower characteristics differ, and so on. A primary reason that leadership experience isn't strongly related to leadership performance is undoubtedly due to variability of situations. However, where previous experience has been in substantially similar situations, and that experience is qualitatively relevant, past leadership experience should be a reasonably good predictor of future leadership performance.

Do Effective Leaders Use a Common Leadership Style?

Mark Willes, CEO at Times-Mirror Corp. and former head of General Mills (where he was known as "the Cereal Killer"), has been very successful in leading his companies through difficult times.[18] And his leadership style? Tough-talking, intense, autocratic. Does this

Mark Willes, CEO at publisher Times-Mirror, has developed a successful leadership record, but there is nothing subtle about his style. He has no qualms making tough decisions—like closing unprofitable operations or laying off hundreds of employees.

suggest that autocratic behavior is a preferred style for *all* leaders? Maybe not! Bob Eaton, former CEO at Chrysler, used a very different style.[19] This soft-spoken leader purposely avoided making major product decisions. He delegated those decisions to teams. The result was a string of hot cars and record earnings.

How many behavioral options do leaders have? And what is the relationship between these various options and leadership effectiveness?

STYLE OPTIONS Numerous efforts have been made to identify the primary dimensions of leader behavior. Studies typically emphasize just a few, and rarely does the list extend beyond four. A careful review finds that there seems to be considerable convergence around two dimensions: task-oriented behavior and people-oriented behavior.[20] And, as we will show, there is encouraging new evidence indicating the importance of a third dimension—development-oriented behavior.

The case for a **two-dimensional view of leadership behavior**—one focusing on tasks and the other on people—can be traced back to the late 1940s. Independent work at Ohio State University and the University of Michigan found that two categories substantially accounted for most of the leadership behavior described by subordinates.[21] The *task* dimension refers to actions such as emphasizing the accomplishment of group goals, defining and structuring group-member work assignments, and emphasizing the meeting of deadlines. The *people* dimension encompasses actions such as developing good interpersonal relationships, being friendly and approachable, and being concerned with workers' personal problems.

Looking at leadership style along two dimensions was popularized for leadership training in the 1960s by way of a graph called the **managerial grid**.[22] As shown in Exhibit 14-2, the managerial grid depicts "concern for people" and "concern for production" (which is synonymous with a task focus) on separate axes. The grid has nine possible positions along each axis, creating eighty-one different positions in which a leader's style may fall. Proponents of the grid focus their attention at its extremes—1,1; 1,9; 9,1; and 9,9—and claim that the most effective leaders use a 9,9 style. From a training perspective, grid advocates test individuals to find their inherent leadership style and, if it is less than 9,9, try to get them to move toward the northeastern corner of the grid.

The search to identify the primary behavioral dimensions of leadership evolved during a time—nearly 50 years ago—when the world was a far more stable and predictable place. In the belief that a task-people focus might be dated and fail to capture the more dynamic realities of today, researchers have conducted updated studies.[23] What they have found is that, in addition to task and people dimensions, there is a third style that effective leaders exhibit. This is **development-oriented behavior**—characterized by experimentation, originating new approaches to problems, pushing new ways of doing things, and encouraging change.

STYLE EFFECTIVENESS The evidence is mixed on the relationship between leadership style and group effectiveness.[24] For instance, a strong people focus generally results in high job satisfaction. But not always. Similarly, a strong task focus often leads to high productivity, but it also leads to greater rates of grievances, absenteeism, turnover, and lower job satisfaction. The evidence just doesn't allow us to generalize across a variety of workers, jobs, organizational cultures, and countries. In fact, in organizations whose culture heavily emphasizes aggressiveness, end results, and downplays the importance of people, leaders who rate high on people orientation are likely to get negative performance ratings by their superiors and not survive the long-term.

The Managerial Grid

EXHIBIT 14-2

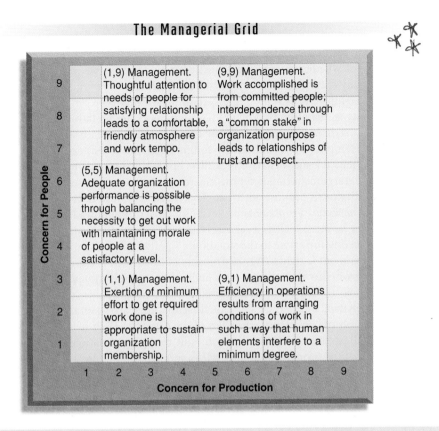

(1,9) Management. Thoughtful attention to needs of people for satisfying relationship leads to a comfortable, friendly atmosphere and work tempo.

(9,9) Management. Work accomplished is from committed people; interdependence through a "common stake" in organization purpose leads to relationships of trust and respect.

(5,5) Management. Adequate organization performance is possible through balancing the necessity to get out work with maintaining morale of people at a satisfactory level.

(1,1) Management. Exertion of minimum effort to get required work done is appropriate to sustain organization membership.

(9,1) Management. Efficiency in operations results from arranging conditions of work in such a way that human elements interfere to a minimum degree.

Concern for People

Concern for Production

The initial evidence relating to development-oriented behavior is encouraging. We find that leaders who demonstrate development-oriented behavior have satisfied subordinates and are seen as competent by those subordinates.[25] There is additional evidence demonstrating the increasing importance of development-oriented behavior.[26] The ability of leaders to adapt and develop in the face of change is more important now than ever before.

The managerial grid is more useful as a framework for conceptualizing leadership style than as a guide for managers. The reason is that there is little substantive evidence to support the conclusion that a 9,9 style is most effective in all situations.[27]

The missing links in the work on leadership styles have been follower characteristics and contextual factors. What works well with construction workers may not work with a team of research scientists. And a style that is highly effective and receives rave reviews in one organizational culture can be disastrous in another. Should you expect there to be a common effective leadership style that would embrace organizations as diverse as Exxon, Friends of the Earth, the Irish Republican Army, the Bank of England, the Christian Coalition, Intel, and The Body Shop? Clearly, follower characteristics and contextual factors need to be added to the equation if leadership styles are to be meaningful.

Are Leadership Styles Fixed?

The question of whether leaders can adjust their leadership style or whether leadership style is essentially fixed is an ongoing debate. On one hand, some argue that style is fixed.[28] They see leadership style as reflecting a certain personality type. And just as an individual's personality is relatively fixed before reaching his or her tenth birthday, it is assumed that leadership style is similarly fixed. Any changes will take place within a very narrow range. If, for example, you are inherently comfortable with a task-oriented style, you will rely on task-oriented leader behavior regardless of the situation or conditions.

The counterargument builds on the inherent flexibility of human beings to adjust to changing conditions. It proposes that people are free to choose their leadership style and can alter it as needed.[29] Proponents of flexibility recognize that leaders will undoubtedly tend to favor or be more skilled in certain behaviors, but they contend that people are still capable of adjusting their style to the situation.

Which argument is right? They're probably both correct! It depends on the leader—specifically, on whether that person rates high or low on self-monitoring.[30] As we know, individuals differ in their behavioral flexibility. Some people show considerable ability to adjust their behavior to external, situational factors; they are adaptable. Others, however, exhibit high levels of consistency regardless of the situation. High self-monitors are generally able to adjust their leadership style to suit changing situations. Unfortunately, we don't know what the proportion of high self-monitors is among the population. If we did, we could better directly answer the question of whether leadership style is fixed or not.

If You Can't *Be* a Leader, Can You at Least *Look* Like One?

In our discussion of leadership traits, we noted that traits predict the *appearance* of leadership better than distinguishing between actual effectiveness and ineffectiveness. Given that leadership outcomes aren't always objective, we should consider the issue of leader attributions. Specifically, we want to show how attribution theory (discussed in chapter 12) can help explain the perception of leadership, or "What can you do to *look* like a leader?"

Attribution theory, as you remember, deals with the ways in which people try to make sense out of cause-and-effect relationships. When something happens, they want to attribute it to something else. In the context of leadership, attribution theory says that leadership is merely an attribution that people make about other individuals.[31] The attribution framework has shown that people characterize leaders as having such traits as intelligence, outgoing personality, strong verbal skills, aggressiveness, understanding, and industriousness.[32] Similarly, the high-high leader (high on both task and people dimensions) has been found to be consistent with attributions of what makes a good leader.[33] That is, regardless of the situation, a high-high leadership style tends to be perceived as best. At the organizational level, the attribution framework accounts for the conditions under which people use leadership to explain organizational outcomes. Those conditions are extremes in organizational performance. When an organization has either extremely negative or extremely positive performance, people are prone to make leadership attributions to explain the performance.[34] This tendency helps to account for the vulnerability of CEOs when their organizations suffer a major financial setback, regardless of whether they had much to do with it. It also accounts for why these CEOs tend to be given credit for extremely positive financial results—again, regardless of how much or how little they contributed.

One of the more interesting findings in the **attribution model of leadership** literature is the perception that effective leaders are generally considered consistent or unwavering in their decisions.[35] That is, one of the explanations for why Ronald Reagan (during his first term as president) was perceived as a leader was that he was fully committed, steadfast, and consistent in the decisions he made and the goals he set. It can also help explain some of the criticism regularly targeted at President Bill Clinton. He is seen by many as "wishy-washy" on the issues and as someone who continually changes his mind.

What are the practical implications of these findings for individuals who want to be leaders? Do what you can to help foster the perception that you are smart, personable, verbally adept, aggressive, understanding, and hard-working. Focus your behavior on emphasizing both tasks and people. And maintain the appearance of consistency.

When someone was once asked what it took to be a great leader, he responded, "Great followers!" Although this response may have seemed sarcastic, it has some truth.

FOLLOWER CHARACTERISTICS

▶ Do Followers Really Matter?

Followers are important in the leadership equation because: (1) They differ in the qualities they bring to the job and therefore require adjustments by leaders; and (2) there is evidence that "good" followers exhibit common characteristics that make it easier for leaders to succeed. In addition, focusing on followers makes increasing sense today, as organizations flatten hierarchies and introduce self-managed teams. Followers have become more important as they have gained increased autonomy and accountability.[36]

▶ What Characteristics of Followers Seem to Be Important?

Studies have found that certain follower characteristics influence the actions of leaders. These include the follower's locus-of-control personality dimension, experience, and perceived ability.[37] For instance:

- Followers with an internal locus of control (those who believe that they control their own destiny) will be most satisfied with a participative leadership style. Those with an external locus of control will be most satisfied with a directive style.
- A task-oriented style of leadership is likely to be perceived negatively by followers with considerable experience. They already know what needs to be done and how to do it, so they see the task-oriented behavior as redundant or even insulting. Conversely, followers with minimal experience tend to appreciate the structure and guidance provided by task-oriented leadership.
- Followers who perceive that they have strong abilities are likely to view task-oriented leadership negatively. They consider such behavior as demeaning to their abilities.
- Followers who lack both ability and motivation need clear and specific directions. Followers who have ability but lack motivation will perform best with a supportive, nondirective, participative style of leadership.

In addition, the quality of the leader-member relationship has been found to be important.[38] For instance, when followers have a high degree of confidence, trust, and respect for their leader, they are more willing to accept a task-oriented approach. When

EXHIBIT 14-3

leader-member relations are poor, a task-oriented approach is very likely to lead to reduced group performance.

Since leadership is the process of helping people achieve a common goal, to the degree that followers have certain qualities, leaders are more likely to be effective. We find that effective followers have these common qualities:[39]

1. *They manage themselves well.* Effective followers are able to think for themselves. They can work independently and without close supervision.
2. *They are committed to a purpose outside themselves.* Effective followers are committed to something—a cause, a product, a work team, an organization, an idea—in addition to the care of their own lives. Most people like working with colleagues who are emotionally, as well as physically, committed to their work.
3. *They build their competence and focus their efforts for maximum impact.* Effective followers master skills that will be useful to their organizations, and they hold higher performance standards than their job or work group requires.
4. *They are courageous, honest, and credible.* Effective followers establish themselves as independent, critical thinkers whose knowledge and judgment can be trusted. They hold high ethical standards, give credit where credit is due, and aren't afraid to admit their mistakes.

▶ Can Great Leadership Overcome Mediocre Followers?

Even if we acknowledge that effective followers can make effective leaders, we still run into cause-and-effect issues. It may be that effective followers result from effective leaders. In fact, leaders who are development-oriented might be likely to turn mediocre followers into effective followers over time!

The attitudes and behaviors of followers are not fixed. Followers can and do respond to the actions of their leaders. So individuals with superior leadership skills—what we call transformational or outstanding leadership in the next chapter—can successfully inspire mediocre followers and transform them into effective followers.

▶ Do Leaders Treat All Followers Alike?

Think about your experiences in groups. Did you notice that leaders often act very differently toward different subordinates? Did the leader tend to have favorites who made up his or her "in" group? If you answered yes to these questions, you are confirming what an increasing amount of evidence supports—leaders *don't* treat everyone alike![40]

Leaders almost always differentiate among subordinates. The result is a dichotomization of in-group and out-group members.[41] Leaders establish a special relationship with a small set of their subordinates who make up the in-group—they are trusted, get a disproportionate amount of the leader's attention, and are likely to receive special privileges. Other subordinates fall into the out-group. They get less of the leader's time, fewer of the preferred rewards that the leader controls, and have superior-subordinate relations based on formal authority interactions. This is called the **leader-member exchange model**.

Apparently, early in the history of the interaction between a leader and a given subordinate, the leader implicitly categorizes the subordinate as an "in" or an "out," and that relationship holds relatively steady over time.[42] Just precisely how the leader chooses who falls into each category is unclear, but there is evidence that leaders tend to choose in-group members because they have attitude and personality characteristics that are similar to the leader's or a higher level of competence than out-group members.[43] (See Exhibit 14-4 on page 454.) A key point to note here is that even though it is the leader who is doing the choosing, it is the follower's characteristics that are driving the leader's categorizing decision.

Overall, there is substantial evidence that leaders do differentiate among subordinates; that these disparities are far from random; and that subordinates with in-group status will have higher performance ratings, lower turnover intentions, greater satisfaction with their superior, and higher overall satisfaction than will the out-group.[44] These positive findings for in-group members shouldn't be totally surprising given our knowledge of the self-fulfilling prophecy (see chapter 12). Leaders invest their resources with those they expect to perform best. And "knowing" that in-group members are most competent, leaders treat them as such and unwittingly fulfill their prophecy.[45]

◀ LEADER BEHAVIOR

In addition to traits and experience, the behavior of a leader is a critical factor in determining overall leadership effectiveness (see Exhibit 14-1, page 443). Let's begin our look at leader behavior by considering the various styles that leaders can exhibit.

EXHIBIT 14-4

EXHIBIT 14-4 — **Leader-Member Exchange Model**

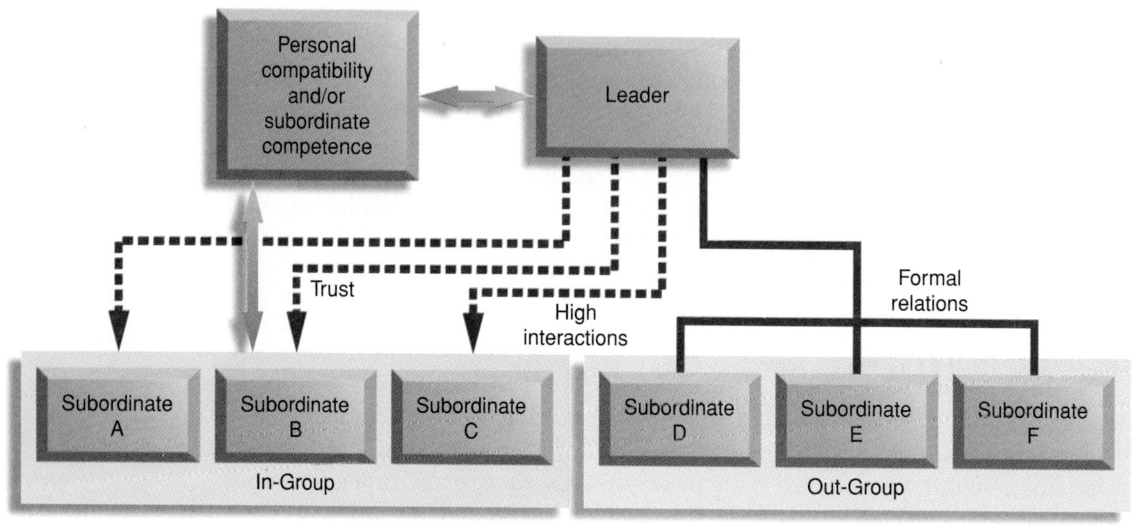

How Do Follower Characteristics Influence the Effectiveness of a Leader's Style?

We've already shown how follower characteristics influence the effectiveness of a leader's style. We identified three styles that leaders tended to exhibit: task-oriented, people-oriented, development-oriented, or some combination of the three. We also said that these styles might not be fixed, but rather that leaders could make decisions about which style to use. As also previously noted, studies have found that certain follower characteristics appear to influence the leader's choice of style. These include the follower's personality, experience, ability, and motivation.[46]

How Much Involvement Should Followers Be Given?

Leaders need to determine how much involvement they should allow followers to have in the group's decision-making process. For instance, at one extreme, the leader can make the decision by herself, without any consultation with others in the group. Or, at the other extreme, she could turn the decision over completely to the group and empower them to make the choice.

The most comprehensive and meaningful framework for dealing with this issue is the **leader-participation model**.[47] It provides a set of rules for leaders to follow in determining the amount and form of participative decision making that should be encouraged in different situations.

The model identifies five leadership behaviors. As we describe each, note that they progressively trade off leader control for increased employee involvement (see Exhibit 14-5).

The leader-participation model can guide leaders in choosing how much involvement they should allow followers to have in the decision-making process.

1. The leader makes the decision alone.
2. The leader asks for information from group members but makes the decision alone. Group members may or may not be informed as to what the situation is.
3. The leader shares the situation with each group member individually and asks for information and evaluation. Members do not meet as a group, and the leader alone makes the decision.
4. The leader and group members meet to discuss the situation, but the leader makes the decision.
5. The leader and group members meet to discuss the situation, and the group makes the decision.

Which of the five styles should a leader use? The evidence indicates that eight situational variables should guide the leader: (1) the quality of the decision, (2) the importance of subordinate commitment to the decision, (3) whether the leader has sufficient information, (4) how well structured the problem is, (5) whether subordinates would still be committed to the decision if the leader made the decision alone, (6) the degree to which subordinates share the organizational goals to be attained in solving the problem, (7) whether there is conflict among subordinates over preferred solutions, and (8) whether subordinates have sufficient information to make a high-quality decision.

Employee-Involvement Continuum

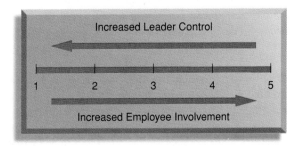

Increased Leader Control

1   2   3   4   5

Increased Employee Involvement

EXHIBIT 14-5

A substantial amount of evidence supports the following general propositions.[48] Leaders should increase group participation when:

- They lack sufficient information to solve a problem by themselves.
- The problem is unclear, and help is needed to clarify the situation.
- Acceptance of the decision by others is necessary for its successful implementation.
- Adequate time is available to allow for true participation.

On the other hand, leaders should maintain control and rely on more unilateral behaviors when:

- They personally have the expertise needed to solve the problem.
- They are confident and capable of acting alone.
- Others are likely to accept the decision they make.
- Little or no time is available for discussion.

In summary, since leaders actually lead followers, leadership effectiveness is influenced by how well the two parties interact. Leaders have to make decisions about the style they will exhibit to the followers, along with the amount of interaction in decision making they will promote. Understanding how the follower's characteristics influence those leader-behavior choices brings leaders a step closer to being effective.

LEADERSHIP CONTEXT

It seems as if almost every time we try to make a definitive conclusion on some leadership issue, we have to qualify our statement to reflect one or more situational factors. It is obvious that the effect of a leader's traits and behavior, as well as follower characteristics, on a group's performance almost always depends on the context in which leadership is happening. Many of these situational factors have already shown up at numerous points throughout this chapter, since it's almost impossible to draw meaningful conclusions about leadership concepts without taking the situation into account. In this section, we identify the more potent elements of this context and also consider those conditions under which formal leaders take on minimal importance.

Leadership needs to reflect the situation. Military battles almost always call for autocratic, hierarchical leadership. In contrast, research groups tend to be more effective under democratic leadership.

What Situational Factors Influence Leader Effectiveness?

Several leadership models have sought to identify the key situational factors in leadership effectiveness. Because these models often include follower characteristics and contextual factors, they could actually be described as integrative approaches to leadership effectiveness. But, in this section, our interest is with situational factors. So we look at these models from that perspective. Then we briefly review a couple of additional studies that suggest other pertinent situational factors.

THE FIEDLER MODEL The first comprehensive attempt to develop a situational approach to leadership was presented by Fred Fiedler in the mid-1960s.[49] The **Fiedler leadership model** proposed that effective group performance depends on the proper match between the leader's style and the degree to which the situation gives control and influence to the leader. From our perspective, we are specifically interested in the situational variables he identified that provided control to the leader.

Fiedler identified three variables that, he argued, determine leadership effectiveness. The first variable, leader-member relations, we have discussed already. Fiedler combined this variable with task structure and position power. They are all defined as follows:

1. *Leader-member relations.* The degree of confidence, trust, and respect subordinates have in their leader. (Rated as either good or poor.)
2. *Task structure.* The degree to which the subordinate's job assignments are structured. (Rated as either high or low.)
3. *Position power.* The degree of influence a leader has over variables such as hiring, firing, discipline, promotions, and salary increases. (Rated as either strong or weak.)

Fiedler stated that the better the leader-member relations, the more highly structured the job, and the stronger the position power, the more control or influence the leader will have. For example, a very favorable situation (in which the leader would have a great deal of control) might involve a payroll manager who is well respected and whose subordinates have confidence in her (good leader-member relations); where the activities to be done—such as wage computation, check writing, report filing—are specific and clear (high task structure); and the job provides considerable freedom for her to reward and punish her subordinates (strong position power). On the other hand, an unfavorable situation might be the disliked chairman of a voluntary United Way fund-raising team. In this job, the leader has very little control. Altogether, by mixing the three contingency variables, there are potentially eight different situations or categories in which leaders can find themselves.

Fiedler studied over 1,200 groups. He compared people- versus task-oriented leadership styles in each of the eight situational categories, and he concluded that task-oriented leaders tend to perform better than people-oriented leaders in situations that are *very favorable* to them and in situations that are *very unfavorable* (see Exhibit 14-6). So Fiedler would predict that when faced with a category I, II, III, VII, or VIII situation,

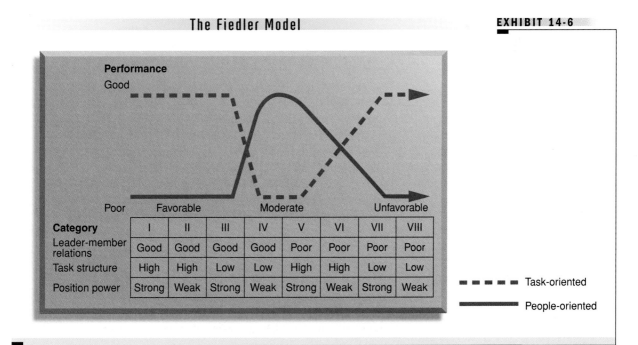

The Fiedler Model

EXHIBIT 14-6

Category	I	II	III	IV	V	VI	VII	VIII
Leader-member relations	Good	Good	Good	Good	Poor	Poor	Poor	Poor
Task structure	High	High	Low	Low	High	High	Low	Low
Position power	Strong	Weak	Strong	Weak	Strong	Weak	Strong	Weak

- - - - Task-oriented

——— People-oriented

task-oriented leaders perform better. People-oriented leaders, however, perform better in moderately favorable situations—categories IV through VI.

Many studies have tested Fiedler's model, and the overall evidence is generally supportive.[50] The model's predictions work particularly well when the eight situational categories are collapsed into three. That is, task-oriented leaders perform best in situations of high and low control, whereas relationship-oriented leaders perform best in moderate control situations.[51] Although Fiedler may not have definitively identified all the situational variables that affect leadership, the ones he did identify do seem to contribute substantially to our understanding of situational factors.

THE PATH-GOAL MODEL   The other major situational approach to leadership is the path-goal model.[52] The essence of the **path-goal model of leadership** is that it is the leader's job to assist his or her followers in attaining their goals and to provide the necessary direction and support to ensure that their goals are compatible with the overall objectives of the group or organization. The term *path-goal* is derived from the belief that effective leaders clarify the path to help their followers get from where they are to the achievement of their work goals and make the journey along the path easier by reducing roadblocks.

The path-goal model proposes two classes of so-called situational variables—those in the environment that are outside the control of the subordinates (task structure, the formal authority system, and the work group) and those that are part of the personal characteristics of the subordinate (locus of control, experience, and perceived ability). (Note that these "situational variables" are respectively synonymous with what we have called "leadership context" and "follower characteristics.") Environmental factors determine the type of leader behavior required as a complement if the subordinate outcomes are to be maximized; personal characteristics of the subordinate determine how the environment and leader behavior are interpreted (see Exhibit 14-7). So the model proposes that leader behavior will be ineffective when it's redundant with sources of environmental structure or incongruent with subordinate characteristics. For example, the following are illustrations of predictions based on the path-goal model (note that because the path-goal model takes into consideration characteristics of the subordinate, some of these predictions repeat findings previously discussed in the section "Follower Characteristics," on page 451):

- Task-oriented leadership leads to greater employee satisfaction when tasks are ambiguous than when they are highly structured and well laid out.
- People-oriented leadership results in high employee performance and satisfaction when subordinates are performing structured tasks.
- Task-oriented leadership is likely to be perceived as redundant among subordinates with high perceived ability or with considerable experience.
- The clearer and more structured the formal authority relationships, the more leaders should exhibit people-oriented behavior and deemphasize task-oriented behavior.
- Task-oriented leadership will lead to higher employee satisfaction when there is substantial conflict within a work group.
- Subordinates with an external locus of control will be more satisfied with a directive style.

The evidence generally supports the logic underlying the path-goal model.[53] That is, employee performance and satisfaction are likely to be positively influenced when the leader compensates for things lacking in either the employee or the work setting. However, the leader who spends time explaining tasks when those tasks are already clear or

Path-Goal Model

EXHIBIT 14-7

```
                    ┌──────────────────────────┐
                    │ Subordinate Characteristics│
                    │  • Locus of control       │
                    │  • Experience             │
                    │  • Perceived ability      │
                    └──────────────────────────┘
                                │
                                ▼
┌──────────────────────┐                    ┌──────────────────────┐
│ Leader Behavior      │                    │ Subordinate Outcomes │
│  • Directive         │ ─────────────────▶ │  • High performance  │
│  • Supportive        │                    │  • High satisfaction │
│  • Participative     │                    │                      │
│  • Achievement-oriented│                  └──────────────────────┘
└──────────────────────┘                    
                                ▲
                    ┌──────────────────────────┐
                    │ Environmental Factors     │
                    │  • Task Structure         │
                    │  • Formal authority system│
                    │  • Work group             │
                    └──────────────────────────┘
```

when the employee has the ability and experience to handle them without interference is likely to be ineffective because the employee will see such task-oriented behavior as redundant or even insulting.

Does the path-goal model contradict Fiedler? No. In fact, there is considerable overlap. For instance, both directly recognize the importance of the employee's task in determining the best leadership behavior, and both recognize the moderating influence of the leader's formal position power.

COGNITIVE RESOURCE MODEL   In the search for a better explanation of leadership effectiveness, Fiedler and an associate, Joe Garcia, have reconceptualized Fiedler's original contingency model to include the effect of situationally induced stress on leaders and followers.[54] This reconceptualized explanation is called the **cognitive resource model**. This new model has received surprisingly strong support.[55]

The model is built on two assumptions. First, intelligent and competent leaders formulate more effective plans, decisions, and action strategies than less intelligent and competent leaders. Second, leaders communicate their plans, decisions, and strategies through directive behavior. Fiedler and Garcia then show how stress and cognitive resources such as experience, tenure, and intelligence act as important influences on leadership effectiveness.

One of the more important predictions from the cognitive resource model is that, under low stress, intelligence is positively related, and experience negatively related, to performance. In contrast, under high stress, intelligence is negatively related with performance, and experience is positively related. What this means, essentially, is that when subordinates report high job- or boss-related stress, bright individuals perform worse in the leadership role than dull people. When job- or boss-related stress is low, more experienced individuals perform worse than do less experienced people.

The leadership of executives from countries such as Peru, Mexico, and Brazil tends to be autocratic, reflecting their culture's high power distance scores. As an example, Enrique Razon, chairman of International Container Terminal Services, is a Mexican businessman who is well known for his tough, autocratic style.

So, according to this theory, stress is the enemy of rationality. Under conditions of high stress, a highly intelligent leader should rely on experience, rather than intelligence, to be effective. Or, put another way, those leaders required to undertake tasks that require intelligence rather than experience for effective performance (which tends to include many nonroutine and creative activities) should be chosen for their ability to handle stress or be trained in stress-reduction techniques.

CULTURAL VARIABLES We conclude our discussion of situational variables by mentioning two additional factors that seem to play an important role in determining leadership effectiveness—national and organizational culture.

National culture affects leadership style in two ways. It shapes the preferences of leaders. It also defines what is acceptable to subordinates.[56] Leaders cannot choose their styles at will. They are constrained by the cultural conditions in which they have been socialized and that their subordinates have come to expect. For example, a manipulative or autocratic style is compatible with high power distance, and we find high power distance scores in Arab and Latin countries. Arab leaders are expected to be tough and strong. To show kindness or to be generous without being asked to do so is perceived as a sign of weakness. In Mexico, with its strong paternalistic tradition and the presence of the machismo principle, leaders are expected to be decisive and autocratic. Power distance rankings should also be good indicators of employee willingness to accept participative leadership. Participation is likely to be most effective in such low power distance cultures as exist in Norway, Finland, Denmark, and Sweden. Not incidentally, the participation–low power distance relationship may explain (1) why a number of leadership approaches implicitly favor the use of a participative or people-oriented style, (2) the emergence of development-oriented leader behavior found in Scandinavian organizations, and (3) the recent enthusiasm in North America for empowerment. Remember that most leadership theories were developed by North Americans, using North American subjects, and the United States, Canada, and Scandinavian countries all rate below average on power distance.

An organization's culture shapes a leader's behavior by influencing the selection of leaders and the values that effective leaders are expected to exhibit.[57] When organizations seek to fill leadership positions, they look for individuals whose traits and behaviors are compatible with the organization's culture. In fact, a good part of the selection process, particularly interviews, attempts to identify and reject mismatches. Similarly, the culture conveys to leaders what behaviors are acceptable and unacceptable. The result is that leadership styles in organizations tend to be more alike than different; and "effective leadership" is often assessed in terms of how well a leader's traits and behaviors align with the values that the organization holds. For instance, an autocratic leader may be successful in getting high performance out of his work group. But if the organization's culture values and encourages person-oriented leadership, this autocratic leader is likely to be assessed as ineffective merely because of his incompatible style. So a good culture-leader fit would seem to be important in determining leader effectiveness; and leaders whose style clashes with the organization's culture don't tend to last too long.

▶ When Are Formal Leaders Relatively Unimportant?

Formal leaders may not always be important. Data from numerous studies collectively demonstrate that, in many situations, whatever behaviors leaders exhibit are irrelevant. Certain individual, job, and organizational variables can act as *substitutes* for formal leaders or can *neutralize* the leader's ability to influence his or her subordinates.[58]

Neutralizers make it impossible for leader behavior to make any difference to subordinate outcomes. They negate the leader's influence. Substitutes, on the other hand, make a leader's influence not only impossible but also unnecessary. They act as a replacement for the leader's influence. For instance, characteristics of subordinates such as their experience, training, "professional" orientation, or indifference toward organizational rewards can substitute for, or neutralize the effect of, leaders. Experience and training, for example, can replace the need for a leader's support or ability to create structure and reduce task ambiguity. Jobs that are inherently unambiguous and routine or that are intrinsically satisfying may require little direct attention from formal leaders. Organizational characteristics such as explicit formalized goals, rigid rules and procedures, and cohesive work groups can replace formal leaders (see Exhibit 14-8 on page 462). However, if we go back to our original definition of *leadership* as "a process that influences a group of people toward a common goal," we could argue that although *formal leaders* can be replaced, *leadership* can't be. Instead of formal leaders' exercising leadership, the process of leadership might be happening through informal leaders, through group norms, and so on, rather than being the formal responsibility of one person. In fact, we propose that often, when formal leaders are ineffective, these other forms of leadership emerge to help the organization continue to survive.

Our understanding of leadership has focused on five variables—(1) leader effectiveness, (2) leader characteristics and style, (3) follower characteristics, (4) leader behavior, and (5) leadership context. Let's try to summarize where our journey has taken us in terms of what we currently know about leadership.

THE LEADERSHIP JOURNEY: WHERE WE HAVE BEEN

1. Leadership effectiveness is problematic. In many cases, leadership effectiveness is defined in terms of perception. And that perception may not align with any objective measure of effectiveness.

EXHIBIT 14-8

Substitutes and Neutralizers for Formal Leaders

Defining Characteristic	Effect on People-Oriented Leadership	Effect on Task-Oriented Leadership
Individual		
Experience/training	No effect on	Substitutes for
Professionalism	Substitutes for	Substitutes for
Indifference to rewards	Neutralizes	Neutralizes
Job		
Highly structured task	No effect on	Substitutes for
Provides its own feedback	No effect on	Substitutes for
Intrinsically satisfying	Substitutes for	No effect on
Organization		
Explicit formalized goals	No effect on	Substitutes for
Rigid rules and procedures	No effect on	Substitutes for
Cohesive work groups	Substitutes for	Substitutes for

Source: Based on S. Kerr and J. M. Jermier, "Substitutes for Leadership: Their Meaning and Measurement," *Organizational Behavior and Human Performance*, December 1978, p. 378.

2a. Certain traits do seem to be related to the perception of leadership. But possession of these traits is no guarantee of success. Traits appear to predict leadership more in weak situations than in strong situations.

2b. Prior experience is not a very powerful predictor of leadership effectiveness. This appears to be due to measuring experience in terms of time on the job and failure to adjust for variability across situations.

2c. Regardless of actual effectiveness, people characterize individuals as "leaders" when they have traits such as intelligence, outgoing personality, strong verbal skills, aggressiveness, understanding, and industriousness and when they exhibit both high-people and high-task behaviors.

2d. Some people—those who are low self-monitors—tend to meet every leadership challenge with the same response. People who are high self-monitors are more flexible. They're able to adjust their style to the situation, thus increasing the likelihood of achieving the proper leader-situation match.

3a. Leader effectiveness is enhanced by having followers who exhibit "good follower" behaviors.

3b. Leaders play favorites. They give preferential treatment to those followers in the "in" group. In response, those with favored status tend to have higher performance ratings, less turnover, and greater satisfaction with their leader.

4a. The actions of a leader are influenced by a follower's personality, experience, ability, and motivation.

4b. The proper amount of employee participation in decision making has been found to be heavily influenced by situational factors such as quality requirements, subordinate commitment, and conflict over options.

5a. There is no leadership style that is consistently effective. Contextual factors and follower characteristics must be taken into consideration in the selection of the "best" leadership style.

5b. Key situational variables determining leadership effectiveness include task structure, position power, leader-member relations, the work group, subordinate characteristics, stress level, organizational culture, and national culture.

5c. Formal leaders don't always make a difference. There are substitutes for leadership and neutralizers that can negate the formal leader's influence.

There is a variety of additional material available on the CD-ROM and companion Web site that accompany this text. You can access this information through the CD-ROM or by visiting the Web site at <**www.prenhall.com/robbins**>.

SUMMARY

(This summary is organized by the chapter-opening learning objectives on page 440.)

1. Leadership is about coping with change, whereas management is concerned with bringing about order and consistency. Organizations need both leadership and management. Leadership provides a vision and helps people to move toward that vision; management puts together the plans and structure to achieve specific goals.

2. The five key variables that have shaped our understanding of leadership are leadership effectiveness, the leader's characteristics and style, follower characteristics, leader behavior, and leadership context.

3. Leadership effectiveness essentially refers to success in moving a group to the achievement of a common goal. But success can be an objective outcome or a perception. Moreover, researchers haven't used consistent factors as outcomes. Examples of outcomes used by researchers include group performance, follower satisfaction, and acceptance of the leader. This lack of consistency makes conclusions about what makes an effective leader somewhat dubious, since these conclusions are based on different effectiveness criteria. The result is that we need to specify the effectiveness criteria when we make leadership predictions.

4. The following traits have been found to regularly explain perceptions of leadership: ambition and energy, the desire to lead, self-confidence, intelligence, and a high self-monitoring personality.

5. The three primary leadership styles are task-oriented (emphasizes accomplishing group goals and defining and structuring group-member work assignments); people-oriented (develops good interpersonal relationships; is friendly and approachable); and development-oriented (experiments and encourages change).

6. The leader-participation model provides a set of rules for leaders to follow in determining the degree of participation subordinates should have in decision making. It identifies five leadership behaviors and projects the most effective behavior based on eight situational variables.

7. The leader-member exchange model recognizes that leaders differentiate among subordinates and place them into either an "in" or an "out" group. In-group members are trusted, get more of the leader's attention, and are more likely to receive special privileges. Consistent with the self-fulfilling prophecy, in-group members respond positively, so leaders appear to be more effective with in-group members.

8. Both Fiedler's model and the path-goal model recognize that the "right" leadership style depends on the situation, and both identify the situational variables of task structure and the leader's formal position. Fiedler's model emphasizes leader-member relations. The path-goal model adds the work group and directly recognizes that leaders need to adjust their style to reflect the characteristics of the followers.

1. What role do you think traits play in the selection process for filling most management jobs?

2. What is the managerial grid? What are its implications for leadership?

3. When might leaders be irrelevant?

4. Would you give different recommendations to a person who wanted to be an effective leader than you would to a person who wanted others to think he was a good leader?

5. What is the attribution theory of leadership?

6. How might the leader-member exchange model provide insights into problems that women and minorities often have in being accepted and promoted in organizations?

7. Do you think most managers use a situational approach to increase leader effectiveness? Explain.

8. When average people on the street are asked to explain why a given individual is a leader, they tend to describe the person in terms such as competent, consistent, self-assured, and supportive of his or her followers. Can you reconcile this description with the variables illustrated in Exhibit 14-1 (page 443)?

9. "The essence of effective leadership is matching the leader's personality with the dominant leadership style in the organization." Do you agree or disagree with this statement? Explain.

10. What does the phrase "organizations are overmanaged and underled" mean?

IF I WERE THE MANAGER . . .

The New Job at Connecticut Mutual

You're 22 years old and will be receiving your business degree from the University of Connecticut at the end of this term. You've spent the past two summers working for Connecticut Mutual in Hartford, filling in on a number of different jobs while employees took their vacations. You've received and accepted an offer to join CM on a permanent basis upon graduation, as a supervisor in the policy renewal department.

Connecticut Mutual is a large insurance company. In the headquarters office alone, where you'll work, they employ 3,000 people. The company believes strongly in the personal development of its employees. This translates into a philosophy, emanating from the top executive offices, of trust and respect for all CM employees.

The job you'll be assuming requires you to direct the activities of nine clerical personnel. Their jobs require little training and are highly routine. The primary responsibility of these jobs is to follow up on nonrenewals. Company computers automatically generate renewal notices and your department handles the problem cases. Most interactions are with sales reps in the field and customers calling or writing for clarifications. In some instances the computer-generated notices are in error and your people have to recalculate premiums by referring to standardized tables.

Your group is composed of all females, ranging from 19 to 51 years of age, with a median of 29. For the most part, they are high school graduates with little prior working experience. The salary range for policy renewal processors is $1,525 to $1,880 per month. You'll be replacing a longtime CM employee, Mabel Fincher. Mabel is retiring after 37 years with CM, the last 14 spent as a policy renewal supervisor. Since you had spent a few weeks in Mabel's group last summer, you're familiar with Mabel's style and also knew most of the group members. You anticipated no problems from any of your soon-to-be employees, except possibly for Lillian Lantz. Lillian is the oldest member of the department, has been a policy renewal processor for over a dozen years, and—as the "grande dame"—she carries a lot of weight with group members. You've concluded that without Lantz's support, your job could prove difficult.

You're determined to get your career off on the right foot. What style of leadership would you use in the department? Explain why.

Choosing an Effective Leadership Style

You are a manufacturing manager in a large electronics plant. The company's management is always searching for ways to increase efficiency. They recently installed new machines and set up a new simplified work system, but to the surprise of everyone—including you—the expected increase in productivity was not realized. In fact, production has begun to drop, quality has fallen off, and the number of employee resignations has risen.

You don't think that there is anything wrong with the machines. You have had reports from other companies that are using them, and they confirm your opinion. You have also had representatives from the firm that built the machines go over them, and they report that the machines are operating at peak efficiency.

You know that some aspect of the new work system must be responsible for the change, but you are getting no help from your immediate subordinates—four first-line supervisors,

each in charge of a section, and your supply manager. The drop in production has been variously attributed to poor training of the operators, lack of an adequate system of financial incentives, and poor morale. All of the individuals involved have deep feelings about this issue. Your subordinates do not agree with you or with one another.

This morning you received a phone call from your division manager. He had just received your production figures for the last 6 months and was calling to express his concern. He indicated that the problem was yours to solve in any way that you think best but that he would like to know within a week what steps you plan to take.

You share your division manager's concern with the falling productivity and know that your employees are also concerned. Using your knowledge of leadership concepts, which leadership style would you choose? Justify your choice.

Source: Based on V. H. Vroom, "A New Look at Managerial Decision Making," *Organizational Dynamics*, Spring 1973, pp. 66–80. With permission.

Debate: Do Leaders Really Matter?

Break the class into groups of two. One group member will argue "Leaders are the primary determinant of an organization's success or failure." The other group member will argue "Leaders don't really matter because most of the things that affect an organization's success or failure are outside a leader's control." Take ten minutes to develop your arguments; then you have ten minutes to conduct your debate.

After the dyad debates, form into teams of six. Three from each of these groups should have taken the "pro" argument on leadership and three should have taken the "con" side. The teams have 15 minutes to reconcile their arguments and to develop a unified position. When the 15 minutes are up, each team should be prepared to make a brief presentation to the class, summarizing their unified position.

Can You Argue with Success?

Chuck Mallory graduated near the top of his Harvard Business School class.* His classmates described him with terms such as "brilliant," "ruthless," "ambitious," and "power-hungry." Recruiters were impressed with his polish, intelligence, and leadership potential. He had seven offers. He took a job with a ma-

jor consulting firm. Within two years, he was a project manager in Europe, overseeing a team of six. Five years later, he was a partner in the consulting firm, managing the Atlanta office.

In follow-up interviews with people at his consulting firm, two distinct pictures evolved. Partners in the firm spoke about Chuck's ability to bring in new business and squeeze high productivity from his staff. Several referred to him as "arrogant" and "abrasive," but they were quick to point out that his yearly performance numbers were always among the highest in the firm. The people who worked for Chuck talked differently. They focused on the "relentless pressure he puts us under" and his "unrealistically high expectations." One particularly negative employee offered the following analysis: "He's like a tornado. He whips in with all this energy and takes immediate control. But when he leaves, all that remains is rubble."

While in Atlanta, Chuck caught the eye of the CEO in a Fortune 100 consumer-products company. Chuck was hired as president of one of the company's smaller divisions. In the three years that he ran that division, Chuck posted some incredible numbers. He increased sales nearly 50 percent and profits more than 85 percent. He fired a number of low-performing managers and replaced them with more aggressive types. One of the accomplishments he was most proud of was generating his increase in sales with almost no increase in staff. When some managers complained about people being overworked, Chuck was quoted as saying, "If someone wants to work only 50 hours a week, let them do it for someone else. There's 168 hours in a week. I expect my people to give me at least half of them." In an interview with a business journalist, Chuck was asked about his demanding style. He replied, "Managing isn't a popularity contest. If people don't like working for me, they can leave. Slavery was abolished 130 years ago."

Last year, the same CEO who hired Chuck promoted him to senior executive vice-president for marketing. In announcing that promotion, the CEO emphasized Chuck's impressive accomplishments. But critics continue to attack his "slash-and-burn" style of management. They point out that within 2 weeks after the announcement of Chuck's promotion, three of the eight people who would be reporting to him turned in their resignations and one requested a transfer. Critics also charged that Chuck left his previous divison in shambles. People were exhausted and morale was low. They noted that the division's performance collapsed within 6 months of Chuck's leaving. His supporters, on the other hand, used the large drop in the division following Chuck's departure as prime evidence of how effective he was as a manager.

QUESTIONS

1. Is Chuck Mallory a leader? Explain.
2. Would you want to work for Mallory?
3. What do you think explains Mallory's success?
4. Would you hire Mallory to work for you?

---

*This person's name and organizational affiliations have been disguised for obvious reasons.

NOTES

1. Based on A. Taylor III, "Toyota's Boss Stands Out in a Crowd," *Fortune*, November 25, 1996, pp. 116–22.
2. R. J. House and P. M. Podsakoff, "Leadership Effectiveness: Past Perspectives and Future Directions for Research," in J. Greenberg (ed.), *Organizational Behavior: The State of the Science* (Hillsdale, NJ: Lawrence Erlbaum Associates, 1994), p. 46.
3. G. Capowski, "Anatomy of a Leader: Where Are the Leaders of Tomorrow?" *Management Review*, March 1994, pp. 12–15.
4. J. P. Kotter, "What Leaders Really Do," *Harvard Business Review*, May–June 1990, pp. 103–11; and J. P. Kotter, *A Force for Change: How Leadership Differs from Management* (New York: Free Press, 1990).
5. Cited in Capowski, "Anatomy of a Leader," p. 13.
6. See, for instance, W. Shapiro, "What Debates Don't Tell Us," *Time*, October 19, 1992, pp. 32–33.
7. See, for instance, early reviews in C. A. Gibb, "The Principles and Traits of Leadership," *Journal of Abnormal and Social Psychology*, July 1947, pp. 267–84; R. M. Stogdill, "Personal Factors Associated with Leadership: A Survey of the Literature," *Journal of Psychology*, January 1948, pp. 35–71.
8. See R. J. House and R. N. Aditya, "The Social Scientific Study of Leadership: Quo Vadis?" *Journal of Management*, vol. 23, no. 3, 1997, pp. 417–18.
9. G. H. Dobbins, W. S. Long, E. J. Dedrick, and T. C. Clemons, "The Role of Self-Monitoring and Gender on Leader Emergence: A Laboratory and Field Study," *Journal of Management*, September 1990, pp. 609–18; and S. J. Zaccaro, R. J. Foti, and D. A. Kenny, "Self-Monitoring and Trait-Based Variance in Leadership: An Investigation of Leader Flexibility across Multiple Group Situations," *Journal of Applied Psychology*, April 1991, pp. 308–15.

10. R. G. Lord, C. L. DeVader, and G. M. Alliger, "A Meta-Analysis of the Relation between Personality Traits and Leadership Perceptions: An Application of Validity Generalization Procedures," *Journal of Applied Psychology*, August 1986, pp. 402–10.

11. B. Schneider, "Interactional Psychology and Organizational Behavior," in L. L. Cummings and B. M. Staw (eds.), *Research in Organizational Behavior*, vol. 5 (Greenwich, CT: JAI Press, 1983), pp. 1–31.

12. See W. Mischel, "Toward a Cognitive Social Learning Reconceptualization of Personality," *Psychological Review*, July 1973, pp. 252–83; and M. R. Barrick and M. K. Mount, "Autonomy as a Moderator of the Relationship between the Big Five Personality Dimensions and Job Performance," *Journal of Applied Psychology*, February 1993, pp. 111–18.

13. Lord, DeVader, and Alliger, "A Meta-Analysis of the Relation between Personality Traits and Leadership Perceptions."

14. F. E. Fiedler, "Time-Based Measures of Leadership Experience and Organizational Performance: A Review of Research and a Preliminary Model," *Leadership Quarterly*, Spring 1992, p. 5.

15. Ibid., p. 7.

16. F. E. Fiedler, "Leadership Experience and Leadership Performance: Another Hypothesis Shot to Hell," *Organizational Behavior and Human Performance*, January 1970, pp. 1–14; and F. E. Fiedler, *Leadership Experience and Leadership Performance* (Alexandria, VA: U.S. Army Research Institute, 1994).

17. M. A. Quinones, J. K. Ford, and M. S. Teachout, "The Relationship between Work Experience and Job Performance: A Conceptual and Meta-Analytic Review," *Personnel Psychology*, Winter 1995, pp. 887–910.

18. "The Meaner, the Better," *Working Woman*, September 1997, p. 17.

19. M. Loeb, "Empowerment That Pays Off," *Fortune*, March 20, 1995, pp. 145–46.

20. House and Aditya, "The Social Scientific Study of Leadership," p. 420.

21. R. M. Stogdill and A. E. Coons (eds.), *Leader Behavior: Its Description and Measurement*, Research Monograph No. 88 (Columbus: Ohio State University, Bureau of Business Research, 1951); R. Kahn and D. Katz, "Leadership Practices in Relation to Productivity and Morale," in D. Cartwright and A. Zander (eds.), *Group Dynamics: Research and Theory*, 2nd ed. (Elmsford, NY: Row, Peterson, 1960); and R. Likert, *New Patterns of Management* (New York: McGraw-Hill, 1961).

22. R. R. Blake and J. S. Mouton, *The Managerial Grid* (Houston: Gulf, 1964).

23. See G. Ekvall and J. Arvonen, "Change-Centered Leadership: An Extension of the Two-Dimensional Model," *Scandinavian Journal of Management*, vol. 7, no. 1 (1991), pp. 17–26; M. Lindell and G. Rosenqvist, "Is There a Third Management Style?" *The Finnish Journal of Business Economics* 3 (1992), pp. 171–98; and M. Lindell and G. Rosenqvist, "Management Behavior Dimensions and Development Orientation," *Leadership Quarterly*, Winter 1992, pp. 355–77.

24. See Stogdill and Coons, *Leader Behavior*; and S. Kerr, C. A. Schriesheim, C. J. Murphy, and R. M. Stogdill, "Toward a Contingency Theory of Leadership Based upon the Consideration and Initiating Structure Literature," *Organizational Behavior and Human Performance*, August 1974, pp. 62–82.

25. See references cited in note 21.

26. E. Van Velsor and J. B. Leslie, "Why Executives Derail: Perspective across Time and Culture," *The Executive*, November 1995, pp. 62–72.

27. See, for example, L. L. Larson, J. G. Hunt, and R. N. Osborn, "The Great Hi-Hi Leader Behavior Myth: A Lesson from Occam's Razor," *Academy of Management Journal*, December 1976, pp. 628–41; and P. C. Nystrom, "Managers and the Hi-Hi Leader Myth," *Academy of Management Journal*, June 1978, pp. 325–31.

28. This position is probably most adamantly argued by Fred Fiedler in his contingency theory. See F. Fiedler, *A Theory of Leadership Effectiveness* (New York: McGraw-Hill, 1967).

29. This position is probably best articulated in the Vroom-Yetton-Jago leader-participation model. See V. H. Vroom and A. G. Jago, *The New Leadership: Managing Participation in Organizations* (Upper Saddle River, NJ: Prentice Hall, 1988).

30. See references cited in note 9.

31. See, for instance, J. C. McElroy, "A Typology of Attribution Leadership Research," *Academy of Management Review*, July 1982, pp. 413–17; J. R. Meindl and S. B. Ehrlich, "The Romance of Leadership and the Evaluation of Organizational Performance," *Academy of Management Journal*, March 1987, pp. 91–109; R. G. Lord and K. J. Maher, *Leadership and Information Processing: Linking Perception and Performance* (Boston: Unwin Hyman, 1991); B. Shamir, "Attribution of Influence and Charisma to the Leader: The Romance of Leadership Revisited," *Journal of Applied Social Psychology*, March 1992, pp. 386–407; and J. R. Meindl, "The Romance of Leadership as a Follower-Centric Theory: A Social Constructionist Approach," *Leadership Quarterly*, Fall 1995, pp. 329–41.

32. Lord, DeVader, and Alliger, "A Meta-Analysis of the Relation between Personality Traits and Leadership Perceptions."

33. G. N. Powell and D. A. Butterfield, "The 'High-High' Leader Rides Again!" *Group and Organization Studies*, December 1984, pp. 437–50.

34. J. R. Meindl, S. B. Ehrlich, and J. M. Dukerich, "The Romance of Leadership," *Administrative Science Quarterly*, March 1985, pp. 78–102.

35. B. M. Staw and J. Ross, "Commitment in an Experimenting Society: A Study of the Attribution of Leadership from Administrative Scenarios," *Journal of Applied Psychology*, June 1980, pp. 249–60; J. Pfeffer, *Managing with Power* (Boston: Harvard Business School Press, 1992), p. 194; and M. Loeb, "An Interview with Warren Bennis: Where Leaders Come From," *Fortune*, September 19, 1994, p. 241.

36. T. Brown, "Great Leaders Need Great Followers," *Industry Week*, September 4, 1995, p. 30.

37. R. J. House and T. R. Mitchell, "Path-Goal Theory of Leadership," *Journal of Contemporary Business*, Autumn 1974, pp. 81–97.

38. Fiedler, *A Theory of Leadership Effectiveness*.

39. R. E. Kelley, "In Praise of Followers," *Harvard Business Review*, November–December 1988, pp. 142–48; and I. Chaleff, *The Courageous Follower: Standing Up To and For Our Leaders* (San Francisco: Berrett-Koehler, 1995).

40. See, for instance, R. T. Sparrowe and R. C. Liden, "Process and Structure in Leader-Member Exchange," *Academy of Management Review*, April 1997, pp. 522–52.

41. R. M. Dienesch and R. C. Liden, "Leader-Member Exchange Model of Leadership: A Critique and Further Development," *Academy of Management Review*, July 1986, pp. 618–34; and G. B. Graen and M. Uhl-Bien, "Relationship-Based Approach to Leadership: Development of Leader-Member Exchange (LMX) Theory of Leadership over 25 Years: Applying a Multi-Level Multi-Domain Perspective," *Leadership Quarterly*, Summer 1995, pp. 219–47.

42. R. Liden and G. Graen, "Generalizability of the Vertical Dyad Linkage Model of Leadership," *Academy of Management Journal*, September 1980, pp. 451–65; and R. C. Liden, S. J. Wayne, and D. Stilwell, "A Longitudinal Study of the Early Development of Leader-Member Exchanges," *Journal of Applied Psychology*, August 1993, pp. 662–74.

43. D. Duchon, S. G. Green, and T. D. Taber, "Vertical Dyad Linkage: A Longitudinal Assessment of Antecedents, Measures, and Consequences," *Journal of Applied Psychology*, February 1986, pp. 56–60; Liden, Wayne, and Stilwell, "A Longitudinal Study of the Early Development of Leader-Member Exchanges"; R. J. Deluga and J. T. Perry, "The Role of Subordinate Performance and Ingratiation in Leader-Member Exchanges," *Group & Organization Management*, March 1994, pp. 67–86; T. N. Bauer and S. G. Green, "Development of Leader-Member Exchange: A Longitudinal Test," *Academy of Management Journal*, December 1996, pp. 1538–67; and S. J. Wayne, L. M. Shore, and R. C. Liden, "Perceived Organizational Support and Leader-Member Exchange: A Social Exchange Perspective," *Academy of Management Journal*, February 1997, pp. 82–111.

44. See C. R. Gerstner and D. V. Day, "Meta-Analytic Review of Leader-Member Exchange Theory: Correlates and Construct Issues," *Journal of Applied Psychology*, December 1997, pp. 827–44.

45. D. Eden, "Leadership and Expectations: Pygmalion Effects and Other Self-Fulfilling Prophecies in Organizations," *Leadership Quarterly*, Winter 1992, pp. 278–79.

46. See specifically House and Mitchell, "Path-Goal Theory of Leadership"; Fiedler, *A Theory of Leadership Effectiveness*; and P. Hersey and K. H. Blanchard, *Management of Organizational Behavior: Utilizing Human Resources*, 7th ed. (Upper Saddle River, NJ: Prentice Hall, 1996).

47. Vroom and Jago, *The New Leadership*.

48. Ibid.; and R. H. G. Field and R. J. House, "A Test of the Vroom-Yetton Model Using Manager and Subordinate Reports," *Journal of Applied Psychology*, June 1990, pp. 362–66; and V. H. Vroom and A. G. Jago, "Situation Effects and Levels of Analysis in the Study of Leader Participation," *Leadership Quarterly*, Summer 1995, pp. 169–81.

49. Fiedler, *A Theory of Leadership Effectiveness*; and F. E. Fiedler, M. M. Chemers, and L. Mahar, *Improving Leadership Effectiveness: The Leader Match Concept* (New York: Wiley, 1977).

50. L. H. Peters, D. D. Hartke, and J. T. Pohlmann, "Fiedler's Contingency Theory of Leadership: An Application of the Meta-Analysis Procedures of Schmidt and Hunter," *Psychological Bulletin*, March 1985, pp. 274–85; C. A. Schriesheim, B. J. Tepper, and L. A. Tetrault, "Least Preferred Co-Worker Score, Situational Control, and Leadership Effectiveness: A Meta-Analysis of Contingency Model Performance Predictions," *Journal of Applied Psychology*, August 1994, pp. 561–73; and R. Ayman, M. M. Chemers, and F. Fiedler, "The Contingency Model of Leadership Effectiveness: Its Levels of Analysis," *Leadership Quarterly*, Summer 1995, pp. 147–67.

51. House and Aditya, "The Social Scientific Study of Leadership," p. 422.

52. R. J. House, "A Path-Goal Theory of Leader Effectiveness," *Administrative Science Quarterly*, September 1971, pp. 321–38; House and Mitchell, "Path-Goal Theory of Leadership"; and R. J. House, "Path-Goal Theory of Leadership: Lessons, Legacy, and a Reformulated Theory," *Leadership Quarterly*, Fall 1996, pp. 323–52.

53. J. C. Wofford and L. Z. Liska, "Path-Goal Theories of Leadership: A Meta-Analysis," *Journal of Management*, Winter 1993, pp. 857–76.

54. F. E. Fiedler and J. E. Garcia, *New Approaches to Effective Leadership: Cognitive Resources and Organizational Performance* (New York: Wiley, 1987).

55. F. E. Fiedler, "Cognitive Resources and Leadership Performance," *Applied Psychology—An International Review*, vol. 44, 1995, pp. 5–28.

56. See, for instance, R. S. Bhagat, B. L. Kedia, S. E. Crawford, and M. R. Kaplan, "Cross-Cultural Issues in Organizational Psychology: Emergent Trends and Directions for Research in the 1990s," in C. L. Cooper and I. T. Robertson (eds.), *International Review of Industrial and Organizational Psychology*, vol. 5 (Chichester, England: Wiley, 1990), pp. 79–89; and M. F. Peterson and J. G. Hunt, "International Perspectives on International Leadership," *Leadership Quarterly*, Fall 1997, pp. 203–31.

57. E. H. Schein, *Organizational Culture and Leadership* (San Francisco: Jossey-Bass, 1985); and H. M. Trice and J. M. Beyer, *The Cultures of Work Organizations* (Upper Saddle River, NJ: Prentice Hall, 1993), pp. 254–98.

58. S. Kerr and J. M. Jermier, "Substitutes for Leadership: Their Meaning and Measurement," *Organizational Behavior and Human Performance*, December 1978, pp. 375–403; J. P. Howell, D. E. Bowen, P. W. Dorfman, S. Kerr, and P. M. Podsakoff, "Substitutes for Leadership: Effective Alterna-

tives to Ineffective Leadership," *Organizational Dynamics*, Summer 1990, pp. 21–38; P. M. Podsakoff, B. P. Niehoff, S. B. MacKenzie, and M. L. Williams, "Do Substitutes for Leadership Really Substitute for Leadership? An Empirical Examination of Kerr and Jermier's Situational Leadership Model," *Organizational Behavior and Human Decision Processes*, February 1993, pp. 1–44; P. M. Podsakoff, S. B. MacKenzie, and W. H. Bommer, "Meta-Analysis of the Re-

lationships between Kerr and Jermier's Substitutes for Leadership and Employee Job Attitudes, Role Perceptions, and Performance," *Journal of Applied Psychology*, August 1996, pp. 380–99; and J. M. Jermier and S. Kerr, "Substitutes for Leadership: Their Meaning and Measurement'— Contextual Recollections and Current Observations," *Leadership Quarterly*, vol. 8, no. 2, 1997, pp. 95–101.

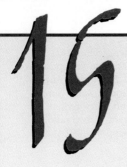
CONTEMPORARY ISSUES IN LEADERSHIP

IT'S HARD TO LOOK UP TO A LEADER WHO KEEPS HIS
EAR TO THE GROUND.

J. H. BOREN

LEARNING OBJECTIVES

After studying this chapter, you should be able to:

1 Contrast transactional with transformational leadership.

2 Define the qualities of a charismatic leader.

3 Identify the skills that visionary leaders exhibit.

4 Explain how framing influences leadership effectiveness.

5 Describe how a leader can make others dependent upon him or her.

6 Identify the four roles that team leaders perform.

7 Explain the role of a mentor.

8 Define what coaching is.

9 Explain whether men and women lead differently.

10 Describe the implications of leadership concepts to management practice.

Richard Branson marches to the beat of a different drummer.[1] He's brash, confident, unconventional, a self-promoter, a bold risk taker, and a man with big ideas. A born maverick, the charismatic, 50-year-old Branson has raised establishment bashing to an art form and built a business with more than $2.5 billion in revenues in the process. His Virgin brand can be found on entertainment mega-stores, two airlines, hotels, radio stations, cafés, cinemas, a publishing company, and even soda pop.

Branson never graduated from high school. But lack of a diploma hasn't stopped him from developing a personal net worth estimated at $2.7 billion—making him the fifth-richest person in Britain, excluding the royal family. He understood the taste of music consumers, created Virgin Records, built it into a megacorporation, and then sold it for nearly a billion dollars. Then he started Virgin Atlantic Airlines. With only eight 747s, it has redefined transatlantic service. First class was replaced with upper class—which includes free limo service. Branson's airline has aggressively captured a large share of the transatlantic business-traveler market by merging technology with service. For instance, he was the first to install multichannel video monitors for every seat on his planes.

One of Branson's more recent ventures is a Coca-Cola clone—Virgin Cola. Why take on Coke? "I believe that if you're going to take someone on, you might as well take on the biggest brand in the world," says Branson. "Besides, most people who have been around as long as Coke have become quite fat. I believe they've got very vulnerable skin."

Richard Branson has amassed a fortune by doing what business strategists strongly advise against: He targets well-established industries with entrenched competitors—airlines, records, retailing—and then attacks head-on. He wins because his businesses are able to do things more efficiently than his competitors and because he has successfully identified consumer needs that his more established competitors have failed to see.

The past decade has seen an explosion of interest in the leadership phenomenon. That interest has gone in several directions. One of those directions, for instance, has been to find out what it is that differentiates charismatic individuals like Richard Branson from the more mundane leaders who oversee most organizations. In this chapter, we present the most recent work in the area of leadership. We begin by differentiating between transactional and transformational leaders and reviewing the evidence demonstrating the superiority of the latter. Then we present evidence that charismatic and visionary leaders have the qualities to transform their organizations or the units they manage. The rest of this chapter addresses recent insights into leadership—for instance, how leaders acquire and use power, the concept of team leadership, and how effective leaders mentor and coach others. We conclude by considering what the findings in this and the previous chapter mean in terms of the selecting and training of leaders.

CREATING TRANSFORMATIONAL LEADERS

Until very recently, most of the discussion on leadership has addressed **transactional leaders**. These kinds of leaders guide or motivate their followers in the direction of established goals by clarifying role and task requirements. Our focus in the previous chapter on leader characteristics and behaviors, follower characteristics, and situational factors represents a transactional view of leadership. But there is another type of leader who inspires followers to transcend their own self-interests for the good of the organization and who is capable of having a profound and extraordinary effect on his or her followers. These are **transformational leaders**.[2] A list of such leaders reads like a Who's Who of successful executives: Jack Welch at General Electric; Ray Kroc at McDonald's; Soichiro Honda at Honda; Michael Eisner at Disney; Anita Roddick at The Body Shop; and Bill Gates at Microsoft.

EXHIBIT 15-1

Characteristics of Transactional and Transformational Leaders

Transactional Leader	Transformational Leader
Contingent reward. Contracts exchange of rewards for effort, promises rewards for good performance, recognizes accomplishments.	*Charisma.* Provides vision and sense of mission, instills pride, gains respect and trust.
Management by exception (active). Watches and searches for deviations from rules and standards, takes corrective action.	*Influence.* Projects self-confidence and success, articulates goals, arouses followers' emotions.
	Inspiration. Communicates high expectations, uses symbols to focus efforts, expresses important purposes in simple ways.
	Intellectual stimulation. Promotes intelligence, rationality, and careful problem solving.
Management by exception (passive). Intervenes only if standards are not met.	*Individualized consideration.* Gives personal attention, treats each employee individually, coaches, advises.

Source: Based on B. M. Bass, "From Transactional to Transformational Leadership: Learning to Share the Vision," Organizational Dynamics, Winter 1990, p. 22; and M. J. Tejeda, T. A. Scandura, and R. Pillai, "Charismatic Leadership: Review, Re-Analysis and Integration of Major Theories," paper presented at the 1997 Academy of Management Conference, Boston, MA, August 1997.

What distinguishes transformational leaders? They pay attention to the concerns and developmental needs of individual followers; they change followers' awareness of issues by helping them look at old problems in new ways; and they are able to excite, arouse, and inspire followers to put out extra effort to achieve group goals. Exhibit 15-1 briefly identifies and defines the characteristics that differentiate these two types of leaders.

A more helpful way to understand transformational leadership may be to think of it as "outstanding leadership."[3] Such leadership is "intended to account for, and differentiate, leaders who accomplish outstanding achievements from ordinary leaders who are either ineffective, or those who meet the normal requirements of their positions, but do not make outstanding achievements."[4] In terms of our discussion of management versus leadership in the preceding chapter, transactional leadership closely parallels the more structured role of managers, and the transformational leader is essentially synonymous with what John Kotter of Harvard defined as "leadership."

Transactional and transformational leadership shouldn't be viewed as opposing approaches to getting things done.[5] Transformational leadership is built on top of transactional leadership—it produces levels of subordinate effort and performance that go beyond what would occur with a transactional approach alone.

The evidence supporting the superiority of transformational leadership over the transactional variety is overwhelmingly impressive. For instance, a number of studies with U.S., Canadian, and German military officers found, at every level, that transformational leaders were evaluated as more effective than their transactional counterparts.[6] And managers at Federal Express who were rated by their followers as exhibiting more transformational leadership were evaluated by their immediate supervisors as higher performers and more promotable.[7] In summary, the overall evidence indicates that transformational leadership is more strongly correlated than transactional leadership with higher productivity, lower turnover rates, and higher employee satisfaction.[8]

▶ Charismatic Leadership

Charismatic leadership is an extension of the attribution model of leadership. It says that followers make attributions of heroic or extraordinary leadership abilities when they observe certain behaviors.[9] Studies on charismatic leadership have been, for the most part, directed at identifying those behaviors that differentiate charismatic leaders from their noncharismatic counterparts. Some examples of individuals frequently cited as being charismatic leaders include John F. Kennedy, Gandhi, Martin Luther King Jr., Walt Disney, Mary Kay Ash (founder of Mary Kay Cosmetics), Ross Perot, Steve Jobs (co-founder of Apple Computer), Ted Turner, Lee Iacocca (former chairman of Chrysler), Jan Carlzon (chairman of SAS Airlines), General Norman Schwarzkopf, and Tony Blair (Britain's prime minister).

What, if any, differences exist between charismatic leadership and transformational leadership? There has been considerable debate on this issue. We propose that charismatic leadership is a subset of transformational leadership. Transformational leadership is the larger concept and includes charisma.

QUALITIES OF THE CHARISMATIC LEADER Several authors have attempted to identify personal characteristics of the charismatic leader. Robert House of the Wharton School has identified three: extremely high confidence, dominance, and strong convictions in his or her beliefs.[10] Warren Bennis, after studying ninety of the most effective and successful leaders in the United States, found that they had four common competencies: They had a compelling vision or sense of purpose; they could communicate that vision in clear terms with which their followers could readily identify; they demonstrated consistency and focus in the pursuit of their vision; and they knew their own strengths and capitalized on them.[11] The most comprehensive analysis, however, has been completed by Jay A. Conger and Rabindra N. Kanungo.[12] Their conclusions propose that charismatic leaders have an idealized goal that they want to achieve, have a strong personal commitment to their goal, are perceived as unconventional, are assertive and self-confident, and are perceived as agents of radical change rather than as managers of the status quo. Exhibit 15-2 on page 474 summarizes the key characteristics that appear to differentiate charismatic leaders from noncharismatic ones.

Attention has recently been focused on trying to determine how charismatic leaders actually influence followers. The process begins by the leader's articulation of an appealing vision. This vision provides a sense of continuity for followers by linking the present with a better future for the organization. The leader then communicates high performance expectations and expresses confidence that followers can attain them, thereby enhancing follower self-esteem and self-confidence. Next, the leader conveys, through words and actions, a new set of values and, by his or her behavior, sets an example for followers to imitate. Finally, the charismatic leader makes self-sacrifices and engages in unconventional behavior to demonstrate courage and convictions about the vision.[13]

What can we say about the charismatic leader's effect on his or her followers? An increasing body of evidence shows impressive correlations between charismatic leadership and high performance and satisfaction among followers.[14] People working for charismatic leaders are motivated to exert extra work effort and, because they like their leader, express greater satisfaction than do people working for transactional leaders.

ARE CHARISMATIC LEADERS BORN OR MADE? If charisma is desirable, can people learn to be charismatic leaders? Or are charismatic leaders born with their qualities? Although a small minority of researchers still think charisma cannot be learned, most experts believe that

Key Characteristics of Charismatic Leaders

1. *Self-confidence.* They have complete confidence in their judgment and ability.
2. *A vision.* This is an idealized goal that proposes a future better than the status quo. The greater the disparity between this idealized goal and the status quo, the more likely that followers will attribute extraordinary vision to the leader.
3. *Ability to articulate the vision.* They are able to clarify and state the vision in terms that are understandable to others. This articulation demonstrates an understanding of the followers' needs and, hence, acts as a motivating force.
4. *Strong convictions about the vision.* Charismatic leaders are perceived as being strongly committed, willing to take on high personal risk, incur high costs, and engage in self-sacrifice to achieve their vision.
5. *Behavior that is out of the ordinary.* Those with charisma engage in behavior that is perceived as being novel, unconventional, and counter to norms. When successful, these behaviors evoke surprise and admiration in followers.
6. *Perceived as being a change agent.* Charismatic leaders are perceived as agents of radical change rather than as caretakers of the status quo.
7. *Environment sensitivity.* These leaders are able to make realistic assessments of the environmental constraints and resources needed to bring about change.

Source: Based on J. A. Conger and R. N. Kanungo, "Behavioral Dimensions of Charismatic Leadership," in J. A. Conger, R. N. Kanungo and Associates (eds.), *Charismatic Leadership* (San Francisco: Jossey-Bass, 1988), p. 91.

individuals can be trained to exhibit charismatic behaviors and can thus enjoy the benefits that accrue to being labeled a charismatic leader.[15] For instance, it has been shown that a person can learn to become charismatic by following a three-step process.[16] First, an individual needs to develop the aura of charisma by maintaining an optimistic view, using passion as a catalyst for generating enthusiasm, and communicating with the whole body, not just with words. Second, an individual draws others in by creating a bond that inspires others to follow. And third, the individual brings out the potential in followers by tapping into their emotions. This approach seems to work, as evidenced by success that researchers have had in actually scripting undergraduate business students to "play" charismatic.[17] The students were taught to articulate an overarching goal, to communicate high performance expectations, to exhibit confidence in the ability of subordinates to meet those expectations, and to empathize with the needs of their subordinates. They learned to project a powerful, confident, and dynamic presence, and they practiced using a captivating and engaging voice tone. To further capture the dynamics and energy of charisma, the leaders were trained to evoke charismatic nonverbal characteristics: They alternated between pacing and sitting on the edges of their desks, leaned toward the subordinates, maintained direct eye contact, and had a relaxed posture and animated facial expressions. These researchers found that these students could learn how to project charisma. Moreover, subordinates of these leaders had higher task performance, task adjustment, and adjustment to the leader and to the group than did subordinates who worked under groups led by noncharismatic leaders.

WHEN CHARISMA IS A LIABILITY One last word on this topic: Charismatic leadership may not always be needed to achieve high levels of employee performance. It may be most appropriate when the follower's task has an ideological component.[18] This may explain why, when charismatic leaders surface, it is most likely to be in politics, religion, wartime, or when a business firm is introducing a radically new product or facing a life-threatening crisis. Such conditions tend to involve ideological concerns. Franklin D. Roosevelt offered a vision to get Americans out of the Great Depression. Steve Jobs achieved unwavering loyalty and commitment from the technical staff he oversaw at Apple Computer during the late 1970s and early 1980s by articulating a vision of personal computers that would dramatically change the way people lived. General "Stormin' Norman" Schwarzkopf's blunt, passionate style, absolute confidence in his troops, and a vision of total victory over Iraq made him a hero in the free world after Operation Desert Storm in 1991. A charismatic leader, in fact, may become a liability to an organization once the crisis and need for dramatic change subside.[19] Why? Because when there is no crisis, the charismatic leader's overwhelming self-confidence probably isn't needed. Nor is unconventional behavior needed. And a charismatic leader often is unable to listen to others, becomes uncomfortable when challenged by aggressive subordinates, and holds a rigid belief in his or her "rightness" on issues. Philippe Kahn's charismatic style, for instance, was an asset in his position as CEO during the rapid-growth years of the software-database company Borland International. But he became a liability as the company matured. His dictatorial style, arrogance, and reckless decision making put the company's future in jeopardy.[20]

▶ Visionary Leadership

The term *vision* has recurred throughout our discussion of charismatic leadership. But visionary leadership goes beyond charisma. In this section, we review recent revelations about the importance of visionary leadership.

DEFINING VISIONARY LEADERSHIP **Visionary leadership** is the ability to create and articulate a realistic, credible, attractive vision of the future that grows out of and improves upon the present.[21] This vision, if properly selected and implemented, is so energizing that it "in effect jump-starts the future by calling forth the skills, talents, and resources to make it happen."[22]

A review of various definitions finds that a vision differs from other forms of direction setting in several ways: "A vision has clear and compelling imagery that offers an innovative way to improve, which recognizes and draws on traditions, and connects to actions that people can take to realize change. Vision taps people's emotion and energy. Properly articulated, a vision creates the enthusiasm that people have for sporting events and other leisure-time activities, bringing the energy and commitment to the workplace."[23]

Keep in mind what a vision is not. It's not a dream, it's not a mission statement, and it's not synonymous with goals. A vision is not some nebulous prophecy—it is a reality that has yet to come into existence. A mission statement conveys an organization's purpose, not its direction. A well-designed vision provides direction; that is, it offers means as well as ends. Finally, a vision is not a statement of goals. Goals point to a desired end and rarely consider values. They don't contain an innovative solution possibility that shows the way with a clear and compelling picture of the future. A vision contains values and the actions to take to achieve the desired result.

THE CASE FOR AND AGAINST VISIONARY LEADERSHIP The case for visionary leadership has been made by many writers. For instance: "The twenty-first-century organization virtually demands visionary leadership. It cannot function without it, for an organization driven by accelerating technological change, staffed by a diverse, multicultural mix of highly intelligent knowledge workers, facing global complexity, a vast kaleidoscope of individual customer needs, and the incessant demands of multiple constituencies would simply self-destruct without a common sense of direction."[24] Another article argues that vision is "the glue that binds individuals into a group with a common goal.... When shared by employees, [it] can keep an entire company moving forward in the face of difficulties, enabling and inspiring leaders and employees alike."[25]

A survey of 1,500 senior leaders, 870 of them CEOs from twenty different countries, additionally attests to the growing importance of visionary leadership.[26] The leaders were asked to describe the key traits or talents desirable for a CEO in the year 2000. The dominant characteristic most frequently mentioned was that the CEO convey a "strong sense of vision." Ninety-eight percent rated this trait as "most important." Another study contrasted eighteen visionary companies with eighteen comparable nonvisionary firms over a 65-year period.[27] The visionary companies were found to have outperformed the comparison group by six times on standard financial criteria, and their stocks outperformed the general market by fifteen times.

But not everyone buys into the importance of visionary leadership.[28] Louis Gerstner, after taking over the top job at IBM, said that a vision was the last thing IBM needed at the moment. Robert Eaton, former CEO of Chrysler, said that inside his company they didn't use the word *vision*. He said the concept is too vague and esoteric and wanted Chrysler people to focus on quantifiable short-term results. Microsoft's Bill Gates says "being a visionary is trivial."

Gerstner, Eaton, and Gates are in the minority. And Gates is clearly a visionary leader, regardless of whether he accepts the title or thinks it is trivial. Why? Because Gates has created a direction for Microsoft that is defining the future of information technology.

The debate on the importance of vision can best be reconciled by recognizing that visionary leadership needs to be supported by detailed plans. An outstanding organization needs both a vision and a high level of attention to daily operations. A strong vision can't substitute for good day-to-day management. Both are necessary.

QUALITIES OF A VISION The key properties of a vision seem to be inspirational possibilities that are value-centered, realizable, and communicated with superior imagery and articulation.[29] Visions should be able to create possibilities that are inspirational, unique, and offer a new order that can produce organizational distinction. A vision is likely to fail if it doesn't offer a view of the future that is clearly and demonstrably better for the organization and its members than is the status quo. Desirable visions fit the times and circumstances and reflect the uniqueness of the organization. People in the organization must also believe that the vision is attainable. It should be perceived as challenging yet doable. Visions that have clear articulation and powerful imagery are easily grasped and accepted.

What do visions look like? They are typically easier to talk about than to actually create. In practice, they often lack the direction that differentiates them from mere mission statements. But, given this caveat, here are a few examples: "To be the single source software provider to the financial services industry." "To be the leading African American–owned promotional and public relations firm in the USA." "To become the most customer-responsive producer of automobile interior trim in North America."[30] Here are some additional organization-specific examples.[31] Walt Disney single-handedly reinvented the idea of an amusement park when he described his vision of Disneyland in the early 1950s. Rupert Murdoch was one of the first people to see the future of the communications industry by combining entertainment and news media around a global vision. Through his News Corporation, Murdoch has successfully integrated a broadcast network, TV stations, movie studio, publishing, and global satellite distribution. Mary Kay Ash's vision of women as entrepreneurs selling products that improved their self-image gave impetus to her cosmetics company. Scandinavian Airlines CEO Jan Carlzon used the notion of "50,000 daily moments of truth" to depict the emphasis to be placed on customer service. Carlzon wanted every employee to ensure that each "moment of truth"— those instances when customers come into contact with employees—would be a positive experience for SAS customers. Charles Schwab is currently attempting to redefine financial services by combining discount prices with comprehensive offerings.

QUALITIES OF A VISIONARY LEADER The *content* of a vision is important. But the evidence indicates that the *delivery* of the vision is even more important.[32] This begs the question: What skills do visionary leaders exhibit? These leaders appear to have three qualities that are related to effectiveness in their visionary roles.[33]

The first quality is the ability to explain the vision to others. The leader needs to make the vision clear in terms of required actions and aims through clear oral and written communication. The best vision is likely to be ineffective if the leader isn't a strong communicator. Second is the ability to express the vision not just verbally but also through the leader's behavior. The leader must behave in ways that continually convey and reinforce the vision. Herb Kelleher, CEO at Southwest Airlines, lives and breathes his commitment to customer service. He is famous within the company for jumping in, when needed, to help check in passengers, load baggage, fill in for flight attendants, or do anything else to make the customer's experience more pleasant. The third skill is being able to extend the vision to different leadership contexts. This is the ability to sequence activities so that the vision can be applied in a variety of situations. For instance, the vision has to be as meaningful to the people in accounting as to those in marketing, to employees in Prague as well as in Pittsburgh.

Gordon M. Bethune has brought a single-minded vision to his job as CEO at Continental Airlines. The new focus is on performance. "We had a crappy product, and we were trying to discount ourselves into profitability. Nobody wants to eat a crummy pizza, no matter if it's 99 cents," he says. Under Bethune, Continental is now among the leaders in on-time performance and lack of customer complaints.

Let's now move to important issues that every effective leader today is, and will continue to be, concerned about. How do I get others to see the world from my perspective? How do I acquire power? What demands does team leadership place on me? How can I be an effective mentor and coach? And what can I do to help people manage and lead themselves?

CONTEMPORARY LEADERSHIP ROLES

Framing Issues

Martin Luther King Jr.'s "I Have a Dream" speech largely shaped the civil rights movement. His words created an imagery of what a country would be like where racial prejudice no longer existed; that is, King *framed* the civil rights movement in a way that others would see it the way he saw it. In this section, we demonstrate the importance of framing to effective leadership and how successful leaders frame issues.

WHAT IS FRAMING? **Framing** is a way to use language to manage meaning.[34] It's a way for leaders to influence how events are seen and understood. It involves the selection and highlighting of one or more aspects of a subject while excluding others.

Framing is analogous to what a photographer does. The visual world that exists is essentially ambiguous. When the photographer aims her camera and focuses on a specific shot, she frames her photo. Others then see what she wanted them to see. They see her

> **Trial lawyers make their living by framing issues**

point of view. That is precisely what leaders do when they frame an issue. They choose which aspects or portion of the subject they want others to focus on and which portions they want to be excluded.

Political leaders live or die on their ability to frame problems and their opponent's image. In an age of language wars, political victory often goes to those who win the battle over terminology. As a case in point, the increase in the U.S. minimum wage in 1997 was largely won because of the ability of those who favored the increase to shape information to support their case. They used U.S. Labor Department data, for instance, to show that 40 percent of minimum-wage workers "are the sole breadwinners of their family." What they didn't say was that the department counted single people living alone as family heads.[35]

Trial lawyers make their living by framing issues. Defense attorneys, for instance, shape their arguments so as to get the jury to see their client in the most favorable terms. They include "facts" that might help the jury find their client "not guilty." They exclude facts that might reflect unfavorably on their client. And they try to provide alternative interpretations to the "facts" that the prosecution argues makes their client guilty.

Lobbying groups also provide rich illustrations of the framing concept. The leadership of the National Rifle Association (NRA) has historically been very successful in limiting gun controls in the United States. They've done this not by focusing on shootings, deaths, or even self-defense. They've succeeded by framing gun control as a First Amendment "freedom" issue. To the degree that the NRA can shape public opinion to think of gun controls as taking away a citizen's right to bear arms, they have been able to minimize gun control regulations. In a similar vein, original opponents of abortion rallied their cause by describing themselves as "anti-abortion" advocates. In response, and realizing the negative imagery from using the label "pro-abortion," supporters reframed the issue by referring to themselves as "pro-choice."

WHY IS IT IMPORTANT? In the complex and chaotic environment in which most leaders work, there is typically considerable manueverability with respect to "the facts." What is real is often what the leader says is real. What's important is what he or she chooses to say is important. Leaders can use language to influence followers' perceptions of the world, the meaning of events, beliefs about causes and consequences, and visions of the future. So a leader's effectiveness is strongly influenced by his or her ability to frame issues.

People need to make sense of a situation before they know to respond. Interestingly, many people prefer to look to others to define what is real, what is fair, or what is preferred. Those "others" are often leaders. It's through framing that leaders determine whether people notice problems, how they understand and remember problems, and how they act upon them.[36] Thus, framing is a powerful tool by which leaders influence how others see and interpret reality.

Framing influences leadership effectiveness in numerous ways. It largely shapes the decision process in that frames determine the problems that need attention, the causes attributed to the problems, and the eventual choices for solving the problems.[37] Framing also increases a leaders's success in implementing goals and getting people's agreement, because once the right frames are in place, the right behavior follows.[38] Additionally, framing is critical to effective leadership in a global context because leaders must frame problems in common ways in order to prevent cultural misunderstandings. Finally, of course, framing is a vital element in visionary leadership. Shared visions are achieved through common framing. And shared visions transform individuals "from robots blindly following instructions to human beings engaged in a creative and purposeful venture."[39]

HOW EFFECTIVE LEADERS FRAME ISSUES As part of your quest to be an effective leader, you want to enhance your skills at framing issues. What tools are at your disposal and how do you use them? It has been suggested that there are five language forms that you can use to build memorable frames—metaphors, jargon, contrast, spin, and stories.[40]

Metaphors help us to understand one thing in terms of another. They work well when the standard of comparison is well understood and links logically to something else. When the manufacturing executive describes his goal of having "our production process running like a fine Swiss watch," he is using a metaphor to help his employees envision his ideal.

Organizational leaders are fond of using *jargon.* This is language that is peculiar to a particular profession, organization, or specific program. It conveys accurate meaning only to those who know the vernacular. Bell Atlantic used exercises such as "breaking the squares" and "finding the blue chips" in employee-training sessions, and they became symbols within the company for finding new ways of thinking and identifying priority assignments, respectively.[41] When a manager at Bell Atlantic says that "this project is a blue chip assignment," people know that it's important and should take priority.

When leaders use the *contrast* technique, they illuminate a subject in terms of its opposite. Why use an opposite to make a point? Sometimes its easier to say what a subject is *not* more easily than what it is. The ad campaign, "This is not your father's Oldsmobile" was meant to say more about what the new Olds wasn't than what it was. It was *not* conservative. It was *not* pedestrian. It was *not* just another GM brand. When an executive at a small software company was frustrated by his employees' lack of concern with keeping costs down, he constantly chided them with the phrase, "we're not Microsoft." The message he wanted to convey was that his company didn't have the financial resources of the software giant and they needed to reduce costs.

Presidential politics has created a new term—*spin.* Those who practice the art are called *spin doctors.* The objective of this technique is to cast your subject in a positive or negative light. Leaders who are good at "spinning" get others to interpret their interests in positive terms and opposing interests in negative terms. They emphasize their strengths and their opponent's weaknesses. When executives at British Air and American Airlines announced plans to cooperate on U.S.-U.K. routes, they gave it a positive spin by promoting the advantages to consumers. Richard Branson, head of Virgin Airlines and a direct competitor on these routes, responded with a negative spin—emphasizing the monopolistic implications and the downside effects on consumers.

Finally, leaders use *stories* to frame issues with examples that are larger than metaphors or jargon. You'll remember in Chapter 11 that we described the power of stories to convey an organization's culture. Well they also are powerful means to frame images. When leaders at 3M Co. continually retell the story of how the Post-it Note was discovered, they remind people of the importance the company places on creativity and serendipity in the innovation process.

▶ Acquiring Power

In the first *Godfather* film, Marlon Brando plays the part of Don Corleone, the head, or "Godfather," of a prominent Mafioso family. In one classic scene, the Godfather is told about an individual who doesn't want to comply with a family "request." The Godfather states this now-famous line (and perfect illustration of power): "I'm gonna make him an offer he can't refuse." The not-so-subtle message was that either you comply or you'll "be taking a swim with cement shoes"!

Leaders need power. Why? As a means to facilitate goal attainment. **Power** is the capacity for a leader to influence the behavior of another individual or group of individuals so that the individual or group does something it wouldn't otherwise do.[42] Probably the most important aspect of power is that it is a function of dependence.[43] The more someone is dependent on a leader, the greater the leader's power in the relationship. If your boss has the authority to fire you, if you desperately need your job to pay your bills, and if you don't think it would be possible to find a comparable job, your boss is likely to have considerable power over you. The Godfather could expect compliance with his request because he knows that people value their life!

Both leadership and power involve the attempt to influence others. But power doesn't require goal congruence nor is it singularly focused on downward influence. Power does not require goal compatibility; it merely requires dependence. Leadership, on the other hand, requires some congruence between the goals of the leader and the led. Moreover, leadership tends to focus on the leader's downward influence. It minimizes the importance of lateral and upward influence patterns. Power does not. The concept of power recognizes that peers and subordinates frequently attempt to influence the leader. It's not unusual, for instance, for a low-ranking member of an organization to filter information he gives to his boss so as to make certain decision options appear more attractive. This action, in essence, is an attempt to use upward influence to get the boss to behave in a way that favors the low-ranking member.

HOW DO YOU ACQUIRE POWER? There are two primary sources of power: an individual's *position* in an organization and the *personal characteristics* of the individual.[44] In formal organizations, managerial positions come with authority. As noted in chapter 8, this authority is the right to give orders and expect the orders to be obeyed. In addition, a managerial position typically comes with the discretion to allocate rewards and enact punishments. Managers can give out desirable work assignments, appoint people to interesting or important projects, provide favorable performance reviews, and recommend salary increases. But they also can dish out undesirable work shifts and assignments, put people onto boring or low-profile projects, write up unfavorable appraisals, recommend undesirable transfers or even demotions, and limit merit raises.

> You don't have to be a manager or have formal authority to have power.

You don't have to be a manager or have formal authority to have power. You can influence others through personal characteristics such as your expertise or personal charisma. In today's high-tech world, expertise has become an increasingly powerful source of influence. As jobs have become more specialized and complex, organizations and members have become dependent on experts with special skills or knowledge to achieve goals. Specialists such as software analysts, tax accountants, environmental engineers, and industrial psychologists are examples of individuals in organizations who can wield power as a result of their expertise. If a director of human resources needs valid selection tests to help identify high-potential candidates, and if the human resources director relies on the industrial psychologist on staff to provide these valid tests, that industrial psychologist has expert power. Of course, as we already discussed earlier in this chapter, charisma is a powerful source of influence. If you possess charismatic traits, you can use this power to get others to do what you want.

CREATING DEPENDENCY We said earlier that probably the most important aspect of power is that it is a function of dependence. When you possess a resource that others require but you alone control, you make them dependent on you, and, therefore, you gain power over them. That resource could be information, money, status, expertise, friends in high places, or anything else that others desire. Dependence is increased when the resource you control is both important and scarce.[45]

If nobody wants what you have, it is not going to create dependency. To create dependency, therefore, the thing or things you control must be perceived as being *important*. It has been found, for instance, that organizations actively seek to avoid uncertainty.[46] We should, therefore, expect that those individuals or groups who can absorb an organization's uncertainty will be perceived as controlling an important resource. For instance, a study of industrial organizations found that the marketing departments in these firms were consistently rated as the most powerful.[47] It was concluded by the researcher that the most critical uncertainty facing these firms was selling their products. This finding might suggest that, during a labor strike, the organization's negotiating representatives have increased power, or that engineers, as a group, would be more powerful at Intel than at Procter & Gamble. These inferences appear to be generally valid. Labor negotiators do become more powerful within the human resources area and the organization as a whole during periods of labor strife. An organization such as Intel, which is heavily technologically oriented, is highly dependent on its engineers to maintain its products' technical advantages and quality. And, at Intel, engineers are clearly a powerful group. At Procter & Gamble, marketing is the name of the game, and marketers are the most powerful occupational group. These examples support not only the view that the ability to reduce uncertainty increases a group's importance and, hence, its power but also that what is important is situational. It varies between organizations and undoubtedly also varies over time within any given organization.

As noted previously, if something is plentiful, possession of it will not increase your power. A resource needs to be perceived as *scarce* to create dependency. Scarcity can help to explain how low-ranking members in an organization who have important knowledge not available to high-ranking members gain power over the high-ranking members. Possession of a scarce resource — in this case, important knowledge — makes the high-ranking member dependent on the low-ranking member. The scarcity-power relationship also helps make sense out of behaviors of low-ranking members that otherwise might seem illogical, such as destroying the procedure manuals that describe how a job is done, refusing to train people in their jobs or even to show others exactly what they do, creating specialized language and terminology that inhibits others from understanding their jobs, or operating in secrecy so that an activity will appear more complex and difficult than it really is. Interestingly, technology has both increased and decreased the power of information in today's organizations. As mentioned earlier, expertise has become an increasingly potent power base in organizations. At the same time, computerized networks have widened the availability of information and, ironically, have thereby reduced leader power. When the leaders were the ones who knew things, they could use that knowledge to control followers. They no longer can. The democratization of information has lessened the power of many leaders by making information more plentiful.

IMPLICATIONS For managers, the message behind an understanding of power is that it is more than formal authority. As a manager of a group, you are not the only one with power. Your ability to get things accomplished depends, to a considerable degree, on learning who has power in your group and working to get them to use their power in ways that will help the group achieve its goals. A subordinate whom others admire or who has skills that your work group needs has the capacity to have power over you. Many managers have found themselves captive to subordinates who have no formal authority but who have power and who have learned to use it in ways to make their managers dependent upon them. As one young supervisor commented, "I'm very careful how I treat Sharon. She's been in the department longer than anyone. She knows everyone's job, backwards and forwards. People in the department look up to her. They follow her example. If

Sharon didn't think I was treating her right, she could turn the whole department against me. And make my life miserable." In addition, this discussion of power tells us that managers within an organization can expand their own power by increasing their alternatives, gaining control over specific scarce resources, or some combination of both.

▶ Providing Team Leadership

Leadership is increasingly taking place within a team context. As teams grow in popularity, the role of the leader in guiding team members takes on heightened importance. And the role of team leader is different from the traditional leadership role performed by first-line supervisors. J. D. Bryant, a supervisor at Texas Instruments' Forest Lane plant in Dallas, found that out.[48] One day he was happily overseeing a staff of fifteen circuit-board assemblers. The next day he was informed that the company was moving to teams and that he was to become a "facilitator." "I'm supposed to teach the teams everything I know and then let them make their own decisions," he said. Confused about his new role, he admitted, "There was no clear plan on what I was supposed to do." In this section, we consider the challenge of being a team leader, review the new roles that team leaders take on, and offer some tips on how to increase the likelihood that you can perform effectively in this position.

THE CHALLENGE OF TEAM LEADERSHIP   Many leaders are not equipped to handle the change to teams. As one prominent consultant noted, "Even the most capable managers have trouble making the transition because all the command-and-control type things they were encouraged to do before are no longer appropriate. There's no reason to have any skill or sense of this."[49] This same consultant estimated that "probably 15 percent of managers are natural team leaders; another 15 percent could never lead a team because it runs counter to their personality. [They're unable to sublimate their dominating style for the good of the team]. Then there's that huge group in the middle: Team leadership doesn't come naturally to them, but they can learn it."[50]

EXHIBIT 15-3

Source: Dilbert, by Scott Adams. Dilbert reprinted by permission of United Feature Syndicate, Inc.

The challenge for most managers, then, is to learn how to become an effective team leader. They have to learn skills such as sharing information, trusting others, giving up authority, and understanding when to intervene. Effective leaders have mastered the difficult balancing act of knowing when to leave their teams alone and when to intercede. New team leaders may try to retain too much control at a time when team members need more autonomy, or they may abandon their teams at times when the team needs support and help.[51]

TEAM LEADERSHIP ROLES A study of twenty organizations that had reorganized around teams found certain common responsibilities that all leaders had to assume. These included coaching, facilitating, handling disciplinary problems, reviewing team and individual performance, training, and communication.[52] Many of these responsibilities apply to managers in general. A more meaningful way to describe the team leader's job is to focus on two priorities: managing the team's external boundary and facilitating the team process.[53] We have broken these priorities down into four specific roles.

First, team leaders are *liaisons with external constituencies*. These include upper management, other internal teams, customers, and suppliers. The leader represents the team to other constituencies, secures needed resources, clarifies others' expectations of the team, gathers information from the outside, and shares this information with team members.

Second, team leaders are *troubleshooters*. When the team has problems and asks for assistance, team leaders sit in on meetings and help try to resolve the problems. This role is rarely related to technical or operation issues. Why? Because the team members typically know more about the tasks being done than does the team leader. The leader is most likely to contribute by asking penetrating questions, helping the team talk through problems, and getting needed resources from external constituencies. For instance, when a team in an aerospace firm found itself short-handed, its team leader took responsibility for getting more staff. He presented the team's case to upper management and got the approval through the company's human resources department.

Third, team leaders are *conflict managers*. When disagreements surface, they help process the conflict. What is the source of the conflict? Who is involved? What are the issues? What resolution options are available? What are the advantages and disadvantages of each? By getting team members to address questions such as these, the leader minimizes the disruptive aspects of intrateam conflicts.

Finally, team leaders are *coaches*. They clarify expectations and roles, teach, offer support, cheerlead, and do whatever else is necessary to help team members improve their work performance.

SUGGESTIONS FOR BEING AN EFFECTIVE TEAM LEADER If you want to be an effective team leader, what can you do?[54] Let's begin with the obvious: You need to develop your team-leadership skills. Specifically, these include coaching, conflict resolution, listening, feedback, and oral persuasion.

You need to overcome any fears you may have about admitting ignorance. Accept the reality that you don't have, and are unlikely to acquire, the level of technical skills held by the people on your team. The skills you bring are of another sort. Your job is to get people to focus on goals, provide motivation, and reduce barriers that the team may come across. A team leader at Honeywell's defense avionics division in Albuquerque quickly made this discovery: "My most important task was not trying to figure out everybody's job. It was to help this team feel as if they owned the project by getting them whatever information, financial or otherwise, they needed."[55]

When Nancy Toro, 33, was promoted to project leader at PictureTel, she faced new challenges in trying to coordinate a team of 6 engineers. "I've been an individual contributor for most of my career, so when PictureTel asked me to become project leader, I was very excited. But I had no experience. I'd been on plenty of teams, but I'd never led a team."

You need to learn to share authority. You need to empower your team. Doing so is a lot easier said than done. Most experienced managers have come to link responsibility and authority. If they're going to be held responsible for their team's performance, they want control over the decisions that will shape that performance. But effective leaders understand their teams' need to be given autonomy and that giving it to them won't necessarily result in disaster. Quite the contrary. Team norms can be powerful devices to control slackers and maintain high levels of performance.

Effective team leaders do not associate empowerment with abdication. The leader monitors the team's progress and lets the team solve its own problems. But as one consultant noted, "Too little help and direction is just as paralyzing as too much."[56] When the team is struggling, the effective leader knows when to let the team find its own solution and when to intervene. This distinction requires leaders to maintain ongoing communication and feedback on the team's progress.

▶ Mentoring

Many leaders create mentoring relationships. A **mentor** is a senior employee who sponsors and supports a less-experienced employee (a protégé). The mentoring role includes coaching, counseling, and sponsorship.[57] As a coach, mentors help to develop their protégés' skills. As counselors, mentors provide support and help bolster protégés' self-confidence. And as sponsors, mentors actively intervene on behalf of their protégés, lobby to get their protégés visible assignments, and politic to get their protégés rewards such as promotions and salary increases.

Successful mentors are good teachers. They can present ideas clearly, listen well, and empathize with the problems of their protégés. They also share experiences with the protégé, act as role models, share contacts, and provide guidance through the political maze of the organization. They provide advice and guidance on how to survive and get ahead in the organization and act as a sounding board for ideas that a protégé may be hesitant to share with his or her direct supervisor. A mentor vouches for a protégé, answers for him or her in the highest circles within the organization, and makes appropriate introductions.

SELECTION OF MENTORS   Some organizations have formal mentoring programs. New employees or young managers for whom the organization has high expectations are assigned to senior managers who play mentoring roles. Or employees might select a candidate from a set of volunteer mentors. At DuPont, for instance, 7,000 of the company's 60,000 U.S. employees have chosen a mentor from a list of volunteers whose skills and experience the protégés seek to tap.[58] More typically, senior managers informally select an employee and take that employee on as a protégé.

The most effective mentoring relationships exist outside the immediate boss-subordinate interface.[59] The boss-subordinate context has tension and an inherent conflict of interest, mostly attributable to managers directly evaluating the performance of subordinates, that limit openness and meaningful communication.

Why would a leader want to be a mentor? There are personal benefits to the leader as well as benefits for the organization. The mentor-protégé relationship gives the mentor unfiltered access to the attitudes and feelings of lower-ranking employees. Protégés can be an excellent source of potential problems by providing early warning signals. They provide timely information to upper managers that short-circuits the formal channels. So the mentor-protégé relationship is a valuable communication channel that allows mentors to have news of problems before they become common knowledge to others in upper management. In addition, in terms of leader self-interest, mentoring can provide personal satisfaction to senior executives. In the latter stages of their career, managers are often allowed the luxury of playing the part of elder states-person. They are respected for their judgment, built up over many years and through varied experiences. The opportunity to share this knowledge with others can be personally rewarding for the mentor.

VALUE OF MENTORS A major organizational benefit of mentoring is its influence in shaping and sustaining the organization's culture.[60] Mentors play a critical role in the socialization process, especially for new and inexperienced employees. They help reinforce strong cultures by conveying those stories, myths, and rituals that identify the organization's core values. In addition, mentors provide a support system for high-potential employees. Where mentors exist, protégés are often more motivated, better politically grounded, and less likely to quit. For instance, one study found that where a significant mentoring relationship existed, the protégés had more favorable and frequent promotions, were paid significantly more than those who were not mentored, had a greater level of commitment to the organization, and had greater career success.[61]

POTENTIAL BIASES Are all employees in an organization equally likely to participate in a mentoring relationship? Unfortunately the answer is no.[62] Evidence indicates that minorities and women are less likely to be chosen as protégés than are white males and thus are less likely to accrue the benefits of mentorship. Mentors tend to select protégés who are similar to themselves on criteria such as background, education, gender, race, ethnicity, and religion. "People naturally move to mentor and can more easily communicate with those with whom they most closely identify."[63] In the United States, for instance, upper-management positions in most organizations have been traditionally staffed by white males, so it is hard for minorities and women to be selected as protégés. In addition, in terms of cross-gender mentoring, senior male managers may select male protégés to minimize problems such as sexual attraction or gossip. Organizations have responded to this dilemma by increasing formal mentoring programs and providing training and coaching for potential mentors of special groups such as minorities and women.

Women often prefer to have another woman as a mentor. And minorities typically identify better with other minorities.

Coaching

We first introduced the topic of coaching in chapter 1 when we described how the "manager as boss" is changing to the "manager as coach." In this section, we want to offer some suggestions on how managers can improve their coaching skills.

WHAT IS COACHING? **Coaching** is a day-to-day hands-on process of helping employees recognize opportunities to improve their work performance.[64] A coach analyzes the employee's performance, provides insights as to how that performance can be improved, and offers the leadership to help the employee achieve that improvement. As a coach, you provide instruction, guidance, feedback, and encouragement to help employees improve their job performance.[65]

Coaching requires you to suspend judgment and evaluation. Managers, in the normal routine of carrying out their jobs, regularly express judgments about performance against previously established goals. As a coach, you focus on accepting employees the way they are and help them to make continual improvement toward the goal of developing their full potential.

THE TRANSITION FROM "BOSS" TO "COACH" Jim Chartrand, a plant manager with International Paper, provides some interesting insights into the transformation from "boss" to "coach."[66] Chartrand took over IP's Philadelphia liquid-packaging plant in 1984. The 130-person plant was struggling when he came in. His natural autocratic style—"I was a kick-ass-and-take-names manager whose job it was to tell people what they were doing wrong"—only made the situation worse. In 2 years, under his leadership, the plant's costs were excessive, quality was substandard, union relations were terrible, and customers were unhappy. Something had to change. Chartrand decided the changes had to begin with him.

"He had absolutely no empathy for employees," says Pat Kerner, a plate-room operator. Dennis Hughes, supervisor of the converting department, added that "Jim used to go to the supervisors and pound the heck out of them, leaving them no choice but to do the same to others." Chartrand's change program touched almost every part and person in the liquid-packaging plant. He reorganized the plant around teams. He empowered the teams to make operating decisions. Chartrand began regular strolls around the plant floor, looking for examples of workers doing positive things—so that he could provide recognition. He initiated an open-door policy and encouraged people to come into his office at any time and discuss anything. He reconfigured his office, replacing the visitor's chair in front of his desk with a round table. Now he could talk with people more informally, face-to-face. But, maybe most important, Chartrand changed the way he managed his people. He considers his transition from autocrat to coach as critical to his plant's success:

> Almost every individual in the organization, myself included, is capable and willing to perform at a higher level. To do that, we need coaching.
>
> A good coach listens to what people are saying, trying to get all the information available about a situation. The good coach then asks questions, prompting the person to work through the possibilities and come up with solutions. After all, the person closest to the problem likely has a better feel than I do for what will handle the problem. It's also important not to confuse being an expert with being a good coach. Many great athletic coaches weren't particularly good athletes, but they know how to build on others' successes.
>
> To become a great coach, I have to overcome my own ego and the feeling that no one else can do something as well as I can. I can never withhold knowledge or worry that helping someone else succeed will somehow threaten me.[67]

The results speak for themselves. After 3 years under the "new" Jim Chartrand, production quality at the Philadelphia plant has greatly improved while the scrap rate has dropped more than 15 percent; labor productivity is up significantly; cost per ton produced has dropped to one of the lowest in the industry; and customer complaints have decreased by 20 percent. Chartrand's performance resulted in his being promoted to facility manager at IP's folding-cartons plant in Richmond, Virginia.

GENERAL COACHING SKILLS There are three general coaching skills that leaders can apply to help their employees generate breakthroughs in performance.[68]

1. *Ability to analyze ways to improve an employee's performance and capabilities.* A coach looks for opportunities for an employee to expand his or her capabilities and improve performance. To do this you need to observe your employee's behavior on a day-to-day basis. You can also ask questions of the employee: Why do you do a task this way? Can it be improved? What other approaches might be used? Then listen to the employee.

You need to understand the world from the employee's perspective. Finally, show genuine interest in the person as an individual, not merely as an employee. Respect his or her individuality. More important than any technical expertise you can provide about improving job performance is the insight you have into the employee's uniqueness.

2. *Ability to create a supportive climate.* It is the coach's responsibility to reduce barriers to development and to foster a climate that encourages performance improvement. Through intensive listening and empowering employees to implement appropriate ideas they suggest, you can create a climate that contributes to a free and open exchange of ideas. You can also offer help by being available for assistance, guidance, or advice if asked. By being positive and upbeat, you can encourage your employees. Effective coaches do not use threats, because threats create a climate of fear and inhibition. Focus on mistakes as learning opportunities. Change implies risk, and employees must not feel that they will be punished for mistakes. When failure occurs, ask: What did we learn that can help us in the future?

   Analyze the factors that you control and reduce all obstacles that you can to help the employee to improve his or her job performance. Validate employees' efforts when they succeed, and point to what was missing when they fail. But never blame employees for poor results. Express to the employee the value of his or her contribution to your unit's goals.

3. *Ability to influence employees to change their behavior.* The ultimate test of coaching effectiveness is whether an employee's performance improves. But this is not a static concept. The concern is for ongoing growth and development. Consequently, you should help employees continually work toward improvement and encourage them by recognizing and rewarding even small improvements. Continual improvement, however, means that there are no absolute upper limits to an employee's job performance.

Your concern as a coach is to enable your employees to accomplish tasks independently at a high level of effectiveness when you're not there to assist. Your task is education and training so that employees can solve their own problems and perform effectively independently in the future.

> **More important than any technical expertise you can provide about improving job performance is the insight you have into the employee's uniqueness.**

Self-Leadership

In the previous chapter, we discussed situations where formal leaders are relatively unimportant. An extension of this idea is **self-leadership**. This is a set of processes through which individuals control their own behavior.[69] That is, effective leaders, or what proponents of self-leadership call *superleaders*, focus primarily on their followers and help them to lead themselves.

What can you do if you want to help create self-leaders? The following points have been suggested:[70]

1. *Model self-leadership.* Practice self-observation, setting challenging personal goals, self-direction, and self-reinforcement. Then display these behaviors and encourage others to rehearse and then produce them.

2. *Encourage employees to create self-set goals.* Having quantitative, specific goals is the most important part of self-leadership.

3. *Encourage the use of self-rewards to strengthen and increase desirable behaviors.* In contrast, self-punishment should be limited only to occasions when the employee has been dishonest or destructive.

4. *Create positive thought patterns.* Encourage employees to use mental imagery and self-talk to further stimulate self-motivation.

5. *Create a climate of self-leadership.* Redesign the work to increase the natural rewards of a job and focus on these naturally rewarding features of work to increase motivation. This would include suggestions offered by the Job Characteristics Model described in chapter 7.

6. *Encourage self-criticism.* Encourage individuals to be critical of their own performance.

The underlying assumptions behind self-leadership are that people are responsible, capable, and able to exercise initiative without the external constraints of bosses, rules, or regulations. Given the proper support, individuals can monitor and control their own behavior.

The importance of self-leadership has increased with the expanded popularity of teams. Empowered, self-managed teams need individuals who are themselves self-directed. Management can't expect individuals who have spent their organizational lives under boss-centered leadership to suddenly adjust to self-managed teams. Training in self-leadership is an excellent means to help employees make the transition from dependence to autonomy.

THE GENDER ISSUE: DO MEN AND WOMEN LEAD DIFFERENTLY?

An extensive review of the evidence suggests two conclusions regarding gender and leadership.[71] First, the similarities between men and women tend to outweigh the differences. Second, what differences there are seem to be that women prefer a more democratic leadership style, while men feel more comfortable with a directive style.

The similarities among men and women leaders should not be completely surprising. Almost all the studies looking at this issue have used managerial positions as being synonymous with leadership. Consequently, gender differences apparent in the general population do not tend to be evident. Why? Because of career self-selection and organization selection. Just as people who choose careers in law enforcement or civil engineering have a lot in common, individuals who choose managerial careers also tend to have commonalities. People with traits associated with leadership—such as intelligence, confidence, and sociability—are likely to be perceived as leaders and encouraged to pursue careers in which they can exert leadership. This is true regardless of gender. Similarly, organizations tend to recruit and promote people into leadership positions who project leadership attributes. The result is that, regardless of gender, those who achieve formal leadership positions in organizations tend to be more alike than different.

Despite the previous conclusion, studies indicate some differences in the inherent leadership styles between women and men. Women tend to adopt a more democratic leadership style. They encourage participation, share power and information, and attempt to enhance followers' self-worth. They prefer to lead through inclusion and rely on their charisma, expertise, contacts, and interpersonal skills to influence others. Men, on the other hand, are more likely to use a directive command-and-control style. They rely on the formal authority of their position for their influence base. These differences are typically attributed to early socialization experiences. Most young girls are socialized to display care and consideration, while boys are socialized to compete. However, consistent with our first conclusion, these findings need to be qualified. The tendency for female leaders to be more democratic than males declines when women are in male-dominated jobs. Apparently, group norms and masculine stereotypes of leaders override personal preferences so that women abandon their feminine styles in such jobs and act more autocratically.

Given that men have historically held the great majority of leadership positions in organizations, it is tempting to assume that the existence of the noted differences between men and women would automatically work to favor men. It doesn't. In today's organizations, flexibility, teamwork, trust, and information sharing are replacing rigid structures,

Catherine Good Abbott, CEO

Catherine Good Abbott is a woman in a once macho industry. She has a direct, businesslike style. But the head of Columbia Energy Group, Oliver G. Richard III, thinks she's just the right person to head up two key subsidiaries—Columbia Gas Transmission and Columbia Gulf Transmission. They encompass a natural gas pipeline network with revenues in excess of $1 billion a year.

Abbott has a bachelor's degree from Swarthmore College and a master's from the Kennedy School at Harvard. From 1976 to 1982, as an analyst with the Environmental Protection Agency in Washington, D.C., she helped shape deregulation policies in the Jimmy Carter White House. In 1982, she jumped to a trade group, the Interstate Natural Gas Association, as a policy analyst. Then in 1985, Abbott moved to Houston as a vice president at Enron, a major energy producer, where she marketed gas nationwide. There she honed her negotiation skills. In late 1995, when Oliver Richard took over the helm of Columbia Energy Group, he offered Abbott the $300,000-a-year post as CEO of his two biggest subsidiaries.

According to insiders, Abbott's rise to become CEO in an industry dominated by males is a sign of how the industry's old utilitylike, engineer-dominated culture is giving way to one where marketing, deal making, and financial innovation reign. Says Richard: "It's a time for change in our business. It's a time to make a difference, and it's a time to have new leadership. She represents all those things."

Cathy Abbott is seen by many as "hard as nails" because of her direct style and ability to be a tough negotiator. But Abbott also impresses foes and friends alike with her passionate but non-ideological advocacy. "Any discomfort I cause has more to do with my personality and style than the fact that I am a woman," she says.

Source: Based on J. Weber, "Cathy Abbott Is No Good Ol' Boy," *Business Week*, February 12, 1996, pp. 94–96.

---

competitive individualism, control, and secrecy. The best managers listen, nurture, share power, and provide support to their people. And many women seem to do those things better than men. As a specific example, the expanded use of cross-functional teams in organizations means that effective managers must become skillful negotiators. The leadership styles women typically use can make them better at negotiating, as they are less likely than men to focus on wins, losses, and competition. They tend to treat negotiations in the context of a continuing relationship—trying hard to make the other party a winner in his or her own and others' eyes.

The topic of leadership and ethics has received surprisingly little attention. Only very recently have ethicists and leadership researchers begun to consider the ethical implications in leadership.[72] Why now? One reason may be the growing general interest in ethics throughout the field of management. Another reason may be the discovery by probing

THE ETHICS ISSUE: IS THERE A MORAL DIMENSION TO LEADERSHIP?

biographers that many of our past leaders—such as Martin Luther King Jr., John F. Kennedy, and Franklin D. Roosevelt—suffered from ethical shortcomings. Regardless, no contemporary discussion of leadership is complete without addressing its ethical dimension.

Ethics touches on leadership at a number of junctures. Transformational leaders, for instance, have been described by one authority as fostering moral virtue when they try to change the attitudes and behaviors of followers.[73] Charisma, too, has an ethical component. Unethical leaders are likely to use their charisma to enhance power over followers, directed toward self-serving ends. Ethical leaders are considered to use their charisma in a socially constructive way to serve others.[74] There is also the issue of abuse of power by leaders, for example, when they give themselves large salaries and bonuses while, at the same time, they seek to cut costs by laying off longtime employees. And, of course, the topic of trust explicitly deals with honesty and integrity in leadership.

Leadership effectiveness needs to address the means that a leader uses in trying to achieve goals as well as the content of those goals. GE's Jack Welch, for instance, is consistently described as a highly effective leader because he has succeeded in achieving outstanding returns for shareholders. But Welch is also widely regarded as one of the world's toughest managers. He is regularly listed high on Fortune's annual list of the most hated and reviled executives. Similarly, Bill Gates's success in leading Microsoft to domination of the world's software business has been achieved by means of an extremely demanding work culture. Microsoft's culture demands long work hours by employees and is intolerant of individuals who want to balance work and their personal life.

In addition, ethical leadership must address the content of a leader's goals. Are the changes that the leader seeks for the organization morally acceptable? Is a business leader effective if he builds his organization's success by selling products that damage the health of its users? This question might be asked of tobacco executives. Or is a military leader successful if he wins a war that should not have been fought in the first place?

Leadership is not value-free. Before we judge any leader as effective, we should consider both the means used by the leader to achieve his or her goals and the moral content of those goals.

FINDING AND CREATING EFFECTIVE LEADERS

We have covered a lot of ground in these two chapters on leadership. But the ultimate goal of our review is to answer this question: How can organizations find or create effective leaders? Let's use our review to try to answer that question.[75]

Selection

The entire process that organizations go through to fill management positions is essentially an exercise in trying to identify individuals who will be effective leaders. You might begin by reviewing the job specification for the position to be filled. What knowledge, skills, and abilities are needed to do the job effectively? You should try to analyze the situation in order to find candidates who will make a proper match.

Testing is useful for identifying and selecting leaders. Personality tests can be used to look for traits associated with leadership—intelligence, aggressiveness, industriousness, self-confidence, persistence. Testing to find a leadership candidate's score on self-monitoring also makes sense. High self-monitors are likely to outperform their low-scoring counterparts because the former are better at reading situations and adjusting their behavior accordingly. You can additionally use simulation tests such as the assessment-center exercises described in chapter 9. Having candidates act out leadership situations, and observing their behavior in those situations, has been found to be an effective selection device.[76]

Interviews additionally provide an opportunity to evaluate leadership candidates. For instance, we know that experience, per se, is a poor predictor of leader effectiveness, but situation-specific experience is relevant. You can use the interview to determine if a candidate's prior experience fits with the situation you are trying to fill. Similarly, the interview is a reasonably good vehicle for identifying the degree to which a candidate has leadership traits such as an outgoing personality, strong verbal skills, a vision, or a charismatic physical presence.

We know the importance of situational factors in leadership success. And we should use this knowledge to match leaders to situations. Does the situation require a change-focused leader? If so, look for transformational qualities. If not, look for transactional qualities. You might also ask: Is leadership actually important in this specific position? There may be situational factors that substitute for or neutralize leadership. If there are, then the leader essentially performs a figurehead or symbolic role, and the importance of selecting the "right" person is not particularly crucial.

TODAY ? or TOMORROW ?

Leadership Software

Knowledge of what makes an effective leader continues to be translated into the design of training materials.

In the mid-1970s, Fred Fiedler and his associates took their findings (see chapter 14) and created a self-teaching guide, *Improving Leadership Effectiveness*.[a] This 220-page paperback reviews Fiedler's contingency model, provides a rating form to assess an individual's style, and supplies a series of rating scales for evaluating situational characteristics. It was an early attempt to help individuals improve their leadership skills.

By the 1980s, leadership advocates had begun to utilize the capabilities of computers to help individuals sort out the complexities in choosing a leadership style. Foremost among these were Vroom and Jago's computerization of their leader-participation model.[b] To aid managers in assessing 12 contingency variables and selecting from among five decision-making styles, they developed software to facilitate an individual's ability to define their situation, answer the questions about problem attributes, and arrive at a strategy for decision-making participation.

The latest degree of sophistication is illustrated in Kouzes and Posner's Leadership Practices Inventory (LPI).[c] The LPI facilitator's guide contains a 30-item inventory to evaluate your performance and effectiveness as a leader plus scoring software. An accompanying workbook teaches you how to interpret your score, how to compare your scores with other leaders, and how to improve upon your leadership skills with more than 140 suggested action steps.

Researchers have only scratched the surface in the creation and availability of leadership-training software. In the not so distant future, virtual-reality simulations will undoubtedly allow managers and aspiring managers to develop their leadership skills in an environment not unlike the way today's airlines train pilots. Leadership simulators will allow individuals to test themselves in situations where errors and misjudgments turn into learning experiences rather than disgruntled employees.

Sources: (a) F. E. Fiedler, M. M. Chemers, and L. Mahar, *Improving Leadership Effectiveness*: The Leader Match Concept (New York: Wiley, 1976); (b) V. H. Vroom and A. G. Jago, *The New Leadership* (Upper Saddle River, NJ: Prentice Hall, 1988); and (c) J. M. Kouzes and B. Z. Posner, *The Leadership Practices Inventory* series (San Francisco: Jossey-Bass, 1997).

The Center for Creative Leadership in North Carolina conducts training exercises (like that shown) to help individuals develop their leadership skills.

Training

Organizations, in aggregate, spend billions of dollars, yen, and marks on leadership training and development. And these efforts take many forms—from $20,000 executive leadership programs offered by universities such as Harvard, to the hiring of executive coaches, to rock-climbing experiences at the Outward Bound School. Although much of the money spent on training may provide dubious benefits, our review suggests that there are some things management can do to get the maximum effect from their leadership-training budgets.[77]

First, let's recognize the obvious. People are not equally trainable. Leadership training of any kind is likely to be more successful, for instance, with high self-monitors than with low self-monitors. Such individuals have the flexibility to change their behavior.

What kinds of things can individuals learn that might be related to higher leader effectiveness? It may be a bit optimistic to believe that we can teach "vision-creation," but we can teach implementation skills. We can train people to develop "an understanding about content themes critical to effective visions."[78] We also can teach skills such as coaching and mentoring. The evidence is mixed on whether we can teach people to have a greater need for power, but we can certainly train individuals on how to use power, especially in a positive way. And leaders can be taught situational-analysis skills. They can learn how to evaluate situations, how to modify situations to make them fit better with their style, and how to assess which leader behaviors might be most effective in given situations.

On an optimistic note, there is evidence suggesting that behavioral training through modeling exercises can increase individuals' ability to exhibit charismatic leadership qualities. The success of the researchers mentioned earlier (in "Are Charismatic Leaders Born or Made?" on page 474) in actually scripting undergraduate business students to "play" charismatic is a case in point.[79]

There is a variety of additional material available on the CD-ROM and companion Web site that accompany this text. You can access this information through the CD-ROM or by visiting the Web site at <**www.prenhall.com/robbins**>.

SUMMARY

(This summary is organized by the chapter-opening learning objectives on page 470.)

1. Transactional leaders guide and motivate their followers in the direction of established goals by clarifying role and task requirements. Transformational leaders provide outstanding leadership by inspiring followers to transcend their self-interests for the good of the organization. Transformational leaders are capable of having a profound and extraordinary effect on followers.

2. Charismatic leaders have self-confidence, a vision, ability to articulate the vision, strong convictions about the vision, and behavior that is out of the ordinary. They are perceived as change agents and are environmentally sensitive.

3. Visionary leaders have the ability to express the vision through their behavior, to explain the vision to others, and to extend the vision in a variety of situations.

4. Framing shapes the decision process because it determines the problems that need attention, the causes attributed to

problems, and the eventual choices for solving the problems. Framing also shapes goals and behavior, and is critical to creating shared visions.

5. Leaders increase follower dependence by controlling resources that are important, scarce, and nonsubstitutable.

6. Team leaders play four roles: liaisons with external constituencies, troubleshooters, conflict managers, and coaches.

7. Mentors coach, counsel, and support a protégé who is lower in the organization.

8. Coaching is a day-to-day hands-on process of helping employees recognize opportunities to improve their work performance.

9. The leadership styles of men and women are more alike than different. However, in general, men are more comfortable with a directive style, and women prefer a more democratic style.

10. Leadership concepts can help practicing managers make selection decisions and design training programs that will increase the effectiveness of managers.

REVIEW QUESTIONS

1. Are transformational leaders always more effective than transactional leaders? Explain.

2. What could you do if you wanted others to perceive you as a charismatic leader?

3. "Great leaders have a vision." Do you agree or disagree with this statement? Explain.

4. How does a leader increase self-leadership among his or her followers?

5. Contrast positional and personal sources of power.

6. Give some examples of things you could do to frame issues in your favor.

7. How does one become an effective team leader?

8. As a new employee in an organization, why might you want to acquire a mentor? Why might women and minorities have more difficulty in finding a mentor than would white males?

9. Describe general coaching skills.

10. Why do you think successful leaders of both genders in specific organizations tend to have a common leadership style?

IF I WERE THE MANAGER . . .

Ian Campbell's Dilemma

It's hard to find anyone who doesn't like Sherm Hayes. Hired as plant manager for the ESS Plastics facility in Parkersburg, West Virginia, Hayes immediately won over the plant's 330 employees by learning everyone's name after he had worked there only a week. Friendly, outgoing, and upbeat, Sherm Hayes is a charmer. The problem is, he doesn't seem to get much done.

Workers regularly describe Hayes in terms such as "charismatic," "visionary," and "inspiring." They appreciate his informality, his friendliness, and his availability to even the lowest-ranking employees. As one machine operator put it, "Mr. Hayes has been here only a year but he's really changed this place. The previous plant manager was aloof and autocratic. He didn't care about his people. But Mr. Hayes cares. He's always walking around the plant, answering questions, and talking with everyone. He's a regular guy."

In spite of Hayes's popularity, two facts suggest that there are problems that many don't see. First, three of the four department heads who oversee operations and report directly to Hayes have resigned recently. All three complained about Hayes's tendency to procrastinate and his inability to make decisions. They also felt that his "hands-on" style of managing preempted their own attempts to run their departments. Second, ESS Plastics division manager Ian Campbell—the person to whom Sherm Hayes reports—has been very disappointed with the performance of the Parkersburg plant. Month-to-month comparisons of this year's productivity figures against the previous year's show declines of between 2.3 percent and 7.7 percent. Meanwhile, the other five plants under Campbell have all shown consistent month-to-month productivity improvements.

If you were Ian Campbell, what would you do?

Coaching

You work for a large mortgage brokering company. The company has thirty offices in California. You are supervisor of the Napa Valley office and have seven mortgage brokers, an assistant, and a secretary reporting to you. Your business entails helping home buyers find mortgages and acting as a link between lenders and borrowers in getting loans approved and processed.

Todd Corsetti is one of your brokers. He has been in the Napa Valley office for two and a half years. Before that, he sold commercial real estate. You have been in your Napa Valley job for 14 months; before that you supervised a smaller office for the same company.

You have not been pleased with Todd's job performance. So you decide to review his personnel file. His first 6-month review stated: "Todd is enthusiastic. He is a bit disorganized but willing to learn. Seems to have good potential." After a year, his previous supervisor had written, "Todd seems to be losing interest. Seems frequently disorganized. Often rude to clients. Did not mention these problems to him. Hope he'll improve. His long-term potential now much more in question."

You have not spent much time with Todd, perhaps because your offices are far apart. But probably the real reason is that he is not easy to talk to and you have little in common. When you took the Napa Valley job, you decided that, to make sure you had a good grasp of the people and the situation, you would wait some time before attacking any problems.

But Todd's problems have gotten too visible to ignore. He is consistently missing his quarterly sales projections. On the basis of mortgages processed, he is your lowest performer. In addition, his reports are constantly late. After reviewing last month's performance reports, you made an appointment yesterday to meet him today at 9:00 A.M. But he didn't show up and wasn't in his office. You waited 15 minutes and gave up. Your secretary tells you that Todd regularly comes in late for work in the morning and takes extra-long coffee breaks. Last week, Valerie Oleata, who has the office next to Todd's, complained to you that Todd's behavior was demoralizing for her and some of the other brokers.

You don't want to fire Todd. It wouldn't be easy to find a replacement. Moreover, he has a lot of contacts with new-home builders, which brings in a number of borrowers to your office. In fact, maybe 60 percent of the business generated by your entire office comes from builders who have personal ties to Todd. If Todd were to leave your company and go to a competitor, he would probably be able to convince the builders to take their business somewhere else.

Directions: Break into groups of two. One person plays the role of the supervisor. The other plays the role of Todd. You have up to 15 minutes to simulate how a supervisor could use his or her coaching skills to deal with Todd's problem.

Projecting Charisma

People who are charismatic engage in specific behaviors.

1. *They project a powerful, confident, and dynamic presence.* This has both verbal and nonverbal components. They use a captivating and engaging voice tone. They convey confidence. They also talk directly to people, maintaining direct eye contact, and holding their body posture in a way that says they're sure of themselves. They speak clearly, avoid stammering, and avoid sprinkling their sentences with non-content phrases such as "uhhh" and "you know."
2. *They articulate an overarching goal.* They have a vision for the future, unconventional ways of achieving the vision, and the ability to communicate the vision to others. The vision is a clear statement of where they want to go and how they're going to get there. They are able to persuade others how the achievement of this vision is in the others' self-interest. They look for fresh and radically different approaches to problems. The road to achieving their vision is novel but also appropriate to the context. They not only have a vision but they're able to get others to buy into it. The real power of Martin Luther King Jr. was not that he had a dream, but that he could articulate it in terms that made it accessible to millions.
3. *They communicate high performance expectations and confidence in others' ability to meet these expectations.* They demonstrate their confidence in people by stating ambitious goals for them individually and as a group. They convey absolute belief that they will achieve their expectations.
4. *They are sensitive to the needs of followers.* Charismatic leaders get to know their followers individually. They understand their individual needs and are able to develop in-

tensely personal relationships with each. They do this through encouraging followers to express their points of view, being approachable, genuinely listening to and caring about their followers' concerns, and by asking questions so they can learn what is really important to them.

Now that you know what charismatic leaders do, here's an opportunity to practice projecting charisma.

1. The class should break into groups of four or five. Two students should be chosen and identified as Leader A and Leader B.
2. Leader A's task is to lead his or her group through a new-student orientation to your college. The orientation should last about 10 to 15 minutes. Leader A should assume that group members are new to your college and are unfamiliar with the campus. Remember, Leader A should attempt to project himself or herself as charismatic.

3. Now, Leader B will lead the group in a 10- to 15-minute program on how to study more effectively for college exams. Leader B should take a few minutes to think about what has worked well for him or her and assume that the rest of the group are new students interested in improving their study habits. Again remember that Leader B should attempt to project himself or herself as charismatic.
4. When both role plays are complete, the group should assess how well each did in projecting charisma and how they might improve.

Source: This exercise is based on J. M. Howell and P. J. Frost, "A Laboratory Study of Charismatic Leadership," *Organizational Behavior and Human Decision Processes*, April 1989, pp. 243–69.

CASE EXERCISE

Matt Scott at Fore Systems, Inc.

Pressure. Deadlines. It comes with the job. Matt Scott learned that working on a team and leading one are two different tasks.

About a year after joining Fore Systems, Inc., a Pittsburgh-based software company, Matt was placed in charge of six software engineers. Their job was to develop—from conception to near delivery—a major computer program. Almost a year has passed, and Matt, now age 29, is working with his team, in nearly round-the-clock shifts, to work out some bugs in a subprogram.

Matt is finding that running a team is a tumultuous process. He's tried to be coach, referee, cheerleader, and player. He's also sought to create an informal atmosphere that would "let my enthusiasm flow over." The experience hasn't been an altogether happy one. He's grown frustrated at his mounting paperwork and crowded meeting schedule. While he wants to be a peer to his team members, he has often had to be their boss, handing out performance reviews during the project's final weeks. And he's found his management duties stealing time away from doing what he loves most—sitting in front of his computer, designing and writing computer code.

When Matt took the job with Fore Systems, he was lured by the chance to write long computer codes. It would allow him to combine the creative thrill of composing short stories with the mental challenge of solving a tough crossword puzzle. "My mind loves solving these problems," he says. But the company

has grown rapidly. It was founded by four teachers and researchers in 1990. By 1994, it employed about 200 people. Today it employs more than 1,400. And most of these people are working on teams, since company projects tend to be too big for any one person.

As this project comes to a close, Matt has decided to give up his manager's title. His bosses speak of his performance and that of his team in glowing terms. Matt knew he was good at leading the team, but he wasn't happy. He felt he had failed at handling a lot of the minutiae associated with managing. And he missed writing code.

Returning to his code-writing job, Matt's salary will remain at $62,000. He'll be giving up his corner cubicle and some perks. But he'll have more time to devote to his wife and newborn baby. "And I'll never have to do a review again," he says.

QUESTIONS

1. What does this case say about managerial versus nonmanagerial jobs?
2. What, if anything, could management have done to make Matt Scott's transition to team leader less traumatic for him?
3. What are the implications of this case for selecting team leaders?

Source: Based on M. Murray, "A Software Engineer Becomes a Manager, with Many Regrets," *Wall Street Journal*, May 14, 1997, p. A1.

Casting a Long Shadow

"All companies are shadows of their leader." This is a statement made by Tom Velez of CTA, who has proven to have a huge shadow indeed. He has provided the strong leadership that guided his company as it grew from nothing to $150 million in sales revenues. What can Velez teach us about leadership?

The Velez family emigrated from Ecuador to the United States, and both of Tom's parents were uneducated. However, his father strongly believed in education and also believed in music. With these family values, it's not surprising that Velez attended the Julliard School of Music. However, he soon realized that, although he was a good violinist, he would never be great. He began to look at other possibilities. At the time, there weren't many opportunities for Hispanics, but Velez knew that mathematics was easy for him and this self-knowledge guided him in his job search. He eventually ended up in a job at the National Aeronautics and Space Administration (NASA) and went on to get his Ph.D. in mathematics at Georgetown University. Mathematics was a core skill that NASA needed in writing computer programs and understanding the physical phenomena coming from the data being gathered from space exploration, so Velez's skills seemed tailor made. However, in addition to his study of mathematics, Velez had studied philosophy. One of the philosophical ideas he took to heart was the idea of the creative genius—that is, a person who makes things happen. Because of NASA's mission and reputation, he expected to find many creative geniuses there; instead, he found

that it was only a few people who made the biggest difference. From NASA, Velez went on to work at Martin Marietta, a large defense contractor.

Velez soon left Martin Marietta to form CTA with a partner. What does CTA do? It provides information systems and resource management capabilities to the U.S. government. How has Velez encouraged, in his organization, the type of creative genius he considers so important to success? His leadership approach has been based on the belief that people aren't always attracted to paychecks. Instead, they're attracted to challenge, to opportunities, and to culture. He advises finding a way to build a team incrementally and to be a leader. As a leader, admit you're not the best. Admit you need their help and then reward those creative geniuses. How? Give them ownership in the business; give them freedom. And, he says, remember that creating the culture you want your business to have is a day-by-day, month-by-month, year-by-year process.

QUESTIONS

1. What role do you think Velez's pursuit of creative genius plays in the way he leads CTA? Explain.
2. At NASA, what types of power do you think Velez might have had? Explain.
3. Do you agree with Velez's philosophy that people aren't always attracted to paychecks? Discuss.
4. What can you learn about leadership from Tom Velez?

Source: Based on *Small Business Today, Show 107.*

1. See D. Sheff, "Richard Branson," *Forbes ASAP,* February 24, 1997, pp. 95–102; and M. F. R. Kets de Vries, "Charisma in Action: The Transformational Abilities of Virgin's Richard Branson and ABB's Percy Barnevik," *Organizational Dynamics,* Winter 1998, pp. 7–21.
2. See, for example, B. M. Bass, *Leadership and Performance Beyond Expectations* (New York: Free Press, 1985); B. M. Bass, "From Transactional to Transformational Leadership: Learning to Share the Vision," *Organizational Dynamics,* Winter 1990, pp. 19–31; F. J. Yammarino, W. D. Spangler, and B. M. Bass, "Transformational Leadership and Performance: A Longitudinal Investigation," *Leadership Quarterly,* Spring 1993, pp. 81–102; P. Bycio, R. D. Hackett, and J. S. Allen, "Further Assessments of Bass's

(1985) Conceptualization of Transactional and Transformational Leadership," *Journal of Applied Psychology,* August 1995, pp. 468–78; and B. S. Pawar and K. K. Eastman, "The Nature and Implications of Contextual Influences on Transformational Leadership: A Conceptual Examination," *Academy of Management Review,* January 1997, pp. 80–109.
3. R. J. House and P. M. Podsakoff, "Leadership Effectiveness: Past Perspectives and Future Directions for Research," in J. Greenberg (ed.), *Organizational Behavior: The State of the Science* (Hillsdale, NJ: Lawrence Erlbaum Associates, 1994), p. 55.
4. Ibid.
5. B. M. Bass, "Leadership: Good, Better, Best," *Organizational*

Dynamics, Winter 1985, pp. 26–40; and J. Seltzer and B. M. Bass, "Transformational Leadership: Beyond Initiation and Consideration," *Journal of Management*, December 1990, pp. 693–703.

6. Cited in B. M. Bass and B. J. Avolio, "Developing Transformational Leadership: 1992 and Beyond," *Journal of European Industrial Training*, January 1990, p. 23.

7. J. J. Hater and B. M. Bass, "Supervisors' Evaluation and Subordinates' Perceptions of Transformational and Transactional Leadership," *Journal of Applied Psychology*, November 1988, pp. 695–702.

8. Bass and Avolio, "Developing Transformational Leadership."

9. J. A. Conger and R. N. Kanungo, "Behavioral Dimensions of Charismatic Leadership," in J. A. Conger, R. N. Kanungo and Associates (eds.), *Charismatic Leadership* (San Francisco: Jossey-Bass, 1988), p. 79.

10. R. J. House, "A 1976 Theory of Charismatic Leadership," in J. G. Hunt and L. L. Larson (eds.), *Leadership: The Cutting Edge* (Carbondale: Southern Illinois University Press, 1977), pp. 189–207.

11. W. Bennis, "The Four Competencies of Leadership," *Training and Development Journal*, August 1984, pp. 15–19.

12. Conger and Kanungo, "Behavioral Dimensions of Charismatic Leadership," pp. 78–97; and J. A. Conger and R. N. Kanungo, "Charismatic Leadership in Organizations: Perceived Behavioral Attributes and Their Measurement," *Journal of Organizational Behavior*, September 1994, pp. 439–52.

13. B. Shamir, R. J. House, and M. B. Arthur, "The Motivational Effects of Charismatic Leadership: A Self-Concept Theory," *Organization Science*, November 1993, pp. 577–94.

14. R. J. House, J. Woycke, and E. M. Fodor, "Charismatic and Noncharismatic Leaders: Differences in Behavior and Effectiveness," in Conger, Kanungo, et al. (eds.), *Charismatic Leadership*, pp. 103–04; and D. A. Waldman, B. M. Bass, and F. J. Yammarino, "Adding to Contingent-Reward Behavior: The Augmenting Effect of Charismatic Leadership," *Group & Organization Studies*, December 1990, pp. 381–94.

15. J. A. Conger and R. N. Kanungo, "Training Charismatic Leadership: A Risky and Critical Task," in Conger, Kanungo, et al. (eds.), *Charismatic Leadership*, pp. 309–23.

16. R. J. Richardson and S. K. Thayer, *The Charisma Factor: How to Develop Your Natural Leadership Ability* (Upper Saddle River, NJ: Prentice Hall, 1993).

17. J. M. Howell and P. J. Frost, "A Laboratory Study of Charismatic Leadership," *Organizational Behavior and Human Decision Processes*, April 1989, pp. 243–69.

18. House, "A 1976 Theory of Charismatic Leadership."

19. J. A. Conger, *The Charismatic Leader: Behind the Mystique of Exceptional Leadership* (San Francisco: Jossey-Bass, 1989); R. Hogan, R. Raskin, and D. Fazzini, "The Dark Side of Charisma," in K. E. Clark and M. B. Clark (eds.), *Measures of Leadership* (West Orange, NJ: Leadership Library of America, 1990); and D. Sankowsky, "The Charismatic Leader as Narcissist: Understanding the Abuse of Power," *Organizational Dynamics*, Spring 1995, pp. 57–71.

20. G. P. Zachary, "How 'Barbarian' Style of Philippe Kahn Led Borland into Jeopardy," *Wall Street Journal*, June 2, 1994, p. A1.

21. This definition is based on M. Sashkin, "The Visionary Leader," in Conger, Kanungo, et al. (eds.), *Charismatic Leadership*, pp. 124–25; B. Nanus, *Visionary Leadership* (New York: Free Press, 1992), p. 8; and N. H. Snyder and M. Graves, "Leadership and Vision," *Business Horizons*, January–February 1994, p. 1.

22. Nanus, *Visionary Leadership*, p. 8.

23. P. C. Nutt and R. W. Backoff, "Crafting Vision," *Journal of Management Inquiry*, December 1997, p. 309.

24. Nanus, *Visionary Leadership*, pp. 178–79.

25. Snyder and Graves, "Leadership and Vision," p. 2.

26. Cited in L. B. Korn, "How the Next CEO Will Be Different," *Fortune*, May 22, 1989, p. 157.

27. J. C. Collins and J. I. Porras, *Built to Last: Successful Habits of Visionary Companies* (New York: HarperBusiness, 1994).

28. See, for instance, D. Lavin, "Robert Eaton Thinks 'Vision' Is Overrated and He's Not Alone," *Wall Street Journal*, October 4, 1993, p. A1.

29. Nutt and Backoff, "Crafting Vision," pp. 308–28. See also J. R. Lucas, "Anatomy of a Vision Statement," *Management Review*, February 1998, pp. 22–26.

30. Cited in L. Larwood, C. M. Falbe, M. P. Kriger, and P. Miesing, "Structure and Meaning of Organizational Vision," *Academy of Management Journal*, June 1995, pp. 740–69.

31. Cited in Nanus, *Visionary Leadership*, pp. 141, 173, 178; and Nutt and Backoff, "Crafting Vision," pp. 1, 3.

32. See S. J. Holladay and W. T. Coombs, "Speaking of Visions and Visions Being Spoken: An Exploration of the Effects of Content and Delivery on Perceptions of Leader Charisma," *Management Communication Quarterly*, November 1994, pp. 165–89; R. Awamleh and W. L. Gardner, "Perceptions of Leader Charisma and Effectiveness: The Effects of Vision Content, Vision Delivery and Organizational Performance," paper presented at the 1997 Southern Management Association Meetings, Atlanta, GA, August 1997; and J. R. Baum, E. A. Locke, and S. A. Kirkpatrick, "A Longitudinal Study of the Relation of Vision and Vision Communication to Venture Growth in Entrepreneurial Firms," *Journal of Applied Psychology*, February 1998, pp. 43–54.

33. Based on Sashkin, "The Visionary Leader," pp. 128–30.

34. See R. M. Entman, "Framing: Toward Clarification of a Fractured Paradigm," *Journal of Communication*, Autumn 1993, pp. 51–58; and G. T. Fairhurst and R. A. Sarr, *The Art of Framing: Managing the Language of Leadership* (San Francisco: Jossey-Bass, 1996), p. 21.

35. J. Leo, "Opinions Were Expressed," *U.S. News & World Report*, February 17, 1997, p. 23.

36. Fairhurst and Sarr, *The Art of Framing*, p. 4.

37. Entman, "Framing," p. 52.

38. Fairhurst and Sarr, *The Art of Framing*, p. 22.

39. W. Bennis and B. Nanus, *Leaders: The Strategies for Taking Charge* (New York: Harper & Row, 1985), p. 91.

40. Fairhurst and Sarr, *The Art of Framing*, pp. 100–21.

41. R. M. Kanter, "Championing Change: An Interview with Bell Atlantic's CEO Raymond Smith," *Harvard Business Review*, January/February 1991, pp. 119–30.

42. See, for instance, H. Mintzberg, *Power in and around Organizations* (Englewood Cliffs, NJ: Prentice Hall, 1983); J. Pfeffer, *Managing with Power* (Boston: Harvard Business School Press, 1992); and R. I. Dilenschneider, *On Power* (New York: HarperBusiness, 1994).

43. R. E. Emerson, "Power-Dependence Relations," *American Sociological Review* 27 (1962), pp. 31–41.

44. Based on J. R. P. French Jr. and B. Raven, "The Bases of Social Power," in D. Cartwright (ed.), *Studies in Social Power* (Ann Arbor: University of Michigan, Institute for Social Research, 1959), pp. 150–67; and N. W. Biggart and G. G. Hamilton, "The Power of Obedience," *Administrative Science Quarterly*, December 1984, pp. 540–49.

45. Mintzberg, *Power in and around Organizations*, p. 24.

46. R. M. Cyert and J. G. March, *A Behavioral Theory of the Firm* (Upper Saddle River, NJ: Prentice Hall, 1963).

47. C. Perrow, "Departmental Power and Perspective in Industrial Firms," in M. N. Zald (ed.), *Power in Organizations* (Nashville, TN: Vanderbilt University Press, 1970).

48. S. Caminiti, "What Team Leaders Need to Know," *Fortune*, February 20, 1995, pp. 93–100.

49. Ibid., p. 93.

50. Ibid., p. 100.

51. N. Steckler and N. Fondas, "Building Team Leader Effectiveness: A Diagnostic Tool," *Organizational Dynamics*, Winter 1995, p. 20; and E. Matson, "Congratulations, You're Promoted. Now What?" *Fast Company*, June–July 1997, pp. 116–30.

52. R. S. Wellins, W. C. Byham, and G. R. Dixon, *Inside Teams: How 20 World-Class Organizations Are Winning through Teamwork* (San Francisco: Jossey-Bass, 1994), p. 318.

53. Steckler and Fondas, "Building Team Leader Effectiveness," p. 21.

54. This is largely based on Caminiti, "What Team Leaders Need to Know," pp. 94–98; and E. Matson, "Congratulations, You're Promoted."

55. Caminiti, "What Team Leaders Need to Know," p. 94.

56. Ibid.

57. See, for example, K. E. Kram, *Mentoring at Work: Developmental Relationships in Organizational Life* (Glenview, IL: Scott, Foresman, 1985); and E. O. Welles, "The Mentors," *Inc.*, June 1998, pp. 48–63.

58. F. Jossi, "Mentoring in Changing Times," *Training*, August 1997, p. 50.

59. J. A. Wilson and N. S. Elman, "Organizational Benefits of Mentoring," *The Executive*, November 1990, p. 90.

60. Ibid., p. 89; and A. H. Geiger-DuMond and S. K. Boyle, "Mentoring: A Practitioner's Guide," *Training & Development Journal*, March 1995, pp. 51–54.

61. G. F. Dreher and R. A. Ash, "A Comparative Study of Mentoring among Men and Women in Managerial, Professional, and Technical Positions," *Journal of Applied Psychology*, October 1990, pp. 539–46.

62. See, for example, J. Clawson and K. Kram, "Managing Cross-Gender Mentoring," *Business Horizons*, May–June 1984, pp. 22–32; D. A. Thomas, "The Impact of Race on Managers' Experiences of Developmental Relationships: An Intra-Organizational Study," *Journal of Organizational Behavior*, November 1990, pp. 479–92; and K. E. Kram and D. T. Hall, "Mentoring in a Context of Diversity and Tur-

bulence," in E. E. Kossek and S. A. Lobel, *Managing Diversity* (Cambridge, MA: Blackwell, 1996), pp. 108–36.

63. Wilson and Elman, "Organizational Benefits of Mentoring," p. 90.

64. See S. P. Robbins and P. L. Hunsaker, *Training in InterPersonal Skills: TIPS for Managing People at Work*, 2nd ed. (Upper Saddle River, NJ: Prentice Hall, 1996), p. 151.

65. See R. Zemke, "The Corporate Coach," *Training*, December 1996, pp. 24–28.

66. R. Wellins and J. Worklan, "The Philadelphia Story," *Training*, March 1994, pp. 93–100.

67. Ibid., p. 95.

68. C. D. Orth, H. E. Wilkinson, and R. C. Benfari, "The Manager's Role as Coach and Mentor," *Organizational Dynamics*, Spring 1987, p. 67.

69. See C. C. Manz, "Self-Leadership: Toward an Expanded Theory of Self-Influence Processes in Organizations," *Academy of Management Review*, July 1986, pp. 585–600; C. C. Manz and H. P. Sims Jr., "Superleadership: Beyond the Myth of Heroic Leadership," *Organizational Dynamics*, Spring 1991, pp. 18–35; C. C. Manz, *Mastering Self-Leadership: Empowering Yourself for Personal Excellence* (Upper Saddle River, NJ: Prentice Hall, 1992); H. P. Sims Jr. and C. C. Manz, *Company of Heroes: Unleashing the Power of Self-Leadership* (New York: Wiley, 1996); and M. Uhl-Bien and G. B. Graen, "Individual Self-Management: Analysis of Professionals' Self-Managing Activities in Functional and Cross-Functional Work Teams," *Academy of Management Journal*, June 1998, pp. 340–50.

70. Based on Manz and Sims, "Superleadership."

71. The material in this section is based on G. H. Dobbins and S. J. Platz, "Sex Differences in Leadership: How Real Are They?" *Academy of Management Review*, January 1986, pp. 118–27; S. Helgesen, *The Female Advantage: Women's Ways of Leadership* (New York: Doubleday, 1990); A. H. Eagly and B. T. Johnson, "Gender and Leadership Style: A Meta-Analysis," *Psychological Bulletin*, September 1990, pp. 233–56; A. H. Eagly and S. J. Karau, "Gender and the Emergence of Leaders: A Meta-Analysis," *Journal of Personality and Social Psychology*, May 1991, pp. 685–710; A. H. Eagly, M. G. Makhijani, and B. G. Klonsky, "Gender and the Evaluation of Leaders: A Meta-Analysis," *Psychological Bulletin*, January 1992, pp. 3–22; L. R. Offermann and C. Beil, "Achievement Styles of Women Leaders and Their Peers," *Psychology of Women Quarterly*, March 1992, pp. 37–56; G. N. Powell, *Women & Men in Management*, 2nd ed. (Thousand Oaks, CA: Sage, 1993), pp. 158–80; C. Lee, "The Feminization of Management," *Training*, November 1994, pp. 25–31; H. Collingwood, "Women as Managers: Not Just Different–Better," *Working Woman*, November 1995, p. 14; J. L. Berdahl, "Gender and Leadership in Work Groups: Six Alternative Models," *Leadership Quarterly*, Spring 1996, pp. 21–40; and B. S. Moskal, "Women Make Better Managers," *Industry Week*, February 3, 1997, pp. 17–19.

72. See J. B. Ciulla, "Leadership Ethics: Mapping the Territory," *Business Ethics Quarterly*, January 1995, pp. 5–28; E. P. Hollander, "Ethical Challenges in the Leader-Follower Relationship," *Business Ethics Quarterly*, January 1995, pp. 55–65; J. C. Rost, "Leadership: A Discussion about Ethics,"

Business Ethics Quarterly, January 1995, pp. 129–42; and R. N. Kanungo and M. Mendonca, *Ethical Dimensions of Leadership* (Thousand Oaks, CA: Sage, 1996).

73. J. M. Burns, *Leadership* (New York: Harper & Row, 1978).

74. J. M. Howell and B. J. Avolio, "The Ethics of Charismatic Leadership: Submission or Liberation?" *Academy of Management Executive*, May 1992, pp. 43–55.

75. For one prominent scholar's view on this topic, see F. E. Fiedler, "Research on Leadership Selection and Training: One View of the Future," *Administrative Science Quarterly*, June 1996, pp. 241–50.

76. B. J. Avolio, D. A. Waldman, and W. O. Einstein, "Transfor-mational Leadership in a Management Game Simulation," *Group & Organization Studies*, March 1988, pp. 59–80.

77. See, for instance, A. A. Vicere, "Executive Education: The Leading Edge," *Organizational Dynamics*, Autumn 1996, pp. 67–81; and J. Barling, T. Weber, and E. K. Kelloway, "Effects of Transformational Leadership Training on Atti-tudinal and Financial Outcomes: A Field Experiment," *Journal of Applied Psychology*, December 1996, pp. 827–32.

78. Sashkin, "The Visionary Leader," p. 150.

79. Howell and Frost, "A Laboratory Study of Charismatic Leadership."

Chapter

16

BUILDING TRUST

A VERBAL CONTRACT ISN'T WORTH THE PAPER IT'S
WRITTEN ON.

S. GOLDWYN

Pilots at American Airlines didn't trust the company's management, especially the company's combative CEO, Robert Crandall.[1] That lack of trust had been building for a number of years and eventually led to the pilots' strike in February 1997. Only intervention by President Bill Clinton, just minutes into the strike, kept American's 9,300 pilots on the job.

The long-standing animosity between Crandall (who retired in 1998) and his pilots was due to a number of factors. In order to help American deal with huge financial losses, the pilots made concessions throughout the early and mid-1990s. For example, to minimize layoffs, the pilots had gone since 1993 without a raise. But in 1995, Crandall gave himself a 25 percent pay hike. And in 1996, the company surprised nearly everybody by reporting record earnings of $1 billion. The pilots thought it was time for the company to share its good fortune with them. In early 1997, when the Allied Pilots Association (APA) began negotiating with American for a new contract for its pilots, Crandall took his typical tough stance. The pilots asked for an 11 percent pay hike over 4 years and 7.25 million shares of the company's stock at a $10 per share discount. Crandall's best counteroffer was a 5 percent raise over 4 years, 5.75 million shares, and limited profit-sharing incentives. Additionally, Crandall sought to buy new fifty-seat jets for the company's regional-commuter subsidiary, American Eagle, and staff them with non-APA pilots. To compete more effectively against United Shuttle and Delta Express, Crandall wanted to replace American Eagle's slower and noisy turboprops. But American Eagle pilots, which are represented by another union, make only $35,000 a year. In contrast, American's APA members average $120,000 a year. The APA and its pilots saw this as a direct threat to their job security and wanted Crandall to agree to let APA pilots fly these small jets. The pilot's union feared that Crandall's real intention was to turn the company's short-haul routes over to lower-cost American Eagle.

Crandall viewed American's pilots as whiners who were already the best paid in the industry. The pilots, meanwhile, saw Crandall as greedy and someone who didn't keep his promises. "We just don't trust Mr. Crandall," said Captain Tom Kachmar, a union spokesman. James G. Sovich, president of the pilots' union, concurred: "The pilots don't trust management, including the CEO, Mr. Crandall."

Trust, or lack of trust, is an increasingly important issue for today's managers. In this chapter, we define what trust is, explain why the topic is more relevant today than in the past, and provide you with some guidelines for helping build credibility and trust.

WHAT IS TRUST?

We say we *trust* a friend to pick us up in his car at a specified time. We *trust* our spouse to be faithful. We *trust* our stockbroker to give us good advice. And we *trust* our boss to treat us fairly. Based on these usages of the term, does *trust* mean *dependability*? Is it synonymous with *honesty* or *loyalty*? Let's clarify what we mean when we discuss the term *trust*.

A Definition

Trust is a positive expectation that another will not—through words, actions, or decisions—act opportunistically.[2] Our definition is purposely broad to cover a wide range of applications. And as you'll see, the two most important elements of our definition is that it implies familiarity and risk.

Most discussions of trust focus at the interpersonal level. For instance, our previous examples all relate to interpersonal trust—between an individual and his or her friend, spouse, stockbroker, or boss. But in a management context, trust also is relevant to group or team interactions and the organization as a whole. The pilots at American Airlines not only didn't trust Robert Crandall; they didn't seem to trust American Airlines' entire senior management team. And when people say they don't trust the FBI, the CIA, the IRS, or the North Korean government, they cast suspicions on an entire organization.

The phrase *positive expectation* in our definition assumes knowledge and familiarity about the other party. Trust is a history-dependent process based on relevant but limited samples of experience.[3] It takes time to form, building incrementally and accumulating. Most of us find it hard, if not impossible, to trust someone immediately if we don't know anything about them. At the extreme, in the case of total ignorance, we can gamble but we can't trust.[4] But as we get to know someone, and the relationship matures, we gain confidence in our ability to make a positive expectation.

The term *opportunistically* refers to the inherent risk and vulnerability in any trusting relationship. Trust involves making oneself vulnerable as when, for example, we disclose intimate information or rely on another's promises.[5] By its very nature, trust provides the opportunity for disappointment or to be taken advantage of.[6] But trust is not taking risk per se; rather it is a *willingness* to take risk.[7] So when I trust someone, I expect that they will not take advantage of me. This willingness to take risks is common to all trust situations.[8]

If you don't trust someone, does that mean that you distrust them? Not necessarily. An absence of trust does not imply distrust. **Distrust** occurs when you become suspicious of someone because you anticipate that he or she will (1) make unreliable representations with respect to themselves or information; (2) violate formal or informal understandings, commitments, or norms; or (3) take advantage of another's vulnerability.[9] So you can have neutral situations where there is an absence of trust but no epectations of opportunistic behavior.

▶ Identifying Its Key Dimensions

What are the key dimensions that underlie the concept of trust? Recent evidence has identified five: integrity, competence, consistency, loyalty, and openness[10] (see Exhibit 16-1).

Integrity refers to honesty and truthfulness. Of the five dimensions, this one seems to be most critical when someone assesses another's trustworthiness. "Without a perception of the other's 'moral character' and 'basic honesty,' other dimensions of trust [are] meaningless."[11]

Competence encompasses an individual's technical and interpersonal knowledge and skills. Does the person know what he or she is talking about? You're unlikely to listen to or depend upon someone whose abilities you don't respect. You need to believe that the person has the skills and abilities to carry out what he or she says they will do.

Consistency relates to an individual's reliability, predictability, and good judgment in handling situations. "Inconsistencies between words and action decrease trust."[12] This dimension is particularly relevant for managers. "Nothing is noticed more quickly . . . than a discrepancy between what executives preach and what they expect their associates to practice."[13]

Loyalty is the willingness to protect, and save face for, another person. Trust requires that you can depend on someone not to act opportunistically.

Openness is the final dimension of trust. Can you rely on the person to give you the full truth?

EXHIBIT 16-1

Trust Dimensions

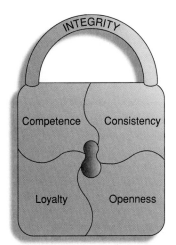

Does High Trust Imply Gullibility?

In most cultures, it's socially desirable to trust a fellow human being. People who don't trust others are viewed as skeptics or cynics. And if trust begets trust, those who don't trust others can't be expected to be trusted themselves. On the other hand, most of us are cautious in trusting *everyone*. In some situations, distrust may be highly functional. In fact, it has been suggested that distrust may be an evolutionary mechanism protecting us from being taken advantage of by others.[14]

But if cultural norms advocate exhibiting trust, is it possible to be too trusting? The answer is yes.

We would be naive to ignore the reality that there are people who will take advantage of us. Hopefully, as a result of experience, we can identify such individuals and act accordingly. In some cases, however, high trust implies gullibility. This is specifically true in situations where the rules assume that there will be some deception, game playing, and an absence of complete openness. An obvious example is the process of negotiation.

I have a friend who recently told me he bought a new car. Because we share quite a bit, I asked him what he paid for it. He looked a bit surprised at the question. "I paid the price listed on the window sticker," he said. I told him that with few exceptions (those being brand models where demand far exceeds supply and a few "no-haggling" dealers or manufacturers that prediscount their cars), dealers expect you to negotiate a lower price. My friend then began lecturing me on the topic of honesty and trust. He told me, for instance, how the dealership had been around for more than 20 years and how friendly and helpful the salesman was. I didn't argue those facts. What I pointed out to him was that the dealer *expected* him to bargain. And the salesman would try to get the highest price he could for the car. The fact that negotiations were expected, and that neither party would reveal everything it knew (for instance, dealers don't let buyers know the absolute lowest price they'll accept for a specific car), did not mean the dealer was deceiving him. My friend was supposed to know the rules of the game.

Another friend recently reminded me that she never trusts real estate agents when she buys property. She pointed out that agents, by law, are responsible to the seller. As my friend noted, "I tell the agent only what I would want the seller to know. If I confide in that agent, I can expect that information to go directly back to the seller and be used against me in the negotiation process."

In organizations, managers engage in negotiations all the time. If they believe everything the other party says, they put themselves in a situation where they can be taken advantage of. At the other extreme, if they disbelieve everything the other party says, it would be very difficult to reach an agreement.[15] Therefore, negotiations represent situations where complete openness and honesty is unlikely to occur and where managers need a basic level of distrusting belief. They should expect the other party to make unreliable statements and, if given the opportunity, to take advantage of their vulnerability.

WHY HAS TRUST BECOME SO IMPORTANT TODAY?

The concept of trust can help explain why business executives favor hierarchies over markets, why firms vertically integrate, the primary reason organizations have accountants, and the continued growth in employment opportunities for corporate lawyers. Yet, surprisingly, a management textbook from only a few years ago is unlikely to include any discussion of trust. It wasn't that trust was unimportant in the past; rather, both practicing managers and those who wrote books on management essentially took it for granted. That's no longer the case. We've identified at least half a dozen reasons why trust is so important today.

General Loss of Trust in Institutions

The 1950s was a time when there was undying belief in the integrity of those in authority. We know better today. The hippies, in the 1960s, questioned authority, but most citizens ignored their message. But beginning with the Watergate burglary in the 1970s, and its subsequent cover-up by the president of the United States, much of the public's confidence in government has eroded. Today, we aren't surprised to learn that elected officials, law-enforcement personnel, business executives, academics, journalists, researchers, and prominent attorneys don't always tell the truth. Few of us are surprised nowadays when we see government officials or business executives acting in their blatant self-interest. We've become skeptical of authority figures, and as a result, trust has been lost in institutions as a whole.

Employer-Employee Relations Have Suffered in Many Organizations

The loss of trust in institutions in general has filtered down to employers. In 1996, 40 percent of employees surveyed by a firm in Chicago agreed with the statement: "I often don't believe what management says." That was up from 33 percent in 1988.[16] Similarly, in another survey conducted in 1995, 47 percent of respondents said that lack of trust was a problem in their organizations.[17]

Many organizations are paying the price for sloppy managment practices. They are suffering from management's lack of open communication and straight talk. Employees have lost trust as a result of such practices as failing to confront poor performers, underrewarding high performers, ignoring charges of workplace harassment, and turning promotion decisions into political contests. Additionally, the downsizing movement has undermined trust.[18] The problem is not so much the laying off of people (although that certainly is relevant), but the way the process has been handled. Too often, individuals learn about cuts in their company from the media rather than from management. Or management says the cutbacks have ended, and then a few months later, additional layoffs occur.

Change and Instability

Trust is more important under conditions of change and instability.[19] And, as we've seen throughout this book, *change* and *instability* are terms increasingly describing today's workplace. When rules, policies, cultural norms, and traditional practices are in flux, people turn to personal relationships for guidance. And the quality of these relationships are largely determined by level of trust.

The New Psychological Contract

The **psychological contract** is an unwritten agreement that sets out what management expects from the employee, and vice versa. From an employee's standpoint, the psychological contract is their perceptions of what they think they are entitled to receive as a result of what they believe their employer has promised them.[20]

As we noted in chapter 1, and which has been reiterated repeatedly, loyalty bonds between employers and employees have loosened significantly over the previous decade. In the past, employers essentially guaranteed workers long-term job security; in return, employees responded with hard work, commitment, and loyalty. When employers broke the covenant, employees responded in kind.

The new psychological contract is more ambiguous than its predecessor. Contractual transgressions are less clear. People look for ways to protect themselves against the possibilities of opportunistic actions by colleagues, managers, and others with whom they work. With the bonds of security broken—and if levels of trust are low—employees tend to avoid taking risks, demand greater protections against the possibility of betrayal, and increasingly insist on costly sanctioning mechanisms to defend their interests.[21]

In this new climate, managers that can actively establish and maintain trusting relationships with their employees lessen the likelihood that those employees will perceive a contract breach. And because psychological contract breach is associated with a number of negative outcomes—such as less willingness to exceed the formal requirements of their jobs, as well as reduced commitment and satisfaction—high levels of trust should lead to improved organizational performance.

New Structural Relationships

New structural design options and the practice of empowerment require increased trust within organizations. For instance, organization theorists have noted that trust reduces "the necessity for continually making provisions for the possibility of opportunistic behavior among participants. . . . Trust lubricates the smooth, harmonious functioning of the organization by eliminating friction and minimizing the need for bureaucratic structures that specify the behavior of participants who do not trust each other."[22] Another author suggests that contemporary management practice requires trust as "a key organizing principle."[23]

When the San Francisco 49ers won the 1995 Super Bowl, owner Eddie De-Bartolo (far left, with quarterback Steve Young) and team president Carmen Policy had been close friends for 30 years. Even though Policy was the architect of the NFL's winningest organization in the 1980s and 1990s, lack of communication between the two led to a loss of trust, and the eventual resignation of Policy in 1998. He now heads up the Cleveland Browns.

We noted the growing popularity of virtual and boundaryless organizations in chapter 8. In these structures, top management must have faith in members at all levels to make independent decisions, they must believe that the organization's information system provides the appropriate information individuals need, and they must be able to rely on people in other organizations to perform outsourcing functions and fulfill interdependent responsibilities. Trust, then, is an essential part of these new organizational forms.[24]

The trend toward empowering individuals, creating self-managed work teams, and telecommuting reduce or remove many of the traditional control mechanisms used to monitor employees. For instance, if a group of workers are free to schedule their own work, evaluate their own performance, and even make their own team hiring decisions, trust becomes critical. Employees have to trust management to treat them fairly, and management has to trust workers to conscientiously fulfill their responsibilities. And the trend toward expanding nonauthority relationships within and between organizations widens the need for interpersonal trust. Managers increasingly have to direct others who are not in their direct line of authority or whom they may even rarely see—members of cross-functional teams, individuals who work for suppliers and customers, and people who represent other organizations through strategic alliances, joint ventures, and partnerships. These situations don't allow managers to fall back on their formal positions to enact compliance. Many of the relationships, in fact, are fluid and fleeting. So the ability to quickly develop trust may be crucial to the success of the relationship.

▶ Building Commitment

Finally, we argue that trust is important because of the evidence indicating a positive relationship between high trust and high commitment in organizations. As noted in chapter 12, employees that demonstrate high commitment identify with their particular organization and its goals, and seek to maintain membership in that organization. Managers obviously prefer committed employees because, in addition to showing loyalty to the organization, they also tend to have fewer absences and are less likely to resign.

Managers who are seen as credible and trusting appear to create commitment among their employees.[25] One study, for instance, divided 186 managers into high and low credibility groups based on scores on a credibility questionnaire. Comparisons between the two groups found that employees who perceived their managers as having high credibility felt significantly more positive about and attached to their work and organizations than did those who perceived their managers as low on credibility. In another, smaller study, individuals who reported that their manager was honest, competent, and inspiring were significantly more likely to feel a strong sense of teamwork and commitment to their organization than were those who reported their managers as not honest, competent, or inspiring.

LEADERSHIP AND TRUST ▶ Trust appears to be a primary attribute associated with leadership. "Part of the leader's task has been, and continues to be, working with people to find and solve problems, but whether leaders gain access to the knowledge and creative thinking they need to solve problems depends on how much people trust them. Trust and trustworthiness modulate the leader's access to knowledge and cooperation."[26] As the dean of the business school at New York University put it, "Trust, and especially the processes that lead to its growth and dissipation, deserve a prominent place in the training of leaders whose actions will do so much to sustain or extinguish it."[27]

When followers trust a leader, they are willing to be vulnerable to the leader's actions—confident that their rights and interests will not be abused.[28] People are unlikely to look up to or follow someone who they perceive as dishonest or who is likely to take advantage of them. Honesty, for instance, consistently ranks at the top of most people's list of characteristics they admire in their leaders. "Honesty is absolutely essential to leadership. If people are going to follow someone willingly, whether it be into battle or into the boardroom, they first want to assure themselves that the person is worthy of their trust."[29]

Warren Bennis, an international expert on leadership, confirms the importance of trust to effective leadership.[30] However, his argument is shaped in the context of the empowerment and downsizing movements. Bennis sees the problem for leaders as one of striving to achieve three conflicting goals: empower their organizations, increase competitiveness by cutting staff and restructuring processes, and generate trust. "How do you create an empowered organization in a time of radical reengineering and layoffs?"[31] When people don't know from one day to the next whether they'll have a job or not, "how do you generate the necessary trust to lead in an environment like this?"[32] Bennis has no quick answers, but he concludes that this is "the major challenge" for leaders of today and tomorrow.[33]

> Honesty consistently ranks at the top of most people's list of characteristics they admire in their leaders.

TRUST TYPOLOGIES AND STAGES

All trust-based relationships aren't the same. Some can be characterized as "thick" while others are "thin."[34] Thick forms of trust are relatively resilient and durable. Once this form of trust is established, it's not easily disrupted. And once it's shattered, it's not easily restored. In contrast, thin forms of trust are fragile. They're conferred easily and withdrawn quickly. These latter forms are typically made with reservations, and with built-in safeguards to protect against violations.

Three Types of Trust

A more detailed typology characterizes three types of trust in organizational relationships: deterrence-based, knowledge-based, and identification-based.[35] The first is synonymous with the "thin" variety, while the latter two are thick forms of trust.

DETERRENCE-BASED TRUST   The most fragile relationships are contained in **deterrence-based trust.** One violation or inconsistency can destroy the relationship. This form of trust is based on fear of reprisal if the trust is violated. Individuals who are in this type of relationship do what they say because they fear the consequences from not following through on their obligations.

Deterrence-based trust will work only to the degree that punishment is possible, consequences are clear, and the punishment is actually imposed if the trust is violated. To be sustained, the potential loss of future interaction with the other party must outweigh the profit potential that comes from violating expectations. Moreover, the potentially harmed party must be willing to introduce harm (for example, "I have no qualms about speaking badly of you if you betray my trust") to the person acting distrustingly. Not surprisingly, this type of trust is often characterized by protections such as contracts and other legal arrangements.

Most new or very brief relationships begin on a base of deterrence. Take, as an illustration, a situation where you're selling your car to a friend of a friend. You don't know the buyer. You might be motivated to refrain from telling this buyer all the problems with the car that you know about. Such behavior would increase your chances of selling the car and securing the highest price. But you don't withhold information. You openly share the car's flaws. Why? Probably because of fear of reprisal. If the buyer later thinks you deceived him, he is likely to share this with your mutual friend. If you knew that the buyer would never say anything to the mutual friend, you might be tempted to take advantage of the opportunity. If it's clear that the buyer would tell and that your mutual friend would think considerably less of you for taking advantage of this buyer-friend, your honesty could be explained in deterrence terms.

Another example of deterrence-based trust is a new manager-employee relationship. As an employee, you typically trust a new boss even though there is little experience to base that trust on. The bond that creates this trust lies in the authority held by the boss and the punishment he or she can impose if you fail to fulfill your job-related obligations.

KNOWLEDGE-BASED TRUST Most organizational relationships are rooted in **knowledge-based trust**. That is, trust is based on the behavioral predictability that comes from a history of interaction. It exists when you have adequate information about someone to understand them well enough to be able to accurately predict their likely behavior.

Knowledge-based trust relies on information rather than deterrence. Knowledge of the other party and predictability of his or her behavior replaces the contracts, penalties, and legal arrangements more typical of deterrence-based trust. This knowledge develops over time, largely as a function of experience that builds confidence of trustworthiness and predictability. The better you know someone, the more accurately you can predict what he or she will do. Predictability enhances trust—even if the other is predictably untrustworthy—because the ways that the other will violate the trust can be predicted! The more communication and regular interaction you have with someone else, the more this form of trust can be developed and depended upon.

Interestingly, at the knowledge-based level, trust is not necessarily broken by inconsistent behavior. If you believe you can adequately explain or understand another's apparent violation, you can accept it, forgive the person, and move on in the relationship. However, the same inconsistency at the deterrence level is likely to irrevocably break the trust.

In an organizational context, most manager-employee relationships are knowledge-based. Both parties have enough experience working with each other that they know what to expect. A long history of consistently open and honest interactions, for instance, is not likely to be permanently destroyed by a single violation.

IDENTIFICATION-BASED TRUST The highest level of trust is achieved when there is an emotional connection between the parties. It allows one party to act as an agent for the other and substitute for that person in interpersonal transactions. This is called **identification-based trust**. Trust exists because the parties understand each other's intentions and appreciate the other's wants and desires. This mutual understanding is developed to the point that each can effectively act for the other.

Controls are minimal at this level. You don't need to monitor the other party because there exists unquestioned loyalty.

The best example of identification-based trust is a long-term, happily married couple. A husband comes to learn what's important to his wife and anticipates those actions. She, in turn, trusts that he will anticipate what's important to her without having to ask. Increased identification enables each to think like the other, feel like the other, and respond like the other.

You see identification-based trust occasionally in organizations among people who have worked together for long periods of time and have a depth of experience that allows

The best fire-fighting teams have members who have learned they can depend on each other and have developed trust relationships that are identification based.

them to know each other inside and out. This is also the type of trust that managers ideally seek in teams. Team members are so comfortable and trusting of one another that they can anticipate one another and freely act in each's absence. Realistically, in the current work world, most large corporations have broken the bonds of identification trust they may have built with long-term employees. Broken promises have led to a breakdown in what was, at one time, a bond of unquestioned loyalty. It's likely to have been replaced with knowledge-based trust.

Stages of Trust Development

The previous typology can be better understood by looking at the trust development model depicted in Exhibit 16-2.

In organizational relationships, trust develops gradually as the parties move from one stage to another. If a relationship reaches full maturity, it will move from deterrence-based, to knowledge-based, to identification-based trust. But not all relationships develop fully. Trust may not develop past the first or second stage. In reality, only a few will reach the third stage.[36]

What determines whether a relationship will reach the third stage? The answer is that it must first successfully go through the two earlier stages. All relationships begin with deterrence-based trust activities. If these confirm the validity of the trust, the parties will begin developing a knowledge base about the other's needs, preferences, and priorities. At point A in Exhibit 16-2, the transition from the first to the second stage has been made. However, the relationship may go no further than Stage I because it doesn't necessitate more than "arm's-length" transactions; the interdependence between the parties is heavily bounded and regulated; the parties have already gained enough information about each other to be aware that any further information gathering is unnecessary or likely to be unproductive; or one or more violations of deterrence-based trust occurred.

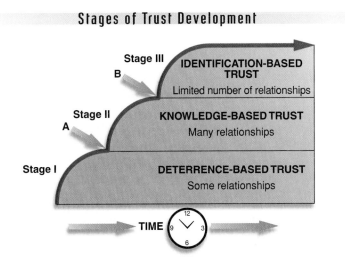

Stages of Trust Development

EXHIBIT 16-2

- **Stage III** — B — **IDENTIFICATION-BASED TRUST** / Limited number of relationships
- **Stage II** — A — **KNOWLEDGE-BASED TRUST** / Many relationships
- **Stage I** — **DETERRENCE-BASED TRUST** / Some relationships

TIME

Source: Adapted from R. J. Lewicki and B. B. Bunker, "Developing and Maintaining Trust in Work Relationships," in R. M. Kramer and T. R. Tyler (eds.), *Trust in Organizations* (Thousand Oaks, CA: Sage, 1996), p. 124.

Once the relationship makes it to Stage II and the level of knowledge-based trust, it has the potential to move further. As the parties interact and gain experience about each other, they may also begin to identify strongly with each's needs, preferences, and priorities and come to see them as their own. If this occurs, the relationship moves to the next stage at point B in Exhibit 16-2. As noted, however, few relationships reach Stage III. Why? The parties may not have the time, energy, or desire to invest in the relationship. Or the knowledge gained in Stage II may make it clear that the relationship lacks the common values and chemistry needed to reach the final stage.

Our three typologies can be thought of as analogous to three stages in the development of a romantic relationship. Two people meet and begin dating. Neither party has enough information or experience about the other to create a strongly bonded trust. They fall back on deterrence-based trust; in fear of the other ending the relationship, they take limited risks. Repeated dates provide opportunities to gain knowledge. They ask questions of each other; learn each's backgrounds, interests, fears, and goals; watch each perform in social situations; and build a history with each other. What began as cautious and protected behavior can build into knowledge-based trust. And as we noted, in some cases, it can lead to a stage of deep understanding of the partner and complete confidence that he or she would do nothing to harm the relationship.

▶ Violations and Consequences

It's important to keep in mind that violations of trust are treated differently at different stages. At the deterrence stage, because trust is fragile, a seemingly minor violation can lead to immediately classifying someone as "untrustworthy." The assumption is, based on limited information, that this minor episode is typical of the person and therefore can be extrapolated to the full range of his or her behaviors.

At the knowledge stage, violations are a concern but they don't necessarily mean that trust is irrevocably damaged. Disconfirmation of expectations will typically be unsettling for two reasons. First, the person has failed to act as expected. Second, it calls into question your own perceptual skills. Someone you thought is a friend, for instance, acts in a way that suggests he betrayed you. Does that mean that the person is untrustworthy? Not necessarily. Consistent with attribution theory, trust is perceived violated only when the person's actions are interpreted as freely chosen. If situational factors can attribute the betrayal to external causations, you may perceive that no violation actually occurred, and the trusting relationship may remain intact. So the same violation that destroys a relationship early on, may be only a slight disruption in an established relationship.

To seriously undermine identification-based trust, violations typically have to be major. They have to go against the common interests or agreements established between the parties. They have to tap into the values that underlie the relationship and create a sense of moral violation. Infidelity of a spouse is an obvious example. So, too, was how many longtime admirers of O. J. Simpson felt when he was charged with the murders of his ex-wife and her friend Ron Goldman. Simpson was a football hero and celebrity. They interpreted the fact that he might have perpetrated the brutal crime as a betrayal. A betrayal of just *what* isn't so clear. But this example illustrates that one of the hard parts of an identification-based violation is that it requires us to acknowledge that our decision to trust the other person was ill-founded. It requires us to admit, at least to ourselves, that we were foolish in trusting at this level.

When violations of trust occur, what are the consequences? Intellectually, the individual who feels violated thinks about how important the situation is and where the responsibility for it lies. Emotionally, individuals typically experience strong feelings of anger, hurt, fear, and frustration.[37] But because much of the interaction that occurs in the workplace is organizationally determined and not voluntary, employees or managers who feel violated typically must continue to work with each other. The result is that trust violations tend to surface as communication problems.[38] The amount and type of information shared between the parties changes. The steady flow of information that previously existed may be impeded. Information is reshaped and "sanitized" so it doesn't reflect unfavorably on the sender. And the information that is shared tends to be less accurate. In anticipation that anything "can and will be used against you," the violated party is likely to assume opportunistic behavior on the part of the violator and act so as to minimize his or her risk.

BASIC PRINCIPLES OF TRUST

Before we get to a discussion of techniques for managing trust, we want to review some basic principles. The following points lay a foundation from which we can assess ways to build or rebuild trust.[39]

Mistrust drives out trust. People who are trusting demonstrate their trust by increasing their openness to others, disclosing relevant information, and expressing their true intentions. People who mistrust do not reciprocate. They conceal information and act opportunistically to take advantage of others. To defend against repeated exploitation, trusting people are driven to mistrust. A few mistrusting people can poison an entire organization.

Trust begets trust. In the same way that mistrust drives out trust, exhibiting trust in others tends to encourage reciprocity. Effective leaders increase trust in small increments and allow others to respond in kind. By offering trust in only small increments, leaders limit penalty or loss that might occur if their trust is exploited.

Growth often masks mistrust. Growth gives leaders opportunities for rapid promotion and for increased power and responsibility. In this environment, leaders tend to solve problems with quick fixes that elude immediate detection by higher management and leave the problems arising from mistrust to their successors. Leaders can take a short-term perspective because they are not likely to be around to have to deal with the long-term consequences of their decisions. The lingering effects of mistrust become apparent to the successors when the growth slows.

Decline or downsizing tests the highest levels of trust. The corollary to the previous growth principle is that decline or downsizing tends to undermine even the most trusting environment. Layoffs are threatening. Even after layoffs have been completed, those who survive feel less secure in their jobs. When employers break the loyalty bond by laying off employees, there is less willingness among workers to trust what management says.

Trust increases cohesion. Trust holds people together. Trust means people have confidence that they can rely on each other. If one person needs help or falters, that person knows that the others will be there to fill in. When faced with adversity, group members that display trust in one another will work together and exert high levels of effort to achieve the group's goals.

Mistrusting groups self-destruct. The corollary to the previous principle is that when group members mistrust one another, they repel and separate. They pursue their own interests rather than the group's. Members of mistrusting groups tend to be

An increasing number of organizations are participating in programs such as those offered by Outward Bound, because they help work teams build cohesiveness and trust.

suspicious of one another, are constantly on guard against exploitation, and restrict communication with others in the group. These actions tend to undermine and eventually destroy the group.

Mistrust generally reduces productivity. While we cannot say that trust necessarily *increases* productivity, though it usually does, mistrust almost always *reduces* productivity. Mistrust focuses attention on the differences in member interests, making it difficult for people to visualize common goals. People respond by concealing information and secretly pursuing their own interests. When employees encounter problems, they avoid calling on others, fearing that those others will take advantage of them. A climate of mistrust tends to stimulate dysfunctional forms of conflict and retard cooperation.

HOW DO YOU BUILD TRUST?

Managers who have learned to build trusting relationships engage in certain common practices. The following items highlight what you can do to emulate these successful managers.[40]

Practice openness. Mistrust comes as much from what people don't know as from what they do know. Openness leads to confidence and trust. So keep people informed, make the critieria on how decisions are made overtly clear, explain the rationale for your decisions, be candid about problems, and fully disclose relevant information.

Be fair. Before making decisions or taking actions, consider how others will perceive them in terms of objectivity and fairness. Give credit where it's due, be objective and impartial in performance appraisals, and pay attention to equity perceptions in reward distributions.

Speak your feelings. Managers who convey only hard facts come across as cold and distant. If you share your feelings, others will see you as real and human. They will know who you are, and their respect for you will increase.

Tell the truth. Because integrity is critical to trust, you must be perceived as someone who tells the truth. People are generally more tolerant of learning something they "don't want to hear" than finding out that their manager lied to them.

Show consistency. People want predictability. Mistrust comes from not knowing what to expect. Take the time to think about your values and beliefs. Then let them consistently guide your decisions. When you know your central purpose, your actions will follow accordingly, and you will project a consistency that earns trust.

Fulfill your promises. Trust requires that people believe that you are dependable. So you need to ensure that you keep your word and commitments. Promises made must be promises kept.

Maintain confidences. You trust people who are discreet and upon whom you can rely. So if people make themselves vulnerable by telling you something in confidence, they need to feel assured that you will not discuss it with others or betray that confidence. If people perceive you as someone who leaks personal confidences or someone who can't be depended on, you won't be perceived as trustworthy.

Demonstrate competence. Develop the admiration and respect of others by demonstrating technical and professional ability. Pay particular attention to developing and displaying your communication, negotiating, and other interpersonal skills.

Creating a Trusting Climate at Rhino Foods

Rhino Foods, Inc., is a specialty-dessert manufacturer. (One of the things they make is the chocolate-chip cookie dough that goes into Ben & Jerry's ice cream.) The company employs 83 people, all working in a single facility in Burlington, Vermont.

Founded in 1981, the company is still led by its founder and president, Ted Castle. From the beginning, Castle was determined to create a company that had an empowered and committed workforce. A climate of trust was crucial. Castle included an Employee Principle section into his original purpose statement:

> The employees and families of Rhino Foods are its greatest assets. The company's relationship with its employees is founded on a climate of mutual trust and respect within an environment for listening and personal expression. Rhino Foods declares that it is a vehicle for its people to get what they want.

These words might sound more fantasy than fact. But they're not! "We do what we can to get people to trust us," says Castle. "At our company meetings, we're being as honest as we can with people. Trust is a huge thing. People don't come to work for a company and trust that company right off the bat. It takes a number of years for people to develop trust for their employer. We also try to create an environment for listening. We work hard at listening to what our people are saying, and we work hard to get people to express what they think."

What other kinds of practices, beside listening, does Rhino Foods try to do to build trust? It shares information with employees and offers them generous profit-sharing programs. It empowers employees. Cross-functional work teams, for instance, are involved in most key decisions. And it practices openness, honesty, and participation. As a case in point, during a slowdown in 1993, management openly discussed its overstaffing problem with employees. There was no whispering behind closed doors about who would stay and who would go. Instead, a team composed of over half the workforce at the time worked out a solution—ten employees voluntarily "jobbed themselves out" to other employers in the community on a temporary basis. Management responded by guaranteeing the volunteers they would have their jobs upon return.

Rhino Foods' trusting climate seems to be working. Since 1993, the company has doubled its number of employees. Sales and profits are up. And employee commitment is high. Stephen Mayo, a four-year employee, summed it up pretty well. "I can be honest, I'm not wild about working. But working at Rhino, I can get out of bed, and I don't have the work knots. I look forward to being here the time I need to be here. It's unlike any company I've ever worked for. And Ted [Castle] knows I'll be here until I retire. As long as the company needs what I'm giving it and it's giving me what I need, I'll be here without a doubt."

Source: Based on G. Flynn, "Why Rhino Won't Wait 'til Tomorrow," *Personnel Journal*, July 1996, pp. 36–43.

REBUILDING LOSS OF TRUST

Layoffs, per se, need not destroy trust. But they often do because they're handled poorly.

To this point, we've basically looked at building trust as if managers operate from a positive or neutral starting point. We've assumed there already exists some basis of trust or, at least, an absence of mistrust. Unfortunately, managers can find themselves in situations where mistrust is already firmly established. A manager, for instance, may be new and coming into an organization or unit that has a history of dishonest and manipulative relations between managers and employees. Or a manager may have said or done things in the past that have undermined trust with his or her work group. In either case, a manager isn't working from a neutral state. There is already a climate of mistrust. In such cases, what can a manager do?

The place to begin is assessing what the source of mistrust is. If it's the organization itself, and if you're not part of the senior executive group, there isn't much you can do. For instance, Apple Computer was a difficult place for most employees to work in the mid-1990s. Sales had fallen, losses piled up, employees were laid off, and management turnover was high. For managers at Apple, there wasn't much they could do to rebuild employees' mistrust of management. This conclusion probably goes a long way toward explaining *why* there was so much turnover among managerial personnel.

What if you're part of senior management? Use your authority to change organizational policies and practices that have undermined trust. Downsizing provides a good example. Layoffs, per se, need not destroy trust. But they often do because they're handled poorly. Evidence indicates that practices such as making layoff decision criteria clear, providing social support, offering counseling and group grievance sessions, and treating layoff victims fairly and with dignity can result in downsized workplaces that still maintain high levels of trust.[41]

The more relevant situation is where you, as a manager, have individually acted so as to have destroyed what may have been at least knowledge-based or even identification-based trust. If it's a single event that has destroyed the trust relationship, move quickly to rectify it. Admit that the event was destructive. Engage in a full discussion of the event itself and the consequences with the other party. And be willing to accept responsibility for the violation. "Denying that the act happened, claiming that there weren't any consequences, denying any responsibility for it, or claiming that the act was unimportant and should have no impact on the trust level will likely intensify the other's anger and contribute to further trust deterioration rather than to trust repair."[42]

What if the problem is bigger? What if the problem relates to a number of events or practices, engaged in over a long period of time. What if you've reached a point where employees question your honesty and truthfulness; they see you as inconsistent and unreliable; they expect you to withhold important information from them; or they see you as self-serving and fearful that you'll use your position to exploit them? When trust has deteriorated to this point, the best you can probably hope for—at least in the short-term—is a minimal amount of deterrence-based trust emanating from your position of power. Employees aren't likely to give you any more than the minimal level of trust needed to maintain professional relations.

For the longer term, you need to reassess what you've said in the past, who you've said it to, and practices you've engaged in which were handled poorly. You can't begin changing a deeply mistrusting climate until you know and understand clearly what you've done to create it.

Once you understand what you've done wrong, look back to our discussion of how to build loyalty. Particularly notice the importance of good communication skills—being open and candid; sharing your feelings; telling the truth, even when it hurts; conveying who you are and what you stand for; and knowing what information needs to be held in strict confidence.

Serious deteriorations of trust will take a long time to overcome. It takes a lot of time and experiences to develop thick levels of trust. Similarly, it takes a long time and a lot of new experiences to rebuild them. And, remember, once bitten, twice shy. People who have lost trust in you will be watching you very closely for signs of backtracking. You can destroy months of progress by a single inappropriate action. You'll find that the task of rebuilding trust in a climate where it has been deeply damaged will be onerous, but it's not impossible.

Ian Baker is director of compensation at the *Toronto Sun* Publishing Corp. When the newspaper recently began bargaining preparation for a new labor contract with its printers union, Ian was selected by senior management to head up the "prenegotiation" team. Made up of people from six different departments at the *Toronto Sun*, the team's objective was to gather facts that would help the company's negotiators when the serious bargaining began. For instance, the team would look at internal information such as grievance and accident records, overtime figures, and turnover rates, as well as external data including statistics on the local economy, economic forecasts for Toronto and Ontario, cost of living data, and copies of recently negotiated contracts by the union with other employers to determine what issues the union considers important.

TRUST ON TEMPORARY TEAMS: THE CASE OF "SWIFT TRUST"

Because the *Toronto Sun* is a big company and people don't tend to interact much with others outside their functional areas, Ian found he knew only one other member on this prenegotiation team. And since she had been with the company for less than six months, he didn't know her very well. He had never previously met three of the team's appointees, and contact with the final member was limited to a brief introduction at last year's Christmas party.

Ian found his circumstances uncomfortable. Here he was directing a company team. They would have to work closely together for at least a month. Yet he didn't know these people. As assignments were made, could he depend on each member to carry out their responsibilities? Could he trust these people to hold information he shared with them in confidence?

As we've stated many times in this book, work in organizations is increasingly being done by teams. While some of these teams are ongoing and staffed by a relatively constant set of members, many work teams today are temporary in nature. Like the team Ian had, they typically cut across functions within the organization. And they are often composed of an ever-changing set of individuals. Even so-called "permanent" teams frequently have to deal with new members and replacements. If trust relies heavily on experience, temporary teams have a major dilemma in trying to increase trust among members: Members frequently don't know enough about one another to permit them to trust. Given the widespread acceptance of temporary teams and the desire by people to develop trust with their co-workers, what do people like Ian Baker do? The answer appears to be: They develop **swift trust**.[43] That is, they act as if trust were present even though there is a lack of history that precludes its development.

Temporary teams need to exhibit behavior that presupposes trust. They have to depend on each other, take risks, demonstrate confidences, and make themselves vulnerable. Yet traditional sources of trust—familiarity, shared experiences, reciprocal disclosure, fulfilled promises, and demonstrations of nonexploitation of vulnerability—don't exist. Temporary teams lack the requisite history on which incremental and accumulative confidence-building measures are built. Moreover, they typically don't provide the time or opportunity for the kind of experiences necessary for thicker forms of trust to emerge. So swift trust seeks substitutes for history. What are those substitutes? We can suggest four.

First is the creation of the temporary team itself. There is substantial evidence indicating that the mere process of group formation alone may provide an initial foundation for the emergence of swift trust. The fact, for instance, that Ian and five other *Toronto Sun* employees were selected by senior management for the prenegotiation team suggests that the company's top executives believed these people were capable of working together and doing the job.

Second is a leader's reputation. Team leaders with strong reputations can act as useful substitutes for interpersonal history. Film directors such as Woody Allen, Steven Speilberg, George Lucas, and Francis Ford Coppola have established reputations for assembling remarkable and successful ensemble casts. The cast "trusts" these directors to do what is necessary to make the movie work.

A third substitute is choosing temporary teams made up of close friends. Doing so allows each member of the team to focus on the task at hand and not worry about problems of trust. This provides insight into why new CEOs, brought into a company from the outside, often fill key senior positions with people they have worked with before. Old bonds create swift trust in new situations.

Finally, swift trust can be created by reliance on referred contacts. "I don't know you, but a mutual friend tells me that you're OK." These implicit recommendations of others reduce risk when you otherwise don't have firsthand experience to draw upon. Recommendations are widely used for checking on job applicants, assessing candidates who seek to join prestigious country clubs, and determining who gets into fraternities and sororities. They also are relied on for allowing people to make swift-trust judgments.

These criteria, incidentally, can help explain why group class projects in college are typically disliked by students and often unsuccessful in creating outstanding work. They are temporary groups with thin trust. Especially where the groups are put together by the instructor, there is typically no leader whom members respect enough to give their "undying" confidence to, and there is a lack of history that might indicate that members can trust one another. Additionally, with more and more students commuting to campus and having part-time jobs, the opportunity to build friendships or make contacts who can "vouch" for others' reliability has been dwindling. The result is that students find few appropriate substitutes and hence are reluctant to exhibit swift-trust behaviors.

THE ROLE OF TRUST IN DIFFERENT CULTURES

In many parts of the world, business transactions won't take place until the parties are acquainted and a trusting relationship has been established.[44] For instance, in Saudi Arabia, you don't do much business during a first business meeting. The time is used to become acquainted and build trust. Similarly, Western executives often get frustrated in trying to do business with Asians. The Westerners want to begin business negotiations immediately, while their Asian counterparts are more concerned with developing a relationship. It's not unusual for an American company to spend months, even years, building a relationship with a Japanese firm before the latter will give the Americans one yen worth of business. Asian managers also tend to select family and friends to fill positions in their organizations. Consistent with our previous discussion on swift trust, Asians prefer to recruit family and friends for vacancies because they believe they can be depended upon. Such nepotistic practices are typically frowned upon by Western managers, who prefer more impersonal sources of recruitment.

We conclude this chapter by considering the role of trust in different countries.[45] To give you a flavor of the differences you're likely to encounter, we look at practices in Africa, Canada, the People's Republic of China, and France.[46]

Friendship and trust must come before an African enters a business deal. A close bond must develop between the two people involved. And friendships often continue after specific business activities end. Once a person is accepted as a friend, that person is automatically a member of the family. Not surprisingly, formal invitations and appointments are uncommon. In African societies, a friend can drop into a friend's place anytime.

Canadians believe that trust is an important component in achieving organizational goals. They believe this even when dealing with people from cultures where trust may even be a competitive liability. In negotiations, Canadians tend to trust the information that is communicated to them as long as the other party uses a cooperative negotiating strategy that emphasizes the free exchange of information. If Canadians perceive that the other party is not using a cooperative strategy, then trust is damaged. It's assumed that the other person is more interested in achieving individual outcomes than in joint outcomes.

The Chinese rely heavily on **guanxi.** This term means personal connections or social networking, and it is endemic in Chinese business.[47] For instance, when Chinese executives were shown a list of 11 factors and asked to rank them in order of importance to long-term business success, *guanxi* was consistently rated highest.[48] Additionally, evidence indicates that companies that have developed the right *guanxi* networks tended to perform better financially than those which had not.[49] The primary explanation of why *guanxi* is important to managers in China is that it acts as a substitute for reliable government and unambiguous laws.[50] Business executives in China build trusting relationships with government officials to defend themselves against threats like appropriation or extortion. So while managers in Western countries can accept thinner levels of trust because laws and reliable government lessen business risks, the Chinese look to thicker levels of trust as a substitute.

The French are very status conscious. Social class is very important to them. While an American trusts a person according to past personal accomplishments and upon other people's recognition and ranking of that person, the French rely heavily on social class stereotypes when making trust determinations. It's very difficult for French people to earn respect from members of other social classes merely through work accomplishments and performance. So whether you are trusted or not is influenced more by who your parents were, your level of education, your professional title, and the furnishings in your home than on past experiences in dealing with you.

Chinese executives in the building materials business rely on guanxi *to jointly develop plastic homes for the Shanghai market.*

There is a variety of additional material available on the CD-ROM and companion Web site that accompany this text. You can access this information through the CD-ROM or by visiting the Web site at <**www.prenhall.com/robbins**>.

SUMMARY

(This summary is organized by the chapter-opening learning objectives on page 500.)

1. Trust is a positive expectation that another will not—through words, actions, or decisions—act opportunistically.

2. The five dimensions making up trust are integrity, competence, consistency, loyalty, and openness.

3. Trust has become so important to today's managers because there has been a general loss of trust in institutions (such as government and business); poor management practices have undermined good employer-employee relationships in many organizations; in times of change and instability, which describes today's workplace, trust becomes more important for maintaining relationships; trust stabilizes the new psychological contract; new structural designs are more ambiguous and rely on trust rather than bureaucratic hierarchy; and trust leads to higher organizational commitment, which managers see as desirable.

4. The most fragile form of trust is deterrence-based. It relies on fear of punishment and is highly vulnerable. One violation or inconsistency can destroy it. Knowledge-based trust relies on behavioral predictability. It characterizes most organizational relationships. The third and most highly developed form of trust is based on identification. Here there is an emotional connection that allows parties to act for and substitute for one another.

5. You can build trust by being open, fair, speaking your feelings, telling the truth, showing consistency, fulfilling your promises, maintaining confidences, and demonstrating competence.

6. You can begin to rebuild lost trust by identifying the source of mistrust; if possible, change organizational policies and practices that have undermined it; admit mistakes and openly accept responsibility for the violation; and share your feelings.

7. Swift trust is a state where people act as if trust were present even though there is no history to support it. As organizations have moved to teams and other temporary structural devices, people are forced to work together who have no history upon which to build substantive trust. They rely on swift trust.

8. *Guanxi* refers to personal connections, and it is endemic in Chinese business. Strong social contacts create trusting relationships, and they substitute for ambiguous laws and unreliable government.

REVIEW QUESTIONS

1. Do you think trust evolves out of an individual's personal characteristics or out of specific situations? Explain.

2. What role do you think training plays in an individual's ability to trust others? For instance, does the training of lawyers, accountants, law-enforcement personnel, and social workers take different approaches toward trusting others? Explain.

3. What is the psychological contract and what are its implications for trust building?

4. Is is possible for a leader to be effective if he or she is not perceived as trustworthy? Explain.

5. What type of trust relationship do you have with your current best friend? How does it compare with previous "best friend" relationships? Give examples of behaviors that could permanently shake that trust. How have you handled past violations of trust from a close friend?

6. How might an understanding of knowledge-based trust explain the reluctance of a person to change jobs?

7. "It's not possible to be both a trusting boss and a politically astute leader. One requires openess and the other requires concealment." Do you agree or disagree with this statement? Explain.

8. What are four substitutes that swift trust relies on in place of history?

9. If you were a Canadian manager trying to build a trusting relationship with a group of French executives, what would you do?

10. Contrast thin versus thick trust in the United States, the United Kingdom, and China.

Taking Over Burnaby Auto Supply

"I don't know much about the automotive supply business, but then I don't need to," was one of Karen Chung's favorite phrases. Unfortunately for Karen, those words would prove to be untrue.

Karen's dad founded Burnaby Auto Supply outside Vancouver, British Columbia, before she was born. By high school, her father had her helping out in the store. She worked most weekends and during the summer months. But Karen always made it clear to her dad that her work career would lie elsewhere. After graduating from college in 1994, she joined Procter & Gamble as a sales representative. Since then, she's had two promotions. Events of last month, however, have changed those career plans.

Karen's father died of a sudden heart attack 4 weeks ago, leaving her mother to run the family business. An only child, Karen knew her obligations. Her mother had little knowledge of business and wasn't equipped to run the store. When her mother said, "Karen, you have to come back and take over the store. If not you, there is no one. And I can't think of selling your dad's legacy," Karen fulfilled her duty. She gave notice to P&G and began preparing for taking over the business.

As part of the transition, Karen asked the store's five full-time employees to come in early last Saturday for a meeting. She wanted to use this time to meet the staff and allow them to get to know her. After all, except for Charley Waterton, who had worked for her dad for nearly 20 years, no one really knew Karen. And she wanted to hear their ideas and any problems they thought needed attention. Karen wasn't prepared for what she heard.

The meeting started with Karen thanking everyone for coming in. She briefly described her background and what she had been doing during her 26 years. Then she talked about her plans. "I have a lot to catch up on. I've been away from the business for a number of years. But I want to continue the things my dad did. I want us to function as a team. I want to make this a good place to work." Karen wasn't prepared for the response that her remarks created.

"I certainly hope you run this place better than your father," opined Al Hall. "I don't want to bad-mouth the dead, but your father was a very tough guy to work for."

Flo Murray added, "I'll be honest with you. I was planning on leaving this place. I was gonna start looking for another job. Your father's death put that on hold. I decided I'd wait and see if things changed around here. But if they don't, I'm gonna leave. No one should be treated the way your father treated us."

"I don't think you have any idea what a ruthless tyrant your father was," added an angry Michael Wong. "In the past year, your father drove off four different people. I've worked here only six months. If my wife hadn't recently lost her job, I wouldn't be here either."

Finally, Charley Waterton spoke. "Karen, I've known you since you were a pip-squeak. I know you loved your dad, but I have to tell you, he was an impossible guy to work for. I don't think a week has gone by that I haven't thought about quitting. Maybe I'm just too passive. It was easier to take the s*** from your dad than to go out looking for another job. What made working here the most difficult was . . . your dad was never straight with us. He'd promise us something, and then never follow through. He was that way from day one. In 1988, he told me he was going to set up a pension plan. He never did. Last year he said he was going to close the store one weekend in August and take us all up to the lake at his expense. It never happened. He promised me a raise for three straight years. More baloney."

"Charley's right," added Flo. "Mr. Chung couldn't be trusted. It's hard for me to say this to you, but lying came easy to your father."

Karen's first reaction was to deny what she was hearing. But why would all these people say these things if they weren't true? She remembered, during her high school days, how people in the store seemed to fear her dad. But she thought that was just because he was the boss. Now things seemed to be clearer. She understood how her father's drive and "win at any cost" attitude might have led him to promise things he couldn't deliver. And he was always a poor communicator. Karen realized she had to accept the perceptions of her employees. Regardless of whether they were true or not, if they thought they were true, they were. She needed to change this climate and change it fast. She needed these people's knowledge and experience if she was going to keep the store going.

If you were Karen, what, if anything, could you do to erase this climate of mistrust that your father had created?

Getting Others to Trust Me

Is there someone with whom you would like to improve their level of trust in you? Maybe it's a parent, a sibling, a romantic interest, a friend, a business associate, or a college instructor. With this person in mind, ask yourself: On a 1-to-5 scale (1 being low), to what degree does this person perceive me as:

Open _____
Fair _____
Speaking my feelings _____
Telling the truth _____
Being consistent _____

Fulfilling my promises _____
Maintaining confidences _____
Demonstrating competence _____

Review your responses. Focus on items where you scored less than 4. These are the areas that need your attention. Now ask yourself: What can I do in these areas to improve my score? Prepare a specific plan and detailed set of behaviors that can help you improve in these weaker areas. Remember that trust takes time to build. So don't expect overnight results. But the first step toward building a more trusting relationship begins by identifying weak areas and taking action to improve them.

Affirmation of Trust

Break into groups of eight to 12 members each.

A. Each group has 20 minutes to discuss the following four topics:
  1. What kind of situations cause you to be afraid?
  2. What kind of situations cause you to feel insecure?
  3. What makes you happy?
  4. What makes you cry?
B. Each group member should remove a shoe and place it alongside the shoes of other members in a designated place, outside the group's meeting area. Each member should identify his or her shoe by putting his or her name on a slip of paper and putting it in front of the shoe.
C. Review the 5-item "Affirmation of Trust" listing that follows this exercise. Each member should:
  1. Write down the name of a person in your group on a slip of paper. Under his or her name, write the letters A through E in a vertical column. Next to each letter rate your perception of that person (based on your experience in class as well as their responses in this activity) on a scale of 1 to 5 (1 being low) using the "Affirmation of Trust" listing. Sign your name to the bottom of the slip.

Deposit this slip of paper in the other member's shoe.
  2. Repeat the above for all the other members of the group.
D. After all members have distributed their slips, each one retrieves his or her own shoe with the slips left in. Read each of the slips directed to you by the other members of your group and record the summary results.
E. Group members now discuss their reactions to their slips with the group. To what degree do they align with your self-perceptions? To what degree do the various statements converge and agree? What have you learned from this feedback that could help you build trust with others?

AFFIRMATION OF TRUST LIST

A. Open
B. Speaks his or her feelings
C. Tells the truth
D. Consistent
E. Demonstrates competence

Source: Based on J. W. Pfeiffer and J. E. Jones, (eds.), *A Handbook of Structured Experiences for Human Relations Training*, vol. VI (La Jolla, CA: University Associates, 1977), pp. 110–13.

CASE EXERCISE

The Motoman-Stillwater Relationship

Motoman Inc. was created in 1989 as a joint venture between Hobart Brothers Co., a welding-equipment firm based in Ohio, and Yaskawa Electric, a Japanese firm that is a world leader in robotics, factory automation, and related control systems. In 1994, Yaskawa bought out Hobart's interests. Motoman, today, is a $100 million a year business and holds a major share of the North American market for arc-welding, laser-welding, laser-cutting, and water-jet-cutting robots and robotic systems.

Stillwater Technologies Inc. began in the 1950s as a tool-and-die shop. Today it is a contract tooling and machining company doing $9.5 million a year in sales.

The two companies do business with each other. About one-quarter of Stillwater's income comes from doing work for Motoman. But what's unique about this relationship is that the two companies are physically linked like few joint ventures are. They occupy office and manufacturing space in the same 165,000-square-foot facility. Their telephone and computer systems are linked. They also share a common lobby, a conference room, training rooms, and an employee cafeteria. This is a relationship that clearly goes beyond the typical customer-supplier partnership.

The two companies had worked together since the early 1990s. When each had outgrown their facilities near Troy, Ohio, a suggestion by a mutual friend led to their current sharing of leased space in a new facility. While the arrangement is unique, it seems to make sense because the two companies have developed strong bonds of trust with each other. For instance, Stillwater's original contract with Motoman had been based on a percentage-above-cost commitment for so many hours a month. And Stillwater opened their books to Motoman so they could accurately know Stillwater's cost.

The current relationship is based on trust and a handshake, not a written contract. "No one piece of paper defines this arrangement," says Motoman's CEO. "This is a virtual partnership. It's like a joint venture without all the paperwork. We are two independent companies cooperating as close to the line of intimacy as you can get."

The shop-floor areas of the two companies are separated by a 12-inch thick wall. When it is time for Stillwater to "ship" a pallet of parts, a 14-foot overhead door is raised and a forklift truck passes through the wall—often delivering directly to the Motoman assembly line. It's the ultimate in just-in-time delivery. This allows Stillwater not only to be able to make speedy deliveries to Motoman, but employees of both companies have ready access to one another to share information and are able to solve mutual problems jointly. The linking of computers even allows the companies to send design drawings back and forth to each other, which saves critical turnaround time.

"We never sat down and said that we trust each other," says Motoman's CEO. "We just trust each other."

QUESTIONS

1. What is the basis for the trust between Motoman and Stillwater?
2. What advantages do you see from this arrangement for each?
3. What disadvantages do you see?
4. To what degree do you think this model of a "virtual partnership" is transferable for use by other companies? Explain.

Source: Based on J. H. Sheridan, "An Alliance Built on Trust," *Industry Week*, March 17, 1997, pp. 67–70.

NOTES

1. See A. Bryant, "American Air's Pilots: Holding the Trump Card," *New York Times*, February 15, 1997, p. Y23; W. J. Holstein and D. McGraw, "Can Crandall Keep Control?" *U.S. News & World Report*, February 17, 1997, pp. 46–49; and W. Zellner, "Bob Crandall: An American Gladiator," *Business Week*, April 27, 1998, p. 44.
2. Based on S. D. Boon and J. G. Holmes, "The Dynamics of Interpersonal Trust: Resolving Uncertainty in the Face of Risk," in R. A. Hinde and J. Groebel (eds.), *Co-operation and Prosocial Behavior* (Cambridge, England: Cambridge University Press, 1991), p. 194; D. J. McAllister, "Affect- and Cognition-Based Trust as Foundations for Interpersonal Cooperation in Organizations," *Academy of Management Journal*, February 1995, p. 25; and D. M. Rousseau, S. B. Sitkin, R. S. Burt, and C. Camerer, "Not So Different After All: A Cross-Discipline View of Trust," *Academy of Management Review*, July 1998, pp. 394–95.

3. J. B. Rotter, Interpersonal Trust, Trustworthiness, and Gullibility," *American Psychologist*, January 1980, pp. 1–7.

4. J. D. Lewis and A. Weigert, "Trust as a Social Reality," *Social Forces*, June 1985, p. 970.

5. J. K. Rempel, J. G. Holmes, and M. P. Zanna, "Trust in Close Relationships," *Journal of Personality and Social Psychology*, July 1985, p. 96.

6. M. Granovetter, "Economic Action and Social Structure: The Problem of Embeddedness," *American Journal of Sociology*, November 1985, p. 491.

7. R. C. Mayer, J. H. Davis, and F. D. Schoorman, "An Integrative Model of Organizational Trust," *Academy of Management Review*, July 1995, p. 712.

8. C. Johnson-George and W. Swap, "Measurement of Specific Interpersonal Trust: Construction and Validation of a Scale to Assess Trust in a Specific Other," *Journal of Personality and Social Psychology*, December 1982, p. 1306.

9. D. L. Ferren, K. T. Dirks, and L. L. Cummings, " 'Must You Speak of One That I Love Not Wisely But Too Well': A Theory of Interpersonal Distrust." Paper presented at the Annual Conference of the Academy of Management, Cincinnati, Ohio, 1996.

10. P. L. Schindler and C. C. Thomas, "The Structure of Interpersonal Trust in the Workplace," *Psychological Reports*, October 1993, pp. 563–73; and M. C. Clark and R. L. Payne, "The Nature and Structure of Workers' Trust in Management," *Journal of Organizational Behavior*, May 1997, pp. 205–24.

11. J. K. Butler Jr. and R. S. Cantrell, "A Behavioral Decision Theory Approach to Modeling Dyadic Trust in Superiors and Subordinates," *Psychological Reports*, August 1984, pp. 19–28.

12. D. McGregor, *The Professional Manager* (New York: McGraw-Hill, 1967), p. 164.

13. B. Nanus, *The Leader's Edge: The Seven Keys to Leadership in a Turbulent World* (Chicago: Contemporary Books, 1989), p. 102.

14. D. L. Ferrin, K. T. Dirks, and L. L. Cummings, " 'Must You Speak of One That I Loved Not Wisely But Too Well.'"

15. R. J. Lewicki, J. A. Litterer, J. W. Minton, and D. M. Saunders, *Negotiations*, 2nd ed. (Burr Ridge, IL: Irwin, 1994), p. 32.

16. Cited in C. Lee, "Trust Me," *Training*, January 1997, p. 32.

17. Ibid.

18. See, for instance, D. M. Noer, *Healing the Wounds: Overcoming the Trauma of Layoffs and Revitalizing Downsized Organizations* (San Francisco: Jossey-Bass, 1993); and A. K. Mishra and G. M. Spreitzer "Explaining How Survivors Respond to Downsizing: The Roles of Trust, Empowerment Justice, and Work Redesign," *Academy of Management Review*, July 1998, pp. 567–88.

19. D. Krackhardt and R. Stern, "Informal Networks and Organizational Crisis: An Experimental Simulation," *Social Psychology Quarterly*, June 1988, pp. 123–40.

20. D. M. Rosseau, *Psychological Contracts in Organizations* (Thousand Oaks, CA: Sage, 1995); S. L. Robinson, "Trust and Breach of the Psychological Contract," *Administrative Science Quarterly*, December 1996, pp. 574–99; and E. W. Morrison and S. L. Robinson, "When Employees Feel Betrayed: A Model of How Psychological Contract Violation Develops," *Academy of Management Review*, January 1997, pp. 226–56.

21. T. R. Tyler and R. M. Kramer, "Whither Trust?" in R. M. Kramer and T. R. Tyler (eds.), *Trust in Organizations* (Thousand Oaks, CA: Sage, 1996), p. 4.

22. D. Limerick and B. Cunnington, *Managing the New Organization* (San Francisco: Jossey-Bass, 1993), pp. 95–96.

23. A. K. Mishra, "Organizational Responses to Crises: The Centrality of Trust," in R. M. Kramer and T. R. Tyler (eds.), *Trust in Organizations*, p. 283.

24. See C. Handy, "Trust and the Virtual Organization," *Harvard Business Review*, May–June 1995, pp. 40–50; H. C. Lucas Jr., *The T-Form Organization* (San Francisco: Jossey-Bass, 1996), p. 7; J. H. Sheridan, "Bonds of Trust," *Industry Week*, March 17, 1997, pp. 52–62; and R. Garud, "Trust and Virtual Systems," *SternBusiness*, Spring–Summer 1997, pp. 33–35.

25. These two studies are cited in J. M. Kouzes and B. Z. Posner, *Credibility: How Leaders Gain and Lose It, and Why People Demand It* (San Francisco: Jossey-Bass, 1993), pp. 278–83.

26. D. E. Zand, *The Leadership Triad: Knowledge, Trust, and Power* (New York: Oxford University Press, 1997), p. 89.

27. G. G. Daly, "Trust and Prosperity," *SternBusiness*, Spring–Summer, 1997, p. ii.

28. See L. T. Hosmer, "Trust: The Connecting Link between Organizational Theory and Philosophical Ethics," *Academy of Management Review*, April 1995, p. 393; R. C. Mayer, J. H. Davis, and F. D. Schoorman, "An Integrative Model of Organizational Trust," p. 712; and K. Ohlson, "Leadership in an Age of Mistrust," *Industry Week*, February 2, 1998, pp. 37–46.

29. Kouzes and Posner, *Credibility*, p. 14.

30. R. M. Hodgetts, "A Conversation with Warren Bennis on Leadership in the Midst of Downsizing," *Organizational Dynamics*, Summer 1996, pp. 72–78.

31. Ibid., p. 74.

32. Ibid., p. 73.

33. Ibid., p. 74.

34. D. Meyerson, K. E. Weick, and R. M. Kramer, "Swift Trust and Temporary Groups," in R. M. Kramer and T. R. Tyler (eds.), *Trust in Organizations*, p. 184.

35. This section is based on D. Shapiro, B. H. Sheppard, and L. Cheraskin, "Business on a Handshake," *Negotiation Journal*, October 1992, pp. 365–77; and R. J. Lewicki and B. B. Bunker, "Developing and Maintaining Trust in Work Relationships," in R. M. Kramer and T. R. Tyler (eds.), *Trust in Organizations*, pp. 119–24.

36. This section is based on R. J. Lewick and B. B. Bunker, "Developing and Maintaining Trust in Work Relationships," pp. 124–25.

37. Ibid., p. 125

38. See, for example, G. D. Mellinger, "Interpersonal Trust as a Factor in Communication," *Journal of Abnormal and Social Psychology*, May 1959, pp. 304–09; C. A. O'Reilly III and K. H. Roberts, "Information Filtration in Organizations: Three Experiments," *Organizational Behavior and Human Performance*, April 1974, pp. 253–65; and C. A. O'Reilly III, "The Intentional Distortion of Information in Organizational Communication: A Laboratory and Field Investigation," *Human Relations*, February 1978, pp. 173–93.

39. This section is based on D. E. Zand, *The Leadership Triad*, pp. 122–34; and A. M. Zak, J. A. Gold, R. M. Ryckman, and E. Lenney, "Assessments of Trust in Intimate Relationships and the Self-Perception Process," *Journal of Social Psychology*, April 1998, pp. 217–28.

40. This section is based on F. Bartolome, "Nobody Trusts the Boss Completely—Now What?" *Harvard Business Review*, March–April 1989, pp. 135–42; and J. K. Butler Jr., "Toward Understanding and Measuring Conditions of Trust: Evolution of a Condition of Trust Inventory," *Journal of Management*, September 1991, pp. 643–63.

41. J. Brockner, "Managing the Effects of Layoffs on Survivors," *California Management Review*, Winter 1992, pp. 21–33; and D. M. Noer, *Healing the Wounds* (San Francisco: Jossey-Bass, 1993).

42. R. J. Lewicki and B. B. Bunker, "Developing and Maintaining Trust in Work Relationships," in R. M. Kramer and T. R. Tyler, *Trust in Organizations*, p. 132.

43. This section is based on D. Meyerson, K. E. Weick, and R. M. Kramer, "Swift Trust and Temporary Groups," in R. M. Kramer and T. R. Tyler (eds.), *Trust in Organizations*, pp. 166–95.

44. P. R. Harris and R. T. Moran, *Managing Cultural Differences*, 4th ed. (Houston: Gulf Publishing, 1996), p. 3.

45. See, for example, K. Strong and J. Weber, "The Myth of the Trusting Culture," *Business and Society*, June 1998, pp. 157–83; and P. M. Doney, J. P. Cannon, and M. R. Mullen, "Understanding the Influence of National Culture on the Development of Trust," *Academy of Management Review*, July 1998, pp. 601–20.

46. This section is largely based on P. R. Harris and R. T. Moran, *Managing Cultural Differences*, pp. 208, 315, 372–73.

47. See I. Y. M. Yeung and R. L. Tung, "Achieving Business Success in Confucian Societies: The Importance of *Guanxi* (Connections)," *Organizational Dynamics*, Autumn 1996, p. 55; K. R. Xin and J. L. Pearce, "*Guanxi*: Connections as Substitutes for Formal Institutional Support," *Academy of Management Journal*, December 1996, p. 1642; C. Hui and G. Graen, "Guanxi and Professional Leadership in Contemporary Sino-American Joint Ventures in Mainland China," *Leadership Quarterly*, Winter 1997, pp. 453–56; and E. W. K. Tsang, "Can Guanxi Be a Source of Sustained Competitive Advantage for Doing Business in China?" *Academy of Management Executive*, May 1998, pp. 64–73.

48. I. Y. M. Yeung and R. L. Tung, "Achieving Business Success in Confucian Societies," p. 59.

49. Ibid., p. 61.

50. K. R. Xin and J. L. Pearce, "*Guanxi* Connections as Substitutes for Formal Institutional Support," pp. 1641–58.

DEVELOPING INTERPERSONAL SKILLS

EXTREMISTS THINK "COMMUNICATION" MEANS
AGREEING WITH THEM.

L. ROSTEN

LEARNING OBJECTIVES

After studying this chapter, you should be able to:

1 Describe the communication process.

2 Contrast gender differences in interpersonal communications.

3 Exhibit effective active-listening skills.

4 Provide effective performance feedback.

5 Describe five conflict resolution behaviors.

6 Contrast distributive and integrative bargaining.

7 Engage in effective negotiation.

8 Effectively delegate authority.

9 Contrast directive, nondirective, and participative counseling.

10 Describe how a manager can become more politically adept.

Deborah S. Kent's rise in the automotive industry is a success story built on strong people skills.[1] It's also a striking example of a manager who breaks stereotypes.

Kent entered the auto industry, first with General Motors and then with Ford Motor Co., after finishing her master's degree in industrial psychology from Washington University in St. Louis. Unlike many of her contemporaries who chose careers in marketing or accounting, Kent sought out manufacturing management. Dave Gorman, her boss and Ford's vehicle operations manager, said "three things stood out" when he hired her in 1988: "She was a female, she had great people skills, and she worked in production. . . . We were extremely impressed with her floor savvy, and she had come from a plant that had a reputation as being difficult to run and she had been good at it."

In 1994, at age 41, Deborah Kent became the plant manager of Ford's Avon Lake, Ohio, 3.3-million-square-foot assembly plant. The first woman to head a vehicle assembly plant at Ford, and the only African-American woman ever to rise to this post, she oversees 3,700 workers. Her plant's 19.5

miles of assembly line produces more than 216,000 Ford Econo-line vans and 115,000 Mercury Villager and Nissan Quest mini-vans a year.

Kent is aware she doesn't fit the stereotype of the typical auto plant manager. A petite woman, with horn-rimmed glasses and a preference for white silk blouses, she's a white-collar woman in a brawny blue-collar man's world. But don't let her looks fool you. "One of the first things I did when I arrived here was to hold a meeting with the area managers," she recalled. "I said, 'Let's assume you guys know I got this job because of my competency and proven successes with this company and you're just as happy to have me here as I am to be here, and I won't ever think anything other than that." And her directness was well received by those area managers. As one put it, "Nobody looks at it as if, 'She's a woman, can she do the job?' It's: 'She's the manager, so she can do the job.'"

Kent recognizes the importance of treating her employees right and creating a constructive climate for communication. "It does no good to have a diverse workforce if you don't listen to their opinions and thoughts," she says. "When I talk to my area managers, I say, 'Give me some feedback and some eye contact.' Don't look away from me and say, 'O.K. we have to do this because she says so.' Let's talk about it. If I had all the answers, surely I'd be someplace on high, so when I call you into my office, I'm looking for feed-back." Daniel Jowiski, body and assembly operations manager for the Econoline vans, speaks of his boss in glowing terms, "She's open to our opinions, and she's accessible."

Good communication skills are increasingly important to a manager's success. In this chapter, we review the communication process and provide some suggestions on how you can improve your listening and feedback skills. Then we address several other interpersonal skills—specifically, conflict management, negotiating, delegating, counseling, and politicking.

THE IMPORTANCE OF INTERPERSONAL SKILLS

Would it surprise you to learn that more managers are fired because of poor interpersonal skills than for lack of technical ability on the job? The evidence suggests that this is true.[2] There are abundant data indicating that many managers suffer deficiencies in their interpersonal skills. For instance, the Center for Creative Leadership in North Carolina esti-mates that half of all managers and 30 percent of all senior managers have some type of difficulty working with people.[3] And a survey of nearly 200 top executives at six Fortune 500 companies found that, according to these executives, the single biggest reason for fail-ure was poor interpersonal skills.[4]

If you need further evidence of the importance of interpersonal skills, we would point to a comprehensive study of the people who hire students with undergraduate busi-ness degrees and depend on these hires to fill future management positions. This study found that the area in which graduates were most deficient was in leadership and interpersonal skills.[5]

These findings shouldn't surprise you. They are consistent with our view of the manager's job. Because managers integrate the work of others, competencies in leadership, communication, and other interpersonal skills must be a prerequisite to managerial effectiveness.

INTERPERSONAL COMMUNICATION

A lot of managers pay little attention to communication. Why? Some explanations include: "I'm already a good communicator." "Good communication skills can't be taught. You either have 'em or you don't." "People hear what they want to hear. I can't do much about that." The truth is that effective communication is critical to a manager's success, that there are specific techniques that can be learned to improve communication skills, and that being an effective communicator requires managers to maneuver through a field of land mines. "There are probably a million ways to screw up communication in your company and only a few ways to get it right."[6] In this section, we'll try to give you some tools you can use to "get it right."

What Is Communication?

Communication involves the transfer of meaning from one person to another. If no information or ideas have been conveyed, communication hasn't taken place. If no one hears what you say or reads what you write, you haven't communicated. In addition, for communication to be successful, the meaning must be understood. If you speak to me in Mandarin Chinese, but I don't know this language, there won't be any understanding on my part. So **communication**, the transference of meaning, involves a sender's transmitting a message and a receiver's understanding it.

Communication is obviously not limited to merely speaking words. Memos, when read and understood, constitute a form of communication. So, too, do e-mail, bulletins, and visual displays. And communication also encompasses nonverbal messages and symbols. Body language, gestures, and facial expressions often "say" more than any words. Similarly, the clothes we wear, our hairstyles, the way we arrange our offices, the cars we drive, and other symbols communicate information to others.

Our focus in this chapter is on **interpersonal communication**, that is, communication between two people, either one-to-one or in face-to-face or group settings, in which the parties are treated as individuals rather than as objects. This type is in contrast to **organizational communication**, which encompasses communication among several individuals or groups. Because our interest here is in interpersonal skills, our attention will be directed at interpersonal communication.

The Communication Process

Exhibit 17-1 depicts the **communication process**. This model is made up of seven parts: (1) the communication source, (2) encoding, (3) the message, (4) the channel, (5) decoding, (6) the receiver, and (7) feedback. The source is the sender. He or she initiates the communication process by converting a thought or message to symbolic form. We call this conversion **encoding**. The **message** is the actual physical product from the source en-

The Communication Process

EXHIBIT 17-1

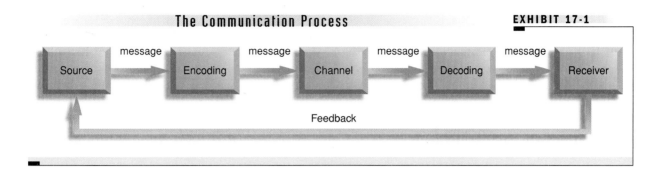

Source → message → Encoding → message → Channel → message → Decoding → message → Receiver

Feedback

coding. "When we write, the writing is the message. When we paint, the picture is the message. When we gesture, the movements of our arms, the expressions on our faces are the messages."[7] In interpersonal communication, the message is typically words and nonverbal cues. The **channel** is the medium through which the message travels. Interpersonal communications rely heavily on face-to-face talk, the telephone, and increasingly e-mail as primary channels. The receiver is the object to whom the message is directed. But before the message can be received, the symbols in it must be translated into a form that can be understood by the receiver. This is the **decoding** of the message. The final link in the communication process is a feedback loop. **Feedback** is the check on how successful we have been in transferring our messages as originally intended. It seeks to determine whether understanding has been achieved.

If communication were perfect, messages would be transferred so that the receiver understood them exactly as they were envisioned in the mind of the sender. Unfortunately that rarely happens, because there are deviations or blockages in the flow of the communication process. Most of the seven components in Exhibit 17-1 have the potential to create distortion and, therefore, impinge on the goal of communicating perfectly. If the encoding is done carelessly, the message encoded by the sender will be distorted. The message itself can also cause distortion. The poor choice of symbols and confusion in the content of the message are frequent problem areas. The channel can distort communication if a poor one is selected or if the "noise level" is high. And, of course, the receiver represents a potential source for distortion. His or her prejudices, knowledge gaps, perceptual skills, attention span, and care in decoding are all factors that can result in interpreting the message somewhat differently than intended by the sender.

Contemporary Communication Issues

In this section, we address six contemporary issues: (1) Contrary to what some people think, not all problems in organizations are caused by poor communication. (2) Sometimes communication distortions are purposeful and even functional. (3) Nonverbal communications may be more powerful than the verbal variety. (4) The explosive growth of e-mail is creating new types of communication problems. (5) Men and women generally use talk for different reasons, thus creating cross-gender communication difficulties. (6) And cross-cultural communication is becoming a major challenge to managers in today's global environment.

THE "BLAME GAME" Poor communication is an obvious problem in organizations. But poor communication gets blamed for a lot of problems that aren't its doing.[8] If a TQM program fails, inevitably someone is going to attribute it to lack of communication. When work teams have trouble developing positive synergy, it's likely to be blamed on a communication problem. If a manager has trouble motivating his or her work group, it's probably a communication problem. When conflicts arise between two employees, we tend to assume that the culprit, again, is poor communication. Well, communication isn't necessarily the source of all these problems. It *may* be, but not necessarily!

Communication is a convenient, all-encompassing source of blame for organizational problems. Why? We can offer three possible explanations. First, many people call everything under the sun a communication problem because they find it too painful to confront what is often the real problem—competence. It's difficult to tell someone that he or she is incompetent in doing the job. So we say the person has a communication problem, which is a far less sweeping indictment. Second is the growing credibility problem in organizations. For instance, a recent study found that 61 percent of U.S. employees don't believe that management tells them the truth, and this number has been increasing in recent years.[9] In this distrustful climate, employees aren't likely to believe that management is open or honest in what it says, so what appear to be communication problems develop. Finally, many so-called communication problems are really value differences. Interpersonal conflicts, for example, are often called communication problems but are actually caused by basic differences in beliefs. If a manager believes that fair compensation means tying pay to productivity, but a union member believes that fair compensation means linking pay to seniority, discussions between the two parties may seem to be one of communication problems. In reality, the parties fully understand each other. It's just that they disagree as to what characterizes "fair compensation."

This shouldn't be construed as suggesting that communication problems aren't real or that they don't create serious problems for managers. Poor communications *do* frequently undermine a manager's or unit's effectiveness. Our point, however, is to emphasize that a lot of dilemmas that masquerade as communication problems are, under closer scrutiny, caused by something else.

PURPOSEFUL MISCOMMUNICATION   A basic fact about communication is often overlooked: It is frequently in the interest of one or both parties in a communication exchange to avoid clarity.[10] While rarely admitted in public, most of us recognize that ambiguity in communication has its benefits. Keeping communications fuzzy can cut down on questions, reduce opposition, make it easier to deny one's earlier statements, help to preserve mystique and hide insecurities, allow one to say several things at the same time, permit one to say "no" diplomatically, and help to avoid confrontation and anxiety.

If you want to see the fine art of ambiguous communication up close, all you have to do is watch a television interview with a politician who is running for office. The interviewer attempts to get specific information; the politician tries to retain multiple possible interpretations. Such ambiguous communications allow the politician to approach his or her ideal image of being "all things to all people."

NONVERBAL COMMUNICATION   Your boss can tell you that his office door is always open and that he wants you to come to him with any problem any time. Yet every time you take him up on his offer he fidgets with his pen, seems to be distracted by papers on his desk, and constantly glances at his watch. Are you getting a different message than the one he verbally conveyed? Probably. What you are experiencing is the power of nonverbal communication. You are learning that actions frequently speak louder (and more accurately) than words. Or, as so aptly put by the industrialist Andrew Carnegie, "As I grow older, I pay less attention to what men say. I just watch what they do."[11]

The telephone, voice mail, e-mail, electronic meetings, faxes, and personal communicators have lessened the importance of nonverbal communication. But the majority of interpersonal communication in organizations still takes place through face-to-face interaction. This means that every verbal message also comes with a nonverbal component. And, if you are going to be an effective communicator, you need to make sure that your verbal and nonverbal messages are in alignment.

Receivers interpret messages by taking in meaning from all channels that are available to them. So when they are communicating face-to-face with someone, they listen to words, interpret symbols such as appearance, and watch for facial expressions, body positions, eye contact, physical distancing, and other nonverbal cues in their effort to extract meaning.[12] To the degree that your nonverbal cues are consistent with your verbal message, they act to reinforce the message. But when they are inconsistent, they create confusion for the receiver. And, as we noted earlier, most of us tend to put more stock in the nonverbal messages we receive than the words we hear.

ELECTRONIC MAIL Few technological breakthroughs have become as rapidly accepted and widely used as electronic mail. For instance, it's been estimated that in 1994, approximately 776 billion e-mail messages moved through U.S.-based computer networks. In 1997, that number was 2.6 trillion. The estimate for the year 2000 was 6.6 trillion.[13] Currently, more than 40 percent of the American workforce uses e-mail.

> Currently, more than 40 percent of the American workforce uses e-mail.

E-mail, of course, offers some very positive advantages. It's convenient, inexpensive, and highly democratic. But it has the potential to create a number of problems. The downside of convenience, for instance, is that it's as easy to send a message to 200 people as it is to one. This encourages inclusion of addressees who have little interest in your message and information overload on the receiving end. It's not unusual for employees to find they've received 20 or more messages in a given day, of which maybe only two or three are actually relevant to them. Other communication-related problems include misunderstandings, maintenance of privacy, lack of responsibility, and failure to align e-mail and personal styles.

As noted previously, e-mails come without a nonverbal component. This makes it easy for e-mail messages, especially critical or complex ones, to be misconstrued. E-mail messages are not private. Most organizations have the capability of reading employee messages and many do so regularly. E-mail has made it easier for middle managers to shun responsibility by bucking decisions up to higher levels of management. It's also used by some managers to avoid direct confrontations. They'll say things on e-mail that they would never say to that person's face. Finally, many e-mail users exploit the impersonal nature of this mechanism to "speak" in aggressive or threatening tones. Their e-mail style doesn't align with their personal style. People who are always polite and sensitive in person can become curt, even rude, on e-mail. In some cases, this is purposeful. In many cases, however, it's attributable to a failure to understand the power of e-mail. A written word, even on a screen, has decidedly more staying power than a mere verbal comment. Similarly, many users forget that the thoughtless use of ALL CAPS is the electronic equivalent of verbal shouting.

E-mail users need to refrain from using electronic mail as a means to hide from confronting people. If you can't say to someone's face what you're writing him or her by e-mail, you need to rethink the message or rethink whether e-mail is the right medium for the message. Additionally, care needs to be used in constructing e-mail messages. The written word carries greater weight than the spoken word. So even though e-mail is an easy and convenient channel of communication, it's also an extremely powerful mechanism that if misused can be an ineffective way to transmit meaning.

CROSS-GENDER COMMUNICATION Differences in speech styles are not always related to gender. But there is increasing evidence of general differences between men and women in terms of their conversational styles.[14] And these differences can create real barriers when men and women attempt to communicate with one another.

The most interesting finding is that men use talk to emphasize status, whereas women use it to create connection. You can think of communication as a continual balancing act, juggling the conflicting needs for intimacy and independence. Intimacy emphasizes closeness and commonalities. Independence emphasizes separateness and differences. Interestingly, the sexes tend to give different emphasis to these two forces. Women speak and hear a language of connection and intimacy; men speak and hear a language of status and independence. So, for many men, conversations are primarily a means to preserve independence and maintain status in a hierarchical social order. For many women, conversations are negotiations for closeness in which people try to seek and give confirmation and support.

For example, men frequently complain that women talk on and on about their problems. Women criticize men for not listening. What's happening is that when men hear a problem, they frequently assert their desire for independence and control by offering solutions. Many women, however, view telling a problem as a means to promote closeness. The women present the problem to gain support and connection, not to get the male's advice. Mutual understanding is symmetrical. But giving advice is asymmetrical—it sets the advice giver up as more knowledgeable, more reasonable, and more in control. This attitude contributes to distancing men and women in their efforts to communicate.

CROSS-CULTURAL COMMUNICATION Effective communication is difficult under the best of conditions. Cross-cultural factors clearly create potential for increased communication problems. Four specific problems have been identified that are related to language difficulties in cross-cultural communications.[15]

First, there are *barriers caused by semantics*. Words mean different things to different people, particularly people from different national cultures. Some words, for instance, don't translate between cultures. Understanding the word *sisu* will help you in communicating with people from Finland, but this word is untranslatable into English. It means something akin to "guts" or "dogged persistence." Similarly, the new capitalists in Russia may have difficulty communicating with their British or Canadian counterparts because English terms such as *efficiency*, *free market*, and *regulation* are not directly translatable into Russian.

Second, there are *barriers caused by word connotations*. Words imply different things in different languages. Negotiations between American and Japanese executives, for instance, are made more difficult because the Japanese word *hai* translates as "yes," but its connotation may be "yes, I'm listening," rather than "yes, I agree."

Third are *barriers caused by tone differences*. In some cultures, language is formal, in others it's informal. In some cultures, the tone changes depending on the context: People speak differently at home, in social situations, and at work. Using a personal, informal style in a situation where a more formal style is expected can be embarrassing and off-putting.

Fourth, there are *barriers caused by differences among perceptions*. People who speak different languages actually view the world in different ways. Eskimos perceive snow differently from people in milder climates because they have many words for it. Thais perceive "no" differently from Americans because Thais have no such word in their vocabulary.

In The News

Boeing's Philip Condit Works on Communication

The Boeing Co. is one big organization. It has sales of nearly $20 billion a year. And because you don't build aircraft in limited quarters, Boeing owns and leases around 76 million square feet of floor space. The company is also geographically dispersed. For example, helicopters are produced in Philadelphia, commercial aircraft in Seattle, and defense and space projects are located in Oak Ridge, Tennessee. The physical size of Boeing's operations makes a favorite activity of Philip M. Condit, the company's president and CEO, just that more challenging. Condit likes to walk Boeing's factory floors and talk with the workers. "It helps you to have a complete picture of what's going on," Condit says of the practice. "It isn't that [the workers'] view is right and others are wrong. But it *is* their view. It *is* what they are seeing."

These walkarounds are nothing new to Condit. Although he has been CEO at Boeing only since April 1996, he's been walking through company factories and talking to workers for at least 20 years. He considers it essential to effective communication and a means for him to learn, firsthand, the problems and concerns of those on the factory floor.

To put workers at ease and to lessen the influence of factory supervisors and managers, Condit has created a standard *modus operandi*. He arrives at a plant unannounced and wearing casual clothes. "I can have a much better conversation, faster, if I have a pair of khakis on than if I go into the factory with my tie on," he says. He doesn't ask workers for their names. He excludes supervisors and other in-plant managers from the

conversations. And he encourages candor. What he wants to know is what problems are hindering their ability to do a first-rate job.

What has Condit learned from his walkarounds? Most recently, workers have been complaining about the quality of incoming work. Condit has responded by working with plant management to improve quality and to streamline production processes.

Source: Based on J. S. McClenahen, "Condit Takes a Hike," *Industry Week*, December 2, 1996, pp. 12–16.

When communicating with people from different cultures, what can you do to minimize misperceptions, misinterpretations, and misevaluations? Following these four rules can be helpful:[16]

1. *Assume differences until similarity is proved.* You are far less likely to make an error if you assume that others are different from you rather than assuming they are similar.
2. *Emphasize description of what someone has said or done rather than interpretation or evaluation.* Interpretations are highly culture-sensitive. So delay judgment until you have had sufficient time to observe and interpret the situation from the differing perspectives of all the cultures involved.

3. *Practice empathy.* Before sending a message, put yourself in the recipient's shoes. Try to see the other person as he or she really is.

4. *Treat your interpretations as a working hypothesis.* Once you have developed an explanation for a new situation or think you empathize with someone from a foreign culture, treat your interpretation as a hypothesis that needs further testing rather than as a certainty. And be ready to modify your interpretation as new information arises.

Key Oral Communication Skills

Two of the most important skill elements for effective oral communication are the ability to be an active listener and the ability to provide feedback. Each of these skills is associated with a set of specific behaviors. In this section, we review those specific behaviors.

ACTIVE LISTENING Most people take listening skills for granted.[17] They confuse hearing with listening. What's the difference? Hearing is merely picking up sound vibrations. Listening is making sense of what we hear. Listening requires paying attention, interpreting, and remembering sound stimuli.

Effective listening is active rather than passive. In passive listening, you are like a tape recorder. You absorb the information given. **Active listening**, in contrast, requires you to "get inside" the speaker's head so that you can understand the communication from his or her point of view.

The average person normally speaks at the rate of 125 to 200 words per minute. However, the average listener can comprehend up to 400 words per minute. This difference leaves a lot of time for idle mind wandering while listening. The active listener works to fill in this idle time. The active listener concentrates intensely on what the speaker is saying and tunes out the thousands of miscellaneous thoughts (about money, sex, vacations, parties, friends, bills, getting the car fixed, and the like) that create distractions. As an active listener, you try to understand what the speaker wants to communicate rather than what you want to understand. You also demonstrate acceptance of what is being said. You listen objectively without judging content. Finally, as an active listener, you take responsibility for completeness. You do whatever is necessary to get the full intended meaning from the speaker's communication.

The following eight behaviors are associated with effective active-listening skills. If you want to improve your listening skills, look to these behaviors as guides:

1. *Make eye contact.* How do you feel when somebody doesn't look at you when you're speaking? If you're like most people, you're likely to interpret this behavior as aloofness or lack of interest. We may listen with our ears, but others tend to judge whether we're really listening by looking at our eyes.

2. *Exhibit affirmative head nods and appropriate facial expressions.* The effective listener shows interest in what is being said. How? Through nonverbal signals. Affirmative head nods and appropriate facial expressions, when added to good eye contact, convey to the speaker that you're listening.

3. *Avoid distracting actions or gestures.* The other side of showing interest is avoiding actions that suggest that your mind is somewhere else. When listening, don't look at your watch, shuffle papers, or engage in similar distractions. They make the speaker feel as if you're bored or uninterested. Maybe more important, they indicate that you aren't fully attentive and may be missing part of the message the speaker wants to convey.

Pilgram Fund manager Howard Tiffen illustrates that a key element of effective active listening is maintaining eye contact. It demonstrates interest in what the other party is saying.

4. *Ask questions.* The critical listener analyzes what he or she hears and asks questions. This behavior provides clarification, ensures understanding, and assures the speaker that you're listening.

5. *Paraphrase.* Paraphrasing means restating what the speaker has said in your own words. The active listener uses phrases such as "What I hear you saying is . . ." or "Do you mean . . .?" Why rephrase what has already been said? Two reasons! First, it's an excellent control device to check on whether you're listening carefully. You can't paraphrase accurately if your mind is wandering or if you're thinking about what you're going to say next. Second, it's a control for accuracy. By rephrasing what the speaker has said in your own words and feeding it back to the speaker, you verify the accuracy of your understanding.

6. *Avoid interrupting the speaker.* Let the speaker complete his or her thought before you try to respond. Don't try to second-guess where the speaker's thoughts are going. When the speaker is finished, you'll know it!

7. *Don't overtalk.* Most of us would rather speak our own ideas than listen to what someone else says. Too many of us listen only because it's the price we have to pay to get people to let us talk. Although talking may be more fun and silence may be uncomfortable, you can't talk and listen at the same time. The active listener recognizes this fact and doesn't overtalk.

8. *Make smooth transitions between the roles of speaker and listener.* In most situations, you're continually shifting back and forth between the roles of speaker and listener. The active listener makes transitions smoothly from speaker to listener and back to speaker. From a listening perspective, this means concentrating on what a speaker has to say and practicing not thinking about what you're going to say as soon as you get your chance.

PROVIDING FEEDBACK There are abundant data that indicate that managers do a pretty poor job of providing employees with performance feedback. For instance, a recent survey found that 60 percent of U.S. and European companies identified poor or insufficient performance feedback as a primary cause of deficient employee performance—by far the highest percentage of any response in the study.[18]

We can make six specific suggestions to help you be more effective in providing feedback.[19] Since our focus is on management, these suggestions, for the most part, are directed at performance issues in work situations. However, you can modify them to improve feedback on any type of communication.

1. *Focus on specific behaviors.* Feedback should be specific rather than general. Avoid such statements as "You have a bad attitude" or "I'm really impressed with the good job you did." They are vague, and although they do provide information, they do not tell the recipient enough to correct the "bad attitude" or on what basis you concluded that a "good job" had been done.

    Suppose you said something like, "Todd, I'm concerned with your attitude toward your work. You were a half-hour late to yesterday's staff meeting and then told me you hadn't read the preliminary report we were discussing. Today you tell me you're taking off 3 hours early for a dental appointment." Or, "Laura, I was really pleased with the job you did on the Phillips account. They increased their purchases from us by 22 percent last month, and I got a call a few days ago from Dan Phillips complimenting me on how quickly you responded to those specification changes for the MJ-4 microchip." Both of these statements focus on specific behaviors. They tell the recipient why you are being critical or complimentary.

2. *Keep feedback impersonal.* Feedback, particularly the negative variety, should be descriptive rather than judgmental or evaluative. No matter how upset you are, keep the feedback job-related and never criticize someone personally because of an inappropriate action. Telling people they're "stupid," "incompetent," or the like is almost always counterproductive. It provokes such an emotional reaction that the performance deviation itself is apt to be overlooked. When you are criticizing, remember that you are censuring a job-related behavior, not the person. You might be tempted to tell someone he or she is "rude and insensitive" (which might well be true), but that's hardly impersonal. It's better to say something like, "You interrupted me three times, with questions that were not urgent, when you knew I was talking long-distance to a customer in Scotland."

3. *Keep feedback goal-oriented.* Feedback should not be given primarily to "dump" or "unload" on another. If you have to say something negative, make sure it's directed toward the recipient's goals. Ask yourself whom the feedback is supposed to help. If the answer is essentially you—"I've got something I need to get off my chest"—bite your tongue. Such feedback undermines your credibility and lessens the meaning and influence of future feedback.

4. *Make feedback well timed.* Feedback is most meaningful to a recipient when there is a very short interval between his or her behavior and the receipt of feedback about that behavior. To illustrate, a new employee who makes a mistake is more likely to respond to his manager's suggestions for improvement right after the mistake or at the end of that working day, rather than during a performance-review session several months later. If you have to spend time re-creating a situation and refreshing someone's memory of it, the feedback you're providing is likely to be ineffective.

5. *Ensure understanding.* Is your feedback concise and complete enough that the recipient clearly and fully understands your communication? Remember that every successful communication requires both transference and understanding of meaning. If feedback is to be effective, you need to ensure that the recipient understands it. Consistent with the previous discussion of active-listening techniques, you should have the recipient rephrase the content of your feedback to find out whether it fully captures the meaning you intended.

6. *Direct negative feedback toward behavior that the recipient can control.* There is little value in reminding a person of some shortcoming over which he or she has no control. Negative feedback should be directed toward behavior the recipient can do something about. For example, to criticize an employee who is late because she forgot to set her alarm clock is valid. To criticize her for being late when the subway she takes to work every day had a power failure, trapping her underground for half an hour, is pointless. There is nothing she could have done to correct what happened.

   In addition, when negative feedback is given concerning something that the recipient can control, it's a good idea to indicate specifically what can be done to improve the situation. Giving suggestions takes some of the sting out of the criticism and offers guidance to recipients who understand the problem but don't know how to correct it.

CONFLICT MANAGEMENT SKILLS

We briefly discussed conflict, as it is related to teams, in chapter 10. We defined conflict as perceived incompatible differences that result in interference or opposition. In this section, we address conflict management. What is it? Why is it important? And how can you improve your conflict management skills?

What Is Conflict Management?

The term *conflict management* is often used synonymously with *conflict resolution*. But they are not the same. If all conflicts were dysfunctional, then the manager's job would be solely to eliminate or resolve conflicts. However, as we noted in chapter 10, conflict can have a positive side. It keeps work groups viable, self-critical, and creative. A group that is totally void of conflict is prone to becoming static, apathetic, and nonresponsive to needs for change and innovation.

Conflict management entails maintaining the optimum level of conflict in a group. Too little conflict creates stagnation. Too much creates disruption and infighting. Both are dysfunctional because they undermine group performance. The job of the manager, therefore, is to balance these forces by using conflict resolution and stimulation techniques.[20]

Why Is Conflict Management Important?

The ability to manage conflict is undoubtedly one of the most important skills a manager needs to possess. A study of middle- and top-level executives by the American Management Association revealed that the average manager spends approximately 20 percent of his or her time dealing with conflict.[21] The importance of conflict is reinforced by a survey of what topics practicing managers consider most important in management development programs. Conflict management was rated as being more important than decision making, leadership, or communication skills.[22] In further support of this claim, another study looked at twenty-five skill and personality factors to determine which, if any, were related to success (defined in terms of ratings by one's boss, salary increases, and promotions) among a group of managers.[23] Of the twenty-five measures, only one—the ability to handle conflict—was positively related to managerial success.

Developing Effective Conflict Resolution Skills

If you're a manager and have too much dysfunctional conflict in your unit, what can you do? This section reviews conflict resolution skills. Essentially, you need to know your basic conflict-handling style, as well as those of the conflicting parties, to understand the situation that has created the conflict, and to be aware of your options.

WHAT IS YOUR UNDERLYING CONFLICT-HANDLING STYLE? Most of us have the ability to vary our conflict response according to the situation, but each of us has a preferred style for handling conflicts.[24] You might be able to change your preferred style to suit the context in which a certain conflict exists; however, your basic style tells you how you're *most likely* to behave and the conflict-handling option on which you *most often rely*.

BE JUDICIOUS IN SELECTING THE CONFLICTS THAT YOU WANT TO HANDLE Not every conflict justifies your attention. Some might not be worth the effort; others might be unmanageable.

Not every conflict is worth your time and effort to resolve. Although avoidance might appear to be a "cop-out," it can sometimes be the most appropriate response. You can improve your overall management effectiveness, and your conflict-management skills in particular, by avoiding trivial conflicts. Choose your battles judiciously, saving your efforts for ones that count.

> Conflict keeps work groups viable, self-critical, and creative.

Regardless of your desires, reality tells us that some conflicts are unmanageable.[25] When antagonisms are deeply rooted, when one or both parties wish to prolong a conflict, or when emotions run so high that constructive interaction is impossible, your efforts to manage the conflict are unlikely to meet with much success.

Don't be lured into the naive belief that a good manager can resolve every conflict effectively. Some aren't worth the effort. Some are outside your realm of influence. Still others may be functional and, as such, are best left alone.

EVALUATE THE CONFLICT PLAYERS If you choose to manage a conflict situation, it's important that you take the time to get to know the players. Who is involved in the conflict? What interests does each party represent? What are the players' values, personalities, feelings, and resources? Your chances of success in managing a conflict will be greatly enhanced if you can view the conflict situation through the eyes of the conflicting parties.

ASSESS THE SOURCE OF THE CONFLICT Conflicts don't pop out of thin air. They have causes. Because your approach to resolving a conflict is likely to be determined largely by its causes, you need to determine the source of the conflict. Sources of conflict can generally be separated into three categories: communication differences, structural differences, and personal differences.[26]

Communication differences are disagreements arising from semantic difficulties, misunderstandings, and noise in the communication channels. People are often quick to assume that most conflicts are caused by lack of communication, but there is usually plenty of communication going on in most conflicts. The mistake many people make is equating good communication with having others agree with their views. As noted earlier in this chapter, what might at first look like an interpersonal conflict based on poor communication is usually found, upon closer analysis, to be a disagreement caused by different value systems, role requirements, unit goals, personalities, or other factors. As a source of conflict for managers, poor communication probably gets more attention than it deserves.

As we discussed in chapter 8, organizations are typically horizontally differentiated through specialization and departmentalization and vertically differentiated by creation of management levels. This *structural differentiation* creates problems of integration. The frequent result is conflict. Individuals disagree over goals, responsibilities, decision alternatives, performance criteria, and resource allocations. These conflicts are not due to poor communication or personal animosities. Rather, they are rooted in the structure of the organization itself.

The third conflict source is *personal differences*. Conflicts can evolve out of individual idiosyncrasies and personal value systems. The chemistry between some people makes it hard for them to work together. Factors such as background, education, experience, and training mold each individual into a unique personality with a particular set of values. The result is people who may be perceived by others as abrasive, untrustworthy, strange, or difficult to work with. These personal differences can create conflict.

KNOW YOUR OPTIONS What resolution tools or techniques can a manager call upon to reduce conflict when it's too high? Managers essentially can draw upon five conflict resolution options: avoidance, accommodation, forcing, compromise, and collaboration.[27] Each has particular strengths and weaknesses, and no one option is ideal for every situation. You should consider each a "tool" in your conflict management "tool chest." You will have a preferred style and might be better at using some tools than others, but the skilled manager knows what each tool can do and when each is likely to be most effective.

As previously noted, not every conflict requires an assertive action. Sometimes **avoidance**—just withdrawing from or suppressing the conflict—is the best solution. When is avoidance a desirable strategy? When the conflict is trivial, when emotions are running high and time is needed to cool them down, or when the potential disruption from a more assertive action outweighs the benefits of resolution.

The goal of **accommodation** is to maintain harmonious relationships by placing another's needs and concerns above your own. You might, for example, yield to another person's position on an issue. This option is most viable when the issue under dispute isn't that important to you or when you want to build up credits for later issues.

In **forcing**, you attempt to satisfy your own needs at the expense of the other party. In organizations this is most often illustrated by a manager's using his or her formal authority to resolve a dispute. Forcing works well when you need a quick resolution on important issues, when unpopular actions must be taken, and when commitment by others to your solution is not critical.

A **compromise** requires each party to give up something of value. Typically this is the approach taken by management and labor in negotiating a new labor contract. Compromise can be an optimum strategy when conflicting parties are about equal in power, when it is desirable to achieve a temporary solution to a complex issue, or when time pressures demand an expedient solution.

Collaboration is the ultimate win-win solution. All parties to the conflict seek to satisfy their interests. It is typically characterized by open and honest discussion among the parties, active listening to understand differences, and careful deliberation over a full range of alternatives to find a solution that is advantageous to all. When is collaboration the best conflict option? When time pressures are minimal, when all parties seriously want a win-win solution, and when the issue is too important to be compromised.

> For most people the term *conflict* has a negative connotation, and the idea of purposely creating conflict seems to be the antithesis of good management.

▶ Don't Forget about Conflict Stimulation

What about the other side of conflict management—situations that require managers to *stimulate* conflict? The notion of stimulating conflict is often difficult to accept. For most people the term *conflict* has a negative connotation, and the idea of purposely creating conflict seems to be the antithesis of good management. Few of us personally enjoy being in conflict situations. Yet the evidence demonstrates that there are situations in which an increase in conflict is constructive.[28] Given this reality and the fact that there is no clear demarcation between "good" conflicts and "bad" ones, Exhibit 17-2 on page 538 lists a set of questions that might help you. Although there is no definitive method of assessing the need for more conflict, an affirmative answer to one or more of the questions in Exhibit 17-2 suggests a need for conflict stimulation.

We know a lot more about resolving conflict than about stimulating it. That's only natural, since human beings have been concerned with the subject of conflict reduction for hundreds, maybe thousands, of years. The dearth of ideas on conflict stimulation techniques reflects the relatively recent interest in the subject. The following are some preliminary suggestions that managers might want to utilize.[29]

CHANGE THE ORGANIZATION'S CULTURE The initial step in stimulating conflict is for managers to convey to employees the message, supported by actions, that conflict has its legitimate place. Individuals who challenge the status quo, suggest innovative ideas, offer divergent opinions, and demonstrate original thinking need to be rewarded visibly with recognition, promotions, salary increases, and other positive reinforcers.

EXHIBIT 17-2

Is Conflict Stimulation Needed?*

1. Are you surrounded by "yes" people?
2. Are subordinates afraid to admit ignorance and uncertainties to you?
3. Is there so much concentration by managers on reaching a compromise that they lose sight of values, long-term objectives, or the organization's welfare?
4. Do managers believe that it's in their best interest to maintain the impression of peace and cooperation in their unit, regardless of the price?
5. Is there an excessive concern by decision makers for not hurting the feelings of others?
6. Do managers believe that popularity is more important for obtaining organizational rewards than competence and high performance?
7. Are managers unduly enamored of obtaining consensus for their decisions?
8. Do employees show unusually high resistance to change?
9. Is there a lack of new ideas?
10. Is there an unusually low level of employee turnover?

*An affirmative answer to any or all of these questions suggests the need for conflict stimulation.
Source: From S. P. Robbins, "'Conflict Management' and 'Conflict Resolution' Are Not Synonymous Terms," *California Management Review,* Winter 1978, p. 71. Copyright 1978 by The Regents of the University of California. Reprinted from *California Management Review,* vol. 21, no. 2. By permission of The Regents.

USE COMMUNICATION In the United States, as far back as Franklin D. Roosevelt's administration (in the 1930s), and probably before, the White House consistently has used communication to stimulate conflict. Senior officials "plant" possible decisions with the media through the infamous "reliable source" route. For example, the name of a prominent judge is "leaked" as a possible Supreme Court appointment. If the candidate survives the public scrutiny, his or her appointment will be announced by the president. However, if the candidate is found lacking by the media and public, the president's press secretary or other high-level official will make a formal statement such as, "At no time was this individual under consideration." Regardless of party affiliation, occupants of the White House have regularly used the reliable source as a conflict stimulation technique. It's all the more popular because of its handy escape mechanism. If the conflict level gets too high, the source can be denied and eliminated.

Mike McCurry, White House press secretary under President Bill Clinton, regularly used communication to stimulate and manage conflict.

Ambiguous or threatening messages also encourage conflict. Information that a plant might close, that a department is likely to be eliminated, or that a layoff is imminent can reduce apathy, stimulate new ideas, and force reevaluation—all positive outcomes that result from increased conflict.

Another way communication can stimulate conflict is to draw attention to differences of opinion that individuals themselves didn't previously recognize. People often cover up or sublimate potential differences in order to keep the peace. When these differences are overtly addressed, parties are forced to confront conflicts.

BRING IN OUTSIDERS   A widely used method for shaking up a stagnant unit or organization is to bring in—either by hiring from outside or by internal transfer—individuals whose backgrounds, values, attitudes, or managerial styles differ from those of present members. Many large corporations have used this technique during the last several decades in filling vacancies on their boards of directors. Women, minority group members, consumer activists, and others whose backgrounds and interests differ significantly from those of the rest of the board have been purposely selected to add a fresh perspective.

RESTRUCTURE THE ORGANIZATION   We know that structural variables are a source of conflict. It is therefore only logical that managers look to structure as a conflict stimulation technique. Centralizing decisions, realigning work groups, introducing teams into a highly individualistic culture, increasing formalization, and increasing interdependencies between units are all structural devices that disrupt the status quo and can act to increase conflict levels.

APPOINT A DEVIL'S ADVOCATE   A **devil's advocate** is a person who purposely presents arguments that run counter to those proposed by the majority or against current practices. He or she plays the role of the critic, even to the point of arguing against positions with which he or she actually agrees.

A devil's advocate acts as a check against groupthink and practices that have no better justification than "that's the way we've always done it around here." When thoughtfully listened to, the advocate can improve the quality of group decision making. On the other hand, others in the group often view advocates as time wasters, and their appointment is almost certain to delay any decision process.

Managers often need to negotiate. For instance, they may have to negotiate salaries for incoming employees, cut deals with superiors, work out differences with associates, and resolve conflicts with subordinates. For our purposes, we'll define **negotiation** as a process in which two or more parties exchange goods or services and attempt to agree on the exchange rate for them.[30] Note that we use the terms *negotiation* and *bargaining* interchangeably.

NEGOTIATION SKILLS

▶ Bargaining Strategies

There are two general approaches to negotiation—distributive bargaining and integrative bargaining.[31] These are compared in Exhibit 17-3.

DISTRIBUTIVE BARGAINING   You see a used car advertised for sale in the newspaper. It seems to be just what you've been looking for. You go to see the car. It's great and you want it. The

EXHIBIT 17-3

Distributive versus Integrative Bargaining

Bargaining Characteristic	Distributive Bargaining	Integrative Bargaining
Available resources	Fixed amount of resources to be divided	Variable amount of resources to be divided
Primary motivations	I win, you lose	I win, you win
Primary interests	Opposed to each other	Convergent or congruent with each other
Focus of relationships	Short-term	Long-term

Source: Based on R. J. Lewicki and J. A. Litterer, *Negotiation* (Homewood, Il: Irwin, 1985), p. 280.

owner tells you the asking price. You don't want to pay that much. The two of you then negotiate over the price. The negotiating strategy you're engaging in is called **distributive bargaining**. Its most identifying feature is that it operates under zero-sum conditions. That is, any gain the seller makes is at your expense, and vice versa. Referring to the used car example, every dollar you can get the seller to cut from the car's price is a dollar you save. Conversely, every dollar more he can get from you comes at your expense. So the essence of distributive bargaining is negotiating over who gets what share of a fixed pie.

Probably the most widely cited example of distributive bargaining is in labor–management negotiations over wages. Typically, labor's representatives come to the bargaining table determined to get as much money as possible out of management. Since every cent more that labor negotiates increases management's costs, each party bargains aggressively and treats the other as an opponent who must be defeated.

The essence of distributive bargaining is depicted in Exhibit 17-4. Parties A and B represent two negotiators. Each has a *target point* that defines what he or she would like to achieve. Each also has a *resistance point*, which marks the lowest outcome that is acceptable—the point below which they would break off negotiations rather than accept

EXHIBIT 17-4

Staking Out the Bargaining Zone

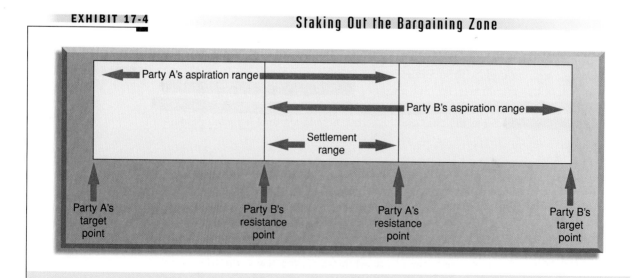

a less-favorable settlement. The area between these two points makes up the aspiration range of each. As long as there is some overlap between A's and B's aspiration ranges, there exists a settlement range where each one's aspirations can be met.

When engaged in distributive bargaining, your negotiation tactics should focus on trying to get your opponent to agree to your specific target point or to get as close to it as possible. Examples of such tactics are persuading your opponent of the impossibility of getting to his or her target point and the advisability of accepting a settlement near yours; arguing that your target is fair, while your opponent's isn't; and attempting to get your opponent to feel emotionally generous toward you and thus accept an outcome close to your target point.

INTEGRATIVE BARGAINING A sales representative for a women's sportswear manufacturer has just closed a $15,000 order from a small clothing retailer. The sales rep calls in the order to her firm's credit department. She is told that the firm can't approve credit to this customer because of a past slow-pay record. The next day, the sales rep and the firm's credit manager meet to discuss the problem. The sales rep doesn't want to lose the business. Neither does the credit manager, but he also doesn't want to get stuck with an uncollectible debt. The two openly review their options. After considerable discussion, they agree on a solution that meets both their needs: The credit manager will approve the sale, but the clothing store's owner will provide a bank guarantee that will assure payment if the bill isn't paid within 60 days.

This sales–credit negotiation is an example of **integrative bargaining**. In contrast to distributive bargaining, integrative problem solving operates under the assumption that there exists one or more settlements that can create a win-win solution.

In general, integrative bargaining is preferable to distributive bargaining. Why? Because it builds long-term relationships and facilitates working together in the future. It bonds negotiators and allows each to leave the bargaining table feeling that he or she has achieved a victory. Distributive bargaining, in contrast, leaves one party a loser. It tends to build animosities and deepen divisions when people have to work together on an ongoing basis.

Why, then, don't we see more integrative bargaining in organizations? The answer lies in the conditions necessary for this type of negotiation to succeed. These conditions include parties who are open with information and candid about their concerns, a sensitivity by both parties to the other's needs, the ability to trust one another, and a willingness by both parties to maintain flexibility.[32] Because many organizational cultures and interpersonal relationships aren't characterized by openness, trust, and flexibility, it is not surprising that negotiations often take the approach of "win at any cost."

▶ Developing Effective Negotiation Skills

The essence of effective negotiation can be summarized in the following eight recommendations.[33]

RESEARCH YOUR OPPONENT Jerry Anderson, president of Apogee Enterprises, a Minneapolis-based architectural-glass fabricator, is constantly negotiating with architects, engineers, and building contractors—three groups whose agendas clash more often than not. Yet he's consistently successful at reaching a consensus.[34] He attributes a large amount of his success to forethought. "Always try to figure out where the other guy is coming from," he says. "If you think enough about it, you can usually come up with a reading."

Much of the 1998–99 NBA season was lost because members of the NBA players' union (see photo) could not reach an acceptable contract with the owners' negotiating committee.

Start negotiations by acquiring as much information as you can about your opponent's interests and goals. What constituencies must he or she appease? What is his or her strategy? Understanding your opponent's position will help you to better understand his or her behavior, to predict his or her responses to your offers, and to frame solutions in terms of his or her interests.

BEGIN WITH A POSITIVE OVERTURE A substantial amount of evidence shows that concessions tend to be reciprocated and lead to agreements. So begin bargaining with a positive overture—perhaps a minor concession—and then reciprocate your opponent's concessions.

ADDRESS PROBLEMS, NOT PERSONALITIES Concentrate on the negotiation issues, not on the personal characteristics of your opponent. When negotiations get tough, avoid the tendency to attack your opponent. It's your opponent's ideas or position that you disagree with, not him or her personally. Separate the people from the problem, and don't personalize differences.

PAY LITTLE ATTENTION TO INITIAL OFFERS Treat an initial offer as merely a point of departure. Everyone has to have an initial position. Such positions tend to be extreme and idealistic. Treat them as such.

EMPHASIZE WIN-WIN SOLUTIONS Inexperienced negotiators often assume that their gain must come at the expense of the other party. As noted with integrative bargaining, that needn't be the case. There are often win-win solutions. But assuming a zero-sum game means missed opportunities for trade-offs that could benefit both sides. So if conditions are supportive, look for an integrative solution. Frame options in terms of your opponent's interests and look for solutions that can allow your opponent, as well as yourself, to declare a victory.

CREATE AN OPEN AND TRUSTING CLIMATE Skilled negotiators are good listeners, ask questions, focus their arguments directly, are not defensive, and have learned to avoid words and phrases that can irritate an opponent (for example, "generous offer," "fair price," "reasonable arrangement"). In other words, they are adept at creating the open and trusting climate necessary for reaching an integrative settlement.

BE OPEN TO ACCEPTING THIRD-PARTY ASSISTANCE When stalemates are reached, consider using a neutral third party. *Mediators* can help parties come to an agreement, but they don't impose a settlement. *Arbitrators* hear both sides of the dispute and then impose a solution. *Conciliators* are more informal and act as a communication conduit, passing information between the parties, interpreting messages, and clarifying misunderstandings.

DON'T FORGET CULTURE DIFFERENCES! Negotiation practices are heavily influenced by national culture. The approach that the typical Chinese take in negotiating a contract, for example, isn't the same as the typical American.[35] So if you're negotiating with someone from a different cultural background, take into consideration how cultural influences are likely to shape their negotiating tactics. For instance, the Chinese place a strong emphasis on relationships. They don't like to negotiate with people they don't know well or trust. So don't expect a Chinese negotiator to quickly jump into bargaining with you if he or she doesn't know you. In addition, be aware that the Chinese position on an issue is likely to become rigid if they feel their goals are being compromised. And nothing should be considered final in negotiations with Chinese until it has been actually realized.

American negotiators tend to use a combination of tactics that reflect their cultural background. Here are a few examples:[36] Americans value informality and equality in interactions. So they try to make people feel comfortable by playing down status distinctions. Americans also get frustrated easily and are famous for their impatience. Actions that particularly irk Americans include small talk (they want to get right to the issues), dishonesty (Americans expect their opponent to be open and honest), silence (Americans expect others to speak up), intermingling issues (Americans like to approach complex negotiation tasks sequentially, one at a time), inability to bring closure (comments like "I have to check with my boss back in Paris" frustrates Americans), and backing out on an agreement (Americans expect bargainers to honor any agreement that is reached no matter what the circumstances).

Savvy negotiators from Asia and Latin America have learned how to turn cultural preferences to their favor when bargaining with Americans. To return to the Chinese example, many consciously stall the bargaining process and inject long periods of silence when negotiating with Americans to purposely exploit the latter's propensity for impatience.

There are limits to any manager's time and knowledge. So effective managers rely on others to help them achieve their unit's objectives. This section describes the value of delegating and shows how effective managers do it.[37]

DELEGATION SKILLS

▶ What Is Delegation?

Delegation is the assignment of authority to another person to carry out specific activities. It allows a subordinate to make decisions—that is, it is a shift of decision-making authority from one organizational level to another, lower one.[38]

Delegation should not be confused with participation. In participative decision making, there is a sharing of authority. With delegation, subordinates make decisions on their own.

▶ Barriers to Delegation

Many managers, especially inexperienced ones and those new to the managerial ranks, have a tough time delegating. They would rather do the work themselves, and then complain about how overworked they are. Why don't managers delegate more often? Five reasons have been suggested:[39]

1. Managers think they are giving up power and control when they delegate. But they aren't. By delegating, managers increase their influence through their employees' efforts. Managers who delegate widen their span of control and, by doing so, ultimately have more people reporting to them and become more powerful.

2. A lot of managers think delegation is abdication. When properly done, it isn't. The key word here is *properly*. If a manager dumps tasks on an employee without clarifying the exact job to be done, the range of the employee's discretion, the expected level of performance, the time the tasks are to be completed, and similar concerns, he or she is abdicating responsibility and inviting trouble. Proper delegation also includes establishing controls that will quickly advise the manager if an employee acts outside his or her delegated authority.

3. Many managers lack confidence in their employees or fear that they will be criticized for their employees' mistakes. So they try to do everything themselves. It's often true that a manager is capable of doing tasks better, faster, or with fewer mistakes. The catch is that a manager's time and energy are limited. It is not possible for managers to do everything themselves. What effective managers do is determine the acceptable level of performance in a task, and then delegate that task to someone who can achieve that level. And they accept some mistakes by their employees. Mistakes are part of delegation. As long as their costs aren't excessive, mistakes are often good learning experiences for employees.

4. Many managers tend to do those things that are interesting, quick, and easy. They take the "fun tasks" for themselves. Ironically, these are the tasks that often are easiest to delegate. If a manager insists on doing all the interesting or easy tasks, he or she will never get to the important work managers are supposed to be doing.

5. A lot of managers are insecure and fear that delegation could undermine their own job. They think that if they delegate important tasks to their employees, those employees will become better skilled, more experienced, and eventually steal their jobs from them. Quite the contrary is typically true. The best managers, and the ones who get promoted fastest, are often the ones who build a reputation for developing the people below them.

▶ Developing Effective Delegating Skills

If you're a manager and want to delegate some of your authority to someone else, how do you go about it? The following summarizes the primary steps you need to take.[40]

CLARIFY THE ASSIGNMENT The first thing to do is to determine what is to be delegated and to whom. You need to identify the person best capable of doing the task, and then determine if he or she has the time and motivation to do the job.

Assuming you have a willing and able employee, it is your responsibility to provide clear information on what is being delegated, the results you expect, and any time or performance expectations you hold.

Unless there is an overriding need to adhere to specific methods, you should delegate only the end results. That is, get agreement on what is to be done and the end results expected, but let the employee decide on the means.

Are there any activities that managers should *never* delegate? Yes![41] Don't delegate feedback. Feedback should be given only by the direct manager. Don't delegate disciplinary action. Reprimands, suspensions, dismissals, and similar disciplinary actions should be made and conveyed by the direct manager. And never delegate politically sensitive matters. It's not fair to subordinates to burden them with decisions that are certain to be highly controversial.

SPECIFY THE SUBORDINATE'S RANGE OF DISCRETION Every act of delegation comes with constraints. You are delegating authority to act, but not unlimited authority. What you are delegating is authority to act on certain issues and, on those issues, within certain parameters. You need to specify what those parameters are so that subordinates know, in no uncertain terms, the range of their discretion. When this has been successfully communicated, both you and the subordinate will have the same idea of the limits to the latter's authority and how far he or she can go without further approval.

ALLOW THE SUBORDINATE TO PARTICIPATE One of the best sources for determining how much authority will be necessary to accomplish a task is the subordinate who will be held accountable for that task. If you allow employees to participate in determining what is delegated, how much authority is needed to get the job done, and the standards by which they'll be judged, you increase employee motivation, satisfaction, and accountability for performance.

Be aware, however, that participation can present its own set of potential problems as a result of subordinates' self-interest and biases in evaluating their own abilities. Some subordinates might be personally motivated to expand their authority beyond what they need and beyond what they are capable of handling. Allowing such people too much participation in deciding what tasks they should take on and how much authority they must have to complete those tasks can undermine the effectiveness of the delegation process.

INFORM OTHERS THAT DELEGATION HAS OCCURRED Delegation should not take place in a vacuum. Not only do you and the subordinate need to know specifically what has been delegated and how much authority has been granted, but anyone else who may be affected by the delegation act also needs to be informed. The people affected include those outside the organization as well as those inside it. Essentially, you need to convey what has been delegated (the task and the amount of authority) and to whom. Failure to inform others makes conflict likely and decreases the chances that your employee will be able to accomplish the delegated task efficiently.

WHEN PROBLEMS SURFACE, INSIST ON RECOMMENDATIONS FROM THE SUBORDINATE Many managers fall into the trap of letting subordinates reverse the delegation process: The subordinate runs into a problem and then comes back to the manager for advice or a solution. Avoid being sucked into reverse delegation by insisting from the beginning that when subordinates want to discuss a problem with you, they come prepared with a recommendation. When you delegate downward, the subordinate's job includes making necessary decisions. Don't allow the subordinate to push decisions back upward to you.

ESTABLISH FEEDBACK CONTROLS To delegate without instituting feedback controls is to invite problems. There is always the possibility that an employee will misuse the discretion that

> By allowing employees to participate in the delegation process, you increase employee motivation, satisfaction, and accountability for performance.

he or she has been delegated. The establishment of controls to monitor the employee's progress increases the likelihood that important problems or expensive mistakes will be identified early and that the task will be completed on time and to the desired performance level.

Ideally, controls should be determined at the time of the initial assignment. Agree on a specific time for completion of the task and then set progress dates when the employee will report back on how well he or she is doing and any major problems that have surfaced. These controls can be supplemented with periodic spot checks to ensure that authority guidelines are not being abused, organization policies are being followed, proper procedures are being met, and the like.

Too much of a good thing can be dysfunctional. If the controls are too constraining, the employee will be deprived of the opportunity to build self-confidence and much of the motivational aspect of delegation will be lost. A well-designed control system permits your employees to make small mistakes but quickly alerts you when big mistakes are imminent.

COUNSELING SKILLS

Counseling is discussion of a problem (usually one with emotional content) with an employee in order to resolve the problem or, at a minimum, to help the employee to cope with it better.[42] Examples of problems that might require you to counsel an employee include divorce, serious illness, difficulty in getting along with a co-worker, a drinking problem affecting work performance, or frustration over a lack of career progress in the organization.

Counseling is not the same thing as coaching. *Coaching*, as discussed in chapter 15, addresses ability issues. As a coach, you provide instruction, guidance, advice, and encouragement to help employees improve their job performance. Counseling deals with personal problems. When employee personality or attitudes are the problem, you need to provide counseling.

Types of Counseling

How much direction should a manager provide during a counseling session? The answer to this question reveals three types of counseling: directive, participative, and nondirective. As you move to the right along the continuum shown in Exhibit 17-5, you will find yourself doing more of the talking and taking a more assertive role in solving the problem.

DIRECTIVE COUNSELING Historically, many managers used **directive counseling**. They listened to employee problems, decided what should be done, and then told employees what to do. In directive counseling, the manager is in control. However, directive counseling has

EXHIBIT 17-5

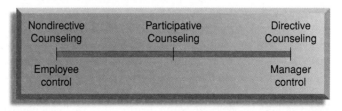

Three Types of Counseling

Nondirective Counseling	Participative Counseling	Directive Counseling
Employee control		Manager control

fallen out of favor in recent years. It assumes that managers fully understand the employee's problem, the options, and what is best for the employee. Clearly, these assumptions are unrealistic. And even if they were realistic, a manager telling an employee what they should do is no guarantee that they will follow that manager's advice. Most employees today prefer to have a say in decisions that directly affect them. They don't look kindly on managers who tell them what they should do. When confronted by such a boss, they aren't likely to accept his or her advice with much enthusiasm or conviction.

NONDIRECTIVE COUNSELING Whereas directive counseling gives control to the manager, nondirective counseling puts control in the hands of the employee. That is why the latter is also known as client-centered counseling.[43]

Nondirective counseling is based on the belief that people can solve their own problems with the aid of a sympathetic listener. The manager listens, repeats, synthesizes, understands, and gives feedback; however, the employee determines the alternatives and makes the decision. Most important, the manager avoids passing judgment.

When an employee is frustrated, nondirective counseling can help in two ways: First, the employee has the opportunity to vent frustrations; second, when frustrations are not reduced, the employee can still improve his or her ability to adjust to the problems when they are stated and listened to and solutions are formulated.

PARTICIPATIVE COUNSELING The middle ground between the two extremes of directive and nondirective counseling is called **participative counseling**. In this approach, the manager is an active listener but plays a more assertive role than in nondirective counseling by offering insights and advice. For example, because of the knowledge and experience you have acquired, you can often discuss the situation from a broader perspective and give your employee a different view of the problem.

In terms of management practice, the participative approach tends to be more widely used nowadays than either directive or nondirective counseling. Directive counseling has become increasingly inconsistent with the needs of today's employees and the values of today's organization. And nondirective counseling ignores the insights that an experienced manager can contribute as a result of his or her knowledge of the organization. Participative counseling has filled an important role in the 1990s because it is consistent with the view that managers empower their people rather than boss them.

▶ Effective Counseling Skills

The following twelve points provide you with specific guidelines to make you more effective in counseling employees.[44]

1. *Create a nonthreatening and supportive atmosphere for discussion.* The first thing you need to do is create a climate in which the employee will be comfortable and that will encourage him or her to be open and honest. Pick a time and place that provides privacy and where you won't be interrupted. Then greet the employee in a friendly and open manner.
2. *Emphasize confidentiality.* Convey early in the counseling session that everything the employee says will be treated in confidence. Effective counseling requires that the employee trust you.
3. *Listen patiently.* Listen to what the employee has to say before making any comments on your own.
4. *Avoid offering hasty advice.* Hold your tongue. Let the employee get his or her concerns and frustrations out on the table.

5. *Use your active-listening skills.* Paraphrase. Ask questions such as "Tell me about . . ." Avoid questions that can be answered with a mere yes or no. Watch for negative non-verbal messages. And don't interrogate the employee.

6. *Provide supportive responses.* Show empathy rather than sympathy. By your comments and gestures, show your support and concern. Withhold criticism. Don't argue with the employee, even if you disagree with what he or she is saying. And display confidence in the employee. Show that you believe that he or she can solve the problem.

7. *Focus on job performance expectations.* The purpose of the counseling session is to deal with some problem or problems that are affecting the employee's job performance. Keep the focus on those attitudes or behaviors that are undesirable. Don't pry into your employee's personal life. And don't moralize. Explain in very specific terms your job performance expectations.

8. *Help the employee to identify and articulate the problem.* It is not your role to define the problem. You should focus on job expectations. Make the employee responsible for identifying the problem. Don't allow yourself to be distracted or swayed by emotional pleas or hard-luck stories.

9. *Help the employee to look at several alternatives for solving the problem.* Individuals frequently limit their search for alternatives. In many cases, they quickly focus on a single option and discontinue the search for other alternatives. Encourage the employee to search for a wide range of possible solutions to his or her problem.

10. *Don't solve the problem for the employee.* It is the employee's problem, and he or she needs to take responsibility for it. If you provide a solution, the employee is not likely to accept ownership for it. Moreover, if your solution doesn't work out, you are the natural person for the employee to blame.

11. *Encourage the employee to articulate an action plan.* Conclude the counseling session by encouraging the employee to describe, in clear and specific language, the course of action he or she plans to take to solve the problem.

12. *Refer problems that are beyond your expertise.* You are not a trained therapist. Severe emotional or behavioral problems should be referred to a professional.

POLITICKING SKILLS

In the real world of organizations, the "good guys" don't always win. Demonstrating openness, trust, objectivity, support, and similar humane qualities in relationships with others doesn't always lead to improved managerial effectiveness. There will be times when, to get the resources you want or to have decisions go your way, you will need to engage in politics. This section can help you develop your politicking skills.

▶ What Is Politicking?

Politics is related to who gets what, when, and how. **Politicking** is the actions you can take to influence, or attempt to influence, the distribution of advantages and disadvantages within your organization.[45]

Politics is closely intertwined with the concept of power. When managers (or any organizational members, for that matter) convert their power into action, they are engaging in politics. Those with good political skills have the ability to use their power bases effectively.

Why Is There Politics in Organizations?

Can you conceive of an organization that is free of politics? It's possible, but not likely. Organizations are made up of individuals and groups with different values, goals, and interests. Therefore they have the potential for conflict over resources. Department budgets, space allocations, project responsibilities, and salary adjustments are just a few examples of the resources about whose allocation organizational members will disagree.

Resources in organizations are also limited, so potential conflict often turns into real conflict. If resources were abundant, then all the various internal constituencies within the organization could satisfy their goals. But because resources are limited, not everyone's interests can be provided for. Further, whether true or not, gains by one individual or group are often *perceived* as being at the expense of others within the organization. These factors create a competition among members for the organization's limited resources.

Maybe the most important factor leading to politics within organizations is the realization that most of the "facts" that are used to allocate the limited resources are open to interpretation. What, for instance, is good performance? What's a *good* job? What's an *adequate* improvement? The manager of any major league baseball team knows that a .400 hitter is a high performer and a .125 hitter is a poor performer. You don't need to be a baseball genius to know that you should play your .400 hitter and send the .125 hitter back to the minors. But what if you have to choose between players who hit .280 and .290? Then other factors—less objective ones—come into play: fielding, attitude, potential, ability to perform in the clutch, and so on. Most managerial decisions in organizations more closely resemble choosing between a .280 and a .290 hitter than deciding between a .125 hitter and a .400 hitter. It's in this large and ambiguous middle ground of organizational life—where the facts don't speak for themselves—that politics takes place.

Finally, because most decisions have to be made in a climate of ambiguity—where facts are rarely fully objective, and thus are open to interpretation—people within organizations will use whatever influence they can to taint the facts to support their goals and interests. That tendency, of course, creates the activities we call *politicking*.

Effective Politicking Skills

Forget, for a moment, the ethics of politicking and any negative impressions you may have of people who engage in organizational politics. If you wanted to be more politically adept in your organization, what could you do? The following suggestions are likely to improve your political effectiveness.[46]

Conveying the right image in terms of dress and appearance is an important element in the development of political skills.

FRAME ARGUMENTS IN TERMS OF ORGANIZATIONAL GOALS Effective politicking requires covering up self-interest. It doesn't matter that your objective is self-serving; all the arguments you marshal in support of it must be framed in terms of the benefits that will accrue to the organization. People whose actions appear to blatantly further their own interests at the expense of the organization's are almost universally denounced, are likely to lose influence, and often suffer the ultimate penalty of being expelled from the organization.

DEVELOP THE RIGHT IMAGE If you know your organization's culture, you understand what the organization wants and values from its managers—in terms of dress, associates to cultivate and those to avoid, whether to appear to be risk-taking or risk-aversive, the preferred leadership style, the importance placed on getting along with others, and so forth. Then you are equipped to project the appropriate image.

Because effectiveness in an organization is not a fully objective outcome, style as well as substance must be attended to. **Impression management**—that is, attempting to shape the image you project during an interaction—is an important part of political success.[47] People who are good at impression management tend to favorably shape how others see and evaluate them. Exhibit 17-6 summarizes some impression management techniques and provides an example of each.

GAIN CONTROL OF ORGANIZATIONAL RESOURCES The control of organizational resources that are scarce and important is a source of power. Knowledge and expertise are particularly effective resources to control. They make you more valuable to the organization and therefore more likely to gain security, advancement, and a receptive audience for your ideas.

CREATE OBLIGATION People believe in reciprocity. They try to repay, in kind, what another has provided them. Use this fact to build your influence base by creating obligation. Do favors for people, whether they request them or not. By so doing, they'll feel obligated to return that favor. The more favors you do for people, the more people you'll have indebted to you. And when the time comes that you ask *them* for a favor, it's more likely they'll comply.

MAKE YOURSELF APPEAR INDISPENSABLE Because we are dealing with appearances rather than objective facts, you can enhance your power by appearing to be indispensable. That is, you don't have to really be indispensable as long as key people in the organization believe that you are. If the upper management believes that there is no ready substitute for what you are giving the organization, they are likely to go to great lengths to ensure that your desires are satisfied. How do you make yourself appear indispensable? The most effective means is to develop expertise through experience, contacts, secret techniques, natural talents, and the like—that is, attributes that are perceived as critical to the organization's operations and that upper management believes no one else possesses to the extent that you do. In today's competitive climate, where managers are increasingly overseeing teams, the ability to display team leadership and build strong team loyalty can be seen as indispensable qualities.

It can also help for others in your organization to perceive you as mobile and to believe you have ready employment options available at other organizations. Combining perceived mobility with perceived indispensability lessens the likelihood that your rise in your present organization will be stalled by the excuse that "we can't promote you right now because your current unit can't afford to lose your expertise."

BE VISIBLE Because the evaluation of managerial effectiveness has a substantial subjective component, it is important that your boss and those in power in the organization be made aware of your contribution. If you are fortunate enough to have a job that brings your accomplishments to the attention of others, it may not be necessary to take direct measures

Impression Management Techniques

EXHIBIT 17-6

Conformity. Agreeing with someone else's opinion in order to gain his or her approval.

Example: A manager tells his boss, "You're absolutely right on your reorganization plan for the western regional office. I couldn't agree with you more."

Excuses. Explanations of a predicament-creating event aimed at minimizing the apparent severity of the predicament.

Example: Sales manager to boss, "We failed to get the ad in the paper on time, but no one responds to those ads anyway."

Apologies. Admitting responsibility for an undesirable event and simultaneously seeking to get a pardon for the action.

Example: Employee to boss, "I'm sorry I made a mistake on the report. Please forgive me."

Acclaiming. Explanation of favorable events to maximize the desirable implications for oneself.

Example: A salesperson informs a peer, "The sales in our division have nearly tripled since I was hired."

Flattery. Complimenting others about their virtues in an effort to make oneself appear perceptive and likable.

Example: New sales trainee to peer, "You handled that client's complaint so tactfully! I could never have handled that as well as you did."

Favors. Doing something nice for someone to gain that person's approval.

Example: Salesperson to prospective client, "I've got two tickets to the theater tonight that I can't use. Take them. Consider it a thank-you for taking the time to talk with me."

Association. Enhancing or protecting one's image by managing information about people and things with which one is associated.

Example: A job applicant says to an interviewer, "What a coincidence. Your boss and I were roommates in college."

Sources: Based on B. R. Schlenker, *Impression Management: The Self-Concept, Social Identity, and Interpersonal Relations* (Monterey, CA: Brooks/Cole, 1980); W. L. Gardner and M. J. Martinko, "Impression Management in Organizations," *Journal of Management*, June 1988, p. 332; and R. B. Cialdini, "Indirect Tactics of Image Management: Beyond Basking," in R. A. Giacalone and P. Rosenfeld (eds.), *Impression Management in the Organization* (Hillsdale, NJ: Lawrence Erlbaum Associates, 1989), pp. 45–71.

---

to increase your visibility. But your job may require you to handle activities that are low in visibility, or your specific contribution may be indistinguishable because you are part of a team. In such cases—without creating the image of a braggart—you will want to call attention to yourself by giving progress reports to your boss and others, being seen at social functions, being active in professional associations, developing powerful allies who speak positively about your accomplishments, and similar tactics. Of course, the skilled politician actively and successfully lobbies to get those projects that will increase his or her visibility.

GET A MENTOR We discussed the benefits of mentors in the preceding chapter on leadership. From a political perspective, they offer two very positive benefits. First, they are a valuable communication source. A mentor can relay inside information that you might otherwise not have access to. And second, they send a message to others in the organization. Just the fact that you have a mentor provides a signal to others that you have the resources of a powerful higher-up behind you. Obviously, the more powerful your mentor, the stronger the signal.

But how do you get a mentor? Typically, at least where mentoring is an informal process, the mentors do the choosing. They spot someone lower in the organization with whom they identify and take that person on as a protégé. The more contacts you make with higher-ups—both formally and informally—the greater chance you have of being singled out as someone's protégé. Participating in company sports tournaments, going out with colleagues after work, taking on visible projects, and assignments to cross-functional teams are examples of activities that are likely to bring you to the attention of a potential mentor.

DEVELOP POWERFUL ALLIES It helps to have powerful people in your camp. In addition to a mentor, you can cultivate contacts with potentially influential people above you, at your level, and in the lower ranks. They can provide you with important "grapevine" information not available through formal channels. In addition, there will be times when decisions will be made by those with the greatest support. Sometimes—though not always—there is strength in numbers. Having powerful allies can provide you with a coalition of support if and when you need it.

AVOID "TAINTED" MEMBERS In almost every organization, there are fringe members whose status is questionable. Their performance or loyalty is under close scrutiny. Such individuals, while they are under the microscope, are "tainted." Carefully keep your distance from them. We all tend to judge others by the company they keep. Given the reality that effectiveness has a large subjective component, your own effectiveness might be called into question if you are perceived as being too closely associated with tainted people.

SUPPORT YOUR BOSS Your immediate future is in the hands of your current boss. Since he or she evaluates your performance, you will typically want to do whatever is necessary to have your boss on your side.

You should make every effort to help your boss succeed, make her look good, support her if she is under siege, and spend the time to find out what criteria she will be using to assess your effectiveness. Don't undermine your boss. Don't speak negatively of her to others. If she is competent, visible, and in possession of a power base, she is likely to be on the way up in the organization. By being perceived as supportive, you increase the likelihood of being pulled along too. At the worst, you will have established an ally higher up in the organization. If your boss's performance is poor and her power low, it is difficult to distance yourself from her without her perceiving you as a traitor. The most effective solution in such a situation is to quietly lobby for a transfer. It's better to switch than fight.

▶ Is It Unethical to Act Politically?

We conclude our discussion of politics by providing some ethical guidelines for political behavior. While there are no clear-cut ways to differentiate ethical from unethical politicking, there are some questions you should consider.

Exhibit 17-7 illustrates a decision tree to guide ethical actions. The first question you need to answer addresses self-interest versus organizational goals. Ethical actions are consistent with the organization's goals. Spreading untrue rumors about the safety of a new product introduced by your company, in order to make that product's design group look bad, is unethical. However, there may be nothing unethical if a department head exchanges favors with her division's purchasing manager in order to get a critical contract processed quickly.

The second question concerns the rights of other parties. If the department head described in the previous paragraph went down to the mailroom during her lunch hour and read through the mail directed to the purchasing manager—with the intent of "getting something on him" so he will expedite her contract—she would be acting unethically. She would have violated the purchasing manager's right to privacy.

The final question that needs to be addressed is related to whether the political activity conforms to standards of equity and justice. The department head who inflates the performance evaluation of a favored employee and deflates the evaluation of a disfavored

Is a Political Action Ethical?

EXHIBIT 17-7

Question 1
Is the political action motivated by self-serving interests to the exclusion of the organization's goals?

Yes → Unethical

No →

Question 2
Does the political action respect the rights of the individuals affected?

Yes →

No → Unethical

Question 3
Is the political activity fair and equitable?

Yes → Ethical

No → Unethical

Source: Adapted from G. Cavanagh, D. Moberg, and M. Valasquez, "The Ethics of Organizational Politics," *Academy of Management Review*, July 1981, p. 368.

employee—and then uses those evaluations to justify giving the former a big raise and nothing to the latter—has treated the disfavored employee unfairly.

Unfortunately, the answers to the questions in Exhibit 17-7 are often argued in ways to make unethical practices seem ethical. Powerful people, for example, can become very good at explaining self-serving behaviors in terms of the organization's best interests. Similarly, they can persuasively argue that unfair actions are really fair and just. Our point is that immoral people can justify almost any behavior. Those who are powerful, articulate, and persuasive are most vulnerable because they are likely to be able to get away with unethical practices. When faced with an ethical dilemma regarding organizational politics, try to answer the questions in Exhibit 17-7 truthfully. And if you have a strong power base, recognize the ability of power to corrupt. Remember, it's a lot easier for the powerless to act ethically, for no other reason than that they typically have very little political discretion to exploit.

There is a variety of additional material available on the CD-ROM and companion Web site that accompany this text. You can access this information through the CD-ROM or by visiting the Web site at <**www.prenhall.com/robbins**>.

SUMMARY

(This summary is organized by the chapter-opening learning objectives on page 524.)

1. The communication process is made up of seven parts: the source, encoding, the message, the channel, decoding, the receiver, and feedback.

2. Men and women tend to use talk differently. For women, conversation provides intimacy and connection. For men, it is primarily a means to preserve independence and maintain status.

3. As an effective active listener, you will exhibit eye contact, affirmative head nods and appropriate facial expressions, an absence of distracting actions or gestures, the asking of questions, paraphrasing, avoiding interrupting the speaker, an absence of overtalking, and smooth transitions between the roles of speaker and listener.

4. To provide effective performance feedback, you will focus on specific behaviors and keep feedback impersonal. Your feedback will be goal-oriented and well-timed, be understood, and you will direct negative feedback toward behavior that is controllable by the recipient.

5. Five conflict resolution behaviors are avoidance, accommodation, forcing, compromise, and collaboration.

6. Distributive bargaining operates under zero-sum conditions. Any gain for one party is a loss to the other. In contrast, integrative bargaining seeks win-win solutions.

7. As an effective negotiator, you will research your opponent, begin with a positive overture, focus on problems rather than personalities, pay little attention to initial offers, emphasize win-win solutions, create an open and trusting climate, accept third-party assistance when needed, and adjust for cultural differences.

8. To effectively delegate authority, you will clarify the assignment, specify the employee's range of discretion, allow the employee to participate, inform others that delegation has occurred, insist on recommendations from the employee when problems surface, and establish feedback controls.

9. Directive counseling places control for solving the problem in the hands of the manager. Nondirective counseling places that control with the employee. Participative counseling is a compromise, with the manager listening and providing advice and insights, but relying on the employee to solve the problem.

10. A manager can become more politically adept by framing arguments in terms of organizational goals, developing the right image, gaining control of organizational resources, creating obligation, appearing to be indispensable, increasing visibility, getting a mentor, developing powerful allies, avoiding "tainted" members, and supporting the boss.

REVIEW QUESTIONS

1. Why do you think interpersonal skills may be more important to a manager's success than technical skills?

2. Explain how each of the various parts of the communication process can cause distortion and limit the ability to achieve perfect communication.

3. "The medium is the message." What do you think this phrase means?

4. How can you improve your listening skills, at the same time recognizing that not everything people have to say is worth the effort of active listening?

5. What are the three sources of conflict? Which one do you think is most prevalent in organizations? In families? Explain your answers.

6. When, if ever, would a manager want to increase conflict?

7. Why might managers be reluctant to delegate?

8. What could you do to improve your counseling skills?

9. Why is there politics in organizations? Can it be completely eliminated? Explain.

10. How can you assess whether a political action you might take is unethical?

IF I WERE THE MANAGER . . .

The Trouble with Harry

You gotta like Harry! Harry Crombie has been an accountant at your Dallas-based manufacturing plant for more than 20 years.

Born and raised in Perth, Australia, his outgoing personality and endearing accent make him the favorite "mate" of everyone in the office. But Harry has his quirks. Number one on that list would be his macho attitude toward women. While no one has ever accused him of sexual harassment, he does have difficulty dealing with women as equals. His department has 14 members, three of whom are women. In meetings, you've noticed Harry's tendency to downgrade suggestions made by women. Others in the department have made similar observations.

You're the plant manager at Dallas. Your chief plant accountant has notified you that he is planning to retire at the end of the current quarter. You didn't think anyone in your accounting department was prepared to fill this position. So you contacted the corporation's human resources group in New York. They suggested a highly qualified female candidate now the head of accounting at one of the company's smaller plants in Phoenix. You talked to the candidate on the phone several times. Last Monday you flew to Phoenix to interview her. You were impressed and, although you haven't made a firm offer, you're close to doing so. Then your problem surfaced.

This morning, Harry came into your office. (He does this occasionally.) But it was clear he hadn't come by for a social call. He was angry. His face was red and his speech rapid. "Tell me it's not true," Harry began. "I hear a rumor that our new boss is going to be a woman! Let me tell you something. I've never worked for a woman and I never will. Our department is a close-knit group. But there are a couple of us who feel like I do. And it's not all guys! One or two women in the department agree that they don't want to work for a female. Don't get me wrong. I respect women. I have no problem with them in the workplace. But not in a leadership position. And not as my boss!" On that final comment, Harry turned and was out of the office before you had a chance to respond.

What do you do now?

SKILL EXERCISE

Active Listening

This exercise is a debate. Break into groups of two. Party A can choose any contemporary issue. Some examples: business ethics, value of labor unions, prayer in schools, stiffer college grading policies, gun control, money as a motivator. Party B then selects a position on that issue and presents his or her argument. Party A must automatically take the counterposition. The debate is then to proceed, with only one catch. Before Party A speaks, he or she must first summarize, in his or her

own words and without notes, what Party B said. If the summary doesn't satisfy Party B, it must be corrected until it does. Then Party A presents the counterposition, and Party B must summarize Party A's argument. This format should be continued until both parties have made all their points.

This exercise should not exceed 10 minutes in length. Remember that each debater has to paraphrase the other's statements until acknowledged as correct before stating his or her own points.

TEAM ACTIVITY

Nonverbal Communication

Break into groups of five or six. You have 15 minutes to rank-order the importance of the following ten factors in terms of their ability to control employee behavior:

_____ Employee selection process
_____ New employee orientation
_____ Employee training
_____ Formal organization rules and regulations
_____ Direct supervision
_____ Performance appraisals
_____ Organizational rewards
_____ Discipline
_____ Group norms
_____ Organizational culture

However, during the ranking procedure, the group may communicate *only verbally*. They may *not* use gestures, facial movements, body movements, or any other nonverbal communication.

When the group has completed its task, members should answer the following questions: (1) How effective was communication? (2) What purpose does nonverbal communication serve? In this last part of the exercise, group members are free to communicate both verbally *and* nonverbally.

CASE EXERCISE

Stan Whitley's Problem

Stan Whitley had been a bit nervous about accepting the job at ProElecTronix. Although he had an engineering degree and quite a bit of summer work experience, he was only 23 years old and his entry-level job would be as the line supervisor of the assembly production unit. But he took the job and made it a high priority to gain the respect and trust of the older workers he was supervising.

Stan started his job four months ago. So far, everything has gone well. Just last week, in fact, he was praised by his boss for the good job he was doing with building morale in his unit. That is, everything went well until this morning's staff meeting.

Company policy states that workers have to use their annual vacation by December 31 or lose it. Stan knew this policy. He was also aware that in past years many workers timed their vacations to coincide with holidays. So, during the past two months, as employees brought their vacation cards to him for his signature, he approved a number of requests for December vacations. He even gave verbal approvals to several requests. He didn't run any of these requests by his boss, since approving vacations was an area where he had full authority.

You can imagine Stan's surprise at the morning staff meeting, when his boss said in an off-handed way that the company would need to maintain full production in December, and that "it will be Stan's responsibility to make sure line scheduling is balanced." Stan left the meeting in a daze. Even ignoring the verbal agreements he had approved, over one-third of his line was going to be out on vacation at different times during the month of December. For at least one week, almost half the line could potentially be gone.

Trying to keep his cool, Stan first went to the human resources department to find out exactly what the rules were about vacations. Tina Chen, the HR manager, explained that it was a long-standing company policy not to allow vacations to be carried over into the next year. "What's the logic of that?" Stan asked. He learned management was concerned about the potential impact to scheduling production if people were permitted to take vacations lasting more than four weeks. Tina also told Stan that his particular Christmas scheduling problem had happened not only last year, but the year before as well. Apparently, it was common practice for management to promise too many vacations and leave the employees and human resources to pick up the mess. Tina obviously wasn't too excited about the news that it might happen again.

Tina's information on past practices made Stan feel as if he had been blindsided. Why hadn't his boss warned him earlier about this problem? Why hadn't the employees said anything as they asked for their vacations?

Stan is now sitting at his desk pondering his dilemma. It's the middle of November. If he turns the problem over to his boss and admits defeat, he thinks he would undermine his credibility with both management and his work group. But he needs to do something.

QUESTIONS

1. Discuss Stan's dilemma in political terms.
2. What do you think Stan should do?

Source: Based on "Vacation Blues," prepared by P. S. Heath for classroom usage at the University of Washington.

NOTES

1. L. Williams, "A Silk Blouse on the Assembly Line? (Yes, the Boss's)," *New York Times*, February 5, 1995, p. F7.
2. See, for instance, J. D. Pettit Jr., B. C. Vaught, and R. L. Trewatha, "Interpersonal Skill Training: A Prerequisite for Success," *Business*, April–June 1990, pp. 8–14; D. Milbank, "Managers Are Sent to 'Charm Schools' to Discover How to Polish Up Their Acts," *Wall Street Journal*, December 14, 1990, p. B1; and E. Van Velsor and J. B. Leslie, "Why Executives Derail: Perspectives across Time and Cultures," *Academy of Management Executive*, November 1995, pp. 62–72.
3. Milbank, "Managers Are Sent to 'Charm Schools' to Discover How to Polish Up Their Acts."
4. C. Hymowitz, "Five Main Reasons Why Managers Fail," *Wall Street Journal*, May 2, 1988, p. 25.
5. L. W. Porter and L. E. McKibbin, *Future of Management Education and Development: Drift or Thrust into the Twenty-First Century?* (New York: McGraw-Hill, 1988).
6. B. Filipczak, "Obfuscation Resounding: Corporate Communication in America," *Training*, July 1995, p. 36.
7. D. K. Berlo, *The Process of Communication* (New York: Holt, Rinehart & Winston, 1960), p. 54.
8. Filipczak, "Obfuscation Resounding," p. 30.
9. Ibid.
10. See, for instance, C. O. Kursh, "The Benefits of Poor Communication," *The Psychoanalytic Review*, Summer–Fall 1971, pp. 189–208; and E. M. Eisenberg and M. G. Witten, "Reconsidering Openness in Organizational Communica-

tion," *Academy of Management Review*, July 1987, pp. 418–26.

11. Cited in L. E. Boone, *Quotable Business* (New York: Random House, 1992), p. 60.

12. See, for instance, M. L. Kapp and J. A. Hall, *Nonverbal Communication in Human Interaction* (Fort Worth: Holt, Rinehart & Winston, 1992).

13. This section, and these statistics, are based on information in S. C. Gwynne and J. F. Dickerson, "Lost in the E-Mail," *Time*, April 21, 1997, pp. 88–90.

14. This section is based on D. Tannen, *You Just Don't Understand: Women and Men in Conversation* (New York: Ballantine Books, 1991); D. Tannen, *Talking from 9 to 5* (New York: William Morrow, 1994); and D. Tannen, "The Power of Talk: Who Gets Heard and Why," *Harvard Business Review*, September–October 1995, pp. 138–48.

15. See M. Munter, "Cross-Cultural Communication for Managers," *Business Horizons*, May–June 1993, pp. 69–77.

16. N. Adler, *International Dimensions of Organizational Behavior*, 3rd ed. (Cincinnati, OH: Southwestern, 1997), pp. 87–88.

17. This section is based on S. P. Robbins and P. L. Hunsaker, *Training in InterPersonal Skills: TIPS for Managing People at Work*, 2nd ed. (Upper Saddle River, NJ: Prentice Hall, 1996), pp. 33–39; and data in R. C. Husman, J. M. Lahiff, and J. M. Penrose, *Business Communication: Strategies and Skills* (Chicago: Dryden Press, 1988), pp. 380, 425.

18. Cited in M. Hequet, "Giving Good Feedback," *Training*, September 1994, p. 72.

19. This section is based on Robbins and Hunsaker, *Training in InterPersonal Skills*, pp. 70–75.

20. See S. P. Robbins, *Managing Organizational Conflict: A Nontraditional Approach* (Englewood Cliffs, NJ: Prentice Hall, 1974); and K. M. Eisenhardt, J. L. Kahwajy, and L. J. Bourgeois III, "How Management Teams Can Have a Good Fight," *Harvard Business Review*, July–August 1997, pp. 77–85.

21. K. W. Thomas and W. H. Schmidt, "A Survey of Management Interests with Respect to Conflict," *Academy of Management Journal*, June 1976, pp. 315–18.

22. Ibid.

23. J. Graves, "Successful Management and Organizational Mugging," in J. Papp (ed.), *New Directions in Human Resource Management* (Upper Saddle River, NJ: Prentice Hall, 1978).

24. M. A. Rahim and N. R. Magner, "Confirmatory Factor Analysis of the Styles of Handling Interpersonal Conflict: First-Order Factor Model and Its Invariance across Groups," *Journal of Applied Psychology*, February 1995, pp. 122–32.

25. L. Greenhalgh, "Managing Conflict," *Sloan Management Review*, Summer 1986, pp. 45–51.

26. Robbins, *Managing Organizational Conflict*, pp. 31–55.

27. K. W. Thomas, "Conflict and Negotiation Processes in Organizations," in M. D. Dunnette and L. M. Hough (eds.), *Handbook of Industrial and Organizational Psychology*, 2nd ed., vol. 3 (Palo Alto, CA: Consulting Psychologists Press, 1992), pp. 666–77.

28. See, for instance, E. van de Vliert and C. K. W. de Dreu, "Optimizing Performance by Conflict Stimulation," *International Journal of Conflict Management*, July 1994, pp. 211–22.

29. Robbins, *Managing Organizational Conflict*, pp. 78–89.

30. J. A. Wall Jr., *Negotiation: Theory and Practice* (Glenview, IL: Scott, Foresman, 1985).

31. R. E. Walton and R. B. McKersie, *A Behavioral Theory of Labor Negotiations: An Analysis of a Social Interaction System*, (New York: McGraw-Hill, 1965).

32. Thomas, "Conflict and Negotiation Processes in Organizations."

33. These suggestions are based on J. A. Wall Jr. and M. W. Blum, "Negotiations," *Journal of Management*, June 1991, pp. 278–82.

34. D. J. McConville, "The Artful Negotiator," *Industry Week*, August 15, 1994, p. 40.

35. See L. Pye, *Chinese Commercial Negotiating Style* (Cambridge, MA: Oelgeschlager, Gunn & Hain Publishers, 1982).

36. J. Graham and R. Herberger, "Negotiating Abroad—Don't Shoot From the Hip," *Harvard Business Review*, July–August 1983, pp. 160–69.

37. B. K. Hackman and D. C. Dunphy, "Managerial Delegation," in C. L. Cooper and I. T. Robertson, eds., *International Review of Industrial and Organizational Psychology*, vol. 5 (Chichester, England: Wiley, 1990), pp. 35–57.

38. C. R. Leana, "Predictors and Consequences of Delegation," *Academy of Management Journal*, December 1986, pp. 754–74.

39. Adapted from S. Caudron, "Delegate for Results," *Industry Week*, February 6, 1995, pp. 27–28.

40. This section is adapted from Robbins and Hunsaker, *Training in InterPersonal Skills*, pp. 93–95.

41. Caudron, "Delegate for Results," p. 30.

42. See, for example, R. Walsh, "Basic Counseling Skills," *Supervisory Management*, July 1977, pp. 2–9; G. D. Cook, "Employee Counseling Session," *Supervision*, August 1989, pp. 3–5; and J. Wisinski, "A Logical Approach to a Difficult Employee," *HR Focus*, January 1992, pp. 15–18.

43. C. Rogers, *Counseling and Psychotherapy* (Boston: Houghton Mifflin, 1942).

44. Based on R. L. Knowdell and E. N. Chapman, *Personal Counseling*, rev. ed. (Los Altos, CA: Crisp Publications, 1986).

45. D. Farrell and J. C. Petersen, "Patterns of Political Behavior in Organizations," *Academy of Management Review*, July 1982, p. 405.

46. This section is from Robbins and Hunsaker, *Training in InterPersonal Skills*, pp. 131–34; and R. B. Cialdini, *Influence: The Psychology of Persuasion*, rev. ed. (New York: Morrow, 1993).

47. See, for example, B. R. Schlenker, *Impression Management: The Self-Concept, Social Identity, and Interpersonal Relations* (Monterey, CA: Brooks/Cole, 1980); J. Tedeschi and V. Melburg, "Impression Management and Influence in the Organization," in S. Bacharach and E. J. Lawler (eds.), *Research in the Sociology of Organizations*, vol. 3 (Greenwich, CT: JAI Press, 1984), pp. 31–58; M. R. Leary and R. M. Kowalski, "Impression Management: A Literature Review and Two-Component Model," *Psychological Bulletin*, January 1990, pp. 34–47; and B. R. Schlenker and M. F. Weigold, "Interpersonal Processes Involving Impression Regulation and Management," in M. R. Rosenzweig and L. W. Porter (eds.), *Annual Review of Psychology*, vol. 43 (Palo Alto, CA: Annual Reviews Inc., 1992), pp. 133–68.

MANAGEMENT: FROM A CROSS-DISCIPLINARY PERSPECTIVE

Humanities and Social Sciences

ECONOMICS A primary topic in economics is labor markets. For instance, an understanding of demand curves, supply curves, and market equilibrium are helpful in designing compensation systems that can maximize motivation.

PSYCHOLOGY The topics you've covered in chapters 12 through 17 are largely drawn from research conducted by psychologists. Specialty areas that are particularly relevant to the discipline of management include personality psychology, social psychology, and industrial/organizational psychology.

Some of the questions that personality psychologists have shed light on are: Is personality shaped by genetics or the environment? Is an individual's personality stable over his or her lifetime? What role does personality play in affecting job performance?

Some of the relevant questions that social psychologists have addressed include: How can we change an employee's attitude? How do attributions shape judgments? What's the best way to structure teams? How do roles influence behavior? What are the roots of prejudice and discrimination? How can man-

agers build trust with employees? How can individuals improve their negotiating skills?

Finally, industrial/organizational psychology has been a major source for guiding managers in areas such as selection, motivation, performance evaluation, and training. Some of the questions that I/O psychologists have studied include: What differentiates functional from dysfunctional emotions? How much importance should managers place on intelligence and mental abilities in employee selection? What's the most effective leadership style? How do you motivate today's workers? What's the most effective way to structure training programs? What effect, if any, can a manager have on reducing employee stress?

SOCIOLOGY Much of what we know today about managing conflict, organizational politics, and power dynamics in organizations has evolved out of sociology.

POLITICAL SCIENCE Closely paralleling the contributions of sociology, political science provides managers with insights into power and power elites, organizational politics, conflict, and the role of trust in organizations.

ENGLISH Courses in English composition are typically taken by students during their first year of college. And the importance of these courses is often lost on students. But it's not lost on practicing managers! Every manager quickly recognizes the importance of written communication to doing his or her job. Effective managers know the importance of being able to organize their ideas, selecting the proper words to convey their message, and being able to present those ideas with clarity.

SPEECH COMMUNICATION Speech communications and linguistics provide a rich source of information to help managers better understand how language can hinder or facilitate employee communication. For instance, research on linguistic differences between genders clarifies historic communication problems between men and women. What one sex intends by a comment is not always what the other sex hears in the words. In addition, courses in speech help future managers to improve their communication skills by focusing on tone, presentation, enthusiasm, emotion, persuasiveness, and nonverbal messages.

Business Disciplines

ACCOUNTING The field of behavioral accounting has evolved to offer managers insights into how budgets, performance reports, audits, and other accounting and financial controls influence the behavior of employees. In many universities, for example, faculty members are evaluated almost exclusively on their publication records. Should we be surprised when faculty at these schools slight their teaching responsibilities in order to devote more time to their research and publication efforts? Not if we recognize the role that evaluation criteria play in shaping behavior.

MARKETING A major objective of any marketing course is to introduce students to consumer behavior. Issues typically addressed include perception, personality, learning, attitudes, decision-making processes, and motivation. Clearly, much of the knowledge gained about consumer behavior is easily transferable and valuable in the manager's quest to understand employee behavior.

MANAGING CHANGE: REVISITING THE CHANGING WORLD OF WORK

CHANGE IS INEVITABLE, EXCEPT FROM
A VENDING MACHINE.

ANONYMOUS

LEARNING OBJECTIVES

After studying this chapter, you should be able to:

1 List sources of individual and organizational resistance to change.

2 Describe force-field analysis.

3 Contrast first-order and second-order change.

4 Identify strategies for reducing resistance to change.

5 List tactics for reducing resistance to change.

6 Describe what it is that managers can change.

7 Define *organizational development*.

8 Identify techniques for reducing employee stress.

9 Explain how managers can increase innovation.

10 Describe a learning organization.

Xerox Business Services (XBS) is the fastest-growing, fastest-moving part of Xerox.[1] This unit, which employs 15,000 people, has taken advantage of business firms' emphasis on core competencies to become the world leader in document outsourcing. It has more than 4,000 customers in 36 countries, and it provides its services to as many as 4 million businesspeople per day. Over the past few years, XBS has been growing at the startling rate of 40 percent a year. That means the company anticipates sales going from $1 billion to $5 billion in four years! The person charged with managing the people side of this growth is 15-year XBS veteran Chris Turner (see photo).

Turner started her career at XBS in sales management. Today she has the unique title of Learning Person. Her job is to manage change. Specifically, she oversees a series of simulations, seminars, events, and experiences that are designed to ensure that XBS people will have the skills to handle an intense level of growth and change.

According to Turner, her biggest challenge is managing what she calls *organizational knowledge*. "We're bringing in tons of new people, and the people we already have are constantly changing jobs to keep up with growth. That creates three big issues. First, we've got business context issues. What kind of business do we have? Second, we've got community issues. How can our people participate in this large, unwieldly thing we call XBS? And third, we've got skills issues. What are the knowledge and infrastructure systems we need to develop?"

While XBS has grown up in a functionally driven machine hierarchy, Turner sees XBS as a dynamic, living system. "You can't treat a natural system like a machine. All you can do is create experiences that disturb a natural system, and then it decides how to respond. My job is to disturb the system. I give people new ways to think."

How does Turner get XBS people to think in new ways? Early on, she ran workshops where employees helped create a shared vision for change. Out of these workshops came the recognition that change requires trust. "Trust is one of the essentials for learning," Turner says. "Wherever you have a trusting environment, you have a much more productive, much more humane organization." This insight has guided the creation of all her learning activities.

Probably the most visible vehicle for learning at XBS is Turner's annual Camp Lur'ning. These 5-day conferences are meant to make learning fun. They'll include 300 to 400 XBS people, plus a number of real live customers. They'll spend their days in small teams developing plans for ways to get closer to specific customers. Each team is assigned a customer—for instance, TRW, Estee Lauder, Dow Chemical, Microsoft, or Florida Power & Light—and they have four days to develop a plan and then report back to the entire camp. To help the teams do a more effective job, Turner puts on seminars and brings in guest speakers who provide guidance and suggestions. But the real learning part of this exercise is that employees have to work together and they get to perfect their detective skills. Through questions and a series of interactive group exercises, the teams learn how to gather evidence, formulate a theory, test it, modify it, and craft a solution. Essentially, Turner has found a way to teach employees how to use the scientific method and to make the process fun.

Turner summarizes what she's learned about learning: "Learning is like anything else. The more we do it, the better and quicker people get. People make connections very fast. Learning enables the organization to have a fighting chance to keep up with change."

As Turner and XBS recognize, in today's economy, you snooze, you lose! Led by globalization and technological advances, managers of almost every organization are feeling intense competitive pressures. XBS, for instance, has plenty of competition in the market to service the outsourcing needs of business.

It's the rare manager today who has the luxury to operate in a stable and predictable environment. *Chaotic*, in fact, is the adjective that managers are increasingly using to describe their world. Bill Gates (CEO at Microsoft) and Andrew Grove (former CEO at Intel) have become posterboys for paranoia. "Only the paranoid survive," says Grove in an oft-quoted line.[2] Gates and Grove see new competitors coming from every direction. And they turned their paranoia into corporate cultures in which employees feel intense pressures to create new and innovative products at an ever-faster rate. Microsoft and Intel are two companies that have learned to thrive on change.

Management guru Tom Peters aptly captures this world of chaotic change: "Today's winners, and especially tomorrow's, will have a penchant for disruption, a love of disorder—and even a willingness to throw baby parts (e.g., cherished 'core competencies') out with the bathwater . . . again and again."[3]

THE CHANGING WORLD OF WORK REVISITED

This book has spent seventeen chapters describing to you the new world of management. In truth, we probably should say that we have described the ongoing transition toward the new world of management. Even the best-managed organizations are still in the process of making the needed changes to adjust to the new economy and the new rules of competition. And the number of organizations that have fully transformed their work systems is still rather small. For instance, recent data suggest that less than one-third of U.S. companies have undertaken some significant work organization reforms.[4] This finding tells us that the vast majority of organizations will undoubtedly be going through wrenching transformations during the coming years as they attempt to become more flexible and quicker on their feet.

Managing change is a challenge facing every organization. How organizations manage—or mismanage—change will inevitably mean the difference between victory and defeat in an ultracompetitive new world.[5] Those managers who are able to exploit change will be able to capitalize on the unlimited opportunities that change creates. This chapter provides guidelines to help you better manage change.

RESISTANCE TO CHANGE

The manager's job would be a lot easier if most people embraced change. But they don't. One of the best-documented findings from studies of individual and organizational behavior is that organizations and their members resist change. In a sense, this resistance is positive. It provides a degree of stability and predictability within organizations. If there weren't some resistance, organizational behavior would take on characteristics of chaotic randomness. Resistance to change can also be a source of functional conflict. For example, resistance to a reorganization plan or a change in a product line can stimulate a healthy debate over the merits of the idea and result in a better decision. But there is a serious downside to resistance to change. It hinders adaptation and progress.

Ironically, organizations that have historically experienced lengthy periods of success tend to be particularly resistant to change.[6] The declining fortunes in the late 1990s of such formerly illustrious companies as Apple Computer, Toyota, and Motorola illustrate that success often leads to arrogance and loss of touch with the environment. But success need not breed failure. General Electric, for example, presents a strong case that, with first-rate management, big and successful organizations can adapt to changing environments. Nevertheless, resistance to change remains a basic barrier that managers must recognize and be prepared to overcome.

Resistance to change doesn't necessarily surface in standardized ways. Resistance can be overt, implicit, immediate, or deferred.[7] It is easiest for management to deal with resistance when it is overt and immediate. For instance, a change is proposed and employees quickly respond by voicing complaints, engaging in a work slowdown, threatening to go on strike, or the like. The greater challenge is managing resistance that is implicit or deferred. Implicit resistance efforts are more subtle—loss of loyalty to the organization, loss of motivation to work, increased errors, increased absenteeism due to "sickness"—and hence more difficult to recognize. Similarly, deferred actions cloud the link between the source of the resistance and the reaction to it. A change may produce what appears to be only a minimal reaction at the time it is initiated, but then resistance surfaces weeks, months, or even years later. Or a single change that in and of itself might have little impact becomes the straw that breaks the camel's back. Reactions to change can build up and then explode in some response that seems totally out of proportion to the change action it follows. The resistance, of course, has merely been deferred and stockpiled. What surfaces is a response to an accumulation of previous changes.

Let's look at the sources of resistance. For analytical purposes, we have categorized them by individual and organizational sources. In the real world, the sources often overlap.

Individual Resistance

Individual sources of resistance to change reside in basic human characteristics such as perceptions, personalities, and needs. The following summarizes five reasons why individuals may resist change (see Exhibit 18-1).

HABIT Every time you go out to eat, do you try a different restaurant? Probably not. If you're like most people, you find a couple of places you like and return to them on a somewhat regular basis.

Sources of Individual Resistance to Change

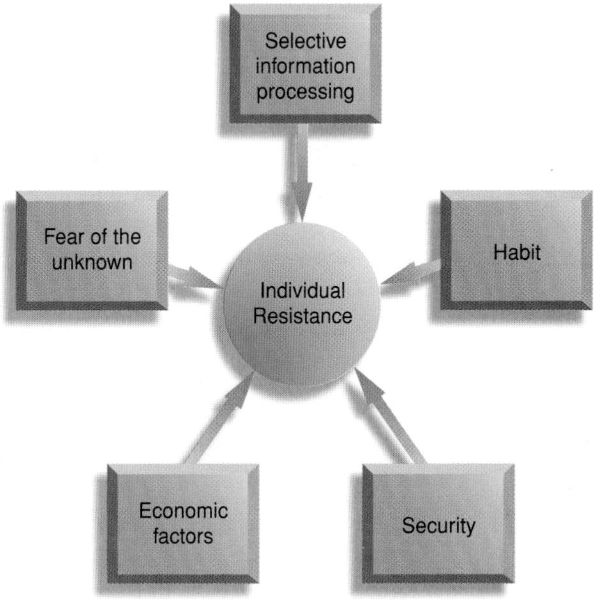

EXHIBIT 18-1

As human beings, we are creatures of habit. Life is complex enough; we don't need to consider the full range of options for the hundreds of decisions we have to make every day. To cope with this complexity, we all rely on habits, or programmed responses. But when we are confronted with change, this tendency to respond in our accustomed ways becomes a source of resistance. When your department is moved to a new office building across town, you're likely to have to change many habits: waking up 10 minutes earlier, taking a new route to work, finding a new parking place, adjusting to the new office lay-out, developing a new lunchtime routine, and so on. Making so many changes in your routine will require effort, and you might resist the change.

SECURITY People with a high need for security are likely to resist change because it threatens their feeling of safety. When Levi Strauss announces that it's laying off 6,000 people or when Nissan introduces new robotic equipment, many employees at these firms may fear that their jobs are in jeopardy, and those people are not likely to welcome the change.

ECONOMIC FACTORS Another source of individual resistance is concern that changes will lower one's income. Changes in job tasks or established work routines also can arouse economic fears if people are concerned that they won't be able to perform the new tasks or routines to their previous standards, especially when pay is closely tied to productivity.

FEAR OF THE UNKNOWN Changes substitute ambiguity and uncertainty for the known. The transition from high school to college is typically such an experience. By the time we're seniors in high school, we understand how things work. You might not have liked high school, but at least you understood the system. Then you move on to college and face a whole new and uncertain system. You have traded the known for the unknown and the fear or insecurity that goes with it.

Employees in organizations hold the same dislike for uncertainty. If, for example, the introduction of TQM means production workers will have to learn statistical process control techniques, some may fear they'll be unable to do so. They may, therefore, develop a negative attitude toward TQM or behave dysfunctionally if required to use statistical techniques.

SELECTIVE INFORMATION PROCESSING As we learned in chapter 12, individuals shape their world through their perceptions. Once they have created this world, it resists change. So individuals are guilty of selectively processing information in order to keep their perceptions intact. They hear what they want to hear. They ignore information that challenges the world they have created. The production workers who are faced with the introduction of TQM may ignore the arguments their bosses make in explaining why a knowledge of statistics is necessary or the potential benefits the change will provide them.

Organizational Resistance

Organizations, by their very nature, tend to be characterized by inertia.[8] They actively resist change. You don't have to look far to see evidence of this phenomenon. Government agencies want to continue doing what they have been doing for years, whether the need for their service changes, remains the same, or no longer exists. Organized religions are deeply entrenched in their history. Attempts to change church doctrine require great persistence and patience. Educational institutions, which exist to open minds and challenge established doctrine, are themselves extremely resistant to change. Most school systems

Sources of Organizational Resistance to Change

EXHIBIT 18-2

are using essentially the same teaching technologies today as they were 50 years ago. The majority of business firms, too, appear to be highly resistant to change.

Six major sources of organizational resistance have been identified.[9] They are shown in Exhibit 18-2.

STRUCTURAL INERTIA Organizations have built-in mechanisms to produce stability. For example, the selection process systematically selects certain people in and certain people out. Training and other socialization techniques reinforce specific role requirements and skills. Formalization provides job descriptions, rules, and procedures for employees to follow.

The people who are hired into an organization are chosen for fit; they are then shaped and directed to behave in certain ways. When an organization is confronted with change, this structural inertia acts as a counterbalance to sustain stability.

LIMITED FOCUS OF CHANGE Organizations are made up of interdependent subsystems. You can't change one without affecting the others. For example, if management changes the technological processes without simultaneously modifying the organization's structure to match, the change in technology is not likely to be accepted. So limited changes in subsystems tend to get nullified by the larger system.

GROUP INERTIA Even if individuals want to change their behavior, group norms may act as a constraint. An individual union member, for instance, may be willing to accept changes in his job suggested by management. But if union norms dictate resisting any unilateral change made by management, he's likely to resist.

THREAT TO EXPERTISE Changes in organizational patterns may threaten the expertise of specialized groups. The introduction of decentralized personal computers, which allow managers to gain access to information directly from a company's mainframe, is an example of a change that was strongly resisted by many information systems departments in the early 1980s. Why? Because decentralized end-user computing was a threat to the specialized skills held by those in the centralized information systems departments.

THREAT TO ESTABLISHED POWER RELATIONSHIPS Any redistribution of decision-making authority can threaten long-established power relationships within the organization. The introduction of participative decision making or self-managed work teams is the kind of change that is often seen as threatening by supervisors and middle managers.

THREAT TO ESTABLISHED RESOURCE ALLOCATIONS Those groups in the organization that control sizable resources often see change as a threat. They tend to be content with the way things are. Will the change, for instance, mean a reduction in their budgets or a cut in their staff size? Those that most benefit from the current allocation of resources often feel threatened by changes that may affect future allocations.

MANAGERS AS CHANGE AGENTS

Changes within an organization need a catalyst. Those people who act as catalysts and assume the responsibility for managing the change process are called *change agents*. IBM's CEO, Lou Gerstner, is such a person. Since taking over the top spot at IBM in 1993, he has completely remade the company.[10] But you don't have to be a CEO to be a change agent. Bob Knowling, when a vice president of network operations at US West, led more than 20,000 employees in a large-scale change effort to improve service to the company's 25 million customers. Mark Maletz was recruited by computer giant Siemens Nixdorf to create a school for change and train a cadre of change agents who could, like a virus, infect the company. Mark Maletz is a middle-manager change agent. And David Clarke is a lower-level manager acting as a change agent. He's leading a team at W. L. Gore & Associates, the maker of Gore-Tex, that is introducing a comprehensive new manufacturing system in one of the company's plants.[11]

We introduced change agents in chapter 2. We said that, today, many managers play the role of change agent. We also said, preempting our discussion of transformational leadership, that today's managers need to implement quantum change and reinvent their organizations. As organizations enter the twenty-first century, they need transformational leaders who can reengineer workplaces and to get employees to "buy into" the upheavals that come with quantum change.

Managers who can effectively play the role of change agent are in high demand and can accelerate their ascendency into executive positions.[12] For major change programs, senior management frequently looks outside to find people who have experience in promoting change and who have no vested interest in the current system. Those individuals who can exhibit visionary leadership and charismatic qualities additionally have characteristics that organizations associate with successful change agents. So if a manager wants to assume bigger responsibilities and move onto the fast track, he or she should focus on the change-agent aspects of the manager's job.

MANAGING PLANNED CHANGE

Managers are concerned with **planned change**. These are change activities that are intentional and goal-oriented. In this section, we'll briefly introduce a three-step model of planned change, differentiate change efforts in terms of magnitude, describe techniques for overcoming resistance to change efforts, and consider the politics of change.

A Three-Step Model of Planned Change

It's generally acknowledged that successful change in organizations should follow three steps: *unfreezing* the status quo, *movement* to a new state, and *refreezing* the new change to make it permanent. This is called **force-field analysis**.[13] That is, successful change requires analyzing the forces that are driving change and those that are holding it back so the former can be increased and the latter reduced.

The status quo can be considered to be an equilibrium state. To move from this equilibrium—to overcome the pressures of both individual and organizational resistance—unfreezing is necessary. It can be achieved in one of three ways. (See Exhibit 18-3.) The *driving forces*, which direct behavior away from the status quo, can be increased. The *restraining forces*, which hinder movement from the existing equilibrium, can be decreased. A third alternative is to combine the first two approaches.

Once a change has been implemented, if it is to be successful, the new situation needs to be refrozen so that it can be sustained over time. Unless this step is taken, there is a very high chance that the change will be short-lived and that employees will attempt to revert to the previous equilibrium state. The objective of refreezing, then, is to stabilize the new situation by balancing the driving and restraining forces.

What might this model look like in practice? When the management at a Connecticut-based insurance company decided to reorganize its claims department around teams, many employees expressed concern about the change. Some feared their job might be eliminated. Others weren't sure if they'd like being part of a team. Still others were concerned about having to learn new skills and take on new responsibilities. Management responded first by increasing driving forces. They did this by putting on presentations discussing the value of empowered teams, with particular emphasis on how most workers prefer team-based jobs once they got used to them. To reduce restraining forces, the company talked-up the frustrations of doing narrow and repetitive tasks, and then provided team-building workshops to help employees overcome their fear of taking on team tasks. Finally, management sought to refreeze the change by restructuring the performance

Bob Knowling, president and chief executive officer at COVAD Communications, led more than 20,000 employees in a large-scale change effort to improve service to U.S. West's 25 million customers when he was their vice president of network operations.

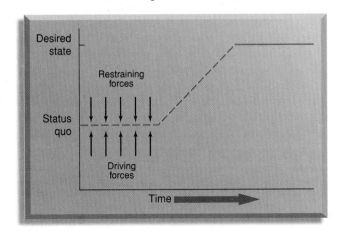

Unfreezing the Status Quo

EXHIBIT 18-3

appraisal and pay systems to reward team cooperation, and introduced semi-annual three-day retreats where employees updated their team-building skills.

First-Order versus Second-Order Change

Historically, managers pursued **first-order change**.[14] This is change that is of the linear variety. It implies no fundamental shifts in the assumptions that organizational members hold about the world or how the organization can improve its functioning. Rather, it strives to make minor improvements while essentially "staying the course." Examples of first-order change include onetime cost-cutting initiatives, short-term programs to improve quality, and efforts to improve productivity incrementally by "trying harder." Mikio Kitano, director of all production engineering at Toyota, is introducing first-order change in his company.[15] He is pursuing slow, subtle, incremental changes in production processes to improve the efficiency of Toyota's plants.

There is nothing inherently wrong with first-order change. When organizations face relatively benign competitive conditions, making small incremental changes makes sense. Unfortunately, such conditions are becoming increasingly rare. And the risk of playing it safe—making small changes at the margin—have become quite high. Companies such as Kodak, the CBS television network, and Wang have learned the hard way that first-order changes can be disastrous when competitors are aggressively redefining products and markets. In a dynamic environment, managers who pursue first-order changes are doing the organizational equivalent of "rearranging the deck chairs on the Titanic." They give the appearance of doing something when, in reality, they are doing nothing toward dealing with the real problems.

Second-order change is a multidimensional, multilevel, discontinuous, radical change involving a reframing of assumptions about the organization and the world in which it operates. One author uses the term *transformation* to differentiate it from incremental improvement.[16] Boeing is a good case in point. Boeing's management, responding to a massive airline slump, aggressive competition from Airbus, and the threat of Japanese competitors, radically reinvented the company.[17] They slashed costs by up to 30 percent, reduced the time it takes to make a 737 from 13 months to 6 months, dramatically cut inventories, put the company's entire workforce through a 4-day course in "competitiveness," renegotiated labor contracts to give the company more flexibility in outsourcing production, and brought customers and suppliers into the once-secret process of designing new planes.

Managing change in the twenty-first century will be less of the first-order variety and increasingly of the second-order. And this shift will make the manager's job more difficult. Resistance to change will be greater. And managers themselves will be required to show a level of courage that wasn't required before. They will be venturing into new territory. They will be attempting to do what has never been done before. So risks of failure will be considerably higher. Yet, ironically, the risks inherent in pursuing first-order changes are probably greater. The manager's job today may be more challenging and stressful than at any time in the past. Following the road that led to past successes is increasingly the path to failure. And pursuing new roads is scary and full of uncertainty and potholes of resistance.

> **Following the road that led to past successes is increasingly the path to failure.**

Overcoming Resistance to Change

What can managers do to overcome the resistance that transformational change creates? There is no easy or surefire approach that will guarantee that changes can be implemented smoothly and painlessly. However, proper planning and execution can increase your odds.

ASSESSING THE CLIMATE FOR CHANGE Why do some change efforts succeed and others fail? One major factor is readiness to change.[18] That is, to what degree is there a supportive climate for change? Research has identified seventeen key elements to successful change. The more affirmative answers a manager gives to the following questions, the greater the likelihood that change efforts will succeed.

1. Is the sponsor of change high up enough to have power to effectively deal with resistance?
2. Is day-to-day leadership supportive of the change and committed to it?
3. Is there a strong sense of urgency from senior management about the need for change, and is it shared by the rest of the organization?
4. Does management have a clear vision of how the future will look different from the present?
5. Are there objective measures in place to evaluate the change effort, and are reward systems explicitly designed to reinforce them?
6. Is the specific change effort consistent with other changes going on within the organization?
7. Are functional managers willing to sacrifice their personal self-interest for the good of the organization as a whole?
8. Does management pride itself on closely monitoring changes and actions taken by competitors?
9. Is the importance of the customer and a knowledge of customer needs well accepted by everyone in the workforce?
10. Are managers and employees rewarded for taking risks, being innovative, and looking for new solutions?
11. Is the organization structure flexible?
12. Are communication channels open both downward and upward?
13. Is the organization's hierarchy relatively flat?
14. Has the organization successfully implemented major changes in the recent past?
15. Are employee satisfaction and trust in management high?
16. Is there a high degree of cross-boundary interactions and cooperation between units in the organization?
17. Are decisions made quickly, taking into account a wide variety of suggestions?

STRATEGIES FOR REDUCING RESISTANCE Given that the climate supports change, managers need to prepare a strategy for change. Six suggestions have been offered as crucial in preparing the organization and its members for the trauma of seismic change.[19]

1. *Conduct an organizational identity audit before undertaking any major change.* This audit should include all departments and levels affected by the change, and it should focus on members' beliefs about the organization. What do they see as the organization's core beliefs—current and ideal states?
2. *Tailor the change to fit the organization.* Different organizations and subunits within organizations have different concerns and identities. One size doesn't fit all! Use the audit to identify those differences, and then use change tactics that fit best.
3. *Present the change as significant (to overcome organizational inertia) while tying it to valued aspects of organizational identity.* The change agent needs to convince employees of the critical importance and need for change. This phase is essentially the task of providing visionary leadership.
4. *Introduce change in a series of midrange steps.* Comprehensive changes are very threatening to people. They are less likely to resist if changes are presented in steps. And each successful step increases momentum and widens the distance to the past.

5. *Take the path of least resistance.* In complex organizations, members in separate units are likely to have distinct identity beliefs that are held with varying levels of conviction. This diversity of beliefs creates entry points at which change can be implemented with relative ease. Managers should select those units in which the probability that change will be readily accepted is highest. Then, successes in these units can be leveraged to build momentum for expanding the change to more-resistant units.

6. *Know how much change your organization can handle.* Organizations differ in their willingness to accept change. So do subunits within a large organization. What is perceived as radical and threatening in one organization or subunit may be viewed as incremental in others. There is an upper limit to how much change is acceptable. You need to keep this limit in mind as a constraint on how much change your organization can absorb at any one time.

TACTICS FOR REDUCING RESISTANCE Six specific tactics have been suggested for use by change agents in dealing with resistance to change.[20]

1. *Education and communication.* Resistance can be reduced through communicating with employees to help them see the logic of a change. This tactic basically assumes that the source of resistance lies in misinformation or poor communication: If employees receive the full facts and get any misunderstandings cleared up, resistance will subside. Communication can be achieved through one-on-one discussions, memos, group presentations, or reports. Does it work? It does, provided that the source of resistance is inadequate communication and that management-employee relations are characterized by mutual trust and credibility. If these conditions don't exist, the change is unlikely to succeed.

2. *Participation.* It's difficult for individuals to resist a change decision in which they participated. Before a change is made, those opposed can be brought into the decision process. If the participants have the expertise to make a meaningful contribution, their involvement can reduce resistance, obtain commitment, and increase the quality of the change decision. However, against these advantages are the negatives: potential for a poor solution and great time consumption.

3. *Facilitation and support.* Change agents can offer a range of supportive efforts to reduce resistance. When employee fear and anxiety are high, employee counseling and therapy, new-skills training, or a short paid leave of absence may facilitate adjustment. The drawback of this tactic is that, as with the others, it is time-consuming. In addition, it is expensive, and its implementation offers no assurance of success.

4. *Negotiation.* Another way for the change agent to deal with potential resistance to change is to exchange something of value for a lessening of the resistance. For instance, if the resistance is centered in a few powerful individuals, a specific reward package can be negotiated that will meet their individual needs. Negotiation as a tactic may be necessary when resistance comes from a powerful source. Yet one cannot ignore its potentially high costs. There is also the risk that, once a change agent negotiates with one party to avoid resistance, he or she is open to the possibility of being blackmailed by other individuals in positions of power.

5. *Manipulation and cooptation.* Manipulation refers to covert influence attempts. Twisting and distorting facts to make them appear more attractive, withholding undesirable information, and creating false rumors to get employees to accept a change are all examples of manipulation. If corporate management threatens to close down a particular manufacturing plant if that plant's employees fail to accept an across-the-board pay cut, and if the threat is actually untrue, management is using manipulation. Coopta-

tion, on the other hand, is a form of both manipulation and participation. It seeks to "buy off" the leaders of a resistance group by giving them a key role in the change decision. The leaders' advice is sought, not to seek a better decision, but to get their endorsement. Both manipulation and cooptation are relatively inexpensive and easy ways to gain the support of adversaries, but the tactics can backfire if the targets become aware that they are being tricked or used. Once discovered, the change agent's credibility may drop to zero.

6. *Coercion.* Last on the list of tactics is coercion: that is, the application of direct threats or force upon the resisters. If the corporate management mentioned in item 5 really is determined to close a manufacturing plant if employees don't acquiesce to a pay cut, then coercion would be the label attached to its change tactic. Other examples of coercion are threats of transfer, loss of promotions, negative performance evaluations, and a poor letter of recommendation. The advantages and drawbacks of coercion are approximately the same as those mentioned for manipulation and cooptation.

The Politics of Change

No discussion of resistance to change would be complete without a brief mention of the politics of change. Because change invariably threatens the status quo, it inherently implies political activity.[21]

Internal change agents typically are managers high in the organization who have a lot to lose from change. They have, in fact, risen to their positions of authority by developing skills and behavioral patterns that have, so far, been favored by the organization. Change is a threat to those skills and patterns. What if they are no longer the ones the organization values? Any change creates the potential for others in the organization to gain power at their expense.

Politics suggests that the impetus for change is most likely to come from individuals who are new to the organization (and have less invested in the status quo) or from executives slightly removed from the main power structure. Those managers who have spent their entire careers with a single organization and eventually achieve a senior position in the hierarchy are often major impediments to change. Change, itself, is a very real threat to their status and position. Yet they may be expected to implement changes to demonstrate that they are not merely caretakers. By acting as change agents, they can symbolically convey to various constituencies—stockholders, suppliers, employees, customers—that they are on top of problems and adapting to a dynamic environment. Of course, as you might guess, when forced to introduce change, these longtime power holders tend to implement first-order changes. Radical change is typically too threatening.

Power struggles within the organization will determine, to a large degree, the speed and quantity of change. You should expect that longtime career executives will be sources of resistance. This, incidentally, explains why boards of directors who recognize the imperative for the rapid introduction of second-order change in their organizations frequently turn to outside candidates for new leadership.[22]

This suggests that all managers should tread carefully in their roles as change agents. It's a good idea, for instance, to assess how much support you have from above. For top executives, this means having the board in your corner. For mid- and lower-level managers, you need to know that you will be backed up by the people above you. Once you have support, you should consider who will have a vested interest in the change. This group might include specific departments and teams, staff units, suppliers, key customers,

> **Because change invariably threatens the status quo, it inherently implies political activity.**

unions, and informal employee leaders. Then focus on these vested interests. Winning their support will be crucial to the change effort's success or failure. The techniques discussed previously for dealing with resistance—education and communication, participation, facilitation, negotiation, manipulation and cooptation, and coercion—can be used to build this support.

WHAT CAN MANAGERS CHANGE?

What can managers change? The options essentially fall into five categories: structure, culture, technology, the physical setting, and people[23] (see Exhibit 18-4). Changing *structure* involves making an alteration in authority relations, coordination mechanisms, job redesign, or similar structural variables. Changing *culture* requires reshaping the organization's core values. Changing *technology* encompasses modifications in the way work is processed and in the methods and equipment used. Changing the *physical setting* covers altering the space and layout arrangements in the workplace. Changing *people* refers to changes in employee attitudes, skills, expectations, perceptions, or behavior.

Changing Structure

In chapter 8, we discussed structural issues such as work specialization, span of control, and various organizational designs. But organizational structures are not set in stone. Changing conditions demand structural changes. As a result, managers might need to modify the organization's structure.

An organization's structure is defined as how tasks are formally divided, grouped, and coordinated. Managers can alter one or more of the key elements in an organization's design. For instance, departmental responsibilities can be combined, vertical layers removed, and spans of control widened to make the organization flatter and less bureaucratic. More rules and procedures can be implemented to increase standardization. An increase in decentralization can be made to speed up the decision-making process.

Management can also introduce major modifications in the actual structural design. Modifications might include a shift from a simple structure to a team-based structure or

EXHIBIT 18-4

Change Options

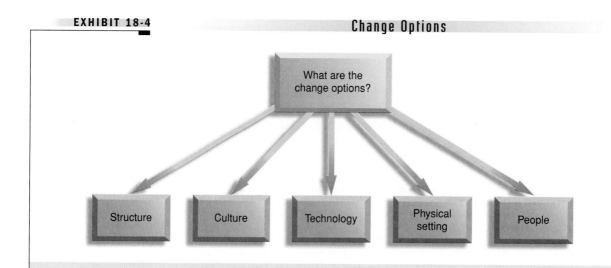

the creation of a matrix design. Managers might also consider redesigning jobs or work schedules; jobs can be redefined or enriched, or flexible work hours can be introduced. Still another option is to modify the organization's compensation system. Employee motivation could be increased by, for example, introducing performance bonuses or profit sharing.

Changing Culture

We discussed cultural change in chapter 11. In that discussion, we drew on a number of studies to conclude that cultures are highly resistant to change. And when change does come, it comes slowly. Jack Welch, CEO at General Electric, characterized his company's cultural transformation as a 7- to 10-year effort.[24] It is probably accurate to say that it is a lot easier to change an organization's structure or technology than it is to transform its culture.

This doesn't mean that culture can't be changed. Again, as we noted in chapter 11, certain conditions increase the likelihood that cultural change can be successfully accomplished. These include a dramatic crisis, new top leadership, a fairly new and small organization, and a weak dominant culture.

The typical challenges management faces in trying to change its organization's culture are captured in the experiences of IBM Canada.[25] Like its parent, in the early 1990s, IBM Canada had become cocky, arrogant, and removed from its customers. The company was oblivious to its environment and rewarded its employees for conformity. Between 1991 and 1993, IBM Canada lost $125 million. The company brought in a new CEO who reduced the workforce by almost one-third and did away with the company's practice of promoting exclusively from within. But change has come very slowly. This isn't completely surprising given that fourteen of the company's current top fifteen executives are longtime IBM veterans, still enmeshed in the company's old country-club mentality. You can understand the problem when the most visible and most talked-about evidence of cultural change in the company is the dumping of its rigid, dark suit and white shirt dress code.

Changing Technology

Most of the early studies in management dealt with efforts aimed at technological change. At the turn of the century, for example, scientific management sought to implement changes based on time-and-motion studies that would increase production efficiency (see Appendix A). Today, major technological changes usually involve the introduction of new equipment, tools, methods, or processes; automation; or computerization.

Competitive factors or innovations within an industry often require managers to introduce new equipment, tools, methods, or operations processes. For example, many aluminum companies have significantly modernized their plants in recent years to compete more effectively. More efficient handling equipment, furnaces, and presses have been installed to reduce the cost of manufacturing a ton of aluminum.

Automation is a technological change that replaces people with machines. It began in the industrial revolution and continues as a change option today. Examples of automation are the introduction of address scanners by the U.S. Postal Service, robots on automobile assembly lines, and flexible manufacturing systems in production operations.

As noted in previous chapters, the most visible technological change in recent years has been expanding computerization. Many organizations now have sophisticated man-

Changing office design and layout can influence behavior patterns in the workplace. Chiat/Day, a large advertising agency, has introduced an open office design to facilitate open and informal communication.

agement information systems. Large supermarkets have converted their cash registers into input terminals and linked them to computers to provide instant inventory data. The office of 1999 is dramatically different from the office of 1979, predominantly because of computerization. Now desktop microcomputers can run hundreds of business software packages, and network systems allow these computers to communicate with one another.

Changing the Physical Setting

The layout of work space should not be a random activity. Typically, management thoughtfully considers work demands, formal interaction requirements, and social needs when making decisions about space configurations, interior design, equipment placement, and the like.

For example, when an office design is opened up by eliminating walls and partitions, employees can more easily communicate with one another. Similarly, management can change the quantity and types of lights, the level of heat or cold, the levels and types of noise, the cleanliness of the work area, and interior design dimensions such as furniture, decorations, and color schemes.

The evidence indicates that changes in the physical setting, in and of themselves, do not have a substantial impact on organizational or individual performance.[26] But they can make certain employee behaviors easier or harder to perform. In this way, employee and organizational performance may be enhanced or reduced.[27]

Changing People

The final area in which management or change agents operate is in helping individuals and groups within the organization to work more effectively together. This category typically involves changing the attitudes and behaviors of organizational members through processes of communication, decision making, and problem solving. A good part of our discussion of learning, in chapter 12, reflects efforts to understand the most effective ways to change employee attitudes and behaviors.

In recent years, practicing managers and academics have tended to focus their attention on three variables: structure, culture, and people. Structural change has been subsumed within the reengineering movement. We will return to reengineering later in this chapter. We have already discussed cultural change in chapter 11. So that leaves the topic of people change. In this section we will review the most popular techniques for changing employee attitudes and behaviors.

▶ Organizational Development

The umbrella term used most frequently to encompass methods for changing employees is **organizational development (OD)**. Essentially, this term refers to a collection of techniques for understanding, changing, and developing an organization's workforce in order to improve its effectiveness.[28] It builds on humanistic, democratic values. It emphasizes confronting problems and conflicts between individuals in work groups and between work groups.

OD techniques emphasize a set of underlying values. OD places a high degree of importance on human and organizational growth, collaborative and participative processes, and a spirit of inquiry.[29] For example, OD techniques assume that individuals are responsible and conscientious; that effective relationships are based on trust and equality; that problems should be openly confronted; and that the more people that participate in the decisions surrounding a change, the more they will be committed to implementing those decisions. Popular OD techniques include survey feedback, team building, and intergroup development.

▶ Survey Feedback

A tool for assessing attitudes held by organizational members, identifying discrepancies among member perceptions, and solving these differences is the **survey feedback** approach. Everyone in an organization can participate in survey feedback, but of key importance is the organizational family—the manager of any given unit and those employees who report directly to him or her. A questionnaire is usually completed by all members in the organization or unit. Organization members may be asked to suggest questions or may be interviewed to determine what issues are relevant. The questionnaire typically asks members for their perceptions and attitudes on a broad range of topics, including decision-making practices; communication effectiveness; coordination between units; and satisfaction with the organization, job, peers, and their immediate supervisor.

The data from this questionnaire are first cross-tabulated with data pertaining to an individual's specific "family" and to the entire organization and then distributed to employees. These data then become the springboard for identifying problems and clarifying issues that may be creating difficulties for people. In some cases, the manager may be counseled by an external change agent about the meaning of the responses to the questionnaire and may even be given suggested guidelines for leading the organizational family in group discussion of the results. Particular attention is given to the importance of encouraging discussion and ensuring that discussions focus on issues and ideas and not on attacking individuals.

Finally, group discussion in the survey feedback approach should result in members identifying possible implications of the questionnaire's findings. Are people listening? Are new ideas being generated? Can decision making, interpersonal relations, or job assignments be improved? Answers to questions such as these, it is hoped, will result in the group's agreeing upon commitments to various actions that will remedy the problems that are identified.

Team Building

As we have noted in numerous places throughout this book, organizations are increasingly relying on teams to accomplish work tasks. **Team building** utilizes high-interaction group activities to increase trust and openness among team members.[30]

Team building can be applied within groups or at the intergroup level where activities are interdependent. For this discussion, we'll emphasize the intragroup level and leave intergroup development to the next section. So our interest concerns applications to organizational families (command groups), as well as to committees, project teams, self-managed teams, and task groups.

Not all group activity has interdependence of functions. For example, consider a football team and a track team:

> Although members on both teams are concerned with the team's total output, they function differently. The football team's output depends synergistically on how well each player does his particular job in concert with his teammates. The quarterback's performance depends on the performance of his linemen and receivers, the ends on how well the quarterback throws the ball, and so on. On the other hand, a track team's performance is determined largely by the mere addition of the performances of the individual members.[31]

Team building is applicable to the case of interdependence, such as in football. The objective is to improve coordinative efforts of members in such a way that the team's performance will also improve.

The activities considered in team building typically include goal setting, development of interpersonal relations among team members, role analysis to clarify each member's role and responsibilities, and team process analysis. Of course, team building may emphasize or exclude certain activities depending on the purpose of the development effort and the specific problems with which the team is confronted. Basically, however, team building attempts to use high interaction among members to increase trust and openness.

It may be beneficial to begin by having members attempt to define the goals and priorities of the team. This exercise will bring to the surface different perceptions of what the team's purpose may be. Next, members can evaluate the team's performance—how effective are they in structuring priorities and achieving their goals? This step should identify potential problem areas. This self-critique discussion of means and ends can be done with all members of the team present, or, if large size impinges on a free interchange of views, it may initially take place in smaller groups, which can later share their findings with the total team.

Team building can also address itself to identifying and clarifying each member's role on the team. Previous ambiguities can be brought to the surface. It may offer one of the few opportunities some individuals have had to think through thoroughly what their job is all about and what specific tasks they are expected to carry out if the team is to optimize its effectiveness.

Still another team-building activity is to analyze key processes that go on within the team to identify the way work is performed and how these processes might be improved to make the team more effective.

Employees at Harvard Pilgrim Health Care act out roles in a team-building training exercise.

Intergroup Development

A major area of concern in OD is the dysfunctional conflict that exists between groups. This has been a subject to which change efforts have been directed.

Intergroup development seeks to change the attitudes, stereotypes, and perceptions that groups have of one another. For example, in one company, the engineers saw the accounting department as composed of shy and conservative types and the human resources department as having a bunch of "ultra-liberals, who are more concerned that some protected group of employees might get their feelings hurt than with the company's making a profit." Such stereotypes can have an obvious negative impact on the coordinative efforts between the departments.

Although there are several approaches for improving intergroup relations,[32] one popular method emphasizes problem solving.[33] In this method, each group meets independently to develop lists of its perception of itself and of the other group and how it believes the other group perceives it. The groups then share their lists and discuss similarities and differences. Differences are clearly articulated, and the groups look for the causes of the disparities.

Are the groups' goals at odds? Were perceptions distorted? On what basis were stereotypes formulated? Have some differences been caused by misunderstandings of intentions? Have words and concepts been defined differently by each group? Answers to questions such as these clarify the exact nature of the conflict. Once the causes of the difficulty have been identified, the groups can move to the integration phase—working to develop solutions that will improve relations between the groups. Subgroups, with members from each of the conflicting groups, can now be created for further diagnosis and to begin to formulate possible alternative actions that will improve relations.

We wrap up this chapter, and the text itself, by discussing some contemporary issues related to managing change. These are: the importance of adjusting change practices to reflect national differences, the reengineering revolution, employee stress, dealing with the aftermath of downsizing, building innovative organizations, and creating a learning organization.

◁ **CONTEMPORARY ISSUES IN MANAGING CHANGE**

Managing Change Needs to Reflect National Culture

A number of the issues addressed in this chapter are culture-bound. To illustrate, let's briefly look at four questions: (1) Do people believe that change is possible? (2) If it is possible, how long will it take to bring it about? (3) Is resistance to change greater in some cultures than in others? (4) Does culture influence how change efforts will be implemented?

Do people believe change is possible? Remember that cultures vary in terms of beliefs about their ability to control their environment. In cultures in which people believe that they can dominate their environment, individuals will take a proactive view of change. This would, for example, describe the United States and Canada. In other countries, such as Iran and Saudi Arabia, people see themselves as subjugated to their environment and thus will tend to take a passive approach toward change.

If change is possible, how long will it take to bring it about? A culture's time orientation can help us answer this question. Societies that focus on the long-term, such as Japan, will demonstrate considerable patience while waiting for positive outcomes from change efforts. In societies with a short-term focus, such as the United States and Canada, people expect quick improvements and will seek change programs that promise fast results.

Is resistance to change greater in some cultures than in others? Resistance to change will be influenced by a society's reliance on tradition. Italians, as an example, focus on the past, whereas Americans emphasize the present. Italians, therefore, should generally be more resistant to change efforts than are Americans.

Does culture influence how change efforts will be implemented? Power distance can help answer this question. In high power distance cultures, such as the Philippines or Venezuela, change efforts will tend to be autocratically implemented by top management. In contrast, low power distance cultures value democratic methods. We would predict, therefore, a greater use of participation in countries such as Denmark and Israel than in the Philippines or Venezuela.

▶ The Reengineering Revolution

Reengineering was a popular management tool for implementing change through much of the 1990s. But it was a tool for second-order change. Reengineering, as you remember, refers to redesigning the organization's core processes by essentially starting with a blank sheet of paper. It entails ignoring the way things have historically been done and completely redesigning everything the organization does—from product development to customer service. But it has little relevance for first-order or incremental change efforts.

Reengineering has been widely applied in tens of thousands of U.S. and European organizations. In fact, it is the unusual organization today whose management *hasn't* tried reengineering. However, not surprisingly, given the magnitude of change inherent in reengineering and our knowledge of resistance pressures, many of these efforts have failed or at least fallen well short of original expectations. Many companies undertook reengineering efforts "only to abandon them with little or no positive result."[34]

Reengineering had a high failure rate because of both the extent of change it imposed and because it emphasized processes over people. The CEO of Aetna Life & Casualty noted, reengineering is "agonizingly, heartbreakingly tough."[35] Lots of people typically lose their jobs, and those who don't find that their jobs aren't the ones they used to do. Most successful reengineering efforts leave little intact. Such drastic change is extremely threatening to everyone in the organization. Moreover, reengineering programs forgot about people. Managers found that simply cutting staff, rather than reorganizing the way people in different functions work, didn't yield the expected quantum leaps in performance. Disillusioned by large layoffs, overwork, and the uncertainty created by massive change, employee morale and productivity suffered. Levi Strauss, for instance, used reengineering to cut the time it takes to fill orders from 3 weeks to 36 hours. But when managers demanded that 4,000 white-collar workers reapply for their jobs as part of a reorganization into process groups, employees rebelled. To bring the turmoil under control, management put the brakes on its reengineering effort.[36]

In spite of mounting skepticism, reengineering isn't likely to go away. But it'll be modified to better recognize its effect on people. It'll focus on getting *more* out of people rather than getting *rid* of people. And it will give more attention to culture change. One of the two consultants who originally launched the idea of reengineering, in fact, now uses the label of "business transformation" to describe his more people-focused approach.[37]

▶ Reducing Employee Stress

Today's new work environment is increasingly characterized by employees' assuming larger work loads, putting in longer hours, having fewer resources to work with, confronting more day-to-day ambiguities, and facing less job security. And these changes are a major cause of employee stress. In a sample of 600 U.S. workers, 46 percent said that their jobs were highly stressful, and 34 percent reported that the stress was so bad they were thinking of quitting.[38] A similar poll of German workers found 60 percent saying they suffered from work-related stress.[39] What are the costs to organizations from work-related stress? One estimate for the United States alone places the figure at $150 billion a year based on increased absenteeism, reduced productivity, increased compensation claims, and higher health insurance costs and direct medical expenses.[40]

These statistics beg the question: What, if anything, can management do to help employees reduce stress or better cope with it?

Not all sources of stress are controllable by management.[41] Some people, for instance, are naturally high-strung and stress-prone. And employees often have dilemmas outside their work — such as financial and family problems — that management can't control but that employees bring with them to their jobs. The good news is that stress isn't necessarily all bad. Low levels of stress can make work more interesting for employees and stimulate higher performance.

Yet there are things management can do to lessen the negative impact of work stress on employees. They include improved personnel selection and job placement, the use of realistic goal setting, training in time management, redesign of jobs, increased employee involvement, expanded social support networks, improved organizational communication, and creation of organizationally supported wellness programs.[42]

Certain jobs are more stressful than others, and individuals differ in their response to stress situations. For example, individuals with little experience in their job tend to be more stress-prone than are experienced jobholders. Similarly, people with a highly anxious personality are not likely to do well in jobs, such as air traffic controllers and emergency-room physicians, that are inherently stressful. *Selection and placement* decisions should take these factors into consideration.

We discussed *goal setting* in chapter 5. On the basis of an extensive amount of research, we concluded that individuals perform best when they have specific and challenging goals and receive feedback on how well they are progressing toward those goals. The use of goals can reduce stress. Specific goals that are perceived as attainable clarify performance expectations. In addition, goal feedback reduces uncertainties as to actual job performance. The results are less employee frustration, less job uncertainty, and less stress.

A frequent cause of stress is poor use of time. So management should consider providing *time-management* training. The well-organized employee can often accomplish twice as much as the person who is poorly organized. An understanding and utilization of time-management principles can help individuals better cope with job demands.

Redesigning jobs to give employees more responsibility, more-meaningful work, more autonomy, and increased feedback can reduce stress, because these factors give the employee greater control over work activities and lessen dependence on others. But as we noted in our discussion of work design, not all employees want enriched jobs. The right job redesign, then, for employees with a low need for growth might be *less* responsibility and *increased* specialization. If individuals prefer structure and routine, reducing skill variety should also reduce uncertainties and stress levels.

> In a sample of U. S. workers, 46 percent said that their jobs were highly stressful . . . A similar poll of German workers found 60 percent saying they suffered from work-related stress.

Job stress occurs to a large extent because employees feel uncertain about goals, expectations, how they will be evaluated, and the like. By giving these employees a voice in those decisions that directly affect their job performances, management can increase employee control and reduce this cause of stress. So managers should consider increasing *employee involvement* in decision making.

Having friends, family, or colleagues to talk to provides an outlet when stress levels become excessive. Helping employees expand their *social support networks* can be a means of reducing tension. Having someone else to hear a problem can provide an objective perspective on a given situation. Interestingly, the value of social support in lessening stress may be an important, but rarely mentioned, advantage provided by work teams.

Increasing formal *organizational communication* with employees reduces uncertainty by lessening ambiguity. If uncertainty creates stress, then improving internal communication and lessening uncertainty and ambiguity can reduce it.

A final suggestion is to offer organizationally supported *wellness programs*. These programs focus on the employee's total physical and mental condition. For example, they typically provide workshops to help people quit smoking, control alcohol use, lose weight, eat better, and develop a regular exercise program. The assumption underlying most wellness programs is that employees need to take personal responsibility for their physical and mental health. The organization is merely a vehicle to facilitate this end.

Organizations, of course, aren't altruistic. They expect a payoff from their investment in wellness programs. And most of those firms that have introduced wellness programs have found that the benefits exceed the costs. For instance, Du Pont saw a 14 percent decline in sick days among employees at forty-one plants, nonhospital health-care costs shrank 43 percent at Tenneco Inc., and the average annual employee health claim at Steelcase Inc. fell from $1,155 to $537.[43]

▶ Helping Employee "Survivors" Cope with Downsizing

Joyce Colbert-Jones is a casualty, although most people wouldn't think so. An employee of AT&T for 14 years, she has evaded numerous corporate layoffs. Unlike many of her former co-workers who have lost their jobs and moved on, Colbert-Jones struggles daily to cope with the anxiety created by job insecurity. Although she still has a job, she describes her attempt to survive at AT&T as a "duck-and-dodge game."[44]

People like Joyce Colbert-Jones don't get much attention. When we read about corporate downsizing, typically the focus is on those who have been laid off. But there is another side to these layoffs—the side experienced by the Joyce Colbert-Joneses of the world. For every "victim" who is laid off, there are probably five to ten remaining "survivors." So, while AT&T may have cut 40,000 jobs in a recent two-year period, there is a tendency to overlook the 270,000 damaged survivors who are left at the company. The merger of Chase Manhattan and Chemical Bank eliminated 12,000 jobs but left 63,000 to cope with the aftermath.

Many organizations have done a fairly good job of helping layoff victims through outplacement services, psychological counseling, support groups, severance pay, extended benefit programs, and detailed communications. Unfortunately, very little has been done for those who have been left behind and have the task of keeping the organization going or revitalizing it.

LAYOFF-SURVIVOR SICKNESS The evidence shows that both victims and survivors experience similar feelings of frustration, anxiety, and loss.[45] But layoff victims get to start over with a

TODAY ? or TOMORROW ?

Organizational Psychopharmacology and Stress Reduction

Du Pont used to describe itself as seeking "better living through chemistry." It appears that an increasing number of workers are doing the same—that is, improving their lives through chemistry. We propose, therefore, that one solution to the increase in employee stress is likely to be the application of **organizational psychopharmacology**—the use of drugs to influence behavior in the work environment.[46]

Psychopharmacology is a discipline that has been studied in medical schools for 40 years. It's not a topic studied or discussed at any typical business school. But the linkage between the chemistry lab and the workplace is tighter than many people think.

We know that drugs are widely used by individuals to deal with psychological and behavioral problems. Any such list would include popular social drugs—caffeine, nicotine, and alcohol—as well as the expanding choice of over-the-counter and prescription drugs. Prozac, as a case in point, is used by more than 21 million people worldwide to raise mood levels and lessen anxiety.

Many of these drugs are used by workers to deal with the anxiety, frustration, and stress they experience as a result of their jobs. In some cases, this drug use is under a doctor's care. But people use cigarettes, alcoholic beverages, tranquilizers, and similar products as personal mechanisms for coping with work-related and personal problems. Is this wrong? That's an ethical question. What is clearly beyond dispute, however, is that a large proportion of the workforce use drugs as a way to cope with job-related pressures. The more relevant questions, then, are: At what point do organizations acknowledge this use? And if employees choose to use drugs to cope, should management actively involve itself in helping workers decide what chemicals they should put in their bodies?

Most people consider the idea of organizational psychopharmacology as something out of a science-fiction novel. It's not. A factory employee complains of a headache and he's sent to the plant infirmary. The company nurse gives him a couple of aspirin. That nurse is practicing organizational psychopharmacology. Or an employee complains of stress symptoms to the company doctor and that doctor responds by writing a prescription for a tranquilizer. That doctor, too, is proactively prescribing drugs to influence an employee's work-related behavior. Most importantly, these somewhat benign examples—or incidences very much like them—occur in thousands of work settings every day.

As management becomes more aware of the escalating costs of work-related stress to both employees and organizations, and as the relationship between employers and health providers (specifically HMOs) becomes more intertwined, we should expect to see wider acceptance of drugs as a means for coping with work-related problems such as stress.

clean slate. This isn't true of survivors. As one authority suggested, "the terms could be reversed; those who leave become survivors, and those who stay become victims."[47] A new syndrome seems to be popping up in more and more organizations: **layoff-survivor sickness**. It's a set of attitudes, perceptions, and behaviors of employees who remain following involuntary employee reductions.[48] Symptoms of this sickness include job insecurity, perceptions of unfairness, depression, stress from increased work loads, fear of change, loss of loyalty and commitment, reduced risk taking and motivation, unwillingness to do anything beyond the required minimum, feelings of not being kept well informed, and a loss of confidence in upper management.

STEPS FOR HELPING SURVIVORS COPE What should organizations do to deal with layoff-survivor sickness? A four-step approach has been suggested:[49]

Step 1: *Get the process right.* Well-designed processes won't cure survivor sickness, but they keep survivors from sinking into deeper survivor symptoms. Characteristics of a well-designed process include: Make the cuts clear and quick. Provide abundant information to both victims and survivors. Give layoff victims adequate prior notification. Be emotionally honest and authentic in all communications. Explain decisions openly and in terms of fairness. And, if possible, allow employees to participate.

Step 2: *Let people grieve to deal with repressed feelings and emotions.* Even in the best-handled layoffs, survivors feel violated. They must release their feelings before they can go on. They need to go through the same grieving process that one goes through after a death in the family. Use of groups is one of the most effective and efficient means of bringing survivor emotions to the surface. In a relatively short time, most natural work teams can make a great deal of progress in unblocking and addressing their survivor feelings. Often survivor feelings must be teased out through structured exercises and nontraditional processes such as drama. Confession is cathartic and bonding as people learn that others harbored the same set of feelings that they do. This process of confession tends to lead to sharing and acceptance.

Step 3: *Break the chain of organizational dependence.* This step tries to help survivors recapture their sense of control and self-esteem. While Steps 1 and 2 react to existing layoff survivor symptoms, this step offers the possibility of preventing the sickness in the first place by moving people from organizational dependency to self-directed careers.

A primary symptom of this dependency is that employees' sense of value and identity is based on pleasing not himself or herself but someone or something else. Employees need to become detached. "If who you are is where you work, you will do almost anything to hang on".[50]

The new workplace requires employees to build transferable skills and have independence from their employers. An employee's loyalty is no longer to the organization but to his or her own career. The breaking of this dependency relationship is essentially an individual effort.

Step 4: *Reshape the organization's systems to lessen dependency-creating processes.* This final step seeks to help people immunize themselves against survivor sickness.

Organizations historically did a lot to create co-dependency: seniority systems for promotions and rewards, loyalty expectations, promotion from within, long-term socialization processes to shape people into "desired employees," long-term career planning, and nontransferable corporate pension plans.

Organizations have to detach themselves from their paternalistic practices. The following are some suggestions for management to take: Shape a new culture of employee independence by explicitly conveying that there is no such thing as lifetime caretaking; introduce transferable, 401(k)-type benefit plans and tenure-free recognition systems; downplay differences between full-time, part-time, and temporary employees; offer job enrichment and participation; use self-directed work teams; facilitate social support with open and honest communication; develop nonhierarchical performance and reward systems; stop "taking care" of employees; discontinue providing detailed long-term career planning; provide counseling and processing exercises for survivors; and support and celebrate interorganizational mobility.

Building an Innovative Organization

Innovativeness stimulates opportunities and growth. Without it, organizations "eventually wither and die."[51] But how does an organization become innovative?

The standard toward which many organizations strive is that achieved by the 3M Co.[52] It has built a reputation as one of the most innovative organizations in the world by consistently developing new products over a very long period of time. The company currently markets some 60,000 different products. 3M has historically sought to have 25 percent of its annual sales come from products developed in the previous 5 years. And it always reached that goal. More recently, top management challenged the company by increasing the goal to 30 percent for products introduced in the previous 4 years and 10 percent for those introduced in the past year. In 1996, a typical year at 3M, the company introduced 500 new products.

3M is obviously doing something right. What can other organizations do to achieve 3M's track record for innovation? There is no guaranteed formula, but certain characteristics surface again and again when researchers study innovative organizations such as 3M, Intel, Hewlett-Packard, and Compaq. Here, they are grouped into structural, cultural, and human resource categories. Our message to top management is that they should consider introducing these characteristics into their organization if they want to create an innovative climate. Before we look at these characteristics, however, let's clarify what we mean by innovation.

DEFINITION Innovation is a special kind of change. Whereas *change* refers to making things different, **innovation** refers to a new idea applied to initiating or improving a product, process, or service.[53] So all innovations involve change, but not all changes necessarily involve new ideas or lead to significant improvements. Innovations in organizations can range from small incremental improvements, such as RJR Nabisco's extension of the Oreo product line to include double stuffs and chocolate-covered Oreos, up to radical breakthroughs, such as Otis Elevator's Odyssey system, which replaces lift cables with vertical tracks and horizontal turnouts that could make mile-high skyscrapers possible. Keep in mind that, although our examples are mostly of product innovations, the concept of innovation also encompasses new production process technologies, new structures or administrative systems, and new plans or programs pertaining to organizational members.

SOURCES OF INNOVATION *Structural variables* have been the most-studied potential source of innovation.[54] A comprehensive review of the structure-innovation relationship leads to the following conclusions.[55] First, organic structures positively influence innovation. Because they are low in vertical differentiation, formalization, and centralization, organic organizations have the flexibility, adaptiveness, and cross-fertilization that facilitate the adoption of innovations. Second, long tenure in management is associated with innovation. Managerial tenure apparently provides legitimacy and knowledge of how to accomplish tasks and obtain desired outcomes. Third, innovation is nurtured where resources are abundant. Having an abundance of resources allows an organization to afford to purchase innovations, bear the cost of instituting innovations, and absorb failures. Finally, interunit communication is high in innovative organizations.[56] These organizations are high users of committees, task forces, new-venture teams, and other mechanisms that facilitate interaction across departmental lines.

Innovative organizations tend to have similar *cultures*. They encourage experimentation. They reward both successes and failures. They celebrate mistakes. At Hewlett-

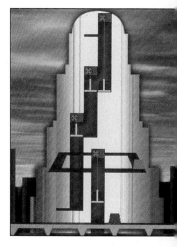

Otis Elevator's Odyssey system replaces lift cables with vertical tracks and horizontal turnouts, making mile-high skyscrapers possible.

Packard, for instance, CEO Lewis Platt has successfully built a corporate culture that supports people who try something that doesn't work out.[57] Platt, himself, protects people who stick their necks out, fearful that to do otherwise would stifle the risk-taking culture he encourages among his managers. Unfortunately, in too many organizations, people are rewarded for the absence of failures rather than for the presence of successes. Such cultures extinguish risk taking and innovation. People will suggest and try new ideas only when they feel that such behaviors will exact no penalties. Managers in innovative organizations recognize that failures are a natural by-product of venturing into the unknown. When Babe Ruth set his record for home runs in one season, he also led the league in strikeouts. And he is remembered for the former, not the latter!

Within the *human resources* category, we find that innovative organizations actively train and develop their members so that they can keep current. They offer high job security so that employees won't fear getting fired for making mistakes, and they encourage individuals to become champions of change. Once a new idea is developed, **idea champions** actively and enthusiastically promote the idea, build support, overcome resistance, and ensure that the innovation is implemented.[58] Recent research finds that idea champions have common personality characteristics: extremely high self-confidence, persistence, energy, and a tendency to take risks. Bernard Meyerson, one of IBM's forty-five research fellows, spent more than a dozen years persistently wheeling and dealing to keep his development team working on a novel chip technology called silicon-germanium alive.[59] Meyerson's efforts paid off in the mid-1990s with a profitable new product. Idea champions also display characteristics associated with transformational leadership. They inspire and energize others with their vision of the potential of an innovation and through their strong personal conviction in their mission. They are also good at gaining the commitment of others to support their mission. In addition, idea champions have jobs that provide considerable decision-making discretion. This autonomy helps them introduce and implement innovations in organizations.[60]

Given the status of 3M as a premier product innovator, we would expect it to have most or all of the properties we have identified. It does. The company is so highly decentralized that it has many of the characteristics of small, organic organizations. Employees are encouraged to communicate across departmental lines to combine ideas from different disciplines. All of 3M's scientists and managers are challenged to "keep current." Idea champions are created and encouraged by allowing scientists and engineers to spend up to 15 percent of their time on projects of their own choosing. The company encourages its employees to take risks—and rewards the failures as well as the successes. 3M management exhibits high patience. The company invests nearly 7 percent of its sales revenue (more than $1 billion a year) in research and development, yet management tells its R&D people that not everything is going to work. And 3M doesn't hire and fire with the business cycle. For instance, during the last recession, while nearly all major companies cut costs by firing employees, 3M initiated no layoffs. When reductions in staff have been necessary, 3M has averted layoffs by relying on early retirement incentives and transfers of full-time employees to jobs filled by temporary or part-time workers.

▶ Creating a Learning Organization

What TQM was to the 1980s and reengineering was to the early and mid-1990s, the learning organization has become to the late 1990s. It has developed a groundswell of interest from managers looking for new ways to successfully respond to a world of interdependence and change.[61] In this section, we describe what a learning organization looks like and methods for managing learning.

Innovation at NEC Corp.

The general view used to be: In electronics, U.S. companies lead in innovation while their Japanese counterparts have the edge in production technology. This view is no longer accurate. U.S. production facilities can compete with anyone in the world. And Japanese companies are learning to innovate. NEC Corp., the Japanese electronic giant, illustrates the latter.

In today's fast-moving global technology market, few electronics manufacturers have the luxury to follow the crowd. New product innovations are coming from major U.S. players like Hewlett-Packard and IBM, as well as manufacturers in Japan, South Korea, Taiwan, Singapore, and Hong Kong. To survive in this free-for-all, NEC has had to drastically reengineer its research capabilities.

The reengineering began in 1993. Some of the changes included less reliance on group consensus, and the introduction of flexible work hours and a relaxed dress code. To place particular emphasis on individual achievement, a special bonus system was created to reward the most productive researchers. And superstars are recognized by having their pictures on display in the research center's hall of fame.

For a company that was historically very rigid and tradition-bound, these changes were considered nothing short of revolutionary. Today, NEC researchers can come and go at any time they want and wear whatever they please. They don't even have to report to work at all if they don't want to. Says the company's R&D vice president, "We believe that people can think better in their chosen environment. What we're interested in are results."

And what about those results? In just a couple of years, NEC has gone from sixth to third on the list of Japanese companies

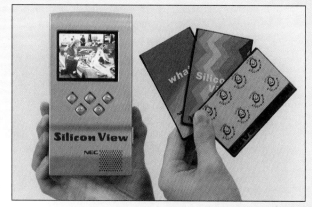

with the highest number of patents registered in Japan. In the United States, NEC moved from fifteenth to fourth. An example of what this new innovative climate has produced is shown in the photo. What looks like a pocket-sized TV is a two-inch, color liquid crystal display panel, called Silicon View, which is actually a multimedia appliance. It uses electronic cards (also in photo) no bigger than a credit card for storing information. These cards can store about four minutes of video and sound each. When the Silicon View's built-in modem is connected to a mobile phone, it becomes a versatile tool for the traveling business-person.

Source: Based on P. Gloster and J. Leung, "Innovators Spearhead Global Drive by Techno Giants," *Asian Business*, May 1996, pp. 28–34.

WHAT IS A LEARNING ORGANIZATION? A **learning organization** is an organization that has developed the continuous capacity to adapt and change. Just as individuals learn, so too do organizations. "All organizations learn, whether they consciously choose to or not—it is a fundamental requirement for their sustained existence."[62] However, some organizations—such as Xerox, Corning, Federal Express, Ford, General Electric, Nucor, and Applied Materials—just do it better than others.

Most organizations engage in what has been called **single-loop learning**.[63] When errors are detected, the correction process relies on past routines and present policies. In contrast, learning organizations use **double-loop learning**. When an error is detected, it is corrected in ways that involve the modification of the organization's objectives, policies, and standard routines. Like second-order change, double-loop learning challenges deep-

■

EXHIBIT 18-5

Characteristics of a Learning Organization

1. There exists a shared vision upon which everyone agrees.
2. People discard their old ways of thinking and the standard routines they use for solving problems or doing their jobs.
3. Members think of all organizational processes, activities, functions, and interactions with the environment as part of a system of interrelationships.
4. People openly communicate (across vertical and horizontal boundaries) without fear of criticism or punishment.
5. People sublimate their personal self-interest and fragmented departmental interests to work together to achieve the organization's shared vision.

Source: Based on P. M. Senge, *The Fifth Discipline* (New York: Doubleday, 1990).

rooted assumptions and norms within an organization. In this way, it provides opportunities for radically different solutions to problems and dramatic jumps in improvement.

Exhibit 18-5 summarizes the five basic characteristics of a learning organization. It is an organization in which people put aside their old ways of thinking, learn to be open with one another, understand how their organization really works, form a plan or vision that everyone can agree upon, and then work together to achieve that vision.[64]

Proponents of the learning organization envision it as a remedy for the three fundamental problems inherent in traditional organizations: fragmentation, competition, and reactiveness.[65] First, fragmentation based on specialization creates "walls" and "chimneys" that separate different functions into independent and often warring fiefdoms. Second, an overemphasis on competition often undermines collaboration. Members of the management team compete with one another to show who is right, who knows the most, or who is most persuasive. Divisions compete with one another when they ought to cooperate to share knowledge. Team project leaders compete to show who is the best manager. And third, reactiveness misdirects management's attention to problem solving rather than to creation. The problem solver tries to make something go away, whereas a creator tries to bring something new into being. An emphasis on reactiveness pushes out innovation and continuous improvement and, in its place, encourages people to run around "putting out fires."

It may help to better understand what a learning organization is if you think of it as an ideal model that builds on a number of contemporary management concepts. No company has successfully achieved (or probably ever will achieve) all the characteristics described in Exhibit 18-5. You should think of a learning organization as an ideal to strive toward rather than a realistic description of structured activity. Notice, too, how learning organizations draw on previous concepts such as TQM, organizational culture, the boundaryless organization, functional conflict, and transformational leadership. For instance, the learning organization adopts TQM's commitment to continuous improvement. Learning organizations are also characterized by a specific culture that values risk taking, openness, and growth. It seeks "boundarylessness" through breaking down barriers created by hierarchical levels and fragmented departmentalization. A learning organization supports the importance of disagreements, constructive criticism, and other forms of functional conflict. And transformational leadership is needed in a learning organization to implement the shared vision.

MANAGING LEARNING How do you change an organization to make it into a continual learner? What can managers do to make their firms learning organizations?

Establish a strategy. Management needs to make explicit its commitment to change, innovation, and continuous improvement.

Redesign the organization's structure. The formal structure can be a serious impediment to learning. Flattening the structure, eliminating or combining departments, and increasing the use of cross-functional teams reinforce interdependence and reduce boundaries between people.

Reshape the organization's culture. As noted earlier, learning organizations are characterized by risk taking, openness, and growth. Management sets the tone for the organization's culture both by what it says (strategy) and what it does (behavior). Managers need to demonstrate by their actions that taking risks and admitting failures are desirable traits. That means rewarding people who take chances and make mistakes. And management needs to encourage functional conflict. "The key to unlocking real openness at work," says one expert on learning organizations, "is to teach people to give up having to be in agreement. We think agreement is so important. Who cares? You have to bring paradoxes, conflicts, and dilemmas out in the open, so collectively we can be more intelligent than we can be individually."[66]

AN APPLICATION: THE U.S. ARMY? The U.S. Army isn't the typical example that comes to mind when you think of what a learning organization might look like. But think again.[67] The Army's environment has changed dramatically since the days of the Vietnam conflict. For one thing, the Soviet threat, which was a major justification for the Army's military buildup, is largely gone. Army soldiers are more likely to be involved in feeding children in Somalia, keeping peace in Haiti, or helping put out forest fires in the Pacific Northwest than fighting a war. And its new mission is reflected in its budget. The Army's annual appropriation dropped from $90 billion in 1989 to $64 billion in 1998. Meanwhile, the number of active troops in uniform has been downsized from 780,000 to 480,000. Clearly, it's no longer "business as usual" in the U.S. Army.

The Army's high command has redesigned its structure to reflect its new mission. The old Army was said to be an organization "designed by geniuses to be run by idiots."[68] That rigid, hierarchical, command-and-control structure was fine when the Army's single purpose was combat-related. Authority was centralized at the Pentagon, and orders were passed down to the field. Officers weren't expected to innovate or make adjustments. But that type of structure doesn't fit with the changing role of the military. The new Army is putting into place an adaptive and flexible structure to match its more-varied objectives.

Along with the new structure is a major program to make the Army's culture more egalitarian. Everyone, from PFCs to brigadier generals, has gone through team training to learn how to make decisions in the field and even to question authority (a previously unheard-of idea). Senior officers are required to go through something called the After Action Review—a public performance appraisal—where decisions are openly critiqued by subordinates. The potential for public embarrassment in an AAR would never have been allowed in the old Army.

The bottom line is that the U.S. Army is becoming a learning organization. It is developing soldiers, especially officers, who can adapt rapidly to different tasks and missions. The new Army seeks to be able to quickly improvise in complex and ambiguous situations. Its soldiers will be prepared to play a multiple set of changing roles—fighting, peacekeeping, peacemaking, humanitarian rescue, nation building, or whatever—and be able to change those roles quickly as needed.

There is a variety of additional material available on the CD-ROM and companion Web site that accompany this text. You can access this information through the CD-ROM or by visiting the Web site at <**www.prenhall.com/robbins**>.

SUMMARY

(This summary is organized by the chapter-opening learning objectives on page 560.)

1. Sources of individual resistance to change include habit, security, economic factors, fear of the unknown, and selective information processing. Sources of organizational resistance include structural and group inertia, limited focus, and threats to expertise, power relationships, and established resource allocations.

2. Force-field analysis is a process of balancing the forces that drive and resist a proposed change.

3. First-order change involves minor incremental improvements. Second-order change is a multidimensional, multilevel, discontinuous, radical change involving a reframing of assumptions.

4. Strategies for reducing resistance to change include conducting an identity audit, identifying key differences so change will fit properly, presenting the change as significant and tying it to valued aspects of the organization's identity, introducing the change as a series of midrange steps, taking the path of least resistance, and keeping the amount of change within tolerable limits.

5. Tactics for reducing resistance include education and communication, participation, facilitation and support, negotiation, manipulation and cooptation, and coercion.

6. Change options available to a manager include structure, culture, technology, the physical setting, and people.

7. Organizational development refers to a collection of techniques for understanding, changing, and developing an organization's workforce to improve its effectiveness.

8. Stress-reduction techniques include improved personnel selection and job placement, use of realistic goals, time management, job redesign, increased employee involvement, expanded social support networks, improved organizational communication, and wellness programs.

9. Managers can increase innovation by implementing an organic structure, facilitating long tenure in the management ranks, providing abundant resources, expanding interunit communication, creating cultures that reward risktaking and tolerate mistakes, promoting employee training and development, offering job security, and encouraging idea champions.

10. A learning organization is one that has developed the continuous capacity to adapt and change.

REVIEW QUESTIONS

1. What are the forces reshaping the changing world of work?

2. "Resistance to change isn't all bad." Build an argument to support this statement.

3. It is commonly assumed that an individual's resistance to change increases with age. Do you think this is true? Defend your position.

4. What is the transformational leader's role in planned change? What is the role of the transactional leader?

5. As a low-level manager acting as a change agent, what can you do to deal with the political aspects of implementing change?

6. How can managers get people to more readily accept a major organizational change—such as the redesign of jobs from individual work activities to teams?

7. How does national culture influence change agents?

8. Do you think it is unethical for managers to try to help employees deal with stress that is nonwork-related? Explain.

9. Describe the characteristics of a learning organization. Relate the learning organization to the concepts of reengineering, TQM, team building, and organization design.

10. Organizations typically have limits to how much change they can absorb. As a senior manager, what signs would you look for that might suggest that your organization has exceeded its change capacity?

Michael Volkema at Herman Miller

In July 1995, Michael Volkema, age 39, was promoted to CEO at office furniture manufacturer Herman Miller. Volkema was selected because of his successful record at running the company's profitable file cabinet division.

Upon assuming his new job, Volkema sat down to look at the problems he faced. The company had built its reputation by producing only premium office furniture. It justified its high prices on the grounds that the furniture paid for itself in higher employee productivity. That strategy worked fine in the 1970s and 1980s. It didn't in the 1990s because businesses were cutting costs and downsizing. In 1992, Herman Miller's sales dropped from $879 million the previous year to $804 million. Its earnings sank from $37 million to $17 million. The company's expenses were growing faster than its sales. And companies like Steelcase were successfully attacking Herman Miller's argument that better design equals productivity gains. Compared to Herman Miller, competitors were developing more new designs, more choices, and greater style options. Customers found these attributes more appealing than the "increased productivity" argument.

One of the few bright spots in the company was a small division that built cheaper furniture. Called SQA, for Simple, Quick, and Affordable, this division had grown from nothing to annual revenues of $200 million in just half a dozen years. What was the appeal of SQA? Many small businesses knew the Herman Miller name and wanted to own their furniture, but the price was too high. Whereas a fully furnished Herman Miller cubicle costs $10,400, SQA could provide comparable quality—but with fewer frills and fabric choices—for $8,300. It also prided itself on using technology to provide rapid delivery. The industry standard for lead time is 5 weeks. SQA cut it to 2 weeks and sometimes to 2 days!

Assume you're Michael Volkema. The head of SQA thinks Volkema should redirect company resources his way. Volkema, on the other hand, doesn't want to lose the reputation Herman Miller has as the Rolls Royce of the office furniture business. If you were Volkema, would you focus on building lower-cost furniture like SQA? Would you focus on cost cutting? Would you focus on investing in technology? Can you manage change without tossing out everything from the past? And once you've decided what you are going to do, how would you go about implementing your change program?

Source: Based on B. Upbin, "A Touch of Schizophrenia," *Forbes*, July 7, 1997, pp. 57–59.

Managing Resistance to Change

Almost from its inception, Prentice Hall's college division (which produces textbooks and educational materials for use in colleges and universities) had been located in Englewood Cliffs, New Jersey. This location proved convenient for a wide range of employees. City types were only 20 minutes from the Upper West Side of New York City. Suburbanites could choose from dozens of small New Jersey communities that were only minutes from the office. And employees who preferred a rural lifestyle could have it and still be less than a 40-minute commute to work.

Prentice Hall's senior management decided in the early 1990s that the company had outgrown its present Englewood Cliffs facility, but local officials resisted management's efforts to expand on its current site. After much analysis, management bought the former headquarters of Western Union in Upper Saddle River, New Jersey. After remodeling of the Upper Saddle River location, a final moving date was set for all Prentice Hall operations.

Upper Saddle River repositioned Prentice Hall in terms of hiring and retaining employees. The major difference between Upper Saddle River and Englewood Cliffs was proximity to New York City. The latter was just a few miles away and a short commute by car or bus. The former was 35 miles from the city—taking nearly an hour each way to commute and accessible only by car.

The relocation had little impact on managers in the production area, because most production employees lived in New Jersey and drove to work. But it caused problems for managers of creative departments such as advertising and design. Most employees in those departments lived in New York City, had no desire to live anywhere else, and did not own cars.

Linda Wilson manages a small group at Prentice Hall that exclusively works on designing books. All six of her people live in New York City. When Linda was officially informed of the move to Upper Saddle River (about 9 months prior to the actual move), she immediately relayed the information to her people. No one immediately resigned. But as the official moving date got closer, she was hearing more and more rumors that most of her people were looking for jobs in the city.

Assume that you are Linda Wilson. It's now only two months away from moving day. You don't want to lose any of the skilled and talented people you have in your group. What will you do? Be specific.

TEAM ACTIVITY

Managing a Cutback

Break into teams of five or six students. You have 60 minutes to complete the following task:

Your instructor has been asked to present the same course you are currently taking (and in which you're using *Managing Today!*) but in a short format. Specifically, your instructor will have to teach the course in exactly half the current time. So, for instance, if your present class met for 75 minutes, twice a week, for 16 weeks, your instructor had 40 hours to cover the course material. The short course would allow only 20 hours.

Your instructor feels too close to the problem to be able to decide what should be retained and what should be omitted. In response, your team has been asked to solve the problem. Beginning with the course objectives, your team will need to prioritize lectures, topics, chapters, in-class activities, outside assignments, and exams.

When teams have completed this project, be prepared to discuss processes and results with the entire class. Specific attention should be paid to how various teams determined priorities, dealt with resistance to change, and whether teams pursued first-order or second-order change strategies.

CASE EXERCISE

What Went Wrong at Levi Strauss?

It began in 1993. Management called it "the biggest change program in the history of the company." Levi Strauss, the clothing manufacturer (in addition to jeans, the company produces western wear, leisure clothing, and casual working clothes), had decided that the company needed to change. Was there a problem? Nothing major. But management wasn't satisfied.

According to Tom Kasten, who headed up the change program: "We had great products—always have. We had great marketing—nobody can touch us. But customers were telling us our service wasn't good enough. We were slow. It could take us 30 days to restock a store. In Womenswear . . . it could take a year to source a new product. We weren't reliable, either. We shipped less than 40 percent of our orders when we said we would."

The change program Kasten set up looked like it was taken right out of a management textbook. Kasten created a team of hundreds to become a flying wedge for change. They took over the third floor of Levi's headquarters in San Francisco. They created a plan to totally redesign the company: new business processes, systems, facilities. They ran workshops for managers and employees in order to get them to participate in the change effort. They developed mechanisms to respond to pockets of resistance. And they carefully addressed the human side of

change. By 1995, management was basking in the positive results of its efforts. The company generated record sales of nearly $7 billion and profits of more than $700 million.

Two years later, all was not well at Levi Strauss. The competition was eating Levi's market share at a rapid rate. This was most evident in the blue jeans market. In 1990, Levi had a 31 percent market share. In 1997, it was down to 18 percent. In November 1997, in an announcement that shook the company, management announced that it would close 11 U.S. factories in four states and lay off 34 percent of its North American workforce.

What went wrong? In spite of all the focus on change, the company got out of step with young customers. The company focused on reliability. Young buyers wanted fashion. Private-label designer jeans and upstarts responded with stylish cuts attractive to teens and buyers in their twenties. Jeans didn't go out of style, but styles changed and Levi was slow to respond to fashion trends like the wide-legged pants. "It's a fair assessment to say we were behind in fashion," says a senior executive of Levi Strauss. "Levi's strength is that it is never the most fashionable but the most relevant." Unfortunately, "relevant" isn't what buyers have been looking for. Once hopelessly unhip J. C. Penney and Sears were grabbing market share with their Arizona and Canyon River brands, respectively. The Gap's store brand was well received by young buyers. And designers Donna

Karan, Tommy Hilfiger, Ralph Lauren, and Versace all successfully introduced their own line of jeans. Even mainstream VF Corp, maker of Lee and Wrangler, revitalized its fashion line and created a hip new line, Lee Riveted. Riveted now accounts for about 40 percent of Lee's $1 billion jeans business.

QUESTIONS

1. What does this case say about change programs?
2. What, if anything, did Levi Strauss do wrong in 1993? in 1995?

3. In addition to the plant closings and layoffs, if you were a senior executive at Levi today, what recommendations would you make to help restore the company's dominance in the jean business?

Source: Based on D. Sheff, "Levi's Changes Everything," *Fast Company*, Greatest Hits, Vol. 1, 1997, pp. 24–31; and S. Perman, "Levi's Gets the Blues," *Time*, November 17, 1997, p. 66.

VIDEO CASE EXERCISE

Slam Dunk!

ABCNEWS

Sex sells. Just as promoters of men's sports aim to do, women's sports promoters are looking to get sports fans to spend dollars, and lots of them. Savvy marketers have long known that sex appeal gets attention in an overcrowded marketplace, and until the summer of 1997, sex appeal was often used to promote women's sports. Starting with the initial season of the WNBA, the Women's National Basketball Association, that approach is changing. But getting people to see women sports stars as more than just sexy athletes won't be easy!

The 1990s boom in figure skating provides a lesson about the good things that can happen when people get interested in a sport. As televised figure skating events became more and more popular, fans of the sport flocked to ice rinks around the country. From group lessons to private lessons, from purchasing new skating equipment to repairing broken equipment, the dollars spent on ice skating took off. However, as a sport, figure skating features lithe, slender females in short, skimpy, and often sexy costumes. And even though the sport hasn't been actively promoted with sex appeal, it would appear to be the underlying aura surrounding figure skating. With the debut of the WNBA, this approach to women's sports changed.

After watching the first promotions for the WNBA, Jeff Jensen of *Advertising Age* concluded that a three-cornered women's sports industrial complex was being built. Its components included performers, presenters, and producers of equipment. He said "You need all of those things working in unison and concert for . . . something like women's sports to really take off. And that's exactly what we're seeing right now." Val Ackerman, the WNBA president, knows that changing the perception of women's sports isn't going to be easy. Yet she says that her league's survival depends on their ability to deliver an audience: actually, three primary target audiences. One is existing basketball fans, who are probably predominantly male. The second is active women 18 to 34 who have some connection to sports. The third is younger women who are just starting to play sports. There's a feeling among the supporters of the WNBA that the new professional women's basketball league will send a signal that women athletes can take themselves more seriously. That attitude helps legitimize all women's sports whether it's roller blading, swimming, or mountain climbing. Even some businesses are pushing for the changed attitude toward women's sports. For instance, Nike aims to increase its sales to women. Nike spokeswoman Sue Levin says, "This is an opportunity where what's good for Nike's business is also the right thing to do because we really believe strongly as a company that sports are good for girls and women."

QUESTIONS

1. Would you characterize this situation as more like first-order change or second-order change?
2. Describe some other organizations that might be affected by the changing view of women's sports and how they might be affected.
3. Of the three primary target audiences for the WNBA, whose attitudes do you think will be the most difficult to change? Why? How would you suggest tackling this challenge?
4. What implications for change management do you see from the statement that the new professional women's basketball league will send a signal that women athletes can take themselves more seriously and will help legitimize *all* women's sports?

Source: Based on "The WNBA and the Changing Role of Women's Sports," *ABC Nightline*, June 24, 1997.

NOTES

1. Based on A. M. Webber, "XBS Learns to Grow," *Fast Company*, October–November 1996, pp. 113–24.

2. Cited in T. Peters, "The Peters Principles," *Forbes ASAP*, October 9, 1995, p. 184.

3. Ibid.

4. E. Appelbaum and R. Batt, *The New American Workplace: Transforming Work Systems in the United States* (Ithaca, NY: ILR Press, 1994).

5. D. Bottoms, "Facing Change or Changing Face?" *Industry Week*, May 1, 1995, p. 17.

6. D. Miller, "What Happens after Success: The Perils of Excellence," *Journal of Management Studies*, May 1994, pp. 325–58; and E. E. Lawler III and J. R. Galbraith, "Avoiding the Corporate Dinosaur Syndrome," *Organizational Dynamics*, Autumn 1994, pp. 5–17.

7. See, for instance, A. B. Fisher, "Making Change Stick," *Fortune*, April 17, 1995, pp. 121–29.

8. See, for instance, P. S. Tolbert, "Institutional Environments and Resource Dependence: Sources of Administrative Structure in Institutions of Higher Education," *Administrative Science Quarterly*, March 1985, pp. 1–13.

9. D. Katz and R. L. Kahn, *The Social Psychology of Organizations*, 2nd ed. (New York: Wiley, 1978), pp. 714–15.

10. E. Ransdell, "IBM's Grassroots Revival," *Fast Company*, October–November 1997, pp. 183–99.

11. These examples are cited in C. Fishman, "Change," *Fast Company*, April–May 1997, pp. 64–75.

12. H. Lancaster, "Quick-Change Artists May Find Fast Route to Executive Positions," *Wall Street Journal*, May 9, 1995, p. B1.

13. This was originally proposed by K. Lewin, *Field Theory in Social Science* (New York: Harper & Row, 1951).

14. See A. Levy, "Second-Order Planned Change: Definition and Conceptualization," *Organizational Dynamics*, Summer 1986, pp. 4–20; J. H. Want, "Managing Radical Change," *Journal of Business Strategy*, May–June 1993, pp. 21–28; and D. A. Nadler, R. B. Shaw, and A. E. Walton, *Discontinuous Change* (San Francisco: Jossey-Bass, 1995).

15. K. L. Miller, "The Factory Guru Tinkering with Toyota," *Business Week*, May 17, 1993, pp. 95–97.

16. R. Pascale, cited in T. Brown, "Re-Invent Yourself," *Industry Week*, November 21, 1994, pp. 21–26.

17. D. J. Yang and A. Rothman, "Reinventing Boeing: Radical Change and Crisis," *Business Week*, March 1, 1993, pp. 60–67.

18. As described in T. A. Stewart, "Rate Your Readiness to Change," *Fortune*, February 7, 1994, pp. 106–10.

19. R. K. Reger, J. V. Mullane, L. T. Gustafson, and S. M. DeMarie, "Creating Earthquakes to Change Organizational Mindsets," *The Executive*, November 1994, pp. 38–41.

20. J. P. Kotter and L. A. Schlesinger, "Choosing Strategies for Change," *Harvard Business Review*, March–April 1979, pp. 106–14.

21. See J. Pfeffer, *Managing with Power: Politics and Influence in Organizations* (Boston: Harvard Business School Press, 1992), pp. 7, 318–20.

22. See, for instance, W. Ocasio, "Political Dynamics and the Circulation of Power: CEO Succession in U.S. Industrial Corporations, 1960–1990," *Administrative Science Quarterly*, June 1994, pp. 285–312.

23. Based on H. J. Leavitt, "Applied Organization Change in Industry," in W. Cooper, H. Leavitt, and M. Shelly (eds.), *New Perspectives on Organization Research* (New York: Wiley, 1964); and P. J. Robertson, D. R. Roberts, and J. I. Porras, "Dynamics of Planned Organizational Change: Assessing Empirical Support for a Theoretical Model," *Academy of Management Journal*, June 1993, pp. 619–34.

24. Cited in T. D. Jick, "Accelerating Change for Competitive Advantage," *Organizational Dynamics*, Summer 1995, p. 78.

25. T. Tillson, "Be It Ever So Humble," *Canadian Business*, Special Technology Issue, June 1995, pp. 26–32.

26. F. Steele, *Making and Managing High-Quality Workplaces: An Organizational Ecology* (New York: Teachers College Press, 1986).

27. J. I. Porras and P. J. Robertson, "Organizational Development: Theory, Practice, and Research," in M. D. Dunnette and L. M. Hough (eds.), *Handbook of Industrial & Organizational Psychology*, 2nd ed., vol. 3 (Palo Alto, CA: Consulting Psychologists Press, 1992), p. 734.

28. This definition is adapted from T. G. Cummings and C. G. Worley, *Organizational Change and Development*, 5th ed. (St. Paul, MN: West, 1993).

29. L. D. Brown and J. G. Covey, "Development Organizations and Organization Development: Toward an Expanded Paradigm for Organization Development," in R. W. Woodman and W. A. Pasmore (eds.), *Research in Organizational Change and Development*, vol. 1 (Greenwich, CT: JAI Press, 1987), p. 63; and W. A. Pasmore and M. R. Fagans, "Participation, Individual Development, and Organizational Change: A Review and Synthesis," *Journal of Management*, June 1992, pp. 375–97.

30. See, for instance, P. F. Buller, "The Team Building–Task Performance Relation: Some Conceptual and Methodological Refinements," *Group and Organization Studies*, September 1986, pp. 147–68; and D. Eden, "Team Development: Quasi-Experimental Confirmation among Combat Companies," *Group and Organization Studies*, September 1986, pp. 133–46.

31. N. Margulies and J. Wallace, *Organizational Change: Techniques and Applications* (Glenview, IL: Scott, Foresman, 1973), pp. 99–100.

32. See, for example, E. H. Neilsen, "Understanding and Managing Intergroup Conflict," in J. W. Lorsch and P. R. Lawrence (eds.), *Managing Group and Intergroup Relations* (Homewood, IL: Irwin-Dorsey, 1972), pp. 329–43.

33. R. R. Blake, J. S. Mouton, and R. L. Sloma, "The Union-Management Intergroup Laboratory: Strategy for Resolving Intergroup Conflict," *Journal of Applied Behavioral Science*, no. 1 (1965), pp. 25–57.

34. M. Hammer and S. A. Stanton, "Beating the Risks of Reengineering," *Fortune*, May 15, 1995, p. 106; and J. B.

White, "Re-Engineering Gurus Take Steps to Remodel Their Stalling Vehicles," *Wall Street Journal*, November 26, 1996, p. A1.

35. Hammer and Stanton, "Beating the Risks of Reengineering," p. 106.

36. J. B. White, "Re-Engineering Gurus Take Steps to Remodel Their Stalling Vehicles."

37. Ibid.

38. Cited in A. Farnham, "Who Beats Stress Best—and How," *Fortune*, October 7, 1991, p. 71.

39. "Stress On the Job in Germany," *Manpower Argus*, February 1997, p. 7.

40. Cited in R. Karasek and T. Theorell, "*Healthy Work: Stress, Productivity and the Reconstruction of Working Life* (New York: Wiley, 1990).

41. S. Parasuraman and J. A. Alutto, "Sources and Outcomes of Stress in Organizational Settings: Toward the Development of a Structural Model," *Academy of Management Journal*, June 1984, pp. 330–50; and R. L. Kahn and P. Byosiere, "Stress in Organizations," in Dunnette and Hough (eds.), *Handbook of Industrial & Organizational Psychology*, 2nd ed., vol. 3, pp. 573–80.

42. Adapted from J. M. Ivancevich and M. T. Matteson, "Organizational Level Stress Management Interventions: A Review and Recommendations," *Journal of Organizational Behavior Management*, Fall–Winter 1986, pp. 229–48; J. M. Ivancevich, M. T. Matteson, S. M. Freedman, and J. S. Phillips, "Worksite Stress Management Interventions," *American Psychologist*, February 1990, pp. 252–61; and S. Cartwright and C. L. Cooper, *Managing Workplace Stress* (Thousand Oaks, CA: Sage, 1997).

43. C. E. Beadle, "And Let's Save 'Wellness.' It Works," *New York Times*, July 24, 1994, p. F9.

44. D. L. Boroughs, "Winter of Discontent," *U.S. News & World Report*, January 22, 1996, p. 52.

45. D. M. Noer, *Healing the Wounds* (San Francisco: Jossey-Bass, 1993).

46. See S. P. Robbins, "Organizational Psychopharmacology: Drugs, Behavior and the Work Environment," *Proceedings of the 17th Annual Midwest Academy of Management Conference*, Kent, Ohio, April 1974, pp. 143–61; M. Chase, "More Are Listening to Prozac to Keep Their Business Edge," *Wall Street Journal*, March 27, 1995, p. B1; R. Spiegel, R. Markstein, P. Baumann, and T. Weston, *Psychopharmacology: An Introduction*, 3rd ed. (New York: Wiley, 1996); S. M. Stahl, *Essential Psychopharmacology*, (London: Cambridge University Press, 1996); and W. S. Appleton, *Prozac and the New Antidepressants* (Boston: Plume, 1997).

47. Ibid., p. 11.

48. Ibid., p. 13.

49. Ibid., pp. 87–185.

50. Ibid., pp. 138–39.

51. D. L. Day, "Raising Radicals: Different Processes for Championing Innovative Corporate Ventures," *Organization Science*, May 1994, p. 148.

52. Discussions of the 3M Co. in this section are based on T. Stevens, "Tool Kit for Innovators," *Industry Week*, June 5, 1995, pp. 28–31; T. A. Stewart, "3M Fights Back," *Fortune*, February 5, 1996, pp. 94–99; B. O'Reilly, "The Secrets of America's Most Admired Corporations: New Ideas, New Products," *Fortune*, March 3, 1997, pp. 60–64; and B. Filipczak, "Innovation Drivers," *Training*, May 1997, p. 36.

53. See, for instance, A. Van de Ven, "Central Problems in the Management of Innovation," *Management Science* 32 (1986), pp. 590–607; R. M. Kanter, "When a Thousand Flowers Bloom: Structural, Collective, and Social Conditions for Innovation in Organizations," in B. M. Staw and L. L. Cummings (eds.), *Research in Organizational Behavior*, vol. 10 (Greenwich, CT: JAI Press, 1988), pp. 169–211; and R. A. Wolfe, "Organizational Innovation: Review, Critique, and Suggested Research Directions," *Journal of Management Studies*, May 1994, pp. 405–29.

54. F. Damanpour, "Organizational Innovation: A Meta-Analysis of Effects of Determinants and Moderators," *Academy of Management Journal*, September 1991, p. 557.

55. Ibid., pp. 555–90.

56. See also C. K. Bart, "New Venture Units: Use Them Wisely to Manage Innovation," *Sloan Management Review*, Summer 1988, pp. 35–43; and P. R. Monge, M. D. Cozzens, and N. S. Contractor, "Communication and Motivational Predictors of the Dynamics of Organizational Innovation," *Organization Science*, May 1992, pp. 250–74.

57. J. H. Sheridan, "Lew Platt: Creating a Culture for Innovation," *Industry Week*, December 19, 1994, pp. 26–30; and E. Nee, "What Have You Invented for Me Lately?" *Forbes*, July 28, 1997, pp. 76–82.

58. J. M. Howell and C. A. Higgins, "Champions of Change," *Business Quarterly*, Spring 1990, pp. 31–32; and Day, "Raising Radicals."

59. O. Port and J. Carey, "Getting to 'Eureka!'" *Business Week*, November 10, 1997, pp. 72–75.

60. Howell and Higgins, "Champions of Change."

61. See, for example, P. M. Senge, *The Fifth Discipline* (New York: Doubleday, 1990); M. Dodgson, "Organizational Learning: A Review of Some Literatures," *Organization Studies* 14, no. 3 (1993), pp. 375–94; D. Miller, "A Preliminary Typology of Organizational Learning: Synthesizing the Literature," *Journal of Management*, vol. 22, no. 3, 1996, pp. 485–505; and T. T. Baldwin, C. Danielson, and W. Wiggenhorn, "The Evolution of Learning Strategies in Organizations: From Employee Development to Business Redefinition," *Academy of Management Executive*, November 1997, pp. 47–58.

62. D. H. Kim, "The Link between Individual and Organizational Learning," *Sloan Management Review*, Fall 1993, p. 37.

63. C. Argyris and D. A. Schon, *Organizational Learning* (Reading, MA: Addison-Wesley, 1978).

64. B. Dumaine, "Mr. Learning Organization," *Fortune*, October 17, 1994, p. 148.

65. F. Kofman and P. M. Senge, "Communities of Commitment: The Heart of Learning Organizations," *Organizational Dynamics*, Autumn 1993, pp. 5–23.

66. Dumaine, "Mr. Learning Organization," p. 154.

67. L. Smith, "New Ideas from the Army (Really)," *Fortune*, September 19, 1994, pp. 203–12.

68. Ibid., p. 203.

Humanities and Social Sciences

PSYCHOLOGY Psychology has long been interested in why and how people resist change. For example, the subject of organizational development is largely built on the work of psychologists. Additionally, almost everything we know today about stress and its management has come from psychologists. If you took a course in introductory psychology, you undoubtedly spent considerable time reading about sources of stress, how stress affects health, and how people cope with stress.

SOCIOLOGY Every introductory sociology course spends time on the topic of social change: What is social change? What causes it? And how does change in one segment of society initiate changes elsewhere? Much of this analysis is transferable to organizations. So, for example, demographic changes in populations have largely fueled organizations' interest in managing diversity.

In addition, sociologists have long been concerned with the dispersion of innovation within organizations and increasing the willingness of employees to accept change. Force-field analysis, socio-technical systems, and early insights into the value of worker participation have helped managers understand how to stimulate innovation and change.

ANTHROPOLOGY How do language, rituals, ceremonies, stories, and the like facilitate and hinder changes in an organization's culture? The answer can be found in the work of anthropologists.

Business Disciplines

ACCOUNTING Because accounting data influences and shapes behavior, effective change efforts need to include modifications in what information is collected, the ways the information is organized and displayed, and to whom it is distributed.

MANAGEMENT INFORMATION SYSTEMS Similarly, information systems should be modified when organizations are undergoing significant change programs. As with accounting data, information systems are not neutral influences on behavior or processes. Through the decisions that managers make in what information is gathered, how it's presented, and who gets it, past practices can be strengthened or weakened.

The Historical Roots of Current Management Practice

When I want to understand what is happening today or try to decide what will happen tomorrow, I look back.

— O. W. Holmes Jr.

Hans Becherer, chief executive of John Deere & Co., thinks he has introduced some innovative changes at his company. When he took over the top spot at Deere in 1990, sales and profits were both falling. He needed to cut costs, reduce design time, and increase productivity. He decided to reach out to his workforce for solutions.[1] "It's often the people at the root of the company, on the shop floor, who will provide the best answers," said Becherer. He believed that employees would be more receptive to improving efficiency if they felt part of the process.

So Becherer restructured jobs around teams and brought Deere's blue-collar workers into the decision-making process. Hourly workers now routinely offer advice on everything from cutting production costs to improving product quality. Cost-reduction teams composed of production workers at Deere's Davenport, Iowa, plant, for example, meet weekly to figure out ways to simplify parts or eliminate production problems. One of these teams found that two engine brackets could be eliminated from a new line of earth-moving equipment. The savings? Sixteen dollars per vehicle. Suggestions such as these have cut Deere's design times by 33 percent over 3 years. Another work team in the company's East Moline, Illinois, factory helped overhaul assembly-line methods. That team cut assembly costs by over 10 percent. Overall, Becherer's innovations are paying big dividends. In 1991, the company lost $20 million on sales of $7 billion. In 1997, Deere made $987 million profits on sales of $13 billion.

Although Becherer may think that the changes he has made at Deere are innovative, the truth is that his ideas were being advocated more than 80 years ago by a prominent Boston business philosopher and lecturer.[2] Her name was Mary Parker Follett.

As early as 1918, Follett was extolling the benefits of participative management and teams. Follett advocated tapping into workers' firsthand experience. She warned that in most large organizations, one loses "what we might learn from the man actually on the job." She also argued that command-style, hierarchical organizations "ignore one of the fundamental facts of human nature, namely, the wish to govern one's own life." Follett advocated what she called "cross-functioning," in which "a horizontal rather than a vertical authority" would foster a freer exchange of knowledge within organizations. Her cross-functioning groups are essentially the same thing that we, today, call cross-functional work teams.

The purpose of this appendix is twofold. First, it illustrates, as we showed with the John Deere example, that things that may seem new and innovative often aren't. Second, it can help you better understand current management practices. This appendix will introduce you to the origins of many contemporary management concepts and demonstrate how they evolved, over time, to reflect the changing needs of organizations and society as a whole.

THE PREMODERN ERA

Organized endeavors and management have existed for thousands of years. The Egyptian pyramids and the Great Wall of China are current evidence that projects of tremendous scope, employing tens of thousands of people, were undertaken well before modern times. The pyramids are a particularly interesting example. The construction of a single pyramid occupied over 100,000 people for 20 years.[3] Who told each worker what he or she was supposed to do? Who ensured that there would be enough stones at the site to keep workers busy? The answer to questions such as these is *management*. Regardless of what managers were called at the time, someone had to plan what was to be done, organize people and materials to do it, and provide direction for the workers.

When you hear the name Michelangelo, what comes to your mind? *Renaissance artist? Genius?* How about *manager?* Recent evidence tells us that the traditional image of Michelangelo—the lonely genius trapped between agony and ecstasy, isolated on his back on a scaffold, single-handedly painting the ceiling of the Sistine Chapel—is not exactly accurate.[4] Some 475 years ago, Michelangelo was actually running a medium-sized business. Thirteen people helped him paint the Sistine ceiling; about twenty helped carve the marble tombs in the Medici Chapel in Florence, and he supervised a crew of at least 200 to build the Laurentian Library in Florence. Michelangelo personally selected his workers, trained them, and assigned them to one or more teams. And he kept detailed employment records. For example, he recorded the names, days worked, and wages of every employee, every week. Meanwhile, Michelangelo played the role of the troubleshooting manager. He would daily dart in and out of the various work areas under his supervision, check on workers' progress, and handle any problems that arose.

These examples from the past demonstrate that organized activities and managers have been with us since ancient times. However, it has been only in the past several hundred years, particularly in the last century, that management has undergone systematic investigation, acquired a common body of knowledge, and become a formal discipline of study.

Scene from Sistine Chapel ceiling fresco. While this work is attributed to Michelangelo, in reality it was done by others under his managerial leadership.

Adam Smith's name is typically cited in economics courses for his contributions to classical economic doctrine. But his discussion in *The Wealth of Nations,* published in 1776, included a brilliant argument on the economic advantages that organizations and society would reap from division of labor.[5] He used the pin-manufacturing industry for his examples. Smith noted that ten individuals, each doing a specialized task, could produce about 48,000 pins a day among them. However, if each were working separately and independently, those ten workers would be lucky to make 200—or even 10—pins in one day. If each worker had to draw the wire, straighten it, cut it, pound heads for each pin, sharpen the point, and solder the head and pin shaft, it would be quite a feat to produce ten pins a day!

Smith concluded that division of labor increased productivity by increasing each worker's skill and dexterity, by saving time that is commonly lost in changing tasks, and by the creation of labor-saving inventions and machinery. The wide application today of job specialization—in service jobs such as teaching and medicine as well as on assembly lines in manufacturing plants—is undoubtedly due to the economic advantages cited over 200 years ago by Adam Smith.

Possibly the most important pre-twentieth-century influence on management was the **industrial revolution.** Begun in the eighteenth century in Great Britain, the Revolution had crossed the Atlantic to America by the end of the Civil War. Machine power was rapidly being substituted for human power. This change, in turn, made it more economical to manufacture goods in factories than in homes. For instance, before the industrial revolution, an item such as a blanket was made by one person, typically at home. The worker would shear wool from his or her sheep, twist the wool into yarn, dye the yarn, weave the blanket manually on a home loom, and then sell the finished product to merchants who would travel to farms buying merchandise that then would be sold at regional fairs or markets. The introduction of machine power, combined with the division of labor, made it possible to have large, efficient factories using power-driven equipment. A blanket factory with 100 people doing specialized tasks—some making wool into yarn, some dyeing, others working on the looms—could manufacture large numbers of blankets at a fraction of their previous cost. But these factories required managerial skills. Managers were needed to forecast demand, ensure that enough wool was on hand to make the yarn, assign tasks to people, direct daily activities, coordinate the various tasks, ensure that the machines were kept in good working order and that output standards were maintained, find markets for the finished blankets, and so forth. When blankets were made individually at home, there was little concern with efficiency. Suddenly, however, when the factory owner had 100 people working for him or her and a regular payroll to meet, it became important to keep workers busy. The performing of management skills became necessary.

The advent of machine power, mass production, the reduced transportation costs that followed the rapid expansion of the railroads, and almost no governmental regulation also fostered the development of big corporations. John D. Rockefeller was putting together the Standard Oil monopoly. Andrew Carnegie was gaining control of two-thirds of the steel industry, and similar entrepreneurs were creating other large businesses that would require formalized management practices. The need for a formal theory to guide managers in running their organizations had arrived. However, it was not until the early 1900s that the first major step toward developing such a theory was taken.

◀ CLASSICAL CONTRIBUTIONS ▬

The roots of modern management lie with a group of practitioners and writers who sought to create rational principles that would make organizations more efficient. Because they set the theoretical foundation for a discipline of management, we call their contributions the classical approach to management. We can break the **classical approach** down into two subcategories: scientific management and general administrative theorists.

SCIENTIFIC MANAGEMENT

If you had to pick a specific year that modern management theory was born, you could make a very strong case for 1911. That was the year that Frederick Winslow Taylor's book *The Principles of Scientific Management* was published.[6] Its contents would become widely accepted by managers throughout the world. The book described the theory of **scientific management**—the use of the scientific method to define the "one best way" for a job to be done. The studies conducted before and after the book's publication would establish Taylor as the father of scientific management. And it set the groundwork for to-

day's assembly lines, where tasks are timed to a fraction of a second; law offices, where attorneys record their time by fractions of a minute; and fast-food restaurants that carefully standardize the production of burgers and french fries.

FREDERICK TAYLOR Frederick Taylor did most of his work at the Midvale Steel Company in Pennsylvania. As a mechanical engineer with a Quaker-Puritan background, he was consistently appalled at the inefficiency of workers. Employees used vastly different techniques to do the same job. They were prone to "take it easy" on the job. Taylor believed that worker output was only about one-third of what was possible. Therefore, he set out to correct the situation by applying the scientific method to jobs on the shop floor. He spent more than two decades pursuing with a passion the "one best way" for each job to be done.

It is important to understand what Taylor saw at Midvale that aroused his determination to improve efficiency in the plant. At the time, there were no clear concepts of worker and management responsibilities. Virtually no effective work standards existed. Workers purposely worked at a slow pace. Management decisions were of the "seat-of-the-pants" nature, based on hunch and intuition. Workers were placed on jobs with little or no concern for matching their abilities and aptitudes with the tasks they were required to do. Most important, management and workers considered themselves to be in continual conflict. Rather than cooperating to their mutual benefit, they perceived their relationship as a zero-sum game—any gain by one would be at the expense of the other.

Taylor sought to create a mental revolution among both the workers and management by defining clear guidelines for improving production efficiency. He defined four principles of management, listed in Exhibit A-1. He argued that following these principles would result in the prosperity of both management and workers. That is, workers would earn more pay, and management more profits.

Probably the most widely cited example of scientific management has been Taylor's pig iron experiment. Workers loaded "pigs" of iron, weighing 92 pounds each, onto rail cars. Their average daily output was 12.5 tons. Taylor believed that scientifically analyzing the job to determine the one best way to load pig iron could increase the output to between 47 and 48 tons per day.

EXHIBIT A-1 ■

Taylor's Principles of Management

1. Develop a science for each element of an individual's work, which replaces the old rule-of-thumb method.
2. Scientifically select and then train, teach, and develop the worker. (Previously, workers chose their own work and trained themselves as best they could.)
3. Heartily cooperate with the workers so as to ensure that all work is done in accordance with the principles of the science that has been developed.
4. Divide work and responsibility almost equally between management and workers. Management takes over all work for which it is better suited than the workers. (Previously, almost all the work and the greater part of the responsibility were thrown upon the workers.)

Taylor began his experiment by looking for a physically strong subject who placed a high value on the dollar. The individual Taylor chose was a big, strong Dutch immigrant, whom he called Schmidt. Schmidt, like the other loaders, earned $1.15 a day, which even at the turn of the century was barely enough for a person to survive on. Taylor offered Schmidt $1.85 a day if he would do exactly what Taylor told him.

Using money to motivate Schmidt, Taylor then went about having him load the pig irons, alternating various job factors to see what impact the changes had on Schmidt's daily output. For instance, on some days Schmidt would lift the pig irons by bending his knees; on other days he would keep his legs straight and use his back. Taylor experimented with rest periods, walking speed, carrying positions, and other variables. After a long period of scientifically trying various combinations of procedures, techniques, and tools, Taylor succeeded in obtaining the level of productivity he thought possible. By putting the right person on the job with the correct tools and equipment, by having the worker follow his instructions exactly, and by motivating the worker through the economic incentive of a significantly higher daily wage, Taylor was able to reach his 48-ton objective.

Using scientific management techniques, Taylor was able to define the one best way for doing each job. He could then, after selecting the right people for the job, train them to do it precisely in this one best way. To motivate workers, he favored incentive wage plans. Overall, Taylor achieved consistent improvements in productivity in the range of 200 percent or more. And he reaffirmed the role of managers to plan and control and that of workers to perform as they were instructed.

The impact of Taylor's work cannot be overstated.[7] During the first decade of the 20th century, Taylor delivered numerous public lectures to convey scientific management to interested industrialists. Between 1901 and 1911, at least eighteen firms adopted some variants of scientific management. In 1908, the Harvard Business School declared Taylor's approach the standard for modern management and adopted it as the core around which all courses were to be organized. Taylor, himself, began lecturing at Harvard in 1909. Between 1910 and 1912, two events catapulted scientific management into the limelight. In 1910, the Eastern Railroad requested a rate increase from the Interstate Commerce Commission. Appearing before the commission, an efficiency expert claimed that railroads could save a million dollars a day (equivalent to about $17 million a day in 1999 dollars) through the application of scientific management. This claim became the centerpiece of the hearings and created a national audience for Taylor's ideas. Then in 1911, Taylor published *The Principles of Scientific Management.* It became an instant best-seller and was eventually translated into at least a dozen languages. By 1914, Taylor's principles had become so popular that an "efficiency exposition" held in New York City, with Taylor as the keynote speaker, drew a crowd estimated at 69,000! And, although Taylor spread his ideas not only in the United States but also in France, Germany, Russia, and Japan, his greatest influence was on U.S. manufacturing. It gave U.S. companies

Frederick Taylor was the father of scientific management. His ideas were instrumental in redefining the roles of workers and managers, and in leading to huge increases in production efficiency.

a comparative advantage over foreign firms that made U.S. manufacturing efficiency the envy of the world—at least for 50 years or so.

FRANK AND LILLIAN GILBRETH Taylor's ideas inspired others to study and develop methods of scientific management. His most prominent disciples were Frank and Lillian Gilbreth.[8]

A construction contractor by background, Frank Gilbreth gave up his contracting career to study scientific management after hearing Taylor speak at a professional meeting. Along with his wife Lillian, a psychologist, he studied work arrangements to eliminate wasteful hand and body motions. The Gilbreths also experimented in the design and use of the proper tools and equipment for optimizing work performance. Frank Gilbreth is probably best known for his experiments in reducing the number of motions in bricklaying.

By carefully analyzing the bricklayer's job, he reduced the number of motions in the laying of exterior brick from eighteen to four and a half. On interior brick, the eighteen motions were reduced to two. He developed a new way to stack bricks, utilized the scaffold to reduce bending, and even devised a different mortar consistency that reduced the need for bricklayers to level the brick by tapping it with a trowel. The importance of these productivity improvements become meaningful when you recognize that most quality buildings at that time were constructed of brick, that land was cheap, and that the major cost of a factory or home was the cost of the materials (bricks) and the labor cost to lay them.

The Gilbreths were among the first to use motion picture films to study hand and body motions. They devised a microchronometer that recorded time to $\frac{1}{2000}$ second, placed it in the field of study being photographed, and thus determined how long a worker spent enacting each motion. Wasted motions missed by the naked eye could be identified and eliminated. The Gilbreths also devised a classification system to label seventeen basic hand motions—such as "search," "select," "grasp," "hold"—which they called **therbligs** (*Gilbreth* spelled backward with the *th* transposed). This system allowed the Gilbreths a more precise way of analyzing the exact elements of any worker's hand movements.

GENERAL ADMINISTRATIVE THEORISTS

The general administrative theorists were individuals who looked at the subject of management from the perspective of the entire organization. They are im-

portant because they developed early general theories of what managers do and what constitutes good management practice. The most prominent of the general administrative theorists were Henri Fayol and Max Weber.

HENRI FAYOL Henri Fayol wrote during the same time as Taylor.[9] However, whereas Taylor was concerned with management at the shop level (or what we today would describe as the job of a supervisor) and used the scientific method, Fayol's attention was directed at the activities of *all* managers, and he wrote from personal experience. Taylor was a scientist. Fayol, the managing director of a large French coal-mining firm, was a practitioner.

Fayol described the practice of management as something distinct from accounting, finance, production, distribution, and other typical business activities. He argued that management was an activity common to all human undertakings in business, in government, and even in the home. He then proceeded to state fourteen principles of management—fundamental or universal truths—that could be taught in schools and universities. These principles are listed in Exhibit A-2.

MAX WEBER Max Weber (pronounced Vay-ber) was a German sociologist. Writing in the early 1900s, Weber developed a theory of authority structures and described organizational activity based on authority relations.[10] He described an ideal type of organization that he called a bureaucracy. It was a system characterized by division of labor, a clearly defined hierarchy, detailed rules and regulations, and impersonal relationships. It also acknowledged a separation of owners from managers, thus legitimizing the status of career or professional managers. The detailed features of Weber's ideal bureaucratic structure are outlined in Exhibit A-3.

Weber recognized that this "ideal bureaucracy" didn't exist in reality but, rather, represented a selective reconstruction of the real world. He meant it as a basis for theorizing about work and how work could be done in large groups. But Weber sincerely believed that his model could remove the ambiguity, inefficiencies, and patronage that characterized most organizations at that time. This model became the design prototype for most large organizations until less than a decade ago.

Bureaucracy, as described by Weber, is not unlike scientific management in its ideology. Both emphasize rationality, predictability, impersonality, technical competence, and authoritarianism. Although Weber's writings were less operational than Taylor's, the fact that his "ideal type" still describes many contemporary organizations attests to the importance of his work.

Job selection tests. Pay-for-performance reward systems. Benefit programs. Designing jobs to improve employee motivation. Participative leadership. Using teams to increase productivity. These contemporary management concepts have evolved out of ideas and research efforts contributed by followers of the **human resources approach** to management. This approach looks at management by focusing on factors that influence and explain human behavior at work.

EARLY CONTRIBUTORS

There were undoubtedly a number of people in the nineteenth and early part of the twentieth centuries who recognized the importance of the human factor to an organization's success, but four individuals stand out as early advocates of the human resources approach. They were Robert Owen, Hugo Münsterberg, Mary Parker Follett, and Chester Barnard.

ROBERT OWEN   Robert Owen was a successful Scottish businessman who bought his first factory in 1789 when

---

EXHIBIT A-2

Fayol's Fourteen Principles of Management

1. *Division of work.* This principle is the same as Adam Smith's "division of labor." Specialization increases output by making employees more efficient.

2. *Authority.* Managers must be able to give orders. Authority gives them this right.

3. *Discipline.* Employees must obey and respect the rules that govern the organization.

4. *Unity of command.* Every employee should receive orders from only one superior.

5. *Unity of direction.* Each group of organizational activities that have the same objective should be directed by one manager using one plan.

6. *Subordination of individual interests to the general interest.* The interests of any one employee or group of employees should not take precedence over the interests of the organization as a whole.

7. *Remuneration.* Workers must be paid a fair wage for their services.

8. *Centralization.* Whether decision making is centralized with management or decentralized to subordinates is a question of proper proportion. The task is to find the optimum degree of centralization for each situation.

9. *Scalar chain.* Communication should follow the line of authority from top management to the lowest ranks. However, if following this chain creates delays, cross-communications can be allowed if agreed to by all parties and superiors are kept informed.

10. *Order.* People and materials should be in the right place at the right time.

11. *Equity.* Managers should be kind and fair to their subordinates.

12. *Stability of tenure of personnel.* High employee turnover is inefficient. Management should provide orderly personnel planning and ensure that replacements are available to fill vacancies.

13. *Initiative.* Employees who are allowed to originate and carry out plans will exert high levels of effort.

14. *Esprit de corps.* Promoting team spirit will build harmony and unity within the organization.

EXHIBIT A-3

Weber's Ideal Bureaucracy

1. *Division of labor.* Jobs are broken down into simple, routine, and well-defined tasks.

2. *Authority hierarchy.* Offices or positions are organized in a hierarchy, each lower one being controlled and supervised by a higher one.

3. *Formal selection.* All organizational members are to be selected on the basis of technical qualifications demonstrated by training, education, or formal examination.

4. *Formal rules and regulations.* To ensure uniformity and to regulate the actions of employees, managers must depend heavily on formal organizational rules.

5. *Impersonality.* Rules and controls are applied uniformly, avoiding involvement with personalities and personal preferences of employees.

6. *Career orientation.* Managers are professional officials rather than owners of the units they manage. They work for fixed salaries and pursue their careers within the organization.

he was just 18. Repulsed by the harsh practices he saw in factories across Scotland—such as the employment of young children (many under the age of 10), 13-hour workdays, and miserable working conditions—Owen became a reformer. He chided factory owners for treating their equipment better than their employees. He said that they would buy the best machines, but then buy the cheapest labor to run them. Owen argued that money spent on improving labor was one of the best investments that business executives could make. He claimed that showing concern for employees was both highly profitable for management and would relieve human misery.

Owen proposed a utopian workplace. As one author noted, Owen is not remembered in management history for his successes, but rather for his courage and commitment to reducing the suffering of the working class.[11] He was more than a hundred years ahead of his time when he argued, in 1825, for regulated hours of work for all, child labor laws, public education, company-furnished meals at work, and business involvement in community projects.[12]

HUGO MÜNSTERBERG Hugo Münsterberg created the field of industrial psychology—the scientific study of individuals at work to maximize their productivity and adjustment. His text, *Psychology and Industrial Efficiency,*[13] was published in 1913. In it, he argued for the scientific study of human behavior to identify general patterns and to explain individual differences. Münsterberg suggested the use of psychological tests to improve employee selection, the value of learning theory in the development of training methods, and the study of human behavior in order to understand what techniques are most effective in motivating workers. Interestingly, he saw a link between scientific management and industrial psychology. Both sought increased efficiency through scientific work analyses and through better alignment of individual skills and abilities with the demands of various jobs. Much of our current knowledge of selection techniques, employee training, job design, and motivation is built on Münsterberg's work.

MARY PARKER FOLLETT We mentioned Mary Parker Follett at the opening of this appendix when we discussed her early advocacy of participative management and teams. Follett is important because she was one of the first to recognize that organizations could be viewed from the perspective of individual and group behavior.[14]

She lived, lectured, and wrote around the same time that scientific management's ideas were flourishing, but Follett proposed more people-oriented ideas. She thought that organizations should be based on a group ethic rather than on individualism. Individual potential, she argued, remained only potential until released through group association. The manager's job was to harmonize and coordinate group efforts. Managers and workers should view themselves as partners—as part of a common group. As such, managers should rely more on their expertise and knowledge to lead subordinates than on the formal authority of their position. Her humanistic ideas influenced the way we look at motivation, decision making, leadership, teams, power, and authority.

One of the strongest cases for Follett's importance to management practice is the recent comment made by London School of Economics chairman Sir Peter Parker: "People often puzzle about who is the father of management. I don't know who the father was, but I have no doubt about who was the mother. Mary Parker Follett."[15]

CHESTER BARNARD Like Fayol, Chester Barnard was a practitioner—he was president of New Jersey Bell Telephone Company. He had read Weber's work and was influenced by his writings. But unlike Weber, who had a mechanistic and impersonal view of organizations, Barnard saw organizations as social systems that require human cooperation. He expressed his views in his book *The Functions of the Executive,*[16] published in 1938.

Barnard believed that organizations were made up of people who have interacting social relationships. The manager's major roles were to communicate and stimulate subordinates to high levels of effort. A major part of an organization's success, as Barnard saw it, depended on obtaining cooperation by emphasizing common goals. Barnard also argued that success depended on maintaining good relations with people and institutions outside the organization with whom the organization regularly interacted. By recognizing the organization's dependence on investors, suppliers, customers, and other external stakeholders, Barnard introduced the idea that managers had to examine the external environment and then adjust the organization to maintain a state of equilibrium. Regardless of how efficient an organization's production might be, if management failed either to ensure a continuous input of materials and supplies or to find markets for its outputs, then the organization's survival would be threatened.

The current interest in building cooperative work groups, making business firms more socially responsible, and matching organizational strategies to opportunities in the environment can be traced to ideas originally proposed by Barnard.

THE HAWTHORNE STUDIES

Without question, the most important contribution to the human resources approach to management came out of the **Hawthorne studies,** undertaken at the Western Electric Company's Hawthorne Works plant outside Chicago, Illinois, between 1924 and 1932. Originally initiated by Western Electric officials and later overseen by Harvard professor Elton Mayo, the Hawthorne studies concluded that behavior and sentiments were closely related, that group influences significantly affected individual behavior, that group standards established individual worker output, and that money was less a factor in determining output than were group standards, group senti-

These five women, under the direction of their supervisor, were part of the experiments conducted at the Hawthorne Works plant of Western Electric between 1924 and 1932. The Hawthorne studies dramatized that a worker was not a machine and that scientific management's "one best way" had to be modified to recognize the effects of group behavior.

ments, or security.[17] Hawthorne dramatized that workers were primarily social beings driven by a need for belonging and acceptance. These conclusions led to a new emphasis on the human factor in the functioning of organizations. They also led to increased paternalism by management.

The Hawthorne researchers began by examining the relation between the physical environment and productivity. Illumination and other working conditions were selected to represent this physical environment. The researchers' initial findings contradicted their anticipated results. They began the illumination experiments with various groups of workers. The researchers manipulated the intensity of illumination upward and downward, while at the same time noting changes in group output. Results varied, but one thing was clear: In no case was the increase or decrease in output in proportion to the increase or decrease in illumination. So the researchers introduced a control group: An experimental group worked under varying illumination intensities, and the control group worked under a constant illumination intensity. Again, the results were bewildering to the Hawthorne researchers. As the light level was increased in the experimental unit, output rose for both the experimental and the control groups. To the further surprise of the researchers, as the light level was dropped in the experimental group, productivity continued to increase in both. In fact, the experimental group's productivity decreased only when the light intensity had been reduced to that of moonlight. The Hawthorne researchers concluded that illumination intensity was only a minor influence among the many influences that affected an employee's productivity, but they could not explain the behavior they had witnessed.

As a follow-up to the illumination experiments, the researchers began a second set of experiments in the relay assembly test room at Western Electric. A small group of women were isolated from the main work group so that their behavior could be more carefully observed. They went about their job of assembling small telephone relays in a room laid out to resemble their normal department. The only significant difference was that there was a research assistant in the room who observed; kept records of output, rejects, and working conditions; and kept a daily log describing everything that happened. Records covering a multiyear period showed that this small group's output increased steadily. The number of personal absences and those due to sickness were approximately one-third of those taken by women in the regular production department. What became evident was that this group's performance was significantly influenced by its status as a "special" group. The women in the test room thought that being in the experimental group was fun, that they were in sort of an elite group, and that management showed it was interested in them by engaging in such experimentation.

A third study in the bank wiring observation room was introduced to ascertain the effect of a sophisticated wage incentive plan. The assumption was that individual workers would maximize their productivity when they saw that it was directly related to economic rewards. The most important finding coming out of this study was that employees did not individually maximize their outputs. Rather, their output became controlled by a group norm that determined what was a proper day's work. Output was not only being restricted, but individual workers were giving erroneous reports. The total for a week would check with the total week's output, but the daily reports showed a steady, level output regardless of actual daily production. What was going on? Interviews determined that the group was operating well below its capability and was leveling output in order to protect itself. Members were afraid that if they significantly increased their output, the unit incentive rate would be cut, the expected daily output would be increased, layoffs might occur, or slower workers would be reprimanded. So the group established its idea of a fair output—neither too much nor too little. They helped one another out to ensure that their reports were nearly level.

The first published results from Hawthorne appeared in 1930 and then were followed, over the next decade, by a stream of articles and books written by Mayo and his colleagues.[18] A number of these publications received considerable attention. Mayo's *The Human Problems of an Industrial Civilization*,[19] which came out in 1933, became a best-seller and was reviewed favorably in both the popular and academic presses. Another book on Hawthorne, *Management and the Worker*,[20] was considered important enough to be abstracted by *Reader's Digest* in 1939.

The legacy of Hawthorne is still with us today. Current organizational practices that owe their roots to the Hawthorne studies include attitude surveys, employee counseling, management training, participative decision making, and team-based compensation systems.

You should be aware that the Hawthorne studies' research methods and conclusions have been widely criticized.[21] However, from a historical standpoint, it's of little importance whether the studies were academically sound or their conclusions justified. What is important is that they stimulated an interest in human factors. The Hawthorne studies went a long way in changing the dominant view at the time that people were no different from machines; that is, you put them on the shop floor, cranked in the inputs, and they produced a known quantity of output.

THE HUMAN RELATIONS MOVEMENT

Another group within the human resources approach is important to management history for its unflinching commitment to making management practice more humane. Members of the **human relations movement** uniformly believed in the importance of employee satisfaction—a satisfied worker was believed to be a productive worker. For the most part, names associated with this movement—Dale Carnegie, Abraham Maslow, and Douglas McGregor—were individuals whose views were shaped more by their personal convictions than by substantive research evidence. The common thread that united human relations supporters was an unshakable optimism about people's capabilities. They believed strongly in their cause and were inflexible in their beliefs, even when faced with contradictory evidence. Despite their lack of objectivity, their beliefs found a large following, and they had a significant influence on management practice, especially from the late 1930s through the early 1970s.

DALE CARNEGIE Dale Carnegie is often overlooked by management historians, yet his ideas and teachings had an enormous effect on management practice. His book *How to Win Friends and Influence People*[22] was read by millions in the 1930s, 1940s, and 1950s. In addition, during this same period, tens of thousands of managers and aspiring managers attended his management speeches and seminars.

What was the theme of Carnegie's book and lectures? Essentially, he said that the way to success was through winning the cooperation of others. Carnegie advised that the path to success resided in: (1) making others feel important through a sincere appreciation of their efforts; (2) making a good first impression; (3) winning people to your way of thinking by letting others do the talking, being sympathetic, and "never telling a man he is wrong"; and (4) changing people by praising good traits and giving the offender the opportunity to save face.[23]

ABRAHAM MASLOW In 1943, Abraham Maslow, a humanistic psychologist, proposed a theoretical hierarchy of five categories of needs: physiological, safety, social, esteem, and self-actualization.[24] In terms of motivation, Maslow argued that each step in the hierarchy must be satisfied before the next can be activated and that once a need was substantially satisfied it no longer motivated behavior. Moreover, Maslow believed that self-actualization—that is, achieving one's full potential—was the summit of a human being's existence. On the basis of Maslow's theory, millions of managers altered their organizations' policies and practices to reduce barriers that stood in the way of employees' being able to self-actualize.

A survey of management professors in the early 1970s found that Maslow's 1943 publication on the need hierarchy was cited as the second most influential article in all of management.[25] The need hierarchy is arguably still the best-known theory of general motivation, despite the fact that "the available research does not support the Maslow theory to any significant degree."[26] Even today, no author of an introductory textbook in management, organizational behavior, psychology, or marketing is likely to omit discussion of Maslow's hierarchy of needs.

DOUGLAS McGREGOR Douglas McGregor is best known for a book in which he formulated two sets of assumptions—Theory X and Theory Y—about human nature.[27] Theory X presents an essentially negative view of people. It assumes that they have little ambition, dislike work, want to avoid responsibility, and need to be closely directed to work effectively. On the other hand, Theory Y offers a positive view. It assumes that people can exercise self-direction, accept responsibility, and consider work to be as natural as rest or play. McGregor believed that Theory Y assumptions best captured the true nature of workers and should guide management practice.

A story about McGregor does a good job of capturing the essence of the human relations perspective. McGregor had taught for a dozen years at the Massachusetts Institute of Technology. Then he became president of Antioch College. After 6 years at Antioch, he decided to return to his professorship at MIT. In his farewell address at Antioch, McGregor seemed to recognize that his philosophy had failed to cope with the realities of organizational life.

I believed, for example, that a leader could operate successfully as a kind of advisor to his organization. I thought I could avoid being a "boss." Unconsciously, I suspect, I hoped to duck the unpleasant necessity of making difficult decisions of taking the responsibility for one course of action among many uncertain alternatives, of making mistakes and taking the consequences. I thought that maybe I could operate so that everyone would like me—that "good human relations" would eliminate all discord and disagreement. I couldn't have been more wrong. It took a couple of years but I finally began to realize that a leader cannot avoid the exercise of authority any more than he can avoid responsibility for what happens to his organization.[28]

The irony in McGregor's case was that he went back to MIT and began preaching his humanistic doctrine again. And he continued doing so until his death.

The key point here is that, like Maslow's, McGregor's beliefs about human nature have had a strong following among management academics and practitioners. For instance, the previously cited survey on important contributions to management identified McGregor's book as the number one most influential book.[29]

BEHAVIORAL SCIENCE CONTRIBUTIONS

Our final category within the human resources approach encompasses primarily psychologists and sociologists (but also economists, political scientists, and social anthropologists) who relied on the scientific method for the studying of organizational behavior. Unlike proponents of the human relations movement, **behavioral science theorists** engaged in *objective* research of human behavior in organizations. They carefully attempted to keep their personal beliefs out of their work. They sought to develop rigorous research designs that could be replicated by other behavioral scientists. In so doing, they hoped to build a science of organizational behavior. And they succeeded. As human relations began to appear outmoded, a science of organizational behavior rose.[30]

A list of important behavioral science theorists and their contributions would number into the hundreds. But beginning after World War II and continuing on to today, they have created a wealth of studies that allow us to make fairly accurate predictions about behavior in organizations. Our current understanding of such issues as leadership, employee motivation, personality differences, the design of jobs and organizations, organizational cultures, high-performance teams, performance appraisals, conflict management, and negotiation techniques are largely due to the contributions of these behavioral scientists. Parts III through V of this book are based almost completely on the work of these scientists.

QUANTITATIVE APPROACHES

Quantitative approaches to management (also sometimes referred to as *operations research* or *management science*) evolved out of the development of mathematical and statistical solutions to military problems. During World War II, the British and American military employed teams of mathematicians, physicists, and statisticians to devise methods for solving complex logistical problems. For instance, when the British confronted the problem of how to get the maximum effectiveness from their limited aircraft capability against the massive forces of the Germans, they turned to their mathematicians to devise an optimum allocation model. Similarly, U.S. antisubmarine warfare teams used operations research (OR) techniques to improve the odds of survival for Allied convoys crossing the North Atlantic and for selecting the optimal depth-charge patterns for aircraft and surface vessel attacks on German U-boats.

Working with early computers, these OR teams were so successful that after the war each of the services established its own OR unit. In addition, many of the quantitative techniques that had been applied to solve military problems began to be used in the business sector. One group of military officers, labeled the "Whiz Kids," joined Ford Motor Company in the mid-1940s and immediately began using statistical devices to improve decision making at Ford. Two of the most famous Whiz Kids were Robert McNamara and Charles "Tex" Thornton. McNamara rose to the presidency of Ford and then became U.S. secretary of defense. At the Department of Defense, he sought to quantify resource allocation decisions in the Pentagon through cost-benefit analysis. He concluded his career as head of the World Bank. Tex Thornton founded the conglomerate Litton Industries, again relying on OR techniques to make acquisition and allocation decisions. Dozens of other operations researchers from the military went into consulting. The consulting firm of Arthur D. Little, for instance, began applying OR tech-

niques to management problems in the early 1950s. By 1954, at least twenty-five firms had established formal OR groups and as many as 300 OR analysts worked in industry.[31]

What are these quantitative techniques, and how have they contributed to current management practice? The **quantitative approaches** to management include applications of statistics, optimization models, information models, and computer simulations. Linear programming, for instance, is a technique that managers can use to improve resource allocation choices. Work scheduling can be made more efficient as a result of critical-path scheduling analysis. Decisions on optimum inventory levels have been significantly influenced by the economic order quantity model. In general, the quantitative approaches have contributed the most directly of all the approaches discussed to management decision making, particularly to planning and control decisions.

CONTEMPORARY APPROACHES

During the past 30 years there have been several additional approaches to management. These include the systems, contingency, and cultural perspectives. In this section, we briefly introduce these different perspectives on organizations and the manager's job.

THE SYSTEMS PERSPECTIVE

The idea that organizations could be analyzed in a systems framework became popular in the mid-1960s.[32] The **systems perspective** defines a system as a set of interrelated and interdependent parts arranged in a manner that produces a unified whole. Societies are systems, and so too are automobiles, animals, and human bodies.

There are two basic types of systems: closed systems and open systems.[33] **Closed systems** are not influenced by and do not interact with their environment. Frederick Taylor's machine view of people and organizations was essentially a closed-systems perspective. In contrast, an **open-systems** approach recognizes the dynamic interaction of the system with its environment. In the 1930s, Barnard fostered the idea that organizations are open systems, but widespread acceptance of the notion took another 30 years. Today, when we talk of organizations as systems, we mean open systems; that is, we acknowledge the organization's constant interaction with its environment.

Using a systems perspective, we envision the organization as being made up of "interdependent factors, including individuals, groups, attitudes, motives, formal structure, interactions, goals, status, and authority."[34] The job of a manager is to ensure that all parts of the organization are coordinated internally so that the organization's goals can be achieved. A systems view of management, for instance, would recognize that, regardless of how efficient the production department might be, if the marketing department doesn't anticipate changes in consumer tastes and work with the product development group in creating what consumers want, the organization's overall performance will be hampered.

In addition, the open-systems approach recognizes that organizations are not self-contained. They rely on their environment for life-sustaining inputs and as outlets to absorb their outputs. No organization can survive for long if it ignores government regulations, supplier relations, or the myriad external constituencies upon which the organization depends. The discussion in chapter 2 of the role of stakeholders in assessing an organization's effectiveness clearly builds on this notion of organizations as open systems.

THE CONTINGENCY PERSPECTIVE

Management, like life itself, is not based on simplistic principles. Insurance companies know that not all people have the same probability of being in an accident. Factors such as age, gender, past driving record, and number of miles driven per year are *contingencies* that influence accident rates. The **contingency perspective** sought to apply this same logic to the management of organizations. This approach recognizes that management practices need to be modified to reflect situational factors.[35]

People such as Taylor, Fayol, and Weber offered universal principles of management and organization. But these principles failed to reflect the full complexity involved in managing organizations and people. An increasing body of research has told us that, in certain situations, these universal principles don't lead to the most effective outcomes. Contrary to Taylor's ideas, managers are not always better qualified than employees to do the jobs of planning and control. Fayol's axiom that division of labor increases employee output is not universally applicable. And managers are increasingly rejecting Weber's belief that bureaucracy is the most efficient design for large organizations. *Sometimes* managers should do the

planning and controlling. *Sometimes* division of labor is the best way to increase productivity. And *sometimes* bureaucracy is the best organization design. But *sometimes* isn't *always*.

Since organizations are diverse—in size, objectives, the type of people employed, tasks being done, and the like—it would be surprising to find principles that would work in all situations. But, of course, it's one thing to say, *"It all depends,"* and another to say *what* it depends upon. Advocates of the contingency perspective—which includes almost all management scholars and practitioners today—have been working to identify these "what" variables. Some of the more popular of these variables include an organization's size; the degree of routineness in an employee's job; the degree of uncertainty in the organization's environment; and individual differences among employees such as skill levels, tolerance for ambiguity, need for growth, or desire for autonomy.

THE CULTURAL PERSPECTIVE

It began in the late 1970s and by the mid-1980s it was the hottest thing in management. "It," in this case, was the recognition that organizations had cultures and the belief that an understanding of a specific organization's culture could provide valuable insights into the behavior of people in that organization.[36]

Every organization has its own unique personality. But instead of calling it personality, we call it *organizational culture*. Organizations seek to hire people who will fit into their culture. In addition, they will go to extreme efforts to promote only people who accept and support what the organization values. So managers, for the most part, have been prescreened—in the selection or promotion process—to ensure that their attitudes and style fit with those sought by the organization. Nonmanagerial personnel also are hired, judged, and rewarded on the basis of their acceptance of the organization's culture. The software programmer, for instance, who is competent but believes that a job shouldn't consume more than 40 to 45 hours a week is unlikely to be hired at Microsoft. And if hired, he or she isn't likely to last long. Why? Microsoft's culture values workaholic behaviors. Seventy- and eighty-hour workweeks are the norm. If you're not willing to work long hours, you're not likely to survive at Microsoft.

The cultural perspective proposes that (1) successful organizations have cultures that fit well with their environments; (2) senior management should proactively seek to ensure a proper culture-environment fit; (3) "successful" employees will be those whose attitudes and styles fit with their cultures; and (4) strong cultures act as informal mechanisms for shaping employee behaviors. Regarding this last point: If you understand the shared values of an organization, you should be able to significantly improve your ability to predict the behavior of employees in that organization.

ANALYSIS: HOW TIMES SHAPE MANAGEMENT APPROACHES

We conclude this appendix by showing you how the times shape what theorists write about and what practicing managers focus on. Although some management historians may quarrel with the following cause-effect analysis, few would disagree that societal conditions are the primary driving force explaining the emergence of the different management approaches.

WHAT STIMULATED THE CLASSICAL APPROACH?

The common thread in the ideas offered by people such as Taylor, the Gilbreths, Fayol, and Weber was *increased efficiency*. The world that existed in the late nineteenth and early twentieth centuries was one of high inefficiency. Most organizational activities were unplanned and unorganized. Job responsibilities were vague and ambiguous. Managers, when they existed, had no clear notion of what they were supposed to do. There was a crying need for ideas that could bring order out of this chaos and improve productivity. And the standardized practices recommended by the classicists offered a means of achieving that increased productivity.

Take the specific case of scientific management. At the turn of the 20th century, the standard of living was low. Wages were modest, and few workers owned their own homes. Production was highly labor-intensive. It wasn't unusual, for instance, for hundreds of people to be doing the same repetitive, back-breaking job, hour after hour, day after day. Midvale Steel may have employed twenty or thirty workers who did nothing but load pig iron onto rail cars. Today, of course, their entire daily tonnage could probably be done in several hours by one person with a hydraulic lift truck. But they didn't have such mechanical conveniences. So Taylor could justify spending 6 months or more studying one job and perfecting a standardized "one best way" to do it because the labor-intensive procedures of the time had so many people performing the same task. And the efficiencies on the production floor could be passed on in lower prices for steel, thus expanding markets, creating more jobs, and making products such as stoves and refrigerators more accessible to working families. Similarly, Gilbreth's breakthroughs in improving the efficiency of bricklayers and standardizing bricklaying techniques significantly lowered the cost of putting up factories and homes. So more factories could be built, and more people could own their own homes. The end result: The application of scientific management principles contributed to raising the standard of living of entire countries.

WHAT STIMULATED THE HUMAN RESOURCES APPROACH?

The human resources approach really began to roll in the 1930s. Two related forces in that decade were instrumental in fostering this interest. First was a backlash to the overly mechanistic view of employees held by the classicists. Second was the emergence of the Great Depression.

The classical view treated organizations and people as machines. In this view, managers were the engineers. They ensured that the inputs were available and that the machine was properly maintained. Any failure by the employee to generate the desired output was viewed as an engineering problem: It was time to redesign the job or grease the machine by offering the employee an incentive wage plan. Unfortunately, this kind of thinking created an alienated workforce. Human beings were not machines and did not necessarily respond positively to the cold and regimented work environment of the classicists' perfectly designed organization. The human resources approach offered managers solutions for lessening this alienation and for improving worker productivity.

The Great Depression swept the globe in the 1930s and brought forth a dramatic increase in the role of government in individual and business affairs. For instance, in the United States, Franklin D. Roosevelt's New Deal sought to restore confidence to a stricken nation. Between 1935 and 1938 alone, the Social Security Act was created to provide old-age assistance, the National Labor Relations Act was passed to legitimize the rights of labor unions, the Fair Labor Standards Act introduced the guaranteed hourly wage, and the Railroad Unemployment Insurance Act established the first national unemployment protection. This New Deal climate raised the importance of the worker. Humanizing the workplace had become congruent with society's concerns at the time.

WHAT STIMULATED THE QUANTITATIVE APPROACHES?

The major impetus to the quantitative approaches was World War II. Government-funded research programs were created to develop mathematical and statistical aids for solving military problems. The success of these operations research techniques in the military was impressive. After the war, business executives became more open to applying these techniques to their organizational decision making. And, of course, as these techniques proved successful in improving the quality of decisions and increasing profits in those firms that used them, managers in competing firms were forced to adopt these same techniques.

New organizations were additionally being created to disseminate information to managers on these quantitative techniques. "The Operations Research Society of America was founded in 1952, and began publishing its journal, *Operations Research.* In 1953, The Institute of Management Science stated its objectives as to identify, extend, and unify scientific knowledge that contributes to the understanding of the practice of management' and began publishing the journal *Management Science.*"[37]

By the late 1960s, coursework in mathematics, statistics, and operations management had become required components of most business school curricula. The new generation of managers would be knowledgeable in such techniques as probability theory, linear programming, queuing theory, and game theory.

WHAT STIMULATED THE OPEN-SYSTEMS PERSPECTIVE?

The open-systems perspective exploded in the 1960s. By the early 1970s, it seemed as if almost every management textbook had "systems" in its title.[38] Why *then?*

The anti–Vietnam War and activism movements of the 1960s and 1970s included heavy criticism of business. Business was portrayed as a closed system—insensitive to its social responsibilities. Critics attacked business for creating shoddy products and unsafe working conditions, for discriminating against minorities, and for insensitivity to the communities in which they were located.[39] Management academics and practitioners realized that business needed to take a proactive stance. If it didn't act to strategically respond to the increasing demands placed on it by external stakeholders—particularly consumers and government—then those stakeholders would use political pressures to limit business's influence. The open-systems perspective focused managers' attention on the world outside their organization and the need to respond to their critics.

WHAT STIMULATED THE CULTURAL PERSPECTIVE?

The cultural perspective owes its emergence to global competition and particularly to the tremendous success post–World War II Japan had in world commerce. How was it that Japanese companies could turn out high-quality products at significantly lower prices than their American and European competitors? Although the Japanese had more-modern factories and newer equipment, researchers kept coming back to the unique cultures of Japanese organizations.[40]

Japanese organizations provided lifetime employment, emphasized long-term rather than short-term performance, relied heavily on teamwork and collective team responsibility, and had strong mission statements that defined the organization and provided clarity of direction for employees. These cultural characteristics explained a great deal of the success of companies such as Sony, Honda, and Matsushita. American, Canadian, and European managers responded by trying to emulate the Japanese. This environment largely explains the interest in the past two decades in creating strong organizational cultures that emphasize quality, utilize teams, and value flexibility and rapid response to change.

NOTES

1. K. Kelly, "The New Soul of John Deere," *Business Week,* January 31, 1994, pp. 64–66.

2. M. P. Follett, *The New State: Group Organization, the Solution of Popular Government* (London: Longmans, Green, 1918); D. A. Wren, *The Evolution of Management Thought,* 4th ed. (New York: Wiley, 1994); and D. W. Linden, "The Mother of Them All," *Forbes,* January 16, 1995, pp. 75–76.

3. C. S. George Jr., *The History of Management Thought,* 2nd ed. (Englewood Cliffs, NJ: Prentice Hall, 1972), p.4.

4. W. E. Wallace, "Michelangelo, C.E.O.," *New York Times,* April 16, 1994, p. Y11.

5. A. Smith, *An Inquiry into the Nature and Causes of the Wealth of Nations* (New York: Modern Library, 1937). Originally published in 1776.

6. F. W. Taylor, *The Principles of Scientific Management* (New York: Harper, 1911).

7. These facts about the dissemination of Taylor's ideas are from S. R. Barley and G. Kunda, "Design and Devotion: Surges of Rational and Normative Ideologies of Control in Managerial Discourse," *Administrative Science Quarterly,* September 1992, pp. 369–71. See also M. Banta, *Taylored Lives: Narrative Productions in the Age of Taylor, Veblen, and Ford* (Chicago: University of Chicago Press, 1993); and R. Kanigel, *The One Best Way* (New York: Viking, 1997).

8. F. B. Gilbreth, *Motion Study* (New York: D. Van Nostrand, 1911); and F. B. Gilbreth and L. M. Gilbreth, *Fatigue Study* (New York: Sturgis and Walton Co., 1916).

9. H. Fayol, *Industrial and General Administration* (Paris: Dunod, 1916).

10. M. Weber, *The Theory of Social and Economic Organizations,* ed. T. Parsons, trans. A. M. Henderson and T. Parsons (New York: Free Press, 1947).

11. W. J. Duncan, *Great Ideas in Management* (San Francisco: Jossey-Bass, 1989), p. 137.

12. R. A. Owen, *A New View of Society* (New York: E. Bliss and White, 1825).

13. H. Münsterberg, *Psychology and Industrial Efficiency* (Boston: Houghton Mifflin, 1913).

14. Follett, *The New State.*

15. Linden, "The Mother of Them All," p. 76.

16. C. I. Barnard, *The Functions of the Executive* (Cambridge, MA: Harvard University Press, 1938).

17. E. Mayo, *The Human Problems of an Industrial Civilization* (New York: Macmillan, 1933); and F. J. Roethlisberger and W. J. Dickson, *Management and the Worker* (Cambridge, MA: Harvard University Press, 1939).

18. The facts in this paragraph are from Barley and Kunda, "Design and Devotion," p. 374.

19. Mayo, *The Human Problems of an Industrial Civilization.*

20. Roethlisberger and Dickson, *Management and the Worker.*

21. See, for example, A. Carey, "The Hawthorne Studies: A Radical Criticism," *American Sociological Review,* June 1967, pp. 403–16; R. H. Franke and J. Kaul, "The Hawthorne Experiments: First Statistical Interpretations," *American Sociological Review,* October 1978, pp. 623–43; B. Rice, "The Hawthorne Defect: Persistence of a Flawed Theory," *Psychology Today,* February 1982, pp. 70–74; J. A. Sonnenfeld, "Shedding Light on the Hawthorne Studies," *Journal of Occupational Behavior,* April 1985, pp. 111–30; S. R. G. Jones, "Worker Interdependence and Output: The Hawthorne Studies Revisited," *American Sociological Review,* April 1990, pp. 176–90; and S. R. G. Jones, "Was There a Hawthorne Effect?" *American Journal of Sociology,* November 1992, pp. 451–68.

22. D. Carnegie, *How to Win Friends and Influence People* (New York: Simon & Schuster, 1936).

23. Wren, *The Evolution of Management Thought,* p. 336.

24. A. H. Maslow, "A Theory of Human Motivation," *Psychological Review,* July 1943, pp. 370–96. See also A. H. Maslow, *Motivation and Personality* (New York: Harper & Row, 1954).

25. M. T. Matteson, "Some Reported Thoughts on Significant Management Literature," *Academy of Management Journal,* June 1974, pp. 386–89.

26. J. B. Miner, *Theories of Organizational Behavior* (Hinsdale, IL: Dryden, 1980), p. 41.

27. D. McGregor, *The Human Side of Enterprise* (New York: McGraw-Hill, 1960).

28. Wren, *The Evolution of Management Thought,* p. 372.

29. Matteson, "Some Reported Thoughts on Significant Management Literature."

30. M. Warner, "Organizational Behavior Revisited," *Human Relations,* October 1994, p. 1153.

31. Cited in E. Burack and R. B. D. Batlivala, "Operations Research: Recent Changes and Future Expectations in Business Organizations," *Business Perspectives,* January 1972, pp. 15–22.

32. See, for example, E. J. Miller and A. K. Rice, *Systems of Organizations* (London: Tavistock Publications, 1967); C. W. Churchman, *The Systems Approach* (New York: Dell, 1968); and F. E. Kast and J. E. Rosenzweig, "General Systems Theory: Applications for Organization and Management," *Academy of Management Journal,* December 1972, pp. 447–65.

33. D. Katz and R. L. Kahn, *The Social Psychology of Organizations,* 2nd ed. (New York: Wiley, 1978), pp. 23–30.

34. K. B. DeGreene, *Sociotechnical Systems: Factors in Analysis, Design and Management* (Upper Saddle River, NJ: Prentice Hall, 1973), p. 13.

35. See, for example, R. J. Mockler, "Situational Theory of Management," *Harvard Business Review,* May–June 1971, pp. 146–55; F. E. Kast and J. E. Rosenzweig, *Contingency Views of Organization and Management* (Chicago: Science Research Associates, 1973); and H. L. Tosi Jr. and J. W. Slocum Jr., "Contingency Theory: Some Suggested Directions," *Journal of Management,* Spring 1984, pp. 9–26.

36. See, for example, J. J. O'Toole, "Corporate and Managerial Cultures," in C. L. Cooper (ed.), *Behavioral Problems in Organizations* (Upper Saddle River, NJ: Prentice Hall, 1979), pp. 7–28; A. Pettigrew, "On Studying Organizational Cultures," *Administrative Science Quarterly,* December 1979, pp. 570–81; T. E. Deal and A. A. Kennedy, *Corporate Cultures* (Reading, MA: Addison-Wesley, 1982); and R. T. Pascale, "Fitting New Employees in the Company Culture," *Fortune,* May 28, 1984, pp. 28–43.

37. Wren, *The Evolution of Management Thought*, p. 395.

38. See, for example, F. E. Kast and J. E. Rosenzweig, *Organization and Management Theory: A Systems Approach* (New York: McGraw-Hill, 1970); H. G. Hicks, *The Management of Organizations: A Systems and Human Resources Approach,* 2nd ed. (New York: McGraw-Hill, 1972); D. I. Cleland and W. R. King, *Management: A Systems Approach* (New York: McGraw-Hill, 1972); E. F. Huse and J. L. Bowditch, *Behavior in Organizations: A Systems Approach to Managing* (Reading, MA: Addison-Wesley, 1973); T. E. Vollmann, *Operations Management: A Systems-Model Building Approach* (Reading, MA: Addison-Wesley, 1973); H. G. Hicks and C. R. Gullett, *Modern Business Management: A Systems and Environmental Approach* (New York: McGraw-Hill, 1974); M. S. Wortman and F. Luthans (eds.), *Emerging Concepts in Management: Process, Behavioral, Quantitative, and Systems,* 2nd ed. (New York: Macmillan, 1975); and H. Koontz and C. J. O'Donnell, *Management: A Systems and Contingency Analysis of Managerial Functions,* 6th ed. (New York: McGraw-Hill, 1976).

39. See, for example, T. A. Petit, *A Moral Crisis in Management* (New York: McGraw-Hill, 1967).

40. See W. Ouchi, *Theory Z: How American Business Can Meet the Japanese Challenge* (Reading, MA: Addison-Wesley, 1981) and R. Pascale and A. Athos, *The Art of Japanese Management: Applications for American Executives* (New York: Simon & Schuster, 1981).

WELCOME TO MAD DOGS & ENGLISHMEN, A FAST-GROWING AD AGENCY

In the first part of your text, you were introduced to the changing world of work and the foundations of managing organizations and people. Now you are ready to view the first of five video segments showing how some of the management concepts and practices you have been examining are actually applied in a fast-growing ad agency, Mad Dogs & Englishmen, in New York City. Bear in mind that these videos are intended to show several management concepts in action, rather than focusing on only one or two. Because the videos reflect management in the real world, the concepts may be mixed together, and some may not be exactly in order (as in your textbook chapters).

In this video case for Part 1, you will meet Mad Dogs & Englishmen's founder and chairman, Nick Cohen, and hear how he and his managers are riding the crest of Alvin Toffler's third wave, defined in chapter 1 as an economy based on information rather than agriculture or machinery. Influences on the new economy—including globalization, diversity, entrepreneurial spirit, social responsibility, and ethics—also play a major role in the management of this business. The agency's staff members exemplify the new employee discussed in chapter 1, with multiple skills, a teamwork orientation, and the ability to cope with all kinds of pressures. And, as you will see, the agency's managers carry out the functions, roles, and skills described in chapter 2.

AN AGENCY WITH ENTREPRENEURIAL SPIRIT

Founded in 1991, Mad Dogs & Englishmen is a young, hip agency that has already grown to $5 million in annual revenues and won more than 150 awards for its extraordinarily creative, often hilarious advertisements. Cohen started his own company not because he wanted to make more money, but because he wanted to make more creative ads and have more fun doing it. Although leaving an established agency to become an entrepreneur meant coping every day with possible failure, Cohen found the opportunities both exciting and rewarding. "In a little agency, you tend to work more by the skin of your teeth," he says, comparing the stripped-down, fast-paced environment at Mad Dogs & Englishmen with the multiple layers and longer approval process typical of larger agencies. "We'll do a piece of work and three weeks later, it'll be out there."

As the agency grew to 30 full-time managers and employees, its reputation for creativity attracted a diverse workforce from England, Scotland, Holland, Germany, and Australia. College interns and entry-level employees flock to Mad Dogs & Englishmen to gain hands-on experience and learn skills that increase their market value. The salary levels are lower than at larger agencies, but employees have more responsibility and more opportunities to see their work incorporated into television, radio, or print advertisements.

Because Mad Dogs & Englishmen is a small business, its employees have to juggle multiple duties. "I wear about five or six different hats," says David Drucker, the agency's finance director, "including finance, accounting, operations, facilities management, contract negotiations, dealing with outside accountants and lawyers, and getting involved in budgeting." Similarly, Dave Cook is more than a creative director. "I'm an art director by trade, but . . . I have to write as much copy as I have to do art direction," he says. In addition to completing his own work, he coaches others, "In a small agency, it's a mixture of doing and showing other people how to do it."

The agency is a good example of Alvin Toffler's third wave, because it employs knowledge workers who use computers to acquire and apply information—specifically, the information about products, markets, and customers used to develop creative advertising. To date, the agency has worked on campaigns for many clients, including Movie-Fone, Yoo-hoo chocolate drink, the *Village Voice* newspaper, the *Economist* magazine, Thom McAn shoe stores, the New York Islanders hockey team, and Friends of Animals.

A COMMITMENT TO ETHICS AND SOCIAL RESPONSIBILITY

Since the start, Nick Cohen and his colleagues at Mad Dogs & Englishmen have been on a crusade to help their clients build their brands and connect with customers—but not at the expense of ethics. The chairman opposes advertising that is deceptive, sexist, or condescending. Advertising, he says, should be honest and sincere to effectively "make a relationship between the brand and the public."

In keeping with society's changing expectations of business, social responsibility is also on the agency's business agenda. About 20 percent of the work done by Mad Dogs & Englishmen is produced free or at very low cost for nonprofit groups. These campaigns give Mad Dogs & Englishmen personnel a chance to showcase their talents and help causes in which they believe. Still, with the agency's image on the line, management takes care when selecting the cause and the creative approach.

In a recent anti-fur campaign for Friends of Animals, for example, the agency decided against a confrontational approach to this controversial topic, opting instead for a lighter tone to get the point across. The creative staff came up with the tagline "Fur Is a Thing of the Past. Evolve" and used arresting visuals and humorous headlines to reinforce a more subtle anti-fur message in this campaign.

KEEPING THE AGENCY ON TRACK

The top managers at Mad Dogs & Englishmen are responsible for the basic management functions of planning, organizing, leading, and controlling. As shown in the video, Nick Cohen performs various interpersonal roles such as leader; informational roles such as spokesperson; and decisional roles such as entrepreneur. Robin Danielson, the agency's president, complements Cohen by serving as a liaison with internal sources of information, disseminating this information, and allocating resources as needed.

Despite the free-wheeling atmosphere, the agency takes a total quality management approach to giving its clients the best possible service by consistently delivering creative, effective advertising—on time and within budget. Danielson and Cohen work with other senior managers to integrate the work of the various departments and to coordinate the activities of the creative teams.

Good management skills are critical for guiding growth in a young agency like Mad Dogs & Englishmen. Top managers also need a keen understanding of organiza-

tional behavior, says Robin Danielson. "I really believe an organization is an organism," she observes. "You can't turn an organism into a machine. Organizations are about people, and they develop their own shape and their own neurotic qualities and their own fabulous, wonderful qualities that are about the weird chemical interaction of alive things. You can't be a leader without understanding that what you've got is something that's alive, and if you want something alive to do well, you have to love it."

DISCUSSION QUESTIONS

1. How is Mad Dogs & Englishmen basing its business on the characteristics of the new economy, as shown in Exhibit 1-1 on page 4?

2. Which of the groups shown in Exhibit 2-5 on page 49 are the agency's key stakeholders? Why?

3. From the client's perspective, what criteria would be appropriate for measuring this agency's effectiveness? From the employees' perspective? Explain.

4. Political skills are one of the general skills identified in chapter 2 as being necessary for management proficiency. Why are political skills as important in a small organization like Mad Dogs & Englishmen as they are in a larger organization?

5. Visit the Mad Dogs & Englishmen's Internet Web site (**www.maddogsandenglishmen.com**). How is the agency portraying its capabilities on the Web site? Based on this case, on the Web site, and on your knowledge of the new organization from chapter 1, what do you think are the agency's core competencies?

PART TWO: DECISION, PLANNING, AND MONITORING SYSTEMS

A LOOK INSIDE MAD DOGS & ENGLISHMEN

ON LOCATION! In the second part of your text, you learned how managers make decisions, monitor the environment, use planning systems, and monitor performance through control systems. This video case for Part 2 takes you back to the offices of Mad Dogs & Englishmen, where

managers discuss how they make decisions about agency issues and client issues.

For everyday issues, founder Nick Cohen and his managers often use intuitive decision making, defined in chapter 3 as an unconscious process created out of distilled experience. When considering decisions that affect their clients, however, the agency tends to use the rational decision process, a more formal, criteria-driven method of choosing the optimal alternative to solve a particular problem.

As you will see in the video, Cohen and other agency managers are constantly monitoring the environment, as discussed in chapter 4, to stay abreast of competitive moves and overall trends that can affect the agency's performance. In addition, they complete a SWOT analysis of each client to better understand its strengths, weaknesses, opportunities, and threats, a process you learned about in chapter 5. Like any well-managed business, the agency sets objectives and tracks performance through budgets and other control systems, as discussed in chapter 6.

DECISIONS, DECISIONS, DECISIONS

Given all the uncertainty in the highly pressured, ever-changing world of advertising, it is not surprising that managers at Mad Dogs & Englishmen apply both rational and intuitive processes when making decisions. Often, Cohen and his management team will invite different members of the staff to help make decisions about agency matters. And he works hard at maintaining a culture that fosters creativity and risk-taking, two elements that contribute to good decisions.

Many decisions are made informally, says David Drucker, the finance director, by "walking around, talking to other partners, talking to staff people, making decisions on the fly." Major decisions are made during more formal partners meetings. "The partners meet probably every month and a half or so, sometimes on site or sometimes we'll go off site so we can think and talk in private, for several hours at a time," he explains. "Sometimes we'll have a formal agenda, sometimes we'll just talk about the morale issues or how people feel."

However, when managers at Mad Dogs & Englishmen are making decisions about which strategy to recommend to a client, they tend to follow the rational decision-making model. First, the agency's account planners conduct research to identify the client's problem(s), which might be low audience awareness or inaccurate perception of the product. The account team also uses environmental scanning to understand that client's unique environment and to develop a SWOT analysis of the client and its brand. "We will look at what they've done in the past," says Robin Danielson, the agency's president, "but usually we're looking at the brand in toto and asking about strengths, weaknesses, opportunities, and threats to that brand, which can be a very helpful way to figure out what we're going to do."

After considering decision criteria such as the client's top priorities and the size of the advertising budget, the creative team—a copywriter and an art director—comes up with a number of alternatives for reaching customers. These alternatives are ranked, and only the top few are presented to the client. At this point, the decision-makers on the client side have a chance to react to the alternatives and, where necessary, ask for a change or two before deciding on the optimal choice.

DEALING WITH ENVIRONMENTAL UNCERTAINTY AND INSTABILITY

Because the advertising industry is both complex and volatile, top managers at Mad Dogs & Englishmen have to stay on top of the latest trends and competitive moves. In fact, a lot of competitive intelligence and leads for new business come directly from Nick Cohen's contacts within other New York agencies. "When you have larger and middle-sized and smaller agencies, it's very common that an account may just not fit right at that agency, or there may be a conflict," points out David Drucker. It is therefore not unusual for Cohen to wind up with a referral to a new client when he calls his counterpart at another agency or sees a competitor at an industry meeting.

Although Mad Dogs & Englishmen's staff is extremely knowledgeable about the creative side of advertising, the agency is too small to keep experts on the payroll who are knowledgeable in planning and buying print and broadcast media. Yet the successful implementation of every advertising plan depends, in part, on decisions about media. For this reason, the agency handles media decisions through coalescing, joining forces with another firm. Mad Dogs & Englishmen's in-house media expert, Zander Riese, works alongside the Wilson Media Group, an independent media buying service that knows all media. Working with this outside firm allows Mad Dogs & Englishmen to concentrate on its creative niche and still gain access to the media resources needed to plan and execute clients' advertising campaigns.

CONTROLS FOR BUSINESS AND FOR CREATIVITY

Making money is only one of Mad Dogs & Englishmen's objectives. The agency's real mission—the reason Nick Cohen started his own business—is to create exceptional advertising and have fun at the same time. Still, to keep the agency going strong, its managers have to be concerned about control, the process of monitoring activities to be sure they are accomplished as planned and of correcting any significant deviations.

Budgeting is part of this control process, explains the chairman. "Every year, at the beginning of the year, we project earnings and we . . . have to predict what we're going to spend," he says. "We have a payroll and we have percentages [for certain expense categories]. We analyze things quarterly, and we have to make adjustments if we don't think we're going to make our numbers."

Measuring the creativity of an ad can be difficult. Yet Mad Dogs & Englishmen's managers are able to get a sense of their agency's creative performance by competing against other agencies for industry awards. To date, the agency has captured more than 150 awards, showing that advertising experts recognize its creativity.

For clients, the ultimate measure of an ad's effectiveness is its ability to achieve specific goals such as changing the public perception of a product or boosting sales. Here again, Mad Dogs & Englishmen has methods in place to measure performance. For example, the agency recently created television commercials for Yoo-Hoo chocolate drink, which wanted to change its image and expand consumption among teenagers.

After the ads began to appear in two test markets, the agency hired a research firm to survey local teens about their perceptions of Yoo-Hoo. The agency also tracked product sales in the test markets to see whether teens' perceptions were being translated into purchases. The results: Yoo-Hoo's sales rose more than 60 percent in the test markets, driven by much more positive attitudes on the part of the target audience. This information helped the agency and its client finalize plans for rolling out the campaign in more markets.

DISCUSSION QUESTIONS

1. Does Mad Dogs & Englishmen appear to be using a cost-leadership strategy, a differentiation strategy, or a focus strategy? How do you know?

2. How is the making of an ad subject to project management?

3. If Mad Dogs & Englishmen's top managers were conducting a SWOT analysis of their agency, what strengths and weaknesses might they identify? Explain.

4. Should Mad Dogs & Englishmen use benchmarking to improve its competitive position? Why or why not?

5. Select one of the major sources of environmental uncertainty, such as government regulation or competition. Then, using a search tool such as Yahoo! (www.yahoo.com) or a specialized site such as a government or an industry Web site, locate at least two recent pieces of information about your selected factor. Why do you think it is important for Mad Dogs & Englishmen to monitor this factor?

PART THREE: ORGANIZING TASKS, PEOPLE, AND CULTURE

ORGANIZATION AT MAD DOGS & ENGLISHMEN

In the third part of your text, you learned about organizing tasks, managing people and teams, and sustaining organizational culture. Now you're ready to view the video case for Part 3, showing how Nick Cohen, Robin Danielson, and all the managers apply these principles at Mad Dogs & Englishmen. Information technology drives many of the agency's activities and, as discussed in chapter 7, reduces the cycle time in producing advertising materials. Along with the open floor-plan design of the office, this emphasis on technology improves the flow of work while speeding internal communications among staff members.

As shown in the video, the agency organizes tasks by departmentalization, defined in chapter 8 as the grouping of jobs according to function, product, geography, process, or customer. Although Mad Dogs & Englishmen uses functional departmentalization, its organization design is organic, deliberately loose and flexible for maximum adaptability. Recruiting of interns and employees, covered in chapter 9, relies mainly on referrals and word-of-mouth, but growth is prompting the agency to formalize more of its HR activities, including performance appraisals. In the video, you will see that cross-functional teams—defined in chapter 10 as teams of employees from different departments—are the backbone of the agency. Finally, as you watch one of the agency's clients describe the culture at Mad Dogs & Englishmen, listen for some of the primary characteristics of culture that are covered in chapter 11.

LET THE INFORMATION FLOW

The free flow of information—business as well as personal—is a way of life at Mad Dogs & Englishmen, thanks to its completely open floor plan and its highly organic structure. No one has a private office or even a walled-in cubicle, because founder Nick Cohen did not want his employees to work in isolation.

"We decided, let's turn everything just inside out," he remembers. Now he and each of his employees have a designated work area with a desk, storage space, and a computer, but no doors or walls. As a result, he says, "everyone can see each other and everyone can see each other's struggle. Everyone can see each other's effort. So everyone becomes a bit more understanding of each other." In fact, the office seems specifically designed "to encourage collaboration and the breakdown of those layers in the creative process," adds Sandi Bachom, director of broadcast production. "It's a very family atmosphere."

Mad Dogs & Englishmen is organized according to functional departmentalization, with separate departments for account planning (consumer research), account management (client contact), creative (art direction and copywriting), broadcast production (for television and radio advertising), print production (for newspaper, magazine, and other print advertising), and finance (accounting and related tasks). When needed, the agency complements its staff expertise by hiring suppliers such as freelance writers, Web site designers, and film producers to work on specific client projects.

TEAMING UP AT MAD DOGS

Work on each client's advertising materials is shared by a cross-functional team. A typical team consists of a strategic planner, a creative team, a media specialist, and print/broadcast production personnel, who collaborate on the advertising strategy and tactics. In general, managers assign employees to teams based on their skills, their experience with the product category, and their current work load.

At times, Mad Dogs & Englishmen management uses cross-hierarchical teams to inject more creativity into its already highly creative process. Cohen recently assembled a cross-hierarchical team for a presentation to a prospective client in the clothing business. Reasoning that "fashion is something that touches so many different people in so many different ways," he put together a team of eight employees from many departments who were "really interested in clothes and fashion." This team not only came up with original advertising ideas, it also decided on a fresh approach to presenting the ideas to the clothing company. Instead of handing out pieces of paper describing their concepts, the employees painted the ideas onto ceramic picnic plates and made the presentation in a conference room transformed into a mountain meadow, complete with real grass.

HANDLING HUMAN RESOURCE MANAGEMENT

Many advertising agencies simply hire employees when they take on a new client and then let them go when they lose a client. But top managers at Mad Dogs & Englishmen do not want to get locked into a continual cycle of growth and retrenchment, preferring to maintain the cohesiveness of its 30-person staff through controlled growth. With such a small and close-knit group, says Cohen, recruiting is "not just about finding people, it's about creating a group of people that work together well."

This is why agency managers, who are responsible for staffing their own departments, look for more than exceptional technical skills when they evaluate applicants. Explains Valerie Hope, the director of print production, "We are very conscientious about who we hire and whether the chemistry is right." The best applicants are asked to come back several times for two or three months for meetings with a number of people from each department. In some cases, prospective employees start out working as interns or as freelancers on selected projects, and if they fit in, they are invited to join the company as full-time employees.

Sandi Bachom got her start at Mad Dogs & Englishmen in just this way, working freelance on production projects for two years until she was offered a full-time job. Like many of the employees, she was introduced by a friend who was working at the agency. College interns are another recruitment source. During the summer, the agency hires as many as 20 college students as interns; after graduation, some are invited to return as full-timers.

Once on staff, employees are encouraged to enhance their skills by attending seminars and other industry events. In addition, employees can and do develop their careers within the agency by shifting from one department to another. The reason, says Paul Levine, the general manager, is that "we'd rather keep good people and give them the opportunity to learn different disciplines."

The performance appraisal process at Mad Dogs & Englishmen is becoming more formalized as the agency grows. In the past, the president would conduct periodic reviews of individual employees. Now the agency is revamping the process, aiming for 360-degree feedback every six months to "give employees a better sense of how they're doing," says Paul Levine. This will help the agency "get a better understanding of what [employees'] aspirations are and how the organization can help them more in terms of getting a rounded education," he adds.

A STRONG CULTURE

Creating great advertising *and* having fun doing it has always been Nick Cohen's vision. The agency's organizational culture (the system of shared meaning held by staff members that distinguishes this agency from others) definitely reflects the founder's vision as well as his entrepreneurial spirit. Clients notice the difference. For example, Andrew R. Jarecki, CEO of MovieFone, recognizes that Mad Dogs & Englishmen is "a fun place to be, a very good environment for creativity." At the same time, he says, "they're aggressive, they're creative, they're pretty brash" and, unlike MovieFone's former agency, they're willing to take risks such as criticizing their clients when it seems appropriate.

Just as important, Jarecki is pleased that the agency's culture attunes employees to the need for balancing the artistic and the commercial sides of the advertising process. "They know that [the advertising] is not going to work if it's just artistic," he explains. "This is an agency that knows . . . they've got to meet somewhere in the middle."

DISCUSSION QUESTIONS

1. Why would Mad Dogs & Englishmen have functional departmentalization even though work for clients is accomplished through cross-functional teams?
2. What skills and abilities would Mad Dogs & Englishmen look for in a new employee? Why are current and former employees good sources for referrals to (and communication with) potential job applicants?
3. Why do you think the agency's cross-functional teams are likely to be highly productive?
4. How does the agency's highly selective, sometimes lengthy, hiring process affect its culture?
5. Stories, rituals, symbols, and language are all ways of communicating an organization's culture. Browse the Web site of Kirshenbaum Bond & Partners (**www.kb.com**), another New York City ad agency, looking for clues to the organization's culture. Based on its Web site, what kind of culture do you think this agency has? Support your answer.

PART FOUR: LEADING AND EMPOWERING PEOPLE

EXPLORING PEOPLE AT MAD DOGS & ENGLISHMEN

ON LOCATION!

In the fourth part of your text, you investigated the concepts and processes involved in leading and empowering people. Now get ready to view the video case for Part 4, which shows these techniques in action at the Mad Dogs & Englishmen ad agency. When hiring employees and matching them to jobs, Nick Cohen and other managers pay close attention to the personality dimensions discussed in chapter 12, including self-esteem—the degree to which people like or dislike themselves—and risk taking.

As you will see in the video, management is well aware that the agency attracts employees seeking to satisfy higher-order needs such as esteem and self-actualization. These employees exhibit commitment to the agency's goals, as well as self-direction, eagerness for more responsibility, and the desire to participate in decisions. Cohen, as chairman, has many of the leadership traits discussed in chapter 14, and his participative style means a minimum of leader control.

President Robin Danielson is more of a transactional leader, defined in chapter 15 as guiding and motivating employees toward goals by clarifying role and task requirements. In contrast, employees see Cohen as a transformational leader, inspiring employees to transcend their self-interests for the good of the agency. Watch the video for Danielson's statement about Cohen's visionary leadership—his ability to create and articulate a vision of the future that improves on the present. You will also see that Cohen and his managers believe in honest advertising, which builds trust among employees and the consumers who see the agency's ads—an issue explored in chapter 16. Above all, this is an agency and an industry where good interpersonal skills, like those described in chapter 17, are a must.

MASLOW'S HIERARCHY AT WORK

Employees at Mad Dogs & Englishmen earn both salary and benefits—enough to take care of the basic needs identified in Maslow's hierarchy—but money is less of a motivational factor than the opportunity to develop their talents and create good advertising. Cohen is especially excited about seeing younger employees pitch in and come up with creative ideas that "empower them so much in their career" and, ultimately, boost their confidence. Danielson sees the agency as "a wonderful canvas for the personal expression" of the employees, where all members of the staff can "make their own impression and be truly seen, not invisible." This aspect of their work helps employees satisfy higher-order needs such as esteem and self-actualization.

At the same time, the mix of personalities and the organizational culture add another dimension to job satisfaction. "It's really fun," explains Jamie Palmiotti, a creative assistant. "These are really good people who really work hard and love their jobs. Because they love their jobs, they're going to do the best they can at them and spend the extra time." Danielson concurs: "We do have probably a more flexible, humanistic, enjoyable culture than almost any place anybody will work in their lifetime."

THE DYNAMIC LEADERSHIP DUO

Behind the scenes, Mad Dogs & Englishmen thrives on the complementary leadership approaches taken by the chairman and the president. Both Cohen and Danielson have necessary leadership traits such as high energy, the desire to lead, self-confidence, and intelligence. And both encourage increased employee participation rather than relying on increased leader control. As Danielson says, "Those of us who are running the place have a tremendous interest in the opinions of those who are not running the place."

As the transformational leader in this dynamic duo, Cohen inspires employees with his strong vision of what the agency should be and the high level of work it should pro-

duce for clients and consumers. "Nick is a visionary," says Danielson. "He is a wonderful communicator in terms of imparting to everybody in the organization a desire for [the work] to be really right." Mikal Reich, one of the agency's creative directors, says that Cohen "totally takes the ceiling away and wants you to keep finding better ways, more interesting ways to communicate."

Just as important, Cohen's leadership allows employees to take more risks in their work. "You're not afraid to try things for fear that maybe they won't be successful," comments Valerie Hope, the director of print production. "He brings a freedom . . . that helps you be more creative." As a result, agency personnel feel free to look beyond the obvious solutions to the slightly off-beat, unexpected alternatives that can result in more creative advertisements.

Danielson is the agency's transactional leader, providing motivation for employees tackling the day-to-day tasks. "I believe that as a leader, I'm pretty straightforward and pretty efficient," she says, "and probably rather intellectual in a problem-solving way." Employees appreciate and welcome both Danielson's and Cohen's leadership styles. Whereas Cohen will show respect and "sit quietly and contemplate your work," Danielson helps employees get the job done through a more hands-on, engaging style, notes Michael Fanuele, deputy planning director. "Robin will grab a red pen and dive into your work. And in some ways, it's a faster process."

BUILDING TRUST AND A SUPPORTIVE CULTURE

Cohen sets high standards for advertising produced by Mad Dogs & Englishmen, outlawing ideas that are deceptive, sexist, or condescending. His insistence on honesty and sincerity—backed up by a supportive organizational culture that allows people to speak openly—builds trust among staff members, clients, and companies that work with the agency.

Tom Wilson, president of the Wilson Media Group, is impressed by the agency's honesty. "I've seldom worked with a company that has the respect for the consumer that they do," he says, "and a respect for honesty in telling the client about what the consumer thinks about their business. Honesty and respect are two things that are incredibly valuable in the business of advertising."

Employees can speak their minds because the organizational culture actively encourages sharing thoughts and feelings. David Drucker, the finance director, says he has to describe the culture using "words that aren't typically used for a corporation: loving, caring, nurturing, supportive." Conflicts occur, but airing differences openly and listening actively to the viewpoints of others makes for "a healthy outcome from our conversations."

DISCUSSION QUESTIONS

1. How is the agency's supportive organizational culture likely to affect employee involvement and satisfaction?

2. Why is it important for Mad Dogs & Englishmen to have both transactional and transformational leadership?

3. Why are trust and an open, supportive culture important for effective cross-functional teamwork at this agency?

4. In the context of communication and conflict, what are the positives and negatives of the agency's open floor-plan design (lacking doors and private offices)?

5. Some companies have candidates take a personality test before making a hiring decision. Go to the on-line Keirsey Temperament Sorter II (**www.keirsey.com/cgi-bin/keirsey/newkts.cgi**). Read about the test and answer the questions. Would you recommend that Mad Dogs & Englishmen have candidates take such a test? Why or why not?

PART FIVE: ORGANIZATIONAL RENEWAL

MANAGING CHANGE & INNOVATION WHILE HOLDING ON TO THE FUN AT MAD DOGS & ENGLISHMEN

In the final part of your text, you learned about organizational renewal, focusing on the ever-changing world of work. Now you are ready to view the video case for Part 5. In this video, you will find out how the managers at Mad Dogs & Englishmen apply a variety of techniques to effectively handle change and keep the agency successful now and into the future.

Change, especially planned change—defined in chapter 18 as intentional and goal-oriented change—has played a pivotal role in the young agency's growth and development. Chairman Nick Cohen likes to push the envelope on technological change, acquiring state-of-the-art computerized equipment and software to enhance and support the agency's creativity and to streamline implementation. In the pursuit of planned change, he has also changed the agency's organizational structure, people, and physical setting.

Going beyond change, Cohen is a champion of innovation, constantly searching for new ideas to apply to each client's advertising. As you have seen in all these video cases, innovation in advertising is what draws clients to Mad Dogs & Englishmen and what distinguishes the agency from rivals in this highly competitive industry. To continue its success in a dynamic industry and an uncertain environment, Cohen has molded the agency into a learning organization, one with the continuous capacity to adapt and change.

MANAGING THE CHALLENGE OF CHANGE

Mad Dogs & Englishmen is not the only ad agency facing the challenge of change, but it has been one of the most successful in achieving the kind of planned change needed to operate in the new economy and under the new rules of competition (described in chapter 1). Its success is partly due to its size and age: as a relatively small, entrepreneurial young company, the agency has had little time to build up the structural inertia, group norms, power relationships, and resource allocations that work against change.

In particular, the founder and his management team have made changes to four of the five categories that can be changed by managers:

▶ *Technology*. From the ubiquitous laptop computers to the electronic editing equipment, Mad Dogs & Englishmen keeps investing in the latest hi-tech tools. These allow employees to create new and unusual advertising concepts—and produce the ads more efficiently as well, an important advantage when schedules are tight.

▶ *Structure*. As the agency has grown, so too has the structure, with more formal grouping of jobs and more deliberate coordination of responsibilities throughout the organization. Still, the structure has remained flat, in contrast to larger agencies, where "it just takes a lot longer and there is more chance that your ads aren't going to happen or they're going to get watered down," says Dave Cook, creative director.

- ➤ *Physical Setting*. Mad Dogs & Englishmen was originally located in Cohen's loft apartment. Once the agency outgrew that space, Cohen took over the entire floor of a lower Fifth Avenue building and had an architect design a flexible, entirely open floor-plan to enhance communication and collaboration. A few revolving walls help define the space, and everything—right down to the kitchen equipment—can be quickly shifted into a new layout as needed.
- ➤ *People*. The agency helps employees develop their skills through participation in seminars and industry events. It also applies team building activities, emphasizing interpersonal relations and clarifying each member's team role and responsibilities.

What has not been changed so far is the organizational culture. Valerie Hope, the director of print production, says that despite steady growth, the agency has "the same feeling and the same camaraderie. It's just as much fun now with thirty people as when there were four people." The culture also points the way to the kinds of products and advertising the agency will continue to take on, says Paul Levine, the general manager. "We're not going to advertise anything we don't believe in," he says, "and we feel that advertising should do some good."

INNOVATION, LEARNING, AND GROWTH

Innovative organizations such as Mad Dogs & Englishmen are organic rather than mechanistic, and they tend to place a premium on communication across departmental lines.

The agency's organizational culture—which has grown up around the founder's vision of more creative advertising—fosters experimentation and risk taking, two key ingredients for innovation.

Although Cohen is determined to control his agency's growth and stick close to his vision of creating great advertising while having fun, Mad Dogs & Englishmen must remain a learning organization if it is to enjoy sustained future success. He and his managers know that the shared vision is only part of the answer, and they're already looking ahead to ways of addressing internal fragmentation, competition, and reactiveness—three problems that cause problems in traditional organizations.

DISCUSSION QUESTIONS

1. Which of the six tactics for reducing resistance to change are likely to be the *least* effective at Mad Dogs & Englishmen? Why?

2. Given that the agency is strictly controlling its growth, what are the implications for the politics of change at Mad Dogs & Englishmen?

3. Under what circumstances might Nick Cohen and his top managers want to consider changing the culture at Mad Dogs & Englishmen?

4. Based on what you know about Mad Dogs & Englishmen, how does the agency embody the characteristics of a learning organization shown in Exhibit 18-5?

5. What is happening at Mad Dogs & Englishmen right now? Use your favorite Internet search tool, such as Metacrawler (**www.metacrawler.com**) or Hotbot (**www.hotbot.com**) to locate news releases and articles about the agency. Also check the *Advertising Age* Web site for agency news (**www.adage.com**). What kinds of changes are taking place, and how is the agency managing those changes? What other changes would you expect to see within a few years? Why?

Photo Credits

Name and Organization Index

Z

The Prentice Hall Self-Assessment Library CD-ROM License Agreement

Prentice-Hall, Inc.

READ THIS LICENSE CAREFULLY BEFORE OPENING THIS PACKAGE. BY OPENING THIS PACKAGE, YOU ARE AGREEING TO THE TERMS AND CONDITIONS OF THIS LICENSE. IF YOU DO NOT AGREE, DO NOT OPEN THE PACKAGE. PROMPTLY RETURN THE UNOPENED PACKAGE AND ALL ACCOMPANYING ITEMS TO THE PLACE YOU OBTAINED THEM FOR A FULL REFUND OF ANY SUMS YOU HAVE PAID FOR THE SOFTWARE. THESE TERMS APPLY TO ALL LICENSED SOFTWARE ON THE DISK EXCEPT THAT THE TERMS FOR USE OF ANY SHAREWARE OR FREEWARE ON THE DISKETTES ARE AS SET FORTH IN THE ELECTRONIC LICENSE LOCATED ON THE DISK:

1. GRANT OF LICENSE and OWNERSHIP: The enclosed computer programs ("Software") are licensed, not sold, to you by Prentice-Hall, Inc. ("We" or the "Company") and in consideration of your payment of the license fee, which is part of the price you paid and your agreement to these terms. We reserve any rights not granted to you. You own only the disk(s) but we and/or our licensors own the Software itself. This license allows you to use and display your copy of the Software on a single computer (i.e., with a single CPU) at a single location for academic use only, so long as you comply with the terms of this Agreement. You may make one copy for back up, or transfer your copy to another CPU, provided that the Software is usable on only one computer.

2. RESTRICTIONS: You may not transfer or distribute the Software or documentation to anyone else. Except for backup, you may not copy the documentation or the Software. You may not network the Software or otherwise use it on more than one computer or computer terminal at the same time. You may not reverse engineer, disassemble, decompile, modify, adapt, translate, or create derivative works based on the Software or the Documentation. You may be held legally responsible for any copying or copyright infringement which is caused by your failure to abide by the terms of these restrictions.

3. TERMINATION: This license is effective until terminated. This license will terminate automatically without notice from the Company if you fail to comply with any provisions or limitations of this license. Upon termination, you shall destroy the Documentation and all copies of the Software. All provisions of this Agreement as to limitation and disclaimer of warranties, limitation of liability, remedies or damages, and our ownership rights shall survive termination.

4. LIMITED WARRANTY AND DISCLAIMER OF WARRANTY: Company warrants that for a period of 60 days from the date you purchase this SOFTWARE (or purchase or adopt the accompanying textbook), the Software, when properly installed and used in accordance with the Documentation, will operate in substantial conformity with the description of the Software set forth in the Documentation, and that for a period of 30 days the disk(s) on which the Software is delivered shall be free from defects in materials and workmanship under normal use. The Company does not warrant that the Software will meet your requirements or that the operation of the Software will be uninterrupted or error-free. Your only remedy and the Company's only obligation under these limited warranties is, at the Company's option, return of the disk for a refund of any amounts paid for it by you or replacement of the disk. THIS LIMITED WARRANTY IS THE ONLY WARRANTY PROVIDED BY THE COMPANY AND ITS LICENSORS, AND THE COMPANY AND ITS LICENSORS DISCLAIM ALL OTHER WARRANTIES, EXPRESS OR IMPLIED, INCLUDING WITHOUT LIMITATION, THE IMPLIED WARRANTIES OF MERCHANTABILITY AND FITNESS FOR A PARTICULAR PURPOSE. THE COMPANY DOES NOT WARRANT, GUARANTEE OR MAKE ANY REPRESENTATION REGARDING THE ACCURACY, RELIABILITY, CURRENTNESS, USE, OR RESULTS OF USE, OF THE SOFTWARE.

5. LIMITATION OF REMEDIES AND DAMAGES: IN NO EVENT, SHALL THE COMPANY OR ITS EMPLOYEES, AGENTS, LICENSORS, OR CONTRACTORS BE LIABLE FOR ANY INCIDENTAL, INDIRECT, SPECIAL, OR CONSEQUENTIAL DAMAGES ARISING OUT OF OR IN CONNECTION WITH THIS LICENSE OR THE SOFTWARE, INCLUDING FOR LOSS OF USE, LOSS OF DATA, LOSS OF INCOME OR PROFIT, OR OTHER LOSSES, SUSTAINED AS A RESULT OF INJURY TO ANY PERSON, OR LOSS OF OR DAMAGE TO PROPERTY, OR CLAIMS OF THIRD PARTIES, EVEN IF THE COMPANY OR AN AUTHORIZED REPRESENTATIVE OF THE COMPANY HAS BEEN ADVISED OF THE POSSIBILITY OF SUCH DAMAGES. IN NO EVENT SHALL THE LIABILITY OF THE COMPANY FOR DAMAGES WITH RESPECT TO THE SOFTWARE EXCEED THE AMOUNTS ACTUALLY PAID BY YOU, IF ANY, FOR THE SOFTWARE OR THE ACCOMPANYING TEXTBOOK. BECAUSE SOME JURISDICTIONS DO NOT ALLOW THE LIMITATION OF LIABILITY IN CERTAIN CIRCUMSTANCES, THE ABOVE LIMITATIONS MAY NOT ALWAYS APPLY TO YOU.

6. GENERAL: THIS AGREEMENT SHALL BE CONSTRUED IN ACCORDANCE WITH THE LAWS OF THE UNITED STATES OF AMERICA AND THE STATE OF NEW YORK, APPLICABLE TO CONTRACTS MADE IN NEW YORK, AND SHALL BENEFIT THE COMPANY, ITS AFFILIATES AND ASSIGNEES. HIS AGREEMENT IS THE COMPLETE AND EXCLUSIVE STATEMENT OF THE AGREEMENT BETWEEN YOU AND THE COMPANY AND SUPERSEDES ALL PROPOSALS OR PRIOR AGREEMENTS, ORAL, OR WRITTEN, AND ANY OTHER COMMUNICATIONS BETWEEN YOU AND THE COMPANY OR ANY REPRESENTATIVE OF THE COMPANY RELATING TO THE SUBJECT MATTER OF THIS AGREEMENT. If you are a U.S. Government user, this Software is licensed with "restricted rights" as set forth in subparagraphs (a)-(d) of the Commercial Computer-Restricted Rights clause at FAR 52.227-19 or in subparagraphs (c)(1)(ii) of the Rights in Technical Data and Computer Software clause at DFARS 252.227-7013, and similar clauses, as applicable.

Should you have any questions concerning this agreement or if you wish to contact the Company for any reason, please contact in writing:

Director New Media
Higher Education Division
Business Publishing Group
Prentice Hall, Inc.
One Lake Street
Upper Saddle River, NJ 07458

Should you have any questions concerning technical support of this product, please contact our Technical Support staff in writing at:

New Media Production and Technical Support
Higher Education Division
Prentice Hall, Inc.
One Lake Street
Upper Saddle River, NJ 07458

or call:

201-236-3477

or email:

tech_support@prenhall.com